C000225485

THE WORLD'S MERCHANT FLEETS

1939

THE WORLD'S MERCHANT FLEETS

1939

The Particulars and Wartime Fates of 6,000 Ships

Roger W Jordan

CHATHAM PUBLISHING

LONDON

For Jennifer
For her support and encouragement

Frontpiece: Umtali, one of three sisterships built for the Natal Line service. (Alex Duncan)

Copyright © Roger W Jordan 1999

First published in Great Britain in 1999 by
Chatham Publishing,
61 Frith Street,
London W1V 5TA

Chatham Publishing is an imprint of Gerald Duckworth & Co Ltd

British Library Cataloguing in Publication Data
A catalogue record for this book is available from the British Library

ISBN 1 86176 023 X

All rights reserved. No part of this publication may be reproduced or transmitted in any form or by any means, electronic or mechanical, including photocopying, recording, or any information storage and retrieval system, without prior permission in writing from the publisher or a licence permitting restricted copying.
The right of Roger W Jordan to be identified as the author of this work has been asserted by him in accordance with the Copyrights, Designs and Patents Act 1988

Typeset and designed by Trevor Ridley
Printed and bound in Great Britain by WBC Book Manufacturers Limited

Contents

Introduction

In common with scores of other authors and researchers over the years I had become increasingly irritated by the lack of easily located information concerning the world's ocean-going merchant fleet as it existed at about the time of the start of the Second World War. Company histories in print abound and with some delving it is often not too difficult a task to obtain information concerning a large number of vessels of this era, but by no means all of them.

Encouraged by others I embarked on this task to endeavour to rectify many of the shortcomings which have appeared in print postwar and present the results of my research in a familiar style.

The contents of this book are, under national and company headings, listings of ocean-going fleets as they existed at the end of 1939.

A large part of the book is devoted to vessels lost during the Second World War by both war causes and marine hazard. This part also includes listings of ocean-going vessels scuttled for war purposes (usually as blockships), vessels sunk as breakwaters in the Mulberry harbours following D-Day, vessels lost postwar through striking mines, and the many vessels which were sunk postwar laden with surplus war materials, including poison gas ammunition.

Further sections also list vessels which changed name, flag, role or otherwise disposed of during the war years.

Roger W Jordan

Acknowledgements

During the past few years I have consulted many people both in the United Kingdom and overseas on many aspects of this book, and I would particularly thank Barbara Jones and Anne Cowne of Lloyd's Register Information Group for their greatly appreciated help.

Especial thanks also to the staff at the Information Centre of the Institute of Marine Engineers, and David Burrell, Anthony Cooke, Paul Louden-Brown, and Alan Peake, who have helped with regard to specific items of text; Paul and Penny Dalton with regard to photograph research. From outside of the United Kingdom, I have received much help from Peter Simonsen (Denmark), Torbjørn Larsson-Fedde (Farsund, Norway), Paolo Piccione (Genoa, Italy), and from many shipowners, shipbuilders and individuals who have readily supplied information and photographs.

Explanatory notes

The contents of this book are, under national and company headings, listings of ocean-going fleets as they existed at the end of 1939.

Sales which occurred at any time during 1939, for either further trading or for breaking up, are annotated in footnotes at each entry. Also listed are vessels which were on order but not commenced or in the course of contruction, either listed under their eventually-decided names or shown as 'Newbuilding', the latter usually in cases where they were either not proceeded with or became casaulties of war before completion.

Shipowners/managers

Under each national heading will be found shipowner and manager headings. These are largely based on entries as found in the 1939–40 edition of the Register of Ships, published by Lloyd's Register of Shipping and are thus those most familiar. At the heading is to be found the principal trading address(es) of that shipowner/manager.

Funnel and hull colours

The funnel and hull colours, identified for most owners and groups, are also shown, as are the principal services and trades operated.

The vessels listed are shown under various types, including
Passenger
Passenger/general cargo
General cargo
Fruit carrier
Tanker
Whale oil factory
and others.

Where no description is shown the entire listing for that company, or group of companies, comprises general cargo vessels, which were the most numerous type in service at the time.

Column 1

Vessel name is followed by
◊ type of machinery and number of screws. Where there is no type listed this should be read as steam-reciprocating single-screw (see Abbreviations).
◊ where applicable, by the number of passengers carried (see Abbreviations); for example, (st2,P50/1,50/2) denotes steam turbines, twin screw, 50 first-class and 50 second-class passengers.

Column 2

◊ Year of build (completion).

Column 3

◊ Name of builder (names of builders are abbreviated and coded, with a full listing at Names of Shipbuilders, where successions of shipbuilding company titles are also shown).

Columns 4 and 5

◊ Gross register tons (column 4); and
◊ deadweight tons (column 5)
are those applicable at about the end of 1939 and which appeared in either the *Register of Ships* published by Lloyd's Register of Shipping or the register books of other classification societies or other authoritative contemporary publications.

Columns 6, 7 and 8

Dimensions, in feet or feet and inches, are
◊ length, overall or registered (column 6);
◊ breadth (column 7);
◊ draught or registered depth (column 8).
Overall length is shown, eg, 400–6 (feet–inches), whereas registered length is shown, eg, 400.5 (feet); draught is shown, eg, 25–6 (feet–inches) and registered depth is shown, eg, 25.5 (feet).

I have endeavoured to trace overall length and draught wherever possible due to the variations in methods of calculation of registered length and registered depth among different countries. For example, for Finnish and Italian vessels, registered length is, in fact, overall length.

Column 9
Speed is service speed, extracted from authoritative contemporary publications and based largely on information provided by shipowners and shipbuilders.
Former names
Former names with year of change are shown under each vessel entry, and where applicable major conversions, lengthenings, etc, are shown

Footnotes
Many entries have footnotes in which brief mention is made of smaller vessels which occasionally undertook ocean voyages in 1938–39. Names are followed by (year of build/gross tons). Also appearing here are details of sales and transfers which occurred during 1939.

Abbreviations

Vessels		
Machinery	(m)	motor vessel
	(s)	steam-reciprocating (only shown if vessel had two or more screws)
	(st)	steam turbine
	(r/t)	steam reciprocating with exhaust turbine
	(me)	diesel-electric
	(te)	turbo-electric
	2	two screws
	3	three screws
	4	four screws
Passengers	(P–)	passengers, numbers not located; and preceded by number:
	/1	first class
	/2	second class
	/3	third class
	/4	fourth class
	/cab	cabin class
	/d	deck passengers
	/int	interchangeable
	/st	steerage class
	/t	tourist class
	/tr	troops
	/Ch	Chinese
	/nat	native
	/pilg	pilgrims (Hadj)
Other	BU	broken up
	conv	converted
	gt	gross tons
	LU	laid up
	mv	motor vessel

See also list of abbreviations used in the Losses section

SHIPBUILDERS

This is a list of shipbuilders, the abbreviated form of which appears in column 3 of the fleet listings

Aalb1	P Ph Stuhr's Maskin & Skibs, Aalborg; later
Aalb2	Aalborg Skibsværft A/S; later
Aalb3	Aalborg Maskin & Skibsbyggeri A/S, Aalborg, Denmark; later
Aalb4	Aalborg Værft A/S
Ailsa1	Ailsa Shipbuilding Co, Troon; later
Ailsa2	Ailsa Shipbuilding Co Ltd
AISB	American International Shipbuilding Corp, Hog Island, Pennsylvania, USA
Akers	Akers Mekaniske erksted A/S, Oslo, Norway
Alabam	Alabama Drydock & Shipbuilding Co, Mobile, Alabama, USA
Albina	Albina Engine & Machine Works Inc, Portland, Oregon, USA
A&M	Aitken & Mansell, Glasgow
AllisC	Canadian Allis Chalmers Ltd, Bridgeburg, Ontario, Canada
Ames	Ames Shipbuilding & Dry Dock Co, Seattle, Washington, USA
AmSB	American Shipbuilding Co, USA (Cl) Cleveland, Ohio, (Lo) Lorain, Ohio
AnsG	Giorgio Ansaldo & Co, Genoa-Sestri, Italy; later
AnsGC	Società Anonima Italiana Giorgio Ansaldo & Co; later
AnsSA	Ansaldo SA
Anvers	Chantiers Navals Anversois, Antwerp (later – see AwpEng)
Ardrsn	Ardrossan Dockyard & Shipbuilding Co Ltd, Ardrossan; later
ArdDk	Ardrossan Dockyard Ltd
ArmMit	Sir W G Armstrong, Mitchell & Co Ltd, Walker, Newcastle upon Tyne; later
ArmWh1	Sir W G Armstrong, Whitworth & Co Ltd; later
ArmWh2	Sir W G Armstrong, Whitworth & Co (Shipbuilders) Ltd
ArsnBr	Arsenal de la Marine, Brest (French Government Yard, Brest)
ArsnCh	Arsenal de la Marine, Cherbourg (French Government Yard, Cherbourg)
ArsnLo	Arsenal de la Marine, Lorient (French Government Yard, Lorient)
Asaki	Asaki Shipbuilding Co Ltd, Osaka, Japan
Asano	Asano Shipbuilding Co Ltd, Tsurumi, Japan (later – see Tsurmi)
AtlC	Atlantic Corporation, Portsmouth, New Hampshire, USA
Austin	S P Austin & Son Ltd, Sunderland
AwpEng	Antwerp Engineering Co Ltd, Hoboken (previously – Anvers)
AyrDk	Ayrshire Dockyard Co Ltd, Irvine
Baanhk	NV Scheepsbouwwerf 'Baanhoek' Voorheen T Nederlof, Sliedrecht, Netherlands
Bacini	Società Anonima Bacini e Scali Napoletani, Naples, Italy
Baltca	Baltica-Varftet A/S, Copenhagen, Denmark
Baltic	Baltic Shipbuilding & Engineering Works, Leningrad, USSR
Baltmr	Baltimore Dry Docks & Shipbuilding Co, Baltimore, Maryland, USA
Bartm1	Bartram & Sons, Sunderland; later
Bartm2	Bartram & Sons Ltd
Bath	Bath Iron Works Ltd, Bath, Maine, USA
Beardm	W Beardmore & Co Ltd, Dalmuir (previously – see Napier)
Bergen	Bergens Mekaniske Verksteder A/S, Bergen, Norway (previously – see Laxe)
Beth	Bethlehem Shipbuilding Corp, USA
BethB	Bethlehem Shipbuilding Corp, Baltimore, Maryland
BethFR	Fore River Shipbuilding Co (later Corp), Quincy, Massachusetts; later
BethQu	Bethlehem Shipbuilding Corp
BethMS	Maryland Steel Co, Sparrow's Point, Maryland; later
BethSP	Bethlehem Steel Co; later styled Bethelehem Shipbuilding Corp
BethU1	Union Iron Works, San Francisco, California; later
BethSF	Bethlehem Shipbuilding Corp
BethU2	Union Iron Works, Alameda, California; later
BethAl	Bethlehem Shipbuilding Corp
BethSW	South Western Shipbuilding Co, San Pedro, California
BethHH	Harlan & Hollingsworth Corp, Wilmington, Delaware; later
BethWi	Bethlehem Shipbuilding Corp
BethEl	Bethlehem Shipbuilding Corp, Elizabeth, New Jersey
Blohm	Blohm & Voss, Hamburg
Blumr1	J Blumer & Co, Sunderland; later
Blumr2	J Blumer & Co Ltd
Blyth	Blyth Shipbuilding & Dry Docks Co Ltd, Blyth (previously – see Cowpen)
Blythw	Blythswood Shipbuilding Co Ltd, Glasgow
Boele	Boele's Scheepwerven en Machine Fabriek NV, Bolnes, Netherlands
Bonn&M	NV Scheepswerf v/h Bonn & Mees, Rotterdam, Netherlands
Bremer	Schiffbau & Maschinefabrik Bremer Vulkan, Vegesack, Germany
Bretgn	Ateliers & Chantiers de Bretagne, Nantes, France
BritAm	British American Shipbuilding Co, Welland, Ontario, Canada
Brodin	E Brodins Varvs A/B, Gefle, Sweden
BrownG	George Brown & Co, Greenock
BrownJ	John Brown & Co Ltd, Clydebank
Brys&G	Brys & Gylsen Ltd, Whiteinch, Glasgow (later part of – see Curle)
Bufflo	Buffalo Dry Dock Co, Buffalo, new York, USA
Burger	NV Burgerhout's Maschinefabriek & Scheepswerf, Rotterdam, Netherlands
Burntd	Burntisland Shipbuilding Co Ltd, Burntisland
B&W	Burmeister & Wain's Maskin & Skibsbyggeri A/S, Copenhagen, Denmark
B&W,K	Kjobenhavns Flydedok & Skibsværft A/S
Caen	Chantiers Navals Français, Caen, France
Caird	Caird & Co Ltd, Greenock (later – see H&WGk)
Caledn	Caledon Shipbuilding & Engineering Co Ltd, Dundee (previously – see ThmpsD)
Cammel	Cammell Laird & Co Ltd, Birkenhead
Camp1	Campbeltown Shipbuilding Co, Campbeltown, Argyllshire; later
Camp2	Campbeltown Shipbuilding Co Ltd
CanVic	Canadian Vickers Ltd, Montreal, Canada
Cargll	Cargill Inc, Albany, New York, USA
Cerusa	Società Anonima Santieri Cerusa, Genoa-Voltri, Italy

CFCN	Cantiere Federale per Costruzioni Navale, Pietra Ligure, Italy
Chepst	Chepstow Shipbuilding Works, Chepstow, Monmouthshire (formerly – see Monmth)
Chestr	Chester Shipbuilding Co, Chester, Pennsylvania, USA (later – see Merch)
Chicgo	Chicago Shipbuilding Co, Chicago, Illinois, USA
Chick	Chickasaw Shipbuilding & Car Co, Chickasaw, Alabama, USA
Clyde	Clyde Shipbuilding & Engineering Co Ltd, Port Glasgow
CNOM	Cantieri Navali e Officine Meccaniche di Venezia, Venice, Italy
CNR	Cantieri Navali Riuniti, Italy
CNR1	Cantiere Navale di Muggiano SA, Muggiano D'Arcola, Spezia; later
CNR2	Cantiere Navale Riuniti, Muggiano
CNR3	Cantiere Navale Bacino e Stabilimenti Meccanici Siciliani, Palermo; later
CNR4	Cantiere Navale Riuniti
CNR5	Cantiere Navale Riuniti, Ancona
Cockll	John Cockerill SA, Antwerp and Hoboken, Belgium
Collwd	Collingwood Shipbuilding Co Ltd, Collingwood, Toronto, Ontario, Canada
Columb	Columbia River Shipbuilding Corp, Portland, Oregon, USA
COM	Cantieri ed Officine Meridionali, Società Italiana per Costruzioni Navali & Meccaniche, Baia, Italy
CommSy	Commonwealth Government Shipbuilding & Dockyard, Sydney, NSW, Australia
Conn1	C Connell & Co, Glasgow; later
Conn2	C Connell & Co Ltd
Conrad	NV Conrad Werf, Zaandam, Netherlands
ConsSt	Consolidated Steel Corp, Wilmington, California, USA
Coughl	J Coughlan & Sons Ltd, Vancouver, British Columbia, Canada
Cowpen	Cowpen Dry Docks & Shipbuilding Co Ltd, Blyth (previously – see Blyth)
Cragg1	R Craggs & Sons, Tees Dockyard, Middlesbrough; later
Cragg2	R Craggs & Sons Ltd
Craig1	Craig, Taylor & Co, Stockton-on-Tees; later
Craig2	Craig, Taylor & Co Ltd
Cramp	Wm Cramp & Sons Ship & Engine Building Co, Philadelphia, Pennsylvania, USA
CRDA	Cantieri Riuniti Dell'Adriatico, Italy
CRDA1	Cantiere Navale Triestino, Monfalcone; later
CRDA2	Cantiere Riuniti Dell'Adriatico
CRDA3	Cantieri San Rocco (SA), Trieste
CRDA4	Stabilimento Tecnico Triestino, Trieste; later
CRDA5	Cantiere Riuniti Dell'Adriatico
CrichV	A/B Crichton-Vulcan O/Y, Åbo (Turku), Finland
Crown1	John Crown & Sons Ltd, Sunderland; previously
Crown2	John Crown; previously
Crown3	The Strand Slipway Co
Curle	Barclay, Curle & Co Ltd, Whiteinch, Glasgow
Daniel	O Daniels Shipbuilding Co, Tampa, Florida, USA
Davie	Davie Shipbuilding & Repairing Co, Levis, Quebec, Canada; previously
DavieG	G T Davie & Sons
DeBies	NV Scheepswerf en Machinefabrik 'De Biesbosch', Dordrecht, Netherlands
DeHaan	De Haan & Oerlermans Scheepsbouwwerf, Heusden, Netherlands
DeKlop	NV Scheepsbouwwerf & Machinefabrik 'De Klop', Sliedrecht, Netherlands
DeMaas	NV Internationale Scheepsbouwmaatschappij 'De Maas', Slikkerveer, Netherlands
Delwre	Delaware River Iron Shipbuilding & Engine Works, Chester, Pennsylvania, USA
DeMwde	NV Scheepsbouwwerf 'De Merwede' voorheen Van Vliet & Co, Hardinxveld, Netherlands
Denny1	W Denny & Bros, Dumbarton; later
Denny2	W Denny & Bros Ltd
Desch1	Deutsche Schiff-und Maschinenbau AG (Deschimag), Germany
Desch2	Deutsche Schiffs-und Maschinebau Akt Werk Joh C Tecklenborg AG (previously – see Teckl)
Desch3	Deutsche Schiffs-und Maschinebau AG Werk AG 'Weser' (previously – see Weser)
Desch4	Deutsche Schiff-und Maschinebau AG 'Vulcan', Hamburg (previously – see VulcH)
DeutsH	Deutsche Werft AG, Betrieb Finkenwärder, Hamburg, Germany
DeutsK	Deutsche Werke AG, Kiel, Germany
DeutsR	Deutsche Werft, Betrieb Reiherstiegwerft, Hamburg, Germany (previously – see Reiher)
DGroot	NV Scheepsbouwwerf v/h de Groot & Van Vliet, Slikkerveer, Netherlands
Dijvdk	NV Scheepswerf voorheen de Wwe a Van Dijvendijk, Papendrecht, Netherlands
Dixon1	Sir Raylton Dixon & Co, Middlesbrough; later
Dixon2	Sir Raylton Dixon & Co Ltd
DNoord	NV Scheepsbouwwerf 'De Noord', Alblasserdam, Netherlands
Dobson	W Dobson & Co, Walker-on-Tyne (later part of Sir W G Armstrong-Whitworth & Co (Shipbuilders) Ltd)
Domnn	Dominion Shipbuilding Co Ltd, Toronto, Ontario, Canada
Dordr	NV Scheepswerf Dordrecht, Dordrecht, Netherlands (later – see DeBies)
DoultW	Doullut & Williams Shipbuilding Co Inc, New Orleans, Louisiana, USA
Downey	Downey Shipbuilding Corp, Arlington, New York, USA (previously Downey Shipyard Corp)
Doxfrd	William Doxford & Sons Ltd, Sunderland
Dtroit	Detroit Shipbuilding Co, Wyandotte, Michigan, USA
Dubign	Société Anonyme des Anciens Chantiers Dubigeon, Nantes-Chantenay, France
Dublin	Dublin Dockyard Co Ltd, Dublin, Ireland
Duncan	R Duncan & Co Ltd, Port Glasgow
Dundee	Dundee Shipbuilding Co Ltd, Dundee
DunlpB	Dunlop, Bremner & Co Ltd, Port Glasgow; previously
DunlpD	David J Dunlop & Co
Duthie	J F Duthie & Co, Seattle, Washington, USA
Dyle&B	Société Anonyme de Travaux Dyle & Bacalan, Bordeaux, France (later – see SOuest)
Earles	Earle's Shipbuilding & Engineering Co Ltd, Hull
Ech&L	Echevarrieta y Larrinaga, Cadiz, Spain

Edwrds	Edwards Shipbuilding Co Ltd, Newcastle upon Tyne
Eider1	Eiderwerft AG, Tönning, Germany; previously
Eider2	Schömer & Jensen
Eltrgm	Eltringhams Ltd, Willington Quay-on-Tyne
Eriksb	Eriksbergs Mekaniske Verkstads A/B, Gothenburg, Sweden
Esp	Sociedad Española de Construccion Naval, Spain, (B) Bilbao, (C) Cadiz, (Ca) Carthagena, (F) Ferrol
Eusk	Compañia Euskalduna, Bilbao, Spain
Fairfd	Fairfield Shipbuilding & Engineering Co Ltd, Glasgow
Fed2	Federal Shipbuilding & Dry Dock Co, Kearny, New Jersey, USA; previously
Fed1	Federal Shipbuilding Co
Fergsn	Ferguson Bros (Port Glasgow) Ltd, Port Glasgow
Fevigs	Fevigs Jernskibsbyggeri, Fevig, near Arendal, Norway (later – Sörlan)
Finch	E Finch & Co (1916) Ltd, Chepstow, Monmouthshire (later part of – see Chepst)
Finnb	Finnboda Varf A/B, Stockholm, Sweden
Flensb	Flensburger Schiffsbau-ges, Flensburg, Germany
Forth	Forth Shipbuilding & Engineering Co (1921) Ltd, Alloa
Framns	Framnes Mek Verksted A/S, Sandefjord, Norway
France	Ateliers & Chantiers de France, Dunkirk, France
Fredst	Frefriksstad Mek Verksted A/S, Fredrikstad, Norway
Fredsv	Fredrikshavns Værft & Flydedok A/S, Fredrikshavn, Denmark
Freric	Frerichswerft AG, Einswarden a/d Weser, Germany; previously
FrerJ	J Frerichs & Co AG
Fuji	Fujinagata Shipbuilding Co, Osaka, Japan
Fullr1	George A Fuller Co, Wilmington, North Carolina, USA; previously
Fulllr2	The Carolina Shipbuilding Co
FurnH	Furness Shipbuilding Co Ltd, Haverton Hill, Middlesbrough
Fyenrd	NV Maatschappij voor Scheeps-en Werktuigbouw 'Fyenoord', Fyenoord, Rotterdam, Netherlands (later merged into – see WiltnF)
G&G	Greenock & Grangemouth Dockyard Co Ltd, Greenock and Grangemouth
G&G1	Grangemouth Dockyard Co, Grangemouth (later – see G&G4)
G&G2	Grangemouth & Greenock Dockyard Co, Greenock; later
G&G3	Greenock & Grangemouth Dockyard Co Ltd, Greenock (later – see GrkDY)
G&G4	Grangemouth & Greenock Dockyard Co, Grangemouth; later
G&G5	Greenock & Grangemouth Dockyard Co Ltd, Grangemouth (later – see Grgmth)
Giessn	C Van der Giessen & Zonen's Scheepswerven NV, Krimpen, Netherlands
Girnd	Forges et Chantiers de la Gironde, France, (B) Bordeaux, (H) Harfleur
GLake	Great Lakes Engineering Works, USA, (A) Ashtabula, Ohio, (E) Ecorse (River Rouge), Michigan
Goole	Goole Shipbuilding & Repairing Co Ltd, Goole
Göta1	Götaverken A/B, Gothenburg, Sweden; previously
GöteN	Göteborgs Nya Verkstads A/B; previously
GöteM	Göteborgs Mekaniska Verkstads A/B
Gourly	Gourlay Brothers & Co (Dundee) Ltd, Dundee; previously Gourlay Brothers & Co
Graysn	H & C Grayson Ltd, Garston, Liverpool
GrayWH	W Gray & Co Ltd, West Hartlepool; previously
Gray18	W Gray & Co (1918) Ltd, West Hartlepool; previously
GrayX	W Gray & Co Ltd (before 1918); previously W Gray & Co
GraySd	W Gray & Co Ltd, Sunderland; previously
GrayWr	Wear Shipyard of W Gray & Co Ltd, Sunderland
GrayXX	W Gray & Co (1918) Ltd
Grgmth	Grangemouth Dockyard Co Ltd, Grangemouth (previously G&G5)
GrkDY	Greenock Dockyard Co Ltd, Greenock (previously G&G3)
Groton	Groton Iron Works, Groton, Connecticut, USA
Gusto	NV Werf Gusto v/h Firma A F Smulders, Schiedam, Netherlands
Halifx	Halifax Shipyards Ltd, Halifax, Nova Scotia, Canada
HallR	Hall, Russell & Co Ltd, Aberdeen
Hamtn1	Wm Hamilton & Co, Port Glasgow; later
Hamtn2	Wm Hamilton & Co Ltd; later
Hamtn3	Wm Hamilton & Co (1928) Ltd; later
Hamtn4	Wm Hamilton & Co Ltd
Hanlon	Hanlon Dry Dock & Shipbuilding Co, Oakland, California, USA
HarbrM	Harbour Marine Co Ltd, Victoria, British Columbia, Canada
Harim1	Harima Dockyard, Harima, Japan; later
Harim2	Harima Shipbuilding & Engineering Co Ltd
Harkes	W Harkess & Son Ltd, Middlesbrough
Helsbg	Helsingborgs Varfs A/B, Helsingborg, Sweden
Helsgr	Helsingörs Jernskibs-og Maskinbyggeri A/S, Helsingör (Elsinore), Denmark
Hendn1	D & W Henderson & Co, Partick, Glasgow; later
Hendn2	D & W Henderson & Co Ltd
Hill	C Hill & Sons (later Ltd), Bristol
HK&Wh	Hong Kong & Whampoa Dock Co Ltd, Kowloon, Hong Kong
HMDYDv	HM Dockyard Devonport, Devonport
HMDYPm	HM Dockyard Pembroke, Pembroke
Hølens	Hølens Verksted A/S, Larvik, Norway
H&W,B	Harland & Wolff Ltd, Belfast
H&WGk	Harland & Wolff Ltd, Greenock (previously – see Caird)
H&WGw	Harland & Wolff Ltd, Govan, Glasgow
H&WIrv	Harland & Wolff Ltd, Irvine
HwldtH	Howaldtswerke AG, Hamburg (previously – see SMvJS)
HwldtK	Howaldtswerke AG, Kiel (previously Howaldtswerke)
Ilv2	Cantiere Navali 'Ilva', Naples, Italy
Ingall	Ingalls Ship Building Corp, Pascagoula, Mississippi, USA
Ingls1	A & J Inglis, Glasgow; later
Ingls2	A & J Inglis Ltd
IntDzg	International Shipbuilding & Engineering Co Ltd, Danzig
IntPas	International Shipbuilding Co, Pascagoula, Mississippi, USA
Irvin1	Irvine's Shipbuilding & Dry Docks Co Ltd; previously

Irvin2	Irvine & Co
Irvin3	Irvine's Shipbuilding & Dry Docks Co Ltd, Middleton Shipyard, West Hartlepool; previously
Irvin4	Furness Withy Co Ltd
Ishkwa	Ishikawajima Shipbuilding & Engineering Co Ltd, Tokyo, Japan
Jonker	NV Scheepswerf en Gashouderbouw voorheen Jonker & Stans, Hendrik Ido Ambacht, Netherlands
Kaldns	Kaldnes Mek Verksted, Tønsberg, Norway
Kawami	Kawaminami Kogyo KK, Koyagi Island, Nagasaki, Japan
Kiang	Kiangnan Dock & Engineering Works, Shanghai, China
Kingst	Kingston Shipbuilding Co Ltd, Kingston, Ontario, Canada
KobeSW	Kobe Steel Works, Harima Dockyard, Kobe, Japan
Koch	Schiffswerft von Henry Koch (later AG), Lübeck, Germany
Kockum	Kockums Mekaniska Verksteds A/B, Malmö, Sweden
Köge	Köge Værft Skibs og Maskinbyggeri A/S, Kjöge, Denmark
Krupp	Fried Krupp Germaniawerft AG, Kiel, Germany
Kuy&R	Van der Kuy & Van der Rees NV (Werf Maasdijk), Schiedam, Netherlands
Kwsaki	Kawasaki Dockyard Co Ltd, Kobe, Japan
Laing	Sir James Laing & Sons Ltd, Sunderland; previously Sir James Laing
Langsd	Langesunds Mek Verksted A/S, Langesund, Norway
Laport	Laporte & Compagnie, Rouen, France
Larvik	Larvik Slip & Verksted A/S, Larvik, Norway
Laxe	Laxevaags Maskin & Jernskibsbyggeri, Bergen, Norway (later – see Bergen)
LBeach	Long Beach Shipbuilding Co, Long Beach, California, USA
Lderry	Londonderry Shipbuilding & Engineering Co Ltd, Londonderry
Leslie	R & W Hawthorn, Leslie & Co Ltd, Hebburn
Limham	Limhamns Skeppsvarv A/B, Limhamn, Sweden
Lindhm	Lindholmens Verkstads A/B, Gothenburg, Sweden; later
LindMo	A/B Lindholmen Motala; later
LindVv	A/B Lindholmens Varv
Lithgw	Lithgows Ltd, Port Glasgow; previously
LithR	Russell & Co
LivCpr	Livingstone & Cooper Ltd, Hessle
LloydA	Lloyd Austriaco, Trieste, Austria-Hungary; later
LloydT	Arsenale del Lloyd Triestino, Trieste, Italy
LloydR	Lloyd Royal Belge (Great Britain) Ltd, Whiteinch, Glasgow (later absorbed into – see Curle)
Lobith	'Lobithsche' Scheepsbouw Maatschappij v/h Gebroeder Bodewes NV, Lobith, Netherlands
Loire	Ateliers et Chanters de la Loire, France (N) Nantes, (S) St Nazaire
Lond&G	London & Glasgow Engineering & Iron Shipbuilding Co Ltd, Govan, Glasgow
LosAng	Los Angeles Shipbuilding & Drydock Corp, San Pedro, California, USA
Lübec1	Lübecker Flender-Werke AG, Lübeck/Siems, Germany; previously
Lübec2	Schiffs u Dockbauwerft Flender AG
LübecM	Lübecker Maschinenbau Gesellschaft, Lübeck, Germany
McDoug	McDougall-Duluth Shipbuilding Co, Duluth, Minnesota, USA
Mackay	Mackay Bros, Alloa
Mackie	Mackie & Thomson, Govan, Glasgow
McL&S	McLeod & Sons, Alloa
McMlln	A McMillan & Son Ltd, Dumbarton
Manito	Manitowoc Shipbuilding Corp, Manitowoc, Wisconsin, USA
Marine	Marinewerft (Navy Shipyard), Wilhelmshaven, Germany
MartiL	Shipbuilding & Engineering Works 'Andre Marti', Leningrad, USSR
MartiN	Shipbuilding Yard 'Andre Marti', Nicolaieff, USSR
Matsuo	Matsuo Iron Works & Dockyard, Nagasaki, Japan
Médit	Société Anonyme des Forges et Chantiers de la Méditerranée, France, (H) Havre, (S) La Seyne
Merch	Merchant Shipbuilding Corp, USA (C) Chester, Pennsylvania, (H) Harriman, Pennsylvania
Merril	Merrill-Stevens Shipbuilding Corp, Jacksonville, Florida, USA
Meyer	Meyer & Co's Scheepsbouw Maatschappij NV, Zaltbommel, Netherlands
Mitsu	Mitsubishi Zosen Kaisha, Japan (H) Hikoshima, (K) Kobe, (N) Nagasaki, (Y) Yokohama
MM	Messageries Maritimes, La Ciotat (later – see Provçle)
Mobile	Mobile Shipbuilding Co, Mobile, Alabama, USA
Monmth	Monmouth Shipbuilding Co Ltd, Chepstow, Monmouthshire (later – see Chepst)
Moore1	Moore & Scott Iron Works, Oakland, California, USA; later
Moore2	Moore Shipbuilding Co; later
Moore3	Moore Dry Dock Co
Moss	A/S Moss Værft & Dokk, Moss, Norway
Mtsui1	Mitsui Bussan Kaisha, Tama, Japan; later
Mtsui2	Tama Shipbuilding Co Ltd
Murdo1	Murdoch & Murray, Port Glasgow; later
Murdo2	Murdoch & Murray Ltd
Nakskv	Nakskov Skibsværft A/S, Nakskov, Denmark
Napier	R Napier & Sons Ltd, Dalmuir (later – see Beardm)
Napr&M	Napier & Miller Ltd, Old Kilpatrick, Glasgow
Nat3R	National Shipbuilding Corp, Three Rivers, Quebec, Canada
Nbskrg	Werft Nobiskrug GmbH, Rendsburg, Germany
Nburgh	Newburgh Shipyards Inc, Newburgh, New York, USA
NedDok	Nederlandsche Dok Maatschappij NV, Amsterdam, Netherlands
NedSM	Nederlandsche Scheepsbouw Maatschappij NV, Amsterdam, Netherlands
Neptn1	AG Neptun, Rostock, Germany; later
Neptn2	Neptunwerft Rostock Schiffswerft und Maschinenfabrik GmbH
Nervn	Sociedad Anonima de Los Astilleros Del Nervion, Bilbao, Spain (later – see EspB)
Nevsky	Nevsky Shipbuilding & Mechanical Works, Leningrad, USSR
NewEng	New Engineering & Shipbuilding Works Ltd, Shanghai, China
NewWat	New Waterway Shipbuilding Co, Schiedam, Netherlands

Nitta	Nitta Shipbuilding Yard, Osaka, Japan
NNews	Newport News Shipbuilding & Dry Dock Co, Newport News, USA
NofIre	North of Ireland Shipbuilding Co Ltd, Londonderry
Norddt	Norddeutsche Werft GmbH, Wesermünde, Germany (previously – see Rickmr)
NordsE	Nordseewerke Emden GmbH, Emden, Germany
NordUW	Norddeutsche Union Werke AG, Tonning, Germany
Normnd	Chantier de Normandie, Grand Quévilly, Rouen, France (a subsidiary of Chantier et Ateliers de Saint Nazaire (Penhoët) SA)
NovaSC	Nova Scotia Steel & Coal Co Ltd, New Glasgow, Nova Scotia, Canada
Nthmb1	Northumberland Shipbuilding Co Ltd, Howden-on-Tyne; later
Nthmb2	Northumberland Shipbuilding Co (1927) Ltd
Nüscke	Nüscke & Co AG, Stettin-Grabow, Germany
NWBrdg	Northwest Bridge & Iron Co, Portland, Oregon, USA; previously
NWStl	Northwest Steel Co
Nyland	Nylands Verksted, Oslo, Norway
NYHbr	New York Harbor & Dry Dock Corp, Port Jefferson, New York, USA
NYSB3	New York Shipbuilding Co, Camden, New Jersey, USA; previously
NYSB2	American Brown Boveri Electric Corp; previously
NYSB1	New York Shipbuilding Corp
Odense	Odense Staalskibsværft ved A P Møller, Odense, Denmark
Odero1	N Odero fu A, Sestri-Ponente, Italy; later
Odero2	Nicolo Odero fu A & Co
Orlogs	Orlgosværftet, Copenhagen
Örsnd1	Nya Varvsaktiebolaget Öresund, Landskrona, Sweden; later
Örsnd2	Öresundsvarvet A/B
Osaka	Osaka Iron Works, Japan (I) Innoshima, (O) Osaka
OsbGr1	Osbourne, Graham & Co, Hylton, Sunderland; later
OsbGr2	Osbourne, Graham & Co Ltd
Oskar	Oskarshamns Varv A/B, Oskarshamn, Sweden
Ostsee	Ostsee-Werft, Schiffbau und Maschinenfabrik AG, Frauendorf, Stettin, Germany
OTO	Odero-Terni-Orlando Societa per la Costruzione di Navi, Italy (G) Genoa, (L) Leghorn, (M) Muggiano, Spezia; from amalgamation of (and successors to)
OTO1	N Odero & Co, Genoa; later
OTO2	Cantieri Navali Odero SA
OTO3	Fratelli Orlando (later & Co), Leghorn
OTO4	Cantieri Navali Della Spezia, Muggiano, Spezia
OTO5	Fiat San Giorgio, Muggiano, Spezia
OTO6	Ansaldo San Giorgio, Muggiano, Spezia
OTO7	Società Odero-Terni Orlandi, Muggiano, Spezia
Ouse	Ouse Shipbuilding Co Ltd, Goole
PacC	Pacific Coast Shipbuilding Co, Bay Point, California, USA
Palmer	Palmers Shipbuilding & Iron Co Ltd, Jarrow and Hebburn-on-Tyne
PenhtS	Chantiers de l'Atlantique (Penhoët), St Nazaire, France (see also Normnd)
Penns	Pennsylvania Shipyards Inc, Beaumont, Texas, USA
Pensac	Pensacola Shipbuilding Co, Pensacola, Florida, USA
Pgill1	William Pickersgill & Sons, Sunderland; later
Pgill2	William Pickersgill & Sons Ltd
Polson	Polson Iron Works Co Ltd, Toronto, Ontario, Canada
Porsgr	Porsgrund Mek Verksted, Porsgrunn, Norway
Pot	NV Scheepsbouwwerf Gebr Pot, Bolnes, Netherlands
Poutlv	Poutilov Shipyard, Leningrad, USSR
Provçl	Société Provençale de Constructions Navales, La Ciotat, France (previously – see MM)
ProvPB	Société Anonyme des Chantiers et Ateliers de Provence, Port de Bouc, France
PrRup	Prince Rupert Dry Dock & Repair Co, Prince Rupert, British Columbia, Canada
Prstm1	J Priestman & Co, Sunderland; later
Prstm2	Sir John Priestman & Co
PtArth	Port Arthur Shipbuilding Co Ltd, Port Arthur, Ontario, Canada
Pusey	Pusey & Jones Co, USA (G) Gloucester, New Jersey, (W) Wilmington, Delaware
Qurnro	Cantieri Navali del Quarnaro SA, Fiume, Italy
Ramage	Ramage & Ferguson Ltd, Leith
RDuck1	Richardson, Duck & Co, Stockton-on-Tees; later
RDuck2	Richardson, Duck & Co Ltd
Reid	John Reid & Co Ltd, Whiteinch, Glasgow
Reiher	Reiherstieg Schiffswerfte & Maschinenfabrik, Hamburg, Germany (later – see DeutsR)
Rennld	Chas Rennoldson & Co, South Shields
Rhead1	J Readhead & Co, South Shields; later
Rhead2	J Readhead & Sons; later
Rhead3	J Readhead & Sons Ltd
Rickmr	Rickmers Reismuhlen Rhederi & Schiffsbau AG, Bremerhaven, Germany (later – see Norddt)
Rijkee	NV Werf Voorheen Rijkee & Co, Rotterdam, Netherlands
Rødby	Rødbyhavns Dok og Skibsværft AS, Rødby Havn, Denmark
Rodger	A Rodger & Co, Port Glasgow
Ropnr3	Ropner Shipbuilding & Repairing Co (Stockton) Ltd, Stockton-on-Tees (later – see SmithS); previously
Ropnr2	Ropner & Sons Ltd; previously
Ropnr1	Ropner & Son
Rosenb	A/S Rosenberg Mekaniske Verksted, Stavanger, Norway
RottDD	NV Rotterdamsche Droogdok Maatschappij, Rotterdam, Netherlands
Saginw	Saginaw Shipbuilding Co, Saginaw, Michigan, USA
Sandvk	Sandvikens Skeppsdocka & Mekaniska Verkstad A/B, Helsingfors (Helsinki), Finland
Savoia	Cantieri Officine Savoia, Genoa-Cornigliano, Italy
Scheld	NV Koninklijkemaatschappij, Scheepsbouw-en Werktuigenfabriek 'De Schelde', Vlissingen, Netherlands
Schich	F Schichau GmbH, Elbing, Danzig, Germany

Schuyt	J & A Van der Schuyt Scheepswerf & Maschinefabriek, Papendrecht, Netherlands
Scott1	Scott & Co, Greenock; later
Scott2	Scott's Shipbuilding & Engineering Co Ltd
SeatCD	Seattle Construction & Dry Dock Co, Seattle, Washington, USA (later – see ToddDD)
SeatNP	Seattle-North Pacific Shipbuilding Co, Seattle, Washington, USA
Seebk1	G Seebeck AG, Wesermünde, Germany; later
Seebk2	Deutsche Schiff-und Maschinenbau AG Werke Seebeck Wesermünde
Seine	Ateliers et Chantiers de la Seine Maritime Worms & Co, Le Trait, Seine Inférieure, France
Sevast	Sevastopol Marine Works, Sevastopol, USSR
Sevrny	Severney Shipbuilding Yard 'A Jdanov', Leningrad, USSR
SH	C S Swan & Hunter, Wallsend; later
SH1	C S Swan & Hunter Ltd (see SHWR)
Shangh	Shanghai Dock & Engineering Co Ltd, Shanghai, China
Short1	Short Bros, Pallion, Sunderland; later
Short2	Short Bros Ltd
SHWR	Swan, Hunter & Wigham Richardson Ltd, Wallsend, (Sd) Sunderland (an amalgamation of Wighm1 and SH1)
61Komm	Shipbuilding Yard '61 Kommunar', Nicolaieff, USSR
Skinnr	Skinner & Eddy Corp, Seattle, Washington, USA
Smit	J & K Smit's Scheepswerven, Netherlands, (K) Kinderdijk, (Kr) Krimpen
SmitJ	NV Scheepswerf Voorheen Jan Smit Czn, Alblasserdam, Netherlands
SmitK	J & K Smit's Scheepswerven, Netherlands (K) Kinderdijk, (Kr) Krimpen a/d Lek
SmitL	NV L Smit & Zoon Scheeps-en Werktuig Bouw, Kinderdijk, Netherlands
SmitP	P Smit Jnr, Rotterdam
SmithM	Smith's Dock Co Ltd, South Bank, Middlesbrough
SmithS	Smith's Dock Co Ltd, Stockton-on-Tees (previously – see Ropnr3)
SMvJS	Schiffswerf und Maschinenfabrik (vormals Janssen & Schmilinsky) AG, Hamburg, Germany (later – see HwldtH)
Sörlan	Sörlandets Skibsbyggeri A/S, Fevig, near Arendal, Norway (previously – see Fevigs)
SOuest	Ateliers et Chantiers Maritimes du Sud-Ouest, Bordeaux, France (previously – see Dyle&B)
SouthW	South Western Shipbuilding Co, San Pedro, California, USA (see under BethSW)
Standd	Standard Shipbuilding Corp, Shooter's Island, New York, USA
Standf	G M Standifer Construction Corp, Vancouver, Washington, USA
Staten	Staten Island Shipbuilding Co, Richmond, New York, USA (later part of Bethlehem Steel Co, Shipbuilding Division)
Steph1	A Stephen & Sons, Linthouse, Glasgow; later
Steph2	A Stephen & Sons Ltd
StephR	R Stephenson & Co Ltd, Newcastle upon Tyne
StettO	Stettiner Oderwerke AG, Stettin-Grabow, Germany
Stülck	H C Stülcken Sohn, Hamburg, Germany
SubmBC	Submarine Boat Corp, Newark, New Jersey, USA
Sundld	Sunderland Shipbuilding Co Ltd, Sunderland
SunSB	Sun Shipbuilding Co, Chester, Pennsylvania, USA; later
SunSBD	Sun Shipbuilding & Dry Dock Co
Superr	Superior Shipbuilding Co, West Superior, Wisconsin, USA
Svndbg	Svendborg Skibsværft og Maskinbyggeri A/S, Svendborg, Denmark
Tacoma	Seattle Tacoma Shipbuilding Corp (Todd Pacific Shipyard Inc), Tacoma, Washington, USA
Taikoo	Taikoo Dockyard & Engineering Co of Hong Kong Ltd, Hong Kong
Tampa	Tampa Shipbuilding & Engineering Co, Tampa, Florida, USA
Teckl	Joh C Tecklenborg AG Schiffswerft u Maschinefabrik, Wesermünde, Germany (later – see Desch2)
Teikku	Teikoku Steamship Co Ltd, Tokyo, Japan
Terry	Terry Shipbuilding Co, Savannah, Georgia, USA
Texas	Texas Steamship Co, Bath, Maine, USA
ThmpR1	Robert Thompson & Sons, Bridge Dockyard, Sunderland; later
ThmpR2	Robert Thompson & Sons Ltd
ThmpsD	W B Thompson & Co Ltd, Dundee (later – see Caledn)
ThmpsJ	J L Thompson & Sons Ltd, North Sands, Sunderland
Thorny	John I Thornycroft & Co Ltd, Woolston, Southampton
Tidew	Tidewater Shipbuilders Ltd, Three Rivers, Quebec, Canada
Tirr2	Cantieri Del Tirreno, Riva Trigoso, Genoa, Italy; previously
Tirr1	Società Esercizio Bacini
Toba	Toba Dockyard, Toba, Japan
ToddDD	Todd Drydock & Construction Corp, Tacoma, Washington, USA
Toledo	Toledo Shipbuilding Co, Toledo, Ohio, USA
Tosi	Cantieri Navali Franco Tosi SA, Taranto, Italy
Trigg	W R Trigg Co, Richmond, Virginia, USA
Trondh	Trondhjems Mekaniske Verksted, Trondheim, Norway
Tsurmi	Tsurumi Seitetsu Zosen KK, Tsurumi, Japan (previously – see Asano)
TurnbT	Thomas Turnbull & Son, Whitby
TyneIr	Tyne Iron Shipbuilding Co Ltd, Willington Quay-on-Tyne (later part of – see ArmWh1)
UnionC	Union Construction Co, Oakland, California, USA
UnionN	Union Naval de Levante SA Astilleros de Valencia, Valencia, Spain
UnionS	Union Shipbuilding Co, Baltimore, Maryland, USA
Uraga	Uraga Dock Co Ltd, Uraga, Japan
VanD1	T van Dijvendijk, Lekkerkerk, Netherlands; later
VanD2	NV T van Dijvendijk Scheepswerf
Versch	Verschure & Co's Scheepswerf & Maschinefabriek, Amsterdam, Netherlands
Vick1	Vickers Armstrongs Ltd, (B) Barrow in Furness, (N) Newcastle upon Tyne (previously – see ArmWh1); previously
VickB2	Vickers Ltd; previously
VickB3	Vickers, Son & Maxim Ltd; previously
VickB4	Naval Construction & Armaments Co Ltd
VirgAl	Virginia Shipbuilding Corp, Alexandria, Virginia, USA

VSE2 Vereinigte Stahlwerke AG, Abteilung Nordseewerke, Emden, Germany; later
VSE1 Nordseewerke Abteilung der Deutsche-Luxemburgischen Bergwerks und Hutten AG (later – see NordsE)
Vuijk A Vuijk & Zonen, Capelle a/d Ijssel, Netherlands
VulcH Stettiner Maschinebau AG 'Vulcan', Hamburg, Germany; later – see Desch4
VulcSt Stettiner Maschinebau AG 'Vulcan', Stettin, Germany

WallSB Wallace Shipbuilding & Dry Dock Co Ltd, Vancouver, British Columbia, Canada
WallSY Wallace Shipyards Ltd, North Vancouver, British Columbia, Canada
Weldng Welding Shipyards Inc, Norfolk, Virginia, USA
Weser AG 'Weser', Bremen, Germany; later – see Desch3
White J Samuel White & Co Ltd, East Cowes
Wigham Wigham Richardson & Co, Walker, Newcastle upon Tyne; later
Wighm1 Wigham Richardson & Co Ltd (see SHWR)
WiltnF Wilton-Fyenoord NV, Netherlands, (R) Rotterdam, (S) Schiedam
Wilton NV Wilton's Maschinefabriek & Scheepswerf, Rotterdam, Netherlands (later merged into – see WiltnF)
WoodS1 Wood, Skinner & Co, Newcastle upon Tyne; later
WoodS2 Wood, Skinner & Co Ltd
Workmn Workman, Clark & Co Ltd, Belfast; later
Work28 Workman, Clark (1928) Ltd
WPipe Western Pipe & Steel Co, San Francisco, California. USA

Yarrow Yarrow & Co Ltd, Scotstoun
YokoDk Yokohama Dock Co Ltd, Yokohama, Japan
YokoIW Yokohama Iron Works, Yokohama, Japan; previously
YokoU Uchida Shipbuilding & Engineering Co Ltd
Yoshi Yoshiura Dockyard, Yoshiura, Japan

Zeelnd NV Werf 'Zeeland', Hansweert, Netherlandst

Losses

This section includes
◊ Losses through marine hazard,
◊ Losses through Second World War causes, including Axis states' vessels ceded to or prizes of Allied nations
◊ Losses through Spanish Civil War causes
◊ Vessels scuttled for war purposes (mainly as blockships)
◊ Vessels sunk as breakwaters at Mulberry harbour, Normandy, in 1944
◊ Vessels lost postwar through striking mines
◊ Vessels sunk postwar with surplus war materials
◊ Changes of name, flag, role and disposals

In these sections events occurring between January 1 1939 and December 31 1945 are included, and additional information, taken beyond 1945, for example to indicate final disposition of sunken vessels which were raised and broken up or repaired, even as late as the 1960s.

Japanese names

In 1937 the Japanese government adopted the Romaji spelling system instead of the Latin version of Japanese names. This spelling was used in the Register of Ships of Lloyd's Register of Shipping from the 1938–39 edition to the 1949–50 edition, although the system had been discarded much earlier. For consistency with the leading reference, the spelling style adopted by Lloyd's Register is used in the Japanese listing in this book. For company names the former style is also indicated.

Publications consulted

British Standard Ships of World War I, W H Mitchell and L A Sawyer
British Vessels Lost at Sea 1939–45, HMSO
Casualty Returns 1939–1950, Lloyd's Register of Shipping
Chronology of the War at Sea, J Rohwer
Conway's All the Worlds Fighting Ships
Dictionary of Disasters at Sea in the Age of Steam, Lloyd's Register of Shipping, 1969
Directory of Shipowners, Shipbuilders and Marine Engineers, various editons 1930–1960
Empire Ships of World War II, W H Mitchell and L A Sawyer
From America to United States, L A Sawyer and W H Mitchell, volumes 1–4
Lloyd's War Losses, published by Lloyd's of London press Ltd 1989
Lloyd's Register, *Register of Ships,* various issues
Lloyd's Shipping Index, various issues 1938–1953
Marine News, various editions 1947–1998
Merchant Ships, E C Talbot-Booth, various editions 1934–1950
North Atlantic Seaway, N R P Bonsor, volumes 1–5
Register of Ships, various editions 1890–1956, Lloyd's Register of Shipping
Sea Breezes, various editions 1946–1998
Ships of the Royal Navy, J J Colledge; volumes 1 and 2
South Atlantic Seaway, N R P Bonsor
U-Boat Operations of the Second World War, K Wynn, volumes 1 and 2
Victory Ships and Tankers, W H Mitchell and L A Sawyer
Various company histories, published by World Ship Society

THE WORLD'S MERCHANT FLEETS

Argentina

Funnel: Yellow, black top, narrow black band
Hull: Black
Services: General tramping; oil and petroleum trades

Note: Also a large fleet of vessels employed on R Plate local services
Note: This company controlled Compañía Uruguaya de Navegación Ltda (*qv* in Uruguay section)

COMPAÑÍA ARGENTINA DE NAVEGACIÓN MIHANOVICH LTDA,
Calle Cangullo 300, esquina Calle 25 de Mayo, Casilla 1593, Buenos Aires

General cargo vessels								
Parana	1915	TyneIr	3286	4876	349–7	46–11	21–2	10.0
ex Gaboon 33								
Riogrande	1921	Clyde	3564	7700	350.0	50–2	25–10	9.0
ex Tivy 35, ex Foldenfjord 29, ex Remus 28								
Uruguay (P18)	1921	DeMaas	3425	7010	359.4	50–2	24–1	9.0
ex Star of Alexandria 36, ex Anjer 34, laid down as Maristo								
Tankers								
Juncal	1923	ArmWhl	5810	8869	423–8	52–2	26–5	10.0
ex San Quirino 39								
Los Pozos	1924	ArmWhl	5805	8890	423–9	52–2	26–6	10.0
ex San Salvador 39								

Funnel: Yellow with black top and blue over white over blue bands
Hull: Black
Services: Whaling

Note: Also a fleet of whalers and other small vessels

COMPAÑÍA ARGENTINA DE PESCA, SOCIEDAD ANÓNIMA,
Calle Bartolomé Mitre 559, Buenos Aires

Whale factory vessel								
Ernesto Tornquist	1897	Connl	6547	8000	450.0	52–6	26–4	10.0
ex Kommandören I 27, ex Hampstead Heath 23, ex Craftsman 19; conv general cargo 23								
Whale oil carrier (barrels)								
Harpon	1897	Blohm	4940	6200	401.5	46–5	26–0	9.0
ex Zaandijk 26, ex Silesia 20, ex Wally 98; conv general cargo 26								

Trades: Oil and petroleum, mainly West Indies–Argentina
Note: This company, a subsidiary of Compañía Italo-Argentina de Electricidad, also owned small tankers

COMPAÑÍA GENERAL DE COMBUSTIBLES SOCIEDAD ANÓNIMA,
Calle Tucuman 141, Buenos Aires

Tankers								
Juvenal (s2)	1928	CRDA1	9459	13,700	556–0	74–1	29–11	11.5
Tacit	1924	Nthmbl	4783	7200	441–9	57–0	26–1	9.5

Funnel: Yellow with blue Ω (omega) black top;
Ariston – orange with yellow Ω
Hull: Black or grey
Services: General tramping; oil and petroleum trades

Notes: *, ** Sold Greece 1939, renamed *Miramare* and *Miraflores* respectively; † sold Norway when building

ONASSIS, ARISTOTELES S, Calle Reconquista 336, Buenos Aires

Under Panamanian flag								
General cargo vessels								
Onassi Pinelopi*	1919	CanVic	5404	8393	413–1	52–5	25–3	10.5
ex Canadian Spinner 33								
Onassi Socratis**	1919	CanVic	5439	8390	413–1	52–4	25–3	10.5
ex Canadian Miller 33								
Tanker								
Aristophanes† (m2)	bldg	Göta	10,224	15,360	515–2	64–5	29–8	13.0

A/B A S ONASSIS,
Norra Hamngatan 6, Gothenburg, Sweden (manager Gustav E Sandström) (Swedish flag)

Tanker								
Ariston (m2)	1938	Göta	10,566	15,360	515–10	64–4	29–8	13.0

Funnel; Grey with black top or yellow, with YPF emblem
Hull: Black, red boot-topping
Trades: Oil and petroleum, mainly in R Plate region; West Indies–R Plate
Note: YPF, controlled by the Government of Argentina, also owned tankers engaged in R Plate trade

YACIMIENTOS PETROLIFÉROS FISCALES, (YPF), Buenos Aires

Tankers								
Ministro Frers	1927	GirndB	8868	11,350	485–7	63–5	24–8	11.5
San Jorge (m,P–)	1938	Blohm	10,006	11,620	542–5	61–11	25–6	13.0
San Matias	1928	CRDA1	5518	7500	396.4	55–3	23–6	10.0
ex Astra III 37								
13 de Diciembre (P80)	1935	DeutsH	9503	11,070	522–6	60–10	24–6	13.5

A S Onassis: *Although not Argentinean-flagged,* Onassi Socratis *was one of two sisterships beneficially owned by Aristoteles S Onassis, then based in Buenos Aires. Built in Canada in 1919, this vessel was sold to Greek interests in 1939 and renamed* Miraflores. *In 1941 she passed to Japanese owners as* Enzyu Maru, *and in 1944 was sunk by USN carrier-based aircraft (Alex Duncan)*

Petrofina: Laurent Meeus *was completed at the Rotterdam Drydock shipyard in March 1930 for this Belgian oil company. She was fitted with a Harland & Wolff oil engine manufactured in Glasgow.* Laurent Meeus *tanker served the Allied cause throughout the Second World War, which it survived, and after a few years trading postwar arrived at Ghent in November 1953 to be broken up (Courtesy Petrofina, Brussels; photograph by Damienne de Harbez)*

Compagnie Maritime Belge: Elisabethville, *built for the passenger and mail service from Antwerp to the Belgian Congo, was completed in November 1921 by John Cockerill at Hoboken. She was continuously involved in that service until the occupation of Belgium, when she passed to Ministry of Shipping control and was under Lamport & Holt management. During the war years she carried over 85,000 Allied military personnel. CMB vessels made an important contribution to the Allied effort, and the company lost 294 seagoing personnel and many of its ships as a result of enemy action. In 1946* Elisabethville *was returned to CMB, but only for a few months, as in May 1947 she was sold to the Ministry of Transport, refitted at Liverpool for trooping duty, and renamed* Empire Bure. *She completed this duty in 1949 and was laid up in early 1950. Sold the same year to the Chandris group she was renamed* Charlton Star, *and in 1958 became* Maristrella *under the Liberian flag. She was broken up at Osaka two years later (CMB archives)*

Belgium

Funnel: Yellow, black top
Hull: Light grey, red boot-topping
Trades: Oil and petroleum

BELGIAN GULF OIL CO SA, Avenue de France 97–99, Antwerp

Tankers

Name	Year	Builder	GRT	DWT	Length	Beam	Draught	Speed
Alexandre André (m)	1928	Burger	5261	7341	392–10	54–5	24–4	10.5
Belgian Gulf (m2)	1929	Burger	8401	11,686	468–10	61–4	27–10	10.5
Good Gulf (m)	1938	HwldtK	7874	11,190	498–4	59–6	26–6	11.5
Lubrafol (m2)	1924	ArmWh1	7138	10,850	455–0	57–5	26–4	9.5
Spidoleïne (m2)	1928	France	6190	8470	403.1	52–6	26–1	10.0

Funnel: Black with emblem on white disc surrounded by blue ring, superimposed on red over white bands
Hull: Grey, red boot-topping
Trades: Oil and petroleum

Note: See also Société Anonyme Purfina Transports in France section

COMPAGNIE FINANCIÈRE BELGE DES PETROLES (PETROFINA) SA, 11 Rue du Commerce, Brussels

Tankers

PURFINA-ARMEMENT SOCIÉTÉ ANONYME, Rue Wuppers 4, Antwerp

Name	Year	Builder	GRT	DWT	Length	Beam	Draught	Speed
President Francqui (m)	1928	NewWat	5077	7000	401.0	53–0	23–0	9.5
lengthened 38								

SOCIÉTÉ PURFINA-MARITIME, Rue Wuppers 4, Antwerp

Name	Year	Builder	GRT	DWT	Length	Beam	Draught	Speed
Laurent Meeus (m)	1930	RottDD	6429	8900	401.7	55–2	26–11	10.0

Funnel: Yellow
Hull: Light grey, red boot-topping
Services: Antwerp–Rio de Janeiro–Rosario–Pernambuco–Montevideo–Bahia Blanca–Santos–Buenos Aires–Santa Fé; Antwerp–New York; Antwerp–W Africa–Matadi; Antwerp–Suez–E Africa–Beira

COMPAGNIE MARITIME BELGE (LLOYD ROYAL) SA, Rempart Ste Cathérine 16, Antwerp

Name	Year	Builder	GRT	DWT	Length	Beam	Draught	Speed
Passenger/general cargo vessels								
Albertville (r/t2,P352/1,/2)	1928	LoireS	10,629	7285	537–3	62–0	26–4	16.0
lengthened 37								
Baudouinville (m2,P179/1,116/2,100/3)	1939	Cockll	13,544	6990	541–9	67–8	25–11	16.0
Copacabana (m,P174/cab)	1938	Cockll	7246	7750	459–9	61–6	26–8	15.0
Elisabethville (s2,P165/1,114/2)	1921	Cockll	8300	7280	459–0	57–0	25–6	14.0
Grisarville (m2,P179/1,116/2,100/3)	bldg	Cockll	13,550	6990	541–9	67–8	25–11	16.0
Leopoldville (r/t2,P177/1,178/2)	1929	Cockll	11,439	7154	501.8	62–2	25–11	16.0
lengthened 37								
Mar del Plata (m,P174/cab)	1938	Cockll	7246	7721	459–9	61–6	26–8	15.0
Piriapolis (m,P174/cab)	1938	Cockll	7246	7750	459–9	61–6	26–8	15.0
Thysville (s2,P165/1,114/2)	1922	Cockll	8300	7280	459–0	57–0	25–7	14.0
General cargo vessels								
Alex Van Opstal (m,P12)	1937	Nakskv	5833	8170	447–4	57–1	26–1	15.0
Alex Van Opstal (m,P12)	order	Cockll	6157	8202	448–2	57–1	26–11	14.0
Armand Grisar (m,P12)	order	Cockll	6150	8205	448–0	57–1	26–11	14.0
Astrida (P–)	1929	RottDD	3405	5075	339.9	48–6	21–7	12.0
Atlantier (m,P8)	bldg	Örsnd2	4911	9400	453–9	57–1	25–7	15.0
Carlier (P–)	1915	Flensb	7217	11,850	471.1	60–11	28.6	11.0
ex Itauri 21								
Eglantier* (P–)	1918	Workmn	5355	8100	412–0	52–4	25–3	12.0
ex War Beetle 19								
Emile Francqui (P–)	1929	Flensb	5783	9300	443.7	57–4	25–9	13.0
Félicien Cattier (m,P12)	order	Cockll	6157	8189	448–0	57–1	26–11	14.0
Gouverneur Galopin (m,P12)	order	Cockll	6157	8189	448–0	57–1	26–11	14.0
Henri Jaspar (P30)	1929	RottDD	5719	9285	460–0	57–2	25–9	13.0
Indier	1918	Prstm1	5257	8110	412–9	52–4	25–3	11.0
ex War Redcap 19								

Jean Jadot (P–)	1929	Flensb	5783	9300	443.7	57–4	25–9	13.0
Josephine Charlotte (P–)	1929	RottDD	3405	5075	339.9	48–6	21–7	12.0
Kabalo	1917	Cammel	5051	7950	412–9	52–5	25–3	11.0
ex Caledonier 27, ex War Myrtle 19								
Kabinda	1917	H&W,B	5051	7950	412–9	52–5	25–1	11.0
ex Belgier 27, ex War Shamrock 19								
Kasongo	1918	Steph2	5112	7906	412–9	52–4	25–3	11.0
ex Trevier 26, ex War Hunter 19								
Katanga (P9)	1917	SHWR	5052	7950	412–10	52–4	25–4	11.0
ex Keltier 26, ex War Daffodil 19								
Londonier** (P–)	1919	LloydR	5355	8150	412–9	52–4	25–4	11.0
Macedonier (P–)	1921	LloydR	5136	8160	412–8	52–4	25–3	11.0
Mayumbé†	1929	AwpEng	3567	5300	347.1	49–0	21–8	10.5
Mercier	1915	Bremer	7886	11,850	476.2	60–9	28–6	10.5
ex Erfurt 22								
Moanda (m)	1937	Cockll	4511	7415	409–11	54–0	24–8	13.0
Mobeka (m)	1937	Flensb	5086	8250	449–5	55–9	25–2	13.0
Moero (m)	1937	Flensb	5086	8220	449–5	55–9	25–2	13.0
Mokambo (m)	1938	Flensb	4878	8500	414.3	55–9	25–3	13.0
Olympier (P–)	1920	LloydR	5174	8170	412–5	52–2	25–3	11.5
Persier (P–)	1918	Nthmbl	5232	8200	412–4	52–4	25–3	11.5
ex War Buffalo 19								
Pionier*** (P–)	1919	HK&Wh	5226	8260	412–4	52–4	25–5	11.5
launched as War Bomber								

Charterers of
ÉTABLISSEMENT VAN HEYGHEN FRÈRES
General cargo vessel

Gandia (s2)	1907	SHWR	9626	13,586	480–0	59–11	29–7	13.5
ex Königstein 39, ex Arawa 28; conv passenger/general cargo 39								

Note: * Sold Yugoslavia 1939, renamed *Sréca*; **sold Greece 1939, renamed *Illenao* (Panamanian flag); *** sold Greece 1939, renamed *Carmar* (Panamanian flag); † sold Adriatica Soc Anon di Nav, Italy, 1939, renamed *Bosforo*

DENS-OCÉAN SOCIÉTÉ ANONYME, COMPAGNIE,
Place de Meir 52, Antwerp

Funnel: Yellow with black top separated by yellow lion on broad blue band
Hull: Grey, red boot-topping
Services: Antwerp–London–Newcastle–Spain–Genoa–Naples–Sicily–Greece–Tunisia–Algeria–Morocco

Fruit carriers

Prince de Liège (m,P12/1)	1938	Cockll	2480	4215	323–2	45–2	20–6	12.5
Prinses Maria-Pia (m,P12/1)	1938	Cockll	2480	4215	323–2	45–2	20–6	12.5

DEPPE, ARMEMENT, Rue de Bordeaux 8–10, Antwerp

Funnel: Yellow or yellow, black top
Hull: Black, red boot-topping
Services: Antwerp–Canada; Antwerp–Marseilles; Antwerp, Dunkirk–Portugal–Spain–Morocco–W Africa–Algeria–Tunisia–Alexandria–Tripoli (Syria)–Beirut–Haifa–Greece–Turkey–Bulgaria–Romania–S Russia; Antwerp–Rio de Janeiro–Rosario–Buenos Aires–Santa Fé; Rotterdam, Antwerp–New Orleans–Havana–Tampico–Veracruz; Antwerp–China–Japan–Siberia

Bruges	1904	Teckl	4984	7800	400.9	52–2	25–5	9.5
ex Kybfels 21								
Bruxelles	1919	Bartm2	5085	8268	412–8	52–4	25–4	10.5
ex Southern 21, launched as War Beagle								
Florida (m)	bldg	Cockll	5542	8100	448–2	57–1	26–1	16.0
Gand	1919	Bartm2	5086	8268	412–8	52–5	25–4	10.5
ex Langley								
Ostende	1903	SHWR	4438	6732	375.1	50–6	25–6	8.0
ex Ehrenfels 21								

COMPAGNIE DE NAVIGATION SUD ATLANTIQUE BELGE

Antverpia	1908	SHWR	4932	7515	401.2	52–6	25–3	8.75
ex Fangturm 21								

COMPAGNIE NATIONAL BELGE DE TRANSPORTS MARITIMES

Brabant (m)	1938	Cockll	2483	1710	307.6	45–2	20–0	11.0
Egypte	1905	Eiderl	2538	4232	283.4	41–11	24.9	8.5
ex Mars 21								
Espagne	1911	Neptnl	1749	2987	299–6	41–1	18–0	8.0
ex Turin 21								
Gironde	1920	AwpEng	1770	2913	261–3	38–2	19–5	9.0
Liège	1908	Flensb	4322	7185	383.7	52–1	24–0	8.5
ex Erhard 14, ex Adelheid Menzell 12								
Louis Sheid (P6)	1920	Norddt	5945	9185	418.5	55–8	25–7	10.0
ex Kendal Castle 31, ex Ultor 21								
Luxembourg	1915	Weser	5809	8888	421.8	56–0	26–0	10.0
ex Sonnenfels 21								
Lys	1908	Neptnl	1609	2623	273–10	38–1	18–5	9.0
ex Bremen 21, ex Minna Cords –								
Portugal	1906	Neptnl	1550	2400	268–9	37–6	16.0	8.0
ex Barmen 22, ex Consul Cords –, ex Minna Boldt –								

Compagnie Maritime Belge: Mar del Plata *was launched on July 1 1938 and delivered on September 17 and was used on her owner's service between northwest Europe and South America. With the German occupation of France she was captured at Bordeaux in June 1940 and placed under the management of the Hamburg-Süd company. Earmarked for the aborted Seelöwe operation, she was given the designation H15. In January 1942* Mar del Plata *became an ambulance carrier for the VTS organisation, and three years later under the same banner was involved in the evacuation of refugees from East Prussia. Badly damaged through striking a mine in May 1945, she was repaired, and returned to CMB. After 12 years further service, she was sold to the DDR and renamed* Heinrich Heine. *She was broken up in Taiwan in 1973 following five years service as the Cypriot-flagged* Cleo 2 *(CMB archives)*

Compagnie Maritime Belge: Mobeka *was completed at Flensburg in August 1937 and was placed on CMB's service from Antwerp to the Belgian Congo. She was fitted with a MAN 5-cylinder oil engine of 3400bhp. Withdrawn from CMB's service upon the German occuption of Belgium,* Mobeka *became available to the Allies, and North Atlantic voyages. On January 19 1942 she ran ashore at Carskey Point, Mull of Kintyre and became a total loss (CMB archives)*

Compañia Sud Americana: Copiapó *was one of three sisterships completed at Nakskov, Denmark, during 1937–38 and used on her owner's service between Chile and northwest Europe via the US. With her two sisterships,* Copiapó *was sold to the US in August 1943 and converted to a troop transport. Laid up after the war, she was sold to Turkey in 1948 and renamed* Ordu. *She was operated on Mediterranean services for over 20 years and was broken up at Halic, Turkey, in 1970 (Compañia Sud Americana)*

Roumanie	1906	Flensb	3563	5502	341.7	48–9	17.2	11.0
ex Pyrgos 21, ex Horncap 20, ex Haimon –								

COMPAGNIE ROYALE BELGO-ARGENTINE

Anvers	1908	Flensb	4322	7023	383.3	52–1	24–0	8.5
ex Ekkehard 14, ex Elsa Menzell 12								
Belgique	1902	Ropnrl	4932	8056	391.0	51–8	26–3	10.0
ex Courtfield 21								
Elisabeth van Belgie	1909	Flensb	4241	7067	387.0	51–0	24–8	10.0
ex Elisabeth von Belgien 11								
Flandres	1914	Weser	5802	8888	437–0	56–2	26–1	10.5
ex Greiffenfels 21								
Hainaut	1905	Blohm	4277	6275	403–11	51–8	22–7	10.0
ex Marksburg 21								
Léopold II	1906	Dobson	2893	5069	331.2	44–2	21–11	9.5
Limbourg (m)	1938	Cockll	2483	1710	307.6	45–2	20–0	11.0

Note: This company also owned/operated vessels under 1500gt

STANDARD AMERICAN PETROLEUM CO SA, 101 Avenue de France, Antwerp

Funnel: Black with white over blue over white bands
Hull: Black, red boot-topping
Trades: Oil and petroleum, mainly Aruba–Antwerp
Note: This company, which was renamed from American Petroleum Co Société Anonyme Belge in May 1939, was controlled by Standard Oil Co of New Jersey (*qv* in United States section)

Tankers

Ampetco (m2)	1926	HwldtK	8718	13,175	490–0	63–2	27–5	11.0
ex Urania 29								
Esso Belgium (m2)	1937	B&W	10,568	15,250	506–0	74–11	29–10	12.5

Brazil

COMPANHIA DE NAVEGAÇÃO LLOYD BRASILEIRO (PATRIMONIO NACIONAL), Praça Servulo Dourado, Rio de Janeiro

Funnel: White, black top
Hull: Black, red boot-topping with white dividing line
Services: Brazilian ports to Montevideo, Buenos Aires, Corumba, Lisbon, Leixoes, Vigo, Havre, Antwerp, Rotterdam, Hamburg; Santos–Rio de Janeiro–New York–Hampton Roads–Baltimore; Rio de Janeiro–New Orleans; Buenos Aires–Rio de Janeiro–Manaus

Passenger/general cargo vessels

Alegrete (P–)	1906	H&W,B	5786	7600	392.0	50–4	25–11	9.0
ex Salamanca 17								
Almirante Alexandrino (P90/1,500/3)	1900	Reiher	5786	5800	426–10	48–4	26–6	10.0
ex Itú 26, ex Cap Roca 17								
Almirante Jaceguay (P111/1,58/2,48/3)	1912	Reiher	6079	6200	408–2	52–5	25–1	12.0
ex General San Martin 26, ex Edmund Wagenknecht 22, ex Professor 21, ex Professor Woermann 15								
Aracajú	1914	Flensb	3569	5000	381–1	51–0	22–8	10.5
ex Persia 17								
Atalaia (P–)	1910	Bremer	5555	8800	419.7	54–6	25–11	10.5
ex Carl Woermann 17								
Ayuruoca	1912	Weser	6872	11,400	468.4	58–5	29–0	12.0
ex Roland 17								
Bagé (s2,P–)	1912	VulcSt	8235	8500	458–0	56–0	23–7	11.5
ex Sierra Nevada 17								
Barbacena	1909	Teckl	4772	–	392.5	51–11	27.3	9.5
ex Gundrun 17								
Cabedello	1912	Flensb	3557	5000	381–1	51–0	22–8	10.5
ex Prussia 17								
Camamú	1911	VulcSt	4613	8000	413–4	52–9	25–2	10.0
ex Steiermark 17								
Caxambú	1909	Teckl	5546	7280	399.3	54–2	22–5	11.0
ex Minneburg 17								
Cuyabá (P356)	1906	Bremer	6489	7520	427–0	52–8	26–0	11.0
ex Hohenstaufen 17								
Iguassú	1912	Flensb	3797	6328	351–0	50–2	24–0	9.0
ex Santa Rosa 17								
Jaboatão	1907	Bremer	4526	6000	386.7	51–9	26–0	10.0
ex Arnold Amsinck 17								
Joazeiro (P40/cab,500/3)	1907	Teckl	4238	5389	350.2	47–3	23–4	10.0
ex Santa Lucia 17								
Lagés	1907	SHWR	5472	8620	421.9	55–4	28.4	9.5
ex Rauenfels 17								
Mandú	1913	Bremer	6588	11,200	491–1	59–2	26–4	12.0
ex Belmonte 19, ex Posen 17								

Parnahyba	1913	Flensb	6692	–	460.5	59–1	28.8	10.0
ex Alrich 17								
Poconé (P32/1,200/3)								
	1908	Bremer	6750	7900	436–4	54–6	25–8	11.0
ex Coburg 17								
Raul Soares (P87/1,500/3)								
	1900	Flensb	6003	7190	425–0	48–4	26–8	10.0
ex Madeira 25, ex Cap Verde 22								
Sabará (m2)	1912	HwldtK	3693	6324	364–0	50–1	23–0	10.0
ex Monte Penedo 17								
Santarém (P32/1,200/3)								
	1908	Bremer	6757	8100	436–4	54–6	25–8	11.0
ex Eisenach 17								
Santos (P80/1,430/3)								
	1898	Reiher	4855	6030	390–5	46–7	24–4	11.5
Siqueira Campos (s2,P–)								
	1907	Reiher	6456	8000	415.6	50–9	26–0	11.5
ex Cantuaria Guimarães 31, ex Curvello 27, ex Gertrud Woermann 17								
Taubaté	1905	Bremer	5099	7800	409.6	52–9	27–0	10.5
ex Franken 17								

Note: Also vessels under 3000gt on coastal services

Bulgaria

Funnel: Black, or white with black top
Hull: Grey or black
Services: Varna–Bourgas–Antwerp–Hamburg; Varna–Italy; Varna–Piræus–Alexandria–Port Said, and other E Mediterranean ports

SOCIÉTÉ COMMERCIALE BULGARE DE NAVIGATION À VAPEUR,
Rue Tzarigrad 1, Varna

Balkan (P31)	1914	ProvPB	3838	5030	353.5	46–8	21–2	11.5
ex Louis Fraissinet 34								
Bourgas	1900	LloydA	2940	3680	315.3	40–10	20–5	12.0
ex Carniolia 28								
Chipka (r/t,P–)	1938	Neptn2	2304	3200	321–0	43–7	18–1	12.0
Knyaguinya Maria Louisa (P28)								
	1919	ProvPB	3821	5075	353.5	46–8	21–2	11.5
ex Félix Fraissinet 33								
Rodina (P12)	1922	VulcSt	4159	6510	377–0	51–0	23–5	10.5
ex Eisenach 35								
Varna (r/t,P–)	1937	Neptn2	2141	3200	321–0	43–7	18–1	12.0

Note: Also vessels under 2000gt

Chile

Funnel: Red, black top, separated by white over blue bands
Hull: Black
Services: Valparaíso and other Chilean ports–R Plate–Santos–Rio de Janeiro

COMPAÑÍA CHILENA DE NAVEGACIÓN INTEROCEANICA,
Casilla 1410, Calle Almirante Señoret 47, Valparaíso

Angol	1923	Workmn	5215	7820	400.1	52–4	25–5	11.5
ex Torr Head 33								
Antofagasta	1921	Palmer	4798	7000	398.5	53–10	23–0	11.5
ex Plum Branch 33								
Arauco (P22/1,28/2)								
	1921	Gray18	5414	6773	363–3	52–6	25–1	10.5
ex Boussole 35, ex Saint Eloi 30, ex Registan 28, ex Saint Roger 22								
Arica (P–)	1931	Duncan	4583	6300	354–0	53–2	23–4	12.0
Punta Arenas (P–)	1920	Earles	4452	6950	388–2	51–9	24–0	10.5
ex Apple Branch 33, launched as War Bobtail								
Tarapacà (P–)	1895	Reiher	3832	4500	343.2	42–5	26.1	11.5
ex President Mitre 23, ex Argentina 07								

Note: Also vessels under 2000gt

Funnel: Red, black top
Hull: Black, red boot-topping
Services: Hamburg–Antwerp–Baltimore–Panama–Callao–Valparaíso

COMPAÑÍA SUD AMERICANA DE VAPORES,
Casilla 49-V, Calle Blanco 895, Valparaíso

Passenger/general cargo vessels

Aconcagua (m,P32/1,132/t)								
	1938	Nakskv	7237	6050	440–6	58–4	23–7	15.5
Copiapó (m,P32/1,132/t)								
	1937	Nakskv	7216	6050	440–6	58–4	23–7	15.5
Imperial (m,P32/1,132/t)								
	1938	Nakskv	7217	6050	440–6	58–4	23–7	15.5

Note: Also coastal vessels

Denmark

ANDRESEN, CHR, Amaliegade 33, Copenhagen

A/S D/S DANIA

Birgit	1924	LübecM	1971	3200	280.0	40–5	18–0	10.0
Bonita (m)	1930	Aalb3	3198	5500	325.6	50–1	20.7	11.0
ex Skule 31								
Cyril	1925	LübecM	2116	3436	292–0	41–9	18–7	9.5
Elie	1921	AwpEng	1873	3200	289–5	40–2	17–9	9.5
Irene Maria	1922	AwpEng	1862	3200	289–5	40–2	17–9	9.5
Tovelil	1925	NewWat	2214	3745	304–1	45–0	18–7	10.0
ex Monica Seed 29								

Funnel: Black with two broad red bands separated by narrow white band, white C on upper red band, white A on lower
Hull: Black or grey
Services: General tramping

Note: Also short-sea vessels

ANGLO-DANISH SHIPPING CO LTD, 8 French Bund, Shanghai

Under Danish flag

Johanne Justesen	1909	Dixon2	4471	7400	372–7	52–0	24–2	9.0
ex Fiona 33								

Funnel: Black
Hull: Black
Services: Tramping in Japan/China/ Far East

BROWN JUN & CO, P, Amaliegade 49, Copenhagen

D/S NORDEN A/S

M C Holm*	1924	Helsgr	2814	5115	335–6	48–5	21–5	9.0
Nordbo (m2)	1923	B&W	4472	8365	380.0	53–11	25–3	11.0
Norden (m2,P7)	1937	Nakskv	4700	8380	429–11	57–4	24–11	13.0
Nordfarer (m2)	1929	Nakskv	4605	8300	401–0	54–5	24–7	11.0
Nordhavet (m2)	1930	B&W	4617	8325	385.6	54–11	24–7	11.0
Nordhval (m2)	1924	B&W	4473	8320	380.0	53–11	25–2	11.0
Nordkap (m2)	1930	Nakskv	4553	8300	401–0	54–5	24–7	11.0
Nordkyn (m)	order	Nakskv	4684	8350	418–0	56–4	24–8	13.0
Nordlys	1916	B&W	3726	6846	378–0	51–6	23–9	10.0
Nordpol (m2)	1926	B&W	4480	8300	380.0	53–11	25–2	11.0
Nordvest (m2,P7)	1938	Nakskv	4702	8380	429–11	57–4	24–11	13.0

Funnel: Black with red band bordered by two white bands
Hull: Light grey, red boot-topping
Services: General tramping

Note: * Sold Germany 1939, renamed *Irmtraut Cords*

CARL, MARTIN, Stockholmsgade 55, Copenhagen

A/S D/S HEIMDAL

Kalø (r/t)	1937	Helsgr	1973	3200	271.8	42–1	19.8	10.5

Funnel: Black with red H on white band
Hull: Grey, red boot-topping
Services: General tramping
Note: Also *Aarø* (built 1925/1426gt), *Askø* (20/1308), *Manø* (25/1415), *Martin Carl* (24/1412), *Sejrø* (29/1489), *Samsø* (30/1494) on ocean voyages

CHRISTENSEN, T C, Amaliegade 33, Copenhagen

D/S HAFNIA A/S

Alssund	1920	SmitJ	3222	5377	345–0	48–9	21–11	9.5
ex Sierra Leone 29								
Brosund	1916	OsakaO	2939	5100	314–11	43–9	23–0	9.0
ex Danevirke 25, ex Winneconne 24, ex Aslaug 20, ex General Wergeland 17, ex Yesaki Maru 16								

Funnel: Black, blue band, white Maltese cross
Hull: Black
Services: General tramping

DANSKE PETROLEUMS A/S, DET, Sankt Annæ Plads 13, Copenhagen K

Tankers

Christian Holm (m2)	1927	B&W	9119	14,026	488–6	64–4	27–10	10.5
ex Christian 29								
Danmark (m2)	1931	B&W	10,517	16,400	490.8	67–10	29–4	12.0
Scandia	1918	NNews	8571	12,760	477–9	60–2	27–8	9.5
ex F D Asche 22								

Funnel: Yellow, black top and red '+' on white band
Hull: Black, red boot-topping
Trades: Oil and petroleum
Note: Det Danske Petroleums A/S, managed by C F Holm, and a subsidiary of Standard Oil Co of New Jersey (*qv* in United States section), also owned vessels of under 2000gt

FORENEDE DAMPSKIBS SELSKAB, DET (United Steamship Co),

Sankt Annæ Plads 30, Copenhagen K

Funnel: Black with red band
Hull: Black, red boot-topping (vessels registered Copenhagen); grey, red boot-topping (vessels registered Esbjerg)
Services: Copenhagen–Oslo–Montreal–New York–Philadelphia–Baltimore–Savannah–New Orleans–Galveston; Scandinavia–Las Palmas–Tenerife–Madeira–Rio de Janeiro–Santos; Copenhagen (various services to)–Casablanca–Cadiz–Tarragona–Valencia–Denia–Malaga–Almeria–Tangier–Algiers–Tunis–Ceuta–Melilla–Oran–Marseilles–Leghorn–Genoa–Bari–Naples–Catania–Messina–Palermo

Alabama (st,P6/1)	1921	Örsndl	4575	8462	417–8	53–8	25–5	9.5
ex Atlantic 30								
Algier (m,P12/1)	1938	Helsgr	1654	2520	288–0	40–5	18–3	13.0
Argentina (m2,P4)	1921	B&W,K	5375	8590	390–0	52–2	24–9	10.5
ex Polarhavet 24								
Arizona (m2,P11/1)	1922	Nakskv	6385	9900	422–4	54–0	28–1	10.5
Brasilien (st,P3/1)	1921	B&W,K	5334	8600	390–0	52–2	24–9	11.0
ex Atlanterhavet 24								
Broholm (r/t,P9/1)	1925	Fredsv	1544	2125	293–3	37–9	17–10	8.5
lengthened 37								
Brynhild	1907	Sundld	2195	3560	295–5	43–6	18–5	8.5
ex Leif 14								
California (m2,P11/1)	1913	B&W	4576	8090	423–6	54–2	25–1	10.5
Delaware (st,P2/1)	1919	Örsndl	2280	4460	323–0	44–6	21–0	9.0
ex Copenhagen 29								
Ebro (P4/1)	1920	HallR	1547	1565	248–0	36–1	16–1	11.0
Frode (P1)	1918	Nyland	2140	3843	300–0	44–3	19–1	9.5
Georgia (st,P2/1)	1920	Örsndl	2272	4460	323–0	44–9	21–0	9.0
ex Yokohama 29								
Gorm	1916	Nyland	2156	3800	300–0	44–3	19–1	9.5
Ivar	1917	Nyland	2145	3810	300–0	44–3	19–1	9.5
Kentucky	1905	Clyde	2136	3860	305–6	42–0	19–11	9.0
ex Generalkonsul Pallisen 23								
Louisiana (m2,P6/1)	1921	Ardrsn	6513	8100	423–9	55–2	28–1	10.5
Marocco (m,P12/1)	1936	Helsgr	1641	2549	288–0	40–5	18–3	13.0
Maryland (P6/1)	1921	HallR	4895	7590	375–0	50–2	26–7	10.5
Nevada (r/t,P2/1)	1917	Helsgr	3766	6925	377–6	50–2	25–2	11.0
Oregon (m2,P3/1)	1916	B&W	4774	8720	422–0	54–2	25–7	10.5
Sicilien (m,P12/1)	1938	Helsgr	1654	2525	288–1	40–5	18–3	13.0
Svanhild (P2)	1919	Nyland	2147	3810	300–6	44–3	19–1	9.5
Tennessee (P2)	1921	Baltca	2342	4225	315–4	44–2	20–11	11.0
ex Fredensbro 29								
Texas (m,P8/1)	1939	Helsgr	2328	4080	346–10	45–10	20–6	12.5
Tunis (m,P10/1)	1936	Helsgr	1641	2530	288–1	40–5	18–3	13.0
Uffe (P2)	1906	GrayX	1889	2930	289–2	40–0	17–8	8.5
Virginia (st,P2)	1920	B&W,K	4088	7550	389–4	52–2	26–0	10.0
ex Pacific 30								

Note: This company also owned a large fleet of vessels on short-sea and coastal trades and ferry services

HANSEN, C K, Amaliegade 35, Copenhagen K

Funnel: Yellow with black top and Danish flag on blue band
Hull: Black or grey
Services: General tramping

A/S D/S DANNEBROG

Christiansborg (st)	1922	SmitJ	3270	5240	343–0	48–9	22–2	10.0
Flynderborg	1930	GrayWH	1999	3320	290–0	40–1	18–9	8.75
Fredensborg	1922	SmitJ	2094	3300	295–2	42–1	19–4	9.0
Frederiksborg	1916	Sørlan	1816	3038	277–7	42–2	17–5	9.0
Nordborg	1930	GrayWH	1998	3267	290–4	40–1	18–7	9.0
Ørneborg	1919	Wilton	1775	2895	282–7	39–0	18–3	8.75
Rosenborg	1914	GrayX	1997	3250	280.0	40–0	18–6	8.75
Silkeborg	1915	Fredst	1806	3060	278–6	42–1	17–7	8.75
Søborg	1924	GrayWH	1993	3270	290–7	40–1	18–6	8.5
Stjerneborg (m2)	1929	B&W	4551	8475	380.0	53–11	25–2	11.0
Uranienborg (st)	1922	B&W,K	3300	6310	360–2	50–2	22–10	10.5
Viborg	1919	SmitJ	2028	3450	295–0	42–2	19–4	8.75

Note: Also *Skodsborg* (built 1919/1450gt) and short-sea vessels

HOLM & WONSILD, Amaliegade 36, Copenhagen

Funnel: Black with blue eight-pointed star on white band
Hull: Light grey, red boot-topping
Services: General tramping

D/S A/S MYREN

Asbjörn (m2,P–)	1935	B&W	4387	8000	399–5	54–9	24–6	13.0
Astrid	1924	B&W,K	1735	2950	273–0	40–1	18–6	9.0
Birte	1921	B&W,K	1741	3000	272–10	40–1	18–6	9.0
Chr Sass (m2)	1931	B&W	3812	7170	380–0	53–7	23–4	11.0
Kai	1921	B&W,K	1746	3000	273–0	40–1	18–6	9.0
Margit	1924	B&W,K	1735	2950	273–0	40–1	18–6	9.0
Stal (st)	1921	Baltca	2242	4275	313–10	44–2	20–10	9.5

Note: Also *Clara* (built 1925/1398gt), *Inga* (21/1494) on ocean voyages

JEBSEN A/S, RHEDERI M, Aabenraa

Funnel: Black
Hull: Black with white band
Services: General tramping

Gustav Diederichsen (P–)	1930	HwldtK	2332	3380	281.2	41–11	20–0	11.0
Heinrich Jessen (P*c*825/d)	bldg	HK&Wh	3335	3320	319–6	46–7	19–6	11.5
Michael Jebsen (P–)	1929	HwldtK	2318	3380	281.2	41–11	20–0	11.0

JENSEN A/S, ALBERT, Islands Brygge 22, Copenhagen

Funnel: White with two narrow red bands with red star between, black top
Hull: White or light grey
Services: Fruit trade – Puerto Armuelles–Los Angeles–San Francisco (charter)

D/S GLORIA A/S

Fruit carriers

Knud Rasmussen (P12)	1929	Curle	5399	4878	405–6	53–2	23–7	15.0
ex Toltec 38								
Peter Lassen (P12)	1929	Curle	5383	4878	405–3	53–2	23–8	15.0
ex Aztec 38								
Vitus Bering (P12)	1929	Curle	5383	4878	405–6	53–2	23–7	15.0
ex Mazatec 38, ex Maya 31								

JENSEN, C P, (Otto Jelstrup), Amaliegade 36, Copenhagen K

Funnel: Black with red eight-pointed star on yellow band
Hull: Black
Services: General tramping

A/S D/S ORION

Astra	1920	Clyde	2398	3800	305–3	44–4	20–0	8.0
ex Ferm 29, ex Saphir 22								
Orion	1919	WoodS2	2405	3950	315–6	43–0	19–10	9.5
Venus	1920	WoodS2	2456	3950	315–6	43–0	19–10	9.5

JENSEN, CHR, Chr IX's Gade 10, Copenhagen

Funnel: Black with red Maltese cross on white band
Hull: Black
Services: General tramping
Note: Also short-sea vessels
Note: See also in Latvia section

D/S BALTIC A/S

Fanø	1922	DeHaan	1889	3269	268.1	42–2	18–0	9.5

LAURITZEN, J, Hammerensgade 1, Copenhagen K

Funnel: Black with two broad red bands separated by narrow white band, white J on upper red band, white L on lower
Hull: Black or white, red boot-topping
Services: Finland–France–N Spain; Memel–Pasajes–Bilbao; Italy–Sicily–Liverpool–Manchester; Spain–UK; Finland–Spain; fruit trades

A/S D/S OCEAN

Fruit carriers and general cargo vessels

African Reefer (m,P4)	1935	Helsgr	1771	2420	318–0	42–8	18–7	13.5
ex Yrsa 36, launched as Pacific Reefer								
American Reefer (m,P4)	1936	Nakskv	2328	2600	354–2	47–10	18–11	15.0
Argentinean Reefer (m,P8/1)	bldg	Aalb4	2826	3355	374–0	51–8	19–4	15.5
Australian Reefer (m,P4)	1937	Aalb4	2321	2600	354–2	47–10	18–11	15.0
Brazilian Reefer (m,P4)	1936	Nakskv	1831	2349	311–4	44–8	18–6	13.5
Canadian Reefer (m,P4)	1936	Nakskv	1831	2400	311–4	44–8	18–6	13.5
Chilean Reefer (m,P4)	1936	Nakskv	1831	2400	311–4	44–8	18–6	13.5

P Brown Jun & Co: Nordvest *was in 1939 a recent addition to the fleet of D/S Norden A/S. With accommodation for seven passengers, and powered by a 2300bhp oil engine, she and her sistership Norden had been completed at Nakskov during 1937–38. In July 1942 she was transferred to USMC ownership, and raised the Panamanian flag as* Alan-A-Dale. *In December 1944, when on voyage from New York to Antwerp with government stores, she was sunk in the Schelde estuary. Her crew of 42 and 23 armed guards were all saved*
(Photograph courtesy D/S Norden A/S)

J Lauritzen: The fruit carrier Australian Reefer, *launched February 6 and delivered March 22 1937 was one of several 'reefers' which this owner introduced in the mid to late 1930s. She had a varied wartime career, which included a USN commission. She was laid up in the James River in August 1945 and at the end of the year was deleted from the Danish register. She was laid up at Baltimore in 1948*
(Photograph courtesy J Lauritzen)

J Lauritzen: Marna, *built by the Helsingør shipyard and completed in May 1936, was powered by a triple-expansion engine with exhaust turbine with a total power of 1750ihp. Under the Ship Requisition Act (US) she was acquired by the USMC, and renamed* Azra *under Panamanian registry. She was in collision with the Canadian destroyer* Saguenay *in November 1942, when on voyage from Botwood to Sydney NS with a cargo of paper and pulp. Following the collision two depth charges fell from the destroyer, one exploded underneath it causing considerable stern damage, and another exploded under* Marna, *causing her to sink.* Saguenay *was towed to St John NB*
(Photograph courtesy J Lauritzen)

Egyptian Reefer (m,P8/1)	1936	Odense	3159	3235	361–6	48–8	22–8	15.5
ex Francine 37								
Frida (r/t)	1936	Helsgr	1700	2900	306–0	41–9	18–7	12.0
Helga (r/t)	1937	Helsgr	1700	2900	306–0	40–6	18–7	14.0
Indian Reefer (m,P8/1)	1939	Helsgr	2815	3400	374–0	51–8	19–4	15.5
Jonna (r/t)	1933	Nakskv	1517	2180	271.8	39–9	15.7	13.5
Laila (r/t)	1936	Helsgr	1700	2825	306–7	41–8	18–7	12.0
Marna (r/t)	1936	Helsgr	1700	2900	306–0	41–9	18–7	12.0
Sessa (r/t)	1936	Helsgr	1700	2900	306–0	41–9	18–7	12.0
Ulla (r/t)	1931	Helsgr	1575	2425	253.5	39–1	17–0	12.0
launched as Kirsten								

D/S VESTERHAVET

Betta	1931	Nakskv	1567	2200	254.2	39–2	17–0	12.0
ex Betty 37								
Else	1906	Helsgr	1970	2200	281.7	42–1	17.9	8.5
ex Kotonia 35								
Erna (r/t)	1930	Helsgr	1590	2460	253.5	39–1	17–1	12.0
Grete (r/t)	1931	Helsgr	1563	2200	253.5	39–1	17–1	12.0
Helene	1922	Koch	2414	4165	296.4	42–6	20–0	8.0
ex Ceres 32, ex Mimi Horn 26								
Johanne	1919	Oskar	2257	3400	285–6	41–2	20–7	10.0
Jutta (r/t)	1934	Helsgr	1549	2700	304–0	39–8	16–6	12.0
Lotta (r/t)	1938	Aalb4	1858	3400	298–10	43–6	19–3	11.0
Maja	1922	Ostsee	2203	3200	263.5	41–1	19–0	9.0
ex Mira 29								
Najaden*	1906	Helsgr	2203	3730	292–4	42–1	20–6	8.0
ex Örkild 28, ex Boscia 10								
Nora (m)	bldg	Aalb4	2937	4500	373–7	51–11	20–2	15.5
Paula (r/t)	1934	Helsgr	1549	2700	304–0	39–9	16–6	12.0
Randa	1930	Nakskv	1555	2430	266–4	39–5	16–11	12.0
ex Basse Terre 37, ex Else 34								

Note: Also *Alfa* (built 1922/844gt), *Anna* (24/1220), *Britta* (21/1146), *Carmen* (20/1206), *Dagmar* (22/844), *Gerda* (21/1151), *Harriet* (22/1144), *Inger* (22/1208), *Jenny* (17/843), *Karla* (20/941), *Laura* (33/1471), *Lilian* (24/1271), *Linda* (36/962), Maria (33/1369), *Nancy* (21/1193), *Nerma* (21/1210), *Niobe* (21/1153), *Selma* (37/1392), *Stella* (33/1394), *Tanja* (37/1392) on ocean voyages, and several short-sea vessels
Note: * Sold Finland 23.11.39

MØLLER, A P, Kongens Nytorv 8, Copenhagen

Funnel: Black with white eight-pointed star on blue band
Hull: Grey or black with name of vessel in large letters amidships, red boot-topping
Services: Regular line – Far East–Los Angeles–Panama–New York; general tramping; oil and petroleum trades

D/S SVENDBORG A/S

General cargo vessels

Cornelia Mærsk (r/t,P–)	1925	Schich	1892	3125	293–5	40–2	18–9	9.0
Jessie Mærsk	1920	Vuijk	1972	3285	292–0	40–2	18–4	8.5
ex Marsdiep 22								
Leise Mærsk (m)	1921	Odense	3136	4915	334–8	44–2	22–3	10.5
lengthened 32								
Lica Mærsk (r/t)	1927	LübecM	2480	4325	308.7	43–11	20–7	10.0
Marit Mærsk	1938	Fredst	1894	3330	301.3	44–8	18–9	13.5
Mathilde Mærsk	1921	Yarrow	2088	3579	296–8	43–5	19–5	9.5
ex Peter Mærsk 31, ex Haderslev 24								
Rita Mærsk (r/t)	1939	Helsgr	1918	3493	299–8	43–6	19–10	11.5
Tanker								
Inge Mærsk (m)	1939	Odense	9397	14,580	501–1	65–6	28–0	12.0

D/S A/S AF 1912

General cargo vessels

Agnete Mærsk	1921	Yarrow	2088	3579	296–8	43–5	19–5	9.5
ex Aabenraa 24								
Arnold Mærsk	1914	GrayX	1966	3250	291–1	40–0	18–6	9.0
Betty Mærsk (r/t)	1922	Odense	2357	3980	311–5	42–8	19–7	9.5
Elisabeth Mærsk (r/t,P–)	1925	Schich	1892	3125	294–1	40–2	18–9	9.0
Emilie Mærsk (r/t)	1922	Odense	2212	3297	297–9	42–5	19–11	9.5
Gunvor Mærsk	1931	GrayWH	1984	3295	286–1	42–4	18–5	10.5
ex Josephine Gray 34								
Hans Mærsk	1916	Vuijk	1937	3250	292–8	40–2	18–6	9.0
Herta Mærsk (r/t)	1939	Fredsv	1890	3450	299–6	43–6	19–10	11.5
Jakob Mærsk (r/t)	1921	Odense	2245	3750	297–9	42–5	19–11	9.5
Johannes Mærsk (r/t,P–)	1925	Schich	1899	3125	292–4	40–2	18–9	9.0
Kirsten Mærsk (r/t)	1920	Odense	2410	3780	311–0	42–5	19–4	9.5
lengthened 34								

Nicoline Mærsk (m2)	1925	Odense	4194	8065	374.8	52–2	24–8	10.5
Oluf Mærsk	1916	Vuijk	1950	3265	292–6	40–2	18–6	9.5
Sally Mærsk (m)	1923	Odense	3252	5230	332.1	44–2	22–3	10.5
Sonja Mærsk	1921	Nüscke	1909	3150	266.8	42–2	17–7	9.5
ex Thekla 29, ex Baldur 25; lengthened 30								
Susan Mærsk	1923	Odense	2355	3990	311–5	42–8	19–8	9.5

D/S SVENDBORG A/S & D/S A/S AF 1912

General cargo vessels

Anna Mærsk (m,P12/1)	1932	Odense	5339	8805	462–2	57–2	25–9	15.0
Chastine Mærsk (m2)	1923	Odense	5177	8015	378.0	50–2	25–7	10.5
Gertrude Mærsk (m2,P6/1)	1930	Odense	5038	8665	437–6	54–9	25–7	13.5
Grete Mærsk (m2,P12/1)	1937	Bremer	6576	9205	497–4	59–5	26–9	16.0
Hulda Mærsk (m,P12/1)	1938	Odense	5601	8690	466–4	57–9	25–5	14.5
Laura Mærsk (m,P12/1)	1939	Odense	6599	9100	483–10	59–1	26–10	15.5
Lexa Mærsk (m,12/1)	1939	Odense	5614	8690	466–4	57–9	25–5	14.5
Marchen Mærsk (m2,P12/1)	1937	Bremer	6580	9205	497–0	59–5	26–9	16.0
Niel Mærsk (m2,P6/1)	1931	Odense	5086	8465	437–6	54–9	25–7	14.0
Peter Mærsk (m,P12/1)	1932	Odense	5476	8805	462–2	57–0	25–9	15.0
Trein Mærsk (m,P12)	bldg	Odense	6706	9430	473–10	60–8	27–1	15.0

Refrigerated cargo vessels

Gudrun Mærsk (m,P4/1)	1937	Odense	2294	4050	341–8	46–2	19–11	14.0
Robert Mærsk (m,P4/1)	1937	Odense	2294	4050	341–9	46–2	19–11	14.0

Tankers

Aase Mærsk (m)	1930	Odense	6184	9605	424–1	54–8	26–10	10.5
Anglo Mærsk (m)	1930	ArmWh2	7705	11,306	461.1	59–11	27–1	11.5
ex Anglo Swede 32								
Bente Mærsk (m)	1928	Odense	5722	8625	411–11	53–9	26–6	11.0
ex Anna Mærsk 32								
Caroline Mærsk (m2)	1928	Odense	7691	12,725	483–7	59–0	27–2	11.0
Caroline Mærsk (m)	bldg	Odense	10,043	15,530	522–6	65–11	28–6	13.0
Eleonora Mærsk (m)	1936	DeutsH	10,694	15,900	523–0	68–8	29–1	12.0
Emma Mærsk (m2)	1928	B&W	8278	13,580	484–5	61–10	28–1	10.5
Henning Mærsk* (m)	1936	Odense	9386	14,650	501–1	65–6	28–0	12.0
Henning Mærsk (m)	bldg	Nakskv	10,106	15,500	513–6	66–9	28–8	12.0
Jane Mærsk (m2)	1928	Odense	7691	12,675	483–7	59–9	28–0	11.0
Katrine Mærsk (m)	1928	Odense	5530	8635	411–8	55–2	25–8	11.0
ex Varg 36								
Marie Mærsk (m2)	1928	B&W	8271	13,580	484–5	61–10	28–2	11.0

Note: * Sold France 1939, renamed *Saintonge*
Note: Also vessels under 1500gt, and short-sea vessels

NIELSEN & SØN, MARIUS, Kalvebod Brygge 4, Copenhagen

Funnel: Black with red seven-pointed star on white band
Hull: Black, red boot-topping
Services: General tramping
Note: Also *Henry Tegner* (built 1914/1457gt), *Knut* (24/1274), *Lily* (31/1281), *Margrete* (17/1196), *Rigmor* (20/1278), *Robert* (24/1272), *Sigrid* (17/1196), *Skagerak* (31/1283), and short-sea vessels

D/S A/S PROGRESS

Absalon	1898	GrayX	2144	3080	290.3	42–1	18–7	8.0
ex Joseph Merryweather 07								
Hans Broge	1922	Köge	2095	3100	289.9	43–1	19.5	9.0
Kejserinde Dagmar	1905	Duncan	1597	2410	273–10	37–3	18–1	7.5
Martin Goldschmidt	1922	Köge	2094	3100	289.9	43–1	19.5	9.0
Ulrik Holm	1905	SmitJ	1502	2463	260–3	37–10	19–4	8.0
Wilh Colding	1905	SmitJ	1510	2463	260–0	37–10	19–4	8.0

A P Møller: Inge Mærsk *was completed by the Odense shipyard in May 1939, being typical of the many tankers which were interoduced into service in the later 1930s. In April 1940 she was requisitioned by South Africa and for much of the war years was voyaging between the Persian Gulf and Durban. In 1946 she rturned to Danish registry. In November 1957 she was sold to a Swedish company, renamed* Tosterö, *and remained in service until 1966 when sold to breakers at Castellon, Spain*
(Photograph courtesy A P Møller)

A P Møller: Nicoline Mærsk *was completed at Odense in November 1925. In June 1940 she was seized at Marseille by the Vichy authorities and later that year was renamed* St Felix *under the French flag. It is reported she was renamed* Nicoline Mærsk *in 1941 under German flag. On December 24 1943 she was found off Tortosa by the French destroyer* Le Fantasque *and to avoid capture was run aground off San Carlos de la Rapita, Spain, where she became a total loss*
(Photograph courtesy A P Møller)

A P Møller: Robert Mærsk *was completed at Odense in February 1937, and was fitted with a B&W 6-cylinder oil engine of 3000ihp. With the occupation of Denmark she passed to the Ministry of Shipping (later Ministry of War Transport) in June 1940. She returned to the Danish register in 1946. In June 1955* Robert Mærsk *was sold to a Danish company as* Birgitte Toft, *and on May 20 1957 was badly damaged as a result of an engine room fire while off Rangoon. The following year she was sold to a Singapore company and renamed* Ever Glory, *and after more changes of name and owner was broken up at Hong Kong in 1970 as the Panamanian-flagged Tandjung Layang*
(Photograph courtesy A P Møller)

Østasiatiske Kompagni: Amerika *was completed by Burmeister & Wain in January 1930. She was powered by a B&W 6-cylinder oil engine of 6400bhp and originally had accommodation for 56 first class passengers. In 1936 the passenger accommodation was altered and increased 70 first class. East Asiatic company passengers travelled in what was then considered to be among the most stylish accommodation afloat. In 1940, with the occupation of Denmark,* Amerika *was transferred to the Ministry of Shipping and managers were United Baltic Corporation, a London company in which East Asiatic had an interest. In April 1943* Amerika *was eastbound on the North Atlantic in convoy HX234, when she was torpedoed and sunk by* U306. *Her voyage was from Halifax to Liverpool with a general cargo. Of the 130 passengers, crew and gunners on board, there were only 44 survivors (Photograph courtesy East Asiatic Co)*

Østasiatiske Kompagni: Selandia, *completed in October 1938 and powered by a B&W 5-cylinder oil engine of 7300bhp, was the latest in a series of three- or four-masted and funnelless motor ships built for this company. She was built for the service between Denmark and northwest Europe and Bangkok. With the occupation of Denmark,* Selandia *came under firstly French and then British and South African control, and for much of the war served as an Allied troopship. Returning to East Asiatic service in 1945,* Selandia *continued in service until 1962 and was broken up the following year at La Spezia (RW Jordan collection)*

Det Forenede: Arizona, *powered by two B&W 6-cylinder oil engines of 2100bhp, was one of several vessels owned by this company and named after US states. She was involved in the company's regular service between Scandinavia and the east coast of Canada and USA and US Gulf ports. In April 1940 she was laid up at Vitoria, Brazil, and two years later taken over by the Brazilian government. From 1942 to August 1945 she was under the Brazilian flag as* Gavealoide. *She was returned to Denmark in 1945 and as* Arizona *continued in service until she was laid up at Esbjerg in March 1958. About one year later she was sold to a Netherlands company and renamed* Ari *for a single voyage to Japan with delivery to breakers at Osaka (Alex Duncan)*

Det Forenede: Marocco, *together with her sisterships* Sicilien *and* Tunis, *operated on the DFDS service between northwest Europe and Mediterranean ports. On April 9 1940 at the time of the German occupation she was at Oslo, and by the end of the same month had arrived at Copenhagen where she was laid up until the end of the war. In early postwar years she was trading between Denmark, the UK and western Mediterranean, but during 1949–64 was mainly operating between Denmark and London. Marocco was sold to a Greek owner in 1966 and changed hands again in 1971 under the name* Dimitra M. *She was reported broken in Greece in 1978 (Alex Duncan)*

Holm & Wonsild: Chr Sass *was completed by Burmeister & Wain at Copenhagen in January 1931, and was fitted with two B&W 6-cylinder oil engines of 2400bhp. In 1941 she was seized by Uruguay and sailed under that flag as* Colonia *until 1946 when she was returned to Denmark and again traded her original name. In 1959 she was sold to a Greek company and as* Taxiarchis *was in service until 1967 when she was broken up at Split, Yugoslavia (Alex Duncan)*

A/S D/S Orient: Columbia *was completed at Nakskov in December 1928, her machinery consisting of two B&W 6-cylinder oil engines of 2200bhp. In 1941 she was requisitioned by the US, passed to ownership of the USMC, and under the Panamanian flag was renamed* Sir Huon. *On August 30 1942 she was torpedoed and sunk by U66 when on voyage from Suez and Port Elizabeth for Trinidad and Baltimore with a cargo mainly of manganese ore and with a deck cargo of former German and Italian tanks. Her 38-man crew and 8 gunners were all saved (Alex Duncan)*

ORIENT, A/S D/S, Ved Stranden 14, Copenhagen

Funnel: Black with white band
Hull: Black with white band, red boot-topping
Services: General tramping

Astoria (m2,P–)	1926	Nakskv	4454	8370	390–4	53–4	24–1	11.5
Columbia (m2,P–)	1928	Nakskv	4488	8280	400–1	54–5	24–6	11.5
Olympia (m2,P–)	1930	Nakskv	4488	8270	400–1	54–5	24–6	11.0
Tacoma (m2,P–)	1926	Nakskv	4482	8330	390–4	53–4	24–2	11.5
Tasmania (m2,P–)	1935	Nakskv	4460	8400	415–4	56–5	24–9	12.5
Westralia (m2,P–)	1937	Nakskv	4568	8400	415–4	56–5	24–10	13.0

ØSTASIATISKE KOMPAGNI, A/S DET, (The East Asiatic Company), Holbergsgade 2–4, Copenhagen

Funnel: Yellow
Hull: Black with white band, or light grey, or white with blue band, red boot-topping
Services: Japan–China Line – Copenhagen, Oslo, Gothenburg, Antwerp, Rotterdam, Hamburg–Suez–Hong Kong–Shanghai–Yokohama–Kobe–Moji–Dalny–Vladivostok; Bangkok Line – Copenhagen, Gothenburg, Oslo, Middlesbrough, Hamburg, Rotterdam, Antwerp, Southampton, La Rochelle–Suez–Colombo–Penang–Port Swettenham–Singapore–Bangkok; Netherlands–Indies Line – Copenhagen, Gothenburg, Oslo, Hamburg–Suez–Batavia, Samarang, Sourabaya; West India and North Pacific Line – Copenhagen, Gothenburg, Oslo, Newcastle, Hamburg, Antwerp–St Thomas–Cristobal–Los Angeles–San Francisco–Portland–Seattle–Vancouver; South African Line – Copenhagen, Gothenburg, Oslo–Cape Town–Mossel Bay–Algoa Bay–East London–Durban–Delagoa Bay–Beira; Australia Line – Copenhagen, Gothenburg, Oslo, Hamburg–Fremantle–Adelaide–Melbourne–Sydney–Brisbane; Baltic America Line – Danzig, Copenhagen–Halifax–New York

Passenger/general cargo vessels and general cargo vessels

Afrika (m2,P10)	1920	B&W	8597	13,275	462–5	60–4	31–10	12.0
Alsia (m2,P40/1)	1929	Nakskv	5812	8100	439–8	57–4	24–9	14.0
Amerika (m,P70/1)	1930	B&W	10,218	10,830	484–2	62–2	28–5	15.0
Annam (m2,P4)	1913	B&W	6636	10,075	427–0	55–2	28–1	11.5
Asia (m2,P10/1)	1919	B&W	7014	10,800	442–0	55–2	28–10	11.5
Australien (m2,P10)	1915	B&W	6652	9815	427–1	55–2	28–1	11.5
Bintang (m2,P–)	1922	Nakskv	2779	3401	284.8	44–2	20–11	10.5
Boringia (m2,P40/1)	1930	B&W	5821	8150	442–0	57–1	24–8	15.0
Canada (m,P55/1)	1935	Nakskv	11,108	10,950	493–0	64–4	28–8	15.0
Chile (m2)	1915	B&W	6956	10,325	442–0	55–2	28–0	11.0
Danmark (m2,P12/1)	1925	B&W	8391	12,350	477–0	59–9	28–0	12.5
Erria (m2,P74/1)	1932	Nakskv	8786	8500	463–0	62–2	27–4	16.5
Europa (m,P70/1)	1931	B&W	10,224	10,850	482–5	62–2	28–5	15.0
Falstria (m,P54/1)	order	Nakskv	8299	8400	453–0	63–2	25–0	16.0
Fionia (m2,P42/1)	1914	B&W	5219	6820	414–4	53–2	24–6	12.5
India (m2,P12/1)	1930	Nakskv	9549	13,550	488–0	63–8	29–8	14.5
Java (m2,P12)	1921	Nakskv	8681	13,160	461–10	60–3	31–10	12.0
Jutlandia (m2,P59/1)	1934	Nakskv	8457	7950	460–2	61–2	25–1	15.0
Kina (m,P12/1)	1939	Nakskv	9823	12,350	508–4	65–2	29–8	16.0
Korea (m,P12/1)	1939	Nakskv	9945	12,350	510–11	65–2	29–8	16.0
Lalandia (m2,P28/1)	1927	Nakskv	4913	7480	405–4	53–5	24–11	13.5
Malaya (m2,P12)	1921	B&W	8654	13,400	464–6	60–4	31–10	12.0
Meonia (m2,P28/1)	1927	Nakskv	5218	7480	419–0	54–5	24–10	13.5
Muinam (m2,P34/cab,300/d)	1931	Nakskv	3113	3325	346–0	48–11	18–3	13.0
Panama (m2,P10/1)	1915	B&W	6650	9825	427–1	55–2	28–1	11.5
Peru (m2,P10/1)	1916	B&W	6962	10,325	442–0	55–2	28–0	11.5
Selandia (mP54/1)	1938	B&W	8482	8400	452–4	63–1	25–1	15.0
Siam (m2,P10/1)	1913	B&W	6637	10,075	427–1	55–2	28–1	11.5

PETERSEN, A N, & E HAHN-PETERSEN, Store Kongensgade 49, Copenhagen

Funnel: White with black D-F, black top
Hull: Black or grey, red boot-topping
Services: Scandinavia–France; general tramping

Note: Also short-sea vessels under 1500gt

A/S DET DANSK-FRANSKE D/S

Bornholm (m)	1930	B&W	3177	5500	340–10	50–1	20–6	10.5
Bretagne (m)	1928	B&W	3177	5588	340–10	50–1	20–6	10.5
Irland (m)	1927	B&W	3173	5500	340–10	50–1	20–6	10.5
Lifland (st)	1920	Odense	2254	3900	297–0	42–4	19–11	10.0
Normandiet (m,P–)	1935	Nakskv	3161	5800	345.6	50–2	21–11	11.0
Slesvig (m,P–)	1938	Helsgr	3098	5800	373–0	50–6	21–11	12.0

REIMANN, A E, Stensbygaard, Stensved

Funnel: Black with red stylised M on white diamond
Hull: Black with white band
Services: General tramping

A/S MOTORTRAMP

Lundby (m) *ex Saga 31*	1926	Örsndl	4150	6850	357.0	51–4	25.4	11.0
Stensby (m)	1926	Eriksb	3953	6850	365–7	50–10	23–3	11.0

Tureby (m2,P–)	1936	B&W	4372	7350	382–0	56–5	23–3	12.5
Vedby (m)	order	B&W	4446	7270	382–2	56–5	23–3	12.5

SCHMIEGELOW, A, & AXEL KAMPEN, Holmens Kanal 42, Copenhagen K

D/S TORM A/S

Fruit carriers and general cargo vessels

Almena (m)	1933	Nakskv	1554	2580	283–6	41–2	16–10	12.5
Anne	1928	HwldtK	1593	2560	264–0	38–6	16–10	10.0
Aslaug	1927	B&W	1509	2465	261–9	38–9	17–0	10.0
Birgitte	1930	Helsgr	1595	2550	266–6	39–1	16–6	11.0
Gerd (r/t)	1934	Helsgr	1700	2880	306–6	41–9	18–3	13.0
Gertrud (m,P8/1)	1938	Helsgr	2282	3940	345–6	45–10	20–0	14.0
Gyda (r/t)	1934	Helsgr	1695	2880	306–6	41–8	18–3	13.0
Helvig (m,P8/1)	1937	Helsgr	2252	3950	345–6	45–10	20–0	14.0
Herdis (m)	1935	Helsgr	1659	2860	301.9	42–9	18–8	14.0
Hilde	1930	Helsgr	1595	2550	266–6	39–1	16–6	11.0
Olga S (m,P8/1)	1938	Helsgr	2252	3950	345–6	45–10	20–0	14.0
Ragnhild (m,P8/1)	1938	Helsgr	2252	3950	345–6	45–10	20–0	14.0
Thyra S (m,P2)	1936	Nakskv	1738	2940	322–0	42–9	18–8	14.0
Viola	1929	Helsgr	1595	2550	266–6	39–1	16–6	11.0

Funnel: Black with blue T on white band between two narrow red bands
Hull: White, red boot-topping
Services: Fruit trades, mainly Mediterranean–NW Europe; Las Palmas/Tenerife–Cadiz, Barcelona; NW Africa–Marseilles; Torm Italian Line – Antwerp–Leghorn–Genoa–Naples–Palermo
Note: Also *Aase* (built 1924/1206gt), *Agnete* (21/1458), *Alice* (24/1196), *Estrid* (33/1397), *Freya* (24/1207), *Gudrun* (24/1498), *Ingeborg S* (24/1200), *Kirsten* (19/1196), *Tekla* (20/1469), and short-sea vessels

SCHMITH, L R, Amaliegade 33, Copenhagen

Paris	1927	B&W	1509	2450	250.1	38–9	17–0	10.0
Stockholm	1930	Fredsv	1596	2500	253.5	39–1	17–0	10.0

Funnel: Black with white cross (+) on red band
Hull: Black, red boot-topping
Services: General tramping
Note: Also *Kjøbenhavn* (built 1923/1264gt), *London* (24/1260), Oslo (20/1412), *Prins Knud* (22/1340)

SKOU A/S, D/S OVE, Lindevej 3, Copenhagen V

D/S AF 1937 A/S

Mette	1906	HwldtK	1909	3600	296–8	42–2	19–10	8.5
ex Jelling 37, ex Frumentia 29								

Funnel: Black with white S on blue band
Hull: Black, red boot-topping
Services: General tramping
Note: Also *Hanne* (built 1905 /1080gt), *Jytte* (84/1877), *Lotte* (05/1420), *Rikke* (07/1432)

STORE NORDISKE TELEGRAF-SELSKAB, A/S DET, Kongens Nytorv 28, Copenhagen

Cable vessels

Edouard Suenson	1922	Orlogs	1552	1105	260–0	35–2	16–1	11.0
Pacific (s2)	1903	B&W	1570		264.6	35–10	21.5	10.0
Store Nordiske	1922	Nakskv	1456	800	264–0	35–2	16–8	11.0

Funnel: Yellow, narrow black top
Hull: Black or white *Services:* Cable laying/maintenance

SVENDSEN & CHRISTENSEN, Frederiksgade 1, Copenhagen K

A/S D/S VENDILA

Chr J Kampmann	1924	B&W,K	2281	4255	305.6	45–5	18.6	10.0
E M Dalgas	1930	Helsgr	2836	4965	342–8	48–4	20–6	11.0
Edv Nissen	1921	Aalb1	2062	3600	282.5	42–9	19.0	9.5
ex Thorsdal 28								
Erik Boye	1924	Nakskv	2238	4130	319–3	45–5	19–3	10.0
Lars Kruse	1923	Aalb2	1807	3232	287–6	42–1	17.8	9.5
Otto Petersen	1930	Helsgr	2832	4965	342–8	48–4	20–6	11.0
P Madsen*	1924	Aalb2	1804	3230	287–6	42–1	17.8	9.5
P N Damm	1930	Helsgr	2832	4965	342–8	48–4	20–6	11.0
Svend Pii	1923	Aalb2	1809	3232	287–6	42–4	19–0	9.5

Funnel: Black with emblem consisting of white stylised Maltese cross on red ground
Hull: Black, red boot-topping
Services: General tramping
Note: * Sold Estonia 1939, renamed *Signe*

TOFT, JENS, Ny Toldbodgade 5, Copenhagen

A/S D/S JUTLANDIA

Gerda Toft	1930	AwpEng	1960	3628	307–0	43–9	18–10	9.0
Inger Toft	1920	SHWRSd	2190	3560	285.6	41–6	19–6	10.0
ex Elphinston 36, ex Van Dyck 25, ex Phyllis Seed 23, ex Langford 22								
Karen Toft	1920	SHWR	2220	3550	285.6	41–6	19–6	10.0
ex Flotterston 34, ex Starkad 27								

Funnel: Black with white band bearing blue J in blue diamond frame
Hull: Black
Services: General tramping

Société Misr: The passenger vessel Zamzam *(pictured here as originally built as Bibby Line's* Leicestershire*) had an interesting career. Completed in September 1909 by Harland & Wolff, Belfast, as* Leicestershire, *she was involved in a great deal of trooping duty during the First World War before returning to Bibby and refitted in 1919. This refit included conversion from coal burning to oil fuel. With the introduction of new vessels in the mid to late 1920s* Leicestershire *became surplus to Bibby requirements and was sold to British National Exhibition Ship Co and renamed* British Exhibitor. *It was intended that following a £100,000 conversion by Cammell, Laird, at Birkenhead, she would undertake a series of voyages promoting British export goods. However, the slump caused these plans to be abandoned, the owning company went into liquidation, and the vessel was laid up. In September 1933 she was sold to Egypt, renamed* Zamzam, *and made voyages from Egypt to Jeddah with Hadj pilgrims. The start of the Second World War saw her laid up at Suez, where she remained until February 1941 when placed into service between Alexandria, Cape Town, Recife and New York. However on her first such voyage she was intercepted by the German auxiliary cruiser* Atlantis, *and although flying the colours of a neutral state was shelled, and received 55 hits. Later she was sunk by bombs placed along the waterline. Reports vary, but it seems to be largely accepted that 24 persons on board lost their lives during the shelling from* Atlantis. *The survivors were put aboard the Norddeutscher Lloyd vessel* Dresden *and landed at St Jean de Luz. Later the captain of* Atlantis *admitted that he recognised the vessel as a Bibby liner and decided she must be a disguised troopship (Bibby Line)*

Merilaid & Co: Osmussar *was completed in April 1909 by Craig, Taylor & Co as* Magdalena. *She remained under the British flag until 1936, latterly as* Duddingston *(owned by James Cormack & Co, Leith) when purchased by this Estonian owner. In the Second World War she passed to Russian control and at the end of 1945 was voyaging between US Pacific ports and Vladivostok. As was the case with many Soviet vessels acquired about this time,* Osmussar *seems to have dropped out of international trade soon after 1945 and is believed to have been scrapped in the 1950s (Alex Duncan)*

Tallinn Shipping Co: The 1902-built steamer Piret *had been owned in Estonia since 1930 having been then purchased from a Belgian company. Under Allied control, she was chartered to Irish Shipping Co from January 12 1942 and renamed* Irish Alder. *In August 1946 she was returned to her former owners, but soon took up Panamanian registration as* Trebol, *owned by Compania Maritima La Ciguena SA. She traded in northwest Europe until 1952 when she was sold to be broken up at Blyth (Alex Duncan)*

Maria Toft	1928	AwpEng	1991	3190	289–8	40–2	17–9	9.0
Ove Toft	1921	Dundee	2135	3500	286.0	43–6	19.1	8.5
ex Hav 35, ex Putten 35, ex Dagfin 30, ex Aarstad 22								

Egypt

ALEXANDRIA NAVIGATION CO LTD, (Red Rose Line),
1 Rue de l'Ancienne Bourse, PO Box 72), Alexandria

Star of Alexandria	1928	SHWRSd	4329	7928	388–8	52–6	24–2	10.5
ex Toftwood 36								
Star of Cairo (r/t)	1924	Hamtn3	4579	7750	387.6	52–0	23–11	10.5
ex Golden Sea 37								
Star of Egypt	1921	Palmer	4372	7035	386.7	52–10	23–4	11.0
ex General Smuts 34, ex Phoebus 24								
Star of Luxor	1919	GrayX	5219	8150	412–4	52–4	25–3	10.5
ex Fostat 39, ex Tartar Prince 33, ex War Jackdaw 19								
Star of Ramleh	1920	Ropnr3	3683	6900	346.7	51–0	24–2	9.0
ex Alness 33								
Star of Suez	1926	Hendn2	4999	8246	415–4	52–3	24–5	9.5
ex Marthara 38								

Funnel: Black with white over green over white bands
Hull: Black, red boot-topping
Services: Egypt–Mediterranean ports–UK–NW Europe; Alexandria–Karachi–Indian ports

Note: Fleet managed by Watts, Watts & Co Ltd (*qv* in Great Britain section)

KLAT, ALBERT, 2 Rue Tewfik, Alexandria

Memphis	1920	AllisC	2085	3500	261–0	43–6	20–2	9.5
ex Siren 35, ex Iside 29, ex Città di Palermo 20, ex War Magic 20								
Radames	1903	McMllan	3672	5900	351–10	45–0	23–9	8.5
ex Fernand Colignon 32, ex Winslow 30, ex Overdale 26, ex Dumbarton 07								

KLAT NAVIGATION CO LTD SAE

Sesostris	1915	Blumr1	2962	5648	340.0	47–9	21–10	8.5
ex Middlemoor 36, ex Arranmead 22, ex Arranmoor 19								

Funnel: Black with white 'star and K' emblem on green band
Services: General tramping

MABRO, TEWFICK, 1 Rue Antoniadis, PO Box 219, Alexandria

Angele Mabro	1898	GrayX	3154	5130	330.1	48–6	20–4	7.0
ex PLM 10 28, ex Easingwold 17								
Georges Mabro	1918	Forth	2477	4444	305.3	42–10	20–1	10.0
ex Bordeaux 32								

Services: General tramping

MISR DE NAVIGATION MARITIME (SAE), SOCIÉTÉ,
151 Rue Emad el Din, Cairo, and 14 Rue Fouad 1er, Alexandria

El Nil (s2,P48/1,52/2,1067/d)								
	1916	Reiher	7769	6800	442–0	55–11	25–0	14.0
ex Tjerimai 33, ex Wadai 21, ex Marie 17, ex Marie Woermann 16								
Fostat*	1919	GrayX	5219	8150	412–4	52–4	25–3	10.5
ex Tartar Prince 33, ex War Jackdaw 19								
Kawsar (st2,P–)	1924	AnsGC	7778	4400	445–0	52–8	27–0	14.0
ex Ammiraglio Bettolo 34								
Rod-el-Farag (P110/1,–/d)								
	1910	Denny1	6369	8600	445.5	55–2	25–1	13.0
ex Chindwin 37								
Zamzam (s2,P–/1,–/2,–/d)								
	1909	H&W,B	8299	8890	467.2	54–2	27–8	12.5
ex British Exhibitor 33, ex Leicestershire 30								

Funnel: Yellow with green and white emblem
Hull: White, green boot-topping
Services: Mediterranean–UK–NW Europe; Alexandria–Genoa–Naples–Marseilles; N Africa–Jeddah (for Mecca) (Hadj pilgrims)

Note: * Sold Alexandria Navigation Co Ltd (*qv* above) 1939, renamed *Star of Luxor*
Note: Also vessels under 1000gt

PHARAONIC MAIL LINE SAE, 5 Rue Adib, Alexandria

Khedive Ismail (st2,P155/1,88/3,–/d)								
	1922	Scott2	7289	6372	422.8	56–3	28–3	16.0
ex Aconcagua 35								
Mohamed Ali El-Kabir (st2,P155/1,88/3,–/d)								
	1922	Scott2	7289	6372	422.8	56–3	28–3	16.0
ex Teno 35								

Funnel: Black
Hull: Black or greenish-grey, green boot-topping
Services: Mediterranean and Black Sea; Egypt–Jeddah (for Mecca, Hadj pilgrims)

SOCIÉTÉ ORIENTALE DE NAVIGATION, Immeuble Sebai, Rue Foch, BP183, Beirut, Syria (French flag)

Al Rawdah (P–/d) 1911 Cammel 3549 4189 350.2 44–3 24–2 11.5
ex Ville de Beyrouth 39, ex Chenab 31

Funnel: V Bassili – black with houseflag, green with white diagonal stripe
Services: General tramping
Note: * This vessel was operated by D Georgopoulos, Syra, Greece; registered owner was V Bassili
Note: See Rethymnis & Kulukundis Ltd in Greece section

RETHYMNIS & KULUKUNDIS LTD, Holland House, 1–4 Bury St, London EC3, and Odos Tritis Septemvriou 136, Athens, Greece

Manager and/or agent for
VICTOR BASSILI, Alexandria; and Galatz, Romania (Egyptian flag)
Samir* 1909 Ropnr2 3700 6260 346.5 51–0 21–6 8.0
ex Poseidonia 39, ex Holtby 36

Estonia

Funnel: Black with yellow over red over white bands
Hull: Black
Services: General tramping
Note: Also vessels under 2000gt in Baltic/UK/NW Europe trade

BERGMANN, ERNST, Vabaduseplats 7, Postkast 158, Tallinn

Kadri 1897 Irvin2 2775 4450 314.0 44–0 19–10 7.5
ex Ellind 35, ex Jacob Bright 14
Keila 1905 ThmpsJ 3621 6150 361–0 50–11 21–5 8.0
ex Brockabeck 32, ex Zamora 27
Liina 1896 RDuck1 2480 4100 310.0 44–0 18–10 7.5
ex Lina Peronne 31, ex Simeto 25, ex Kinsale 24
Manager for
MIHKEL MÄNNAPSO AND OTHERS
Koidula 1909 ThmpsJ 3741 6270 364.5 50–10 22–5 9.0
ex Lundy Light 32, ex Scottier 22, ex Kingsgate 16

Services: General tramping
Note: Also vessels under 2000gt
Note: See T Liimann and Others also under A/S Tallinna Laevaühisus (below)

JURISON, JAKOB, S Roosikrantsi 16, Tallinn

THEODOR LIIMANN, JAKOB JURISON AND OTHERS
Eestirand 1910 McMlln 4688 8160 390–0 52–2 23–0 8.5
ex Glenbeath 32, ex Harold Dollar 27, ex Strathardle 16

Services: General tramping

JURNAS AND OTHERS, KRISTJAN, Brackmanni 46, Pärnu

Otto 1918 Toledo 1954 2930 261–0 43–6 18–7 9.5
ex Nestor 39, ex Frank Lynch 37, ex Lake Sunapee 22, launched as War Flag; conv mv 38, conv steamer 22
Peet 1913 G&G5 2111 3048 283–3 42–9 18–0 9.0
ex Moorfoot 37

Funnel: Yellow with emblem bearing KLO superimposed on blue over white over black bands, narrow black top
Hull: Black
Services: General tramping
Note: Also short-sea vessels

KASMU LAEVA OMANIKUD, (Oskar Tiedemann, K Kristenbrun and H Pahlberg), Vabaduse Valjak 10, Tallinn

G KRISTENBRUN, A ALTENBRUN AND G PRUUN
Sigrid 1910 Vuijk 1809 2815 284–0 39–1 17–3 8.5
ex Boomberg 32
OSKAR TIEDENMANN
Hildur 1914 Fredst 1856 3050 277–6 42–1 18–0 9.0
ex Monark 38, ex Helgøy 28, ex Freda 19, launched as Gemma
OSKAR TIEDEMANN AND M ANDREJEV
Elna 1903 Dixon2 3195 5370 325.0 47–4 21–8 9.0
ex Lennuk 35, ex Remenham 32, ex Arlon 26, ex Carol 1er 23
OSKAR TIEDEMANN, I KRISTENBRUN, M EINMANN AND E KRISTENBRUN
Maia 1917 Chicgo 1932 3100 261–0 43–9 17–11 9.5
ex Scandia 34, ex Danebrog 25

Services: General tramping

MÄGI, ARVAD, FERDINAND PAJOMÄGI, EDOUARD RISNA AND JURI LAURI, Tallinn

Neme 1914 OsbGr1 1914 3350 279.3 42–0 18.4 8.5
ex Erland 39, ex Vedamore 28, ex Wingate 22

MERILAID & CO, A/S, Aia tänaw 5a, Tallinn

Funnel: Black, blue band
Services: General tramping

Kuressaar	1914	Mackay	2283	3735	296–0	42–10	19–7	8.5
ex Inverawe 35								
Merisaar	1900	CRDA4	2136	3700	299–4	42–1	18–10	7.5
ex Anna Goich 30								
Naissaar	1911	Crown1	1893	2800	277–6	37–11	18–0	8.0
ex Ford Castle 33								
Osmussar	1909	Craig2	2229	3565	298–2	44–0	18–3	9.0
ex Duddingston 36, ex Magdalena 22								

Note: This company also owned and managed short-sea vessels

TALLINNA LAEVAÜHISUS, A/S, (Tallinn Shipping Co Ltd)
Suur Karja 18, Tallinn

Funnel: Black with blue over black over white bands, white TLU on black band; or yellow TK monogram
Hull: Black
Services: General tramping; Baltic

Kajak	1902	Duncan	3234	5000	325.2	48–9	20–4	8.0
ex Gagara 19, ex Zandbergen 13, ex Bacchus 12								
Vapper	1913	Ropnr2	4549	8220	379.0	56–0	23–2	9.0
ex Pilcot 39, ex Seapool 36								
A/S TALLINNA LAEVAÜHISUS AND OTHERS								
Piret	1902	Cockll	2598	4200	299–11	45–0	21.6	8.5
ex Reine Elisabeth 30, ex Princesse Elisabeth 10								
Sulev	1908	Bremer	2233	3250	307.3	42–2	18–1	9.0
ex Borinage 30, ex Clara Blumenfeld 21								
Torni	1918	PtArth	2044	3300	261–0	43–9	20–2	9.5
ex Claudegallus 29, ex War Isis 20								
A/S TALLINNA LAEVAÜHISUS, THEODOR LIIMANN AND OTHERS*								
Maret	1910	Blumr1	3025	4870	315.5	46–7	20–3	8.5
ex Llangorse 30, ex Boverton 28								

Note: This company also owned and managed vessels under 2000gt
Note: * See T Liimann and Others also under J Jurison (above)

TRUBERG, ANTON, L Koidula 2, Tallinn

Funnel: Black
Hull: Black
Services: General tramping

Manager for
MISS MARIA INKAPÖÖL & OTHERS

Lake Hallwil	1907	Rodger	3165	5600	330.5	49–0	21–0	8.0
ex Carol Dorian 38, ex Carol 32, ex Helmsdale 31								

Operator for
A INKAPÖÖL, E JAKOBSON & OTHERS

Lake Lucerne	1909	WoodS2	2317	3250	295.3	40–6	18–6	9.0
ex Barmoor 38								

Note: Also vessels under 2000gt on Baltic/NW Europe/UK trade

Finland

ABRAHAMSEN, S, Sveavågen 34–36, Stockholm

Funnel: Black with white band
Hull: Black
Services: General tramping

REDERI-A/B IRIS, Mariehamn (Maarianhamina), Åland (Finnish flag)

Rigel	1905	Doxfrd	3779	6450	362–10	48–2	22–1	8.0
ex Nordland 30								
Virgo	1902	GrayX	2959	5080	335–8	47–0	20–9	8.0
ex Adriatico 36, ex Adriatic 31, ex Trumf 29, ex Newlands 24								

REDERI-A/B PLUTO, Mariehamn (Maarianhamina), Aland (Finnish flag)

Pluto	1907	RDuck1	3496	6450	362–11	49–2	23.6	8.0
ex Bolivia 31, ex Yankalilla 29, ex Lady Lewis 12								

REDERI-A/B TAURI, Alandsgatan 20, Mariehamn (Maarianhamina), Åland (Finnish flag)

Tauri	1909	ThmpsJ	2517	4855	330–10	47–2	20–8	8.0
ex Norden 36								

Note: Also vessels under 2000gt
Note: See S Abrahamsen also in Sweden section

ANDERSSON, ARTHUR, Södra Esplanadgatan, Mariehamn (Maarianhamina), Åland

Funnel: Black with yellow 'reindeer' emblem on blue band between narrow white bands
Services: General tramping

REDERI-A/B ASKÖ								
Askö	1897	Neptn1	2122	2980	290–10	40–9	17–11	7.5
ex Erik B 36, ex Ursus 23, ex Dora 06								
REDERI-A/B ASTA								
Asturias	1912	Sørlan	1829	3050	277–2	42–1	17–7	9.0
ex Ærø 15								
REDERI-A/B BARBRO								
Barbro*	1902	Murdo1	2155	–	296–9	43–0	18–7	8.0
ex Polarhavet 33, ex Atlanten 27								

Note: * Sold Lovisa Rederi-A/B (manager A/B R Nordström & Co O/Y), 1939, renamed *Margareta*

AVELLAN, TORSTEN, Unionink 15, Helsinki (Helsingfors)

O/Y SUOMI SHIPPING A/B

Zephyr	1907	Eider2	2556	4200	302–10	42–8	18–6	7.5
ex Deva 38, ex Levensau 21								

Services: General tramping
Note: Also *Trio* (built 1884/1451gt), *Zilos* (84/1711)
Note: See I Barthen also in Sweden section

BARTHEN, IVAR, Nybrokajen 7vii, Stockholm, Sweden

LEMLANDS REDERI-A/B, Mariehamn (Maarianhamina), Åland (Finnish flag)

Ferrum	1918	Meyer	2089	3200	293–7	41–4	19.3	9.0
ex Stad Zalt-Bommel 36								

Services: General tramping

CADENIUS & GRAHN, A/B, Skepparegatan 7, Kotka

A/B ODDVAR

Oddvar II	1918	Collwd	1897	2900	261–0	43–6	18–6	9.5
ex Bracciano 37, ex Citta di Lecce 25, ex War Wizard 20								

Services: General tramping

CARLBOM & CO LTD, JOHN,
Yorkshire Insurance Bldg, Lowgate, Hull, Yorkshire

Chartering agent for
REDERI-A/B EUROPA, Slottsgatan 45, Turku (Åbo), Finland (Finnish flag)

Fidra	1918	Fredst	1827	3060	277–6	42–1	18–0	9.5
ex Eidsfos 27, ex Lisa Brodin 22								

REDERI-A/B HANÖ, Helsinki (Helsingfors), Finland (Finnish flag)

Hanö*	1900	G&G3	1813	3000	279–6	42–2	16–10	8.0
ex Småland 24, ex Drott 17, ex Alexey Goriainow 03								

O/Y POHJANMERI, Slottsgatan 45, Turku (Åbo), Finland (Finnish flag)

Rosenborg	1919	Sørlan	1512	2500	254–11	39–5	17.0	9.0
ex Fagernes 21								

Note: * Sold N Lapato, Estonia, 1939, renamed *Hanonia*

Services: General tramping

EKLÖF, PAUL, Mechelinink, Helsinki (Helsingfors)

O/Y MARGARITA STEAMSHIP CO A/B, Porvoo (Borgå)

Margarita	1904	GrayX	3016	5500	336–1	47–1	20–10	8.0
ex Atlantic 39								

Funnel: Black with blue E on white band
Hull: Black
Services: General tramping; sailing vessels – grain, mainly Australia–UK–NW Europe

ERIKSON, GUSTAF, Mariehamn (Maarianhamina), Åland

Sailing vessels (barques)

Killoran (3 mast)	1900	Ailsa1	1817	3050	288–5	39–1	20–1	–
Lawhill (4 mast)	1892	ThmpsD	2816	4600	333–0	45–0	22–9	–
Moshulu (4 mast)	1904	Hamtn1	3117	5000	338–2	46–11	23–8	–
ex Kurt 17								
Olivebank (4 mast)	1892	Mackie	2795	4400	326.0	43–1	21–9	–
ex Caledonia 24, ex Olivebank 22								
Pamir (4 mast)	1905	Blohm	2799	4500	330–11	46–0	23–5	–
Passat (4 mast)	1911	Blohm	3137	4223	343–8	46–11	23–3	–
Penang (3 mast)	1905	Rickmr	2019	3300	285–10	40–2	24.3	–
ex Albert Rickmers 11								
Pommern (4 mast)	1903	Reid	2376	4050	310–7	43–5	24.5	–
ex Mneme 06								
Viking (4 mast)	1907	B&W	2670	4000	319–4	45–10	23–5	–
Winterhude (3 mast)	1898	Rickmr	1980	3060	285–6	40–6	24.1	–
ex Selma Hemsoth 26, ex Winterhude 23, ex Mabel Rickmers 12								

REDERI-A/B ARCHIBALD RUSSELL

Archibald Russell (4 mast)	1905	Scott2	2354	3950	304–11	43–2	20–11	–

General cargo steamers
REDERI-A/B HERZOGIN CECILIE

Kirsta	1906	Neptn1	1694	2550	267–5	37–5	18–0	7.0
ex Glenisla 28, ex Bonn 20, ex Heinrich Diestel –, ex Lena Petersen –								

MARIEHAMNS REDERI-AB

Agnes	1912	RottDD	2983	5150	337–9	47–5	20–4	8.5
ex Blairlogie 36, ex Oostdijk 22								

REDERI-A/B PONAPE

Argo	1898	Napier	2513	4300	321–0	44–3	19–7	8.0
ex Odessa 24, ex Elizabeth 19, ex Camperdown 12								

Note: Also steamers under 2000gt, sailing vessels under 1500gt, and short-sea vessels

FINSKA ÅNGFARTYGS A/B, Etelä Makasiinik 4, Helsinki (Helsingfors)

Funnel: Black with two white bands
Hull: Black or white, red boot-topping; Finland-Amerika – light grey, red boot-topping
Services: Finland and Baltic ports–Spain–Italy; Finland-Amerika – Helsinki–South America; Helsinki–South Africa

General cargo vessels

Hektos	1903	Cragg2	2108	3048	290–3	40–1	19–0	10.5
Najaden	1906	Helsgr	2203	3730	292–4	42–1	20–6	8.0
ex Örkild 28, ex Boscia 10								
Orion (P6/1)	1935	Sandvk	2408	2720	285–5	41–0	19–11	10.5
Pohjanmaa (m)	1929	Eriksb	2063	3240	305–2	43–0	18–9	10.5
ex Nordland 38, ex Manhem 31								
Saimaa (m,P2/1)	1922	Eriksb	2001	3230	302–8	43–4	18–7	11.0
ex Erland 37								
Sirius (P6/1)	1929	Helsgr	2197	2600	273–0	40–2	19–5	11.0
A/B FINLAND-AMERIKA LINJEN O/Y								
Equator*	1901	Irvin4	3985	6780	361.1	48–1	25–2	9.5
ex Manchester Exchange 25								
Equator	1911	GrayX	4595	7350	384–11	50–1	24–7	11.5
ex Atlanta 39, ex Shahristan 34, ex Ninive 25, ex Turkistan 13								
Mercator	1904	Irvin4	4260	6900	366–8	48–0	25–0	9.5
ex Manchester Mariner 25								
Navigator (P12)	1921	H&W,B	5656	8276	424–6	54–4	24–8	10.5
ex Tower Dale 35, ex Bompata 35								

Note: * Sold Italy 1939, renamed *Caporto*; resold for BU
Note: Finska Ångfartygs A/B, managed by Birger Krogius (*qv*), also owned passenger vessels operating in the Baltic Sea and short-sea general cargo vessels

HACKLIN, WERNER, Pori (Björneborg), and Reposaari (Räfsö)

Funnel: Black with blue H on white diamond on blue band
Services: General tramping

Edit H	1905	GrayX	3470	6200	342.0	49–6	22–2	8.0
ex Aristides L Goulandris 39, ex Calimeris 25, ex Harlech 14								
REPOSAAREN LAIVA O/Y								
Flora H	1899	Flensb	2025	3000	284–0	39–6	18–0	8.5
ex Jupiter 34								
BJÖRNEBORG SHIPPING CO								
Otto H	1897	Flensb	2158	3100	285–2	39–8	18–0	8.2
ex Helga Ferdinand 31, ex Goslar 22, ex Sprogö 21, ex Tertia 21								
LAIVA O/Y JUSSI H								
Jussi H	1910	France	2216	3620	299–6	42–11	19–9	8.0
ex Ospringe 37, ex Homecourt 31								
PORIN LAIVA O/Y								
Betty H	1902	TurnbT	2478	3946	310–9	44–0	19–8	9.0
ex Kirktown 32, ex Broomfield 19								

Note: Also vessels in Baltic Sea trade and Baltic/UK/NW Europe trade

HANSEN O/Y, A/B KRISTIAN, Esplanadgatan 27, Helsinki (Helsingfors)

Funnel: Black with blue band between two narrow white bands
Hull: Grey
Services: General tramping

REDERI-A/B DEEPSEATRADER O/Y								
Karin	1904	Blumrl	2791	4715	323–10	46–9	19–10	9.5
ex Johanne 35, ex Johanne Dybwad 28, ex Nepos 20, ex Arranmore 14								
REDERI-A/B GARRYVALE								
Garryvale	1907	Doxfrd	4067	6720	349.8	49–1	23–0	8.0
REDERI-A/B GERTRUD								
Gertrud*	1914	ThmpR2	3396	5660	350–1	48–5	21–9	9.0
ex Randsfjord 34, ex Kongsfos 21								
A/B TRANSPORT								
Vicia	1896	Irvin4	2660	4200	326–2	43–1	20.4	7.0
ex Sigrid 19, ex Carham 12								
A/B TRÆTRAMP								
Smut**	1896	Austin	1703	2640	276–8	37–9	17–11	7.0
ex Harbury 12								
REDERI-A/B TURRET								
Tilda	1903	Blumrl	2768	4680	326–0	46–6	19–10	9.0
ex Margarita 36								

Note: Also vessels under 2000gt
Note: * Sold A Wihuri 1939, renamed *Wilja*; ** sold A Kalm, Estonia, 1939, renamed *Aarne*

JOHANSSON, ALGOT, Torggatan 1, Mariehamn (Maarianhamina), Åland

Funnel: Black with white over blue over white bands
Hull: Black
Services: General tramping

REDERI-A/B ADVANCE								
Advance	1917	Chicgo	1839	3100	260–11	43–10	17–11	9.0
ex Benito 36, ex Binab 35, ex Cap la Hève 32, ex Serbier 24, ex Lake Huron 20, launched as War Hound								

REDERI-A/B HAVNIA								
Havnia	1888	LithR	1571	2350	264–6	36–0	16.8	7.0
ex Bertil 23, ex Schiehallion 99								
REDERI-A/B SALLY								
Sally	1896	GrayX	2533	4250	325–3	44–1	19–6	8.5
ex Oswal 37, ex Norrköping 23, ex Edmond-Gustave 17, ex Greylands 99								
REDERI-A/B SNABB								
Snabb	1904	Rhead2	2317	3650	299–8	43–6	18–6	8.0
ex Mari Chandris 36, ex Frank Delmas 33, ex Tregarthen 11								

Funnel: Black
Services: General tramping

Note: * Sold Finska Fiskeri A/B, Finland, 1939, renamed *Jäämeri*; ** managed for John E Sandstrom, Nybrokajen 7, Stockholm, Sweden

KARLSSON, ARTHUR, Mariehamn (Maarianhamina), Åland

ÅNGFARTYGS-A/B ALFA								
Charterhague*	1920	Monmth	2522	4050	312–9	43–0	19–10	9.0
ex Silverway 25, ex War Fig 22								
Thornbury	1905	StettO	2163	3050	288–7	41–11	18–4	8.0
ex Elwine Köppen 20								
REDERI-A/B DAGMAR								
Dagmar	1900	Helsgr	2149	3534	301–9	42–10	18–9	7.5
REDERI-A/B HILDEGAARD								
Hildegaard	1906	RDuckl	2362	4330	322–11	44–0	19–9	8.5
ex Butetown 24, ex Eda 18								
Pandia	1903	GrayX	2368	3850	313–0	43–2	18–11	7.5
ex Diamando 37, ex Nirefs 26, ex Pandia A Ralli 22								
REDERI-A/B MARGA								
Margareta**	1919	Fredst	1860	3060	277–5	42–1	18–0	9.0
ex Bella Gaditana 29, ex Eidsvaag 26, ex Altair 22								

Funnel: Black with black K◊L on white band with white over blue bands above and red over white bands below
Services: General tramping

KNUDSEN & LINDFORS A/B, O/Y, Unionink 18, Helsinki (Helsingfors)

REDERI-A/B ESBJÖRN								
Esbjörn	1904	Craig2	1905	2850	290–2	38–2	17–9	8.0
ex Maderas 26, ex Richard 15								

Funnel: Bore – black with broad blue band bordered by two narrow white bands; some vessels on Finland South America Line (*qv* below) service – white AL on blue band; Mare – black with houseflag
Hull: Black or grey
Services: Turku–Helsinki–Gdynia–Rotterdam–Antwerp–Havre–Montevideo–Bahia Blanca–Buenos Aires–Rosario; general tramping

Note: Also vessels under 2000gt

KRAMER, THR, Slottagatan 36, Turku (Åbo)

ÅNGFARTYGS-A/B BORE								
Bore VIII	1907	Beardm	4528	7210	406–4	50–3	25–6	9.0
ex Frank Sutton 26, ex Huanchaco 25								
Bore IX	1910	McMlln	4512	7200	390–0	52–6	23–0	9.5
ex Queensbury 28, ex Yonne 25, ex Strathan 16								
Bore X (m)	1938	Göta	5058	7750	442–7	56–8	25–9	15.0
A/B-MARE								
Karhula	1909	Flensb	2103	3500	305–2	42–5	18–0	9.0
ex Clyne Rock 38, ex Franz Dahl 20, ex Glückauf 19								
Myllykoski (P4)	1909	Bremer	2702	3925	336–0	45–2	18–4	9.5
ex Willem René 33, ex Tervaete 24, ex Adeline Hugo Stinnes 3 21								
ORIENT A/B								
Orient	1914	Nthmbl	4160	7350	373–5	51–4	24–7	9.5
ex Brage 34, ex Natal 30								

Funnel: Black with white AL on blue band between two narrow white bands
Hull: Grey
Services: Finland South America Line – Helsinki, Kotka, Danzig, Antwerp–Rosario–Buenos Aires–Santos–Necochea (see also above under Thr Kramer); general tramping

Note: See Birger Krogius also under Finska Ångfartygs A/B

KROGIUS, BIRGER, Etelä Makasiinik 4, Helsinki (Helsingfors)

REDERI-A/B ATLANTA								
Angra	1920	Lithgw	4660	7560	398–0	52–0	23–11	10.5
ex Maudie 37; conv bulk whale oil carrier; laid down as tanker								
Anja	1914	Flensb	4836	7930	412–2	54–10	25–1	11.0
ex Airthria 38, ex Trelevan 29, ex Lübeck 21, ex Gera 14								
Atlanta (m,P10)	1939	CrichV	4956	7200	427–2	54–8	25–5	16.0
Aura	1907	SHWR	4763	7240	411–1	52–8	22–3	9.0
ex Tenbury 33, ex Löwenburg 21								
Aurora (m,P10)	1938	CrichV	4956	7200	427–2	54–8	25–5	16.0
A/B OCEANFART								
Herakles	1910	LithR	4881	8213	423–5	52–3	24–3	10.0
ex Vinstra 36, ex Drumcraig 13								

Gustaf Erikson: Kirsta *had been owned by Gustaf Erikson's Rederi-A/B Herzogin Cecilie, a company title perpetuating the name of a well-known sailing vessel owned earlier by Erikson. During the war she was trading mainly in Finnish and Norwegian waters and in January 1944 was reported at Lübeck. After a postwar refit* Kirsta *found herself in regular employment, voyaging on many occasions to the Mediterranean. She remained in service until 1960 when she was broken up (Photograph courtesy Gustaf Erikson)*

Gustaf Erikson: Four years before the start of the Second World War, Gustaf Erikson made his last sail purchase, Moshulu. *In 1939 she made a 91-day passage from Port Victoria to Queenstown with a cargo of grain, and in January 1940 loaded grain in Buenos Aires for Scandinavia. She was approaching the Norwegain coast unwittingly on the night of the German invasion and on April 10 put into Farsund. She was captured there by the Germans, and during the war was at Kristiansund and Kirkenes, and in May 1945 at Narvik. In 1945 she was seized by Russia, but returned to Erikson. Upon delivery to Erikson she was found to be in poor condition, having been roughly used by the Germans.* Moshulu *served as a grain store for a number of years after the war in Finland and Sweden. In 1996 she opened as a floating museum in Philadelphia (Photograph courtesy Gustaf Erikson)*

K Hansen: Dating from 1896, this steamer was completed by Furness, Withy & Co at West Hartlepool for British owners as Carham. *She became the Swedish owned* Sigrid *in 1912, and raised the Finnish flag in 1919 as* Vicia. *In April 1942 shed was sold to the then recently-formed Irish Shipping, to become* Irish Spruce. *She was repairing for nearly three years because of lack of steel and spare parts and did not make her first voyage under Irish control until April 1945. In September 1949 she became the Turkish-owned* Osman, *and in 1952 was renamed* Kaptan Uzunoglu, *also Turkish. On February 18 1956 she ran aground near Eregli, Turkey when on voyage from Istanbul to Zonguldak, was abandoned, and became a consructive total loss (RW Jordan collection)*

T Kramer: Bore IX *started her career in 1910 as the British-owned* Strathan, *and was sold to Finland in 1928 after three years' service with Alexander Shipping Co as* Queensbury. *During the war she was under German control and voyages in the Baltic and North Sea. In July–August 1944 received some damage at Danzig. Postwar, she was seemingly low on the priority list for repair, but did eventually re-enter service for Bore, remaining with the company until May 1959 when she arrived at Hong Kong to be broken up (Photograph courtesy Bore Line)*

Services: General tramping

LOFGREN A/B, EMIL,
Västra Trädgardsgatan 11a, Postfack 1209, Stockholm, Sweden

ÅNGFARTYGS-A/B SIGGY, Mariehamn (Maarianhamina), Åland (Finnish flag)

Siggy	1921	Nüscke	1792	2975	279–0	42–2	17–9	9.5
ex Carl 35, ex Artensis 34, ex Gustav Fischer 24								

Funnel: Black with black M on white band
Hull: Black
Services: General tramping

MATTSON, CURT G, Aurorank 5, Helsinki (Helsingfors)

CURT MATTSON REDERI-A/B

Hammarland	1911	ThmpsJ	3875	6412	363–8	50–2	21–8	11.0
ex Jurko Topic 37, ex Wien 36, ex Jurko Topic 34, ex Cento 30								
Hogland	1914	Rhead3	4360	7700	374–10	51–0	23–7	10.0
ex Kingswood 28, ex Rumney 24, ex Onwen 20								

A/B NAXOS PRINCE

Kastelholm	1907	Bremer	5417	8738	437–1	54–6	25–6	9.5
ex Woron 27, ex Naimes 20								

Funnel: Black with white T on red band
Services: General tramping
Note: Also vessels trading in the Baltic Sea

MERITOIMI O/Y, Turku (Åbo)

LAIVA O/Y ANSIO

Aura	1908	Irvine	1912	3200	289–3	40–5	18–0	9.5
ex Mary 33, ex Grovehill 15								
Vienti	1911	Nyland	1715	2800	274–11	40–0	17–0	9.0
ex Bris 36, ex Bruse 33								

TURUN LAIVA O/Y

Airisto	1907	Austin	2410	4000	295.0	43–5	19–9	9.0
ex Ragni 35, ex Sixty-Four 33, ex Sommen 20, ex St Thomas 16, ex Vikingen 15								

Funnel: Black with red star emblem on white disc surrounded by red circle superimposed on narrow red band, all on broad white band
Services: General tramping
Note: Also vessels under 1500gt

NIELSEN & THORDÉN O/Y, A/B,
Eteläranta 12, Postbox 88, Helsinki (Helsingfors)

A/B BRITANNIA STEAMSHIP CO LTD

Britannic	1899	WoodS1	2242	3450	300–6	42–5	18–5	7.5
ex Oceanic 33, ex Franz Haubuss 26, ex Ferro 24, ex Falkanger 16, ex Brynhild 15, ex Hirundo 11								
Scandinavic	1903	Irvin2	2320	4000	311–6	45–1	18–8	8.5
ex H Pontoppidan 32, ex Olympic 13								

A/B HELSINGFORS STEAMSHIP CO LTD

Delaware	1902	Dobson	2441	4135	307–10	43–6	19–7	8.0
ex Newa 30, ex Mickley 07								
Nidarholm	1920	Thorny	2588	4265	304–7	43–10	20–4	9.0
ex Meandros 25								

A/B OHLSON STEAMSHIP CO O/Y

Carolus	1919	OsbGr2	2245	3500	296–2	43–4	19–0	9.0
Ericus	1919	OsbGr2	2214	3500	296–9	43–5	19–0	9.0

Funnel: Yellow with black N on white diamond superimposed on red over green bands
Hull: Black
Services: General tramping
Note: Also vessels in Baltic/NW Europe/UK trade

NORDSTROM & CO O/Y, AKTIEBOLAG R, Lovisa (Loviisa)

LOVISA REDERI-A/B

Immo-Ragnar	1914	Clyde	2342	3500	299–8	42–4	19–0	8.5
ex Inga 36, ex Lynntown 32, ex Capelcourt 19, ex Hermia 17								
Karl-Erik	1923	Trondh	1945	3100	265.8	42–3	18–0	8.5
ex Salamis 39, ex Oddvar 37								
Margareta	1902	Murdo1	2155		296–9	43–0	18–7	8.0
ex Barbro 39, ex Polarhavet 33, ex Atlanten 27								
Martti-Ragnar	1912	Neptn1	3989	6000	361–5	50–0	23–0	10.0
ex Ähtäri 39, ex Mimis Chandris 38, ex Oueme 36, ex Ingo 21								
Veli-Ragnar	1914	Craig2	2158	3700	298–11	44–0	19–0	8.5
ex Torgny Lagman 38, ex Banchory 31								

Funnel: Blue with yellow Y on red band
Services: General tramping

NYLUND, E, Mariehamn (Maarianhamina), Aland

REDERI-A/B YILDUM

Yildum	1913	RottDD	3300	5600	345–3	48–2	20–7	9.5

REDERI-A/B YRSA

Yrsa	1914	GrayX	2803	4820	330–8	46–6	20–0	9.0
ex Blairadam 36, ex Ubier 22								

NYMAN, HARALD, Lonnrotsink 39c, Helsinki (Helsingfors)

Services: General tramping

O/Y SEA FREIGHT A/B

Aagot	1906	GrayX	3939	6085	350–4	48–0	22–7	8.5

PAULIN, J W, Uudenportink 2, Viipuri (Viborg)

Funnel: Yellow with black top and white JWP on red band, with yellow band above and yellow over black bands below
Services: General tramping

Note: Also vessels under 1500gt

Imatra	1912	RottDD	3259	5600	342–4	48–1	20–7	9.0
ex Alcor 15								
Modesta	1917	Prstm1	3830	6250	357–9	50–10	21–6	9.5
Nagu	1927	Napr&M	3393	5777	352–2	48–9	21–6	10.0
ex Bradesk 36								

SEPPINEN & KEMPPI O/Y (A K Seppinen and Alb Kemppi), Koivisto

Funnel: Black with red bordered black diamond at centre of blue cross (+) on white band
Services: General tramping
Note: Also short-sea vessels

O/Y SARMATIA

Sarmatia	1901	GrayX	2417	3750	312–9	43–3	18–11	8.0

SLOTTE, ALEXANDER, Sändögatan 3, Vaasa (Vasa)

Funnel: Black with three white bands
Services: General tramping
Note: * Sold Lovisa Rederi-A/B (manager A/B R Nordström & Co O/Y), Finland, 1939, renamed *Martti-Ragnar*

ÄHTÄRI O/Y								
Ähtäri*	1912	Neptn1	3989	6000	361–5	50–0	23–0	10.0
ex Mimis Chandris 38, ex Oueme 36, ex Ingo 21								
O/Y WASA STEAMSHIP CO LTD								
Elle	1913	ThmpR2	3868	6250	350.0	50–1	21–9	8.5
ex Ellerdale 38								

THORDÉN, GUSTAF B, Brandön Huvilakaupunki (Brandö Villastad), Kulosaari (Brandö)

Funnel: Black with white star on red band
Hull: Light grey, red boot-topping; fruit carriers: white
Services: Fruit trades; oil and petroleum trades; general tramping

General cargo vessels and fruit* carriers

Kristina Thordén* (m,P12/1)	order	CrichV	3501	5985	388–2	51–5	23–10	15.0
Selma Thordén* (m,P12/1)	order	CrichV	3503	5985	388–2	51–5	23–10	15.0
REDERI-A/B ASTRID THORDÉN								
Astrid Thordén* (m,P12/1)	1937	CrichV	1816	3000	305–10	42–4	18–7	14.5
REDERI-A/B ESTER THORDÉN								
Ester Thordén	1921	Fredst	1940	3050	264–9	42–2	18–0	9.0
ex C G Thulin 32								
A/B FINSKA NORDAMERIKA LINIEN								
Mathilda Thordén* (m,P12/1)	1938	CrichV	3641	5985	388–2	51–5	23–9	15.0
REDERI-A/B PEGGY THORDÉN								
Marisa Thordén	1920	ThmpsJ	4536	6900	376–10	52–10	23–3	10.0
ex Starck 35, ex Stakesby 29								
Peggy Thordén	1922	Nüscke	1784	2997	280–10	42–3	17–10	9.5
ex Nervion 34, ex Hans Fischer 24, ex Erik Larsen 23								
REDERI-A/B STEAM								
Brita Thordén	1920	Sørlan	1866	3050	277–2	42–1	17–6	9.5
ex Gerdrun 35, ex Eidsbotten 27, ex Aries 21								
Karin Thordén	1919	Sørlan	1789	3050	277–7	42–1	17–8	9.0
ex Eda 34, ex Antares 21								
REDERI-A/B SUOMI								
Björneborg	1894	Ropnr1	2466	3700	305–1	40–5	20–2	7.0
ex Arnøy 23, ex Vestland 16, ex St Andrew 16, ex Maria 97								
Carolina Thordén* (m,P12/1)	1937	CrichV	3645	5985	388–3	51–5	23–9	14.5
REDERI-A/B THOR								
Greta Thordén	1906	Eider1	2084	3150	287–1	39–10	18–8	9.0
ex Greta 29, ex Frieda Fahrenheim 26, ex Regnator 13, ex Rendsburg 11								
Hulda Thordén	1900	Blyth	2255	3925	312–10	43–2	19–3	8.0
ex Herbert Fischer 28, ex Woodburn 22								
Ingrid Thordén	1920	LindMo	1869	3330	277–8	42–9	19–2	8.5
ex Knäppingsborg 31								

Note: Also *Maud Thordén* (built 1921/1335gt) and short-sea vessels

Tanker

REDERI-A/B SUOMI TANKER

Josefina Thordén (m2)	1931	Eriksb	6549	9765	422–6	55–1	26–9	11.5

Funnel: Black with white U
Hull: Black
Services: General tramping

ULFF A/B, TORE, Norrlandsgatan 2, Stockholm, Sweden

REDERI-A/B DAPHNE, Brandön (Brandö) (Finnish flag)								
Daphne	1920	deKlop	1939	3000	267.7	42–1	17–9	9.0
ex Granheim 36, ex Avecappelle 26, ex Yselveer 22								
REDERI-A/B DIANA, Brandön (Brandö) (Finnish flag)								
Diana	1908	OsbGr1	1892	3200	289–1	40–1	18–0	8.0
ex Blenda 34, ex Kennington 24, ex Grantley 24								

Services: General tramping

VAASEN LAIVA O/Y, Vaasa (Vasa)

Kemi	1900	Neptn1	2462	4000	302–1	41–0	23.3	7.5
ex Spessart 32, ex Westfalen 21								
Kurikka	1918	Irvin3	3106	5050	342–0	46–10	23–2	10.0
ex Newaster 33, ex War Hamlet 19								
KOURAN LAIVA O/Y								
Koura	1907	GrayX	3335	5250	341–11	48–4	20–10	8.5
ex Mimis 36, ex Aghios Vlasios 34, ex Budapest 33, ex Sszterényi 25								
KUURTANES O/Y								
Kuurtanes	1906	GrayX	3026	5000	342–0	47–7	20–0	7.5
ex Dirphys 36, ex Ioannis Carras 29, ex Dirphys 26								

Funnel: Yellow with white W on blue band between two narrow white rings, black top
Hull: Black
Services: General tramping

WIHURI, ANTTI, Kulosaari, Helsinki (Helsingfors)

Wiima	1897	GrayX	3232	5080	336–4	47–2	20–8	7.5
ex Everilda 28, ex Aldersgate 06, ex Britannic 98								
WAPPU O/Y								
Wirta	1909	Leslie	4028	7210	393–2	49–0	24–9	10.0
ex Nippon 36								
WIIDES O/Y								
Wiides	1904	Nthmb1	2324	4026	305–2	46–0	18–7	7.5
ex Ladykirk 32								
Wisa	1907	Prstm1	3846	6230	356–8	49–1	23–0	9.5
ex Dagmar Salén 36, ex Valdivia 34, ex Österdal 29, ex Alden 15								
WIIRI O/Y								
Wiiri	1912	Craig2	3525	6100	373–11	50–1	21–5	9.5
ex Charterhulme 31, ex Northway 25, ex Tempestuous 22, ex Hornfels 20								
WILKE O/Y								
Wilke	1909	ThmpR2	2598	4060	300–0	46–0	18–10	8.0
ex Relillio 32								
WINHA O/Y								
Winha	1904	Leslie	3331	5550	352–0	49–0	20–11	8.5
ex Atlantic 35								
WIPU O/Y								
Wilja	1914	ThmpR2	3396	5700	350–1	48–5	21–9	9.0
ex Gertrud 39, ex Randsfjord 34, ex Kongsfos 21								
Wipunen	1913	GrayX	4103	6100	362–11	50–0	22–8	10.0
ex Tabarka 32								
WIRMA O/Y								
Wirma	1903	ThmpR1	2609	3940	310–2	44–6	18–10	9.0
ex Rhio 32								

Note: Also short-sea vessels

Funnel: Black with two white Zs crossing, resembling a Swastika, on red band
Services: General tramping

ZACHARIASSEN & CO, J A, (Mimi and Berndt G Zachariassen), Munkkiniemi (Munksnäs)

Kronoborg	1920	Workmn	8287	11,270	461–11	58–5	29–3	10.5
ex Tower Dale 37, ex Port Curtis 36								
Marieborg	1920	B&W,K	1737	3010	272–9	40–1	18–9	9.5
ex Olga S 37								
Olovsborg	1912	Short2	5758	11,350	443–0	56–4	26–11	10.0
ex Anglo-Egyptian 27								
Saint Stephen	1911	Hamtn2	4746	7322	389–1	52–2	23–0	9.5

Note: Also short-sea vessels

France

ASSOCIATION PÉTROLIÈRE, 19–21 Rue de la Bienfaisance, Paris

Funnel: Black with yellow over green over yellow bands
Hull: Black or grey, red boot-topping
Trades: Oil and petroleum
Note: * Sold French navy 1939, hulked
Note: This company, a subsidiary of Anglo-Iranian Oil Co Ltd (controllers of British Tanker Co Ltd – *qv* in Great Britain section), also owned tankers under 500gt

Tankers								
Bahram (st)	1922	Caen	7765	12,021	452.0	57–2	29–0	10.0
ex Saint Boniface 29								
Firuz	1929	Caen	7327	11,410	467–10	56–11	27–10	11.0
Kobad	1930	Caen	7329	11,404	467–10	56–11	27–10	11.0
Shapur*	1922	Beardm	4121	5970	363–3	49–4	23–2	9.5
ex Saint Jerome 29, ex British Industry 23								

BERTIN, OSCAR E,
c/o Turner, Sturrock & Brown, Avenue Edward VII, Shanghai, China

Hull: Black
Services: Tramping Far East/Indian Ocean

Under French flag								
Hortensia Bertin	1912	Weser	3721	6077	355.1	50–5	22–10	9.0
ex King David 38, ex Gundomar 21								
Yolande Bertin	1915	Prstml	4524	7450	380.0	50–0	23–9	10.0
ex Stanthorpe 38, ex Kambole 37, ex Malvern Range 22								

CHARGEURS RÉUNIS, COMPAGNIE FRANÇAISE DE NAVIGATION À VAPEUR,
3 Boulevard Malsherbes, BP 98, Paris, and 99 Boulevard de Strasbourg, Havre

Funnel: Yellow with row of red five-pointed stars on white band; Sud Atlantique – yellow, black top
Hull: Black, red boot-topping; fruit carriers – grey, red boot topping
Services: France–Singapore–Indo-China–China; France–South America; France–French West Africa; fruit carriers – W Africa–NW Europe; Sud Atlantique – Bordeaux–Vigo–Lisbon–Rio de Janeiro–Santos–Montevideo–Buenos Aires

Passenger/general cargo vessels								
Asie (s2,P159/1,80/2,96/3)	1914	France	8561	5160	439.3	55–11	25–0	14.5
Aurigny (s2,P74/1,32/2,78/3)	1918	MéditS	9589	8150	481.6	58–2	27–11	13.5
Belle Isle (s2,P74/1,32/2,78/3)	1918	MéditH	9591	8150	479.0	58–4	27–7	13.5
Brazza (m2,P179/1,94/2,90/3)	1923	LoireN	10,387	6650	492–0	59–1	24–0	16.0
ex Camranh 27; lengthened 36, conv general cargo 27								
Cap Padaran (st,P154/1,70/2,618/3)	1922	LoireS	8009	8850	417.7	55–1	27–9	13.0
ex D'Iberville 25; conv general cargo 25								
Cap Saint Jacques (st,P117/1,610/4)	1921	LoireN	8009	8850	417.7	55–1	27–9	13.0
ex Guichen 25; conv general cargo 26								
Cap Tourane (st,P117/1,610/4)	1924	LoireN	8009	8850	417.7	55–1	27–9	13.0
ex Jouffroy D'Abbans 25; conv general cargo 25								
Cap Varella (st,P117/1,610/4)	1922	LoireN	8009	8850	417.7	55–1	27–9	13.0
ex Kersaint 25; conv general cargo 26								
Désirade (s2,P97/1,16/2,84/3,803/4)	1921	France	9645	8200	501–0	58–11	27–9	13.5
Formose (s2,P100/1,36/2,84/3,782/4)	1921	MéditS	9975	8400	501–0	58–11	27–10	13.5
Foucauld (s2,P258/1,133/2,62/3,512/4)	1922	MéditS	11,028	5710	501–0	58–11	27–10	14.5
ex Hoedic 29								
Groix (s2,P100/1,36/2,84/3,782/4)	1922	MéditS	9975	8400	501–0	58–11	27–10	13.5
Jamaique (st2,P103/1,150/2,150/3,400/4)	1922	SHWR	10,123	8750	499–0	59–5	27–8	13.5
ex Mosella 28								
Kerguelen (st2,P103/1,150/2,150/3,400/4)	1922	SHWR	10,123	8750	499–0	59–5	27–8	13.5
ex Meduana 28								
Lipari (st2,P111/1,35/2,84/3,774/4)	1922	LoireS	9954	8400	478.5	59–3	27–11	13.5
General cargo vessels								
Aden (s2,P6)	1918	Asano	8033	11,420	461–8	58–0	28–8	11.0
Ango (P–)	1913	MéditH	7110	9178	414.0	53–10	27–5	12.0
Bangkok (s2,P6)	1919	Uraga	8056	11,360	461–8	58–0	28–8	10.5
Baoulé (P12)	1921	LoireN	5874	7500	393.6	55–11	25–5	11.5
Bougainville (P)	1913	MéditH	7110	9178	414.0	53–10	27–5	12.0

CGT: Île-de-France *was launched at St Nazaire on March 14 1926 and made her maiden voyage from Havre to New York in June 1927. Fitted with four screws and four St Nazaire/Parsons steam turbines developing 52,000ship she voyaged successfully on the North Atlantic, but with the start of war in September 1939 made her last prewar Havre–New York crossing. She went from New York to Marseilles in May 1940, but soon left that port and was heading for Saigon via Cape Town when diverted to Singapore. In July she was taken over by the British at Singapore, and while many of her crew were persuaded to join the Allied cause, the majority did not stay with the vessel. In November 1940* Île-de-France *was requisitioned as a troopship with accommodation for about 8000 troops, being managed and largely crewed by P&O. In January 1944 management was transferred to Cunard. From the start of her trooping duties until May 1945* Île-de-France *travelled over 500,000 miles and carried 485,000 military personnel. In September 1945 she was returned to France, and was used immediately on voyages from Cherbourg and Southampton to the US repatriating US and Canadian troops. At the end of 1945 the liner went to the Far East to bring home 3500 former POWs. She was released to CGT in 1947 and refitted for re-entry into North Atlantic service. Her postwar service took her to 1958 when she was laid up pending sale, and the following year she was sold to Okada Gumi of Japan for breaking up. She made the delivery voyage to Japan under the name* Furanzu Maru, *but before scrapping was used by Metro-Goldwyn-Mayer and temporarily renamed* Claridon *for use in the film The Last Voyage. This involved a controlled explosion scuttling off Japan (RW Jordan collection)*

Lamy: Danaé, *built at Le Trait in 1936, was taken over by the Ministry of Shipping in 1940 and renamed* Danae II *under the British flag. In 1945 she was returned by the Ministry of War Transport to France and renamed* Danaé. *In her owner's service she continued until 1966 when sold to a company based in Haiti and renamed* Pangloss. *Later the same year she raised the Panamanian flag as* Stelios. *She was broken up in 1968 (RW Jordan collection)*

Chargéurs Reunis: Kerguelen *was completed in 1923 as* Meduana *for the Sud-Atlantique company. She was launched on September 30 1920 and on November 23 while fitting-out was on fire and sank at the berth. She was raised in April 1921, and it was not until February 1923 that she made her maiden voyage from Bordeaux to South America. In May 1928* Meduana *was transferred to Chargeurs Réunis and renamed* Kerguelen *for service from Hamburg, Antwerp and French ports to South America. She became a transport in 1940, and on August 6 1940 was seized at Bordeaux by the occupying Germans. She was renamed* Winrich von Kniprode, *and was prepared as transport H20 for the later to be abandoned Operation 'Seelöwe'. On October 16 1940 she was commissioned as a transport for carrying German troops to and from Norway. In January 1945 it was intended that the vessel be used for accommodation purposes, but the plans were changed and she was handed over to the VTS organisation. In March 1945 at Pillau she was bombed and damaged by Allied aircraft. She was recovered at Kiel in May 1945 and after temporary repairs at Rotterdam was returned to Chargeurs Réunis in November 1945 as* Kerguelen. *Following a 1947–48 refit at Bordeaux she resumed service between that port and South America and was broken up in 1955 at Antwerp (RW Jordan collection)*

Casamance	1921	LoireS	5817	7500	390.6	55–11	25–5	11.0
D'Entrecasteaux (P12)	1922	MéditH	7291	9470	417.8	55–4	27–9	12.0
Dahomey (P12)	1920	LoireS	5851	7500	393.6	55–11	25–5	11.0
Dalny	1914	Bremer	6672	11,450	472.3	58–11	27–0	10.5
ex Waldeck 20								
Dupleix (P12)	1914	LoireN	7135	9182	417.9	54–0	27–6	12.0
Forbin (P12)	1922	MéditH	7291	9470	417.8	55–2	27–9	12.0
Fort Archambault	1918	H&W,B	5549	8247	412–6	52–4	25–4	10.5
ex Ariano 29, ex War Python 19								
Fort Binger	1919	Craig2	5250	8247	412–6	52–4	25–4	10.5
ex Cornish City 29, launched as War Ferret								
Fort de Douaumont	1918	Doxfrd	5266	8339	412–5	52–2	25–4	10.5
ex War Deer 19								
Fort de Souville	1918	Craig2	5228	8230	412–6	52–4	25–4	10.5
ex War Finch 19								
Fort de Troyon	1919	BrownJ	5206	8264	417–7	52–4	25–4	10.5
ex War Rider 19								
Fort de Vaux	1918	Ropnr2	5186	8248	412–6	52–3	25–4	10.5
ex War Gnat 19								
Fort Lamy	1919	Craig2	5234	8230	412–6	52–4	25–4	10.5
ex Portfield 29, launched as War Peacock								
Fort Médine	1919	Craig2	5355	8247	412–6	52–5	25–4	10.5
ex Bradford City 29, launched as War Fox								
Linois	1907	Blohm	7472	9362	434.4	54–11	26–11	11.0
ex Santa Elena 22								

COMPAGNIE DE NAVIGATION SUD ATLANTIQUE, 3 Boulevard Malsherbes, BP 98, Paris, and 1 Allées de Chartres, Bordeaux

Passenger and passenger/general cargo vessels

Massilia (r/t4,231/1,71/2,88/3,456/st)	1920	MéditS	15,363	6100	600–1	64–1	26–6	20.0
Pasteur (st4,P216/1,906/t)	1939	PenhtS	29,253	9689	696–10	88–2	30–7	23.0

COMPAGNIE DES TRANSPORTS MARITIMES DE L'AFRIQUE OCCIDENTALE FRANÇAISE

Fruit carriers

Kakoulima* (P11)	1933	ProvPB	3723	1907	341–7	48–8	18–0	14.5
Katiola* (st,P12)	1936	MéditS	3891	1869	350–1	49–4	18–10	15.5
Kilissi* (P11)	1934	ProvPB	3723	1907	341–7	48–8	18–0	14.5
Kindia	1919	Napr&M	1972	2060	282–0	37–10	17–6	10.0
ex Haworth 29, launched as War Stour								
Kita* (st,P12)	1936	MéditS	3894	1870	350–1	49–4	18–10	15.5
Kolenté* (P11)	1932	ProvPB	3723	1907	341–7	48–11	18–0	14.5

Note: * Registered owner Compagnie Française de Navigation à Vapeur Chargeurs Réunis

CHASTELLAIN & COMPAGNIE, J,

27 bis, Rue de Buffon, and 11 Rue Vignon, Paris

Funnel: Black with houseflag
Services: N France and NW Europe to Mediterranean

COMPAGNIE DE TRANSPORTS MARITIMES ET FLUVIAUX

Formigny	1915	Nüscke	2166	4300	310.8	42–6	26.1	11.0
ex Frida Horn 21, ex Stettin 17								

COMPAGNIE DES AFFRÊTEURS FRANÇAIS

Cérès	1918	Eltrgm	3073	5550	330.6	47–9	21–4	10.0
Rabelais	1921	SOuest	4999	7000	386.4	52–5	23–1	10.5
ex Jean Stern 25								
Villiers	1923	SMvJS	2548	4095	344–6	45–6	18–11	10.0
ex Barmbek 28								

COMPAGNIE MARITIME NORMANDE

Gonneville	1912	Koch	2285	3100	291–0	38–11	20–0	9.0
ex Tetuan 28								

COMPAGNIE AUXILIAIRE DE NAVIGATION, 48 Rue La Bruyère, Paris 9e

Funnel: Black with band of blue and white vertical stripes
Hull: Tankers – black, red boot-topping; *Pierre-Claude* – white, red boot-topping
Trades: Oil and petroleum; fruit trades

Tankers

Henry Desprez (m2)	1932	B&W	9895	14,948	489.9	65–2	28–8	12.5
La Saône (st2)	order	France	12,202	16,850	506.1	72–8	33–0	13.0
La Seine (st2)	order	France	12,202	16,850	506.1	72–8	33–0	13.0
Melpomene	1923	GirndB	7011	10,646	426–11	56–9	26–0	10.5
Monique	1922	GirndB	7011	10,705	425.0	56–9	26–0	10.5
Omphale*	1922	PenhtS	6477	9396	442.5	57–6	24–0	10.5
Ophélie	1922	PenhtS	6477	9396	421.6	57–6	24–0	10.5

Chargeurs Réunis: The liner Massilia *was launched on April 30 1914 and construction ceased upon the outbreak of war. She was delivered on October 8 1920 and at the end of the month started her maiden voyage from Bordeaux to the River Plate. Her triple expansion engines and low pressure turbines were originally coal burning, but in 1928 she was converted at Penhoët to an oil burner. Two years later her original accommodation for 464 first, 129 second, 98 third and 350 steerage passengers was altered to 231, 71, 88 and 456 respectively. In April 1940* Massilia *was used as a troop transport and in June took 150 members of the French government from Bordeaux to Casablanca. She was then laid up at Marseilles. In August 1944 she was scuttled by the retreating Germans off the Mirabeau Basin, Marseilles, in order to block the harbour entrance. The wreck was raised and broken up postwar (RW Jordan collection)*

Fabre Line: Patria, *fitted with two triple expansion engines of 9500ihp, was completed at the Méditerranée shipyard, La Seyne, in March 1914. She made her first voyage in April 1914 from Marseilles to New York and apart from wartime interruptions remained on this service until 1931. She was then chartered to Messageries Maritimes for its Marseilles–Egypt– Levant service.* Patria *was sold to Messageries Maritimes on January 1 1940, and delivered to them at Haifa in July that year. She was requisitioned by Great Britain at Haifa in August 1940, and was sunk there on November 25 1940 following an explosion on board believed to have been caused by sabotage. There were many casualties. The wreck was raised in 1952 and broken up (RW Jordan collection)*

CGT: The liner Mexique *was launched as Île de Cuba on May 27 1914 and was intended for the Havre–Mexico–Central America service. It was then decided she should transfer to the Bordeaux–New York service and she was renamed Lafayette in 1915, making her maiden voyage in November. She was given the name* Mexique *in 1928. In June 1939 she was laid up pending sale for scrapping, but in July re-entered service carrying Jewish refugees to Mexico. With the outbreak of war it was at first intended she should be converted to an armed merchant cruiser, but instead she became an armed transport, and as such went from Brest to Norway in April–May 1940 with troops of the ill-fated expeditionary force.* Mexique *later went to the Mediterranean and came under Vichy control. On June 19 1940 she was struck by a magnetic mine and sunk at Le Verdon, River Gironde. There were no fatalities and the 178 persons on board were all rescued (RW Jordan collection)*

CGT: The quadruple-screw liner Paris *was laid down at St Nazaire in September 1913 and launched in 1916 only for work to be suspended because priority was being given to wartime construction and repairs. After the war work recommenced and* Paris *was completed in June 1921. She entered CGT's Havre–New York service. In August 1929 she was damaged by fire, but was repaired and resumed service in January 1930. In 1937 she was withdrawn from the regular service to New York, making only occasional voyages. During the evening of April 18 1939, while preparing for departure she was on fire at Havre. The following morning* Paris *heeled over on her side in 40 feet of water after the accommodation and superstructure had been gutted. Her engines were largely intact. At the time she had on board several valuable works of art, most of which were removed safely. The wreck was removed after the end of the Second World War (RW Jordan collection)*

Pallas	1925	SOuest	5260	8446	389.9	53–0	24–0	10.5
Rhea (m2)	1928	SOuest	7813	11,548	462–7	62–2	26–8	11.0
Roxane (m2)	1929	SOuest	7813	11,632	462–7	62–1	26–8	11.0
Salomé (m2)	bldg	France	13,140	18,530	574–2	71–6	30–11	13.0
Shéhérazade (m2)	1935	Seine	13,467	18,530	574–0	71–11	30–11	13.0
COMPAGNIE AFRICAINE D'ARMEMENT								
Mérope	1922	Provçl	7011	10,705	426.0	56–8	26–0	10.5
Theodora (m2)	bldg	B&W	10,765	15,452	534–0	65–9	29–2	12.5
Fruit carrier								
COMPAGNIE DE NAVIGATION FRUITIÈRE								
Pierre-Claude (m,P4)	1934	B&W	1787	2560	310–0	42–9	18–4	14.0
ex Asta 35								

Note: BU Belgium 1939

COMPAGNIE DE NAVIGATION FRAISSINET, 3–5 Rue Beauvau, Marseilles

Funnel: White, black top
Hull: Black or white, red boot-topping
Services: Marseilles–Constantinople–Bourgas–Constanta–Sulina–Galatz–Braila; Marseilles–Senegal–French Guinea–Sierra Leone–Ivory Coast–Dahomey–Nigeria–Cameroons

Note: Also vessels owned and on operated Mediterranean services, particularly Marseilles–Corsica

Passenger and passenger/general cargo vessels								
Hoggar (P44/1,44/2,586/3)	1923	MéditS	5146	5132	390.2	50–2	22–11	13.0
Touareg (P650)	1924	ProvPB	5135	5920	390.3	50–2	22–11	13.0
Fruit carriers								
Cap des Palmes (m,P12/1)	1935	Helsgr	3082	1950	351–1	44–0	18–1	15.0
Tamara (r/t,P12/1)	1937	ProvPB	3747	2630	344–11	47–11	18–10	15.0
General cargo vessel								
Tombouctou (P–)	1919	Workmn	5302	8163	412–6	52–5	25–3	10.0
ex Kepwickhall 30, ex Ballygally Head 24, launched as War Peewit								

COMPAGNIE DE NAVIGATION MIXTE, (COMPAGNIE TOUACHE)

1 La Canabière, Marseilles

Funnel: Black with black 'NM' on white band between two narrow red bands
Hull: Black, red boot-topping
Services: Marseilles–N Africa; oil and petroleum trades (managed tankers)
Note: Also owned and operated vessels in service between Marseilles and N Africa and others under 2000gt

Passenger/general cargo vessel								
Kairouan (te2,P133/1,287/t,957/4)	bldg	MéditS	8602	2040	467–7	60–2	20–8	22.5
SOCIÉTÉ ANONYME MAZOUT TRANSPORTS								
Tankers								
Capitaine Damiani	1921	Nat3R	4854	6729	380.7	51–10	23–0	11.0
CIP	1922	Normnd	6587	9365	422.5	57–8	24–10	11.5
Motrix	1922	Normnd	6587	9365	422.5	57–8	24–10	11.5

COMPAGNIE DE NAVIGATION PAQUET,

90 Boulevard des Dames, Marseilles

Funnel: Black
Hull: Passenger vessels – most white, red boot-topping; other vessels – black, red boot-topping
Services: Marseille–Tangier–Agadir–Casablanca–Dakar

Note: * Sold 1939, wrecked 9.9.39 near Itu Aba, Spratley Archipelago
Note: Also vessels under 2000gt, and others in service Marseilles–Algiers

Passenger/general cargo vessels								
Asni* (P70)	1929	SHWR	2800	3130	330.3	43–0	21–3	12.0
Azrou (st,P26/1,24/2,48/3)	1931	Bretgn	2998	3174	330.6	43–1	22–1	13.5
Chella (st2,P178/1,188/2,102/3)	1935	MéditS	8920	2950	453–0	62–1	22–0	20.0
Djenné (st2,P168/1,148/2,96/3)	1931	MéditS	8790	4893	449–2	58–8	23–10	17.0
Iméréthie II (P46/1,41/2,30/3)	1925	MéditS	3713	3776	330.5	43–5	22–5	12.0
Koutoubia (st2,P168/1,148/2,96/3)	1931	MéditS	8790	4971	443–7	58–6	23–10	17.0
Maréchal Lyautey (st2,P173/1,149/2,80/3)	1924	MéditS	8256	4132	428.0	56–10	21–10	14.5
Médie II (P81/1,60/2,40/3)	1922	MéditS	5078	5111	385.9	46–0	24–3	14.5
General cargo vessels								
Arcturus (P7)	1914	Neptnl	2532	4881	331–5	46–0	21–0	10.5
Bamako (m,P4)	1930	B&W	2357	4064	303–2	45–1	21–3	12.0
Le Rhin (P21)	1920	Graysn	2456	3120	275–0	41–4	20–2	12.0
Oued Fes (P6)	1913	StettO	2633	4907	345–8	46–2	20–10	9.5
ex Paz 29, ex Bath 25, ex Andromeda 17								
Oued Sebou II (P24/1,24/2)	1925	MéditS	2448	3257	279.2	42–1	19–4	10.5

COMPAGNIE DELMAS VIELJEUX, 29 Rue Galilée, Paris

Funnel: Black with white 'ship's wheel' emblem
Hull: Black, red boot-topping, white dividing line
Services: France–UK, Belgium, Netherlands (coal trade); Nantes, La Rochelle-Pallice, Bordeaux–Morocco, Algeria, Tunisia (general cargo and passenger); N Africa–Italy (ore, mineral, grain trades); Hamburg, Rotterdam, Antwerp, Dunkirk and other French ports–French W Africa

André Thome	1920	ArsnBr	2012	3100	281–10	39–5	19–10	8.0
ex Député André Thome 25								
Argonne	1920	White	2115	3200	280.0	40–2	18–9	8.0
Auvergne	1921	White	2114	3200	280.0	40–2	18–9	8.0
Cévennes (st)	1921	Bretgn	2509	3800	302–0	43–4	19–6	9.0
Cornouaille	1928	AwpEng	3324	5105	336–4	48–2	21–4	10.0
ex Mahagi 38								
Maurice Delmas	1919	Dobson	3161	4785	338–9	47–6	21–8	10.5
ex Mateba 37, launched as War Crater								
Medjerda	1923	GirndH	4578	6850	377–0	49–1	23–3	10.5
ex Capitaine Charles Boivin 24								
2 Newbuildings (m)	order	7300	408–2	51–8	23–8	14.0		

Registered owner –

COMPAGNIE DU CHEMIN DE FER DE PARIS À ORLEANS

Agen	1921	Pgill2	4186	6920	380–4	52–11	22–11	10.0
Albi	1920	Pgill2	4191	6925	380–4	52–10	22–11	10.0
Aurillac	1921	Pgill2	4248	6935	380–4	52–10	22–11	10.0
Bourges	1919	Forth	2910	4976	324.4	44–4	21–8	9.0
Châteauroux	1921	TyneIr	4185	6960	380–4	52–10	23–0	9.5
Lorient	1921	TyneIr	4185	6960	380–4	52–10	23–0	9.5
Montauban	1920	Forth	4191	6960	380–4	52–10	23–0	9.5
Poitiers	1921	TyneIr	4185	6965	380–4	52–10	23–0	9.5
Psyché*	1904	Blumrl	2951	5000	315.0	46–0	23–1	9.0
Saint Nazaire	1919	Forth	2910	4890	324.5	44–4	21–8	9.0
Saumur	1920	Forth	2955	4890	324.4	44–4	21–8	9.0
Tours	1920	Forth	4158	6980	380–4	52–10	22–11	10.0
Vendôme	1920	TyneIr	4192	6945	380–4	52–10	22–11	10.0

COMPAGNIE COMMERCIALE DE L'AFRIQUE EQUATORIALE FRANÇAISE

Mécanicien Principal Carvin	1920	GirndB	4282	6742	362.9	49–2	24.4	9.5

Note: * Sold Marine National (French navy) 1939, for conversion to storeship

COMPAGNIE FLUVIALE ET MARITIME DE L'OUEST AFRICAIN, 22 Rue de l'Arcade, Paris

Services: Hamburg, NW European–Dakar–W Africa

Elima	1920	Koch	5264	7814	386.7	52–8	24–0	10.0
ex Ingeborg 28, ex Progress 27								

COMPAGNIE FRANÇAISE DES PÉTROLES, Rue du Docteur Lancereaux II, Paris

Funnel: Yellow with black top, blue band and emblem
Hull: Black, red boot-topping
Trades: Oil and petroleum

COMPAGNIE NAVALE DES PÉTROLES

Tankers

Emile Miguet (m2)	1937	France	14,115	21,735	577–2	73–11	32–6	13.5
Palmyre (m2)	bldg	PenhtS	14,120	21,735	577–2	73–11	32–5	13.0

COMPAGNIE FRANCE-NAVIGATION, 21 Rue de l'Arcade and 18 Rue Pasquier, Paris 8e

Funnel: Black with white IO monogram
Hull: Black
Services: N and S France–N Africa

Aïn el Turk	1925	SHWR	2477	4650	315.9	45–1	21–6	10.0
ex Koningen Elisabeth 37								
Bonifacio	1918	Blumrl	3566	6200	356.3	48–9	23–5	9.5
ex Craggan Hill 37, ex Wulsty Castle 36; conv mv 36, conv steamer 26								
Bougaroni	1919	Blumrl	3050	5125	342–0	46–10	21–9	10.0
ex Sheaf Spear 37, launched as War Sun								
Grand Quévilly	1914	Blumrl	2844	4940	348–0	48–10	21–6	12.0
ex San Carlos 38, ex Rio de la Plata 24								
Gravelines	1925	SHWR	2477	4650	315.9	45–1	21–6	10.0
ex Roi Albert 38								
Guilvinec	1920	LloydR	3273	5020	342–0	46–6	21–9	9.0
ex Stanmore 37, ex Mambika 37, ex Asier 25, ex War River 20								
Perros Guirec	1921	ArsnCh	2012	3100	281–10	39–5	19–10	8.0
ex Edimbourg 37, ex Commandant Rabot 24								
Saint Malô	1917	Kwsaki	5779	9163	381.9	51–2	27–1	10.5
ex Commandant Mages 38, ex War Wolf 19								
Winnipeg (s2)	1918	France	8379	8150	495–0	59–10	26–8	12.5
ex Paimpol 39, ex Winnipeg 38, Jacques Cartier 31								

Note: In Sept 1939 company wound up and vessels transferred – *Bonifacio, St Malô, Winnipeg,* to Compagnie Générale Transatlantique (*qv*), *Aïn el Turk, Bougaroni, Gravelines* to Cie Française de Nav à Vapeur Chargeurs Reunis (*qv*), *Grand Quévilly, Guilvinec, Perros Guirec* to Worms & Cie (*qv*)
Note: Also vessels under 2000gt

Les Petroles: The tanker Aragaz *was completed by Armstrong, Whitworth at Newcastle in May 1914, and together with her two sisterships was involved in carrying oil mainly from the US Gulf and Curaçao to northwest Europe during 1938–39. After the war* Aragaz *was sold to Sociedade Geral de Comércio of Portugal and renamed* Monchique. *In 1950 she was sold to Bisco, and renamed* Bisco 1 *for the delivery voyage in tow to Rosyth, where she was broken up (R Sherlock)*

Louis-Dreyfus: Jean L-D *was built at Dunkirk in 1936 for this Paris merchants company which owned its first steamers in 1891. She was powered by a CCM/Sulzer 8-cylinder oil engine of 3300bhp. After Allied service during the Second World War she was sold in 1945 to Compagnie Marseillaise de Navigation Coloniale, Paris, and renamed* Betelgeuse. *She returned to Louis-Dreyfus in 1947 and was once again name* Jean L-D. *The London subsidiary Buries Markes took over the vessel in 1954 and she was renamed* La Laguna *under the British flag. She was then sold to a Greek company in 1958 and renamed* Achaean, *to another Greek company in 1965 and renamed* Transrodopi I, *and finally to Bulgaria in 1968 and renamed* Alphacca. *She was broken up in Japan in 1968 (Alex Duncan)*

Messageries Maritimes: Eridan *was completed at the Provençale shipyard, La Ciotat, in November 1929 for Services Contractuels des Messageries Maritimes, this company's state-aided associate. In June 1940 she was under Vichy control, but on November 8 1942 was captured by vessels of the covering force for Operation 'Torch'. She was taken over by the Ministry of War Transport and placed under the management of British India. In March 1946* Eridan *was returned to Messageries Maritimes and after a brief period of trooping in the Mediterranean, was in 1946–47 refitted at Toulon. She was broken up at La Seyne in 1956 (Alex Duncan)*

Messageries Maritimes: Well-known to many Allied troops during the Second World War was the liner Felix Roussel. *She was transferred to the UK in July 1940 after the fall of France, and under the British flag and Bibby management undertook trooping duty for most of the war. She suffered slight damage from Japanese aircraft attacks when embarking evacuees at Singapore in April 1942.* Felix Roussel *was returned to Messageries Maritimes at Durban on April 15 1946, and was refitted at Dunkirk during June 1948–September 1950. In 1955 she was sold to Arosa Line and renamed* Arosa Sun *for an Italy–New York emigrant service, but when the owning company went into bankruptcy in 1958, the vessel was laid up. In 1960 she was sold for use as a workers' hostel near Ijmuiden, and while employed in this role was damaged by fire in April 1963. In March 1974 she was towed to Bilbao to be broken up.* Felix Roussel *was built at St Nazaire in 1930 and was fitted with two CCM 10-cylinder oil engines of 10,900ihp. In February 1931 she made her maiden voyage from Marseilles to the Far East. During 1935–36 she was lengthened by 27 feet and re-engined with two CCM/Sulzer 10-cylinder oil engines of 14,700ihp. The result was a 4 knot increase in speed (RW Jordan collection)*

Messageries Maritimes: Leconte de Lisle *was completed in 1922 at the Provençale shipyard in La Ciotat. She was fitted originally with steam turbines, but these were found to be unsatisfactory on trials and delivery was delayed while two sets of Provençale triple expansion engines, totalling 7000ihp, were fitted. In September 1939 the vessel was transferred from Marseilles–East Africa to the Marseilles–Indo-China service, and on April 10 1942 was seized in Indo-China by the Japanese. She was renamed* Teiritsu Maru *and used as a transport mainly between Japan and Korea. In July 1945 she was bombed by US aircraft off Maizuru naval base, the bombs missed, but in the course of escaping* Teiritsu Maru *struck a mine and sank in shallow water. Salvage was started in 1947 and Japan was ordered to return the vessel in a condition similar to that when seized, with Messageries Maritimes bearing the cost of modernisation and improvements. In August 1948 she was refloated and taken to Maizuru for rebuilding. This was completed in December 1950 and she was put on to the Marseilles–Indian Ocean service under her former name. During the French colonial problems she carried troops to Indo-China in 1954 and returned with evacuees. She resumed commercial service in 1955, and was trooping for a short time between Marseilles and Oran in 1956. She was sold to breakers at Spezia later that year (RW Jordan collection)*

COMPAGNIE GÉNÉRALE DE NAVIGATION À VAPEUR (Fabre Line),
15 Rue Beauvau, Marseilles

Funnel: Red, blue top, white band
Hull: Black or white, red boot-topping
Services: Mail, passenger, cargo – Marseilles–Naples–Palermo–New York; Marseilles–Algeria–Palermo–Naples–Monaco; Marseilles–Lisbon–Azores–New York; Marseilles–Dakar–Duala–Lome–Port Gentil–Conakry–Takoradi and other W Africa ports; Marseilles–Beirut–Jaffa; Marseilles–Red Sea ports; fruit – French W Africa–Marseilles

Note: * Chartered Cie des Messageries Maritimes for Marseilles–Alexandria–Levant service

Passenger/general cargo vessels								
Banfora (s2,P127/1,127/2,82/3,548/4)								
	1914	Scheld	9347	6413	497–2	57–2	25–11	15.5
ex Insulinde 33								
Canada (s2,P120/1,196/2,–/4)								
	1912	MéditS	9684	5437	476.0	56–6	33.8	15.5
laid down as Santa Lucia								
Patria* (s2,140/1,250/2,1850/3)								
	1914	MéditS	11,885	5000	512–2	59–2	26–6	15.0
Providence* (s2,P140/1,250/2,1850/3)								
	1915	MéditS	11,996	5660	511–10	59–9	27–0	15.0
Sinaia (s2,P132/cab,522/3)								
	1922	Curle	8567	9220	459–0	56–1	28–0	13.5
Fruit carriers								
Benty (m,P12/1)	1938	Helsgr	2983	1950	351–0	44–0	18–1	16.0
Edea (r/t,P12/1)	1936	ProvPB	3747	2030	344–11	47–11	18–9	15.0
General cargo vessels								
Chelma (P)	1920	Palmer	4968	6795	386–5	52–6	23–4	10.5
ex Bacchus 26								
Sinfra (m2)	1929	Akers	4470	8230	402–0	54–10	25–6	11.0
ex Sandhamn 39, ex Fernglen 34								

COMPAGNIE GÉNÉRALE TRANSATLANTIQUE, (French Line),
6 Rue Auber, Paris

Funnel: Red, black top
Hull: Black, red boot-topping; *Colombie, Cuba* – white, green boot-topping; fruit carriers – white, red boot-topping
Services: Mail, passenger and cargo – Havre–Southampton–Plymouth–New York; Bordeaux–Vigo–Halifax–New York; Havre–Cuba–Mexico; Havre–Gdynia–Leningrad; Havre–Havana–Venezuela–Colombia–Panama–Pacific ports; Marseilles–Morocco–Algeria–Tunis; Bordeaux–Casablanca; Rouen–French Antilles; fruit trades – mainly French West Indies–France–NW Europe

Passenger and passenger/general cargo vessels								
Bretagne (st2,P440/cab)								
	1922	Curle	10,108	6950	472–0	59–2	26–10	14.5
ex Flandria 36								
Champlain (st2,P623/cab,308/t,122/3)								
	1932	PenhtS	28,124	7940	641–11	83–0	30–4	19.0
Colombie (st2,P201/1,146/2,144/3)								
	1931	France	13,391	5270	508–6	66–7	26–4	16.0
Cuba (st2,P450)	1923	SHWR	11,337	7290	495–1	62–4	24–0	15.5
De Grasse (st2,P536/cab,410/3)								
	1924	Cammel	18,435	6280	573–10	71–5	28–0	16.0
laid down as Suffren								
De la Salle (s2,P163/cab,128/3)								
	1921	Curle	8400	7900	459–0	56–9	26–6	13.0
Duc d'Aumale (s2,P159/1,82/2,56/3)								
	1912	ProvPB	4464	1035	378.8	49–4	17–6	15.5
Flandre (r/t4,P550)	1914	PenhtS	8571	2614	480–0	57–0	23–7	16.0
Île-de-France (st4,P670/cab,408/t,508/3)								
	1927	PenhtS	43,450	8460	792–11	91–11	32–0	23.0
Lamoricière (st3,P135/1,116/2,130/3)								
	1921	SHWR	4713	1070	387–0	50–0	29.8	17.0
Marrakech (r/t2,P106/1,56/2,76/3)								
	1914	ProvPB	6179	2115	414.3	51–8	20–4	13.0
ex Haïti 29								
Meknès (r/t2,P112/1,32/2,406/3)								
	1913	PenhtS	6127	2270	413.8	51–2	20–8	13.0
ex Puerto Rico 29								
Mexique (r/t4,P336/1,110/2,90/3,400/4)								
	1915	ProvPB	12,220	2940	563–0	64–2	24–3	18.0
ex Lafayette 28, launched as Île de Cuba								
Normandie (te4,P848/1,670/t,454/3)								
	1935	PenhtS	83,423		1029–0	118–0	57.6	28.5
Paris* (st4,P565/1,530/t,844/3)								
	1921	PenhtS	34,569	6420	764–4	85–4	31–0	21.0
General cargo vessels								
Alabama	1931	Normnd	5645	8170	442–10	54–11	25–5	13.0
Alaska	1922	Sundld	5399	8460	425.0	55–0	25–6	10.0
Arica	1921	Sundld	5390	8460	423.6	54–9	25–6	10.0
ex Zenon 21								
Arizona	1925	Sundld	5457	8460	425.0	55–0	25–6	10.0
Aveyron	1923	GirndH	4785	6850	377–0	49–2	23–3	10.5
ex Pasteur 28								
Cambronne	1919	Grgmth	3059	5100	342–0	46–9	21–9	8.5
launched as War Horizon								

Cantal	1916	OsakaO	3178	5061	305.2	43–9	23–2	9.0
ex Unkai Maru No 6 17								
Carbet	1920	Napr&M	3689	6240	377–3	49–0	23–4	11.5
Carimaré (P78)	1920	Napr&M	4459	5840	364.6	49–1	23–4	11.5
ex Saint Aygulf 22								
Floride	1921	Normnd	7030	9800	429.5	58–4	25–3	10.5
ex La Marseillaise 29								
Grandlieu	1919	HK&Wh	3290	5010	325.0	45–2	21–6	8.0
ex War Drummer 19								
Indiana (P9/1)	1915	Bremer	5751	8330	420.2	56–2	26–2	11.5
ex Kagera 22								
Loire	1928	Lithgw	4285	6800	370.0	51–0	23–1	10.5
ex Irrawaddy 38								
Louisiane	1921	PenhtS	6903	10,000	427.5	58–5	25–3	11.0
ex Notre Dame de Fourvière 29								
Martinière	1911	GrayX	3871	5320	360.0	47–1	20–10	10.0
ex Duala 21, ex Armanistan 12								
Michigan	1920	ThmpsJ	6419	10,480	427–4	55–6	28–6	12.5
Nevada (P9/1)	1915	Bremer	5693	8330	420.2	56–2	26–2	11.5
ex Rovuma 19								
Orégon (m2,P38/1)	1929	Bremer	7706	9940	493–7	61–3	26–2	14.0
Saint Domingue (P96)	1911	Laing	3159	2125	324.9	44–0	16–10	11.0
ex Pologne 32, ex Orégon 21, ex Rawson 17								
San Antonio (P11)	1930	H&W,B	6013	7700	447–0	57–5	25–7	13.0
San Diégo (P11)	1930	H&W,B	6013	7700	447–0	57–5	25–7	13.0
San Francisco (P11)	1930	H&W,B	6013	7700	447–0	57–5	25–7	13.0
San José (P11)	1931	H&W,B	6013	7675	447–0	57–5	25–7	13.0
San Mateo (P11)	1931	H&W,B	5947	7900	447–0	57–5	25–7	13.0
San Pedro (r/t,P11)	1931	H&W,B	5947	7840	447–0	57–5	25–6	13.5
Sèvre	1920	Napr&M	3689	6400	377–3	49–0	22–6	10.0
Vermont	1919	Bartm2	5186	8010	412–6	52–4	28–5	10.5
ex Easterly 21, launched as War Collie								
Winnipeg (s2)	1918	France	8379	12,800	495–0	59–10	32–0	12.0
ex Paimpol 39, ex Winnipeg 38, ex Jacques Cartier 29								
Wisconsin (P38/1)	1930	Bremer	8062	9398	493–7	61–3	26–2	14.0
Wyoming (P38/1)	1930	Bremer	8062	9350	493–7	61–3	26–2	14.0

Cattle carrier

Marigot (st)	1932	PenhtS	4048	2800	344–0	52–6	25–0	14.5
ex Ardèche 35; conv fruit carrier 39, conv sheep carrier 35								

Operated by

COMPAGNIE GÉNÉRALE D'ARMEMENTS MARITIMES (*qv* below)

Fruit carriers

Barfleur (m,P12)	1938	B&W	3259	2464	336–5	45–8	18–11	16.0
Fort de France (m2,P12)	1935	Odense	4278	2950	356–9	48–7	20–3	16.0
Fort Richepanse (m2,P12)	1935	Odense	3485	2950	356–10	48–7	20–3	16.0
Fort Royal (m2,P12)	1935	Göta	3485	2950	356–10	48–7	20–4	16.0
Maurienne (m,P12)	1938	B&W	3260	2463	336–5	45–8	18–11	16.0
Quercy (m,P12)	1938	B&W	3043	2250	336–6	45–7	18–11	16.0

COMPAGNIE GÉNÉRALE D'ARMEMENTS MARITIMES

Fruit carriers• and general cargo vessels

Caraïbe• (st)	1932	France	4048	2800	344–0	52–6	20–0	14.5
ex Allier 35; conv sheep carrier 35								
Enseigne Maurice Préchac	1924	GirndH	4578	6851	377–0	49–1	23–3	10.5
Ésterel• (m,P12)	1938	Göta	3331	2850	335–6	46–2	19–6	15.0
Grande Terre•†	1932	SHWR	1920	2500	266.2	40–0	19–4	12.0
ex Anatolian 33								
Guadeloupe• (m,P–)	1936	Eriksb	2778	4267	322–5	50–4	24–0	15.0
ex Croisine 37								
Guyane• (m,P12)	1934	B&W	1794	2562	313–6	41–6	18–4	14.5
ex Dora 36								
Penerf	1930	Napr&M	2151	3319	278.6	42–8	18–0	11.0
Penthièvre	1922	Dubign	2382	3960	300–2	42–8	20–0	9.0
ex Crucy 32, ex Cybèle 25								
Petite Terre•††	1931	Bergen	1699	2200	256.8	39–3	18–0	12.0
ex Donator 33								
Saint Clair (r/t)	1929	SHWRSd	3824	6300	347.5	48–4	25.6	11.5

Sainte Maxime	1911	Weser	4051	6000	354–2	48–2	20.4	9.0
ex Parnassos 21								

Note: This company also owned and operated vessels under 2000gt, and others on Mediterranean services, particularly Marseilles–Algeria

Note: * Capsized in port after fire 18.4.39; † sold Norway 1939, renamed *Pasat*; †† sold Charles Schiaffino & Cie 1939, renamed *Prosper Schiaffino*

Operator for

GOVERNMENT OF FRANCE (MINISTÈRE DE LA MARINE MARCHANDE)

Fruit carrier

Charles Plumier (m2,P12)	1938	ProvPB	4504	2365	377–4	52–4	19–8	16.0

General cargo vessels

Calédonien (m,P12/cab)	bldg	Provçl	7960	8500	469.3	61–8	26–0	15.5
Indochinois (m,P12/cab)	1939	GirndB	6966	8900	487–0	61–5	26–4	14.5

Services: Antwerp, Dunkirk, Rouen–Algiers–Oran–Alexandria–Haifa–Beirut

COMPAGNIE MARITIME FRANCO-BELGE,

142 Boulevard de Strasbourg, Havre

COMPAGNIE NAVALE-AFRIQUE DU NORD

Congo	1914	France	5202	7650	352.5	52–6	25–5	12.0
ex Saint Michel 38								
Maroc	1908	France	2456	3540	288.8	38–11	19–8	9.5
ex Saint Paul 37								
Syrie	1909	France	2460	3540	288.8	38–11	19–8	9.5
ex Saint Thomas 37								

Funnel: Black with band of blue and white vertical stripe;
Hull: Black
Services: France–UK; N France–Mediterranean; France–West Indies; France–W Africa

Note: * Sold Compagnie Générale Transatlantique 1939
Note: This company, a 1939 amalgamation of Compagnie Nantaise de Navigation à Vapeur and Chargeurs de l'Ouest Société Anonyme de Navigation, also owned vessels under 2000gt

COMPAGNIE NANTAISE DES CHARGEURS DE L'OUEST,

2 Rue de Bréa, BP 329, Nantes

Beaumanoir	1920	Murdo2	2324	4050	290.2	44–2	20–0	9.0
Cens	1926	PenhtS	2384	3530	280–11	42–0	19–9	9.0
Divatte	1918	Crown2	2266	3085	298–6	42–0	19–3	9.0
ex War Weapon 19								
Graslin	1925	Dubign	2323	3307	288–11	41–5	18–2	9.0
Isac	1926	PenhtS	2385	3530	280–11	42–1	19–9	9.0
Kervegan	1922	Dubign	2018	3139	270.3	39–6	19–10	9.0
ex Capitaine Winckler 24								
Martinière*	1911	GrayX	3871	5320	360.0	47–1	20–10	10.0
ex Duala 21, ex Armanistan 12								
Monselet	1929	ThmpR2	3372	5450	358–6	47–6	20–5	10.0
Rhuys	1920	LoireN	2921	4620	313.8	46–5	20–2	9.5
Surville	1919	Eltrgm	2318	4050	290.2	44–0	19–11	9.0

Funnel: Black with houseflag
Hull: Grey, red boot-topping
Trades: Oil and petroleum

COMPAGNIE NATIONALE DE NAVIGATION,

83 Rue de Faubourg St Honoré, Paris

Tankers

Frimaire	1929	DeutsR	9242	13,940	487–7	61–10	28–8	11.0
Vendémiaire	1929	DeutsH	9228	13,850	487–7	61–10	28–8	11.0

Funnel: Black with black VW monogram on white band
Hull: Black, red boot-topping
Services: Oil supply/bunkering at Algiers
Note: This company was associated with Andrew Weir & Co Ltd (*qv* in Great Britain section)

COMPAGNIE VENTURE-WEIR SA,

28 Rue de Châteaudun, Paris, and 2 Blvd Laferrière, Algiers

Fuel depot tankers

Françunion V	1912	ArmWh1	5805	7580	392.7	51–10	25–2	10.0
ex Comanchee 33								
Françunion VI	1915	Laing	4667	7056	383–0	50–1	23–5	9.5
ex Winnebago 35								

Trades: Oil and petroleum

COURTAGE ET TRANSPORTS, SOCIÉTÉ ANONYME,

36 Rue Vignon, Paris 9e

Tanker

Phénix	1920	Lithgw	5907	8800	412–0	51–3	25–6	10.5
ex Henri Desmarais 35, ex Oriflamme 26								

Cie de Nav Paquet: Chella *was completed at the Méditerranée shipyard, La Seyne, in 1934, and was fitted with six steam turbines of 14,300shp manufactured by the shipbuilders. Her career was relatively short, as on June 2 1940 she was bombed by German aircraft at Marseilles and badly damaged.* Chella *was moved to outside of the harbour where she was shelled and sunk by coastal artillery. The wreck was eventually broken up (RW Jordan collection)*

Delmas Vieljeux: The steamer Medjerda *came under the British flag and Ministry of Shipping control in 1940 following the fall of France. She sailed from Pepel on March 7 1941, and from Freetown (in northbound convoy SL68) on March 13 for Middlesbrough with a cargo of iron ore. On March 18* Medjerda *was torpedoed by* U105 *and sunk with the loss of 54 crew.* U105 *sank five vessels from the convoy in four days*
(Alex Duncan)

ÉTABLISSEMENTS ODON DE LUBERSAC, 20 Rue de l'Arcade, Paris

Funnel: Red with black top, separated by white band
Services: General tramping

Name	Built	Builder	GT	DWT	Length	Beam	Draught	Speed
Capitaine Edmond Laborie	1923	Seine	3087	4700	330–8	46–5	20–2	9.0
Gallois	1917	WoodS2	2687	3922	321.2	43–3	19–2	8.5
ex Lord Aberconway 30, ex Tynemouth 29								
Normand	1917	Blyth	1764	2525	255.3	38–5	17–11	8.5
ex William Griffiths 30, ex Elwick 29								

FRANCE, GOVERNMENT OF, Paris

MINISTÈRE DES POSTES, TÉLEGRAPHES ET TELÉPHONES, 20 Avenue de Ségur, Paris

Services: Cable laying and maintenance

Note: This ministry owned vessels listed under managers/operators – Compagnie Générale Transatlantique, Nouvelle Compagnie Havraise Peninsulaire de Navigation à Vapeur, Société Française de Transports Pétrolièrs (SFTP)

Cable vessels

Name	Built	Builder	GT	DWT	Length	Beam	Draught	Speed
Alsace (s2)	bldg	Normnd	2092	1250	288–10	39–9	17–6	14.0
Ampère (s2)	1930	Provçl	2435	1600	291.6	41–2	23.7	15.0
Arago	1914	Goole	901	–	208.4	30–1	15–8	11/5
ex Transmitter 30								
Emile Baudot (s2)	1917	SHWR	1049	1016	222.5	32–2	19.2	11.0

MINISTÈRE DE LA MARINE MARCHANDE

Tanker

Name	Built	Builder	GT	DWT	Length	Beam	Draught	Speed
Beauce	1926	Duncan	4870	6945	375.1	51–9	24–8	9.5
ex Peterjo 39, ex Maryad 39, ex Vitruvia 38								

LAMY & COMPAGNIE, G, 19 Quai Caffarelli, Caen

Funnel: Black with white SNC on red band between two narrow white bands
Hull: Black, red boot-topping
Services: France–NW Europe–Baltic; France–Mediterranean–NW Africa

Note: Also vessels under 2000gt

SOCIÉTÉ NAVALE CAENNAISE

Name	Built	Builder	GT	DWT	Length	Beam	Draught	Speed
Astrée	1921	Blyth	2147	3100	285.3	42–0	18–1	10.0
ex Bellbro 33								
Circe	1926	Caen	2031	3000	280–6	39–11	18–0	9.0
Colleville	1922	ArsnCh	2012	3100	281–10	39–6	19–10	8.0
ex Matelot Huguen 23								
Danaé	1936	Seine	2660	3450	322–6	43–7	18–2	11.5
Dioné	1936	Seine	2660	3450	322–6	43–7	18–2	11.5
Egeé	bldg	Seine	2667	3487	322–6	43–7	18–2	11.5
Phryné	1939	Normnd	2660	3450	322–6	43–7	18–2	11.5
Senneville	1922	GirndH	4578	6800	377–0	49–3	23–3	10.5
ex Capitaine Baudouin 24								
Thésée	1921	Fergsn	2088	3300	274.2	41–0	18–11	9.0
ex Harlyn 33, ex Elizabeth Ann Slater 22								

LE BORGNE, COMPAGNIE CHARLES,

97 Avenue des Champs Elysées, Paris, and 53 Boulevard de la République, Fécamp

Funnel: Black with diamond emblem on white band between two blue bands
Hull: Black
Services: Rouen–Algiers
Note: Also several vessels under 2000gt operating in the Mediterranean

Name	Built	Builder	GT	DWT	Length	Beam	Draught	Speed
Alberte le Borgne (s2,P–)	1915	Weser	3921	6553	356.3	50–5	23–0	10.0
ex Kribi 21, ex Primus 14								

LES CARGOS ALGÉRIENS, SOCIÉTÉ ANONYME

96 Avenue du Mont Riboudet, Rouen, and 20 Rue de la Liberté, Algiers, Algeria

Funnel: Black with houseflag bearing letters CA
Hull: Black
Services: Rouen–Algiers–Bona – Tunis

Name	Built	Builder	GT	DWT	Length	Beam	Draught	Speed
Capitaine Maurice Eugène	1921	SOuest	4499	7280	400–0	52–8	23–0	9.0
ex Westminster 37, ex Capitaine Maurice Eugène 34								
Djurdjura	1922	Ardrsn	4070	6500	351.8	50–2	23.6	9.5
ex Penrith Castle 27								
Dunkerque	1925	SHWR	2477	4650	315.9	45–1	21–6	10.0
ex Duc de Brabant 38								
Jean et Jacques (P10)	1921	FurnH	3493	5858	363.3	52–3	22–8	11.5
ex Corsican Prince 38, ex Chickahominy 23, ex Persiana 22								
Madali	1911	Neptn1	3014	5600	337.1	48–2	22–0	8.5
ex Rialto 28, ex Olympos 21								
Marie José	1925	SHWR	2477	4650	315.9	45–1	21–6	10.0
ex Princess Marie-José 38								
Menhir Bras	1906	Neptn1	2834	4483	291.2	43–11	24.2	9.0
ex Emmi Arp 22								
Mitidja	1906	Hamtn2	3351	5600	358.0	45–2	24.3	8.5
ex Mundale 23, ex Luristan 14								

Tlemcen	1912	France	4425	6200	361.9	48–10	23–3	9.0
ex Edouard Shaki 28								
Vulcain	1911	France	4362	6200	361.9	48–10	25.0	9.0

LES PÉTROLES D'OUTRE-MER, SOCIÉTÉ ANONYME,
73 Avenue des Champs Elysées, Paris

Trades: Oil and petroleum

Tankers								
Aragaz	1914	ArmWhl	5009	7323	385.3	50–4	25–1	9.5
Massis	1914	ArmWhl	5022	7320	385.3	50–4	25–1	9.5
Sunik	1915	ArmWhl	5009	7320	385.0	50–4	25–1	9.5

LOUIS-DREYFUS & COMPAGNIE,
2–4 Rue de la Banque, Paris, and Holland House, 1–4 Bury St, London EC3

Funnel: Black with blue LD&C on white band between two narrow red bands
Hull: Black with white band, white boot-topping
Services: General tramping, mainly grain trade
Note: Controllers of Buries Markes Ltd (*qv* in Great Britain section)

Charles L-D (m,P–)	1934	Göta	5267	9060	446–2	56–8	25–0	12.5
François L-D (m,P–)	1938	Seine	5800	8760	479–1	57–7	25–0	13.0
Jean L-D (m,P–)	1936	France	5795	9130	464–11	57–1	29–0	13.0
Leopold L-D (m,P–)	1933	Göta	5267	9060	446–2	56–8	25–0	12.5
Louis L-D (m,P–)	1936	France	5833	9130	464–11	57–1	29–0	13.0
Pierre L-D (m,P–)	1936	France	5795	9130	465–0	57–1	25–0	13.0

MARTIN S A R L, LOUIS, 56 Rue de la Victoire, Paris 9e

Funnel: Yellow with white disc on blue band
Hull: White
Services: Fruit trades

Fruit carriers								
ARMEMENT NICOLARDOT								
Felix Henri (P–)	1933	Fredst	2526	3575	300.9	46–8	22.5	13.0
COMPAGNIE FRANCO-COLONIALE DE NAVIGATION S.A.R.L.								
Alice Robert (P8)	1934	Nakskv	2588	3400	310–4	48–1	25.7	13.0

MAUREL & PROM, ÉTABLISSEMENTS, 18 Rue Porte-Dijeaux, Bordeaux

Funnel: Black with white MP monogram
Hull: Black
Services: Antwerp, Dunkirk, Bordeaux–Dakar; Marseilles–Dakar

Montaigne	1920	PuseyW	2770	4350	314–11	44–1	21–3	9.5
ex Livonier 28, ex Shelter Island 20								
Montesquieu (P25)	1922	Krupp	3325	3710	305–0	46–10	20–1	10.5
ex Dominic 32, ex Claus Horn 27, ex Nord Friesland 23								
Tourny	1920	PuseyW	2769	4350	314–11	44–1	21–3	9.5
ex Argentinier 28, ex Long Island 20								

MESSAGERIES MARITIMES, COMPAGNIE DES,
3 Rue de Sèze, Paris, and 3 Place Sadi Carnot, Marseilles

Funnel: Black or white
Hull: Black, red boot-topping, or white, green boot-topping
Services: Marseilles–Egypt–E Mediterranean–Black Sea; Near East; Ceylon; Malaya; Indo-China; China; Japan; Australasia; E Africa, Madagascar, Mauritius; Marseilles–Panama–Tahiti–Noumea

Passenger/general cargo vessels								
Claude Chappe* (s2,P59/1,47/2,548/3)								
	1909	Nthmbl	4353	3898	370.0	47–0	24–0	12.0
ex Patris 25								
Khai Dinh (s2,P81/1,60/2,68/3)								
	1914	Dennyl	5110	5100	381.1	51–10	26–1	13.0
ex Lamartine 39, ex Imperator Eleksander III 21								
General cargo vessels								
Anadyr	1930	Nthmb2	5278	9290	412.8	55.3	25–5	10.0
ex Redsea 38								
Commandant Dorise (P4)								
	1917	MitsuK	5529	8422	400.4	54–6	25–0	10.5
ex Kureha Maru 17								
Espérance (P22/1,28/2,12/3)								
	1923	GrayWH	5072	6570	364–3	52–6	25–3	11.0
ex Saint Luc 30, ex Kohistan 28, ordered as Saint Timothee								
Lieutenant de la Tour (P12)								
	1917	Kwsaki	5700	9150	385.3	51–2	27–1	10.5
ex War Queen 19								
Lieutenant Saint Loubert Bié (r/t)								
	1911	Teckl	6126	9590	451.0	57–3	25–10	12.0
ex Mannheim 22								
Min (r/t,P–)	1913	Bremer	7997	11,627	484.0	62–6	26–2	14.0
ex Java 21								
Si-Kiang (r/t)	1914	Teckl	7014	10,932	473.9	59–0	31–2	11.5
ex Meiningen 20								

Yalou (r/t)	1914	Weser	8564	10,443	477.9	58–5	27–7	11.5
ex Raimund 20								
Yang-Tsé (r/t,P4)	1915	HwldtK	8150	11,466	492–1	60–6	27–7	12.5
ex Remscheid 20								

SERVICES CONTRACTUELS DES MESSAGERIES MARITIMES

Passenger and passenger/general cargo vessels

André Lebon (s2,205/1,184/2,107/3)								
	1915	MM	13,682	8400	523–0	61–8	29–5	14.5
Aramis (m2,P196/1,110/2,89/3,650/4)								
	1932	MéditS	17,537	–	574–0	69–9	28–0	17.0
lengthened 36								
Athos II (st2,P84/1,108/2,112/3)								
	1926	Weser	15,276	9225	565–7	66–2	28–3	17.0
Bernardin de Saint Pierre (st2,P141/1,90/2,68/3)								
	1926	Teckl	10,086	7170	455.8	60–10	25–5	14.0
Champollion (r/t2,188/1,257/2,480/3)								
	1924	Provçl	12,546	5043	550–0	62–9	26–3	17.5
lengthened 34								
Chantilly (st2,P134/1,84/2,116/3,254/4)								
	1923	LoireS	9986	8779	500–8	59–2	27–11	13.0
laid down as Kerguelen								
Chenonceaux (s2,P106/1,118/2,100/3)								
	1922	GirndB	14,825	9830	565–0	65–2	24–7	14.0
ex Aramis 26								
Commissaire Ramel (r/t,58/1,78/2,416/3)								
	1920	Provçl	10,061	10,877	500–4	59–3	33.3	12.5
Compiègne (st2,P136/1,84/2,116/3,250/4)								
	1923	LoireS	9986	8385	500–9	59–2	27–8	13.0
launched as Jamaique								
D'Artagnan (s2,P163/1,152/2,102/3)								
	1925	GirndB	15,105	10,700	574–0	65–0	24–7	14.5
Eridan (m2,P56/1,86/2,436/3)								
	1929	Provçl	9928	6575	476–0	61–1	27–0	15.0
Explorateur Grandidier (s2,P141/1,90/2,68/3)								
	1925	PenhtS	10,268	5700	455.8	60–9	25–5	13.0
Félix Roussel (m2,P196/1,113/2,89/3)								
	1930	LoireS	17,083	8500	597–11	68–3	27–11	18.0
lengthened 36								
Général Metzinger (s2,P98/1,112/2,87/3)								
	1906	Blohm	9312	7514	476.6	55–2	30.8	13.0
ex Sobral 23, ex Cap Vilano 17								
Jean Laborde (m2,P136/1,90/2,72/3,590/4)								
	1930	Provçl	11,591	5684	517–0	61–10	26–4	18.0
lengthened 36								
Leconte de Lisle (s2,P88/1,72/2,72/3)								
	1922	Provçl	9877	7650	470–0	61–0	26–3	13.0
Maréchal Joffre (m2,P138/1,92/2,76/3,590/4)								
	1933	Provçl	11,732	6100	495–6	64–0	25–11	17.0
Maréchal Pétain (m3,P344/1,75/2,318/3)								
	order	Provçl	17,280	6825	593–10	75–7	26–11	19.5
Mariette Pacha (s2,P188/1,133/2,128/3,498/4)								
	1926	Provçl	12,239	6200	522–0	62–9	26–9	16.0
Pierre Loti (s2,P77/1,60/2,68/3)								
	1913	BrownJ	5114	5230	381.1	51–10	26–0	13.0
ex Avjator (seaplane tender) 20, ex Imperator Nicholas I 17								
Porthos (s2,P112/1,96/2,90/3,–/4)								
	1915	GirndB	12,692	9341	527–11	61–8	28–6	13.5
President Doumer (m2,P138/1,92/2,76/3,570trps)								
	1935	Provçl	11,898	6100	492–0	64–0	25–9	17.0
Sagittaire (m2,P58/1,47/2,38/3,358trps)								
	1930	Bremer	8254	9940	493–7	61–3	26–2	12.5
ex Washington 38								
Sphinx (s2,P188/1,95/2,111/3)								
	1915	LoireS	11,375	6508	503–0	60–9	28–0	14.5
Théophile Gautier (m2,P107/1,98/2,82/3)								
	1926	France	8195	4570	445–0	56–4	22–0	12.5
Ville d'Amiens (r/t,P32/1,478/3)								
	1924	NofIre	6975	8540	425–0	53–9	27–9	12.5
Ville de Strasbourg (P38/1,50/2,290/3)								
	1920	NofIre	7138	8530	425–0	53–6	27–9	11.0
Ville de Verdun (P38/1,50/2,230/3)								
	1921	NofIre	7007	8500	425–0	53–6	27–9	11.0

Manager for
UNION MARITIME MÉDITERRANÉENNE (a subsidiary of Union Industrielle – *qv*)

Ship	Built	Builder	GRT	DWT	Length	Beam	Draught	Speed
Sontay (r/t, P16/1,750/tr)	1921	Bremer	8917	9970	486–11	58–2	24–10	12.0
ex Bayern 36								

Note: * BU Hong Kong 1939
Note: Also vessels under 2000gt
Note: See also under Compagnie Générale de Navigation à Vapeur (Fabre Line)

MORY ET COMPAGNIE, SOCIÉTÉ À LA RESPONSIBILITE LTÉE, 96 Quai du Bassin, Boulogne

Ship	Built	Builder	GRT	DWT	Length	Beam	Draught	Speed
Lieutenant Robert Mory	1922	Caen	3176	4800	330–8	45–11	20–2	9.0
ex Capitaine Henri Rallier 30								

Funnel: Grey, black top
Services: UK/Baltic/NW Europe/Mediterranean

NOUVELLE COMPAGNIE HAVRAISE PÉNINSULAIRE DE NAVIGATION, 10 Rue de Châteaudun, Paris

Ship	Built	Builder	GRT	DWT	Length	Beam	Draught	Speed
Bourbonnais	1914	G&G3	4484	7086	388–4	52–8	23–6	10.0
ex Port de Boulogne 22, ex Baytigern 21, ex Saint Kentigern 16								
Condé (P16)	1915	MéditH	7202	8470	418.2	53–10	26–10	11.0
Malgache* (m,P12/cab)	1939	Seine	6903	8960	487–5	61–11	26–8	14.5
Ville d'Oran (st2,P20)	1912	MéditH	4861	6650	351.5	46–8	26–2	12.0
Ville de Majunga (P22/cab)	1931	Seine	4972	7065	392.9	53–6	24–5	13.0
Ville de Metz (P54)	1920	NofIre	7007	9498	427–9	53–10	27–9	10.0
Ville de Reims (P22/–,1600/3)	1918	Hamtn2	4617	7355	375–8	52–2	24–1	9.0
Ville de Rouen (P24)	1919	NofIre	5083	7037	384–4	51–2	25–1	10.0
Ville de Tamatave (P22/cab)	1931	Seine	4993	7065	392.9	53–6	24–5	13.0
Ville du Havre (P24)	1919	NofIre	5083	7037	384–4	51–2	24–10	10.0

Funnel: Black with broad red band
Hull: Black, red boot-topping
Services: Dunkirk, Rouen, Havre–Algeria, Tunisia; Havre, Cardiff, Pauillac, Marseille–Port Said–Suez–Port Sudan–Djibouti–Diego Suarez–Tamatave–Vatomandry–Mananjary–Farafanga–Fort Dauphin–Port Louis–Saint Denis–Pointe des Galets

Note: * Registered owner Ministère de la Marine Marchande (*qv* under Government of France)
Note: This company was controlled by Worms & Cie (*qv*)

ORBIGNY, COMPAGNIE DE NAVIGATION D', 81 Rue Taitbout, Paris

Ship	Built	Builder	GRT	DWT	Length	Beam	Draught	Speed
Arijon	1938	GrayWH	4374	7500	425–0	55–0	23–1	12.0
Criton	1927	GrayWH	4564	8420	400.0	53–0	24–9	10.0
Fauzon	1938	GrayWH	4376	7500	425–1	55–0	23–1	12.0
Gazcon	1932	Steph2	4131	7530	394.5	53–0	23–0	12.0
Lyon	bldg	Normnd	4533	7500	425–0	54–11	23–1	12.0
Moron	1930	Napr&M	4128	7560	394.5	53–0	23–0	11.5
Myson	1927	GrayWH	4564	8420	400.0	53–0	24–9	10.0
Pavon	1930	Napr&M	4128	7560	394.5	53–0	23–0	11.5
Platon	1925	GraySd	4550	8420	400.0	53–0	24–9	10.0
Solon	1925	GraySd	4550	8420	400.3	53–3	24–9	10.0
Strabon	1928	GrayWH	4572	8420	400.0	53–0	24–9	10.0

Funnel: Black with blue over red over green bands
Hull: Black
Services: NW Europe, France–Argentina (some called at Brazilian ports)

OUEST, SOCIÉTÉ NAVALE DE L', 8 Rue Auber, Paris

Ship	Built	Builder	GRT	DWT	Length	Beam	Draught	Speed
Saint Ambroise	1920	Gray18	3075	4776	310.0	46–6	22–4	11.0
Saint Basile	1920	LivCpr	2778	4790	323.8	44–1	21–10	10.5
laid down as Saint Benoit								
Saint Camille	1920	Gray18	3274	4776	310.2	46–6	22–4	11.0
Saint Cyrille	1920	Gray18	3075	4776	310.1	46–6	22–4	11.0
Saint Didier	1920	LivCpr	2778	4895	323.8	44–1	21–10	10.5
Saint Firmin	1920	Gray18	4356	6876	364–2	52–6	24–4	9.5
Saint Louis	1913	France	5202	6940	352.5	52–6	25–5	11.0
Saint Octave	1922	France	5099	7650	352.8	52–8	25–5	10.5
Saint Prosper	1920	Gray18	4330	6876	364–2	52–6	23–11	9.5

Funnel: Yellow, black top
Hull: Black, red boot-topping
Services: Hamburg, Antwerp, Dunkirk, Boulogne, Havre, Rouen, Brest, St Nazaire, Nantes, Bordeaux, Bayonne–Algeria, Tunisia, Morocco, Portugal, Spain, Italy, Canary Islands, Senegal, French Guinea, Ivory Coast, Gold Coast, Togo, Dahomey, Cameroons, Congo

SCHIAFFINO ET COMPAGNIE, CHARLES, Anciens bureau de la Douane, Quai Nord, Algiers, Algeria

SOCIÉTÉ ALGÉRIENNE DE NAVIGATION POUR L'AFRIQUE DU NORD

Ship	Built	Builder	GRT	DWT	Length	Beam	Draught	Speed
Ange Schiaffino	1929	HwldtK	3236	5250	354–1	48–1	22–0	10.0

Funnel: Red with black top separated by red band over narrow black band, white S on red band
Hull: Black, red boot-topping with white dividing line

Services: N France (Rouen)–Algeria–N Africa; Marseilles–Mediterranean ports

Note: Also vessels under 2000gt operating in the Mediterranean

Charles Schiaffino	1930	Seine	3664	6100	379–7	51–7	21–8	10.0
Louis Charles Schiaffino	1919	Prstml	3089	4860	342–0	46–10	21–9	10.0
ex Algerian Prince 37, launched as War Isthmus								
Marcel Schiaffino	1930	HwldtK	3482	5600	383–11	48–2	21–8	10.0
Monique Schiaffino	1929	HwldtK	3236	5250	354–1	48–1	22–0	10.0
Nicole Schiaffino	1920	Palmer	4974	6795	386–5	52–8	23–3	10.5
ex Muirton 37, ex Silène 26								
Rose Schiaffino	1920	Blyth	3349	4900	342–0	46–9	21–9	10.0
ex Notton 23, launched as War Minaret								
Schiaffino	1920	Eltrgm	3236	5462	339–7	47–11	21–0	9.0
ex Flore 29								
Schiaffino Frères	1910	Neptnl	3314	4550	317.0	48–2	21–0	9.0
ex Procida 22								

SOCIÉTÉ ANONYME DE GÉRANCE ET D'ARMEMENT (SAGA),

9 Rue de Montchanin, Paris

Funnel: Black with houseflag
Hull: Black or white, red boot-topping
Services: Antwerp, Dunkirk–Casablanca, Kenitra, Tangier, Mogador and other Moroccan ports; NW Europe–French N Africa; general itramping

General cargo vessels

André Moyrand (m)	1927	France	2471	3520	300–4	45–9	18–1	9.5
Cap Blanc	1932	Seine	3317	3553	338–0	46–1	19–11	11.0
Cap Cantin	1933	Seine	3317	3553	337–11	46–1	19–11	11.0
Cap El Hank	1920	Burntd	2307	4000	311–0	43–9	21–0	11.5
ex Ardennes 38, ex Nelly Lasry 31								
Cap Guir	1927	Duncan	1536	2700	282–9	41–0	17–1	10.0
ex Almazora 36								
Cap Tafelneh	1920	Burntd	2266	4000	311–0	43–10	21–0	11.5
ex Ariège 38, ex Sydney Lasry 31								
Paul Emile Javary (m)	1926	France	2471	3520	300–3	45–7	18–1	9.5

Fruit carriers

Cap Hadid (r/t)	1938	Fredsv	1689	2945	294.9	41–4	18–11	13.5
Cap Sim (m2)	1929	LindMo	1906	2480	281–11	37–6	20–8	13.5
ex Genale 37, ex I K Ward 34								

General cargo vessels

COMPAGNIE DES BATEAUX À VAPEUR DU NORD

Algérie	1910	France	3386	4920	331.0	46–6	21–0	10.5
Alsacien	1923	FurnH	3819	5988	363.5	52–1	23–0	12.0
ex Quernmore 37								
Amiénois	1932	FurnH	3713	5300	345–0	53–3	20–10	10.0
Artésien	1921	Rhead3	3152	5340	331.2	47–3	22–1	10.0
Cambraisien	1921	Ardrsn	3151	5235	331.4	47–4	22–1	10.0
Champenois	1921	FurnH	3482	5890	363.3	52–1	22–8	11.0
ex Lancastrian Prince 38, ex Tunisiana 22								
Douaisien	1920	NordsE	2954	5500	338.7	48–3	22–1	10.0
ex Miliana 36, ex Mont Aigoual 34, ex Sunhaven 25, ex Danzig 21								
Dunkerquois	1920	Ardrsn	3145	5250	331.2	47–4	22–1	10.0
Lillois	1910	Conn2	3681	5870	349.6	45–11	24–7	10.0
ex Student 30								
Lorrain	1923	FurnH	3819	5991	363.5	52–1	22–7	12.0
ex Kenmore 37								
Nancéen	1929	ThmpR2	2895	5250	347–10	48–11	21–6	10.5
ex Athen 36, ex Sandö 31								
Rémois	1932	FurnH	3713	5300	345–0	53–2	20–10	10.0
Roubaisien	1921	Rhead3	3152	5340	331.2	47–2	22–1	10.0
Sahel* (m)	1939	Fredsv	2470	3030	318–2	41–7	19–2	14.0
Strasbourgeois	1929	ThmpR2	2895	5300	347–10	48–11	21–6	10.5
ex Ankara 36, ex Vegö 31								

COMPAGNIE FRANCO-AFRICAINE DE NAVIGATION 'FRANCAFRICA'

Brestois	1919	ThmpR2	3094	5030	342–0	46–10	21–9	9.5
ex Lyras N 37, ex Matadi 37, launched as War Ravine								

Manager for

UNION MARITIME AUXILIAIRE SOCIÉTÉ ANONYME

Tabarka	1909	Rijkee	2624	3915	327.5	44–2	18–8	8.5
ex Pollux 31								

UNION MARITIME SOCIÉTÉ ANONYME

Rouennais	1911	Dobson	3777	6400	354.4	48–0	26–0	9.0
ex Malgache 37, ex Port de Cherbourg 22, ex Malgache 21, ex Baymano 21, ex Cayo Romano 16								

Note: * Wine in tanks
Note: Also vessels under 1500gt, and the Calais–Dover ferries *Côte D'Argent* and *Côte D'Azur*

SOCIÉTÉ ANONYME PETROTANKERS, 8 Rue de Berri, Paris

Funnel: Black with white emblem
Hull: Black
Trades: Oil and petroleum

Tanker

Pluviôse	1931	Normnd	9561	14,300	467.4	61–10	27–0	11.0

SOCIÉTÉ ANONYME PURFINA TRANSPORTS, 14 Rue Le Peletier, Paris

Hull: Black, red boot-topping
Trades: Oil and petroleum
Note: This company was a subsidiary of Compagnie Financière Belge des Petroles (Petrofina) SA (*qv* in Belgium section)

Tanker

President Sergent	1923	France	5344	7650	352.9	52–8	26–7	9.5
ex Saint Quentin 24								

SOCIÉTÉ DES TRANSPORTS MARITIMES PÉTROLIÈRS, 27 Avenue Matignon, Paris

Funnel: Black with white emblem
Hull: Black
Trades: Oil and petroleum

Tanker

Brumaire	1930	Normnd	7638	10,942	427.3	58–9	33.8	11.0

SOCIÉTÉ EUROPÉENNE DE NAVIGATION, 1 bis, Cité Paradis, Paris

Services: General tramping
Note: * Manager/agent for this vessel was P B Pandelis Ltd, 13 St Mary Axe, London EC3

Calvados*	1909	Irvin3	2993	5335	336–0	47–0	21–1	9.0
ex Eftychia Vergotti 38, ex Rowtor 14, ex Asiana 10								

SOCIÉTÉ FRANÇAISE DE TRANSPORTS PÉTROLIÈRS (SFTP), 41 Blvd Hausmann, Paris

Funnel: Black
Hull: Grey, green boot-topping
Trades: Oil and petroleum

Tankers

Bourgogne (m)	1937	Odense	9357	14,620	501–1	65–9	28–0	12.0
ex Høegh Ray 38								
Champagne (m)	1938	DeutsH	9946	14,883	510–8	66–1	28–4	12.5
ex Marietta 38								
Franche-Comté (m)	1936	Odense	9314	14,620	501–2	65–4	27–11	12.0
ex Loosdrecht 39								
Languedoc (m2)	1937	B&W	9512	15,010	501–1	65–5	28–5	12.5
ex Actor 38								
Limousin* (m)	1930	SHWR	7619	12,478	471–2	59–6	27–7	11.0
ex Nore 39								
Lorraine (m2)	1937	B&W	9512	15,010	501–1	65–5	28–5	12.5
ex Argus 38								
Picardie* (m)	1936	Eriksb	8263	12,650	486–8	61–1	26–10	12.5
ex Kollgrim 39								
Roussilon (m)	1936	Bremer	9967	14,820	510–8	66–1	28–5	12.5
ex Harald Brøvig 38								
Saintonge (m)	1936	Odense	9386	14,650	501–1	65–5	28–4	12.0
ex Henning Mærsk 39								
Touraine (m2)	1934	Göta	6589	9850	422–0	55–2	26–6	11.0
ex Senator 39								
Vendée* (m2)	1928	B&W	9153	14,386	488–6	64–5	28–2	11.5
ex H G Wagon 39, ex Sir Osborn Holmden 39								

Note: * Registered owner Ministère de la Marine Marchande (*qv* under Government of France)
Note: When formed in 1937 the main shareholders in this company were Worms & Cie (*qv*) (also manager of this fleet), Compagnie Auxiliaire de Navigation (*qv*), Louis-Dreyfus & Cie (*qv*) and Établissement Démarais

SOCIÉTÉ GÉNÉRALE DE TRANSPORTS MARITIMES À VAPEUR SA, 70 Rue de la République, Marseilles, and 5 Rue de Surène, Paris

Funnel: Black with red band
Hull: Black, red boot-topping
Services: Mail, passenger, cargo – Marseilles–Barcelona–Valencia–Alicante–Almeria–Dakar–Rio de Janeiro–Santos–Montevideo–Buenos Aires; Marseilles–Spain–Montevideo–Buenos Aires–Santos; cargo only – Marseilles–Spain–New Orleans

Passenger/general cargo vessels

Alsina (st2,P74/1,128/2,48/3,–/4)								
	1922	SHWR	8404	6518	450.5	58–5	24–3	15.0
Campana (st2,P107/1,96/2,56/ec,230/3,816/4)								
	1929	SHWR	10,186	7025	536–7	67–0	23–1	15.0
Florida (st2,P1500)	1926	LoireS	9331	6738	490–5	60–8	24–3	15.0
Mendoza (st2,P74/1,128/2,46/3,–/4)								
	1920	SHWR	8199	6571	450.5	58–5	24–3	15.0

General cargo vessels

Capitaine Paul Lemerle								
	1921	SOuest	4945	7275	399–8	52–6	23–2	11.0
Mont Agel	1920	GrkDY	4572	7417	377.0	52–2	23–5	10.5
Mont Everest	1918	Hendn2	5120	8200	412–6	52–4	25–3	10.5
ex Mount Everest 23, ex War Drake 18								
Mont Viso	1921	Dixon2	4531	7930	369.9	53–4	24–10	11.0

Fruit carrier

Victor Schœlcher (m2,P11)	1938	MéditS	4510	2400	381–0	51–11	19–8	16.0

Note: Also several vessels operating Marseilles–N Africa

COMPAGNIE DE NAVIGATION FRANCE-AMERIQUE

Passenger/general cargo vessel

Ipanema (te)	1921	MéditS	4282	5147	360.2	45–11	23–2	13.0

Funnel: Black
Hull: Black
Services: UK/NW Europe/Mediterranean/NW Africa

SOCIÉTÉ MARITIME NATIONALE, 3 Rue Godot de Mauroy, Paris

Cabourg	1918	Austin	2423	3041	298–6	41–10	19–3	9.5
ex Sierra Madre 24, ex War Fife 19								
Paramé	1918	GrayX	2423	3041	298–6	41–10	19–3	9.5
ex Sierra Negra 25, ex War Torpedo 19								
Portrieux	1918	H&W,B	2257	3041	298–6	41–10	19–3	9.5
ex War Buckler 20								
Saint Enogat	1918	Forth	2245	3120	298–6	41–10	19–3	9.5
ex War Clarion 20								
Saint Palais	1918	Forth	2257	3120	298–6	41–8	19–3	9.5
ex War Pibroch 20								

SOCIÉTÉ MARITIME DE TRANSPORTS ET D'AFFRÊTEMENTS

Capitaine Le Bastard	1923	Caen	3176	4527	330–8	45–11	20–2	9.0
Capitaine Luigi	1922	Caen	3176	4527	330–8	45–11	20–2	9.0

Funnel: Black with emblem on white band
Hull: Black, red boot-topping
Trades: Oil and petroleum
Note: Also tankers under 3000gt
Note: This company was a subsidiary of Standard Oil Co of New Jersey (*qv* in United States section)

STANDARD FRANÇAISE DES PÉTROLES,
82 Avenue de Champs Elysées, Paris

Tankers

	1926	GirndB	5011	6550	400–0	52–8	21–2	10.0
Marguerite Finaly (m2)	1933	CRDA2	12,309	17,963	542–4	70–2	30–5	13.0

Funnel: Black with red UIM on blue and white diagonally halved disc on broad black band between two narrow white bands
Hull: Black, red boot-topping
Services: UK, NW Europe and Mediterranean

UNION INDUSTRIELLE ET MARITIME, SOCIÉTÉ FRANÇAISE D'ARMEMENT, 36 Rue de Naples, Paris

Capitaine Augustin	1922	Caen	3137	4780	330–8	45–11	20–2	9.0
Capitaine Le Diabat	1922	Seine	3107	4600	330–11	46–4	20–1	9.0
Capitaine Prieur	1922	Seine	3087	4670	330–11	46–4	20–1	9.0
Capitaine Saint Martin (r/t)	1939	SmithM	3439	5150	373–0	48–6	20–4	12.0
Chef Mécanicien Armand Blanc	1922	Seine	3070	4600	330–8	46–5	20–2	9.0
Dalila	1923	Caen	3176	4670	330–8	45–11	20–2	9.0
ex Capitaine Catinchi 26								
Dorine	1923	Caen	3176	4670	330–8	45–11	20–2	9.0
ex Capitaine Pierre Allee 23								
Enseigne Marie Saint-Germain	1923	Caen	3139	4788	330–8	45–10	20–2	9.0
launched as Enseigne de Vaisseau Marie Saint-Germain								
Gabriel Guist'hau	1918	Forth	2352	3230	298–6	41–11	19–3	10.5
ex Gorgona 30, ex Giuseppina Ilardi 28, ex War Platoon 19								
Henri Mory (st)	1920	Bretgn	2564	3800	302–0	43–6	20–0	10.0
ex Martine 35, ex Thoriu 26, ex Les Hurlus 20								
Janine	1918	Hill	2358	3065	298–6	42–0	19–0	10.0
ex Sierra Leone 25, ex War Musket 19								

Note: Also vessels under 2000gt
Note: See also subsidiary company Union Maritime Méditerranéenne under Cie des Messageries Maritimes

Funnel: Black
Hull: Black with white line, red boot-topping
Services: Dunkirk–Rouen–Havre–Marseilles; Havre–Oran–Algiers
Note: Also vessels under 2000gt
Note: See also Nouvelle Compagnie Havraise Peninsulaire de Navigation à Vapeur and Société Française de Transports Pétroliers (SFTP)

WORMS & COMPAGNIE,
138 Blvd de Strasbourg, Havre, and 43–45 Blvd Hausmann, Paris

Château Larose	1930	Hendn2	2047	2450	286–2	39–1	18–9	10.5
Château Pavie	1930	Hendn2	2047	2450	286–2	39–1	18–9	10.5
Château Yquem	1925	Seine	2536	3258	279.8	39–6	19.7	9.5

Germany

AHRENS DAMPFSCHIFFSREEDEREI, ERICH,
Stephanstraße 14, Postfach 322, Seestadt Rostock

Ernst Brockelmann	1927	Neptn1	1900	3010	278–10	42–2	18–0	9.5
Manager for								
ERIK LARSEN								
Ellen Larsen	1900	GrayX	1936	3050	289–6	40–1	18–0	8.5
ex Erik 26, ex Erik II 23								

Funnel: Black with white over red over white bands
Hull: Black
Services: Baltic ports, UK–Mediterranean
Note: Also smaller vessels

ALBRECHT KG, DR MAX, Wallhof, Glockengiesserwall 2–4, Hamburg 1

Tankers								
ALBRECHT GEBRÜDER & CO KG								
Max Albrecht (m2)	1929	Kockum	5824	8786	402–5	55–1	26–11	11.5
PARTENREEDEREI D RUDOLF ALBRECHT								
Rudolf Albrecht	1922	Krupp	3817	5640	390–6	45–8	21–6	10.0
lengthened 34								

Funnel: Black with red A on white disc bordered by a black circle, all superimposed on black over white over red bands, bordered by narrow white bands
Hull: Black
Trades: Oil and petroleum

ARGO REEDEREI RICHARD ADLER & CO,
Argohaus, Langenstraße 104–6, Postfach 82, Bremen

Antares (P8)	1937	LübecM	2593	4100	319.9	46–9	19–0	12.0
Arcturus (P8)	1937	LübecM	2596	4100	319.9	46–9	19–0	12.0

Funnel: Yellow, separated from black top by white eight-pointed star on green band
Hull: Black, red boot-topping
Services: Hamburg–Bremen–Mediterranean; NW Europe– Canada
Note: Also a large fleet of short-sea vessels

ARP DAMPSCHIFFS-REEDEREI, HEINRICH F C,
(S Öllgaard and Thoersen), Rolandhaus, Mönckebergstraße 9, Hamburg 1

Hans Arp	1926	Rødby	1645	4550	316.6	44–0	21.2	8.5
ex Anna 26								

Funnel: Yellow with red A, black top
Services: General tramping
Note: Also *Cronshagen* (built 1904/1787gt), *Heinrich Arp* (24/1428)

ATLANTIC-RHEDEREI (F & W JOCH)
Stella Haus, Rödingsmarkt 52, Hamburg 11

Tankers								
Thalatta (m)	1921	DeutsH	3145	4896	385–5	45–6	20–11	9.0
ex Julius Schindler 39; lengthened 34								
HANSA TANK REEDEREI GMBH								
Winnetou	1913	HwldtK	5113	7840	399–11	52–5	24–0	9.5
ex Corning 27, ex Mohican 14								

Funnel: Black with white over blue bands
Hull: Black
Trades: Oil and petroleum
Note: Also small tankers

BALTISCH-AMERIKANISCHE PETROLEUMS IMPORT GMBH
Neuer Jungfernstieg 21, Hamburg 36

Note: The fleet of this company was removed from the German register in 1939 and transferred to Panama Transport Co (*qv* under Standard Oil Co of New Jersey in United States section)

BLUMENTHAL, JOHANN M K, Stella Haus, Rödingsmarkt 52, Hamburg 11

Hannah Böge (r/t)	1938	Neptn2	2337	–	302–6	45–1	18–4	10.5
Helga Böge	1925	LübecM	2181	3350	292–0	41–9	18–6	9.5
Henry Böge	1938	Trondh	1995	3400	302–9	44–1	19–0	11.0
Ida Blumenthal	1921	LübecM	1549	2796	262.6	37–11	16–0	9.0
Ina Lotte Blumenthal	1921	LübecM	1549	2771	262.2	37–11	16–0	9.0
Johann Blumenthal	1927	LübecM	1626	2500	263.3	38–3	16–0	9.5
Magdalena Reith*	1905	SmitJ	2130	3630	280.4	41–2	20–0	9.0
ex Anneliese 23, ex Alioth 21								

Funnel: Black with black B on broad white band with narrow white over red bands above and red over white bands below
Hull: Black
Services: General tramping
Note: * Sold Robert Bornhofen 1939, renamed *Hans Bornhofen*
Note: Also vessels under 1500gt

A Bolten: The flagship of this company's fleet in 1939 was August Bolten, *completed by Neptun at Rostock in 1936. On August 16 1940 she was commissioned by the Kriegsmarine for use in Operation 'Seelöwe' and was given the designation* H50. *This operation was abandoned and she was returned to Bolten on July 4 1942. Service in the war was mainly to Norway, and it was in Korsfjord on November 20 1944 that* August Bolten *was attacked by an MTB, stranded, and sunk (Photograph August Bolten archives)*

Bugsier: Friedenau *was completed at St Nazaire in November 1920 as* Adrar *for French owner Chargeurs Reunis. With a single screw, she was fitted with a Loire triple expansion engine of 2800ihp.* Adrar *stranded in a storm on the island of Sylt on October 20 1935. On August 17 1936 operations were commenced by the salvage department of Bugsier, and following refloating* Adrar *was at the Seebeck Werft in Bremerhaven for repairs. She was purchased by Bugsier in September 1937. On April 8 1940 she was commissioned by the Kriegsmarine as a transport for Operation 'Weserubung', the invasion of Norway, but two days later when carrying troops of the 196th Infantry Division, was torpedoed and sunk by the British submarine* Triton *(Photograph courtesy Bugsier archives)*

DOAL: Usambara *was delivered in April 1923 for service between Germany and East Africa. On September 17 1939 she was commissioned by the Kriegsmarine as an accommodation vessel at the Mürwik torpedo school. She became a depot ship for the 7th U-boat flotilla in February 1940, and in July 1941 was based at Stettin as depot ship for the 4th U-boat flotilla. On March 20 1945* Usambara *was bombed and badly damaged at Stettin and the wreck was scuttled off Kranichwerder (DAL)*

Frigga: Frigga *was completed at Lübeck in 1924. During the war she was mainly involved in carrying coal from Germany to Norway, and in March 1945 was bombed by Allied aircraft and sunk at Schulau. The wreck was raised in 1945 and found to be in repairable condition.* Frigga *was returned to her former owners and by 1950 was involved in the European ore trades. She served the* Frigga *company until February 1962 when she arrived at Bremerhaven to be broken up (R Sherlock)*

Fritzen: The turret deck steamer Erika Fritzen *was built by Doxford in 1905 as* Ryton *for British owners. After some changes of name and owner she was purchased by Fritzen in 1926 and renamed* Erika Fritzen. *During the war she was employed mainly in the Germany–Norway coal trade. On February 26 1945 she struck a mine and was sunk (RW Jordan collection)*

Hamburg-Amerika: Hamburg *was built by Blohm & Voss and completed in March 1926, and during the next few years saw much improvement. During a 1929–30 refit her original steam turbines were replaced by eight Blohm & Voss SR geared turbines with a total 28,000shp. In 1933 she underwent another extensive refit, was modernised, and lengthened. Soon after the outbreak of the Second World War she was taken over by the Kriegsmarine and became an accommodation vessel at Gotenhafen, and in January 1945 was transferred to VTS for use in the evacuation of East Prussia. In the course of three voyages* Hamburg *evacuated over 23,000 persons, but on way to embark a fourth complement struck two mines on March 7 1945, and sunk off Sassnitz. She was salved by the Russians in 1950, and was refitted at Warnemünde, DDR, as a passenger vessel with accommodation for 900 passengers. When work was almost completed it was decided that she should be converted to a whale factory ship. She entered service as the factory vessel* Yuri Dolgoruky *in 1960. She was broken up in 1977 (Hamburg-Amerika)*

BOLTEN, AUG, (WM MILLER'S NACHFOLGER),
Boltenhof, Admiralitätstraße 36, Hamburg 11

Funnel: Black with black B on white stylised Maltese cross on red band or that design in form of houseflag on white band
Hull: Black
Services: General tramping
Note: Also vessels under 2000gt

Adolf Binder (r/t)	bldg	Neptn2	3535	6075	357–7	51–7	22–1	12.0
August Bolten (r/t)	1937	Neptn2	3665	5700	363.1	51–10	22–0	12.0
Bolheim	1913	RottDD	3324	5500	345–3	48–1	20–7	8.0
ex Arundo 28								
Bollwerk	1917	Craig2	4173	7535	369.2	51–6	23–9	9.0
ex Söderham 37, ex Nailsea Moor 37, ex David Lloyd George 32								
Boltenhagen	1912	RottDD	3335	5500	345–3	48–2	20–7	8.0
ex Dubhe 29								
Boltenhof	1911	RDuck1	3307	5450	352–0	49–0	20–5	8.5
ex Dorie 35								

Manager for
WACHSMUTH & KROGMAN, Zippelhaus 2, Hamburg

Helios	1912	Irvin3	3821	6596	362–2	51–1	21–9	9.0
ex Boscombe Chine 37, ex Nailsea Brook 35, ex Cymric Queen 32, ex Apsleyhall 20, ex Newfield 18								

BORNHOFEN, ROBERT, Slomanhaus, Steinhöft 11, Hamburg 11

Funnel: Black with white Maltese cross on red band between two narrow white bands
Hull: Black
Services: General tramping; Baltic trade
Note: Also vessels under 1500gt in NW Europe/UK/Baltic trade

Elisabeth Bornhofen	1923	FrerJ	2289	4095	296.2	42–10	20–3	9.0
ex Konya 39, ex Angora 37, ex Elsbeth Kimme 25								
Hans Bornhofen	1905	SmitJ	2130	3630	280.4	41–2	20–0	8.5
ex Magdalena Reith 39, ex Anneliese 23, ex Alioth 21								
Luise Bornhofen	1906	Clyde	2860	4614	330.2	43–2	20–11	9.0
ex Traunstein 39, ex Siptah 30, ex Shahristan 11								
Robert Bornhofen	1919	Doxfrd	6643	10,950	427–6	55–6	25–10	11.0
ex Mount Ossa 39, ex Tower Crown 37, ex Bothwell 34, ex War Beryl 20								

BUGSIER-, REEDEREI-U BERGUNGS AG,
Johannisbollwerk 10, Hamburg 3

Funnel: Black with white band
Hull: Black, red boot-topping
Services: General tramping
Note: Also a large fleet of short-sea and coastal vessels, salvage vessels and tugs
Note: Also a large fleet of short-sea and coastal vessels, salvage vessels and tugs

Birkenau (m)	1926	Weser	1990	2830	293–7	43–5	18–5	10.0
ex Barbara (rotor ship) 33								
Friedenau	1920	LoireS	5219	7500	393.3	55–11	25–5	10.0
ex Adrar 37								

CHRISTOPHERSEN, H W, Schiffbrücke 24, Postfach 148, Flensburg

Funnel: Yellow with white C on blue band between two narrow white bands
Hull:
Services: General tramping
Note: Also *Inge Christophersen* (built 1905/1353gt)

Annelis Christophersen	1927	Flensb	1581	2600	272–0	40–4	16–11	9.0
ex Sexta 38, ex Marquardt Petersen 35								
Hans Christophersen	1928	Flensb	1599	2600	272–0	40–2	16–11	9.0
ex Quinta 38								
Helene	1898	Blumr1	2160	3535	290.0	42–0	18–6	8.0
ex Druidstone 14, ex Queenmoor 04								

CORDS, AUG, Strandstraße 79–81, Postfach 183, Seestadt Rostock

Funnel: Black with white AC on white bordered red diamond on blue band
Hull: Black
Services: General tramping
Note: Also vessels under 1000gt

Charlotte Cords	1923	Neptn1	1779	2990	266.3	40–2	18–0	9.0
Hanna Cords	1926	Neptn1	1891	3000	266.3	42–2	18–0	9.0
Irmtraut Cords	1924	Helsgr	2814	5115	320.4	48–5	21–5	9.0
ex M C Holm 39								
Margarethe Cords (r/t)	1927	Neptn1	1912	3000	266.9	42–1	18–0	9.0
Rostock	1922	SMvJS	2542	3885	344–6	45–4	18–11	9.5

DEUTSCHE ARBEITSFRONT GMBH, Berlin

Funnel: Yellow with symbol containing Swastika at centre, narrow brown top with narrow yellow over red bands
Hull: White or cream
Services: Workers' cruises for Kraft Durch Freude ('Strength Through Joy') organisation

Cruise vessels

Der Deutsche* (s2,P1000/oc)	1924	Bremer	11,453	10,412	511–0	66–3	30–4	14.5
ex Sierra Morena 34								
Oceana** (s2,P516)	1913	Bremer	8791	3248	452–9	56–0	23–8	12.0
ex Meteor 27, ex Neptunia 27, ex Peer Gynt 25, ex Avaré 24, ex Sierra Salvada 17								

Robert Ley** (me2,P1774/oc)								
	1938	HwldtH	27,288	–	668-8	78-8	24-10	16.0
Sierra Cordoba* (s2,P1000/oc)								
	1924	Bremer	11,492	10,300	511-0	66-3	30-4	14.5
Stuttgart* (s2,P990/oc)								
	1923	VulcSt	13,387	8870	550-6	65-0	28-0	15.0
Wilhelm Gustloff*** (m2,P1465/oc)								
	1938	Blohm	25,484	5747	684-0	77-5	27-0	15.5

Notes: * Manager Norddeutscher Lloyd (*qv*); ** manager Hamburg-Amerika Linie (*qv*); *** manager Hamburg-Südamerikanische Dampfs Ges (*qv*)

DEUTSCHE LEVANT LINIE GMBH, Ferdinandstraße 56, Hamburg 1

Funnel: Black with red and white houseflag bearing black letters 'DLL
Hull: Grey, red boot-topping
Services: Stettin, Hamburg, Bremen, Antwerp to most important Mediterranean ports except France, W Italy

DEUTSCHE LEVANT-LINIE HAMBURG AG

Adana (P12)	1922	VulcSt	4205	6570	360.7	51-0	23-7	11.0
ex Atto 36								
Andros	1910	Neptn1	2995	4547	320.9	46-2	21-0	8.5
ex Ascensione 26, ex Catania 12								
Athen (m,P12)	1936	DeutsR	4450	7072	424-11	55-10	23-0	14.0
Belgrad (m,P12)	1937	DeutsR	4418	7100	424-10	55-10	23-0	14.0
Bukarest (m)	1939	DeutsR	4446	6380	424-10	55-8	23-3	14.0
Chios	1912	Koch	1731	3041	277.7	39-2	18-6	9.0
ex Ceuta 27								
Delos (P–)	1922	Neptn1	2589	4527	311.0	45-2	20-0	9.5
ex Donau 27, ex Osterndorf 25								
Derindje	1916	VSE1	3063	5452	336.1	48-4	21-11	10.0
ex Chief Scout 22, ex Derindje 21								
Galilea	1922	Lübec2	1927	3292	287.7	41-9	19-5	10.0
Heraklea	1922	Lübec2	1927	3292	287.7	41-9	19-5	10.0
Kreta (P2)	1923	HwldtK	2359	4281	309.3	44-1	21-2	10.0
Macedonia	1922	Lübec2	2875	5414	337.8	48-6	22-0	9.5
ex Cuba 32, ex Olinda 24, ex Gutfeld 24								
Milos	1906	Flensb	2702	4330	290.3	44-0	21-10	9.0
ex Main 27, ex Maria 24, ex Regina 21								
Morea	1922	Lübec2	1927	3292	287.7	41-9	19-5	10.0
Pompeji (r/t)	1939	Flensb	2916	5167	361-6	52-6	20-7	13.5
Samos (P–)	1922	Neptn1	2576	4429	311.1	46-1	20-0	9.5
ex Saar 24, ex Otto Zelck 22								
Sivas	1928	ThmpR2	3831	7498	380.8	52-0	22-10	10.5
ex George M Livanos 38								
Sofia (m)	1939	DeutsR	4446	7100	421-0	55-8	23-0	14.0
Thessalia	1921	Lübec2	2875	5442	337.7	48-6	22-0	9.5
ex Mexico 32, ex Orissa 24, ex Freifeld 24								
Tinos (P–)	1914	Blumr1	2826	5148	332.5	48-9	21-1	10.5
ex Rio de Janeiro 25								
Yalova (P10)	1920	FrerJ	3750	6345	362.7	50-4	22-7	11.0
ex Winfried 36								

ATLAS LEVANT-LINIE AG

Achaia	1921	NordUW	1778	3285	283.2	39-10	20-3	9.0
ex Aquila 36, ex Deutschland 30; lengthened 28								
Akka	1924	StettO	2646	4810	346-0	46-0	20-2	10.0
ex Stettin 30								
Ankara (m,P12)	1937	NordsE	4768	7280	434-0	56-5	23-7	14.0
Arkadia (P4)	1927	Neptn1	1756	2585	276.1	42-2	17-0	10.0
Arta	1922	Weser	2452	4610	315.8	46-0	21-0	10.0
ex Naimes 24, ex Ægina 22								
Cairo (m,P12)	1936	Krupp	4778	7245	434-0	56-8	23-2	14.0
Cavalla*	1912	Bremer	1570	2460	260.5	37-1	19-0	12.0
ex Frankfurt 20								
Ithaka	1921	NordUW	1773	3385	283.2	39-9	20-3	9.0
ex Alaya 36, ex Vaterland 30; lengthened 28								
Konya**	1923	FrerJ	2289	4095	296.2	42-10	20-3	9.0
ex Angora 37, ex Elsbeth Kimme 25								
Kythera	1901	SH1	3727	6020	348.8	45-2	24-6	9.5
ex Alimnia 36, ex Ostsee 31, ex Themisto 21								
Larissa	1923	NordUW	1819	3285	283.1	39-10	20-3	9.0
ex Avola 36, ex Oderland 30; lengthened 28								
Levante (m,P12)	1939	NordsE	4769	7344	437-2	56-7	23-6	14.0
Smyrna***	1912	Bremer	1663	2499	260.5	37-1	19-0	10.0
ex Heidelberg 20, ex Ije 18, ex Heidelberg 14								
Sparta	1927	FrerJ	1724	2601	275.5	42-2	17-3	11.5
ex Star 36								

Note: * Sold Aug Bolten 1939, renamed *Falkenberg*; ** sold Robert Bornhofen 1939, renamed *Elisabeth Bornhofen*; *** sold Aug Bolten, 1939, renamed *Sullberg*

Hamburg-Amerika: Milwaukee *was completed in June 1929 for the Hamburg–Boulogne–Southampton–New York service. This twin screw vessel was fitted with two Blohm & Voss/MAN 12-cylinder oil engines of 12,000bhp. She underwent an extensive refit in 1935–36 for seasonal cruising. In 1940 the Kriegsmarine employed her as an accommodation ship at Kiel, where she was seized on May 9 1945.* Milwaukee *passed to the Ministry of War Transport under the management of Cunard White Star and was renamed* Empire Waveney. *While at Liverpool undergoing conversion for use as a regular troopship, she was on fire on March 1 1946, and by the 3rd was partially submerged. On May 4 she was refloated and it was decided that repairs would be uneconomical. On January 25 1947 she left Liverpool in tow for Dalmuir to be broken up, and in September that year her substantial remains were towed to Troon for final breaking up.* Milwaukee's *sistership* St Louis *was in the headlines in May–June 1939 in a widely-publicised Nazi propaganda exercise. She carried about 900 Jewish refugees from Hamburg to Cuba, but the authorities at Havana refused to allow them to disembark at that port, and eventually they were disembarked at Antwerp after several European countries agreed to accept them (RW Jordan collection)*

Hamburg-Amerika: A model of the liner Vaterland, *the first of a series of three, which had been launched on August 24 1940, at Hamburg. She was intended for service from Hamburg, Southampton and Cherbourg to New York and seasonal cruising. In 1941 title of the vessel was transferred to Deutsche Amerika Line of Bremen. On July 25 1943 Vaterland was badly damaged during a USAAF and RAF raid on Hamburg, and her fore deck was curled back over the bridge. After the war the wreck, which was lying in the Kaiser Wilhelm Haven, was found to be so badly damaged that repairs would be uneconomical and was scrapped.* Vaterland, *a twin screw vessel, was to be fitted with turbo-electric machinery and had a contracted 62,000shp and 24 knots trials speed (RW Jordan collection)*

Hamburg-Amerika: The cargo liner Amasis *was completed by Bremer Vulkan for the Kosmos company, which was taken over by Hamburg-Amerika on November 24 1926. On April 9 1940 she was torpedoed and sunk off Lysekil by the British submarine* Sunfish *(RW Jordan collection)*

DEUTSCHE LUFTHANSA AG,
Flughafen, Berlin and Lindenstraße 35, Berlin SW68

Funnel: Yellow or grey with black top and houseflag *Hull:* Grey
Services: Vessels stationed in S Atlantic as floating aerodromes for Lufthansa aircraft

Aircraft service vessels (seadromes)								
Friesenland (m2)	1937	HwldtK	5434		455–4	54–4	19–8	16.0
Schwabenland (m2)	1925	DeutsK	8631		468.2	60–5	27–9	12.0
ex Schwarzenfels 34; conv general cargo 34								
Westfalen	1906	Teckl	5367		409.4	52–10	26–4	10.0
conv general cargo 33								

Note: These vessels were managed by Norddeutscher Lloyd (*qv*); also *Ostmark* (built 1936/1280gt)

DEUTSCHE OST-AFRIKA LINIE,
Afrika Haus, Grosse Reichenstraße 25–27, Hamburg

Funnel: Yellow with black top separated by yellow over black over white over red over white over black bands
Hull: Silver grey, red boot-topping
Services: Hamburg, NW Europe–W Africa–South Africa–E Africa (via Canary Islands or Suez)

Passenger/general cargo vessels								
Njassa (st,P108/1,57/2,128/3)	1924	Blohm	8754	7775	432.4	58–2	25–6	14.0
Pretoria (st2,P152/1,338/t)	1936	Blohm	16,662	9754	576–9	72–4	26–6	18.0
Ubena (st,P124/1,78/2,132/3)	1928	Blohm	9523	7350	468.7	60–4	25–7	15.5
lengthened 34								
Usambara (st,P108/1,57/2,120/3)	1923	Blohm	8690	7900	433.5	58–2	25–6	14.0
Usaramo (st,P101/1,62/2,98/3)	1921	Blohm	7775	7150	418.6	56–2	23–8	14.0
Ussukuma (st,P101/1,61/2,102/3)	1921	Blohm	7834	7130	418.6	56–2	23–8	14.0
General cargo vessels								
Livadia	1922	Lübec2	3094	5360	354.4	48–0	22–0	10.0
Muansa (P60)	1911	Bremer	5472	8970	419.8	54–6	25–11	11.0
Urundi (st,P60)	1920	Blohm	5791	9500	418.6	56–2	25–8	11.5

Note: This company, associated with Woermann Linie AG (*qv*), also owned the coastal vessel *Rufidji* (1400gt)

EMDER DAMPFERKOMPAGNIE AG, Altermarkt 5, Postfach 231, Emden

Funnel: Black, two white bands
Hull: Black
Services: General tramping

Bernlef	1919	Ardrsn	2482	3950	311–6	43–0	19–10	10.0
ex Seven Seas Sound 37, ex Hunstanworth 37, launched as War Olive								
Radbod	1910	Nthmbl	4354	7525	378.0	49–1	23–8	9.5
ex Victoria W Kunstmann 36, ex Crawford Castle 30, ex Hova 19								
Tagila	1906	Bonn&M	2682	4425	305.7	44–9	20–0	8.5
ex Frithjof 26, ex Hildegard 25, ex Phecda 21								
Wittekind	1906	TyneIr	4028	6600	351.2	50–1	23–0	9.0
ex Tricolor 25								

Note: The manager of this company was Wilhelm Nubel

ESSBERGER, JOHN T, Palmaille 49, Postfach 941, Hamburg-Altona

Funnel: Black with blue E on white band
Hull: Black or grey with white band, red boot-topping
Services: General tramping; oil and petroleum trades

General cargo vessels								
Anneliese Essberger (m)	1935	DeutsH	5173	9153	440–0	57–3	25.3	13.0
Elsa Essberger (m2)	1938	HwldtH	6103	9425	476–9	61–4	24–0	13.0
Tankers								
Adria (m)	1927	Weser	6358	9349	430–11	55–1	26–2	10.5
Biscaya (m)	1927	Weser	6369	9349	430–6	55–4	26–2	10.5
Karibisches Meer	1917	Laing	6864	10,975	424.1	57–0	26–0	10.0
ex Mendocino 39								
Kattegat (m)	1928	Schich	6031	9275	428–4	55–2	26–2	12.0
Mittelmeer (m)	1927	Weser	6370	9349	430–11	55–1	26–2	10.5
Nord Atlantic (m)	1938	DeutsH	9897	14,600	510–8	65–11	28–5	13.0
Nordmeer	1917	ArmWh1	5671	9100	420–0	52–2	25–4	10.0
ex Mantilla 39								
Schwarzes Meer	1923	Monmth	3371	5172	330.3	46–10	22–7	10.0
ex Cynthiana 26								
Skagerrak (m)	1928	Schich	6044	9275	428–0	55–2	26–2	12.0

Note: Also short-sea tankers occasionally involved in ocean voyages

EUROPÄISCHE TANKREEDEREI GMBH, 6 Esplanade, Hamburg 36

Trades: Oil and petroleum
Note: This company, controlled from 1937 by Crusader Petroleum Industries Ltd, London, also owned tankers under 1500gt

Tanker								
Eurofeld	1917	RDuck2	5863	9000	380.8	50–11	28–4	9.5
ex Stanbridge 39, ex Ch N Kahan 37, ex Limicana 27, ex Beechleaf 22								

Deutsche Arbeitsfront: Wilhelm Gustloff *was launched on May 5 1937 and delivered on March 16 1938 to Deutsche Arbeitsfront to operate workers' cruises for the Kraft durch Freude ('Strength Through Joy') association. She was managed by Hamburg-Süd. She had accommodation for 1465 tourist class passengers and in peacetime carried a crew of 426. During the war she served mainly as an accommodation vessel at the 2nd U-boat training base at Gotenhafen (Gdynia). On January 30 1945 she sailed from Gotenhafen with over 6100 refugees and wounded who had been evacuated from East Prussia. At 2106 hours that day when off Stolpmünde* Wilhelm Gustloff *was hit by three torpedoes from the Russian submarine S-13. Several German warships and the cargo vessel* Göttingen *were on the scene shortly afterwards but were only able to rescue 904 persons from among those on board.* Wilhelm Gustloff *capsized at 2218 and sank at 2258 (RW Jordan collection)*

Deutsche Arbeitsfront: Oceana *was completed in 1913 as Sierra Salvada for Norddeutscher Lloyd, and after various changes of owner and name, was sold to Hamburg-Amerika in 1927 and renamed* Meteor. *In 1936 she was chartered to the Kraft durch Freude ('Strength Through Joy') association for workers' cruises, and in in 1939 came under the ownership of Deutsche Arbeitsfront with Hamburg-Amerika retaining management of the vessel. After the start of the Second World War* Oceana *was taken over by the Kriegsmarine and was used as an accommodation vessel and a U-boat depot ship. In June 1945 she was transferred to the Ministry of War Transport, and renamed* Empire Tarne, *and in 1946 was passed to Russia as* Sibir. *Her area of operation was then on the western Pacific coast, and she was broken up at her home port, Vladivostok, in 1963 (RW Jordan collection)*

Deutsche-Levant: The cargo liner Cairo *was completed at the Krupp shipyard in Kiel in 1936. She was fitted with a Krupp Germaniawerft/MAN 7-cylinder oil engine of 3750bhp. In 1942 she was commissioned as the auxiliary cruiser* Stier *(HSK6), being designated 'Raider J' by the Admiralty, and additionally known as Schiff 23 by the Germans. In her conversion she was given 6 150mm, 2 37mm and 4 20mm guns, 2 533mm torpedo tubes, and also carried two Ar231 floatplanes. Her complement was 324. In her short career she was responsible for the sinking of four Allied merchant ships, but remarkably was sunk in action in bad weather with the US Liberty ship* Stephen Hopkins *in the South Atlantic on September 27 1942.* Stephen Hopkins *was badly damaged and also sunk (Alex Duncan)*

Hansa: Drachenfels *was interned at Mormugao (Goa) in October 1939, and on September 9 1943 was set on fire and scuttled by her own crew to prevent seizure by the Portuguese authorities. Title to the wreck passed to Portugal, but it was not until December 1948 that it was sold to salvors for removal. Upon refloating the wreck was beached in December 1950, and broken up in situ (Alex Duncan)*

Laiesz: Pelikan *was built in 1935 and was fitted with a Bremer Vulkan 5-cylinder oil engine of 2750ihp. She was intended for the Cameroons–Europe banana trade and continued in this until the outbreak of the Second World War. In 1940 she was requisitioned by the Kriegsmarine as an auxiliary vessel and in May 1945 was seized by Great Britain. She passed to the ownership of the Ministry of War Transport, and was renamed* Empire Alde. *In 1946 she was sold to Elders & Fyffes and the following year renamed* Pacuare, *and under this name went to breakers at Troon in 1959 (Alex Duncan)*

Sloman: Sardinien *is pictured here as the British-flagged Helmstrath owned by Strath Steamship Co and managed by ER Management Co Ltd. She was sold to Sloman in 1937. She was largely involved in Germany–Norway trade following the occupation, and in May 1945 was seized at Bergen. She passed to Yugoslav owners in 1946 and was renamed* Losinj. *She remained under Yugoslavian flag until 1963 and was broken up during 1963–64 (RW Jordan collection)*

FERDINAND, HUGO, Kossfelderstraße 10, Seestadt Rostock

Funnel: Black with blue HF with narrow blue bands above and below, all on broad yellow band
Hull: Black
Services: General tramping

Helga Ferdinand	1897	GrayX	2566	4300	314.0	44–1	20–0	8.0
ex Ursula Fischer 33, ex Ambassador 24								
Marie Ferdinand	1911	ThmpR2	1757	2630	267.4	38–6	18–0	8.0
ex Wrotham 30, ex Bearwood 27, ex Garesfield 19								

FISSER & V DOORNUM, Hindenburgstraße 43, Emden

Funnel: F&VD – black with white F&D on green diamond on red bend between two narrow white bands; HFAG – as last but white HF
Hull: Black
Services: Mainly NW Europe –Mediterranean, –W Africa, –Canada, –US; general tramping
Note: Also vessels under 2000gt

FISSER & V DOORNUM REEDEREI GMBH								
Bertha Fisser	1919	Flensb	4110	7000	399–5	52–9	22–10	10.5
ex Hesperides 37, ex Parthia 19								
Christoph v Doornum	1928	ThmpR2	3751	7200	371–9	50–0	23–2	10.0
ex Goodleigh 37								
HENDRIK FISSER AG								
Elisabeth Hendrik Fisser	1924	Duncan	5145	8875	426–11	53–0	24–7	10.0
ex Dunrobin 37								
Erika Hendrik Fisser	1924	VSE1	3347	4850	332.7	46–6	20–0	10.0
ex Ursula Siemers 36								
Konsul Carl Fisser	1914	Weser	5843	8935	421.6	56–2	26–0	10.0
ex Jacatra 36, ex Westmark 20								
Konsul Hendrik Fisser	1928	Lithgw	4458	8380	385.0	52–0	24–9	10.0
ex Aelybryn 37								
Martha Hendrik Fisser	1911	Ropnr2	4879	8273	387.7	52–1	24–5	9.5
ex Blackheath 37								

FRIEDERICH, REEDEREI EUGEN, Schillerstraße 3, Bremen

Funnel: Black with red F inside black circle on white band
Hull: Black *Trades:* Oil and petroleum
Note: * Managed by Carl F Peters GmbH, Rödingsmarkt 28, Hamburg 11

Tankers								
Emmy Friederich	1904	LithR	4327	6800	374.5	48–11	27.2	8.5
ex Borderer 29; conv general cargo 30								
Pauline Friederich*	1912	NedSM	4733	6950	375.0	51–0	29.0	9.0
ex Vassos 39, ex Emanuel Nobel 35; conv mv 20								

'FRIGGA' AG, SEEREEDEREI, Kirdorfhaus, Alsterdamm 16–18, Hamburg 1

Funnel: Black with red F on white disc superimposed on white cross (**X**) between narrow white bands
Hull: Black
Services: General tramping

Aegir	1924	Reiher	4500	6447	351.8	50–4	24–0	9.5
August Thyssen	1924	Flensb	2342	3445	297.0	42–8	19.1	9.5
Baldur (r/t)	1929	Flensb	5805	10,266	411.9	58–3	26–0	9.5
Brage (r/t)	1938	NordsE	5954	9154	437.1	58–9	24–0	12.0
Frigga (r/t)	1924	Lübec2	5831	8297	436–4	53–4	24–1	10.0
Heimdal	1921	VSE1	2186	3100	283.0	40–11	20.5	9.5
ex Minna Horn 21								
Hermod	1922	Schich	5210	8323	405–0	52–8	24–7	9.5
ex Essex Envoy 38, ex Therese Horn 24								
Hödur	1913	Hendn2	5386	9710	424.5	54–10	25–0	9.5
ex Haggersgate 36, ex Chalister 24								
Odin	1929	VSE2	5806	9150	432.5	59–0	24–0	10.0
Thor	1922	DeutsH	2526	4096	291.8	44–4	22–0	9.5
Vale (r/t)	1939	NordsE	5950	9150	443.6	59–0	24–0	11.5
Widar (r/t)	1936	NordsE	5972	9291	437.1	58–11	24–0	11.5
FRACHTCONTOR GMBH								
Albert Janus	1928	Flensb	1598	2682	272–0	40–4	16–11	9.0
ex Heinrich Schuldt 33, ex Anna Marquardt Petersen 32								

FRITZEN & SOHN Vorm Lexzau, Scharbau & Co, Skagerrakstraße 37, Emden

Funnel: Black with red F on broad white band between narrow red bands
Hull: Black, red boot-topping
Services: General tramping, mainly ore trades

Carl Fritzen (st)	1920	Chepst	6594	11,000	428–0	55–10	28–0	10.0
ex Taifun 38, ex Fiume 26, ex War Genius 20								
Erika Fritzen	1906	Doxfrd	4169	7244	349.0	50–11	23–0	8.5
ex Dampfem 26, ex Hogland 23, ex Ryton 13								
Jacobus Fritzen	1909	Doxfrd	4090	7200	348.8	51–1	23–0	8.5
ex Dekade, ex Ruth 26, ex Dalemead 23, ex Dalemoor 20								
Jantje Fritzen (st)	1920	Chepst	6582	11,000	428–0	55–10	28–0	10.0

ex Passat 37, ex Sile 26, ex War Iliad 20

Theda Fritzen 1905 GrayX 2882 5000 342–0 47–6 20–0 9.0

ex Ostfriesland 39, ex Vigor 37, ex Sheaf Dart 29, ex Leander 16

JOHS FRITZEN & SOHN vorm W Kunstmann, Bollwerk 1, Stettin, and Swinemünde

Antje Fritzen 1916 Pgill1 4330 7350 365.0 51–0 23–7 9.0

ex Meopham 39, ex Gibraltar 38, ex Maplemore 21

Dora Fritzen 1914 Ropnr2 6888 10,135 419.4 56–9 25–0 10.0

ex Adamastos 37, ex Richmond Hill 37, ex Great City 36

Gerrit Fritzen 1910 Irvin3 4128 7462 377–6 51–4 24–7 9.0

ex Aylsham 38, ex Star of Cairo 36, ex Chatham 31, ex Lingfield 29

Gertrud Fritzen 1906 Blumr1 2999 5300 325.0 46–9 21–5 9.0

ex Arthur Kunstmann 38, ex Sortehavet 23, ex St Andrews 20

Harm Fritzen 1915 RDuck2 4818 8100 389.6 53–5 23–9 9.0

ex Laleham 39, ex Dorington Court 37

Hermann Fritzen (turret)
1906 Doxfrd 3845 6800 366–0 50–2 22–4 8.5

ex Werner Kunstmann 38, ex Efstathios 25, ex Clearway 25, ex Nonsuch 14

Herta Engeline Fritzen
1906 RDuck1 5100 8700 377.6 52–1 24–9 8.0

ex Heinz W Kunstmann 38, ex Seven Seas Transport 29, ex Picton 27

Jürgen Fritzen 1912 Rodger 4465 8600 410.0 54–4 24–9 8.5

ex Peckham 39, ex Ioannis Vatis 37, ex Baron Jedburgh 30

Katharina Dorothea Fritzen
1916 Doxfrd 7843 12,500 455.0 58–2 26–11 11.0

ex Daghild 37

Klaus Fritzen 1922 VulcH 2936 4650 328–6 45–1 19–5 9.5

ex Wilhelm Kunstmann 38

Reimar-Edzard Fritzen
1922 VulcH 2936 4650 328–6 45–1 19–5 9.5

ex Lina Kunstmann 38

Note: Also small vessels
Note: This company was reconstituted in 1938 from W Kunstmann, Stettin, and Lexzau, Scharbau & Co, Emden

GLÄSSEL, ERNST, Schlachte 29, Bremen

Funnel: Black with red arrowhead emblem on white band
Trades: Oil and petroleum

Tanker

Rekum 1919 Lithgw 5540 8300 412–0 52–2 25–1 10.5

ex Heron 39, ex Chiton 26, ex War Shikari 21

GRAMMERSTORF, KARL, Kiel-Holtenau

Funnel: Black with white KG on broad red band between two narrow white bands
Hull: Black
Services: General tramping
Note: Also coastal vessels

Käte Grammerstorf 1915 Rickmr 5088 8080 418–0 53–1 24–0 10.0

ex Ditmar Koel 39, ex Merriwa 28, ex Gertrud 21, ex Sperrbrecher 10 18, ex Gertrud 17, ex Willy Rickmers 17

HALTERMANN, JOHANN, 55–57 Ferdinandstraße, Hamburg 1

Funnel: Black with houseflag
Trades: Oil and petroleum

Tanker

Tine Asmussen 1919 Doxfrd 6795 10,040 429–4 55–4 28–2 10.0

ex Radix 39, ex Linerton 21; conv general cargo 21

HAMBURG-AMERIKA LINIE,
Ferdinandstraße 58–62, Hamburg 1; Alsterdamm 25, Hamburg 1

Funnel: Yellow with black top separated by white over red bands
Hull: Black, red boot-topping; *Milwaukee, Oceana* and *Reliance* – white, red boot-topping
Services: Passenger, mail, cargo: Germany, NW Europe–E and W coasts North America, –US and Gulf of Mexico, Cuba, Mexico, Central America, West Indies, Cristobal, Colón, and W coast Central America and Mexico via Panama; –W coast South America via Panama and Magellan Strait, –Far East; passenger, cargo – Germany, NW Europe–Netherlands East Indies, –Australia via South Africa, –Levant; cruising; cargo only – Germany, NW Europe–Canada, –West Indies, –South Africa

Passenger and passenger/general cargo vessels

Caribia (m2,P206/1,103/2,110/t)
1933 Blohm 12,049 7696 524–1 65–10 24–8 17.0

Cordillera (m2,P206/1,103/2,110/t)
1933 Blohm 12,055 7834 524–1 65–9 24–8 17.0

Deutschland (st2,P200/1,360/t,400/3)
1923 Blohm 21,046 12,806 676–11 78–9 32–8 19.5

lengthened 34

Hamburg (st2,P200/1,350/t,400/3)
1926 Blohm 22,117 13,257 677–6 79–0 32–8 19.0

lengthened 34

Hansa (st2,P204/1,361/t,400/3)
1923 Blohm 21,131 12,845 676–11 78–9 32–8 19.5

ex Albert Ballin 35; lengthened 34

Iberia (m2,P320) 1928 Schich 9829 6289 504–9 60–10 24–7 15.0

ex Magdalena 34; lengthened 34

Hamburg-Amerika: Bitterfeld *was at Padang in the Netherlands East Indies when German forces occupied Holland. She was promptly seized and under the Netherlands flag and Batavia registration was renamed* Mariso. *On March 20 1942 she was torpedoed by* U518 *and sunk when on voyage from New York and Trinidad to Saldhana Bay, Durban and Alexandria with 11,079 tons of genral cargo (Alex Duncan)*

Hamburg-Amerika: The twin-screw motor vessel Spreewald *was completed in 1923. In 1935 she was renamed* Anubis *and reverted to* Spreewald *in 1939. When serving as a naval supply ship she was torpedoed sunk in error by* U333 *on January 31 1942 (RW Jordan collection)*

Hamburg-Amerika: Tacoma *was completed in 1930 for the service between Hamburg and Pacific coast ports of the United States. She had accommodation for 49 passengers and carried a crew of 66. In September 1939 she was requisitioned as a supply ship for the battleship* Admiral Graf Spee, *and following the Battle of the River Plate was interned at Montevideo. In 1942 she was seized by Uruguay, and with the national shipping company saw much postwar service trading between the River Plate and northwest Europe. Eventually* Tacoma *became uneconomical to operate, and in 1974 was reported as being in service as a floating prison (RW Jordan collection)*

Hamburg-Süd: Monte Pascoal *was launched on September 17 1930, and delivered on January 15 1931. She was fitted with four Blohm & Voss/MAN 6-cylinder oil engines totalling 6800bhp. On September 9 1939 she sailed from Buenos Aires, painted grey, trying to beat the Allied blockade and arrived in Hamburg on October 14 with about 80 tons of oil fuel remaining in her bunkers. In January 1940 she was requisitioned by the Kriegsmarine for use as an accommodation vessel at Wilhelmshaven, where, on February 3 1944, she was bombed, burnt out and sunk, in an Allied air raid. In May 1944 the wreck was raised and then repaired.* Monte Pascoal *was seized by British forces in May 1945, and she became one of the many vessels which were scuttled in various locations loaded with surplus war materials, mainly poison gas ammunition (EH Cole)*

Milwaukee (m2,P559/1)	1929	Blohm	16,754	10,157	574–5	72–5	29–1	16.0
New York (st2,P210/cab,350/t,400/3)	1927	Blohm	22,337	13,257	677–6	79–0	32–8	19.0
lengthened 34								
Orinoco (m2,P140/1,100/2,100/3)	1928	Bremer	9660	6535	475–0	60–9	29–0	14.5
Patria (me2,P185/1,164/t)	1938	DeutsH	16,595	8500	597–8	74–1	23–4	16.0
St Louis (m2,P767)	1929	Bremer	16,732	9901	574–5	72–5	29–1	16.0
Vaterland (te2,P354/1,435/t,533/3)	bldg	Blohm	36,000		827–0	98–5	41.9	23.5
Newbuilding (te2)	bldg	Blohm	36,000		827–0	98–5	41.9	23.5
Newbuilding (te2)	order	Blohm	36,000		827–0	98–5	41.9	23.5
General cargo vessels								
Adalia	1921	Neptn1	3199	5590	351–7	48–2	21–11	10.0
Altona (st)	1921	Blohm	5892	9576	450.0	58–3	25–2	12.0
Amasis (r/t,P84)	1923	Bremer	7129	9439	457–8	55–4	25–3	12.0
Ammon (P82)	1922	Bremer	7134	9478	457–8	55–4	25–3	12.0
Antilla (te,P12)	1939	DeutsH	4363	6500	398–4	55–8	22–9	15.0
Antiochia	1921	Neptn1	3106	5531	351–7	48–4	21–11	10.0
Arauca (te,P12)	1939	Bremer	4354	6500	398–4	55–8	22–9	15.0
Baden (st,P90)	1922	Bremer	8204	9370	468.7	58–4	27–10	12.5
Bitterfeld (st)	1930	Krupp	7659	10,797	477.5	63–3	22–7	15.0
Böchum (r/t,P78)	1922	VulcH	6121	9350	450.0	58–2	25–1	13.0
Burgenland (m,P24/1,24/3)	1928	Flensb	7320	9916	483–4	61–2	26–3	13.0
Cassel (st,P27)	1922	Blohm	6047	9448	450.0	58–2	25–2	12.0
Dortmund (st,P24)	1926	Blohm	5138	8207	425–0	56–0	26–9	12.0
Duisburg (m,P24/1,24/3)	1928	DeutsH	7389	10,034	483–4	60–1	26–1	13.0
Ermland (m2,P69)	1922	Blohm	6528	9475	449.1	58–5	25–1	11.0
Essen (st,P84)	1923	Blohm	5158	8139	425–0	56–0	24–9	12.0
Feodosia	1922	Neptn1	3075	5590	351–7	48–4	21–11	10.0
Frankenwald (P66)	1922	DeutsH	5062	8735	415–8	54–2	26–3	10.0
Freiburg (st,P24)	1923	Blohm	5165	8130	425–0	56–0	24–9	12.0
Friesland (m,P83)	1925	Blohm	6310	10,285	449.1	58–4	25–8	11.5
Gera (st,P24)	1923	Blohm	5155	8120	425–0	56–0	24–9	12.0
Hagen (r/t)	1921	VulcH	5988	9478	450.0	58–4	25–2	13.0
Halle (st,P–)	1921	Blohm	5889	9621	449.4	58–2	25–2	12.0
Hamm (st,P–)	1921	Blohm	5874	9650	449.4	58–2	25–2	12.0
ex Hannover 26								
Hanau (st,P–)	1921	Blohm	5892	9621	450.0	58–2	25–2	12.0
Havelland (m2,P12)	1921	Blohm	6334	9667	449.0	58–4	25–1	11.0
Havenstein (P18/1)	1921	Flensb	7974	12,096	471.2	58–2	26–9	12.0
Heidelberg (m,P30)	1925	VulcH	6530	9252	450.3	58–2	25–1	12.0
ex Duisburg 26								
Hermonthis (m,P20)	1935	Bremer	4833	6702	436–0	54–8	22–0	14.0
laid down as Hannover								
Hindenburg	1921	Bremer	7880	12,086	468.8	58–4	26–11	11.0
Huascaran (me,P58)	1939	Blohm	6951	8819	487–6	60–4	26–11	15.0
Idarwald (P66)	1923	DeutsH	5033	8681	415–8	54–2	26–3	10.0
Ionia	1922	Neptn1	3102	5590	351–7	48–4	21–11	10.0
Iserlohn	1922	Krupp	3704	6255	338.7	47–9	24–4	10.0
Itauri (P83)	1923	Flensb	6838	9281	439.0	55–7	24–10	11.5
Karnak (P21)	1926	Flensb	7209	9143	439.6	55–9	25–7	11.5
Kellerwald (P60)	1923	DeutsH	5032	8681	415–8	54–2	26–3	10.0
Kiel	1922	Krupp	3703	6255	338.7	47–5	24–4	10.0
Kulmerland (m,P24)	1929	DeutsH	7363	10,034	483–4	60–1	26–0	13.0
Kurmark (st)	1930	Blohm	7021	9950	485–7	61–1	26–6	14.5
Kyphissia	1923	Lübec2	2964	5568	337.7	48–2	22–0	10.0
Leuna (st)	1928	Flensb	6856	9670	484–0	61–1	25–9	13.5
Leverkusen (m,P24)	1928	DeutsH	7386	10,034	483–4	60–1	25–10	13.0
Lübeck	1923	Krupp	3703	6170	338.7	47–4	24–4	10.0
Lüneburg (r/t)	1914	Teckl	5828	9404	451.1	57–3	25–2	13.0
ex City of Sydney 23, ex Freiburg 21								

Magdeburg (m)	1925	Blohm	6128	9237	449.4	58–2	25–2	13.0
Mecklenburg	1921	Bremer	7892	12,086	468.8	58–4	26–11	11.5
ex Ludendorff 29								
Menes (P69)	1926	Bremer	5609	8548	457–8	55–4	24–4	12.0
Monsérrate (m,P28)								
	1938	Bremer	5578	7456	459–0	56–4	23.1	14.0
Münsterland (m2,P12)								
	1921	Blohm	6408	9763	449.0	58–4	25–1	11.0
Naumburg (r/t)	1920	Flensb	5878	9434	449.6	58–3	25–3	13.0
ex Hamburg 26								
Neumark (st)	1930	HwldtK	7851	11,269	499–2	63–1	27–2	14.5
Nordmark (st)	1930	Flensb	7750	11,289	477.4	63–2	27–0	14.5
Oakland (m,P48)	1929	DeutsH	6757	8705	451–3	59–2	25–6	13.5
Odenwald (m2,P42)								
	1923	DeutsH	5098	8550	399.6	54–2	26–3	11.0
ex Assuan 38, ex Odenwald 35								
Oldenburg (r/t,18/1)								
	1923	Flensb	8537	12,057	471.7	58–2	27–5	12.0
Orizaba (te)	1939	DeutsH	4354	6500	398–4	55–8	22–9	15.0
Osorno (me,P58)	1938	Blohm	6951	8819	487–6	60–4	26–11	15.0
Ostmark (me2,P66)	order	HwldtK	8730	12,305	524–9	66–4	30–6	17.0
Palatia (m)	1928	Koch	3979	6210	392–10	53–9	22–10	12.5
Patricia (m)	1929	Koch	3979	6200	392–10	53–8	22–10	12.5
Phœnicia (m)	1928	HwldtK	4124	6274	393–0	53–8	22–3	12.5
Phrygia (m)	1928	HwldtK	4137	6274	393–0	53–8	22–3	12.5
Portland (m,P24/1,24/3)								
	1928	Bremer	7132	9408	483–4	61–2	26–1	14.0
Preussen (P18/1)	1922	Flensb	8230	11,958	471.1	58–2	27–10	12.0
Ramses (m,P73)	1926	Flensb	7983	11,565	481.5	62–9	26–9	12.5
Rendsburg (m,P47)	1926	VulcH	6200	9330	450.3	58–2	25–1	12.0
Rhakotis (m,P24/1,24/3)								
	1928	DeutsH	6753	8809	451–3	59–2	25–6	13.5
ex San Francisco 35								
Rhein (m,P73)	1926	Weser	6031	9384	453.8	58–2	24–6	11.5
Rheinland (m)	1927	DeutsH	6622	10,295	452.3	59–4	25–8	13.0
Roda (m,P24/1,24/3)								
	1928	DeutsH	6780	8750	451–3	59–2	25–6	13.5
ex Los Angeles 35								
Ruhr (m,P73)	1926	Bremer	5954	9498	454.0	58–4	24–5	11.5
Saarland (st,P36)	1924	Blohm	6725	9468	449.1	58–4	25–8	12.0
Sauerland (m,P24/1,24/3)								
	1929	Schich	7087	8517	483–4	61–1	26–1	13.5
Scheer	1915	Flensb	8298	12,377	477.9	62–4	27–8	12.0
ex St Lawrence River 21, ex Kronenfels 20								
Seattle (m,P24/1,24/3)								
	1928	DeutsH	7369	9619	461.6	61–8	25–11	14.0
Sesostris (P69)	1923	Reiher	3987	5708	365.3	50–4	22–7	11.0
Spreewald (m2,P60)	1922	DeutsH	5083	8550	399.6	54–3	26–3	11.0
ex Anubis 39, ex Spreewald 35								
Stassfurt (st)	1930	Bremer	7395	10,728	498–5	63–1	27–4	14.5
Steiermark (me2,P66)								
	1939	Krupp	8736	12,305	524–9	66–4	30–6	17.0
Tacoma (st,P49)	1930	DeutsH	8268	10,491	499–8	63–0	26–11	14.5
Tirpitz (P18/1)	1921	Flensb	7970	12,096	471.2	58–3	26–9	11.5
Troja (P2)	1922	HwldtK	2390	4158	309.3	44–1	21–2	11.0
Uckermark (st)	1930	Blohm	7021	9822	485–7	61–1	26–6	14.5
Vancouver (st,P49)	1930	DeutsH	8269	10,492	499–0	63–0	27–4	14.5
Vogtland (me2,P122)								
	1924	Blohm	6608	9600	449.0	58–1	25–6	12.0
Wasgenwald (P59)	1923	DeutsH	4990	8710	415–8	54–0	26–3	11.0
Wuppertal (me,P10)	1936	DeutsH	6737	9790	498–0	61–9	27–11	15.0
AG FÜR SEESCHIFFAHRT								
Oliva	1921	Bremer	7885	12,057	468.8	58–4	26–11	11.5

Note: Also *Alemania* (built 1921/1383gt), *Cerigo* (22/1120), *Durazzo* (22/1153), *Frisia* (30/561) operating in the West Indies area

HAMBURG-SÜDAMERIKANISCHE DAMPFSCHIFFAHRTS GESELLSCHAFT, Holzbrücke 8, Hamburg 8

Funnel: White with red top, or white with red top and black 'key' (key of Bremen) emblem for vessels registered Bremen
Hull: Black, red boot-topping
Services: Mail, passenger, cargo – variety of services covering

Passenger/general cargo vessels

Antonio Delfino (r/t2,P184/1,334/2,1368/st)								
	1922	VulcH	13,589	9650	526–3	64–0	29–10	15.0
ex Sierra Nevada 34, ex Antonio Delfino 32								

Hamburg, Bremen, Antwerp, Boulogne–Spain–Portugal–Brazil–Uruguay–Argentina (R Plate)

Cap Arcona (st2,P575/1,275/2,465/3)	1927	Blohm	27,561	11,319	675–8	86–8	28–5	20.0
Cap Norte (r/t2,P184/1,334/2,1368/st)	1922	VulcH	13,615	12,057	526–0	64–0	29–10	15.0
ex Sierra Salvada 34, ex Cap Norte 32								
España (r/t,P148/3)	1922	HwldtK	7465	9129	428–4	55–2	27–8	12.0
General Artigas (st,P169/cab,392/3)	1923	HwldtK	11,254	9055	495–1	60–9	27–11	13.5
ex Westphalia 29, laid down as Ammerland								
General Osorio (m2,P228/2,752/3)	1929	Bremer	11,590	9931	527–6	66–0	28–0	13.5
General San Martin (st,P169/cab,392/3)	1922	HwldtK	11,251	9133	495–1	60–9	27–11	13.0
ex Thuringia 30, laid down as Havelland								
La Coruña (r/t,P146/3)	1922	Reiher	7414	9036	428–4	55–2	27–8	12.0
Madrid (s2,P221/2,209/3,302/st)	1922	VulcSt	8777	8000	439.6	56–9	27–6	12.0
ex Sierra Nevada 25								
Monte Olivia (m2,P1372/2,1156/st)	1925	Blohm	13,750	10,876	524–0	65–10	26–9	14.0
Monte Pascoal (m2,P1372/3,1156/st)	1931	Blohm	13,870	10,896	524–0	65–9	26–9	14.0
Monte Rosa (m2,P1372/3,1036/st)	1931	Blohm	13,882	10,896	524–0	65–9	26–9	14.0
Monte Sarmiento (m2,P1372/3,1036/st)	1924	Blohm	13,625	10,876	524–0	65–10	26–9	14.0
Vigo (r/t,P190/3)	1922	HwldtK	7358	9129	428–4	55–1	27–8	12.0
General cargo vessels								
Asuncion (r/t)	1921	DeutsH	4626	6939	414.4	50–4	24–7	12.5
ex Niederwald 37								
Babitonga (m2)	1922	DeutsH	4422	7165	376.3	51–10	24–0	12.0
ex Osiris 38								
Bahia (m)	1927	Kockum	4117	7618	397–10	54–2	24–0	12.0
Bahia Blanca	1918	Short	8558	10,990	449.3	57–2	27–11	11.0
ex Schönfels 38, ex Celtic Prince 26								
Bahia Camarones	1918	Palmer	8551	10,740	448.1	57–2	27–11	11.0
ex Sonnenfels 39, ex Gothic Prince 27								
Bahia Castillo	1918	Short	8580	10,740	449.2	57–2	27–11	11.0
ex Rheinfels 39, ex Gaelic Prince 26								
Bahia Laura	1918	Palmer	8561	10,740	447.9	57–2	27–11	11.0
ex Rabenfels 38, ex Slavic Prince 26								
Belgrano (m)	1936	HwldtH	6095	9627	476–0	61–4	23–0	13.0
Buenos Aires	1912	Flensb	6097	9205	469–9	58–2	25–5	13.0
ex Witram 37, ex Boonah 25, ex Melbourne 14								
Campinas	1921	DeutsH	4541	7225	391.2	50–5	24–7	10.0
ex Westerwald 37								
Cordoba	1919	Lithgw	4611	7421	397–11	52–0	24–0	10.0
ex Taunus 37, ex Lisa 29, ex Galtymore 27, launched as War Sable								
Corrientes	1921	FurnH	4565	7040	380–7	52–2	24–11	11.0
ex Münster 38, ex Nord-Friesland 31, ex Louisiana 28								
Curityba	1911	Flensb	4969	8520	402.3	54–0	25–8	12.0
ex Holstein 38								
Entrerios	1923	Schich	5179	8120	386.2	52–9	25–0	10.0
Esmeralda (m,P12/1)	order	NedSM	6446	9100	475–10	59–3	24–8	13.0
Florida (m)	1939	Bremer	6148	9425	449.8	59–5	24–0	13.0
João Pessôa	1922	Flender	3023	5580	351–8	48–2	22–1	10.0
ex Georgia 37								
La Plata (P20/1)	1922	Bremer	8056	11,343	468.7	58–4	27–10	12.0
ex Sachsen 37								
Maceio	1920	Neptnl	3252	5531	351–9	48–4	21–11	10.0
ex Amassia 37								
Mendoza	1920	Dobson	5193	8390	413–5	52–4	25–3	10.0
ex Mount Ida 37, ex Ballena 33								
Montevideo (m)	1936	HwldtH	6075	9450	476–0	61–4	23–0	13.0
Natal	1921	Neptnl	3172	5590	337.7	48–4	21–11	10.0
ex Eupatoria 36								
Olinda	1927	HwldtK	4576	7052	349.5	50–4	23–7	10.5
ex Hohenstein 37								
Paranà	1921	VulcH	6038	10,470	450.0	58–2	25–1	13.0
ex Edmund Siemers 22								

Paranagua (m)	1939	HwldtH	6062	9425	476–0	61–4	23–0	13.0
Patagonia	1912	Teckl	5898	10,110	450.9	57–2	25–2	12.0
ex Grandon 38, ex City of Boston 27, ex Düsseldorf 21								
Pernambuco (m)	1925	Kockum	4121	7749	397–10	54–0	24–7	12.0
ex Skåneland 28								
Petropolis	1911	Bremer	4845	8890	399.2	53–9	26–10	11.0
ex Berengar 38, ex General Botha 26, ex Berengar 22								
Porto Alegre (m)	1936	Flensb	6105	9690	476–0	61–4	24–0	13.0
Rio de Janeiro	1914	Bremer	5261	9331	401.9	55–0	26–4	10.5
ex Santa Inés 21								
Rio Grande (m)	1939	HwldtH	6062	9450	476–0	61–4	23–0	13.0
Rosario (P12/1)	1913	Flensb	6079	9280	469–9	58–4	25–5	13.0
ex Witell 37, ex Bakara 25, ex Cannstatt 14								
Santa Fé (r/t)	1921	DeutsH	4627	7101	414.4	50–5	24–7	12.5
ex Steigerwald 37; lengthened 33								
Santos	1923	Krupp	5943	9330	408–0	54–4	26–7	11.0
ex Rapot 38								
Sao Paulo (P10/1)	1922	Schich	4977	7750	361.7	51–5	25–7	10.0
ex Alrich 38, ex Glücksburg 23								
Tenerife	1922	Schich	4996	7771	361.8	51–5	25–7	10.0
Tijuca	1923	Krupp	5918	9040	408–0	54–4	26–7	11.0
ex Ludwigshafen 38								
Tucuman	1918	LithR	4621	7735	397–6	51–10	24–0	11.0
ex Eifel 37, ex Doris 29, ex Comino 29, ex Ardgorm 19								
Uruguay	1922	Krupp	5846	9180	408–0	54–3	26–7	11.0
ex Optima 25, ex Einfeld 23								
Viktoria (m)	bldg	HwldtH	6111	9450	476–3	61–1	24–1	14.0

Note: See also under Deutsche Arbeitsfront GmbH

HAMBURGER WALFANG-KONTOR GMBH, Jungfernstieg 7, Hamburg 36

Funnel: Yellow
Hull: Black with white band, or grey
Services: Whaling
Note: * Sold Norway (in part exchange for *Vikingen*) 1939, renamed *Norness*
Note: This company controlled Hvalfslsk Blaahval A/S and Hvalfslsk Finnhval A/S (*qv* under Jorgen Krag and Yngvar Hvistendahl respectively in Norway section), and also owned whalers

DEUTSCHE ÖLMÜHLEN ROHSTOFFE GMBH, Roonstraße 5, Berlin

Tanker								
Newbuilding* (m)	1939	DeutsH	9577	14,800	510–9	65–9	28–4	12.5
Whale factory vessels								
Südmeer (s2)	1902	Wighml	8133	10,810	487.3	56–0	29–4	9.5
ex Sydis 37, ex Torodd 34, ex Colonia 27; conv cable vessel 27								
Wikinger (s2)	1929	SHWR	14,772	19,730	493.2	71–1	35–4	11.0
ex Vikingen 38								

'HANSA', DEUTSCHE DAMPFSCHIFFAHRTS GESELLSCHAFT, Schlachte 6, Bremen

Funnel: Black with black 'Iron Cross' on white band between narrow red bands
Hull: Black, red boot-topping
Services: Bremen, Hamburg, Antwerp–Persian Gulf, India; Bremen, Hamburg–Burma, Ceylon; Bremen, Hamburg–Aden, Port Sudan, Djibouti; Bremen–South America; Hamburg–Spain–Portugal; Bombay–Philadelphia, New York; New York–South Africa, E Africa; New York–Australia, New Zealand

Altenfels (m,P10)	1925	VulcH	8132	11,870	469.1	60–5	29–1	12.0
Bärenfels (r/t,P4)	1921	Teckl	7569	11,000	491–3	58–8	27–2	12.0
Birkenfels (r/t,P4)	1922	Weser	6322	9190	431.6	56–6	26–6	12.0
Braunfels (m,P7)	1927	Desch3	7847	11,200	488–2	60–6	27–11	12.0
Drachenfels (r/t,P4)	1921	HwldtK	6342	9250	430.3	56–6	26–6	12.0
Ehrenfels (m,P12)	1936	Desch3	7752	10,250	508–6	61–2	27–4	16.0
Falkenfels (r/t,P4)	1921	Weser	6318	9190	431.6	56–5	26–6	12.0
Frauenfels (r/t,P4)	1920	Teckl	7487	11,050	495–4	58–6	27–3	12.0
Freienfels (r/t,P12)	1929	Desch3	7563	10,550	527–7	62–2	25–7	14.0
Geierfels (r/t,P12)	1931	Desch3	7605	10,340	527–7	62–2	25–7	14.0
Goldenfels (m,P12)	1938	Bremer	7862	10,340	508–6	61–4	27–2	16.0
Hohenfels (m,P12)	1938	Bremer	7862	10,340	508–6	61–4	27–2	16.0
Kandelfels (m,P12)	1937	Desch3	7766	10,450	508–6	61–4	27–4	16.0
Kybfels (m,P12)	1937	Desch3	7764	10,450	508–6	61–4	27–4	16.0
Lauterfels (r/t,P4)	1921	Weser	6310	9190	431.6	56–4	26–6	12.0
Lichtenfels (r/t,P12)	1929	Desch3	7566	10,550	527–7	62–2	25–7	13.0
Liebenfels (r/t,P4)	1922	Weser	6318	9190	431.6	56–5	27–0	12.0
Lindenfels (r/t,P8)	1928	Teckl	8457	12,215	510–2	62–2	28–2	13.0
Marienfels (r/t,P4)	1921	Teckl	7575	11,010	491–3	58–7	27–2	12.0
Moltkefels (m,P12)	bldg	Bremer	7862	10,340	508–6	61–1	27–2	16.0
Neidenfels (m,P12)	1939	Desch3	7838	10,375	508–6	61–2	27–2	16.0
Neuenfels (m2,P10)	1925	Weser	8096	11,600	469.9	60–6	29–1	12.0
Ockenfels (r/t,P4)	1921	Teckl	7574	11,000	491–3	58–6	27–2	12.0
Rauenfels (r/t,P8)	1928	Bremer	8460	12,065	510–2	62–2	28–2	13.0
Reichenfels (m,P12)	1936	Desch3	7744	10,250	508–6	61–11	27–4	16.0

Hamburg-Süd: The steamer Bahia Blanca *was completed in 1918 as* Celtic Prince *for Prince Line. She was sold to Hansa in November 1926 and renamed* Schönfels, *and June 9 1938 was sold to Hamburg-Süd and renamed* Bahia Blanca. *In an effort to break through the Allied blockade, she sailed from Rio de Janeiro on December 9 1939 for Germany with a cargo of coffee and minerals. On January 10 1940 she struck an iceberg in the Denmark Strait and sank (Hamburg-Süd)*

Hamburg-Süd: Launched on January 17 1939, the cargo liner Rio Grande *was delivered in April. She was fitted with an Howaldtswerke/MAN 8-cylinder oil engine of 3350bhp. On September 3 1939 she was requisitioned at Rio Grande, Brazil, by the Kriegsmarine, and commenced conversion for use as a supply vessel for surface raiders. On October 31 1940 she sailed from Rio Grande to meet in mid Atlantic the auxiliary cruiser* Thor. *In mid November* Thor *transferred to* Rio Grande *350 survivors from Allied merchant ships which she had sunk. In December 1940 she arrived in Bordeaux and during 1941–43 eluded the Allied blockade on three occasions on voyages Bordeaux–Kobe–Bordeaux. On October 4 1943 she sailed from Kobe for Germany with a valuable cargo and was intercepted on January 4 1944 by US warships and scuttled to avoid capture (Hamburg-Süd)*

Leonhardt & Blumberg: Lotte Leonhardt *was completed in 1937 at Rostock and was fitted with a Weser triple expansion engine with low pressure turbine. On August 8 1940 she was commissioned by the Kriegsmarine as a transport for the aborted Operation 'Seelöwe' and was given the designation* O11. *After the abandonment of 'Seelöwe' she was released to her owner.* Lotte Leonhardt *was then making the short voyages from Germany to occupied Norway. On April 26 1944 she was bombed and sunk by Allied aircraft south of Bodø, Norway (Leonhardt & Blumberg)*

Rheinfels*	1918	Short	8579	10,740	449.2	57–2	26–5	11.0
ex Gaelic Prince 26								
Rolandseck (P11)	1937	StettO	1845	2875	280.1	42–4	19–0	11.5
Rotenfels (m,P7)	1927	Desch3	7854	11,200	488–2	60–10	27–11	12.0
Schwaneck (r/t,P12)	1939	Desch5	2193	2900	329–8	44–10	19–10	12.0
Soneck (r/t,P12)	1939	Desch5	2191	2900	329–8	44–10	19–10	12.0
Sonnenfels**	1918	Palmer	8552	10,740	448.1	57–2	27–11	11.0
ex Gothic Prince 27								
Stolzenfels (r/t,P4)	1916	Teckl	7512	10,780	469.4	58–6	27–1	12.0
ex Eastern Prince 26, ex Altenfels 20								
Sturmfels (P4)	1921	Weser	6288	9190	431.5	56–2	27–0	12.0
Tannenfels (m,P12)	1938	Desch5	7840	10,200	508–6	59–1	27–2	16.0
Trautenfels (r/t,P4)	1921	Flensb	6418	9450	430.5	56–6	27–0	12.0
Treuenfels (r/t,P8)	1928	Desch3	8457	12,215	510–2	62–4	28–2	14.0
Trifels (r/t,P4)	1922	Teckl	6198	9080	450–11	56–6	26–6	12.0
Uhenfels (r/t,P12)	1931	Desch3	7603	10,340	527–7	62–2	25–6	13.0
Wachtfels (r/t,P8)	1928	Desch2	8467	12,125	510–2	62–2	28–2	13.0
Wartenfels (r/t,P8)	1921	Teckl	6181	9080	450–11	56–5	26–6	12.0
Weissenfels (m,P10)	1925	Teckl	7861	11,405	468.4	60–5	29–1	12.0
Werdenfels (r/t,P4)	1921	Weser	6318	9190	431.6	56–5	27–0	12.0
Wildenfels (r/t,P4)	1922	Teckl	6224	9200	450–11	56–6	26–5	12.0
Wolfsburg	1916	Teckl	6201	10,020	469.6	62–1	24–6	11.5
ex Baron Lovat 25, ex Wolfsburg 21								

Note: *, ** Sold Hamburg-Südamerikanische DG 1939, renamed *Bahia Castillo, Bahia Camarones*, respectively
Note: Also *Hundseck* (built 1923/1456gt), *Lahneck* (23/1663), *Rolandseck* (37/1845), *Stahleck* (23/1663)

HANSEATISCHE REEDEREI EMIL OFFEN & CO, Alsterdamm 8, Hamburg 1

Funnel: Black with white bordered black 'Iron Cross' on red band between two narrow white bands
Hull: Black, red boot-topping
Services: General tramping

Ditmar Koel*	1915	Rickmr	5088	8080	401.0	53–1	24–0	10.5
ex Merriwa 28, ex Gertrud 21, ex Willy Rickmers 17								
Hein Hoyer (r/t,P6)	1937	Lübecl	5836	9940	464–4	59–9	25–0	12.0
Karpfanger (st)	1922	DeutsK	4974	9350	425–10	54–5	26–7	10.0
ex Luise Hemsoth 26								
Kersten Miles (st)	1922	DeutsK	4971	9350	425–10	54–5	26–7	10.0
ex Martha Hemsoth 26								
Klaus Schoke (r/t)	1938	Lübecl	5848	9940	464–4	59–9	25–0	12.0
Memphis	1918	Dtroit	1996	2805	261–10	43–10	17–9	10.0
ex Vera 32, ex Virginia Express 30, ex Lake Stirling 21, launched as War Thrush								
Sesostris	1918	Dtroit	2013	2805	261–10	43–10	17–9	10.0
ex Valentine 32, ex Virginia Limited 30, ex Lake Arthur 21, launched as War Palm								
Simon von Utrecht (st)	1922	DeutsK	4949	9350	425–10	54–5	26–7	10.0
ex Wilhelm Hemsoth 26								

Note: * Sold Karl Grammerstorf 1939, renamed *Käte Grammerstorf*

HANSEN, A, Schiffbrücke 24, Postfach 147, Flensburg

Funnel: Yellow
Services: General tramping

Iris (r/t)	1921	Örsndl	3323	5000	311.8	44–10	24–0	9.5
ex Herøy 39, ex Adour 34								
Juno	1903	Neptnl	2038	3300	292.1	41–3	19–0	9.0
ex Romö 24, ex Elisabeth 21								
Thetis	1909	Neptnl	2788	4560	304–0	44–0	21–10	9.0
ex Genua 29, ex Lissabon 21								

HENKEL & CO GMBH, Düsseldorf

ERSTE DEUTSCHE WALFANG GMBH, Alsterdamm 16–17, Hamburg 1

Funnel: Yellow with green and white diagonally quartered house-flag bearing letters 'E D W G'
Services: Whaling

Tanker								
Antarktis (m)	1939	HwldtK	10,711	15,000	488.3	69–7	29–0	12.5
Whale factory vessel								
Jan Wellem (r/t)	1921	Bremer	11,776	9463	487–0	71–5	25–6	10.5
ex Württemberg 35; conv passenger/general cargo 35								

Note: Also whalers

HORN, H C, Slomanhaus, Baumwall 3, Hamburg 11

Ship	Built	Builder	GRT	DWT	Length	Beam	Draught	Speed
Claus Horn (m,P32/1)	1926	Reiher	3177	4520	326–10	46–4	24–2	11.0
ex Minna Horn 30								
Consul Horn (s2,P190/t)	1904	H&W,B	7772	6200	453.8	56–5	23–0	11.0
ex Gerolstein 39, ex Mamari 28								
Frida Horn (m,P32/1)	1925	Flensb	3184	4250	326–10	45–10	24–2	11.0
Gravenstein (P4)	1906	B&W	3505	6500	369.0	47–6	23–0	10.0
ex Hansa 29, ex Tranquebar 22								
H C Horn (m,P30/1)	1932	Flensb	4132	4950	343–6	49–9	24–6	15.0
Heinz (m,P32/1)	1928	Schich	3994	5166	329–1	48–9	24–4	13.0
ex Heinz Horn 39								
Henry Horn (m,P32/1)	1926	Reiher	3164	4100	326–10	46–0	24–2	11.0
ex Presidente Gomez 36, ex Waldtraut Horn 36								
Ingrid Horn (m,P32/1)	1928	Schich	4006	5200	329–1	48–9	24–2	13.0
Mimi Horn (m,P32/1)	1928	Schich	4007	5200	329–1	48–9	24–2	13.0
Waldtraut Horn (m,P38/1)	1929	Schich	3995	5200	329–1	48–9	24–2	13.0
ex Presidente Gomez 36								

Funnel: Black with white H superimposed on blue over red bands
Hull: Black with white band, red boot-topping
Services: Hamburg, Antwerp, London–West Indies
Note: Also smaller vessels

HOWALDT, BERNARD, Norderhofenden 23, Postfach 70, Flensburg

Ship	Built	Builder	GRT	DWT	Length	Beam	Draught	Speed
Edith Howaldt	1903	Neptnl	2067	3650	291.3	41–2	19–0	8.5
ex Most 27, ex Julius Zelck 21, ex Wangard 13, ex Ingo 11, ex Elsa Menzell 07								
Klaus Howaldt (r/t)	1938	NordsE	5956	9600	437.4	59–0	24–0	11.5
Sabine Howaldt (r/t)	1938	NordsE	5956	9600	437.4	59-0	24–0	11.5

Funnel: Black with red H on white diamond on blue band
Hull: Black
Services: General tramping

JOST, J, (Otto Brink), Hafendamm 5, Postfach 3, Flensburg

Ship	Built	Builder	GRT	DWT	Length	Beam	Draught	Speed
Constantia	1909	Neptnl	1777	2900	266.2	40–4	19–0	9.0
ex Hanna Larsen 24, ex Cilondia 21, ex Anna Dorette Boog 20								
Gratia	1905	EiderW	2068	3200	274.0	39–9	15.8	8.5

Funnel: Black with blue and white houseflag
Services: General tramping

JURGENS VAN DEN BERGH MARGARINE-VERKAUFS UNION GMBH, Unionhaus, Berlin

Ship	Built	Builder	GRT	DWT	Length	Beam	Draught	Speed
Tanker								
Brake* (m)	1937	Bremer	9925	14,550	510–9	66–0	28–0	12.0
Whale factory vessel								
Unitas** (r/t2)	1937	Desch3	21,846	28,500	635–0	80–2	39–7	12.0

OELFABRIK GROSS GERAU–BREMEN

Ship	Built	Builder	GRT	DWT	Length	Beam	Draught	Speed
Tanker								
Germania* (m)	1938	DeutsH	9851	14,560	510–9	66–0	28–0	12.0

Funnel: Grey with white U on white bordered blue diamond superimposed on blue over white over blue bands, separated from black top and grey base by narrow white bands
Services: Whaling; oil and petroleum trades
Note: * Manager Schiffahrts & Speditionskontor Elbe GmbH, Messberghof, Hamburg 1: ** manager Unitas Deutsche Walfang GmbH, Ballinhaus, Postfach 791, Hamburg
Note: This company, which was a member of the Unilever group, also owned a fleet of whalers

KAUFFAHRTEI SEEREEDEREI ADOLF WIARDS & CO, Alsterufer 10, Hamburg 11

Ship	Built	Builder	GRT	DWT	Length	Beam	Draught	Speed
Emshörn	1913	Rhead3	4301	7913	369.6	51–1	24–1	8.0
ex Karin 36, ex Antje Catharina 33, ex Trevethoe 32								
Emsland	1901	HwldtK	5170	7680	405.3	52–5	22–0	8.5
ex Heinrich Hugo Stinnes 7 28, ex Drottning Sophia 21								
Emsriff	1912	RDuck2	4935	8100	379.0	50–11	24–8	8.0
ex Jolanthe 36, ex Finchley 35, ex Westra 26, ex Nantwen 21								
Emsstrom	1900	HwldtK	4517	6550	388.9	52–1	21–0	8.0
ex Fritz Hugo Stinnes 5 28, ex Oscar Fredrik 21								

Funnel: Black with white K inside white circle
Hull: Black
Services: General tramping

Monsun (st)	1920	Monmth	6590	10,735	428–0	55–6	28–0	10.5
ex Adige 26, ex War Epic 20								
Stadt Emden	1901	HwldtK	5180	7750	406.2	52–6	22–0	8.5
ex Adeline Hugo Stinnes 3 28, ex Kronprins Gustaf 21								

Funnel: Black with blue disc on white band
Hull: Black, red boot-topping
Services: General tramping

KNÖHR & BURCHARD NFL, Neptunhaus, Hamburg 11

Barmbek	1929	Flensb	2446	4350	322–1	45–6	20–4	10.5
Dalbek	1939	LübecM	2884	4745	345–4	48–2	20–1	12.0
Eilbek	1936	LübecM	2185	3315	295–4	44–2	18–1	11.5
Flottbek	1926	Schich	1930	3130	293–2	40–2	19–0	10.0
Goldbek	1939	LübecM	2815	4745	345–4	48–2	20–1	11.0
Jersbek	1938	LübecM	2804	4745	344–6	48–2	20–1	12.0
Lasbek (P–)	1930	LübecM	2159	3250	295–4	44–2	18–1	10.0
Reinbek	1938	LübecM	2804	4745	344–6	48–1	20–1	12.0
Schiffbek	1930	LübecM	2159	3300	295–4	44–2	18–1	10.0
Schürbek	1930	Flensb	2448	4350	322–1	45–6	20–4	10.5
Steinbek (P–)	1936	LübecM	2185	3315	295–4	44–1	18–1	11.5
Thielbek	1927	Ostsee	1883	2950	266.9	41–1	18–0	10.0
ex Siegmund 28								
Wandsbek (r/t)	1938	Moss	2388	4010	317–0	47–8	19–0	11.0

Funnel: Stinnes – black with black 'HSt' on white band over black crossed hammer emblem on red band
Hull: Black, red boot-topping
Services: General tramping

KOHLEN-IMPORT-U. POSEIDON SCHIFFAHRT AG
Postfach 88, Lizenstraße 13, Königsberg

Felix Heumann	1921	LivCpr	2468	4075	294.4	43–8	20.3	9.0
ex B A Sanne 33, ex England 28, ex Thorhild 22								
Königsberg-Preussen	1924	Krupp	2530	3628	277.8	44–2	19–0	10.0
Masuren (r/t)	1935	Schich	2383	3507	292–0	44–6	19–5	10.5
Ostpreussen	1920	Boeles	3030	5429	324.8	47–4	21.9	8.5
ex Merak 27								
Poseidon	1918	Conrad	3911	6238	345.8	54–6	24.4	8.5
ex Berk 29, ex Nieuwe Maas 22								
Rheinland	1920	Dijvdk	2570	4224	300.3	45–2	19–2	8.5
ex Willem van Driel Sr 27								
Manager for								
Albert Jensen (m,P8)	1939	Flensb	5450	7500	443–3	60–2	24–0	14.0
ex Flensburg 39								
'BRENNTAG' BRENNSTOFF-CHEMIKALIEN U TRANS AG								
Mathias Stinnes (m,P8)	1937	Flensb	5337	7975	443–3	60–2	24–0	14.0
Mulheim-Ruhr (m,P8)	1938	Flensb	5350	7975	443–3	60–2	24–0	14.0
HUGO STINNES GMBH								
Cläre Hugo Stinnes 1 (m)	1935	Flensb	5295	7921	444–0	60–2	24–0	13.0
Johannes Molkenbuhr (m)	1936	Flensb	5294	8035	443–0	60–2	24–0	13.0
Welheim (m)	1939	Flensb	5455	7500	443–0	60–2	24–0	14.0
HUGO STINNES REEDEREI GMBH								
Dieter Hugo Stinnes 12	1924	Krupp	2545	3400	277.8	44–2	19–0	10.0
Else Hugo Stinnes 15	1928	Nüscke	3291	4600	316–7	47–9	21–2	10.0
Ernst Hugo Stinnes 11	1928	Nüscke	3295	4600	316–7	47–9	21–2	10.0
Julius Hugo Stinnes 27	1924	Krupp	2530	3400	277.8	44–2	19–0	10.0

Funnel: Black with three interlocking white circle
Hull: Black
Services: Mainly carrying ore to Germany; general tramping

KRUPP AG, FRIED, Essen

Borbeck	1923	Workmn	6002	10,200	419.0	56–4	26–8	10.0
ex Berwindmoor 29								
Frielinghaus	1922	Krupp	4339	6980	380.1	47–5	24–0	9.5
lengthened 32								
Gillhausen (st)	1921	Krupp	4339	6980	380.1	47–5	24–0	9.5
lengthened 32								

NDL: Europa *was a consort to the record-breaking* Bremen *and was delivered by her builders on March 21 1930. She was fitted with 12 Blohm & Voss single reduction geared turbines with a maximum rating of 130,000shp. In September 1939 she was laid up at Bremerhaven and was earmarked to be a headquarters ship for Operation 'Seelöwe'. This planned invasion of England did not materialise, nor did a later plan to convert* Europa *to an aircraft carrier. Eventually she became an accommodation ship at Wesermünde. On May 8 1945 she was seized by US forces, repaired, refitted, and in August commissioned as the USN troop transport* AP 177. *In September 1945 she voyaged from Bremen and Southampton to New York with 6500 troops and in November and December made two voyages from Southampton to New York with a total 11,793 troops. In June 1946 she was allocated to France, and after a refit emerged eventually as CGT's* Liberté, *under which name she made her first voyage for CGT in 1950. She was withdrawn from service in November 1961 and broken up at La Spezia in 1962–63 (Blohm & Voss)*

NDL: The twin-screw liner Scharnhorst *was launched on December 14 1934 and started her maiden voyage in May 1935 from Bremerhaven and Southampton to Mediterranean ports, Suez, Hong Kong and Japan. She was fitted with 26,000shp turbo-electric machinery, and had a Maierform hull.* Scharnhorst *was in Japan upon the outbreak of the Second World War, and it was decided she should remain there. In February 1942 she was sold to the Japanese navy for conversion to a troop transport, but plans for this were cancelled and she was converted at the Kure naval yard to an escort carrier. On December 15 1943 she was commissioned as* Shinyo, *and less than a year later was torpedoed and sunk by the US submarine* Spadefish *(RW Jordan collection)*

Oslebshausen	1923	Seebck	4989	7360	370.6	51–0	24–3	10.0
ex Zembra 37								
Rheinhausen	1912	Doxfrd	6298	11,285	439.1	57–11	25–0	8.0
ex Stiklestad 28								

Note: Also short-sea vessels

KRUPP REEDEREI UND KOHLENHANDEL GMBH, Chilehaus B, Fischertwiete 1, Hamburg

Carl Jüngst	1921	Eltrgm	2879	4450	304.8	44–2	20–7	8.5
ex Bernhard Blumenfeld 38, ex Dalewood 23								

Note: This fleet was managed by Fried Krupp AG Schiffsbetrieb, Atlantic Haus, PO Box 655, Westplein 2, Rotterdam, Netherlands

NORDDEUTSCHE KOHLEN-U COKESWERKE AG, Chilehaus B, Fischertwiete 1, Hamburg

Hammonia	1910	WoodS2	2543	3650	304.4	42–2	19–0	8.0
ex Clara Blumenfeld 38, ex Marsden 23								
Nordcoke	1936	LübecM	2491	3200	311–0	44–6	18–3	10.0

LAEISZ, F, Laeiszhof, 1 Trostbrücke, Hamburg 11

Funnel: Black with two white bands separated by narrow red band
Hull: Grey or white, red boot-topping
Services: African fruit trades; general tramping

AFRIKANISCHE FRUCHT COMPAGNIE AG

Fruit carriers

Palime (m,P12)	1937	DeutsR	2863	2800	362.6	47–1	17–0	15.0
Panther (m)	1939	DeutsH	4876	4020	422–6	52–8	20–2	15.5
Pelikan (m,P12)	1935	Bremer	3264	2558	378–1	44–10	17–0	15.0
Pionier (m,P12)	1933	Bremer	3285	2750	378–1	44–10	17–0	15.0
Pomona (m)	1938	DeutsH	3457	2970	422–9	52–8	17–10	15.5
Pontos (m,P12)	1935	Bremer	3410	3843	392–8	44–10	17–0	15.0
Python (m,P12)	1936	DeutsH	3664	3415	362.6	47–1	17–0	15.0

REEDEREI F LAEISZ GMBH

General cargo vessels

Planet (st,P12)	1922	Teckl	5821	9480	450.8	57–2	25–4	13.0
Poseidon (st,P12)	1922	Teckl	5864	9520	450.8	57–2	25–4	13.0

Sailing vessels (4-masted barques)

Pádua	1926	Teckl	3064	4600	344–6	46–1	23–6	–
Priwall	1920	Blohm	3185	4600	323.1	47–1	23–6	–

Note: Also smaller vessels

LEONHARDT & BLUMBERG, Alterwall 10, Hamburg 11

Funnel: Black with houseflag – red diagonal cross (**x**) and black horizontal cross (+) with white square at centre
Hull: Black, red boot-topping
Services: General tramping

Adolf Leonhardt	1921	VSE1	2990	5400	339.9	47–11	22–0	8.5
ex Theben 25								
August Leonhardt	1922	StettO	2593	4775	342–5	46–1	20–3	10.5
ex Johanna Blumberg 23								
Hans Leonhardt (r/t)	1938	Neptn2	4174	7185	429–8	55–10	22–3	12.0
Karl Leonhardt	1913	Craig2	6042	9500	415.0	55–10	24–8	8.5
ex Marietta 39, ex W I Radcliffe 35, ex Clarissa Radcliffe 17								
Lotte Leonhardt (r/t)	1937	Neptn2	4167	7185	429–8	55–10	22–3	12.0
Luise Leonhardt	1932	GrayWH	4816	8700	421–0	54–10	24–10	10.0
ex Siltonhall 38								
Marie Leonhardt	1922	StettO	2594	4775	342–5	46–1	20–3	10.5
Otto Leonhardt	1911	ThmpR2	3682	6250	361–5	50–0	22–1	9.0
ex Arethusa 37, ex Darnholme 32								

LÜBECK-LINIE AG, Untertrave 107-1, Lübeck

Funnel: Black with two elongated Ls on white band
Services: Germany–UK, –Baltic, –Mediterranean, –NW Africa
Note: Also *Hansestadt Lübeck* (built 1925/1704gt), *Travemünde* (07/1756)

Ostland	1920	Koch	2152	4010	286.6	42–9	19–0	9.0
ex Asta 37, ex Gustav Vigeland 30, ex Christian Horn 22, ex Proximus 21								
Possehl	1921	HwldtK	2369	3475	317–0	42–4	18–9	9.0
Schleswig-Holstein	1921	Koch	2369	4180	310–0	42–8	20–5	9.0
ex Hansburg 38, ex Yalta 31, ex Horncap 26								

NEPTUN, DAMPFSCHIFFAHRTS GESELLSCHAFT, Langenstraße 98–9, Bremen

Funnel: Black with blue over yellow bands
Hull: Black or grey, red boot-topping
Services: Bremen, Antwerp–Portugal, N and S Spain, Balearic Islands, N and NW Africa

Ajax (r/t,P31)	1927	Desch3	2297	4340	297–4	46–0	21–0	10.0
Apollo (r/t,P31)	1927	Desch3	2297	4340	297–4	46–0	21–0	10.0
Arion (r/t,P31)	1927	Desch3	2297	4340	297–4	46–0	21–0	10.0
Atlas (r/t,P31)	1927	Desch3	2297	4340	297–4	46–0	21–0	10.0
Bessel (m,P35)	1925	Weser	1878	2810	283.7	41–8	17–10	11.0
ex Sorrento 26								

Euler (m,P35)	1925	Weser	1879	2810	283.7	41–8	17–10	11.0
ex Amalfi 28								
Helios (r/t,P12)	1929	Desch3	2883	4350	296.9	46–0	20–11	11.0
Hercules (r/t,P12)	1929	Desch3	2883	4350	296.9	46–0	20–11	11.0
Hestia (r/t,P12)	1929	Desch3	2883	4350	296.9	46–0	20–11	11.0
Mars (m,P12)	1939	Seebk2	3494	4300	364–2	47–11	22–8	14.0
Minerva (m,P12)	1939	Bremer	2446	3065	360–9	47–10	22–8	14.0
Nestor (m,P12)	1939	Bremer	2446	3065	360–9	47–10	22–8	14.0
Triton	1921	Weser	1620	2055	256–5	36–4	17–8	10.0
Vesta	1921	Weser	1620	2055	256–5	36–2	17–8	10.0
Zeus (m,P12)	1939	Seebk2	3494	4300	364–2	47–11	22–8	14.0

Note: Also short-sea vessels

NIMTZ, FRANZ L, Bollwerk 1, Stettin

Funnel: Black with black FLN on white band between two red bands *Hull:* Black
Services: General tramping, including voyages to West Indies and South America

Brigitte	1924	Blyth	2740	4050	319.6	43–0	19–3	10.0
ex Tullochmoor 36								
Franz Jürgen	1910	StettO	2166	3430	283.6	41–3	18–10	8.0
ex Vasco 29, ex Brandenburg 20								
Marianne	1924	Blyth	2743	4050	319.6	43–0	19–3	8.0
ex Uskmoor 36								
Stettiner Greif (r/t)	1938	StettO	2214	3140	296.8	42–9	18–0	10.5

Note: Also vessels under 2000gt

NORDDEUTSCHE SEEKABELWERKE AG, Nordenham

Funnel: Yellow
Hull: Grey
Services: Cable laying/maintenance
Note: Also cable vessel Norderney (built 1915/1487gt)

Tanker and cable vessel								
Neptun (s2)	1926	Blohm	7250	10,250	473–0	57–4	28–6	11.0

NORDDEUTSCHER LLOYD, (North German Lloyd), Papenstraße 5–13, Bremen

Funnel: Yellow
Hull: Black, red boot-topping – most passenger vessels have white dividing line; some passenger vessels white, red boot-topping
Services: Mail, passenger cargo – Bremen, Southampton, Cherbourg–New York; passenger,cargo – Bremen–Halifax NS; Bremen, Hamburg–W coast North America; Bremen–Central America; Bremen–Spain, Portugal; Hamburg–Australasia; Hamburg–Far East, China, Japan

Passenger and passenger/general cargo vessels								
Berlin (s2,P424/cab,285/t,513/3)	1925	Bremer	15,286	9045	571–11	69–2	29–8	16.5
Bremen (st4,P800/1,500/2,300/t,600/3)	1929	Desch3	51,732	13,000	939–1	101–11	33–11	27.0
Columbus (st2,P513/1,574/2,705/3)	1923	Schich	32,581	10,790	775–0	83–1	49.1	22.0
laid down as Hindenburg								
Europa (st4,P687/cab,830/t,507/3)	1930	Blohm	49,746	12,800	936–9	102–1	33–8	27.0
Fulda (m2,P89/cab,159/2)	1924	Weser	7744	9000	478–0	62–4	28–1	13.0
Gneisenau (st2,P149/1,144/2)	1935	Desch3	18,160	10,535	652–3	74–1	29–0	20.0
Potsdam (te2,P126/1,160/2)	1935	Blohm	17,528	11,976	633–10	74–1	27–2	21.0
Scharnhorst (te2,P149/1,144/2)	1935	Desch3	18,184	11,000	652–0	74–1	28–11	20.0
Cruise vessel								
Steuben (r/t2,P484/cab)	1923	VulcSt	14,660	9310	550–6	65–0	28–0	16.0
ex General von Steuben 38, ex München 30								
General cargo vessels								
Aachen (r/t,P12)	1923	Teckl	6388	9165	459.8	56–5	26–2	14.0
lengthened 37								
Ægina	1922	Weser	2447	4610	315.8	46–1	21–0	9.5
ex Arkadia 23								
Aller (P16/cab)	1927	Bremer	7627	12,145	527–0	63–1	26–10	13.5
Alster (r/t,P16/cab)	1928	Desch4	8514	12,880	535–9	63–8	27–9	14.0
Anatolia	1923	Weser	2446	4610	315.8	46–1	21–0	9.5
Anhalt (P14/1)	1922	Krupp	5870	9632	408–0	54–3	26–6	11.0
ex Angsir 36								
Arucas (P48)	1927	Flensb	3369	3381	319.9	46–10	19–3	12.0
Augsburg (P4)	1915	Nthmb1	6512	9274	419.8	53–4	28–3	12.0
ex Northwestern Miller 27								
Borkum	1922	VSE1	3670	6650	369.7	50–10	22–7	9.5
ex Ingram 36, ex Antares 23								

NDL: Following derequisition from the aborted Operation 'Seelöwe' the cargo liner Donau *was employed on voyages between Germany and Norway and Germany and Finland for much of the Second World War. She was lost in January 1945 (RW Jordan collection)*

Red Star Line: The liner Westernland *was first in German service in 1935 following her sale in August that year to Arnold Bernstein under whose Red Star Line banner, after a refit, she was employed in service from Antwerp and Southampton to New York. In June 1939 the Red Star Line name together with* Westernland *and her sister* Pennland *were sold to Holland America Line. She made her last voyage from Antwerp to New York in April 1940, after which she was at Falmouth and used temporarily as the seat of the Netherlands government in exile. She then became an Allied troop-ship, and later served as a destroyer depot ship. She was decommissioned in 1945 and for a short while was under Cunard White Star management during a planned conversion for Canadian passenger service. This plan was abandoned and* Westernland *was laid up in the River Blackwater. In October 1946 she was sold to Chr Salvesen for conversion to a whale factory ship, but this project was also abandoned, and on July 30 1947 she left lay up and arrived at Blyth two days later for scrapping (RW Jordan collection)*

Hugo Stinnes: Pictured here postwar as Professor Popov, *the 1939-built* Flensburg *was renamed* Albert Jensen *in the same year, being one of a series of sisterships built for this owner during 1935–39. She was fitted with two 8-cylinder MAN oil engines of 4600bhp. During the war she made iron ore voyages from Sweden to Germany, but for much of the period of hostilities was laid up. On April 9 1945 shed was bombed by Allid aircraft and sunk off Hela, but was later raised and put into Russian service as* Professor Popov. *She put in many years postwar service and is believed to have been voyaging well into the 1970s (RW Jordan collection)*

Chemnitz (r/t,P4)	1929	Bremer	5522	9315	471–0	56–5	25–5	13.0
Coburg (m,P12/cab)	1928	Schich	7400	11,000	504.0	61–2	26–11	16.0
ex Havel 38; lengthened 38								
Crefeld	1922	Flensb	8045	11,865	474.2	60–11	28–6	12.0
Dessau (P14/1)	1923	Krupp	5933	9632	408–0	54–4	26–5	10.0
ex Wido 36								
Donau (r/t,P12)	1929	Desch4	9035	12,300	546–6	63–8	27–10	14.0
Dresden (m,P28)	1937	Bremer	5567	7510	452–0	56–4	24–9	15.0
Düsseldorf (m,P20)	1935	Bremer	4930	6750	430–3	54–8	24–1	14.5
Eider (m,P12)	1937	Desch3	3288	4420	377–3	50–2	21–4	14.0
Eisenach (st,P12/cab)	1921	VulcSt	4177	6675	407–6	51–2	23–7	13.5
ex Alda 36; lengthened 39								
Elbe (m2, P18)	1929	DeutsK	9179	10,350	510–2	60–8	29–0	17.0
ex Holstein 33, ex Wenatchee Star 31, ex Sud Expreso 30; lengthened, rebuilt 34								
Ems (m,P12)	1937	Desch3	3287	4420	377–3	50–2	21–4	14.0
Erfurt (m,P12/cab)	1923	VulcSt	4201	6200	360.7	51–0	23–7	11.0
Erlangen (st,P6)	1929	Blohm	6101	9860	449.6	57–8	26–3	13.0
Este (r/t,P16)	1930	Desch3	7915	11,530	495.7	63–11	27–10	14.5
Franken (P12/2)	1926	Bremer	7789	12,500	491.5	63–11	27–1	13.5
Frankfurt (r/t,P4)	1929	Bremer	5522	9315	471–0	56–2	25–5	13.0
Friderun (P8)	1922	FrerJ	2464	3825	296.2	42–10	20–2	10.0
Goslar (st,P8)	1929	Blohm	6040	9860	449.6	57–8	26–3	13.0
Gottingen (m,P–)	bldg	Lübecl	6267	9800	476–0	60–8	27–6	14.0
Greifswald (m,P–)	order	Lübecl	6112	980	476–0	60–8	27–6	14.0
Hameln (st,P14/1)	1921	VulcSt	4351	6675	388.4	51–0	23–6	13.5
ex Roland 36; lengthened 39								
Hannover (m,P28)	1939	Bremer	5537	8500	475–0	56–4	24–7	15.0
Helgoland (P2)	1922	VSE1	3664	6650	369.7	50–10	22–8	9.5
ex Riol 36, ex Arcturus 22								
Iller (m,P12)	1938	Desch3	3290	4400	377–3	50–2	21–4	14.0
Inn (r/t,P12)	1929	Desch3	2867	4070	306–5	46–1	18–1	11.0
ex Abana 36								
Isar (r/t,P12)	1929	Desch4	9026	12,295	546–6	63–6	27–10	14.0
Köln	1922	Bremer	7881	11,470	474.0	60–9	28–8	12.5
Königsberg (m2,P10/cab)	1924	Weser	6466	9235	431.3	56–5	26–3	12.0
Lahn (r/t,P14/cab)	1927	Teckl	8498	12,850	535–9	63–8	27–9	14.0
Lech (m,P12)	1939	Desch3	3290	4570	377–3	50–2	21–4	14.0
Leipzig (m,P28)	1938	Desch3	5898	7500	428.1	56–1	24.6	15.0
Linz (m)	bldg	IntDzg	3562	4560	336–5	45–8	18–0	14.0
Lippe (P6)	1917	Bremer	7849	11,890	475.3	60–9	27–4	12.0
ex City of Dunedin 28, ex Porta 21								
Main (r/t,P14/cab)	1927	Bremer	7624	12,145	503.1	63–1	26–10	14.0
Marburg (m,P16)	1928	Schich	7564	10,940	503.6	61–2	28–1	16.0
ex Saale 38; lengthened 38								
Memel (m,P12)	1934	Desch3	3183	4620	378–0	50–2	21–4	14.0
ex Cairo 35								
Minden (P12/cab)	1921	VulcSt	4301	6513	399–6	51–0	23–7	13.5
lengthened 39								
Mosel (r/t,P14/cab)	1927	Desch3	8428	12,870	535–9	63–7	27–9	14.0
München (m,P20)	1936	Bremer	5619	7770	452–0	56–4	24–9	15.0
Mur (m,P12)	1939	Desch3	3250	4600	377–3	50–2	21–4	12.0
Neckar (r/t,P14/cab)	1928	Desch3	8417	12,870	535–9	63–9	27–9	14.0
Nienburg (P12/cab)	1922	VulcSt	4318	6513	399–7	51–0	23–6	13.5
lengthened 38								
Norderney (P2)	1922	VSE1	3667	6650	369.7	50–10	22–8	9.5
ex Raimund 36, ex Altair 22								
Nürnberg (m,P20)	1936	Bremer	5635	7770	452–0	56–4	24–9	15.0
Oder (r/t,P14/cab)	1927	VulcH	8516	12,900	535–9	63–8	27–9	14.0
Orotava (P48/cab)	1927	Krupp	3344	3470	319.5	46–10	18–11	12.0

Note: Also *Bogota* (built 1938/1230gt), *Bremerhaven* (20/1615), *Quito* (38/1230)
Note: See also under Deutsche Arbeitsfront GmbH, Deutsche Lufthansa AG

Ship	Built	Builder	GT	DWT	Length	Beam	Draught	Speed
Osnabrück (m,P20)	1935	Desch3	5095	7500	415.1	54–6	24–0	14.5
Porta (P12/cab)	1921	VulcSt	4162	6527	399–6	51–0	23–8	13.5
lengthened 39								
Regensburg (m,P14/cab)	1927	VulcSt	8063	11,650	506.7	60–2	28–6	16.0
ex Trave 38; lengthened 38								
Saar (m,P12)	1935	Desch3	3261	4620	377–3	50–2	21–4	14.0
Schwaben (r/t,P12/cab)	1926	Bremer	7773	12,245	511–8	63–11	27–1	13.5
Spree (r/t,P12)	1930	Desch3	2867	4062	306–5	46–1	18–1	11.0
ex Agira 36								
Weser (m2,P18)	1929	DeutsK	9179	10,350	510–2	60–8	29–0	17.0
ex Yakima Star 34, ex Sud Americano 30; lengthened, rebuilt 34								
Wiegand (P14/1)	1922	Krupp	5869	9632	408–4	54–4	26–5	10.0
Fruit carrier								
Ulm (m,P12)	1938	IntDzg	3071	2960	336–0	45–9	21–1	16.0
launched as Rapide								
Training ship (m auxiliary 4-masted barque)								
Kommodore Johnsen	1921	Krupp	3572	5300	328.8	48–2	26.9	–
ex Magdalene Vinnen 36								

Funnel: Yellow with blue over red bands
Hull: Grey, red boot-topping
Services: Hamburg, Bremen, Rotterdam–Spain, Portugal, N Africa, Canary Islands

OLDENBURG-PORTUGIESISCHE DAMPFSCHIFFS-RHEDEREI

Mönckebergstraße 27, Hamburg 1

Ship	Built	Builder	GT	DWT	Length	Beam	Draught	Speed
General cargo vessels								
Casablanca (r/t,P–)	1936	DeutsR	2313	3180	314–0	45–10	19–11	12.0
Ceuta (P10)	1929	DeutsH	2719	4100	297–0	45–11	21–2	11.0
Gijon* (st,P12)	order	DeutsH	2700	3200	311–0	49–2	19–6	14.0
Gran Canaria* (st,P12)	order	DeutsH	3900	5200	400–0	54–8	23–4	14.5
Larache (P–)	1923	SMvJS	1999	4100	267–10	38–5	18–1	10.0
Las Palmas (P–)	1926	DeutsH	2317	3400	270.5	41–8	21–0	11.0
Lisboa	1911	Koch	1799	3200	277.7	39–2	18–6	9.0
Melilla	1923	Stülck	2653	4100	279.3	40–11	23–0	10.0
Oldenburg (r/t,P–)	1936	DeutsR	2312	3180	314–0	45–10	19–11	12.0
Pasajes (P–)	1923	SMvJS	1996	4100	267–5	38–5	18–1	10.0
Plus** (P–)	1922	Norddt	2449	3000	278.6	40–6	20–0	10.5
ex Kamerun 38, ex Bilbao 32								
Porto	1922	Ostsee	2185	3150	278–10	41–11	19–3	10.0
ex Neckar 27, ex Magdalena Fischer 24, ex Georg Zelck 24								
Rabat (P10)	1929	DeutsH	2719	4100	297–0	45–11	21–2	11.0
Santa Cruz (st,P12)	1938	DeutsH	3862	5170	400–3	54–6	23–4	16.0
Santander* (st,P12)	order	DeutsR	2700	3200	311–0	49–2	19–6	14.0
Sebu	1921	Limnhm	1894	2640	242.1	38–0	18–0	9.5
Sevilla	1923	SMvJS	1995	4100	267–5	38–5	18–1	10.0
Tanger	1923	Giessn	1742	3350	270.0	41–2	17.6	9.5
Telde (m)	1934	DeutsR	2978	4618	375–0	50–2	21–4	14.5
ex Sofia 38								
Tenerife (r/t,P–)	1922	Norddt	2436	3860	278.4	40–6	22–0	10.5
ex Hermann Burmester 27								
Tanker								
Newbuilding*	order	DeutsH	10,600	15,000	505.9	68–8	29–2	13.0

Note: * Order cancelled 1939; ** chartered F Laeisz (*qv*) from 1938
Note: Also vessels under 1000gt

FRACHTSCHIFFAHRT GMBH

Ship	Built	Builder	GT	DWT	Length	Beam	Draught	Speed
General cargo vessel								
Ammerland	1923	Irvin3	5381	8340	374.4	51–2	25–11	9.0
ex Kilnsea 36								

Funnel: Black with white EO on blue band
Hull: Black
Services: General tramping

OLDENDORFF, EGON, Ostseehaus, Untertrave 84, Lübeck

Ship	Built	Builder	GT	DWT	Length	Beam	Draught	Speed
Dora Oldendorff	1896	Short1	2730	4450	314.0	43–1	20–3	7.5
ex Erik Larsen 38, ex Karl Leonhardt 28, ex Gustav Salling 26, ex Eskasoni 23, ex Wilhelmina 13								
Erna Oldendorff	1900	Prstm1	2095	3300	301–0	42–2	19–5	8.5
ex Lena Petersen 39, ex Svend 27, ex Svend II 24								
Henning Oldendorff	1916	Vuijk	3648	5950	360.0	48–3	20–11	8.5
ex Leersum 39								
Hugo Oldendorff	1904	Craig1	1876	2900	278.5	38–5	17–10	8.0
ex Baltia 39, ex Harald 33								

Note: Also short-sea vessels

ORION SCHIFFAHRTS GMBH,
10 Kossfelderstraße, Seestadt Rostock, Rostock

Baltia*	1904	Craig1	1876	2900	278.5	38–5	17–10	7.5
ex Harald 33								
Fortuna	1906	Neptn1	2700	4240	291.1	44–0	20–5	9.0
ex Imbros 33, ex Isar 26, ex Helene 25, ex Erika 21								
Gloria	1917	RDuck2	5896	8875	400.3	51–8	24–9	10.5
ex Mount Pentelikon 39, ex Illinois 34, ex Farnworth 34								
Lena Petersen**	1900	Prstm1	2095	3300	301–0	42–2	19–5	8.5
ex Svend 27, ex Svend II 24								
Patria	1901	GrayX	3845	6485	338.6	49–6	23–3	9.0
ex Scottish Rover 30, ex Westborough 28, ex Beechley 12								

Funnel: Black with houseflag – red with white cross (**x**) and black O on white disc at centre
Hull: Black
Services: General tramping

Note: *, ** Sold Egon Oldendorff 1939, renamed *Hugo Oldendorff* and *Erna Oldendorff* respectively
Note: Also vessels under 2000gt

OSSAG MBH, TANKDAMPFER-GES, Shell Haus, Alsterufer 4–5, Hamburg

Tanker

Ossag (m)	1922	DeutsH	2793	4016	309.7	45–6	20–0	9.0

Funnel: Yellow, black top
Trades: Oil and petroleum
Note: This company was controlled by Anglo-Saxon Petroleum Co Ltd (*qv* in Great Britain section)

RABIEN & STADTLANDER,
Drei-Kaiserhaus, General Ludendorffstraße 132-B8, Postfach 50, Bremen

Rhön	1921	HwldtK	1778	3100	261.0	40–11	19–0	9.0
ex Selma 23								

Funnel: Black with houseflag
Services: General tramping
Note: Also Eifel (built 1924/1429gt)

RAU NEUSSER OELWERKE AG, WALTER, Neuss-am-Rhein

Whale factory vessel

Walter Rau (s2)	1937	DeutsH	13,751	21,600	574–4	74–6	34–9	12.0

Funnel: Black with white RAU on red band between two narrow white bands *Hull:*
Services: Whaling
Note: Also whalers

RED STAR LINIE GMBH, Ferdinandstraße 64–48, Hamburg 1

Passenger/general cargo vessels

Gerolstein* (s2,P190/t)								
	1904	H&W,B	7772	6200	453.8	56–5	23–0	11.0
ex Mamari 28								
Ilsenstein** (s2,P190/t)								
	1904	Workmn	8216	10,500	447.6	56–2	28–10	11.0
ex Matatua 29								
Königstein*** (s2,P290)								
	1907	SHWR	9626	11,570	480–0	59–11	29–7	13.5
ex Arawa 28								
Pennland† (r/t3,P486/t)								
	1922	H&W,B	16,082	16,800	600–1	67–10	33–11	16.0
ex Pittsburgh 26								
Westernland† (r/t3,P486/t)								
	1918	H&WGw	16,231	16,800	600–1	67–10	33–11	16.0
ex Regina 30								
General cargo vessels								
Eberstein (P–)	1904	Blohm	5226	8500	410.8	50–11	26–0	10.5
ex Maldonado 28, ex Thuringia 16, ex California 06								
Gravenstein††	1906	B&W	3505	6360	384–6	47–6	23–6	10.5
ex Hansa 29, ex Tranquebar 22								
Traunstein‡	1906	Clyde	2860	4614	330.2	43–2	20–11	9.0
ex Siptah 30, ex Shahristan 11								

Funnel: Black with five-pointed red star on white band
Hull: Black
Services: Antwerp, Havre, Southampton–New York; Hamburg, Antwerp–New York

Notes: * Sold H C Horn 1939, renamed *Consul Horn*; ** sold breakers at Blyth 1939, towed Scapa Flow 1940, sunk as blockship, BU *in situ* 1951; *** sold Belgium 1939, renamed *Gandia*; † sold Netherlands 1939; †† sold H C Horn 1939; ‡ sold R Bornhofen 1939, renamed *Luise Bornhofen*

RICKMERS RHEDEREI AG (Rickmers Linie),
2 Barkhof, Mönckebergstraße 8–10, Postfach 690, Hamburg 11

Bertram Rickmers	1923	Norddt	4188	6684	367.8	49–9	23–10	11.0
Claus Rickmers	1924	Norddt	5165	8040	417–9	53–2	25–3	12.0
Hans Rickmers	1919	Rhead3	5226	8210	414–4	52–5	25–4	12.0
ex Trelyon 38, launched as War Plover								
Moni Rickmers	1920	Rhead3	5272	8210	413–10	52–5	25–4	12.0
ex Trewyn 37, launched as War Gannet								
R C Rickmers (P25/1)								
	1921	Norddt	5198	8022	417–9	53–2	24–0	12.0

Funnel: Black with white band bearing houseflag
Hull: Green, red boot-topping
Services: Hamburg, Antwerp–Philippines–China–Japan–Siberia

Sophie Rickmers (P25/1)	1920	Norddt	7033	10,770	441.4	57–8	26–4	12.0
Ursula Rickmers	1917	Irvin3	5050	8602	418.7	53–5	27–1	12.0
ex Wheatmore 27, ex Thistlemore 23								

Funnel: Black with red ER and small red five-pointed star on white band
Hull: Black, with name of vessel in white amidships
Services: Germany, NW Europe–Mediterranean, NW Africa and W Africa; NW Europe short-sea

Note: Also *Lorenz L-M Russ* (built 1925/1448gt), *Reinhart L-M Russ* (23/1478) and short-sea vessels under 1500gt

RUSS, ERNST, Mönckebergstraße 7, Postfach 936, Hamburg

Georg L-M Russ (r/t,P4)	1938	Flensb	2980	5118	361–6	52–8	20–0	11.5
Walter L-M Russ	1927	Neptn1	1538	2264	246.9	40–1	17–0	10.0
SCHIFFAHRT-U. ASSEKURANZGES E RUSS & CO								
Anita L-M Russ	1926	Neptn1	1712	2657	271–11	41–1	17–6	10.0
Clara L-M Russ	1927	Flensb	1600	2510	272–0	41–11	16–11	10.0
Ernst L-M Russ (r/t,P4)	1937	Flensb	2957	5100	361–6	52–8	20–0	11.5
Helga L-M Russ	1926	Neptn1	1709	2677	269–0	41–1	17–9	10.0
Ilse L-M Russ	1926	Flensb	1600	2569	272–0	41–11	16–11	10.0
Theresia L-M Russ	1927	Neptn1	1694	2667	268–10	41–10	17–7	10.0
Tilly L-M Russ	1926	Flensb	1600	2564	272–0	41–11	16–11	10.0
Wolfgang L-M Russ (m)	1939	Lübec1	3750	5600	341.2	52–6	18.2	11.0

Funnel: Black with narrow red band over broad yellow band
Hull: Black
Services: General tramping

SAUBER & CO, Senator Hayn-Haus, Alsterdamm 26, Hamburg 1

Emily Sauber	1939	Flensb	2475	3325	290–0	44–5	19–9	11.5
Emma Sauber	1922	DeutsH	2548	4105	312–8	44–4	20–2	9.75
Herman Sauber	1936	Flensb	2474	3327	290–0	44–5	19–9	11.5
Robert Sauber	1910	RDuck1	2515	3860	313–0	42–6	19–0	9.5
ex Rotherhill 25								

Funnel: Yellow with black top separated by white band bearing red S
Hull: Black
Trades: Oil and petroleum
Note: * Sold Atlantic-Rhederei (F & W Joch), 1939, renamed *Thalatta*
Note: This subsidiary of Oelwerke Julius Schindler GmbH, also owned *Gustav Schindler* (built 1935/1533gt)

SCHINDLER GMBH, TANKSCHIFF-REEDEREI JULIUS, Hohe Bleichen 28, Hamburg 36

Tankers

Julius Schindler* (m)	1921	DeutsH	3145	4896	385–5	45–6	20–11	9.0
lengthened 34								

Funnel: Black with white circle bordered by black circle superimposed on narrow red band separating two white bands
Trades: Oil and petroleum

SCHLIEMANN & MENZELL AG, Esplanade 6, Hamburg

Tanker

Charlotte Schliemann (m2)	1928	Nakskv	7747	11,180	450.5	59–2	25–9	11.5
ex Sir Karl Knudsen 39								

Funnel: Yellow with blue 7-pointed star
Services: General tramping

SCHMIDT GMBH, HEINRICH, Schiffbrücke 41–2, Flensburg

Hans Schmidt	1920	NewWat	4427	7863	370.0	50–1	23–10	10.5
Pollux	1905	Cragg2	3161	5150	329.7	47–0	21–0	8.0
ex Kurt 24, ex Sliedrecht 22								
FLENSBURGER SCHIFFSPARTEN VEREINIGUNG AG								
Diana	1924	Flensb	1551	2600	262.5	39–5	17–0	10.0
Heinrich Schmidt	1936	Flensb	1560	2438	262.6	41–4	17–0	10.5
Neptun	1928	Flensb	1594	2680	272–0	40–0	16–11	9.0

Funnel: Black with houseflag – white with black S
Hull: Black
Services: Hamburg–Madeira–Rio de Janeiro–Santos–Buenos Aires; Baltic, NW Europe, UK–Mediterranean

SCHUCHMANN, W, H H Meierstraße, Postfach 111, Bremerhaven

Bugsee	1927	Nüscke	2307	3380	270.4	42–8	19–0	9.5
ex Swinemünde 31								
Hochsee	1926	Koch	2245	3550	282.8	45–4	18–0	10.0
ex Rheinland 31								
Leesee	1922	Nüscke	2624	4400	322.9	46–0	19–0	9.5
ex Robert Köppen 33; lengthened 36								
Luvsee	1898	Craggs	2373	4080	298.5	43–4	19–5	9.5
ex Elsa Köppen 33, ex Westsee 26, ex Earlswood 24								

Weissesee	1905	Teckl	5066	8230	409.4	52–9	26–5	11.5
ex Bulla 26, ex Hessen 15								
Westsee	1914	Weser	5911	9100	421.6	56–2	26–0	11.5
ex Ehrenfels 32, ex Baron Cawdor 26, ex Neumark 20								

Note: Also short-sea vessels

SCHULDT, H, Alsterdamm 8, Hamburg 1

Funnel: Yellow with red S on white triangle on blue band
Hull: Grey or black
Services: General tramping; fruit trades

FLENSBURGER DAMPFERCOMPAGNIE HARALD SCHULDT & CO

General cargo vessels								
Donau (r/t)	1939	Neptn2	2931	4980	332.1	49–0	19.1	12.0
Duburg	1922	Krupp	2675	4950	328.7	44–2	19–5	9.0
ex Hazelpark 29, ex Sayn 21; lengthened 34								
Glücksburg	1922	Krupp	2680	4950	328.7	44–2	19–5	9.0
ex Heathpark 28, ex Mühlhofen 21; lengthened 35								
Maritza (r/t)	1936	Neptn1	2910	4979	332.1	49–0	19.1	12.0
Norburg	1922	Koch	2392	4200	295.6	42–8	20–0	9.5
ex Pera 31, ex Hornsund 26								
Salzburg	1922	DGroot	1756	3000	279.4	39–4	17.8	10.0
ex Jonge Anthony 39, ex Slot Loevestein 24								
Troyburg	1923	FrerJ	2288	4150	290.2	42–10	20–3	9.5
ex Achaia 31, ex Hanna Kimme 23								
Fruit carriers								
Ahrensburg (m,P12)	1939	B&W	2988	2413	337–2	45–10	19–5	15.5
launched as Prinsdal								
Angelburg (m)	1938	Örsnd2	3053	2255	336–5	45–8	18–11	16.0
ex Viator 39								

SCHULTE & BRUNS, Hindenburgstraße 2, Postfach 207, Emden

Funnel: Atlas – black with white A on red disc on green band
Services: General tramping

Konsul Schulte	1898	GrayX	2975	4600	318.0	46–0	19–9	8.5
ex Cardiff 24								

ATLAS REEDEREI AG

Afrika	1920	Doxfrd	6503	10,800	420.0	54–0	28–4	12.0
ex Lavington Court 37, ex Vincenzo Florio 27								
Amerika	1911	SHWR	7463	11,140	467.9	58–4	27–1	12.0
ex Goldenfels 36, ex Brocktown 23, ex Goldenfels 20								
Asien	1905	ThmpsJ	3894	6450	344.7	49–4	23–0	9.0
ex Hermes 29								
Elise Schulte	1913	Nthmb1	4613	8010	384.1	52–2	24–3	10.0
ex Rounton Grange 34								
Europa	1899	GrayX	3767	6350	338.5	51–0	23–0	8.5
Godfried Bueren	1911	Doxfrd	4664	8520	390.0	53–6	26.1	10.0
ex Atna 25								
Heinrich Schulte	1918	H&WGw	5056	8136	412–8	52–4	25–3	10.0
ex Mount Ossa 37, ex Grelbank 32, ex War Legate 19								
Johann Schulte	1921	WallSB	5334	8390	413–0	52–2	25–3	10.0
ex Mount Parnassus 39, ex Canadian Scottish 37								
Johann Wessels	1913	Irvin3	4601	8050	384.1	52–1	24–2	10.0
ex Royal Transport 29								

SIEMERS & CO, G J H, Dornbusch 12, Hamburg

Funnel: Black with white star and moon emblem on red band
Hull: Black *Services:* General tramping
Note: Also *Kurt Hartwig Siemers* (built 1918/1100gt)

Ilona Siemers	1923	VSE1	3243	4850	332.5	46–6	21–0	10.0
Olga Siemers	1923	VSE1	3347	4850	332.7	46–8	21–0	10.0

SLOMAN JNR, ROB M, (Mittelmeer Linie), Slomanhaus, Baumwall 3, Hamburg 11

Funnel: Black with green band
Hull: Black with white band, red or green boot-topping
Services: Hamburg, Bremen–Spain, Italy; Hamburg, Bremen–E coast US/Canada, South America; fruit trades

General cargo vessels								
Alicante (r/t,P–)	1934	DeutsH	2140	3180	321–0	43–8	18–10	12.5
Barcelona (P6)	1921	Neptn1	3101	5640	351–8	49–4	21–11	10.0
Capri (P10)	1927	Neptn1	1846	2980	287.9	41–1	18–1	11.0
Castellon (r/t,P–)	1935	DeutsH	2086	3210	321–6	43–8	18–10	12.5
Catania (r/t,P–)	1935	Neptn2	2148	3140	321–7	43–9	18–10	12.5
Genua	1930	Flensb	1949	3180	313–10	42–9	18–5	12.0
Lipari	1930	Flensb	1943	3180	313–10	42–8	18–5	12.0
Livorno (P10)	1924	Neptn1	1829	2990	287.1	41–4	18–1	11.0
Malaga (r/t,P–)	1936	Neptn2	2146	3140	321–7	43–8	18–10	12.5

Messina (r/t,P–)	1937	Neptn2	2192	3040	321–7	43–8	18–10	12.5
Procida (P10)	1927	Neptn1	1843	2980	287.9	41–1	18–1	11.0
Sardinien	1928	ThompJ	4292	7590	399–6	52–6	22–11	12.0
Helmstrath 37								
Savona (r/t,P–)	1934	Stülck	2120	3170	321–0	43–8	18–10	12.5
Sizilien	1930	Rhead3	4647	8119	395.0	54–2	23–9	10.5
ex Harpagus 38								
Spezia (P10)	1924	Neptn1	1825	2990	287.1	41–4	18–1	11.0
Trapani (P10)	1926	Neptn1	1855	2990	287.5	41–3	18–1	11.0
Valencia (P6)	1922	Neptn1	3096	5640	351–8	49–4	21–11	10.0
Fruit carriers								
Alstertor (m,P12)	1938	Örsnd2	3063	2250	334–2	45–10	18–10	15.0
ex Rose 39								
Alsterufer (m,P12)	1939	Eriksb	2729	4300	314.4	50–4	24–2	15.0

Note: Also *Palermo* (built 1922/1461gt)

Woermann: Tanganyika *was completed in October 1922 for the DOAL service between Hamburg and East Africa. In January 1935 she was transferred to Hamburg-Amerika ownership and on June 30 1936 was sold to Woermann. On April 19 1939* Tanganyika *was requisitioned and served as an accommodation ship at the Kriegsmarine shipyard at Kiel; she was later similarly employed at Wilhelmshaven. On November 4 1943* Tanganjika *was bombed by Allied aircraft and was burnt out. In 1948 the wreck was towed to Dover to be broken up (DAL)*

Woermann: The twin-screw liner Windhuk *made her maiden voyage from Hamburg to Walvis Bay and Cape Town in April 1938 and upon the outbreak of war in September 1939 was at Lobito. In November she left Lobito disguised as the Japanese liner* Santos Maru *and headed for Santos where she was laid up. She was seized in January 1942 when Brazil severed relations with the Axis states, and was sold to the US in May. After a refit, during which the second funnel was removed,* Windhuk *became the USN troop transport* Lejeune *(AP 74), with capacity for 4660 troops. She was laid up at Tacoma in February 1948, and in August 1966 was sold for breaking up at Portland, Oregon (DAL)*

TRABER & CO, W, Mönckeberghaus, Lilienstraße 36, Hamburg

Adele Traber	1930	Flensb	2575	3650	293–6	46–1	18–9	11.0
Marion Traber	1923	Burntd	2434	4460	297.4	43–11	20–2	10.5
ex Uskhaven 33								
Olga Traber	1921	ArmWh1	3124	5050	329.9	46–11	22–0	9.0
ex Vindeggen 39								
Wilhelm Traber	1935	Flensb	3093	4350	310–7	48–8	19–10	12.5

Funnel: Black with white T superimposed on band quartered diagonally red top and bottom, blue left and right
Hull: Black
Services: General tramping

'UNION' HANDELS UND SCHIFFAHRTS GMBH, Fruchthof, Breitenweg 21–22, Bremen

Fruit carriers

MIDGARD DEUTSCHE SEEVERKEHRS-AG, Nordenham

Nordenham (P10)	1914	Teckl	4592	4800	386.7	49–1	23–1	14.0
ex Miami 33, ex Pionier 21								
Oldenburg (P10)	1914	Teckl	4595	4640	386.7	49–2	23–0	14.0
ex Greenbrier 33, ex Pungo 21, ex Möwe 19, ex Vineta, ex Möwe, ex Pungo								

UNIDA SCHIFFSTREUHAND GMBH

Brake (P12)	1920	Cammel	5347	6240	417–0	51–1	27–0	13.5
ex Zent 36								
Bremerhaven (P12)	1921	Workmn	5355	6260	417–0	51–3	27–0	13.5
ex Reventazon 36								
Vegesack (P12)	1911	Steph	4061	4900	375.5	48–2	25–8	13.5
ex Manzanares 36								
Wesermünde (P12)	1920	Workmn	5357	6260	417–0	51–4	26–11	13.5
ex Chirripo 36								

Funnel: Yellow with houseflag
Hull: Grey, red boot-topping
Services: Fruit trades, mainly Caribbean–NW Europe

Note: This company was associated with United Fruit Co (*qv* in United States section)

UNTERWESER REEDEREI, AG, Blumenthalstraße 16, Bremen

Bockenheim	1924	Rhead3	4902	8618	403–8	53–8	28–6	9.5
ex Kieldrecht 32, ex Anboto Mendi 24								
Fechenheim	1922	Bremer	8116	11,545	468.7	58–4	27–9	11.5
ex Hessen 35, ex Westfalen 22								
Ginnheim	1937	Burntd	4798	9535	422–0	56–0	25–2	11.0
Gonzenheim	1930	ArmWh2	4574	8795	394.1	53–9	25–2	10.5
ex Jo Taylor 33								
Heddernheim (r/t)	1921	Schich	4947	7490	361.0	51–5	25–7	10.0
ex Fridericus Rex 27, ex Stad Delft 24								
Schwanheim (m)	1936	Bremer	5339	9055	423.8	55–10	25–0	11.0

Manager for

LEHNKERING & COMPAGNIE AG

Eschersheim	1913	RottDD	3303	5460	330.3	48–2	20–9	8.5
ex Westerdijk 23								
Kelkheim	1920	Schich	4943	7582	362.0	51–4	25–7	10.0
ex Marie Mærsk 27								

Funnel: Black with houseflag on white band *Hull:* Black, red boot-topping
Services: General tramping

VINNEN & CO, F A, Altenwall 23, Bremen

General cargo vessels

Magdalena Vinnen	1922	Lithgw	4525	7800	398–2	52–0	23–11	10.0
ex Dunstaffnage 39								

CHR J W VINNEN

Werner Vinnen (m)	1922	Krupp	2342	3830	305.5	44–4	20–0	10.0
conv from aux schooner, lengthened, 37								

F A VINNEN

Christel Vinnen (m)	1922	Krupp	1874	2940	256.3	44–5	20–0	10.0
conv from 5-masted aux schooner 34								

Sailing vessel (5-masted m auxiliary schooner)

C R H VINNEN

Carl Vinnen (m aux)	1922	Krupp	1827	2500	261.8	44–4	19.1	–

Funnel: Black with blue V on white band
Services: General tramping

VITH, H P, Schiffbrücke 21, Flensburg

Peter Vith	1928	Flensb	1598	2680	272–0	40–4	16–11	9.0

Funnel: Black with red V superimposed on blue over yellow bands
Services: General tramping
Note: Also smaller vessels

Funnel: Yellow with white V on red band
Services: General tramping

VOGEMANN, H, Rathaus Hörn, Mönckebergstraße 22, Hamburg

Rheingold (st)	1922	DeutsH	5055	8809	415–8	54–5	27–9	10.5
ex Schwarzwald 35								
Vogesen	1904	Irvin4	4240	6889	359.8	47–11	25–0	9.5
ex Manchester Port 25								
Walküre	1914	Doxfrd	4251	8160	388.4	51–11	24–0	10.0
ex Lisa 37, ex Gonzenheim 33, ex Cornish Point 26, ex Bland Hall 16								

Funnel: Black with red R interrupting band consisting of black to left and red to right on broad white band
Hull: Black
Trades: Oil and petroleum
Note: This company, a subsidiary of Standard Oil Co of New Jersey (*qv* in United States section) also owned smaller tankers; it was also associated with Baltisch-Amerikanische Petroleums Import GmbH (*qv*)

WARIED TANKSCHIFF RHEDEREI GMBH, Neuer Jungfernstieg 21, Hamburg 36

Tankers								
Gedania (r/t)	1919	HwldtK	8923	13,940	516–6	64–7	27–6	9.5
Wilhelm A Riedemann (m2)	1920	Krupp	10,326	16,665	525.7	66–6	29–0	10.5
ex Zoppot 24, ex Wilhelm A Riedemann 20								

DEUTSCH-AMERIKANISCHE PETROLEUM GES

Friedrich Breme (m)	1936	Desch3	10,397	15,265	506–4	69–11	29–11	12.0
Paul Harneit (m)	1936	Schich	10,391	15,320	506–4	70–0	29–11	12.0

Funnel: Black with green band and white over blue over white bands above and below
Hull: Silver grey, red boot-topping
Services: Mail, passenger, cargo – Hamburg–W Africa; Hamburg–South Africa and E Africa

WOERMANN LINIE AG, Afrika Haus, Grosse Reichenstraße 25–27, Hamburg 8

Passenger/general cargo vessels								
Adolph Woermann (st,P100/1,57/2,134/3)	1922	Blohm	8577	8080	433.5	58–2	25–6	12.0
Tanganjika (st,P123/1,82/2,110/3)	1922	Blohm	8540	7598	449.1	58–4	23–6	14.0
Wadai (P60/1)	1922	Reiher	4696	5070	375–6	50–4	22–6	10.5
launched as Marie Woermann								
Wahehe (P60/1)	1922	Reiher	4709	5070	375–6	50–4	22–6	10.5
laid down as Wadigo								
Wangoni (st,P101/1,61/2,102/3)	1921	Blohm	7848	7130	418.6	56–2	23–11	13.0
Watussi (st,P124/1,78/2,132/3)	1928	Blohm	9521	7350	468.7	60–4	25–7	14.0
lengthened 34								
Windhuk (st2,P152/1,338/t)	1937	Blohm	16,662	9600	576–9	72–6	26–6	17.5
General cargo vessels								
Kamerun (m,P12)	1938	Bremer	5042	6950	438–6	58–7	24–0	15.0
Togo (m,P12)	1938	Bremer	5042	6890	438–7	58–8	24–1	15.0
Ulanga (m2,P12)	bldg	Bremer	6860	9420	492–0	63–7	26–0	15.0
Wagogo (P50)	1914	Neptn1	3118	5560	341–0	48–1	22–0	9.0
ex St Andrews 25, ex Sofia 20								
Wakama	1922	VSE1	3771	6560	369.7	50–10	22–8	10.0
ex Odin 26								
Wameru	1920	Flensb	4076	7060	384.7	52–6	23–0	10.5
ex Porthia 28, ex Polaria 20								

Note: * Sold Hochseefischerei Ges, Hamburg, 1939, for conversion to fish factory ship, renamed *Hamburg*
Note: Hamburg–Bremer Afrika Linie GmbH was jointly owned by Woermann Linie AG and Deutsche Ost-Afrika Linie (*qv*)

HAMBURG–BREMER AFRIKA LINIE GMBH, Lloydgebäude, Papenstraße 8, Bremen

General cargo vessels								
Ilmar* (P6)	1911	Bremer	5470	8800	419.8	54–6	25–11	11.5
ex Sunheath 27, ex Polladern 22, ex Emir 16								
Ingo (P2)	1926	FrerJ	3950	5725	382.4	50–2	22–0	11.0
Tübingen (P4)	1920	FurnH	5453	8465	401.5	52–2	25–0	10.0
ex Delaware 29; lengthened 29								
Wigbert (P11)	1921	FrerJ	3648	6110	361.0	49–11	22–7	10.0
Wolfram (P11)	1921	FrerJ	3648	6110	362.7	50–4	22–7	10.0

Great Britain, Dominions and Colonies

ABERDEEN & COMMONWEALTH LINE LTD,
New Zealand Chambers, 34 Leadenhall St, London EC3

Passenger/general cargo vessels

Esperance Bay (st2,P512/t)	1922	VickB2	14,204	14,849	549–0	68–4	33–2	15.0
ex Hobson's Bay 36								
Jervis Bay (st2,P542/t)	1922	VickB2	14,164	14,480	549–0	68–4	33–2	15.0
Largs Bay (st2,P542/t)	1922	Beardm	14,182	14,621	549–0	68–4	33–2	15.0
Moreton Bay (st2,P542/t)	1922	VickB2	14,193	14,867	549–0	68–4	33–2	15.0

Funnel: Yellow
Hull: Green with white band, red boot-topping
Services: London–Port Said–Aden–Colombo–Fremantle–Adelaide–Melbourne–Sydney–Brisbane

Note: This company, managed by Geo Thompson & Co Ltd, had been jointly owned by P&O (*qv*) and Shaw, Savill & Albion Co Ltd (*qv*) from 1932

ADELAIDE STEAMSHIP CO LTD, THE,
Currie St, Adelaide, South Australia, and 101 Leadenhall St, London EC3

Passenger/general cargo vessels

Manoora (m2,P250/1,130/2)	1935	Steph2	10,856	5190	482–0	66–2	23–11	16.0
Manunda (m2,P176/1,136/2)	1929	Beardm	9115	5020	447–9	60–2	24–11	16.0
Moonta (m,P140/–,–/d)	1931	B&W	2693	1365	298–4	43–9	15–8	13.0

Funnel: Yellow, black top
Hull: Black, red boot-topping
Services: Adelaide–Spencer's Gulf–W coast Australia; Queensland–Sydney–Newcastle–Melbourne–Adelaide–Albany–Fremantle

Note: Also general cargo vessels on Australian coastal services

ADELLEN SHIPPING CO LTD, Cory Bldgs, 117 Fenchurch St, London EC3

Tanker

Adellen (m)	1930	Blythw	7984	12,650	459.7	60–0	27–10	11.5

Funnel: Black with broad white band containing two narrow red bands
Hull: Black, red boot-topping
Trades: Oil and petroleum
Note: This company was a subsidiary of BL Shipping Co Inc (*qv* in United States section)

ADMIRALTY, THE, (Royal Fleet Auxiliary), Whitehall, London SW1

Hospital ship								
Maine (s2)	1902	Fairfd	5981		401.2	52–4	23–6	13.0
ex Panama 21								
Oilers								
Abbeydale (m)	1937	SHWR	8299	12,235	481–7	61–11	27–7	12.0
Aldersdale (m)	1937	Cammel	8402	12,250	481–8	61–11	27–6	12.0
Appleleaf (s2)	1917	Workmn	5892	7200	425–3	54–8	28–8	12.0
ex Texol 17								
Arndale (m)	1937	SHWR	8296	12,250	481–7	61–11	27–7	12.0
Belgol	1917	Irvin3	2648	2000	342–6	41–6	22–4	12.0
Bishopdale (m)	1937	Lithgw	8406	12,160	481–6	61–8	27–7	12.0
Black Ranger (m)	bldg	H&WGw	3417	3031	365–10	47–0	22–2	14.5
Blue Ranger (m)	order	H&WGw	3417	3031	365–9	47–0	22–3	14.5
Boardale (m)	1937	H&WGw	8334	12,250	481–6	61–11	27–5	12.0
Brambleleaf (s2)	1917	LithR	5917	7300	425–3	54–6	28–8	12.0
ex Rumol 17								
Broomdale (m)	1937	H&WGw	8334	12,250	483–1	61–8	27–6	12.0
Brown Ranger (m)	order	H&WGw	3400	3031	365–10	47–0	22–2	14.5
Cairndale (m)	1939	H&W,B	8129	12,100	482–10	59–6	27–6	12.0
launched as Erato 38								
Cedardale (m)	1939	Blythw	8132	12,100	482–10	59–6	27–6	12.5
Celerol	1917	Short2	2649	2000	342–6	41–6	22–4	12.0
Cherryleaf (s2)	1917	Dixon2	5934	7200	425–5	54–6	28–8	12.0
ex Persol 17								
Darkdale (m)	bldg	Blythw	8145	12,100	482–10	59–6	27–6	12.5
Fortol	1917	McMlln	2629	2000	342–6	41–6	22–4	12.0
Francol	1917	Earles	2607	2000	342–6	41–6	22–4	12.0
Gold Ranger (m)	order	Caledn	3313	3788	355–4	48–4	20–2	14.5
Gray Ranger (m)	order	Caledn	3313	3788	355–4	48–4	20–2	14.5

Funnel: Grey, or grey with black top
Hull: Dark grey, grey, or black
Services: Supplies and oil to fleet and fleet bases; operators of hospital ship

Aberdeen & Commonwealth Line: Moreton Bay *was launched on April 23 1921, and was the first of five sisterships completed in 1922 for Australian Commonwealth Line of Steamers. Each vessel cost £1.68m to build. In 1928 she was sold to White Star Line, and in 1933 with the collapse of the Kylsant group, of which White Star Line was part,* Moreton Bay *and her four sisters were transferred to the newly-formed Aberdeen & Commonwealth Line. In October 1939 she was commissioned as an armed merchant cruiser, and converted to a troopship in 1941, she took part in several campaigns, including Madagascar, North Africa and European operations. She was released and reverted to commercial service in 1946. She was broken up in 1957–58 at Barrow after making her last voyage at the end of 1956 to early 1957 (RW Jordan collection)*

Adelaide Steamship Co: Manunda *was completed by the Glasgow shipyard of Wm Beardmore in April 1929 and operated on Australian passenger services. In September 1939 she was requisitioned for use as an hospital ship, being commissioned on May 25 1940. At Darwin in February 1942, although her hospital ship markings were clearly visible, she was bombed by Japanese aircraft, resulting in several deaths, many injuries and some damage to the ship. After more front line action* Manunda *was released to her owners in September 1946. She was withdrawn from service 10 years later and sold to a Japanese company with the intention of putting her into service from Japan to Far Eastern countries. Although renamed* Hakone Maru, *the proposed service did not materialise and she was broken up in Japan in 1957 (RW Jordan collection)*

The Admiralty: One of the many Fleet oilers operated by the Royal Fleet Auxiliary was Abbeydale, *completed in March 1937 by Swan, Hunter & Wigham Richardson at Newcastle. She was powered by a 4-cylinder Doxford oil engine.* Abbeydale *survived the Second World War and was broken up at Barrow during 1960–61 (Alex Duncan)*

Anchor Line: California *started her career in August 1923 on the Anchor Line Glasgow–Liverpool –New York service, carrying over 1,100 passengers in three classes. In August 1939 she was requisitioned by the Admiralty to become the armed merchant cruiser HMS* California *and continued in this role until April 1942, when she was converted to a troopship. On July 11 1943, in company with* Duchess of York, *she was bombed from high level by German FW200 Kondor aircraft, set on fire, and eventually sunk by HMS* Douglas, *one of the escorting destroyers.* Duchess of York *was also lost in the same attack (RW Jordan collection)*

Green Ranger (m)	order	Caledn	3313	3788	355–4	48–4	20–2	14.5
Montenol	1917	GrayX	2646	2000	342–6	41–6	22–5	12.0
Olcades	1918	Workmn	6891	10,675	444–1	57–1	27–2	10.0
ex British Beacon 36								
Oleander	1922	HMDYPm	7048	10,950	444–0	57–1	27–5	11.0
Oligarch	1918	Workmn	6897	10,675	444–1	57–1	27–2	10.0
ex British Lantern 37								
Olna	1921	HMDYDv	7026	10,820	444–0	57–1	27–3	11.0
Olwen	1917	Palmer	6470	9760	435–9	54–4	27–0	10.0
ex British Light 37								
Olynthus	1918	SHWR	6888	10,683	444–1	57–1	27–3	10.0
ex British Star 37								
Orangeleaf (s2)	1917	ThmpsJ	5983	7200	425–3	54–6	28–2	12.0
ex Bornol 17								
Pearleaf (s2)	1917	GrayX	5911	7200	425–3	54–6	28–8	12.0
ex Gypol 17								
Plumleaf (s2)	1917	SHWR	5916	7200	425–3	54–6	28–7	12.0
ex Trinol 17								
Prestol	1917	Napr&M	2629	2000	342–6	41–8	22–4	12.0
Rapidol	1917	GrayX	2648	2000	342–6	41–6	22–4	12.0
Serbol	1917	Caledn	2669	2000	342–6	41–6	22–4	12.0
Slavol	1918	G&G3	2623	2000	342–6	41–8	22–4	12.0
War Afridi	1920	Duncan	5570	8320	412–0	52–2	25–7	10.0
War Bahadur*	1918	ArmWh1	5559	8320	412–0	52–5	25–7	10.0
War Bharata	1920	Palmer	5604	8320	412–0	52–4	25–7	10.0
War Brahmin	1920	Lithgw	5567	8320	412–0	52–3	25–7	10.0
War Diwan	1919	Lithgw	5551	8450	412–0	52–2	25–7	10.0
War Hindoo**	1919	Hamtn2	5565	8320	412–0	52–2	25–7	10.0
War Krishna	1919	SHWR	5760	8380	412–0	52–4	25–7	10.0
War Mehtar	1920	ArmWh1	5502	8380	412–0	52–5	25–7	10.0
War Nawab***	1919	Palmer	5586	8472	412–0	52–4	25–7	10.0
War Nizam*	1918	Palmer	5605	8510	412–0	52–4	25–7	10.0
War Pathan	1919	Laing	5581	8585	412–0	52–5	25–7	10.0
War Pindari	1920	Lithgw	5559	8585	412–0	52–3	25–7	10.0
War Sepoy	1919	GrayX	5574	8472	412–0	52–4	25–7	10.0
War Sirdar	1920	Laing	5542	8395	412–0	52–5	25–7	10.0
War Sudra	1920	Palmer	5627	8280	412–0	52–5	25–7	10.0
Store carriers								
Bacchus	1936	Caledn	3154	3300	338–5	49–4	18–0	12.0
Reliant (st)	1923	FurnH	7938	11,340	471–6	58–0	30–2	14.0
ex London Importer 33								

Note: Storage depots from 1939 – * at Devonport, ** at Milford Haven, *** at Plymouth; the Royal Fleet Auxiliary fleet included tankers under 2000gt, and oil storage hulks also at Alexandria and Singapore

ALEXANDER & SONS, DAVID, 95 Bothwell St, Glasgow C2

Funnel: White with black top
Hull: Black, white band around sheer
Services: General tramping

GROVE LINE (GLASGOW) LTD

Oakgrove	1906	OsbGr1	1985	3040	279.5	40–1	17–9	8.5
ex Needwood 25								
Olivegrove	1929	Lithgw	4060	7550	375.0	52–6	23–1	10.0

ALLAN, BLACK & CO, Midland Bank Chambers, St Thomas St, Sunderland

Funnel: White with black thistle emblem, black top
Hull: Black with white band, red boot topping
Services: General tramping

ALBYN LINE LTD

Thistlebrae	1928	ThmpsJ	4747	8580	420–0	55–10	24–7	10.0
Thistleford	1928	Laing	4764	8664	420–0	55–10	24–1	10.0
Thistlegarth	1929	Laing	4747	8509	421–0	56–0	24–1	10.0
Thistleglen	1929	Laing	4748	8509	421–0	56–0	24–1	10.0
Thistlegorm	bldg	ThmpsJ	4898	9050	431–10	58–2	26–0	10.5

AMBROSE, DAVIES & MATTHEWS LTD, Coleridge House, Swansea

Funnel: Black with white band bearing 'A.D.M.'
Hull: Black with white band, red boot-topping
Services: General tramping

BRYNYMOR STEAMSHIP CO LTD

Aelybryn	1938	Laing	4986		428–0	57–9	24–6	11.0
Brynymor	1936	Burntd	4771	9500	410.0	56–0	25–11	10.5
Dan-y-Bryn	bldg	Burntd	5117	9940	436–0	58–8	25–9	11.0
Ger-y-Bryn	order	Burntd	5108	9940	436–0	58–8	25–9	11.0

COOK SHIPPING CO LTD

Cefn-y-Bryn	1939	Burntd	5164	10,000	436–0	58–0	25–9	11.0

Note: This company was associated with Jugoslavenska Plovidba DD (*qv* in Yugoslavia section)

Anchor Line: Circassia *was one of two sisterships completed during 1937–38 for the Anchor Line Glasgow–Liverpool–Bombay – Karachi service. After war service as an armed merchant cruiser, troopship, and infantry landing ship, she returned to commercial service in August 1947. In January 1966* Circassia *left Liverpool on Anchor Line's final passenger voyage to Bombay, a service which had been inaugurated 110 years previously. In April arrived at Alicante, Spain, to be broken up (RW Jordan collection)*

Anglo-Saxon Petroleum: Circe Shell *was one of several similar tankers built during the early 1930s for this owner. Prior to the outbreak of the Second World War she was voyaging between UK oil refineries and islands in the West Indies. In the evening of February 21 1942* Circe Shell *was torpedoed and damaged by* U161 *WNW of Port of Spain. Soon after this attack* U161 *was bombed by an Albacore aircraft, was not damaged, and proceeded to make a second attack on* Circe Shell, *in which the tanker was torpedoed and sunk.* Circe Shell *was on voyage from Glasgow to Curaçao in ballast, and had been diverted to Trinidad (Alex Duncan)*

Anglo-Saxon Petroleum: Daronia *was one of several almost identical tankers built for Anglo-Saxon during the late 1930s in European shipyards. She was completed by Hawthorn, Leslie at Newcastle in February 1939 and was powered by a Hawthorn, Leslie/Werkspoor 8-cylinder oil engine of 3500bhp and carried a crew of 57. She survived the Second World War, although on August 20 1944 when a part of convoy DN68, she was torpedoed by* U861 *about 400 miles east of Durban and damaged. She reached Durban four days later and was repaired.* Daronia *was broken up during 1960–61 at Hong Kong (Alex Duncan)*

B & S Shipping: St Helena *and four sisterships were completed in 1936–38 and operated on the South American Saint Line service. On April 12 1941 she was torpedoed and sunk by* U124 *when on voyage from Montevideo and Bahia for Hull with 7600 tons canned meat, and general cargo including grain, cotton, rice and wet hides (RW Jordan collection)*

ANCHOR LINE (HENDERSON BROS) LTD,
12–16 St Vincent Place, Glasgow C1, and 52–54 Leadenhall St, London EC3

Passenger/general cargo vessels

Britannia (r/t,P175/1)	1926	Steph2	8799	9690	460.0	59–0	26–7	15.0
Caledonia (st2,P206/cab,440/t,485/3)	1925	Steph2	17,046	10,400	578–6	70–4	29–0	16.0
California (st2,P206/cab,440/t,485/3)	1923	Steph2	16,792	10,400	579–1	70–4	29–0	16.0
Cameronia (st2,P290/cab,431/t,698/3)	1920	Beardm	16,297	11,580	578–4	70–5	29–0	15.5
Castalia (P102/cab)	1906	Curle	6601	8120	453–6	53–2	26–0	12.5
Cilicia (m2,P300/1,80/st)	1938	Fairfd	11,136	10,370	506–0	66–5	27–5	16.0
Circassia (m2,P300/1,80/st)	1937	Fairfd	11,136	10,370	506–0	66–5	27–5	16.0
Elysia (P90/cab)	1908	Hendn2	6757	8600	453–6	53–4	26–0	12.5
Transylvania (st2,P279/cab,461/t,248/3)	1925	Fairfd	16,923	10,060	578–6	70–4	29–0	16.0
Tuscania* (st2,P206/cab,439/3,485/st)	1922	Fairfd	16,991	10,400	578–6	70–4	28–11	16.0

Funnel: Black
Hull: Black, red boot-topping, white dividing line
Services: Glasgow, Liverpool–New York–Boston; Glasgow, Liverpool, Manchester, Newport–Gibraltar–Marseilles–Port Said–Suez–Port Sudan–Bombay–Karachi

Note: * Sold Greece 1939, renamed *Nea Hellas*
Note: This company was acquired by the Runciman Group in 1935. Runciman Group also controlled W Runciman Shipping Co Ltd (*qv*)

ANGEL, SON & CO LTD, Boston Bldgs, James St, Cardiff

General cargo vessels								
Bramwell	1921	Blyth	1927	2606	271–10	38–9	18–2	10.0
ex Sheaf Garth 37								
Hillfern	1920	Rennld	1535	2435	240.0	36–2	18–8	9.0
Kaolack* (s2)	1917	LoireS	1837	2343	278–11	35–10	17–1	9.0
Tanker								
Miocene	1911	AmSBCl	2153	3100	250.0	43–1	20.7	8.0
ex Eocene 30								

Services: General tramping (voyages to Spain during Spanish Civil War); Mediterranean/Black Sea oil and petroleum trades

Notes: * Sold Zubi Shipping Co Ltd (*qv* under Harris & Dixon Ltd) 7.7.39

ANGLO-AMERICAN OIL CO LTD, 36–38 Queen Anne's Gate, London SW1

Tankers								
Appalachee (m)	1930	Palmer	8826	13,265	477.0	63–10	28–3	12.0
Cadillac	1917	Palmer	12,062	17,235	530.5	66–6	30–3	10.5
Chesapeake (m)	1928	Workmn	8955	13,550	476.8	63–8	28–3	11.0
Cheyenne (m)	1930	Palmer	8826	13,265	477.0	63–10	28–3	12.0
Comanchee (m)	1936	BrownJ	6837	10,310	469–3	61–3	26–4	12.5
Housatonic	1919	Hamtn2	5559	8503	412–0	52–2	25–7	10.5
ex War Dogra 20								
Iroquois (s2)	1907	H&W,B	8937	11,890	476.3	60–4	28–8	11.0
Kennebec	1919	Duncan	5548	8335	412–0	52–2	25–7	10.5
ex War Mogul 20								
Robert F Hand (m2)	1933	Krupp	12,197	18,025	542–1	70–4	30–5	12.0
Saranac	1918	Palmer	12,049	17,235	530.5	66–4	30–2	10.5
Schuylkill (m)	1928	Laing	8964	13,775	492–11	63–6	28–4	10.5

BRITISH MEXICAN PETROLEUM CO LTD,
Waterloo House, 16 Charles St, Haymarket, London SW1

Beaconstreet	1927	Palmer	7467	12,337	450.3	59–9	27–0	11.0
Inverarder	1919	Laing	5578	8335	412–0	52–5	25–7	10.5
ex War Hagara 20								
Narragansett (m)	1936	Krupp	10,389	14,800	506–9	69–11	29–11	12.5
Seminole (m)	1936	Blohm	10,389	14,815	506–8	69–11	29–11	12.5

Funnel: Red, black top; British Mexican – yellow, black top
Hull: Black, red boot-topping
Trades: Oil and petroleum

Note: These companies, subsidiaries of Standard Oil Co of New Jersey (*qv* in United States section), also owned vessels under 3000gt and the associate company Lago Shipping Co Ltd owned tankers employed in the Lake Maracaibo area

ANGLO-AMERICAN TELEGRAPH CO LTD,
Winchester House, Old Broad St, London EC2

Cable vessel								
Lord Kelvin (s2)	1916	SHWR	2641	3338	333–2	41–2	22–2	12.0

Funnel: Yellow, black top
Hull: Grey
Services: Cable laying/maintenance

Funnel: Yellow, black top
Hull: Black, red boot-topping
Trades: Oil and petroleum

ANGLO-SAXON PETROLEUM CO LTD ('Shell Oil'),

St Helen's Court, Leadenhall St, London EC3

Tankers

Acavus (m)	1935	Work28	8010	12,320	483–2	59–5	27–6	12.5
Adula (m)	1937	Blythw	8040	12,053	482–6	59–2	27–7	12.5
Agnita (m)	1931	Leslie	3561	4959	317–0	50–6	24–0	9.0
Alexia (m)	1935	Bremer	8016	12,145	483–10	59–5	27–6	12.5
Amastra (m)	1935	Lithgw	8031	12,180	483–10	59–2	27–7	12.5
Anadara (m)	1935	H&WGw	8009	12,284	483–10	59–5	27–6	12.5
Ancylus (m)	1935	SHWR	8017	12,190	483–10	59–5	27–6	12.5
Arinia (m)	1936	Lithgw	8024	12,100	483–10	59–2	27–7	12.5
Auris (m)	1935	CRDA2	8030	12,262	483–10	59–5	27–5	12.5
Bullmouth (m)	1927	Leslie	7519	10,532	455–10	59–6	26–9	11.5
Bulysses (m)	1927	Leslie	7519	10,532	455–10	59–6	26–9	11.5
Caprella (m2)	1931	Leslie	8230	12,585	467–0	62–0	27–7	12.5
Capsa (m2)	1931	Leslie	8229	12,585	467–0	62–0	27–7	12.5
Cardita (m2)	1931	SHWR	8237	12,585	467–0	62–0	27–7	12.5
Cardium (m2)	1931	SHWR	8236	12,585	467–1	62–0	27–7	12.5
Carelia (m)	1938	NedSM	8030	12,070	484–4	59–4	27–6	12.0
Cerion* (m)	1938	SmithM	2588	3846	321–4	42–0	21–1	10.5
Chama (m)	1938	RottDD	8028	12,070	483–4	59–4	27–6	12.0
Circe Shell (m2)	1931	HwldtH	8207	12,596	467–0	62–1	27–7	12.5
Clam (m)	1927	NedSM	7404	10,567	455–10	59–6	26–8	11.5
Clausina (m)	1938	RottDD	8028	12,100	483–4	59–4	27–6	12.5
Clea (m)	1938	RottDD	7987	12,032	483–4	59–4	27–6	12.5
Cliona (m2)	1931	H&WGw	8375	12,718	472–0	62–0	27–8	11.0
Conch (m2)	1931	H&WGw	8376	12,698	472–0	62–0	27–8	11.0
Conus (m2)	1931	Work28	8132	12,623	468–8	62–0	27–7	12.5
Corbis (m2)	1931	Work28	8132	12,623	468–8	62–1	27–7	12.5
Cowrie (m2)	1931	CRDA2	8198	12,613	467–3	62–1	27–7	12.5
Crista* (m)	1938	Gusto	2590	3831	320–8	42–0	21–2	10.5
Cymbula (m)	1938	NedSM	8033	12,046	483–4	59–4	27–6	12.5
Daphnella (m)	1938	Leslie	8078	12,163	483–4	59–4	27–7	12.0
Darina (m)	1939	Blythw	8113	11,884	482–10	59–4	27–6	12.0
Daronia (m)	1939	Leslie	8139	12,068	483–4	59–3	27–6	12.0
Davila (m)	1938	Lithgw	8053	12,150	483–4	59–2	27–7	12.0
Delphinula (m)	1939	Lithgw	8120	12,150	483–4	59–3	27–6	12.0
Desmoulea (m)	1939	Lithgw	8120	12,150	483–4	59–3	27–7	12.0
Diala (m)	1938	Bremer	8106	12,150	483–4	59–4	27–7	12.0
Diloma (m)	1939	Cammel	8146	12,088	483–4	59–4	27–7	12.0
Discina (m)	bldg	DeutsH	8152	12,100	483–4	59–4	27–7	12.0
Dolabella (m)	1939	Leslie	8142	11,925	483–4	59–4	27–7	12.0
Donacilla (m)	1939	Blythw	8113	11,884	482–10	59–4	27–6	12.0
Donax (m)	1938	H&WGw	8036	12,127	483–4	59–6	27–7	12.0
Donovania (m)	order	Leslie	8149	12,100	483–4	59–6	27–7	12.0
Dorcasia (m)	1938	Lithgw	8053	12,100	484–0	59–3	27–7	12.0
Dorsanum (m)	bldg	DeutsH	8050	12,100	483–4	59–5	27–7	12.0
Doryssa (m)	1938	Leslie	8078	12,163	483–4	59–4	27–7	12.0
Dosinia (m)	1938	Lithgw	8053	12,100	484–0	59–2	27–7	12.0
Dromus (m)	1938	H&WGw	8036	12,079	483–4	59–6	27–6	12.0
Drupa (m)	1939	DeutsH	8102	11,830	483–4	59–4	27–7	12.0
Elax (m)	1927	NedSM	7403	10,592	456–6	59–6	26–8	11.5
Elona (m)	1936	SHWR	6192	9185	446–4	54–6	25–7	12.0
Ensis (m)	1937	RottDD	6207	9140	446–4	54–8	25–8	12.0
Erodona (m)	1937	Giessn	6207	9093	446–10	54–8	25–9	12.0
Eulima (m)	1937	WiltnF	6207	9121	446–4	54–8	25–9	12.0
Faunus (m2)	1914	Caledn	3800	5388	360–0	46–2	22–10	9.0
ex Selene 39								
Felania (m2)	1914	NedSM	3882	5365	360–0	46–9	22–10	9.0
ex Artemis 38								
Gold Shell (m2)	1931	Bremer	8208	12,546	467–5	62–2	27–7	12.5
Goldmouth (m)	1927	Fyenrd	7402	10,479	456–9	59–6	26–9	11.5
Harpa (m2)	1931	Leslie	3007	3868	315–10	50–1	17–8	9.0
Havre	1905	GrayX	2073	3190	288–0	39–0	19–3	8.0
Horn Shell (m2)	1931	DeutsH	8272	12,382	474–0	62–1	27–7	12.5
Mactra (m)	1936	SHWR	6193	9185	446–4	54–6	25–7	12.0
Maja (m2)	1931	Giessn	8248	12,640	467–11	62–1	27–7	12.0
Megara (m2)	1929	Seine	7992	12,600	440–0	65–1	27–1	12.0
Miralda (m)	1936	NedSM	8003	12,100	483–4	59–4	27–5	12.0
Opalia (m)	1938	NedDok	6195	9090	446–5	54–8	25–8	12.0
Otina (m)	1938	Odense	6217	9150	446–4	54–8	25–9	12.0
Patella (m)	1927	Palmer	7468	9600	458–6	59–3	26–10	11.5

Pecten (m)	1927	Palmer	7468	10,579	458–6	59–4	26–10	11.5
Pellicula (m)	1936	Cammel	6254	9235	446–4	54–6	25–9	12.0
Pinna	1910	Teckl	6121	8265	436–8	55–1	25–1	10.0
ex Polshannon 22, ex Tandem 15, ex Birkenfels 14; conv gen cargo 22								
Pleiodon**	1922	HK&Wh	5878	8800	412.0	53–4	25–8	10.0
Pomella (m)	1937	Cammel	6766	9770	457–4	57–6	26–6	12.0
Rapana (m)	1935	WiltnF	7986	12,267	481–0	59–4	27–5	12.0
San Tirso***	1913	SHWR	6236	9890	435–9	54–8	26–11	10.0
San Zeferino***	1914	Palmer	6430	10,080	435–10	54–8	26–11	10.0
Scalaria†	1921	SHWR	5683	8370	426–0	53–5	25–6	10.0
Sepia (m)	1936	SHWR	6213	9210	446–4	54–6	25–8	12.0
Simnia (m)	1936	H&WGw	6197	9233	446–4	54–8	25–7	12.0
Sitala (m)	1937	H&WGw	6218	9232	446–4	54–8	25–7	12.0
Solarium (m)	1936	CRDA2	6239	9152	446–4	54–6	25–7	12.0
Solen**	1922	SHWR	5693	8370	426–0	53–5	25–6	10.0
Spirila**	1922	SHWR	5695	8370	426–0	53–5	25–6	10.0
Spondilus (m)	1927	Fyenrd	7402	10,489	456–8	59–6	26–9	11.5
Standella (m)	1936	H&WGw	6197	9233	446–2	54–8	25–7	12.0
Taron (m)	1936	DeutsH	8054	11,910	483–3	59–4	27–6	12.0
Telena (m)	1927	NewWat	7406	10,529	456–0	59–6	26–8	12.0
Thiara (m)	1939	SHWR	10,364	15,150	525–4	64–3	29–7	13.0
Torinia (m)	1939	SHWR	10,364	15,150	525–4	64–3	29–7	13.0
Tornus (m)	1936	Bremer	8054	11,960	483–4	59–5	27–6	12.0
Tricula (m)	1936	HwldtK	6221	8926	446–5	54–6	25–7	12.0
Trigonia** (m2)	1916	VickB2	7496	10,280	456–8	54–4	29–4	10.5
ex Marinula 31, ex Santa Margherita 19								
Trocas (m)	1927	RottDD	7406	10,522	456–7	59–6	26–8	11.5
Turbo	1912	Laing	4782	7000	387–0	50–9	24–4	10.0

Note: * Case oil carrier; ** storage hulk Singapore, 1939; *** storage hulk Gibraltar; † storage hulk Ras Gharib, Gulf of Suez, 1939
Note: This company also owned tankers under 3000gt engaged mainly on coastal voyages, and tankers which were withdrawn before 1939 to become storage hulks, and was controller of Tankdampfer-ges Ossag mbH (*qv* in Germnay section) and 'La Corona' Petroleum Maatschappij NV (*qv* in Netherlands section)

ANNING BROTHERS, Cymric Bldgs, West Bute St, Cardiff

Funnel: Black with red band bearing white A
Hull: Grey, red boot-topping
Services: General tramping

EXMOUTH STEAMSHIP CO LTD

Starcross	1936	ThmpsJ	4662	9050	411.0	57–9	25–1	10.0

ASIATIC STEAM NAVIGATION CO LTD,
5–7 St Helen's Place, London EC3

Funnel: Yellow
Hull: Black with white band, red boot-topping
Services: *Maharaja* (passenger and mail service) – Calcutta–Rangoon–Madras–Port Blair (Andaman Islands); cargo services – Calcutta–Rangoon–Akyab–W India–Ceylon–Bombay; Java–Burma–Coromandel–Calcutta–Ceylon–Malabar–Kathiawar–Karachi

Passenger/general cargo vessel								
Maharaja (P–)	1927	Lithgw	2895	3880	348–3	47–6	21–9	12.0
General cargo vessels								
Bahadur (P–)	1929	Lithgw	5424	8841	405.0	54–0	25–5	12.0
Begum (P–)	1922	Lithgw	5843	9250	423.2	56–0	25–6	12.0
Havildar	bldg	Lithgw	5407	8350	425–0	53–11	25–5	12.0
Kohinur (P–)	1922	Lithgw	5168	8150	404.3	52–2	24–7	12.0
Nawab	1915	Conn2	5430	8530	404.4	52–10	25–7	12.0
Nizam	1914	Conn2	5322	8530	404.4	52–10	25–7	12.0
Nurjehan (P–)	1923	Conn2	5424	8528	405.0	52–11	25–8	12.0
Nurmahal (P–)	1923	Conn2	5419	8547	405.2	52–11	25–8	12.0
Pasha (P–)	1919	SHWR	5307	8238	413–0	52–5	25–3	12.0
launched as War Chamois								
Pundit (P–)	1919	SHWR	5305	8238	413–0	52–5	25–3	12.0
launched as War Moose								
Rajput (P–)	1925	Lithgw	5497	8650	405.7	54–0	25–9	12.0
Ranee (P–)	1928	Lithgw	5060	8150	400.0	52–0	24–6	12.0
Risaldar	order	Lithgw	5407	8350	425–0	53–11	25–5	12.0
Subadur (P–)	1929	Lithgw	5424	8840	405.0	54–0	25–6	12.0

Note: Manager of this company was Turner & Co; British India Steam Navigation Co Ltd (*qv*) held a controlling interest in Asiatic Steam Navigation Co Ltd from 1935

ATLANTIC TRANSPORTATION CO LTD,
1155 Beaver Hall Sq, Montreal, Canada, and 220 E 42nd St, New York, USA

Services: US and Canada E coast and Gulf ports
Note: This vessel was managed by A H Campbell, 220 E 42nd St, New York, USA

Philip T Dodge	1910	Bremer	5047	7800	384.0	51–7	23–2	9.5
ex Cläre Hugo Stinnes 1 21								

AUSTRALASIAN UNITED STEAM NAVIGATION CO LTD,
122 Leadenhall St, London EC3

Funnel: Black with two white bands separated by thin black band
Hull: Black with white band, red boot-topping
Services: Melbourne to Australian main ports; Sydney–Noumea–Fiji

Passenger/general cargo vessels								
Ormiston (st,P199/oc)	1922	Steph2	5832	6155	406–0	55–2	25–5	13.0
ex Famaka 27								

Orungal (st,P199/oc)								
	1923	Steph2	5826	6155	406–0	55–2	25–5	13.0
ex Fezara 27								
General cargo vessels								
Corinda (m,P12)	1937	Short	3376	4952	356–10	48–4	22–6	12.0
Mareeba	1921	Walker	3472	6155	341–0	47–2	24–0	9.5
ex Echuca 24								
Mildura	1920	NSWGov	3478	6155	340–10	47–11	23–11	9.5
ex Enoggera 24								
Mungana	1920	NSWGov	3351	6170	341–1	47–11	23–11	9.0
ex Eurelia 26								
Murada	1921	CommWV	3345	6170	341–1	47–11	23–11	9.0
ex Erriba 26								

Note: This company, a member of the P&O Group, also owned vessels under 3000gt

Funnel: Yellow
Hull: Black with white band, red boot-topping
Service: Melbourne–Sydney–Brisbane–Townsville–Cairns–Thursday Is–Manila–Hong Kong
Note: Manager of these vessels was G S Yuill & Co Ltd, Sydney

AUSTRALIAN–ORIENTAL LINE LTD, 3 Queens Rd, Central, Victoria, Hong Kong, and Box 524b GPO, 6 Bridge St, Sydney NSW, Australia

Passenger/general cargo vessels								
Changte (P40/1,30/2,26/Ch,–/d)								
	1925	HK&W	4324	4215	367–11	48–2	23–6	12.0
Taiping (P40/1,30/2,26/Ch,–/d)								
	1926	HK&W	4324	4215	367–11	48–2	23–6	12.0

Funnel: White, black top
Hull: Black, red boot-topping
Services: Passenger and cargo – Melbourne–Sydney–Newcastle–Brisbane–Townsville
Note: This company, controlled and managed by Howard Smith Ltd, also owned general cargo vessels and colliers in Australian coastal trade

AUSTRALIAN STEAMSHIPS PROPRIETARY LTD, 269–71 George St, Sydney, NSW, Australia, and 33 Cornhill, London EC3

Passenger/general cargo vessel								
Canberra (s2,P170/1,180/2,60/3)								
	1913	Steph2	7710	4525	426–6	57–2	22–8	15.0

Services: Tramping, mainly Mediterranean
Note: Also smaller vessels

AVGHERINO & APERGUIS, Marmora House, 13 St Mary Axe, London EC3

MEDITERRANEAN STEAMSHIP CO LTD								
Toussika	1903	Campl	1818		272.2	40–0	19–1	8.0
ex Brompton Manor Maru 26, ex Brompton Manor 25, ex Horseferry 24, ex Hero 17								

Funnel: Red, bearing white flag with red diagonal cross, black top
Hull: Black with white band, red boot-topping
Services: SASL – Hull–Antwerp–Santos–Pernambisco–Montevideo–Buenos Aires–Rosario (service commenced May 1939); general tramping
Note: * Title changed from Barry Shipping Co Ltd May 1939
Note: See also *Toltén* under Trinder, Anderson & Co

B & S SHIPPING CO LTD, Merthyr House, James St, Cardiff

ST QUENTIN SHIPPING CO LTD								
St Helena (r/t,P2)	1936	ThmpsJ	4313	7910	414–3	56–0	23–4	10.0
St Lindsay	1920	WallSY	5370	8390	413–0	52–5	25–4	10.5
ex Canadian Highlander 38								
St Margaret (r/t,P2)								
	1936	ThmpsJ	4312	7910	414–3	56–0	23–4	10.0
ex Nailsea Belle 37, ex Hellenic 36								
SOUTH AMERICAN SAINT LINE LTD*								
St Clears (r/t,P2)	1936	ThmpsJ	4312	7910	414–3	56–0	23–4	10.0
St Elwyn (r/t,P2)	1938	ThmpsJ	4940	9150	431–10	58–3	25–0	10.0
St Essylt (m,P–)	bldg	ThmpsJ	5634	9600	442.5	58–1	27–0	12.0
St Glen	1907	ArmWh1	4647	8470	400.0	52–1	26–3	10.0
ex City of Swansea 37, ex Katuna 29								
St Merriel	1925	Curle	4980	9175	411.8	55–4	25–7	10.0
ex Hopetor 37, ex Prunus 32, ex City of Stockholm 27, laid down as Frederick Gilbert; conv mv 27								
St Rosario (r/t,P2)	1937	ThmpsJ	4312	7910	414–3	56–0	23–4	10.0
TRITON STEAMSHIP CO LTD								
St Usk	1909	Leslie	5472	7860	380.2	52–0	26–5	10.0
ex Nailsea Belle 37, ex Hellenic 36								

Funnel: Black with red crossed hammer and torch on broad white band
Hull: Grey, red boot-topping
Trades: Oil and petroleum

BALTIC TRADING CO LTD, 55 Bishopsgate, London EC2

Tankers								
OVERSEAS OIL & TRANSPORT CO LTD								
Caspia	1928	ArmWh1	6018	8660	427–2	53–5	26–3	11.0
WESTERN OIL SHIPPING CO LTD								
Karabagh (m)	1932	Blythw	6427	9500	426.4	57–2	26–6	11.5

Bibby Brothers & Co: Bibby had been owners and operators of troopships since 1921, and a short time before the start of the Second World War commissioned the new Devonshire, *which was a near sister of British India's* Dunera. *Apart from use during 1943–44 as an infantry landing ship, service as such including the Salerno landings, she spent the rest of her Bibby career in trooping.* Devonshire, *with three other Bibby troopships, carried 10,000 troops to Normandy on June 7 1944. She was sold to British India in 1962 to become the educational cruise ship* Devonia, *and was broken up at La Spezia in 1968 (EH Cole)*

Blue Star Line: One of five sisterships built in the mid 1920s, Andalucia Star *was engaged on Blue Star Line's regular service from London to Buenos Aires. She was built by Cammell, Laird, at Birkenhead, and ran trials in March 1927. At the Swan, Hunter shipyards she was lengthened by 66ft in 1935. Like all her sisters she became a war loss, being torpedoed and sunk by* U107 *when on voyage from Buenos Aires to the River Mersey with 5374 tons of frozen meat and 32 tons of eggs (RW Jordan collection)*

Blue Star Line: Trojan Star *had no sisters in the Blue Star Line fleet, but was much the same as British India's* Devon *and* Cumberland *owned by Federal Steam Navigation Co. Delivered in November 1916, she was laid down in 1914 and launched in 1916 as* Aberdeenshire *for Scottish Shire Line intended for the Federal-Houlder-Shire service. However, she was completed for a French Line subsidiary as* La Pérouse. *She was designed to have accommodation for 300 third class passengers and as such was put to use in the First World War as a troop carrier. In 1924 she was sold to become* Trojanstar *and passenger capacity was reduced to 12. In 1929 she was renamed* Trojan Star. *She ran on most Blue Star Line services, but in 1935 was refitted for the Australian service at Smith's Dock, South Shields, and two Bauer-Wach exhaust turbines were added to each screw together with superheated boilers. She was given additional bunker capacity and the overall result was a 2-knot increase in service speed. Her final voyage was in August 1954, during which she suffered a fire off Colombo, a leaking stern gland, heavy weather damage and engine failure. She was broken up at Blyth in 1955 (Alex Duncan)*

Kars (m)	1939	Blythw	8888	13,478	495–5	63–8	27–6	12.5
Shirak	1926	ArmWhl	6023	8660	427–2	53–5	26–4	11.0
Shirvan	1925	ArmWhl	6017	8660	427–2	53–5	26–4	11.0
Varand	1927	ArmWhl	6023	8660	427–2	53–5	26–4	11.0

BARNETT, DAVID P, Bury Court House, 7–8 Bury Court, London EC3

Funnel: Black with red triangle on white band; A&M – black with white T on red band
Hull: Black, red boot-topping
Services: General tramping, and voyages to Spain during Spanish Civil War

Notes: '& Trading' added to African & Continental title May 1939; * sold Italy 1939, renamed *Capo Rosa*; **, †, ††, sold Italy 1939, renamed *Paolo*, *San Leonardo*, and *Zenobia Martini*, respectively; †††, *** sold Board of Trade (*qv*) 1939, renamed *Botavon* and *Botusk* respectively; ‡ sold Charles Strubin & Co Ltd 1939
Note: Atlantic & Mediterranean Trading Co Ltd was associated with Charles Strubin & Co Ltd (*qv*)

Manager for

AFRICAN & CONTINENTAL STEAMSHIP & TRADING CO LTD, London

African Explorer*	1919	Lithgw	4663	7730	397–11	52–0	24–0	10.0
ex Musician 38, ex Saint Bede 24								
African Mariner (st)	1919	FurnH	6581	10,146	428–0	55–10	28–2	11.0
ex Bois-Soleil 37, ex Scheldemonde 28, ex Wolhandel 28, ex Andalusier 25, ex War Vigour 20								
African Trader**	1908	Rhead2	3825	5830	371–6	47–8	23–6	9.0
ex Laurent Schiaffino 37, ex Scientist 25, ex Sargasso 20								
Lulca†	1907	ArmWhl	4658	8616	400.0	52–1	26–3	10.5
ex Kabinga 38								
Lutine††	1911	StettO	1479	2213	231.7	36–5	17–0	9.0
ex Torcello 38, ex Stahlhof 20								

ATLANTIC & MEDITERRANEAN TRADING CO LTD, London

Atlantic Guide	1924	Grgmth	1943	3150	291–9	41–11	18–3	9.5
ex Albatross 39								
Atlantic Scout‡	1912	Ropnr2	4575	8140	391–9	56–0	23–2	9.0
ex Fishpool 38								

CONTINENTAL TRANSIT CO LTD, London

Cemenco	1927	ThmpsJ	1887	2890	281–3	38–0	18–5	10.0
ex Baytree 34, ex Byrness 29								
Emerald Wings	1920	ArsnCh	2139	3100	281–9	39–8	19–10	9.0
ex Nicolaos Baikas 36, ex Député Pierre Goujon 34								
Trade†††	1912	Conn2	5848	8900	430.0	54–0	27–6	9.0
ex Eurypylus 38, ex Indrakuala 15								
Transeas	1924	SHWRSd	1499	2450	248–4	37–2	17–3	9.5
ex Polmela 38, ex Lilburn 37, ex Islington 27								
Transit***	1919	Ropnr3	3091	5150	342–0	46–9	21–9	10.0
ex Molton 38								

BARR, CROMBIE & CO LTD, 109 Hope St, Glasgow C2

Funnel: Black with broad white band bearing two blue bands
Hull: Black, red boot-topping
Services: General tramping

BARR SHIPPING CO LTD

Barrdale	1925	GrkDY	5072	8463	400.3	54–5	24–1	10.5
Barrgrove	1918	Nthmbl	5222	8300	412–10	52–4	25–3	10.0
ex Stromboli 27, ex War Anemone 19								
Barrhill	1912	Duncan	4972	8350	419–3	53–0	24–3	10.0
ex Queen Margaret 25								
Barrwhin (r/t)	1929	GrkDY	4998	9100	421–0	55–9	25–0	10.5

BIBBY BROTHERS & CO, Martin's Bank Bldgs, Water St, Liverpool

Funnel: Pink, black top
Hull: Black with gold band, red boot-topping; troopships – white with broad blue band, red boot-topping
Services: First class passenger, mail and cargo – London, Middlesbrough, Hamburg, Rotterdam, Antwerp, Liverpool–Gibraltar–Marseilles–Port Said–Port Sudan–S India–Colombo–Rangoon (passengers embarked Liverpool outward, homeward disembarked Plymouth or London); trooping from Southampton

BIBBY LINE LTD

Passenger/general cargo vessels

Cheshire (m2,P275/1)								
	1927	Fairfd	10,552	10,192	500–6	60–4	29–9	16.0
Derbyshire (m2,P291/1)								
	1935	Fairfd	11,660	10,412	501–6	66–3	29–5	16.0
Oxfordshire (s2,P210/1)								
	1912	H&W,B	8646	9290	494–0	55–4	24–9	15.0
Shropshire (m2,P265/1)								
	1926	Fairfd	10,549	10,192	500–6	60–2	29–8	15.5
Staffordshire (m2,273/1)								
	1929	Fairfd	10,683	10,440	500–6	62–2	29–7	16.0
Worcestershire (m2,286/1)								
	1931	Fairfd	11,402	10,139	501–6	64–2	29–9	16.0
Yorkshire (st2,P280/1)								
	1920	H&W,B	10,183	12,209	504–0	58–4	32–0	15.0

Troopships

Devonshire (m2,P104/1,90/2,1150/trp)								
	1939	Fairfd	11,275	9500	516–10	63–3	23–8	15.5
Dorsetshire (m2,P112/1,108/2,1450/trp)								
	1920	H&W,B	9656	4500	468–10	57–4	22–3	13.0
conv general cargo 27								

Lancashire (s2,P320,1200/trp)	1917	H&W,B	9557	9520	502–0	57–4	24–8	15.0
conv passenger/general cargo 30								
Somersetshire (m2,P112/1,108/2,1450/trp)	1921	H&W,B	9659	4500	468–10	57–4	22–3	13.0
conv general cargo 27								

BILLMEIR & CO LTD, J A, 9 St Helen's Place, London EC3

STANHOPE STEAMSHIP CO LTD

Funnel: Black with white B, or black with broad white band
Hull: Black, red boot-topping
Services: General tramping; Grimsby–Hull–Newcastle–Antwerp–Rotterdam–Valencia–Barcelona–Tarragona–Alicante–Cartagena; voyages to Spain

General cargo vessels

Stanburn	1924	WoodS2	2881	4450	333.8	44.6	20–1	9.0
ex Hebburn 38								
Stancliff (r/t)	1936	Lithgw	4511	8250	385.0	53–6	24–1	10.5
ex Huncliff 39, ex Dornoch 37								
Stanfleet* (s2)	1920	Curle	7951	9410	465–0	58–2	29–3	11.0
ex Clan Robertson 38, ex Otaki 34, launched as War Jupiter								
Stanford	order	Pgill2	5969	8800	415–0	54–0	25–9	10.5
Stanforth	1915	SmitJ	1817	2600	262.2	38–2	18–1	9.0
ex Foreland 37, ex Dirksland 29								
Stangrant	1912	Leslie	5817	9350	443–3	54–1	27–7	10.5
ex Clan Grant 39, ex Cambrian Marchioness 38, ex Port Macquarie 27								
Stanhall	1932	GrayWH	4831	8700	423–8	54–10	24–9	10.5
ex Kepwickhall 38								
Stanholme	1927	Burntd	2473	4500	298.5	43–11	20–3	9.5
ex Goleta 36								
Stanhope	1919	Caledn	2337	3194	298–6	42–0	19–3	8.5
ex Corwen 37, ex War Dagger 19								
Stanlake	1923	SHWR	1742	2640	253.0	37–2	18–1	9.0
ex Mortlake 38, ex Ruckinge 36, ex Courcelles 29, ex Marjorie S 28								
Stanland	1912	Curle	1753	2660	271–0	36–0	21–1	10.5
ex Borderland 38								
Stanleigh	1912	Seebk1	1802	2600	259.7	38–1	18–1	8.5
ex Prekla 37, ex Corpath 34, ex Ernst Hugo Stinnes 11 21								
Stanmore**	1911	Denny1	5525	8640	425.0	54–2	24–5	10.0
ex Arracan 38								
Stanmore	bldg	Pgill2	4970	9400	442–0	56–10	25–0	10.5
Stanwell	1914	Laing	5767	9050	425.0	53–11	26–3	12.0
ex Stockwell 38								
Stanwood	1915	Reiher	4158	7500	361.6	51–2	25–5	10.0
ex Hesione 37, ex Itajahy 21								

Tankers

Stanbridge†	1917	RDuck2	5863	9000	380.9	50–11	28–4	9.5
ex Ch N Kahan 37, ex Limicana 28, ex Beechleaf 21								
Stanfield††	1892	ArmMit	2432	3850	295.0	39–0	21–7	7.0
ex Trinidadian 37, ex Augusta 12, ex Cadagua 07								
Stanmount	1914	GrayX	4468	6930	365.0	50–9	23–4	9.5
ex Bratton 37, ex Wyneric 37, ex Ricardo A Mestres 19, launched as Anerley								

Notes: * Sold Blue Star Line Ltd 1939, renamed *Pacific Star*; ** Sold Latvia 1939, renamed *Everest*; † sold Germany 1939, renamed *Eurofeld*; †† BU 1939
Note: Also coastal and short-sea vessels under 1500gt

BLUE STAR LINE LTD, 40 St Mary Axe, London EC3

Funnel: Red with blue star on white disc, separated from black top by white over black bands
Hull: Black or black with white band, red boot-ropping; *Arandora Star* – white with dark green band, dark green boot-topping
Services: UK–Lisbon–Madeira–South America; UK–Australia–New Zealand; UK–NW Europe–Malaya–Hong Kong–China–Japan; UK–W coast North America; *Arandora Star* cruising only

Passenger/refrigerated cargo vessels

Almeda Star (st2,P162/1)	1926	Cammel	14,935	9530	597–9	68–4	28–1	16.0
ex Almeda 29; lengthened 35								
Andalucia Star (st2,P162/1)	1927	Cammel	14,943	9530	597–9	68–4	28–7	16.0
ex Andalucia 29, launched as Andalusia; lengthened 35								
Avila Star (st2,P162/1)	1927	BrownJ	14,443	9530	569–3	68–3	28–1	16.0
ex Avila 29; lengthened 35								

General cargo/refrigerated cargo vessels

Adelaide Star (m2,P12/1)	bldg	B&W	12,636	12,812	554–4	71–0	27–7	17.0
Afric Star (st2,P12/1)	1926	Palmer	11,900	11,940	494–0	67–4	30–0	15.0
ex Africstar 29								
Avelona Star (st2,P12/1)	1927	BrownJ	13,376	9710	530–0	68–3	28–7	16.0
ex Avelona 29; conv passenger/general cargo 31								

Blue Star Line: The twin-screw motor vessel Australia Star *was one of a series of large capacity refrigerated cargo liners built for Blue Star Line group companies in the mid to late 1930s. Completed by Harland & Wolff at Belfast in April 1935, she could carry 12 passengers and had 557,487 cubic feet of refrigerated cargo space and was involved in the Australia and New Zealand services. She survived the Second World War and was broken up at Faslane in 1964 (RW Jordan collection)*

Blue Star Line: Arandora Star *was the company's best-known vessel, thanks to her career as a cruise ship which started in 1929. She was one of nine vessels ordered in 1925 from British shipbuilders, being one of five sisterships which each cost £303,300 (excluding refrigeration plant) to build. From January to May 1929 she was at the Fairfield shipyard, Govan, for conversion to a cruise ship, and was improved by several refits in the 1930s. With the outbreak of the Second World War she arrived at Dartmouth at the end of September 1939 for transfer to Admiralty service. On July 2 1940* Arandora Star *was torpedoed by* U47 *when carrying from Liverpool to Canada 1178 German and Italian internees together with an armed guard of 254 and 176 crew. When the vessel sank 805 lives were lost (RW Jordan collection)*

Booth Steamship Co: The 1934-built steamer Clement *is well-known as one of the victims of the infamous and short wartime career of the German pocket battleship* Admiral Graf Spee. *She was found southeast of Pernambuco on September 30 1939 when on voyage from New York to Bahia with a general cargo including large quantities of gasoline and kerosene. She had left Pernambuco the previous day on the final part of her voyage.* Clement *sent a raider report by wireless, which was relayed to the Admiralty, and marked the beginning of the operation which was to end with the battle of the River Plate a few weeks later.* Clement *was not only the first merchant ship sunk by* Graf Spee, *but was also the first Allied merchant ship of the war sunk by a German surface vessel. A seaplane from* Graf Spee *at first shelled* Clement. *The crew took to the boats, some picked up by another vessel, and the others landing in Brazil; the master and chief engineer were taken aboard the German ship, later being transferred to a neutral steamer.* Clement *was shelled and sunk by* Graf Spee *(RW Jordan collection)*

British India SN Co: Amra, *launched on April 29 1938 and completed in October the same year was one of two sisterships built by Swan, Hunter & Wigham Richardson shortly before the start of the Second World War for the Calcutta–Rangoon express service. A third sistership was completed in February 1941. Amra had a large passenger capacity, mostly for short journey deck passengers. In December 1940 she was taken over and converted into Hospital Ship* No 41, *with 385 patient beds and carrying 107 medical staff. In July 1943 she was involved in the Sicily invasion and three months later was at Salerno. Upon release to British India after the war was refitted with accommodation for 222 cabin class and 737 deck passengers, and went back to the Calcutta–Rangoon service. Later she was well-known on the company's services from India to East Africa. She was sold in 1966 for breaking up in Taiwan (RW Jordan collection)*

British India SN Co: Karanja *was completed in March 1931 by Alexander Stephen at Glasgow. She was fitted with six Stephen/Parsons single reduction geared turbines of 8800shp and could attain 18 knots in service. In June 1940 she was requisitioned by the Admiralty for use as a troop transport, but on June 10, during her final commercial voyage from Bombay to Durban, a time bomb exploded in the baggage room and set fire to the cargo. The hold was flooded to extinguish the fire and the vessel made Durban. In July 1941* Karanja *was converted into a landing ship, carried 24 landing craft, and had a maximum complement of 297 crew and 1500 troops. In May 1942 she was at the Madagascar landings, and during Operation 'Torch' was one of the assault vessels at Algiers. She was bombed by enemy aircraft and sunk off Bougie with the loss of 50 lives (RW Jordan collection)*

California Star (m2,P12/1)								
	1938	B&W	8300	9798	463–11	60–2	29–9	13.0
Canadian Star (m2,P12/1)								
	1939	B&W	8293	9741	463–11	60–2	29–9	13.0
Columbia Star (m2,P12/1)								
	1939	B&W	8334	9816	463–11	60–2	29–9	13.0
Imperial Star (m2,P12/1)								
	1935	H&W,B	10,733	11,500	542–11	70–5	29–8	16.0
Ionic Star	1917	LithR	5602	6985	406–5	53–3	27–1	11.0
ex Ionicstar 29, ex Rubiera 20								
Napier Star (st2,P12)								
	1927	Lithgw	10,116	12,080	476.0	67–4	30–0	15.0
ex Napierstar 29, launched as Raleighstar								
New Zealand Star (m2,P12/1)								
	1935	H&W,B	10,941	11,503	542–11	70–5	29–8	16.0
Pacific Star (s2)	1920	Curle	7951	10,150	465–0	58–3	29–3	12.0
ex Stanfleet 39, ex Clan Robertson 38, ex Otaki 34, launched as War Jupiter								
Rodney Star (st2,P12)								
	1926	Lithgw	11,803	12,080	476.0	67–4	30–0	16.0
ex Rodneystar 29								
Scottish Star	1917	H&WGw	7224	10,100	434.9	55–4	29–3	11.5
ex Millais 38								
Trojan Star (r/t2)	1916	France	9257	12,600	495–0	60–0	30–7	12.5
ex Trojanstar 29, ex La Pérouse 24, launched as Aberdeenshire								
Viking Star	1920	Napr&M	6445	7600	400.0	52–4	27–4	10.0
ex Vikingstar 29, launched as Lusiada								

F LEYLAND & CO LTD

Cruising vessel

Arandora Star (st2,P354/1)								
	1927	Cammel	15,501	6800	535–0	68–4	28–1	16.0
ex Arandora 29; conv pass/gen cargo 29								

General cargo/refrigerated cargo vessels

Australia Star (m2,P12/1)								
	1935	H&W,B	11,122	11,448	542–11	70–3	29–7	16.0
Empire Star (m2,P12/1)								
	1935	H&W,B	11,093	11,800	535–6	70–5	29–7	16.0
Fresno Star (s2)	1919	Curle	7998	10,020	449–1	58–3	29–3	11.5
ex Woodarra 29, launched as War Apollo								
Sultan Star (st2,P12)								
	1930	Cammel	12,306	11,400	506–1	70–3	31–10	15.0
Sydney Star (m2,P12/1)								
	1936	H&W,B	11,219	11,303	542–10	70–5	29–8	16.0
Tacoma Star (s2)	1919	Workmn	7924	10,150	465–0	58–6	29–3	11.5
ex Wangaratta 29, launched as War Theseus								
Tuscan Star (m2,P12)								
	1930	Palmer	11,449	10,900	491–0	68–4	30–0	15.0

UNION COLD STORAGE CO LTD

General cargo/refrigerated cargo vessels

Albion Star (s2)	1919	Workmn	7946	10,170	449–0	58–6	29–3	11.5
ex Albionstar 29, launched as War Hecuba								
Auckland Star (m2,P12/1)								
	1939	H&W,B	12,382	12,800	555–0	70–4	30–11	16.0
Brisbane Star (m2,P12/1)								
	1936	Cammel	11,076	11,519	548–11	70–3	29–6	16.0
Celtic Star	1918	DunlpB	5575	6985	406–5	53–3	27–1	11.0
ex Celticstar 29, ex Camana 18								
Doric Star (st2,P12)								
	1921	Lithgw	10,086	13,550	529–10	64–0	30–9	13.0
ex Doricstar 29; lengthened 34								
Dunedin Star (m2,P12/1)								
	1936	Cammel	12,891	11,800	542–10	70–5	29–8	16.0
Gaelic Star	1917	LithR	5595	6985	406–5	53–3	27–1	11.0
ex Gaelicstar 29, ex Montilla 20								
Melbourne Star (m2,P12/1)								
	1936	Cammel	12,086	11,800	542–10	70–5	29–8	16.0
Norman Star (r/t)	1919	DunlpB	6817	8925	415.6	56–3	28–2	11.0
ex Normanstar 29, launched as Almeda								
Royal Star (s2)	1919	Workmn	7900	10,030	465–0	58–6	29–3	13.0
ex Royalstar 29, ex War Charon 19								
Tudor Star	1919	Lithgw	7199	9200	423.4	56–0	28–4	11.5
ex Empire Star 35, ex Empirestar 29								
Wellington Star (m2,P12/1)								
	1939	H&W,B	12,382	12,800	555–0	70–4	30–11	16.0

Notes: Also short-sea vessel *Britanica* (built 1913/1350gt)

BOARD OF TRADE, Great George St, London SW1

Botavon*	1912	Conn2	5848	8900	430.0	54–0	27–6	10.0
ex Trade 39, ex Eurypylus 38, ex Indrakuala 15								
Botlea*	1917	AyrDk	5119	8000	400.7	53–5	24–1	10.0
ex Pentridge Hill 39, ex African Prince 36, ex Glennevis 21								
Botusk*	1919	Ropnr3	3091	5150	342–0	46–9	21–9	10.5
ex Transit 39, ex Molton 38								
Botwey**	1916	Laing	5106	8820	432–6	53–6	29–6	10.0
ex Manchester Producer 39, ex Start Point 21								

Services: Under government control

Note: Manager * Sir William Reardon Smith & Sons Ltd (*qv*); ** P Henderson & Co (*qv*)

BOLTON STEAM SHIPPING CO LTD, 23-24 Bevis Marks House, Bevis Marks, London EC3

Ramsay	1930	Duncan	4855	8790	409–0	53–5	24–5	10.0
Rembrandt	order	Lithgw	5559	9750	447–2	58–0	25–9	11.0
Reynolds	1927	Duncan	5024	9060	418–9	53–6	24–9	10.0
Ribera	bldg	Lithgw	5559	9750	447–2	58–0	25–9	11.0
Romney	1929	Duncan	5840	10,320	434–10	57–0	25–11	10.0

Funnel: Black
Hull: Black, red boot-topping
Services: General tramping

BOOKER BROS, MCCONNELL & CO LTD, 6 Old Hall St, Liverpool 3

ARAKAKA STEAMSHIP CO LTD

Amakura (P–)	1924	Caledn	1987	3400	280.1	42–3	20–0	11.0
Arakaka (P–)	1933	Lithgw	2379		322.5	43–6	20–0	11.5

Funnel: Yellow with black top
Hull: Black, red boot-topping
Services: Liverpool–Demerara (direct)
Note: Also a fleet of small vessels in British Guiana

BOOTH STEAMSHIP CO LTD, Cunard Bldg, Pier Head, Liverpool 3

Passenger/general cargo vessels								
Anselm (st,P150/1)	1935	Denny2	5954		412.3	55–9	25–7	14.0
Hilary (r/t,P80/1,250/3)	1931	Cammel	7403	5750	442–0	56–2	24–8	14.5
General cargo vessels								
Basil (P12/1)	1928	Leslie	4913	7940	422–4	53–10	25–5	12.0
Benedict (P12/1)	1930	Cammel	4949	7940	422–4	53–10	25–5	12.0
Boniface (r/t,P12/1)	1928	Leslie	4928	7880	422–4	53–8	25–5	12.5
Clement (r/t,P20)	1934	Cammel	5051	7870	412.2	55–9	25–7	12.5
Crispin (r/t,P20)	1935	Cammel	5051	7920	412.2	55–8	25–7	12.5
Dunstan	1925	Duncan	5149	8700	404.9	53–0	24–7	9.0
ex A D Bordes 35, ex Saint Oswald 29								
Polycarp (P12)	1918	Curle	3577	5250	340.7	46–10	23–4	10.5

Funnel: Black
Hull: Black, red boot-topping
Services: Liverpool–London–NW Europe–Oporto–Lisbon–Madeira–Para–Manaos–Iquitos–Maranam–Parnahyba–Ceará; New York–Brazil–Para–Manaos–Iquitos–Maranam–Parnahyba–Ceará–New York–Amazon ports; cruises 1000 miles of Amazon river

BOWATER'S NEWFOUNDLAND PULP & PAPER MILLS LTD, Corner Brook, Newfoundland, Canada

Corner Brook (P10)	1925	ArmWh1	5767	9080	439–5	56–4	27–4	11.5
Humber Arm (P10)	1925	ArmWh1	5758	9080	439–5	56–4	27–4	11.5

Services: Corner Brook, Newfoundland–US, and UK (newsprint reels)

Note: This company's title changed from International Power & Paper Co of Newfoundland Ltd in 1939

BOWRING & CO LTD, C T, 52 Leadenhall St, London EC3, and 209 India Bldgs, Water St, Liverpool 2

BOWRING STEAMSHIP CO LTD

General cargo vessels								
Anthea	1924	Ardrsn	5186	8344	398–11	53–2	25–6	10.0
Cape Breton	bldg	GrayWH	6044	9280	448–2	57–1	25–2	10.0
Urla	1924	Ardrsn	5198	8457	391.1	53–3	25–3	10.0
Tankers								
Regent Lion (m)	1937	SHWR	9551	14,540	510–2	66–3	28–5	12.0
Regent Panther (m)	1937	SHWR	9556	14,540	510–2	66–3	28–4	12.0
Regent Tiger (m)	1938	SHWR	10,177	15,150	525–1	68–4	29–0	12.5
Manager for								
Tankers								
BEAR CREEK OIL & SHIPPING CO LTD								
Benedick (m)	1928	Blythw	6978	11,040	446–0	58–2	26–11	11.5
Capulet (m)	1932	SHWR	8190	12,469	460.4	59–6	28–2	11.0

Funnel: Black with broad white band bearing red diagonal cross (**x**); Lobitos Oilfields only – black
Hull: Black with white top line, red boot-topping, or grey, red boot-topping
Services: General tramping; oil and petroleum trades

LOBITOS OILFIELDS LTD

El Aleto (m2)	1927	ArmWh1	7203	11,034	454–11	57–6	27–7	11.0
El Ciervo	1923	ArmWh1	5841	8968	420–0	52–2	26–5	10.5
ex Tricentrol 26								
El Grillo	1922	ArmWh1	7264	11,025	454–11	57–6	27–5	11.0
El Mirlo (m)	1930	Blythw	8092	12,455	459.7	60–0	27–10	11.5
El Oso	1921	ArmWh1	7267	11,012	454–11	57–6	27–5	11.0

OIL TANK STEAMSHIP CO LTD

Cordelia (m)	1932	SHWR	8190	12,469	460.4	59–6	28–2	11.0
Cymbeline	1927	Hamtn2	6317	10,121	420.0	54–5	26–10	11.0

BRITISH INDIA STEAM NAVIGATION CO LTD,

122 Leadenhall St, London EC3

Funnel: Black with two white bands separated by thin black band; troopships - yellow
Hull: Black with white band; red boot-topping; troopships – white with broad blue band, red boot-topping
Services: Antwerp, Middlesbrough, London–Calcutta; Antwerp, Middlesbrough, London–Karachi–Bombay; Antwerp, Middlesbrough, London–Mombasa–Beira; London–Australia; Bombay–Kathiawar coast–Karachi; Bombay–Karachi–Persian Gulf; Bombay–Seychelles–E Africa–South Africa; Burma–Ceylon–India–E Africa; Calcutta–Rangoon; Calcutta–Rangoon–Penang–Port Swettenham–Singapore; Calcutta–Rangoon–Malaya–Singapore–China–Japan; Calcutta–Chittagong–Arracan–Burma; Calcutta–Persian Gulf; Calcutta–Australia–New Zealand; Colombo–Tuticorin; Madras–Negapatam–Port Swettenham–Singapore; Rangoon–Mergui; Rangoon–Madras; Rangoon–Coromandel coast; Bangkok–Singapore; seasonal voyages to Jeddah (for Mecca) with pilgrims

Passenger/general cargo vessels

Amra (st2,P45/1,68/2,154/t,2327/d)	1938	SHWR	8314	6326	461–1	61–3	23–9	16.5
Aronda* (s2,P50/1,47/2,1250/d)	1912	Steph2	4062	3000	390.2	50–0	21–3	15.0
Aronda (st2,P45/1,118/2,154/t,2278/d)	order	SHWR	9031	6326	461–1	61–2	23–9	16.5
Aska (st2,P45/1,118/2,154/t,2327/d)	1939	SHWR	8323	6326	461–1	61–2	23–9	16.5
Bamora (P12/1,24/2,1156/d)	1914	Curle	3291	4265	342–6	46–2	21–9	12.0
Bandra (P12/1,24/2,1105/d)	1914	Curle	3194	4300	342–9	46–2	21–8	12.0
Bankura (P30/cab,1008/d)	1912	Curle	3185	4310	342–9	46–2	21–8	12.0
Barala (P12/1,24/2,1100/d)	1912	Curle	3148	4318	342–9	46–2	21–8	12.0
Barjora (P12/1,24/2,1000/d)	1912	Curle	3164	4318	342–9	46–2	21–8	12.0
Baroda (P12/2,24/2,1100/d)	1911	Curle	3205	4318	342–6	46–2	21–8	12.0
Barpeta (P12/1,24/2,1189/d)	1914	Curle	3194	4265	342–6	46–2	21–10	12.0
Chakdina (P12/1,24/2,1000/d)	1914	Ramage	3033	3366	330.7	46–1	21–5	14.0
Chakla (P12/1,24/2,1000/d)	1914	Steph2	3081	3570	330.5	46–2	21–9	14.0
Chantala (P10/1,38/2,1503/d)	1920	Curle	3129	3450	330.2	46–0	21–9	14.0
Chilka (st2,P22/1,15/2,3031/d)	1922	Denny2	4360	4429	390.0	52–7	21–10	14.0
Domala (m2,P138/oc)	1921	Curle	8441	10,438	464–0	58–4	28–0	12.0
launched as Magvana								
Dumana (m2,P140/oc)	1923	Curle	8427	10,400	464–0	58–4	28–0	12.0
launched as Melma								
Dumra (m2,P20/1,24/2,306/d)	1922	Hill	2304	3050	294–0	43–8	20–9	11.0
Durenda (m2,P130/1,/2)	1922	Duncan	7241	11,150	464–3	58–4	27–10	12.0
Egra (s2,P50/1,36/2,2182/d)	1911	Workmn	5108	4620	410.0	52–10	23–4	16.0
Ekma (s2,P51/1,39/2,2257/d)	1911	Workmn	5101	4620	410.0	52–8	23–5	16.0
Ellenga (s2,P50/1,36/2,1800/d)	1911	Steph2	5196	4920	410.0	52–5	23–5	16.0
Erinpura (s2,P51/1,39/2,2359/d)	1911	Denny1	5143	4750	426–0	52–6	23–5	16.0
Ethiopia (st2,P50/1,49/2,2257/d)	1922	Denny2	5574	4670	410.6	53–5	23–3	16.0
Juna (s2,P10/1,12/2,742/d)	1927	SHWR	2190	2265	280.0	43–8	18–0	13.0
Karagola (s2,P58/1,64/2,1050/d)	1917	SHWR	7053	6770	425.0	55–10	26–5	16.0
Karanja (st2,P66/1,180/2,2329/d)	1931	Steph2	9891	8370	487–1	64–2	26–11	18.0

British India SN Co: Dumana *was laid down in March 1923 as* Melma, *but completed as* Dumana *for service from London to Karachi and Bombay. Like her sister* Domala, *she was given a 'D for diesel' name, being among the first major British passenger ships with such propulsion. In 1934 she was transferred to the Calcutta service and her previous accommodation for 100 first class and 50 second class passengers was altered for 140 one-class. In 1939* Dumana *was taken over by the Air Ministry as a floating base ship for 500 airmen, was given workshops for aircraft overhaul, and was based at Port Said, Alexandria, Malta and Gibraltar. In 1941 she evacuated RAF personnel from Crete, and the following year moved to Bathurst with two Sunderland flying boat squadrons. She was on voyage from Port Etienne to Takoradi with a Royal Air Force contingent on board, when on December 24 1943 she was torpedoed by by* U515. Dumana *sank in a short time, dragging some of the lifeboats down with her before they could be released. Three officers, one engine room hand and 20 lascars were killed, as well as seven RAF personnel (RW Jordan collection)*

British India SN Co: Among the company's orders in the late 1930s were a series of sisterships which included the triple expansion engined coal burner Itinda, *completed by Wm Gray & Co, West Hartlepool, in January 1938. When completed her crew complement was 98. In March 1949 she was converted for oil fuel and the crew complement was reduced to 65. She continued in British India service until December 1958 when she was sold to Hong Kong owners, and later the People's Republic of China (Alex Duncan)*

British Tanker Co: One of a very large class built by various British shipyards, the turbine tanker British Commodore *was completed by Caledon Shipbuilding at Dundee in March 1923. She was fitted with two Metropolitan Vickers double reduction geared steam turbines giving 3200shp. Her peacetime service, like that of most of the British Tanker Co fleet, was carrying oil from Abadan to various European locations. She was broken up in 1953 (Alex Duncan)*

British Tanker Co: British Premier *was one of two sisters built by Palmers Shipbuilding, and was completed in December 1922. She was fitted with two Palmers double reduction geared steam turbines of just over 3200shp. On December 24 1940 she was torpedoed about 200 miles southwest of Freetown by* U65 *and sunk with the loss of 31 of her crew and a gunner.* British Premier *was on voyage from Abadan and Table Bay to Freetown and Swansea with 8000 tons of crude oil (Alex Duncan)*

Karapara (s2,P44/1,64/2,1490/d)
1915 SHWR 7117 6820 425.0 55–10 26–5 16.0
ordered as Karunga
Karoa (s2,P44/1,64/2,1471/d)
1915 SHWR 7009 6820 425.0 55–8 26–5 16.0
Kenya (st2,P66/1,180/2,1981/d)
1930 Steph2 9890 8740 487–1 64–2 26–11 18.0
Khandalla (s2,P60/1,68/2,1061/d)
1923 SHWR 7108 6662 425.2 55–11 26–5 16.0
Madura (st2,P170/oc)
1921 Curle 9032 11,080 485–0 58–4 28–4 13.0
Malda (st2,P133/oc)
1922 Curle 9066 11,080 485–0 58–4 28–4 13.0
Manela (st2,P135/oc)
1921 Curle 8303 10,695 465–2 58–4 28–0 13.0
Mantola (st2,P168/oc)
1921 Curle 9065 11,080 485–0 58–4 28–4 13.0
Mashobra (s2,P129/oc)
1920 Curle 8324 10,724 465–2 58–4 28–0 13.0
Matiana (st2,P168/oc)
1922 Curle 9045 11,080 485–0 58–4 28–4 13.0
Modasa (st2,P178/oc)
1921 SHWR 9070 11,045 485–0 58–4 28–4 13.0
Mulbera (st2,P158/oc)
1922 Steph2 9100 10,950 483–0 60–1 28–5 13.0
Rajula (s2,P30/1,30/2,92/3,3622/d)
1926 Curle 8478 9420 476–9 61–8 26–2 13.0
Rohna (s2,P28/1,33/2,100/3,3851/d)
1926 Leslie 8602 9400 476–5 61–9 26–5 13.0
Santhia (s2,P23/1,24/2,2842/d)
1925 SHWR 7754 9610 436.1 57–10 27–1 13.0
Shirala (s2,P30/1,32/2,2950/d)
1925 Leslie 7841 9552 437.2 57–10 27–1 13.0
Sirdhana (s2,P30/1,32/2,2914/d)
1925 SHWR 7745 9539 436.1 57–10 27–1 13.0
Sirsa (P9/cab,650/d)
1920 Leslie 5445 7960 412–0 52–5 25–3 10.5
Surada (P9/cab,650/d)
1920 Leslie 5427 7995 412–0 52–5 25–4 10.5
Tairea (s2,P56/1,80/2,3262/d)
1924 Curle 7933 8250 466–0 60–2 27–3 16.0
Takliwa (s2,P56/1,80/2,3302/d)
1924 Curle 7936 8250 466–0 60–2 27–3 16.0
Talamba (s2,P56/1,72/2,2777/d)
1924 Leslie 8018 8525 466–0 60–4 27–8 16.0
Talma (s,P62/1,74/2,3136/d)
1923 Leslie 10,000 9422 471–1 59–4 27–1 12.0
Tilawa (s,P62/1,74/2,3156/d)
1924 Leslie 10,006 9429 471–1 59–4 27–1 12.0
Varela (s2,32/1,24/2,1291/d)
1914 SHWR 4651 5160 404–3 53–4 22–10 12.5
Varsova (s2,P32/1,24/2,1160/d)
1914 SHWR 4701 5160 404–3 53–4 22–10 12.5
Vasna (s2,29/1,27/2,1605/d)
1917 Steph2 4820 4900 404–3 53–4 22–10 15.5
Vita (s2,P32/1,24/2,1575/d)
1914 SHWR 4691 5160 404–3 53–4 22–10 12.5
Waroonga (s2,P5/1,1066/d)
1914 Denny1 9178 10,325 529–11 64–2 30–9 13.5
ex Hororata 39

Troopships

Dilwara (m2,P104/1,100/2,164/3,1157/trp)
1936 Curle 11,080 3430 517–0 63–3 23–4 17.0
Dunera (m2,P104/1,100/2,164/3,1157/trp)
1937 Curle 11,162 5912 516–10 63–2 23–4 17.0
Neuralia (s2,P50/cab,1050/trp)
1912 Curle 9182 9920 499–0 58–1 28–4 14.0
Nevasa (s2,P50/cab,1050/trp)
1913 Curle 9213 9920 499–0 58–1 28–4 14.0

General cargo vessels

Binfield 1919 Dixon2 5181 8230 412–0 52–5 25–4 11.0
launched as War Acacia
Cranfield 1919 Pgill2 5332 8471 412–0 52–5 25–4 11.0

launched as War Verbena								
Dalgoma (m2,P6)	1923	Steph2	5953	8260	430.0	54–9	25–8	12.0
Devon†† (s2)	1915	France	9036	11,307	495–0	59–11	30–4	13.0
Fultala (m)	bldg	Doxfrd	5051	8860	441–10	54–4	25–6	11.0
Gairsoppa (P4)	1919	Palmer	5237	8160	412–4	52–3	25–3	10.5
launched as War Roebuck								
Gamaria (P4)	1920	Palmer	5255	8120	412–4	52–3	25–3	10.5
launched as War Llama								
Gambhira	1919	Short2	5257	8241	412–6	52–5	25–3	10.5
ex War Merlin 19								
Gandara	1919	Craig2	5281	8241	412–6	52–5	25–4	10.5
launched as War Peahen								
Garbeta††	1920	GrayXX	5327	8210	412–6	52–5	25–4	10.5
launched as War Fly								
Garmula (P4)	1920	Palmer	5254	8120	412–6	52–5	25–3	10.5
launched as War Reynard								
Gazana	1920	Craig2	5284	8240	412–6	52–5	25–4	10.5
Gharinda	1919	Sundld	5306	8180	412–6	52–5	25–3	10.5
launched as War Mavis								
Goalpara	1919	Sundld	5314	8191	412–6	52–5	25–4	10.5
launched as War Thrush								
Gogra	1919	Workmn	5190	8120	412–6	52–4	25–3	10.5
launched as Gorissa, laid down as War Tomtit								
Golconda	1919	GrayXX	5316	8230	412–6	52–4	25–4	10.5
launched as War Owl								
Gurna	1919	Palmer	5248	8130	412–6	52–2	25–3	10.5
launched as War Zebra								
Haresfield	1919	Doxfrd	5299	8330	412–4	52–5	25–3	10.5
launched as War Aster								
Hatarana (s2,P6)	1917	Kwsaki	7522	10,474	461–8	58–4	26–5	11.0
ex War Sailor 19								
Hatimura	1918	ThmpsJ	6690	10,950	426–6	55–6	28–6	11.0
ex War Opal 19								
Hatipara** (s2)	1918	Asano	7764	10,400	461–8	58–0	28–7	11.0
ex War Lance 19								
Homefield	1919	Doxfrd	5324	8270	412–6	52–5	25–4	11.0
launched as War Balsam								
Howra	1922	ArmWht	6709	10,424	412.2	55–10	28–3	10.5
Ikauna	order	GrayWH	6793	8420	442–10	57–7	25–0	11.0
Indora (r/t)	1938	GrayWH	6622	8700	443–0	57–7	25–0	11.0
Ismaila (r/t)	bldg	GrayWH	6793	8420	442–10	57–7	25–0	11.0
Itaura (r/t)	bldg	GrayWH	6793	8420	442–10	57–7	25–0	11.0
Itinda (r/t)	1938	GrayWH	6619	8700	442–10	57–7	25–0	11.0
Itola (r/t)	bldg	GrayWH	6793	8420	442–10	57–7	25–0	11.0
Itria (r/t)	bldg	Curle	6845	8420	442–6	57–6	25–6	11.0
Masula (s2,P12)	1919	Curle	7324	11,360	449.7	58–2	28–0	12.0
Mundra (s2,P12)	1920	Curle	7341	11,360	450.2	58–1	28–0	12.0
Nagina (st,P8)	1921	GrayXX	6551	10,818	433.0	57–5	28–6	11.0
Nalgora (st,P8)	1922	GrayXX	6579	10,840	433.0	57–5	28–6	11.0
Nardana (r/t2)	1919	Curle	7974	10,680	465–0	58–2	29–2	14.0
launched as War Sybil								
Naringa (st,P8)	1923	GrayWr	6607	10,880	433.0	57–5	28–6	10.0
Nirpura (P6)	1921	GrayWH	5961	10,125	450.5	56–0	25–9	12.0
Nirvana	1914	GrayX	6044	10,012	450.5	56–0	25–8	12.0
Nowshera (s2)	1919	Workmn	7920	11,250	465–0	58–5	29–4	14.0
launched as War Ceres								
Orna (m)	1938	Curle	6779	9180	441–8	57–3	25–6	12.0
Ozarda (m)	bldg	Curle	6895	9180	441–10	57–2	25–6	12.0
Queda (P10)	1925	GrayWH	7766	12,336	501–10	60–8	27–9	12.0
Querimba (P12)	1925	GraySd	7769	12,336	501–10	60–9	27–9	12.0
Quiloa (P12)	1925	GrayWH	7765	12,336	501–10	60–8	27–9	12.0
Tanfield	1916	Nthmbl	4548	7500	396–11	52–11	23–5	10.0
ex Corsham 16								
Warfield	1917	LithR	6070	9800	415.0	52–9	28–1	10.5
launched as Frankmount								
Warialda	1918	ArmWhl	3135	5050	342–6	46–10	21–9	11.5
ex War Mansion 19								
Warina	1918	Craig2	3120	5050	342–6	46–10	21–9	11.5
ex War Loch 19								
Warora*	1918	OsbGr2	2334	3050	285.0	41–10	19–3	11.0
ex War Cuirass 19								
Winkfield	1919	Pgill2	5279	8482	412–0	52–3	25–3	10.5
launched as War Violet								

Notes: * BU 1939; ** BU Rotterdam 1939; † sold Calcutta breakers Dec 1939; †† cadet training

Note: This company also owned vessels of under 2000gt mainly in coastal services

Note: British India Steam Navigation Co Ltd became a member of the P&O Group in 1914; British India was controller of Eastern & Australian Steam Ship Co Ltd (*qv*)

British Tanker Co: British Renown, *fitted with a Richardsons, Westgarth 4-cylinder oil engine, was completed by Laing, Sunderland, in April 1928. She survived the Second World War, but had at least two lucky escapes. The first was on April 21 1941 when she was bombed by German aircraft three miles southeast of Dartmouth, and the second was on November 21 1942, when she was torpedoed and damaged by* U518 *about 200 miles south of Placentia Bay, Newfoundland. She was a part of westbound convoy ON145. Also torpedoed and damaged by the same U-boat was the tanker* British Promise. *Both tankers made port and were repaired.* British Renown *was broken up during 1954–55 (Alex Duncan)*

T & J Brocklebank: Wm Hamilton & Co completed Marwarri *in July 1935. She was fitted with three single reduction geared turbines of 5200shp. At the beginning of the Second World War,* Marwarri *was converted into a military vehicle transport and took on armament. On October 5 1939 she was on voyage from Belfast to Newport when she was struck by a magnetic mine in the Bristol Channel, west-southwest of Porthcawl. The mine was one of several which had been laid by* U32 *on September 17. This exploded under the vessel and stopped her engines. She was beached, made watertight, and at Swansea it was necessary to replace her three turbines as these had been blown out of alignment. She was back in service in January 1940 and was used for transporting vehicles between South Wales and France.* Marwarri *reverted to general cargo carrying for the next two years, but was taken up again as a vehicle carrier for the Normandy invasion. She was able to carry 185 vehicles and 570 troops. Returned to Brocklebank in 1945, she gave this company several more years service and was broken up at Hong Kong in 1963 (R Sherlock)*

Burns, Philp & Co: One of the best-known Australian passenger ships, Bulolo *was requisitioned in September 1939 to become the armed merchant cruiser HMS* Bulolo. *Later she became landing ship headquarters for part of the Operation 'Torch' landings in the Algiers area. She also saw service at Sicily, Anzio and Normandy and the Netherlands East Indies.* Bulolo *was returned to her owner in December 1946, and after an extensive refit returned to commercial service in May 1948. She was broken up at Kaohsiung in 1968 (Alex Duncan)*

BRITISH PHOSPHATE COMMISSIONERS, THE,
499 Little Collins St, Melbourne, Victoria, Australia, and Bush House, Aldwych, London WC2

Triadic (m,P12)	1938	Lithgw	6378	9650	457–6	60–0	25–9	12.0
Triaster (m)	1935	Lithgw	6032	8150	423.2	58–2	24–8	10.5
Trienza (m,P12)	1938	Lithgw	6378	9650	457–6	60–0	25–9	12.0
Triona	1931	H&WGw	4413	6851	389.5	54–1	24–5	10.5

Funnel: Black
Hull: Black, red boot-topping
Services: Phosphate trade, Nauru/Ocean Island –Melbourne –Adelaide–Hobart–Sydney–Newcastle NSW

BRITISH TANKER CO LTD, Britannic House, Finsbury Circus, London EC2

Funnel: Red, black top, separated by broad green band bordered by two narrow white bands
Hull: Dark 'topside grey', red boot-topping
Trades: Oil and petroleum; mainly Persian Gulf–UK, NW Europe

Tankers

British Advocate (st)	1922	Laing	6994	10,925	456–4	57–1	27–9	10.0
British Ambassador	1924	Laing	6940	11,008	448–6	57–4	27–8	10.0
British Architect	1922	Blythw	7388	11,624	440.4	56–1	27–10	10.0
British Ardour	1928	Palmer	7124	11,196	456–8	57–1	27–8	10.0
British Aviator (m)	1924	Palmer	6998	10,762	456–0	57–1	27–8	10.0
British Captain (st)	1923	Palmer	6968	10,822	456–0	57–1	27–8	10.0
British Chancellor (st)	1921	Laing	7085	10,925	456–4	57–1	27–9	10.0
British Chemist (m)	1925	Palmer	6997	10,762	456–0	57–1	27–8	10.0
British Chivalry	1929	Palmer	7118	11,220	456–0	57–1	27–8	10.0
British Colonel (st)	1921	Laing	6999	10,995	456–4	57–1	27–9	10.0
British Colony	1927	SHWR	6917	10,840	455–0	57–0	27–9	10.0
British Commander (st)	1922	Caledn	6901	11,028	456–0	57–0	27–9	10.0
British Commodore (st)	1923	Caledn	6865	11,028	456–0	57–0	27–9	10.0
British Confidence (m)	1936	Cammel	8494	11,262	482–7	62–0	27–6	12.0
British Consul	1924	Laing	6940	11,008	448–6	57–4	27–8	10.0
British Corporal (st)	1922	Palmer	6972	10,817	454–11	57–1	27–8	10.0
British Councillor (st)	1922	Laing	7048	10,925	455–0	57–1	27–9	10.0
British Courage (m)	1928	Lithgw	6952	10,959	454–5	57–0	27–10	10.0
British Destiny (m)	1937	H&WGw	8470	12,177	483–1	61–9	27–5	12.0
British Diligence (m)	1937	SHWR	8408	12,235	481–7	62–0	27–6	12.0
British Diplomat (m2)	1926	BrownJ	6498	9692	420.2	54–5	26–9	10.0
British Dominion (m)	1928	SHWR	6983	10,912	455–0	57–0	27–10	10.0
British Duchess	1924	ThmpsJ	5973	9405	420–10	54–10	27–4	10.0
British Emperor	1916	ArmWhl	3663	5796	345.0	49–1	21–10	9.0
British Endeavour	1927	ArmWhl	4580	6906	381.2	50–5	23–4	10.0
British Endurance (m)	1936	SHWR	8406	12,275	483–0	61–11	27–7	12.0
British Energy (m)	1931	GrkDY	7209	11,186	454–5	59–5	27–3	10.0
British Engineer (st)	1922	Workmn	6993	10,898	454–11	57–0	27–9	10.0
British Faith (m)	1928	Caledn	6955	10,887	441.8	56–11	27–8	10.0
British Fame (m)	1936	SHWR	8406	12,275	483–0	61–11	27–7	12.0
British Fidelity (m)	1939	H&WGw	8465	12,201	483–1	61–8	27–6	12.0
British Fortitude (m)	1937	Cammel	8482	12,265	482–11	62–0	27–6	12.0
British Fortune	1930	Lithgw	4696	6913	384.6	50–2	23–4	10.0
British Freedom (m)	1928	Palmer	6985	11,148	456–8	57–1	27–8	10.0
British Fusilier (st)	1923	SHWR	6943	10,873	454–11	57–0	27–10	10.0
British General (st)	1922	Palmer	6989	10,822	454–10	57–1	27–8	10.0
British Genius (m)	1939	Doxfrd	8553	12,416	481–8	62–0	27–8	12.0
British Glory (m)	1928	Laing	6993	10,867	435.0	57–4	27–8	10.0
British Governor	1926	SHWR	6840	10,904	455–5	57–0	27–10	10.0
British Grenadier (st)	1922	SHWR	6857	10,750	454–11	57–0	27–7	10.0
British Gunner (st)	1922	SHWR	6894	10,750	454–11	57–0	27–7	10.0

Name	Built	Builder	GRT	DWT	Length	Beam	Draught	Speed
British Honour (m)	1928	Palmer	6991	11,135	456–8	57–1	27–8	10.0
British Hope (m)	1928	Caledn	6951	10,830	441.8	56–11	27–7	10.0
British Hussar (st)	1923	SHWR	6955	10,929	454–11	57–0	27–10	10.0
British Industry	1927	Palmer	4297	6631	366.2	49–2	23–4	10.0
British Influence (m)	1939	SHWR	8431	12,250	481–6	61–9	27–6	12.0
British Integrity (m)	1937	H&WGw	8412	12,145	483–1	61–8	27–5	12.0
British Inventor	1926	Palmer	7101	11,693	430.0	58–1	27–10	10.0
British Isles	1917	ArmWh1	7108	10,240	430.0	57–0	27–4	10.0
British Judge	1921	Laing	6735	10,573	420.5	56–5	27–8	10.0
British Justice (m)	1928	Palmer	6982	11,174	456–8	57–1	27–8	10.0
British Liberty (m)	1939	FurnH	8485	12,490	481–6	61–9	27–8	12.0
British Lord (st)	1922	ThmpsJ	6098	9517	427–0	54–10	27–5	10.0
British Loyalty (m)	1928	Palmer	6993	11,150	456–8	57–1	27–8	10.0
British Mariner (st)	1922	Palmer	6996	10,772	454–11	57–1	27–8	10.0
British Merchant (st)	1922	Beardm	6994	10,729	455–0	57–2	27–8	10.0
British Motorist (m)	1924	SHWR	6891	10,772	453–3	57–0	27–10	10.0
British Officer (st)	1922	Palmer	6990	10,822	453–3	57–1	27–9	10.0
British Petrol (m)	1925	SHWR	6891	10,784	453–3	57–0	27–10	10.0
British Power (m)	1936	H&WGw	8451	12,177	483–1	61–9	27–6	12.0
British Premier (st)	1922	Palmer	5872	9132	416–0	53–9	27–5	10.0
British Prestige (m)	1931	Lithgw	7106	11,040	455–8	59–6	27–3	10.0
British Pride (m)	1931	Lithgw	7106	11,040	455–8	59–6	27–3	10.0
British Princess	1917	ArmWh1	7019	10,860	430.0	57–0	27–4	10.0
British Progress	1927	ArmWh1	4581	6906	381.2	50–5	23–4	10.0
British Prudence (m)	1939	Laing	8620	12,451	481–6	61–9	27–8	12.0
British Reliance (m)	1928	GrkDY	7000	11,066	454–5	57–0	27–10	10.0
British Renown (m)	1928	Laing	6997	10,950	435.0	57–4	27–8	10.0
British Resolution (m)	1937	SHWR	8408	12,235	481–7	62–0	27–7	12.0
British Resource (m)	1931	GrkDY	7209	11,186	454–5	59–5	27–3	10.0
British Sailor *ex War Rajah 21*	1918	SHWR	5576	8450	412–0	52–4	25–7	10.0
British Science (m)	1931	Palmer	7138	11,082	456–0	59–9	27–1	10.0
British Security (m)	1936	H&WGw	8470	12,121	483–1	61–9	27–5	12.0
British Sergeant (st)	1922	Palmer	5868	9122	416–0	54–2	27–5	10.0
British Sincerity (m)	1939	Cammel	8533	12,207	482–6	62–0	27–8	12.0
British Soldier *ex War Sikh 19*	1918	GrayX	5564	8460	412–0	52–4	25–7	10.0
British Sovereign	1917	ArmWh1	3657	5796	345–2	49–1	21–10	9.0
British Splendour (m)	1931	Palmer	7138	11,095	456–0	59–9	27–1	10.0
British Statesman (st)	1922	Laing	6991	10,925	457–6	57–1	27–9	10.0
British Strength (m)	1931	Palmer	7139	11,095	456–0	59–9	27–1	10.0
British Tenacity (m)	1939	SHWR	8439	12,254	481–8	62–0	27–7	12.0
British Trader	1921	Beardm	4204	6089	363–3	49–3	23–2	9.0
British Triumph (m)	1936	Lithgw	8501	12,200	483–1	61–9	27–7	12.0
British Trust (m)	1939	H&WGw	8466	12,416	483–1	61–9	27–7	12.0
British Union (m)	1927	SHWR	6987	10,912	454–0	57–0	27–10	10.5
British Unity (m)	1939	Lithgw	8407	12,250	481–6	61–9	27–7	12.0
British Valour (m)	1927	Lithgw	6952	10,959	454–0	57–0	27–10	10.5
British Venture	1930	Lithgw	4696	6922	384.6	50–2	23–4	10.0
British Viscount (st)	1921	SHWR	6895	10,873	456–0	57–0	27–7	10.0
British Workman (st)	1922	Workmn	6994	10,898	456–0	57–0	27–9	10.0
British Yeoman (st)	1923	Palmer	6990	10,822	456–0	57–1	27–8	10.0
British Zeal (m)	1937	Lithgw	8532	12,180	481–6	61–9	27–6	12.0

Note: Many of the above vessels carried up to eight passengers or supernumeries

Note: British Tanker Co Ltd was

Manager for
MINISTRY OF TRANSPORT

British Lady (st)	1923	ThmpsJ	6098	9517	427–0	54–10	27–5	10.0

controlled by Anglo-Iranian Oil Co Ltd, which was also associated with Burmah Oil Co Ltd (*qv*)

BRITISH WESTERN UNION LTD, 22 Great Winchester St, London EC2

Cable vessel

Cyrus Field (s2)	1924	PenhtS	1288	1022	223–7	34–2	17–2	10.5

Funnel: Yellow
Hull: White
Services: Cable laying/maintenance

BROCKLEBANK LTD, THOS & JNO, Cunard Bldg, Pier Head, Liverpool 3

Macharda (st)	1938	Hamtn4	7998	10,975	493–7	62–8	27–10	14.5
Magdapur (st)	1920	Lithgw	8641	13,000	493–5	64–0	30–4	13.5
shortened 35								
Mahanada (st)	1914	Conn2	7181	10,960	485–2	58–0	27–3	13.0
Mahout (st)	1925	Hamtn2	7921	11,636	488–3	62–1	27–6	13.0
Mahratta	1917	Duncan	6690	10,320	462–0	58–2	26–11	12.0
Mahronda (st)	1925	Hamtn2	7926	11,600	488–3	62–1	27–6	13.0
Mahseer (st)	1925	Conn2	7911	11,575	488–3	62–2	27–8	13.0
Mahsud	1917	LithR	7540	11,214	490–8	58–2	27–3	12.0
Maidan (st)	1925	Conn2	7908	11,500	488–3	62–2	27–8	13.0
Maihar	1917	LithR	7563	11,214	490–6	58–2	27–3	12.0
Makalla	1918	Duncan	6677	10,350	462–0	58–2	26–11	12.0
Malabar (st)	1938	Hamtn4	7976	11,310	494–11	62–9	27–9	14.5
Malakand	1919	Lithgw	7649	11,200	490–6	58–2	27–3	12.0
Malancha (st)	1937	Hamtn4	8124	10,975	493–7	62–8	27–10	14.5
Manaar (st)	1917	Conn2	7242	10,910	490–0	58–0	27–3	13.0
Mandasor	1920	Hamtn2	5144	7917	412–4	52–4	25–4	12.0
launched as War Genista, laid down as War Gorse								
Mangalore (st)	1920	Conn2	8886	13,450	501–0	63–11	30–2	13.5
shortened 35								
Manipur (st)	1920	Lithgw	8652	13,000	493–0	64–0	30–4	13.5
shortened 35								
Markhor (st)	1929	Hamtn2	7917	11,330	488–1	62–4	27–7	14.0
Martand (st)	1939	Hamtn4	7967	11,310	494–10	62–8	26–9	14.5
Marwarri (st)	1935	Hamtn4	8063	11,153	488–0	62–9	27–10	14.5
Masirah	1919	Conn2	6578	10,781	448.0	56–0	28–6	12.5
Matheran	1919	Lithgw	7653	11,200	489–6	58–2	27–3	12.0
Mathura (st)	1920	Conn2	8890	13,450	501–0	63–11	30–2	13.5
shortened 35								
Matra (st)	1926	Hamtn2	8003	11,675	488–3	62–3	27–6	13.0

Funnel: Black with blue over white bands
Hull: Black with white band on topsides, red boot-topping
Services: Swansea, Newport, Manchester, Glasgow, Liverpool–Calcutta; NW Europe–Middlesbrough–London–Colombo–Madras–Calcutta; Calcutta–Colombo–Boston–New York–Philadelphia–Baltimore; US ports–London, Avonmouth

Note: This company was a member of the Cunard Steam Ship Co Ltd group from 1911

BROWN, ATKINSON & CO LTD, WM, Commercial Bldgs, Scale Lane, Hull

SEA STEAMSHIP CO LTD

Chelsea	1925	Nthmbl	4804	8300	396.1	52–10	24–4	10.0
Portsea	1938	Burntd	1583	2470	274–6	40–2	16–0	11.0

Funnel: Black with white band
Hull: Black, red boot-topping
Services: General tramping

BRUCE & CO, JOHN, 70 Wellington St, Glasgow C2

BALMORE STEAMSHIP CO LTD								
Balmore	1920	Grgmth	1925	3200	291–3	41–11	18–3	9.0
ex Kirkliston 37, ex Rowanpark 30								
MOSSGIEL STEAMSHIP CO LTD								
Almenara	1922	OsbGr2	1851	2920	260.2	41–2	19–0	8.0
ex Papelera 29								
Alpera	1920	Graysn	1777	3150	275–0	41–2	20–4	9.0
ex Cabo del Agua 24, ex Coria 23								

Funnel: Red, black top
Hull: Black, red boot-topping
Services: Glasgow–Genoa–Leghorn–Naples–Sicily; Glasgow–Marseilles; Glasgow–Huelva–Valencia–Seville–Barcelona; Glasgow–Dublin–Alexandria; Italy–Sicily–Spain–Dublin, Belfast
Note: Also *Alcira* (built 1923/1387gt), *Alcora* (19/1381), *Alhama* (38/1352)

BULLARD, KING & CO LTD, 14 St Mary Axe, London EC3

Operator of
NATAL LINE OF STEAMERS
Passenger/general cargo vessels

Umgeni (r/t2,P108/1)	1938	SHWR	8180	8320	468–0	61–2	25–6	15.0
Umkuzi* (s2,P75)	1903	Curle	5175	7270	419.1	50–2	24–9	10.5
ex Cluny Castle 24								

Funnel: Yellow, black top, with yellow over brown bands
Hull: Grey, red boot-topping
Services: Middlesbrough–Antwerp–London–(occasionally called Cape Town)–Durban–Mauritius–Lourenço Marques–Beira–London–Hull–Hamburg

Umona	1910	Laing	3767	5450	356.0	44–6	23–9	11.5
Umtali (r/t2,P108/1)	1936	SHWR	8162	8357	468–0	61–2'	25–6	15.0
Umtata (r/t2,P108/1)	1935	SHWR	8141	8357	468–0	61–2	25–6	15.0
Umvoti (s2,P75)	1903	Curle	5183	7270	419.3	50–2	24–9	10.5
ex Comrie Castle 24								
Umvuma (P50)	1914	Laing	4419	6730	365.0	49–2	25–5	13.0

Note: * BU 1939
Note: This company was acquired by Union-Castle Mail Steamship Co Ltd (*qv*) in May 1919

BURIES MARKES LTD, Holland House, 1–4 Bury St, London EC3

Funnel: Black with blue BM on broad white band bordered by two narrow red bands
Hull: Black with white line, white boot-topping
Services: General tramping, mainly grain trade
Note: This company was a subsidiary of Louis-Dreyfus & Cie (*qv* in France section)

La Cordillera (m)	bldg	Doxfrd	5185	9340	444–9	56–6	25–11	13.0
La Estancia (m)	bldg	Doxfrd	5185	9340	444–9	56–6	25–11	13.0
La Pampa (m)	1938	Göta	4149	8170	397–0	55–2	24–10	11.0

BURMAH OIL CO LTD,
175 West George St, Glasgow C2 and Britannic House, Finsbury Circus, London EC2

Funnel: White, black top
Hull: Light grey, red boot-topping
Trade: Rangoon–India oil and petroleum
Note: Burmah Oil Co Ltd which also owned small tankers, was associated with Anglo-Iranian Oil Co Ltd, controllers of British Tanker Co Ltd (*qv*)

Tankers

Badarpur	1922	Leslie	8079	11,764	454–5	57–1	29–10	10.5
Masimpur	1927	Laing	5586	8449	410–0	54–4	26–2	11.0
Singu	1931	SHWR	4927	7405	381.5	55–4	24–1	11.0
Yenangyaung (m)	1937	SHWR	5447	8020	400–9	54–2	26–2	12.5

BURNETT STEAMSHIP CO LTD,
Milburn House, Dean St, Newcastle upon Tyne

Funnel: Black, yellow band
Hull: Black, red boot-topping
Services: General tramping

Birtley	1923	WoodS2	2873	4550	334.3	44–8	20–1	10.5
Holmside	1930	Cowpen	3433	5550	338.0	48–0	21–10	10.5
Towneley	1923	WoodS2	2888	4550	334.3	44–8	20–1	10.5
Tynemouth	bldg	Laing	3168	4903	357–0	48–0	20–4	11.0
Wallsend	1937	Laing	3157	4935	356–11	48–0	20–4	11.0

BURNS, PHILP & CO LTD,
5–11 Bridge St, Sydney, NSW, Australia, and 35 Crutched Friars, London EC3

Funnel: Black with black and white chequered band between two white rings
Hull: Black with white band, red boot-topping, or white, red boot-topping
Services: Australia E coast –Java–Singapore; Australia E coast–New Guinea–Papua–Solomon Is–Norfolk Is–New Hebrides; Sydney–Pacific Islands–Mexico–W coast US, Canada; Australia coastal

Passenger/general cargo vessels

Bulolo (m2,P223/1,16/2,–/nat)	1938	Curle	6267	4375	412–6	58–2	23–0	15.0
Macdhui (m,P167/1,–/nat)	1931	Curle	4561	3200	341.9	51–2	22–1	15.0
Malaita (m,P77/1,24/2,8/Ch,–/nat)	1933	Curle	3310	3660	328–0	47–0	21–1	12.0
Marella (P100/1,50/2)	1914	Reiher	7474	7290	441–10	55–10	26–11	12.0
ex Wahehe 21, ex Hilda Woermann 14								
Merkur (m2,P85/1,20/2)	1924	Krupp	5952	4900	410–10	51–11	21–8	12.0
ex Rio Bravo 34								
Montoro (P100/1)	1911	Clyde	4088	4800	373–6	47–5	23–0	12.0
Morinda (P58/1,14/2))	1913	G&G5	2025	1950	271–8	38–1	18–0	11.0
Neptuna (m2,P85/1,20/2)	1924	Krupp	5952	4900	410–10	51–11	21–8	12.0
ex Neptun 35, ex Rio Panuco 34								
Tulagi (m2,P12/1,200/d)	1939	HK&Wh	2281	2550	254–6	44–2	19–6	12.0

General cargo vessels

Burnside (r/t,P12)	bldg	Curle	5659	8800	442–6	57–2	25–6	12.0
Mangola	1920	CommSy	3352	6194	341–1	47–11	23–11	9.0
ex Eudunda 26								

Note: This company also owned vessels of under 2000gt

CABLE & WIRELESS LTD, Electra House, Victoria Embankment, London WC2

Cable vessels

Recorder (s2)	1902	DunlpD	2276	–	311–6	40–9	20–6	13.0
ex Iris 29								
EASTERN TELEGRAPH CO LTD								
Cambria (s2)	1905	SHWR	1959	2370	283.0	37–1	22–3	11.0
Lady Denison-Pender (s2)	1920	Fairfd	1984	1940	282–8	38–2	18–1	12.0
Mirror (s2)	1923	BrownJ	1850	1689	271–3	37–2	18–1	12.0
WEST COAST OF AMERICA TELEGRAPH CO LTD								
Retriever	1909	Goole	674	881	190.2	28–3	15–3	9.5
WESTERN TELEGRAPH CO LTD								
Cable Enterprise	1924	Ingls2	943	697	212–7	30–1	14–2	10.5
Norseman (s2)	1923	BrownJ	1844	1684	271–3	37–2	18–0	12.0

Funnel: Yellow
Hull: White or light grey, blue or black band, dark green boot-topping
Services: Cable laying/maintenance

CAIRNS, NOBLE & CO LTD,

Milburn House, Dean St, Newcastle upon Tyne 1 and 38 Great St Helen's, London EC3

CAIRN LINE OF STEAMSHIPS LTD								
Cairnesk (st,P12)	1926	Pgill2	5007	8010	418–10	55–4	25–8	12.0
Cairnglen (st,P12)	1926	Pgill2	5019	8010	418–10	55–4	25–6	12.0
Cairnmona	1918	Sundld	4666	7485	390.2	53–1	25–0	12.0
Cairnross (st)	1921	Sundld	5494	8493	425.0	55–0	25–8	12.0
Cairnvalona (P10)	1918	Sundld	4929	7853	430–0	53–1	24–10	12.0

Funnel: Red with broad red band bordered by two narrow white bands, white triangle on red band, black top
Hull: Black, red boot-topping
Services: R Tyne, Leith, Dundee–Montreal–Quebec (summer), Portland ME (winter); Mediterranean ports–Quebec –Montreal (spring, autumn)
Note: This company was purchased by Furness, Withy & Co Ltd (*qv*) in 1928

CAMPBELL BROS & CO, 33 High Bridge, Newcastle upon Tyne 1

AYRSHIRE NAVIGATION CO LTD								
River Afton	1935	Lithgw	5479	9970	433.2	58–3	25–6	10.5
River Lugar (r/t)	1937	Lithgw	5423	9970	457–11	58–3	25–5	11.0
UNITED STEAM NAVIGATION CO LTD								
Dalblair	1926	Scott2	4608	8643	420–6	54–1	24–2	10.5
Dalcairn	1927	Scott2	4608	8643	420–6	54–1	24–2	10.5
Dalcross	1930	Scott2	4557	8561	420–0	54–1	24–4	10.5
Dalcroy	1930	Scott2	4558	8561	420–0	54–1	24–4	10.5
Dalfram	1930	Scott2	4558	8561	420–0	54–1	24–4	10.5
Dalmore	1927	Scott2	5193	8483	419–4	52–4	24–10	10.5
Dalryan	1930	Scott2	4558	8561	420–0	54–1	24–4	10.5
Dalveen	1927	Scott2	5193	8483	419–4	52–4	24–10	10.5

Funnel: United – black with red C on broad black band bordered by two narrow red bands; Ayrshire – similar, but red A instead of C
Hull: Black, salmon pink boot-topping
Services: General tramping

CAMPBELL & SON, JOHN M, 98 West George St, Glasgow C2

STEAMSHIP DALDORCH CO LTD								
Daldorch (r/t)	1930	Beardm	5571	8831	420–10	55–2	25–3	11.5
STEAMSHIP DALHANNA CO LTD								
Dalhanna (r/t)	1930	Beardm	5571	8831	420–10	55–1	25–3	11.5

Funnel: Black, light blue band
Hull: Black, red boot-topping
Services: General tramping

CANADIAN NATIONAL STEAMSHIPS LTD

384 St James St, Montreal, Quebec, Canada, and 17–19 Cockspur St, London SW1

Passenger/general cargo vessels

LADY DRAKE LTD								
Lady Drake (st2,P103/1,32/2,102/3)	1929	Cammel	7985	6700	437–2	59–1	24–0	14.0
LADY HAWKINS LTD								
Lady Hawkins (st2,P103/1,32/2,102/3)	1929	Cammel	7988	6456	437–2	59–1	24–0	14.0
LADY NELSON LTD								
Lady Nelson (st2,P103/1,32/2,102/3)	1929	Cammel	7970	6456	437–2	59–1	24–1	14.0
LADY RODNEY LTD								
Lady Rodney (st2,P107/1)	1929	Cammel	8194	4665	438–0	60–2	23–0	14.0
LADY SOMERS LTD								
Lady Somers (st2,P107/1)	1929	Cammel	8194	4620	438–0	60–2	23–0	14.0

Funnel: Red with blue top separated by broad white band
Hull: Lady vessels – white, red boot-topping; MANZ vessels – black, green boot-topping; others black, red boot-topping
Services: Passenger, mail and cargo – Halifax–Boston–Bermuda–St Kitts–Nevis–Antigua–Martinique–Dominica–St Lucia–Barbados–St Vincent–Grenada–Trinidad–Demerara–Boston–St John NB; Montreal–Halifax–Boston (summer); Halifax–Boston (winter) –Bermuda–Nassau–Kingston (connection for Belize); cargo only – Montreal (summer) –Halifax (summer, winter) –Kingston; cargo – Montreal

Campbell Bros & Co: Built by Scott's of Greenock, Dalcairn *was one of two sisterships completed in 1926–27 for the subsidiary company United SN Co. While part of eastbound convoy HX72, she was torpedoed and sunk by* U100 *on September 21 1940 when on voyage from Montreal to Hull with 8000 tons of wheat.* U100 *had sunk the previous month the sistership* Dalblair *during a successful attack on a westbound convoy, in which she sank four vessels and damaged another. Campbell Bros, which was formed in 1902, changed its title in 1940 to Mungo Campbell & Co Ltd (Alex Duncan)*

Canadian National Steamships: Lady Rodney *was one of five passenger vessels completed for this owner by Cammell, Laird, Birkenhead, in 1929. The five vessels ran a passenger and cargo service from Halifax, Nova Scotia, and Boston to Bermuda, Caribbean ports, Trinidad and Demerara. On return voyages they were usually loaded with bananas. During 1942–45* Lady Rodney *was in service as a troopship and afterwards made repatriation and 'war brides' voyages. She was refitted at St John, New Brunswick, and in July 1947 resumed the Caribbean service, but was sold in 1953 when this was discontinued. As the Egyptian-owned* Mecca, *she was converted for North Africa–Egypt–Jeddah Hadj pilgrim voyages and for charter trade. On May 5 1965 she was in collision with the British mv* Fremantle Star *in the Gulf of Suez, and was laid up damaged at Port Said. In June 1967* Mecca *was scuttled in the Suez Canal during the Israel–Egypt war, and by September 1974 the wreck was being demolished (RW Jordan collection)*

PRINCE DAVID LTD
Prince David (st2,P334/1,70/3)
1930 Cammel 6892 1050 384–6 57–1 16–9 20.0

PRINCE ROBERT LTD
Prince Robert (st2,P334/1,70/3)
1930 Cammel 6892 1050 384–6 57–1 16–9 20.0

General cargo vessels

CANADIAN AVIATOR LTD
Cavelier (P–) 1919 WallSB 3663 4910 343–3 46–8 22–9 13.0
ex Canadian Aviator 29

CANADIAN HUNTER LTD
Cathcart (P–) 1920 DavieG 3708 4915 343–3 46–8 22–9 13.0
ex Canadian Hunter 29

CANADIAN PATHFINDER LTD
Chomedy (P–) 1921 Coughl 6136 8390 414–0 52–5 26–3 11.0
ex Canadian Pathfinder 32, ex Canadian Freighter 27

CANADIAN SKIRMISHER LTD
Colborne (P–) 1921 WallSB 6230 8390 413–0 52–5 26–3 11.0
ex Canadian Skirmisher 32

CANADIAN TRANSPORTER LTD
Cornwallis (P6) 1921 Coughl 5458 8390 414–0 52–5 26–3 11.0
ex Canadian Transporter 32

MONTREAL AUSTRALIA NEW ZEALAND LINE LTD (MANZ)
Canadian Challenger (P6)
1921 Davie 5439 8399 414–0 52–2 25–5 11.0
Canadian Constructor* (P9)
1922 Halifx 7178 10,550 430.0 56–2 29–2 12.0
Canadian Cruiser (P9)
1921 Halifx 7178 10,550 430.0 56–2 29–2 12.0

(summer), Halifax (summer, winter)–Bermuda–Porto Rico–Guadeloupe–Martinique–Barbados–Trinidad–Demerara: MANZ – Montreal (summer), Halifax (summer, winter)–Panama–Australia–New Zealand–Panama–New York–Boston–Canada

Note: * Sold Ernels Shipping Co Ltd (Counties Ship Management Co Ltd) 1939, renamed *Argos Hill*
Note: This company owned smaller vessels and ferries

CANADIAN PACIFIC STEAMSHIPS LTD, 8 Waterloo Place, London SW1

Funnel: Yellow
Hull: Empresses – white with (blue band), green boot topping; others – black, red boot-topping
Services: Mail, passenger and cargo – Liverpool, Belfast, Glasgow, Southampton–Quebec–Montreal (summer)–St John NB (winter); Vancouver–Honolulu–Yokohama–Kobe–Shanghai–Manila–Hong Kong; Vancouver–Suva–Australia–New Zealand; cargo only – London, NW Europe–Quebec–Montreal (summer)–St John NB (winter); cruising

Managers for
CANADIAN PACIFIC RAILWAY CO

Passenger vessels (North Atlantic)
Duchess of Atholl (st2,P573/cab,480/t,510/3)
1928 Beardm 20,119 10,148 601–3 75–2 27–7 17.5
Duchess of Bedford (st2,P573/cab,480/t,510/3)
1928 BrownJ 20,123 10,148 601–3 75–3 27–7 17.5
Duchess of Richmond (st2,P573/cab,480/t,510/3)
1928 BrownJ 20,022 9718 601–3 75–2 27–7 18.0
Duchess of York (st2,P573/cab,480/t,510/3)
1928 BrownJ 20,021 9718 601–3 75–2 27–7 18.0
ordered as Duchess of Cornwall
Empress of Australia (st2,P387/1,394/t,358/3)
1920 VulcSt 21,833 7520 615–0 75–2 29–3 18.0
ex Empress of China 21, ex Tirpitz 21, launched as Admiral von Tirpitz
Empress of Britain (st4,P452/cab,260/t,470/3)
1931 BrownJ 42,348 9532 758–0 97–10 32–8 24.0
Montcalm (st2,P542/cab,1268/3)
1921 BrownJ 16,418 8094 575–2 70–2 28–1 17.0
Montclare (st2,P544/cab,1252/3)
1922 BrownJ 16,314 8030 575–2 70–2 28–1 17.0
Montrose (st2,P544/cab,1252/3)
1922 Fairfd 16,402 8050 575–2 70–2 28–1 17.0

Passenger vessels (North Pacific)
Empress of Asia (st4,P398/1,66/t,820/3)
1913 Fairfd 16,909 9135 590–0 68–2 29–0 20.0
Empress of Canada (st2,P453/1,126/2,168/3,926/st)
1922 Fairfd 21,517 9580 653–0 77–11 30–0 21.0
Empress of Japan (st2,P400/1,164/2,100/3,510/st)
1930 Fairfd 26,032 10,300 666–6 83–10 30–7 22.0
Empress of Russia (st4,P1250/1,2,st)
1913 Fairfd 16,810 9135 590–0 68–2 29–0 20.0

General cargo vessels (North Atlantic)
Beaverbrae (st2) 1928 ArmWh1 9956 12,910 512–0 61–11 30–0 15.5
Beaverburn (st2) 1927 Denny2 9874 12,750 512–0 61–10 30–0 15.5
Beaverdale (st2) 1928 ArmWh1 9957 12,910 512–0 61–11 30–0 15.5
Beaverford (st2) 1928 Curle 10,042 12,840 520–8 61–10 29–11 15.5
Beaverhill (st2) 1928 Curle 10,041 12,840 520–8 61–10 29–11 15.5

Canadian Pacific Steamships: Completed by John Brown, Clydebank, in August 1922, Montclare *was built for her owner's service from Liverpool to Quebec and Montreal. On August 28 1939 she was requisitioned to become the armed merchant cruiser HMS* Montclare, *and continued in this role until 1942. She was sold in June 1942 to the Admiralty and became a submarine depot ship. In 1944 she became flagship of Rear-Admiral Fisher's Pacific Fleet supply train. In 1946 she acted as submarine base ship at Rothesay, and in 1954 was decommissioned and put into reserve at Gareloch.* Montclare *was later transferred to Portsmouth under care and maintenance, and in September 1955 was for disposal. She was broken up at Inverkeithing in 1958*
(RW Jordan collection)

Canadian Pacific Steamships: Empress of Canada *was completed by Fairfield, Govan, in April 1922 for her owner's Vancouver–Far East trans-Pacific service. Prewar she made at least one round-the-world cruise and one Southampton–Quebec–Southampton round voyage. In November 1939, after completing 200 trans-Pacific voyages, she was requisitioned for service as a troopship. In March 1943 she left Durban with 1800 persons on board, including 200 Poles released by Russia when that country entered the war, 400 Italian POWs, and several hundred naval personnel. She was ordered to Takoradi to pick up 300 more Italians. On March 13 she was torpedoed by the Italian submarine* Leonardo da Vinci *with the loss of 392 lives, which included about half the Italians on board, 8 gunners and 44 crew members (EH Cole)*

Canadian Pacific Steamships: Operating on North Atlantic service was Beaverdale, *one of five sisterships completed in the late 1920s. All five were twin-screw with six Parsons single reduction steam turbines of 8000shp. They could carry 12 passengers and had a crew of 79.* Beaverdale *is pictured here in Tilbury docks with a deck cargo of railway coaches. On September 13 1939 she was requisitioned by the Ministry of Shipping for the carriage of essential war cargoes and on April 1 1941 while in eastbound convoy SC26 was torpedoed and sunk by* U48. *Her voyage was St John NB to Liverpool with general cargo (RW Jordan collection)*

James Chambers & Co: Muncaster Castle, *fitted with two NEME 6-cylinder oil engines of 4200bhp, was one of the nine-strong Lancashire Shipping Co fleet which operated regular cargo liner services. On March 30 1942 she was torpedoed and sunk by* U68 *when on voyage from Glasgow and Freetown to Table Bay and Alexandria with 3000 tons of government stores (Alex Duncan)*

R Chapman & Son: Carlton *was one of 17 tramp steamers operated by this company, which had been shipowners since 1880. On December 20 1940, while in convoy OB260, she was torpedoed and shelled by the Italian submarine* Pietro Calvi *and sunk with most of her crew.* Carlton *was on voyage from Newport to Buenos Aires with 6545 tons of coal. On January 7 1941 four survivors were picked up by the British steamer* Antiope *about 200 miles southwest of Iceland (Alex Duncan)*

CAPPER, ALEXANDER & CO, 4 St Mary Axe, London EC3

Funnel: Black
Hull: Black, red boot-topping
Services: General tramping

ALEXANDER SHIPPING CO LTD

Ashbury	1924	GrayWH	3901	6500	356.5	50–0	22–8	10.5
ex Cairnhill 35, ex Nitedal 25								
Aylesbury	1932	Burntd	3944	7910	385–0	52–6	24–4	11.0
Bibury	1929	Duncan	4616	9517	420–6	55–0	25–1	10.5
Charlbury	bldg	Burntd	4836	9366	430–4	57–0	25–4	10.5
Holmbury	1925	Lithgw	4566	8000	397–9	52–0	24–0	11.5
ex Wirral 34								
Kingsbury	1937	Burntd	4898	9450	430–2	56–11	25–4	10.5
Ledbury	1912	Neptnl	3528	6354	366.0	50–10	22–5	8.5
ex Podesta 24, ex Odessa 21								
Newbury	1927	Duncan	5012	8920	418–5	53–0	24–7	10.5
Queensbury	1931	Burntd	3911	7900	385–0	52–4	24–4	11.0
Shaftesbury	1923	Curle	4284		370.6	53–0	24–0	10.0
ex Crown of Galicia 35, ex Hopeland 29								
Shrewsbury	1924	RDuck2	4542	8314	399.5	53–0	24–8	10.0
ex Southborough 35								
Tewkesbury	1927	Craig2	4601	8533	425–0	53–6	24–8	10.0
ex Glocliffe 32								
Westbury	1928	Burntd	4712	9350	417–0	54–4	24–10	10.5
Woodbury (r/t)	1936	Burntd	4434		400.0	55–1	24–10	10.5

CARPENTER & CO LTD, W R, 19 O'Connell St, Sydney NSW, Australia

Funnel: Yellow with blue and white star emblem bearing white T
Hull: Black with white band, red boot-topping
Services: Australia–New Guinea–London; Australia–New Guinea–S Pacific islands; Australia–Honolulu–British Columbia

W R CARPENTER OVERSEA SHIPPING LTD, Rabaul, New Guinea

Rabaul (m2)	1916	B&W	5618	9475	444–4	55–4	26–9	10.0
ex George Washington 34								
Salamaua (m2,P12)								
	1920	H&WGw	6676	9030	420–9	54–2	27–10	10.0
ex Milverton 34, ex Glentara 28								
Suva (P12)	1938	Bartm2	4873	9150	436–11	56–8	25–6	10.0

CARRICK & CO LTD, F, Milburn House, Dean St, Newcastle upon Tyne 1

Funnel: Black with red band bearing white six-pointed star in white circle
Hull: Dark grey with white band, red boot-topping
Services: General tramping

Langleebrook	1930	Palmer	4246	8101	410–0	54–8	23–3	10.0

MEDOMSLEY STEAM SHIPPING CO LTD

Langleecrag	1929	Palmer	4909	9312	431–0	55–10	25–1	10.0
Langleeford	1925	Palmer	4622	7758	370.0	56–2	23–7	10.0
Langleegorse	1927	Palmer	4524	8165	399–11	52–9	24–7	10.0
ex Hedgehope 29								
Langleetarn	1929	Palmer	4908	9312	431–0	55–10	25–1	10.0

CATSELL & CO LTD, S, (Selman Catsell), 36 Camomile St, London EC3

Funnel: Red with black top separated by five-pointed blue star on broad white band
Hull: Black
Services: Tramping, mainly Mediterranean; oil and petroleum trades

General cargo vessels

Noemijulia	1895	Ropnr3	2490	3750	302–0	43–0	19–0	7.5
ex Noemi 30, ex Barlby 26								

BRODWAL STEAMSHIP CO LTD

Brodwal	1900	ThmpR1	3385	5640	326.0	48–0	22–3	8.0
ex Katerina 33, ex Immacolata 30								

NOEMIJULIA STEAMSHIP CO LTD

Kenfig Pool	1908	France	2390	3540	288.8	38–11	19–8	9.0
ex Saint Marc 37								

Tankers

ESTURIA STEAMSHIP CO LTD

Esturia*	1914	Laing	6968	10,360	425.1	57–0	27–1	10.0
ex Apache 37, ex La Habra 36								

Note: * Sold Harris & Dixon Ltd 1939

NAPHTHA TANKERS LTD

Naphtha Shipper	1916	Rhead3	5897	9100	393.5	51–1	28–4	9.5
ex Dovrefjell 38, ex Lacuna 28, ex Briarleaf 22								

Note: * See also in Turkey section

CHAMBERS & CO, JAMES, 3–5 King St, Liverpool 1

Funnel: Red, black top
Hull: Black, red boot-topping
Services: Castle Line – Antwerp–Ghent–Galveston–Houston; Barber Line – New York–China–Japan–Philippines–Malaya;

LANCASHIRE SHIPPING CO LTD

Bolton Castle	1939	Laing	5203	9250	454–4	57–1	24–9	11.0
Greystoke Castle (m2,P12/1)								
	1928	Cammel	5853	8944	440–0	56–3	26–11	13.5

Lancaster Castle	1937	Laing	5172	9250	454–2	57–1	24–9	11.0
Lowther Castle	1937	Laing	5171	9250	454–2	57–1	24–9	11.0
Muncaster Castle (m2,P12/1)	1928	Cammel	5853	8944	440–0	56–1	26–11	13.5
Penrith Castle (m2,P12/1)	1929	Cammel	6369	9816	481–0	60–4	27–5	13.5
Raby Castle (m,P12/1)	1925	Caledn	4996	8345	412–3	52–5	25–10	11.5
Thurland Castle (m2,P12/1)	1929	Cammel	6372	9816	480–10	60–4	27–4	13.5
Wray Castle	1938	Hamtn4	4253	7785	392–8	56–3	23–9	12.0

Dodwell–Castle Line – Japan–China–Philippines–Batavia–Malaya–Colombo–New York–Boston; Cuban Line – Antwerp–London–Cuba–Mexico

CHAPMAN & SON, R, Maritime Bldgs, King St, Newcastle upon Tyne 1

Funnel: Black with red and white diagonally quartered houseflag on broad black band bordered by two narrow white bands
Hull: Grey, pink boot-topping
Services: General tramping

Carlton	1924	Short2	5162	8870	402–0	53–6	25–7	10.0
Clearton	1919	RDuck2	5219	8240	412–0	52–4	25–3	11.0
Innerton *launched as War Scilla*	1919	Ropnr2	5276	8335	412–4	52–4	25–3	11.0
Koranton	1920	Doxfrd	6695	11,050	429–4	55–6	28–6	11.5
Mabriton	1920	Doxfrd	6694	10,990	429–4	55–6	28–6	11.5
Peterton	1919	RDuck2	5221	8200	414–5	52–5	25–3	11.0
Tiberton	1920	RDuck2	5225	8200	414–5	52–5	25–3	11.0
CARLTON STEAMSHIP CO LTD								
Amberton	1928	Short2	5377	8979	409.6	54–0	25–8	10.0
Brighton	1928	Short2	5359	8958	409.6	54–0	25–8	10.0
Demeterton	1926	Short2	5251	8820	410–10	54–0	25–7	10.0
Frumenton	1930	Short2	6675	11,715	452–9	60–4	27–9	10.0
Generton	1936	Short2	4797	8120	439–2	54–0	24–2	10.5
Grainton	1929	Short2	6341	10,200	439–0	58–5	26–7	10.0
Nurtureton	1929	Short2	6272	10,200	439–0	58–5	26–7	10.0
Riverton	1928	Short2	5378	8979	409.6	54–0	25–8	10.0
CARLTON STEAMSHIP CO LTD AND CAMBAY STEAMSHIP CO LTD								
Hermiston	1939	Short2	4813	8120	439–2	54–0	24–2	10.5
Scorton	1939	Short2	4813	8120	439–2	54–0	24–2	10.5

CHARLTON, MCALLUM & CO LTD,
St Nicholas Chambers, Amen Corner, Newcastle upon Tyne 1

Funnel: Yellow, black top
Hull: Black, red boot-topping
Services: General tramping

CHARLTON STEAM SHIPPING CO LTD

Hazelside	1928	Short2	4646	8300	395.0	52–9	24–4	10.0
Hazelside	bldg	Short2	5297		441–6	57–0	26–2	11.0
Hollinside	1930	Short2	4172	6750	365.0	52–4	22–2	10.0
Homeside	1924	Short2	4617	7850	396–5	52–3	23–8	10.0

CHELLEW STEAMSHIP MANAGEMENT CO LTD,
47 Stuart St, Cardiff, and 69 Dock St, Newport, Monmouthshire

Funnel: Black, white band
Hull: Black, red boot-topping
Services: General tramping

CHELLEW NAVIGATION CO LTD, Bevis Marks House, Bevis Marks, London EC3

Auretta (r/t)	1935	Burntd	4564	9100	424–0	56–0	24–11	11.0
Justitia	1935	Burntd	4562	9100	424–0	56–0	24–11	10.0
Pencarrow	1921	Irvin3	4841	8008	402–0	52–0	24–3	10.0
Pendeen	1923	Irvin3	4174	7357	375.0	51–2	23–10	10.0
Pengreep	1914	Irvin3	4806	8100	402–0	52–0	24–3	8.5
Penhale	1924	Prstm2	4071	6650	377–6	51–6	21–5	9.5
Penolver	1912	GrayX	3721	6300	350.0	50–0	21–6	9.5
Penrose	1928	Dobson	4393	8500	412–2	53–0	24–10	10.5
Pensilva *ex Brynymor 31*	1929	Burntd	4258	7937	382–3	51–5	24–1	9.5
Statira	1929	Doxfrd	4852	7937	439–2	54–2	25–6	9.5

CHINA NAVIGATION CO LTD, 8 Billiter St, London EC3

Funnel: Black
Hull: Black with white band, red boot-topping
Services: Hong Kong and China–Bangkok–Singapore; Hong Kong–Chinese ports

Anhui (st,P8/1,34/2,1748/d)	1925	Taikoo	3494	4620	351–0	49–4	21–8	12.0
Anking (st,P8/1,34/2,1748/d)	1925	Scott2	3472	4619	351–0	49–2	21–8	12.0
Anshun (m,P52/1,1750/d)	1930	Scott2	3188	4445	351–0	50–2	22–6	12.0

China Nav Co: Taiyuan, *completed in 1929, was one of several similar vessels owned by this company operating regular passenger and cargo services in the China Seas and Far East. In 1941 she was requisitioned by the Ministry of War Transport and on December 10 that year was bombed by Japanese aircraft at Manila.* Taiyuan *escaped further attention of the enemy for a short time, being transferred to US forces for special service on February 15 1942. Just over two weeks later she was sunk off Sourabaya by Japanese surface craft (RW Jordan collection)*

China Nav Co: The steamer Anking *was launched in February 1925 and delivered the following month by Scotts of Greenock. When built she had accommodation for 8 first class, 34 saloon and 1748 unberthed passengers. These numbers changed slightly over the years, but by 1939 were much the same. In 1941* Anking *was hired by the Royal Navy for service as a depot ship at Malta, and she continued in this role until early 1942 when transferred to Tjilatjap to become a communications centre for Batavia (Java). With the imminent Japanese invasion she sailed in convoy escorted by the sloop HMAS* Yarra, *attempting to get to Fremantle to avoid capture by the enemy, but after leaving Tjilatjap she was found by Japanese surface vessels on March 3 1942 and sunk about 200 miles east of Christmas Island. There were three survivors (China Navigation Co archives)*

Ship	Year	Builder	GRT	DWT	Length	Beam	Draught	Speed
Hoihow (P17/1,28/3,243/d)	1933	Taikoo	2798	2700	312–0	44–2	17–6	12.0
Hunan (P17/1,28/3,243/d)	1932	Scott2	2827	2710	312–0	44–2	17–6	12.0
Hupeh (P15/1,28/3,290/d)	1933	Taikoo	2801	2710	312–0	44–2	17–6	12.0
Kalgan (st,P12/1,1319/d)	1921	Scott2	2655	3150	310.3	44–3	18–2	11.0
Kweiyang (st,P12/1,1319/d)	1921	Scott2	2644	3150	310.3	44–2	18–2	11.0
Nanning (P–/d)	1923	Taikoo	2486	2330	295.8	44–3	18–4	10.0
Newchwang (P–/d)	1922	Scott2	2482	2330	295.8	44–3	18–4	10.0
Shengking (st,P45/1,82/2,54/3)	1931	Scott2	2999	1706	314–0	46–1	16–1	15.0
Shuntien (st,P41/1,30/cab,54/unb,52/stg)	1934	Taikoo	3059	2300	314–0	46–1	16–1	15.0
Taiyuan (P8/1,32/cab,40/3,426/d)	1929	Taikoo	2994	3345	329–10	45–2	18–2	13.0
Tsinan (P8/1,32/cab,40/3,426/d)	1930	Taikoo	2994	3345	329–10	45–2	18–2	13.0
Yochow (m,P21/1,329/d)	1933	Scott2	2810	1278	312–0	44–3	17–6	12.0
Yunnan (m,P16/1,3154/d)	1934	Scott2	2812	2778	312–0	44–2	17–6	12.0

Note: This company, was managed and controlled by John Swire & Sons Ltd, owned *Kaying* (built 1922/2626grt), *Kiangsu* (21/2661), *Kingyuan* (21/2653), *Kiungchow* (21/2653), *Kwangchow* (21/2626), *Kwangtung* (21/2626), *Nanchang* (22/2489) *Shantung* (15/2549), *Sinkiang* (15/2646), *Soochow* (20/2604), *Suiyang* (17/2590) and *Szechuen* (20/2604) and a large fleet of river and smaller vessels

CHINE SHIPPING CO LTD, 72 The Exchange, Mount Stuart Sq, Cardiff

Funnel: Black with white C on broad blue band bordered by two narrow white bands
Hull: Black, red boot-topping
Services: General tramping
Note: This company was managed by Harper, Matthews & Co Ltd

Ship	Year	Builder	GRT	DWT	Length	Beam	Draught	Speed
Canford Chine *ex Bryntawe 36*	1917	RDuck2	3364	5500	356–4	47–10	20–9	9.0

CHINESE ENGINEERING & MINING CO LTD, 3 London Wall Bldgs, London EC2

Services: China Seas

Ship	Year	Builder	GRT	DWT	Length	Beam	Draught	Speed
Kaiping	1905	SHWR	2563	3540	312.0	44–4	20.8	9.0

CLAN LINE STEAMERS LTD, THE, 2 St Mary Axe, London EC3, 109 Hope St, Glasgow C2, and 114 Royal Liver Bldg, Liverpool 3

Funnel: Black with two red bands
Hull: Black, red boot-topping
Services: Newport, Glasgow, Liverpool–Mossel Bay–Algoa Bay–East London; Newport, Glasgow, Liverpool–Durban–Lourenço Marques–Beira, also Mauritius, E Africa, Red Sea ports; Newport, Glasgow, Manchester, Liverpool–Bombay–Malabar Coast–Tuticorin–Colombo–Madras–Calcutta; Australia, India, S Africa, E Africa to UK, NW Europe, US; Clan Line Steamers Ltd also ran joint services with Harrison Line (*qv* under T & J Harrison), Ellerman Lines Ltd (*qv*), and Strick Line (*qv* under F C Strick & Co Ltd)

Ship	Year	Builder	GRT	DWT	Length	Beam	Draught	Speed
Clan Alpine (r/t)	1918	G&G3	5442	8933	410.2	53–6	26–2	11.0
Clan Buchanan (r/t2)	1938	GrkDY	7266	10,160	487–8	63–0	28–4	16.0
Clan Cameron (r/t2)	1937	GrkDY	7243	10,160	487–8	63–0	28–4	16.0
Clan Campbell (r/t2)	1937	GrkDY	7255	10,160	487–8	63–0	28–4	16.0
Clan Chattan (r/t2)	1937	GrkDY	7262	10,160	487–8	63–0	28–4	16.0
Clan Chisholm (r/t2)	1937	GrkDY	7256	10,180	487–8	63–0	28–4	16.0
Clan Colqhoun (s2) *ex Gallic 33, ex War Argus 19*	1918	Workmn	7914	9900	462–0	58–6	29–3	13.0
Clan Cumming (r/t2)	1938	GrkDY	7264	10,160	484–8	63–0	28–4	16.0
Clan Farquhar (s2) *ex Delphic 33, ex Mesaba 25, ex War Icarus 19*	1918	H&W,B	7958	10,000	462–0	58–4	29–3	13.0
Clan Ferguson (r/t2)	1938	GrkDY	7347	10,160	484–6	63–0	28–4	16.0
Clan Forbes (r/t2)	1938	GrkDY	7529	9997	487–7	63–0	28–4	16.0
Clan Fraser (r/t2)	1939	GrkDY	7529	9997	487–8	63–0	28–4	16.0
Clan Lamont (r/t2)	1939	GrkDY	7268	10,453	487–8	63–0	29–1	16.0
Clan Macalister (r/t)	1930	GrkDY	6787	11,155	453.8	62–4	27–6	13.0
Clan Macarthur (r/t2)	1935	GrkDY	10,528	10,975	498–8	66–2	30–0	16.0
Clan Macaulay (r/t2)	1936	GrkDY	10,492	10,945	498–8	66–2	30–0	16.0

Clan Macbean	1918	Bartm2	5000	8120	411–10	52–5	24–10	11.5
Clan Macbrayne	1916	Ropnr2	4818	7825	402–0	50–6	24–10	11.0
Clan Macdonald (m2)	1939	GrkDY	9653	9300	505–4	64–8	28–6	16.0
Clan Macdougall (m)	1929	GrkDY	6843	10,010	472–0	62–4	27–1	14.0
Clan Macfadyen (r/t)	1923	AyrDk	6191	8850	432–6	53–5	27–9	13.0
Clan Macfarlane (r/t)	1922	AyrDk	6193	8845	432–6	53–5	27–9	13.0
Clan Macgillivray	1911	ArmWh1	6464	9510	430.6	53–8	27–3	13.0
Clan Macilwraith (r/t)	1924	GrkDY	4839	7400	402–0	52–2	24–8	11.0
Clan Macindoe (r/t)	1920	Lithgw	4635	7309	397–6	52–0	24–1	11.0
Clan Macinnes	1920	Lithgw	4672	7520	397–6	52–0	24–0	11.0
Clan Maciver	1921	Lithgw	4500	7350	397–6	52–0	24–1	11.0
Clan Mackinlay (r/t)	1918	Hamtn2	6365	9994	433–0	53–6	27–10	13.0
Clan Macnab (r/t)	1920	AyrDk	6076	8785	425–0	53–4	27–9	11.0
Clan Macnair (r/t)	1921	AyrDk	6096	8795	425–0	53–4	27–9	11.0
Clan Macnaughton (r/t)	1921	AyrDk	6088	8795	425–0	53–4	27–9	11.0
Clan Macneil (r/t)	1922	AyrDk	6111	8795	424–10	53–4	27–9	11.0
Clan Macphee	1911	Irvin3	6628	9266	430.0	53–6	27–3	13.0
Clan Macpherson (r/t)	1929	GrkDY	6940	10,740	472–0	62–4	27–6	13.0
Clan Macquarrie	1913	Steph2	6471	9365	429.2	53–9	26–11	13.0
Clan Mactavish (st)	1921	AyrDk	7631	10,420	468–0	57–9	27–9	13.0
Clan Macwhirter	1918	LloydR	5941	10,200	437–0	55–10	26–7	10.5
ex Willcasino 23, ex Halizones 20, ex Ypresville 18								
Clan Matheson	1919	Hamtn2	5613	8327	410–0	51–5	27–5	11.0
launched as Clan Morgan								
Clan Menzies (r/t2)	1938	GrkDY	7336	10,160	487–8	63–0	28–4	16.0
Clan Monroe	1918	AyrDk	5952	8488	426–8	53–5	26–8	12.0
Clan Morrison	1918	AyrDk	5936	8500	426–8	53–6	26–8	12.0
Clan Murdoch (r/t)	1919	AyrDk	5950	8489	426–8	53–6	26–8	12.0
Clan Murray (r/t)	1918	AyrDk	5954	8433	426–8	53–6	26–4	12.0
Clan Ranald	1917	Napr&M	5447	8766	421–4	54–0	25–6	10.5
Clan Skene (r/t)	1918	Conn2	5214	8195	412–6	52–4	25–4	11.0
ex Halocrates 24, ex Clan Skene 20, launched as War Adder								
Clan Stuart (r/t)	1916	LithR	5760	9247	423.5	56–0	25–5	13.0

Note: Clan Line Steamers Ltd, managed by Cayzer, Irvine & Co Ltd, controlled Houston Line (London) Ltd (*qv*) and Scottish Shire Line Ltd (*qv* under Turnbull, Martin & Co Ltd); Cayzer, Irvine & Co were managers of *Empire Song*

Manager for

MINISTRY OF SHIPPING

Empire Song (r/t2)	bldg	GrkDY	9228	10,145	487–7	63–0	29–10	15.0

CLARK & SERVICE, 21 Bothwell St, Glasgow C2

Funnel: Black
Hull: Grey, red boot-topping
Services: General tramping

ARDAN STEAMSHIP CO LTD

Ardanbhan	1929	Hendn2	4980	8487	402.9	52–2	24–4	10.0
Ardangorm	1930	Conn2	5200	8625	405.0	54–0	24–4	10.0

CLARKE STEAMSHIP CO LTD,

Canada Cement Bldg, Phillip's Sq, Montreal, PQ, Canada

Funnel: Yellow with four blue bands (black cowl top)
Hull: White, red boot-topping
Services: Cruising – Canada, New York–West Indies cruising; Miami –Havana, Miami–Nassau

Passenger vessels

New Northland (P175/1)	1926	SHWR	3445	2000	287.7	47–2	18–0	13.0
ex Northland 26								
North Star (st2,335/1)	1930	Cammel	6893	1300	385–6	57–2	16–6	18.0
ex Prince Henry 37								

Note: Also smaller vessels

CLAYMORE SHIPPING CO LTD, 60 Mount Stuart Sq, Cardiff

Funnel: Black
Hull: Black, red boot-topping
Services: General tramping

Daydawn	bldg	Pgill2	4768	8650	421–0	54–10	25–3	10.2
Dayrose	1928	ThmpR2	4113	7730	391–10	53–1	23–1	10.0
Seringa	1913	Ropnr2	4729	7950	391–8	51–6	24–4	7.5
ex Falls City 29								

Clan Line: The twin-screw motor vessel Clan Macdonald, *powered by two Kincaid/B&W 10-cylinder oil engines with a total 11,100bhp, was launched on August 15 1939 by Greenock Dockyard Co and entered service in December. In January 1941 her only major brush with the enemy was when she was commodore ship of a UK–Piræus ammunition convoy, surviving several aircraft attacks. Her postwar career was relatively uneventful, apart from picking up a few survivors following the Red Sea collision involving the tankers* World Liberty *and* Mosli. *She arrived at Shanghai in August 1970 to be broken up (R Sherlock)*

Clan Line: Clan Murdoch *was completed by Ayrshire Dockyard Co, Irvine, in 1919. In 1930 she was fitted with a Bauer-Wach exhaust turbine. She had a lucky escape in 1942 when she carried 1000 tons of bombs to Rangoon. Just under 300 tons had been discharged when the Japanese invaders were closing in.* Clan Murdoch *promptly embarked about 1000 Royal Air Force personnel, was directed to Akyab where she embarked 250 Royal Navy personnel, and proceed to Calcutta, where she arrived safely, together with 700 tons of bombs. In 1948 she was transferred to Houston Line and renamed* Halesius. *When on voyage from Macoris to Colombo she ran aground 25 miles from Cape Ténès, Algeria, on May 30 1952. She refloated, but was laid up at Algiers, where she was sold for £155,000 to a Panamanian company and renamed* Jan Kiki. *Her career ended on November 29 1953 when she foundered after her cargo of phosphates shifted in heavy weather about 50 miles north of Lisbon when on voyage from Casablanca to Rotterdam (Real Photographs)*

Constantine Steamship Line: Completed by Northumberland Shipbuilding Co, Howden on Tyne, in January 1930, Wearwood *operated on her owner's regular cargo and passenger services between the UK and USA. She survived the Second World War but had been damaged during a German air raid on Liverpool on March 13 1941. After being sold out of the fleet in 1946, and several changes of name and owner, she was wrecked off Terschelling on October 18 1967 when flying the Lebanese flag as* Margariti *(RW Jordan collection)*

FAIRWATER SHIPPING CO LTD

Fairwater	1928	ThmpR2	4108	7720	391–11	53–1	23–1	10.0

COCKERLINE & CO, W H, Union Bank Chambers, Trinity House Lane, Hull

Funnel: Red, black top
Hull: Black, red boot-topping
Services: General tramping

Albionic	1924	BrownG	2468	4200	290.2	44–1	20–1	9.0
Asiatic	1923	Burntd	3741	6350	350–1	50–0	21–9	9.0
Atlantic*	1904	GrayX	3016	5150	336–1	47–0	20–10	8.5
Britannic	1918	Hill	2490	3860	313–7	43–0	19–10	10.0
ex Mumbles Light 22, ex War Damson 19								
SIR WALTER H COCKERLINE								
Athenic	1937	GrayWH	5351	9360	425–2	57–0	25–1	10.0
Atlantic	1939	GrayWH	5414	9360	425–4	57–0	25–0	10.5
Corinthic	1924	Irvin3	4823	8800	402–8	55–6	24–6	11.5
Germanic	1936	GrayWH	5352	9360	425–2	57–0	25–1	10.0
Pacific	1923	Murdo2	2816	4780	324.0	44–2	21–10	9.0

Note: * Sold Finland 1939, renamed *Margareta*

COLONIAL SUGAR REFINING CO LTD,
1–3 O'Connell St, PO Box 483AA, Sydney NSW, Australia

Funnel: Black, white band bearing pale blue horizontal stripes
Hull: Black, red boot-topping
Services: Australian coastal, molasses

Molasses carriers

Fiona (P8/2)	1933	Caledn	2198	3484	299–0	44–1	20–7	10.5
Rona* (P12/2)	1918	Dixon2	6205	9300	414–7	54–6	26–11	9.5
Tambua* (P6/2)	1938	Caledn	3566	6135	377–4	50–2	22–9	10.0

Note: * Partial tanker

COMMERCIAL CABLE CO, Mackay House, Wormwood St, London EC2

Funnel: Yellow, black top
Services: Cable laying/maintenance

Cable vessels

John W Mackay (s2)	1922	SHWR	4049	4939	361–8	48–1	25–3	12.5
Marie Louise Mackay (s2)	1922	SHWR	1378	1465	246–0	34–2	17–1	12.5

Note: This company was associated with Pacific Cable Co (*qv* in United States section)

COMMON BROTHERS LTD,
Exchange Bldgs, Quayside, Newcastle upon Tyne 1

Funnel: Black with white C on broad red band bordered by narrow white bands above and below
Hull: Black, red boot-topping
Services: General tramping; oil and patroleum trades

HINDUSTAN STEAM SHIPPING CO LTD

General cargo vessels

Badjestan	1928	Bartm2	5573	9075	408–8	54–0	25–6	10.0
Goolistan	1929	Short2	5851	10,732	454–2	57–6	26–2	10.0
Hindustan (m)	bldg	Short2	5245	8980	450–0	56–6	25–6	12.0
Kafiristan	1924	Short2	5193	8870	390.0	53–6	25–7	10.0
Kurdistan	1928	Short2	5844	9400	434–0	54–0	25–7	10.0
Pukkastan	1929	Short2	5809	10,739	454–2	57–6	26–2	10.0
Rajahstan	1929	Bartm2	6391	10,445	440–3	57–0	26–7	10.0
Selvistan	1924	Short2	5136	8870	390.0	53–6	25–7	10.0
Waziristan	1924	Short2	5135	8870	390.0	53–6	25–8	10.0
Tankers								
Daghestan	1921	Short2	5842	9125	405.0	52–0	26–7	11.0
Laristan	1927	Short2	6401	10,500	420.0	55–0	27–7	10.0
NORTHUMBRIAN SHIPPING CO LTD								
General cargo vessels								
Holystone	1927	Short2	5462	9020	397.4	54–0	25–6	10.0
Newbrough (m)	order	Short2	5255	8980	450–0	56–6	25–6	12.0
Simonburn	1925	Short2	5213	8870	390.0	53–6	25–7	10.0

CONNELL & GRACE LTD, 17–29 Side Proctor House, Newcastle upon Tyne 1

Funnel: Black, with white C&G on green band bordered by narrow white bands
Hull: Black, red boot-topping
Services: General tramping
Note: See Quayside Shipping Co Ltd under J Salcmans & K Jansons in Latvia section and Cia de Vapores Ltd in Panama section

QUAYSIDE SHIPPING CO LTD

Akenside	1917	WoodS2	2694	3950	321.1	43–3	19–2	8.0
ex Burnhope 28								
Trident	1917	Sundld	4317	7125	386–6	51–1	23–0	8.5

CONSTANTINE STEAMSHIP LINE LTD, JOSEPH,
York House, Borough Rd, Middlesbrough

Funnel: Red, black top and black band
Hull: Black, pink boot-topping
Services: UK–US; UK–Cuba; general tramping

Briarwood	1930	Nthmb2	4019	6525	377–0	51–0	22–7	10.0
Brookwood (r/t,P12)	1929	GrayWH	5100	8775	408.2	53–6	25–0	10.5
Kingswood (r/t,P12)	1929	Nthmb2	5080	8800	418–7	53–10	25–0	10.0
Kirnwood (P12)	1928	Rhead3	3829	6560	402–6	52–6	21–7	10.0
lengthened 35								
Maplewood (r/t,P12)	1930	Nthmb2	4566	7565	395–6	52–0	23–10	10.5
Wearwood (P12)	1930	Nthmb2	4597	7565	395–5	52–0	23–10	10.5
CONSTANTINE SHIPPING CO LTD								
Balmoralwood (r/t,P12)	1937	Leslie	5834	9200	463–2	56–9	25–9	10.0
Windsorwood (r/t,P12)	1936	Leslie	5395	8550	454–10	55–10	25–1	10.0
Yorkwood (r/t,P12)	1936	Leslie	5401	8540	454–10	55–10	25–1	10.0

Note: Also coastal vessels

CONSTANTS (SOUTH WALES) LTD,
National Provincial Bank Bldgs, Bute St, Cardiff, and 11 Billiter Sq, London EC3

Funnel: Black, red band bordered by two narrow white bands
Hull: Black, red boot-topping
Services: General tramping, mainly to Spain/Mediterranean

Beltinge	1916	WoodS2	1736	2500	269–8	37–9	17–2	8.0
ex Guéthary 31								
Cape Ortegal	1911	LithR	4896	8250	405.0	52–5	24–6	10.0
Garlinge	1918	Finch	2012	3300	293–9	41–9	18–10	8.5
ex Petworth 31								
Hawkinge	1924	Burntd	2475	4400	308–6	44–0	20–3	9.0
ex Pentraeth 31								
Heminge	1919	GrayX	2499	4050	313–6	43–0	19–10	8.5
ex Rudchester 34, ex Leicester 29, ex War Currant 19								
Lottinge	1918	Forth	2468	4350	305.3	42–10	20–1	9.0
ex Orleans 34								
Lyminge	1919	Hill	2500	4050	313–6	43–0	19–10	8.5
ex Neath Abbey 39, ex Baron Herries 34, ex Trevelyan 23, launched as War Quince								
Ottinge	bldg	GrayWH	2870	4700	338–5	46–6	20–6	10.0
Ruckinge	1939	GrayWH	2869	4700	338–4	46–6	20–6	10.0
Sellinge	1916	Prstm2	2327	3350	301–0	40–9	18–7	9.5
ex Ensign 37, ex Wrotham 35, ex Ensign 33, ex Uskmouth 27								
Wrotham	1927	ThmpsJ	1884	2890	280–1	38–0	18–5	9.5
ex Firtree 35, ex Ramshope 29								

Note: Also vessels under 1500grt

CORY & SONS LTD, JOHN, Mount Stuart House, Mount Stuart Sq, Cardiff

Funnel: Black
Hull: Black, red boot-topping
Services: General tramping

BRITISH STEAM SHIPPING CO LTD								
Coryton	1928	GrayWH	4553	8500	412–8	53–0	24–5	10.0
Ramillies	1927	GrayWH	4553	8500	412–8	53–0	24–5	10.0
Ruperra	1925	GrayWH	4548	8500	409–11	53–0	24–5	10.0

COUNTIES SHIP MANAGEMENT CO LTD,
Holland House, 1–4 Bury St, London EC3

Funnel: Yellow with red C inside red ring, black top
Hull: Black
Services: General tramping, and grain trade from North America, R Plate and Black Sea

BRIGHT NAVIGATION CO LTD, 37–45 Creechurch Lane, London EC3								
Muneric	1919	Workmn	5229	8130	412–4	52–5	25–3	10.5
launched as War Spider								
BROCKLEY HILL STEAMSHIP CO LTD								
Brockley Hill	1919	Caird	5287	8150	412–4	52–4	25–3	10.0
ex Penteli 39, ex David Dawson 37, ex Azul 36, ex Burgondier 26, launched as War Burman								
BURY HILL STEAMSHIP CO LTD								
Michael E	order	Hamtn4	7628	9900	434–6	60–5	28–2	10.5
DORSET STEAMSHIP CO LTD								
Lulworth Hill	bldg	Hamtn4	7628	9900	434–6	60–5	28–2	11.0
Pentridge Hill*	1917	AyrDk	5119	8000	400.7	53–5	24–1	10.5
ex African Prince 36, ex Glennevis 22								
Pentridge Hill	order	Bartm2	7579	11,137	434–2	60–5	28–2	11.0
DOVER HILL STEAMSHIP CO LTD								
Dover Hill	1918	Nthmbl	5815	9150	400.1	53–0	26–2	10.0
ex Clan Macvicar 36, launched as Maenwen								

Note: * Sold Board of Trade (*qv*) 1939, renamed *Botlea*
Note: This company was associated with Rethymnis & Kulukundis Ltd (*qv* in Egypt and Greece sections)

ERNELS SHIPPING CO LTD								
Argos Hill	1921	Halifx	7178	10,550	430.0	56–2	29–2	12.0
ex Canadian Constructor 39								
LEITH HILL SHIPPING CO LTD								
Marietta E	1940	Hamtn4	7628	9900	434–6	60–4	28–2	11.0
MILL HILL STEAMSHIP CO LTD								
Mill Hill	1930	Doxfrd	4318	7775	384–7	52–11	23–9	10.0
ex Peebles 36, ex Gracechurch 33								
PUTNEY HILL STEAMSHIP CO LTD								
Kingston Hill	order	Hamtn4	7628	9900	434–2	60–5	28–2	11.0
Primrose Hill	order	Hamtn4	7628	9900	434–6	60–5	28–2	10.5
Putney Hill (m)	bldg	Doxfrd	5216	9490	442–11	56–6	25–11	12.0
Richmond Hill	order	Bartm2	7579	11,137	434–2	60–6	28–2	11.0
SURREY STEAMSHIP CO LTD								
Box Hill	1920	Leslie	5677	9456	450.0	55–0	25–7	10.5
ex Glentworth 34								
TOWER STEAMSHIP CO LTD								
Tower Field	1935	Burntd	4241	7995	372.0	52–5	24–5	10.0
ex Roxburgh 37								
Tower Grange (m)	bldg	Doxfrd	5226	9490	442–11	56–6	25–11	12.0

Services: General tramping

CRAVOS & CO, CHARLES, 146 Bute St, Cardiff

AMPLEFORTH STEAMSHIP CO LTD								
Ampleforth	1929	Craig2	4576	8555	415–0	53–6	24–9	10.5
ex Glofield 32								

Funnel: Black, two blue bands
Hull: Black, red boot-topping
Services: General tramping

CRAWFORD & CO LTD, ANDREW, 166 Buchanan St, Glasgow C1

CRAWFORD SHIPPING CO LTD								
Gogovale	1927	Lithgw	4586	8000	397–7	52–0	23–11	10.0
Gretavale	1928	Lithgw	4586	8000	397–7	52–0	23–11	10.0
GRYFEVALE STEAMSHIP CO LTD								
Gryfevale (r/t)	1929	Lithgw	4434	8350	398–0	53–6	24–1	10.5

Funnel: Black with green band between two narrow white bands
Hull: Black, red boot-topping
Services: General tramping

CREST SHIPPING CO LTD, Stone House, Bishopsgate, London EC2

Aircrest	bldg	Lithgw	5237	9200	447–8	56–2	25–9	11.0
Bancrest	1925	Ropnr3	4450	8341	399.0	53–2	24–8	11.0
ex Ambassador 39								
Belcrest	1925	Nthmb1	4517	8350	399.7	52–11	24–8	9.5
ex Treherbert 39, ex Gardépée 27								
Marcrest	1911	ArmWh1	4224	7280	378.1	52–4	22–8	8.5
ex Marija Racic 39, ex Atlantica 22								
Milcrest	1919	SHWR	5283	8290	412–6	52–5	25–3	10.0
ex Lika 39, ex Kobac 38, ex Cefn-y-Bryn 38, ex Dacre Castle 37								
Suncrest	bldg	Burntd	5117	9660	436–0	58–0	26–9	10.5

Funnel: Black with white band bearing red CS monogram
Hull: Black, white top strakes, red boot-topping
Services: General tramping

CROSBY, SON & CO LTD, Shipping Chambers, George St, West Hartlepool

NORTH OF ENGLAND STEAMSHIP CO LTD								
Hartbridge	1927	GrayWH	5080	9093	390.1	55–0	25–9	9.0
Ousebridge	1929	FurnH	5601	10,428	406.1	56–1	26–6	10.0

Funnel: Red with three narrow black rings, black top; *Britannic, Georgic, Laurentic* – yellow, black top
Hull: Black, red boot-topping with white dividing line (cruising ships (*Carinthia, Lancastria, Laurentic*) white hull, red boot-topping)
Services: Passenger and mail – Southampton–Cherbourg–New York (express); (Southampton–Havre–Cobh/Galway–New York–Boston; (Liverpool Glasgow–

CUNARD WHITE STAR LTD,
Cunard Bldg, Pier Head, Liverpool 3, and Cunard House, Leadenhall St, London EC3

Passenger and passenger/general cargo vessels

Alaunia (st2,P292/cab,880/3)								
	1925	BrownJ	14,030	12,060	538–6	65–2	32–2	15.0
Andania (st2,P239/cab,990/3)								
	1922	Leslie	13,950	11,776	538–1	65–4	31–7	15.0
Antonia (st2,P240/cab,838/3)								
	1921	VickB2	13,867	12,047	539–5	65–4	31–7	15.0
Aquitania (st4,P514/cab,410/t,865/3)								
	1914	BrownJ	44,786	14,200	901–6	97–0	36–2	24.0
Ascania (st2,P215/cab,913/3)								
	1925	ArmWh1	14,013	11,487	538–6	65–4	31–7	15.5

Cunard White Star: Completed by Armstrong, Whitworth, at Newcastle in May 1925, Ascania *was in 1939 operating on her owner's service between London and New York via Halifax. She is pictured here on the River Thames on August 6 1939. On September 4 she was requisitioned by the Admiralty to become the armed merchant cruiser HMS* Ascania. *In 1942 she was converted Southampton to a landing ship infantry (LSI), and saw service at the invasion of Sicily in July 1943 and then at Anzio. In 1944 she was taken up for trooping duty. She was returned to her owner in 1947 and re-entered commercial service in December with austerity accommodation on the Liverpool–Halifax service.* Ascania *was refitted in 1949, and in April 1950 resumed service between Liverpool, Quebec and Montreal. Before final withdrawal from service she made a trooping voyage to Cyprus in November 1956. In 1957 she was broken up at Newport by John Cashmore (RW Jordan collection)*

(Centre)
Cunard White Star: Britannic *was one of the last two vessels ordered for the former White Star Line. She was completed in 1930 by Harland & Wolff, Belfast. In May 1934 she was taken over by Cunard White Star, and together with* Georgic *these were the last two White Star ships in service. On August 29 1939 she was requisitioned for trooping service, originally converted to carry 3000 troops, but later increased to 5000. In March 1947* Britannic *was released from trooping and returned to Cunard-White Star, and refitted at Liverpool. In 1961 she was broken up at Inverkeithing (RW Jordan)*

(Lower)
Cunard White Star: Franconia *was completed by John Brown, Clydebank, in June 1923, and was put into service between Liverpool and New York and also undertook regular winter cruises. In 1933 she was given a white hull for a world cruise which started in New York. In September 1939* Franconia *was refitted at Liverpool for trooping service, and was able to carry 1300 troops. She had a very active wartime career, Norway, Malta, Suez, Madagascar, France, and Sicily being among her destinations. She was the headqaurters ship for the 1944 Yalta Conference. She undertook troop repatriation voyages during 1946–48, and in total carried 149,239 personnel and voyaged 319,284 miles on war service. After a refit she returned to commercial service in 1949 with accommodation for 250 first class and 600 tourist class passengers. After a season of New York cruising* Franconia *was withdrawn from service in 1956, and the following year was broken up at Inverkeithing (RW Jordan collection)*

Cunard White Star: The liner Queen Mary *is pictured here in Cowes Roads before making her first visit to Southampton in May 1936. She was immediately withdrawn from commercial service upon the outbreak of war, and for the duration saw service as a troopship, carrying a total 810,730 military personnel. She was returned to her owners in October 1946 and after an extensive refit re-entered commercial service at the end of July 1947. She was sold by Cunard in 1967 to become a tourist attraction at Long Beach, California, where she remains (EH Cole)*

J & J Denholm: The cargo steamer Grangepark *was completed in November 1919 by Greenock Dockyard, having been launched two months earlier as* War Canna, *a standard 'A' type. On November 20 1942, when in convoy KRS3 on voyage from Barry and the River Clyde to Oran with about 2000 tons of government stores, she was torpedoed and sunk by* U262 *(J & J Denholm Ltd)*

J & J Denholm: The steamer Holmpark, *completed by Lithgows, Port Glasgow, in 1927, was torpedoed and sunk in October 1942 when on voyage from Lourenço Marques and Cape Town for Trinidad and Philadelphia in ballast. A lifeboat with survivors arrived St Lucia after 16 days and travelling 900 miles (J & J Denholm Ltd)*

J & J Denholm: The steamer Mountpark, *completed by C Connell in 1938, was first in contact with the enemy when she was bombed by German aircraft on September 30 1940 in 57 24N 01 35W. She was damaged, but this was soon repaired.* Mountpark *was bombed by German aircraft and sunk on April 26 1941 when on voyage from Bahia Blanca to Manchester with 7720 tons of grain (J & J Denholm Ltd)*

Aurania (st2,P290/cab,890/3)	1924	SHWR	13,984	11,960	540–0	65–4	31–7	15.0
Ausonia (st2,P250/cab,846/3)	1921	ArmWh1	13,912	12,060	538–1	65–4	31–7	15.0
Britannic (m2,P504/cab,551/t,498/3)	1930	H&W,B	26,943	17,010	711–9	82–5	32–10	18.0
Carinthia (st2,P–)	1925	VickB2	20,277	12,936	624–0	73–10	32–8	16.5
laid down as Servia								
Franconia (st2,P261/cab,356/t,296/3)	1923	BrownJ	20,175	12,760	623–9	73–9	32–7	16.5
Georgic (m2,P479/cab,557/t,554/3)	1932	H&W,B	27,759	16,834	711–10	82–5	35–0	18.0
Laconia (st2,P347/1,350/2,1500/3)	1922	SHWR	19,695	13,180	623–5	73–9	32–8	16.5
Lancastria (st2,P580/cab)	1922	Beardm	16,243	11,826	578–5	70–5	31–4	16.5
ex Tyrrhenia 24								
Laurentic (r/t3,P–)	1927	H&W,B	18,724	11,710	603–0	75–5	29–3	16.5
Mauretania (st2,P486/1,392/cab,502/t)	1939	Cammel	35,677	10,275	771–10	89–5	32–11	22.0
Queen Elizabeth (st4,P823/1,662/cab,798/3)	bldg	BrownJ	83,673	15,610	1031–0	118–7	39–0	29.5
Queen Mary (st4,P776/cab,784/t,579/3)	1936	BrownJ	81,235	15,807	1019–6	118–7	38–10	28.5
Samaria (st2,P330/cab,313/t,533/3)	1921	Cammel	19,597	13,144	624–0	73–8	32–8	16.5
Scythia (st2,P330/cab,313/t,533/3)	1920	VickB2	19,761	13,210	624–0	73–10	32–8	16.5
General cargo vessels								
Bactria	1928	ThmpsJ	2402	3550	304–2	45–0	19–8	9.0
Bantria	1928	ThmpsJ	2402	3559	304–2	45–0	19–8	9.0
Bosnia	1928	ThmpsJ	2407	3550	304–2	45–0	19–8	9.0
Bothnia	1928	ThmpsJ	2407	3550	304–2	45–0	19–8	9.0

Belfast–New York); Southampton, London, Liverpool, Glasgow, Belfast, Havre–Quebec–Montreal (summer)/Halifax–St John NB (winter); New York–Nassau; cruising; general cargo – Liverpool –Mediterranean ports

Note: Cunard White Star Ltd was formed through the 1934 merger of Cunard Steam Ship Co Ltd and White Star Line Ltd; Cunard Steam Ship Co Ltd purchased Port Line Ltd (*qv*) in 1916 and T & J Brocklebank Ltd (*qv*) was fully absorbed into the Cunard Group in 1919

CURRIE & CO LTD, JAMES, 16 Bernard St, Leith, Edinburgh 6

THE LEITH, HULL & HAMBURG STEAM PACKET CO LTD

Shetland	1921	Ramage	1846	2810	260.2	40–2	20–0	10.0
ex Kara 27								

Funnel: Black with white band
Hull: Black, red boot-topping
Services: London–Mediterranean ports
Note: Also *Gothland* (built 1932/1286gt), *Kirkland* (34/1361), *Lapland* (36/1330), *Merkland* (34/1363), *Rutland* (35/1437) and *Zealand* (36/1433) engaged in Mediterranean trade, and vessels on services from UK ports to NW Europe and the Baltic Sea

DALGLIESH LTD, R S, Watergate Bldgs, 61 Sandhill, Newcastle upon Tyne 1

DALGLIESH STEAM SHIPPING CO LTD

Backworth*	1919	DunlpB	2481	3950	313–6	42–11	19–10	8.5
launched as War Orange								
Coatsworth**	1919	DunlpB	2555	3400	313–6	42–11	19–10	8.5
Oakworth (m)	1925	McMlln	4968	7910	404–0	53–2	24–2	10.5
Warkworth	1924	Blythw	4941	8070	401.4	53–2	24–2	11.0
Wentworth	1919	RDuck2	5212	8207	413–0	52–5	25–4	11.0
launched as War Phlox								

WATERGATE STEAM SHIPPING CO LTD

Ashworth	1920	Pgill2	5227	8432	412–8	52–4	25–4	10.0
launched as War Spirea								

Funnel: Blue with red D, black top
Hull: Black with white band, red boot-topping
Services: General tramping; and Port Churchill (Hudson Bay) –UK (summer)
Note: * Sold Branch Steam Ship Co Ltd (Reginald Jones & Co Ltd), 1939, renamed *Ogmore Castle*; ** sold Yugoslavia 1939, renamed *Dinaric*
Note: Also coastal vessels

DALHOUSIE STEAM & MOTOR SHIP CO LTD, 26–28 Mark Lane, London EC3

Dalhousie (m)	order	Burntd	7072		431–6	56–6	27–0	11.0

Funnel: Intended – black with red Maltese cross between two narrow red bands on broad white band
Hull: Intended – black, red boot-topping
Services: Intended – general tramping

Funnel: Red with blue D on white diamond inside white ring, black top
Hull: Black, red boot-topping
Services: General tramping

DAWSON LTD, FRANK S, Midland Bank Chambers, Bute St, Cardiff

CORONATION STEAMSHIP CO LTD

Thomas Walton	1917	GrayX	4460	8110	380.3	52–0	24–0	10.0
ex Portgwarra 32, ex Anglesea 22								

JUBILEE STEAM NAVIGATION CO LTD

Alma Dawson	1917	TyneIr	3985	6712	372–6	51–1	22–3	9.5
ex Whinfield 36								

Services: General tramping, particularly coal to South America

DAWSON, F L, Dunford House, Dean St, Newcastle upon Tyne 1

BEVERLEY STEAMSHIP CO LTD

Frances Dawson	1923	Rhead3	3724	6350	347.0	49–1	22–3	9.0
ex Steelville 37								
Leo Dawson	1918	Blyth	4330	7400	363.2	51–0	23–7	9.0
ex Roseden 36								

Funnel: Black with broad white band bearing oblique blue bands
Hull: Black, red boot-topping
Services: General tramping

Note: * Sold Switzerland 1939, renamed *St Cergue*

DENE SHIPPING CO LTD, 25 St Mary Axe, London EC3

Cressdene	1936	GrayWH	4270	7555	396–0	53–2	23–11	10.0
Elmdene	1939	GrayWH	4853	8960	431–6	56–1	25–0	10.5
Eskdene	1934	Bartm2	3829		384–1	51–6	22–2	10.0
Felldene*	1937	GrayWH	4260	7590	395–6	53–2	23–10	10.0
Glendene	1929	GraySd	4412	7980	387.5	52–6	23–10	10.0
Oakdene	1936	GrayWH	4255	7600	396–0	53–2	23–10	10.0
Tordene	1936	GrayWH	4271	7555	396–0	53–2	23–10	10.0

Funnel: Red, black top
Hull: Black, red boot-topping
Services: General tramping

DENHOLM LTD, J & J, 37 Renfield St, Glasgow C2

DENHOLM LINE OF STEAMERS LTD

Broompark	1939	Lithgw	5136	9200	447–6	56–2	24–9	10.5
Clunepark	1928	Lithgw	3491	5900	362–7	49–0	21–8	10.0
Denpark	1928	Lithgw	3491	5900	362–7	49–0	21–8	10.0
Earlspark	1929	Scott2	5250	8634	407.3	53–4	25–0	11.0
Eldonpark	1928	Scott2	5184	8640	407.3	53–4	25–1	11.0
Glenpark	1939	Lithgw	5136	9200	447–6	56–2	24–9	10.5
Grangepark	1919	GrkDY	5132	8250	412–8	52–4	25–3	10.5
launched as War Canna								
Holmpark	1927	Lithgw	5780	9650	423.5	56–0	25–5	10.0
Lylepark	1929	Scott2	5186	8634	407.3	53–4	25–0	11.0
Mountpark	1938	Conn2	4648	8635	419–6	54–9	25–0	11.0
Wellpark	1938	Conn2	4649	8640	419–5	54–9	25–0	11.0

Funnel: Yellow, black top
Hull: Black, red boot-topping
Services: General tramping

DODD, THOMSON & CO LTD, 5 St Helen's Place, London EC3

Manager for

KING LINE LTD

King Alfred	1919	Doxfrd	5275	8381	412–6	52–5	25–4	11.0
launched as War Azalea								
King Arthur (m)	1928	H&W,B	5224	8330	417–2	54–10	23–9	10.0
King Edgar (m)	1927	H&W,B	4536	8211	417–2	54–10	23–6	10.0
King Edward	1919	Workmn	5224	8210	412–6	52–4	25–4	11.0
ex Gorala 24, launched as War Terrier								
King Edwin (m)	1927	H&W,B	4536	8211	417–2	54–10	23–7	10.0
King Egbert (m)	1928	H&W,B	4535	8211	417–2	54–10	23–6	10.0
King Frederick	1920	HK&Wh	5106	8271	412–6	52–4	25–4	11.0
ex Trialos 23, launched as War Sceptre								
King Gruffyd	1919	HK&Wh	5072	8266	412–6	52–4	25–3	11.0
ex Ambatielos 23, launched as War Trooper								
King Idwal	1920	Taikoo	5115	8155	412–8	52–4	25–3	11.0
ex Keramies 23, launched as War Coronet								
King John (m)	1928	H&W,B	5228	8330	417–2	54–10	23–9	10.0
King Lud (m)	1928	H&W,B	5224	8330	417–2	54–8	23–9	10.0
King Neptune (m)	1928	H&W,B	5224	8330	417–3	54–10	23–9	10.0
King Stephen (m)	1928	H&W,B	5274	8189	417–2	54–10	23–9	10.0
King William (m)	1928	H&W,B	5274	8189	417–2	54–10	23–9	10.0

SCOTTISH STEAMSHIP CO LTD

King James (m)	1925	Hendn2	5122	9401	400.3	59–0	25–3	10.0
launched as River Ottawa								

Donaldson Bros: With the unwelcome distinction of being the first British merchant ship sunk in the Second World War, the Donaldson liner Athenia *was torpedoed by* U30 *on September 3 1939. She sank the following day with the loss of 93 passengers and 19 crew, out of 1418 persons on board.* Athenia *and her sistership* Letitia *were built for the service between Glasgow and Liverpool to Quebec and Montreal, with winter sailings to Halifax, and originally accommodated 400 cabin class and 1000 third class passengers. The accommodation on both liners was remodelled in 1927, and* Athenia *then carried 310 cabin class and 928 third.* Letitia *survived the war after service as an armed merchant cruiser, hospital ship and troopship, in 1946 became the Australian emigrant carrier* Empire Brent, *and from 1951 to 1959 carried emigrants to New Zealand under the name* Captain Cook *(Alex Duncan)*

Donaldson Bros: Dorelian *was completed by D & W Henderson at Glasgow in May 1923 for Frederick Leyland & Co. This vessel and four similar ships were running on the Dominion-Leyland joint service from Bristol to Canada. This service and the vessels on it were taken over by Donaldson and T & J Harrison in 1934.* Dorelian *was transferred then to Harrison ownership. In 1936 the Harrison interest in the service was bought by Donaldson and* Dorelian *was transferred to them. She survived the war and was broken up at Dalmuir in 1954*
(RW Jordan collection)

Eagle Oil & Shipping: San Adolfo *was one of several motor tankers completed for this owner in the mid to late 1930s. Built by Furness Shipbuilding at Haverton Hill, she was completed in May 1935, and unlike many of her sisterships came through the war apparently unscathed. She was requisitioned by the Admiralty on November 5 1939 as a Fleet oiler, and was involved as an oiler in convoys to Russia, in the invasion of North Africa and in the Pacific war. After return to her owners in 1945,* San Adolfo *saw a few more years service and was broken up at Grays, Essex, during 1957–58 (Alex Duncan)*

King Malcolm (m)	1925	Hendn2	5120	9401	400.3	59–0	25–3	10.0
laid down as River St Lawrence								
King Robert	1920	FurnH	5886	9171	413–0	53–0	26–2	11.0
ex Città di Messina 26								

Funnel: Black, white band
Hull: Black, red boot-topping with or without white dividing line
Services: Glasgow–Halifax NS –St John NB (winter); Glasgow–Quebec–Montreal (summer); Donaldson South America – Glasgow–Liverpool–Montevideo–Buenos Aires; Anglo-Newfoundland – Botwood–London (newsprint)

DONALDSON BROS & BLACK LTD, 14 St Vincent Place, Glasgow C1, Cunard Bldg, Pier Head, Liverpool 3, and 31–34 Fenchurch St, London EC3

DONALDSON ATLANTIC LINE LTD

Passenger/general cargo vessels

Athenia (st2,P314/cab,310/t,928/3)								
	1923	Fairfd	13,581	9940	538–2	66–5	27–8	15.5
Letitia (st2,P314/cab,310/t,682/3)								
	1925	Fairfd	13,595	9880	538–2	66–5	27–8	15.5

DONALDSON LINE LTD

General cargo vessels

Dakotian (P4)	1922	Hendn2	6426	9595	413–5	52–6	29–2	12.0
Delilian (P4)	1923	Hendn2	6423	9430	412–0	52–6	29–2	12.0
Dorelian (P4)	1923	Hendn2	6431	9480	412–0	52–5	29–3	12.0
Gracia (st,P–)	1921	Scott2	5642	8120	415.5	54–2	27–2	12.0
Gregalia (P–)	1929	Lithgw	5802	9390	439–0	56–0	27–5	12.0
Modavia (m)	1927	VickB2	4858	7250	399–6	53–9	26–8	11.5
Moveria (m,P–)	1927	VickB2	4867	7445	398–4	51–8	27–4	11.5
Norwegian (P12)	1921	Caledn	6366	9493	400.2	52–5	29–1	12.0
Parthenia	1917	LithR	4872	7400	416–0	51–11	24–3	12.0
ex Kirkholm 18								
Salacia (m)	1937	H&WGw	5495	8332	447–11	57–2	27–1	14.0
Sulairia (P–)	1929	Lithgw	5802	9390	439–0	56–0	27–5	12.0

DONALDSON SOUTH AMERICAN LINE LTD

Coracero (r/t)	1923	Lithgw	7252	8925	438–8	56–0	28–6	12.0
Cordillera (st)	1920	Short2	6865	7850	434–11	54–10	27–8	13.0
Corinaldo (st)	1921	Scott2	7131	8505	414.5	55–8	28–9	13.0
Corrientes (st)	1920	Short2	6863	7850	434–11	54–10	27–7	13.0
Cortona (st)	1921	VickB2	7093	8505	414.4	55–9	28–9	13.0

Manager for

ANGLO-NEWFOUNDLAND STEAMSHIP CO LTD, Grand Falls, Newfoundland, Canada

Esmond	1930	Conn2	4976	8750	421–1	53–5	24–10	12.5
ex Traprain Law 33								
Geraldine Mary	1924	VickB2	7244	9056	438–5	56–1	27–1	12.0
Rothermere	1938	Conn2	5356	8840	434–0	56–6	25–8	12.0

DOMINION SHIPPING CO LTD, c/o Dominion Coal Co Ltd, Canada Cement Bldg, Phillips Sq, Montreal, Canada

Lord Strathcona	1915	Doxfrd	7335	11,305	455.0	58–0	25–6	11.5

ROSE CASTLE STEAMSHIP CO LTD, Sydney, Nova Scotia, Canada

Rose Castle	1915	Short2	7803	11,220	455.0	58–0	25–6	11.5

Funnel: Black
Services: General tramping

DOUGLAS & RAMSEY, 45 West Nile St, Glasgow C1

FARCO SHIPPING CO LTD

Darcoila	1928	Lithgw	4084	7000	370.0	50–8	22–7	9.5

TROODOS SHIPPING CO LTD, Famagusta, Cyprus (British flag)

Evagoras	1929	Hamtn3	5197	8850	418–0	52–5	24–6	10.0
ex Darshiel 32								

Funnel: White, black top
Hull: Black, red boot-topping
Services: General tramping

DOVER NAVIGATION CO LTD, 196 London House, Crutched Friars, London EC3

Sea Glory	1919	SHWRSd	1966	3380	300–9	42–6	20–4	10.0
launched as War Wear								
Sea Rambler	1930	SHWRSd	2327		294.1	43–1	18–0	9.0
Sea Valour	1930	Austin	1950	3200	276.0	42–2	18–2	10.0
Sea Venture	1930	SHWRSd	2327	294.1	43–1	18–0	9.0	

Funnel: Yellow, black top and red D on white square
Hull: Black with white line, red boot-topping
Services: General tramping
Note: Manager of this company

DRAKE SHIPPING CO LTD, Baltic Exchange Chambers, 24 St Mary Axe, London EC3

Merchant Prince (m)	1939	Doxfrd	5229	9490	442–11	56–6	25–11	11.5

Merchant Royal *ex Goodwood 36*	1928	Rhead3	5008	8532	416–1	55–0	24–3	9.5

was Lykiardopulo & Co Ltd (*qv* under N D Lykiardopulo in Greece section)

DUNLOP & SONS, THOS, 50 Wellington St, Glasgow C2

CADOGAN STEAMSHIP CO LTD								
Queen Anne (m)	1936	Curle	4937	9450	431–6	55–2	25–8	10.0
LOMOND SHIPPING CO LTD								
Dunkeld (m)	1937	Curle	4944	9450	431–10	55–2	25–8	10.0
QUEEN LINE LTD								
Queen Adelaide (m)	1936	Curle	4933	9450	431–6	55–2	25–9	10.0
Queen Maud (m)	1936	Doxfrd	4976	9225	439–2	54–2	25–6	10.0
Queen Victoria (m)	1936	Curle	4937	9450	431–6	55–2	25–8	10.0

Funnel: Black
Hull: Grey, red boot-topping
Services: General tramping

CHARLES G DUNN SHIPPING CO LTD, 19 St James St, Liverpool 2

Charlton Hall	bldg	Laing	5200	9200	453–8	57–1	24–8	11.0
Haughton Hall	1937	Laing	5103	9250	454–2	57–1	24–8	11.0

Funnel: Yellow with black top separated by white diamonds superimposed on red over blue bands
Hull: Black
Services: General tramping

E R MANAGEMENT CO LTD, Empire House, 51 Mount Stuart Sq, Cardiff

BANTHAM STEAMSHIP CO LTD								
Nailsea Court (r/t)	1936	Bartm2	4946	8950	435–0	56–0	25–1	10.0
Nailsea Meadow (r/t)	1937	Bartm2	4962	8930	435–0	56–0	25–1	10.0
HECTOR STEAMSHIP CO LTD								
Alex *ex Nicos 38, ex Ionia 23, ex Constantinos XII 16*	1914	Prstm2	3907	7160	393–8	51–6	22–7	9.0
NAILSEA STEAMSHIP CO LTD								
Nailsea Lass *ex Specialist 36, ex Santille 20*	1917	Rhead2	4289	6690	382–9	47–8	24–0	10.0
Nailsea Manor (r/t)	1938	Bartm2	4926	8970	435–0	56–0	25–1	10.0
Nailsea Moor (r/t)	1937	Bartm2	4926	8970	435–0	56–0	25–1	10.0
Nailsea River *ex Actor 39*	1917	Hendn2	5548	8455	424–6	52–2	26–7	10.0
STRATH STEAMSHIP CO LTD								
Helmspey	1931	ThmpsJ	4764	8410	401.0	56–4	23–10	10.0

Funnel: Yellow with yellow 'Prince of Wales' emblem on pale blue band; blue band separated from black top by narrow yellow band
Hull: Grey
Services: General tramping

EAGLE OIL & SHIPPING CO LTD, 16 Finsbury Circus, London EC2

Tankers								
San Adolfo (m)	1935	FurnH	7365	11,335	464–7	60–4	26–3	12.0
San Alberto (m)	1935	Lithgw	7397	11,054	464–7	60–2	26–3	12.0
San Alvaro (m)	1935	SHWR	7385	11,235	464–7	60–4	26–2	12.0
San Amado (m)	1935	Blythw	7316	11,190	464–7	60–2	26–2	12.0
San Ambrosio (m)	1935	Leslie	7410	11,254	464–7	60–5	26–2	12.0
San Arcadio (m)	1935	H&WGw	7419	11,275	464–7	60–2	26–2	12.0
San Calisto (m)	1937	Lithgw	8010	12,100	478–8	61–3	27–1	12.0
San Casimiro (m)	1936	Blythw	8046	12,067	483–0	59–2	27–7	12.0
San Cipriano (m)	1937	Blythw	7966	12,080	482–6	59–1	27–6	12.0
San Cirilo (m)	1937	Lithgw	8012	12,150	478–8	61–3	27–0	12.0
San Conrado (m)	1936	Blythw	7982	12,061	478–8	61–3	27–1	12.0
San Delfino (m)	1938	FurnH	8072	12,250	479–0	61–2	27–1	12.0
San Demetrio (m)	1938	Blythw	8073	12,132	479–4	61–2	27–0	12.0
San Elisio (m)	1939	Lithgw	8042	12,100	478–7	61–3	27–0	12.0
San Emiliano (m)	1939	H&WGw	8071	12,152	479–5	61–2	27–0	12.0
San Ernesto (m)	1939	FurnH	8072	12,180	479–0	61–2	27–1	12.0
San Fabian (st)	1922	ArmWh1	13,031	19,800	552–0	69–5	32–2	10.0
San Felix (st)	1921	ArmWh1	13,037	19,800	557–0	69–5	32–2	10.0
San Fernando (st)	1919	ArmWh1	13,056	19,800	557–0	69–5	32–3	10.0
San Florentino (st)	1919	SHWR	12,842	19,540	557–0	68–8	32–3	10.0
San Gaspar (st)	1921	Palmer	12,910	19,225	552–6	68–6	32–4	10.0
San Gerardo (st)	1922	Palmer	12,915	19,245	552–6	68–6	32–4	10.0
San Melito	1914	Palmer	12,286	17,840	553–4	66–6	29–1	10.0
San Quirino*	1923	ArmWh1	5810	8869	423–8	52–2	26–5	10.0
San Roberto	1922	ArmWh1	5890	8620	423–6	52–2	26–5	10.0
San Salvador**	1924	ArmWh1	5805	8890	423–9	52–2	26–6	10.0

Funnel: Black with black eagle and O emblem on broad white band between two narrow yellow bands
Hull: Black, red boot-topping
Trade: Oil and petroleum, mainly Gulf of Mexico ports–UK

Note: *, ** Sold Argentina 1939, renamed *Juncal* and *Los Pozos* respectively
Note: Also tankers under 3000gt

San Tiburcio	1921	Standd	5995	8700	428–2	53–5	25–5	10.0
San Ubaldo	1921	Standd	5999	8700	428–2	53–5	25–5	10.0
San Zotico	1919	SHWR	5582	8865	410–6	52–4	26–4	10.0
ex War Kookri 20								

Funnel: Black
Hull: Black with white band, red boot-topping
Services: Melbourne–Hobart–Sydney–Brisbane–Borneo–Manila–China–Hong Kong–Kobe–Yokohama
Note: This company became a member of the P&O Group in 1919 through acquisition by British India SN Co Ltd (*qv*)

EASTERN & AUSTRALIAN STEAM SHIP CO LTD, 122 Leadenhall St, London EC3, and in Adelaide, Melbourne, Sydney, Brisbane, Fremantle

Nankin (s2,P54/1,40/2)	1912	Caird	7131	9190	466–0	52–0	27–6	12.5
Nellore (s2,P54/1,40/2)	1913	Caird	6942	9160	466–0	52–2	27–6	12.5
Tanda (s2,P–)	1914	Steph2	7174	8748	446–0	58–2	27–4	12.0
ex Madras 20, ex Tanda 14								

Funnel: Black with blue M on white disc on red band
Hull: Black, red boot-topping
Services: General tramping

EELES & CO, THOMAS, 2–4 St Mary Axe, London EC3

MINSTER STEAMSHIP CO LTD

Orminster	1914	Bartm2	5712	8750	385.0	52–1	26–3	10.0
ex Clan Keith 37, ex Hilarius 24, ex Clan Keith 19, ex Etonian 18								

Funnel: Yellow
Hull: Black, red boot-topping
Services: Passenger, mail and cargo – Liverpool, London, Hull, Cardiff, NW Europe–W Africa and South-West Africa; New York, Montreal–W Africa and South-West Africa; Liverpool–Montreal–New Orleans–Galveston

ELDER DEMPSTER LINES LTD, Colonial House, Water St, Liverpool

Passenger/general cargo vessels								
Aba (m2,P221/1,70/2,70/3)	1918	Curle	7937	4108	465–5	55–10	24–3	14.0
ex Glenapp 20								
Abosso (m2,P250/1,74/2,32/3)	1935	Cammel	11,330	7820	460.8	65–2	26–0	15.0
Accra (m2,P243/1,70/2)	1926	H&W,B	9337	6498	468–9	62–4	24–6	14.5
Adda (m2,P225/1,74/2,32/3)	1922	H&WGk	7816	6405	435.3	57–4	24–11	13.5
Apapa (m2,P243/1,70/2)	1927	H&W,B	9333	6488	468–9	62–4	24–6	14.5
General cargo vessels								
Alfred Jones (m,P8)	1930	H&WGw	4022	5933	384–6	51–8	22–9	12.5
Bassa	1918	ArmWh1	5267	8120	412–9	52–4	25–3	11.5
ex War Painter 19								
Bereby	1918	Irvin3	5248	8144	412–9	52–4	25–3	11.5
launched as War Raven								
Biafra	1919	H&WGk	5405	7876	412–9	52–4	25–3	11.5
launched as War Dahlia								
Bodnant	1919	BrownJ	5342	7863	412–9	52–4	25–3	11.5
launched as War Crane								
Boma	1920	H&WGw	5408	7820	412–9	52–4	25–3	11.5
Calgary (st,P12/1)	1921	BrownJ	7206	10,752	454–10	59–2	26–10	11.0
Calumet (st,P8/1)	1923	BrownJ	7268	10,627	454–10	59–2	26–10	11.0
Cochrane (st,P8/1)	1923	BrownJ	7203	10,762	455–0	59–2	26–10	11.0
Dagomba (m,P12/1)	1928	McMlln	3845	5861	367–6	49–2	22–8	10.0
Daru (m,P12/1)	1927	McMlln	3854	5861	367–6	49–2	22–8	10.0
ordered as Duala								
David Livingstone (m,P8)	1919	McMlln	4022	5893	384–6	51–8	22–9	12.5
Deido (m,P12/1)	1928	Ardrsn	3894	5893	370–6	49–2	22–7	11.0
Dixcove (m,P12/1)	1927	McMlln	3790	5836	367–6	49–2	22–8	10.0
Dunkwa (m,P12/1)	1927	McMlln	3789	5786	367–6	49–2	22–8	10.0
Edward Blyden (m,P8)	1930	H&WGw	4022	5933	384–6	51–8	22–9	12.5
Egba (P12)	1914	H&WGw	4989	7358	420–0	54–4	23–7	11.0
Egori* (P12)	1914	H&WGw	4998	7358	420–0	54–4	23–7	11.0
Henry Stanley (m,P8)	1929	Ardrsn	4028	5863	382–0	51–8	22–7	12.5
Macgregor Laird (m,P8)	1930	Hendn2	4015	5850	384–6	51–8	24–3	12.5

Mary Kingsley (m,P8)	1930	Ardrsn	4017	5643	384–6	51–8	22–10	12.5
Mary Slessor (m,P8)	1930	McMlln	4016	5893	384–6	51–8	22–9	12.5
Mattawin (m2,P12/1)	1923	H&WGw	6919	5850	420–0	54–2	27–9	11.5
ex Ediba 29								
New Brooklyn (P4)	1920	H&W,B	6546	10,393	429–0	55–10	28–3	11.0
launched as War Romance								
New Brunswick	1919	H&W,B	6529	10,600	428–0	55–10	28–4	11.0
launched as War Liberty								
New Columbia	1920	H&W,B	6574	10,200	428–0	55–10	28–3	11.0
launched as War Pageant								
New Texas (P4)	1919	H&W,B	6568	10,441	429–0	55–10	28–4	10.5
New Toronto (P4)	1919	H&W,B	6568	10,450	429–0	55–10	28–4	10.5
Sangara (m,P12/1)	1939	Scott2	4124	5927	389–0	52–8	22–9	12.5
Sansu (m,P12/1)	1939	Scott2	4174	5927	389–0	52–8	22–9	12.5
Seaforth (m,P12/1)	1939	Caledn	4199	5957	389–0	52–6	22–9	12.5
Sobo (m,P12/1)	1937	Scott2	4124	5987	389–0	52–9	22–9	12.5
Swedru (m,P12/1)	1937	Scott2	4124	5987	389–0	52–9	22–8	12.5
William Wilberforce (m,P8)	1930	Hendn2	4013	5850	384–6	51–8	24–3	12.5

Note: Also small vessels on West African coastal services
Note: * Sold G E Marden (manager Wheelock & Co Ltd) 1939, renamed *Egorlock*

ELDERS & FYFFES LTD, 31–32 Bow St, Covent Garden, London WC2 (?ok)

Funnel: Yellow, black top
Hull: Silver grey, red boot-topping
Services: Jamaica–Barbados–Trinidad–Panama–Colombia–Costa Rica–Honduras–Avonmouth, Liverpool, Swansea, NW Europe; –Honduras–Rotterdam–Bremerhaven

Passenger/fruit carriers								
Ariguani (s2,P99/1)	1926	Steph2	6746	6375	442–0	54–1	26–0	14.5
Bayano (s2,P99/1)	1917	Steph2	6815	6690	441–6	54–2	27–0	14.5
Camito (s2,P99/1)	1915	Steph2	6833	6750	442–0	54–2	27–2	14.5
Carare (s2,P99/1)	1925	Cammel	6878	6185	442–0	55–1	26–0	14.5
Cavina (s2,P99/1)	1924	Steph2	6907	6375	442–0	54–2	26–0	14.5
Fruit carriers								
Aracataca (P12)	1924	Cammel	5378	6270	400.5	51–5	26–9	13.5
Casanare (P12)	1924	Cammel	5376	6270	400.3	51–5	26–9	13.5
Chagres (P12)	1927	Steph2	5406	6350	417–6	51–2	27–3	13.5
Corrales (P12)	1930	Steph2	5363	6366	417–6	51–2	27–3	13.5
Cristales (P12)	1926	Cammel	5389	6253	400.3	51–5	26–9	13.5
Manistee (P12)	1920	Cammel	5360	6390	400.2	51–1	26–10	13.5
Matina (P12)	1929	Cammel	5389	6253	417–6	51–5	26–9	13.5
Mopan (P12)	1929	Cammel	5389	6253	417–6	51–5	26–9	13.5
Nicoya (P12)	1929	Steph2	5364	6475	417–6	51–2	26–9	13.5
Patia (P12)	1922	Cammel	5355	6374	400.0	51–1	26–10	13.5
Samala (P12)	1928	Cammel	5390	6253	417–6	51–4	26–9	13.5
Sulaco (P12)	1926	Cammel	5389	6253	417–6	51–5	26–9	13.5
Tetela (P12)	1926	Cammel	5389	6253	417–6	51–5	27–2	13.5
Tilapa (P12)	1928	Cammel	5392	6253	417–6	51–5	27–2	13.5
Tortuguero (P12)	1921	Steph2	5285	6330	417–0	51–3	26–11	13.5
Tucurinca (P12)	1926	Steph2	5412	6400	401.0	51–2	26–9	13.5

Note: Elders & Fyffes Ltd was a subsidiary of United Fruit Co (*qv* in United States section)

ELLERMAN & BUCKNALL STEAMSHIP CO LTD, 104–106 Leadenhall St, London EC3

Funnel: Buff, black top separated by white band
Hull: Grey, red boot-topping
Services: Australia–UK–NW Europe; Australia–South Africa; Calcutta and other Indian ports–New York–Boston–Philadelphia; London, South Wales–South Africa; London, South Wales–Persian Gulf; New York–Far East; Canada–India–Java–Levant ports; UK, NW Europe–Far East; UK, NW Europe–US Gulf and Pacific ports

General cargo vessels								
City of Christchurch	1915	Teckl	6009	10,010	491–0	62–1	24–5	12.0
ex Lorenzo 29, ex Aschenburg 20								
City of Derby (st)	1921	GraySd	6616	10,777	450–8	57–5	28–10	12.0
ex Karonga 27								
City of Keelung	1919	Earles	5186	8689	412–0	52–1	26–6	11.0
ex Keelung 36, launched as War Walrus								
City of Kimberley (r/te)	1925	GrayWH	6169	10,190	436–6	56–4	27–9	12.0
City of Lincoln (st2,P4)	1938	Cammel	8039	10,761	516–0	62–5	28–6	15.5
City of Mobile	1912	Workmn	6602	11,030	447.3	56–5	27–7	12.0
ex Kentucky 26								
City of Perth	1913	SHWR	6415	10,964	434.6	55–8	28–1	12.0
ex Kandahar 26								

Note: This company was a member of the Ellerman Lines Ltd (*qv*) group. See also under Ellerman Lines Ltdand Ellerman's Wilson Line Ltd

City of Pretoria (st2,P4)								
	1937	Cammel	8049	10,760	516–0	62–5	28–6	15.5
City of Windsor (r/t)								
	1923	GrayWr	7218	10,550	447.5	57–10	28–7	12.0
ex Knaresbro' 28								

ELLERMAN LINES LTD, 21 Moorgate, London EC2

Funnel: Buff, black top separated by white band
Hull: Grey, red boot-topping
Services: City Line – Glasgow, Liverpool–Colombo–Madras–Calcutta–London; Glasgow, Liverpool–Bombay–Karachi (joint service with Hall Line Ltd – *qv* below); summer cruises to Norwegian fjords; Ellerman & Bucknall – as Ellerman & Bucknall Steamship Co Ltd (*qv* above); Hall Line – London, Glasgow, Liverpool–Suez–Mormogao and Malabar coast; Newport, Glasgow, Liverpool–South Africa (joint service with Harrison Line (*qv* T & J Harrison); Newport, Glasgow, Liverpool–Port Said–Red Sea ports–E Africa; Middlesbrough, NW Europe–Rangoon; India–UK–NW Europe; Ellerman & Papayanni Lines Ltd – Liverpool, Swansea–Genoa–Leghorn–Naples –Palermo–Messina–Catania–Dubrovnik–Bari–Ancona–Trieste–Fiume–Venice; Liverpool, Swansea–Gibraltar–Malta–Patras–Piræus–Volo–Salonica–Smyrna–Constantinople–Bourgas–Varna–Constanta; Liverpool, Swansea–Lisbon–Oporto; Westcott & Laurance Line Ltd – Leith, Tyne, Antwerp, London–Gibraltar–Malta–Alexandria; Leith, Tyne, Antwerp, London–Piræus–Salonica–Smyrna–Constantinople–Bourgas–Varna–Constanta–Sulina–Galatz–Braila; Ellerman Lines Ltd also ran joint services with Clan Line Steamers Ltd (*qv*)

Managed by
THE CITY LINE LTD, 75 Bothwell St, Glasgow C2

Passenger/general cargo vessels

City of Benares (st,P219/oc)								
	1936	Curle	11,081	9756	509–0	62–9	28–6	16.0
City of Canterbury (r/te,P130/1,48/2)								
	1922	SHWR	8331	10,630	467–0	56–5	28–7	13.5
City of Exeter (s2,P194/oc)								
	1914	Workmn	9654	11,476	502–0	58–11	29–0	13.5
City of Hongkong (r/te,P104/1)								
	1924	Earles	9606	12,000	490–0	61–6	29–1	12.5
ordered as Colorado								
City of London (P194/oc)								
	1907	Workmn	8956	10,840	506–0	57–10	28–4	14.0
City of Marseilles (s2,P)								
	1913	Palmer	8317	10,765	483–4	57–0	28–1	13.0
City of Nagpur (P350)								
	1922	Workmn	10,146	11,010	490–6	59–4	30–7	14.0
City of Paris (st,P199/1)								
	1922	SHWR	10,902	13,078	504–0	59–4	32–7	14.5
City of Simla (st2,P)								
	1921	Gray18	10,138	10,697	497–0	58–2	28–7	13.5
City of Venice (r/te,P133/1,32/2)								
	1924	Workmn	8762	10,740	473–4	58–1	28–4	13.5

General cargo vessels

City of Bagdad (r/t)								
	1919	Teckl	7506	11,440	488–11	58–2	27–4	13.0
ex Geierfels 21								
City of Birmingham								
	1917	GrayX	5309	9160	406–6	54–2	27–3	12.0
City of Calcutta (st2,P4)								
	bldg	Cammel	8063	10,622	515–8	62–5	28–6	15.5
City of Delhi (r/t)	1925	GrayWr	7443	11,680	450.5	58–8	29–1	12.5
City of Edinburgh (st2,P4)								
	1938	Cammel	8036	10,533	515–10	62–5	28–6	15.5
City of Karachi (st)	1937	Curle	7139	10,280	464.3	59–2	27–6	13.5
City of Mandalay (r/te)								
	1925	SHWR	7028	11,430	443.2	57–11	28–3	12.0
City of Oran (r/te)	1915	GrayX	7323	12,163	465.5	58–1	28–4	12.5

Managed by
ELLERMAN & BUCKNALL STEAMSHIP CO LTD (*qv*)

General cargo vessels

City of Canberra (r/te,P–)								
	1927	GrayWH	7485	10,437	473–3	57–10	28–4	13.0
City of Dieppe (r/t,P2)								
	1929	GrayWH	7958	10,705	520–3	58–3	28–11	15.0
lengthened 34								
City of Hereford	1927	Curle	5101	8201	385.4	51–8	26–4	12.0

Managed by **HALL LINE LTD**, Tower Bldg, Water St, Liverpool

Passenger/general cargo vessels

City of Baroda* (P113/1)								
	1918	Curle	7129	10,389	433.4	57–2	27–2	12.0
City of Cairo (P133/1,43/2)								
	1915	Earles	8034	10,407	465–2	55–9	28–1	12.5

General cargo vessels

City of Adelaide (st)								
	1920	GrayWr	6589	10,747	450–9	57–5	28–0	11.5
City of Agra (st,P4)								
	1936	Denny2	6361	9500	461–0	56–2	28–0	13.5
City of Athens (r/t)								
	1923	GraySd	6558	10,631	450–9	57–5	28–1	11.5
City of Auckland	1914	Weser	8336	12,169	500–2	62–2	27–8	11.5
ex Weissenfels 21								

Ellerman Lines: The passenger/general cargo liner City of Marseilles *was completed in January 1913. After First World War service, during which she was shelled by an enemy submarine, but escaped, she undertook regular seasonal trooping to India, reverting to her regular service outside the trooping season. This was discontinued in 1930, however, when she was replaced by Bibby's* Lancashire. *She survived the Second World War, although she struck a mine in the Tay estuary on January 6 1940, and on January 22 1942 stranded near Batticaloa, Ceylon, but safely refloated.* City of Marseilles *was broken up in 1947 (EH Cole)*

Ellerman Lines: City of Venice, *completed in April 1924, was torpedoed by* U375 *on July 4 1943. She caught fire and eventually sank. At the time of the attack* City of Venice *was in the UK–Mediterranean convoy KMS18B, carrying troops of the First Canadian Division for Operation 'Husky', the invasion of Sicily (R Sherlock)*

Ellerman Lines: A confiscated German vessel of the First World War, City of Bagdad *was completed in 1919 as* Geierfels *for the Hansa company. She was taken over by the Allies and became* City of Bagdad *in 1921. She was intercepted and shelled by the German auxiliary cruiser* Atlantis *on July 11 1940. Two crew members were killed in the attack and 81 became prisoners of war.* City of Bagdad *was later sunk by explosive charges (R Sherlock)*

City of Barcelona (r/te)	1930	Curle	5787	9292	444–5	58–2	26–4	12.0
City of Bath	1926	GrayWH	5079	8333	408–0	52–2	26–7	11.5
City of Bedford (r/t,P–)	1924	GraySd	6402	10,007	447–6	55–1	27–9	11.5
City of Bombay (st)	1937	Curle	7410	10,280	464.3	59–2	27–6	13.5
City of Brisbane (st)	1920	SHWR	8006	11,059	463.6	58–10	28–0	12.0
City of Canton (st)	1916	SHWR	6692	11,144	466–5	56–11	27–9	12.0
City of Cape Town (st2,P4)	1937	Cammel	8046	10,760	515–6	62–5	28–6	15.5
City of Cardiff	1918	Craig2	5661	9458	419–6	54–5	27–4	11.0
ex Langton Hall 26								
City of Christiania	1921	Earles	4940	8414	396–0	53–0	27–0	11.0
City of Corinth	1918	GrayX	5318	9151	407–0	54–2	27–3	11.5
City of Dundee (st)	1921	Palmer	5273	8664	423–4	52–1	26–8	10.5
City of Dunkirk	1912	Curle	5681	9850	431–6	54–2	26–8	10.5
City of Durban (st)	1921	Earles	5850	8380	394–8	52–1	26–7	11.5
City of Eastbourne (r/te)	1923	GrayWH	5563	9361	421–11	54–2	27–1	11.5
City of Evansville (r/t)	1922	GrayWH	6528	10,384	450–10	57–4	28–1	11.5
City of Florence	1918	GrayX	6862	11,279	467–6	56–2	28–2	11.0
City of Glasgow (st)	1920	Gray18	5321	8616	406–6	54–2	27–3	11.0
City of Guildford	1919	Gray18	5157	8659	414–0	52–4	26–5	11.0
ex Romeo 28, launched as War Midge								
City of Hankow (r/t)	1915	GrayX	7360	11,977	465–5	58–2	28–7	12.5
City of Johannesburg (st)	1920	Curle	5669	9667	417.2	54–10	27–0	12.0
ex Melford Hall 26								
City of Khios (r/t)	1925	Curle	5574	9671	417–6	55–0	27–4	11.0
ex Rydal Hall 25								
City of Kobe	1924	Ramage	4373	7215	367.1	49–9	25–3	11.5
ex Malvernian 27								
City of Leicester (P6)	1926	GrayWH	3351	6033	345.0	47–6	24–0	11.0
City of Lille (m,P4)	1928	Curle	6588	10,394	465–8	57–11	28–7	13.5
City of Lyons (st)	1926	SHWR	7063	11,425	473–6	58–1	28–2	12.5
City of Manchester (st2,P–)	1935	Cammel	8917	11,100	498.5	64–4	28–11	15.0
City of Manila (r/t)	1916	GrayX	7452	12,065	475.0	58–2	28–3	12.5
City of Melbourne	1919	ThmpsJ	6630	10,875	427–6	55–6	28–6	10.5
launched as War Ruby								
City of Newcastle	1915	GrayX	6921	11,420	473–1	56–5	27–10	11.0
City of Norwich	1913	GrayX	6726	10,569	449–0	54–8	27–10	11.0
City of Pittsburg (st)	1922	Palmer	7377	12,264	465.7	58–8	28–10	11.5
City of Rangoon	1914	GrayX	6635	11,070	443.0	55–4	28–2	11.0
City of Roubaix (st)	1928	SHWR	7108	10,998	456.1	58–5	28–6	13.0
City of Shanghai	1917	Earles	5828	9832	418.5	55–0	26–10	11.0
City of Singapore (r/te)	1923	GrayWH	6555	10,826	450–9	57–4	28–1	11.5
City of Sydney (r/t)	1930	Work28	6986	10,720	472–4	58–5	28–8	13.5
City of Tokio (st,P–)	1921	Craig2	6993	11,244	463–4	59–0	28–11	11.5
City of Wellington (r/te)	1925	Curle	5733	9608	427–6	55–0	27–2	11.0
City of Winchester	1917	Palmer	7120	11,202	456.1	57–11	28–4	11.5
City of Worcester	1927	Earles	5469	9143	412–6	53–4	27–3	10.5
City of Yokohama (st)	1922	Gray18	7341	11,990	484–0	58–1	28–6	12.0
Kioto	1918	GrayX	3297	5853	347–6	46–8	24–7	10.5

Managed by

ELLERMAN & PAPAYANNI LINES LTD, Tower Bldg, Water St, Liverpool

General cargo vessels

Algerian (P40)	1924	Curle	2315	4074	295.0	43–9	20–9	10.5
Andalusian	1918	Earles	3082	5462	321.5	45–3	24–2	11.0
Assyrian (s2)	1914	Blohm	2962	4120	332.0	44–10	22–5	9.5
ex Fritz 20; conv mv 25								
Belgravian (r/t,P4)	1937	GrayWH	3136	4275	358–9	50–1	22–2	13.0
City of Lancaster (P6)	1924	Palmer	3041	5173	348–3	45–0	22–4	11.5
City of Oxford	1926	SHWR	2759	5070	336–6	46–5	21–11	10.5
Corinthian (r/t,P4)	1938	GrayWH	3122	4260	358–9	50–1	22–2	13.0
Darino	1917	Ramage	1351	2057	236.3	36–6	17–5	10.0
Destro	1920	DunlpB	3553	5050	327–0	44–10	22–8	10.0
Dido	1920	DunlpB	3554	5050	328–4	45–2	22–8	10.0
Egyptian	1920	Harkes	2866	5082	316.3	44–1	23–1	10.5
Estrellano (P–)	1920	HallR	1983	2569	250.8	38–2	18–11	10.0
Fabian (P–)	1919	GrayWH	3059	5570	343–0	46–10	23–8	10.0
Flaminian	1917	Harkes	2699	4753	315.0	42–5	22–11	10.5
Florian (r/t,P4)	bldg	GrayWH	3174	4275	358–9	50–1	22–2	13.0
Ionian (r/t,P4)	1939	GrayWH	3114	4275	358–9	50–1	22–2	13.0
Lesbian	1923	SHWR	2370	3708	272.1	41–8	21–5	10.0
Lisbon (P–)	1920	HallR	1984	2574	250.8	38–2	18–11	10.0
Malvernian (r/t,P4)	1937	GrayWH	3133	4275	358–9	50–0	22–2	13.0
Mardinian	1919	Austin	2434	4210	313–0	43–0	20–11	10.0
launched as War Almond								
Oporto	1928	Ramage	2352	3091	270.6	40–3	19–6	10.5
Palmella (P–)	1920	Ramage	1578	2358	245.9	38–2	17–11	10.0
Pandorian	order	SHWR	3146	4275	359–6	50–1	22–3	13.0
Serbino	1919	Ramage	4099	5810	342.4	46–0	23–3	10.0
Volturno	1914	Harkes	3424	5120	318.0	42–5	23–8	10.0
ex Bosforo 28, ex Falernian 28								

Managed by

WESTCOTT & LAURANCE LINE LTD, 5 Fenchurch St, London EC3

Castilian (P–)	1919	Dixon1	3067	5440	343–0	46–10	23–5	10.0
launched as War Ocean								

Note: * Registered owner Hall Line Ltd

Note: Ellerman Lines Ltd controlled Ellerman's Wilson Line Ltd, and also owned smaller vessels

ELLERMAN'S WILSON LINE LTD, Commercial Road, Hull

Funnel: Red, black top
Hull: Green, red boot-topping
Services: Liverpool, Manchester, Hull, London, Middlesbrough, R Tyne–Mediterranean, Adriatic, Alexandria, Levant, India; and to USA

Angelo (r/t,P12/1)	bldg	SHWR	2199	2775	306–2	44–2	19–7	13.0
Ariosto (r/t,P12/1)	bldg	SHWR	2176	2775	306–2	44–2	17–9	13.0
Bassano (r/t,P6/1)	1937	SHWR	4834	7205	419–6	55–10	25–7	12.5
Borodino (P27/1)	1911	Earles	2004	3054	318.0	42–2	18–10	9.5
laid down as Tsarskoe Selo								
Carlo	1911	Koch	1737	3046	277.7	39–3	18–6	9.5
ex Las Palmas 21								
Cavallo	1922	Dundee	2268	4064	312.0	44–9	19–10	10.0
City of Ripon	1915	LithR	6368	9300	424–11	53–6	27–2	10.0
ex Lepanto 34								
Consuelo (r/t,P6/1)	1937	SHWR	4847	7010	419–6	55–10	25–7	12.5
Draco	1922	HallR	2018	2888	274.7	39–4	19–7	10.0
Gitano (st)	1921	Goole	3956	5680	345–2	46–8	23–4	10.5
Grodno	1919	Gray18	2458	4215	313–6	43–0	20–9	9.5
Guido (st)	1920	Goole	3921	5680	345–2	46–8	23–3	10.5
Kelso	1924	Goole	3956	5635	345–2	46–8	23–4	10.5
Kyno	1924	Goole	3946	5635	345–2	46–8	23–4	10.5
Mourino (P36/1)	1906	Earles	2165	2400	300.0	41–6	19–0	12.0
Palermo (P4/1)	1938	GrayWH	2928	4494	354–8	48–1	22–1	12.0
Polo	1919	SHWRSd	1950	3388	300–9	42–6	20–3	9.5
launched as War Humber								
Runo	1920	Ramage	1858	2442	262.7	39–0	17–9	10.0
Thurso	1919	Austin	2436	4230	313–6	43–0	20–11	9.5
launched as War Bramble								
Trentino	1919	Dundee	3079	4240	310.0	44–9	20–3	10.0
Urbino*	1918	Earles	5198	8400	412–6	52–3	26–0	10.5
launched as War Seal								
Vasco	1939	GrayWH	2878	4500	354–8	48–1	22–1	12.5

Note: * Manager Ellerman & Bucknall Steamship Co Ltd (*qv*)

Note: Ellerman's Wilson Line Ltd, which became a member of the Ellerman Lines Ltd (*qv*) group in 1916, also owned short-sea vessels, particularly on services to NW Europe and Scandinavia

Funnel: Black with narrow blue band and narrow red band on broad white band
Services: General tramping, oil and petroleum trades

EUXINE SHIPPING CO LTD, Cunard House, 88 Leadenhall St, London EC3

General cargo vessels								
Christine Marie	1919	Flensb	3895	6892	399–6	52–6	22–10	10.0
ex Hesperia 38, ex Patria 19								
W Hendrik	1925	FurnH	4360	7600	377–4	52–2	24–1	9.0
ex Mary Walton 37, ex Tynebridge 34								
Tankers								
Helka	1912	RottDD	3471	4565	325.9	47–2	21–3	9.5
ex Mijdrecht 29								
Myriel	1913	RottDD	3560	4750	331.7	47–4	21–3	9.5
ex Wieldrecht 30								

Services: Whaling

FADUM & WANG, Tønsberg, Norway

Whale factory vessels								
FALKLAND WHALING CO LTD, St Helier, Jersey								
Polar Chief	1897	Palmer	7166	8580	445.0	52–2	26–4	10.0
ex Anglo-Norse 29, ex Rey Alfonso 27, ex Crenella 23, ex Montcalm 16; conv whale depot ship 27, conv tanker 23, conv dummy battleship HMS Audacious 16, conv passenger/general cargo 14								
ST HELIER SHIPOWNERS LTD, St Helier, Jersey								
Svend Foyn (s2)	1931	FurnH	14,795	21,600	538.1	74–4	33–8	11.0

Services: Whaling

Note: Manager of this company was Bruun & Von der Lippe (*qv* in Norway section)

FALKLAND SHIPOWNERS LTD, 15 Moorgate, London EC2

Whale factory vessel								
Anglo Norse	1914	Palmer	7988	10,857	439–0	57–0	27–4	10.0
ex Maricopa 29; conv tanker 29								

Funnel: Red with houseflag, black top
Hull: Black, red boot-topping with white dividing line
Services: UK, US–Australia–New Zealand; Australia, New Zealand–Mediterranean ports–NW Europe–UK; Australia, New Zealand–US

Note: * Owned by Peninsular & Oriental Co (*qv*) and chartered to Federal SN Co Ltd
Note: Federal SN Co Ltd, which became a member of the P&O Group in 1916, was associated with New Zealand Shipping Co Ltd (*qv*)

FEDERAL STEAM NAVIGATION CO LTD, 138 Leadenhall St, London EC3

Cambridge (s2)	1916	Teckl	10,846	13,280	544–6	65–9	29–11	14.0
ex Vogtland 20								
Cornwall (st2)	1920	Hamtn2	10,605	14,502	508–0	63–1	32–11	14.0
Cumberland (r/t2)	1919	Bremer	10,939	15,115	533–0	64–2	31–10	14.0
ex Wendland 21								
Dorset (m2)	1934	Work28	10,624	13,650	513–0	68–8	32–6	16.0
Durham (m2)	1934	Work28	10,893	13,610	513–0	68–7	32–6	16.0
Essex* (m2)	1936	BrownJ	11,063	13,665	551–3	70–5	32–7	17.0
Hertford (r/t2)	1917	Bremer	10,923	15,173	533–0	64–2	31–10	14.0
ex Friesland 21, launched as Rheinland								
Huntingdon (r/t2)	1920	Bremer	10,946	15,120	533–0	64–2	31–10	14.0
ex Munsterland 20								
Kent (st)	1918	Palmer	8694	11,373	480–1	62–10	30–2	14.0
Middlesex (st)	1920	SHWR	8703	11,638	480–1	62–10	30–0	14.0
Norfolk (rt2)	1918	Bremer	10,948	15,177	533–0	64–2	31–10	14.0
ex Sauerland 21								
Northumberland (st2)	1915	SHWR	11,555	14,161	550–5	63–0	31–9	14.0
Somerset (st)	1918	Earles	8790	11,602	480–1	62–10	29–4	14.0
Suffolk (m2)	1939	BrownJ	11,145	14,208	551–4	70–5	32–7	17.0
Surrey (st)	1919	Palmer	8581	11,720	480–1	62–10	30–2	14.0
Sussex* (m2)	1937	BrownJ	11,062	13,539	551–3	70–5	32–7	17.0
Westmoreland	1917	Hendn2	9001	11,957	494–6	60–1	30–7	14.0

Funnel: Yellow
Services: Mediterranean
Note: * Controlled by Callimanoupoulos & Co Ltd (*qv* in Greece section under P G Callimanopoulos)

FENTON STEAMSHIP CO LTD, 18–19 Great St Helen's, London EC3

ANGLO-EGYPTIAN MAIL LINE								
Cairo City (P–)	1906	Steph2	4792		380.4	47–5	22.9	11.5
ex Iphigenia 33, ex Elmina 28, ex Albertville 11, launched as Fulani								

Federal SN Co: Completed for Hamburg-Amerika as Vogtland *by Tecklenborg at Wesermünde in 1916, this vessel was laid up until after the end of the First World War. In January 1919 she was transferred to Britain and was managed by Glen Line for the Shipping Controller. In May 1921 she was sold to Federal SN, had frozen cargo space fitted, and was renamed* Cambridge. *She made her first voyage to new Zealand in September 1922. On November 7 1940 she struck a mine which had been laid by the German auxiliary cruiser* Pinguin, *and sank. She was on voyage from Cardiff to Brisbane with 3500 tons of tinplate, 1000 bags of sawdust and timber (RW Jordan collection)*

Furness, Withy & Co: Completed by Vickers at Barrow in February 1933, the passenger liner Queen of Bermuda *was intended for the New York–Bermuda service. She was requisitioned by the Admiralty on August 30 1939 and following conversion was commissioned as the armed merchant cruiser HMS* Queen of Bermuda. *She commenced service as a troopship in 1943 with accommodation for 4500 troops. She was returned to her owners and during April 1947–February 1949 underwent an extensive refit to resume her original service. After several years both on this and on cruising, she was withdrawn from service in 1966 and broken up at Faslane the following year (EH Cole)*

Furness, Withy & Co Nerissa *was owned by subsidiary company Bermuda & West Indies Steamship Co and was in service between New York and the Caribbean. With the outbreak of war she was chartered to Johnston-Warren Lines and was on service from Liverpool to St John's, Halifax and Boston. On April 30 1941, when on voyage from Halifax and St John's to Liverpool, she was torpedoed by* U551 *and sunk with heavy loss of life (RW Jordan collection)*

Services: General tramping; oil and petroleum trades

Note: Also *Lingfield* (built 1920/1002gt) on short-sea and Mediterranean trade

FINCHLEY STEAMSHIP CO LTD, 91 Bishopsgate, London EC2

General cargo vessel								
Latymer	1919	Polson	2300	3330	261–0	43–8	20–1	9.5
ex Saint Tropez 37								
Tanker								
Oakfield	1918	H&Wg	5244	7860	412–0	52–4	25–4	10.0
ex Salsaas 37, ex Absia 28, ex War African 21								

Funnel: Black with narrow red band above broad red band; B&WI – black with red over white bands
Hull: Black, red boot-topping; *Monarch of Bermuda, Queen of Bermuda* – grey, green boot-topping and white dividing line; B&WI – grey, red boot-topping
Services: Hull, London–St John NB–Halifax NS; Hull, London–Montreal (summer)–Halifax NS; Glasgow, Liverpool–Halifax NS–St John's Nfl–Boston; Glasgow, Manchester–Los Angeles–San Francisco–Victoria–Vancouver–Seattle–Tacoma–Portland; London–Philadelphia–New York–Halifax (winter); London–Philadelphia–New York (summer); Leith, Dundee–Philadelphia – New York; Antwerp, Swansea, Liverpool–Piraeus–Black Sea ports; B&WI, passenger and cargo – New York–Bermuda; New York–Halifax NS–St John's Nfl; New York–St Thomas–St Croix–St Kitts–Antigua–Guadeloupe–Dominica–Martinique–St Lucia–Barbados–Trinidad

Note: See also Cairns, Noble & Co Ltd, Houlder Brothers & Co Ltd and Prince Line Ltd; see Norfolk & North American Steam Shipping Co Ltd also under Shaw, Savill & Albion Co Ltd

FURNESS, WITHY & CO LTD,
Furness House, Leadenhall St, London EC3, and Royal Liver Bldg, Liverpool

Passenger vessels								
Fort Amherst (r/t,P85/1,26/2)	1936	Blythw	3489	2173	325–0	45–1	18–9	13.5
Fort Townshend (r/t,P85/1,26/2)	1936	Blythw	3489	2173	325–0	45–1	18–9	13.5
Monarch of Bermuda (te4,P831/1)	1931	Vick1N	22,424	6100	579–6	76–9	27–1	20.0
Queen of Bermuda (te4,P731/1)	1933	Vick1B	22,575	6100	579–6	76–8	27–1	20.0
General cargo vessels								
Manaquí	1921	Workmn	2802	3920	310–6	47–2	20–3	10.0
Pacific Grove (m2,P12/1)	1928	DeutsK	7117	10,100	470–0	60–10	28–2	13.0
Pacific President (m2,P12/1)	1928	DeutsK	7113	10,100	470–0	60–10	28–2	13.0
Pacific Ranger (m2,P12/1)	1929	B&W	6865	10,000	454–2	60–4	27–10	13.0
Pacific Shipper (m,P10/1)	1924	Doxfrd	6290	9711	436–8	58–0	27–2	11.5
BERMUDA & WEST INDIES STEAMSHIP CO LTD, Hamilton, Bermuda								
Nerissa (P163/1,66/2)	1926	Hamtn2	5583	3300	349.5	54–4	21–0	14.0
JOHNSTON WARREN LINES LTD, Royal Liver Bldg, Liverpool								
Passenger/general cargo vessels								
Newfoundland (P105/cab,80/3)	1925	VickB2	6791	6235	423–9	55–5	25–4	14.5
Nova Scotia (P105/cab,80/3)	1925	VickB2	6796	6250	423–9	55–5	25–4	14.5
General cargo vessels								
Aviemore (P–)	1920	Irvin3	4060	6308	371–5	52–2	23–4	12.0
Dromore (P–)	1920	Irvin3	4096	6317	371–6	52–2	23–3	12.0
Incemore (P–)	1921	Irvin3	4098	6308	371–5	52–2	23–4	12.0
Jessmore (P–)	1921	Irvin3	4099	6308	371–5	52–2	23–4	12.0
ex Peruviana 23								
NORFOLK & NORTH AMERICAN STEAM SHIPPING CO LTD,								
General cargo vessels								
Pacific Enterprise (m2,P12/1)	1927	Blythw	6736	11,050	454–6	60–3	28–0	13.0
Pacific Exporter (m2,P12/1)	1928	Blythw	6734	11,050	454–6	60–3	28–0	13.0
Pacific Pioneer (m2,P12/1)	1928	Blythw	6734	11,050	454–6	60–3	28–0	13.0
Pacific Reliance (m2,P12/1)	1926	Blythw	6717	11,023	454–6	60–3	28–0	13.0

Funnel: Black or black with houseflag (houseflag added to funnel of three vessels listed in 1938)
Hull: Black with white band, red boot-topping
Services: R Tyne, London–W Italy (including Leghorn, Bagnoli, Bastia, Genoa, Naples, Milazzo), Sicily (Messina, Palermo, Syracuse), and other Mediterranean ports (including Malaga, Malta, Patras, Alexandria, Mersin, Mazamet, Smyrna)
Note: Also short-sea vessels, operated mainly between London

GENERAL STEAM NAVIGATION CO LTD,
15 Trinity Square, London EC3

Adjutant	1922	Grgmth	1931	3120	289–7	41–11	18–3	10.0
ex Myrtlepark 24								
Heron (m,P12)	1937	Caledn	2374	3540	314–6	45–2	19–4	12.0
Philomel (r/t,P12)	1936	Caledn	2122	3525	314–0	45–4	19–3	12.0

and NW Europe, and Bordeaux, and seasonal excursion vessels operating on the River Thames to Thames estuary and East Anglia ports
Note: General Steam Nav Co Ltd, which had been a P&O Group company from 1920, purchased Moss Hutchison Line Ltd (*qv*) in 1935

GERARCI, ERNESTO, Billiter House, Billiter St, London EC3

Laleham*	1915	RDuck2	4818	8100	389.6	53–5	23–9	9.0
ex Dorington Court 37								
Peckham**	1912	Rodger	4465	8600	410.0	54–4	24–9	8.5
ex Ioannis Vatis 37, ex Baron Jedburgh 30								
APEX SHIPPING CO LTD								
Meopham***	1916	Pgill1	4330	7350	365.0	51–0	23–7	9.5
ex Gibraltar 38, ex Maplemore 21								

Services: General tramping

Note: *, **, *** Sold Germany 1939, renamed *Harm Fritzen, Jürgen Fritzen* and *Antje Fritzen* respectively

GERMAN & CO LTD, JAMES, 68–69 The Exchange, Mount Stuart Sq, Cardiff

ARLON STEAMSHIP CO LTD,
Creechurch House, 37–45 Creechurch Lane, London EC3

General cargo vessels								
Becheville	1924	Prstm2	4228	8160	377–3	51–6	24–10	9.5
ex Newton Elm 37, ex Westlea 27								
Oregon	1920	VirgAl	6008	9400	402.8	53–4	26–6	10.0
ex Oakridge 27, ex Anna E Morse 24								
Tanker								
Arletta	1925	Duncan	4870	7330	375.1	51–9	24–8	10.5
ex Vanduara 37								

Funnel: Black with blue A inside blue diamond frame on yellow band
Services: General tramping; oil and petroleum trades

GIBBS & CO, Merthyr House, James St, Cardiff

WEST WALES STEAMSHIP CO LTD								
East Wales	1925	Dobson	4358	8450	412–0	53–0	24–9	11.0
South Wales	1929	Bartm2	5619	10,100	446–4	58–2	25–4	10.0
West Wales	1925	Dobson	4353	8450	412–0	53–0	24–9	11.0

Funnel: Red, black top
Hull: Black, red boot-topping
Services: General tramping

GILLESPIE & NICOL,
Station Rd, Grangemouth, and 68 Gordon St, Glasgow C1

RAVELSTON STEAMSHIP CO LTD								
Ravelston	1906	GrayX	2085	3500	296–8	43–1	18–4	9.0

Funnel: Yellow, black top
Hull: Black with white line, red boot-topping
Services: General tramping
Note: Also smaller vessels

GLEN & CO, 165 St Vincent St, Glasgow C2

ADMIRAL SHIPPING CO LTD								
Cara	1929	Burntd	1760	3200	271.5	39–8	18–5	10.5
Jura	1929	Burntd	1759	3200	271.8	39–8	18–5	10.5
CLYDESDALE SHIPOWNERS' CO LTD								
Alva	1934	Burntd	1584	2880	274–0	40–6	18–7	10.0
Elba	1918	G&G5	1974	3320	290–5	41–11	18–1	9.5
ex Glenpark 32								
Lissa	1927	Duncan	1511	2620	264–3	39–3	17–0	9.0
Meta	1931	Burntd	1575	2760	262–6	40–2	17–3	9.5
Ossian	1919	Murdo2	1514	2411	248–9	36–1	18–7	9.0
Runa	1930	Burntd	1575	2760	262–6	40–0	17–0	9.0
Thelma	1935	Burntd	1593	2775	274–0	40–6	17–6	10.0
Winga	1924	NewWat	1478	2480	250.0	37–1	17–1	9.0
GLASGOW SHIPOWNERS' CO LTD								
Jutland	1928	Duncan	6153	9925	430.0	57–0	25–0	11.0
Navarino	1937	Burntd	4841	8260	430–2	56–11	25–0	10.0
Trafalgar	1924	Lithgw	4530	7800	398–2	52–0	23–11	10.0
SCOTTISH NAVIGATION CO LTD								
Dunstaffnage	1922	Lithgw	4525	7800	398–2	52–0	23–11	10.0
Fidra	1936	Burntd	1574	2850	274–0	40–6	18–7	10.0
Narva	1937	Burntd	1575	2850	274–0	40–6	18–7	10.0
Shuna	1937	Burntd	1575	2850	274–0	40–6	18–7	10.0
Ulea	1936	Burntd	1574	2850	274–0	40–6	18–7	10.0

Funnel: Red, black top
Hull: Black, red boot-topping
Services: UK W coast –Mediterranean; general tramping; Glasgow–NW Europe, Scandinavia

Note: Some of these, and other owned vessels, also operated on regular services from UK ports to the Baltic Sea, Scandinavia and NW Europe

General Steam Nav Co: Philomel *was one of the larger vessels in this old-established company's fleet and which operated on its service to Mediterranean ports.* Philomel, *which was completed by Caledon at Dundee in 1936, survived the Second World War and continued in the company's service until 1957 when she was sold to Italy and renamed* Croce Giuseppe. *In 1964 she was sold to Greece and renamed* Anesis, *under which name she ran aground in February 1967, 45 miles E of Lagos, and was abandoned as a total loss (Alex Duncan)*

Glen Line: In the later 1930s, following change of control, this owner placed orders for several fast cargo liners. One of these was Glengarry, *which was laid down at the Copenhagen shipyard of Burmeister & Wain in 1939. In May 1940 she was seized by the invading Germans, and upon completion commissioned by the Kriegsmarine as* Meersburg. *In 1942 she became the auxiliary cruiser* Hansa, *and later served as a training ship. On May 4 1945 she was recovered at Kiel by British forces, and passed to the Ministry of War Transport as* Empire Humber. *In 1946 she was sold to Glen Line and renamed* Glengarry. *As part of inter-group transfers, she was renamed* Dardanus *in 1970, under Blue Funnel Line colours, but a year later reverted to* Glengarry *for a single voyage to Japan, where she was broken up (RW Jordan collection)*

Hain Steamship Co: The general cargo vessel Bangalore *was one of four siterships completed during 1928–29 for charter to P&O which was controller of Hain Steamship Co. On July 20 1941 she was in collision, in convoy, with the motor vessel* Richmond Castle *when on voyage from London and Trinidad to Table Bay and Hong Kong with general cargo, aircraft and horses. The following day she was shelled and sunk by an escort vessel as it was considered she was a danger to navigation (Alex Duncan)*

Haldin & Philipps: The Court Line steamer Tilsington Court *was completed in October 1928 by Armstrong-Whitworth on the River Tyne, and was one of five sisterships built for the company that year. She apparently kept out of harm's way during the Second World War and was sold out of the fleet in the early 1950s (RW Jordan collection)*

GLEN LINE LTD, 20 Billiter St, London EC3

Breconshire (m2,P24/1)	1939	Taikoo	9776	9800	507–0	66–5	30–7	18.0
Denbighshire (m2,P24/1)	1939	NedSM	9100	9800	507–0	66–4	30–7	18.0
Flintshire* (st,P12)	1923	Workmn	7726	9780	477–0	58–5	30–5	14.5
ex Dardanus 35								
Glenaffaric (P12)	1920	Caledn	7782	9595	477–0	56–4	28–3	13.5
ex Machaon 35								
Glenapp (m2,P12/1)	1920	H&WGw	9503	12,205	501–7	62–4	29–8	13.0
ordered as Glenfarne								
Glenartney (m2,P24/1)	bldg	Caledn	9795	9680	507–0	66–4	30–6	18.0
Glenbeg (m2,P12/1)	1922	H&WGw	9461	12,205	501–7	62–4	29–8	14.0
Glenearn (m2,P2411)	1938	Caledn	8986	9500	507–0	66–5	30–6	18.0
Glenfinlas(P12)	1917	Leslie	7572	9425	455.3	56–4	28–2	13.5
ex Elpenor 35								
Glengarry (m2,P23/1)	bldg	B&W	9311	9470	507–0	66–5	30–6	18.0
Glengyle (m2,P24/1)	1939	Caledn	9919	9580	507–0	66–5	30–7	18.0
Gleniffer (s2,P30)	1915	Leslie	9559	13,315	500–1	62–4	29–9	12.0
Glenogle (m2,P12/1)	1920	H&WGw	9513	12,205	501–7	62–4	29–8	13.0
Glenorchy (m2,P24/1)	1939	Taikoo	8982	9500	507–0	66–5	30–7	18.0
Glenroy (m2,P24/1)	1938	Scott2	8997	9585	507–0	66–5	30–6	18.0
Glenshiel (m2,P12)	1924	H&W,B	9415	12,171	501–7	62–4	29–8	13.0
Glenstrae (m2,P12)	1922	H&WGw	9460	12,250	501–7	62–4	29–8	14.0
ex Glengarry 39								
Radnorshire** (m2,P12)	1923	Caledn	7726	9520	477–0	58–3	28–3	13.0
ex Tantalus 36								
Newbuilding*** (m2,P24/1)	bldg	Caledn	9975	9440	512–10	66–5	30–7	18.0

Funnel: Red, black top
Hull: Black, red boot-topping
Services: Hamburg–Middlesbrough–Immingham–Rotterdam–Antwerp–London–Port Said–Penang–Singapore–Hong Kong–Manila–Dairen–Kosichang–Kobe–Yokohama–Vladivostok

Note: * Transferred Ocean SS Co Ltd (A Holt & Co), 1939, renamed *Dardanus*;** transferred Ocean SS Co, 1939, renamed *Tantalus*; *** entered service 1942 as *Priam* for Ocean SS Co Ltd – (*qv* under Alfred Holt & Co)
Note: Glen Line Ltd was acquired by Ocean SS Co Ltd (*qv* under Alfred Holt & Co) in 1935

GLOVER BROTHERS (LONDON) LTD,
Bevis Marks House, Bevis Marks, London EC3

SHAKESPEAR SHIPPING CO LTD

Chaucer	1929	Duncan	5792	10,300	420.0	57.0	25–11	10.0
Shakespear	1926	Duncan	5029	8890	418–9	53–6	24–9	10.0

Funnel: Black
Hull: Grey, red boot-topping
Services: General tramping

GOULD, WALTER T, Merthyr House, James St, Cardiff

CARDIGAN SHIPPING CO LTD

Grelrosa	1914	Nthmbl	4574	8020	385.0	51–11	24–3	10.0
ex Archmel 35, ex Mendip Range 20								

HEANTON SHIPPING CO LTD

Grelhead	1915	RDuck2	4274	7668	380.0	51–0	24–0	10.0
ex Beachy Head 18								

Funnel: Black with black G on blue diamond on narrow red band between two narrow white bands
Hull: Grey, red boot-topping
Services: General tramping

GOW, HARRISON & CO, 8 Gordon St, Glasgow C1

Tankers

VALLDEMOSA STEAMSHIP CO LTD

Valldemosa	1935	Duncan	7222	11,230	446.0	59–6	26–7	12.0

VANCOUVER STEAMSHIP CO LTD

Vancouver	1928	GrkDY	5729	8400	424–0	54–6	24–3	11.0

VENETIA STEAMSHIP CO LTD

Venetia	1927	Duncan	5728	8400	424–0	54–6	24–3	11.0

VIMEIRA STEAMSHIP CO LTD

Vimeira	1927	Duncan	5728	8400	423–10	54–6	24–3	11.0

VIRGILIA STEAMSHIP CO LTD

Virgilia	1927	GrkDY	5723	8400	415–4	54–6	24–3	11.0

VOREDA STEAMSHIP CO LTD

Voreda	1935	GrkDY	7216	11,230	447.7	59–6	26–7	12.0

Funnel: Red, black top
Hull: Black, red boot-topping
Services: Oil and petroleum trades

Services: Trading E coast Canada–US–West Indies; Windsor NS–E coast US ports

Note: Also smaller vessels

GYPSUM PACKET CO LTD, Windsor NS, Canada

Gypsum Empress (P–)	1929	FurnH	4034	6400	357–0	52–10	22–0	10.0
Gypsum King (P–)	1927	FurnH	3915	6412	357–0	52–10	21–11	10.0
Gypsum Prince (P–)	1927	FurnH	3915	6412	357–0	52–10	21–11	10.0
Gypsum Queen (P–)	1927	FurnH	3915	6412	357–0	52–10	21–11	10.0

Funnel: Yellow, black top
Hull: Green, red boot-topping
Services: Oil and petroleum trades; and fruit carrier chartered out
Note: See also under Jamaica Banana Producers Steamship Co Ltd
Note: This company also owned short-sea tankers

HADLEY SHIPPING CO LTD, 53 Leadenhall St, London EC3

Tanker

Cerinthus	1920	Leslie	3878	5875	350–0	48–10	22–7	10.0

Funnel: Black with large white H
Hull: Black with white band, red boot-topping
Services: General tramping

Note: * Operated by Peninsular & Oriental SN Co (*qv*); ** sold Greece 1939, renamed *Agioi Victores*
Note: This company became a member of the P&O group in 1917

HAIN STEAMSHIP CO LTD, THE, Baltic Exchange Chambers, 24 St Mary Axe, London EC3 and Salvage Bldgs, Clarence Rd, Cardiff

Bangalore* (r/t)	1928	Curle	6067	9654	436.0	57–6	29.8	14.0
Behar* (r/t)	1928	H&WGk	6100	9542	436.0	57–7	29.6	14.0
Bhutan* (r/t)	1929	H&WGw	6104	9535	436.0	57–6	29.6	14.0
Burdwan* (r/t)	1928	Curle	6069	9640	436.0	57–6	29.8	14.0
Trebartha	1920	Rhead3	4597	8500	413–4	52–1	25–5	11.0
Trecarrell	1919	Hendn2	5271	8250	412–0	52–4	25–4	11.0
launched as War Lilac								
Tredinnick	1921	Rhead3	4589	8550	413–6	52–1	25–5	11.0
Trefusis	1918	Doxfrd	5299	8250	412–0	52–4	25–3	11.0
ex War Aconite 19								
Tregarthen (r/t)	1936	Lithgw	5201	9130	447–9	56–2	24–9	10.5
Tregenna	1919	Gray18	5242	8300	412–7	52–4	25–4	11.0
launched as War Bulldog								
Trehata	1928	GraySd	4817	8775	413.2	54–2	24–8	12.0
ex Nohata 36								
Trekieve	1919	Rhead3	5244	8210	412–0	52–5	25–4	11.0
launched as War Mallard								
Trelawny	1927	Leslie	4689	8775	419–6	54–9	24–9	12.0
Trelissick	1919	H&WGw	5265	8200	413–6	52–4	25–4	11.0
launched as War Pampas								
Treloske**	1918	Rhead3	4344	8200	413–9	52–1	24–3	11.0
Treminnard	1922	Rhead3	4694	8620	413–0	53–1	25–10	11.0
ex Min 36								
Tremoda	1928	H&WGk	4736	8700	420–0	55–10	24–8	12.0
ex Nimoda 37								
Tresillian	1925	GrayWH	4743	8650	412–6	53–0	25–10	11.0
Trevalgan (m)	1937	Lithgw	5299	9130	448–5	56–2	24–9	10.5
Trevanion (m)	1937	Lithgw	5299	9130	448–6	56–2	24–9	10.5
Trevarrack	1919	Hendn2	5270	8250	413–0	54–4	25–4	11.0
launched as War Laurel								
Trevaylor (m)	bldg	Curle	5257	9080	447–10	56–2	24–9	10.5
Treverbyn	1920	H&WGw	5281	8200	413–6	52–4	25–3	11.0
launched as War Airman, laid down as War Maple								
Trevethoe (m)	bldg	Steph2	5257	9080	447–8	56–3	24–9	10.5
Trevilley (m)	bldg	Lithgw	5296	9080	447–8	56–3	24–9	10.5
Trevorian	1920	Rhead3	4599	8525	413–8	52–1	25–5	11.0
Trewellard	1936	Lithgw	5201	9130	448–5	56–2	24–9	10.5
Treworlas	1922	Rhead3	4692	8620	413–0	53–1	25–10	11.0

Funnel: Yellow, black top
Hull: Black, red boot-topping
Services: General tramping

HALDIN & PHILIPPS LTD, 1 Leadenhall St, London EC3

COURT LINE LTD

Aldington Court (m)	1929	Pgill2	4891	9200	422–4	55–6	25–2	12.5
Arlington Court	1924	Workmn	4915	8080	410–10	53–1	23–8	10.0
Barrington Court	1924	Workmn	4910	8080	410–10	53–1	23–8	10.0
Bonnington Court (m)	1929	Duncan	4909	9200	422–4	55–6	25–1	12.5
Cedrington Court	1918	H&W,B	5160	8175	412–0	52–4	25–3	11.0

ex Cabotia 25, ex War Viper 19								
Cressington Court (m)	1929	Nthmb2	4971	9200	422–4	55–6	25–2	12.5
Darlington Court (m)	1936	Lithgw	4974	9200	431–4	56–2	25–1	11.0
Dorington Court	1939	ThmpsJ	5281	10,860	443–6	59–11	25–6	10.0
Errington Court	1925	Workmn	4913	8050	410–10	53–1	23–8	10.0
Framlington Court	1924	Napr&M	4888	8080	410–0	53–4	23–8	10.0
Geddington Court	1928	Nthmb2	6903	11,088	434–9	56–6	27–1	10.0
Hannington Court (m)	1939	Doxfrd	5449	8450	447–8	57–9	25–9	10.5
Ilvington Court	1919	HK&Wh	5187	8100	412–0	52–4	25–3	10.5
ex Iolcos 24, ex Meandros 20, launched as War Sniper								
Jevington Court	1925	Workmn	4544	8100	410–0	53–2	24–4	10.0
Kensington Court	1927	Napr&M	4863	8080	410–0	53–2	23–8	10.0
Lavington Court (m)	bldg	H&WGw	5372		449–10	57–11	25–9	10.5
Mersington Court	1920	Nthmb1	5141	8000	387–9	51–2	25–2	10.5
ex Giovanna Florio 27								
Nollington Court	1924	RDuck2	6097	9260	400.0	53–0	25–9	9.5
ex Conistone 27								
Ovington Court	1924	RDuck2	6095	9260	400.0	53–0	25–9	9.5
ex Amblestone 27								
Pennington Court	1924	RDuck2	6098	9260	400.0	53–0	25–9	9.5
ex Rochdale 27								
Quarrington Court	1928	Nthmb2	6900	11,060	434–9	56–6	27–1	10.0
Rossington Court	1928	Fairfd	6922	11,060	434–9	56–6	27–1	10.0
Sinnington Court	1928	ArmWh1	6910	11,096	434–10	56–6	27–1	10.0
Tilsington Court	1928	ArmWh1	6910	11,096	434–9	56–6	27–1	10.0
Uffington Court	1929	Pgill2	4976	9281	422–4	55–6	25–2	11.5
Wellington Court	1930	Pgill2	4979	9281	422–4	55–6	25–2	11.5
FRAMLINGTON SYNDICATE LTD								
Dallington Court	1929	Nthmb2	6889	11,088	434–11	56–6	27–1	10.0

HALL BROTHERS, 4 Royal Arcade, Newcastle upon Tyne 1

Funnel: Red with houseflag on broad grey band between two narrow white bands, black top
Hull: Black, pink boot-topping
Services: General tramping

HALL BROTHERS STEAMSHIP CO LTD								
Ambassador*	1925	Ropnrl	4450	8341	399.0	53–2	24–8	11.0
Bretwalda	1939	ThmpsJ	4906	9107	431–10	58–2	25–0	11.0
Caduceus	1927	Dobson	4364	8560	412–2	52–7	24–10	11.0
Embassage	1935	ThmpsJ	4954	9100	409.2	57–9	24–6	11.0
Royal Crown	1927	Dobson	4364	8560	411–10	53–0	24–10	11.0
Royal Emblem	bldg	ThmpsJ	4900	9050	431–10	58–2	26–0	11.0
Royal Sceptre	1937	ThmpsJ	4853	9150	431–10	58–2	25–0	11.0
White Crest	1928	Dobson	4365	8560	411–10	53–0	24–10	11.0

Note: * Sold Crest Shipping Co Ltd 1939, renamed *Bancrest*

HARRIS & DIXON LTD, 81 Gracechurch St, London EC3

Funnel: Yellow with two red bands
Services: Oil and petroleum trades; general tramping

Tankers								
Esturia	1914	Laing	6968	10,360	438–0	57–0	27–1	10.0
ex Apache 37, ex La Habra 36								
REFAST STEAMSHIP CO LTD								
Refast	1914	NYSB1	5189	7790	406–6	51–2	24–7	10.0
ex Nantucket Chief 38, ex Gulflight 37								
General cargo vessel								
ZUBI SHIPPING CO LTD								
Kaolack (s2)	1917	LoireS	1837	2343	278–11	35–10	17–1	9.5

HARRISON LTD, J & C, 66 Mark Lane, London EC3

Funnel: Black with white band bearing black H
Hull: Grey with white band, bright pink boot-topping
Services: General tramping

Harlesden	1932	Leslie	5483	9200	443–0	56–4	24–9	11.0
Harpalion	1932	Leslie	5486	9182	443–0	56–4	24–9	11.0
GOWLAND STEAMSHIP CO LTD								
Harmala (P12)	1935	Lithgw	5730	9370	433.2	58–2	25–10	11.0
Harpagus	bldg	Bartm2	5173		450–10	58–6	25–9	10.5
Harpalyce	bldg	Bartm2	5169		450–10	58–6	25–9	10.5
NATIONAL STEAMSHIP CO LTD								
Harberton	1930	Short2	4585	8160	413–6	54–6	23–6	10.5
Harbledown (r/t)	1933	Lithgw	5414	9200	443–4	56–2	24–10	11.0
Harbury	1934	Lithgw	5081	8450	433–6	56–2	24–0	11.0

Harcalo	1934	Lithgw	5081	8450	433–6	56–2	24–0	11.0
Harlingen (r/t)	1932	Lithgw	5415	9200	443–4	56–2	24–10	11.0
Harmattan	1930	ThmpsR	4558	8130	407–10	54–6	23–8	9.0
Harmonic	1930	ThmpsR	4558	8130	407–10	54–6	23–8	9.0
Harpagon (P12)	1935	Lithgw	5719	9370	428.8	58–2	25–10	11.0
Harpalycus (P12)	1935	Leslie	5629	9550	448–6	58–4	25–9	11.0
Harpasa (r/t)	1934	Lithgw	5082	8450	432–5	56–2	24–0	11.0
Harpathian	1930	Bartm2	4671	8140	416–11	54–6	23–8	10.0
Harpenden	1930	Bartm2	4678	8165	416–11	54–6	23–8	10.5
Harperley	1930	GrayWH	4586	8202	413–6	54–6	23–9	10.5
Hartington	1932	GrayWH	5496	9150	441–8	56–2	24–9	11.0
Hartismere	1933	GrayWH	5498	9150	441–8	56–2	24–9	11.0
Hartlebury (r/t)	1934	Lithgw	5082	8450	432–5	56–2	24–0	11.0
Hartlepool	1932	GrayWH	5500	9150	441–8	56–2	24–9	11.0
WILLIS STEAMSHIP CO LTD								
Harborough	1932	Lithgw	5415	9212	445–0	56–2	24–10	11.0
Hardingham (r/t)	1933	Lithgw	5415	9200	443–4	56–2	24–10	11.0
Harmanteh	1932	Lithgw	5415	9200	443–9	56–2	24–10	11.0
Harmatris	1932	Lithgw	5395	9150	443–2	56–2	24–9	11.0

HARRISON, THOS & JAS, (Harrison Line), Mersey Chambers, Liverpool 2

Funnel: Black with white over red over white bands
Hull: Black, boot-topping pink, below water red
Services: Liverpool–Calcutta; Liverpool–New Orleans–Galveston–Brazil–British West Indies–Venezuela–Curaçao–Colombia–Cristobal–Bahama–Jamaica–Guatemala–Honduras–British Honduras–Mexico; Liverpool, Glasgow, Newport–Red Sea ports –E Africa–South Africa; Glasgow–West Indies–Demerara–Jamaica–Mexico; London, Middlesbrough–West Indies–Demerara–Guianas; London, Middlesbrough–South Africa (Harrison Line operated joint services with Clan Line Steamers Ltd – *qv*, and Ellerman Lines Ltd – *qv*)

CHARENTE STEAMSHIP CO LTD

Passenger/general cargo vessels								
Inanda (P91/1)	1925	SHWR	5985	6925	423–4	52–2	25–8	14.0
Inkosi (P82/1)	1937	SHWR	6618	6940	429–7	56–0	25–7	15.0
General cargo vessels								
Actor*	1917	Hendn2	5548	8461	426–6	52–2	26–7	12.0
Adviser (r/t)	1939	Lithgw	6348	9000	459–8	56–6	25–10	14.0
Astronomer	1917	Hendn2	8401	11,960	502–10	58–4	28–6	13.5
Atlantian	1928	Caledn	6549	9800	431–4	54–8	29–5	13.0
Auditor	1924	Conn2	5444	8380	423–4	52–4	27–0	12.0
Barrister (r/t)	1939	Lithgw	6348	9000	459–9	56–6	25–10	14.0
Chancellor	1916	LithR	4607	7400	385.0	52–0	24–0	12.0
ex Crown of Cadiz 20								
Collegian (st)	1923	FurnH	7886	11,335	471–6	58–0	30–2	14.0
ex Royal Prince 35, ex London Commerce 28								
Colonial	1926	Hendn2	5108	8030	409–0	52–8	25–0	12.0
Comedian	1929	Conn2	5122	8000	409–6	52–6	24–11	12.0
Contractor	1930	Cammel	6004	9150	434–1	54–8	26–6	13.0
Counsellor	1926	Conn2	5068	8030	409–0	52–6	24–11	12.0
Craftsman (st)	1922	FurnH	8022	11,335	472–0	58–0	30–2	14.0
ex Imperial Prince 35, ex London Mariner 28, ex Feliciana 23								
Custodian	1928	Conn2	5881	9150	433–7	54–4	26–6	13.0
Dakarian**	1921	Hendn2	6426	9480	413–6	52–6	29–2	12.0
Dalesman (r/t)	bldg	Lithgw	6443	9000	459–7	56–6	25–9	14.0
Darian***	1922	Hendn2	6434	9480	413–6	52–6	29–2	12.0
Davisian	1922	Hendn2	6433	9480	413–6	52–6	29–2	12.0
Daytonian	1922	Hendn2	6434	9480	413–6	52–6	29–2	12.0
Defender	1915	Conn2	8258	11,960	498–8	58–4	28–7	13.5
Designer	1928	Hendn2	5945	9150	433–8	54–8	26–6	13.0
Diplomat (st)	1921	Conn2	8240	11,960	499–2	58–5	28–7	12.0
Director	1926	Hendn2	5107	8030	409–0	52–8	25–0	12.0
Dramatist	1920	Conn2	5443	8382	423–4	52–4	26–11	12.0
Explorer	1935	SHWR	6235	9310	454–5	56–0	25–8	13.0
Governor	1918	Hendn2	5571	8461	425–0	52–2	26–7	12.0
Historian	1924	Conn2	5074	8030	409–6	52–0	24–11	12.0
Huntsman (st)	1921	Conn2	8196	11,960	499–2	58–4	28–7	12.0
Inventor	1935	Hendn2	6210	9294	453–0	56–0	25–8	13.0
Logician	1928	Cammel	5993	9210	433–8	54–6	26–6	13.0
Magician	1925	NewWat	5105	8065	410–1	52–6	25–0	12.0
Merchant	1935	Lithgw	4615	8800	397–8	52–0	23–11	12.0
Novelist	bldg	H&WGw	6183	9134	438–4	54–6	26–6	13.0
Observer	1928	Conn2	5881	9150	433–8	54–6	26–6	13.0
Planter	1927	Conn2	5887	9150	433–8	54–6	26–6	13.0
Politician (st)	1923	FurnH	7939	11,335	471–9	58–1	30–2	14.0
ex London Merchant 35								
Rancher	1927	Conn2	5882	9150	433–8	54–6	26–6	13.0
Recorder	1930	Cammel	5982	9148	434–6	54–7	26–6	13.0
Scholar	1922	Conn2	3940	6165	378–0	46–11	24–10	10.0
Scientist	1938	Lithgw	6199	8820	453–0	56–0	25–10	14.0
Settler (r/t)	1939	Conn2	6202	8800	453–6	56–6	26–0	14.0

Harrison Line: One of two passenger/general cargo vessels on Harrison Line service in 1939 was Inanda, *completed by Swan, Hunter & Wigham Richardson in 1925. On September 9 1940 during an air raid on London docks, she was bombed and sunk. Later raised, she passed to the ownership of the Ministry of War Transport, being renamed* Empire Explorer. *As such she was torpedoed and shelled on July 8 1942 by* U575 *when on voyage from Demerara for Barbados and the UK with 1000 tons of pitch, 4000 tons of sugar and 200 bags of mail. The vessel was abandoned and sunk the following day. Three crew members were lost, 60 crew and 8 gunners survived (Harrison Line)*

Harrison Line: The steamer Inventor *was completed in September 1935 by D & W Henderson, Glasgow, and was the last ship to be built at this famous yard which was founded in 1857. In March 1943 she survived attacks by enemy torpedo aircraft off Philippeville and survived the war. She was broken up at Ghent in 1960 (R Sherlock)*

P Henderson & Co: The cargo/passenger liner Prome *was completed by Wm Denny & Bros, Dumbarton, in April 1937 and commenced her first voyage from Glasgow and Liverpool to Burma the following month. In November 1940 she was requisitioned for use as a Royal Navy mine depot ship, and on December 21 was hit by a bomb during an air raid on Liverpool docks. During 1941–45 she was based at Trincomalee.* Prome *was returned to commercial service in 1946 and lasted until 1962 when she was broken up at Bruges (RW Jordan)*

Note: * Sold E R Management Co Ltd 1939, renamed *Nailsea River*; ** sold Petrograd Steamers Ltd (Wm Thomson & Co) 1939, renamed *Benvannoch*; *** sold Ben Line Steamers Ltd (Wm Thomson & Co) 1939, renamed *Benvrackie*

Statesman (st)	1923	FurnH	7939	11,335	472–0	58–0	30–2	14.0
ex British Prince 35, ex London Shipper 28								
Strategist	1937	Lithgw	6255	9300	452–4	56–0	25–8	13.0
Tactician	1928	Cammel	5996	9210	433–8	54–8	26–6	13.0
Trader	order	Conn2	6087	9050	435–0	54–7	26–6	13.0
Traveller	1922	Connel	3963	6165	378–0	46–11	24–10	10.0
Tribesman	1937	Lithgw	6242	9200	452–4	55–10	25–8	13.0
Wanderer	1925	Connel	5079	8030	409–0	52–6	24–11	12.0
Wayfarer	1925	Connel	5068	8030	409–0	52–6	24–11	12.0

HEADLAM & SONS, 43 Flowergate, Whitby

Funnel: Black with white band bearing blue cross (+)
Hull: Black, white top strakes, red boot-topping
Services: General tramping

HEADLAM & SONS STEAMSHIP CO LTD

Dunsley	1929	ThmpR2	3862	6750	360.2	50–0	22–6	9.0
Glaisdale	1929	Laing	3777	6550	360.5	49–11	22–6	9.0

ROWLAND & MARWOOD'S STEAMSHIP CO LTD

Barnby	bldg	Short2	4813	8120	439–2	54–0	24–2	10.0
Egton	1938	Pgill2	4363	7390	412–2	53–9	23–3	10.0
Fylingdale	1924	ThmpsJ	3918	6650	366–10	51–2	22–2	9.0
Goathland	1924	ThmpR2	3821	6800	364.8	50–6	22–0	8.5
Kildale	1924	Pgill2	3877	6830	363.5	51–4	22–1	8.5
Larpool	1924	Pgill2	3872	6700	363.5	51–5	22–1	8.5
Runswick	1930	ThmpsJ	3970	6770	379–2	51–0	22–7	9.0
Saltwick	1929	Laing	3775	6550	360.5	49–11	22–6	9.0
Sandsend	1925	Pgill2	3612	5925	361–5	50–0	21–0	9.0
Scoresby	1923	ThmpR2	3843	6750	371–6	50–0	22–7	8.5
Sneaton	1925	ThmpR2	3677	5925	361–5	50–0	20–11	8.5
Stakesby	1930	Pgill2	3900	6700	365.6	51–0	22–7	9.0
Streonshalh	1928	Pgill2	3895	6350	349.4	50–1	21–9	9.0

HECTOR WHALING LTD, 4 St Mary Axe, London EC3

Funnel: Black with houseflag (red over white halved diagonally)
Hull: *Hector* – black, red boot-topping; *United* – black, green boot-topping
Services: Whaling
Note: These companies were associated with N R Bugge (*qv* in Norway section), and also owned whalers

Whale factory vessels

HEKTORIA LTD

Hektoria (s2)	1899	H&W,B	13,797	16,500	565–0	63–4	32.0	10.0
ex Medic 28; conv passenger/general cargo 28								

UNITED WHALERS LTD

Terje Viken (r/t2)	1936	Desch3	20,638	28,000	635–0	80–2	38–6	12.0

HENDERSON & CO, P, 95 Bothwell St, Glasgow C2

Funnel: Black
Hull: Black, red boot-topping with white dividing line
Services: Passenger (1st class only) – Glasgow, Liverpool–Palma–Marseilles–Port Said–Rangoon; cargo – Glasgow–Brazil; Glasgow –Canada

BRITISH & BURMESE STEAM NAVIGATION CO LTD

Passenger/general cargo vessels

Amarapoora (P124/1)	1920	Denny2	8173	10,200	484–6	59–4	26–6	13.0
ordered as Ava								
Burma (P118/1)	1914	Denny1	7821	10,220	484–0	58–1	26–5	13.5
Kemmendine (P139/1)	1924	Denny2	7769	9580	453.8	59–2	26–7	13.0
Pegu (P124/1)	1921	Denny2	8183	10,200	484–6	59–2	26–6	13.0
Prome (st,P76/1)	1937	Denny2	7043	9360	462–0	59–2	27–4	14.0
Sagaing (P137/1)	1925	Denny2	7968	10,330	454.6	61–2	27–11	13.0
Salween (st,P76/1)	1938	Denny2	7063	9360	462–0	59–2	27–4	14.0
Yoma (r/t,P146/1)	1928	Denny2	8139	10,290	460.3	61–2	27–11	14.0

General cargo vessels

Henzada	1934	Hendn2	4161	7830	405–6	53–2	23–9	12.0
Kalewa	bldg	Denny2	4389	8810	421–6	55–2	25–1	10.5
Katha	1938	Denny2	4357	8810	421–6	55–2	25–1	10.5
Kindat	1938	Denny2	4358	8810	421–6	55–2	25–1	10.5
Mandalay (P2)	1911	Denny1	5529	8590	425.0	54–2	24–6	12.0
Martaban	1934	Hendn2	4161	7830	405–6	53–2	23–9	12.0

Note: See also under Board of Trade

HENDRY & SONS, P D, 163 Hope St, Glasgow C2

Funnel: Red, black top
Hull: Grey, red boot-topping
Services: General tramping

KINGSBOROUGH SHIPPING CO LTD

Kingsborough	1928	Lithgw	3368	5840	354–0	48–10	21–3	9.5
Kingsland	1930	Lithgw	3669	6220	366–0	50–2	21–9	10.0

HERCOAL SHIPPING CO LTD,
Farleigh House, 33 Lawrence Lane, London EC2

Herisle	1919	Superr	2640	4155	261–6	43–9	24–6	9.5
ex Fairisle 38, ex Annie Murphy 32, ex Lake Falama 27								
Herland	1920	Dtroit	2649	4155	261–6	43–9	24–5	9.5
ex Fairland 38, ex Lake Treba 33								
Herport	1919	Dtroit	2633	4155	261–6	43–10	24–6	9.5
ex Fairport 38, ex Lake Fairport 31								

Services: General tramping, mainly between French ports and Turkey

HEYN & SONS LTD, G, Head Line Bldgs, 12 Victoria St, Belfast

MOUNTAIN STEAMSHIP CO LTD

Lurigethan	1916	RottDD	3564	6370	373–0	50–1	21–7	9.5
ex Caleano 33								

ULSTER STEAMSHIP CO LTD (Head Line)

Dunaff Head (P12)	1918	Workmn	5258	8390	390.4	51–10	26–4	12.0
Fanad Head (P12)	1917	Workmn	5200	8310	390.4	51–10	26–4	11.0
Fanad Head (r/t,P12/1)	order	H&W,B	5038	8393	424–6	58–11	25–2	12.0
Kenbane Head (P12)	1919	Workmn	5225	8196	412–0	52–4	25–9	11.0
launched as War Whippet								
Melmore Head (st,P12)	1918	Workmn	5273	8450	390.4	51–10	26–4	12.0
ordered as Inishowen Head								
Torr Head (r/t,P12/1)	1937	H&W,B	5021	8489	424–0	58–11	25–2	12.0

Funnel: Black with white shield bearing red hand
Hull: Black, red boot-topping
Services: Belfast, Dublin, Cork, Londonderry–New Orleans, Galveston, Baltimore, Montreal, Quebec, St John NB; general tramping

Note: Also short-sea vessels

HILL & SONS, CHAS, Albion Dockyard, Bristol

BRISTOL CITY LINE OF STEAMSHIPS LTD

Boston City	1920	Hill	2870	4960	329–1	43–10	24–1	10.0
Bristol City	1920	Hill	2864	5000	329–1	43–10	24–1	10.0
Gloucester City	1919	Blumrl	3071	4870	342–2	46–8	21–9	10.0
ex Cyprian Prince 36								
Montreal City	1920	NofIre	3066	4909	342–0	46–8	21–9	10.0
ex Pinar del Rio 33								
New York City	1917	Hill	2722	4660	311.0	42–10	23–9	10.5
Toronto City	1925	Curle	2486	4684	321.8	46–2	20–5	10.0
ex Kyrenia 37, ex Nigerian 35								

Funnel: Black with white band bearing blue five-pointed star
Hull: Black or grey, red boot-topping
Services: Bristol, Cardiff, Swansea–New York and E coast US ports

HO HONG STEAMSHIP CO (1932) LTD,
61 Chulia St, Singapore, Straits Settlements

Hong Kheng (s2,P–/–,–/d)	1903	Reiher	6167	6460	431–10	50–5	26–6	11.5
ex Ling Nam 28, ex Field Marshal 22, ex Feldmarschall 16								
Hong Peng (s2,P–/d)	1899	Dixon2	4055	4890	383–1	46–1	22–5	10.0
ex Bloemfontein 24, ex Dakar 22, ex Anversville 06, launched as Clarence								
Hong Siang (P–/d)	1912	SHWR	3703	4882	371–2	50–1	23–11	12.0
ex Dimboola 35								

Services: Passenger, cargo – Rangoon–Penang–Port Swettenham–Singapore–Hoihow–Hong Kong–Amoy–Swatow

Note: Also smaller vessels

HOGARTH & SONS, H, 120 St Vincent St, Glasgow C2

HOGARTH SHIPPING CO LTD

Baron Ardrossan	1932	Hendn2	3896	6200	376–0	51–8	22–0	11.5
Baron Belhaven	1925	Lithgw	6591	10,250	451–6	57–4	25–10	10.5
Baron Cawdor	1935	Hendn2	3638	7540	401–2	53–2	23–4	10.5
Baron Cochrane	1927	AyrDk	3385	5770	353–7	48–8	21–4	10.5
Baron Dechmont	1929	Ardrsn	3675	6225	366–0	50–2	21–4	11.0
Baron Dunmore	1933	Hendn2	3938	6597	382–0	51–8	22–0	10.0
Baron Elgin	1933	Hendn2	3942	6645	382–0	51–8	22–0	10.0
Baron Elphinstone	1937	Laing	4635	8963	430–0	58–2	25–0	10.5
Baron Fairlie	1925	AyrDk	6706	10,200	456–0	57–5	25–10	10.5
Baron Graham	1925	Napr&M	3242	5620	348–6	48–5	21–3	9.5

Funnel: Yellow, black top
Hull: Black, red boot-topping
Services: General tramping; Glasgow–Lisbon–Huelva

Ho Hong Steamship: Hong Kheng *was completed by Reihersteig, Hamburg, in June 1903 as* Feldmarschall *for Deutsche Ost-Afrika Linie. In 1916 she was captured at Dar-es-Salaam and in 1917 was transferred to the Shipping Controller, renamed* Field Marshal, *and allocated to Union-Castle for management. In 1922 she was sold to Chinese owners and renamed* Ling Nam *(pictured here). After the failure of one owner, and further changes, she became* Hong Kheng *in August 1928. By then she had been refitted for the carriage of large numbers of deck passengers. Having escaped from Singapore before the Japanese occupation, in 1944 she was running between Suez and Jeddah with Hadj pilgrims. After the war she reverted to her former trade in the Far East, but on July 19 1947 stranded at Chilang Point, near Hong Kong, and became a total loss. She was on voyage from Rangoon to Amoy in ballast with 1800 deck passengers, all of whom were saved (RW Jordan collection)*

A Holt & Co: Ulysses *was completed by Workman, Clark at Belfast in October 1913 for service from Glasgow and Liverpool to Australia. She was one of the last vessels to leave Hong Kong before the Japanese occupation, and after calling at Singapore and Australian ports headed home via the Panama Canal. Following a collision with a tanker and reducing speed to 7 knots she headed for Newport News. She was torpedoed by* U160 *and sunk in 34 23N 75 35W fortunately without loss of life (RW Jordan collection)*

Baron Haig	1926	AyrDk	3391	5975	354–0	48–7	21–4	9.5
Baron Inchcape	1917	AyrDk	7005	10,400	441–6	56–2	26–6	10.5
Baron Jedburgh	1936	Lithgw	3656	7540	401–0	53–2	23–4	10.5
Baron Kinnaird	1927	Napr&M	3355	5762	354–0	48–9	21–4	9.5
Baron Lovat	1926	AyrDk	3395	5780	353–7	48–8	21–4	10.0
Baron Maclay	1924	AyrDk	6317	9700	445–6	56–4	25–8	10.0
Baron Minto	1937	Laing	4637	8960	430–0	58–2	25–0	10.5
Baron Napier	1930	Hendn2	3659	6225	366–0	50–2	21–4	10.0
Baron Newlands	1928	AyrDk	3386	5770	353–7	48–8	21–4	10.5
Baron Ogilvy	1926	AyrDk	3391	5780	353–7	48–8	21–4	10.5
Baron Ruthven	1925	DunlpB	3178	5503	348–5	48–6	21–4	9.5
Baron Scott	bldg	Lithgw	4574	9000	431–0	56–5	25–0	10.5
Baron Stranraer	1929	Lithgw	3668	6225	366–0	50–2	21–4	10.0
Baron Tweedmouth	1927	Lithgw	3357	5840	354–0	48–8	21–4	9.5

IBERIA SHIPPING CO LTD

Baron Forbes	1917	Koch	3061	4580	327–0	42–5	22–3	9.0
ex General Napier 22, ex Hamburg 20								
Baron Saltoun	1927	AyrDk	3404	5770	353–7	48–8	21–4	10.5

KELVIN SHIPPING CO LTD

Baron Ailsa	1936	Lithgw	3656	7540	401–0	53–2	23–4	10.5
Baron Blythswood	1929	Lithgw	3668	6225	366–0	50–2	21–4	10.5
Baron Carnegie	1925	DunlpB	3178	5503	348–6	48–6	21–4	10.5
Baron Douglas	1932	Lithgw	3899	6589	376–0	51–8	22–0	10.0
Baron Erskine	1930	Hendn2	3657	6225	366–0	50–2	21–10	10.5
Baron Herries	bldg	Lithgw	4574	9000	431–0	56–5	25–0	10.5
Baron Kelvin	1924	Conn2	3081	5300	332.2	48–2	21–4	10.5
Baron Loudoun	1925	Lithgw	3164	5575	348–6	48–6	21–4	10.5
Baron Nairn	1925	Lithgw	3164	5575	348–6	48–6	21–4	10.5
Baron Pentland	1926	AyrDk	3410	5770	353–9	48–8	21–4	10.0
Baron Ramsay	1929	Hendn2	3650	6290	366–0	50–2	21–10	10.0
Baron Renfrew	1935	Hendn2	3635	7539	401–2	53–2	23–4	10.5
Baron Semple	1939	Conn2	4573	9000	431–0	58–2	25–0	11.0
Baron Vernon	1929	Hendn2	3642	6290	366–0	50–2	21–10	11.0
Baron Yarborough	1928	AyrDk	3388	5770	353–7	48–7	21–4	9.5

HOLT & CO, ALFRED, (Blue Funnel Line), India Bldgs, Water St, Liverpool

Funnel: Blue, black top
Hull: Black, red boot-topping
Services: Passenger (1st class only) and cargo – Liverpool, Glasgow, NW Europe–Netherlands East Indies–China–Japan–Vancouver; Liverpool, Glasgow, NW Europe–Fremantle–Adelaide–Melbourne–Sydney–Brisbane–return to London, Glasgow, NW Europe; New York–Far East; New York–Netherlands East Indies; UK ports–Straits Settlements – Philippines–China–Japan–Korea–E Siberia; Singapore–Java – Fremantle

CHINA MUTUAL STEAM NAVIGATION CO LTD

Passenger/general cargo vessels

Antenor (st2,P155/1)	1925	Palmer	11,174	11,165	517–6	62–2	30–11	15.0
Patroclus (st2,P155/1)	1923	Scott2	11,314	11,405	517–9	62–3	30–8	15.0
Ulysses (s2,P175/1)	1913	Workmn	14,647	16,130	580–0	68–5	33–0	13.5

General cargo vessels

Asphalion (st,P12)	1924	Scott2	6274	7820	449–3	54–9	26–3	13.5
Atreus (P12/–,–/pilg)	1911	Scott2	6546	8625	459–0	52–10	27–5	13.0
Autolycus (st,P12/1)	1922	Leslie	7621	9500	477–6	58–4	28–5	14.5
Demodocus (P12/–,–/pilg)	1912	Workmn	6522	8040	458–11	52–10	27–5	13.5
Diomed (st2,P4/–,–/st)	1922	Workmn	10,374	13,235	513–5	62–5	33–2	14.5
Eurylochus	1912	Lond&G	5723	9050	430.5	53–11	27–6	12.0
ex Indraghiri 15								
Idomeneus (m2,P12/1,800/st)	1926	Workmn	7792	9010	477–6	58–5	28–4	14.5
Ixion (s2,P12/1,1600/st)	1912	Scott2	10,263	13,730	506.0	60–4	27–9	12.5
Laomedon (P12/–,–/pilg)	1912	Workmn	6491	8570	458–11	52–10	27–6	13.0
Lycaon (P12)	1913	Leslie	7350	9610	455.3	56–4	27–6	13.5
Maron (m2,P–,–/pilg)	1930	Caledn	6487	7926	433.0	56–4	27–1	14.0
Memnon (m2,P4)	1930	Caledn	7506	8906	478–0	59–5	28–6	16.0
Meriones (P12)	1922	Palmer	7557	9390	477–6	58–5	28–5	14.5
Neleus (P12/–,–/pilg)	1911	Workmn	6479	8575	458–11	52–9	27–6	13.0
Perseus (st2,P4)	1923	Caledn	10,286	13,485	513–5	62–4	33–2	14.5

Ship	Year	Builder						
Philoctetes (st2,P4/1,–/pilg)	1922	Scott2	11,431	14,525	529–3	63–2	32–0	14.5
Protesilaus (s2,P12)	1910	Leslie	9577	13,105	484.9	60–5	29–6	13.5
Rhesus (P12/–,–/pilg)	1911	Scott2	6530	8630	458–11	52–10	27–5	13.0
Stentor (m,P12)	1926	Caledn	6148	7973	449–0	55–10	26–3	14.5
Troilus (st,P12/1)	1921	Scott2	7422	9670	477–6	56–2	27–6	14.5

OCEAN STEAMSHIP CO LTD

Passenger/general cargo vessels

Ship	Year	Builder						
Aeneas (s2,P180/1)	1910	Workmn	10,058	11,370	509–0	60–5	29–0	13.5
Anchises (s2,P180/1)	1911	Workmn	10,000	11,430	509–0	60–5	29–0	13.5
Ascanius (s2,P180/1)	1910	Workmn	10,048	11,430	509–0	60–5	29–0	13.5
Charon (m,P106/1,12/2,–/d)	1936	Caledn	3703	3160	336–0	51–3	20–8	12.0
Gorgon (m,P132/1,24/2,–/d)	1933	Caledn	3533	3225	336–0	51–3	20–7	12.0
Hector (st2,P155/1)	1924	Scott2	11,198	11,425	517–9	62–4	30–8	15.0
Nestor (s2,P175/1)	1913	Workmn	14,629	15,950	580–0	68–5	33–0	14.0
Sarpedon (st2,P150/1)	1923	Cammel	11,321	11,315	517–9	62–4	30–8	15.0

General cargo vessels

Ship	Year	Builder						
Achilles (st2,P4/1,–/pilg)	1920	Scott2	11,404	14,415	518–1	63–2	32–0	14.0
Adrastus (st,P12/1)	1923	Scott2	7905	9940	477–6	58–1	28–5	14.5
Agamemnon (m2,P4/1,12/3)	1929	Work28	7593	8767	478–4	59–5	28–5	16.0
Agapenor (P12)	1914	Scott2	7392	9497	455.2	56–2	27–6	13.5
Ajax (m2,P5/1)	1931	Scott2	7540	8910	478–4	59–4	28–6	16.0
Antilochus (s2,P12)	1906	Leslie	9082	12,500	485.3	58–4	29–0	12.5
Automedon (st,P12/1,800pilg)	1922	Palmer	7528	9370	477–6	58–5	28–5	14.5
Bellerophon (s2,P12)	1906	Workmn	9019	12,390	485.3	58–5	29–0	12.5
Calchas (st2,P4/1,–/st)	1921	Workmn	10,304	13,205	513–5	62–5	33–2	14.5
Centaur (m,P117/1,44/2)	1924	Scott2	3066	3376	315.7	48–2	20–9	14.0
Clytoneus (m2,P–/–,–/pilg)	1930	Scott2	6278	7940	432.5	56–4	27–1	14.0
Cyclops (P12)	1906	Hendn2	9076	12,390	485.0	58–2	29–0	12.5
Dardanus (st,P12/1)	1923	Workmn	7726	9780	477	58–5	30–5	14.5
ex Flintshire 39, ex Dardanus 35								
Deucalion (m2,P4)	1930	Leslie	7740	8930	478–0	59–5	28–6	16.0
Dolius (sm2,P–)	1924	Scott2	5507	7815	423–0	52–2	25–9	11.0
Eumaeus (st,P12/1)	1921	Caledn	7472	9332	477–0	56–4	28–5	14.5
Euryades	1913	Conn2	5801	8920	430.0	54–0	27–7	12.0
ex Indra 15								
Eurybates (sm2,P4/3)	1928	Scott2	6276	7920	449–3	54–10	26–7	13.5
Eurymedon (m2,P–)	1924	Caledn	6223	7855	449–5	54–9	26–5	13.5
Glaucus (st,P12/1)	1921	Leslie	7586	9280	477–6	56–4	28–3	14.5
Helenus (P12)	1913	Scott2	7366	9670	455.2	56–2	27–6	13.5
Medon (m,P–)	1923	Palmer	5444	7739	423–0	52–2	25–9	12.0
Menelaus (st2,P4/1,–/pilg)	1923	Caledn	10,307	13,340	516–5	62–4	33–2	14.5
Menestheus (m2,P4)	1929	Caledn	7494	8850	478–0	59–5	28–5	16.0
Mentor (P12)	1914	Scott2	7383	9617	455.2	56–2	27–6	13.5
Myrmidon (m2,P–/–,–/pilg)	1930	Scott2	6278	7930	432.5	56–3	27–1	14.5
Orestes (m2,P12/–,800/pilg)	1926	Workmn	7748	9015	477–6	58–5	28–4	14.5
Peisander (m2,P–)	1925	Caledn	6225	7835	449–3	54–10	26–4	13.5
Phemius (st,P12/1)	1921	Scott2	7406	9610	477–6	56–2	27–6	14.5
Priam (m,P12)	bldg	Caledn	9975	9440	512–10	66–5	30–7	16.0
Prometheus (m2,4/1,6/3)	1925	Scott2	6095	8060	449–3	54–10	26–4	13.5
Pyrrhus (P12)	1914	Workmn	7418	9415	455.5	56–6	27–6	13.5

A Holt & Co: The cargo liner Philoctetes *was completed by Scott's of Greenock in December 1922 and used initially on trans-Pacific service. In August 1940 she was acquired by the Admiralty and converted into the destroyer depot ship HMS* Philoctetes. *She was broken up at Newport, Monmouthshire, in 1948* *(R Sherlock)*

A Holt & Co: The passenger/cargo liner Aeneas, *was completed by Workman, Clark at Belfast in November 1910. On July 2 1940 when on voyage in convoy from London to Glasgow to complete discharge, she was attacked and bombed by German aircraft 21 miles off Start Point. She caught fire and after being abandoned sank two days later 11 miles from Portland Bill* *(RW Jordan collection)*

A Holt & Co: Agamemnon *was completed by Workman, Clark at Belfast in 1928 for the Liverpool–Far East and round-the-world services of her owners. In 1940 she was taken over by the Royal Navy, and commissioned as the minelayer HMS* Agamemnon *in October. In 1943 at Vancouver she was converted into a recreation ship for the Pacific Fleet, and had on board a brewery, cinema/theatre and swimming facilities, and served in this role until 1946. She reverted to commercial service in March 1947, and was broken up at Hong Kong in 1963* *(Alex Duncan)*

Houlder Bros: Beacon Grange *was built for service between London and Buenos Aires and other South American ports. She was completed by Hawthorn, Leslie at Newcastle in 1938. On April 27 1941 she was torpedoed and sunk by* U552 *when on voayeg from the River Tyne to Buenos Aires in ballast* *(RW Jordan collection)*

Rhexenor (P12/1)	1922	Taikoo	7957	9860	477–6	58–4	28–5	14.5
Talthybius (s2,P12/1,1600/pilg)	1912	Scott2	10,254	13,725	518–0	60–4	27–9	12.5
Tantalus (m2,P12/1)	1923	Caledn	7726	9520	477–0	58–2	28–3	13.0
ex Radnorshire 39, ex Tantalus 36								
Teiresias (P12)	1914	Leslie	7405	9527	455.3	56–4	27–6	13.5
Telemachus (m2,P12)	order	Caledn	9061	9440	512–10	66–5	30–7	16.0
Teucer (s2,P12)	1906	Leslie	9079	12,590	485.3	58–4	29–0	12.5
Theseus (P12/–,–/pilg)	1908	Workmn	6527	8565	458–11	52–11	27–6	13.0
Titan (s2,P12)	1906	Hendn2	9035	12,395	485.8	58–4	29–0	12.5
Tyndareus (s2,P4/1,600/st)	1916	Scott2	11,361	14,720	518–1	63–2	32–9	13.5

Note: Ocean SS Co Ltd were controllers of Glen Line Ltd (*qv*) from 1935

HOLT & CO (LIVERPOOL) LTD, JOHN, 715 Royal Liver Bldg, Liverpool 3

Funnel: Red, black top
Hull: Grey, white boot-topping
Services: Liverpool–W Africa

Garthorpe* (P12)	1928	SmithM	2922	3690	310.0	44–8	20–2	10.0
ex John Holt 37								
Godfrey B Holt (P12)	1929	Cammel	3585	4152	347–6	47–1	20–4	10.5
John Holt (r/t,P–)	1938	Cammel	3815	5350	390–8	52–10	22–5	12.5
Jonathan Holt (r/t,P–)	1938	Cammel	3793	5350	390–6	52–10	22–5	12.5
Robert L Holt (P12)	1926	SmithM	2918	3685	310.0	44–8	20–2	10.0
Thomas Holt (P12)	1929	Cammel	3585	4152	347–6	47–1	20–4	10.5

Note: * Sold USSR 1939, renamed *Anatoli Serov*

HONEYMAN & CO, 12 Waterloo St, Glasgow C2

Services: General tramping

CARSLOGIE STEAMSHIP CO LTD

Carsbreck	1930	AyrDk	3670	6300	361–5	50–2	21–11	9.5
ex Coulbeg 38								
Carslogie	1924	Rhead1	3786	6300	377–6	50–6	21–6	9.0
ex Hartside 37								

HOULDER BROTHERS & CO LTD, 53 Leadenhall St, London EC3

Funnel: Black with red band bearing white Maltese cross
Hull: Black with white band, red boot-topping
Services: UK ports, Antwerp–Montevideo–Buenos Aires and other R Plate ports; oil and petroleum trades

General cargo and refrigerated cargo vessels

HOULDER LINE LTD

Beacon Grange (m2)	1938	Leslie	10,119	11,160	464–6	65–5	31–5	15.5
Dunster Grange (m2,P12)	1928	Fairfd	9494	9940	452–6	64–6	31–1	15.0
Elstree Grange	1916	Dixon2	6598	7850	420.0	53–6	29–6	12.5
ex Abadesa 28, laid down as Dominion Miller								
Hardwicke Grange (s2)	1921	Hamtn2	9005	9230	430.0	61–1	29–9	15.0
Lynton Grange	1937	Blythw	5029	8714	417.7	55–11	24.3	11.5
Oswestry Grange	1935	Blythw	4684	8492	421–1	55–2	24–0	11.5
ex Rhodesian Prince 37, ex Argentine Transport 36								
Royston Grange (P6)	1918	Leslie	5144	8150	412–6	52–4	25–3	10.0
ex Salado 35, ex Australier 27, ex War Bison 19								
Upwey Grange (m2,P12)	1925	Fairfd	9130	8670	451–2	62–6	29–9	15.0

FURNESS-HOULDER ARGENTINE LINES LTD

Baronesa (s2)	1918	Dixon2	8663	10,000	450–8	61–4	30–8	14.5
Canonesa (st)	1920	Workmn	8286	10,140	465–0	58–4	29–4	14.0
Duquesa (st)	1918	Irvin3	8651	9540	451–0	61–4	29–11	14.5
Marquesa (s2,P12)	1918	Hamtn2	8979	9880	450–5	61–1	30–7	14.5
Princesa (s2,P12)	1918	Steph2	8731	9775	450–5	61–2	30–9	14.5

FURNESS, WITHY & CO LTD

El Argentino* (m2,P12)	1928	Fairfd	9501	10,100	453–2	64–6	31–1	15.0

Note: * Managed by Furness-Houlder Argentine Lines Ltd (*qv* above)

Tankers

BRITISH EMPIRE STEAM NAVIGATION CO LTD

Caroni River (m)	1928	Blythw	7807	11,120	456.0	59–0	26–1	12.0

EMPIRE TRANSPORT CO LTD

Imperial Transport (m)								
	1931	Blythw	8022	12,460	459.7	60–0	27–11	12.0

Note: Houlder Brothers & Co Ltd was a member of the Furness Withy & Co Ltd (*qv*) group.

HOUSTON LINE (LONDON) LTD, 4 St Mary Axe, London EC3

Funnel: Black with two red bands
Hull: Black, red boot-topping
Services: UK–South and E Africa; Canada, New York–South and E Africa; Canada, New York–R Plate

BRITISH & SOUTH AMERICAN STEAM NAVIGATION CO LTD

Banffshire (r/t)	1912	Doxfrd	6479	8895	430.0	53–6	27–3	13.0
ex Clan Macrae 20								
Buteshire (r/t)	1912	Palmer	6590	8910	430.5	53–8	27–3	13.0
ex Clan Macewen 20								
Clan Ogilvy	1914	Doxfrd	5802	8815	430.0	54–2	25–7	12.0
Clan Ross	1914	SHWR	5897	8930	430.0	54–4	25–7	12.0
Halizones	1920	AyrDk	5298	8120	412–6	52–2	25–3	11.5
Harmodius	1919	AyrDk	5229	8074	412–6	52–4	25–3	11.5
launched as Hermione								
Harmonides	1920	AyrDk	5237	8067	412–6	52–4	25–3	11.5
launched as Hesione								

Note: This company was acquired by Clan Line Steamers Ltd (*qv*) in 1918

HUDDART PARKER LTD, 466 Collins St, Melbourne Victoria, Australia

Funnel: Passenger vessels – yellow; cargo vessels – black
Hull: Passenger vessels – black with white band, red boot-topping with white dividing line; cargo vessels – black, red boot-toping with white dividing line
Services: Australia–New Zealand

Passenger/general cargo vessels								
Wanganella (m2,P304/1,104/2)								
	1931	H&W,B	9576	6238	474–0	63–11	24–6	16.5
ex Achimota 32 (proposed name Campaspe not taken up)								
Westralia (m2,P360/1,90/3)								
	1929	H&WGw	8108	6265	448–0	60–2	25–1	16.0
Zealandia (s2,P200/1,120/2,126/3)								
	1910	BrownJ	6683	4485	428–0	54–9	24–4	15.0
General cargo vessels								
Adelong	1936	H&WGw	3577	5379	359–4	48–2	22–9	12.0
Barwon (r/t)	1939	Caledn	4239	5640	378–4	50–4	22–7	11.0
Colac	1920	NSWGov	3341	5600	341–0	47–11	21–10	10.0
ex Dinoga 26								
Corio	1919	NSWGov	3346	5600	341–0	47–11	21–10	10.0
ex Delungra 26								
Goulburn	1915	Sundld	2367	3660	305–5	45–0	19–2	10.0

Note: This company owned vessels of under 2000gt

HUNTER (MANAGEMENT) LTD, FRED, 34 Great St Helen, London EC3

Funnel: Yellow with black H inside black circle, black top
Services: General tramping
Note: * Sold Greece 1939, renamed *Ronin* (Panamanian flag); ** sold Italy 1939, renamed *Fidelitas*

HUNTER SHIPPING CO LTD								
Huntress*	1919	Nthmbl	5704	9000	412–0	53–0	26–3	10.5
ex Tower Ensign 37, ex Waikawa 35, launched as War Donjon								
MINERVA STEAMSHIP CO LTD								
Bolton Castle**	1914	Hamtn2	5826	9250	439–5	53–0	26–3	10.5

HUNTING & SON LTD, B Milburn House, Dean St, Newcastle upon Tyne 1

Funnel: Black with blue seven-pointed star over seven red and six white alternating narrow bands
Hull: Grey, red boot-topping
Services: Oil and petroleum trades

Tankers								
FIELD TANK STEAMSHIP CO LTD								
Clydefield (m)	1928	Hendn2	7365	10,100	450.5	57–9	26–7	11.0
lengthened 35								
Oilfield (m)	1938	Odense	8516	12,540	493–1	61–10	27–6	12.0
Wellfield (m2)	1924	TyneIr	6054	8865	423–0	51–6	26–1	11.0
lengthened 32								
HUNTING STEAMSHIP CO LTD								
Tynefield (m)	1926	Laing	5856	8930	408–0	54–6	26–5	11.0
NORTHERN PETROLEUM TANK STEAM SHIP CO LTD								
Duffield (m)	1938	Odense	8516	12,540	493–1	61–10	27–6	12.0
Gretafield (r/t)	1928	Cammel	10,191	15,550	500.2	67–11	29–8	11.5
Pontfield (m)	1939	Eriksb	8319	12,875	488–10	61–0	26–9	11.5
Sylvafield (m)	1925	Laing	5709	8610	408–0	52–0	26–5	11.0

IMPERIAL OIL SHIPPING CO LTD,
56 Church St, Toronto, Ontario, Canada

Funnel: Black with white over blue over white bands
Hull: Black, red boot-topping
Services: Oil and petroleum trades

Tankers								
Albertolite	1912	ArmWhl	6406	9600	415.0	55–2	27–1	9.0
ex Caddo 29, ex Winnipeg 14, ex Adorna 14								

Calgarolite (m2)	1929	FurnH	11,941	17,144	542–0	70–5	30–4	10.5
Canadolite (m2)	1926	Krupp	11,309	16,000	510.9	68–2	29–2	11.0
Montrolite (m2)	1926	Krupp	11,309	16,000	510.9	68–2	29–2	11.0
Ontariolite (m2)	1925	Krupp	8889	12,515	489–8	63–2	27–2	11.0
Reginolite (m2)	1926	VulcSt	9069	12,495	489–6	63–1	27–1	11.0
Trontolite (m)	1918	Skinnr	7115	9750	428.0	57–0	26–2	10.0
conv steamer 25								
Vancolite (m2)	1928	Steph2	11,404	16,570	510.2	68–2	29–7	11.0
Victolite (m2)	1928	Steph2	11,410	16,535	510.2	68–2	29–7	11.0

Note: This company, which was a subsidiary of Standard Oil Co of New Jersey (*qv* in United States section), also owned tankers under 3000gt

INDO-CHINA STEAM NAVIGATION CO LTD,
Victoria, Hong Kong, and 3 Lombard St, London EC3

Funnel: Red, black top
Hull: Black with white band, red boot-topping
Services: Hong Kong–Chinese ports–Yokohama–Borneo–Malaya–Siam–Calcutta; Chinese coastal

E Sang (P130/1,/2,910/d)	1934	Curle	3370	3200	343–0	47–2	17–6	13.0
ex Hai Heng 38								
Hinsang (m,P–)	bldg	HK&Wh	4644		350.0	53–0	22.7	12.5
Hosang (P26/1,28/2,1662/3)	1922	NofIre	5698	8700	411.0	53–10	27–2	12.5
Kumsang (P6/1,32/2,1680/3)	1920	Laing	5447	7821	420.3	55–0	27–2	12.0
ex Barrymore 25								
Kutsang (P22/1,40/2,2116/d)	1922	SHWR	5869	7820	418.2	54–3	26–8	12.0
Mausang (P10/1,24/2,382/3)	1920	Shangh	3372	5110	331.2	46–10	21–8	11.0
ex Yannis 21								
Ming Sang (P130/1,/2,910/d)	1934	SHWR	3420	3200	343–0	47–2	17–7	13.0
ex Hai Li 38								
Sui Sang (P18/1,222/2,500/3)	1923	HK&Wh	3577	3967	324–6	46–1	22–7	12.0
Taksang (r/t,P20/1–/d)	1935	Lithgw	3471	2800	328–0	48–1	18–6	10.0
Tai Sang (r/t,P20/1,–/d)	1938	HK&Wh	3555	2766	328–0	48–1	18–6	14.0
Wing Sang (r/t,P55/1,16/3,404/d)	1938	HK&Wh	3560	2766	328–0	48–1	18–6	14.0
Wo Sang (P130/1,/2,910/d)	1934	Curle	3373	3200	343–0	47–2	17–7	13.0
ex Hai Chen 38								
Yu Sang (P130/1,/2,910/d)	1934	SHWR	3357	3200	343–0	47–2	17–7	13.0
ex Hai Yuan 38								
Yuen Sang (P12/1,28/2,1285/3)	1923	HK&Wh	3229	3982	324–6	46–1	22–7	12.0

Note: This company, a subsidiary of Jardine, Matheson & Co Ltd, also owned vessels of under 3000gt

IRVIN & JOHNSON (SOUTH AFRICA) LTD,
No 4 Quay, Table Bay Docks, Cape Town, South Africa

Funnel: Black, broad white band
Hull: Black with white band
Services: Whaling
Note: These companies also owned large fleets of whalers and fishing vessels

KERGUELEN SEALING & WHALING CO LTD

Whale factory vessel

Tafelberg (s2)	1930	ArmWh2	13,640	21,021	508.3	72–6	35–2	11.5

JACOBS & CO LTD, JOHN I, 15 St Helen's Place, London EC3

Funnel: Yellow, black top
Hull: Dark grey, red boot-topping
Services: Dry cargo tramping, tanker trades

General cargo vessels

Beechwood	bldg	Laing	4897	8970	431–10	58–2	25–0	10.5
Glenwood	bldg	Laing	4897	8970	431–10	58–2	25–0	10.5

Tankers

MOLASSES & GENERAL TRANSPORT CO LTD

Laurelwood (m2)	1929	ArmWh1	7347	10,225	454–0	59–2	27–8	11.5
Teakwood	1927	ArmWh1	6014	9790	415.1	54–10	26–2	11.0

OIL & MOLASSES TANKERS LTD

Longwood (m2)	1930	Laing	9463	14,230	476.3	66–5	28–7	11.0
Rosewood (m)	1931	ArmWh2	5989	9400	408–0	55–1	26–9	11.0
ex Stegg 34								

Houlder Bros: Imperial Transport *was built by Blythswood Shipbuilding at Glasgow and completed in September 1931. On February 11 1940 she was torpedoed by* U53 *in 59N 12W and broke in two. The stern section was recovered and towed in and a new bow section was built by Wm Hamilton & Co, Glasgow. On March 25 1942 she was again torpedoed, by* U94*, east of Cape Race; although hit by two torpedoes and being abandoned, she remained afloat, and after reboarding was towed in and then proceeded to New York for repairs. After the war, she was sold to Norway in 1947 and renamed* Mesna, *and also within Norway was sold again, in 1949, and renamed* Rona. *She was broken up in Germany in 1958 (RW Jordan collection)*

John I Jacobs & Co: Teakwood *was completed in August 1927 by Armstrong, Whitworth at Newcastle. On September 21 1939, while in convoy OA7, she was torpedoed by* U35 *in 49 39N 06 39W but the damage sustained was repaired and she re-entered service before the end of the year. She survived the war and was broken up during 1955–56 (RW Jordan collection)*

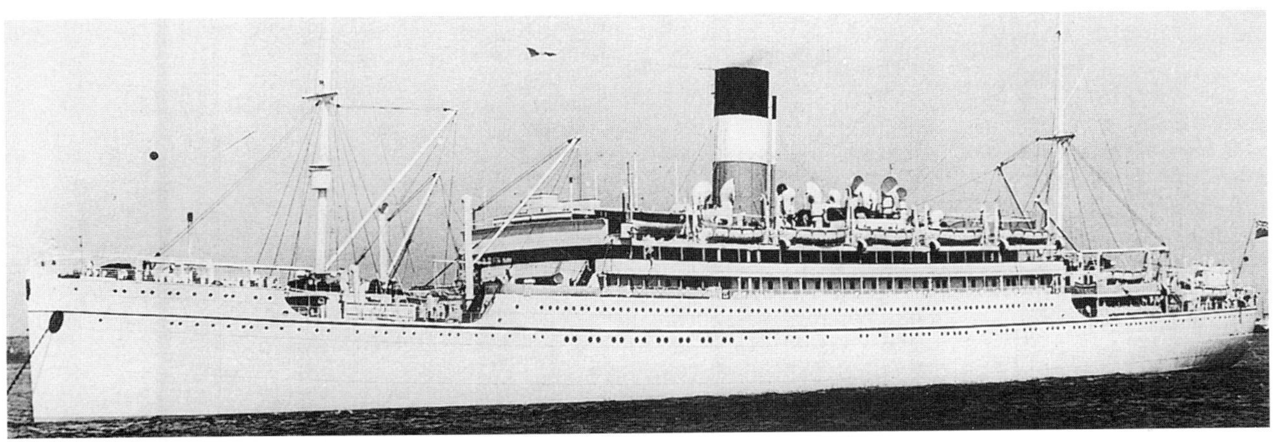

Lamport & Holt: Vandyck *was built by Workman, Clark & Co, Belfast, and originally had accommodation for 300 first class, 150 second class and 230 third class passengers. Later she was used solely for cruising with a much reduced passenger complement. In October 1939 she was converted to the armed boarding vessel HMS* Vandyck. *On June 9 1940* Vandyck *was attacked by a German dive bomber and sunk west of Narvik, Norway. She was en route to take part in the evacuation of Allied troops from Norway. Two officers and five ratings were lost, and 29 officers and 132 ratings having landed, were taken prisoner and were to remain in Germany until the end of the war (RW Jordan collection)*

JAMAICA BANANA PRODUCERS' STEAMSHIP CO LTD, 31–34 Fenchurch St, London EC3

Funnel: Blue with black top and white over blue over white bands
Hull: White, blue boot-topping
Service: Kingston–Plymouth – Rotterdam–London; Kingston–London

Note: * Owned by Hadley Shipping Co Ltd (*qv*) and on long-term charter
Note: The above vessels were managed by Kaye, Son & Co Ltd (*qv*)

Fruit carriers

Jamaica Pioneer (P12)								
	1931	Lithgw	5471	4250	386.2	54–2	22–0	14.5
Jamaica Planter* (m2,P–)								
	1936	Lithgw	4098	3800	370–0	50–2	23–2	15.0
Jamaica Producer (P12)								
	1934	Lithgw	5464	4900	423–0	54–9	23–10	16.0
laid down as Jamaica Perseverence								
Jamaica Progress (P12)								
	1932	Lithgw	5475	4400	393.7	54–2	21–11	15.5

JAMES, R I, Watergate Bldgs, Newcastle upon Tyne 1

Funnel: Black with W on white band between two coloured bands
Services: General tramping

WHITE SHIPPING CO LTD

Biddlestone (r/t)	1937	Short2	4910	8020	414–10	53–11	23–7	10.0

JONES & SONS, FREDERICK, 36 West Bute St, Cardiff

Funnel: Black, red band
Hull: Grey, red boot-topping
Services: General tramping

Note: * Sold Constants (South Wales) Ltd, 1939, renamed *Lyminge*

ABBEY LINE LTD								
Margam Abbey	1938	GrayWH	2470	4350	317–1	45–1	19–11	10.5
Neath Abbey*	1919	Hill	2499	4050	311–6	43–0	19–10	10.5
ex Baron Herries 34, ex Trevelyan 23, launched as War Quince								
Tintern Abbey	1938	GrayWH	2471	4350	317–1	45–1	19–11	10.5
MELROSE ABBEY SHIPPING CO LTD								
Melrose Abbey	1936	GrayWH	2473	4350	317–1	45–1	19–11	10.5

JONES & CO LTD, REGINALD, Empire House, 51 Mount Stuart Sq, Cardiff

Services: General tramping

BRANCH STEAM SHIP CO LTD

Candleston Castle	1920	Burntd	2495	4281	311–0	43–8	20–4	9.0
ex Seven Seas Star 37, ex Antinea 35								
Ogmore Castle	1919	DunlpB	2481	3950	313–6	42–11	19–10	8.5
ex Backworth 39, launched as War Orange								

JONES & CO, RICHARD W, 104 Dock St, Newport, Monmouthshire

Funnel: Yellow
Hull: Black, red boot-topping
Services: General tramping

USKSIDE SHIPPING CO LTD								
Uskside	1937	Burntd	2706	4500	324–2	45–2	20–6	9.5
USKPORT STEAMSHIP CO LTD								
Uskbridge	bldg	Burntd	2715	4500	324–0	45–2	20–6	10.0
Uskmouth	1928	Burntd	2483	4450	310–0	43–11	20–2	9.5
Uskport	1925	Burntd	2462	4450	310–0	44–0	20–2	9.5

KAYE, SON & CO LTD, Plantation House, 31–34 Fenchurch St, London EC3

Funnel: Black with white K inside white diamond frame
Hull: Black, red boot-topping
Services: UK–R Plate; general tramping

General cargo vessels

COOLHAM STEAMSHIP CO LTD								
Joyous (r/t)	1924	Dobson	3585	6650	360.0	50–0	22–10	10.0
ex Jameson 34								
Kayeson	1929	Leslie	4606	8756	393.1	54–4	24–3	10.0
THE 'K' STEAMSHIP CO LTD								
Marina	1935	Lithgw	5088	8500	390.0	55–2	26.5	10.0
Marlene	1920	Curle	6507	10,450	465–0	58–2	27–3	12.0
ex Nogoya 36, ex Highland Warrior 33								
Marsdale	bldg	Lithgw	4890	8500	436–5	56–11	24–0	12.0
Marton	1933	Lithgw	4969	8350	408–0	54–2	23–9	10.0
KAYE TRANSPORT CO LTD								
Marcella	1928	Lithgw	4592	7950	397–6	52–0	23–11	10.0
Marylyn	1930	Lithgw	4555	7950	397–6	52–0	23–11	11.0
MARCONI STEAMSHIP CO LTD								
Marconi (s2)	1917	H&WGw	7402	8270	440.8	56–2	28–3	9.5
WALMAR STEAMSHIP CO LTD								
Margalau	1926	Lithgw	4541	7930	397–6	52–0	23–11	10.0
Margot	1926	Lithgw	4545	7950	397–6	52–0	23–11	10.0
Marslew	1926	Lithgw	4542	7930	397–6	52–0	23–11	10.0

Manager for
MINISTRY OF SHIPPING
Fruit carrier

Empire Merchant (m)								
	1938	DeutsH	4864	2970	422–9	52–7	17–10	16.5
ex Pomona 39								

Note: This company also managed vessels of the Jamaica Banana Producers' SS Co Ltd (*qv*)

LAMBERT BROTHERS LTD, Cunard House, 88 Leadenhall St, London EC3

Huncliff* (r/t)	1936	Lithgw	4511	8250	385.0	53–6	24–1	10.5
ex Dornoch 37								
Terlings	1937	Lithgw	2318	4020	295–6	44–5	20–7	10.5
DORNOCH SHIPPING CO LTD								
Coulbeg	order	Lithgw	5237	9250	447–8	56–3	24–9	10.5
Coulmore	1936	AyrDk	3670	6300	360–0	50–4	21–11	9.5
Coultarn (m)	1938	Lithgw	3759	7500	401–2	53–2	23–4	10.5
Dornoch	1939	Lithgw	5186	9150	448–6	56–3	24–9	10.5
MIDDLETON STEAMSHIP CO LTD								
Middleton (r/t)	1935	Hamtn4	4297	8400	402–9	53–0	24–6	10.0
ex Darcolm 37								
TEMPLE STEAMSHIP CO LTD								
Temple Arch	bldg	Lithgw	5138	9154	447–6	56–2	24–9	10.5
Temple Bar	1928	Hamtn3	4291	8300	402–9	52–0	24–5	10.5
Temple Inn	bldg	Lithgw	5128	9170	447–6	56–2	24–9	10.5
Temple Mead	1928	Pgill2	4427	8383	391.2	53–0	24–6	10.5
Temple Moat	1928	Pgill2	4427	8383	391.2	53–0	24–6	10.5
Temple Pier	1928	Hamtn4	4312	8400	402–8	52–8	24–6	10.5
Temple Yard (r/t)	1937	Hamtn4	5205	9450	447–2	56–2	25–0	10.5
ex Darleny 37								

Funnel: Black with white band bearing red triangle
Hull: Black with white band, red boot-topping
Services: General tramping

Note: * Sold Stanhope Steamship Co Ltd (J A Billmeir & Co Ltd) 1939, renamed *Stancliff*

LAMPORT & HOLT LTD, 101, Royal Liver Bldg, Liverpool

Cruising vessels								
Vandyck (st2,P450)	1921	Workmn	13,241	8600	535–0	64–4	28–4	14.0
Voltaire (st2,P450)	1923	Workmn	13,245	8630	535–0	64–4	28–4	14.0
General cargo vessels								
Balfe (P8)	1920	Hendn2	5369	8082	412–9	52–4	25–4	10.0
launched as War Lupin								
Balzac (P8)	1920	Hendn2	5372	8071	412–9	52–4	25–4	10.5
Biela (P8)	1918	Short	5298	8221	412–8	52–5	25–3	10.5
ex War Mastiff 19								
Bonheur (st,P8)	1920	H&W,B	5327	7603	412–7	52–5	25–4	10.5
Brontë (P8)	1919	McMlln	5317	7955	412–8	52–2	25–3	10.5
launched as War Convoy								
Browning (P8)	1919	McMlln	5332	8060	412–8	52–2	25–3	10.5
launched as War Marten								
Bruyère (P8)	1919	McMlln	5335	8080	412–10	52–3	25–3	10.5
launched as War Mole								
Debrett (m,P10)	bldg	H&W,B	6244	10,090	456–0	62–4	28–1	13.0
Defoe (m,P12)	order	H&W,B	6245	10,090	456–0	62–4	28–0	13.0
Delambre (P–)	1917	MitsuN	7032	10,977	462–0	58–2	26–8	10.5
ex War Dame 19								
Delane (m,P12)	1938	H&W,B	6054	10,214	456–0	62–4	26–9	14.0
Delius (m,P12)	1937	H&W,B	6065	10,210	456–0	62–4	26–8	14.0
Devis (m,P12)	1938	H&W,B	6054	10,203	456–0	62–4	26–9	14.0
Lalande (P9)	1920	Hendn2	7453	10,650	442.6	55–6	28–10	12.5
Laplace (P–)	1919	McMlln	7327	10,510	447–0	56–4	28–7	11.5
Lassell (m2,P–)	1922	McMlln	7417	10,440	430.2	56–2	28–7	11.5
Leighton (m2,P–)	1921	McMlln	7412	10,494	430.1	56–2	28–7	11.5
Linnell* (m2,P–)	1921	McMlln	7424	10,494	430.0	56–2	28–7	11.5
Phidias (P–)	1913	McMlln	5623	9275	415.5	56–0	25–1	10.5
Sheridan (P–)	1918	McMlln	4665	7555	385.6	52–2	24–7	10.5
Swinburne (P–)	1917	McMlln	4659	7565	385.5	52–2	24–7	10.5

Funnel: Blue with black top separated by broad white band
Hull: Black, cruising vessels – white, blue boot-topping
Services: Glasgow, Liverpool – Brazil(direct); Glasgow, Liverpool–R Plate (direct); Liverpool–Lisbon–Brazil; Liverpool–Spain–R Plate; Liverpool–Lisbon–Spain–Brazil–River Plate; Middlesbrough, Antwerp, London–R Plate; New York–West Indies–Brazil–R Plate; New York–Brazil; New York–R Plate; New York–Manchester; R Plate–Canary Islands–UK–NW Europe; R Plate–Brazil–Boston–New York; cruising to Mediterranean, Atlantic islands, West Africa, West Indies, Norwegian fjords, Baltic

Note: * BU Troon 1939

LARRINAGA STEAMSHIP CO LTD, 30 James St, Liverpool

Domingo de Larrinaga								
	1929	Lithgw	5358	9135	415.0	55–0	24–2	10.0
Ena de Larrinaga	1925	Schich	5200	8130	405–0	52–9	24–8	9.5

Funnel: Black with broad yellow containing two red bands
Hull: Black, red boot-topping
Services: Houston–Galveston–Manchester–Liverpool; Liverpool–Cuba; general tramping

José de Larrinaga	1920	CanVic	5303	8242	413–1	52–4	25–3	10.5
ex Loch Tay 27								
Maria de Larrinaga	1929	Duncan	4988	8750	407.0	53–6	24–5	10.5
Miguel de Larrinaga	1924	Schich	5230	8130	405–6	52–8	24–8	9.5
Minnie de Larrinaga	1914	LithR	5046	9060	420.0	54–0	25–1	10.0
Niceto de Larrinaga	1916	LithR	5591	9900	456–6	56–0	25–4	10.5
Pilar de Larrinaga	1918	MitsuN	7046	10,988	462–0	58–1	26–9	11.0
ex War Nymph 19								
Ramon de Larrinaga	1920	Duncan	5791	10,050	464–11	57–11	25–5	9.5
Richard de Larrinaga	1929	Lithgw	5358	9135	415.0	55–0	24–2	10.0
Rupert de Larrinaga	1930	Lithgw	5358	9135	415.0	55–0	24–2	10.0
Sylvia de Larrinaga	1925	Schich	5218	8130	405–0	52–9	24–6	9.5
Telesfora de Larrinaga	1920	Duncan	5780	10,050	464–11	57–11	25–5	9.5

Funnel: Black with blue over red bands bearing yellow five-pointed star
Hull: Dark grey, red boot-topping
Services: UK–British Columbia; British Columbia, W coast US–Australia

LAWTHER, LATTA & CO LTD, 20 Billiter Bldgs, Billiter St, London EC3

Manager for

NITRATE PRODUCERS' STEAMSHIP CO LTD

Anglo African (P12)	1929	Short2	5601	10,066	439–8	58–0	25–2	11.5
Anglo Canadian (m,P12)	1928	Short2	5268	9746	439–9	58–0	25–3	11.5
Anglo Indian (P12)	1938	Short2	5609	9850	447–5	61–6	25–6	12.0
Anglo Peruvian (P12)	1926	Short2	5457	10,138	439–9	58–0	25–2	11.5
Anglo Saxon (P12)	1929	Short2	5596	10,066	440–2	58–0	25–2	11.5

Funnel: Yellow with blue L, black top
Services: General tramping

LENSEN, ABRAHAM CORNELIS, 9 Camomile St, London EC3

ARY SHIPPING LTD								
Ary Lensen (m)	1930	B&W	3214	5555	336–0	50–0	20–6	11.0
ex Orla II 34								
ELISABETH LENSEN NAVIGATION LTD								
Elisabeth Lensen	1910	ThmpsJ	4212	7620	365.0	51–5	24–9	9.0
ex Monkswood 35, ex Maresfield 28								

Funnel: Yellow with blue L, black top
Services: General tramping
Note: * Sold Smith, Hogg & Co Ltd 1939

LENSEN, CORNELIS A, 9 Camomile St, London EC3

CLARE SHIPPING CO LTD, 13 St Mary Axe, London EC3								
Clare Lilley	1917	Prstm1	3726	7100	350.0	50–11	23–9	8.5
ex Modig 34, ex Eastcliffe 19, ex Cliffside 18								
FOSS BECK SHIPPING CO LTD								
Foss Beck (r/t)	1930	SmithM	4876	7180	344–4	60–4?	22–10	10.5
ex Beldagny 38, ex Port Alfred 33								
LENSEN SHIPPING LTD								
Magdalena*	1923	Craig2	3118	5010	325.0	48–1	20–8	9.0
LENSEN TRANSPORT LTD								
Frederika Lensen	1912	Rhead1	4283	7910	369.9	51–1	24–1	9.0
ex Trevaylor 34								
TRANSITUS SHIPPING LTD								
Tweed	1926	DunlpB	2697	4970	314.1	47–2	20–1	10.0
ex Quercus 27								

Services: General tramping
Note: * Sold Baltycka Spólka Okretowa Sp z o o, Gydnia, Poland, 1939, renamed *Wigry*
Note: See also in Greece section

LIVANOS & SONS LTD, JOHN, Baltic House, 27 Leadenhall St, London EC3

JENNY STEAMSHIP CO LTD								
River Dart*	1912	Dixon2	1859	2718	265.3	38–9	18–1	7.5
ex Jenny 37, ex Glenbrydan 33, ex Hooton 21								
River Tyne	1920	Ouse	1525	2440	248–5	36–1	18–7	8.5
ex Mary II 37, ex Islington 35, ex Sherburn 28								

Larrinaga SS Co: Telesfora de Larrinaga *was completed by R Duncan & Co in May 1920. She was damaged during an air raid on the London docks during the night of March 19–20 1941, but re-entered service after repairs. She survived the war and in 1949 was sold to Wheelock, Marden, of Hong Kong, and renamed* Oritrin *with Hong Kong registration. She was sold to Japan in 1951 and renamed* Fuzan Maru, *in 1956 sold within Japan and renamed* Shoei Maru, *and broken up during 1960–61 (RW Jordan collection)*

Lykiardopulo & Co: Merchant Prince *was completed by Doxford, at Sunderland, in September 1939, after the start of the Second World War, for the British flag subsidiary of this London-Greek company. On March 16 1943* Merchant Prince *was in convoy ET14 off Oran when she was torpedoed by* U77 *and damaged. The British steamer* Hadleigh *was also torpedoed and damaged, but eventually became a total loss. After the war* Merchant Prince *commenced normal tramping work and remained with her owner until June 1963 when she was sold to Hong Kong breakers (RW Jordan collection)*

MacAndrews & Co: Colon *was one of a series of nine sisterships built by H & C Grayson, Garston, during 1917–22. Built to a pre-First World War design, these became a standard 'War' type, although only two were completed with 'War' names.* Colon *was launched in July 1919, and completed in September. During the Second World War she was largely on government service, and after a few years back in commercial service was broken up at Port Glasgow in 1954 (Alex Duncan)*

Manchester Liners: The turbine steamer Manchester Port *was completed by Blythswood Shipbuilding, Glasgow, in October 1935. She survived the war and was broken up at Bilbao 1965 (RW Jordan collection)*

LIVANOS & CO LTD, S, Bevis Marks House, Bevis Marks, London EC3

Funnel: Black with red L bordered by ornamental blue bands above and below, all on broad white band
Hull: Grey
Services: General tramping

TRENT MARITIME CO LTD

Duke of Athens (m)	bldg	Doxfrd	5217	9475	442–11	56–6	25–11	12.0
Duke of Sparta	bldg	GrayWH	5397	10,550	457–2	57–10	27–0	11.3

LYLE SHIPPING CO LTD, 120 St Vincent St, Glasgow C2

Funnel: Yellow
Hull: Black, red boot-topping with white dividing line
Service: General tramping, and much Vancouver–UK–NW Europe trade

Cape Corso	1929	Lithgw	3807	6500	352.5	50–6	22–7	10.5
ex Knight of St George 34								
Cape Howe	1930	Lithgw	4443	7300	388–0	53–0	22–11	10.5
ex Knight Almoner 34								
Cape Nelson	1929	Lithgw	3807	6500	352.5	50–6	22–7	10.5
ex Knight of St Michael 34								
Cape Race	1930	Lithgw	3807	6500	352.5	50–6	22–7	10.5
ex Knight of St John 34								
Cape Sable	1936	Lithgw	4398	7285	388–0	53–0	22–11	10.0
laid down as Knight Batchelor								

CAPE OF GOOD HOPE MOTORSHIP CO LTD

Cape of Good Hope (m,P–)	1925	Lithgw	4963	8000	405.0	52–2	24–8	10.5
Cape Wrath	bldg	Lithgw	4512	8000	426–7	54–3	23–10	10.0

CAPE YORK MOTORSHIP CO LTD

Cape Clear (m)	1939	Lithgw	5085	8850	447–6	56–2	24–10	10.5
Cape Horn (m)	1929	Lithgw	5643	9450	425.0	56–0	25–6	12.0
Cape Rodney	bldg	Lithgw	4512	8000	426–7	54–3	23–10	10.0
Cape York (m2,P–)	1926	Lithgw	5027	9075	424–0	54–0	26–3	10.5
Lycia (m)	1924	DunlpB	2338	4511	309–6	44–2	22–1	10.5

MACANDREWS & CO LTD, 19 Leadenhall St, London EC3

Funnel: Yellow
Hull: Steamers – black, red boot-topping with white dividing line; motor vessels – white, green boot-topping
Services: Cargo and passenger – London, Liverpool, Glasgow, Swansea, Hull, Middlesbrough, Antwerp–Hamburg–Mosel–Ferrol –Coruna–Villa-Garcia–Vigo–Huelva–Seville–Cadiz–Malaga–Almeria–Cartagena–Alicante–Valencia–Tarragona–Barcelona; London–Gibraltar–Tangier–Rabat –Casablanca–Mazagan–Mogador; Liverpool–Canary Islands
Note: Also *Calderon* (built 1919/1374gt), *Cortes* (19/1374), *Pacheco* (mv, 27/1346), *Palacio* (mv, 27/1346), *Pelayo* (mv, 27/1346), *Pinto* (mv, 28/1346), *Pinzon* (mv, 22/1365), *Pizarro* (mv, 23/1367), *Ponzano* (mv, 28/1346)
Note: This company was acquired by United Baltic Corporation Ltd in Dec. 1935

Carpio (p2)	1921	Graysn	1847	3100	277–0	41–2	20–3	10.5
Cervantes (P2)	1919	Graysn	1810	3178	277–0	41–2	20–4	10.5
Churruca (P2)	1921	Graysn	1847	3100	277–0	41–2	20–3	10.5
Cid (P2)	1922	Graysn	1847	3100	277–0	41–2	20–4	10.5
Ciscar (P2)	1919	Graysn	1809	3178	277–0	41–2	20–4	10.5
Cisneros (P2)	1926	AwpEng	1886	3564	291–0	40–2	19–10	10.0
Colon (P2)	1919	Graysn	1803	3178	277–0	41–2	20–4	10.0
Florentino (P2)	1921	Graysn	1822	3207	277–0	41–2	20–4	10.5
Palomares (m,P12/1)	1938	Doxfrd	1896	2250	306–7	45–0	17–7	15.5
Pozarica (m,P12/1)	1938	Doxfrd	1893	2250	306–8	45–0	17–7	15.5
Ravens Point (P2)	1918	Graysn	1787	3207	277–0	41–2	20–4	10.5

McCOWEN & GROSS LTD, 101 Leadenhall St, London EC3

Hull: *Black*
Services: General tramping

Derrymore (m)	1938	Burntd	4799	9524	431–9	56–11	25–3	11.5
Derrynane	1938	Burntd	4896	9390	430–6	57–0	25–4	11.5
Pilcot*	1913	Ropnr2	4549	8220	379.0	56–0	23–2	9.0
ex Seapool 36								

Note: * Sold Estonia 1939, renamed *Vapper*

McILWRAITH, MCEACHARN LTD, Scottish House, 94–96 William St, Melbourne, Victoria, Australia, and Stevenson House, 154–56 Fenchurch St, London EC3

Funnel: Red, black top
Hull: Black with narrow gold band, red boot-topping
Services: Passenger and cargo – Cairns–Townsville–Mackay–Brisbane–Sydney–Melbourne–Geelong–Adelaide–Albany–Fremantle; cruising to Pacific islands, including Fiji and New Caledonia

Note: This company owned general cargo vessels under 2000gt

Passenger/general cargo vessels

Kanimbla (m2,P203/1,198/2)								
	1936	H&W,B	10,985	5618	483–3	66–4	24–3	17.0
Katoomba (r/t3,P209/1,192/2,156/3)								
	1913	H&W,B	9424	6775	466–0	60–4	26–11	15.0
General cargo vessels								
Kooliga	1928	Caledn	2459	3700	307–10	44–2	19–1	10.0
Koomilya (r/t)	1929	Caledn	2779	4920	339–5	46–8	21–10	11.5
Kooringa (r/t)	1938	Caledn	3291	5680	374–6	49–9	22–8	11.5
Kooyong	1907	Clyde	2296	3765	295.0	44–1	19–3	10.0

McLAREN & CO, J D, 22 St Mary Axe, London EC3

Services: General tramping

CEREAL TRADE & SHIPPING CO LTD								
Start Point	1919	Sundld	5293	8350	412–0	52–5	25–3	10.5
ex Bretwalda 35, launched as War Warbler								
West Point	1920	GrkDY	4999	8850	412–8	53–6	25–4	11.0
ex Elmpark 37, launched as War Coleus								
GOWAN SHIPPING CO LTD								
Whitford Point	1928	Duncan	5026	9089	418–9	53–6	24–10	11.5
ex Benholm 37								

MACLAY & McINTYRE LTD, 21 Bothwell St, Glasgow C2

Funnel: Yellow, black top
Hull: Black, red boot-topping
Services: General tramping

GLASGOW NAVIGATION CO LTD								
Loch Don	1937	ThmpsJ	5249	9480	437–2	58–11	25–11	10.5
Loch Lomond	1934	Hendn2	5452	9135	414.2	56–2	25–0	10.5
Loch Maddy	1934	Lithgw	4996	9150	414.6	56–2	25–2	10.5
GLASGOW UNITED SHIPPING CO LTD								
Janeta	1929	Curle	5312	9155	415–0	54–9	25–3	10.0
Loch Ranza	1934	Steph2	4958	9150	415.0	56–2	25–2	10.5
STEAMSHIP INDUNA CO LTD								
Induna	1925	Steph2	5086	8371	402.0	52–2	24–5	10.0
Ingola	1925	GrayWH	3846	6560	352.0	50–0	22–6	10.0
Invella	1924	Curle	5026	8280	413–2	52–2	25–4	10.0
Loch Dee	1937	ThmpsJ	5252	9480	437–2	58–11	25–11	10.5
STEAMSHIP LIVINGSTONIA CO LTD								
Uganda	1927	Hendn2	4966	8344	415–4	52–2	24–5	10.0
STEAMSHIP MAGDALA CO LTD								
Masunda	1929	Steph2	5250	9190	415–0	54–9	24–5	10.5
STEAMSHIP MOMBASSA CO LTD								
Nyanza	1928	Hendn2	4974	8354	416–3	52–3	24–5	10.0

MAGEE, SON & CO, 65 Church St, West Hartlepool

Funnel: Blue with red M, black top
Services: General tramping

HARTLEPOOL'S STEAMSHIP CO LTD								
Edencrag	bldg	Burntd	1592	2740	264.3	40–4	18–6	10.0

MANCHESTER LINERS LTD,
Manchester Liners House, St Anne's Sq, Manchester 2

Funnel: Red with black top and black band
Hull: Black, red boot-topping
Services: Manchester–Montreal–Quebec (summer), St John NB, Halifax (winter); Manchester–St John NB–Norfolk VA–Baltimore–Philadelphia

Manchester Brigade (P–)								
	1918	Irvin3	6042	9220	438–0	53–6	28–3	12.0
Manchester Citizen (P7)								
	1925	FurnH	5343	8880	438–0	57–0	26–4	13.0
Manchester City (st,P12/1)								
	1937	Blythw	5600	8591	446–6	57–0	26–5	13.5
Manchester Commerce (P7)								
	1925	FurnH	5343	8880	438–0	57–0	26–4	12.5
Manchester Division (P–)								
	1918	Irvin3	6048	9220	438–0	53–4	28–3	13.0
Manchester Exporter (P–)								
	1918	Laing	5277	8588	431–2	55–1	27–2	13.0
ex Rexmore 29								

Manchester Merchant (st,P12/1)	bldg	Blythw	5670	8590	446–6	57–0	27–5	13.8
Manchester Port (st,P12/1)	1935	Blythw	5469	8505	431–7	56–8	27–5	13.5
Manchester Producer*	1916	Laing	5106	8820	432–6	53–6	27–0	13.0
ex Start Point 21								
Manchester Progress (st,P12/1)	1938	Blythw	5620	8591	446–6	57–0	27–5	13.5
Manchester Regiment (st,P–)	1922	FurnH	5989	9420	450.4	58–1	26–8	14.5
Manchester Spinner	1918	Irvin3	4767	8012	385.0	52–1	24–4	10.5
ex Grampian Range 21								
Manchester Trader (st,P12/1)	order	Blythw	5671	8590	446–6	57–0	27–5	13.8

Note: * Sold Board of Trade 1939, renamed *Botwey*

MARITIME NAVIGATION CO LTD, Liverpool NS, Canada

Services: E coast North America

Western Head	1919	AmSBCl	2508	4145	261–0	43–8	26.1	9.5
ex Cumberland 39								

MARKLAND SHIPPING CO LTD, Liverpool, Queen's Co NS, Canada

Funnel: Yellow with emblem of green tree, ground and two anchors on white disc
Hull: Black, red boot-topping
Services: Liverpool NS–New York–Philadelphia (newsprint)
Note: This company was controlled by Mersey Paper Co Ltd

Markland (s2,P6)	1929	Earles	4454	6250	338–6	52–8	24–2	12.0

MARTIS STEAMSHIP CO LTD, Holland House, Bury St, London EC3

Services: Tramping, mainly Mediterranean

Martis	1894	Rhead2	2483	3860	300.3	41–6	19–10	7.5
ex William Balls 29								

MARTYN, MARTYN & CO LTD,
73–74 Exchange Bldgs, Mount Stuart Sq, Cardiff

Funnel: Yellow, black top and white over black bands
Services: General tramping

MERVYN STEAM SHIPPING CO LTD

Marklyn	1918	TyneIr	3090	5150	342–0	46–10	21–8	9.0
ex Watsness 27, ex War Combe 20								
Mervyn	1924	ThmpR2	3402	5570	337.4	48–0	21–5	9.0
Mostyn	1909	RDuck1	1859	2860	260.2	40–0	18–4	8.0
ex Dalveen 13								

MASSEY & SONS LTD, W A, Quay St, Hull

Services: General tramping

Elizabeth Massey	1929	Doxfrd	4323	7718	385–6	51–8	24–2	10.0
ex Reaveley 39, ex Essex Noble 33, ex Juliet 32								
Frances Massey	1927	Prstm2	4212	8150	377–3	51–6	24–10	10.0

Note: This company also owned fishing vessels

MELBOURNE STEAMSHIP CO LTD,
31 King St, GPO Box 4316, Melbourne, Victoria, Australia

Funnel: Black, red band
Hull: Grey, red boot-topping
Services: Australia–New Zealand; Australian coastal

Passenger/general cargo vessel								
Duntroon (m2,P261/1,115/2)	1935	SHWR	10,346	6340	472–0	65–2	25–6	17.0
General cargo vessels								
Coolana	1921	SHWR	2197	3560	294–6	41–7	19–6	11.0
Ellaroo	1921	ThmpsJ	4655	6785	378–11	52–10	23–1	10.5
ex Aslaug Haaland 22								
Lowana	1924	DunlpB	3021	5717	344–6	47–0	23–3	12.0
Mernoo	1926	SHWR	2417	3857	296–0	42–9	20–8	11.0

Note: Also vessels of under 2000gt

MELDRUM & SWINSON LTD, 9 Camomile St, London EC3

Funnel: Black
Hull: Black with white band, red boot-topping
Services: General tramping

ESSEX LINE LTD

Essex Envoy*	1922	Schich	5210	8323	405–0	52–9	24–8	10.0
ex Therese Horn 24								
Essex Lance	1918	ArmWh1	6625	10,815	428–0	55–10	28–2	11.0
ex Glensanda 28, ex War Courage 19								

Note: * Sold Germany 1939, renamed *Hermod*

METCALFE, SON & CO LTD, 54 Church St, West Hartlepool

Funnel: Black with red M on white band
Hull: Black, red boot-topping
Services: General tramping

METCALFE SHIPPING CO LTD

Dunelmia	1929	GrayWH	5207	9230	434–0	54–2	25–3	10.5
Industria	bldg	GrayWH	4861	8960	431–6	56–1	25–1	10.5

MID-ATLANTIC SHIPPING CO LTD, Creechurch House, Bevis Marks, EC3

Services: Oil and petroleum trades

Tanker

English Tanker (st)	1923	TyneIr	5387	8516	365.2	51–4	26–8	10.0
ex Oilfield 37								

MILBURN & CO LTD, WM, Milburn House, Dean St, Newcastle upon Tyne 1

Funnel: Black
Hull: Black with white band, red boot-topping
Services: General tramping

MILBURN LINE LTD

Fowberry Tower	1929	Leslie	4484	8753	414–0	53–4	24–7	11.0

MILLER & CO, WILLIAM S, 31 St Vincent Place, Glasgow C1

Funnel: Black
Hull: Black, red boot-topping
Services: General tramping

GRETASTON STEAMSHIP CO LTD								
Gretaston*	1924	Duncan	5008	8750	404.9	53–0	24–7	10.0
LORNASTON STEAMSHIP CO LTD								
Lornaston	1925	Duncan	4934	8896	418–9	53–6	24–2	10.0
LUCISTON STEAMSHIP CO LTD								
Luciston**	1924	Duncan	5017	8750	404.9	53–0	24–7	10.0
MARISTON STEAMSHIP CO LTD								
Mariston	1924	Lithgw	4557	7950	384–7	51–6	23–11	10.0
WILSTON STEAMSHIP CO LTD								
Wilston	1916	Duncan	3221	5500	335.0	48–0	21–2	10.0

Note: *, ** Sold W A Souter & Co Ltd 1939, to be renamed *Sheaf Mead*; and renamed *Sheaf Mount*, respectively

MITCHELL, COTTS & CO LTD,
Winchester House, Old Broad St, London EC2

Funnel: Saint Line – red with black top separated by white over red over white bands; Sun Shipping – white, black top
Hull: Saint Line – grey, red boot-topping; Sun Shipping – black, red boot-topping
Services: General tramping

Manager for
SAINT LINE LTD

Saint Agnes	1918	G&G5	5183	8000	412–4	52–4	25–3	10.5
ex Cape St Agnes 37, ex Titan 25, ex War Briton 19								
Saint Anselm	1919	Nthmb1	5614	9000	412–9	53–0	26–3	11.0
ex St Andrew 36, launched as War Turret								
Saint Bernard	1939	Hamtn4	5183	9160	447–4	56–2	24–9	10.5
Saint Dunstan	1919	Nthmb1	5661	8950	412–9	53–0	26–3	11.0
launched as War Keep								
SUN SHIPPING CO LTD, 3 St Helen's Place, London EC3								
Cape St Andrew	1928	Duncan	5094	9030	418–10	53–6	24–10	9.5
Cape St George	1928	Duncan	5112	9030	418–10	53–6	24–10	9.5

Note: Saint Line Ltd also owned *Saint Germain* (built 1924/1044gt)

MOGUL LINE LTD, PO Box 194, 16 Bank St, Fort, Bombay, India

Funnel: Black with red band bordered by two white bands
Hull: Black with white band, red boot-topping
Services: Bombay–Karachi –Calcutta–Red Sea–Persian Gulf; Calcutta–Japan; Bombay/ Calcutta/Karachi–Jeddah (with pilgrims (for Mecca) in Hadj season)
Note: In 1939 this company's title was changed from Bombay & Persia Steam Navigation Co Ltd

Akbar (P244)	1921	Lithgw	4043	6540	375.0	52–0	23–2	11.0
Alavi (P38)	1924	Lithgw	3566	5430	365–0	48–0	22–8	11.0
Islami (P98/1,1321/pilg)								
	1934	Lithgw	5879	8350	429–0	56–2	25–9	12.0
Jehangir (P38)	1924	Lithgw	3566	5435	365–0	48–0	22–9	11.0
Khosrou (P44)	1924	Lithgw	4043	6540	375.0	52–0	23–3	11.0
Rahmani (P60/ –,–/pilg)								
	1928	Lithgw	5291	8430	426–0	54–0	25–11	11.0
Rizwani (P60/ –,–/pilg)								
	1930	Lithgw	5448	8220	426–0	54–0	25–11	11.0

Melbourne Steamship Co: Duntroon *was completed by Swan, Hunter & Wigham-Richardson in August 1935. In October 1939 she was requisitioned for conversion to an armed merchant cruiser, but this was not proceeded with, and she returned to commercial service. In February 1942 she was converted for service as a troopship. After postwar repatriation duty* Duntroon *was returned to her owners in April 1946, but was then on RAN charter until March 1949. She was sold in 1960, and after changes of owner, name and service she was broken up at Kaohsiung in 1968 (RW Jordan collection)*

Moller's Ltd: Gladys Moller *was completed in 1906 as Crown of Galicia for Crown Steamship Co, managed by Prentice, Service & Henderson. Together with seven other Crown ships, she was sold to Harrison of Liverpool in May 1920, and in November renamed* Centurion. *She was sold again in May 1925 and renamed* Bito *under the British flag, and became* Etha Rickmers *under the German flag in March 1926. She was sold to Moller in April 1938, joining the company's large fleet of second-hand vessels.* Gladys Moller *stranded on the east coast of Ceylon on November 7 1942 and was abandoned as a total loss four days later (RW Jordan collection)*

Navigation & Coal Trade Co: The tramp steamer Lodestone *was completed by Bartram, Sunderland, in 1938, for this owner, which was the London operating office of A Vlasov, the Romanian shipping magnate.* Lodestone *survived the war and was broken up during 1962–63 (Alex Duncan)*

MOLLER'S LTD,
Hongkong & Shanghai Bank Bldg, 30 Foochow Rd, Shanghai, China

Funnel: Black with white M
Hull: Black or grey, red boot-topping
Services: Mainly China Seas

MOLLER LINE LTD (vessels registered Shanghai, under British flag)

Alice Moller	1914	Irvin3	4986	8200	400.0	52–0	24–6	10.0
ex Rhodesian Transport 33, ex Clutha River 15								
Ariadne Moller (s2,P250/–)	1907	Ramage	1840	940	255.0	40–2	20.7	12.0
ex Hunter 38								
Daisy Moller	1911	Bremer	4087	6600	337.6	48–2	29.2	10.0
ex Wilfred 35, ex Huntscape 20, ex Pindos 14								
Elizabeth Moller	1906	Hamtn2	4353	7180	385–5	52–2	22–11	8.5
ex Torbeath 31, ex Strathfillan 28								
Erica Moller	1906	SHWR	4683	7250	396.7	49–8	25–0	7.5
ex Commercial Pathfinder 28, ex Osage 20, ex Serapis 17								
Gladys Moller	1906	Steph2	5285	8039	400.0	52–0	24–9	10.0
ex Etha Rickmers 38, ex Bito 26, ex Centurion 25, ex Crown of Galicia 20								
Hannah Moller	1911	Camp1	2931	5450	331.4	45–6	21–9	9.5
ex Hexham 32, ex Amphion 11								
Helen Moller	1918	Conn2	5259	8100	412–6	52–4	25–3	10.5
ex Sierentz 33, exWar Cateran 20								
Helga Moller	1912	Rickmr	5546	8200	404.8	53–4	24–0	10.0
ex Deike Rickmers 38, ex Aker 31, ex Istok 28, ex Kurmark 25								
Hilda Moller	1912	LithR	4622	7680	398–0	52–0	24–6	10.0
ex Orator 31, ex Saint Fillans 18, ex Hawkhead 17								
Isabel Moller	1918	GrayX	2834	4016	313–6	43–1	19–10	10.0
ex Loong Hwa 28, ex Warcuta 25, ex War Mango 19								
Jenny Moller	1919	Duncan	3108	5350	342–0	46–9	21–8	9.5
ex Lord Guilford 32, ex Granicos 23, launched as War Quarry								
Joan Moller	1918	HK&Wh	2232	2990	281–6	40–1	18–11	9.0
ex Dumont D'Urville 36, ex Gia-Long 30, ex St Francois Xavier 29, ex Hermelin 28								
Katie Moller	1919	Prstm1	3100	5150	342–0	46–10	21–8	9.5
ex Admiral Hamilton 32, launched as War Globe								
Lilian Moller	1913	Laing	4866	7550	390.0	50–9	24–6	9.0
ex Valhall 33, ex Cambrian Duchess 31, ex Novgorod 23								
Louise Moller	1907	ThmpsJ	3764	6200	346.5	50–10	21–4	9.0
ex Balto 33, ex Björnefjord 26, ex River Plate 13								
Marion Moller	1909	ThmpsJ	3827	6850	346.0	49–6	23–4	9.0
ex Cymric Pride 32, ex Brinkburn 19								
Mary Moller	1902	TyneIr	2698	4813	326.0	45–4	21–3	9.0
ex Dilkera 31								
Nancy Moller	1907	Prstm1	3916	6200	343.5	49–1	23–0	8.5
ex Rowena 39, ex Norfolk 21								
Nils Moller	1922	H&W,B	6647	10,175	429–0	55–10	28–2	9.5
ex Invergoil 36; conv tanker 36								
Norah Moller (m2,P34)	1915	H&WIrv	4433	6700	365.2	50–1	23–5	10.0
ex Kangaroo 38, laid down as Lalandia								
Rosalie Moller (P12/1,100/3)	1910	Curle	3963	6400	355.0	49–2	23–11	9.5
ex Francis 31								
Therese Moller	1905	Prstm1	3930	6383	355.0	48–0	23–8	9.0
ex Maid of Lemnos 31, ex Newton Hall 27, ex Matra 21, ex Drumgeith 15								
Winifred Moller	1912	OsbGr1	2484	3700	308–0	45–4	18–4	9.5
ex Katoa 34								

MONROE BROTHERS, 15 Brunswick St, Liverpool 2

Funnel: Black with red over white bands
Hull: Black
Services: General tramping
Note: Also coastal vessels

KYLE SHIPPING CO LTD

Kyleglen	1917	Conn2	3670	6200	365–5	47–9	24–5	10.0
ex Senator 38								

MOORSOM & CO LTD, F W, Phoenix Bldgs, Mount Stuart Sq, Cardiff

Funnel: Black with M on white band between two narrow red bands
Hull: Black, red boot-topping, with name of vessel in large white letters about centre of hull
Services: General tramping; voyages to Spain during Spanish Civil War

Jeanne M	1919	Ardrsn	2465	3860	313–5	43–0	19–11	10.0
ex Seabank Spray 39, ex Seven Seas Spray 37, ex Baron Elibank 34, ex Glassford 23								

MOORINGWELL STEAMSHIP CO LTD

Philipp M	1924	Burntd	2085	3340	283–2	39–11	18–9	9.0
ex Halbeath 37								

MOREL LTD, 2 Stuart St, Cardiff, and Leadenhall Bldgs, London EC3

Funnel: Black with white band bearing red disc between two narrow red bands
Hull: Black, red boot-topping
Services: General tramping

Note: * Sold Crest Shipping Co Ltd 1939, renamed *Belcrest*

NOLISEMENT STEAMSHIP CO LTD								
Allende	1928	Nthmb2	5081	9150	426–6	55–4	25–5	10.0
Beignon (m)	1939	Doxfrd	5218	9425	442–11	56–5	25–11	10.5
Forest (m)	1937	Doxfrd	4998	9150	439–2	54–2	25–6	10.5
Nolisement	1928	Nthmb2	5084	9150	426–6	55–4	25–5	10.0
PONTYPRIDD STEAMSHIP CO LTD								
Catrine (m)	bldg	Doxfrd	5218	9426	442–11	56–6	25–11	10.5
Pontypridd	1924	Nthmb1	4458	8415	399.6	52–11	24–9	9.5
TREHERBERT STEAMSHIP CO LTD								
Treherbert*	1925	Nthmb1	4517	8350	399.7	52–11	24–8	9.5
ex Gardépée 27								

MORRISON & SON, JOHN, 28 Mosley St, Newcastle upon Tyne 1

Funnel: Black with red Maltese cross on white band
Hull: Black, red boot-topping
Services: General tramping

CLIFFSIDE SHIPPING CO LTD								
Ashlea	1929	Prstm2	4222	8000	380–0	51–6	24–10	10.0
Barbara Marie	1928	Prstm2	4223	8000	377–6	51–6	24–10	10.0
Eastlea	1924	Prstm1	4267	8000	377–6	51–6	24–10	10.0
Glenlea	1930	Prstm2	4252	8000	380–0	51–6	24–10	10.0
Holmelea	1928	Prstm2	4223	8000	377–6	51–6	24–10	10.0
Nestlea	1921	Prstm1	4274	8000	377–6	51–6	24–10	10.0
Stornest	1921	Prstm1	4265	8000	377–6	51–6	24–10	10.0
ex Stornes 21								
Thornlea	1920	Prstm1	4261	8000	380–3	51–6	24–10	10.0
MORRISON STEAMSHIP CO LTD								
Cheldale	1925	Prstm2	4218	8000	377–6	51–6	24–10	10.0
Elmdale	order	Burntd	4872	9225	441–0	57–0	26–11	10.5
Farndale	1928	Prstm2	4235	8000	377–6	51–6	24–10	10.0

MOSS & CO, 26 Chapel St, Liverpool 3 and 43 St Mary Axe, London EC3

Funnel: Yellow with red M on red bordered white diamond, black top
Hull: Grey, red boot-topping
Trades: Oil and petroleum

Tankers

ARAL STEAMSHIP CO LTD								
Lunula	1926	Hamtn2	6363	10,090	420.0	54–5	26–10	11.0
ASTRAKHAN STEAMSHIP CO LTD								
Lucellum (m)	1938	Odense	9425	14,580	501–2	65–6	28–0	12.0
Luminetta	1927	Palmer	6159	9900	420.5	54–6	26–11	11.0
LUCIGEN STEAMSHIP CO LTD								
Lucigen	1909	ArmWh1	4986	7380	388.0	50–6	24–11	11.0
Luculus (m)	1929	Palmer	6546	10,470	446–6	56–7	26–10	11.3
LUMINA STEAMSHIP CO LTD								
Lucerna (m)	1930	Palmer	6556	10,480	446–8	56–7	26–11	11.3
LUSTROUS STEAMSHIP CO LTD								
Lustrous	1927	Palmer	6156	9910	420.5	54–6	26–11	11.0
H E MOSS & CO'S TANKERS LTD								
Lumen (m2)	1925	BrownJ	6483	9630	420.1	54–6	26–11	11.3
Luxor (m)	1930	Palmer	6554	10,470	446–6	56–7	26–10	11.3

MOSS HUTCHISON LINE LTD, 31 James St, Liverpool 2

Funnel: Black with white band
Hull: Black, red boot-topping
Services: Glasgow, Liverpool, Avonmouth–Bordeaux–Mediterranean (including Algiers, Oran, Malta, Piræus, Salonika, Alexandria, Limassol, Famagusta, Haifa, Jaffa, Beirut, Tripoli (Syria), Syra, Smyrna)–Black Sea ports

Note: This company, controlled by General Steam Navigation Co Ltd (*qv*), also owned short-sea vessels

Esneh	1919	SHWRSd	1931	3493	300–9	42–6	19–11	10.5
ex Western Coast 22								
Etrib	1919	SHWRSd	1943	3300	300–9	42–6	19–11	10.5
ex British Coast 22, launched as War Shannon								
Hatasu	1921	Blumr2	3198	6040	352.7	50–5	22–10	10.0
Kana	1929	McMlln	2783	4515	347–9	47–2	20–9	10.5
Kantara	1925	Curle	3237	4830	330.9	46–9	21–9	10.0
Kavak	1929	McMlln	2782	4515	347–9	47–2	20–9	11.0
Kheti (m,P10/1)	1927	H&WGk	2734	4370	345–0	47–4	20–9	10.5
Kufra (m,P10/1)	1929	H&WGw	2724	4364	345–0	47–3	20–9	11.0
Meroë (P12/1)	1928	Curle	3832	4933	331.2	48–2	20–10	10.0
ex Lafian 36								

MUIR, YOUNG LTD, Creechurch House, Creechurch Lane, London EC3

Funnel: Grey with white CSC on blue band
Hull: Grey
Services: General tramping

CREE STEAMSHIP CO LTD

Cree	1919	CommSy	4791	6735	372.0	54–4	25.6	8.5
ex Yoh Hsing 37, ex Ivanhoe 37, ex Wollert 32, ex Biloela 31								
Creekirk	1912	Duncan	3917	6800	366–11	51–1	21–10	8.0
ex Hyphaestos 38, ex Milcovul 33, ex Mariston 13								

MUIR STEAMSHIP CO LTD

Creemuir	1924	Palmer	3997	6591	360.2	51–0	22–3	10.0
ex Langleemere 38, ex Medomsley 29								

Note: See also under Saguenay Terminals Ltd

MURRELL & SON, JOSEPH E, 2 Victoria Terrace, West Hartlepool

Funnel: Black
Hull: Black, red boot-topping
Services: General tramping

MURRELL STEAMSHIP CO LTD

Thurston	1918	Blumr2	3072	5050	342–0	46–10	21–9	10.5
ex Vera Kathleen 27, ex War Sky 19								

NAPIER, JOHN, 116 Hope St, Glasgow C2

Services: General tramping

GLENEDEN STEAMSHIP CO LTD

Gleneden	1909	Scott2	4772	7744	400.0	52–0	24–1	9.5

NAVIGATION & COAL TRADE CO LTD, 22 Billiter St, London EC3

Funnel: Yellow with blue V
Hull: Black with white line, red boot-topping
Services: General tramping

ALVA STEAMSHIP CO LTD

Gemstone	1938	Laing	4986	9000	428–0	57–8	24–6	10.5
Lodestone	1938	Bartm2	4877	9100	430–10	55–7	25–3	10.5
Starstone	1938	Doxfrd	5702	9965	447–8	57–6	25–11	10.5

Note: See also in Romania section

NEILL & PANDELIS LTD, Bevis Marks House, Bevis Marks, London EC3

Services: General tramping

Marionga	1912	RDuck2	4214	7585	380.0	51–0	23–10	9.5
ex Grelstone 31, ex Eddystone 17								
Mariposa	1914	Prstm1	3807	7130	350.0	50–11	23–8	9.0
ex Greek Mariner 38, ex Galeb 35, ex Cefnybryn 35, ex Galeb 34, ex Dedinje 34, ex Cefnybryn 31, ex Theofano 28, ex Ioannis Vatis 23								
Maritima	1912	Leslie	5785	9350	426.0	54–1	27–7	10.0
ex Clan Graham 38, ex Cambrian Baroness 29, ex Port Lincoln 27								

Note: Manager of the above vessels was Gordon O Till (*qv*); see also in Greece section

NEW EGYPT & LEVANT SHIPPING CO LTD,
Izmir, Asia Minor, and 25 Boulevard Saad Zaghoul, Box 1741, Alexandria, Egypt

Funnel: Red, black top
Hull: Black, red boot-topping
Services: General tramping

Under British flag

Antar (m)	order	Doxfrd	5222	9440	442–11	56–6	25–11	11.0
Antigone	1928	Napr&M	4545	8630	415–10	54–2	24–11	10.0
Antiope	1930	Napr&M	4545	8630	415–10	54–2	25–0	10.0
Antonio	1918	ThmpsJ	5225	8250	412–6	52–4	25–3	10.5
ex Western 24, ex War Fijian 19; conv tanker 19								

Note: Manager of this fleet was T Bowen Rees & Co Ltd, Alexandria

NEW ZEALAND SHIPPING CO LTD, 138 Leadenhall St, London EC3

Funnel: Yellow
Hull: Black, red boot-topping with white dividing line
Services: Passenger – London/Southampton–Panama–Wellington–Auckland; refrigerated and general cargo – London/Liverpool–New Zealand and Australian ports; E coast Canada, US–New Zealand–Australia

Passenger/general cargo vessels

Rangitane (m2,P100/1,498/t)								
	1929	BrownJ	16,712	13,388	552–5	78–9!	33–8	16.0
Rangitata (m2,P100/1,498/t)								
	1929	BrownJ	16,737	13,418	552–5	78–9	33–8	16.0
Rangitiki (m2,P100/1,498/t)								
	1929	BrownJ	16,698	13,198	552–5	78–9	33–8	16.0
Remuera (s2,P200/cab)								
	1911	Denny1	11,445	9760	502–0	62–4	29–5	14.0
Rimutaka* (st2,P272/t)								
	1923	ArmWh1	16,576	8755	573–0	72–0	30–0	15.5
ex Mongolia 38								
Rotorua (s2,P400/t)								
	1911	BrownJ	10,890	12,250	544–0	61–5	30–0	14.0
ex Shropshire 11								

Notes: * Owned by Peninsular & Oriental SN Co (*qv*) and on bareboat charter; ** sold British India SN Co Ltd (*qv*) 1939, renamed *Waroonga*; *** managed by Trinder, Anderson & Co Ltd (*qv*); † relegated to non-passenger carrier in 1938, but passenger carriage reintroduced after Sept. 1939
Note: New Zealand Shipping Co Ltd, a member of the P&O Group, controlled Federal SN Co Ltd (*qv*)

Ruahine (s2,P220/cab†)								
	1909	Denny1	10,870	8975	497–0	60–4	29–6	14.0
Refrigerated and general cargo vessels								
Hororata** (s2,P39/cab,1000+/st)								
	1914	Denny1	9178	10,325	529–11	64–2	30–9	14.0
Hurunui (st)	1920	Dixon2	9315	13,320	482–0	62–5	31–2	13.0
Kaikoura*** (m)	1937	Steph2	5852	9820	460–0	59–0	26–4	13.0
Kaimata*** (m)	1931	Denny2	5237	9350	430–4	56–2	26–8	13.0
ex Ardenvohr 37								
Kaipaki*** (m)	1939	Steph2	5862	9733	458–6	58–9	26–4	13.0
Kaipara*** (m)	1938	Doxfrd	5882	9950	454–7	58–11	26–4	13.0
Kaituna*** (m)	1938	Eriksb	4907	9165	432–2	56–7	25–10	13.0
Opawa (m2)	1931	Steph2	10,354	12,825	490–0	67–4	32–5	16.0
Orari (m2)	1931	Steph2	10,350	12,853	490–0	67–4	32–5	16.0
Otaio (m2)	1930	VickB1	10,298	12,851	490–0	67–3	32–3	16.0
Piako (st)	1920	Steph2	8283	10,920	465–0	58–2	29–0	13.0
launched as War Orestes								
Tekoa (st)	1922	Earles	8689	11,527	483–0	62–10	29–2	14.0
Tongariro (st)	1925	Hamtn2	8719	12,545	480–8	62–8	31–3	14.0
Turakina (st)	1923	Hamtn2	8706	11,780	480–8	62–9	30–1	14.0

Funnel: Red with black top separated by white band
Hull: Black, red boot-topping
Services: General tramping

NISBET & CO, GEORGE, 109 Hope St, Glasgow C2

CLYDESDALE NAVIGATION CO LTD								
Blairangus	1930	Craig2	4409	7825	392–6	52–0	24–1	10.0
ex Portregis 34								
Blairbeg	1917	Blumr1	3509	6025	365–8	48–9	21–10	9.0
ex Wynburn 31, ex Clifftower								
Blairclova	1938	Rhead1	5083	9050	439–2	56–8	25–0	11.0
ex Sutherland 39								
Blairlogie	1929	Craig2	4425	7825	392–6	52–0	24–1	10.0
ex Grovedene 36, ex Portfield 35								
Blairmore	1928	AyrDk	4141	6180	385–3	51–3	22–11	11.0
NISBET SHIPPING CO LTD								
Blairatholl	1925	Napr&M	3319	5620	351–6	48–9	21–10	9.5
Blairdevon	1925	Napr&M	3282	5630	351–6	48–9	21–10	9.5
Blairnevis	1930	Ardrsn	4155	6800	385–3	51–2	22–11	11.0
NORTHERN NAVIGATION CO LTD								
Blairesk	1925	Napr&M	3300	5675	351–6	48–8	21–10	9.5
Blairspey	1929	Ardrsn	4155	6800	385–3	51–3	22–11	10.0

Funnel: Yellow with black top separated by band of yellow over red interlocking triangles
Hull: Grey, red boot-topping
Services: Calcutta–Rangoon–Colombo–Guayanilla–Barbados–Kingston–Havana (native workers and general cargo); US Gulf ports–Japan
Note: This company became a member of the P&O Group in 1917

NOURSE LTD, JAMES, (The Nourse Line), 122 Leadenhall St, London EC3

Bhima (m)	1939	Conn2	5280	9320	431–6	55–2	27–3	10.0
Ganges (r/t,P1000+/d)								
	1930	H&WGw	6246	8869	424.6	56–0	25–8	12.0
Indus (m)	bldg	Conn2	5187	9320	431–6	55–2	27–3	10.0
Jhelum (r/t)	1936	Curle	4038	7510	395–5	52–9	23–8	11.0
Johilla (r/t)	1937	Curle	4042	7510	395–5	52–9	23–8	11.0
Jumna (r/t,P/nat)	1929	Steph2	6078	9340	423.9	55–11	24–5	12.0
Saugor (P/nat)	1928	H&WGk	6303	9450	424.0	56–0	25–4	12.0
Sutlej (m)	bldg	Conn2	5189	9320	431–6	55–2	27–3	10.5

Funnel: Yellow with cowl top
Hull: Black, red boot-topping; *Orama, Orcades, Orion* – deep cream, green boot-topping
Services: London (Tilbury) –Gibraltar–Palma–Toulon–Naples –Port Said–Suez–Aden–Colombo–Fremantle–Adelaide–Melbourne–Sydney–Brisbane; cruising to northern capitals, fjords, Mediterranean, Atlantic islands

Note: P&O SN Co acquired a

ORIENT STEAM NAVIGATION CO LTD, 3–5 Fenchurch Ave, London EC3

Passenger/general cargo vessels								
Orama (st2,P1700)								
	1924	VickB2	19,840	10,150	658–4	75–2	30–5	18.0
Orcades (st2,P463/1,605/t)								
	1937	VickB1	23,456	11,800	664–6	82–2	30–2	20.0
Orford (st2,P590/1,1240/t)								
	1928	VickB2	20,043	9893	659–2	75–5	30–2	18.0
Orion (st2,P486/1,653/t)								
	1935	VickB1	23,371	11,800	665–0	82–6	30–2	20.0
Ormonde (st2,P777/t)								
	1917	BrownJ	14,982	8113	598–9	66–9	29–10	17.0
Oronsay (st2,P592/1,1244/t)								
	1925	BrownJ	20,043	10,640	658–6	75–2	30–5	18.0

New Egypt: This motor vessel was completed in February 1941 as Antar *for the New Egypt company. She was a single-screw vessel fitted with a 3-cylinder Doxford economy engine. In January 1948* Antar *was sold to British India and renamed* Garbeta *(as pictured here). She had an uneventful career, serving on British India's liner services, mainly from London, and was sold to Hong Kong breakers in 1963 (RW Jordan)*

New Zealand Shipping Co: Rangitiki *was one of three sister-ships completed by J Brown, Clydebank, in 1929.* Rangitiki *was in the '*Jervis Bay*' convoy attacked by* Admiral Scheer, *but escaped during the heroic engagement of the German ship by* Jervis Bay. *In December 1940* Rangitiki *was requisitioned and converted for service as a troopship with a capacity of 2600. During her trooping duties she travelled over 600,000 miles. In 1947 she was returned to her owners and following an extensive refit, re-entered commercial service in September 1948. She was broken up at Santander in 1962 (New Zealand Shipping Co)*

New Zealand Shipping Co: Remuera, *originally a coal burner, completed by Denny at Dumbarton in September 1911, was fitted with triple expansion machinery with a low pressure exhaust turbine. In 1920 during her then extensive postwar refit she was converted to burn oil fuel. These developed a total 14,000ihp. She continued in the New Zealand trade after the outbreak of the Second World War, under government control. She had been engaged similarly during the First World War. On August 26 1940 while in convoy HX65A, and nearing the end of her 74th voyage, from Wellington to London via Panama, she was torpedoed by German He115 aircraft and sunk.* Remuera *was carrying 4801 tons of refrigerated produce and 1646 tons of general cargo. Her 93 crew and a gunner were all rescued (EH Cole)*

Orient Line: Orama *was completed by Vickers Armstrongs at Barrow in October 1924. In 1940 she was converted for trooping and was one of the vessels used to transport the British Expeditionary Force to Norway following the German invasion. On June 8 1940* Orama *was sunk by* Admiral Hipper *during the evacuation of troops Norway.* Hipper *and escorting destroyers picked up 280 survivors (Vickers-Armstrongs)*

Orient Line: Orcades *was completed by Vickers Armstrongs, Barrow, in September 1937, being a near-sister of* Orion, *completed in 1935. In 1939 she was requisitioned as a troopship. On October 10 1942 when about 300m WSW of Cape Town, with 1000 persons on board, she was torpedoed by* U172. *Most passengers and crew left the ship and were rescued by the Polish steamer* Narwik. *A volunteer skeleton crew of 55 men stayed on board to try to take the vessel back to Cape Town at 5 knots, but later she was struck by two more torpedoes, heeled over, and sank (RW Jordan collection)*

Orontes (st2,P456/1,518/t)								
	1929	VickB1	20,097	10,000	663–8	75–4	30–2	18.0
Otranto (st2,P521/1,476/t)								
	1925	VickB2	20,026	9700	663–9	75–2	30–6	18.0

controlling interest in this company in 1919
Note: manager of this company was Anderson, Green & Co Ltd

PACIFIC STEAM NAVIGATION CO LTD, Goree, Water St, Liverpool

Passenger/general cargo vessels								
Orbita (r/t3,P227/1,187/cab)								
	1915	H&W,B	15,495	12,110	569–2	67–4	35–10	14.0
Orduña (r/t3,P234/1,186/cab,458/3)								
	1914	H&W,B	15,507	11,430	569–2	67–4	35–10	14.0
laid down as Ormeda								
Oropesa (st2,P141/1,131/2,360/3)								
	1920	Cammel	14,118	14,000	551–11	66–4	31–9	13.5
Oroya* (st2,P150/1,123/2,450/3)								
	1921	H&W,B	12,257		541–8	62–10	32–11	13.5
Reina del Pacifico (m4,P280/1,162/2,446/3)								
	1931	H&W,B	17,702	9910	574–0	76–4	31–3	18.0
General cargo vessels								
La Paz (m2,P12/1)	1920	H&WGw	6548	9190	406.3	54–2	26–11	10.5
Lagarto (m2,P12/1)								
	1917	H&WGw	5072	7520	398–6	52–2	26–9	10.5
ex Glenavy 24, laid down as Lobos								
Laguna (m2,P12/1)								
	1923	H&WGw	6466	8700	420.5	54–2	28–1	10.0
Lautaro (m2,P12/1)								
	1915	H&WGw	6240	9550	412–1	52–2	28–11	10.0
ex Glengyle 23, ex Bostonian 16								
Lobos (m2,P12/1)	1921	H&WGk	6479	9190	420–9	54–2	26–11	10.0
Loreto (m2,P12/1)								
	1919	H&WGw	6682	9090	420–9	54–2	26–11	10.0
ex Glenade 24								
Loriga (m2,P12/1)	1919	H&WGw	6665	9030	420–8	54–2	27–0	10.0
ex Glenariffe 24								
Losada (m2,p12/1)	1921	H&WGw	6520	9190	420–9	54–2	27–0	10.0

Funnel: Yellow
Hull: Black, green boot-topping; *Reina del Pacifico* – white, green boot-topping
Services: Passenger, mail and cargo – Liverpool–La Pallice – Spain–Bermuda–Havana–Cristobal–Callao–Talcahuano–Valparaiso; Liverpool–France–Spain–E coast South America–Magellan Strait–W coast South America; Central America–W coast South America

Note: * BU Spezia 1939

PALESTINE MARITIME LLOYD LTD

PO Box 960, 19 Boulevard Rothschild, Tel Aviv, Palestine

Under British flag								
Har Zion (P28/1,4/2,24/3)								
	1907	B&W	2508	3209	324–5	40–9	19–8	10.5
ex Risveglio 35, ex Nickerie 32, ex St Jan 13								
PALESTINE MARITIME LLOYD LTD (CYPRUS) (British flag)								
Miriam	1912	Earles	1903	3897	300.0	44–9	19–0	9.5
ex Sorrento 38								

Services: Passenger and general cargo in E Mediterranean and Black Sea

PALLAS OIL & TRADING CO LTD

Imperial House, Dominion St, Moorgate, London EC2

Tankers								
Maryad*	1926	Duncan	4870	6945	375.1	51–9	24–8	9.5
ex Vitruvia 38								
Stratford	1913	LithR	4753	7290	376.0	51–2	24–6	9.0
ex Luminous 38, ex Vitruvia 25								

Trades: Oil and petroleum

Note: *Sold Belgium 1939, renamed *Peterjo*; resold France 1939, renamed *Beauce*
Note: Manager of this company was Oscar Margulies

PENINSULAR & ORIENTAL STEAM NAVIGATION CO

122 Leadenhall St, London EC3

Passenger/general cargo vessels								
Canton (st2,P260/1,220/2)								
	1938	Steph2	15,784	7826	563–4	73–4	29–6	19.0
Carthage (st2,P175/1,196/2)								
	1931	Steph2	14,182	8898	543–0	71–5	29–9	18.0
laid down as Canton								
Cathay (s2,P203/1,103/2)								
	1925	Curle	15,225	9748	523.5	70–2	30–8	16.5

Funnel: Black; *Ettrick* and *Straths* – yellow
Hull: Black with white band, red boot-topping; *Straths* – white, red boot-topping; *Ettrick* – white with broad blue band, red boot-topping
Services: Passenger, mail and general cargo – London–Gibraltar–Tangier–Marseilles–Port Said–Aden–Bombay–Karachi; London–

Colombo–Madras–Calcutta; London–Fremantle–Melbourne–Sydney; London–Marseilles–Malta–Port Said–Ceylon–Straits Settlements–China–Japan; London–Marseilles–Malta; Mediterranean, Baltic Sea and northern capitals cruises

Chitral (r/t2,P203/1,103/2)	1925	Steph2	15,346	9645	526.3	70–4	30–8	17.0
Comorin (r/t2,P203/1,103/2)	1925	Curle	15,241	9498	523.5	70–2	30–8	17.0
Corfu (st2,P175/1,196/2)	1931	Steph2	14,170	8909	543–0	71–5	29–9	17.5
laid down as Chefoo								
Maloja (s2,327/1,329/t)	1923	H&W,B	20,914	9663	625–0	73–5	34–10	17.0
Mooltan (s2,327/1,P329/t)	1923	H&W,B	20,952	9663	625–0	73–5	34–10	17.0
Narkunda (s2,P426/1,247/2)	1920	H&W,B	16,632	6984	606–0	69–5	29–3	17.5
Rajputana (s2,P310/1,290/2)	1926	H&WGk	16,644	7521	570–0	71–3	28–9	17.0
Ranchi (r/t2,P310/1,290/2)	1925	Leslie	16,738	7616	570–0	71–4	28–9	17.5
Ranpura (s2,P310/1,290/2)	1925	Leslie	16,688	7616	570–0	71–4	28–9	17.0
Rawalpindi (s2,P308/1,282/2)	1925	H&WGk	16,697	7616	570–0	71–4	28–9	17.0
Strathaird (te2,P1170)	1932	VickB1	22,281	6230	664–0	80–2	29–2	21.0
Strathallan (st2,P526/1,453/t)	1937	VickB1	23,722	8569	664–5	82–2	30–2	20.0
Stratheden (st2,P526/1,453/t)	1935	VickB1	23,722	8719	664–6	82–2	30–2	20.0
Strathmore (st2,P1110)	1935	VickB1	23,428	8376	665–1	82–3	30–2	20.0
Strathnaver (te2,P1170)	1931	VickB1	22,547	6283	664–0	80–2	29–2	21.0
Viceroy of India (te2,P415/1,258/2)	1929	Steph2	19,627	7035	612–0	76–2	28–3	19.0
Troopship								
Ettrick (m2,P100/1,100/2,160/3,1150/trp)	1938	Curle	11,279	5900	516–9	63–2	23–3	15.0
General cargo vessels								
Alipore	1920	Palmer	5273	7818	412–6	52–4	25–3	11.5
Jeypore	1920	GrayWr	5318	7916	412–6	52–4	25–3	11.5
launched as War Moth								
Kidderpore*	1920	SHWR	5334	7997	412–6	52–5	25–3	11.5
Lahore	1920	ThmpR2	5304	7826	412–6	52–4	25–3	11.5
Mirzapore** (st,P4)	1921	ArmWh1	6745	10,092	412.2	55–10	28–2	11.5
Nagpore	1920	Earles	5283	8239	412–6	52–3	25–3	11.5
Peshawur (s2,P12)	1919	Curle	7934	9875	465–0	58–2	29–3	13.0
launched as War Diana								
Shillong (m)	1939	Steph2	5529	8820	459–6	57–11	25–1	12.0
Somali (r/t)	1930	H&Wg	6809	9881	459.0	60–9	29.7	15.0
Soudan (r/t)	1931	Curle	6677	9631	459.0	60–9	29.7	15.0
Surat (m)	1939	Steph2	5529	8820	459–6	57–11	25–1	12.0

Note: * Broken up Genoa 1939; ** broken up Briton Ferry 1939
Note: See also under Federal SN Co, Hain SS Co and New Zealand Shipping Co; P&O also controlled Asiatic SN Co, British India SN Co, Federal SN Co, General Steam Nav Co, Hain SS Co, Moss Huthinson Line, New Zealand Shipping Co, J Nourse Ltd, Orient SN Co, and Union SS Co of New Zealand (all of which – *qv*)

PHOENIX SHIPPING CO LTD, 4 Lloyd's Ave, London EC3

Services: General tramping

Redstone	1918	GrayX	3110	5100	342–4	46–10	21–9	9.5
ex Margari 37, ex Orbe 28, ex Wye Crag 24, ex War Crag 19								

POPE, ALFRED J, 59 Mount Stuart Sq, Cardiff

Services: General tramping (voyages to Spain during Spanish Civil War)
Note: * Sold Mooringwell Steamship Co Ltd (F W Moorsom & Co Ltd), 1939, renamed *Jeanne M*

Seabank Spray*	1919	Ardrsn	2465	3860	313–5	43–0	19–11	10.0
ex Seven Seas Spray 37, ex Baron Elibank 34, ex Glassford 23								

PORT LINE LTD, Cunard House, 88 Leadenhall St, London EC3

Funnel: Red with three narrow black rings, black top
Hull: Silver grey, red boot-topping
Services: Hull, Antwerp, Hamburg, London–Australia–New Zealand; E coast Canada–New York–Australia–New Zealand; Glasgow, Liverpool–New Zealand direct via Panama

Port Adelaide (st2,P12)	1919	Leslie	8422	11,720	499–0	62–4	30–2	13.0
Port Alma (m2,P12/1)	1928	SHWR	8400	10,750	495–0	63–2	29–7	14.5
Port Auckland (r/t2,P12)	1922	Workmn	8789	11,520	499–0	62–5	30–0	13.0

Orient Line: Otranto *was completed by Vickers Armstrongs, Barrow, in December 1925. She was converted for trooping in 1939, and in November 1942 became an assault ship, with her lifeboats replaced by landing craft. She was involved in the landings in North Africa, Sicily and Salerno and later reverted to trooping. Postwar, after further trooping,* Otranto *was involved in Australian emigrant voyages and was broken up at Faslane in 1957 (RW Jordan collection)*

Pacific SN Co: Reina del Pacifico *was completed in March 1931 by Harland & Wolff, Belfast, and the following month made her maiden voyage from Liverpool to Valparaiso. In early 1940 she commenced conversion for service as a troopship and in 1946 became a repatriation ship. In January 1947 she went back to Harland & Wolff for an extensive refit, but her redelivery was delayed due to an engine room explosion with heavy loss of life. She re-entered commercial service in 1948, and 10 years later was broken up at Newport, Monmouthshire (RW Jordan collection)*

Pacific SN Co: Laguna *was completed in 1923 by Harland & Wolff, Glasgow. She was involved in the company's service from the UK to the west coast of South America. On August 17 1942 when in convoy PG6, she was torpedoed by* U658 *west of Anse d'Hainaut, Haiti, and damaged. She made port, was repaired, and continued through the war apparently without further mishap.* Laguna *was broken up at Barrow in 1952 (R Sherlock)*

P&O: Mooltan *was completed by Harland & Wolff, Belfast, in the autumn of 1923. Completed with quadruple expansion reciprocating engines, in 1929 together with her sister* Maloja, *she had fitted a low pressure exhaust turbine which transmitted power through electric motors. After war service firstly as an armed merchant cruiser, then as a troopship,* Mooltan *was returned to P&O in 1947 and re-entered commercial service the following year. She was broken up in 1954 (P&O)*

P&O: Ranpura *was completed by Hawthorn Leslie, Glasgow, in April 1925, for service from London to India and the Far East. In 1930 during a refit she was fitted with a Bauer-Wach exhaust turbine. On September 6 1939 she was requisitioned to become the armed merchant cruiser HMS* Ranpura, *being fitted with eight 6in and two 3in guns. Her conversion took place at Calcutta, and during this her fomer two funnels were reduced to one.* Ranpura *was sold to the Admiralty in 1943 to become a fleet repair ship, and was broken up at Spezia, Italy, in 1961 (Cliff Parsons)*

P&O: Shillong *was in 1939 one of the latest additions to P&O's relatively small cargo fleet. Like her sistership* Surat *had been completed that year by Alexander Stephen at Linthouse and her first voyage in March–April 1939 took her from Middlesbrough, Immingham, Antwerp and London to Calcutta. As part of eastbound convoy HX231, on April 4 1943 she was torpedoed by* U635 *in 57 10N 35 30W. She sank the following day.* Shillong *was on voyage from Port Lincoln and New York to Belfast Lough and Swansea with 8000 tons of zinc concentrates and 3000 tons of grain and general cargo.* Shillong *was manned by 65 crew and 8 gunners, of which 63 and 3 respectively were lost (RW Jordan collection)*

Port Line: Port Huon *was one of five similar vessels completed during 1927–28. Completed by Swan, Hunter & Wigham-Richardson in October 1927, her Wallsend/Sulzer oil engines developed a total 6600bhp and she could carry 378,500 cubic feet of frozen cargo.* Port Huon *was to remain bringing frozen produce to Britain throughout the war, and following several years of postwar service, was broken up at Yokosuka, Japan, in 1961–62 (Port Line)*

Port Line: Port Quebec *was launched on August 17 1939 and delivered in November. She cost £208,000 to build. Soon after delivery she was requisitioned by the Admiralty for conversion to the minelayer HMS* Port Quebec, *and with four others formed the 1st Minelaying Squadron. In 1943 she was purchased outright by the Admiralty and converted to the aircraft repair ship* Deer Sound. *After the war, in 1947, she was sold back to Port Line and renamed* Port Quebec *for her originally intended service. When ordered, she had been intended for the MANZ Line (Montreal, Australia and New Zealand Line) service, which was formed by Port Line, Ellerman & Bucknall and New Zealand Shipping, to take over the loss-making Canadian National Steamship's Australasian service. This service commenced because the Canadian government had many surplus First World War standard ships which they had difficulty in selling. After several years on this service,* Port Quebec *was broken up at Kaohsiung in 1968 (RW Jordan)*

Prince Line: Palestinian Prince, *completed by Wm Hamilton, Glasgow, in December 1936, was one of a series of similar vessels built for the Mediterranean service.* Palestinian Prince *survived the war and in 1960 was sold to Lebanese owners and renamed* Happy Med. *After a further sale in 1965, she became the Panamanian-registered* Mimi. *In October 1966 she was badly damaged by fire when repairing at Perama, Greece, but this damage was repaired and she went back into service. However, her career came to an end in 1970 when she was sold to Brodospas for breaking up at Split, Yugoslavia (RW Jordan collection)*

Port Bowen (st2,P12)	1919	Workmn	8267	11,665	500–6	62–5	30–2	14.0
Port Brisbane (r/t2,P12)	1923	Workmn	8739	11,500	500–8	62–5	30–2	13.5
Port Campbell (r/t2,P12)	1922	Workmn	8751	11,330	500–8	62–5	30–1	13.5
Port Caroline (st2,P12)	1919	Workmn	8263	11,695	500–8	62–5	30–1	13.5
Port Chalmers (m2,P12/1)	1933	SHWR	8535	11,610	506–10	65–4	29–10	15.0
Port Darwin (r/t2,P12)	1918	Workmn	8063	11,410	500–6	60–4	29–5	13.0
Port Denison (r/t2,P12)	1918	Workmn	8043	11,360	500–0	60–4	29–6	13.0
Port Dunedin (m2,P12/1)	1925	Workmn	7441	10,250	484–5	59–10	30–0	14.0
Port Fairy (m2,P12/1)	1928	SHWR	8337	11,060	495–0	63–3	29–7	14.5
Port Fremantle (m2,P12/1)	1927	Workmn	8496	11,060	494–8	63–5	29–7	14.5
Port Gisborne (m2,P12/1)	1927	SHWR	8390	11,060	494–9	63–4	29–7	14.5
Port Halifax (m)	1937	SHWR	5820	9621	456–6	59–0	26–3	14.0
Port Hardy (r/t2,P12/1)	1923	Leslie	8897	11,050	499–0	62–4	30–2	13.5
Port Hobart (m2,P12/1)	1925	SHWR	7448	10,235	484–5	59–9	29–11	14.0
Port Hunter (st2,P12)	1922	Leslie	8802	11,435	500–0	62–4	30–2	13.0
Port Huon (m2,P12/1)	1927	SHWR	8432	10,990	496–6	63–4	30–7	14.5
Port Jackson (m2,P12/1)	1937	SHWR	9687	10,905	521–2	68–2	28–5	16.5
Port Melbourne (r/t2,P12)	1914	Workmn	9142	12,400	501.3	63–4	30–6	13.5
ex Star of Victoria 16								
Port Montreal (m,P–)	1937	Doxfrd	5882	9620	456–6	58–11	26–4	13.0
Port Napier (m2,P12/1)	order	SHWR	9847	11,930	523–11	68–2	28–6	16.5
Port Nicholson (st2,P12)	1918	Leslie	8402	11,630	481.2	62–4	30–1	13.0
Port Quebec (m)	1939	ThmpsJ	5936	9602	468–0	59–9	26–6	14.5
Port Saint John (m)	1938	ThmpsJ	5668	9250	465–1	59–0	26–3	13.0
Port Sydney (r/t2,P12)	1914	Workmn	9129	12,400	501.3	63–4	30–6	13.5
ex Star of England 16								
Port Townsville (m2,P12/1)	1935	SHWR	8661	12,325	516–6	65–2	29–10	16.5
Port Wellington (r/t2,P12/1)	1924	Workmn	8301	10,915	489–0	60–5	29–7	14.0
Port Wyndham (m2,P12/1)	1935	BrownJ	8580	11,400	511–0	65–2	29–11	16.5

Note: The title of this company was changed on 11 Nov 1937 from Commonwealth & Dominion Line Ltd. The company was purchased in 1916 by Cunard Steam Ship Co Ltd

POST OFFICE, (Telegraph Department), London

Services: Cable laying and maintenance

Cable vessels

Alert (s2)	1918	SHWR	941		196.7	31–5	20.1	10.5
Ariel (s2)	1939	SHWR	1479	1150	250–6	35–2	16–4	12.0
Iris (s2)	bldg	SHWR	1479	1152	250–6	35–2	16–4	12.0
Monarch (s2)	1916	SHWR	1150		222.7	32–3	19.1	11.0

PRINCE LINE LTD, Furness House, Leadenhall St, London EC3

Funnel: Black with narrow red band over broad red band; white Prince of Wales' feathers on broad band
Hull: Grey, red boot-topping
Services: Prince Line – New York–Halifax–Norfolk VA–Los Angeles–Japan–China–Philippines–Netherlands East Indies–Straits

Passenger/general cargo vessels

Eastern Prince (m2,P102/1)	1929	Napr&M	10,926	8663	516–5	64–10	26–6	17.0
Northern Prince (m2,P102/1)	1929	Lithgw	10,927	8663	516–5	64–11	26–6	17.0
Southern Prince (m2,P102/1)	1929	Lithgw	10,917	8663	516–5	64–11	26–6	17.0

Ship	Year	Builder	GRT	DWT	Length	Beam	Draught	Speed
Western Prince (m2,P102/1)	1929	Napr&M	10,926	8663	516–5	64–10	26–6	17.0
General cargo vessels								
African Prince (m)	1939	FurnH	4653	9366	437–5	56–8	25–1	11.5
Arabian Prince	1936	Hamtn4	1960	2970	306–0	44–3	18–11	12.0
Cyprian Prince	1937	FurnH	1988	2900	306–0	44–3	18–11	12.0
Egyptian Prince (P10)	1922	FurnH	3490	5858	382–6	52–1	22–7	12.0
Italian Prince	1921	FurnH	3478	5850	381–10	52–1	22–8	12.0
ex Lancastrian Prince 22								
Lancastrian Prince	bldg	SmithM	1914	3400	315–0	44–2	19–11	12.0
Norman Prince	bldg	SmithM	1913	3400	315–0	44–2	19–11	12.0
Palestinian Prince	1936	Hamtn4	1960	2970	306–0	44–2	18–11	12.0
Siamese Prince (m2,P12)	1929	Blythw	8456	10,625	458–0	60–4	29–3	14.5
Stuart Prince	order	SmithM	1911	3137	315–0	44–3	18–11	12.0
Syrian Prince	1936	FurnH	1990	2970	306–0	44–2	18–11	12.0
Tudor Prince	bldg	SmithM	1914	3246	315–0	44–3	18–11	12.0
Welsh Prince	bldg	Blythw	5148	8700	432–6	56–0	25–9	10.5
RIO CAPE LINE LTD								
British Prince (m)	1935	Doxfrd	4979	9215	426–6	54–2	26–6	11.0
ex Sutherland 36								
Chinese Prince (m2,P12)	1926	DeutsH	8593	10,770	458–0	60–4	27–11	15.0
Cingalese Prince (m2,P12)	1929	Blythw	8474	10,625	458–0	60–4	28–0	14.5
Indian Prince (m2,P12)	1926	DeutsH	6376	10,770	458–0	60–4	27–11	15.0
ex Wave 38, ex Japanese Prince 37								
Javanese Prince (m2,P12)	1926	DeutsH	8593	10,770	458–0	60–4	27–11	15.0
Malayan Prince (m2,P12)	1926	DeutsH	8593	10,770	458–0	60–4	27–11	15.0
Sardinian Prince (P10)	1922	FurnH	3491	5858	363.3	52–2	22–8	12.0
ex Appomotox 30								
Sicilian Prince (P10)	1922	FurnH	3489	5858	363.3	52–2	22–8	12.0
ex Castilian Prince 33, ex Alleghany 23								

Settlements–Colombo–Suez–Boston–New York (round-the-world service); Middlesbrough–Antwerp–London–River Plate; Boston–New York–Philadelphia–R Plate; New York–Brazil; New York–South Africa–E Africa–Philadelphia–Boston–New York; Manchester, Leith, Tyne, Middlesbrough, Antwerp, London–Tunis–Malta–Alexandria–Palestine–Syria–Cyprus–Liverpool–Manchester; Rio Cape Line – Brazil–South Africa

Note: Prince Line Ltd was controlled by Furness, Withy & Co Ltd (*qv*)

PYMAN BROTHERS LTD, 16 St Helen's Place, London EC3

Ship	Year	Builder	GRT	DWT	Length	Beam	Draught	Speed
Parracombe	1928	GrayWH	4698	8815	425–0	54–2	24–10	11.0
Welcombe	1930	GrayWH	5122	9208	421.8	55–0	25–0	11.0

Funnel: Black with white band bearing black disc
Hull: Light grey, red boot-topping
Services: General tramping

RADCLIFFE & CO, EVAN THOMAS, Baltic House, Mount Stuart Sq, Cardiff

Ship	Year	Builder	GRT	DWT	Length	Beam	Draught	Speed
ANNE THOMAS STEAMSHIP CO LTD								
Llanover	1928	Bartm2	4959	8640	415–0	53–5	24–7	10.0
ANTHONY RADCLIFFE STEAMSHIP CO LTD AND ETHEL RADCLIFFE STEAMSHIP CO LTD								
Ethel Radcliffe	1920	Craig2	5673	9525	415.2	55–6	25–1	10.0
Vera Radcliffe	1925	Craig2	5587	9325	431–9	55–6	25–2	10.0
CLARISSA RADCLIFFE STEAMSHIP CO LTD								
Clarissa Radcliffe	1915	Craig2	5754	9570	415.0	55–6	25–1	10.0
ex Gwent 17, launched as Windsor								
Llanashe (r/t)	1936	Bartm2	4836	9150	432–9	56–8	25–0	10.0
Llanwern	1928	Bartm2	4966	8450	412–10	53–5	24–7	10.0
GWENLLIAN STEAMSHIP CO LTD								
Llandilo	1928	Bartm2	4966	8640	415–0	53–5	24–7	10.0
LLANBERIS STEAMSHIP CO LTD								
Llanberis	1928	Leslie	5055	8640	415–1	53–8	24–9	10.0
LLANGOLLEN STEAMSHIP CO LTD								
Llangollen	1928	Leslie	5056	8640	415–0	53–8	24–9	10.0
LLANGORSE STEAMSHIP CO LTD								
Peterston	1925	Bartm2	4680	7740	400–0	52–0	24–10	10.0
PICTON STEAMSHIP CO LTD								
Flimston	1925	Bartm2	4674	7740	400–0	52–0	24–10	10.0
Llanarth	1929	Bartm2	5053	8640	415–0	54–0	25–2	10.0
W I RADCLIFFE STEAMSHIP CO LTD AND WYNNSTAY STEAMSHIP CO LTD								
Llanishen	1929	Bartm2	5053	8640	415–0	54–0	25–2	10.0

Funnel: Black with two white bands
Hull: Black, red boot-topping
Services: General tramping

WIMBORNE STEAMSHIP CO LTD

Llandaff (r/t)	1937	Bartm2	4825	9150	432–9	56–7	25–0	10.0
Llanfair	1928	Bartm2	4966	8490	415–0	53–5	24–7	10.0

Funnel: Red, black top
Hull: Black with white band, pink boot-topping
Services: General tramping

RAEBURN & VÉREL LTD, 45 West Nile St, Glasgow C1

MONARCH STEAMSHIP CO LTD

British Monarch	1923	Napr&M	5661	9185	420.6	54–2	25–4	11.0
Caledonian Monarch	1928	Napr&M	5851	9315	445–2	56–2	24–4	10.0
Celtic Monarch	1929	Hendn2	5824	9335	445–0	56–2	24–6	11.0
Imperial Monarch	1926	Napr&M	5831	9430	445–2	56–2	24–4	10.0
Norman Monarch	1937	Caledn	4718	9250	432.7	56–9	23.8	11.0
Scottish Monarch	1938	Caledn	4719	9250	432.7	56–9	23.8	11.0

Funnel: Black with black R on white over blue bands
Hull: Black, red boot-topping
Services: Oil and petroleum trades

RAPP, ARTHUR A, 48 Fenchurch Street, London EC3

Manager for
BRITISH OIL SHIPPING CO LTD
Tankers

Oilpioneer (m)	1928	SHWR	5666	9100	424–0	53–6	25–8	11.0
Oilreliance (m)	1929	SHWR	5666	9100	424–0	53–6	25–8	11.0
Oiltrader	1927	SHWR	5550	9275	424–0	53–6	25–9	10.5

Funnel: Black with white band bearing red R
Hull: Black, prink boot-topping
Services: General tramping

READHEAD & CO, GEORGE T,
Akenside House, Akenside Hill, Newcastle upon Tyne

THE CLIFFE STEAMSHIP CO LTD

Highcliffe	1927	Rhead3	3847	6350	363.9	50–6	21–7	9.0

Funnel: Black with white triangle on black band between two narrow white bands
Services: General tramping

RICHLEY, HALVORSEN & SAMPLE,
Milburn House, Dean St, Newcastle upon Tyne 1

HARTLEY STEAMSHIP CO LTD

Hamsterley	1925	SmithM	2160	3520	280.0	41–6	19–5	9.0

Funnel: Black with red cross and circle emblem on white band
Hull: Black with white band, red boot-topping
Services: Tramping, mainly Welsh coal to Mediterranean

RIDGE STEAMSHIP CO LTD, Phoenix Bldgs, Mount Stuart Sq, Cardiff

Menin Ridge	1924	Burntd	2474	4396	298.5	44–0	20–2	9.0
ex Pentiron 30								

Funnel: Black with black and white chequered band
Hull: Black, red boot-topping
Services: General tramping

RIDLEY, SON & TULLY, JOHN, Milburn House, Dean St, Newcastle upon Tyne

TYNESIDE LINE LTD

Newton Ash	1925	Pgill2	4625	7689	372.8	54–8	23–10	10.0
Newton Beech	1925	Pgill2	4651	7690	372.8	54–8	23–10	10.0
Newton Pine	1925	Prstm2	4212	8120	377–3	51–6	24–10	9.5
ex Fernlea 27								

Funnel: Black with white GL on blue band between two narrow white bands
Hull: Black, red boot-topping
Services: General tramping (voyages to Spain during Spanish Civil War)

ROBERTS, CHARLES ALAN, Atlantic Bldgs, Mount Stuart Sq, Cardiff

GUARDIAN LINE LTD

Macbrae	1924	Burntd	2117	3420	274.5	39–11	18–9	9.5
ex Carlbeath 37								
Macgregor	1918	Forth	2498	4020	303.3	43–0	19–8	10.0
ex Baron Garioch 36, ex War Melon 19								
Maclaren	1915	RDuck2	2330	4000	313–1	43–0	19–3	9.5
ex Singleton Abbey 36								

Funnel: Red with white N, black top
Hull: Grey, red boot-topping
Services: General tramping

ROBERTS & SON, HUGH, St Nicholas Chambers, Newcastle upon Tyne 1

THE NORTH SHIPPING CO LTD

North Britain	bldg	Rhead3	4635	8300	405.6	53–7	24.4	10.5
North Cornwall	1924	Rhead3	4304	7750	380.8	52–0	24–0	9.5
North Devon	1924	Rhead3	3658	6682	374–6	50–0	22–8	9.5

ROBINSON & SONS, JOSEPH, 1 Howard St, North Shields

Funnel: Black with red band bearing white 'stag' emblem
Hull: Black, red boot-topping
Services: General tramping

STAG LINE LTD

General cargo vessels								
Clintonia	1917	Dobson	3106	5342	331.0	48–0	20–6	10.0
Cydonia	1927	Blumr2	3517	6526	365–0	48–9	23–0	9.5
Euphorbia	1924	Sundld	3380	5700	331.0	48–0	21–8	10.0
Gardenia	1928	ArmWh1	3745	6495	360.8	48–4	22–8	10.0
Linaria	1924	Sundld	3385	5700	331.0	48–0	21–8	10.0
Photinia	1929	SHWRSd	4010	6750	376–1	50–10	22–5	10.0
ex Hopedene 38								
Oil/molasses tanker								
Gloxinia	1920	TyneIr	3336	5522	341–4	47–11	21–11	10.0

RODNEY STEAMSHIP CO LTD, Milburn House, Dean St, Newcastle upon Tyne 1

Funnel: Black with broad white band bearing four narrow red bands
Hull: Black with white band, redboot-topping
Services: General tramping

GRAINGER SHIPPING CO LTD

Alice Marie	1920	Austin	2206	3250	280.0	40–6	18–7	9.5

ROPNER & CO LTD, SIR R,
Mercantile Chambers, Mainsforth Terrace, West Hartlepool

Funnel: Black with red and white chequered houseflag
Hull: Grey, red boot-topping
Services: General tramping

POOL SHIPPING CO LTD

Alderpool	1936	Pgill2	4313	8275	382.1	53–5	24–9	10.4
ex Northwick 36								
Boulderpool	1928	SmithM	4805	8765	417–4	53–6	24–11	9.5
Bridgepool	1924	Ropnr3	4845	8670	402–10	55–6	24–6	9.5
Clearpool (st)	1935	GrayWH	5404	9370	441–0	55–2	26–0	10.5
Cragpool	1928	Cowpen	5133	9120	432–8	54–1	25–1	10.0
Deerpool	1930	GrayWH	5167	9310	438–5	54–2	25–3	10.0
Drakepool	1924	Ropnr3	4838	8670	402–10	55–6	24–6	9.5
Fishpool (m)	bldg	Laing	4950		418.0	58–10	25.8	10.5
Gullpool	1928	Cowpen	4868	8750	416–6	53–8	24–11	9.0
Heronspool	1929	GrayWH	5202	9235	438–5	54–3	25–3	10.0
Hindpool	1928	GrayWH	4897	8770	417–8	53–6	24–11	9.5
Kirkpool	1928	Laing	4842	8765	418–6	53–8	24–11	9.5
Mansepool	1928	GrayWH	4894	8745	417–8	53–6	24–11	9.5
Otterpool	1926	GrayWH	4876	8760	402–4	55–0	24–6	9.5
Pikepool	1909	Ropnr2	3683	6260	346.5	51–0	21–6	8.0
Reedpool	1924	Ropnr3	4838	8670	402–10	55–6	24–6	9.5
Rockpool	1927	GrayWH	4897	8750	417–8	53–6	24–11	10.0
Rushpool	1928	Cowpen	5125	9100	432–8	54–1	25–1	10.0
Salmonpool	1924	Irvin3	4803	8674	402–10	55–6	24–6	9.5
Seapool (P4)	bldg	Burntd	4820	9230	425–0	56–10	25–5	10.5
Sedgepool	1918	Ropnr3	5556	9470	433–10	55–6	25–1	8.5
Stagpool	1905	Doxfrd	4560	7370	370.3	52–11	23–1	8.5
ex Iron Chief 35								
Stonepool	1928	SmithM	4803	8765	417–4	53–6	24–11	9.5
Swiftpool	1929	GrayWH	5205	9215	438–5	54–2	25–3	10.0
Troutpool	1927	GrayWH	4886	8770	402–4	55–0	24–6	9.5
Ullapool	1927	GrayWH	4891	8745	417–8	53–6	24–11	9.5
Wearpool (m,P4)	1936	Doxfrd	4982	9160	439–4	54–2	25–6	10.5
Willowpool	1925	Ropnr3	4815	8670	402–10	55–6	24–6	9.5

ROPNER SHIPPING CO LTD

Ainderby	1925	GrayWH	4860	8760	402–6	55–0	24–6	9.5
Ashby	1927	Cowpen	4868	8755	418–6	53–6	24–11	9.5
Carperby	1928	GrayWH	4890	8745	417–8	53–6	24–11	9.5
Daleby	1929	ArmWh1	4640	8775	395.1	53–10	25–2	9.5
ex Kitty Taylor 34								
Danby	1937	GrayWH	4258	7600	396–5	53–2	23–10	10.0
Domby (P1)	1932	GrayWH	5582	9060	435–0	55–5	24–9	9.5
Firby	1926	GrayWH	4869	8760	402–6	55–0	24–6	9.5
Hawnby (st)	1936	GrayWH	5404	9370	441–0	55–2	26–0	10.5
Haxby	1929	GrayWH	5207	9230	438–5	54–2	25–3	10.0
Lackenby	1928	GrayWH	5112	9140	412.1	54–2	25–3	9.5
Moorby (m,P4)	1936	Doxfrd	4992	9160	440–0	54–3	25–6	10.0
Romanby	1927	GrayWH	4887	8770	402–6	55–0	24–6	10.0
Roxby	1923	Ropnr3	4252	7710	389–10	53–0	24–1	9.5
Rudby	1929	GrayWH	4846	8760	402–6	55–0	24–6	9.5
Somersby	1930	GrayWH	5170	9310	438–5	54–2	25–3	9.5
Swainby	1917	Ropnr2	4935	8880	390.0	55–8	24–5	9.0

Thirlby	1928	GrayWH	4887	8750	417–8	53–6	24–11	9.5
Wandby (m)	bldg	Laing	4947		418.0	58–10	25.8	10.5
Warlaby	1927	GrayWH	4876	8760	402–4	55–0	24–6	9.5
Yearby (P4)	1929	GrayWH	5666	10,295	447–6	55–6	26–2	9.5

ROYAL MAIL LINES LTD, Royal Mail House, Leadenhall St, London EC3

Funnel: Yellow
Hull: Black, red boot-topping; *Atlantis* – white
Services: London–Lisbon–Las Palmas–Rio de Janeiro–Santos–Montevideo–Buenos Aires–La Plata; Southampton–Lisbon–Las Palmas–Buenos Aires; Liverpool–Brazil–Argentina; London–Central America; London–Caribbean; cruising

Passenger/general cargo vessels								
Alcantara (st2,P401/1,232/2,768/3)	1926	H&W,B	22,209	13,120	665–11	78–6	31–1	18.0
laid down as Amazon; lengthened, conv mv 34								
Almanzora (r/t3,P1300)	1915	H&W,B	15,551	9110	590–0	67–4	28–0	16.0
Andes (st2,P349/1,204/2)	1939	H&W,B	25,689	10,257	669–4	83–0	29–3	21.0
Asturias (st2,P331/1,220/2,768/3)	1925	H&W,B	22,048	13,853	665–9	78–6	31–1	18.0
lengthened, conv mv 34								
Highland Brigade (m2,P150/1,70/2,500/3)	1929	H&W,B	14,134	9430	544–8	69–5	28–9	15.5
Highland Chieftain (m2,P150/1,70/2,500/3)	1929	H&W,B	14,135	9470	544–8	69–5	28–9	15.5
Highland Monarch (m2,P150/1,70/2,500/3)	1928	H&W,B	14,139	9510	544–6	69–5	28–9	15.5
Highland Patriot (m2,P150/1,70/2,500/3)	1932	H&W,B	14,172	9331	544–8	69–5	28–9	15.5
Highland Princess (m2,P150/1,70/2,500/3)	1930	H&W,B	14,133	9410	544–6	69–5	28–9	15.5
Cruise vessel								
Atlantis (r/t3,P450/oc)	1913	H&W,B	15,135	–	590–0	67–4	28–0	16.0
ex Andes 29								
General cargo vessels								
Araby (m,P–)	1923	McMlln	4936	7923	380.0	53–2	26–3	11.0
Brittany (m)	1928	McMlln	4772	7585	400.4	55–2	24–11	12.0
Culebra	1919	Irvin3	3044	4853	342–0	46–10	21–8	10.0
ex Riposto 22, ex War Mirage 19								
Gascony (m,P12/1)	1925	McMlln	4716	7328	400–6	53–3	26–0	10.5
Lochavon (m2)	1938	H&WGw	9205	10,000	498–0	66–2	28–6	16.0
Lochgoil (m2,P12/1)	1924	H&WGw	9462	11,667	502–0	62–4	29–8	12.5
Lochkatrine (m2,P12/1)	1924	BrownJ	9419	11,510	502–0	62–4	29–9	12.5
Lochmonar (m2,P52/1)	1924	H&W,B	9412	11,767	502–0	62–2	29–8	12.5
Lombardy (P8/1)	1921	RDuck2	3379	6030	394–2	48–1	23–8	11.0
Nagara (s2)	1919	SHWR	8791	10,426	450–5	61–4	30–4	13.0
Nalon (s2)	1915	LithR	7222	8250	455–1	56–2	28–4	12.5
ex Murillo 33								
Narenta* (st)	1920	Workmn	8266	10,447	465–0	58–4	29–3	12.0
laid down as Neganti								
Nariva (s2)	1920	Steph2	8714	9948	450–5	61–4	30–7	13.0
Natia (s2)	1920	Steph2	8715	9707	450–5	61–4	30–7	13.0
Navasota (s2)	1917	SHWR	8795	10,426	450–5	61–4	30–4	13.0
Nebraska (st)	1920	Workmn	8261	10,360	465–0	58–4	29–3	12.0
Nela (s2)	1916	LithR	7221	8280	455–1	56–2	28–4	12.5
ex Molière 33								
Palma (m)	order	H&W,B	5419	8434	450–4	61–4	25–0	15.0
Pampas (m)	bldg	H&W,B	5400	8414	450–4	61–4	25–0	15.0
Pardo (m)	bldg	H&W,B	5405	8434	450–4	61–4	25–0	15.0
Potaro (m)	bldg	H&W,B	5410	8434	450–4	61–4	25–0	15.0
Sabor	1920	Earles	5212	8135	412–0	52–2	25–3	10.5
launched as War Whale								
Sambre	1919	Short2	5260	8150	412–4	52–5	25–3	10.5
launched as War Swift								
Sarthe	1920	Gray18	5271	8200	412–0	52–4	25–3	10.5
Siris	1919	H&WGk	5242	7994	412–0	52–4	25–4	10.5
Somme	1919	Short2	5265	8150	412–0	52–5	25–3	10.5
launched as War Toucan								

Note: * Sold Japan 1939, renamed *Kosei Maru*
Note: This company also owned vessels under 1500gt

Royal Mail Lines: Highland Patriot *was one of six sisterships built by Harland & Wolff at Belfast during 1928–32 for the Nelson Line. One of the original series of five vessels,* Highland Hope, *was wrecked in November 1930. She was replaced by* Highland Patriot, *ordered after that loss and completed in May 1932. With the collapse of the Kylsant Group in 1932 Nelson Line vessels were transferred to the newly-constituted Royal Mail Lines. It was under Royal Mail colours that Highland class liners became well-known up to 1959–60 when they were withdrawn. On October 1 1940* Highland Patriot *was torpedoed by* U38 *when on voyage from Buenos Aires to the River Clyde for orders. She was carrying 5700 tons of refrigerated and general cargo. Of the 143 crew, 3 were lost (EH Cole)*

Royal Mail Lines: Gascony *was built on the Clyde and completed in November 1925, survived the Second World War, and served in this fleet until 1958, when she was broken up. She was originally built for David MacIver & Co Ltd, a company which with others was absorbed into the newly formed Royal Mail Lines Ltd following the collapse of the Kylsant Group in 1932 (Alex Duncan)*

Shaw, Savill & Albion: Completed in June 1922 for Australian Commonwealth Line as Esperance Bay, *and transferring to Shaw, Savill in 1936, the liner* Arawa *saw wartime service firstly as an armed merchant cruiser and then as a troopship. In 1945 she repatriated former prisoners of war from the eastern Mediterranean, and then went to Bombay for use in the Pacific war.* Arawa *was returned to her owners in 1945 and after a refit went back into commercial service in February 1946 with accommodation for 274 tourist class passengers.She made her last voyage starting in December 1954 and was broken up at Newport in 1955*
(RW Jordan collection)

Funnel: Black with blue R on white band
Hull: Black with white band, red boot-topping
Services: General tramping

RUNCIMAN SHIPPING CO LTD, W, 56 Pilgrim St, Newcastle upon Tyne 1

MOOR LINE LTD

Alnmoor	1922	Doxfrd	6573	10,810	433–9	54–0	28–4	10.0
Blythmoor	1922	Doxfrd	6582	10,725	433–9	54–0	28–4	10.0
Castlemoor	1922	Doxfrd	6574	10,785	433–9	54–0	28–4	10.0
Dalemoor	1922	Nthmbl	5796	9165	413–0	52–11	26–4	10.0
Eastmoor	1922	Nthmbl	5812	9195	413–0	52–11	26–4	10.0
Fernmoor (m)	1936	Doxfrd	4972	9185	423–0	54–2	25–6	10.5
Glenmoor (m)	1928	Doxfrd	4393	8220	391–2	52–8	25–5	10.0
Innesmoor (m)	1928	Doxfrd	4392	8220	391–0	52–7	25–5	10.0
Jedmoor (m)	1928	Doxfrd	4392	8220	391–0	52–8	25–5	10.0
Kirriemoor (m)	1935	Doxfrd	4970	9185	428–1	54–2	25–6	10.5
Northmoor (m)	1928	Doxfrd	4392	8220	391–0	52–8	25–5	10.0
Orangemoor	1923	Nthmbl	5775	9040	413–0	53–0	26–4	10.0
Pearlmoor	1923	Rhead3	4581	8495	415–0	52–1	25–6	10.0
Vinemoor (m)	1924	Doxfrd	4359	8235	390–10	52–8	25–5	10.0
Westmoor (m)	1924	Doxfrd	4359	8235	390–10	52–8	25–5	10.0
Yorkmoor	1925	Rhead3	4457	7510	386–2	52–5	23–7	10.5
Zurichmoor	1925	Rhead3	4455	7500	386–2	55–4	23–8	10.5

Note: This company was a member of the Runciman Group, which also controlled Anchor Line (Henderson Bros) Ltd (*qv*)

Funnel: Black with green S on broad white band between two narow green bands
Hull: Green
Services: General tramping
Note: Manager of these vessels was Muir, Young Ltd (*qv*)
Note: Saguenay Terminals Ltd was controlled by Aluminium Co of Canada

SAGUENAY TERMINALS LTD,
1000 Dominion Square Bldg, Montreal PQ, Canada

Corabella	1937	ThmpsJ	5682	9050	425–4	57–8	25–0	11.0
Sire	1938	ThmpsJ	5664	9050	425–4	57–8	25–0	11.0

BESPIAN STEAMSHIP CO LTD, Aldwych House, Aldwych, London WC2

Newton Moore	1937	ThmpsJ	5673	9050	425–4	57–7	25–0	11.0

Funnel: Red with blue top separated by white band
Hull: Black or grey, red boot-topping
Services: Whaling, general tramping

SALVESEN & CO, CHR, 29 Bernard St, Leith, Edinburgh 6

POLAR WHALING CO LTD

Whale factory vessel								
Sevilla	1900	Prstml	7022	7675	397.0	52–2	27–0	10.0
conv general cargo 28								

SEVILLA WHALING CO LTD

Whale factory vessel								
New Sevilla (s2)	1900	H&W,B	13,801	16,536	565–0	63–4	35–1	10.5
ex Runic 30; conv passenger/general cargo 30								

THE SOUTH GEORGIA CO LTD

General cargo vessels								
Albuera	1921	Burntd	3477	6200	331.3	48–8	23–7	10.0
ex Sierra Nevada 31								
Brandon	1917	ThmpsJ	6668	10,250	427–1	55–6	27–11	10.5
ex Bredon 23, ex Holbrook 23								
Fintra	1918	Finch	2089	3200	293–9	41–9	18–10	9.5
ex Carcavellos 27, ex Tutshill 19								
Saganaga	1935	Hendn2	5452	9255	407.5	55–8	28.0	11.0
Seringa*	1913	Ropnr2	4729	7950	391–8	51–6	24–4	8.5
ex Falls City 29								
Shekatika	1936	Caledn	5458	9250	407.0	55–9	28.0	11.0
Sirikishna	1936	Caledn	5458	9240	407.0	55–9	28.0	11.0
Tanker								
Peder Bogen	1925	Dordr	9741	13,440	495–0	62–4	29–8	10.0
Whale factory vessels								
Coronda	1899	SH	7503	10,530	482–0	56–5	27–0	11.5
ex Politician 22; conv general cargo 22								
Saluta	1906	Weser	6261	7635	409.6	52–9	26–6	9.5
ex Southern King 36, ex Moora 23, ex Lothringen 15; conv gen cargo 23								
Salvestria (s2)	1913	Workmn	11,938	13,000	520–0	62–5	29–8	12.0
ex Cardiganshire 29; conv general cargo 29								
Sourabaya	1915	Workmn	10,107	11,000	470.2	58–4	27–11	12.0
ex Carmarthenshire 29; conv general cargo 29								

Manager for
MINISTRY OF SHIPPING

Crown Arun (r/t)	1938	Neptn2	2372	–	302–6	45–2	18–4	9.5
ex Hannah Böge 39								

Note: * Sold Claymore Shipping Co Ltd 1939
Note: Also short-sea vessels and whalers

SCINDIA STEAM NAVIGATION CO LTD,
Scindia Ho, Dougall Rd, Ballard Estate, Bombay, India, and
Scindia Steamships (London) Ltd, Africa House, 44–46 Leadenhall St, London EC3

Funnel: Black with yellow band
Hull: Black with white band, red boot-topping; *El Madina* – grey, red boot-topping
Services: Rangoon–Bombay–Karachi; Rangoon–Madras–Calcutta–Colombo–Karachi; Rangoon–Calcutta; India–Karachi–Jeddah (for Mecca) with Hadj pilgrims; BBSN – passenger and general cargo Rangoon–Calcutta

Passenger/general cargo vessels								
El Hind (P)	1938	Lithgw	5319	7700	414–9	52–0	25–2	12.5
El Madina (r/t2,P12/1,1000 pilg)	1937	Curle	3962	3160	374–5	50–2	20–6	15.0
Jaladurga (s2,P20/1,15/2,2800/3)	1910	Curle	3958	4180	390.5	50–2	20–11	13.0
ex Coconada 33								
Jalagopal (s2,P21/1,89/2,1687/3)	1911	Curle	5284	5060	400.4	52–6	24–0	13.5
ex Edavana 33								
General cargo vessels								
Jalabala	1927	Lithgw	3610	5946	384–7	52–0	23–11	10.0
Jaladuta	1927	Lithgw	4966	8050	415–0	52–0	25–0	10.0
Jalaganga	1936	Lithgw	4981	8032	414–8	52–0	24–11	11.0
Jalajyoti	1918	GrayWH	4430	7104	388–2	51–11	24–0	10.0
ex Vindelia 24, ex War Wagtail 19								
Jalakrishna	1937	Lithgw	4991	8046	414–8	52–0	24–10	11.0
Jalamani	1929	Prstm2	3944	6530	371–0	50–6	22–8	10.5
ex Gambian 36, ex Knight of the Rose 33								
Jalamohan	1925	Bartm2	5100	8280	413–0	52–2	25–3	10.5
ex Buckleigh 33								
Jalapadma	1929	Prstm2	3935	6400	371–0	50–6	22–8	10.5
ex Knight of the Cross 35								
Jalapalaka	1917	Dixon2	4215	7400	364.9	51–1	23–5	8.5
ex Frankby 20, ex William Wallace 18								
Jalaputra	1906	Conn2	4856	8110	400.0	52–2	25–9	9.0
ex Frankdale 20								
Jalarajan	1925	Bartm2	5102	8280	413–0	52–2	25–3	10.5
ex Chulmleigh 33								
Jalarashmi	1918	Earles	4449	7020	388–2	51–9	24–0	10.0
ex Vitellia 23, ex War Pintail 19								
Jalaratna	1930	Prstm2	3942	6528	371–0	50–6	22–8	10.5
ex Knight of the Realm 33								
Jalatarang	1921	Thorny	2498	4287	300.5	43–9	20–4	9.0
ex Elizabeth Stoner 22								
Jalaveera	1927	Lithgw	4966	8050	415–0	52–0	25–0	10.5
Jalavihar	1911	Conn2	5330	8530	410.0	52–2	25–7	10.0
ex Frankmere 21								
Jalavijaya	1918	Prstm1	3756	7157	365.0	51–6	22–4	8.5
ex Franktor 20								
Jalayamuna	1936	Lithgw	4981	8032	414–10	52–0	24–11	11.5

Manager for
BENGAL BURMA STEAM NAVIGATION CO LTD,
644 Merchant St, Rangoon, Burma

Passenger/general cargo vessel								
Englestan (P90)	1910	HallR	4808	6100	386.1	48–2	25–0	12.0
ex Intaba 27								

SEAGER & CO LTD, W H, 109 Bute St, Cardiff

Funnel: Black with white S on black band between two narrow white bands
Hull: Black, red boot-topping
Services: General tramping

TEMPUS SHIPPING CO LTD

Amicus (P–)	1925	Nthmb1	3660	6646	362.5	50–11	21–10	10.0
Beatus	1925	Ropnr3	4885	8656	390.0	55–6	24–7	10.0
Campus (P–)	1925	Nthmb1	3667	6646	362.5	50–11	21–10	10.0
Fiscus (P–)	1928	Nthmb2	4815	8903	399.0	54–6	24–10	10.0
Salvus (P–)	1928	Nthmb2	4815	8903	399.0	54–6	24–10	10.0

SHARP & CO, Milburn House, Dean St, Newcastle upon Tyne 1

Funnel: Black with two white bands
Hull: Black, red boot-topping
Services: General tramping

SHARP STEAMSHIP CO LTD

Glanton	1929	SmithM	2822	4660	317–0	45–6	20–6	9.5
Kyloe	1930	SmithM	2820	4660	317–0	45–6	20–7	9.5

Services: China seas

Note: Also smaller vesssels

SHAW, GEORGE L, No 1 Hwa nan Rd, Tsung Chew, Foochow, China

Under British (Canadian) flag

Shinai	1920	Collwd	2410	3972	261–0	43–8	22–6	9.0
ex Canadian Beaver 34								
Shinkuang	1920	Collwd	2410	3945	261–0	43–8	22–6	9.0
ex Wester 35, ex Canadian Farmer 34								

Funnel: Buff, black top
Hull: Black with white band, red boot-topping
Services: London–Panama–New Zealand–Australia; R Tyne, Hamburg, London–New Zealand–Australia; New Zealand–Panama–Hull; New Zealand–London; New Zealand–Australia–NW Europe–W coast UK

Note: * Sold breakers 1939, repurchased by Ministry of Shipping, to be renamed *Empire Trader* (Br)
Note: Shaw, Savill & Albion Co Ltd became a member of the Furness, Withy & Co Ltd (*qv*) group in 1936, and had been joint owner of Aberdeen & Commonwealth Line Ltd (*qv*) since 1932
Note: See Norfolk & North American Steam Shipping Co Ltd also under Furness, Withy & Co Ltd

SHAW, SAVILL & ALBION CO LTD, 34 Leadenhall St, London EC3

Passenger/general cargo vessels

Akaroa (r/t3,P198/cab)	1914	H&W,B	15,130	13,560	569–9	67–5	32–11	15.5
ex Euripides 32								
Arawa (st2,P292/t)	1922	Beardm	14,462	14,621	548–11	68–4	33–2	15.5
ex Esperance Bay 36								
Ceramic (r/t3,P336/cab)	1913	H&W,B	18,713	19,140	675–0	69–5	34–9	15.0
Dominion Monarch (m4,P517/1)	1939	SHWR	27,155	22,721	682–1	84–10	34–1	21.0
Mataroa (st2,P158/cab)	1922	H&W,B	12,369	11,796	518–9	63–2	32–10	15.0
ex Diogenes 26								
Tainui* (s2,P200/t)	1908	Workmn	9965	11,301	477.8	61–1	31–1	13.5
Tamaroa (st2,P130/cab)	1922	H&W,B	12,405	11,870	518–9	63–2	32–10	15.0
ex Sophocles 26								

General cargo vessels

Coptic (m2,P6/cab)	1928	SHWR	8533	10,725	499–6	64–2	29–2	15.0
Fordsdale (s2)	1924	CommSy	9949	11,527	520–0	63–2	30–2	15.0
Karamea (m2,P6/cab)	1928	Fairfd	8457	10,797	499–6	64–2	29–2	15.0
Mahana (st2)	1917	Workmn	8740	10,412	520–9	63–4	28–11	13.5
Maimoa (s2)	1920	Palmer	8011	11,070	494–0	63–0	29–0	13.5
Matakana (st2)	1921	Steph2	8048	11,020	494–0	63–0	29–0	14.0
Pakeha (s2)	1910	H&W,B	7909	10,680	494–0	63–1	29–0	13.5
Tarananki (m2,P6/cab)	1928	Fairfd	8448	10,797	499–5	64–3	29–2	15.0
Waimarama (m2)	1938	H&W,B	12,843	13,000	535–6	70–5	29–7	16.5
Waiotira (m2)	1939	H&W,B	12,823	13,000	535–6	70–5	29–7	16.5
Waipawa (m2,P12)	1934	H&W,B	10,801	12,320	535–6	70–5	29–7	17.0
Wairangi (m2,P12)	1935	H&WGw	10,796	12,313	535–6	70–5	29–8	17.0
Waiwera (m2,P12)	1934	H&W,B	10,800	12,320	535–6	70–5	29–7	17.0
Zealandic (m2,P6/cab)	1928	SHWR	8443	11,200	499–6	64–2	29–2	15.0

NORFOLK & NORTH AMERICAN STEAM SHIPPING CO LTD

Passenger/general cargo vessel

Themistocles (s2,P103/1,242/3)	1911	H&W,B	11,231	11,920	520–0	62–4	31–6	14.0

General cargo vessels

Mahia (st2)	1917	Workmn	7926	11,010	494–0	63–1	28–11	13.5
Mamari (s2)	1911	H&W,B	7924	10,198	494–0	63–1	28–6	13.0
Raranga (s2)	1916	ArmWh1	7956	10,971	494–0	63–2	29–0	13.0
Tairoa (s2)	1920	ArmWh1	7983	10,935	494–0	63–2	29–0	13.0
Waimana (s2)	1911	Workmn	7870	10,800	494–0	63–1	29–1	13.0
ex Herminius 32, ex Waimana 26								

Funnel: Yellow, blue N on broad white band between two narrow blue bands
Hull: Black with white band, red boot-topping
Services: General tramping

SHIPS FINANCE & MANAGEMENT CO LTD,
Bevis Marks House, Bevis Marks, London EC3

NORFOLK STEAMSHIP CO LTD

Lord Byron	1934	Lithgw	4118	7080	377–4	57–6	22–7	10.0
ex Arcgow 36								

NORWICH STEAMSHIP CO LTD

Lord Cochrane	1934	Short2	4157	7068	377–4	57–6	22–7	10.0
ex Arcwear 37								

Shaw, Savill & Albion: Tamaroa *was completed in February 1922 as Sophocles for Aberdeen Line and was transferred on charter to Shaw, Savill in 1926. She was requisitioned as a troopship from November 1940 and converted for this role at Liverpool. In November 1942* Tamaroa *was the first troopship to enter the port of Bone during the Operation 'Torch' landings. After return to her owners she was refitted at Liverpool during 1947–48, emerging with accommodation for 372 tourist class passengers. After nine years of commercial service she was broken up at Blyth in 1957*
(RW Jordan collection)

Shaw, Savill & Albion: Mahana *was delivered by Workman, Clark, Belfast in July 1917, and was put under the government's Liner Requisition Scheme. Upon entering commercial service in 1919 she was fitted with accommodation for 12 first class and 450 third class passengers, the latter being emigrants. In 1925 the emigrant accommodation was removed, and the vessel was modified as a cargo vessel. During the Second World War she continued on her peacetime service and apparently came through the conflict unscathed. In 1949* Mahana *was chartered by the Ministry of Food as a frozen meat store ship, and was broken up at Dalmuir in 1953*
(RW Jordan collection)

Shaw, Savill & Albion: Waiwera *was one of several motorships built in the mid to late 1930s for the refrigerated cargo trades from New Zealand and Australia. Her large refrigerated cargo space was considered as large and proved valuable during the war years. In May 1940* Waiwera *was damaged during an air raid on Liverpool docks and was later taken over as a munitions carrier. She made one voyage to Malta loaded with stores and munitions. She was torpedoed and sunk by* U754 *in June 1942 when on voyage from Auckland to Liverpool via Panama with 12,933 tons of foodstuffs*
(RW Jordan collection)

Silver Line: This owner's fleet was involved in regular liner services and many had accommodation for a few passengers. Silverteak *was one of three sisters completed by Harland & Wolff at Belfast in September 1930. She was fitted with two Harland & Wolff 6-cylinder oil engines of 5500bhp.* Silverteak *was one of seven vessels in the 1939 fleet to survive the war. With a reduction of the Silver Line fleet in the 1950s, she was sold in 1954 to Panama and renamed* Gardigan, *and was broken up during 1959–60 (RW Jordan collection)*

Reardon Smith: The motor vessel East Lynn *was built by Doxford and delivered in August 1928. In April 1931 she was renamed* Santa Clara Valley, *being involved in regular service from northwest Europe to the Pacific coast of North America. On April 23 1941 she was bombed by enemy aircraft at Nauplia, and sunk. She had arrived at the port with a cargo of ammunition and mules.* Santa Clara Valley *had a crew of 34 and two naval gunners, and also on board were 14 military personnel and 47 muleteers. One crew member, one military serviceman and five muleteers were lost. On October 1 1952 the wreck was raised and was towed to Trieste to be scrapped (RW Jordan collection)*

Steel Bros: Shwedagon *was completed by Armstrong, Whitworth in May 1912 and was typical of tankers of that era built for service in the Far East. Management of the tanker was transferred to British Tanker Co in 1947, and she was broken up in 1953 at Sunderland (RW Jordan collection)*

SIEMENS BROTHERS & CO LTD, Woolwich, London SE18

Funnel: Yellow, black top
Hull: Grey, red boot-topping
Services: Cable laying and maintenance

Cable vessel

Faraday (s2)	1923	Palmer	5533	7342	394.3	48–4	27–6	10.0

SILVER LINE LTD, Bishopsgate House, 80 Bishopsgate, London EC2

Funnel: White with blue top and white over blue bands
Hull: Silver-grey, red boot-topping
Services: Round-the-world line; Pacific ports–Java–Calcutta; Los Angeles–San Francisco–Manila–Malaya–India; Boston–New York–Far East (Kerr-Silver Lines); US Gulf ports–NW Europe; US Atlantic and Gulf of Mexico ports–Persian Gulf and India (American-Persian Gulf Line); services also operated with Leif Høegh & Co (*qv* in Norway section)

Silverash (m,P6/1)	1926	ThmpsJ	5311	9109	441–10	58–4	25–10	13.5
Silveray (m,P–)	1925	ThmpsJ	4535	8142	395.7	57–0	23–8	10.5
Silverbeech (m,P6/1)	1926	Laing	5311	9109	441–10	58–4	25–10	13.5
Silverbelle (m,P6/1)	1927	ThmpsJ	5302	8927	441–10	58–4	25–10	13.5
Silvercedar (m)	1924	Doxfrd	4354	8255	395–0	52–10	25–5	10.5
Silverelm (m)	1924	Doxfrd	4351	8205	395–0	52–8	25–5	10.5
Silverfir (m)	1924	Doxfrd	4347	8225	395–0	52–8	25–5	10.5
Silverguava (m,P6/1)	1927	Laing	5294	8927	441–10	58–4	25–10	13.5
Silverlarch (m,P–)	1924	SHWR	5064	8540	417–2	55–4	25–9	13.5
Silverlaurel (st,P12/1)	1939	ThmpsJ	6142	9600	465–1	59–0	26–3	14.0
Silvermaple (m,P6/1)	1927	Laing	5313	8927	441–10	58–4	25–10	13.5
Silverpalm (m2,P6/1)	1929	ThmpsJ	6373	9766	471–0	61–4	26–6	14.5
Silverpine (m,P–)	1924	SHWR	5066	8540	417–2	55–4	25–10	13.5
Silversandal (m2,P6/1)	1930	H&W,B	6770	10,086	475–0	62–0	26–9	14.5
Silverteak (m2,P6/1)	1930	H&W,B	6770	10,086	475–0	62–0	26–9	14.5
Silverwalnut (m2,P6/1)	1930	H&W,B	6770	10,086	475–0	62–0	26–9	14.5
Silverwillow (m2,P6/1)	1930	ThmpsJ	6373	9766	471–0	61–4	26–6	14.5
Silveryew (m2,P6/1)	1930	ThmpsJ	6373	9766	471–0	61–4	26–6	14.5

Note: Silver Line Ltd was managed by Stanley & John Thompson Ltd.

SMITH, ALFRED HARRIS, 34 Lime St, London EC3

Services: General tramping

SEA & LAND SECURITIES LTD

Alresford	1922	BrownG	2472	4150	290.2	44–1	20–0	9.0
ex Terneuzen 38								
Ulmus	1926	DunlpB	2733	5350	314.1	47–2	20–1	9.5
ex Rákóczi Ferenc 33, ex Ulmus 31								

SMITH, HOGG & CO LTD, 6 Victoria Terrace, West Hartlepool

Funnel: Black with white Maltese cross
Hull: Black with white band
Services: General tramping

Arkleside	1924	OsbGr2	1567	2575	258.0	38–3	17–3	9.0
Magdalena	1923	Craig2	3118	5010	325.0	48–1	20–8	9.0
Roseburn	1922	Craig2	3103	5010	325.0	48–0	20–8	9.0
ex Helena Lensen 35, ex Helena 31								

SMITH & SONS LTD, SIR WILLIAM REARDON, Merthyr House, James St, Cardiff

Funnel: Red with black S, black top
Hull: Black with white band, red boot-topping
Services: UK–W coast North America; general tramping

LEEDS SHIPPING CO LTD

Bradburn*	1930	GrayWH	4736	8770	415–0	54–4	25–3	10.0
Bradfyne*	1928	GrayWH	4740	8740	415–0	54–2	25–3	10.0
Bradglen*	1930	GrayWH	4741	8770	415–0	54–2	25–3	10.0
Cornish City* (m)	1936	FurnH	4952	9543	426.5	56–2	25.3	12.0
Leeds City	1927	GraySd	4758	8740	415–0	54–4	25–1	10.0
Orient City*	bldg	FurnH	5095	8850	438–0	56–10	26–1	11.5

REARDON SMITH LINE LTD

Bradford City (m)	1936	FurnH	4952	9543	426.5	56–2	25.3	12.0
Dallas City (m)	1936	FurnH	4952	9543	426.5	56–2	25.3	12.0
Devon City (m)	1933	FurnH	4928	9295	442–0	56–4	25–1	12.0
Fresno City (m)	1929	Doxfrd	4955	8980	415.6	55–0	25–0	12.0
Houston City (m)	1933	FurnH	4935	9555	442–0	56–4	25–1	12.0
laid down as Bradaire								

Imperial Valley	1924	Workmn	4573	8570	416–8	54–4	25–0	11.0
ex Buchanness 31								
Jersey City	1920	ThmpsJ	6322	9900	411.8	55–0	27–9	10.5
King City	1928	GraySd	4744	8740	415–0	54–4	25–3	10.5
Madras City	bldg	FurnH	5092	8850	438–0	56–10	25–0	11.0
New Westminster City	1929	GraySd	4747	8800	416–6	54–4	25–0	10.5
Prince Rupert City	1929	GraySd	4749	8800	415–0	54–4	25–1	10.5
Quebec City	1927	GraySd	4745	8740	415–0	54–4	25–1	10.5
Queen City	1924	ThmpsJ	4814	8720	412.1	55–0	24–6	11.0
ex Cragness 31								
Sacramento Valley	1924	Workmn	4573	8576	416–8	54–4	24–8	11.0
ex Skegness 31								
Santa Clara Valley (m)	1928	Doxfrd	4665	8610	401.1	54–4	24–11	11.0
ex East Lynn 31								
Tacoma City	1929	GrayWH	4738	8800	415–0	54–3	25–1	10.5
Vancouver City (m)	1929	Doxfrd	4955	8980	415.6	55–0	25–0	12.0
Vernon City	1929	GraySd	4748	8800	415–0	54–4	25–1	10.5
Victoria City	1929	GrayWH	4739	8770	415–0	54–4	25–1	10.5
Willamette Valley (m)	1928	Napr&M	4702	8705	401.1	54–3	24–11	12.0
ex West Lynn 31								

Note: * Manager Sir William Reardon Smith & Partners Ltd (associate company)
Note: See also under Board of Trade

Funnel: Black with blue band bearing yellow 'sheaf' emblem
Hull: Black, red boot-topping
Services: General tramping

SOUTER & CO LTD, W A, Sheaf House, 24–26 The Side, Newcastle upon Tyne 1

HEBBURN STEAMSHIP CO LTD

Hylton (m)	1937	Pgill2	5197	9285	445–0	56–2	25.9	12.0

SHEAF STEAM SHIPPING CO LTD

Gretaston	1924	Duncan	5008	8750	404.9	53–0	24–7	10.0
to be renamed Sheaf Mead								
Sheaf Crest	1924	Blyth	2730	4085	320.2	42–11	19–3	10.5
Sheaf Crown	1929	GrayWH	4868	8911	418–5	54–6	25–1	10.5
Sheaf Don	1924	Burntd	2480	4450	308–5	44–0	20–3	10.0
ex Seven Seas Sun 39, ex Porthkerry 35								
Sheaf Field	1923	Blyth	2719	4095	320.3	42–11	19–3	10.5
Sheaf Holme (m)	1929	Pgill2	4814	8858	422–0	54–6	24–11	10.0
Sheaf Mount	1924	Duncan	5017	8750	404.9	53–0	24–7	10.0
ex Luciston 39								
Sheaf Water	1925	Blyth	2730	4065	320.2	42–11	19–3	10.5

Funnel: Yellow with green band and narrow green bands above and below
Hull: Grey, green boot-topping
Services: South African ports–Straits Settlements, Australia, Netherlands East Indies, mainly with coal

SOUTH AFRICA, GOVERNMENT OF, (Railways & Harbours Administration), Durban, South Africa

Aloe	1925	Duncan	5047	8865	419–10	53–0	24–7	10.0
Dalia	1931	Duncan	5188	8904	421–0	55–0	25–1	10.5
Erica	1926	Duncan	5112	8870	419–10	53–0	24–8	10.0

Funnel: Yellow, black top
Hull: Grey
Services: Whaling

Note: This company, a member of the Lever Bros group, also owned a fleet of whalers

SOUTHERN WHALING & SEALING CO LTD, Unilever House, Blackfriars, London EC4

Whale factory vessels

Southern Empress	1914	Doxfrd	12,398	16,000	539–2	66–6	29–7	11.0
ex San Jeronimo 28; conv tanker 28								
Southern Princess	1915	ArmWh1	12,156	16,000	553–4	66–8	29–3	11.0
ex San Patricio 29; conv tanker 29								

Funnel: Black with black triangle on white disc on broad blue band between two narrow white bands
Hull: Black
Services: General tramping

SPRINGWELL SHIPPING CO LTD, 27 Creechurch Lane, London EC3

Springdale	1937	Short2	1579	2550	259–11	40–4	17–7	10.5
Springfjord	bldg	Trondh	2072	3450	286.2	44–1	19–1	10.5
Springtide	1937	Short2	1579	2550	259–11	40–4	17–7	10.5

STANDARD FRUIT & STEAMSHIP CORP (Vaccaro Line),
American Bank & Trust Co Bldg, 200 Carondelet St, Postbox 830, New Orleans LA, USA and 21 West St, New York, USA

Fruit carriers
LLANRUMNEY LTD, 2 Port Royal St, Kingston, Jamaica, BWI (British flag)

Miraflores (P12/1)	1921	SHWR	2158	2620	280–0	39–0	20–1	12.5
St Mary (P12/1)	1921	SHWRSd	2141	2620	280–0	38–10	20–0	12.5
MORANT STEAMSHIP CO LTD								
Erin (r/te,P12)	1932	Work28	5780	6010	431–3	54–8	24–11	16.0
Eros (r/te,P12)	1936	H&W,B	5888	5840	431–6	54–10	24–11	16.0

Funnel: Black with red V on braod white band between two narrow blue bands
Hull: White with dark green band, dark green boot-topping
Services: Fruit trades
Note: Until May 1939 *Erin* and *Eros* were owned by Erin Steamship Co Ltd (manager Standard Fruit & Steamship Corp); from that date manager was M A Kerwin, Port of London Authority Bldg, London EC3
Note: See also in United States section

STANDARD TRANSPORTATION CO LTD, Union Bldgs, Hong Kong

Tankers

Ahamo	1926	Lithgw	8621	12,770	477–3	62–10	29–3	11.5
ex Plume 33								
Coimbra	1937	HwldtK	6768	10,150	433–6	60–5	27–1	11.0
Eclipse	1931	Scott2	9767	14,025	500–0	66–0	29–7	11.5
Eocene	1922	BethB	4216	6300	340.0	49–2	24–3	10.0
ex Schulau 35, ex Vacoil 29, ex Fort McHenry 23								
Lacklan	1929	Lithgw	8670	12,710	477–3	62–10	29–3	11.5
ex Vacuoline 34								
Pegasus	1913	NYSB1	3597	5075	330.5	46–2	23–2	9.5
ex Vesta 31								
Socony	1936	Bremer	4404	6400	349.7	52–4	24–4	11.0
Sovac	1937	Odense	6724	10,150	433–6	60–5	27–3	11.0
Tahchee	1914	Dixon2	6508	9620	420.5	54–5	26–9	9.0
Tamaha	1914	Dixon2	6496	9620	420.5	54–5	26–9	9.0
Tascalusa	1913	Dixon2	6499	9620	420.5	54–5	26–9	9.0
Toorak	1927	Lithgw	8627	12,770	477–3	62–10	29–3	11.5
ex Voco 34								
Vaclite	1928	ArmWh1	5026	7250	386.0	52–2	25–2	11.0
Vacport	1939	HwldtH	6774	10,150	433–6	60–2	27–1	11.0
Voco	1925	GrkDY	5090	7440	394.3	53–4	24–0	11.0
ex Mobiloil 36								
Winamac	1926	Lithgw	8621	12,770	477–3	62–10	29–3	11.5
Yarraville	1928	Lithgw	8627	12,770	477–3	62–10	28–2	11.5
ORIENTAL TANKERS LTD, Hong Kong								
Arthur F Corwin (m)	1938	Blohm	10,516	15,163	506–8	70–0	29–11	12.0
Charles F Meyer (m)	1938	Krupp	10,516	15,260	506–8	70–0	29–11	12.0
Edward F Johnson (m)	1937	RottDD	10,452	15,260	506–9	70–0	29–11	12.0
Edwy R Brown (m)	1937	CRDA2	10,455	15,345	506–9	70–0	29–11	12.0
Frederick S Fales (m)	1939	CRDA2	10,525	15,260	506–8	70–0	29–11	12.0
G S Walden (m)	1935	RottDD	10,627	15,355	505–2	75–1	30–4	12.0
Henry Dundas (m)	1937	Krupp	10,448	15,400	506–3	70–0	29–11	12.0
James J Maguire (m)	1939	CRDA2	10,525	15,260	506–8	70–0	29–11	12.0
John A Brown (m)	1938	CRDA2	10,455	15,345	506–8	70–0	29–10	12.0
W B Walker (m)	1935	Krupp	10,468	15,260	506–8	70–0	30–0	12.0

Funnel: Black with white band bearing 'Esso' symbol – red 'Esso' inside blue oval
Hull: Grey or black, red boot-topping
Services: Oil and petroleum trades

Note: These companies were subsidiaries of Standard Oil Co of New Jersey (*qv* in United States section)

STEEL BROTHERS & CO LTD, 6 Fenchurch Ave, London EC3

INDO-BURMAH PETROLEUM CO LTD
Tanker

Shwedagon	1912	ArmWh1	3391	5400	300.4	44–1	25–1	8.5

Services: Oil and petroleum trades

STEPHENS, SUTTON LTD, Prudential Bldgs, Newcastle upon Tyne

Reaveley*	1929	Doxfrd	4323	7718	385–6	51–8	24–2	10.0
ex Essex Noble 33, ex Juliet 32								
Reaveley (m)	bldg	Doxfrd	4998	9240	439–4	54–3	25–6	11.0
Ridley (m)	1937	Doxfrd	4993	9240	439–3	54–3	25–6	11.0

Funnel: Black with red R on yellow band
Hull: Black, red boot-topping
Services: General tramping

RED 'R' STEAMSHIP CO LTD

Rawnsley (m)	bldg	Doxfrd	4998	9240	439–4	54–3	25–6	11.0
Rugeley (m)	1936	Doxfrd	4985	9240	439–2	54–4	25–6	11.0

THOMASSON SHIPPING CO LTD

Ripley (m)	1936	Doxfrd	4997	9240	439–6	54–2	25–6	11.0
Rodsley (m)	1939	Doxfrd	5000	9240	439–4	54–3	25–6	11.0
Rookley (m)	bldg	Doxfrd	4998	9240	439–4	54–3	25–6	11.0

Note: * Sold W A Massey & Sons Ltd 1939, renamed *Elizabeth Massey*

WHALTON SHIPPING CO LTD

Riley (m)	1936	Doxfrd	4993	9240	438–8	54–3	25–6	11.0
Rothley (m)	1936	Doxfrd	4996	9240	439–3	54–3	25–6	11.0

STOCKWOOD, REES & CO LTD,
20–24 Pembroke Bldgs, Cambrian Place, Swansea

Funnel: Black with red band between two silver bands
Services: General tramping

DILLWYN STEAMSHIP CO LTD

Josewyn	1919	Crown1	1926	2890	268.0	38–1	18–0	8.5
ex Whitwood 39								
Ronwyn	1918	WoodS2	1894	2470	269–8	37–10	17–2	8.5
ex Tinge 38, ex Ottinge 37, ex Lord Rhondda 28								

Note: Also *Kellwyn* (built 1920/1464gt)

STONE & ROLFE LTD, New Dock Rd, Llanelli, and Burrows Chambers, Swansea

Services: General tramping

S & R STEAMSHIPS LTD

Sarastone	1929	Burntd	2473	4350	300.0	44–10	19–4	9.5

Note: Also smaller vessels

STOTT, MANN & FLEMING LTD,
Milburn House, Dean St, Newcastle upon Tyne 1

Funnel: Black with two yellow bands
Hull: Black, red boot-topping
Services: General tramping

General cargo vessels

CLIVE SHIPPING CO LTD

Hopecrown (m)	1937	SHWR	5180	9780	425–0	57–5	26–0	12.0
Hopetarn (m)	bldg	SHWR	5231	9770	425–0	57–5	26–0	12.0

HOPEMOUNT SHIPPING CO LTD

Hopecrest (m)	1935	Curle	5099	9595	425–0	57–5	26–0	12.0
Hopepeak (m)	1938	SHWR	5178	9780	425–0	57–5	26–0	12.0
Hoperange (m)	1939	SHWR	5177	9745	425–0	57–5	26–0	12.0
Hoperidge (m)	1939	SHWR	5222	9770	425–0	57–5	26–0	12.0

NOVOCASTRIA SHIPPING CO LTD

Hopecastle (m)	1937	SHWR	5178	9780	425–0	57–5	26–0	12.0

WALLSEND SHIPPING CO LTD

Hopestar (m)	1936	SHWR	5267	9875	425–0	57–5	26–0	11.0

Tanker

HOPEMOUNT SHIPPING CO LTD

Hopemount (m)	1929	SHWR	7434	12,130	464–10	61–1	27–1	12.0

Note: Stott, Mann & Fleming Ltd was styled Arthur Stott & Co Ltd to 1939

STRICK & CO LTD, F C, 117–121 Leadenhall St, London EC3

Funnel: Strick – Black with white band bearing alternating red and blue chevrons; Cory & Strick – black with black diamond on red and blue chequered band between two narrow white bands; La Tunisienne – black with red M on white diamond on red and blue chequered band between two narrow white bands
Hull: Black, red boot-topping
Services: UK–NW Europe–Marseilles–Port Said –Suez–Port Sudan–Aden–Persian Gulf ports; South Wales, R Tyne – Algeria–Tunisia; UK, NW Europe–Mediterranean

Nigaristan	1913	Bremer	5993	8950	437–0	56–2	26–0	11.5
ex Diyatalawa 22, ex Rappenfels 15								
Shahristan (r/t,P4)	1938	Rhead3	6935	10,000	472–6	58–6	25–6	12.0

CORY & STRICK STEAMERS LTD

Batna	1928	Rhead3	4399	7380	382–8	52–4	23–1	10.5
Hamla	1929	Rhead3	4416	7380	383–10	52–4	23–1	10.5
Kerma	1928	Hendn2	4333	7474	382–8	52–2	23–2	10.5
Lorca	1931	Rhead3	4875	8010	408–0	53–10	23–7	10.0
Marsa	1928	Rhead3	4405	7380	382–8	52–4	23–1	10.5
Thala	1928	Rhead3	4399	7460	382–8	52–4	23–1	10.5

LA TUNISIENNE STEAMSHIP CO LTD

Brika	1929	Rhead3	4412	7380	383–10	52–1	23–1	10.5
Camerata	1931	Rhead3	4875	8010	408–0	53–10	23–7	10.5
Guelma	1928	Rhead3	4402	7380	383–11	52–4	23–1	10.5
Medjerda	1924	GrayWH	4380	7300	383–6	52–0	22–11	10.0
Tafna	1930	Rhead3	4413	7380	383–10	52–4	23–1	10.5
Tunisia	1927	Rhead3	4337	7380	383–10	52–4	23–1	10.5

STRICK LINE (1923) LTD

Afghanistan (r/t,P8)								
	bldg	Rhead3	6992	10,000	472–6	58–6	25–6	12.0
Arabistan (r/t,P12)								
	1929	Rhead3	5874	8950	440–9	55–0	24–11	13.0

Armanistan (r/t,P–)	1937	Rhead3	6805	9500	471–2	58–6	25–7	14.0
Baharistan (P10)	1928	Rhead3	5479	8500	430–6	54–3	24–3	12.0
Baltistan (r/t,P–)	1937	Rhead3	6803	9500	471–2	58–6	25–7	14.0
Baluchistan (r/t,P8)	bldg	Rhead3	6992	10,000	472–6	58–6	25–6	12.0
Bandar Shahpour (P12)	1927	GrayWH	5236	8050	400.0	53–6	24–1	12.0
ex Arabistan 29								
Floristan (P12)	1928	Rhead3	5478	8500	430–6	54–3	24–4	12.0
Gorjistan (r/t,P10)	1929	Rhead3	5880	8950	440–3	55–0	24–11	13.0
Kohistan (r/t,P10)	1930	Rhead3	5884	8950	440–3	55–0	24–11	13.0
Registan (r/t,P12)	1930	Rhead3	5886	8950	440–3	55–0	24–11	13.0
Tabaristan (P12)	1914	Weser	6251	8930	437–0	56–2	26–2	11.5
ex Frankenfels 25								
Turkistan (r/t,P4)	1939	Rhead3	6935	10,000	472–6	58–6	25–6	12.0

STRUBIN & CO LTD, CHARLES, 27 Creechurch Lane, London EC3

Atlantic Scout	1912	Ropnr2	4575	8140	391–9	56–0	23–2	9.0
ex Fishpool 38								
Lake Neuchatel	1907	Doxfrd	3829	6600	350.0	50–0	21–8	8.0
ex Houstone 38, ex Mari 37, ex Ulversmead 22, ex Renfrew 20, ex Claveresk 19								

Funnel: Black with silver band
Services: General tramping
Note: Charles Strubin Co Ltd was associated with Atlantic & Mediterranean Trading Co Ltd (*qv* under David P Barnett)

SUTHERLAND & CO LTD, B J, 38 Sandhill, Newcastle upon Tyne

SUTHERLAND STEAMSHIP CO LTD

Argyll	1939	ThmpsJ	4897	9015	431–10	58–2	25–0	11.0
Caithness (m)	1935	Doxfrd	4970	9250	427–9	54–3	25–6	11.0
Cromarty (m)	1936	Doxfrd	4974	9115	439–3	54–2	25–6	11.0
ex Skipsea 38								
Dumfries	1935	Leslie	5149	9300	429–6	55–2	25–5	11.0
Inverness	bldg	ThmpsJ	4897	9015	431–10	58–2	25–0	11.0
Kinross (m)	1935	Doxfrd	4956	9125	427–11	54–2	25–6	11.0
Peebles (m)	1936	Doxfrd	4982	9260	439–2	54–3	25–6	11.0
Ross (m)	1936	Doxfrd	4978	9260	439–2	54–2	25–6	11.0
Sutherland*	1938	Rhead3	5083	9260	439–2	56–9	25–0	11.0
Sutherland (m)	bldg	Doxfrd	5172	9520	442–11	56–6	25–11	12.0

Funnel: Yellow with black top and band of red over blue interlocking trianagles
Hull: Black, red boot-topping
Services: General tramping

Note: * Sold G Nisbet & Co 1939, renamed *Blairclova*
Note: This company also owned vessels under 1000gt

SUTTON & CO, E J, Cathedral Bldgs, Dean St, Newcastle upon Tyne 1

CONFIELD STEAMSHIP CO LTD

Confield	bldg	ThmpsJ	4956	9110	431–10	58–3	25–0	10.5
Gracefield (r/t)	1928	SHWR	4631	8250	390.0	53–6	24–2	11.0

Funnel: Black with yellow band bearing band of black diamonds
Hull: Black, red boot-topping line
Services: tramping

TANKERS LTD, 37–41 Gracechurch St, London EC3

Tankers

Scottish American	1920	Laing	6999	10,974	438–0	57–0	27–2	9.5
Scottish Chief	1928	ArmWh1	7006	11,130	440.8	57–5	27–8	10.5
Scottish Heather	1928	ArmWh1	7005	11,131	442.0	57–0	27–8	10.5
Scottish Maiden (m2)	1921	VickB2	6993	9730	441–4	57–0	27–4	10.0
Scottish Minstrel (m2)	1921	VickB2	6998	9730	444–9	57–0	27–4	10.0
Scottish Musician (m2)	1922	VickB2	6999	10,509	444–8	57–0	27–4	10.0
Scottish Standard (m2)	1921	VickB2	6999	9730	441–1	57–0	27–4	10.0

Funnel: Blue with black italic T on white band, black top
Hull: Dark grey, red boot-topping
Trades: Oil and petroleum

TATEM LTD, W J, 113–116 Bute St, Cardiff

Chulmleigh	1938	Pgill2	5445	10,050	447–2	56–2	25–9	10.5
Lady Glanely (m)	1938	Doxfrd	5497	10,050	447–2	56–2	25–9	10.5
ATLANTIC SHIPPING & TRADING CO LTD								
Everleigh	1930	FurnH	5222	10,000	418–8	56–0	25–10	10.0
Filleigh	1928	Pgill2	4856	9100	395.5	55–4	25.9	9.75
Hadleigh	1930	FurnH	5222	10,000	418–8	56–0	25–10	10.0

Funnel: Black with white T on red band
Hull: Black, pink boot-topping
Services: General tramping

Tankers Ltd: Scottish Minstrel *was one of four similar tankers built by Vickers at Barrow during 1921–22. In 1941 Tankers Ltd became a subsidiary of United Molasses, which had another tanker owning subsidiary, Athel Line Ltd, which was incorporated in 1940.* Scottish Minstrel *was torpedoed on July 16 1940 when on voyage from New York and Halifax to London with 9200 tons of fuel oil. The tanker remained afloat for many hours but it proved impossible to save her, and she sank on the 17th (RW Jordan collection)*

Wm Thomson: The steamer Bencruachan *was completed by Charles Connell at Glasgow in March 1928. On July 5 1941 she struck a mine and sank off Alexandria when completing a voyage from Glasgow and Durban with 7500 tons of coal and general cargo. The wreck was removed in parts in 1950, and broken up and removed as scrap to the shore in 1951 (Alex Duncan)*

Turnbull, Martin & Co: The steamer Perthshire, *owned by Scottish Shire Line, was completed in June 1936. In 1940 she was taken over by the Ministry of Shipping, and in November that year was one of the vessels which made up the convoy WS3, supplying Malta. She was at Malta in March 1942 and later received damaged as a result of a bomb hit during an air raid. She was later employed as a store ship and also was involved in troop convoys as an equipment carrier. Postwar she was involved in services to South Africa and to Australia, and in October 1963 was laid up at Glasgow pending disposal.* Perthshire *was sold to a Greek company under the name* Borias *for a single voyage to Japan where she was scrapped (RW Jordan)*

MARITIME SHIPPING & TRADING CO LTD

Appledore	1929	FurnH	5218	10,010	418–8	56–0	25–10	10.0

TATEM STEAM NAVIGATION CO LTD

Iddesleigh	1927	ThmpR2	5205	9750	434–6	55–4	24–11	9.75
Monkleigh	1927	ThmpR2	5203	9750	434–6	55–4	24–11	9.75
Northleigh	1937	Pgill2	5450	10,050	447–2	56–2	25–9	10.0
Umberleigh	1927	GrayWH	4950	9200	411–6	54–2	25–3	9.75
Winkleigh	1927	Pgill2	5055		403.0	55–5	25–0	9.5
Winkleigh	bldg	Pgill2	5468	10,100	447–4	56–2	25–9	10.0

TAYLOR, MATTHEW, 82 East High St, Methil, Fifeshire

Funnel: Black with two yellow bands close together
Hull: Black
Services: General tramping, mainly to West Africa and Mediterranean
Note: Also a fleet of coasters

Aberhill	1915	Vuijk	1516	2518	246.8	38–3	17–1	8.5
ex Flora 22								
Maindy Hill	1911	OsbGrl	1918	3315	279.5	41–10	18.3	8.0
ex Hyltonia 20								

THOMAS (BUTE DOCKS) LTD, J J, Merthyr House, James St, Cardiff

Funnel: Yellow, black top
Services: General tramping

ECLIPSE SHIPPING & TRADING CO LTD

Polzella	1929	GrayWH	4751	8770	415–0	54–2	24–10	9.5

THOMPSON STEAMSHIPPING CO LTD, 50–51 Lime St, London EC3

Funnel: Yellow with red T, black top
Hull: Black with white band, red boot-topping
Services: General tramping

Rio Azul	1921	Blyth	4088	7400	363.1	53–2	24–11	11.0
Rio Blanco	1922	Blyth	4086	7400	363.1	53–2	24–11	11.0
Rio Claro	1922	Blyth	4086	7400	363.1	53–2	24–11	11.0
Rio Dorado	1924	Blyth	4507	8200	390.0	55–4	25–1	12.0

THOMSON, HENRY M, 11–12 Bury St, London EC3

Funnel: Black
Hull: Black with white line, red boot-topping
Services: General tramping

Artemisia	1920	Doxfrd	6507	10,880	433–9	54–0	28–4	10.5
ex Antar 32, ex Kincardine 22								
Bosworth	1919	ThmpsJ	6672	10,950	427–6	55–6	28–6	11.0
ex War Peridot 20								
Orfor	1921	Doxfrd	6578	10,880	433–9	54–0	28–4	10.5
ex Romsdalshorn 37								
Sithonia	1919	ThmpsJ	6723	10,950	427–6	55–8	28–6	11.0
ex Radnorshire 30, launched as War Diamond								

THOMSON & CO, WILLIAM, 28 Bernard St, Leith, Edinburgh 6

Funnel: Yellow
Hull: Black, red boot-topping
Services: Leith, Middlesbrough, Antwerp, London–Penang–Port Swettenham–Singapore–Manila–Hong Kong–Shanghai – Nagasaki–Kobe–Yokohama

BEN LINE STEAMERS LTD

Benalbanach	bldg	Conn2	7153		452–1	56–9	29–1	12.0
Benalder	1919	Irvin3	5161	8120	412–9	52–5	25–3	11.0
ex Tower Bridge 35, ex Badagry 33, launched as War Crow								
Benarty	1926	Conn2	5800	9260	430–0	54–0	26–3	12.0
Benavon	1930	Lithgw	5872	9600	437–8	56–0	25–6	12.0
Bencleuch	1919	Coughl	5562	8800	427–0	54–1	24–2	12.0
ex Willdomino 22, ex War Convoy 19								
Bengloe	1918	Hamtn2	5318	8750	419–0	52–8	24–6	12.0
ex Ardgoil 20								
Benledi	1930	Conn2	5943	9250	441–0	53–11	26–4	12.5
Benlomond	1922	Irvin3	6630	9675	435–2	55–0	29–5	12.0
ex Marionga J Goulandris 38, ex London Corporation 37, ex Hoosac 22, ex Cynthiana 22								
Benmacdhui	1911	Lithgw	6869	10,100	447–2	54–2	27–2	12.5
ex Archimedes 32, ex Den of Airlie 12								
Benmohr	1928	Conn2	5920	9250	445–0	53–11	26–3	12.0
Bennevis	1918	RDuck2	5264	8130	412–8	52–5	25–4	11.5
ex Cutcombe 28, ex War Ostrich 19								
Benreoch	1921	Conn2	5818	9240	426–6	54–0	26–2	12.0
Benvenue	1927	Conn2	5920	9250	440–0	53–11	26–3	12.0
Benvorlich	1919	Conn2	5193	8350	412–8	52–2	25–4	12.0
Benvrackie (P4)	1922	Hendn2	6434	9420	413–6	52–6	29–2	12.0
ex Darian 39								
Benwyvis	1929	Conn2	5920	9250	445–0	53–11	26–3	12.0

PETROGRAD STEAMERS LTD

Bencruachan	1928	Conn2	5920	9250	445–0	53–11	26–3	12.0

Bendoran 1910 Conn2 5567 8550 430.2 50–2 26–6 10.0
ex Cambrian Peeress 31, ex Eurybates 26, ex Indradeo 15
Benlawers 1930 Conn2 5943 9250 443–5 53–11 26–4 12.5
Benrinnes (st) 1921 Irvin3 5415 8515 435–2 55–0 29–4 12.0
ex London Exchange 38, ex Parisiana 22
Benvannoch (P4) 1921 Hendn2 6426 9595 413–6 52–6 29–2 12.0
ex Dakarian 39

Services: Whaling support services

THORLAND LTD, 79 Mark Lane, London EC3

Frozen whale meat carrier
Thorland 1903 LithR 5208 6138 385.0 51–0 24–7 10.5
ex Northland 32, ex Highland Enterprise 30

Funnel: Thamesside – yellow with black top, separated by yellow over blue bands;
Westcliff – yellow, black top
Services: General tramping; voyages to Spain during Spanish Civil War

TILL, GORDON O, 13 St Mary Axe, London EC3

Manager for
THAMESSIDE SHIPPING CO LTD
Marvia 1914 Koch 1989 3144 303–10 41–1 17–10 10.5
ex Castelar 37, ex Orotava 22
WESTCLIFF SHIPPING CO LTD
Thorpebay 1918 Manito 2182 3293 261–0 43–9 20–2 9.5
ex Mary 37, ex Lake Monroe 20, launched as War Comet

Funnel: Black with white band bearing black T inside black ring
Hull: Black with white band, red boot-topping
Services: General tramping, mainly grain trade

TRADER NAVIGATION CO LTD, 71 St Mary Axe, London EC3

English Trader 1934 FurnH 3953 7302 374–0 57–6 23–1 9.0
ex Arctees 36
Scottish Trader 1938 ThmpsJ 4016 7500 406–1 54–8 23–2 9.0
Welsh Trader 1938 ThmpsJ 4974 9300 442–0 58–4 24–5 9.0

Funnel: Yellow with houseflag, black top
Hull: Black, red boot-topping with white dividing line
Services: London and other UK ports to Australia
Note: * Operating on South American Saint Line Ltd (*qv* under B & S Shipping Co Ltd) service
Note: See also under New Zealand Shipping Co Ltd

TRINDER, ANDERSON & CO, 27 Leadenhall St, London EC3

AUSTRALIND STEAM SHIPPING CO LTD
Ardenvohr (m) bldg Denny2 5025 9000 428–10 56–2 26–6 11.5
Armadale (m) 1929 Denny2 5066 9520 425–4 54–2 26–4 11.5
Australind (m) 1929 Denny2 5020 8955 425–4 54–2 26–4 11.5
Toltén* (m,P30) 1930 Lithgw 5348 8915 437–10 56–0 25–0 14.0
ex Glenearn 35, ex Toltén 33

Trades: Oil and petroleum

TRINIDAD LEASEHOLDS LTD, 1 London Wall Bldgs, London EC2

Tanker
La Carriére 1938 SHWR 5685 430–8 53–10 25–9 11.0

Funnel: Black with two red bands
Hull: Black, red boot-topping
Services: New Zealand and Australia to UK (refrigerated cargoes), and on Clan Line (*qv*) services

Note: The Scottish Shire Line Ltd was acquired by Clan Line Steamers Ltd (*qv*) in 1918

TURNBULL, MARTIN & CO LTD, 4 St Mary Axe, London EC3

THE SCOTTISH SHIRE LINE LTD
Berwickshire (r/t) 1912 ArmWh1 7464 9860 450.1 57–1 27–1 12.0
ex Clan Macarthur 19
Clan Mactaggart (st) 1920 AyrDk 7622 10,150 468–0 57–9 27–9 12.0
Lanarkshire (st2) bldg GrkDY 8167 9830 505–4 64–9 28–6 16.0
Perthshire (r/t2) 1936 GrkDY 10,496 11,025 498–6 66–2 30–0 16.0
Stirlingshire (m) 1928 GrkDY 6022 9157 434.2 57–9 27–2 13.0
ex Clan Macdonald 30

Funnel: Black with white TS on white bordered red shield
Hull: Black, red boot-topping
Services: General tramping

TURNBULL, SCOTT & CO,
Baltic Exchange Chambers, 24 St Mary Axe, London EC3

REDGATE STEAMSHIP CO LTD
Baxtergate 1925 Short2 5531 10,020 439–7 59–6 25–1 11.0
ex Anglo Indian 37
Redgate 1929 Doxfrd 4323 7718 385–4 51–8 24–2 10.0
ex Ridley 36, ex Essex Oak 33, ex June 32

Skeldergate	1930	Burntd	4251	7950	383–6	52–5	24–5	11.5
Trongate	1924	Nthmb1	3979	7365	380.3	51–11	23–7	9.5

TURNBULL SCOTT SHIPPING CO LTD

Eastgate (m)	bldg	Burntd	5032	9415	441–0	57–0	25–11	11.5
Eskdalegate	1930	Burntd	4250	7950	383–4	52–5	24–5	11.5
Flowergate	1911	Teckl	5156	7820	400.9	53–8	25–4	10.5
ex Schildturm 21								
Saltersgate	1923	Nthmb1	3940	7385	380.3	51–11	23–8	9.5
ex Overstone 27								
Southgate	1926	Rhead3	4862	8962	415–0	55–2	25–3	10.0
launched as Arabistan								
Stonegate	1928	Doxfrd	5044	9126	410.0	55–6	25–3	11.0
Waynegate	1931	Burntd	4260	7935	383–6	52–5	24–5	11.5

Manager for

A E FURST AND F G BROWNE

Widestone	1920	Tidew	3192	4840	343–0	46–10	21–9	
ex Santurce 37, ex Canadian Rancher 29								

TURNER, BRIGHTMAN & CO, Stone House, Bishopsgate, London EC3

'Z' STEAMSHIP CO LTD

Zitella	1929	Burntd	4254	7912	382–6	51–5	24–1	10.0

ZINAL STEAMSHIP CO LTD

Zouave	1930	Burntd	4256	7912	382–6	51–5	24–1	10.0

Funnel: Black with white band bordered by two narrow red bands and white Z on lower black area
Hull: Light grey, red boot-topping
Services: General tramping

UNION-CASTLE MAIL STEAMSHIP CO LTD, THE,
3 Fenchurch St, London EC3

Passenger vessels from Southampton

Arundel Castle (st2,P184/1,347/t)	1921	H&W,B	19,118	14,440	686–3	72–6	32–10	19.0
lengthened 37								
Athlone Castle (m2,P300/1,490/cab)	1936	H&W,B	25,564	15,920	725–0	82–6	32–0	19.0
Balmoral Castle* (s2,P307/1,206/t)	1910	Fairfd	13,363	11,800	570.0	64–6	31–5	16.5
Capetown Castle (m2,P290/1,500/cab)	1938	H&W,B	27,000	15,087	734–0	82–6	32–0	20.0
Carnarvon Castle (m2,P224/1,376/t)	1926	H&W,B	20,122	15,790	683–3	73–6	32–9	20.0
lengthened 38								
Edinburgh Castle (s2,P510)	1910	H&W,B	13,329	11,590	570.2	64–9	31–5	16.5
Stirling Castle (m2,P246/1,508/t)	1936	H&W,B	25,550	15,920	725–0	82–6	32–0	20.0
Warwick Castle (m2,P260/1,248/2,254/t)	1930	H&W,B	20,107	13,667	677–0	75–6	32–1	20.0
Winchester Castle (m2,P198/1,392/t)	1930	H&W,B	20,012	13,005	657–5	75–6	32–1	20.0
Windsor Castle (st2,P219/1,191/2,194/t)	1922	BrownJ	19,141	14,147	686–0	72–5	32–9	20.0
lengthened 37								

Passenger vessels from London

Dunbar Castle (m2,P200/1,260/t)	1930	H&WGw	10,002	7780	471.2	61–2	29.6	14.5
Dunluce Castle (s2,P460)	1904	H&W,B	8131	8135	490–0	56–11	27–0	13.5
Dunnottar Castle (m2,P234/1,254/2)	1936	H&W,B	15,007	10,489	560–0	71–11	28–2	16.0
Dunvegan Castle (m2,P234/1,254/2)	1936	H&W,B	15,007	10,489	560–0	71–11	28–2	16.0
Durban Castle (m2,P205/1,335/t)	1938	H&W,B	17,388	10,802	594–7	76–5	29–2	18.5
Durham Castle (s2,P460)	1904	Fairfd	8240	8530	490–0	56–9	26–11	13.5
Garth Castle*** (s2,P420)	1910	Curle	7625	9200	452.6	54–4	27–3	12.0
Gloucester Castle (s2,P300)	1911	Fairfd	8006	9235	452.7	56–2	27–4	12.0
Grantully Castle*** (s2,P420)	1910	Curle	7592	9100	450.7	54–4	27–3	12.0

Funnel: Red with black top
Hull: Passenger vessels and fruit carriers – lavender-grey, reddish brown boot-topping; general cargo vessels – black, reddish brown boot-topping
Services: Mail, passenger and some general cargo – Southampton–Madeira–Cape Town–Port Elizabeth–East London–Durban; London–Plymouth–Las Palmas–Tenerife–Ascension–St Helena–Lobito–Cape Town–Port Elizabeth–East London–Durban–Lourenço Marques–Beira, returning by east coast route; London to East African ports; general cargo – New York–South and East Africa and Mauritius

Llandaff Castle (s2,P175/1,168/t)	1926	Workmn	10,786	8870	471.2	61–9	27–4	14.0
Llandovery Castle (s2,P221/1,186/t)	1925	Curle	10,640	8915	471.1	61–9	27–4	14.0
Llangibby Castle (m2,P216/1,198/t)	1929	H&WGw	11,951	8465	0	66–2	27–2	16.5
Llanstephan Castle (s2,P231/1,198/t)	1914	Fairfd	11,299	10,753	500.5	63–4	28–8	13.5
Pretoria Castle (m2,P205/1,335/t)	1938	H&W,B	17,160	10,590	594–6	76–5	29–2	18.5
General cargo vessels								
Dromore Castle (P12)	1919	H&WGk	5242	7930	412–6	52–4	25–3	10.5
launched as War Poplar								
Dundrum Castle (P12)	1919	H&WGk	5259	7930	412–6	52–4	25–3	10.5
Sandown Castle (P12)	1921	Short2	7607	11,224	442–0	56–4	30–6	10.5
Refrigerated (fruit) carriers								
Richmond Castle (m,P12)	1939	H&W,B	7798	9191	474–2	63–4	29–2	16.5
Rochester Castle (m,P12)	1937	H&W,B	7795	9258	474–2	63–4	29–2	16.5
Roslin Castle (m)	1935	H&W,B	7016	7800	443–6	61–4	29–3	14.5
Rothesay Castle (m)	1935	H&W,B	7016	7800	443–6	61–4	29–3	14.5
Rowallan Castle (m,P12)	1939	H&W,B	7798	9182	474–2	63–4	29–2	16.5
Roxburgh Castle (m,P12)	1937	H&W,B	7801	9258	474–2	63–4	29–2	16.5

Note: *BU Newport, Monmouthshire 1939; **sold breakers 1939 (see Appendix); *** BU1939

UNION MARITIME & SHIPPING CO LTD
9–13 Fenchurch Bldgs, Fenchurch St, London EC3

Services: Oil and petroleum tramping

GOTHIC STEAMSHIP CO LTD

Note: See Union Maritime & Shipping Co Ltd also in Greece section

Tanker								
Gothic (st)	1920	Graysn	2444	3175	275–0	41–2	20–2	9.0
ex Rigny 39, ex Clemenceau 38, ex War Mersey 19; conv gen cargo 32								

UNION STEAMSHIP CO OF NEW ZEALAND LTD, 36 Custom House Quay, PO Box 1521, Wellington, New Zealand, and 130 Leadenhall St, London EC3

Funnel: Red with two black rings, black top *Hull:* Black, red boot-topping (white dividing line on some vessels)
Services: Passenger – Sydney – Auckland–Fiji–Honolulu–Vancouver (Canadian Australasian Line Ltd); New Zealand–Australia; New Zealand coastal

Passenger vessels								
Awatea (st2,P377/1,151/2,38/3)	1936	VickB1	13,482	6205	542–0	74–2	25–6	22.0
Maori (st3,P630)	1907	Denny1	3488	1000	364–6	47–2	15–10	19.0
Matua (m2,48/cab,120/d)	1936	Leslie	4192	3112	370–6	50–6	21–6	15.0
Maunganui (s2,P415)	1911	Fairfd	7527	5430	447–1	55–9	25–2	16.0
Monowai (r/t2,P483/oc)	1926	H&WGk	10,852	4968	519–0	63–2	26–1	18.0
ex Razmak 30								
Rangatira (te2,P716/1,236/2)	1931	VickB1	6152	1454	419–6	58–6	17–0	21.5
Wahine (st3,P404/1,1882/2)	1913	Denny2	4436	1220	375.0	52–11	17–5	20.5
General cargo vessels								
Hauraki (m2)	1922	Denny2	7113	10,810	450.3	58–2	28–6	12.0
Waikouaiti	1914	Neptn1	3926	6000	362.4	50–1	22–10	10.0
ex Irmgard 20								
Waiotapu	1913	Flensb	6035	9835	467–0	58–2	25–6	10.0
ex Stolberg 20								
Wairuna	1914	Flensb	5832	8984	437–0	56–2	26–2	12.0
ex Polescar 19, ex Gibraltar 15, ex Schneefels 14								

CANADIAN AUSTRALASIAN LINE LTD, 999 West Hastings St, Vancouver, Canada

Passenger/general cargo vessels								
Aorangi (m4,P248/1,266/cab,125/3)	1924	Fairfd	17,491	8345	600–0	72–2	27–10	17.0
Niagara (r/t3,P261/,210/2,176/3)	1913	BrownJ	13,415	7600	524.7	66–4	28–1	16.0

Union-Castle: Stirling Castle *was delivered by Harland & Wolff at Belfast on January 29 1936. She was requisitioned as a troopship in 1940, being refitted to carry 6000 troops. During 1943 she carried troops mainly from the US to Britain for Operation 'Bolero', the build up of US troops in preparation for D-Day. During trooping service she carried 128,000 troops and travelled over half a million miles. She was released to Union-Castle in 1946, refitted at Belfast, and in the following year resumed the mail service to Cape Town. The competition from air travel had a serious effect on Union-Castle, among many others, and by the early 1960s* Stirling Castle *and other vessels in the fleet were becoming uneconomical. She was put up for sale in 1965 and after a sale to Taiwan breakers fell through she was sold to breakers in Japan*
(Real Photographs)

Union-Castle: Roslin Castle *was one of six fruit carriers completed for this owner in the 1930s for the seasonal trade from southern Africa. They were usually laid up between seasons, but were still operated at a profit.* Roslin Castle *was delivered on May 4 1935 by Harland & Wolff, Belfast. She survived the war and was eventually sold to Taiwan breakers and broken up at Kaohsiung in 1968 (R Sherlock)*

Note: Union SS Co of NZ Ltd, which became a member of the P&O Group in Aug 1917, also owned many cargo vessels in New Zealand coastal trade
Note: Canadian Australian Line Ltd was a joint venture with Canadian Pacific Steamship Ltd (*qv*)

INDO-PACIFIC SHIPPING CO LTD, 130 Leadenhall St, London EC3

General cargo vessel

Narbada (st2)	1915	Dixon2	8988	12,200	470.0	60–2	30–5	12.0
ex Leitrim 29								

IRISH COUNTIES STEAMERS, London

General cargo vessel

Limerick (m2)	1925	Hamtn2	8724	12,902	460.5	62–9	31–3	13.0

Services: Whaling
Note: Also a fleet of whalers

UNION WHALING CO LTD,
Orange Grove Bldgs, Smith St, PO Box 818, Durban, South Africa

Whale factory vessel

Uniwaleco	1905	H&W,B	9755	10,552	485–0	58–5	29–5	10.5
ex Fraternitas 37, ex Sir James Clark Ross 30, ex Mahronda 23; conv general cargo 23								

Funnel: Yellow, black top
Hull: Grey, red boot-topping with white dividing line
Services: UK, NW Europe–West Africa

UNITED AFRICA CO LTD, Unilever House, Blackfriars, London EC4

General cargo vessels

Ashantian (r/t)	1935	Hamtn4	4917	7975	416–0	56–9	23–6	10.0
Dahomian	1929	Nthmb2	5277	7300	390–0	53–0	23–9	10.0
ex Themoni 33								
Ethiopian (r/t,P12)	1936	Seebk2	5424	8080	433–0	57–8	23–11	10.0
Guinean (P12)	1936	HwldtH	5205	8020	422–9	57–8	23–7	10.0
Kumasian (r/t)	1935	Hamtn4	4922	7975	416–0	56–9	23–6	10.0
Lagosian	1930	GrkDY	5414	9452	421.4	59–2	24–9	10.0
ex Melmay 32								
Leonian (r/t,P12)	1936	Seebk2	5424	8080	433–0	57–8	23–11	10.0
Liberian (P12)	1936	HwldtH	5025	8020	422–8	57–9	23–7	10.0
Nigerian (r/t,P12)	1936	Seebk2	5423	8080	433–0	57–9	23–11	11.0
ELMINA LTD								
Conakrian (P)	1937	FurnH	4876	8262	438–4	56–9	24–0	10.5
Lafian (P)	1937	FurnH	4876	8265	438–4	56–9	24–0	11.0
Takoradian (m,P12)	1937	Seebk2	5452	8055	438–11	56–8	24–0	11.0
Zarian (P)	1938	FurnH	4871	8265	438–4	56–9	24–0	11.0
LEVER BROS LTD								
Gambian (m,P12)	1937	Seebk2	5452	8055	438–11	56–9	24–0	11.0
Tankers								
UNITED AFRICA CO LTD								
Congonian (m)	1936	HwldtK	5065	7275	399.8	55–2	22–6	12.0
Matadian (r/t)	1936	SHWR	4275	5904	397–1	50–2	21–0	11.5

Services: General tramping

UNITED MERCHANTS SHIPPING CO LTD
160 Gresham House, Old Broad St, London EC2

Panos	1920	Rhead2	4914	8050	401–3	53–8	24–6	9.0
ex Avon Valley 37, ex Homecliffe 34								

Funnel: Red with blue UMCo in white diamond, black top
Hull: Dark grey, red boot-topping
Trades: Oil and petroleum, and molasses

UNITED MOLASSES CO LTD, Bush House, Aldwych, London WC2

ATHEL LINE

Tankers (molasses or petroleum)

Athelbeach (m)	1931	Cammel	6568	10,166	440–0	55–11	26–9	11.0
Athelchief (m)	1939	Curle	10,000	15,140	519–4	66–8	28–5	12.0
ex Kongsten 39								
Athelcrown (m2)	1929	FurnH	11,999	18,045	545–0	68–10	30–1	12.0
Athelduchess (m2)	1929	Hamtn3	8940	13,998	492–0	63–4	28–4	11.0
Athelduke (m2)	1929	Duncan	8966	13,998	492–0	63–4	28–4	11.0
Athelempress (m2)	1930	Hamtn3	8941	13,998	492–0	63–4	28–4	11.0
Athelfoam (m)	1931	Cammel	6554	10,148	440–0	55–11	26–9	11.0
Athelking (m2)	1927	SHWR	9557	14,780	492–6	64–4	29–4	10.5
Athelknight (m2)	1930	Duncan	8940	13,998	492–0	63–4	28–4	11.0
Athellaird (m2)	1930	Cammel	8999	14,190	492–7	63–4	28–5	11.0
Athelmere	1918	ArmWh1	5566	8340	410–4	52–5	26–6	10.0
ex Realf 37, ex Athelbeach 30, ex Conia 26, ex War Rajput 20								
Athelmonarch (m2)	1928	Hamtn3	8995	13,998	492–0	63–4	28–4	11.0
Athelprince (m2)	1926	FurnH	8782	13,709	488–0	62–5	28–7	11.0
Athelprincess (m2)	1929	Hamtn3	8882	13,998	492–0	63–4	28–4	11.0
Athelqueen (m2)	1928	FurnH	8780	13,694	488–0	62–5	28–7	10.0

Athelregent (m2)	1930	FurnH	8881	14,141	492–7	63–2	28–3	11.0
Athelstane	1918	Irvin3	5571	8300	410–4	52–4	26–6	10.0
ex Hird 36, ex Athelfoam 31, ex Caprella 27, ex War Ghurka 21								
Athelsultan (m2)	1929	Hamtn3	8882	13,998	492–0	63–4	28–4	11.0
Atheltemplar (m2)	1930	Lithgw	8939	13,998	492–0	63–4	28–4	11.0
Athelvictor (m)	order	Caledn	8410	12,200	483–2	59–5	27–11	12.0
ordered as Silenus								
Athelviking (m2)	1926	FurnH	8779	13,709	488–0	62–5	28–7	10.0
ex Java 33								
Athelviscount (m2)	1929	Duncan	8882	13,998	492–0	63–4	28–4	11.0

Note: Also owns tankers under 2000gt

VAUGHAN (CARDIFF) LTD, WALTER,
Cory Bldgs, 60 Mount Stuart Sq, Cardiff

Funnel: Yellow with white band bordered by narrow blue bands
Services: General tramping

GOOD HOPE SHIPPING CO LTD

Seven Seas Sun*	1924	Burntd	2480	4450	310–8	44–0	20–2	9.0
ex Porthkerry 35								

Note: * Sold W A Souter & Co Ltd 1939, renamed *Sheaf Don*

VERGOTTIS LTD, 9 Camomile St, London EC3

Services: General tramping

Manager for
HERMES STEAMSHIP CO LTD

Hermes	1916	Short2	9036	11,090	491–0	58–4	30–6	11.0
ex Heraclides 39, ex Anglo Chilean 30								

Note: See also in Greece section

WALLEM & CO LTD,
Hongkong & Shanghai Bank Bldg, Postbox 40, Victoria, Hong Kong

Grayburn	1938	Laing	6342	12,050	471–5	63–9	28–1	11.0
Lerwick	1938	ThmpsJ	5626	9000	425–4	56–8	25–0	10.5

Funnel: Black with white band bearing white W in blue diamond
Hull: Black with white band
Services: General tramping, particularly in Far East
Note: Wallem & Co Ltd was controlled by Wallem & Co A/S (*qv* in Norway section), and its vessels were managed by Muir, Young Ltd (*qv*)

WALTON, WILLIAM G, 30 Elveston Mews, London SW7

Services: General tramping

Manager for
CYPRIAN SHIPPING CO LTD, Leadenhall Chambers, 4 St Mary Axe, London EC3

Danubian	1898	Ropnr	2728	4550	320.0	44–0	20–5	8.0
ex Haralampos P 29, ex Gileston 26, ex Euston 10								

VERBORMILIA STEAMSHIP CO LTD,
Leadenhall Chambers, 4 St Mary Axe, London EC3

Verbormilia	1907	GrayX	3275	5250	341–11	48–4	20–10	8.5
ex Danubio 32, ex Gróf Serényi Béla 24								

WATTS, WATTS & CO LTD, Regis House, King William St, London EC4

Funnel: Black
Hull: Grey, pink boot-topping
Services: General tramping

BRITAIN STEAMSHIP CO LTD

Beaconsfield	1938	Caledn	4635	9225	434–6	56–8	25–2	10.5
Beckenham	1937	Caledn	4636	9225	434–6	56–9	25–2	10.5
Blackheath	1936	Caledn	4637	9225	434–6	56–9	25–2	10.5
Dartford	1930	SmithM	4023	6740	376–5	52–0	22–6	10.5
Deptford	1931	SmithM	4034	6740	376–5	52–0	22–6	10.5
Dulwich	1931	SmithM	4036	6740	376–5	52–0	22–6	10.5
Teddington	order	Caledn	4762	9200	432–10	56–10	25–3	10.0
Tottenham	bldg	Caledn	4762	9200	432–10	56–10	25–3	10.0
Twickenham	bldg	Caledn	4762	9065	432–10	56–10	25–3	10.0
Wanstead	1928	Caledn	5423	9900	420–6	54–2	24–8	10.5
Wendover	1928	Caledn	5419	9900	420–6	54–2	24–8	10.5
Willesden	1925	Workmn	4563	8600	416–9	54–4	25–1	10.0
ex Antinous 33								

Services: In West Indies and Gulf of Mexico

Note: Also vessels under 2000gt

WEBSTER & SONS, J S, 95 Harbour St, Kingston, Jamaica

MRS A A WEBSTER

Magister	1919	WallSY	3188	4530	320.0	44–2	21–5	11.0
ex Canadian Volunteer 33, ex Cornwallis 31, ex Canadian Volunteer 29								

Funnel: Blue with black top separated by houseflag consisting of red cross (+) with 'W, H, &, Co' in the quadrants
Hull: Grey, red boot-topping
Services: General tramping

WEIDNER, HOPKINS & CO, 34 Dean St, Newcastle upon Tyne 1

ELSWICK STEAM SHIPPING CO LTD

Elswick Park	1920	Blyth	4188	7450	364–0	51–0	24–11	10.0

Funnel: Yellow, black top
Hull: Black, red boot-topping; *Inchanga, Incomati, Isipingo* have white with buff band, green boot-topping
Services: Burma–India–Ceylon–Aden–Port Sudan–W coast North America; New York–California – Philippines–China–Java–Straits Settlements–Suez or Cape–New York; Bombay–New York –Philadelphia; Calcutta–Brazil–R Plate ports; India–East and South Africa (passenger/cargo); Calcutta–Rangoon–W coast South America; Hong Kong–Bangkok–Singapore–Indian Ocean–East and South Africa; US and Gulf of Mexico ports–South and East Africa; Australia–Peru–Chile; oil and petroleum trades

WEIR & CO, ANDREW, 21 Bury St, London EC3, Standard Bldgs, 102 Hope St, Glasgow C2, and Royal Exchange, Middlesbrough

BANK LINE LTD

Passenger/general cargo vessels								
Gujarat (m,P12/1,20/2,400+/d)	1923	H&WGw	4148	6827	384–0	48–3	25–2	11.5
Inchanga (m2,P60/1,25/2,600/nat)	1933	Work28	7069	7520	420–0	57–2	25–3	15.0
Incomati (m2,P60/1,25/2,600/nat)	1934	Work28	7369	7750	435–0	57–2	25–3	15.0
Isipingo (m2,P60/1,25/2,600/nat)	1933	Work28	7069	7520	420–0	57–2	25–3	15.0
Luxmi (m,P12/1,20/2,400+/d)	1924	H&WGw	4148	6827	384–0	48–2	24–11	11.5
General cargo vessels								
Alynbank (m2,P–)	1925	H&WGw	5151	8876	436–0	53–11	25–8	12.0
Araybank (m)	bldg	H&W,B	7258	9690	450–7	57–4	26–10	12.0
Aymeric	1919	ThmpR	5196	8310	412–6	52–3	25–3	11.0
launched as War Nemesia								
Birchbank (m2)	1924	H&WGw	5151	8876	436–0	53–11	25–8	12.0
Cabarita	1915	Hamtn2	4364	6638	376–6	51–5	23–5	10.5
ex Chronos 29								
Cedarbank (m2)	1924	H&WGw	5159	8876	436–0	53–11	25–8	12.0
Clydebank (m2)	1925	H&WGw	5156	8876	433–9	53–11	25–8	12.0
Comliebank (m2)	1924	H&WGw	5149	8876	434–6	53–11	25–8	12.0
Congella (m2)	1914	Blohm	4533	7704	399.3	52–10	24–4	10.5
ex Mindoro 33, ex Sagami 28, ex Secundus 27, laid down as Neumark								
Deebank	1929	Work28	5060	9396	436–10	56–10	25–8	12.0
Elmbank (m2)	1925	H&WGw	5156	8876	436–0	53–11	25–8	12.0
Ernebank (m)	1937	H&W,B	5388	9509	448–5	57–4	26–5	14.0
Forresbank (m2)	1925	H&WGw	5155	8876	436–0	53–11	25–8	12.0
Forthbank	1929	Work28	5057	9396	437–0	56–10	25–8	12.0
Foylebank (m2)	1930	H&W,B	5582	9323	426.8	57–4	25.8	14.0
Glenbank (m2)	1924	H&WGw	5151	8876	434–0	53–11	25–8	12.0
Inverbank (m2)	1924	H&WGw	5149	8876	434–0	53–11	25–8	12.0
Irisbank (m2)	1930	Work28	5627	9010	440–0	57–5	26–4	14.0
Kelvinbank (m2)	1921	Cammel	3872	5875	350–11	49–11	23–2	10.5
ex Daga 34, ex Malia 27								
Larchbank (m2)	1925	H&WGw	5151	8876	434–0	53–11	25–8	12.0
Levernbank (m2)	1925	H&WGw	5150	8876	434–0	53–11	25–8	12.0
Lindenbank (t/l39)	1930	Work28	5057	9395	437–0	56–10	25–8	12.0
Lossiebank (m2)	1930	Work28	5627	9140	440–0	57–5	26–4	14.0
Myrtlebank (m2)	1925	H&WGw	5150	8876	434–0	53–11	25–8	12.0
Nairnbank (m2)	1925	H&WGw	5156	8876	434–0	53–11	25–8	12.0
Oakbank (m2)	1926	H&WGw	5154	8876	434–0	53–11	25–8	12.0
Olivebank (m2)	1926	H&WGw	5154	8876	435–0	53–11	25–8	12.0
Shirrabank (m)	bldg	H&W,B	7274	9690	450–5	57–4	26–10	12.0
Speybank (m2)	1926	H&WGw	5154	8876	434–0	53–11	25–8	12.0
Springbank (m2)	1926	H&WGw	5155	8876	434–0	53–11	25–8	12.0
Taybank (m2)	1930	Work28	5627	9130	440–0	57–5	26–0	14.0
Testbank	1937	Rhead3	5083	8960	439–2	56–8	25–0	12.0
Teviotbank	1938	Rhead3	5087	8960	439–2	56–8	25–0	12.0
Thornliebank	1939	Rhead3	5569	9840	451–10	56–9	26.0	12.0
Thursobank (m)	bldg	Rhead3	5575	9840	451–10	56–9	26.0	12.0
Tielbank	1937	Rhead3	5083	8960	439–2	56–8	25–0	12.0
Tinhow (P–)	1913	Neptn1	5232	7250	381–0	50–8	26–3	11.0
ex Hughli 27, ex Valencia 20								

Andrew Weir: The motor vessel Taybank *was one of a large group built for Bank Line in the 1920s and '30s. She was fitted with two Workman, Clark 5-cylinder oil engines of 4300bhp.* Taybank *survived the war and traded until 1961 when she was broken up in Hong Kong (RW Jordan collection)*

Yeoward Line: This company operated a regular service between Liverpool and the Canary Islands. Aguila *and* Ardeola *are pictured here at Liverpool in the 1930s when Yeoward owned a fleet of four similar ships. Both of these and another Yeoward vessel became war losses, leaving* Alca *to carry on postwar services.* Aguila *was torpedoed by* U201 *and sunk on August 19 1941 when on voyage from Liverpool to Gibraltar and Lisbon with 1288 tons of general cargo including 397 bags of mail.* Ardeola *was captured by the Vichy French and became an enemy war loss (EH Cole)*

Trentbank	1929	Work28	5060	9396	437–0	56–10	25–8	12.0
Tweedbank (m2)	1930	Work28	5627	9076	440–0	57–5	26–0	14.0
Tymeric	1919	Leslie	5228	8170	412–6	52–4	25–4	12.0
launched as War Mammoth								
Tynebank	1934	Readhd	4651	8400	427–8	54–0	24–4	12.0
Weirbank (m2)	1925	H&WGw	5150	8876	434–0	53–11	25–8	12.0
Willowbank (m)	1939	Doxfrd	5041	9140	439–4	54–4	26.1	12.0

INVER TRANSPORT & TRADING CO LTD

General cargo vessels

Eskbank (m)	1937	Doxfrd	5137	9040	438–8	55–6	25–6	13.0
Ettrickbank (m)	1937	Doxfrd	5138	9040	438–7	55–6	25–6	13.0
Rowanbank	1919	Taikoo	5103	8270	412–6	52–4	25–3	10.0
ex King Howel 37, ex Cephalonia 23, ex Stathis 20, launched as War Miner								
Teesbank (m)	1937	Doxfrd	5136	8960	438–8	55–6	25–6	13.0

INVER TANKERS LTD*

Tankers

Note: * Tankers owned by Inver Tankers Ltd were under Irish flag to Sep 1939, when they transferred to British flag

Inverdargle (m)	1938	DeutsH	9456	14,000	522–0	67–3	27–7	12.0
Inverilen (m)	1938	DeutsH	9456	14,000	522–0	67–3	27–7	12.0
Inverlane (m)	1938	Bremer	9141	13,800	497–10	63–9	28–6	12.0
Inverlee (m)	1938	Bremer	9158	13,800	497–10	63–9	28–6	12.0
Inverliffey (m)	1938	DeutsH	9456	14,000	522–0	67–3	27–7	12.0
Invershannon (m)	1938	Bremer	9154	13,800	497–10	63–9	28–6	12.0
Inversuir (m)	1938	DeutsH	9456	14,000	522–0	67–3	27–7	12.0

WEST HARTLEPOOL STEAM NAVIGATION CO LTD, THE,
38 Church St, West Hartlepool, and 7–8 Bury St, London EC3

Funnel: Yellow with black G, black top
Hull: Black with white band, red boot-topping
Services: General tramping

Boltonhall	1935	GrayWH	4823	8700	423–6	54–10	24–9	10.5
Cliftonhall (m)	1938	Doxfrd	5063	9130	441–6	54–4	25–6	11.0
Clumberhall	1930	GrayWH	5198	9335	438–6	55–0	25–2	10.0
Derwenthall (m)	bldg	Doxfrd	4934	8860	441–10	54–4	25–6	11.0
Lindenhall (r/t)	1937	GrayWH	5248	9000	453–10	56–1	25–3	10.5

WESTERN AUSTRALIA, GOVERNMENT OF, (State Shipping Service),
Fremantle, Western Australia

Funnel: Yellow
Hull: Light grey, red boot-topping
Services: Fremantle–Western Australia ports–Darwin; Fremantle–Java–Straits Settlements

Note: Also *Kybra* (26/858gt)

Koolama (m2,P106/1,174/–)	1938	H&WGw	4026	2200	362–2	54–3	18–0	15.0
Koolinda (m2,P162)	1926	H&WGw	4372	2070	344–3	50–2	18–8	15.0

WHEELOCK & CO LTD, 2–3 French Bund, PO Box 963, Shanghai, China

Services: Tramping, mainly in Far East

Manager for

G E MARDEN

Under British flag

Annalock (st)	1919	Fed2	6638	9808	411–6	55–2	27–1	10.0
ex Anaconda 38								
Corlock	1913	Austin	3405	5320	341.0	47–0	20–11	9.0
ex Corton39								
Deslock	1909	Nthmbl	5015	7540	380.0	52–4	22–11	8.5
ex Despina 38, ex Bournemouth, ex Errington Court 20								
Federlock (st)	1918	Fed2	6607	9557	411–6	55–2	27–3	10.0
ex Federal 38								
Gemlock	1914	Blumrl	3194	5550	341–0	47–9	21–0	9.0
ex Hai Yu 38, ex Kelsomoor 37, ex Kelsomead 22, ex Kelsomoor 19								
Hatterlock	1917	BethSP	5138	7467	391–9	52–5	24–0	10.0
ex Hatteras 38, launched as War Dragon								
Jeannette Skinner (st)	1917	Skinnr	5800	8660	424–0	54–4	24–0	10.0
Munlock	1917	NNews	5240	7600	370.3	53–2	24–0	10.0
ex Mundelta 38								
St Quentin	1915	Campl	3528	6480	349.0	49–11	21–11	9.5
ex Bainsizza 26, ex Penrhys 24, ex Lady Plymouth 19								
Vitorlock	1918	SeatCD	5030	7382	395–5	53–2	23–7	10.0
ex Vittorio Emmanuele III 38								

Under Chinese flag

Note: This company also manages vessels under 1500gt

Egorlock	1914	H&WGw	4998	7358	420–0	54–4	23–7	11.0
ex Egori 39								

WHIMSTER & CO, Union Bank Bldg, 37 Renfield St, Glasgow C2

Funnel: Red with black top and red over black bands
Hull: Grey, red boot-topping
Services: Gart Line – Glasgow, Swansea–W Italy

GART LINE LTD								
Gartavon	1921	Graysn	1777	3280	275–0	41–2	20–4	10.0
ex Gelves 27								
Gartbrattan (P–)	1931	Curle	1811	3420	275.5	42–1	18.2	10.0

WHITWILL & SONS LTD, MARK, Mill Avenue, Queen St, Bristol 1

Funnel: Black with blue and white vertically halved disc on red band
Services: General tramping

SEVERN STEAMSHIP CO LTD								
Severn Leigh	1919	Caird	5242	8431	412–4	52–4	25–3	10.5
ex Queen Olga 37, ex Bembridge 24, ex War Anchusa 19								

WILLIAMS & CO, IDWAL, Imperial Bldgs, Mount Stuart Sq, Cardiff

Funnel: Black with red G superimposed on white over green bands
Hull: Black, red boot-topping
Services: General tramping

GRAIG SHIPPING CO LTD								
Graig	1924	Duncan	3683	7080	365.0	51–6	22–1	10.0
Graiglas	bldg	ThmpsJ	4312	7535	404–8	54–8	23–3	10.5
Graigwen	1926	Duncan	3697	7050	365.0	51–6	22–1	10.0

WILLIAMSON & CO, GPO Box 615, Connaught Rd, Victoria Hong Kong

Services: Hong Kong–Singapore; tramping, mainly Far East

Ashridge	1905	Hamtn	2884	4850	337–9	47–0	21–0	8.0
DOUGLAS STEAMSHIP CO LTD								
Haitan (P191)	1909	Schich	3554	2728	347–0	45–4	21–0	12.0
ex Silvia 35, ex Orel 22								
Haiyang (P–)	1908	Dunlop	2360	3200	300.5	38–1	21–0	11.5
FOREIGN INVESTMENTS LTD, The Hongkong & Shanghai Bank Bldg, Hong Kong								
Kenilworth	1918	RDuck2	5457	9377	446–8	55–0	26–10	10.5
Silksworth	1922	RDuck2	4921	8580	415.2	53–4	25–5	11.0
LEANA STEAM SHIP CO LTD								
Leana	1914	Neptn1	4743	7934	399.5	54–1	25–3	10.0
ex Tapti 38, ex Ulm 20								
LING NAM STEAMSHIP CO LTD								
Asian	1900	Short2	2461	4000	299.0	43–0	19.5	8.0
ex Hwah Chong 38, ex Winifred Moller 33, ex Gurth 32, ex Albrecht W Selme 28, ex Saltwell 12								
SHUN HONG STEAMSHIP CO LTD								
Cape St Francis	1908	Conn2	3549	5200	349.1	44–2	24–1	10.0
ex Sutlej 29								
WING NING STEAMSHIP CO LTD								
Forafric (m)	1909	Curle	3475	4950	330.1	47–4	21–1	8.5
ex Landvard 27, ex Songvaar 24, ex Landvard 20, ex Chumpon 16; conv steamer 14								

Note: Also smaller vessels and vessels engaged in China coastal trade

WILSON & HARRISON STEAMSHIPS LTD, Empire House, 51 Mount Stuart Sq, Cardiff

Services: General tramping

Note: * Sold Sea & Land Securities Ltd (manager A H Smith) 1939

Ulmus*	1926	DunlpB	2733	5350	314.1	47–2	20–1	9.5
ex Rákóczi Ferenc 33, ex Ulmus 31								

YEOWARD LINE LTD, 24 James St, Liverpool 2, and 60 Haymarket, London SW1

Funnel: Black with black Y on yellow band between two narrow red bands
Hull: Light grey, white top strakes, red boot-topping
Regular services: Liverpool–North Spain–Portugal–Morocco–Las Palmas–Tenerife; occasional charters out

Passenger/general cargo vessels								
Aguila (P*c*150/1)	1917	Caledn	3255	3600	315.3	44–2	20–9	12.5
Alca (P125/1)	1927	Caledn	3712	4300	319.2	46–2	22–1	13.0
Ardeola (P*c*150/1)	1912	Caledn	2069	3600	310.2	44–2	20–6	12.5
Avoceta (P*c*150/1)	1923	Caledn	3442	4300	319.0	44–2	21–10	12.5

Greece

Services: General tramping

ANASTASSIOU, ATH O, Megaron Electricou Stathmou 22–23, Piræus

Igor 1907 Blumr1 2726 4700 314.0 46–6 21–0 8.0
ex Antzouletta 35, ex Otterstad 21, ex Kristiania 12

Services: General tramping

Note: * Sold E N Vintiadis 1939, renamed *Anna Marcou*

ASSIMOMITIS, GEORGE M, Syra

Tourliani* (st) 1919 Bretgn 2486 3740 301–6 43–7 20–0 9.0
ex Marne 36

Services: General tramping

Note: * Sold P S Antippas (*qv* under Petros M Nomikos Ltd), renamed *Takis*

BALKANS & NEAR EAST SHIPPING AGENCY SOCIETE ANONYME, Megaron Oeconomou, Leoforos Miaouli 40, Piræus

Manager and/or agent for
JOHN STEFANOPOULOS, NICOLAOS M ANDRONICOS AND PH PHILIPPACOPOULOS

Anna S* 1903 Irvin1 2759 4650 320.0 46–0 20–1 8.0
ex Neraida 38, ex Amazon 30, ex Scarpa 22, ex Wilster 19
Evdoxia 1903 Flensb 2018 3600 292.0 41–5 18.8 8.5
ex Dionyssios 38, ex Hesbaye 27, ex Albert Killing 21, ex Captain W Menzell 12

FRANGISCOS TH SIGALIS & PARTNERS, Odos Notara 96, Piræus

Aghia Varvara 1904 Rodger 2425 4350 313.6 43–10 19–9 8.0
ex Matheos 37, ex Akenside 21, ex Glyndwr 19, ex Craigronald 11

Funnel: Black with blue B on white band bordered by two narrow blue bands
Hull: Black
Services: General tramping

BOYAZIDES & CO, THRASYVOULOS L, Odos Tritis Septemvriou 2, Athens

Thrasyvoulos 1912 TyneIr 3693 6500 348.5 50–1 21–6 9.5
ex Forfar 22, ex Thessalia 19

THRASYVOULOS L BOYAZIDES

Leonidas 1928 Lithgw 4573 7900 398–0 52–0 23–11 10.0
ex Bellorado 37

Funnel: Hellenic – black with blue E on white diamond on red band, between two narrow blue bands
Hull: Black, red boot-topping, white dividing line
Services: Palestine–Lebanon–Turkey–Greece–London, Antwerp, Rotterdam, Hamburg, Bremerhaven

Note: See Callimanopoulos & Co Ltd also under Fenton Steamship Co Ltd in Great Britain section

CALLIMANOPOULOS, P G, Megaron Vati, Miaoulis Quay, Piræus; and c/o Callimanopoulos & Co Ltd, 18–19 Great St Helens, London EC3

HELLENIC LINES LTD

Anghyra 1923 Weser 2447 4610 315.8 46–1 21–0 10.5
ex Attika 38
Athinai 1910 Short2 2897 5196 340.6 46–5 21–7 10.5
ex Scottish Prince 37
Belgion 1919 PuseyW 2844 4425 314–11 44–1 21–3 9.5
ex Solhaug 35, ex Fire Island 20
Grigorios C II 1919 Hill 2546 4030 313–0 43–0 19–10 10.5
ex Baron Ailsa 35, ex War Guava 19
Hellas 1916 Nyland 2081 4005 314–5 44–6 19–4 10.0
ex Adele 34, ex Ashantian 32, ex Førdefjord 25, ex Kaggefos 21
Hollandia (P8) 1911 Koch 1759 2950 278.0 39–2 18–7 9.0
ex Cano 36, ex Melilla 21
Patrai 1909 Clyde 1977 3597 307–5 42–0 17.2 7.5
ex Germania 39, ex Saint Chamond 36, ex Luga 23
Turkia 1909 Earles 1911 3670 300.2 42–6 18–11 9.0
ex Livorno 36

Funnel: Black with emblem on white band
Hull: Grey, red boot-topping
Services: General tramping

CAMBANIS, HEIRS OF THE LATE LEONIDAS ZAN, Odos Stournara 32, Athens

LEONIDAS Z CAMBANIS

Perrakis L Cambanis
1910 GrayX 3584 6450 362.2 51–1 21–2 8.0
ex Grelarlie 24, ex Rachel 17
Zannis L Cambanis
1920 Craig2 5317 7900 370.7 51–5 25–4 10.0
ex Evros 23

J D Chandris: Built in 1910 as Rendsburg *for Deutsche Australische, this was one of the hundreds of enemy vessels surrendered after the First World War. She passed to France in 1920 and under the SGTM flag was renamed* Mont Kemmel. *She was purchased by Chandris in 1934 and renamed* Dimitrios Chandris. *Postwar, she resumed tramping, was sold to Finland in 1947 being renamed* Wasa, *and was broken up in 1954 (Alex Duncan)*

J D Chandris: Vassos *was completed in 1912 at Amsterdam as* Emanuel Nobel. *She was an early motor ship, but was converted to steam propulsion in 1920. She was purchased by Chandris in 1935 and renamed* Vassos. *In 1939 she was sold to Germany and renamed* Pauline Friederich, *under which name she had only a few weeks of service before the start of the Second World War. Laid up at Boston in September 1939, she was detained there by the US in March 1941, and requisitioned on November 3 1941. She was transferred to the USMC, and renamed* Ormondale *under the Panamanian flag. She was managed by Keystone Shipping into early postwar years, and was laid up in February 1947. On November 2 1948* Ormondale *was delivered at Wilmington NC to be broken up by Sun Shipbuilding (Alex Duncan)*

S G Embiricos: The steamer George M Embiricos *was completed in September 1921 by Short Bros at Sunderland, and remained with this owner throughout her career. She was in Allied service during the Second World War, resumed tramping in 1945, and arrived at Singapore Roads on November 16 1959 having been sold to Singapore breakers (Alex Duncan)*

MINA L CAMBANIS
Leonidas Z Cambanis
1917 Pgill2 4274 7675 401–0 53–4 22–9 9.0
ex Littleton 32, ex Harpalyce 28, ex Shannonmede 24, ex Linmore 20, ex Llanover 17
Mina L Cambani 1920 Pgill2 5227 8450 412–4 52–4 25–5 10.0
ex Somerton 35, launched as War Smilax

Funnel: A G Vlassopoulos – yellow
Services: General tramping

CARAVIAS, J M, Rue Emanouel Antoniadou, Athens

Manager for
G TRILIVAS & ARISTOTELIS G VLASSOPOULOS
Aghios Markos 1919 Gray18 4515 7020 388–2 51–11 24–1 10.0
ex Homayun 29, launched as War Redtail
ARISTOTELIS G VLASSOPOULOS
Aghios Georgios 1912 Earles 3283 6238 352.0 49–8 21–4 8.0
ex Onaway 25, ex Portsea 23

Hull: Black
Services: General tramping

CARRAS LTD, Bury Court House, 7–8 Bury Court, St Mary Axe, London EC3

Manager and/or agent for
JOHN N ANGELOS, Chios
Nicolas Angelos 1912 G&G3 4351 7200 388–4 52–2 23–2 9.0
ex River Orontes 31
AGENCIA MARITIMA CARMAR LTDA, Panama (Panamanian flag)
Carmar 1919 HK&Wh 5226 8260 412–0 52–4 25–3 10.5
ex Pionier 39, launched as War Bomber
AGENCIA MARITIMA COLON LTDA, Panama (Panamanian flag)
Illenao 1919 LloydR 5355 8150 413–0 52–4 25–3 10.5
ex Londonier 39, launched as War Kochia
MICHAEL J CARRAS & OTHERS, Odos Paul Coundouriotis, Chios
Adelfotis 1917 Nthmb1 5838 9150 400.0 53–0 26–2 10.0
ex Cape St Columba 35, ex Carlow Castle 30
Fotini Carra 1918 Duncan 4452 7020 388–2 51–9 23–11 10.5
ex Arafat 36, ex Jadran 33, ex Danybryn 31, ex Harmattan 28, ex Nilemede 25, ex War Fantail 19
PANAGHIOTIS J CARRAS, Odos Paul Coundouriotis, Chios
Ioannis Carras 1917 Camp1 3527 6800 348.5 49–11 23–2 9.0
ex Southlea 31, ex Lady Charlotte 18
MARCOS J AND CONSTANTINOS J FRANGOS, Odos Iapetou 4, Athens
Ioannis Frangos 1912 RDuck2 3442 6060 375–11 50–0 21–3 8.5
ex Novington 31
JOHN TH GALAKIS, Odos D Kallifrona 3, Athens
Aspasia 1914 Sundld 4211 7482 370.0 53–6 23–6 8.5
ex Theodoros Galakis 31, ex Hornby Castle 29, ex Pacific 16

Funnel: Yellow with black top separated by red band with X on blue diamond
Hull: Black with white band, red boot-topping
Services: General tramping; oil and petroleum trades

CHANDRIS, JOHN D, Leoforos II Merarchias 15A, Piræus

General cargo vessels
Adelfoi Chandri 1919 Standf 6176 9426 417–0 53–0 26–7 10.0
ex Cokesit 38
Aghios Vlasios* 1914 Nthmb1 4297 8386 405.0 53–5 24–11 10.0
ex Tysla 35
Antonios Chandris1918 Kwsaki 5867 9096 385.0 51–0 27–1 10.5
ex Easterling 37
Dimitrios Chandris 1910 Flensb 4643 7150 415.2 54–0 24–10 10.5
ex Mont Kemmel 34, ex Rendsburg 20
Evgenia Chandri 1920 Harim1 5317 10,900 425.1 54–0 25–8 10.0
ex Stadsdijk 32, ex Rocky Maru 20
Ioannis Chandris 1920 Standf 6094 9601 417–0 53–2 26–7 10.0
ex Arcturus 38
Margarita Chandri (st)
1920 Pensac 5401 8611 418–0 54–2 25–5 9.5
ex Rockport 38
Mari Chandris 1918 Kwsaki 5840 9090 385.0 51–0 27–1 11.0
ex Easterner 37, ex Seifuku Maru 18
Rita Chandri** 1914 Irvin3 4648 8044 385.0 52–0 24–2 9.5
ex Helen Moller 37, ex Egyptian Transport 33
Stylianos Chandris 1920 VirgAl 6059 9371 417–0 53–2 26–6 10.0
ex Oakspring 38, ex E A Morse 24
Tonis Chandris 1904 Neptn1 3161 5100 314–0 45–4 22–0 7.5
ex Efxinos 25, ex Karl Leonhardt 21, ex Hornburg 18

MME EVGENIA J CHANDRI, Karaiskou 142, Piræus

Keti Chandri	1918	WallSY	2974	4600	300.0	45–4	22–9	9.5
ex Tristan Vieljeux 33, ex Monnette 25, ex Antoinette 22, ex War Power 20								

JOHN D CHANDRIS & NICHOLAS J PISSIS, Odos Kefallinias 64, Athens

Kosti	1905	ThmpsJ	3933	6730	364.6	50–6	22–11	8.0
ex Marathon 31, ex Birte Jensen 27, ex Allaguash 24, ex Rygja 15								

Tanker

JOHN D CHANDRIS

Vassos†	1912	NedSM	4733	6950	375.0	51–0	29.0	9.0
ex Emanuel Nobel 35; conv mv 20								

Note: * Sold Japan 1939, renamed *Sugiyama Maru*; ** sold Latvia 1939, renamed *Everiga*; † sold Germany 1939, renamed *Pauline Friederich*

COULOURAS, ATH N, Odos Korais 4, Athens

Funnel: Black with blue over white over blue bands
Hull: Grey
Services: General tramping

Cape Corso	1905	LithR	3890	6975	369.7	49–0	24–1	8.0
Coulouras-Xenos	1915	Ropnr2	4914	8100	384.9	53–0	27.0	8.5
ex Wyndyke 32, ex Homer City 29								
Hydraios	1902	Conn2	4476	7520	385.5	50–2	25–4	8.0
ex Parnon 27, ex Isfond 21, ex Lothian 19								

COUMANTAROS LTD, TH & N, Odos Athens-Piraeus, Piræus

Services: General tramping

Ekaterini Coumantarou	1917	BethU2	7777	11,700	410.7	56–2	30–6	10.5
ex Talabot 35								
Panagiotis Th Coumantaros*	1912	Hamtn2	5839	9290	424.4	53–0	26–4	10.5
ex Dryden 33, laid down as Bolton Castle								
Stavros Coumantaros	1912	LithR	5528	9100	423–4	56–0	24–10	10.5
ex Vestalia 33								
Theodoros Coumantaros	1917	Kwsaki	5709	9158	385.3	51–2	27–1	9.0
ex Maleas 39, ex Chef Mécanicien Mailhol 36, ex War Admiral 20								

COMPAÑÍA PANAMENA DE VAPORES LTDA, Panama (Panamanian flag)

Rio Grande	1919	Lithgw	5696	9450	423.5	56–0	25–5	10.0
ex Sokol 39, ex Nile 33								

Note: * Sold John N Vassiliou and Coumantaros Bros (Union Maritime & Shipping Co Ltd) 1939

DAMBASSIS, DEM J, Odos Patission 57, Athens

Funnel: Black with blue band and Greek letters in white
Hull: Grey with white line, red boot-topping
Services: General tramping

Georgios G*	1918	GrayX	4289	7590	392–6	53–6	23–1	9.0
ex Kurdistan 27								
Joannis*	1909	RDuck1	3667	6000	360.0	48–9	24.2	8.0
ex Evelpis 26, ex Salerno 21, ex Edenmore 15								

COMPAÑÍA DE VAPORES PORTOBELLO LTDA, Panama (Panamanian flag)

Culebra	1919	RDuck2	5260	8250	412–11	52–5	25–4	10.0
ex Heleni D 38, ex Peebles 33								

Note: * Operated since 1939 by Goulandris Bros Ltd (*qv*)

DRACOULIS, HEIRS OF GEORGE A, D Callifrona 11, Athens

Funnel: Black with blue five-pointed star on white band between two narrow blue bands
Hull: Black
Services: General tramping

Ekatontarchos Dracoulis	1918	RDuck2	5329	7885	412–0	52–5	25–5	10.0
ex Coniscliffe 32, ex Dayton 27, ex Olympe 22, ex War Anglian 19, laid down as War Flier								

DRACOULIS LTD, Leadenhall House, 101, Leadenhall St, London EC3

Funnel: Dracoulis – black with blue five-pointed star on white band between two narrow white bands; Gratsos – black with white five-pointed star on blue band between narrow white bands
Services: General tramping

Manager for

G C DRACOULIS, Leophoros Amalias 12, Athens

Ithakos	1906	Rhead2	3916	6700	346.0	49–8	23–2	7.5
ex Ellaline 21								
Mentor	1902	Ropnr1	3050	5460	325.0	48–1	21–6	7.5
ex Alva 06								
Niritos	1907	GrayX	3854	6400	345.0	50–1	22–9	8.0
ex Islemoor 27, ex Maymead 22, ex Maylands 20								
Polyktor	1914	Pgill2	4077	7180	391–0	52–5	22–4	8.0
Tilemachos	1911	GrayX	3658	6100	356.3	50–9	21–2	8.5

SOCIEDAD MARITIMA MIRAFLORES LTDA, Panama (Panamanian flag)

Miraflores	1919	CanVic	5439	8390	413–1	52–4	25–3	10.5
ex Onassi Socratis 39, ex Canadian Miller 33								

Miramare	1919	CanVic	5404	8393	413–1	52–5	25–3	10.5
ex Onassi Pinelopi 39, ex Canadian Spinner 33								

GEORGE D GRATSOS CO LTD, Boulevard de l'Université 17, Athens

Kastor (st)	1921	Schich	5497	10,550	398.7	55–11	25–1	12.0
ex Parana 35								
Nestor*	1918	Toledo	1954	2930	261–0	43–6	18–7	9.5
ex Frank Lynch 37, ex Lake Sunapee 22, launched as War Flag; conv mv 38, conv steamer 22								
Triton**	1914	Nthmbl	4211	–	370.0	50–11	23–6	8.5
ex Queen Alexandra 25, ex Elfland 15								

Note: * Sold Estonia 1939, renamed *Otto*; ** sold Italy 1939, renamed *Mariarosa*

Services: General tramping

EMBIRICOS, LEONIDAS A, c/o Naftilos SARL, 41 Rue François 1er, Paris 8e, France, and Plateia Karaiskaki, Tzelepis Quai, Piræus

Dunavis*	1915	LithR	5604	9470	438–6	56–0	25–6	10.0
ex Siberian Prince 33, ex Baron Lovat 17								
Rinos	1919	Prstm1	4649	7300	350.0	50–10	25–0	9.5
ex Ullstad 36, ex Westcliff 20								
Tamesis**	1914	Napr&M	3942	6450	380–0	47–10	24–10	11.0
ex Oranian 34								

Note: * Sold Italy 1939, renamed *Arlesiana*; ** sold M A Embiricos 1939, renamed *Pagatsikos*

Funnel: Black with black E on red disc on blue cross (**x**) on white band (houseflag design)
Hull: Black, red boot-topping
Services: General tramping

EMBIRICOS, MARIS A, (Embiricos Line), c/o Naftilos SARL, 41 Rue François 1er, Paris 8e, France, and 3 Rue Lycourgou, Athens

Argolikos (st)	1921	Palmer	4786	7000	413–0	53–11	23–0	11.0
ex Pear Branch 33								
Corinthiakos	1910	Craig2	3562	6500	362.3	51–0	21–0	8.5
ex North Anglia 33, ex Bideford 21								
Evoikos (st)	1922	Cammel	4792	7380	360.0	50–2	25–10	8.5
ex Maid of Psara 31								
Laconikos	1914	Conn2	3803	6315	365.2	47–1	24–6	10.0
ex Lakonikos 33, ex Navigator 32								
Maliakos	1912	Hamtn2	3903	6440	365.0	47–0	24–3	10.0
ex Intombi 31, laid down as Actor								
Oropos	1913	Rickmr	3475	6400	362.4	50–1	23–8	9.5
ex Maid of Sparta 28, ex Minna Horn 21, ex Hornhöhe 19, ex Madeleine Rickmers 17								
Pagatsikos	1914	Napr&M	3942	6450	380–0	47–10	24–10	11.0
ex Tamesis 39, ex Oranian 34								
Petalli	1917	Doxfrd	5126	6565	420.0	54–0	25–8	9.0
ex Admiral Cochrane 28								
Saronikos	1912	Craig2	3548	6100	360.7	50–0	21–5	8.5
ex Maid of Andros 31, ex Luise Horn 21								

ANDREW MARIS EMBIRICOS AND PERICLES MARIS EMBIRICOS

Thermaïkos	1923	GirndH	4518	6744	377–0	49–3	23–3	10.5
ex Ronsard 36, ex Capitaine Joseph Plisson 29, ex Blaise Pascal 23								

Funnels: S G Embiricos – black with blue E on white band
Hulls: S G Embiricos – grey with white band, red boot-topping
Services: General tramping

EMBIRICOS LTD, S G, Bury Court House, 7–8 Bury Court, St Mary Axe, London EC3, and S G Embiricos, Odos Merlin 8, Athens

S G EMBIRICOS

Ellin	1938	Bartm2	4917	9150	432–4	56–6	25–1	10.0
Eugenie S Embiricos	1920	Short2	4882	8632	419.5	53–8	24–9	9.5
George M Embiricos	1921	Short2	5728	10,483	459–0	56–4	26–11	9.5
Ioannis M Embiricos	1924	GrayWH	3734	6695	360.0	51–0	22–3	9.0
ex Rustington 31								
Irene S Embiricos	1927	Short2	4164	7921	409–6	52–4	24–3	9.5
Michael L Embiricos	1918	Caird	5202	8200	412–0	52–4	25–3	10.5
ex War Malayan 19; conv tanker 19								
Stamatios G Embiricos	1936	Short2	3941	–	400.0	53–0	23–7	10.0

Manager and/or agent and/or chartering agent for

ALBA STEAMSHIP CO LTD, Panama (Panamanian flag)
(beneficial owner Nicolas D Bogiazides & Co)

Alba	1908	Anvers	3444	6020	360–0	48–1	22–7	8.0
ex Dimitris N Bogiazides 39, ex Maid of Corfu 24, ex Orissa 20, ex Ingelfingen 13								

AMARYLIS STEAMSHIP CO LTD, Panama (Panamanian flag)
(beneficial owner Michael E Kydoniefs, Odos Eressou 36, Athens)

Amarylis (st)	1918	NofIre	4215	7110	384–0	51–2	24–0	10.0

ex Maroulio 38, ex Assiout 35

NICOLAS D BOGIAZIDES & CO, Odos Ithakis 32, Athens

Matronna	1902	Caggl	2846	–	339–5	46–0	21–3	8.0

ex Ioannis 23, ex Attiki 13

PANAGIOTIS D CHRISTOPOULOS, Odos Merlin 8, Athens

Hydroussa	1922	Dyle&B	2038	3100	281–10	39–6	19–10	8.0

ex Capitaine Commelin 34

GEORGE N CONDYLIS, Andros

Condylis	1914	AwpEng	4439	7905	400.0	51–10	24–7	10.0

ex Lowther Castle 33

CONSTANTINE E EMBIRICOS, Odos Omirou 18, Athens

Epaminodas C Embiricos	1927	Pgill2	4385	7829	373.2	52–9	24–4	10.0
ex Benton 31								
Koumoundouros	1925	ThmpR2	3598	6505	360.0	50–6	22–0	10.0
ex Daybreak 34								
Olga E Embiricou	1922	Rhead3	4677	8286	400.3	52–1	25–7	9.0
ex Bellview 33								

GEORGE NIC EMBIRICOS, Odos Coumbari 5, Athens

Evgena Cambani	1898	RDuck	3470	–	350–0	46–0	22–9	7.0

ex Nea Ellas 23, ex Sir W T Lewis 13

D J GOULANDRIS, Odos Guilford 4, Athens

Naftilos	1904	ThmpsJ	3531	6176	336.0	49–2	22–6	8.0

ex Leamington 25, ex Tynemede 20, ex Blue Jacket 15

JOHN N GOULANDRIS, Andros

Elpis	1912	RDuck2	3651	6250	352.0	50–2	21–3	9.5

ex Buranda 34

ANTONIOS Z GOUNARIS (manager Giannoulis Z Gounaris – *qv* below)

Zannes Gounaris	1907	Cragg2	4407	7250	376.0	52–4	22–11	9.0

ex Tuscania 29, ex Alexandros 29, ex River Araxes 26, ex Fitzclarence 13

GIANNOULIS Z GOUNARIS, Charilaou Tricoupi 28, Athens

Giannoulis Gounaris*	1901	GrayX	2238	–	302.6	43–2	18–10	7.0

ex Zanos Sifneo 26, ex Armanistan 01

HELLENIC SHIPPING CO TRITON SOCIETE ANONYME, Odos Akademias 44, Athens

Souliotis	1917	Nthmb1	4300	8200	400.0	53–0	24–4	9.0

ex Woodfield 33

KIRTATAS BROS, Andros

Afroessa	1905	Ropnr1	2529	4450	321–3	44–1	20–7	8.0

ex Baron Douglas 29, ex Glenmay 19

SANTIAGO STEAMSHIP CO LTD, Panama (Panamanian flag)
(beneficial owner N D Rallias, Andros)

Santiago	1908	Rhead2	3860	6730	346.1	49–8	23–2	8.0

ex Eirini N Rallia 38, ex Redgate 29, ex Gordonia 19

TUIRA STEAMSHIP CO LTD, Panama (Panamanian flag)
(beneficial owner N A Kydoniefs, Andros)

Tuira	1912	Bartm1	4397	7900	385.0	52–0	23–10	9.5

ex Andriotis 39, ex Bellfield 32, ex Craigwen 20, ex Orpheus 17

Note: * Operated by J P Hadoulis Ltd (*qv*)

EPIPHANIADES & CO, T N, Commercial Bank Bldg, Odos Omirou 16, Piræus

Funnel: Yellow with blue E, black top
Services: General tramping

Manager for

KONSTANTINOS CHRISTOU AND DESPINA PAPADOPOULOU

Konistra	1907	Rodger	3527	6210	350.4	48–0	22–6	8.5

ex Lamington 31

W T EPIPHANIADES AND DEMETRIOS G COUCOUMBANIS

Georgios P	1903	SH1	4052	6800	365.0	46–9	24–0	8.5

ex Crosby Hall 27

Note: Also vessels under 2000gt

EPIROTIKI STEAMSHIP NAVIGATION CO 'GEORGE POTAMIANOS', Megaron Electricou Stathmou, Piræus

Services: General tramping

Georgios Potamianos	1913	AwpEng	4044	7514	370.4	51–11	24–1	9.5

ex Petros Nomikos 39, ex Amasis 33, ex Glenrazan 19

Funnel: Black with white Greek F on blue band
Hull: Black
Services: General tramping

Note: * Sold Norway 1939, renamed *San Antonio*

FAFALIOS, STAMATIOS AND DEMITRIOS, Vrontados, Chios

Ioannis Fafalios	1919	MerchC	5670	8780	400.7	54–2	25–8	10.0
ex Muntropic 37, ex Terre Haute 29								
Nea Tyhi*	1912	Koch	3451	6100	361.4	50–8	21–6	9.0
ex Maid of Syra 31, ex Horncap 21								
Stamos	1914	Nthmbl	3801	7530	388–5	51–4	23–9	9.0
ex Reading 34								

Funnel: Black G on white disc on blue band bordered by two narrow white bands, separating yellow base from black top
Hull: Black
Services: General tramping

GEORGANDIS BROS, Odos Koundouriotou 173, Piræus

Adamandios Georgandis	1916	Blumrl	3443	5950	348.5	48–9	21–5	9.0
ex Portvale 32, ex Portrushton 23, ex Portrush 17								
Aikaterini	1913	Ropnr2	4929	8880	390.0	55–6	24–5	9.0
ex Wearpool 35								
Antonis Georgandis	1915	RottDD	3557	6020	345.6	48–10	21–7	9.5
ex Rijndijk 30								

Funnel: Black with blue gamma (Greek G) on white band bordered by two narrow blue bands or yellow with black top separated by blue band bearing white gamma (Greek G); D A Kydoniefs – red, black top; P A Kydoniefs – yellow
Hull: Black, red boot-topping; Kirtatis, P A Kydoniefs – grey, white band
Services: General tramping

GOULANDRIS BROS,
Megaron Laikis, Navarino St, Piræus, and 59 St Mary Axe, London EC3

Passenger vessel
BASIL J, NICOLAS J AND LEONIDAS J GOULANDRIS (General Steam Navigation Co of Greece)

Nea Hellas (st2,P179/1,404/cab,1399/t)	1922	Fairfd	16,991	10,400	578–4	70–4	28–11	16.5
ex Tuscania 39								

General cargo vessels
GOULANDRIS BROS

Anna N Goulandri	1921	RottDD	4358	7100	387–0	51–7	23–10	10.0
ex Texel 34								
Constantinos Louloudis	1922	Gusto	4697	7205	390–0	51–10	23–9	10.0
ex Vlieland 33								
Frangoula B Goulandri	1918	ThmpsJ	6701	10,250	427–1	55–6	25–9	10.0
ex Brecon 28, ex Dunbridge 23								
George J Goulandris	1913	GrayX	4345	7270	377–0	50–10	23–3	9.5
ex Lyminge 37, ex Portloe 35, ex Nigaristan 19								
Ioannis P Goulandris	1910	Craig2	3750	6500	376–0	51–0	20–11	8.5
ex Maria Stathatos 24, ex Eggesford 23								
Kassandra Louloudi	1919	Gray18	5106	8746	412–6	52–4	26–9	10.5
ex Bondowoso 36, launched as War Lurcher								
Maroussio Logotheti	1913	Irvin3	4669	8044	385.0	52–0	24–2	10.0
ex Queensland Transport 34								
Moscha L Goulandri	1918	Caledn	5199	8035	412–0	52–3	25–4	10.5
ex Ridderkerk 33, ex Kieldrecht 21, ex War Roach 19								
Petros J Goulandris	1923	Gusto	4693	7200	390–0	51–10	23–9	10.0
ex Schouwen 33								
Violando N Goulandris	1919	RottDD	3598	6293	373–0	49–10	21–7	9.5
ex Walcheren 32, laid down as Delfshaven								

Manager for
GEORGE J ANDREOU, Andros

Yiannis	1905	Curle	4391	7250	375.0	47–2	24–11	9.5
ex Newby Hall 30								

CHARALAMBOS TH BULGARIS, Andros

Anna Bulgari	1912	RDuck1	4603	8450	390.0	52–6	25–0	10.0
ex Indianola 30								

N TH BULGARIS, Mantzakou 1, Athens

Katina Bulgari	1912	RDuck2	4567	8450	390.0	52–6	25–0	8.5
ex Katina 33, ex Grelwen 31, ex Tonwen 18, ex Tavian 17								

DIMITRIOS L CONDYLIS, Passage Orphanides 8, Athens								
Leonidas N Condylis	1912	GrayX	3923	6600	360.3	49–1	23–1	8.0
ex Branksome Chine 35, ex Aurora 34, ex Swiftway 33, ex Arachne 21								
EUTHALIA COUMARIANOU & OTHERS, Athens								
Euthalia	1918	RottDD	4770	7190	387–0	51–7	23–10	10.0
ex Marken 32								
E A GOULANDRIS & CO, Odos Agorakritou 5B, Athens								
Aristides L Goulandris*	1905	GrayX	3470	6200	342.0	49–6	22–2	8.0
ex Calimeris 25, ex Harlech 14								
HEIRS OF THE LATE MICHAEL J GOULANDRIS, Odos Patission 72, Athens								
Michael J Goulandris	1921	Doxfrd	6669	10,750	420.0	54–0	28–4	9.0
ex Lina L-D 37, ex Hallgyn 26								
HEIRS OF THE LATE PETROS J GOULANDRIS, Odos Patission 152, Piræus								
Evanthia	1915	RottDD	3551	6350	373–0	49–11	21–7	10.0
ex Algenib 37								
HALCYON STEAMSHIP CO LTD								
Cygnet	1917	RottDD	3530	6367	373–2	49–11	21–7	10.0
ex Mirach 39								
Halcyon	1917	RottDD	3531	6424	373–2	49–11	21–7	10.0
ex Sirrah 39								
LEONIDAS L G KERANIS, Andros								
Aghia Thalassini	1911	Pgill2	3508	6515	348.5	50–2	21–9	9.0
ex Montague Seed 33, ex Erlesburgh 29								
A A KIRTATIS & BROTHERS, Andros								
Marionga D Thermiotis	1904	Ropnr1	4784	7715	351.5	53–1	24–7	8.0
ex Laleham 30, ex Llangorse 26, ex Llanover 16, ex Clarissa Radcliffe 13								
BASIL C AND JOHN C KOUTSOUKOS, Andros								
Panachrandos	1915	Bartm2	4661	8082	400.0	52–1	24–4	9.0
ex Hartfield 33								
DEMETRIOS A KYDONIEFS, Andros								
Moscha D Kydoniefs	1915	Nthmb1	3874	7577	375.2	51–11	23–9	9.0
ex Lady Charlotte 36, ex Noelle 21, ex Bronze Wings 17								
PETROS A KYDONIEFS, Andros								
Elengo A Kydoniefs	1916	Irvin3	4129	7517	380.0	51–5	24–0	9.0
ex Ravenshoe 34, ex Marnetown 23, ex Kepwickhall 22								
G N LOULOUDIS, Avenue Rodin 5, Paris, France (Greek flag)								
Pegasus	1920	FurnH	5762	9190	413–8	52–4	26–2	10.0
ex Lappland 39, ex Benares 34								
BASILIOS G MAVROS AND STAMATIOS N MENDRINOS, Leoforos Socratus 70, Piræus								
Theoskepasti	1911	Craig2	3726	6300	367–5	50–0	21–5	9.5
ex Portreath 32, ex Amicus 19								
M N PIANGOS & PARTNERS, Odos Pipirou 14, Athens								
Nicolaos Piangos	1912	Nthmb1	4499	8020	385.0	52–0	24–3	10.0
ex Oaklands Grange 34								
MICHAEL SPYROS POLEMIS, Andros								
Theomitor	1910	Bartm1	4427	7507	375.0	52–0	23–1	8.5
ex Dailwen 32, ex Haigtown 24, ex Dailwen 19, ex Mozart 16								
ALKIVIADIS M TATAKIS, Odos Averoff 24, Athens								
Dimitrios G Thermiotis	1906	Steph2	4271	7150	385.5	50–0	23–6	8.0
ex Janeta 29								
MICHAEL VALMAS, Odos Grigoriou V 3, Piræus								
Leonidas M Valmas	1914	StettO	2080	3050	258.3	40–6	19–5	9.0
ex Germania 36, ex Leonidas M Valmas 35, ex Gerano 34, ex Stern 21								
LEONIDAS N VLACHAKIS, Odos Lekka 29, Piræus								
Faneromeni	1908	Anvers	3404	6075	345.9	48–1	22–6	8.5
ex Thetis 29, ex Rooke 21, ex Slawentzitz 15								

Note: * Sold Finland 1939, renamed *Edit H*
Note: See also under D J Dambassis

GOUMAS, JOHN GHIKAS, Odos Eressou 35, Athens

Funnel: White, black top, separated by white over blue bands
Services: General tramping

Vassilios A Polemis	1907	Anvers	3429	6020	360–0	48–4	22–7	8.0
ex Oehringen 27								

Funnel: Yellow with emblem – white shield with blue diagonal line, red border
Hull: Black with white band, red boot-topping
Services: General tramping

HADJILIAS & CO LTD,
Bury Court House, 7–8 Bury Court, St Mary Axe, London EC3

Manager for
ELIAS E HADJILIAS, AN D MANTHOS & OTHERS,
Odos Ainianos 6, Athens
Zeus 1920 RDuck2 4279 8919 400.6 52–11 32.2 9.0
ex Emilie L-D 34, ex Dagfred 28, ex Vestheim 21
EMANUEL P, GEORGE P, AND PAUL E HADJILIAS AND MME ANNA P HADJILIA, Syra
Ia 1917 Short2 4860 8157 385.0 53–0 24–4 9.5
ex Adra 33
Julia 1914 RDuck2 4352 7650 380.0 51–0 23–10 10.0
ex Burdale 35
NEREUS STEAM NAVIGATION CO LTD, Odos Ainianos 6, Athens
Doris 1917 ThmpsJ 4604 9120 400.0 53–0 26–2 9.0
ex Eastern City 33
Nereus (r/t) 1937 Hamtn4 5205 9400 447–0 56–2 25–0 11.0
launched as Darlyon
Peleus 1928 GrayWH 4695 8660 400.2 54–2 24–10 9.5
ex Egglestone 28
Thetis 1930 GraySd 4123 7600 403–7 53–8 23–6 9.0

Funnel: Black
Services: General tramping

HADJIPATERAS & SONS, CONSTANTINE,
Chios, and Megaron Yannoulatou, Piræus

JOHN C AND ADAMANTIOS C HADJIPATERAS, Megaron Yannoulatou, Piræus
Aghios Nicolaos 1915 Napr&M 3687 6750 364.8 51–6 22.6 9.0
ex Evgenia 33, ex Iron Age 25, ex Australport 24, ex Ardangorm 16
Konstantinos Hadjipateras
1913 ThmpsJ 5962 8685 388.5 54–1 25–5 10.0
ex Calandplein 35, ex Lesreaulx 27, ex Pinemore 23, ex Den of Ewnie 16
JOHN C, N C AND ADAMANTIOS C HADJIPATERAS
Katingo Hadjipatera
1913 ThmpsJ 3661 6812 364–6 51–0 23–4 9.5
ex Hartland Point 37, ex Avon River 35, ex Harry Walton 34, ex Lady Kathleen 33, ex South Pacific 22
CONSTANTINE N MICHALOS AND JOHN C, N C AND ADAMANTIOS C HADJIPATERAS
Leonidas M 1929 Lithgw 4573 7950 385–0 52–0 24–0 10.0
ex Bellucia 37

Services: General tramping

HADOULIS LTD, J P, 6–8. Fenchurch Bldgs, Fenchurch St, London EC3

NICOLAOS MICHAEL MARIS, Andros
Efthalia Mari (st) 1919 NofIre 4195 7060 384–0 51–2 24–0 10.0
ex Amarna 35
NICOLAS SITINAS & CO, Port Said, Egypt (Greek flag)
Avra 1912 Craig2 4652 7850 385.0 51–6 24–7 10.0
ex Halesius 36, ex Clan Macbeolan 20, ex Lord Cromer 17
Kyma 1912 Short2 3994 6960 363.0 50–0 23–6 8.5
ex Hesleyside 33

Funnel: Yellow with black H inside black circle, black top
Services: General tramping

HUNTER, M C FRED, 34 Great St Helen's, London EC3

Manager and/or agent for
JOHN ANDREAS COSMAS, Syra, Greece (Panamanian flag)
Andreas 1917 Conn2 4933 8000 400.3 53–0 24–2 9.5
ex Indian Prince 36, ex Glenlyon 22
ANDREAS PAPPAS, Greece
Meropi 1911 Rhead3 4181 7740 363.0 51–1 24–2 8.0
ex Tregurno 30
J STAVROU & CO, Greece
Kalliopi S 1918 ThmpsJ 5152 8150 413–1 52–2 25–3 10.0
ex Humanitas 34, ex Humilitas 33, ex Elzasier 32, ex War Wager 19

Services: General tramping

ILIOPOULOS, ILIAS AND ATHANASSIOS, Odos Bucarest 18, Athens

Constantinos H 1905 Neptnl 2527 4350 303–0 43–9 21–0 8.5
ex Anthemis 33, ex Nancéen 30, ex Christian Horn 21

Goulandris Bros: Nea Hellas *was purchased by Goulandris in 1939 from Anchor Line, having been completed as* Tuscania *in September 1922. She was fitted with Brown-Curtis double reduction geared turbines of 12,500shp, and a maximum 13,500shp. During the 1920s and '30s* Tuscania *was in Anchor Line service from Glasgow to New York and Liverpool to Bombay, was on cruising, and at various times was chartered to Cunard. She was laid up at Glasgow on October 8 1938, and following sale she was delivered to General Steam Navigation Co of Greece (later better known as Greek Line) on April 19 1939. As* Nea Hellas *she made her first voyage in May 1939 from Piræus to New York. When Greece was invaded in October 1940, she transferred to British control with Anchor Line as managers, and serving as an Allied troopship became affectionately known as 'Nellie Wallace' by many thousands of troops who travelled in her. In January 1947 she was returned to Greece, and refitted in the UK and at Genoa for North Atlantic service. In March 1955 she was renamed* New York, *and was broken up in Japan in 1961 (RW Jordan collection)*

S H Iossifoglu: Completed in October 1928, the Blyth-built Isleworth *was sold to this owner's Panamanian offshoot in 1938 and eventually renamed* Maria. *She had traded well into 1939 under her old name* Isleworth. *In 1940 she was again renamed, as the Panamanian-flagged* Santa Margarita, *and as such was shelled and sunk by* U29 *on July 2 1940 when on voyage from Barry to Hampton Roads. Twenty-one survivors were picked up by the British vessel* King John *and three of those were missing when* King John *herself was sunk (Alex Duncan)*

N G Livanos: The standard War 'A' type steamer War Cypress *was launched on September 29 and completed in November 1917 by Cammell, Laird, at Birkenhead. She was fitted with a Cammell, Laird triple expansion engine of 2500ihp. In 1920 she was sold to France and renamed* Leopold L-D, *and in 1920 to Greece and renamed* Aliki. *In June 1940 at Dakar,* Aliki *was seized by the Vichy authorities, and the following year renamed* Monaco *under the French flag. In 1942 she was transferred to Italy and renamed* Bologna. *Under that name she was torpedoed and sunk by the British submarine* Unbroken *on May 21 1943 when on voyage from Naples to Messina (Alex Duncan)*

Funnel: Black with red I on white triangle on blue band
Services: General tramping

Note: * Operated by Rethymnis & Kulukundis Ltd (*qv*)

INGLESSI FILS SOCIETE ANONYME, D, Samos, and Protos Ofofos, Megaron Electricou Stathmou, Piræus

NAVIGATION DE SAMOS, Samos

Dimitrios Inglessis*	1918	Sundld	5275	8210	412–4	52–5	25–2	10.0
ex Burutu 34, ex War Swan 20								

Services: General tramping; oil and petroleum trades

Note: * Sold 1939, renamed *Santa Helena*

IOSSIFOGLU, SOCRATES H, Odos Akademias 41, Athens

Manager for
COMPAÑÍA PRIMERA DE NAVIERA LTDA, Panama (Panamanian flag)

General cargo vessel								
Maria	1928	Cowpen	4919	8635	400.2	54–2	25–2	10.0
ex Isleworth 39								
Tankers								
Clairy	1916	Laing	5845	8300	407.0	52–5	25–10	10.0
ex Romford 37, ex Ionia 37, ex Glenfield 35, ex Mirita 34, launched as Zurita								
Yolanda*	1913	G&G3	4680	7200	380.6	51–2	24–6	9.5
ex Ilford 37, ex Iossifoglu 37, ex Nord Atlantic 34, ex Uncas 24								

Services: General tramping

Note: * BU Briton Ferry 1939

KOKOTOS, GEORGES H, Corfu, and 55 Avenue Victor Emmanuel III, Paris

THE 'K' NAVIGATION CO

Atea*	1901	Palmer	3893	6200	365.0	48–2	25.4	7.5
ex Anversoise 37, ex Reigate 11								

Services: General tramping

KOUFOS, DEMETRIUS N, Odos Charilou Tricoupi 21, Piræus

Heron	1906	Rijkee	1516	2250	251.5	34–8	19–0	7.0
ex Hollandia 36, ex Heron 35, ex Neptunus 30								
DEMETRIUS N KOUFOS AND F J SOTERIADES								
Pancration	1920	ArsnBr	2171	3143	281–10	39–5	19–10	8.0
ex Député Charles Nortier 35								

Funnel: Black with white K on red disc at centre of white cross (+) on blue band
Hull: Black
Services: General tramping

KYRIAKIDES, HEIRS OF NICOLAS G, Megaron Spyraki, Piræus

Eirini Kyriakidou	1922	ThmpR2	3781	6650	360.1	50–0	22–7	9.5
Georgios Kyriakides	1911	Rhead3	4201	7710	375–4	51–1	24–2	9.0
ex Trevalgan 29								

Funnel: D J Pateras – black
Services: General tramping

LEMOS & PATERAS LTD, 89 Billiter Bldgs, Billiter St, London EC3

Manager and/or agent for

GEORGE A GEORGILIS, Chios								
Papalemos	1910	TyneIr	3748	6394	348.5	50–0	21–5	8.0
ex Stroma 29, ex Leucadia 16								
G D HALKIAS, Oinoussai, Chios								
Aghios Spyridon	1905	Craigl	3338	5500	340.0	47–10	21–7	7.5
ex Dimitris 38, ex Gyp 24, ex Kylestrome 15, ex Ballochmyle 11								
ANTONIOS G LEMOS' SONS, Oinoussai, Chios								
Antonis	1915	ThmpR2	3729	6693	350.0	50–6	22–6	9.0
ex Ioulia Nicolaou 36, ex Rocio 33								
Garoufalia	1914	Irvin3	4708	8020	397–1	52–0	24–1	9.0
ex Orange River 34								
COSTIS ELIA LEMOS, Kato Giallos, Chios								
Maria L	1912	Ropnr2	4707	8100	391–9	51–6	24–6	8.5
ex Brynmel 35, ex Bradburn 29, ex Atlantic City 20								
GEORGE CHRISTOS LEMOS, Leoforos Alexandras 57, Athens								
Efploia	1911	Irvin3	3862	6600	350.0	51–1	22–0	8.5
ex Podmladak 36, ex Doverton 27, ex Severnmede 25, ex Glendene 18								
ANASTASSIOS PATERAS & SONS, Chios								
Anastassios Pateras	1914	Blumr1	3382	5950	348.5	48–9	21–4	8.5
ex Svorono 26, ex Ennisbrook 21								
Marouko Pateras	1917	Pgill2	4269	7675	401–0	53–4	22–9	9.0
ex Harpagus 28, ex Clydemede 24, ex Oakmore 20								
COSTAS N PATERAS, Chios								
Agioi Victores	1918	Rhead3	4344	8200	413–9	52–1	24–3	10.0
ex Treloske 39								

DIAMANTIS J PATERAS & SONS, Chios

Diamantis 1917 Bartm2 4990 8000 414–6 52–5 24–10 10.0
ex Korean Prince 34, ex Hindustan 18

Kalliopi 1910 Nthmbl 4965 8100 390.0 52–6 24–2 8.0
ex Nymphe 28, ex Oceana 27, ex Kermanshah 22, ex Himalaia 20

PANAGOS D PATERAS, Patras

Diamantis 1919 H&WGk 5253 8200 412–6 52–4 25–3 10.5
ex Kostis 39, ex Bathurst 33

LIVANOS & SONS LTD, JOHN, Baltic House, 27 Leadenhall St, London EC3

Funnel: Black with red L (lambda) with stylised band above and below, all on broad white band
Hull: Grey with white line
Services: General tramping

C CHOREMIS

Anastassia 1905 Bartm1 2883 5120 331.0 48–0 21–3 7.5
ex King City 27, ex Quarrydene 19

JOHN G LIVANOS, Piræus

Evros 1918 ThmpsJ 5283 8100 412–8 52–4 25–4 10.0
ex Ethelfreda 33, ex War Tulip 19

Meandros 1919 LithR 4581 7440 385.3 52–0 24–1 10.0
ex Crosshill 34

JOHN G P LIVANOS, Odos Lemison 6, Athens

Annitsa 1918 Rhead3 4324 8100 413–4 52–1 24–2 10.5
ex Tregantle 39

PROTOPAPAS, PANOS A, Odos Bouboulinas 26, PO Box 168, Athens

Marika Protopapa 1915 GrayX 4447 8170 393–0 52–0 24–9 10.0
ex Darius 33, ex Nolisement 27

Note: Title of company changed 1939 from Livanos Brothers Ltd; see also in Great Britain section

LIVANOS & CO LTD, S, Bevis Marks House, 23–24 Bevis Marks, London EC3

Funnel: N G Livanos, Livanos Bros, Livanos Maritime, Theofano Maritime – black with red lambda (L) with stylised band above and below, all on broad white band
Hull: N G Livanos, Livanos Bros, Livanos Maritime, Theofano Maritime – grey or black with white line, red boot-topping
Services: General tramping

Manager for

N G LIVANOS, Megaron Vati, Miaoulis Quay, Piræus

Aliki 1917 Cammel 5140 8100 412–8 52–5 25–3 10.5
ex Leopold L-D 32, ex War Cypress 20

Evi Livanou 1937 GrayWH 4839 9100 431–1 56–8 25–1 10.5

LIVANOS BROS MARITIME CO LTD

Mary Livanos 1938 GrayWH 4771 9100 431–0 56–9 25–1 10.5

LIVANOS MARITIME CO LTD

Chios 1939 GrayWH 5643 9975 456–10 57–8 26–0 10.5

Evinos 1919 Nthmbl 5267 8100 413–6 53–0 26–3 10.0
ex Waihemo 34, launched as War Bastion

G S Livanos 1937 GrayWH 4835 9100 431–1 56–9 25–2 10.5

George M Livanos 1938 GrayWH 5482 10,010 456–10 57–9 26–0 11.0

Strymon 1919 Palmer 5250 8250 412–2 52–2 25–3 10.0
ex Cairndhu 35, launched as War Camel

THEOFANO MARITIME CO LTD

Alfios 1920 Irvin3 5116 8140 412–6 52–4 25–4 10.0
ex Bolivian 33, launched as War Otter

Aliakmon 1913 Nthmbl 4521 8020 385.1 52–0 24–3 10.0
ex Evi 37, ex Victorian Transport 33, ex Borkumriff 19, ex Victorian Transport 17

Archangelos 1917 Dobson 5692 9200 412–6 52–0 25–9 10.0
ex Bawtry 27, ex Mottisfont 23

Athina Livanos 1936 GrayWH 4824 9100 431–0 56–9 25–1 10.5

Axios 1919 SHWR 5289 8100 412–8 52–5 25–4 10.0
ex Barbadian 33, launched as War Tapir

Evgenia Livanos 1936 GrayWH 4816 9100 431–0 56–9 25–1 10.5

Ilissos 1915 Irvin3 4724 8020 397–9 52–0 24–4 10.0
ex Derwent River 33

Michael Livanos 1938 GrayWH 4774 9100 431–1 56–9 25–1 10.5

Nestos 1919 Pgill2 5764 8955 417–5 52–4 25–8 10.0
ex Zenada 33, ex Arabian Prince 27

Theofano Livanos 1937 GrayWH 4815 9100 431–1 56–8 25–2 10.5

Manager and/or agent and/or chartering agent for

GEORGE F ANDREADIS, Odos Panepistimiou 17, Athens

Thetis A 1910 Nthmbl 4111 7370 365.0 51–5 23–4 8.5
ex Nagos 34, ex Indian Transport 29

ANDREADI BROS (S & F ANDREADIS)

Dioni 1906 Nthmbl 4181 – 360.0 48–0 25–0 8.0
ex Lesvos 27, ex Vassilisa Sofia 23, ex Asgard 21

GEORGIOS K KTISTAKIS, Chios

Pelinaion 1907 LithR 4291 7425 385.0 49–11 23–10 8.0
ex K Ktistakis 39, ex Doonholm 27, ex Hillglen 13

VASSILIOS J PATERAS, Oinoussai, Chios
Dirphys 1917 Pgill2 4240 7675 401–0 53–4 22–7 9.0
ex Theofano 37, ex Harpalion 31, ex Avonmede 24, ex Cottesmore 20, ex Swindon 17
MRS A PERRY (Panamanian flag)
(manager Stam Perivolaris, Odos Michael Nomikou 1, Athens)
Aurora 1913 Pgill2 4584 8240 383.0 51–9 25–3 9.0
ex Margaritis 39, ex Fotinia 32, ex Photinia 17
APOSTOLOS KIOUZE PEZAS, Megaron Vati, Miaoulis Quay, Piræus
Igor* 1907 Blumrl 2726 4900 314.0 46–6 21–0 8.0
ex Antzouletta 35, ex Otterstad 21, ex Kristiania 12
Kyma 1911 Blyth 3959 6880 352.5 50–10 22–8 9.0
ex Rothley 33
FOTINI M PROIOU AND C M PROIOS,
Odos Dimokratou 99, Athens (manager Constantine M Proios, Chios)
Pleiades 1918 NNews 4620 7400 385–0 53–1 24–2 10.0
ex Munaires 37
MICHAEL M XYLAS, Odos Notara 44, Piræus
Aris 1914 RDuck2 4810 8100 380.2 50–11 24–9 9.0
ex Michalis Poutous 36, ex Mount Pindus 35, ex Maindy Grange 32, ex Pontwen 20

Note: * Sold Ath O Anastassiou 1939

Services: General tramping

LUSI LTD, A, 11–12 Bury St, London EC3

Manager and/or agent and/or chartering agent for
C BACALAS, A LUSI AND S P SYNODINOS, Odos Stadiou 46, Athens
Marathon (s2) 1919 H&W,B 6352 10,210 465–0 58–5 27–6 12.0
ex Kumara 37, ex Horatius 33, ex Hostilius 26, ex Bardic 25, laid down as War Priam 19
CONSTANTINE J CARRAS & OTHERS, Odos Paul Coundouriotis, Chios
Alexandra 1913 ThmpsJ 4355 7670 375.0 52–6 23–10 8.0
ex Gerontas 33, ex Pentwyn 32, ex Ariadne Irene 22
Carras 1918 Dixon2 5234 8200 412–0 52–4 25–3 10.0
ex Kinross 34, ex Taxandrier 27, ex War Spartan 20
MIKES N FILINIS, Odos Tinou 10, Athens
Nicolaos Filinis 1904 RDuck1 3111 5350 325.0 47–0 21–9 8.5
ex Glenaster 31, ex Seabank 23, ex Dowgate 15
C P LAIMOS AND J C PONTICOS, Chios
Pantelis 1911 Irvin3 3845 6600 350.0 51–1 22–0 8.0
ex Glenbridge 32
ANDR GEO AND DEM GEO LEMOS, Chios
Kyriakoula 1918 NewWat 4340 7075 370.3 50–2 23–10 10.0
ex Kamir 34, ex Sidlaw Range 22
A LUSI, STEFANOS P SYNODINOS, PAUL B METAXAS AND OTHERS
(manager Synodinos Bros, Megaron Electricou Stathmou, Piræus)
Kolchis 1909 France 2219 3660 288.7 42–10 19–9 8.0
ex Waldinge 38, ex Sybil 31
POLYCHRONIS LYRAS, Charilaou Tricoupi 148, Athens
Orion 1909 Conn2 4798 7727 412–9 52–0 24–1 10.5
ex Highland Prince 36, ex Glenshiel 22
PANAGHIS E AND B B PANAS, Argostoli, Cephalonia
Vassilios Destounis 1912 Earles 3299 6280 352.0 49–7 21–4 9.0
ex Northborough 33, ex Ardenhall 20, ex Bathampton 18, ex Withernsea 16
PINDOS STEAMSHIP CO LTD, Odos Stadiou 46, Athens
Cleanthis 1911 Leslie 4153 7370 375.7 51–4 23–6 9.0
ex Framlington Court 22
Pindos 1908 Leslie 4360 7860 393–9 52–0 25–4 9.0
ex Indianic 36
STEFANOS P SYNODINOS
(manager Synodinos Bros, Megaron Electricou Stathmou, Piræus)
Danapris 1914 OsbGr1 2113 3300 279.2 40–4 22.6 8.5
ex Saima 36, ex Clapton 24, ex Pensacola 22
ZEPHYROS STEAMSHIP CO LTD, Odos Stadiou 46, Athens
Aenos 1910 Bartm1 3554 6100 390.5 51–0 21.3 10.5
ex Cedar Branch 30
Zephyros 1909 Conn2 4796 7725 412–9 51–11 24–0 10.5
ex Cherry Branch 30, ex Dunedin 19

Funnel: NDL – yellow with white square bearing five-pointed red star, black top; CMCL – black with houseflag
Hull: NDL – black with white band; CMCL – black
Services: General tramping

LYKIARDOPULO & CO LTD,
Baltic Exchange Chambers, 24 St Mary Axe, London EC3

Manager for
N D LYKIARDOPULO, Leophoros Amalias 36, Athens
Anna 1919 GrkDY 5173 8282 412–4 52–4 25–4 10.0
ex Mount Athos 22, ex Leapark 20, launched as War Birch

Chloe 1928 GrayWH 4641 8930 400.0 56–2 25–3 11.5
ex Rio Diamante 33
Kate 1918 H&WGw 5197 8020 412–4 52–4 25–3 10.5
ex War Envoy 20
Panaghis 1920 Doxfrd 5187 8340 413–0 52–5 25–4 9.5

CEPHALONIAN MARITIME CO LTD
Daphne 1918 Prstm1 3798 7203 365.0 51–6 22–6 9.5
ex Sunland 34
Keramiai 1917 SH&WR 5085 7980 412–4 52–3 25–4 10.5
ex Baltique 34, ex Gallier 33, ex War Rose 19
Nicolaos D L 1939 GrayWH 5486 10,010 456–10 57–9 26–0 11.0
Nymphe 1921 RDuck2 4504 8105 400.3 52–0 24–8 10.0
ex Inkum 31

Manager and/or agent and/or chartering agent for
HEIRS OF A ANDREATOS, Odos Kyprou 37, Athens
Perseus 1918 H&W,B 5172 8100 412–0 52–4 25–3 10.5
ex Patagonier 32, ex War Bittern 19

ANASTASIOS THEODORE CALLINICOS,
Ithaka, and 47 George St, Bute Docks, Cardiff
Eleni 1918 Napr&M 5655 9080 420.7 54–2 25–6 10.5
ex Polamhall 28, ex Rhode Island 27

D C AND J C MAZARAKIS, Odos Agathoupoleos 14, Athens
Anna Mazaraki 1913 Earles 5411 9650 419.7 53–10 24–10 8.5
ex Royal City 28, ex Gerfrid 20, ex Federiko Glavic 15

A AND C MAZARAKI (manager D C and J C Mazarakis)
Elisavet 1922 Burger 3553 6625 373–10 50–4 22–7 8.5
ex Elisabeth 22

BASILE S ROSSOLIMOS, Odos Aghiou Meletiou 72, Athens
Nicolas 1910 LithR 4540 7600 385.0 52–0 23–11 8.0
ex Copenhagen 29

Note: See also Lykiardopulo & Co Ltd under Drake Shipping Co Ltd in Great Britain section

LYRAS & LEMOS BROS LTD, 9 Camomile St, London EC3

Funnel: Black with white L on blue band
Services: General tramping

Manager for
ADAMAS STEAMSHIP CO LTD, Leoforos 11 Merarchias 33, Piræus
Adamantios 1915 GrayX 4277 7652 392–0 53–6 23–1 9.5
ex Eastgate 37
Adamas 1918 Craig2 4144 7535 370.1 51–5 23–9 9.0
ex Promus 33

GALAXIAS STEAMSHIP CO LTD, Odos Notara 44, Piræus
Galaxias 1918 Rhead3 4393 8150 413–4 52–1 24–2 10.0
ex Treneglos 35

PANAGHOS CONSTANTINE AND GEORGE CONSTANTINE LEMOS, Chios
Danaos* 1906 G&G2 4419 7180 384.0 52–2 22–11 8.0
ex Kostantis Lemos 31, ex Constantinos 25, ex Strathearn 24

Note: * Sold Italy 1939, renamed *Moscardin*

MICHALINOS MARITIME & COMMERCIAL CO LTD,
Odos Philonos 37, Piræus, and c/o (London agents) Michalinos & Co Ltd, 158–164 Gresham House, 24 Old Broad St, London EC2

Funnel: Michalinos – black with red M and stylised bands above and below, all on broad white band; Tachmindji – black with white M on blue band;
Hull: Michalinos – black, red boot-topping
Services: General tramping

Manager and London agent for
MICHALINOS MARITIME & COMMERCIAL CO LTD
Anthippi N Michalos
1905 Bartm1 3298 5210 325.0 48–0 20–6 8.0
ex Cromerton 22, ex Novorossia 20
Despina 1907 Blyth 3016 5060 330.2 47–2 21.8 8.0
ex Angelis Cambitsis 34, ex De Greve 25
Nicolaos Michalos 1913 Doxfrd 4342 8600 404–0 54–1 24–0 8.5
ex Akropolis 35, ex Hermion 30
Zinovia 1906 Short2 2975 5150 336.6 47–1 21–2 8.0
ex Ulefos 20, ex Lysekloster 19, ex Andriana 16

Manager and/or agent and/or chartering agent for
NIKOS CARAVALIS, Piraeus
Okeania 1907 Steph1 4843 7990 400.0 52–0 24–7 10.0
ex Candidate 28, ex Crown of Castille 20, ex Ormiston 15

S CASTANOS & SONS (manager A S Castanos, Odos Thiras 34–36, Athens)
Germaine 1911 Conn2 5217 8515 423–4 52–4 25–6 9.5
ex Ocean Prince 35, ex Glenetive 22

DEMETRIOS E COUMBIS, XENOPHON E XENIOS AND PARTNERS
Kapetan Stratis 1906 Craggl 3574 6450 358–4 50–8 22–2 7.5
ex Helredale 29

P M Nomikos: The steamer Aspasia Nomikou *was launched on May 30 and completed at Burntisland in June 1938. She survived the war and in 1952 was sold to Japan and renamed* Ganges Maru. *A further change of name, to* Daikei Maru, *was made in 1958. She was broken up during 1965–66. She is pictured here postwar with a slight change of name to* Aspasia Nomikos *(Alex Duncan)*

Rethymnis & Kulukundis: The Sunderland-built Elias G Kulukundis, *fitted with a North Eastern Marine Engineering Co triple expansion engine of 1700ihp, was typical of the many tramp steamers which were built for Greek shipowners during the mid to late 1930s. Completed in May 1938, this vessel survived the war and in 1960 was sold to a Lebanese company and renamed* Mariannina. *In 1966 she raised the Panamanian flag as* Raffaella. *She was broken up at Split, Yugoslavia, in 1971 (Alex Duncan)*

Rethymnis & Kulukundis: Pictured here some years earlier when under British ownership and her original name as Union-Castle's Bratton Castle, *the 6696grt* Mount Taurus *was an 'N' War type standard ship built by Armstrong, Whitworth & Co on the River Tyne and completed to owner's requirements. Launched on December 8 1919, and completed in May 1920, this vessel passed to the Greek flag in 1931 as* Proteus *and one year later was renamed* Mount Taurus. *On November 17 1942 she was torpedoed and sunk by* U264 *in westbound convoy* ONS144 *while on voyage from London and Oban to Halifax NS in ballast (Alex Duncan)*

MICHAEL A TACHMINDJI, Odos Coumbari 4, Athens

Alexandros 1906 StephR 4343 7250 355.2 50–1 24–8 8.0
ex Artemissia 35, ex Hohneck 22, ex Bayhowel 21, ex King Howel 16

MICHALOS & CO LTD, C, 40 St Mary Axe, London EC3

Funnel: Angelides – black with white A
Services: General tramping

Manager and/or agent and/or chartering agent for

GEORGE ANGELIDES, Vrontados, Chios

Iacovos 1901 Neptn1 2107 3200 291.2 41–3 18.7 7.5
ex Cavalla 27, ex Bylgia 21

NICOLAOS APODIAKOS AND CHARALAMBOS N PATERAS, 40 St Mary Axe, London EC3 and Odos Philonos 37, Piræus, respectively (manager Nicolaos Apodiakos)

Victoria 1914 Rhead3 4202 7900 370.2 51–8 24–1 9.0
ex Sylvia 37, ex Trewellard 33

NICOLAOS D LAGOUTIS AND MME MARIE N LAGOUTI (manager George Angelides – *qv* above)

Georgios 1910 Krupp 2216 3500 286.3 43–1 19.6 8.0
ex Batna 35, ex Else 29, ex Dr Adolf Schmidt 21

DEMETRIUS P MARGARONIS, Odos Chephallinias 47, Athens

P Margaronis 1913 LithR 4979 8322 405.3 52–2 27.4 8.0
ex Socrates 31

CHARALAMBOS N PATERAS (master of *Lily*) **AND C MICHALOS**, Odos Philonos 37, Piræus, and 40 St Mary Axe, London EC3, respectively

Lily 1920 YokoU 5719 8579 400.0 54–6 24–8 10.0
ex Legie 33, ex Taikai Maru 20

COSTAS N AND ELIAS N PATERAS, Piræus

Nicolas Pateras 1910 Nthmb1 4362 7400 365.0 51–5 23–3 8.0
ex Pente Adelfi 35, ex Maria M Diacaki 34, ex Port de la Pallice 25, ex Bayford 20, ex Brantford 15

ELIAS N PATERAS, Chios

Aghia Eirini* 1909 McMlln 4330 8100 390–0 52–2 23–0 8.5
ex Mary N 39, ex Strathlorne 30

PITHIS BROS & CO, 5 Rue Adib, PO Box 333, Alexandria, Egypt

Under Greek flag

Adamantios J Pithis
1908 Napr&M 4537 7450 385.2 51–2 26.4 8.0
ex Baron Minto 29

PITHIS BROS & CO AND G CORAKIS (manager Pithis Bros & Co – *qv* above)

Parthenon 1908 GrayX 3189 5400 331.0 47–9 21–0 7.5
ex PLM 7 22, ex Ambatielos 17, ex Fameliaris 15

MORAITIS, N G, Odos Byron, Psychiko, Athens

Funnel: Yellow with white M on blue band
Hull: Black
Services: General tramping

Nikoklis 1921 Burger 3576 6640 372–0 50–4 22–7 9.5
ex Nikoklis Moraitis 25, ex Lingedijk 22

NEILL & PANDELIS LTD, Bevis Marks House, Bevis Marks, London EC3

Hull: Black
Services: General tramping

Under Greek flag

Marionga 1912 RDuck2 4214 7585 380.0 51–0 23–10 10.0
ex Grelstone 31, ex Eddystone 17

Note: See also in Great Britain section

NICOLAOU (HELLAS) LTD, GEORGIOS,

Defteros Orofos, Megaron Electricou Stathmou, Piræus, and c/o (London office) George Nicolaou Ltd, Bevis Marks House, 23–24 Bevis Marks, London EC3

Funnel: Yellow with blue N on white band
Hull: Grey, white band
Services: General tramping; oil and petroleum trades

Manager for

MME Z G NICOLAOU AND CHILDREN, Odos Stournara 30, Athens

General cargo vessels

Agios Georgios IV (r/t)
1938 Bartm2 4847 9150 431–0 56–6 25–1 11.0

Nicolaou Georgios 1930 GraySd 4108 7580 403–9 53–9 23–6 10.0
ex Georgios Nicolaou 37, ex Atthis 32

Nicolaou Ourania 1922 ThmpsJ 6397 9820 411.8 55–0 28–0 11.0
ex York City 37

Nicolaou Virginia 1920 Sundld 6869 8860 440–0 55–0 28–5 11.0
ex Virginia Nicolaou 37, ex Vechtdijk 33

Nicolaou Zografia 1913 Teckl 7156 11,980 470.7 60–9 26–8 9.0
ex Zografia Nicolaou 38, ex Pisco 34, ex Luxor 17

Tanker

Nicolaou Maria 1927 SHWR 5525 9275 424–0 53–6 25–9 10.5
ex Maria Nicolaou 37, ex Oilshipper 36

Manager and/or agent for
General cargo vessels

DEM PANTALÉON SONS, (P and O Pantaléon),
Megaron Electricou Stathmou, Piræus

Agios Georgios 1911 GrayX 4248 7150 377–0 50–10 23–1 10.0
ex Bonna 22, ex Hans B 15

YANNAGHAS BROTHERS, Syra

Armathia 1919 Lithgw 4575 7880 399–6 52–0 24–0 10.5
ex Tusker Rock 37, ex Kastalia 36

Funnel: Red, separated from black top by red N at centre of white cross (**X**) on green band
Services: General tramping

NOMICOS, LOUCAS, Odos Bouboulinas 31, Piræus

Flora Nomicou 1921 ArsnCh 2012 3150 281–10 39–5 19–10 8.0
ex Nicolas Jean 34, ex Député Paul Proust 22

Teti Nomicou 1902 Koch 1882 3450 281.0 40–4 18.1 7.5
ex Lakis Nomikos 38, ex Eleni 37, ex Monastir 23, ex Kythnos 18

Funnel: Black with blue Maltese cross between two narrow blue bands, all on broad white band
Hull: Black or grey
Services: General tramping; oil and petroleum trades

NOMIKOS (LONDON) LTD, 6–8 Fenchurch Bldgs, Fenchurch St, London EC3

Manager for
General cargo vessels

PETROS M NOMIKOS LTD, (Thiraiki Line),
Bank of Athens Bldg, Odos Omirou 16, Piræus

Aspasia Nomikou 1938 Burntd 4855 9366 430–0 57–0 25–3 10.5

Petros Nomikos* 1913 AwpEng 4044 7514 370.4 51–11 24–1 9.5
ex Amasis 33, ex Glenrazan 19

Manager and/or agent for

PANAGHIS S ANTIPPAS, Odos Navarinou 14, Piræus

Takis 1903 Irvin1 2759 4650 320.0 46–0 20–1 8.0
ex Anna S 39, ex Neraida 38, ex Amazon 30, ex Scarpa 22, ex Wilster 19

STYLIANOS P ANTIPPAS, Odos Navarino 14, Piræus (Panamanian flag)

Urania 1902 Neptn1 1953 3200 281.7 40–6 19–5 8.0
ex Navarchos Sachtouris 37, ex Maid of Hydra 31, ex Navarchos G Sachtouris 28, ex Lord Broughton 22, ex Patmos 20

MME URANIE ANTIPPAS, Odos Navarino 14, Piræus (Panamanian flag)

Takis 1904 Austin 1698 2600 268.2 37–10 17–11 7.5
ex Longhirst 30

EXECUTORS OF THE LATE CONSTANTINE D CALAFATIS, Odos Pinos 20, Piræus

Calafatis 1917 Uraga 4443 6880 360.0 51–0 23–0 9.5
ex *Syria 27, ex War Syren 20*

Fred 1907 GrayX 4043 7350 360.0 50–0 24–9 8.5
ex Hartington 31

EMMANUEL A KARAVIAS, Odos Kyprou 25, Athens

Marietta Nomikou
1919 Napr&M 5241 8350 412–4 52–5 25–3 10.0
ex Taransay 33, launched as War Teasel

EVANGELOS P NOMIKOS

Flora 1904 Craggl 2980 5150 330.1 46–0 21–4 7.5
ex Panaghis Vaglianos 34

Panaghiotis 1901 Prstm1 3577 6100 339.7 48–0 22–0 8.0
ex Nicolaos Athanassulis 37, ex Portugalete 12, launched as Wearfield

CONST A PETROUTSIS, Megaron Laikis, Odos Navarino 9, Piræus

Paralos 1906 Prstm1 3435 5800 332.0 49–6 21–10 7.5
ex Nicolas Pateras 35, ex Paralos 24

CONST A PETROUTSIS AND TANES BROS

Salaminia 1901 ThmpsJ 3634 6400 342.0 49–6 22–10 7.5
ex Tassos 38, ex Nicolaos 34, ex Roma 23

Tanker

MARKOS P NOMIKOS AND EVANGHELOS P NOMIKOS

Petrakis Nomikos 1914 Laing 7020 10,930 440–3 57–0 27–1 10.0
ex Apache 36, ex Belridge 35

Notes: * Sold Epirotiki Steamship Navigation Co 'George Potamianos', 1939, renamed *Georgios Potamianos*
Note: Also vessels under 2000gt

Services: General tramping

Note: * Sold Coumantaros Bros 1939, renamed *Theodoros Coumantaros*

PAPADEAS, JOHN,
Megaron Electricou Stathmou, Piræus, and Odos Didotou 28, Athens

Maleas* 1917 Kwsaki 5709 9158 385.3 51–2 27–1 9.0
ex Chef Mécanicien Mailhol 36, ex War Admiral 20

PAPADIMITRIOU, THEO, Megaron Spyraki, Piræus

Services: General tramping

Manager for
BATISTAS A SARDIS, BASIL J ANDREADAKIS, ARISTOMENI STAVRIDIS AND J CONDUMAS

Ellinico 1904 G&G2 3059 5359 331.0 48–0 20–8 9.0
ex Luchana 33

Note: Also smaller vessels

PARAMYTHIOTIS LTD, S, (Spyridon Paramythiotis), Creechurch House, 37–45 Creechurch Lane, London EC3

Services: General tramping

Manager and/or agent for
POLAR COMPAÑÍA DE NAVIERA LTDA, Panama (Panamanian flag)

Penelopi 1919 H&W,B 6559 10,400 433–10 55–8 27–7 11.0
ex Penelope 39, ex New Georgia 33, launched as War Triumph 19

Phæax 1915 Flensb 7188 11,700 470.9 60–11 26–4 10.5
ex Oldekerk 34, ex Sesostris 21

PATERAS BROS, Chios

Funnel: Black with white band and row of blue diamonds
Hull: Black
Services: General tramping
Note: Operator of *Aeus* was Rethymnis & Kulukundis Ltd (*qv*)

Aeas 1915 Irvin3 4729 8020 397–9 52–0 25–4 10.0
ex Mount Pentelikon 34, ex Gambia River 33

Aegeus 1920 McMlln 4538 8140 413–10 52–6 24–10 10.5
ex Simonside 37, ex Dalworth 35, laid down as War Stock

PITTAS BROS & CO, G N, Chios, and Odos George Skouzes 9, Piræus

Funnel: Black with red π (pi) on white disc superimposed on blue 5-pointed star on white band
Services: General tramping

Possidon 1909 GrayX 3840 6380 346.3 50–10 23.1 8.0
ex Rossano 21

ARISTIDES PITTAS AND CONSTANTINOS S SCRIVANOS

Styliani 1896 ThmpR1 3256 – 328.1 47–1 21–3 7.0
ex Patra 37, ex Orion 32, ex Hillcrag 07

Note: Also vessels under 2000gt

PORTOLO, GEORGES, Strada Misitii 4, Braila, Romania

Funnel: Black with black π (pi) on broad white band between narrow blue bands
Services: General tramping

Under Greek flag

Max Wolf 1917 RottDD 6694 9895 420.5 54–9 28–1 10.0
ex Bali 32

RETHYMNIS & KULUKUNDIS LTD, 7–8 Bury Court, London EC3 (London representative office of Kulukundis Shipping Co SA and Rethymnis & Kulukundis (Hellas) Ltd, Commercial Bank Bldg, Odos Omirou 16, Piræus)

Funnel: Coulouthros – yellow with blue cross (+) on white band between two narrow blue bands; Eustathiou – white with blue E (epsilon), black top; Kassos – yellow with blue disc; Atlanticos, Mount vessels and Kulukundis vessels – black or yellow with five-pointed red star superimposed on white over blue bands; Lemos and Theseus – black with blue L (lambda) on white diamond on blue band; Oceanos – yellow, black top
Hull: Atlanticos, Mount vessels, Kulukundis vessels, Coulouthros – black; Kassos – black with white band, red boot-topping
Services: General tramping

Manager and/or agent for
ATLANTICOS STEAMSHIP CO LTD, Odos Tritis Septemvriou 136, Athens

Atlanticos 1919 Coughl 5446 8732 427–2 54–1 24–2 11.0
ex Maryland 35, ex War Noble 20

Elias G Kulukundi 1938 Short2 5548 9880 433–6 60–6 25–11 10.5

Helene Kulukundi 1938 Short2 5548 9880 433–6 60–2 25–11 10.5

Master Elias Kulukundis 1938 Short2 5548 9880 433–6 60–6 25–11 10.5

Mount Aetna 1929 Burnt 4230 7933 385–0 51–5 24–1 10.0
ex Leith Hill 37, ex Fife 36, ex Penybryn 32

Mount Atlas* 1916 LithR 5647 9500 423.5 56–0 25–6 11.5
ex Megna 35, launched as Baron Inchcape

Mount Ida 1938 Hamtn4 4202 7775 392–8 56–2 23–9 10.5
launched as Arscott

Mount Lycabettus 1917 Dixon2 4292 7280 364.8 51–1 23–6 10.0
ex Turkestan 35, ex War Flower 19

Mount Olympus 1920 Harim1 6692 9250 425.5 54–0 25–8 10.0
ex Toba 32, launched as Nile Maru

Mount Ossa** 1919 Doxfrd 5252 10,950 427–6 55–6 25–10 11.0
ex Tower Crown 37, ex Bothwell 34, ex War Beryl 20

Mount Prionas 1910 LithR 3986 6820 360.0 49–2 23–3 10.0
ex Dunclutha 35

Mount Taurus 1920 ArmWh1 6696 10,700 428–0 55–10 28–6 10.0
ex Proteus 32, ex Bratton Castle 31

Nicolaos G Culucundis
1917 Doxfrd 3201 5596 352–8 47–1 22–0 10.0
ex Maid of Sparta 31, ex Lord Byron 28

ATLANTICOS STEAMSHIP CO LTD AND GIORGILIS BROS, Odos Tritis Septemvriou 136, Athens
Mount Mycale 1907 TyneIr 3556 5950 348.5 50–1 21–5 8.0
ex Maroussio Coulouthros 37, ex Ryde 29

J A COSMETTO AND KULUKUNDIS SHIPPING CO SA, Chamblandes-dessus, Lausanne, Switzerland, and Commercial Bank Bldg, Odos Omirou 16, Piræus
Mount Hymettus 1921 PenhtS 5821 9230 425.8 57–5 24–8 9.5
ex Union 34
Mount Myrto 1919 CanVic 5403 8444 413–1 52–5 25–4 10.0
ex Alsace II 34, ex Alsace 21
Mount Pera 1918 Cammel 5214 8020 412–8 52–5 25–3 10.0
ex Grelisle 33, ex War Painter 19

J A COULOUTHROS AND N N EMBIRICOS, Odos Georgiou Somi, 4, Athens
Nicolaos M Embiricos
1919 RDuck2 5295 8270 412–5 52–5 25–4 10.0
ex Langton Grange 37, ex Segura 35, ex War Pansy 19
Olympos 1918 Hendn2 5216 8210 412–4 52–4 25–3 10.0
ex Mount Hymettus 34, ex Greldon 32, ex War Kinsman 19
Penteli*** 1919 Caird 5287 8150 412–4 52–4 25–4 10.0
ex David Dawson 37, ex Azul 36, ex Burgondier 26, launched as War Burman
Taygetos 1918 Pgill2 4295 8052 405.0 52–4 23–10 10.0
ex Westhope 35

ELIAS G CULUCUNDIS AND STEPHEN C COSTOMENI, Odos Tritis Septemvriou 136, Athens
Mount Pelion 1917 Kwsaki 5655 8761 385.5 51–4 27–1 10.5
ex Commissaire Pierre Lecocq 33, ex War Prince 19

NICOLAS M EUSTATHIOU & CO, Proatiou Ellinikon, 1st Station, Piræus
Marietta†† 1913 Craig2 6042 9500 415.0 55–8 24–8 9.5
ex W I Radcliffe 35, ex Clarissa Radcliffe 17
Marpessa 1919 Coughl 5476 8732 427–2 54–1 24–2 11.0
ex Ontario 34, ex War Company 19
Michalakis† 1919 ThmpR2 5234 8160 412–4 52–4 25–4 10.5
ex Barracoo 33

KASSOS STEAM NAVIGATION CO LTD, Syra
Agia Marina 1912 McMlln 4151 7800 370.1 51–1 25–3 9.0
ex Australmead 24, ex Kirkoswald 16
Chelatros 1914 Nthmbl 3489 7225 360.0 52–0 23–9 8.5
ex Magdala 23
Hadiotis 1929 Nthmbl 4386 7980 410–1 53–5 24–4 9.5
Kassos††† 1919 Nthmbl 4680 9000 412–0 53–0 26–3 10.0
ex Elveric 33, ex War Capitol 19
Kassos (m) 1939 Doxfrd 5215 9500 442–11 56–6 25–10 10.5
Stavros 1925 FurnH 4853 9217 425–0 53–7 24–11 10.0
ex Kingston Hill 37, ex Ashleigh 36
Themoni 1938 Doxfrd 5719 10,000 447–9 57–6 25–11 11.0

KASSOS STEAM NAVIGATION CO LTD SA ‡, Syra
Nitsa 1915 Irvin3 4732 8012 385.0 52–0 24–4 10.0
ex Sagama River 33

KULUKUNDIS SHIPPING CO SA, Commercial Bank Bldg, Odos Omirou 16, Piræus
Mount Cynthos¶ 1918 Workmn 5188 8380 412–4 52–4 25–4 10.5
ex Zeriba 33, ex Villa Ada 27, ex Fratelli Bianchi 24, ex War Leopard 19
Mount Dirfys¶¶ 1924 H&W,B 6651 10,000 412.6 55–8 28–3 10.5
ex Invergarry 37; conv tanker 37
Mount Helikon 1918 OsakaO 5525 8890 407.3 51–1 26–1 11.0
ex Jagersfontein 32, ex Kaiyei Maru 20
Mount Helmos 1923 BrownJ 6481 10,175 412.9 55–8 25–4 10.5
ex Invergordon 37; conv tanker 37
Mount Kassion (s2)
1918 Uraga 7914 11,743 461–8 58–0 28–1 11.0
ex Docteur Pierre Benoit 37
Mount Kitheron 1912 Rhead3 3876 7075 367.3 53–11 22–1 9.5
ex Bellglade 32, ex Chevington 19
Mount Parnassus• 1921 WallSB 5334 8390 413–0 52–2 25–3 10.0
ex Canadian Scottish 37
Mount Parnes 1917 Moorel 4371 7200 376.2 52–8 22–8 10.0
ex American Eagle 37, ex Thekla 33, ex Hampholm 29, ex Thordis 25
Mount Pentelikon••
1917 RDuck2 5896 8875 400.3 51–8 24–9 10.5
ex Illinois 34, ex Farnworth 24

Mount Pindus 1920 ThmpsJ 5729 8830 400.2 54–10 24–9 10.5
ex Zinal 37

KULUKUNDIS SHIPPING CO SA AND CONSTANTINE SCARVELIS,
Commercial Bank Bldg, Odos Omirou 16, Piræus, and Kardamyla, Chios, respectively

Mount Athos 1913 ThmpR2 3578 6458 350.0 50–0 22–4 9.5
ex Pentowy 32, ex Iossifoglu 23

Mount Ithome 1914 Rhead2 4207 7748 369.9 51–1 24–2 9.0
ex Maidenhead 36, ex Newquay 24

LEMOS BROTHERS AND THESEUS STEAMSHIP CO LTD,
Oinoussai, Chios, and Odos Tritis Septemvriou 151, Athens

Taxiarchis 1913 RDuck2 4221 7585 380.0 51–0 23–8 9.5
ex Grelcaldy 31, ex Caldy 17

SIMON AND CONST M LOS AND E C ANDREADIS, Chios

Delphin 1906 Bartm1 3816 6225 346.5 50–10 21–5 8.0
ex Amersham 29, ex Rochdale 24

MARCOS N & P G LYRAS & CO, Psychiko, Athens

Lyras 1918 Nthmb1 5685 7920 413–0 53–0 26–3 10.0
ex Avon Bridge 37, ex Alma Dawson 35, ex Bradclyde 34, ex War Castle 19

EMMANUEL MARCOU, Syra (Panamanian flag)

Mount Othrys 1919 H&W,B 6509 9350 412.6 55–10 25–7 11.0
ex Newton 33, launched as War Justice

OCEANOS MARITIME STEAMSHIP CO (ISIDOROS, ANASTASSIOS AND GEORGE MARGARONIS), Commercial Bank Bldg, Odos Omirou 16, Piræus

Mount Rhodope 1919 Irvin3 5182 8175 415–0 52–4 25–4 10.0
ex Boutry 34, launched as War Gull

Nellie 1913 ThmpsJ 4826 8883 388.7 54–1 25–6 9.0
ex Tideway 33, ex Vologda 23, ex Mottisfont 16

Pandias 1912 Hendn2 4981 8277 403.5 52–2 24–4 9.0
ex Louis L-D 31, ex Port D'Alger 21, ex Baygola 16, ex Angola 12

ANTONIOS ROUSSOS AND TRAMP SHIPPING DEVELOPMENT CO LTD,
Syra, and Holland House, 1–4 Bury St, London EC3, respectively

Elena R 1917 NNews 4576 7400 385–0 53–2 24–2 10.0
ex Munindies 37

XILAS BROTHERS, Chios

Michalios 1908 Neptn1 3742 6415 351.8 50–2 23–7 9.0
ex Julia 35, ex Nordsee 26, ex Estremadura 25, ex Santa Ursula 16

XILAS BROTHERS AND A CONSTANTINIDIS

Thalia 1917 Kwsaki 5875 8073 385.3 51–2 27–1 10.0
ex Jebba 33, ex War Lion 19

Notes: * Sold Japan 1939, renamed *Kuwayama Maru*; ** sold Germany 1939, renamed *Robert Bornhofen*; *** sold Great Britain 1939, renamed *Brockley Hill*; † sold Japan 1939, renamed *Kusuyama Maru*; †† sold Germany 1939, renamed *Karl Leonhardt*; ††† sold L Fatsis (manager A Lusi Ltd) 1939, renamed *Michalis*; ¶ sold Japan 1939, renamed *Momoyama Maru*; ¶¶ sold Netherlands 1939, renamed *Stad Maastricht*; •, ••, sold Germany 1939, renamed *Johann Schulte*, *Gloria* respectively
Note: See also under D Inglessi Fils SA, Pateras Bros, and in Egypt section
Note: ‡ See under Yannaghas Bros

SIGALIS' SONS, GEORGE, (Alexander and Nomikos Sigalis),
Odos Bouboulinas 56, Piræus

Funnel: Black with red cross (+) on blue diamond on broad white band between narrow blue bands
Services: General tramping
Note: Also *Ais Giorgis* (built 1908/2098gt), *Kadio* (11/1430), *Teti* (03/2747), *Popi S* (04/2083)

MME KADIO G SIGALAS

Tassia 1904 Irvin1 3034 5250 325.0 47–1 21–0 8.5
ex Majestic 38

SOCIÉTÉ ANONYME HELLENIQUE MARITIME TRANSPETROL,
Megaron Linardou, Odos Patission 32, Athens

Trades: Oil and petroleum

Tankers

Atlas 1909 Craggl 4009 6400 345.0 48–1 23–7 7.5
ex Irini 35, ex Conrad Mohr 30

Petroil 1903 G&G2 4634 6775 379–1 50–1 25–2 7.0
ex Queen Maeve 31, ex Oswego 24, ex Gargoyle 21, ex Pennoil 14

Note: Also smaller tankers

SOCIÉTÉ COMMERCIALE ET D'ARMEMENT SA,
Commercial Bank Bldg, Odos Omirou 16, Piræus

Hull: Black
Services: General tramping

Boris 1917 Hendn2 5166 8050 412–8 52–4 25–3 10.5
ex Menapier 33, ex War Heather 19

Mimosa 1905 Craggl 3071 5380 330.1 47–0 21–0 8.0
ex Michael 33, ex Kirnwood 22

Nadin 1904 GrayX 3582 6080 340.0 48–1 22–8 8.0
ex Nadine 34, ex Dragon 32, ex Eastwood 27

Note: This company was controlled by A Vlasov (*qv* under Navigation & Coal trade Co Ltd in Romania section)

Funnel: Black with houseflag – blue S on white square superimposed on white cross (+) on blue ground
Services: General tramping

STATHATOS & CO LTD, Palmerston House, 51 Bishopsgate, London EC2

Manager/agent for

MME BASILIKI E BENIERAKI AND C G MOUSOURAS, Aghiou Andreou 16, Patras

Kostis*	1919	H&WGk	5253	8000	412–4	52–4	25–3	10.5
ex Bathurst 33								

ANASTASE DENIS CALLINICOS, Odos Goura 10, Athens

Neion	1918	SHWR	5154	8200	412–6	52–0	25–3	10.5
ex Mont Genèvre 34, ex Mount Berwyn 25, ex War Puma 19								

DEMETRIOS DENYS STATHATOS, ANTHONY D STATHATOS AND OTHERS, Odos Korais 1, Athens

Ann Stathatos	1918	Pgill2	5685	8750	417–5	52–4	25–8	10.5
ex Persian Prince 33								
Antonios Stathatos**	1920	Duncan	3836	6750	364.9	51–6	22–0	9.0
Dionyssios Stathatos	1919	Cammel	5168	8150	412–8	52–5	25–3	10.5
launched as War Cadet								
Eleni Stathatos	1919	Nthmbl	5625	9000	412–4	53–0	26–3	10.5
ex Seapharer 38, ex Lancaster Castle 36, launched as War Terrace								

GER N AND DEMETRIOS DENYS STATHATOS, Odos Pattision 54, Athens

Maria Stathatou	1922	Ropnr3	6303	9660	411–7	54–6	27–9	9.5
ex Welsh City 38								
Nemea	1919	Conn2	5101	8150	413–0	52–2	25–4	10.0
ex Silarus 31								

Note: * Sold P D Pateras (Lemos & Pateras Ltd) 1939, renamed *Diamantis*; ** sold Latvia 1939, renamed *Everasma*

Services: General tramping

TACHMINDJI, JOHN A, Odos Stadiou 16, Athens

Asteria	1904	Prstm1	3313	6000	336.5	46–6	24–0	7.5
ex Despina Glypti 35, ex Despina 28, ex Sildra 22								

Funnel: Yellow, black top
Services: General tramping

TERYAZOS, THEODORE L, Odos Philonos 39A, Piræus

Aikaterini T	1917	Forth	2560	4444	305.3	42–9	21.5	9.0
ex Nantes 34								
Anna T	1906	Blyth	2728	4580	313.0	45–6	19–9	8.0
ex Sf Nicolae 35, ex Auratan 34, ex Blairholm 33, ex Korsholm 22, ex San Giacomo 21, ex Alexander Kamburoff 20								
Eleni T	1897	LithR	3039	5650	324.6	48–0	20–9	7.0
ex Plateai 32, ex Platea 28								
Leontios Teryazos	1911	LithR	4479	7940	400.0	51–11	24–6	9.0
ex Tarantia 37, ex Kirkfield 16								
Theodoros T	1912	Pgill2	3409	5950	331.0	48–2	21–9	8.5
ex Eskbridge 34								

Note: Also vessels under 2000gt

Services: General tramping

TRICOGLU, E M, Andros

Nikos T	1919	VickB2	5175	8170	415–1	52–5	25–3	10.5
ex Sutherland 34, ex Gasconier 26, launched as War Ruler								
Vassilios T	1920	Nitta	3673	5544	315.9	45–10	26.3	10.0
ex Eastern Temple 38								

Funnel: Black
Hull: Black, red boot-topping
Services: General tramping; oil and petroleum trades

UNION MARITIME & SHIPPING CO LTD, 9–13 Fenchurch Bldgs, Fenchurch St, London EC3

Manager and/or agent for

General cargo vessel

JOHN N VASSILIOU AND COUMANTAROS BROS, 9–13 Fenchurch Bldgs, Fenchurch St, London EC3 and Odos Athens-Piræus, Piræus, respectively Panaghiotis Th Coumantaros

	1912	Hamtn2	5839	9290	424.4	53–0	26–4	10.5
ex Dryden 33, laid down as Bolton Castle								

Tankers

COMPAÑÍA MARITIMA ATLANTICA LTDA, Panama (Panamanian flag)

Loida	1916	Craig2	5505	8300	383–10	51–5	28–4	9.0
ex Lampas 39, ex Laurelleaf 22								

COMPAÑÍA MARITIMA ISTMENIA LTDA, Panama (Panamanian flag)

Myriam	1920	Laing	7012	11,107	440–3	57–1	27–1	10.0
ex Nikitas Roussos 35, ex Myriam 34								
Panam	1925	LivCpr	7277	11,057	438.7	57–3	27–10	9.5
ex Otokia 37								

VASSILIADES, MICHAEL V, Chios

Funnel: Yellow, black top, with yellow over blue, white, red, white bands
Services: General tramping

Under Panamanian flag

Ronin	1919	Nthmb1	5704	9000	412–0	53–0	26–3	10.5
ex Huntress 39, ex Tower Ensign 37, ex Waikawa 35, launched as War Donjon								

VERGOTTIS LTD, 9 Camomile St, London EC3

Funnel: Yellow with red B on white square, narrow black top
Hull: Black
Services: General tramping

Manager and/or agent for

AEGEON STEAMSHIP CO LTD, Odos Notara 53, Piræus

Aegeon	1919	Napr&M	5285	8350	412–4	52–4	25–0	10.5
ex Knockfierna 35, launched as War Poppy								
Icarion	1912	Nthmb1	4013	7500	375.1	51–4	23–5	8.0
ex Pontos 36, ex Geddington Court 27								
Spyros	1918	Doxfrd	6629	10,850	420.0	54–0	28–4	10.5
ex Balgowan 34, ex Admiral Codrington 27								

IONIAN STEAMSHIP CO LTD, Odos Notara 53, Piræus

Andreas	1919	H&W,B	6566	10,660	427–10	55–10	28–4	11.0
ex New Mexico 33, launched as Philadelphian								
Rokos	1918	SHWR	6426	10,750	428–0	55–10	28–2	11.0
ex Banbury Castle 31, ex Glenstrae 20, ex War Climax 19								

MARKETTOS STEAMSHIP CO LTD, Odos Coumbari 2, Athens

Christos Markettos	1919	Taikoo	5209	8202	412–6	52–4	25–3	10.5
ex Queen Maud 36, ex Evangelos 24, launched as War Driver								

MYRTOON STEAMSHIP CO LTD, Odos Notara 53, Piræus

Tasis	1913	Irvin3	4706	8014	385.0	52–1	24–6	10.5
ex Manchester Civilian 33								

ANDREAS CH VERGOTTIS, Argostoli, Cephalonia

Emmy	1914	Dixon2	3895	7200	373–0	52–4	23–1	10.0
ex Tsiropinas 37, ex Wolverton 23								
Memas	1900	Napr&M	4359	6975	375.2	50–1	23–6	9.0
ex Achilles 23, ex Lord Erne 19								

Note: See also in Great Britain section

VERGOTTIS LTD, ADELPHI, 40 St Mary Axe, London EC3

Funnel: Yellow with black top separated by yellow over blue bands, white cross and red B in centre on blue band
Hull: Black, red boot-topping
Services: General tramping

EPTANISOS STEAMSHIP CO LTD, Odos Pesmazoglu 8, Athens

Kalypso Vergotti	1918	McMlln	5686	7900	412–4	52–4	25–4	10.5
ex War Server 19								
Rokos Vergottis	1919	Doxfrd	5637	8100	412–8	52–5	25–4	10.5
launched as War Begonia								

POSSIDON STEAMSHIP & TRADING CO LTD, Odos Pesmazoglu 8, Athens

Gerassimos Vergottis	1920	Craig2	6343	9875	412.2	55–0	27–9	10.0
ex Paris City 38								

VINTIADIS, EMMANUEL N, Greece, and Via Ponte Reale 2/37, Genoa, Italy

Services: General tramping

Under Panamanian flag

Anna Marcou (st)	1919	Bretgn	2486	3740	301–6	43–7	20–0	9.0
ex Tourliani 39, ex Marne 36								

VLASSOPOULOS, ELEFTHERIOS K, Odos Ferron 4, Athens

Services: General tramping

Makis	1906	Prstm1	3546	6000	340.0	48–0	23–2	7.5
ex Yorkmead 22, ex Fife 20, ex Clivegrove 19								

Note: Also smaller vessels

XENIOS, ELIAS, AND CHRISTOFORIDIS BROTHERS, Chios

Services: General tramping

Omonia	1908	ThmpsJ	3699	6134	346.5	50–10	21–5	7.5
ex Keyingham 33								

Services: General tramping

XYDIA, MICHAEL C, 1 Rue Mosqée Attarine, Alexandria, Egypt

Note: * Sold Palestine 1939, renamed *Haifa Trader*

Manager for
BASILE I SAPOVALOU (master of *Tregothnan*) (Greek flag)
Tregothnan* 1903 Rhead2 3074 5325 322–11 47–1 23.7 7.5

Services: Tramping, mainly in China Seas/Far East

YANNOULATOS BROTHERS (CHINA),
55 Yuen Ming Road, Shanghai, China, and Odos Pindarou 32, Athens

Note: * Managed by China Hellenic Line Ltd
Note: These companies also owned and managed several vessels under 2000gt

Under Greek flag
Hellenic City 1917 GLakeA 2486 4150 261–10 43–6 23–8 9.0
ex Win On 39, ex Lake George 37, laid down as Perregaux
Hellenic Trader 1907 NNews 2052 3508 295–9 43–1 17.3 8.0
ex Catherine G Sudden 39, ex Thorbjörg 22, ex George W Fenwick 16
Maro Y (m2) 1924 Odense 3549 – 360.5 51–0 21.5 9.0
ex Hellenic Pioneer 39, ex Gisla 38
IOANNIS K SCARLATIDIS* (Greek flag)
Erato 1918 Napr&M 5904 9148 419.6 54–6 25–4 10.0
ex China Exporter 38, ex Cowden Law 33, ex Scottish Monarch 24
Valentini 1909 LithR 4713 8200 405.0 52–0 25–5 10.5
ex China Importer 38, ex Mineric 33
GERASIMOS M STAMETELATOS* (Greek flag)
Karavados 1913 Crown2 2325 3400 290.0 40–10 18–2 8.0
ex Dah Loh 37, ex Llantwit Major 33, ex Rubens 23, ex Slav 21
Pipina 1904 ArmWh1 2709 4300 318.0 43–9 21–9 7.5
ex Dah Sun 38, ex Pentusker 35, ex Conway 29
IOANNIS D TSOUNIAS* (Greek flag)
Panaghis 1894 VickB4 2744 3848 312.0 40–3 23–0 7.0
ex Chang Teh 38, ex Tung-Tuck 37, ex Ceduna 25, ex Clan Mackay 14

Services: General tramping

YANNOULATOS' SONS, ANT G, Megaron Yannoulatou, Piræus

PANAGHIS ANT YANNOULATOS, Piræus
Odysseus 1913 Short2 4575 7912 405–6 52–0 23–10 9.5
ex Ellin 36

Hungary

Services: General tramping

ANGOL MAGYAR HAJÓZÁSI RÉSZVÉNYTÁRSASÁG, (Anglo-Hungarian Shipping Co Ltd), Otthon utca 10, Budapest

Note: These vessels were managed by Giuseppe Bartha, Via Felice Venezian 1/1, CP 214, Trieste, Italy

Csarda 1917 ThmpR2 3872 6320 371–1 50–0 21–5 8.5
ex Vinocean 31, ex Leominster 29, ex Capelcastle 19
Csikós 1913 ThmpsJ 3938 7670 393–10 53–0 23–2 9.0
ex North Pacific 34

Services: General tramping

MAGYAR HAJÓZÁSI RÉSZVÉNYTÁRSASÁG, (Hungarian Navigation Co Ltd)
Széll Kálmán tér 22, Budapest

Note: This vessel was managed by Felix Brózik

Szent Gellért 1916 BethSP 3379 5810 333.5 48–3 22–8 10.0
ex Munrio 37

Services: General tramping

NEPTUN SEA NAVIGATION CO LTD, Nador-utca 24, Budapest

Note: This company, managed by B Burger, was associated with Société Anonyme Maritime et Commerciale (*qv* in Switzerland section)

Kelet 1913 Rhead3 4295 7780 382–0 51–1 24–1 9.0
ex Tregarthen 33
Nyugat 1912 Rhead3 4323 7780 382–0 51–1 24–1 9.0
ex Treglisson 34
SOCIÉTÉ ANONYME MARITIME ET COMMERCIALE,
66 Rue du Stand, Geneva, Switzerland
Under Hungarian flag
Turul 1916 GLakeE 2478 4100 261–10 43–6 24–1 9.0
ex Warta 35, ex PLM 5 24

Italy

ADRIATICA, SOCIETÀ ANONIMA DI NAVIGAZIONE,
Zattere 1411, Venice, and Via Cadorna 11, Trieste

Funnel: Yellow with bronze 'lion' emblem, red over white bands below narrow black top
Hull: White, green boot-topping, or black, red boot-topping
Services: Venice, Trieste–Red Sea ports; Trieste, Venice–Alexandria–E Mediterranean ports

Passenger/general cargo vessels

Esperia (s2,P205/1,118/2,56/3,100/st)								
	1920	Tirrl	11,398	2854	527–11	61–11	23–7	18.0
Galilea (s2,P148/1,47/2)								
	1918	CRDA3	8040	5845	443–8	53–2	25–11	13.5
ex Pilsna 35								
Gerusalemme (st2,P148/1,47/2)								
	1920	CRDA3	8052	5530	443–8	53–2	25–3	13.5
ex Cracovia 34								
Marco Polo (s2,P236/1,80/2,108/3)								
	1912	CRDA1	12,272	6445	500–0	62–2	29–0	16.0
ex Gange 36, ex Presidente Wilson 30, ex Kaiser Franz Josef 19								
Palestina (s2,Pc800)	1916	CRDA3	7039	5737	411–1	53–2	26–0	12.0
ex Amazzonia 35, ex Aquileia 33, ex Innsbruck 21								

Note: This company, controlled by Finmare Società Finanziaria Marittima, Rome, also owned smaller vessels

ARCITI, RODRIGO,
c/o Farina, Galliano, Raineri & Co, 11–12 Bury St, London EC3

Trades: Oil and petroleum

Under Panamanian flag
Tanker

Cesteriano	1919	SunSB	6664	11,259	445–5	59–3	26–8	9.5
ex Sunbeam 39								

ARRIVABENE, SOCIETÀ ANONIMA TRASPORTI MARITTIME E FLUVIALE, LEONARDO, Palazzo Papadopoli S Silvestro 1364, Venice

Funnel: Black
Hull: Black
Trades: Oil and petroleum

Tanker

C Arrivabene	1909	SHWR	5061	7700	399–0	51–10	25–2	9.5
ex Ranvik 38, ex British Knight 29, ex Danubian 18								

Note: Manager of this vessel was L Salom

AVE, SOCIETÀ ANONIMA DI NAVIGAZIONE, Via Feschi 3, Genoa

Services: Mainly Mediterranean ports–NW Europe

Eridano	1912	ThmpR2	3586	6450	362–8	50–11	21–4	10.0
ex Risano 31, ex Zvir 24, ex Monviso 21, ex Zvir 15								
Tebro	1928	FurnH	4310	7570	374–4	52–2	24–1	9.0
ex Levenbridge 34								

AZIENDA GENERALE ITALIANA PETROLI (AGIP),
Via del Tritone 181, Rome, and Via Petraria 2/7, Genoa

Funnel: White with AGIP in black circled white disc superimposed on green over white over red bands, black top
Hull: Black with white band, red boot-topping
Trades: Oil and petroleum

Tankers

Franco Martelli (m)	1939	CNR4	10,535	14,500	524–0	68–4	29–0	13.0
Giulio Giordani (m)	1939	AnsSA	10,533	14,500	524–0	68–4	29–0	13.0
Iridio Mantovani (m)								
	1939	CRDA2	10,539	14,500	524–0	68–6	29–0	13.0
Rapallo	1922	Tirrl	5812	8500	394–9	52–0	27.3	11.0
Recco	1921	Tirrl	5595	8500	394–3	52–0	27.2	11.0

BARBAGELATA, DITTA G M, Salita Santa Caterina 10/10, Genoa

Funnel: Grey with black top, separated by white over black bands
Trades: Oil and petroleum

Tankers

Americano	1903	Palmer	7008	9800	435–1	54–8	27–3	10.0
ex Chinampa 24, ex Cushing 18, ex Prometheus 14								
Genoano	1914	Leslie	6067	10,000	433–6	54–8	26–10	10.0
ex Oyleric 37, ex Barneson 15								

Note: Also smaller tankers

BERTORELLO, FEBO AMEDEO, FU GIACOMO,
Via N Barabino 27/7, Genoa-Sampierdarena

Funnel: Red, black top
Services: General tramping

Volodda	1915	ThmpsJ	4673	7900	414–10	53–0	24–4	10.0
ex Delphoi 39, ex Foyle 34								

CINC: The steamer Amba Alagi *was completed in 1910 for FC Strick & Co as* Boukadra. *She was sold in 1929 and renamed* Yarrowdale, *and again in 1935 and renamed* Sung Shan *under the Chinese flag. With the Japanese invasion of central China after August 1937, the shipping business was thrown into turmoil and measures were taken by many shipowners to prevent their vessels falling into Japanese hands.* Sung Shan *was one of many re-registered under the Italian flag, with Italian master and officers, and which through complicated beneficial ownership arrangements was able to continue trading in the East for the benefit of her former Chinese owner. As* Amba Alagi *she was requisitioned by the Japanese on December 20 1941 and allocated for management to Teikoku Sempaku KK, being renamed* Aoki Maru. *On November 13 1944 she was bombed and sunk off Manila Bay (RW Jordan collection)*

Cia Genovese: Capo Vado *was completed for British owners in 1906. She was found in a four-ship convoy by the British cruisers* Ajax, Orion *and* Sydney *under Vice-Admiral Pridham-Wippell during the night on November 12 1940 in the Strait of Otranto, proceeding from Valona to Brindisi. They were escorted by the auxiliary cruiser* Ramb III *and torpedo boat* Fabrizi. *The four merchant vessels were shelled and sunk about 12 miles off Saseno, and the two escorts managed to escape (Alex Duncan)*

Italia: Conte di Savoia *was completed in January 1932 for the Genoa–New York service of Italia. She had been ordered by Lloyd Sabaudo. She made her best transatlantic passage with an average speed of 27.53 knots. In June 1940 she was in Italy, and on September 11 1943 was bombed by British aircraft off Alberoni when she had houses and trees painted on her side as camouflage.* Conte di Savoia *sank in shallow water. On October 16 1945 she was refloated and taken to Venice. In November 1946 was reported to be refitted for the Italy–South America emigrant service. This did not materialise, however, as the estimated £8 million reconditioning cost was considered to be too high. In 1949 she was sold at auction and broken up the following year at Monfalcone (Alex Duncan)*

BIBOLINI, GIOVANNI B, Piazza Corvetto 2/5, Genoa

Funnel: Black with white B below white band
Hull: Black
Services: General tramping
Note: Also vessels under 2000gt

Marigola	1906	Denny1	5996	9190	438–9	54–5	27–4	9.0
ex Colaba 25								
Pugliola	1917	Dtroit	2074	3095	261–4	44–1	17–9	9.0
ex Argia 28, ex Ninfa 27, ex War Major 18								
Tellaro	1920	Tirr1	2234	3000	263–3	39–5	18–0	10.0
ex Gabriello 32, ex Gabriello Carnazza 30, ex Deiva 27								

BOZZO, FARUFFINI & ROLLO, Vico Giannini 2–4, Genoa

Services: General tramping

SOCIETÀ ANONIMA DI NAVIGAZIONE LA CAMOGLIESE

Vittorio Veneto	1918	CanVic	4595	7190	393–6	49–4	24–5	10.5
ex War Joy 19								

BOZZO FU LORENZO, GIUSEPPE,
Palazzo Penco, Piazza Cinque Lampardi 14/36, Genoa

Funnel: Black with white band
Services: General tramping

Antonietta	1901	Napr&M	4423	6946	398–11	48–9	24–4	11.0
ex Atholl 29								

GIUSEPPE E FILIPPO FRATELLI BOZZO FU LORENZO

Beppe	1912	McMlln	4859	8055	414–2	52–1	22–4	10.0
ex Kingarth 32, ex Berwyn 28, ex Mattawa 23, ex Franktor 15, ex Saint Hugo 15								
Madda	1919	Cammel	5181	7945	413–5	52–5	25–2	10.0
ex Bogota 32, launched as War Lapwing								

CAMELI, CARLO, Piazza Portello 6, Genoa

Funnel: White with blue and yellow houseflag as band, separated from black top by narrow white band
Trades: Oil and petroleum
Note: Also smaller tankers

Tanker

Antonia C	1921	BethSP	6025	8272	427–9	53–4	24–7	9.5
ex Gundine 39, ex Emile Deutsch de la Meurthe 30								

CAMPANELLA, SOCIETÀ DI NAVIGAZIONE TITO,
Via Garibaldi 12, Genoa

Funnel: Yellow separated from black top by yellow over black bands
Services: General tramping; oil and petroleum trades

General cargo vessels

Mira	1908	Conn2	3615	5450	363–0	46–0	23–0	9.5
ex Gabon 35, ex Milanese 32, ex Merchant 29								
Pietro Campanella	1906	Curle	6140	9530	439–0	54–5	27–4	10.5
ex Chanda 25								

Tankers

Clelia Campanella (s2)								
	1917	Baltmr	3245	5040	306–0	47–2	23–0	9.0
ex Oilvigor 31, ex Oilvigore 28, ex Holden Evans 27; conv mv 27								
Lina Campanella	1893	Palmer	3356	5239	337–2	42–9	24–3	9.0
ex Aras 30								

CAPPIELLO, SALVATORE, Via delle Fontane 10, Genoa

Services: General tramping

PAN-EUROPEAN NAVIGATION, Panama (Panamanian flag)

Mayan	1919	Toledo	2571	4200	261–0	43–9	24–5	9.0
ex Lake Festus 29								

CHIARELLA, GIUSEPPE, Via Banchi 3, Genoa

Funnel: Black with broad blue band between two narrow white bands
Hull: Black
Trades: Oil and petroleum

PETROLEUM SOCIETÀ ANONIMA DI NAVIGAZIONE

Tankers

Alabama	1903	Palmer	6725	9700	442–2	54–9	27–3	11.0
ex Ashtabula 30, ex Graf Stroganoff 06								
Colorado	1911	NNews	5039	7250	386–2	52–1	29.5	10.0
ex Wm F Herrin 28								
Frisco	1906	NNews	4609	6500	395–4	49–8	23–11	10.0
ex W S Porter 25								

Hull: Black
Services: Far East, mainly China Seas
Note: Also several vessels under 3000gt and river boats

COMPAGNIA ITALIANA DI NAVIGAZIONE S A I, (Chinese Italian Navigation Co Ltd), 93 and 163 Canton Road, Shanghai, China

Under Italian flag (vessels registered Shanghai)

Amba Alaga	1910	GrayX	3710	6150	365–0	50–1	21–5	9.5
ex Sung Shan 38, ex Yarrowdale 35, ex Boukadra 29								
Granatiere Padula	1909	Blyth	3904	6050	365–6	50–0	21–8	9.5
ex Hua Shan 38, ex Werribee 33								
Pluto	1914	Reiher	3832	5900	361.2	50–4	22–8	10.0
ex Founder 38, ex Medea 37, ex Doris 25, ex Arnold Waregga 20								

Trades: Oil and petroleum

COMPAGNIA ITALIANA MARITTIMA (CIMAR), Via Sistina 30, Rome, and Campo Sant' Angelo 3555, Venice

Tankers

Burano	1901	ArmWh1	4450	7025	373–4	49–8	24–1	9.0
ex Irma Schindler 36, ex Masconomo 31, ex Winnebago 12, ex Kinsman 05								
Marangona	1914	FrerJ	5357	7065	402–1	51–9	24–5	10.0
ex Queen Tailte 31, ex Westwego 21, ex Steaua Romana 15								
Todaro	1913	HwldtK	5162	7820	398–10	52–5	24–0	9.0
ex Lotte Leonhardt 35, ex Jules Cambon 30, ex Bayway 25, ex Mohawk 14								
Trottiera	1901	ArmWh1	6205	8825	436–11	52–0	26–4	9.0
ex Tankschindler 31, ex British Earl 29, ex Pinna 17								

Funnel: Black with five-pointed white star on orange band between two narrow white bands
Hull: Black
Services: Tramping

COMPAGNIA ITALIANA TRASPORTI MARITTIMI SOCIETÀ ANONIMA, Campetto 1, Genoa

Gianfranco	1915	Bremer	8181	11,910	493–2	60–9	27–10	10.0
ex Ouderkerk 34, ex Orsino 22, ex Gera 18								

Trades: Oil and petroleum

COMPAGNIA ITALIANA TRASPORTO OLII MINERALI (CITOM), Palazzo Nuova Borsa 145, Genoa

Tankers

Annarella (m2)	1913	Krupp	5999	8865	417–8	53–2	26–9	9.0
ex Loki 27								
Gianna M	1913	Reiher	5719	8400	420–0	52–9	23–0	9.0
ex Wotan 27; conv mv 27								
Giorgio	1907	NNews	4887	7350	400–8	49–11	23–2	8.0
ex Sun 26								

Funnel: Yellow, black top, separated by diagonally quartered band with white upper and lower and blue left and right
Hull: Black
Services: Genoa–Mediterranean ports; Genoa–Red Sea ports–India–Ceylon

COMPAGNIA LIGURE DI NAVIGAZIONE, Via XX Settembre 2, Genoa

Passenger/general cargo vessels								
San Giovanni Battista (P114)	1913	Hendn2	5628	6910	415–0	52–2	25–9	12.0
ex Ingoma 37								
Santa Maria (P39)	1914	Earles	3539	5207	337–8	42–5	24–0	10.0
ex Malatian 37								
General cargo vessels								
San Leonardo	1907	ArmWh1	4656	8616	400.0	52–1	26–3	10.0
ex Lulca 39, ex Kabinga 38								
Santa Paola	1913	Rhead3	4262	6650	371–5	50–5	23–10	10.0
ex Giovanni Galli 39, ex Nicole Schiaffino 37, ex Speaker 26, ex Savan 20								

Services: General tramping
Note: * Sold Ruggiero & Merega 1939, renamed *Santa Rita*

COMPAGNIA VENEZIANA DI NAVIGAZIONE, Campo Sant' Angelo 3555, Venice

Veniero*	1908	CNR4	5191	8150	382.1	50–9	26–9	8.0
ex Panormus 39, ex Bohéme 37, ex Veniero 31, ex Monginevro 12								

Funnel: Black with red C on white band
Hull: Black, red boot-topping
Services: General tramping; oil and petroleum trades

'CORRADO', SOCIETÀ ANONIMA DI NAVIGAZIONE, Salita S Nicolosio 1-10, Genoa

General cargo vessels

Albisola	1927	Burntd	4097	7936	381–0	51–6	24–3	10.0
ex Pentor 34								

Andrea	1921	Nthmb1	5151	8000	387–9	51–4	25–2	9.0
ex Germaine L-D 32, ex Eastney 24								
Buccari	1925	Lithgw	4543	7850	397–6	52–0	24–0	10.0
ex Lawbeath 33								
Caterina Madre	1904	RDuck1	4020	7100	365–2	48–9	24–7	7.0
ex Valnoce 27, ex Iddesleigh 23								
Confidenza (st)	1920	FurnH	6458	10,500	426–9	55–7	28–3	9.5
ex Ulisse 29, ex Robilante 23, launched as War Project								
Dante	1914	Bartm2	4901	8000	402–5	50–6	24–9	10.0
ex Cambrian Princess 32, ex Glenearn 20, ex Sperrbrecher 11 18, ex Glatz 17, ex Glenearn 17, launched as Salopian								
Dino	1920	Nthmb1	5592	8825	413–6	53–0	26–3	10.0
ex Hendonhall 32, ex Montes 27, ex Sierra Belgrano 23, ex Condor 20, laid down as War Bailey								
Hermada	1907	Hamtn2	4421	7200	385–5	52–2	22–11	9.0
ex Carventum 23, ex Strathness 16								
Ines Corrado	1918	ArmWh1	5159	8075	412–9	52–5	25–3	10.0
ex River Tigris 31, ex Vellavia 25, ex War Setter 19								
Pollenzo (st)	1920	FurnH	6470	10,500	428–0	55–8	28–3	9.5
launched as War Relief								
Premuda	1907	Hamtn2	4427	7250	385–5	52–4	22–11	9.0
ex Tusculum 23, ex Strathdon 16								
Rina Corrado	1918	H&W,B	5180	8100	413–1	52–4	25–1	11.0
ex River Delaware 31, ex Venusia 23, ex War Snake 18								
Valdarno	1919	Coughl	5696	8750	427–0	54–1	24–2	10.5
ex Attività 31, ex War Column 20								
Valentino Coda	1924	Lithgw	4486	7850	397–6	52–0	24–0	10.0
ex Bellailsa 34								
Zeffiro	1918	Caledn	5165	8100	413–2	52–4	25–1	11.0
ex River Hudson 31, ex Vennonia 23, ex War Carp 19								
Tankers								
Bacicin Padre	1918	Laing	5591	8585	410–1	52–5	25–7	10.0
ex Scottish Bard 30, ex War Pundit 20								
Cesco	1917	Leslie	6138	9990	432–8	54–8	26–11	10.0
ex Gymeric 38								
Laura Corrado	1899	Laing	3645	5700	349–6	45–0	24–0	8.0
ex British Duke 30, ex Terek 18								

Note: This company was associated with Soc Anon Emanuele V Parodi (*qv*) and 'Polena' Soc di Nav (*qv*)

COSTA FU ANDREA, GIACOMO, Portici Vittorio Emmanuele 4/4, Genoa

Funnel: Black with blue C on yellow band
Services: Trieste–Fiume–Buenos Aires; Italy–UK–NW Europe

Antonietta Costa	1913	CRDA4	5900	10,000	451–8	54–6	25–8	11.0
ex Monte Bianco 37, ex Nimrod 15								
Beatrice C	1920	CRDA4	6132	10,070	451–8	54–2	25–9	11.0
ex Clara Camus 35								
Enrico Costa	1928	Burntd	4080	7900	380–10	51–5	24–3	10.0
ex Cerasus 34								
Eugenio C	1928	Burntd	4078	7900	380–10	51–5	24–3	10.0
ex Cedrus 34								
Giacomo C	1920	CRDA3	4638	7799	396–4	52–2	24–0	10.5
ex Generale Petitti 36								

Note: Also smaller vessels

D'ALI & CO, GIUSEPPE, Via Ammiraglio Staiti 29, Trapani, Sicily

Services: Mediterranean–UK–NW Europe; within Mediterranean

Erice	1919	McDoug	2350	3610	261–0	43–6	22–11	9.0
ex Lanital 38, ex Isobel 37, ex Isobel Weems 30, ex Chappell 26								
Motia	1918	Caledn	2473	3000	298–0	42–0	19–0	9.0
ex Sicania 20, ex War Dirk 19								

GALLI FU GIOVANNI, FRANCESCO, Piazza San Siro 10–2, Genoa

Funnel: Blue, black top
Services: General tramping

Giovanni Galli*	1913	Rhead3	4262	6650	371–5	50–5	23–10	10.0
ex Nicole Schiaffino 37, ex Speaker 26, ex Savan 20								
Mariarosa	1914	Nthmb1	4211	–	370.0	50–11	23–6	8.5
ex Triton 39, ex Queen Alexandra 25, ex Elfland 15								

Note: * Sold Compagnia Ligure di Nav 1939, renamed *Santa Paola*

GARIBALDI, SOCIETÀ ANONIMA CO-OPERATIVA DI NAVIGAZIONE, Via Fieschi 3, Genoa

Funnel: Black with green over white over red bands
Hull: Black with white band
Services: Italy–Italian E Africa; general tramping

Adamello	1920	Nthmb1	5785	8500	413–0	52–11	26–4	10.0
Antonio Locatelli	1920	WPipe	5754	8584	427–0	54–0	24–6	10.5
ex West Camak 38								

Barbana G	1915	CRDA4	6561	11,000	449–8	55–8	31.1	10.0
ex Barbana 29, ex Teodo 26								
Fianona	1915	CRDA4	6660	11,000	449–6	55–8	31.1	10.0
ex Pola 26								
Gerarchia	1912	Teckl	5859	8620	439–1	55–8	25–1	12.0
ex Nazareno 26, ex Luigi Rizzo 24, ex Ferrara 20, ex Sturmfels 16								
Goffredo Mameli	1910	Rickmr	4370	6650	376–3	47–9	27.3	9.0
ex Myrza Blumberg 21, ex Hornstein 18, ex Mai Rickmers 17								
Ircania	1910	Hamtn2	4815	8079	413–1	51–6	25–11	12.0
ex Dovenden 35, ex Howick Hall 29								
Luigi Razza	1913	GrayX	4319	7270	377–2	50–8	23–3	9.0
ex Penmorvah 36								
Monte Santo	1920	Nthmb1	5850	9160	413–6	52–11	26–3	10.0
Rosario	1918	SHWR	5468	8100	413–0	52–2	25–4	10.0
ex War Maker 20								
San Marco	1919	WoodS2	3076	5050	342–0	46–11	21–8	10.5
ex War Summit 19								
Titania	1918	Bartm2	5397	8240	413–0	52–4	25–4	10.0
ex Tirso 37, ex Etna 20, ex War Hound 20								
XXI Aprile	1919	Standd	4787	7827	395–9	52–2	23–8	10.0
ex Pan Atlantic 37, ex Willfaro 33, ex Richmond Boro 19								
XXIII Marzo	1927	Lithgw	5003	8000	397–5	52–0	24–0	9.5
ex Congonian 36, ex Quercus 33								
XXIV Maggio	1916	G&G3	5388	8680	425–0	53–6	25–5	10.0
ex Orao 37, ex Pontbriand 35, ex Pennyworth 35, ex Gogovale 17								
XXVIII Ottobre	1929	Conn2	4888	8750	417–10	53–5	24–7	12.0
ex Nairn 34, ex Lammer Law 32								

Note: Also smaller vessels and vessels operated for Italian navy

GAVARONE FU GIOVANNI, DITTA GIOVANNI,

Via Interiano 3–5, Genoa

Funnel: Red with white G, black top
Hull: Black with white band, or grey
Services: General tramping

Africana	1919	Tirr1	5869	8500	391–6	51–8	25–0	10.0
ex Valleluce 35, ex Sestri 23								
Delia	1917	McMlln	5406	8100	413–2	52–0	24–8	10.0
ex Valfiorita 35, ex Buckleigh 23								
Ernani	1910	LithR	6619	10,200	476–5	57–0	27–0	10.0
ex Valacia 31, ex Luceric 16								
Fedora	1910	Doxfrd	5016	8100	387–0	51–9	25–0	8.0
ex Vallescura 35, ex Cloutsham 23								
Giuan	1918	OTO1	5473	–	382–9	51–10	24–0	9.0
ex Valprato 35, ex Nicolò II 23								
Grazia	1923	Cerusa	5857	7700	394–4	51–10	24–0	9.5
ex Valcerusa 35								
Mirella	1918	Conn2	5340	7885	413–0	52–2	25–1	10.0
ex Vallarsa 35, ex War Prophet 19								
INDUSTRIE NAVALI SOCIETÀ ANONIMA (INSA)								
Arlesiana	1915	LithR	5604	9470	438–5	56–0	25–6	9.0
ex Dunavis 39, ex Siberian Prince 33, ex Baron Lovat 17								
Butterfly	1920	Bartm2	5127	8250	412–11	52–4	25–4	10.0
ex Suevier 32								
Favorita	1906	Cragg1	3576	6200	349.8	49–10	21–6	8.0
ex Kossuth 33								
Giorgio Ohlsen	1926	Cerusa	5694	7700	394–2	51–11	24–0	9.5
Manon	1901	Wighm1	5597	8500	428–1	55–2	25–7	9.0
ex Sursum Corda 37, ex Gilgai 25, ex Wildenfels 15								
Traviata	1920	Bartm2	5123	8250	413–0	52–4	25–4	10.0
ex Bolivier 32								
Trovatore	1912	ThmpsJ	4745	8935	403–6	54–2	26–0	9.0
ex Ariadne 38, ex Sonora 34, ex Northern 21								
Valdirosa	1914	ThmpR2	4434	7900	397–0	52–0	22–11	8.0
ex Eggesford 23, launched as Recina								
Valsavoia	1919	Tirr1	5733	8500	385.9	51–6	26–0	8.5
ex Rosolino Orlando 22								
Valverde	1910	Doxfrd	4463	7400	378–9	50–1	24–0	8.0
ex Quantock 23								

Note: Also vessels on Mediterranean trade

GAVARONE FU GIUSEPPE, GIUSEPPE, Salito S Nicolosio 1, Genoa

Funnel: Black with blue band
Hull: Black
Services: General tramping

Maddalena G	1919	Curle	5229	9660	413–0	52–4	25–1	10.0
ex Maria Stathatou 38, ex Piave 25, ex War Norman 20								

Italia: Conte Grande *was completed in March 1928 for Lloyd Sabaudo for service from Genoa and Naples to New York. In January 1932 she was transferred to Italia ownership. On June 10 1940* Conte Grande *was laid up at Rio de Janeiro and in August 1941 seized by Brazil. She was sold to the US in April 1942 and converted to the troopship* Monticello *with accommodation for 7000 troops. Following Allied service she was returned to Italy in July 1947, refitted, and following a few more years of service as* Conte Grande *was broken up at Spezia in 1961 (Italia Line)*

Italia: Neptunia *was launched on December 27 1931 for Cosulich, and on October 5 1932 started her maiden voyage from Trieste to Buenos Aires. In 1937 she was transferred to Italia, remaining on the same service. She made her last commercial voyage, returning from Buenos Aires to Trieste in April 1940, and was requisitioned as a troopship after Italy's entry into the Second World War. She was torpedoed and sunk by the British submarine* Upholder *when in a Taranto–Tripoli troop convoy, together with her sistership* Oceania, *on September 18 1941 (RW Jordan collection)*

Ninetto G	1913	CRDA1	5524	8140	400–1	54–0	24–9	10.0
ex Maiella 39, ex Ambra 15								
Nino Padre	1913	ThmpsJ	4171	7050	366–10	50–10	23–11	9.0
ex Lepanto 34, ex Elvaston 17								
Ninuccia	1910	RDuck1	4583	7400	395–5	50–1	24–0	9.0
ex Valrossa 35, ex Bampton 23								

Services: General tramping

GAZZOLO FU ANGELO, ANGELO, Piazza Cinque Lampadi 14, Genoa

Cor Jesu	1908	LoireN	3993	6500	375–8	50–6	22–2	8.5
ex L'Erdre 25								

Services: General tramping

GAZZOLO FU A, TOMASO, Piazza Cattaneo 30, Genoa

SOCIETÀ ANONIMA MARITTIMA SAN PIETRO

San Luigi	1905	Curle	4356	7260	387–6	50–0	24–0	8.0
ex Balcraig 32, ex Vancouver 27								

Funnel: Black with band
Hull: Black, red boot-topping
Services: Mainly Italy–US/Canada; general tramping

GENOVESE DI NAVIGAZIONE A VAPORE SOCIETÀ ANONIMA, COMPAGNIA, Genoa

Capo Alga	1918	Chestr	4723	7400	403–10	51–2	24–0	10.5
ex Munbeaver 38, ex Sudbury 27								
Capo Arma	1905	Palmer	3195	5000	363–3	48–4	22–10	10.0
ex Assuzione 33, ex Chama 30								
Capo Faro	1905	Workmn	3476	5442	384–9	49–4	21.8	10.0
ex Patani 30								
Capo Lena (P–)	1921	Gray18	4820	7000	363–2	52–9	25–7	10.0
ex Astrolabe 35, ex Saint Augustin 30, ex Avristan 23, ex Saint Rene 22								
Capo Mele	1909	Irvin3	3100	5380	354–4	46–7	23–3	9.5
ex Georges et Henri 37, ex Sulima 27, ex Bassam 21								
Capo Noli	1917	Workmn	3921	5750	385–6	50–4	22–9	11.0
ex Munarden 37								
Capo Olmo	1923	GrayWH	4781	6985	362–9	52–6	25–7	10.5
ex Recherche 35, ex Saint Roch 30, ex Bardistan 28								
Capo Orso	1916	BethMS	2449	4690	327.2	46–3	23–4	10.0
ex Munsomo 38								
Capo Rosa	1919	Lithgw	4663	7730	397–11	52–0	24–0	10.0
ex African Explorer 39, ex Musician 38, ex Saint Bede 24								
Capo Vado	1906	SHWR	4391	7200	376–7	51–0	22–11	10.0
ex Alderney 26, ex Dochra 24								
Capo Vita	1916	Nthmb1	5775	9100	411–10	53–0	25–11	10.5
ex St Winifred 38, ex Manchester Hero 37								

Services: General tramping; oil and petroleum trades

IMPRESE NAVIGAZIONE COMMERCIALE SOCIETÀ ANONIMA (INCSA), Via Raimonde da Capua 2, Rome

General cargo vessels								
Ada	1920	CanVic	5248	8400	413–1	52–4	25–5	10.0
ex Canadian Conqueror 38								
Caterina Gerolimich	1912	CRDA3	5430	7930	396–3	52–2	24–1	11.0
Paolina	1911	Blohm	4894	8050	422–5	55–2	25–3	8.5
ex Commercial Guide 36, ex Nyanza 22, ex Esslingen 17								
Tanker								
Conte di Misurata	1908	Laing	5014	7700	397–1	51–0	25–0	8.0
ex British Marquis 30, ex Servian 17								

Funnel: White with narrow black top separated by broad red band over narrow white and green bands
Hull: Black with red boot topping and white dividing line; cruise vessels white
Services: Mail, passenger, cargo – Genoa, Naples–Gibraltar–New York; Genoa, Nice, Barcelona–Rio de Janeiro–Santos–

ITALIA, SOCIETÀ ANONIMA DI NAVIGAZIONE, Piazza de Ferrari 34, Genoa

Passenger and passenger/general cargo vessels								
Augustus (m4,P375/1,600/2,700/3)								
	1927	AnsSA	30,418	9617	710–11	82–10	30–2	18.5
Conte di Savoia (st4,P343/1,778/t,922/3)								
	1932	CRDA5	48,502	9351	814–8	96–1	31–2	27.0
ordered as Conte Azzuro; later proposed name Dux								
Conte Grande (st2,P578/1,256/2,164/ec,720/3)								
	1928	CRDA4	23,861	7274	652–2	78–4	26–9	19.0

Montevideo–Buenos Aires; Genoa–Marseille –Barcelona–Cadiz–Funchal–Central America; oil and petroleum trades

Neptunia (m4,P175/1,709/2,648/3)	1932	CRDA2	19,475	7200	589–8	76–6	27–6	19.0
Oceania (m4,P175/1,709/2,648/3)	1933	CRDA2	19,507	7200	589–9	76–9	27–6	20.5
Orazio (m2,P110/1,184/2,338/3)	1927	COM	11,619	6582	506–1	61–10	27–1	14.0
Principessa Giovanna (st2,P640/3)	1923	Tosi	8955	7382	459–8	59–4	25–0	13.0
Principessa Maria (st2,P640/3)	1923	Tosi	8918	7382	460–8	59–3	25–0	13.0
Rex (st4,P378/1,788/t,866/3)	1932	AnsSA	51,062	12,222	879–9	97–0	33–0	28.0
ordered as Guglielmo Marconi								
Roma (st4,P375/1,236/2,312.t,716/3)	1926	AnsSA	30,816	9725	705–6	82–10	30–2	20.5
Saturnia (m2,P349/1,409/2,555/3)	1927	CRDA1	24,470	8700	630–1	79–10	29–0	21.5
Virgilio (m2,P108/1,184/2,338/3)	1928	COM	11,718	6506	506–1	61–10	27–1	14.0
Vulcania (m2,P305/1,460/2,310/int,700/3)	1928	CRDA1	24,469	8700	631–5	79–10	29–0	21.5
General cargo vessels								
Alberta	1922	CRDA1	6131	8560	417–9	54–2	25–4	10.0
Arsa (P10/1)	1921	CRDA4	5441	8615	404–1	54–1	24–9	10.5
Atlanta	1908	LithR	4404	6660	399–5	49–10	24–3	12.0
ex Stella Polare 17, ex Atlanta 15								
Aussa (P10/1)	1921	CRDA3	5441	8680	404–1	53–11	25–3	10.5
Barbarigo (m,P12)	1930	CRDA1	5293	7953	440–9	56–2	24–2	13.5
Belvedere	1913	CRDA1	6889	7300	437–10	54–0	25–9	13.0
conv passenger/general cargo 37								
Birmania (m,P12)	1930	CRDA2	5305	7953	440–9	56–2	24–2	13.5
Cellina (m,P43)	1926	CRDA4	6086	9970	448–6	55–5	26–4	13.5
Clara	1922	CRDA1	6131	8560	417–9	54–2	25–4	10.5
Fella (m,P43)	1926	CRDA4	6072	9980	447–9	55–5	26–4	13.5
Giulia (m)	1926	CRDA1	5921	8210	407–8	53–11	26–0	14.0
Ida	1923	CRDA1	6131	8560	417–9	54–2	25–2	10.5
Isarco (P10)	1924	CRDA4	5915	8675	405–8	54–0	25–6	11.0
Istria (P12)	1921	CRDA4	5416	8620	404–1	54–1	25–3	10.5
Laura C	1923	CRDA1	6181	8460	417–9	54–2	25–7	10.5
ex Laura 24								
Leme (m2,P57/1)	1925	CRDA4	8059	10,990	467–8	57–2	27–7	12.0
Livenza (st,P10)	1922	CRDA4	5343	8558	404–3	54–0	25–3	12.0
Lucia C	1922	CRDA1	6123	8560	417–9	54–0	25–4	10.5
ex Lucia 24								
Maria (m)	1926	CRDA1	6339	8300	418–0	53–3	25–1	11.5
Recca (P10)	1921	CRDA4	5441	8615	404–1	53–11	24–9	11.0
Rialto (m,P43)	1927	CRDA4	6099	9945	448–6	55–5	26–4	13.5
Teresa	1922	CRDA1	6131	8290	417–7	54–2	25–4	10.5
Tankers								
Dora C	1922	CRDA1	5843	8600	408–3	53–11	26–9	10.0
ex Dora 24								
Sangro (st)	1925	COM	6466	8317	397–0	52–6	26–2	10.0

Note: This company was controlled by Finmare Società Finanziaria Marittima, Rome

'LA COLUMBIA' SOCIETÀ MARITTIMA PER TRASPORTO DI PETROLIO E DERIVATI, Via XX Settembre 41, Genoa

Funnel: Yellow, black top
Hull: Black, red boot-topping
Trades: Oil and petroleum

Tankers								
Ardor (m2)	1927	OTO6	8960	12,710	489–6	63–0	27–3	11.0
Fulgor	1922	OTO4	6504	8965	420–2	55–1	26–2	10.0
R L Hague (m2)	1932	CRDA2	12,175	17,963	542–4	70–3	30–5	13.0
Vigor	1923	OTO6	6511	8965	418–4	54–10	25–1	10.0

Note: This company, a subsidiary of Standard Oil Co of New Jersey (US), also owned tankers under 2000gt

LA COSTIERA, SOCIETÀ ANONIMA DI NAVIGAZIONE,
Via C Roccatagliata Ceccardi 4, Genoa

Services: Fruit trades, Genoa–UK, NW Europe

G DE CASTRO & CO

Ivorea	1908	NedSM	3234	3455	354–1	42–2	23–3	12.0
ex Suriname 38								

ITALO-BALTICA, SOCIETÀ ANONIMA ITALIANA DI NAVIGAZIONE E COMMERCIO

Argentea	1908	NedSM	3312	3455	354–1	42–2	23–3	12.0
ex Saramacca 38								

Italia: Leme *was completed at Trieste in October 1925 for Navigazione Libera Triestina, and was transferred to Italia upon its formation in 1937. In June 1940 she was interned in the US, seized in December 1941 and in 1942 was transferred to the Ministry of War Transport as* Lowlander *under the British flag. Managers were Port Line. She was returned to Italy in 1948. As* Leme *she was then used as an emigrant carrier between Italy and Argentina, with accommodation for 64 cabin class and 258 third class passengers. In June 1949 she transferred to the North Pacific service, and in 1957, when she ceased to carry passengers, was transferred to Italy–South America service. In 1960* Leme *was laid up at Genoa and broken up the following year (RW Jordan collection)*

Lauro: Gioacchino Lauro *was completed in April 1921 by Canadian Vickers at Montreal and was one of the large number of standard vessels completed in Canada during and following the First World War. As* Canadian Commander *she was owned by Canadian National Steamships. She was sold to Italy in 1932. She was seized by Britain in 1940 and renamed* Empire Engineer *with the Ministry of Shipping as owner and Weidner, Hopkins & Co, as manager. She was on voyage from Sydney, Nova Scotia, and Halifax, from where she sailed on January 22 1941 for Newport with a cargo of steel, when she was torpedoed and sunk by* U123. *There were no survivors from the 40 crew on board at the time (Alex Duncan)*

Lloyd Triestino: The liner Colombo *was launched at the Palmers shipyard in October 1915 for Sicula Americana as the general cargo vessel* San Gennaro. *In 1917 she was sold to the Transoceanic company and completed in July 1917. In 1921 she was sold to Navigazione Generale Italiana of Italy, passenger accommodation was added, and she was renamed* Colombo. Colombo *was transferred to Italia Line in 1932 and to Lloyd Triestino in 1937. On April 4 1941 she was scuttled at Massowah, Eritrea, before the entry of British forces into the port. The wreck was broken up in situ during 1949–51 together with other Italian vessels scuttled at the port (RW Jordan collection)*

Snia Amba	1918	NYSB	2532	3956	309–11	40–0	21–4	9.5
ex Santa Tecla 37								
Sniafiocco	1918	Bufflo	2333	3525	261–0	43–6	21–2	9.5
ex Dora 37, ex Dora Weems 32, ex Lake Galera 25								

LAGORARA, FRATELLI, Piazza Vigne 6, Genoa

Services: General tramping

Honor	1919	Ropnr2	5303	8200	413–4	52–4	25–3	10.0
ex Bakana 29, launched as War Primula								

LAURO, ACHILLE, Via Agostino Depretis 114, Naples

Funnel: Blue, or blue with five-pointed white star, black top
Hull: Black or grey, red boot-topping
Services: Italy–Italian E Africa; general tramping; oil and petroleum trades

General cargo vessels								
Achille Lauro (P6)	1921	Halifx	5209	8390	414–2	52–4	25–3	10.0
ex Canadian Explorer 33								
Aida Lauro	1922	RDuck2	6067	9515	445–4	55–10	26–1	10.0
ex Mina 37, ex Illingworth 34								
Amelia Lauro	1919	SHWR	5335	8350	412–11	52–4	25–4	10.0
ex Belgian 34								
Angelina Lauro (P6)	1913	Teckl	5787	9100	437–1	56–2	25–10	10.0
ex Bowes Castle 32, ex Solfels 20								
Antonietta Lauro	1928	SmitP	5428	9200	435–5	55–2	24–0	11.5
ex Parklaan 33								
Antonio Limoncelli	1924	GrayWH	4574	8300	412–2	52–0	24–0	10.0
ex Aberdare 33, ex Merioneth 27								
Cuma (st)	1920	Workmn	8260	10,800	462–5	58–4	29–3	11.5
ex Nictheroy 37								
Edera	1912	GrayX	5254	8226	412–4	53–6	24–2	9.0
ex Misty Law 32, ex Zuiderdijk 22, ex Shahristan 12								
Elios	1912	Prstm1	5202	8550	413–1	53–6	23–9	9.5
ex Hannington Court 36								
Ercole	1904	Palmer	5027	8542	415–0	50–2	24–5	9.5
ex Waaldijk 32, ex Gramsbergen 14, ex Acara 10								
Erica	1909	Reiher	4704	7750	412–7	53–10	24–0	9.5
ex Wasaborg 35, ex Union City 25, ex Iserlohn 21								
Felce	1910	Teckl	5639	8600	435–4	55–1	25–1	9.0
ex Hadiotis 29, ex Freienfels 25								
Gabbiano (r/t)	1923	Neptn1	6584	9875	462–0	57–1	29.6	10.0
ex Grete 34								
Gioacchino Lauro (P6)	1921	CanVic	5345	8390	413–1	52–2	25–5	10.0
ex Canadian Commander 32								
Guidonia	1913	Doxfrd	5060	8900	434–2	54–1	25–6	9.5
ex Eftychia 38, ex Sheaf Mount 30, ex Gifford 19, ex Sperrbrecher 9 18, ex Gifhorn 17, ex Gifford 17								
Iris	1918	Doxfrd	5175	8207	413–5	52–4	25–3	10.5
ex Tregonnell 35, ex War Stag 19								
Ischia	1907	Hamtn2	5101	8260	414–0	52–0	25–0	9.5
ex Navarino 36								
Laura Lauro	1912	Weser	5787	8650	441–1	55–10	24–11	10.0
ex Koudekerk 31, ex Kirkstall Abbey 21, ex Kandelfels 20								
Liana	1914	Hamtn2	6400	10,107	436–5	54–6	27–10	11.0
ex Giekerk 35, ex Bawean 27								
Lucrino	1917	Sundld	5616	8850	401–11	53–0	25–7	10.0
ex Afghanistan 38, ex Aberdeen 18								
Olimpia (P4)	1920	Rickmr	6040	9330	435–0	55–8	25–7	10.0
ex Wray Castle 32, ex Paria 21, ex Rickmer Rickmers 20								
Pozzuoli (P10)	1920	CRDA1	5345	8465	402–10	54–2	24–9	10.0
ex Salina 33								
Procida (P6)	1921	HarbrM	5366	8390	413–1	52–2	25–2	11.0
ex Canadian Traveller 32								
Rapido	1919	CanVic	5363	8390	413–1	52–5	25–2	11.0
ex Zephyros 36, ex Canadian Pioneer 34								
Santagata	1905	TyneIr	4299	7387	367–4	50–1	24–8	8.0
ex Taurus 35								
Veloce	1911	Steph2	5464	8600	424–5	53–2	26–6	11.0
ex Media 35								
Verbania (s2)	1907	Workmn	6640	9640	463–5	56–4	28–6	11.0
ex Kia Ora 35								
Tankers								
Fede (m)	1938	CRDA5	7884	12,293	490–6	59–2	26–3	13.5
Lavoro (m)	1938	CRDA5	7886	12,293	490–6	59–2	26–3	13.5

LA RIVIERA SOCIETÀ ANONIMA DI NAVIGAZIONE, Piazza Nunziata 17, Genoa

Tanker

Portofino 1916 Dixon2 6424 9250 415–6 54–1 27–11 9.5
ex British Rose 30, ex Roseleaf 19, ex Califol 17, laid down as Rona

SOCIETÀ ANONIMA GIUSEPPE BOZZO ARMAMENTO E TRASPORTI MARITTIMA, Piazza Nunziata 17, Genoa

General cargo vessels

Nita (P6) 1913 Bonn&M 6813 9850 446–0 54–2 29–0 12.0
ex Verbania 35, ex Madioen 33

Tina Primo 1911 Bremer 4853 7650 417–0 53–6 27.6 10.0
ex Valsole 36, ex Argentina 35, ex Elias G Culucundis 31, ex Tenterden 30, ex Elias G Culucundis 29, ex Artigas 27, ex Wiegand 17

Note: Also several smaller vessels

Services: General tramping

LAURO & MONTELLA, Via Agostino Depretis 65, Naples

Sileno 1907 Cragg2 3567 7700 370–9 49–9 21–7 10.0
ex Orvieto 35, ex Orsova 24

Stella 1923 Prstm1 4272 8200 378–0 49–10 24–8 9.0
ex Cipro 37, ex Portsea 33, ex Barbara Marie 24

BIAGIO BORRIELLO FU G

Sagitta 1919 Hendn2 5269 8250 412–6 52–2 25–4 10.0
ex Tremeadow 38

AGOSTINO LAURO

Silvano 1906 Napr&M 4234 7500 385.4 48–9 24–0 10.0
ex Nirvo 38, ex Nibbio, ex Irish Monarch 24

Note: Also vessels under 1500gt

Funnel: Black or yellow
Hull: Passenger vessels – white, green boot-topping; cargo vessels – black, red boot-topping
Services: Trieste–India–Far East; Trieste–non Mediterranean African ports; Trieste–Australia; Genoa–Bombay–Shanghai (Trieste–South Africa service suspended April 1939)

LLOYD TRIESTINO, SOCIETÀ ANONIMA DI NAVIGAZIONE, Palazzo del Lloyd Triestino, Piazza Unite 1, Trieste

Passenger/general cargo vessels

Adria (P50/1,28/2,130/3)
1914 Clyde 3809 3319 347–5 46–5 22–2 14.5
ex Pilsna 36, ex Adria 35, ex Ferencz Ferdinánd 21

Adua (P110) 1922 Ramage 3564 3200 344–4 42–10 22–9 12.0
ex Premjer 35, ex Tasso 29

Aquileja (s2,P140/1,138/2,34/3)
1914 NedSM 9448 7098 498–0 57–2 30–0 14.0
ex Prins der Nederlanden 35

Arno (s2,P69/1,148/2,301/3)
1912 Beardm 8024 4430 428–5 56–9 24–7 15.0
ex Cesarea 38, ex Fort St George 35, ex Wandilla 21

Caffaro (st,P–) 1924 AnsSA 6476 9300 408–10 53–9 27–0 12.0

Calabria (s2,P142/2,812/3)
1922 Weser 9515 12,320 479–9 62–4 28–1 12.0
ex Werra 35

California (st2,P130/1,30/2)
1920 Scott2 13,060 8366 539–0 64–0 31–9 13.0
ex Albania 30

Casaregis (st,P–) 1924 AnsSA 6485 9300 408–10 53–9 27–0 12.0

Colombo (s2,P116/1,212/2,1004/3)
1917 Palmer 11,760 7997 536–4 64–0 23–9 14.0
ex San Gennaro 21; conv general cargo 23

Conte Biancamano (st2,P230/1,481/1,704/3)
1925 Beardm 23,255 7382 665–0 76–4 26–0 19.5

Conte Rosso (st2,P250/1,170/2,220/3)
1922 Beardm 17,879 7900 588–2 74–3 27–9 19.5

Conte Verde (st2,P250/1,170/2,220/3)
1923 Beardm 18,765 6750 592–4 74–2 27–9 19.5

Dalmatia L (P77) 1903 LloydA 3252 3739 337.5 42–2 21–1 12.5
ex Dalmatia 24

Duilio (st4,P757/1,/2,/3)
1923 AnsSA 23,636 8077 635–6 76–4 30–0 19.5

Francesco Crispi (st2,P450)
1926 OTO6 7600 5600 447–1 52–11 27–0 16.0

Giulio Cesare (st4,P168/1,168/2,306/3)
1921 SHWR 21,900 9642 633–11 76–6 30–2 19.5

Giuseppe Mazzini (st2,P450)
1926 OTO6 7669 5600 447–1 51–2 27–0 16.0

Gradisca (s2,P233/1,350/2,706/3)
1913 Steph2 13,870 9700 560–2 65–10 29–3 16.5
ex Gelria 35

Italia (s2,P550/–)	1905	OTO1	5203	3584	393.7	47–10	23–10	15.0
Leonardo da Vinci (st2,P450)	1925	OTO6	7515	5000	447–0	52–2	27–0	16.0
Liguria (r/t3,P206/cab,564/t,588/3)	1918	Curle	15,354	3315	546–6	67–4	34–4	13.0
ex Melita 35								
Lombardia (s3,P103/1,4420/tr)	1920	Weser	20,006	5212	616–6	72–2	28–1	16.0
ex Resolute 35, ex Brabantia 22, ex William O'Swald 20								
Nazario Sauro (st2,P450)	1924	AnsSA	8150	4505	447–1	52–9	27–0	15.5
Piemonte (r/t3,P206/cab,545/t,590/3,or 3000/tr)	1918	Curle	15,209	7460	546–1	67–2	34–4	13.0
ex Minnedosa 35								
Po (s2,P185/1,61/2,54/3)	1911	LloydA	7289	2726	454–0	55–9	22–8	17.0
ex Vienna 38, ex Wien 20								
Remo (m2,P66/cab,330/3)	1927	CRDA4	9780	11,073	506–8	62–4	26–2	12.0
Sardegna (s2,P410/cab,712/3)	1923	Bremer	11,452	10,720	511–9	61–10	30–4	14.0
ex Sierra Ventana 35								
Sicilia (st2,P298/2,140/3)	1924	Weser	9646	9390	479–7	62–4	28–1	11.5
ex Coblenz 35								
Tevere (s2,P86/1,107/2,290/3)	1912	CRDA3	8289	6775	469–5	56–4	27–8	15.5
ex Gablonz 21								
Toscana (s2,P98/2,140/3)	1923	Weser	9442	9350	479–9	62–4	29–7	12.0
ex Saarbrücken 35								
Umbria (s2,P108/2,2300/3)	1912	Reiher	10,076	11,506	510–0	59–4	28–0	12.0
ex Bahia Blanca 35								
Urania (s2,P*c*800)	1916	CRDA3	7099	5737	411–1	53–1	26–0	13.0
ex Genova 33, ex Hungaria 23								
Victoria (m4,P266/1,97/2,100/3)	1931	CRDA5	13,098	3739	540–8	69–11	23–10	22.0
General cargo vessels								
Alberto Treves	1917	H&W,B	5145	8105	413–5	52–4	25–4	10.5
ex War Cobra 19								
Anfora (P10/1)	1922	CRDA3	5452	8504	404–3	54–0	25–3	10.0
Arabia (m,P–)	1926	CRDA3	7025	9348	447–9	55–6	25–3	12.0
Brenta (P10/1)	1920	CRDA3	5400	8404	404–1	54–1	24–9	10.0
ex Brenta II 29, ex Brenta 24								
Caboto	1919	Hamtn2	5225	8260	413–0	52–4	25–4	11.0
ex War Celt 19								
Carignano	1918	Ropnr2	5753	8088	411–9	52–5	25–5	11.0
ex War Pigeon 20								
Carlo del Greco (m)	order	CRDA4	6837	9000	463–11	62–4	25–0	16.0
Carnia (P10/1)	1923	CRDA3	5451	8433	404–2	54–0	25–3	10.0
Carso (P10/1)	1923	CRDA4	6275	9130	419–0	54–0	25–4	10.5
Cherca (P10/1)	1920	CRDA4	5346	8627	404–1	52–1	24–9	10.0
Cortellazzo (m,P12)	1931	CRDA2	5292	7953	440–8	56–2	24–2	13.0
Dandolo	1921	SHWR	4964	8480	413–7	53–2	25–9	9.0
Duchessa d'Aosta (P48/cab,12/3)	1921	CRDA4	7872	9520	464–2	57–5	26–10	12.0
laid down as Zrmanja								
Edda (P10/1)	1924	CRDA4	6107	8327	414–6	53–11	25–3	11.5
Esquilino (m2,P59)	1925	CRDA3	8657	10,260	467–9	57–2	27–3	12.0
Fabio Filzi (m)	bldg	CRDA2	6835	9000	463–11	62–4	25–0	16.0
Fusijama (m,P10)	1929	CRDA4	6244	8430	448–4	55–5	25–9	14.0
Gino Allegri (m)	bldg	CRDA2	6835	9000	463–11	62–4	25–0	16.0
Himalaya (m2,P10)	1929	CRDA4	6240	8430	448–4	55–5	25–9	14.0
India (m,P–)	1926	CRDA4	6367	8947	430–8	53–11	25–10	12.0
Isonzo (P10/1)	1921	CRDA3	5441	8410	404–1	53–11	24–9	10.5
ex Isonzo II 26, ex Isonzo 24								
Laguna* (P10/1)	1913	CRDA3	5400	8700	400–1	54–0	24–9	10.0
Maiella** (P20/1,29/3)	1913	CRDA1	5524	8140	400–1	54–0	24–9	10.0
Marin Sanudo (m)	1926	CRDA1	5081	7943	418–1	53–2	24–5	12.0
Mario Rosselli	order	CRDA2	6830	9035	463–11	62–4	25–0	16.0

Mauly (m2)	1925	CRDA1	5463	8268	430–8	54–0	25–10	12.0
Moncalieri	1918	Craig2	5723	8118	413–0	52–4	25–5	11.0
ex War Linnet 19								
Perla (P20/1)	1926	Clyde	5741	8100	404–4	54–0	25–7	12.0
Piave (P58/cab)	1921	CRDA3	7565	9970	464–2	57–5	26–8	12.0
ex Piave II 26, ex Piave 24								
Reginaldo Giuliani (m)	order	CRDA2	6830	9035	463–11	62–4	25–0	16.0
Romolo (m2,P66/cab)	1926	CRDA4	9780	11,073	506–6	62–3	26–2	12.0
Rosandra (P38/1)	1921	CRDA3	8034	9550	464–2	57–5	26–10	12.0
Sabbia (P20/1,29/3)	1926	Clyde	5788	8300	404–4	54–0	25–8	11.5
Sannio (r/t)	1921	Bremer	9834	10,580	485–9	58–4	29–1	12.0
ex General Mitre 35, ex Artus 27								
Savoia (st,P10/1)	1922	CRDA4	5490	8373	404–0	54–0	25–3	12.5
Sistiana (P48/1)	1924	CRDA4	5827	8010	405–8	54–0	25–7	11.5
launched as Salvore								
Sumatra (m)	1927	CRDA4	6141	8310	425–6	54–2	24–3	12.0
Tagliamento (P10/1)	1922	CRDA3	5448	8419	404–2	54–0	25–3	10.5
Timavo (P58/cab)	1920	CRDA3	7549	9960	464–2	57–4	26–8	12.0
laid down as Ombla								
Tripolitania (P41/2,99/3)	1918	SHWRSd	2722	2980	301–1	42–1	20–5	10.0
ex Marzocco 37, ex War Tank 19								
Viminale (m2,P59/cab)	1925	CRDA3	8657	10,207	467–9	57–2	27–3	12.0
Volpi (m,P12)	1931	CRDA2	5292	7953	440–8	56–2	24–2	13.0

Note: * Sold Azienda Carboni Italiani (Nav Carlo Martinolich & Figlio) 1939, renamed *Valdivagna*; ** sold G Gavarone fu G 1939, renamed *Ninetto G*
Note: Also smaller vessels on Mediterranean and Red Sea services
Note: This company was controlled by Finmare Società Finanziaria Marittima, Rome

LUSSINO, SOCIETÀ ANONIMA DI NAVIGAZIONE A VAPORE, Lussinpiccolo

Funnel: Black
Hull: Grey, red boot-topping
Services: General tramping

Hilda (m)	1927	CRDA3	4901	8360	424–8	54–1	24–2	13.0

MANGIAROTTI, FU GIOCONDO & ENRICO RAVANO, LEONARDO, Via Rodi 10, Genoa

Services: General tramping

Entella	1899	Odero1	2691	4100	311–8	40–11	20–11	8.0
ex Berta 26, ex Livietta 25								

Note: Also smaller vessels in Mediterranean trades

MARESCA & CO, MARIANO, Via San Giorgio 2, Genoa

Funnel: White with black top, separated by white over black bands
Services: General tramping

Mar Glauco	1906	Doxfrd	4690	7740	403–11	51–8	24.5	8.0
ex Aquitania 27, ex S E Calvert 24, ex Lübeck 22, ex Drumcondra 13								

MARITTIMA RAVENATE SOCIETÀ ANONIMA, Via Angelo Mariani 9, Ravenna

Services: General tramping

Rubicone	1905	ArmWh1	4740	7250	399–6	49–2	25–3	10.0
ex Myrmidon 30								

Note: Also vessels under 2000gt

MARTINOLICH & FIGLIO, NAVIGAZIONE CARLO, Via Felice Venezian 1, Trieste

Funnel: Black, broad white band
Services: General tramping

AZIENDA CARBONI ITALIANI, Rome

Carlo Martinolich	1928	SHWRSd	4208	7677	385–4	52–0	23–9	9.0
ex Honvéd 35								
Valdivagna	1913	CRDA3	5400	8700	404–1	54–0	25–3	10.0
ex Laguna 39								

NAVIGAZIONE CARLO MARTINOLICH S A G L

Caterina	1920	ToddDD	4786	7659	396–5	53–1	23–9	10.0
ex Fortunata 39, ex Padnsay 38								
Sant' Antioco	1919	BethSP	5048	7450	393–7	52–4	24–3	9.0
ex San Diego 36, ex Orient 30, ex Gosport 27								

Note: Also vessels under 1500gt

Lloyd Triestino: Conte Rosso *in previous colours under the ownership of Lloyd Sabaudo, from which company she was transferred in January 1932. She was completed in January 1922 by Beardmore at Dalmuir for service from Genoa and Naples to New York. Her Parsons double reduction geared tubines gave 22,000shp, and in 1936 these were improved to give an extra 5000shp. She became a troopship in 1940 and on May 24 1941 was torpedoed and sunk by the British submarine* Upholder *with heavy loss of life (RW Jordan collection)*

Lloyd Triestino: The keel of the liner Duilio *was laid by Ansaldo for NGI on May 30 1914, and she was launched on January 16 1916. Wartime priorities prevented further work on the vessel until the early 1920s, and she was delivered in October 1923 for the Genoa–Naples–New York service. In 1928 she transferred to the Buenos Aires service, and three years later was transferred to Italia Line. She then went on to the service from Genoa and Marseilles to Gibraltar, Dakar, Cape Town and Durban. She was transferred to Lloyd Triestino in 1937.* Duilio *was requisitioned by the Italian navy as a hospital ship in 1940. With the Italian surrender she fell into German hands and on July 10 1944 was bombed by Allied aircraft and sunk at Trieste. The wreck was refloated in 1948 and broken up (RW Jordan collection)*

Lloyd Triestino: The quadruple-screw liner Victoria *was launched on December 6 1930 and delivered by CRDA at Trieste on June 21 1931. Her four CRDA/Sulzer 8-cylinder oil engines developed a maximum 18,660bhp and with a trials speed of 23.25 knots, and service speed of 20.5 knots, this vessel was for a time the world's fastest motor ship.* Victoria *was also the first passenger liner with the dining saloon on the top deck. Her original itinerary took her from Trieste, Venice and Brindisi to Alexandria. In 1932 this was extended to Bombay, and in October 1936 she made her first voyage from Genoa to Bombay, Colombo, Singapore, Hong Kong and Shanghai. With Italy's entry into the Second World War,* Victoria *was requisitioned for use as a troopship. While serving in this role was torpedoed by British aircraft and sunk in 33 30N 17 40E on January 23 1942 when on voyage from Taranto to Tripoli (RW Jordan collection)*

Funnel: Black with white over red bands
Hull: Black
Services: General tramping

MAZZELLA, DITTA PASQUALE, Teresella Spagnoli 59, Naples

Dea Mazzella	1919	ThompJ	3082	4850	342–6	46–10	21–9	10.0
ex Welsh Prince 36, ex Syrian Prince 36, launched as War Rock								
Erminia Mazzella	1917	LithR	5742	9350	437–3	55–11	25–6	10.0
ex Mazic 38, ex Patrician 38, ex Saint Jerome 19								

Funnel: Black with white five-pointed star below narrow white band
Hull: White with black band, red boot-topping
Services: Naples–Libya, Tunisia, Palermo, Tripoli, Benghazi, Cirenaica, Massawah

Note: Also vessels under 2000gt

MESSINA & COMPAGNIA, IGNAZIO, Via Cairoli 11, Genoa

Passenger/general cargo vessel								
Ogaden (P–)	1905	Conn2	4553	6830	391–5	49–9	23–9	10.0
ex Naxos 36, ex Saxon Prince 24, ex Glenaffric 21								
General cargo vessels								
Semien	1898	Leslie	6942	9200	421.4	54–0	22–3	9.5
ex Fortunstar 36, ex Tuscanstar 29, ex Brodliffe 20, ex Morayshire 15								
Tembien	1914	Rickmr	5653	8100	417.0	53–2	24–0	11.0
ex Mouni 36, ex Milluna 33, ex Franziska 21, ex Mabel Rickmers 17								

Services: General tramping

Note: Also smaller vessels in Mediterranean trades

MILANO & CO, E, Via G d'Annunzio 2, Trieste

PASUBIO SOCIETÀ ANONIMA DI NAVIGAZIONE

Pasubio	1903	Neptn1	2216	4000	313–10	43–3	20–0	8.0
ex Trade 35, ex Tivat 34, ex Maid of Crete 31, ex Mimi Horn 21								

Funnel: Black
Hull: Black, red boot-topping
Services: General tramping

MUSSO, UGO, Via Acquarone 28, Genoa

Zena (P)	1914	Caledn	5219	7060	392–11	51–9	26–2	11.0
ex Alban 35								

Funnel: Blue, black top
Hull: Black, red boot-topping
Services: Italy–US and Gulf ports; general tramping; oil and petroleum trades

NAVIGAZIONE ALTA ITALIA SOCIETÀ ANONIMA, Via XX Settembre 28/4, Genoa

General cargo vessels								
Monbaldo	1918	Tirr1	6214	8354	389–5	51–6	26–2	9.0
ex Sori 25								
Monfiore	1920	Duthie	5498	8582	423–8	54–2	24–1	9.5
ex Grazia 26, ex West Hesseltine 25								
Mongioia	1924	OTO3	6113	8320	392.4	51–9	35.1	10.0
ex Terni 31, ex Crispi 27								
Monreale (m)	bldg	Tirr2	5323	8520	438–4	58–4	25–3	12.5
Monrosa	1920	Coughl	6703	9035	428–0	54–4	25–3	10.0
ex Indiano 25, ex Indus 23								
Monstella	1918	Doxfrd	5311	8160	412–4	52–4	25–3	10.0
ex Fert 19, ex War Gazelle 19								
Montello	1927	Tirr2	6117	8365	403–6	54–6	26–0	11.0
Tankers								
Stelvio (m2)	1926	Tirr2	6963	9400	441–2	56–1	27–1	11.0
Superga	1923	Tirr1	6154	8858	397.7	51–9	34.1	10.0

NAVIGAZIONE SOCIETÀ ANONIMA ODERO

General cargo vessels								
Ada O (P–)	1919	OTO3	5234	7731	373–0	45–10	33.3	10.0
Ida Z O	1920	OTO1	4935	8248	403–5	51–6	25–0	10.0
Maddalena Odero (st)	1921	Odero2	5479	8260	394–5	51–9	26–0	11.0
ex Maddalena O 23								
Marina Odero (st)	1918	Odero2	5480	8040	393–9	51–10	26–0	10.0
ex Marina O 26								
Nicolò Odero	1925	OTO1	6003	8070	406–8	51–6	25–0	10.0

Trades: Oil and petroleum

Note: Also vessels under 1500gt

NAVIGAZIONE E COMMERCIO, SOCIETÀ ANONIMA ITALIANA, Piazza Campetto 7, Genoa

Tanker								
Tampico	1908	ArmWh1	4958	7700	399–0	51–0	25–2	8.5
ex British Peer 30, ex Carpathian 18								

NAVIGAZIONE GENERALE GEROLIMICH & COMPAGNIA SOCIETÀ IN AZIONI, Via Dante Alighieri 1, Trieste

Funnel: Black with green G on white diamond on red band
Hull: Black, red boot-topping
Services: General tramping

Col di Lana (m)	1926	CRDA1	5891	8170	416–8	53–2	24–5	12.0
Monte Piana (m)	1926	CRDA1	5890	8171	416–8	53–2	24–5	12.0

ORIENTE, SOCIETÀ ANONIMA DI ARMAMENTO MARITTIMO, Punto Franco Magazzeno 12, Fiume

Funnel: Black with broad red band
Services: General tramping

Burma	1912	GrayX	4675	7906	412–2	52–2	23–7	11.0

PARODI, SOCIETÀ ANONIMA EMANUELE V, Via Assarotti 7, Genoa

Funnel: Black with red AP monogram on white band
Hull: Black, red boot-topping
Services: General tramping
Note: This company was associated with Soc Anon di Nav Corrado (*qv*)

Bainsizza	1930	CRDA4	7933	11,142	446–8	58–5	29.3	11.0
Italo Balbo	1919	Fairfd	5114	8170	413–9	52–4	25–4	10.5
ex Avon Cliff 37, ex Lomas 36, ex Brazilier 26, launched as War Pioneer								
San Pietro	1918	H&WGw	5199	8250	413–0	52–4	25–4	10.5
ex Primola 19, ex War Cowslip 19								

PITTALUGA VAPORI, DITTA LUIGI, Vico Giannini 2, Genoa

Funnel: Black, white band
Hull: Black, red boot-topping
Services: General tramping

General cargo vessels								
Aquitania	1924	Blythw	4971	8050	414–8	53–2	24–2	10.0
ex Farnworth 34								
Campania	1918	Caird	5247	8100	413–0	52–4	25–4	10.5
ex War Bracken 19								
Tankers								
Lucania	1902	GrayX	8106	10,600	483–1	55–0	27–2	8.0
ex Coalinga 27, ex Pectan 14								
Pensilvania	1903	DunlpD	6861	9000	437–1	53–2	30.7	8.0
ex De Soto 24, ex Phoebus 14								
Tuscania	1914	Laing	6903	10,260	441–2	57–0	27–2	9.0
ex Caloric 30								

'POLENA' SOCIETÀ DI NAVIGAZIONE, Salita S Nicolosio 1, CP 1862, Genoa

Funnel: Black with white P on green band
Hull: Black, red boot-topping
Services: General tramping; oil and petroleum trades

General cargo vessels								
Delfin	1918	Scott2	5322	7885	412–6	52–2	25–1	10.0
ex Camogli 35, ex Rovereto 28, ex War Angler 20								
Löasso (m2)	1921	OTO3	5968	8800	394–1	51–9	26–1	9.0
ex Messico 36, ex Vejo 28								
Moscardin	1906	G&G2	4419	7180	384–0	52–2	22–11	11.0
ex Danaos 39, ex Constantinos 25, ex Strathearn 24								
Orata	1910	Conn2	8631	13,000	484–8	58–0	31–0	9.0
ex Emanule Accame 37, ex Reliance 20, ex Knight Companion 13								
Pamia (st)	1922	Savoia	6245	7900	394–6	51–6	26–0	10.5
ex Sebeto 35, ex Cariddi 32, ex Artena 28								
Pampano (st)	1924	Savoia	6232	7900	391–8	51–8	26–0	10.5
ex Cuma 35, ex Ferento 28								
Tankers								
Dentice	1918	Fairfd	5197	7830	413–0	52–4	25–4	10.5
ex Adna 37, ex War Patriot 19								
Pagao (st)	1924	AnsGC	6101	10,000	411–1	51–9	27–6	10.0
ex Formia 35, ex Volsinio 29; conv general cargo 30								
Rondine (m2)	1924	OTO6	6077	8029	395–4	51–8	26–1	9.0
ex Löasso 35, ex Literno 35, ex Predappio 29, ex Lanuvio 29								
Sanandrea	1908	ArmWh1	5077	7570	400–0	50–9	25–6	8.0
ex Hyrcania 32								
Strombo (m2)	1921	Savoia	5232	7900	393–2	51–7	26–2	10.5
ex Laxerto 35, ex Carpena 35, ex Capena 28								

Note: This company was associated with Soc Anon di Nav Corrado (*qv*)

PREMUDA, SOCIETÀ ANONIMA DI NAVIGAZIONE G L, Palazza Tergesteo, Via della Borsa 3, Trieste

Funnel: Black
Services: General tramping

Absirtea	1913	Craig2	4170	7550	385–4	51–6	23–9	8.5
Tergestea (m)	1926	CRDA1	5890	7980	416–8	53–1	24–5	10.0

Funnel: Black
Hull: Black
Services: General tramping

QUERCI, DITTA MARINO, Via San Vincenzo 1, Genoa

Marzocco	1918	H&WGw	5106	7885	413–0	52–2	25–4	10.5
ex Kambove 38, ex Nervier 27, ex War Aryan 19								
Mediceo	1918	Conn2	5248	7874	412–0	52–4	25–1	10.5
ex Akera 39, ex War Singer 21								
Morea	1918	Chicgo	1968	3300	261–4	43–5	17–11	9.0
ex Padilla 37, ex Lake Crescent 26, laid down as War Duty								
Mugnone	1918	H&WGw	5198	7800	413–0	52–4	25–4	10.5
ex Andrea 38, ex Anomia 27, ex War Expert 19; conv tanker 38								
Spartivento	1907	Pgill1	3694	6345	372–0	49–0	23–11	8.0
ex Aboukir 28, ex Saint Michael 22								

Funnel: Black with white R on red band between two narrow blue bands *Hull:* Black or grey
Services: General tramping; oil and petroleum trades

RAVANO FU MARCO, PIETRO, Via alla Nunziata 15, Genoa

SOCIETÀ ANONIMA INDUSTRIA ARMAMENTO

General cargo vessels

Amabilitas	1919	Savoia	5425	7920	395–10	51–8	25–0	10.0
ex Ansaldo Savoia Secondo 28, ex Ansaldo Savoia II 25								
Auctoritas	1918	Savoia	5228	7840	395–10	51–8	25–0	10.0
ex Ansaldo Savoia Primo 28, ex Ansaldo Savoia I 25								
Potestas (m2)	1919	OTO6	5237	7700	392–10	51–6	25–0	10.0
ex Ansaldo San Giorgio Secondo 28, ex Ansaldo San Giorgio II 24								
Probitas (m2)	1918	OTO6	5084	7700	392–11	51–7	25–0	10.0
ex Ansaldo San Giorgio Primo 28, ex Ansaldo San Giorgio I 24								
Securitas (st)	1918	AnsGC	5366	7750	393–2	51–9	24–0	10.0
ex Ansaldo Quarto 28, ex Ansaldo IV 24								
Voluntas	1907	SHWR	5655	8725	437–3	53–1	26–0	9.5
ex City of Batavia 38, ex Ganelon 20								
Tanker								
Utilitas (st)	1918	AnsGC	5342	7700	393–2	51–6	24–0	11.0
ex Ansaldo Terzo 28, ex Ansaldo III 24								

CANDIDA BOMBRINI IN RAVANO AND MARIA LUISA ACCAME IN RAVANO

General cargo vessel

Comitas	1905	StephR	3482	6248	355–4	50–1	22–5	8.0
ex Orminster 36, ex Orebic 35, ex Selonia 28, ex Briarwood 28, ex Deemster 23, ex Grelben 20, ex Reliance 17								

MARE NOSTRUM SOCIETÀ ANONIMA

General cargo vessels

Capacitas (st)	1920	OTO6	5371	7701	393–2	51–10	24–0	11.0
ex Ansaldo San Giorgio Quarto 28								
Fidelitas	1914	Hamtn2	5826	9222	439–5	53–0	26–3	9.0
ex Bolton Castle 39								
Honestas	1920	Schich	4959	7755	374–8	51–4	25–9	11.0
ex Gudrun Mærsk 36								

NOVA GENUENSIS, SOCIETÀ ANONIMA PER l'INDUSTRIA ED IL COMMERCIO MARITTIMO

General cargo vessels

Aequitas	1916	Savoia	5335	7925	395–9	51–8	24–0	11.0
ex Cogne 28								
Integritas	1917	Tirrl	5952	8208	398–0	52–6	25–0	9.0
ex Angelo Toso 28								
San Giuseppe	1917	H&W,B	5074	8250	413–0	52–4	25–3	10.0
ex War Trefoil 19								
Serenitas	1918	Sundld	5171	8217	412–4	52–4	25–3	10.0
ex Sierra Roja 25, ex War Coot 19								
Vesuvio	1914	OTO5	5430	7825	394–9	51–9	24–0	10.0

SOCIETÀ ANONIMA DI NAVIGAZIONE UNIONE

General cargo vessel

Mincio	1921	Cerusa	5404	7700	394–2	51–11	24–0	10.0

Funnel: White, blue top
Hull: White, red boot-topping
Services: Fruit and passenger – Italian Somaliland–Italy–NW Europe

REGIA AZIENDA MONOPOLIO BANANE (RAMB) (Ministero dell'Africa Italiana), Viale Brigata Bisagno 14, Rome

Fruit carriers

Capitano A Cecchi (m2,P12)								
	1934	Eriksb	2321	1800	312–10	40–9	18–2	14.5
Capitano Bottego (m2,P12)								
	1933	Eriksb	2316	1800	312–10	40–9	18–2	14.5

Duca degli Abruzzi (m2,P12)

Duca degli Abruzzi (m2,P12)	1933	Eriksb	2315	1800	312–10	40–9	18–2	14.5
Ramb I (m2,P–)	1937	AnsSA	3667	2410	383–2	47–11	18–0	17.0
Ramb II (m2,P–)	1937	CRDA2	3685	2385	383–2	49–8	18–0	17.0
Ramb III (m2,P–)	1938	AnsSA	3667	2460	383–2	47–9	18–0	17.0
Ramb IV (m2,P–)	1937	CRDA5	3676	2380	383–2	49–8	18–0	17.0

Note: This agency was controlled by the Government of Italy

RIZZUTO, FRATELLI, (Giuseppe and Salvatore Rizzuto),
Piazza Garibaldi 3, Naples

Hull: Black
Services: General tramping

Amsterdam (st)	1921	Lithgw	8673	14,352	492–4	65–5	30–0	10.5
Assunzione	1911	Craig2	4531	7375	396–0	50–0	23–8	9.0
ex Valnegra 34, ex Brendon 23, ex Exford 15								
Fortunstella	1912	Palmer	4866	7450	420–0	54–0	23–5	10.5
ex Eboe 38								
Gloriastella (st)	1922	RottDD	5490	8701	419–0	58–4	27–4	10.0
ex Gloriastar 36, ex Klipfontein 35								
Maristella	1912	Palmer	4862	7450	420–0	54–0	23–5	10.5
ex Ebani 38								
Provvidenza	1913	Doxfrd	8459	12,699	485–1	58–0	29–11	11.0
ex Noorderdijk 32, ex Gernis 18, ex Harlow 14								

ROSASCO, ALBERTO TOMASO, Piazza delle Oche 1, Genoa

Funnel: Black, two red bands
Hull: Black, white band; name of vessel in white amidships
Services: General tramping

Escambia*	1920	Bacini	2710	4500	299–11	39–5	22–0	10.0
ex Ariele 27, ex Vittoria 24								
Etiopia	1918	Polson	2153	3400	261–10	43–8	20–2	9.0
ex Capo Mele 36, ex Francisca 26, ex Asp 20								
Florida II	1905	GrayX	3313	5215	329.5	47–6	20–8	8.0
ex Fortunato Terzo 29, ex Nicolaos Pateras 27, ex Tideway 23, ex Typhoon 22, ex Onega 20, ex Twilight 19								
Santarosa	1924	DunlpB	3027	5500	344–0	48–1	20–8	10.0
ex Baron Wemyss 37								

Note: * Sold Peninsulare Società di Navigazione 1939, renamed *Salpi* (Italian flag)

RUGGIERO & MEREGA SOCIETA ANONIMA DI NAVIGAZIONE & VITTORIO DE CASTRO, Piazza Demarini 4/8, Genoa

Services: General tramping

Santa Rita	1908	CNR4	5191	8150	382.1	50–9	26–9	8.0
ex Veniero 39, ex Panormus 39, ex Boheme 37, ex Veniero 31, ex Monginevro 12								

SCHIAFFINO FU GIUSEPPE, G B, Piazza San Luca 7/3, Genoa

Services: General tramping

SOCIETÀ ANONIMA NAVIGAZIONE DE GREGORI & SCHIAFFINO

Ettore	1912	GrayX	4270	7670	391–11	51–0	23–7	9.0
ex Collington 31, ex Fairwater 28, ex Penthaw 27, ex Flixton 23								

SOCIETÀ ANONIMA DI NAVIGAZIONE 'ASSUNTA DE GREGORI'

Assunta De Gregori	1914	Nthmbl	4219	8300	400.0	53–0	23–8	9.0
ex Tirreno 33								
Teresa Schiaffino	1919	Steph2	5189	7885	412–5	52–4	25–3	10.5
ex Beachcliffe 34, ex Melpo 27, ex War Hussar 19								

SCINICARIELLO, ANGELO, Via Agostino Depretis 145, Naples

Funnel: Red, black top
Hull: Black
Services: General tramping

'NIVOSE' SOCIETÀ DI NAVIGAZIONE

Gaeta	1927	Leslie	4470	8703	414–3	53–2	24–7	11.0
ex Benwell Tower 37								
Luigi	1920	Fredst	4283	7700	383–2	52–1	24–0	9.0
ex Modemi 30, ex Modica 27								
Nirvo	1919	Hendn2	5163	8258	412–10	52–4	25–4	10.0
ex Tremorvah 38, launched as War Palm								

SCUDERI, MATTEO, Via Vecchio Bastione 21, Catania

Funnel: Black with four white and three red alternating bands
Hull: Black
Services: General tramping
Note: * Sold Navigazione Carlo

Fortunata*	1920	ToddDD	4786	7659	396–5	53–1	23–9	10.0
ex Padnsay 38								

Lloyd Triestino: Timavo *was completed at the San Rocco shipyard in August 1920. On June 11 1940 she was overtaken by a South African Air Force aircraft off Cape Vidal, 160 miles north of Durban, and was later scuttled by her own crew to avoid capture (Alex Duncan)*

RAMB: Ramb II *was completed at Monfalcone in 1937, and was fitted with two CRDA 7-cylinder oil engines of 7200bhp. With three sisterships she was built for service between Genoa, Trieste and Fiume and Kismayu and Massowah, her homeward cargo mainly bananas. On April 9 1940 she was requisitioned by the Italian navy to become an auxiliary cruiser.* Ramb II *was later in Japan, and in 1942 was chartered to Japan as* Calitea II *under the Italian flag. When Italy surrendered to the Allies in September 1943, she was scuttled at Kobe by her own crew on the 8th. She was raised by the Japanese, but on January 12 1945 was bombed by USAAF aircraft and sunk at Osaka (Alex Duncan)*

Martinolich & Figlio 1939, renamed *Caterina*
Note: Also *Achille* (built 1890/2415gt), *Erigli* (05/2715), *Oreste* (96/2679), *Salvatore*

SOCIETÀ COMMERCIALE DI NAVIGAZIONE, Via Caserotte 5, Milan

Funnel: Yellow with black top, separated by yellow over blue bands
Hull: Black, red boot-topping
Services: General tramping

Chisone (m)	1922	Ilva	6168	8800	394–4	51–8	28–0	9.0
ex Valtellina 27, ex Bagnoli I 23; conv steamer 28								
Juventus (m)	1920	Tosi	4920	8100	394–3	51–9	25–0	10.0
ex Valdieri 27; conv steamer 27								
Pellice (m)	1920	AnsSA	5360	7900	393–2	51–6	24–0	10.0
ex Ansaldo Ottavo 28, ex Ansaldo VIII 24; conv steamer 28								
Riv (m)	1921	ArmWh1	6630	10,120	425–8	55–10	28–3	11.5
ex Montgomeryshire 31, ordered as War Valour; conv steamer 31								
Villarperosa (m)	1921	Ilva	6255	8800	396–9	51–10	28–0	9.0
ex Valsugana 23, ex Piombino I 23; conv steamer 27								

SOCIETÀ ESERCIZIO ARMAMENTO, Via Garibaldi 2, Piano 3, Genoa

Services: General tramping

Adriana (m2)	1923	CFCN	4346	6594	353–6	51–1	24–4	12.0
(tubular vessel)								
Maria Eugenia	1928	Craig2	4702	8570	414–11	53–6	24–8	9.5
ex Maria D'Al 35, ex Amplegarth 34, ex Eastborough 33								

SOCIETÀ ITALIANA D'ARMAMENTO ('SIDARMA'), Fiume

Funnel: Yellow with blue five-pointed star superimposed on narrow red band
Hull: Black with white band, red boot-topping
Services: General tramping

Andrea Gritti (m,P12)	1939	CRDA2	6338	10,350	470–7	60–8	26–2	16.0
Francesco Barbaro (m,P12)	bldg	CRDA2	6342	10,350	470–8	60–8	26–2	16.0
Marco Foscarini (m,P12)	bldg	CRDA2	6405	10,350	470–8	60–8	26–2	16.0
Pietro Orseolo (m,P12)	1939	CRDA2	6342	10,350	470–8	60–8	26–2	16.0
Vettor Pisani (m,P12)	1939	CRDA2	6339	10,354	470–8	60–8	26–2	16.0
Newbuilding (m,P12)	bldg	CRDA2	6339	10,354	470–8	60–8	26–2	16.0

SOCIETÀ ITALIANA ERNESTO BREDA, CP 3590, Milan, and Mestre, Venice

Services: General tramping

Ernesto	1914	Neptn1	7272	11,737	489–0	61–2	26–7	11.5
ex Arendskerk 35, ex St Alban's Abbey 21, ex Totmes 20								

SOCIETÀ ITALIANA TRASPORTI MARITTIMI SOCIETÀ ANONIMA (SITMAR), Via del Conservatorio 15, Milan

Funnel: Black with white V
Hull: Black
Services: General tramping
Note: This company was associated with Navigation & Coal Trade Co Ltd (*qv* in Great Britain section) and controlled by A Vlasov (*qv* in Romania section under Navigation & Coal Trade Co Ltd)

Castelbianco	1924	Lithgw	4895	8250	413–1	52–0	24–3	10.5
ex Pearlstone 38, ex Ovingdean Grange 36, ex Zapala 35								
Castelverde	1921	H&W,B	6666	10,175	428–10	55–10	28–2	10.5
ex Sunstone 38, ex Inverleith 37; conv tanker 37								

SOCIETÀ ITALIANA TRASPORTI PETROLIFERI (SITP), Via XX Settembre 34, Genoa, and Via Ludovisi 16, Rome

Trades: Oil and petroleum

Tankers

Poseidone	1912	SHWR	6613	10,330	432–1	54–6	26–5	10.0
ex Cordelia 30								

SOCIETÀ PETROLIFERA ESERCIZI MARITTIMI, Corso Vittorio Emanuele 18, Fiume

Lucifero	1912	Palmer	4000	6050	364–0	47–6	23–0	9.0
ex Arminco 29, ex F A Tamplin 21								
Prometeo	1922	GrkDY	4958	7550	388.0	52–2	23–8	9.0
ex Cedarpark 28								

Funnel: Yellow, black top, separated by diagonally quartered band with white upper and lower and blue left and right
Hull: Black, red boot-topping
Services: General tramping; oil and petroleum trades

SOCIETÀ LIGURE DI ARMAMENTO,
Via Ippolito D'Aste 5, CP 1501, Genoa

General cargo vessels								
Euro	1926	CNR4	4687	9002	406–5	51–9	34.4	13.0
Marte	1917	CNR4	5290	7886	394.9	51–9	26–5	10.0
Perseo	1921	CNR5	4857	8277	394.2	52–0	26–5	9.0
Sirio	1921	CNR4	5222	8600	394.5	51–8	26–5	9.0
Teseo	1920	CNR4	4966	8575	394.2	51–10	26–5	9.0
Tanker								
Anteo (m,P4)	1934	CNR4	6772	9750	451–4	56–9	27–4	14.0

Funnel: Black with yellow S and anchor emblem on blue band
Hull: Black
Services: General tramping

SZABADOS, E, CP 587, Venice

Luciano	1913	Earles	3329	5100	332–0	42–5	23–7	9.5
ex Maronian 38								
Paolo	1908	Rhead1	3844	5830	371–6	47–8	23–6	9.5
ex African Trader 39, ex Laurent Schiaffino 37, ex Scientist 25, ex Sargasso 20								

Services: General tramping

TAGLIAVIA & CO, SALVATORE, Via Emerico Amari 4, Palermo

Note: * Sold Compagnia Veneziana di Navigazione 1939, renamed *Veniero*

SOCIETÀ ANONIMA DI NAVIGAZIONE TRANSMEDITERRANEA

Drepanum	1914	Palmer	2736	4805	312.0	43–0	22–6	10.0
ex Roumelian 37								
Panormus*	1908	CNR4	5191	8150	382.1	50–9	26–9	8.0
ex Bohême 37, ex Veniero 31, ex Monginevro 12								
Pelorum	1918	Bartm2	5314	8230	413–0	52–4	25–3	10.0
ex Queen Eleanor 38, ex Sierra Blanca 24, ex War Cygnet 19								

Trades: Oil and petroleum

TIGULLIA SOCIETÀ ANONIMA DI NAVIGAZIONE,
Via Ponte Reale 1, Genoa

Tankers								
Arcola	1929	OTO7	6349	9250	419–10	54–11	26–1	10.0
Teresa Odero (m2)	1927	OTO2	8196	10,990	456–0	57–11	37.0	10.0
conv general cargo 30								

Funnel: White with black top separated by white over black bands
Hull: Black, red boot-topping
Services: Venice, Trieste, Fiume–Bari–Palermo–Milazzo–Messina–Leghorn–Susak–Casablanca–London–Antwerp–Rotterdam–Amsterdam–Hamburg; Genoa, Naples–London–Antwerp–Rotterdam–Hamburg; Trieste–Fiume–Lisbon–Leixoes–Rouen–NW Europe; various services within Mediterranean

Note: This company was controlled by Finmare Società Finanziaria Marittima, Rome

TIRRENIA, SOCIETÀ ANONIMA DI NAVIGAZIONE,
Palazzo Sirignano, Rione Sirignano 2, Naples

Alfredo Oriani	1918	LloydR	3059	4900	342–0	46–9	21–9	9.5
ex Mampoko 34, ex Tongrier 27, ex War Breaker 19								
Ariosto	1902	Wighm1	4116	6115	375–5	48–3	23–3	10.5
ex Báró Fejérváry 21, ex Bulganak 19, ex Báró Fejérváry 18								
Carducci (P8/1)	1902	Dobson	2028	3140	285–10	39–1	20–1	10.5
ex Koloszvar 21								
Firenze (s2,P–)	1912	Tirr1	3952	3500	360–11	44–8	22–0	13.5
ex Roma 25								
Foscolo	1919	LloydR	3059	4900	342–0	46–9	21–9	9.5
ex Maringa 34, ex Rogier 27, launched as War Ripple								
Giovanni Boccaccio	1919	Shangh	3141	4705	342–0	46–9	21–8	9.5
ex Makala 38, ex European 27, ex Panagis 24, launched as War Diadem								
Leopardi	1915	TyneIr	3298	5049	349–7	48–8	21–2	10.0
ex Gambia 33								
Manzoni	1902	Wighm1	3955	6115	375–5	48–3	23–3	10.5
ex Lydia 25, ex Széll Kálmán 19								
Pascoli	1902	Dobson	2939	4515	331–10	44–10	21–0	10.0
ex Szeged 21								
Petrarca (P4/1)	1910	Clyde	3329	4600	350–4	45–6	21–3	10.0
ex Szent István 21								
Ugo Bassi	1902	Dobson	2900	4515	331–10	45–0	21–0	10.0
ex Duna 16								

Funnel: Black with white anchor and SA on red band between two narrow white bands, cowl top
Hull: Black, red boot-topping

TRIPCOVICH, D, Palazzo Tergesteo, Via della Borsa 3, Trieste

Laconia	1912	CRDA1	5932	9600	430–10	54–0	25–9	10.5
Numidia	1913	CRDA3	5339	8170	404–5	52–9	24–2	10.0

D TRIPCOVICH & CI – SOCIETÀ ANONIMA DI NAVIGAZIONE RIMORCHI E SALVATAGGI

Andalusia	1907	Hendn2	4499	7200	399–0	50–1	24–0	10.5
ex Australplain 25, ex Ardanmhor 16								

Services: Adriatic, Mediterranean–Morocco; Adriatic–Tripoli–Benghazi; Adriatic–Tunisia–Algeria–Oran–Spain
Note: Also *Etruria* (built 1906/2633gt), *Fanny Brunner* (25/2366), *Giovinezza* (25/2362), *Silvia Tripcovich* (25/2365)

TRUMPY, HUGO, Piazza San Siro 10, Genoa

Services: General tramping

HUGO TRUMPY, STEEN BOESGAARD, ERNESTO CIURLO AND FAUSTO CIURLO

Fausto	1919	Ropnr2	5263	8345	412–4	52–4	25–2	10.5
ex Nedon 38, ex Heathfield 33, ex Briarwood 21, launched as War Mallow								

VILLAIN & FASSIO, SOCIETÀ ANONIMA ITALIANA DI NAVIGAZIONE MERCANTILE, Via Balbi 2, Genoa

General cargo vessel								
Jole Fassio	1908	Napr&M	5169	7740	395–4	51–9	26–1	8.0
ex Sequoya 25, ex Tamarac 12								
Tanker								
Giorgio Fassio	1920	SunSB	6735	11,223	445–5	59–2	26–10	9.5
ex Atlantic Sun 39								

Funnel: Black and, from top, narrow white, blue, white, blue, white, black, red, blue, yellow bands
Hull: Black
Services: General tramping; oil and petroleum trades
Note: Also tanker *Alberto Fassio* (built 1914/2289gt), general cargo vessel *Franca Fassio* (92/1858)

ZANCHI FU GIOVANNI, ANDREA, Via Vittorio Emanuele 8, Voltri, Genoa

General cargo vessels								
Augusta	1904	Leslie	5702	–	434–6	54–0	27–0	11.0
ex Durham 24								
Capo Nord*	1904	Dixon2	6096	8860	436.3	53–2	27–5	8.5
ex Mar Bianco 38, ex Vega 26, ex Carpentaria 24, ex Vega 05								
Cervino	1913	Prstm1	4363	–	379–1	53–0	23–0	10.0
ex Tatra 16								
Mar Bianco (s2)	1912	Workmn	8443	12,170	506–11	61–5	30–0	12.0
ex Martano 38, ex Martand 38, ex Port Napier 36, ex Hawkes Bay 16								
Norge	1907	Workmn	6511	9860	460–5	55–4	28–1	10.0
ex Port Chalmers 26, ex Whakarua 16								
Tankers								
Bonzo (m2)	1931	CRDA2	8177	5050	483–10	60–2	28–0	11.0
Olterra	1913	Palmer	4995	8082	394–5	52–8	24–4	9.0
ex Baton Rouge 24, ex Osage 14								

Funnel: Blue, white band, black top
Hull: Black
Services: General tramping; oil and petroleum trades

Note: * BU 1939

Japan

AMAKASU SANGYO KISEN KK,
32 Masago-tyo, 3 tyome, Naka-ku, Yokohama

Heian Maru (P6)	1921	PrRup	5346	8090	413–0	52–0	25–5	10.5
ex Ping An 38, ex Canadian Britisher 36								
Koan Maru	1905	Neptn1	4306	7000	376.6	48–9	26–0	9.0
ex Kung Ho 38, ex Viking II 35, ex Kari Skogland 30, ex Solingen 21								
Taian Maru (P6)	1921	CanVic	5411	8326	413–0	52–5	25–5	10.5
ex Ta An 38, ex Canadian Leader 36								

Services: East

ASAHI SEKIYU KK,
Tokyo Kaizyo Bldg, 1 Marunouti, 1 tyome, Kozimati-ku, Tokyo

Tankers								
Manzyu Maru (P–)	1921	KobeSW	6515	9328	440–0	54–0	26–7	10.5
ex Manju Maru 38								
Tatibana Maru (P–)	1921	KobeSW	6515	9345	440–0	54–0	26–7	10.5
ex Tachibana Maru 38								

Trades: Trans-Pacific oil and petroleum, W coast US–Japan

Note: Also smaller tankers

Services: Vessel operated by Taiyo Kaiun KK (*qv*)

ASAHI SYOZI KK, (Asahi Shoji KK),
6 Banti, 6 Ginza Nisi, 8 tyome, Kyobasi-ku, Tokyo

Kyokusei Maru	1920	Coughl	5493	8656	427–0	54–1	24–3	10.5
ex Shun Hwa 38, ex Chilcop 36, ex Margaret Coughlan 25								

Funnel: Black
Hull: Black
Trades: Trans-Pacific oil and petroleum, W coast US–Japan

Note: This company was associated with Toyo Kisen KK (*qv*)

ASANO BUSSAN KK, (Asano Production Co Ltd),
Tokyo Kaizyo Bldg, 6 Marunouti, 1 tyome, Kozimati-ku, Tokyo

Tankers								
Genyo Maru (m)	1938	Kwsaki	10,019	14,500	526–1	65–0	29–11	18.0
Kiyo Maru (m)	1930	DeutsH	7240	11,210	416.6	57–0	27–8	11.0
ex Vigrid 35								

Funnel: Black with white cross (+) inside and joined to white circle
Services: Japan–China–W and E coasts US; Japan–R Plate
Note: * Sold Toa Boeki KK (*qv*) 1939
Note: Also general cargo/passenger vessel *Harada Maru* (built 1903/4109gt) on Japan/Far East voyages
Note: This company became associated with Osaka Syosen KK (*qv*) in 1938

HARADA KISEN KK, Osaka Bldg, 1 Soze-tyo, Kita-ku, Osaka

Kansai Maru (m2,P–)	1930	YokoDk	8614	10,774	461.7	61–6	28–2	16.0
ex Kwansai Maru 38								
Kanto Maru (m2,P–)	1930	YokoDk	8607	10,779	461.7	61–6	28–2	16.0
ex Kwanto Maru 38								
Kyusyu Maru (m2,P–)	1937	MitsuN	8666	10,100	466.9	62–4	29–0	17.0

Funnel: Sinko – yellow with SH on band
Hull: Black, white band
Services: W coast US–Japan lumber trade; Japan–Eastern ports

Note: Also smaller vessels

HASIMOTO KISEN KK, (Hashimoto Kisen KK),
46 Imazaiya-mati, Nishinomiya, Hyogo-ken

Koki Maru	1921	Ishkwa	5290	8593	388.0	53–3	25–7	9.0
RYUO KISEN KK, 200 Yamagata-dori, Dairen, Kwantung Peninsula								
Ryuzin Maru (P*c*15)	1907	Denny1	6243	9350	439–0	54–3	27–4	10.0
ex Ryujin Maru 38, ex Culna 23								
SINKO SYOSEN KK								
Sinko Maru (m,P–)	1935	YokoDk	6480	9400	436.2	58–3	26–0	14.5
ex Shinko Maru 38								

Services: Japan–Malaya–India; Japan–China

Note: Also vessels engaged on Eastern services

HATIUMA KISEN KK, 15 Isizai-tyo, Nishinomiya, Hiogo-ken

Kaisyo Maru (P–)	1918	OsakaO	6070	8825	407.3	50–10	26–1	9.5
ex Kaisho Maru 38								
Tamon Maru (s2)	1919	Asano	8134	13,066	462–0	58–0	30–4	12.5
ex Kaikyu Maru 33								

Funnel: Black with white emblem inside white circle
Hull: Black
Services: Whaling

Note: Also a large fleet of fishing vessels and whalers
Note: This company was associated with Okidori Gyogyo KK (*qv*)

HAYASHIKANE SHOTEN KK, 66 Takezaki-tyo, Shimonoseki

TAIYO HOGEI KK, Tokyo

Whale factory vessels								
Nissin Maru (m)	1936	Kwsaki	16,764	22,190	550–0	74–0	34–2	13.0
ex Nisshin Maru 38								
Nissin Maru No 2 (m)	1937	Kwsaki	17,583	22,200	550–0	74–0	34–2	13.0
ex Nisshin Maru No 2 38								

Funnel: Black with white **x**
Hull: Black
Services: Japan–W coast US and Canada; Japan–E coast US; Japan–E Africa–South Africa; Japan–Eastern ports

Note: Also smaller vessels in Japan local services

HIROUMI SYOZI KK, (Hiroumi Shoji KK),
27 Higasino-tyo, Enokozima, Nisi-ku, Osaka

Koryu Maru (m)	1931	MitsuN	6680	10,100	454–9	58–6	26–1	12.0
Kosei Maru (m,P–)	1933	MitsuN	6668	10,300	454–9	58–5	26–3	12.0
Kosin Maru	1924	OsakaI	5485	8769	407.2	50–10	26–2	11.5
ex Koshin Maru 38								
Kotoku Maru (m,P–)	1937	MitsuN	6702	10,003	453–9	58–6	26–3	13.0
Koyu Maru	1921	MitsuK	5325	8500	400.0	54–8	24–8	11.0

Hayashikane Shoten: The whale factory vessel Nissin Maru *was owned by the subsidiary company Taiyo Hogei KK, and was one of two sisters built during 1936–37 by Kawasaki. These were among several such vessels built in Japan in the mid to late 1930s with the country's increasing involvement in the whaling industry.* Nissin Maru, *renamed from* Nisshin Maru *in 1938, was torpedoed and sunk by the US submarine* Crevalle *on May 6 1944 (Alex Duncan)*

Kawasaki: Holland Maru *was completed in 1920 and was one of a large number of general cargo sisterships built at the Kawasaki shipyard during and immediately after the First World War. She was torpedoed and sunk by the US submarine* Trigger *on October 17 1942 (Alex Duncan)*

Kokusai Kisen: The steamer Atlantic Maru *was completed in 1920 and was one of a large series of standard vessels, the construction of which started during the First World War. She was torpedoed and sunk by the US submarine* Picuda *on March 30 1944 (Alex Duncan)*

Services: Japan–Eastern ports; Japan–Australia

HUKUYO KISEN KK, Meikai Bldg, 32 Akasi-mati, Kobe-ku, Kobe

Kasyu Maru (P–)	1919	Asano	5460	8750	400.0	53–2	25–8	10.5
ex Kashu Maru 38								
SAKA KISEN KK								
Ryoka (Ryoga) Maru (P–)	1903	LithR	5308	9030	411.8	52–4	26–2	9.0
ex Oneka 24, ex Schuylkill 13								

Note: Also smaller vessels

Funnel: Black
Hull: Black with white band
Trades: Trans-Pacific oil and petroleum, W coast US–Japan
Note: Also tankers under 3000gt

IINO SYOZI KK, (Iino Shoji KK), Meiziseimei Bldg, Marunouti, Tokyo

Tankers

Huzisan Maru (m)	1931	Harim2	9524	13,586	493.4	65–0	27–11	11.5
ex Fujisan Maru 38								
Kyokuto Maru (m)	1934	Kwsaki	10,052	13,750	526–0	65–0	29–0	17.0
Toa Maru (m)	1934	Kwsaki	10,052	13,748	526–0	65–0	29–0	17.0
Toho Maru (m)	1936	Kwsaki	9987	13,750	526–0	65–0	29–0	17.0

Funnel: Blue with red emblem on white band
Services: Japan–Malaya; Japan–S Pacific; Japan–China

INUI KISEN KK, 39 Sakae-mati, 2 tyome, Kobe-ku, Kobe

Heiei Maru No 7	1903	SHWR	4815	7160	390.4	51–6	24–0	10.0
ex Heiyei Maru No 7 38, ex Ravenrock 23, ex HMS Raven (seaplane carrier) 17, ex Rabenfels 15								
Kenkon Maru (m)	1935	Mtsui1	4575	6645	362.2	50–0	24–0	12.5
Kenryu Maru (m)	1935	Mtsui1	4576	6643	362.2	50–0	24–0	12.5
Kensyo Maru (m,P–)	1938	Mtsui2	4862	6300	384.4	52–6	30.3	13.0
Kenyo Maru (st)	1938	Harim2	6486	7200	438.8	58–10	32.8	15.0
Unyo Maru	1907	G&G2	4643	7195	376.1	52–2	23–0	8.5
ex Australford 23, ex Strathavon 16								
Zuiko Maru	1904	ThmpsJ	4156	6500	368.0	49–8	14–0	8.0
ex Jaladuta 26, ex Shadwell 20								

Funnel: Black with red vertical stripe on white band
Hull: Black with white –I–S–K– amidships breaking white band
Services: Japan–Singapore; Japan–Eastern ports

ISIHARA SANGYO KAIUN KK, (Ishihara Sangyo Kaiun KK), 30 Kaigan-dori, 2 tyome, Kobe-ku, Kobe

Boston Maru (P–)	1919	Asano	5477	8717	400.0	53–2	25–8	9.5
Havre Maru (P–)	1920	Asano	5467	8583	400.0	53–2	25–8	9.5
Malta Maru (P–)	1919	Asano	5500	8727	400.0	53–2	25–8	9.5
Milan Maru (P–)	1920	Asano	5467	8784	400.0	53–2	25–9	9.5
Nansin Maru	1914	Irvin3	4806	8025	385.0	52–0	24–4	8.5
ex Nanshin Maru 38, ex Koki Maru 30, ex Hemisphere 26, ex Thurland Castle 22, ex Corinthic 16								
Syogen Maru	1917	Uraga	4739	6810	360.0	51–0	23–1	9.5
ex Shyogen Maru 38, ex Kofuku Maru 30								
Syozin Maru	1918	Uraga	4739	6800	360.0	51–0	23–2	9.5
ex Shyojin Maru 38, ex Koyei Maru 30								
DAIREN ISIHARA GOSI KAISYA, 6 Suma-mati, Dairen, Kwantung Peninsula								
Nanko Maru	1916	LithR	4714	7800	385.0	52–0	23–11	8.0
ex Nankoh Maru 38, ex Wigmore 22, ex Ardgrange 19								
HARA SYOZI KK (Hara Shoji KK)								
Sinsei Maru No 1 (P–)	1919	Kwsaki	5863	9098	385.0	51–0	27–1	9.5
ex Shinsei Maru No 1 38, ex Washington Maru 33								

Funnel: Black with red band
Hull: Black, red boot-topping
Services: Japan–Eastern ports; Japan–W coast US and Canada; Japan–New Orleans–E coast US

ITAYA SYOSEN KK, (Itaya Shosen KK – Itaya Mercantile Marine Co), 29 Ironai-tyo, 6 tyome, Otaru

Dainiti Maru (P4)	1922	Mtsui1	5813	8903	385.0	51–0	27–1	11.5
ex Dainichi Maru 38, ex Ibukisan Maru 35								
Hakkai Maru (m)	1939	Mtsui2	5114	8320	422.4	58–1	25–0	12.5
Myoko Maru (m,P–)	1937	Mtsui2	5081	8304	422.4	58–1	25–0	12.5
Yahiko Maru (m2)	1926	KobeSW	5747	9109	417.2	54–6	25–7	12.5
Yoneyama Maru (P–)	1919	MitsuN	5274	8486	400.0	54–6	24–8	9.5
ex Kaian Maru 23								
KUROHIME KISEN GOSHI KAISYA								
Kurohime Maru	1920	Lithgw	4697	8010	384.8	52–0	25–0	9.0
ex Bogstad 24; laid down as tanker, completed as general cargo vessel								

KAWASAKI KISEN KK, ('K' LINE), 47 Sakaemati-dori, 2 tyome, Kobe-ku, Kobe

Funnel: Black or yellow with red deep top bearing white K; Goyo – yellow
Hull: Black, red boot-topping; tanker – grey, red boot-topping
Services: General cargo – Japan–Europe via Suez; Japan, Philippines–Panama–Galveston–Philadelphia–New York; Japan–W coast South America; Japan–Malaya–Calcutta; Japan–S Pacific; Japan–W coast US and Canada; Japan–Australia; trans-Pacific oil and petroleum trades

General cargo vessels								
Bordeaux Maru (st,P–)	1923	Kwsaki	6567	9810	428–6	53–0	28–5	11.0
China Maru (P–)	1920	Kwsaki	5869	9072	385.0	51–0	27–1	10.0
Cuba Maru (m,P–)	1926	Kwsaki	5950	9113	428–6	53–0	27–1	11.0
Florida Maru (m,P–)	1925	Kwsaki	5854	9114	428–6	53–0	26–11	11.0
Hirokawa Maru (m)	bldg	Kwsaki	6872	9680	508–6	62–4	28–1	17.0
Holland Maru	1920	Kwsaki	5869	9090	385.0	51–0	27–1	10.0
India Maru	1920	Kwsaki	5872	9074	385.0	51–0	27–1	10.0
Kamikawa Maru (m)	1937	Kwsaki	6853	9689	508–6	62–4	28–1	17.0
Kimikawa Maru (m)	1937	Kwsaki	6863	9690	508–6	62–4	28–1	17.0
Kiyokawa Maru (m)	1937	Kwsaki	6863	9687	508–6	62–4	28–1	17.0
Kunikawa Maru (m)	1937	Kwsaki	6863	9679	508–6	62–4	28–1	17.0
Montreal Maru (P–)	1922	Kwsaki	6577	9946	428–6	53–0	28–5	11.0
Norfolk Maru (P–)	1921	Kwsaki	6576	9728	428–6	53–0	28–0	11.0
Norway Maru (P–)	1920	Kwsaki	5832	9088	385.0	51–0	27–1	10.0
Oregon Maru	1920	Kwsaki	5873	9037	385.0	51–0	27–1	10.0
Thames Maru	1920	Kwsaki	5872	9084	385.0	51–0	27–1	10.0
Venice Maru (P–)	1921	Kwsaki	6571	9727	428–6	53–0	28–0	11.0
Wales Maru (P–)	1921	Kwsaki	6586	9750	428–6	53–0	28–0	11.0
Yasukawa Maru (m2,P–)	1930	H&W,B	6770	10,086	475–0	62–0	26–9	13.5
ex Silvercypress 38								
Tanker								
Tatekawa Maru (m)	1935	Kwsaki	10,152	13,691	524–1	64–11	29–6	19.0

GOYO SYOSEN KK (Goyo Shosen KK)

General cargo vessels								
Gosyu Maru (st)	bldg	Kwsaki	8592	10,600	443.2	60–0	28–0	14.5
Goyo Maru (st)	1939	Kwsaki	8469	10,600	443.0	60–0	28–0	14.5
Terukawa Maru (m)	1934	Odense	6172	9225	482–4	58–3	26–5	13.0
ex Nora Mærsk 38								

KINRYU KISEN KK, 80 Kaisyo-tyo, Sakae-mati, Saihaku-gun, Tottori-ken

Services: Japan–Far East ports

Kinryu Maru (st)	1920	H&W,B	6524	10,600	428–0	55–5	28–3	11.0
ex Chin Yuen 38, ex New Brighton 34								

KITAGAWA SANGYO KAIUN KK, 78 Taisyo-dori, 9 tyome, Taisyo-ku, Osaka

Services: Japan–Far East ports; trans–Pacific oil and petroleum trades, W coast US–Japan

General cargo vessels								
Hokko Maru	1907	Ropnrl	4471	7300	355.0	51–2	23–0	9.0
ex Athanasios 38, ex Cardigan 14								
Hokutai Maru	1918	H&W,B	5220	8150	413–0	52–4	25–3	10.5
ex Pei Tai 37, ex Galvan 37, ex Foreric 27, ex Verentia 27, ex War Lemur 19								
Hokuzyu Maru	1918	CanVic	4246	7211	393–6	48–8	24–3	10.5
ex Hokuju Maru 38, ex Campden Hill 37, ex Umlazi 36, ex Rosyth Castle 20, ex War Earl 19								
Kitahuku Maru*	1912	ThmpsJ	5977	8850	403–0	54–1	25–7	9.5
ex Kitafuku Maru 38, ex Pei Foo 38, ex Macdonald 37, ex Rhymney 36, ex Maasdijk 22, ex Southern 15								
Tanker								
Hokki Maru	1919	Palmer	5601	8480	412–0	52–4	25–7	10.0
ex War Begum 38, ex Thelma 37, ex Herborg 30, ex Conus 27, ex War Begum 21								

Note: * BU 1939

KOBE SANBASHI KK, (Kobe Pier Co Ltd), 122 Higasi-mati, Kobe-ku, Kobe

Services: Singapore Maru operated by Mitui Bussan KK (*qv*); *Sinkoku Maru* – oil and petroleum trades

General cargo vessel								
Singapore Maru	1919	Kwsaki	5859	9105	385.0	51–0	27–1	10.5
Tanker								
Sinkoku Maru (m)	bldg	Kwsaki	10,020	14,500	526–0	65–0	29–11	18.0

Note: Also coastal vessels

Mitui Bussan: Akasisan Maru, *renamed from* Akashisan Maru *in 1938, was employed on her owner's service from Japan to southeast Asia. She was torpedoed and sunk on March 3 1944 by the US submarine* Sandlance *(Mitsui OSK archives)*

Mitui Bussan: The motor vessel Amagisan Maru *was completed by Mitsui in 1933, and was employed on Mitui's service from Japan and the Philippines to San Francisco, Los Angeles and New York. She was sunk by USN carrier-based aircraft on February 17 1944 during Operation 'Hailstone', the US raid on Truk, Caroline Islands (Mitsui OSK archives)*

Mitui Bussan: Aobasan Maru, *renamed from* Awobasan Maru *in 1938, was completed in 1935 as one of a series of five near sisters. She was sunk by USAAF aircraft on December 30 1944 (Mitsui OSK archives)*

KOKOKU KISEN KK, Syosen Bldg, 5 Kaigan-dori, Kobe-ku, Kobe

Hull: Black, red boot-topping
Services: Japan–India; Japan–W coast US, Canada; Japan–Eastern ports

Anzan Maru (st)	1919	Columb	5493	8624	423–10	54–2	24–1	11.5
ex West Harcuvar Maru 38, ex West Harcuvar 37								
Izan Maru (st)	1918	Columb	5475	8700	423–10	54–2	24–1	11.5
ex Westward Ho Maru 38, ex Westward Ho 37, launched as War Sirdar								
Kenzan Maru	1919	Standd	4705	7249	395–9	52–2	23–8	10.0
ex Shooters Island 38								
Konzan Maru (st)	1919	Columb	5488	8635	423–10	54–2	24–1	11.5
ex West Munham Maru 38, ex West Munham 37								
Ryuzan Maru	1920	Standd	4720	7388	395–9	52–0	23–8	10.0
ex Kerhonkson 38								
Tazan Maru (st)	1919	Columb	5478	8635	423–10	54–2	24–1	11.5
ex West Nosska Maru 38, ex West Nosska 37								
Yuzan Maru (st)	1919	Fed1	6039	9740	411–6	55–0	27–2	12.0
ex Marne Maru 38, ex Marne 38								
KOKOKU SANGYO KK								
Zinzan Maru	1919	Short2	5190	8240	413–0	52–4	25–4	10.0
ex Hindustan 38, launched as War Seagull								
MIYATI KISEN KK (Miyachi Kisen KK)								
Kizan Maru	1918	Duncan	5081	8500	405.3	53–0	24–8	10.0
ex Shang Ho 38, ex Cape Verde 35, ex Balfour 28, ex Bedwyn 23, ex Montezuma 23, launched as Camperdown								
Seizan Maru	1918	CanVic	4233	7290	393–6	49–3	24–5	10.5
ex Shing Ho 38, ex Barunga 35, ex Cape Premier 21, ex War Faith 19								
Operator for								
OGINO (OGIHU) SOTARO								
Victoria Maru	1921	Kwsaki	5876	9009	385.0	51–0	27–1	9.5

KOKUSAI KISEN KK, (Kokusai Steamship Co Ltd),
Kogyo Ginko Bldg, 1–8 Marunouti, 1 tyome, Kozimati-ku, Tokyo

Funnel: Black with white A on broad red band between narrow white bands; *Kurama Maru* had no funnel
Hull: Black or grey, red boot-topping
Services: General cargo, passenger – Japan, Eastern ports–New York; general cargo only – New York–Hamburg–Japan–Australia; Japan–NW Europe; Hamburg–Antwerp–Boston–New York–Philadelphia–Japan–Bombay; Japan–NW Europe; Japan–Africa; Japan–Formosa; Boston–Houston–Los Angeles–Japan

Atlantic Maru	1920	Kwsaki	5873	9009	385.0	51–0	27–1	10.0
Belgium Maru (P–)	1920	Kwsaki	5838	9083	385.0	51–0	27–1	10.0
Glasgow Maru	1919	Kwsaki	5831	9023	385.0	51–0	27–1	10.0
Hohuku Maru (P–)	1918	Kwsaki	5825	9097	385.0	51–0	27–1	10.0
ex Hofuku Maru 38								
Kagu Maru (m,P12)	1936	Harim2	6807	9206	477–0	61–0	27–6	16.5
Kano Maru (m,P12)	1934	Uraga	8572	9383	478–0	60–9	27–11	16.5
Kasii Maru (m,P16)	1936	Harim2	8408	9240	477–0	60–9	27–7	16.5
ex Kashii Maru 38								
Katuragi Maru (m,P12)	1931	Uraga	8033	9087	468–0	60–0	26–11	15.0
ex Katsuragi Maru 38								
Kinka Maru (m,P12)	1938	Kwsaki	9305	10,096	508–7	62–4	28–2	17.0
Kinryu Maru (m,P12)	1938	Kwsaki	9310	10,258	508–7	62–4	28–2	17.0
Kinugasa Maru (m,P16)	1936	Kwsaki	8407	9199	477–0	61–0	27–11	16.5
Kirisima Maru (m,P12)	1931	Kwsaki	8121	9265	442.9	59–9	27–9	15.5
ex Kirishima Maru 38								
Kiyosumi Maru (m,P12)	1934	Kwsaki	8614	9494	478–0	60–9	27–11	16.5
Komaki Maru (m,P12)	1933	Harim2	8525	9501	477–0	60–9	28–0	16.5
Kongo Maru (m,P12)	1935	Harim2	8624	9436	477–0	60–9	27–11	16.5
Kurama Maru (m,P12)	1931	Uraga	6789	10,294	438.0	58–0	26–6	13.0
ex Hokusei Maru 31								
Liverpool Maru	1919	Kwsaki	5865	9105	385.0	51–0	27–1	10.0
Naples Maru	1919	Kwsaki	5824	9093	385.0	51–0	27–1	10.0
Sydney Maru (P–)	1919	YokoDk	4105	6369	380.0	54–6	24–3	8.5
Yae Maru	1919	Harim1	6781	10,978	425.0	53–8	28–7	9.5
ex Yaye Maru 38								

Yuri Maru	1919	Harim1	7210	10,975	425.0	53–8	28–7	9.5
Operator for								
OKADA GUMI KK								
Kogyo Maru (st)	1939	Uraga	6353	9602	423.2	59–0	32.8	14.5
Kosin Maru (st)	1938	OsakaI	6530	9903	424.1	57–0	34.4	14.5
Tasmania Maru	1919	Kwsaki	4106	6365	345.0	48–0	24–2	8.5

Note: This company was purchased by Osaka Syosen KK (*qv*) in 1937

Services: Whaling

Note: Also whalers

KYOKUYO HOGEI KK,
311–13 Marunouti Bldg, 2 Marunouti, 2 tyome, Kozimati-ku, Tokio

Whale factory vessel								
Kyokuyo Maru (m)	1939	Kwsaki	17,549	22,200	550–0	74–0	34–2	13.0

Funnel: Black with broad white band
Hull: Black, red boot-topping
Services: Japan–W coast US; tramping, Eastern region

MEIZI KAIUN KK, (Meiji Kaiun KK – Meiji Shipping Co Ltd),
Meikai Bldg, 32 Akasi-mati, Kobe-ku, Kobe

Meigen Maru	1920	Asano	5435	8797	400.0	53–3	25–9	10.5
Meiko Maru	1918	OsakaI	4383	6789	357–5	49–10	23–8	10.0
Meiten Maru (m)	1938	Mtsui2	4474	6519	363.5	50–0	29.0	12.0
TAISYO KAIUN KK								
Meiu Maru (s2)	1918	Uraga	8230	11,648	461–8	58–0	28–8	11.0
ex Meiwu Maru 38								

Funnel: Black with broad white band bearing emblem of three red diamonds
Hull: Black with white band, red boot-topping
Services: General tramping; lumber trade W coast US–Japan; trans-Pacific oil and petroleum trades, W coast US–Japan

MITUBISI SYOZI KK, (Mitsubishi Shoji KK),
10 Marunouti, 2 tyome, Postbox Central 22, Kozimati-ku, Tokyo

General cargo vessels								
Akiura Maru (m,P–)	1938	MitsuN	6804	10,079	453–9	58–6	26–5	15.5
Kazuura Maru (m,P–)	1938	MitsuN	6804	10,069	453–9	58–6	26–5	15.5
Lumber carriers								
Columbia Maru (m,P–)	1927	MitsuN	5618	9330	405.0	55–0	25–8	11.0
Olympia Maru (m,P–)	1927	MitsuN	5617	9354	405.0	55–0	25–8	11.0
Tankers								
San Clemente Maru (m)	1937	MitsuN	7335	11,118	429.8	57–5	28–6	13.0
San Diego Maru (m)	1928	MitsuN	7269	11,410	447–0	57–0	28–7	11.0
San Luis Maru (m)	1928	MitsuN	7269	11,410	447–0	57–0	28–7	11.0
San Pedro Maru (m)	1927	MitsuN	7269	11,407	447–0	57–0	28–7	11.0
San Ramon Maru (m)	1935	MitsuN	7309	11,200	431.5	57–5	28–6	13.0

Funnel: Mitui – black, three white bands; Toyo – yellow, black top
Hull: Black with MITSUI LINE in large white letters, red boot-topping; Toyo – black with white line, red boot-topping
Services: Japan, China, Philippines–Netherlands East Indies–Straits Settlements–British India; Japan, China, Philippines–Australia; Japan, China, Philippines–South America; Japan, China, Philippines–Africa; Japan, China, Philippines–NW Europe; Japan–Philippines–San Francisco–Los Angeles–New York

MITUI BUSSAN KK, (Mitsui Bussan KK),
3 Kaigan-dori, Kobe-ku, Kobe and 1 Muro-mati, 2 tyome, Nihonbasi-ku, Tokyo

General cargo vessels								
Akagisan Maru (m,P12)	1924	Mtsui1	4634	7012	375.0	50–0	24–4	12.0
Akasisan Maru (m,P5/1)	1935	Mtsui1	4551	6480	362.2	50–0	25–9	13.0
ex Akashisan Maru 38								
Akibasan Maru (P2)	1924	Mtsui1	4607	6913	375.0	50–0	24–6	12.0
Amagisan Maru (m,P–)	1933	Mtsui1	7620	9810	472–6	60–0	27–9	16.0
Aobasan Maru (m,P–)	1935	Mtsui1	8812	9418	477–3	62–0	27–0	16.5
ex Awobasan Maru 38								
Arimasan Maru (m,P6/1)	1937	Mtsui1	8697	10,534	477–5	62–0	27–0	16.5
Asahisan Maru (m,P5/1)	1935	Mtsui1	4551	6478	362.2	50–0	25–9	13.0
Asakasan Maru (m,P6/1)	1937	Mtsui1	8709	8861	477–3	62–0	27–0	16.5
Asosan Maru (m,P–)	1935	Mtsui1	8812	9400	477–3	62–0	27–0	16.5

Mitui Bussan: The motor tanker Otowasan Maru *was completed at the Mitsui shipbuilding yard in 1936 and was one of a large number of tankers built in Japan in the 1930s specially for the oil and petroleum trade from the west coast of the United States to Japan. She was fitted with a Mitsui 6-cylinder oil engine of 7600bhp. During 1938 and 1939, this tanker and her sistership* Omurosan Maru *were regularly voyaging between Los Angeles and Yokoham, Kobe and Osaka.* Otowasan Maru *was torpedoed and sunk by the US submarine* Flasher *on December 22 1944 (Mitsui OSK archives)*

Nippon Sekiyu: The tanker Corabank *(pictured here) was sold in 1937 to Japan and renamed* Rikko Maru. Corabank *had been completed for Bank Line in August 1932 by Workman, Clark, at Belfast. She went through most of the war apparently unscathed, and in March 1945 was wrecked off northern Formosa (RW Jordan collection)*

Nippon Yusen: The general cargo vessel Noto Maru *was one of six sisterships built at Nagasaki and Yokohama in 1934, and was fitted with a Mitsubishi 7-cylinder oil engine of 6700bhp. She was involved in service between Japan and the Philippines to the west coast and east coast of the United States. She was sunk by USAAF aircraft on November 2 1944 (RW Jordan collection)*

Osaka Syosen: The passenger/cargo liner Aikoku Maru *was completed in 1940 and in December 1941 was converted by the Imperial Japanese navy to an auxiliary cruiser. After a career which compared with German auxiliary cruisers was unsuccessful, she was converted for use as a troop transport in October 1943. On February 17 1944, she was sunk by USN carrier-based aircraft during Operation 'Hailstone', the raid on Truk, Caroline Islands, during which US Navy surface craft and aircraft sunk large numbers of Japanese warships and merchant vessels (RW Jordan collection)*

Ship	Year	Builder	GRT	DWT	Length	Beam	Draught	Speed
Atutasan Maru (m,P6/1)	1937	Mtsui2	8662	10,462	477–3	62–0	27–0	17.5
ex Atsutasan Maru 38								
Awazisan Maru (m,P–)	1939	Mtsui2	9794	10,700	482.9	64–0	29–0	17.0
Ayatosan Maru (m,P–)	1939	Mtsui2	9788	10,700	482.9	63–9	29–0	17.0
Azumasan Maru (m,P–)	1933	Mtsui1	7623	9809	472–6	60–0	27–9	16.0
Kinkasan Maru	1911	Dixon2	4980	8205	380.0	53–6	24–2	9.5
Nagisan Maru (m,P–)	1931	Mtsui1	4391	5850	361.5	50–0	23–5	12.0
Nasusan Maru (m,P–)	1931	Mtsui1	4399	5850	361.5	50–0	23–4	12.0
Natisan Maru (m,P–)	1931	Mtsui1	4434	5852	339.5	59–0	23–4	13.0
ex Nachisan Maru 38								
Sikisan Maru (m,P–)	1925	Hendn2	4725	8100	400.2	53–4	23–6	12.0
ex Shikisan Maru 38, ex Thistleros 28								
Tankers								
Omurosan Maru (m)	1937	Mtsui1	9205	11,860	512–0	65–0	29–0	16.5
ex Omrusan Maru 38								
Otowasan Maru (m)	1936	Mtsui1	9205	11,870	512–0	65–0	29–0	16.5
General cargo vessels								
TAIYO KOGYO KK								
Hakonesan Maru (m2,P15)	1929	Mtsui1	6674	9733	437.6	56–6	26–3	13.5
Hakubasan Maru (m2,P15)	1928	Mtsui1	6650	9775	437.6	56–6	26–2	13.5
TOYO KAIUN KK, Takatiho Bldg, Utisaiwai-tyo, 1 tyome, Kozimati-ku, Tokyo								
Getuyo Maru (m,P4)	1934	MitsuN	7509	10,126	454–9	58–6	25–3	13.5
ex Getsuyo Maru 38								
Huzikawa Maru (m)	1938	MitsuN	6938	9100	453–9	58–6	26–5	15.0
Kamogawa Maru (m,P–)	1938	MitsuY	6441	9050	439.4	58–4	27–0	16.0
Kinugawa Maru (m)	1938	MitsuN	6937	9100	453–9	58–6	26–5	15.0
Nitiyo Maru (m,P4)	1934	MitsuN	7509	10,129	454–9	58–6	25–3	13.5
ex Nichiyo Maru 38								
Tamagawa Maru (m,P–)	1938	MitsuY	6441	9050	439.4	58–4	27–0	16.0
Uyo Maru (m,P–)	1933	MitsuN	7503	10,157	454–9	58–6	25–3	13.5
Yodogawa Maru (m,P–)	1939	MitsuY	6441	9050	439.4	58–4	27–0	16.0

Note: Also vessels in local services in Japanese and nearby waters

NANYO KAIUN KK, 6 Marunouti, 2 tyome, Kozimati-ku, Tokyo

Funnel: Black with red N cutting narrow black band bordered by two narrow white bands
Hull: Black with white band
Services: Japan–Malaya–Netherlands East Indies–Batavia

Ship	Year	Builder	GRT	DWT	Length	Beam	Draught	Speed
Bandoeng (Bandon) Maru	1920	YokoDk	4003	6400	357–5	50–0	23–11	12.0
ex Kinno Maru 23								
Burma Maru (P8)	1917	Kwsaki	4585	7873	385.0	51–0	24–11	11.0
Cheribon Maru	1921	MitsuK	4016	6300	358–1	50–0	24–0	12.0
ex Yoro Maru 21								
Clyde Maru (P–)	1920	Asano	5498	8772	400.0	53–2	25–9	10.0
Erie Maru	1920	Asano	5493	8746	400.0	53–2	25–9	10.0
Johore Maru (r/t,P–)	1932	Harim2	6181	8772	411.7	56–0	26–2	13.0
Macassar Maru (P–)	1920	MitsuN	4026	6300	358–1	50–0	24–0	12.0
Madras Maru (P–)	1919	MitsuN	3802	6165	358–1	50–0	23–11	12.0
Maebasi Maru (s2,P6/1)	1921	YokoDk	7005	10,402	461–8	58–0	26–8	12.0
ex Mayebashi Maru 38								
Nagoya Maru (r/t,P–)	1932	MitsuN	6070	8657	406.8	55–6	26–0	13.0
Nissyo Maru (st,P–)	1939	MitsuK	6527	8100	419.9	57–1	27–0	15.5
Nitiran Maru (st,P–)	1939	MitsuK	6504	8100	419.9	57–1	27–0	15.5
Samarang Maru (P–)	1920	MitsuK	4013	6315	358–1	50–0	24–1	12.0

NIPPON KAIUN KK, 12 Marunouti, 2 tyome, Kozimati-ku, Tokyo

Hull: Grey, red boot-topping
Trades: Trans-Pacific oil and petroleum, W coast US–Japan

Tankers								
Akatuki Maru (m)	1938	Harim2	10,216	14,236	526–1	64–11	29–11	19.0
Akebono Maru (m)	1939	Harim2	10,182	14,236	526–1	65–0	29–11	19.0

NIPPON SEKIYU KK, (Japan Oil Co Ltd),
4 Marunouti, 3 tyome, Kozimati-ku, Tokyo

Trades: Trans-Pacific oil and petroleum, W coast US–Japan

Tanker								
Rikko Maru (m)	1932	Work28	9182	13,710	477.0	63–10	28–5	12.0
ex Corabank 37								

NIPPON SUISAN KK, (Japan Marine Products Co Ltd),
8th floor, Marunouti Bldg, 1–2 Marunouti, 2 tyome, Kozimati-ku, Tokyo

Funnel: Black with white disc inside white ring
Hull: Black
Services: Whaling; oil and petroleum trades

General cargo/refrigerated cargo vessel								
Kosei Maru (st)	1920	Workmn	8265	10,447	462–0	58–4	29–3	11.5
ex Narenta 39, laid down as Neganti								
Tanker								
Itukusima Maru (m)	1937	Kwsaki	10,008	13,500	524–3	65–0	29–11	18.0
ex Itsukusima Maru 38								
Whale factory vessels								
Tonan Maru (s2)	1906	Denny1	9866	13,000	460.4	60–3	30–0	11.5
ex Antarctic Maru 35, ex Antarctic 34, ex Opawa 28; conv general cargo vessel 28								
Tonan Maru No 2 (r/t2)	1937	OsakaO	19,262	22,588	534.8	74–0	36–3	12.5
Tonan Maru No 3 (r/t2)	1938	OsakaO	19,209	22,900	534.8	74–0	36–3	12.5

Note: Also trawlers, whalers and crab cannery vessels, and other vessels under 3000gt

NIPPON TANKER KK, 6 Marunouti, 3 tyome, Kozimati-ku, Tokyo

Funnel: Black
Hull: Black with white band, red boot-topping
Trades: Oil and petroleum, mainly trans-Pacific

Tankers								
Hoyo Maru (m)	1936	MitsuY	8692	13,300	494–4	61–0	29–8	13.5
Kaizyo Maru (m)	1937	MitsuY	8637	13,305	494–4	61–0	29–8	13.5
ex Kaijo Maru 38								
Syoyo Maru	1928	YokoDk	7499	11,500	430.6	57–9	28–0	12.0
ex Shoyo Maru 38								
Teiyo Maru (m2)	1931	YokoDk	9850	12,200	512–0	64–0	28–9	17.0
Zuiyo (Duiyo) Maru (s2)	1917	Curle	7368	10,120	465–0	58–2	28–0	9.5
ex Atheltarn 29, ex India 22, ex Olinda 19, ex Boxleaf 19, laid down as Margha								
KANTO TANKER KK								
Eiyo Maru (s2)	1929	YokoDk	8674	12,600	460.9	60–0	29–11	10.5
ex Yeiyo Maru 38								

NIPPON YUSEN KK, (Japan Mail Steam Ship Co Ltd),
Yusen Bldg, Marunouti, Kozimati-ku, Tokyo

Funnel: Black with white over red, white, red, white bands
Hull: Black, white line, red boot-topping
Services: Mail, passenger, general cargo – Japan, Philippines–Los Angeles–San Francisco–Vancouver–Seattle; Japan–Philippines–E coast US; Japan–NW Europe; Japan–Australia; Japan–W coast South America; Japan–Bombay; Japan–S Pacific islands; Japan–China; also services in and around Japan and China

Passenger/general cargo vessels								
Aki Maru (m2,P–)	order	MitsuN	11,409	8500	502.0	65–8	29–0	20.0
Anyo Maru (st2,P32/1,62/2,586/3)	1913	MitsuN	9257	12,462	466.3	58–11	30–3	12.0
Asama Maru (m4,P222/1,96/2,504/3)	1929	MitsuN	16,975	8090	583–9	74–0	28–6	17.5
Atuta Maru (s2,P89/1,25/2,62/3)	1909	MitsuN	7983	9285	473.9	54–9	27–1	14.0
ex Atsuta Maru 38								
Awa Maru (m2,P–)	order	MitsuN	11,249	8500	502.8	65–8	41.3	18.0
Bokuyo Maru (st2,P34/1,53/2,448/3)	1924	Asano	8619	12,237	445.0	58–0	28–0	13.5
Ginyo Maru (st2,P37/1,38/2,456/3)	1921	Asano	8613	11,218	445.0	58–0	28–0	13.5
Hakone Maru (st2,P116/1,55/2,134/3)	1921	MitsuN	10,420	11,530	520–0	62–0	29–2	15.5
Hakozake Maru (st2,P116/1,55/2,134/3)	1922	MitsuN	10,413	11,427	520–0	62–0	29–2	15.5
Hakusan Maru (st2,P116/1,55/2,134/3)	1923	MitsuN	10,380	11,355	520–0	62–0	29–2	15.5

Haruna Maru (st2,P120/1,55/2,134/3)
1922 MitsuN 10,421 11,482 520–0 62–0 29–2 15.5
Heian Maru (m2,P76/1,69/t,183/3)
1930 OsakaO 11,614 10,220 535–9 66–0 30–3 17.0
Heiyo Maru (m2,P45/1,80/2,50/3)
1930 OsakaO 9816 9636 482–0 60–0 30–3 16.0
Hie Maru (m2,P76/1,69/t,186/3)
1930 YokoDk 11,621 10,235 535–9 66–0 30–3 17.0
ex Hiye Maru 38
Hikawa Maru (m2,P76/1,69/t,186/3)
1930 YokoDk 11,621 10,274 535–9 66–1 30–3 17.0
Husimi Maru (s2,P132/1,59/2,55/3)
1914 MitsuN 10,936 12,691 525–0 63–6 29–0 14.5
ex Fushimi Maru 38
Izumo Maru (st2,P220/1,120/2,550/3)
bldg Kwsaki 27,700 719–6 87–8 45.6 22.0
Kamakura Maru (m2,P243/1,95/2,500/3)
1930 YokoDk 17,526 7700 583–9 74–0 28–6 17.5
ex Chichibu Maru 39
Kamo Maru (s2,P54/1,52/2,100/3)
1908 MitsuN 7955 9425 473.4 54–1 27–1 14.0
Kashiwara Maru (st2,P220/1,120/2,550/3)
bldg MitsuN 27,700 719–6 87–8 45.6 22.0
Kasima Maru (s2,P120/1,60/2,200/3)
1913 Kwsaki 9908 11,460 522–0 59–8 28–5 14.5
ex Kashima Maru 38
Kasuga Maru (st2,P115/1,163/2)
1939 MitsuN 17,150 11,800 591–0 73–0 29–0 18.0
Katori Maru (r/t3,[P120/1,60/2,200/3])
1913 MitsuN 9849 11,372 520–0 59–11 28–6 14.5
Kitano Maru (s2,P83/1,32/2,12/3)
1909 MitsuN 7952 9260 473.9 54–9 27–1 14.0
Miike Maru (m2,P–)
order MitsuN 11,738 8500 502.0 65–8 29–0 20.0
Nitta Maru (st2,P115/1,163/2)
bldg MitsuN 17,163 11,800 591–0 73–10 29–0 19.0
Rakuyo Maru (st2,P46/1,51/2,614/3)
1921 MitsuN 9419 12,604 460.0 60–0 30–7 12.0
Suwa Maru (s2,P86/1,72/2,24/3)
1914 MitsuN 10,672 12,680 521–0 62–8 29–0 14.5
Taiyo Maru (s2,P344/1)
1911 Blohm 14,457 6926 580–0 65–4 27–9 19.0
ex Cap Finisterre 21
Tango Maru (s2,P90/1,26/2,158/3)
1905 MitsuN 6893 8260 456.4 50–2 26–7 13.0
Tatuta Maru (m4,P222/1,96/2,504/3)
1930 MitsuN 16,975 7970 583–8 72–0 28–6 19.0
ex Tatsuta Maru 38
Terukuni Maru (m2,P125/1,69/2,60/3)
1930 MitsuN 11,930 9997 526–9 64–0 28–8 16.5
Yasukuni Maru (m2,P125/1,69/2,60/3)
1930 MitsuN 11,933 9981 526–9 64–0 28–9 16.5
Yawata Maru (st2,P115/1,163/2)
bldg MitsuN 17,128 11,800 591–0 73–10 29–0 19.0
Yokohama Maru (s2,P28/1,62/3)
1912 MitsuN 6143 7804 406.4 49–1 27–6 14.0

General cargo vessels

Akagi Maru (m,P4) 1936 MitsuN 7390 9461 482–4 62–3 27–4 16.5
Akita Maru (P2/1) 1916 MitsuN 3817 6329 358–1 50–0 23–11 11.5
Arima Maru (m,P4)
1936 MitsuN 7389 9463 482–4 62–4 27–4 16.5
Asaka Maru (m,P4)
1937 MitsuN 7399 9596 482–4 62–4 27–4 16.5
Asuka Maru (m2,P9/1)
1924 Hendn2 7523 10,652 456–0 57–0 28–3 13.0
Atago Maru (m2,P9/1)
1924 Lithgw 7543 10,510 456–0 57–2 28–3 13.0
Awata Maru (m,P4)
1937 MitsuN 7397 9568 482–4 62–4 27–4 16.5
Azuma Maru (m,P4)
1938 MitsuN 6646 9312 485–5 62–4 27–4 16.5
Bengal Maru (P6/1)
1921 MitsuN 5400 8301 400.0 54–6 24–8 11.0

Osaka Syosen: Buenos Aires Maru *was built by Mitsubishi and fitted with two Mitsubishi/Sulzer oil engines of which gave her a speed of 13.65 knots at 6000bhp and 16.6 knots at 6760bhp. She was delivered on October 31 1929 for service from Japan westbound around-the-world via South Africa and South America. Her last voyage on this service was commenced in October 1941. She was sunk by US aircraft on November 27 1943 (Mitsui OSK archives)*

Osaka Syosen: Bangkok Maru, *which was equipped with a 3140bhp oil engine giving a service speed of 12 knots, was completed by Mitsubishi at Kobe in 1937 and was involved in services in south-east Asia. Her sistership was* Saigon Maru. Bangkok Maru *was requisitioned by the Imperial Japanese Navy in December 1941 for service as an auxiliary cruiser and on May 20 1943 was torpedoed and sunk by the US submarine* Pollack *(Mitsui OSK archives)*

Osaka Syosen: The motor vessel Sydney Maru *was built at Yokohama Dock and completed in 1929. With her sisterships* Brisbane Maru *and* Melbourne Maru, *she was involved in OSK's service from Japan to Australia. Her 3000bhp oil engines gave a speed of 11.92 knots in service, but on trials these achieved 16.136 knots at a maximum 3514bhp. On November 28 1943* Sydney Maru *was torpedoed and sunk by the US submarine* Bowfin *(Mitsui OSK archives)*

Osaka Syosen: Toa Maru *was completed in 1939 at the Kawanami shipyard, and on trials achieved 17 knots. Her 5000bhp oil engine gave her a speed in service of 13.9 knots. She was requisitioned as an Imperial Japanese Navy transport in 1942 and on November 25 1943 was torpedoed and sunk by the US submarine* Searaven *(Mitsui OSK archives)*

Calcutta Maru (P3/1)	1917	MitsuN	5339	8350	400.0	54–6	24–8	11.5
Dakar Maru (P6/1)	1920	MitsuN	7170	10,652	420.0	56–0	28–4	12.0
Delagoa Maru (P6/1)	1919	MitsuN	7148	10,560	420.0	56–0	28–4	12.0
Durban Maru (P6/1)	1919	MitsuN	7164	10,614	420.0	56–0	28–4	12.0
Genoa Maru (P4/1)	1919	MitsuN	6785	10,947	425.0	53–8	28–7	12.0
Hakodate Maru (P6/1)	1919	MitsuK	5303	8256	400.0	54–6	24–8	12.0
Lima Maru (s2,P6/1)	1920	MitsuN	6989	10,577	461–8	58–0	26–8	12.0
Lisbon Maru (s2,P4/1)	1920	YokoDk	7053	10,384	461–8	58–0	26–8	12.0
Lyons Maru (s2, P6)	1920	YokoDk	7018	10,460	461–8	58–0	26–8	12.0
Malacca Maru (P6/1)	1920	MitsuK	5374	8384	400.0	54–6	24–8	12.0
Matue Maru (s2,P6/1)	1921	YokoDk	7061	10,400	461–8	58–0	26–8	12.0
ex Matsuye Maru 38								
Matumoto Maru (s2,P6)	1921	YokoDk	7025	10,439	461–8	58–0	26–8	12.0
ex Matsumoto Maru 38								
Mito Maru (s2,P6/1)	1921	YokoDk	7061	10,407	461–8	58–0	26–8	12.0
Morioka Maru (P6/1)	1920	Uraga	4469	6599	360.0	51–3	23–3	12.0
Muroran Maru (P6/1)	1919	MitsuN	5374	8446	400.0	54–6	24–7	12.0
Nagara Maru (m,P4)	1934	YokoDk	7149	9688	471–0	62–4	27–6	16.0
Nagato Maru (P5/1)	1918	Kwsaki	5901	9013	385.0	51–0	27–1	11.5
Nako Maru (m,P4)	1934	Uraga	7145	9670	471–0	62–4	27–6	16.0
Naruto Maru (m,P4)	1934	YokoDk	7149	9686	471–0	62–4	27–6	16.0
Nosiro Maru (m,P4)	1934	MitsuN	7189	9665	471–0	62–4	27–6	16.0
ex Noshiro Maru 38								
Noto Maru (m,P4)	1934	MitsuN	7190	9667	471–0	62–4	27–6	16.0
Nozima Maru (m,P4)	1934	MitsuN	7189	9649	471–0	62–4	27–6	16.0
ex Nojima Maru 38								
Okitu Maru (st)	1939	Harim2	6666	9700	437.2	58–6	26–0	16.0
Onoe Maru (st)	1939	Harim2	6667	9700	437.2	58–6	26–0	16.0
Penang Maru (P2)	1913	LithR	5214	8320	405.0	52–3	24–7	11.0
Sado Maru (m2,P4)	1939	MitsuN	7180	9400	508–5	62–4	27–8	18.0
Sagami Maru (m2,P4)	bldg	MitsuY	7189	9400	508–5	62–4	27–8	18.0
Sagara Maru (m2,P4)	bldg	MitsuY	7189	9400	508–5	62–4	27–8	18.0
Sakito Maru (m2,P4)	bldg	MitsuN	7158	9400	508–5	62–4	27–8	18.0
Sakura Maru (m2,P4)	1939	MitsuN	7167	9400	508–5	62–4	27–8	18.0
Sanuki Maru (m2,P4)	1939	MitsuN	7158	9400	508–5	62–4	27–8	18.0
Sasako Maru (m2,P4)	bldg	MitsuY	7158	9400	508–5	62–4	27–8	18.0
Takaoka Maru (s2,P6/1)	1920	YokoDk	7007	10,490	461–8	58–0	26–8	12.0
Taketoyo Maru (s2,P6/1)	1920	YokoDk	6965	10,479	461–8	58–0	26–8	12.0
Tatuno Maru (s2,P9/1)	1916	Kwsaki	6960	10,139	461–8	58–0	26–5	12.0
Tazima Maru (s2,P9/1)	1916	Kwsaki	6995	10,287	461–8	58–0	26–5	12.0
ex Tajima Maru 38								
Toba Maru (s2,P9/1)	1916	Kwsaki	6995	10,216	461–8	58–0	26–5	12.0

Tokiwa Maru (st2,P9/1)								
	1916	MitsuN	6972	10,659	461–8	58–0	26–8	12.0
Tokusima Maru (P2/1)								
	1913	LithR	5976	9650	423.0	56–0	25–5	11.0
ex Tokushima Maru 38								
Tottori Maru (P2/1)								
	1913	LithR	5973	9650	423.4	56–0	25–5	11.0
Toyohasi Maru (s2,P12/1)								
	1915	Kwsaki	7031	10,464	461–8	58–0	26–4	12.0
ex Toyohashi Maru 38								
Toyooka Maru (st2,P10/1)								
	1915	MitsuN	7098	10,581	461–8	58–0	26–8	13.0
Turuga Maru (s2,P9/1)								
	1916	MitsuN	6988	10,624	461–8	58–0	26–8	12.0
ex Tsuruga Maru 38								
Tusima Maru (s2,P8/1)								
	1914	LithR	6754	10,450	444.4	58–2	26–11	12.0
ex Tsushima Maru 38								
Tuyama Maru (s2,P6/1)								
	1916	MitsuN	6963	10,395	461–8	58–0	26–8	12.0
ex Tsuyama Maru 38								

Note: Also many vessels in services in and around Japan

NISSAN KISEN KK, 67 Kyo-mati, Kobe-ku, Kobe

Funnel: Black with red S cutting two narrow red bands, all on broad white band
Hull: Grey, red boot-topping
Services: Japan–Netherlands East Indies–Borneo; Japan–India; Japan–Far East ports

Hitati Maru (st)	1939	OsakaI	6540	10,060	424.1	57–5	34.4	15.0
Isin Maru	1909	Napr&M	4955	8070	400.3	52–4	27.4	8.0
ex Ishin Maru 38, ex Baron Napier 26								
Nissan Maru (st)	1938	OsakaO	6534	10,059	424.1	57–5	34.4	15.0
Nissyu Maru	1917	BethU2	7815	11,650	410.9	56–2	30–6	10.0
ex Tamaki Maru 39, ex Binna 39, ex Bessa 36								
Nitiai Maru	1919	Asano	5440	8789	400.0	53–3	25–9	9.0
ex Yayoi Maru 38								
Nitian Maru	1912	Doxfrd	6198	11,185	439.5	57–0	25–3	8.5
ex Orone 38, ex Grena 34								
Nitiho Maru	1913	Doxfrd	6364	11,185	439.7	57–0	25–3	8.5
ex Ortwo 38, ex Strinda 34								
Nitii Maru (st)	1939	OsakaO	6543	10,060	424.1	57–5	34.4	15.0
Nitimei Maru	1912	ArmWhl	4694	9000	400.0	52–2	25–0	9.0
ex Ortri 38, ex Alfred Nobel 34								
Nitiren Maru	1920	Asano	5460	8761	400.0	53–2	25–9	9.0
ex Heiei Maru 38, ex Heiyei Maru 38, ex Heiyei Maru No 12 37, ex Uralsan Maru 25								
Nitiryu Maru	1919	Asano	5447	8794	400.0	53–0	25–9	9.0
ex Karafuto Maru 38, ex Rozan Maru 29								
Nitiyu Maru	1938	Kawami	6817	9829	451.8	58–1	32.8	12.0
Nittai Maru	1921	Doxfrd	6484	10,880	420.0	54–0	28–4	9.5
ex Krone 38, ex Tilthorn 37								

RYUUN KISEN KK, 30 Kaga-mati, Dairen, Kwantung Peninsula

Ryuun Maru	1918	H&W,B	6538	10,500	428–0	55–10	28–3	10.5
ex Hakutatsu Maru 37, ex Grace Dollar 24, ex War Melody 19								

NITTO KOGYO KISEN KK, Tiyoda Bldg, Marunouti, Kozimati-ku, Tokio

Trades: Trans-Pacific oil and petroleum, W coast US–Japan

Tankers

Nitiei Maru (m)	1938	Kwsaki	10,020	14,500	526–0	65–0	29–11	18.0
Toei Maru (m)	1938	Kwsaki	10,023	14,500	526–0	65–0	29–11	18.0

OGURA SEKIYU KK, Kobuna-tyo, 2 tyome, Nihonbasi-ku, Tokio

Trades: Trans-Pacific oil and petroleum, W coast US–Japan

Tankers

Ogura Maru No 1 (m)								
	1929	MitsuN	7270	11,331	430.0	57–0	34.6	12.0
ex Ogura Maru 31								
Ogura Maru No 2 (m)								
	1931	MitsuN	7311	11,257	430.0	57–0	34.6	12.0
Ogura Maru No 3 (s2)								
	1916	Curle	7350	10,127	465–0	58–2	28–0	10.0
ex Koyo Maru 38, ex Athelrill 27, ex California 22, ex Oligarch 19, ex Limeleaf 19, launched as Masula								

OKIDORI GYOGYO KK,
631–33 Marunouti Bldg, 1–2 Marunouti, Kozimati-ku, Tokio

Services: General tramping

Note: This company was associated with Hayasikane Syoten KK (*qv*)

Kosei Maru 1920 HarbrM 5430 8390 414–0 52–2 25–2 10.5
ex Canadian Winner 33

ONO SYOZI GOMEI KAISYA, (Ono Shoji Gomei Kaisha),
28 Senbon-dori, 1 tyome, Nisinari-ku, Osaka

Services: Aden Maru out of commission; others on operator's services
Note: * Operated by Yamasita Kisen KK (*qv*); ** operated by Taiyo Kisen KK (*qv*)
Note: Also vessels under 1500gt

Aden Maru (P–) 1919 Kwsaki 5824 9023 385.0 51–0 27–1 9.5
Brazil Maru* 1919 Kwsaki 5860 9025 385.0 51–0 27–1 9.5
Toyama Maru** (st2,P–)
1915 MitsuN 7090 10,627 461–8 58–0 26–8 11.5

OSAKA SYOSEN KK, (Osaka Shosen KK), Osaka Bldg, 1 Soze-tyo, Kita-ku, Osaka

Funnel: Black with two white bands joined at centre
Hull: Black with white band, red boot-topping
Services: Passenger and general cargo – Japan–NW Europe; Shanghai–Puget Sound ports; Hong Kong–Yokohama–Los Angeles–New York; Japan–South America (round-the-world service); Japan–Australia; Japan–Java–Bombay–Calcutta; Japan–East Africa; Japan–Philippines; Saigon–Bangkok; several services between Japan/Hong Kong/China/Formosa; over 20 services in Japanese waters

Passenger/general cargo vessels

Africa Maru (s2,P42/1,125/3)
1918 MitsuN 9476 11,212 475.0 61–0 28–3 14.0
Aikoku Maru (m2,P–)
bldg Mtsui2 10,437 9600 492.1 66–4 29–0 17.0
Arabia Maru (s2,P42/1,125/3)
1918 MitsuN 9480 11,212 475.0 61–0 28–3 14.0
Argentina Maru (m2,P170/1,630/3)
1939 MitsuN 12,755 8200 544–6 68–11 29–0 20.0
Arizona Maru (s2,P39/1,134/3)
1920 MitsuN 9684 11,112 475.0 61–0 28–3 14.0
Baikal Maru (st2,P89/1,140/2,438/3)
1921 MitsuK 5266 4849 399.4 50–0 23–1 15.0
Batavia Maru (P12/1,183/3)
1919 OsakaI 4393 6563 357–6 49–10 23–8 10.5
Brasil Maru (m2,P101/1,800/3)0
1939 MitsuN 12,752 9200 544–6 68–9 29–0 21.0
Buenos Aires Maru (m2,P60/1,1076/3)
1929 MitsuN 9626 8234 473–0 62–0 26–0 15.0
Chicago Maru (s2,P9/1,72/3)
1910 Kwsaki 5866 7744 419.7 49–6 25–7 13.0
Gokoku Maru (m2,P–)
order Mtsui2 10,438 9600 492.1 66–4 29–0 17.0
Hawaii Maru (s2,P42/1,125/3)
1915 Kwsaki 9467 11,424 475.0 61–0 27–9 14.0
Hokoku Maru (m,P–)
1939 Mtsui2 10,439 9600 492.1 66–4 29–0 17.0
Horai Maru (s2,P51/1,123/2,669/3)
1912 Denny1 9192 6694 470–0 60–1 27–8 14.5
ex Pays de Waes 24, ex Indarra 20
Huso Maru (s2,P42/1,88/2,561/3)
1908 Curle 8198 9217 475.0 57–9 28–0 14.5
ex Fuso Maru 38, ex Latvia 24, ex Russia 21, ex Russ 21, ex Rossija –, ex Russia 17
La Plata Maru (m2,P38/1,768/3)
1926 MitsuN 7267 7314 449–0 56–0 25–3 15.0
Manila Maru (s2,P42/1,125/3)
1915 MitsuN 9486 11,107 475.0 61–0 27–10 14.0
Mexico Maru (s2,P12/1,86/3)
1910 MitsuN 5785 7737 400.0 51–0 26–0 13.0
Mizuho Maru (s2,P41/1,133/2,606/3)
1912 LithR 8506 6572 459.5 58–3 26–1 14.0
ex Midzuho Maru 38, ex Infanta Isabel 26
Montevideo Maru (m2,P38/1,768/3)
1926 MitsuN 7267 7299 449–0 56–0 25–3 15.0
Rio de Janeiro Maru (m2,P60/1,1076/3)
1930 MitsuN 9627 8225 473–0 62–0 26–0 15.0
Santos Maru (m2,P40/1,768/3)
1925 MitsuN 7267 7336 449–0 55–9 25–3 15.0
Seattle Maru (s2,P9/1,167/3)
1909 Kwsaki 5773 7578 419.7 49–6 25–6 13.0
Surabaya Maru (P12/1,184/2)
1919 OsakaO 4391 6573 357–6 49–10 23–8 10.5
Tacoma Maru (s2,P9/1,170/3)
1909 Kwsaki 5772 7667 419.7 49–6 25–6 13.0

Ural Maru (st2,P68/1,128/2,577/3)	1929	MitsuN	6374	5345	405.2	55–0	23–1	15.0
General cargo vessels								
Alaska Maru (P6)	1919	MitsuN	7379	10,712	420.0	56–0	28–5	12.5
Argun Maru (P2)	1920	OsakaO	6650	10,512	415.0	55–6	27–7	10.5
Atlas Maru (P6)	1920	MitsuN	7347	10,744	420.0	56–0	28–4	12.5
Bangkok Maru (m)	1937	MitsuK	5351	6630	376.0	55–10	32.8	15.0
Borneo Maru (P5/1)	1917	Kwsaki	5863	9055	385.0	51–0	27–1	11.0
Brisbane Maru (m,P–)	1930	YokoDk	5425	6722	380.0	54–6	24–3	14.5
Canberra Maru (m,P10)	1936	Mtsui1	6477	7100	446–0	57–5	25–5	17.5
Celebes Maru (P5/1)	1917	Kwsaki	5863	9039	385.0	51–0	27–1	11.0
Ganges Maru (P12/1)	1918	OsakaI	4382	6613	357–6	49–10	23–8	10.5
Hague Maru (P6/1)	1920	OsakaI	5642	8693	407.2	50–10	26–1	12.5
Hamburg Maru (P2/1)	1920	YokoU	5220	8499	400.0	54–6	24–8	12.5
Havana Maru (P6/1)	1920	OsakaI	5652	8633	407.2	50–10	26–1	12.5
Havre Maru (P6)	1920	OsakaI	5652	8784	407.2	50–10	26–1	12.5
Himalaya Maru (P6)	1918	MitsuN	5229	8480	400.0	54–6	24–8	12.5
Hokkai Maru (m2,P6/1)	1933	MitsuN	8416	10,135	463–6	60–6	28–2	16.0
Hokuroku Maru (m2,P6/1)	1930	MitsuN	8360	10,105	463–6	60–6	28–2	16.0
Indus Maru (P1/1)	1918	OsakaI	4361	6731	357–6	49–10	23–8	10.5
Kinai Maru (m2,P6/1)	1930	MitsuN	8360	10,142	463–6	60–6	28–2	16.0
London Maru (st,P20/1)	1921	Cammel	7191	10,681	451.1	56–6	27–10	14.0
Melbourne Maru (m,P–)	1930	YokoDk	5423	6724	380.0	54–6	24–3	14.5
Nana Maru (m,P–)	bldg	Harim2	6764	9600	438.8	58–8	26–0	15.0
Nankai Maru (m2,P6/1)	1933	MitsuN	8416	10,162	463–6	60–6	28–2	16.0
Saigon Maru (m)	1937	MitsuK	5350	6645	376.0	55–10	32.8	15.0
San-Yo Maru (m2, P6/1)	1930	MitsuN	8360	10,111	463–6	60–6	28–2	16.0
ex Sanyo Maru 38								
Sumatra Maru (P5/1)	1917	Kwsaki	5863	9023	385.1	51–0	27–1	11.0
Sydney Maru (m,P–)	1929	YokoDk	5425	6721	380.0	54–6	24–3	14.5
Syunko Maru (P5/1)	1919	Toba	6781	10,871	425.0	53–8	28–7	9.5
ex Shunko Maru 38								
Takao Maru (st,P6/1,48/3)	1927	Uraga	4282	5218	355.6	48–6	23–4	15.0
Toa Maru (m,P–)	1939	Kawami	6732	9600	446.2	58–1	26–8	15.0
Toa Maru No 2 (m,P–)	bldg	Kawami	6732	9600	446.2	58–1	26–8	15.0
Tokai Maru (m2,P6/1)	1930	MitsuN	8360	10,109	463–6	60–6	28–2	16.0
Tokyo Maru (m, P10)	1936	Mtsui1	6486	7100	446–0	57–5	25–5	17.0
Ussuri Maru (st2)	1932	MitsuN	6386	5288	406.6	55–0	23–1	15.5

Note: Also a large fleet of vessels in services in and around Japan

SETTU SYOSEN KK (Settsu Shosen KK)

Tosan Maru (m2)	1938	MitsuN	8666	10,102	466.9	62–4	29–0	17.0

Note: This company was controller of Taiyo Kaiun KK (*qv*)

SIMATANI KISEN KK, (Shimatani Kisen KK – Shimatani Steamship Co Ltd),
18 Akasi-mati, Kobe-ku, Kobe

Lumber carrier								
Syohei Maru (m)	1931	Mtsui1	7256	10,230	437.0	58–0	26–5	14.0
ex Shohei Maru 38								

Funnel: Black with red emblem on white band; *Shokei Maru* had no funnel
Hull: Black with white band, red boot-topping
Trades: US W coast US–Japan lumber trade
Note: Also vessels on services in and around Japan

Services: East

SYORYU KISEN KK, Mihara-tyo, Hirosima-ken

Syoryu Maru	1919	H&W,B	6475	10,780	428–0	55–6	28–3	10.5
ex Chang Lung 38, ex Miltonia 35, ex Glenshane 34, ex Sunshine 34, ex Glenshane 32, ex War Dream 19								

Funnel: Yellow
Hull: Black with white band, red boot-topping
Services: Trans-Pacific lumber trade

SYOWA SYOSEN KK, (Showa Shosen KK),
4 Yagumo-dori, 1 tyome, Fukiai-ku, Kobe

Keisyo Maru (m,P–)	1929	Uraga	5879	9119	417.0	56–0	25–3	12.5
ex Keisho Maru 38, ex Kohwa Maru 35								

Trades: Trans-Pacific oil and petroleum, W coast US–Japan

SYOWA TANKER KK, (Showa Tanker KK),
6 Marunouti, 1 tyome, Kozimati-ku, Tokio

Tanker								
Nissyo Maru (m)	1938	MitsuY	10,526	14,500	528.8	65–8	30–0	18.0

Funnel: Yellow with broad red band with narrow red band near top
Hull: Black, or black with white band, red boot-topping
Services: Japan–India; Japan–E coast US–W coast US; Japan–Eastern ports; *Taihei Maru* – trans-Pacific

Note: This company was controlled by Osaka Syosen Kaisha (*qv*)

TAIYO KAIUN KK, (Ocean Transport Co Ltd), 27 Naniwa-mati, Kobe-ku, Kobe

DAIDO KAIUN KK, SANWA SYOSEN KK AND TAKATIHO SYOSEN KK								
Taihei Maru (m)	1928	Mtsui1	6285	9307	413.4	55–6	26–0	11.5
Manager/operator for								
HUKKO SYOSEN KK								
Hukko Maru (m2)	1924	KobeSW	3834	6042	350.7	50–0	22–5	12.0
ex Fukko Maru 38								
NAMURA KISEN GOSI KAISYA								
Daigen Maru No 3	1908	LithR	5256	8200	400.0	52–0	24–7	8.5
ONO SYOZI GOMEI KAISYA (*qv*)								
Brazil Maru	1919	Kwsaki	5860	9025	385.0	51–0	27–1	9.0
SIMOMURA KISEN KK								
Taian Maru (st)	1916	Skinnr	5655	8750	424–0	54–0	24–0	11.0
ex Hanna Nielsen 26								
Taibun Maru	1920	OsakaO	6581	10,681	415.0	55–6	27–7	10.0
ex Etna Maru 29								
Taigen Maru (st)	1917	Skinnr	5660	8750	424–0	54–0	24–0	11.0
ex Luise Nielsen 26								
Taizin Maru (m2,P–)	1922	Rijkee	5155	7830	375.0	51–3	25–10	10.0
ex Taijin Maru 38, ex Hallfried 28								
SYOKO SYOSEN KK								
Tensyo Maru	1914	Hendn2	5013	–	402.9	51–0	24–3	8.0
ex Tensho Maru 38, ex Loong Hwa 38, ex Kalimba 37								
TAKATIHO SYOSEN KK (Takachiho Shosen KK),								
Koei Maru (m)	1934	MitsuN	6774	10,150	454–6	58–5	26–3	14.0
ex Koyei Maru 38								
Kozui Maru (m)	1937	MitsuN	7072	10,200	453–9	58–6	26–3	12.0
YONEHARA MASUZI, 1212 Minami, Takaisi-mati, Izukita-gun, Osaka-ku								
Asama Maru	1901	Hamtn1	4892	7500	369.5	52–1	24–5	8.5
ex Inveric 21								

Hull: Black
Services: Kobe, Yokohama–Vancouver; Kobe, Yokohama, Osaka–Singapore–India

TAMAI SYOSEN KK, (Tamai Shosen KK),
Meikai Bldg, 32 Akasi-mati, Kobe-ku, Kobe

Aratama Maru (st,P–)	1938	Tsurmi	6784	10,000	446.5	59–1	27–0	15.0
Buyo Maru (P–)	1919	Asano	5447	8796	400.0	53–3	25–9	10.0
Italy Maru (P–)	1919	Kwsaki	5859	9160	385.0	51–0	27–1	11.0
Kiso Maru (P–)	1920	Mtsui1	4071	6404	357–6	50–0	23–11	10.5
Pacific Maru (P–)	1920	Kwsaki	5873	9010	385.0	51–0	27–1	11.0
Tone Maru (P4)	1920	Mtsui1	4070	6422	357–5	50–0	23–11	10.5

Funnel: Black with white over red over white bands
Hull: Grey, red boot-topping
Services: Japan–US Gulf; Japan–Australia; general tramping

TATUUMA KISEN KK, (Tatsuuma Kisen Goshi Kaisha),
32 Hon-mati, Nishinomiya, Hyogo-ken

Ayaha Maru	1917	MitsuK	5287	8465	400.0	54–6	24–8	10.0
Hakusika Maru (s2)	1917	Asano	8151	11,475	461–8	58–0	28–7	11.0
ex Hakushika Maru 38								

Taiyo Kaiun: Koei Maru *was completed in 1934 for subsidiary company Takatiho Syosen and was employed mainly on service between Japan and west coast and east coast US ports. She was fitted with a Mitsubishi oil engine of 4200bhp and achieved 16.283 knots on trials. She survived the war and by 1953 was voyaging again in the service of Daido Kaiun of Kobe. She changed owner again in the 1950s and was broken up during 1962–63 (Alex Duncan)*

Yamasita: Yamagiri Maru *was completed by Mitsubishi at Yokohama in 1938. She was in service from Kobe to Los Angeles, Rio de Janeiro, Santos and Buenos Aires. On February 17 1944 she was sunk by USN carrier-based aircraft during Operation 'Hailstone', the raid on Truk, Caroline Islands, during which large numbers of Japanese warships and merchant vessels were sunk (Yamashita/Navix Line archives)*

Yamasita: Yosida Maru No 1, *renamed from* Yoshida Maru No 1 *in 1938, was a standard vessel completed by Asano in 1919. She was requisitioned as a transport in 1943, and on April 26 1944 was torpedoed and sunk by the US submarine* Jack. *She was in the convoy which was part of Operation 'Take-Ichi', which was to reinforce troops on the Vogelkop peninsula. The convoy set out from Shanghai for Halmahera with 20,000 troops. Four of the transports were sunk by US submarines and nearly half the troops embarked failed to reach Halmahera (Yamashita/Navix Line archives)*

Kuretake Maru	1925	Duncan	5175	8950	404.9	53–0	24–7	10.0
ex Benicia 28								
Miyadono Maru	1918	Craig2	5196	8250	412–8	52–4	25–0	10.0
ex Argalia 27, ex War Kestrel 19								
Oridono Maru	1917	MitsuK	5278	8661	400.0	54–6	24–8	10.0
Siraha Maru	1918	LithR	5693	9600	423.3	56–0	25–5	10.0
ex Shiraha Maru 38, ex Vasconia 27, ex Valverde 18								
Somedono Maru	1917	MitsuN	5154	8462	400.0	54–6	24–8	10.0
Tatukami Maru (st)	1939	MitsuK	7064	10,100	441.5	58–6	27–0	15.0
Tatuha Maru	1918	LithR	5784	9600	423.3	56–0	25–5	10.0
ex Tatsuha Maru 38, ex Corby Castle 27, ex Virgilia 25								
Tatuharu Maru (st)	1939	MitsuK	6344	7835	433–10	56–0	25–4	14.5
Tatumiya Maru (st)	1938	MitsuK	6343	7835	433–10	56–0	25–4	14.5
TATUUMA GOSI KAISYA								
Tatuho Maru (st)	1938	MitsuK	6335	7835	433–10	56–0	25–4	14.5
Tatuwa Maru (st)	1937	MitsuK	6333	7835	433–10	56–0	25–4	14.5
ex Tatsuwa Maru 38								

Note: Also vessels on services in Eastern waters

TOTIGI SYOZI KK, (Tochigi Shoji KK), 68 Kyo-mati, Kobe-ku, Kobe

Services: Japan–Borneo–Netherlands East Indies–Calcutta

France Maru	1919	Kwsaki	5828	9022	385.0	51–0	27–1	9.5
Heimei Maru	1919	OsakaI	4364	6550	357–6	49–10	23–8	9.5
Midori Maru	1919	Kwsaki	5827	9023	385.0	51–0	27–1	9.5
ex Cape Town Maru 36								
Ume Maru	1919	Kwsaki	5860	9020	385.0	51–0	27–1	9.5

Note: Also vessels on services in Eastern waters

TOYO KISEN KK, (Oriental Steamship Co Ltd),

Tokyo Kaizyo Bldg, 1 Marunouti, 1 tyome, Kozimati-ku, Tokyo

Funnel: Yellow
Services: Yokohama, Osaka, Niigata–Baltimore–New York; Japan–Manila–Los Angeles–Olympia–Vancouver; Japan–Singapore–Calcutta–Persian Gulf

Biyo Maru (te)	1921	Asano	5480	8799	400.0	53–2	25–9	11.0
Hayo Maru	1921	Asano	5446	8770	400.0	53–3	25–9	9.5
Hukuyo Maru	1920	Asano	5463	8817	400.0	53–3	25–9	9.5
ex Fukuyo Maru 38								
Keiyo Maru (m,P–)	1937	MitsuY	6442	9392	458–0	58–4	25–9	13.5
Oyo Maru	1921	Asano	5458	8750	400.0	53–3	25–9	9.5
ex Woyo Maru 38								
Reiyo Maru	1920	Asano	5446	8691	400.0	53–3	25–9	9.5
Ryoyo Maru (m)	1931	Kwsaki	5974	9102	433–0	56–0	25–1	11.5
Soyo Maru (m)	1931	Asano	6081	9103	433–0	56–0	25–4	11.5
Tenyo Maru (m)	1935	MitsuN	6843	10,150	454–9	58–6	25–3	13.5
Zenyo Maru (m,P–)	1937	MitsuY	6442	9392	458–0	58–6	25–9	13.5
Zyuyo Maru	1926	Asano	5458	8638	400.0	53–3	25–9	10.0
ex Juyo Maru 38								

Note: Also vessels under 3000gt

TYUGAI KAIUN KK, 2 Marunouti, 2 tyome, Kozimati-ku, Tokio

Trades: Trans-Pacific oil and petroleum, W coast US–Japan

Tanker								
Kurosio Maru (st)	1938	Harim2	10,383	15,500	525–6	66–0	29–8	17.0

YABUKI TEIITIRO, (Yakuki Senpakubu),

1 Utubo Minami-dori, 2 tyome, Nisi-ku, Osaka

Services: Japan–India; Japan–Far East ports

TAIKO SYOSEN KK								
Sinno Maru	1912	SHWR	4888	7700	390.0	50–6	24–7	9.0
ex Shinnoh Maru 38, ex Birma Maru 24, ex Birma 23								
Tohuku Maru	1919	Kwsaki	5857	9091	385.0	51–0	27–1	9.5
ex Tofuku Maru 38								
YABUKI GOMEI KAISYA, 199 Yamagata-dori, Dairen, Kwantung Peninsula								
Kinryo Maru	1905	Rodger	4390	7250	369.7	50–0	24–0	9.0
ex Bessie Dollar 23								

YAMAMOTO KISEN KK, 10 Andozibasi-dori, 1 tyome, Minami-ku, Osaka

Funnel: Black with red emblem on white band
Hull: Black with white band
Services: Japan–Far East ports; Osaka–Australia–New Zealand–Noumea; Yokohama–India–Goa

Karachi Maru	1919	Kwsaki	5860	9160	385.0	51–0	27–1	10.5
Kozan Maru (m)	1935	MitsuK	4180	6700	360.0	50–0	24–0	12.5
Toei Maru (st)	1937	Kwsaki	4004	5800	353.6	50–0	27.6	12.5
ex Toyei Maru 38								

YAMAMOTO SYOZI KK, (Yamamoto Shoji KK),
18 Minami Azikawa-dori, 2 tyome, Minato-ku, Osaka

Funnel: Yellow
Hull: Black with white band, red boot-topping
Services: W coast US, Canada–Japan, mainly lumber trade; Japan–Eastern ports; general tramping

Sunten Maru (m)	1928	MitsuK	5623	9106	405.0	55–0	25–7	13.0
ex Shunten Maru 38								
Syunko Maru (st)	1936	Kwsaki	4027	5800	352.0	50–0	27.5	13.5
ex Shunko Maru 38								
Syunsei Maru	1911	Napr&M	4910	8080	400.2	52–4	24–0	8.0
ex Shunsei Maru 38, ex Baron Polwarth 25								

YAMASITA KISEN KK, (Yamashita Kisen KK),
26 Sakaemati-dori, 3 tyome, Kobe-ku, Kobe

Funnel: Yellow with red stylised Y, black top
Hull: Black with white band, red boot-topping (several vessels had YAMASITA LINE in white amidships interrupting white band)
Services: Worldwide

General cargo vessels

Chile Maru	1919	Kwsaki	5860	9104	385.0	51–0	27–1	9.5
Ehime Maru	1920	Uraga	4655	6696	360.0	51–2	23–3	9.5
ex Yehime Maru 38								
England Maru (P–)	1919	Kwsaki	5830	9024	385.0	51–0	27–1	9.5
Hankow Maru	1919	Kwsaki	4105	6378	345.0	48–0	24–2	9.5
Hoeisan Maru (P4)	1918	OsakaI	6032	8813	407.2	50–10	26–1	10.5
ex Hoyeisan Maru 38								
Kohuku Maru	1918	Kwsaki	5822	9033	385.0	51–0	27–1	9.5
ex Kofuku Maru 38								
Kusuyama Maru	1919	ThmpR2	5234	8160	412–8	52–4	25–4	10.5
ex Michalakis 39, ex Barracoo 33								
Kuwayama Maru	1916	LithR	5647	9500	423.5	56–0	25–6	11.0
ex Mount Atlas 39, ex Megna 35, launched as Baron Inchcape								
Kyokko Maru	1920	Toba	6783	10,691	425.0	53–8	28–7	9.5
ex Kyokkoh Maru 38, ex Ypres Maru 28								
Mansei Maru (s2)	1919	OsakaO	7770	12,136	425.0	56–2	31–1	11.5
ex Amur Maru 34								
Mantai Maru	1919	Kwsaki	5864	9091	385.0	51–0	27–1	9.5
ex Vancouver Maru 34								
Momoyama Maru	1918	Workmn	5188	8380	412–8	52–4	25–4	10.5
ex Mount Cynthos 39, ex Zeriba 33, ex Villa Ada 27, ex Fratelli Bianchi 24, ex War Leopard 19								
Nanman Maru	1921	Kwsaki	6551	9521	405.0	53–0	28–0	11.5
ex Kuma Maru 34, ex Fuji Maru 28								
Saiko Maru (P–)	1919	OsakaI	4365	6669	357–6	49–10	23–8	9.5
ex Saikoh Maru 38, ex Heijin Maru 34								
San Francisco Maru (P–)	1919	Kwsaki	5831	9103	385.0	51–0	27–1	10.0
Shanghai Maru	1919	Kwsaki	4104	6372	345.0	48–0	24–2	8.5
Sugiyama Maru	1914	Nthmbl	4297	8386	405.0	53–5	24–11	10.0
ex Aghios Vlasios 39, ex Tysla 35								
Tosei Maru (st)	1926	Uraga	5484	8689	400.0	53–0	25–0	12.0
ex Tohsei Maru 38								
Tyoko Maru	1920	Toba	6783	10,676	425.0	53–8	28–7	9.5
ex Chokoh Maru 38, ex Seine Maru 28								
Yamabiko Maru (st,P–)	1937	Uraga	6799	10,050	441.7	59–0	27–0	14.0
ex Yamahiko Maru 38								
Yamabuki Maru	1930	Doxfrd	5079	9200	421–8	55–2	24–9	10.0
ex Essex Manor 38								
Yamagiku Maru	1920	Irvin3	5236	8200	412–7	52–4	25–4	10.5
ex Kao Sing 37, ex Brightorian 36, ex Bolivar 35, ex Emlynian 33, launched as War Unicorn								
Yamagiri Maru (m,P–)	1938	MitsuY	6438	9301	458–0	58–4	25–9	13.5
Yamahagi Maru (P2/1)	1919	Sundld	5426	8250	412–4	52–5	25–4	10.0
ex Chi Sing 38, ex Brightcomet 36, ex Cairngowan 35, ex War Oriole 19								
Yamahuku Maru (st)	bldg	OsakaO	4928	6900	365.7	54–1	29.1	14.0
Yamahuzi Maru	1920	Coughl	5360	8399	413–0	52–5	25–4	10.0
ex Chao Sing 38, ex Brightstar 36, ex Canadian Importer 33								
Yamakaze Maru (m,P–)	1938	Mtsui2	6921	10,155	458–0	60–0	25–9	13.5
Yamasimo Maru (st,P–)	1938	Tsurmi	6777	10,009	446.5	59–1	27–0	15.0
Yamaura Maru (st,P–)	1937	Uraga	6798	10,004	441.7	59–1	27–0	14.0
Yamayuri Maru	1913	McMlln	5028	8110	400.8	52–1	24–9	9.0
ex Shou Sing 38, ex Brightvega 36, ex Pavlina 35, ex Pauline 34, ex Strabo 32								

Yamazuki Maru (m,P–)	1937	MitsuY	6439	9302	458–0	58–4	25–9	13.5
Yosida Maru No 1	1919	Asano	5425	8769	400.0	53–2	25–9	10.0
ex Yoshida Maru No 1 38								
Yosida Maru No 3	1918	Uraga	4646	6580	360.0	51–0	23–3	10.0
ex Yoshida Maru No 3 38								
Tanker								
Nippon Maru (m)	1936	Kwsaki	9974	13,339	526–0	64–11	29–0	16.5

Operator for

HUSO KAIUN KK (*qv* under H)

General cargo vessels

Yamazato Maru (m)	1937	Mtsui2	6926	10,193	458–0	60–0	27–0	13.0

KAIYO KISEN KK

Tamahoko Maru	1919	Harim1	6780	10,993	425.0	53–8	28–7	9.5
ex Yone Maru 32								
Tihuku Maru	1919	Kwsaki	5857	9100	385.0	51–0	27–1	9.5
ex Chifuku Maru 38								

KOKUYO KISEN KK, Yaesu Bldg, 8 Marunouti, 1 tyome, Kozimati-ku, Tokio

Tanker

Kokuyo Maru (m)	1939	Kwsaki	10,027	14,500	526–0	65–2	29–11	19.0

TAIHEI KISEN KK

General cargo vessels

Muko Maru	1937	OsakaO	4862	6983	369.8	54–1	29.2	12.0
Naniwa Maru	1937	OsakaO	4858	6971	369.8	54–1	29.2	12.0
Utide Maru	1919	BrownJ	5275	8040	413–0	52–4	25–3	10.5
ex Uchide Maru 38, ex Willandra 38, ex Tower Abbey 35, ex Bata 34								
Tanker								
Mitu Maru	1919	Lithgw	6025	8325	412–4	52–3	25–6	10.5
ex Mitsu Maru 38, ex Concordia 37, ex Cardita 28, ex War Gaekwar 19								

TODAI KISEN KK, 27 Dosyu-mati, 3 tyome, Higasi-ku, Osaka

Asakaze Maru (st)	1938	OsakaI	6517	9600	424.1	57–5	28–0	14.5
Eihuku Maru	1918	Kwsaki	5866	9067	385.0	51–0	27–1	10.0
ex Yeifuku Maru 38								
Kamikaze Maru (st)	1938	OsakaI	4916	6900	369.8	54–1	29.2	14.0

UENO KISEN GOSI KAISYA

Ryuyo Maru	1920	Uraga	6707	10,479	400.0	54–0	29–4	9.5
ex Egypt Maru 29								

UWAZIMA UNYU KK

Turusima Maru (P–)	1919	Uraga	4646	6580	360.0	51–2	23–3	9.5
ex Tsurushima Maru 38								
Yosyu Maru (st)	1916	Skinnr	5711	8500	424–0	54–2	24–3	9.5
ex Yoshu Maru 38, ex Niels Nielsen 26								

YAMASITA KISEN GOSI KAISYA,
199 Yamagata-dori, Dairen, Kwantung Peninsula

Note: See also Ono Syozi Gomei Kaisya

Gyoko Maru	1910	Napr&M	5342	8150	405.0	52–3	24–10	11.0
ex Gyokoh Maru 38, ex Tamaqua 22, ex Den of Glamis 15								
Hokko Maru	1918	Short2	5347	8200	412–8	52–5	25–4	10.5
ex Hokkoh Maru 38, ex Castellano 22, ex War Spaniel 19								

Services: General tramping

YOSIAKI TAMAYA, 82 Sinzakacho, Akasaka-ku, Tokyo

Note: * Sold Nissan Kisen KK 1939, renamed *Nissyu Maru*

Tamaki Maru*	1917	BethU2	7815	11,650	410.9	56–2	30–6	10.0
ex Binna 39, ex Bessa 36								

Latvia

Services: General tramping

APVIENOTA KUGNIECIBAS AKCIJU SABIEDRIBA,
15 Maija laukauma 2, Riga

Hercogs Jekabs (m)	1926	Kockum	4138	7800	397–10	54–0	24–0	11.0
ex Aakre 39, ex Childar 35								

Funnel: Yellow with blue PD monogram, black top
Hull: Black
Services: General tramping

DANNEBERG, P, PO Box 181, Zigfrida Meierovica Bulvaris 14, Riga

Konsuls P Dannebergs	1904	RDuck1	2747	5055	330.8	47–5	19–11	8.0
ex Dungeness 27								

Spidola	1905	RDuck1	2833	5000	337–0	47–7	19–11	8.0
ex Brookvale 28, ex Arvonian 19, ex HMS Bendish (Q-ship) 19, ex USS Santee 18, ex HMS Arvonian (Q-ship) 17, ex Arvonian 17, launched as Rosedale								

Note: Also vessels on Baltic/UK/NW Europe trade

GRAUDS, FRICIS, Valdemara iela 7, Riga

Funnel: Black with red over white over red over white bands
Hull: Black
Services: General tramping

Everagra	1911	Rodger	3702	6370	360.3	49–8	21–9	9.0
ex Curonia 39, ex Glensloy 32								
Everasma	1920	Duncan	3836	6750	364.9	51–6	22–0	9.0
ex Antonios Stathatos 39								
Everest	1911	Denny1	5525	8640	425.0	54–2	24–5	9.0
ex Stanmore 39, ex Arracan 38								
MME ELSA GRAUDS								
Everanna	1908	WoodS2	2880	4300	313.3	45–0	19–9	8.0
ex Disciplina 30, ex Amilcare Cipriani 26, ex Stamboul 20								
Everelza	1921	ThmpsJ	4513	6693	364.5	52–10	23–0	10.0
ex Cape Wrath 37, ex Cycle 36								
Everene	1906	G&G2	4434	7185	370.0	52–0	23–0	7.0
ex Louvain 36, ex Louisiana 21, ex Bellview 20, ex Strathyre 19								
Everiga	1914	Irvin3	4648	8044	385.0	52–0	24–2	9.5
ex Rita Chandri 39, ex Helen Moller 37, ex Egyptian Transport 33								
Everoja	1910	Hamtn2	4539	7300	380.0	50–0	24–4	10.5
ex Bright Wings 39, ex Delia 34, ex Middleham Castle 32								
Everolanda	1908	Anvers	3379	6100	360–0	48–2	22–7	8.0
ex Berkdale 33, ex Wotan 27, ex Oswiga 15, ex St Johann 13								
Everonika	1906	ThmpsJ	3743	6097	350.0	50–4	21–6	8.0
ex Tottenham 30, ex Apsley 25, ex Don Cesar 18								
Everosa*	1912	Camp1	3529	6400	348.0	50–0	22–0	8.5
ex *Munorway 34, ex Progress III 15*								
Evertons	1919	Lindhm	4107	6950	355.6	50–8	23–0	9.0
ex Faxen 36, ex Ovidia 20								
Manager for								
MME ZENIJA HEINRICHSONS								
Dole	1912	Duncan	3811	6800	366–11	51–1	21–10	8.5
ex Everhope 39, ex Maplegrove 33, ex Ben Clune 25, ex Oltul 24, ex Iriston 13								
Everalda	1912	GrayX	3950	6700	350.0	50–0	22–9	8.0
ex Mokta 32								
Everita	1917	Ropnr2	3251	5640	335.0	48–1	21–0	9.0
ex Ethelaric 32								

Note: * Sold J Silberberg and Others, 1939, renamed *Kolga*

JENSEN, CHR, PO Box 218, 11 Novembra Bulvaris 13, Riga

Funnel: Black with red Maltese cross on white band
Hull: Black
Services: General tramping

Manager for								
CHR JENSEN, ANDREAS FRIEDENBERG UN BIEDRI								
Vizma	1905	Blumr1	2875	4750	327–2	46–6	20–0	8.5
ex Blairbeg 30, ex Moerdijk 22, ex Northcliffe 09								
KUGNIECIBAS AKCIJU SABIEDRIBA BALTIC (SS Co Baltic Ltd)								
Dagö	1917	Brys&G	2157	3350	290–6	41–10	18–1	8.0
ex Brodsworth 29, ex Elmpark 19								

Note: See also Chr Jensen in Denmark section

KALNINS, A, Jaun iela 25, Riga

Funnel: Black with green band between narrow white (or grey) bands
Hull: Black
Services: General tramping
Note: Also vessels on Baltic/UK/NW Europe trade

Manager for								
MAKSIS KALNINS UN BIEDRI								
Andrejs Kalnins	1907	Clyde	3002	4750	315.3	47–0	20–0	8.0
ex Vilnis 35, ex Onda 33								

KARKLINS, FRICIS, 15 Maija iela 18, Ventspils

Funnel: Black with blue J superimposed on three narrow white bands
Services: General tramping

KUGNIECIBAS AKCIJU SABIEDRIBA JURA (Jura Shipping Co Ltd)								
Gaisma	1900	Ropnr1	3077	5450	323.9	48–1	21–2	7.5
ex Marietta 29, ex Penare 24								

Funnel: Black with grey U on white band or black with white band between two pale blue bands
Hull: Black
Services: General tramping

Note: * Sold Belgian breakers 1939
Note: Also manager for vessels on Baltic/UK/NW Europe trade

LATVIJAS KUGNIECIBAS SABIEDRIBA, (Latvian Shipping Co),
15 Maija laukuma 2, Riga

Manager for
JOHANN FREYMANN

Regent 1903 Bartm1 3280 5430 324.5 46–11 24.2 7.0

JOHANN FREYMANN, OSWALD ANDERSONS, JANIS SALCMANS AND KARLIS JANSONS

Gundega 1906 TyneIr 3583 6200 348.8 50–0 21–4 8.5
ex Wokingham 31, ex River Trent 24, ex Antar 20

Laimdota* 1899 LithR 3699 5970 340.6 46–1 23–2 7.0
ex Carnac 29, ex Federica 25

JOHANN FREYMANN, JANIS SALCMANS AND KARLIS JANSONS

Abgara 1911 GrayX 4422 7370 374.7 51–4 23–3 9.0
ex Vinodol 36, ex Bisley 33, ex Roselands 20

Arija 1907 Bartm1 3676 6250 346.5 50–10 21–6 9.0
ex North Britain 32, ex Baltic Exchange 09

Ciltvaira 1905 ThmpsJ 3779 6249 346.7 50–10 21–5 8.5
ex Twyford 35, ex President Bunge 24, ex Endsleigh 07

Tautmila 1915 Rhead3 3724 6316 347.4 49–2 22–3 9.0
ex Mount Parnassos 36, ex Headcliffe 32

Valdona 1904 Bartm1 3042 5140 339.0 48–1 21–7 8.5
ex Mortlake 33, ex Antiope 26, ex Cragside 16

Funnel: Black with broad green band between narrow white bands; Quayside – black with white C&G on green band between narrow white bands
Hull: Black
Services: General tramping

Note: * See also under Connell & Grace Ltd in Great Britain section
Note: ** Sold Fricis Grauds (*qv* above), 1939, renamed *Everagra*

SALCMANS, JANIS, & KARLIS JANSONS,
c/o Latvijas Kugniecibas Sabiedriba (*qv*), 15 Maija laukuma 2, Riga

Managing agent in Latvia for
GEORGE W GRACE,
Creechurch House, 37–45 Creechurch Lane, London EC3 (Latvian flag)

Lettonia 1913 Pgill2 4163 7400 391–0 52–2 22–3 8.0
ex Roehampton 38, ex Michael L 34, ex Helmsloch 29

QUAYSIDE SHIPPING CO LTD,*
Proctor House, 17–29 Side, Newcastle-upon-Tyne 1 (Latvian flag)

Curonia** 1911 Rodger 3702 6500 360.3 49–8 21–9 9.5
ex Glensloy 32

Funnel: Black with broad white band with blue JS&C or S&C with two narrow white bands above and two below *Hull:* Black, red boot-topping *Services:* General tramping
Note: *, ** transferred German flag 1939, renamed *Johann Faulbaum* and *Sigurd Faulbaum* respectively
Note: Also vessels on Baltic/UK/NW Europe trade

SIERING & CO, JAMES, Liela Kaleju iela 14–16, Riga

MAX FAULBAUMS

Johann Faulbaums* 1907 RDuck1 2944 4560 317.5 46–8 20–1 7.0
ex Janis Faulbaums 39, ex Dimitrios G Thermiotis 29, ex Vittoria 27

Rolfs Faulbaums 1912 Irvin3 1913 3200 279.0 40–1 18.5 8.0
ex Cornelis Lensen 37, ex Merok 34, ex Ingrid 31, ex Ubbergen 25

Sigurds Faulbaums**
1913 Blumr1 3256 5420 331.0 47–9 21–0 8.0
ex Nordeflinge 37, ex Anglet 31, ex Dingle Bank 13

Funnel: Black with emblem on blue band
Services: General tramping

SILBERBERG AND OTHERS, J, Tallinn

Kolga 1912 Camp1 3529 6400 348.0 50–0 22–0 8.5
ex Everosa 39, ex Munorway 34, ex Progress III 15

Funnel: Black with black STCo on white band between narrow red bands
Hull: Black
Services: General tramping
Note: Also vessels on Baltic/UK/NW Europe trade

TOMSONS, D, Citadele éké 30, Riga

Manager for
A & J KARKLINS, TOMSONS UN BIEDRI

Katvaldis 1907 Blumr1 3206 5300 330.4 47–10 20–10 7.5
ex Odile 29, ex Henry W Breyer 27, ex Hallfried 26, ex Magdalene 15, ex Duke of York 11

Services: General tramping

Note: Also vessels on Baltic/UK/NW Europe trade

VALSTA KUGU PĀRVALDE, (Latvian State Shipping Board),
Smilsu iela 6, Riga

Rasma 1902 Ropnr1 3204 5450 325.6 48–1 21–2 7.5
ex Zemvaldis 30, ex Dickre 30, ex Baltik 29, ex Theodoros 28, ex Wieringen 22, ex Burgermeester Jacob 08

Danneberg: The steamer Spidola *was transferred to the Latvian State on July 22 1940, and on August 5 to the USSR. On June 30 1941 she was seized at Liepaja by the invading Germans, and was taken over by the Kriegsmarine and renamed* Rudau *on February 20 1942. After the war she was taken over by the Allies, and in 1947 was under the registered ownership of the Ministry of Transport and named* Spidola. *She flew the British flag and was managed by Richard W Jones. Her prewar owner Mr P Danneberg, of Riga, left Latvia before the Russian takeover in 1940, and during the war carried on his shipping interests from Britain with other Latvian and Estonian shipowners. In 1947 the vessel reverted to the beneficial ownership of Danneberg, who had formed the Compania P Dannebergs Ltd, originally in Costa Rica, to which registry she was transferred in 1953, and later to Nicaragua.* Spidola *lasted until December 1957 when she arrived at Hamburg to be broken up (Alex Duncan)*

Grauds: The steamer Everene *was torpedoed by* U19 *and sunk on January 25 1940, 5 miles off Longstone, Farne Islands, when on voyage from Blyth to Liepaja. In many accounts this vessel has been referred to incorrectly as the Estonian-flagged* Louvain. Louvain *was a former name of* Everene, *and held by her during 1921–36 when under the Belgian flag and owned by Armement Deppe (Alex Duncan)*

Lithuania

AKC-VĖ LIETUVOS BALTIJOS LLOYDAS, Laidvės Aleja 26, Kaunas

Kaunas	1931	Porsgr	1566	2400	255–0	37–11	17–3	10.5
ex Vardefjell 38, ex Dixie 31								
Panevėzys	1924	Akers	1607	2600	256.9	40–0	17–0	9.0
ex Ulefoss 38, ex Beira 37, ex Dagø 35								

Funnel: Black with white L inside white circle on broad red band between narrow white bands
Hull: Black
Services: General tramping

Mexico

Funnel: Black with houseflag
Hull: Black
Trades: Oil and petroleum, mainly Gulf of Mexico and Pacific coast

PETROLEOS MEXICANOS SOCIEDAD ANÓNIMA, Mexico City

Tankers								
Cuauhtemoc	1914	BethFR	3101	5300	329–6	46–0	20–7	9.0
ex Amolco 38								
Minatitlan (m)	bldg	AnsSA	7599	11,200	464–0	62–10	26–4	12.0
Panuco (m)	order	AnsSA	7600	11,200	464–0	62–10	26–4	12.0
Pozarica (m)	bldg	AnsSA	7599	11,190	464–0	62–10	26–4	12.0
XVIII de Marzo	1913	ArmWh1	6439	9450	432–6	54–8	26–1	9.0
ex San Ricardo 38								
Tacona (m)	order	AnsSA	7600	11,200	464–0	62–10	26–4	12.0

Netherlands

Funnel: Black with houseflag – white with green cross (**x**)
Hull: Black, red boot-topping
Services: General tramping

ERHARDT & DEKKERS, Postbus 313, Van Vollenhovenstraat 29, Rotterdam

NV STOOMVAART MAATSCHAPPIJ OISTERWIJK								
Haulerwijk	1924	Clyde	3278	5580	325.0	48–3	21–11	10.0
NV STOOMVAART MAATSCHAPPIJ WIJKLIJN								
Beverwijk	1909	Bonn&M	2948	4950	327.2	47–4	20–1	9.0
ex Terschelling 23								
Katwijk	1921	Jonker	1589	2575	253.5	38–2	16–11	8.5
Naaldwijk	1921	Baanhk	2041	3162	267.1	42–1	18–1	8.5
Noordwijk (r/t)	1939	SmitJ	3697	5512	343–6	50–4	22–1	10.5
Randwijk	1912	SmitJ	2439	4200	287.4	45–2	20–1	9.0
Stolwijk	1920	DNoord	2489	4175	285.8	45–2	20–6	10.0
ex Kongsgaard 21								
Winterswijk	1914	SmitJ	3205	5420	320.0	47–6	21–6	9.0
Zonnewijk	1928	Clyde	4499	7850	383.9	52–11	24–0	10.5

Funnel: Black with black HL on white diamond on broad green band between narrow white bands
Hull: Black, red boot-topping
Services: European and African iron ore ports–NW Europe; general tramping

HALCYON-LIJN NV, Postbus 415, Veerkade 5, Rotterdam

Flensburg	1922	Flensb	6421	11,200	472–9	60–1	26–1	9.0
Stad Alkmaar	bldg	WiltnF	5750	9093				
Stad Haarlem	1929	Lithgw	4518	8127	397–7	52–0	24–9	10.0
Stad Leiden	bldg	WiltnF	5750	9093				
Stad Maassluis	1918	H&W,B	6541	10,760	425–8	55–10	28–3	11.0
ex King Bleddyn 37, ex Glenspey 20, ex War Music 19								
Stad Maastricht	1924	H&W,B	6651	10,000	412.6	55–8	28–3	10.5
ex Mount Dirfys 39, ex Invergarry 37; conv tanker 37								
Stad Schiedam	1911	Craig2	5918	9626	415.0	55–6	24–7	9.5
ex Wimborne 36								
Stad Vlaardingen	1925	Flensb	8501	12,350	490–0	59–4	28–4	10.0
NV ARNHEMSCHE SCHEEPVAART MAATSCHAPPIJ								
Stad Arnhem	1920	Dordr	3819	6220	341.5	50–1	23–3	9.5
NV STOOMBOOT MAATSCHAPPIJ STAD AMSTERDAM								
Stad Amsterdam	1920	Dordr	3780	6200	341.9	50–0	23–3	9.5
NV STOOMBOOT MAATSCHAPPIJ STAD DORDRECHT								
Stad Dordrecht	1920	Dordr	3781	6200	341.9	50–0	23–3	9.5
NV STOOMBOOT MAATSCHAPPIJ STAD ZALT-BOMMEL								
Stad Zwolle	1920	Meyer	2117	3200	293–0	41–5	19.3	9.0
NV STOOMBOOT REDERIJ 'DE GOEDE VERWACHTING'								
Rozenburg	1918	Rijkee	2068	3200	293–0	41–4	19.2	9.0
SCHEEPVAART & TRANSPORT MAATSCHAPPIJ ATLANTICA NV								
Maasburg	1921	Flensb	6415	11,200	472–9	59–11	26–1	9.0
Vredenburg	1921	Flensb	6419	11,200	472–9	59–11	26–1	9.0

Funnel: Yellow with black top
Hull: Black with gold band or grey, red boot-topping
Services: Jointly with Holland-West-Afrika Lijn (*qv* under Vereenigde Nederlandsche SM NV for full itinerary)

HOLLANDSCHE STOOMBOOT MAATSCHAPPIJ NV, Handelskade, Amsterdam

Jaarstroom (st,P24/1)								
	1922	Meyer	2480	3680	321.7	40–2	20–5	11.0
lengthened 36								
Nigerstroom (m,P34/1,14/2)								
	1939	Giessn	4639	6569	401–5	55–4	26–4	14.0

Erhardt & Dekkers: Zonnewijk *was seized by the Germans in 1940. In August 1940 she was taken over by the Kriegsmarine for use in Operation 'Seelöwe' and was given the designation R24, and later RO24. After the abandonment of 'Seelöwe',* Zonnewijk *was in service with the Luftwaffe at Travemünde. She was torpedoed and sunk by the Russian submarine* SC-310 *near Libau on October 8 1944 (Alex Duncan)*

Hollandsche: Nigerstroom, *pictured here berthed at Bordeaux, was built by Van der Giessen at Krimpen and ran trials on March 29 1939. She was placed in service between northwest Europe and West Africa, and following Allied service during the war, reverted to her intended area of operation. In 1957 she was renamed* Ghanakust, *to conform with a new style of naming adopted by her owners and also recognising the newly-independent former Gold Coast. On October 1 1958, when on voyage from Antwerp to Duala with general cargo, she was in collision between Bordeaux and Pauillac with the Spanish liner* Monte Urbasa, *was on fire, and ran aground in the Gironde estuary, becoming a total loss. The wreck was demolished in situ by the Les Abeilles salvage company (RW Jordan collection)*

Hudig & Veder: Themisto *was completed by Rotterdam Drydock in 1928. She survived the Second World War and continued in Dutch service until 1958 when she was sold to a Costa Rican company and renamed* Spetsai Navigator. *In 1962 she was renamed* Navigator *under the Panamanian flag and was broken up during 1963–64 (Alex Duncan)*

Note: Also short-sea vessels

Reggestroom (st,P12/1)	1923	Fyenrd	3854	5870	331.7	48–2	24–10	12.0

Funnel: Yellow, black top
Services: General tramping

NV HUDIG & PIETERS ALGEMEENE SCHEEPVAART MAATSCHAPPIJ, Calandstraat 49–51, Postbus 521, Rotterdam

Spar	1924	Giessn	3616	–	375–1	50–4	22–8	9.0

Funnel: Black with white band bearing blue star
Hull: Black with white band, red boot-topping
Services: UK, NW Europe–W Africa; general tramping

Note: Also vessels under 1500gt

HUDIG & VEDER, Willemskade 23, Rotterdam

MAATSCHAPPIJ ZEEVAART NV

Arundo	1930	Nthmb2	5079	9150	412.0	55–4	25–5	10.5
ex Cromarty 36, ex Petersfield 33								
Colytto	1926	RottDD	4408	7450	387–7	54–8	23–7	10.5
Leto (P2)	1930	RottDD	4712	8655	417–6	55–4	24–10	10.5
Themisto (P2)	1928	RottDD	4707	8640	417–6	55–4	24–9	10.5

Funnel: Black with black JCJL on white diamond superimposed on red over blue bands
Hull: Black, apple-blossom boot-topping
Services: Batavia–Samarang–Sourabaya–Makassar–Balikpapan–Yokohama–Nagoya–Kobe–Osaka–Moji; Sourabaya–Manila–Hong Kong–Amoy–Shanghai–Chin Wen Tao–Dalny–Keelung; Sourabaya–Samarang–Batavia–Hong Kong–Amoy–Shanghai–Manila–Makassar–Bali–Sourabaya–Java ports

Note: * BU Hendrik-Ido-Ambacht 1939

JAVA–CHINA–JAPAN LIJN NV, Het Scheepvaarthuis, Prins Hendrikkade 108–114, Amsterdam, and Kali Besar Oost 12, Postbus 122, Batavia, Java, Netherlands East Indies

Passenger/general cargo vessels

Tjibadak (st,P65/1,75/2,1520/d)	1929	Giessn	7803	9210	448–0	56–2	28–1	12.5
Tjikarang (P12/1,1920/d)	1922	NedSM	9505	13,175	483.5	60–4	30–6	12.5
Tjikembang* (P12/1,42/2,202/3,1691/d)	1914	Scheld	8013	11,476	493.6	58–4	27–6	12.0
Tjileboet (P11/1,24/2,52/3,1662/d)	1918	Fyenrd	5760	8050	420.3	54–4	25–6	11.5
Tjimanoek (P12/1,18/2,20/3,2130/d)	1911	Fyenrd	5628	8650	420.0	54–2	25–3	11.5
Tjinegara (m,P28/1,42/2,90/3,1600/d)	1931	NedSM	9227	9660	458–4	62–2	29–0	15.0
Tjisadane (m,P28/1,42/2,90/3,1600/d)	1931	NedSM	9228	9607	458–4	62–2	29–0	15.0
Tjisalak (P11/1,24/2,52/3,1380/d)	1917	NedSM	5787	7890	419.9	54–2	25–3	11.5
Tisaroea (st,P12/1,38/2,67/3,1093/d)	1926	NedSM	7089	9345	420.5	55–4	28–1	12.0
Tjisondari* (P12/1,46/2,194/3,1691/d)	1915	Scheld	8039	11,080	494.0	58–4	27–6	12.0
Tjitjalengka (m,P50/2,55/2,100/3,1800/d)	1939	NedSM	10,972	9520	475–7	64–8	28–2	15.0

General cargo vessels

Tjibesar (st,P5/1)	1922	Lithgw	10,836	15,550	519–0	63–8	31–4	12.0
Tjikandi (st,P4/1)	1921	Duncan	7970	11,160	448.7	57–11	28–1	12.0

Services: Tramping in Far East

JAVA CHINA TRADING CO LTD, c/o Java China Handelsmaatschappij NV, Bechstraat 59, Amsterdam, and 150 Kiukiang Rd, Postbox 1303, Shanghai, China

Beatrice	1919	CommWV	4128	5600	331.0	47–9	21–10	9.0
ex Yih Hsing 38, ex Dromana 35								

Funnel: Yellow, black band
Hull: Grey, red boot-topping
Services: Hamburg, Bremen, Amsterdam, UK–Pernambuco–Rio de Janeiro–Santos–Ceara–Bahia–Buenos Aires

KONINKLIJKE HOLLANDSCHEN LLOYD, NV TOT VOORTZETTING VAN DEN, (Royal Holland Lloyd), Oostelijke Handelskade 33, Postbus 132, Amsterdam

Amstelland (st)	1920	SHWR	8156	12,388	470.1	61–6	28–8	12.0
Eemland	1906	Flensb	4188	7196	390–0	48–10	26–3	11.0
ex Linden 20								
Montferland (st,P–)	1921	SHWR	6790	10,422	477–3	60–5	26–3	13.0
Salland (st,P–)	1920	Curle	6447	10,316	464–0	58–2	27–3	13.0
Waterland (st,P–)	1922	Curle	6847	10,392	477–4	60–2	26–2	13.0
Westland (m,P8)	1931	Kockum	5888	9266	449–9	59–8	25–7	14.0
ex Nansenville 38								
Zaanland (st,P–)	1921	Curle	6813	10,392	477–4	60–2	26–3	13.0

Java-China: Completed in April 1915 by De Schelde at Vlissingen, Tjisondari *was one of seven vessels built during 1910–22 to cope with the steady increase in trade between the Netherlands East Indies and China. These vessels all had accommodation for both European passengers and large numbers of Chinese passengers.* Tjisondari *arrived at Rotterdam on February 25 1939 to be broken up (Alex Duncan)*

Hollandschen Lloyd: The steamer Waterland *was delivered by Barclay, Curle, in May 1922 and was a development of the standard War 'G' type, several of which were produced at this shipyard. She was fitted with two Brown Curtis double reduction geared turbines of 4500shp. The first voyage of* Waterland *was from Glasgow and Barry to Buenos Aires and she then traded between Amsterdam, Hamburg and Buenos Aires on the company's regular service.* Waterland *survived the Second World War and made her first voyage from Rotterdam to Buenos Aires in October–November 1945. In 1956 was sold to Greece and renamed* Poulariani, *and later the same year was sold to be broken up at Antwerp (Alex Duncan)*

KNSM: The passenger liner Simón Bolívar *was completed in 1927 by Rotterdam Drydock and operated between Hamburg and Amsterdam and the West Indies. She struck a German mine off Harwich on November 18 1939, the explosion from which killed many persons on deck.* Simón Bolívar *was badly damaged and there was difficulty in getting the boats away while she settled by the stern. Other vessels were soon at the scene and a second mine explosion damaged some of the remaining lifeboats and hastened her sinking with the loss of 84 passengers and 18 crew. She was on voyage from Amsterdam to Paramaribo with 400 passengers and crew and general cargo (RW Jordan collection)*

Funnel: Black, two white bands
Hull: Black or grey, red boot-topping
Services: Passenger, mail, cargo – Colon Line – NW Europe –Barbados–Trinidad–Guianas–Puerto Cabello–Curaçao–Santa Marta–Puerto Colombia–Antigua–Jamaica–Cristobal; Surinam Line – NW Europe –Madeira–Surinam–Demerara–Trinidad–Venezuela–Curaçao–Port au Prince–New York; South Pacific Line – NW Europe –Curaçao–Panama–Colombia–Ecuador–Peru–Chile; Curaçao–Maracaibo; Antwerp-West Indies (service commenced 1939); cargo – New York–Venezuela; Curaçao–Guatemala; Curaçao–Antilles; Netherlands–Baltic–Mediterranean–Adriatic–Black Sea

KONINKLIJKE NEDERLANDSCHE STOOMBOOT MAATSCHAPPIJ NV, (Royal Netherlands Steamship Co),

Het Scheepvaarthuis, Prins Hendrikkade 108–114, Amsterdam

Passenger/general cargo vessels								
Colombia (m2,P152/1,97/2,33/3)	1930	SmitP	10,782	6648	457–1	61–9	26–8	14.5
Costa Rica (s2,P152/1,56/2,54/3)	1910	NedSM	8672	6510	473–0	55–4	26–5	15.5
ex Prinses Juliana 30								
Cottica (P41/1,20/2,16/3)	1927	SmitP	3989	3905	328–0	47–3	21–2	12.0
Crijnssen (P72/1,24/2,24/3)	1919	Fyenrd	4298	3630	355–0	47–9	21–0	12.5
laid down as Prins Maurits								
El Libertador (s2,P58/1)	1929	IntDzg	1713	987	240.6	40–2	12–6	12.0
Oranje Nassau* (P57/1,16/2,21/3)	1911	Scheld	3701	2740	350–6	44–2	23–6	12.0
Simón Bolívar (P131/1,52/2,32/3)	1927	RottDD	8309	8228	419.9	59–1	26–5	14.0
Stuyvesant (P72/1,29/2,24/3)	1918	NedSM	4249	3640	355–0	47–8	21–0	12.5
Van Rensselaer (P75/1,29/2,24/3)	1920	NedSM	4241	3629	355–0	47–9	21–0	12.5
General cargo vessels								
Achilles (P4/1)	1906	NedSM	1815	3105	286.9	40–3	19–3	8.5
Agamemnon (P4/1)	1914	DunlpB	1930	3545	295.6	43–2	18–6	9.5
Alkmaar (P18/1)	1919	RottDD	6982	11,645	447.4	62–10	27–8	10.0
Amor (P8/1)	1911	Rijkee	2325	3185	300.0	42–0	17–10	10.0
Aurora (P4/1)	1920	RottDD	1695	2300	245.2	37–4	17–9	9.0
Baarn (P22/1,16/3)	1927	Giessn	5559	9337	417–4	58–3	26–7	11.0
Bacchus (P8/1)	1911	Fyenrd	2255	3099	313–0	42–3	17–10	9.5
Barneveld (P25/1,19/3)	1928	Giessn	5597	9274	417–4	58–4	26–7	11.0
Bennekom (P13/1)	1917	Flensb	5998	9315	449.7	58–1	25–4	12.0
ex Bourne 21, ex Bürgermeister Schröder 20, launched as Gera								
Bodegraven (P25/1,19/3)	1929	Giessn	5593	9320	417–4	58–4	26–7	11.5
Boskoop (P22/1,18/3)	1927	Giessn	5560	9368	417–4	58–4	26–7	11.0
Breda (st,P16/1,4/3)	1921	NewWat	6941	9850	402.6	58–4	28–1	10.5
Calypso (P8/1)	1911	NedSM	2258	3249	313–0	42–0	17–10	9.5
Castor (m,P12/1)	1939	NedDM	1874	2804	310–4	41–2	17–6	11.5
Ceres (P10/1)	1919	SmitK	2680	4640	348.0	48–2	20–1	9.5
Deucalion (P4/1)	1914	Rijkee	1796	3275	296.8	43–3	17–8	9.0
Ganymedes (P10/1)	1918	SmitK	2682	4745	363–0	48–2	20–1	9.5
Hector (m,P12/1)	1939	Pot	1828	2804	310–10	41–1	17–6	11.5
Helder (P10/1)	1920	RottDD	3629	6343	372–0	49–10	22–8	10.0
Hercules (P4/1)	1914	Vuijk	2317	4316	339–0	45–1	20–0	9.0
ex Canton 19, ex Hercules 18								
Hermes (P10/1)	1920	Boeles	2746	4818	363–0	48–3	20–1	10.0
Jonge Willem (r/t,P3)	1939	Vuijk	1632	3035	304–5	42–3	18–7	10.0
Juno (P4/1)	1908	Rijkee	1763	2741	276.5	39–2	18–7	9.0
Mars (P4/1)	1925	NewWat	1582	2831	267.9	39–1	18–6	9.0
ex Delamere 26								
Oberon (P4/1)	1911	Clyde	1996	3588	295.3	43–3	18–5	9.0
ex Ussa 12								
Orestes (P10/1)	1918	Rijkee	2663	4419	363–0	48–3	20–2	9.5
Orion (P4/1)	1914	Vuijk	1722	3137	310–0	45–3	18–4	9.5
Pericles (m,P12/1)	1938	Giessn	3167	4670	374–6	49–7	22–7	13.5
Poseidon (P12/1)	1921	DunlpB	1928	3400	295.8	43–2	18–6	9.5
Pygmalion (m,P6/1)	1938	Pot	1824	3212	300–0	42–4	19–4	11.0
Saturnus (P4/1)	1909	Fyenrd	2741	4050	328.0	44–2	18–10	9.0

Note: * Sold Hellenic Mediterranean Lines Co Ltd, Greece, Feb 1939, renamed *Corinthia*
Note: Also *Amazone* (built 1922/1294gt), *Ariadne*

Socrates (m,P12/1)	1938	Giessn	3169	4670	374–6	49–7	22–7	13.5
Stella (P4/1)	1909	Hamltn	2818	4050	327.0	44–3	18–11	8.5
Telamon (P6/1)	1928	Neptnl	2078	3758	285.7	44–9	19–6	10.5
Tiberius (P8/1)	1930	Neptnl	1712	2960	273–6	42–7	19–2	10.0
Titus (P8/1)	1930	Neptnl	1712	3005	273–6	42–8	19–2	10.0
Trajanus (P8/1)	1930	Neptnl	1712	2985	273–6	42–8	19–2	10.0
Triton (P6/1)	1928	Neptnl	2078	3758	285.7	44–9	19–6	10.0
Ulysses (P10/1)	1918	Vuijk	2666	4690	346.2	48–3	19–7	10.0
Venus (P4/1)	1907	RottDD	1855	2850	278–4	38–3	19–5	9.0
Vesta (P4/1)	1907	RottDD	1854	2870	278–4	38–1	19–5	9.0
Vulcanus (P4/1)	1907	NedSM	1819	3119	286.7	40–2	19–7	9.0

(19/1170), *Berenice* (19/1177), *Fauna* (12/1254), *Hebe* (16/1140), *Irene* (18/1153), *Luna* (22/1456), *Merope* (18/1162), and *Rhea* (22/1388) on ocean voyages and many smaller short-sea vessels; the KNSM subsidiary West Indische Scheepvaart Maatschappij also operated small vessels in the US, West Indies, Panama and W coast of South America areas

KONINKLIJKE PAKETVAART MAATSCHAPPIJ, (Royal Packet Navigation Co),
Het Scheepvaarthuis, Prins Hendrikkade 108–114, Amsterdam; and Koningsplein Oost 5, Batavia Centrum, Java

Funnel: Yellow, narrow black top
Hull: Black or white, red boot-topping
Services: Between Netherlands East Indies ports; Singapore–Batavia–Brisbane–Sydney–Melbourne–Adelaide; Belawan–Singapore–Amoy; Belawan–Rangoon; Batavia–Siam; Saigon–Moluccas; Batavia–Mauritius–E Africa; Manila–Saigon–Bangkok–Batavia–Mauritius–Beira–Port Natal–Cape Town; Saigon–Singapore–Batavia–Noumea–South Sea islands–Sydney; Manila–Hong Kong–Shanghai–Singapore–Batavia–Zanzibar–Mombasa–Mauritius–Seychelles–Cape Town

Passenger/general cargo vessels

Barentsz (P83/1,1277/d)	1915	NedSM	4819	4965	383.4	48–9	23–0	12.0
Boissevain (m3,P663)	1937	Blohm	14,134	11,950	561–0	72–2	30–2	17.0
Bontekoe (P51/cab,980/d)	1923	SmitK	5033	8175	397–0	49–6	22–7	12.0
Cremer (m,P70/1,2130/d)	1926	NedSM	4608	3790	405–0	52–3	21–4	13.0
Maetsuycker (m,P55/1,–/d)	1937	NedDk	4131	3647	375–6	52–6	20–5	15.0
Melchior Treub (s2,P138/cab,–/d)	1913	Fyenrd	3242	1750	350.3	48–1	17–6	15.0
Nieuw Holland (st2,P123/cab,785/d)	1928	NedSM	11,066	9300	559–5	62–8	26–9	15.0
Nieuw Zeeland (st2,P123/cab,785/d)	1928	RottDD	11,069	9270	559–5	62–6	26–9	15.0
Op ten Noort (s2,P182/–,1218/d)	1927	NedSM	6076	4330	438–0	55–3	21–10	15.0
Ophir (m2,P110/–,900/d)	1928	NedSM	4115	2570	385–2	51–8	20–1	15.0
Plancius (s2,P190/–,1210/d)	1924	NedSM	5955	4355	438–0	55–3	21–10	15.0
Reyniersz (m,P66/cab,–/d)	bldg		4399	4068	375–4	53–2	20–2	13.5
Roggeveen (P87/1,1220/d)	1915	Fyenrd	4782	5140	382.3	48–9	23–0	12.0
Ruys (m3,P664)	1938	Scheld	14,155	11,930	561–0	72–3	30–2	17.0
Swartenhondt (P51/–,980/d)	1924	NedSM	5084	5250	397–0	49–5	23–1	12.5
Tasman (P94/–,650/d)	1921	Earles	4992	5320	407–6	49–3	23–2	12.0
Tegelberg (m3,P664)	1938	NedSM	14,150	11,930	559–5	72–2	30–1	17.0
Van Cloon (P58/–,1090/d)	1912	NedSM	4519	4252	383.6	48–6	20–11	11.5
Van der Hagen (P60/–,–/d)	1909	Fyenrd	3033	3470	325.3	44–1	19–6	11.0
Van Heemskerk (P60/–,–/d)	1909	NedSM	2996	3477	325.5	43–10	19–6	11.5
Ven Heutsz (m2,P16/1,30/2,2130/d)	1926	Scheld	4552	3735	404–11	52–2	20–10	13.0
Van Linschoten* (Pc60/–,–/d)	1910	NedSM	3004	3386	328.5	43–11	19–3	11.5
Van Neck (P60/–,–/d)	1913	NedSM	3027	3370	326.0	44–0	19–6	11.0
Van Overstraten (P66/–,1090/d)	1912	Fyenrd	4482	4425	383.2	48–4	21–2	11.5
Van Rees (P58/–,–/d)	1914	Rijkee	3000	3220	325.6	43–1	20–5	10.0
Van Waerwijk (P60/–,–/d)	1909	Fyenrd	3040	3363	325.3	44–0	19–6	11.0

General cargo vessels

Bantam	1930	PSmit	3322	4646	339–6	48–2	20–2	10.0
Japara	1930	PSmit	3323	4646	339–6	48–2	20–2	10.0

KNSM: Barneveld *was launched on October 22 1928 and completed in 1929 by Van der Giessen at Krimpen. She was fitted for coal or fuel oil burning and had at first accommodation for 50 passengers, which was officially reduced in the 1930s to 40, but increased again with her Allied service from May 1940. On January 20 1941* Barneveld *was captured by* Admiral Scheer *about 1200 miles from Freetown. She was sunk by time bomb the following day after her 49 crew and 51 passengers were taken off and who became prisoners of war.* Barneveld *was on voyage from London to Table Bay, Port Said and Malta via Freetown with a cargo of war stores (Alex Duncan)*

KNSM: The steamer Ganymedes *was completed by J & K Smit at Kinderdijk in 1918, and was in service from northwest Europe to both the Mediterranean and to the West Indies. She survived the Second World War and in 1959 was sold to be broken up at Hamburg (Alex Duncan)*

KPM: Destined to undertake much trooping work for the Allies during the war, the triple-screw moor liner Tegelberg *was launched by Nederlandsche SM, Amsterdam, on June 10 1937 and delivered in 1938 for the service from Yokohama and Hong Kong to Singapore, Durban, Cape Town, Rio de Janeiro and Buenos Aires.* Tegelberg *was fitted with three Werkspoor/Sulzer 8-cylinder oil engines of 10,800bhp. She served as an Allied troopship during 1940–45. Her prewar passenger accommodation of 664 was drastically reduced postwar to 104 first and 62 second class. In 1947, with other KPM vessels,* Tegelberg *was transferred to KJCPL upon the merger of the two largest Netherlands shipping companies operating in southeast Asia and following the nationalisation of Netherlands property in the newly-independent Indonesia. After several more years of service, during which her route was largely unaltered, she was broken up in 1968 (RW Jordan collection)*

KPM: Nieuw Zeeland *was launched on January 6 and completed in May 1928 by Rotterdam Drydock. She had accommodation for 155 cabin class and 785 deck passengers, and was at first fitted with four single reduction geared turbines of 7200shp. She was built for the service from the Netherlands East Indies to Australia, and within a few days of entering this service she suffered turbine damage, which had to be repaired at Singapore. Her engines were apparently unsuccessful as in October 1935 she returned to Vlissingen, Holland, for new Stork turbines which were fitted in 1935–36.* Nieuw Zeeland *was torpedoed on November 11 1942 by* U380 *when on voyage from Britain to French North Africa in ballast. She was carrying 214 crew, 29 gunners and 13 service passengers. A total of 15 lives were lost (RW Jordan collection)*

KPM: Based in the Netherlands East Indies, the passenger/cargo vessel Swartenhondt *was built at Amsterdam and completed in 1924. She was fitted with a Werkspoor triple expansion engine of 3150ihp.* Swartenhondt *survived the Second World War during which she was in Allied service, and continued in service in southeast Asia until January 1959 when she arrived at Hong Kong to be broken up (Alex Duncan)*

KPM: The passenger/general cargo steamer Van Rees, *completed by Rijkee in April 1914, was torpedoed and sunk by the Japanese submarine* I-56 *when on voyage from Macassar and Tjilatjap to Padang (Emmahaven). Her cargo had been discharged at Tjilatjap (RW Jordan collection)*

La Corona: The motor tanker Ceronia, *pictured postwar, was one of a large series of tankers built for this owner during the late 1930s. She was launched on January 28 and completed in April 1939 at the Wilton-Fijenoord shipyard in Schiedam.* Ceronia *was torpedoed on February 5 1940 by* U41 *west-southwest of the Scilly Isles, but made port in damaged condition. She survived the Second World War and was broken up at Hong Kong in 1961 (Alex Duncan)*

Note: * Sold Société Les Affréteurs Maritime Indochinois, Saigon, 1939, renamed *Gouverneur Général A Varenne* (French flag)
Note: This company owned many vessels under 3000gt on services in and around the Netherlands East Indies

Le Maire	1908	Fyenrd	3271	3388	325.5	44–0	19–2	10.5
Ombilin	1916	NedSM	5658	8040	420.4	54–2	23–0	10.5
Sawahloento	1921	Pot	3085	5027	325.3	47–8	20–4	10.0
Straat Malakka (m2,P12/1)								
	1939	Giessn	6439	8639	476–3	62–2	27–4	16.5
Straat Soenda (m2,P12/1)								
	1938	Giessn	6439	8639	476–3	62–2	27–4	16.5
Van Spilbergen	1908	Fyenrd	3237	3388	325.5	44–0	19–2	11.0

Funnel: Yellow, narrow black top
Hull: Black, red boot-topping
Trades: Oil and petroleum

'LA CORONA', NV PETROLEUM MAATSCHAPPIJ,
Carel van Bijlandtlaan 30, The Hague

Note: 'La Corona' and NITM owned many smaller tankers, several of which operated in and around the Netherlands Antilles and Netherlands East Indies
Note: This company was a subsidiary of Anglo-Saxon Petroleum Co Ltd (*qv* in Great Britain section)
Note: The following tankers were transferred to Anglo-Saxon Petroleum Co Ltd (*qv* in Great Britain section), in 1939 – *Agnita* (built 1931/3561gt), *Carelia* (38/8033), *Chama* (38/8028), *Clausina* (38/8028), *Clea* (38/7987), *Cymbula* (38/8033), *Maja* (31/8248), *Megara* (29/7992), *Miralda* (36/8003), *Rapana* (35/8017), *Selene* (14/3737)

Tankers

Ceronia (m)	1939	WiltnF	8096	12,033	483–4	59–4	27–6	12.0
Cistula (m)	1939	WiltnF	8097	12,030	483–4	59–4	27–6	12.0
Clavella (m)	1939	RottDD	8097	12,005	483–4	59–4	27–6	12.0
Cleodora (m)	1938	Scheld	8026	12,023	483–4	59–3	27–6	12.0
Corilla (m)	1939	WiltnF	8096	12,025	483–4	59–4	27–6	12.0
Coryda (m)	1938	RottDD	8028	11,984	483–4	59–4	27–6	12.0
Elusa (m)	1936	WiltnF	6236	9100	446–1	54–6	25–7	12.0
Ena (m)	1936	Odense	6229	9150	446–4	54–6	25–8	12.0
Erinna (m)	1936	Scheld	6233	9110	446–1	54–6	25–7	12.0
Etrema (m)	1936	RottDD	6236	9135	446–1	54–6	25–7	12.0
Eulota (m)	1936	WiltnF	6236	9100	446–1	54–6	25–7	12.0
Gadila (m)	1935	HwldtK	7999	12,060	483–1	59–4	27–6	12.0
Genota (m)	1935	DeutsH	7987	12,060	483–1	59–4	27–7	12.0
Hermes (m)	1914	Palmer	3768	6480	360–0	46–1	22–10	9.0
Macoma (m)	1936	NedSM	8011	12,163	483–0	59–4	27–5	12.0
Macuba (m2)	1931	SmitP	8249	12,609	468–0	62–0	27–7	12.0
Magdala (m2)	1931	Giessn	8248	12,623	468–0	62–0	27–6	12.0
Malvina (m2)	1932	Fyenrd	8245	12,658	468–0	62–0	27–6	12.0
Mamura (m2)	1932	Wilton	8245	12,645	468–0	62–0	27–6	12.0
Manvantara (m2)	1931	NedSM	8237	12,610	468–0	62–0	27–6	12.0
Marisa (m)	1937	NedSM	8029	12,100	483–0	59–4	27–5	12.0
Merula (m2)	1932	NedSM	8228	12,635	468–0	62–0	27–7	12.0
Mirza (m2)	1929	Seine	7991	11,469	440–0	65–2	27–1	12.0
ex Descubridor 35, ex Mirza 35								
Murena (m2)	1931	Burger	8252	12,630	467–10	62–0	27–6	12.0
Ocana (m)	1938	WiltnF	6256	9062	446–6	54–8	25–8	12.0
Olivia (m)	1939	CRDA2	6307	9105	446–4	54–6	25–7	12.0
Omala (m)	1938	CRDA2	6256	9130	446–4	54–6	25–7	12.0
Ondina (m)	1939	NedDok	6341	9070	446–5	54–6	25–8	12.0
Onoba (m)	1938	Giessn	6256	9100	446–6	54–8	25–8	12.0
Oscilla (m)	1939	Giessn	6341	9100	446–6	54–8	25–8	12.0
Ovula (m)	1938	WiltnF	6256	9067	446–6	54–8	25–8	12.0
Perna (m)	1935	Odense	7984	12,220	483–0	59–0	27–5	12.0
Rotula (m)	1935	NedSM	7981	12,200	483–0	59–4	27–5	12.0
Sunetta (m)	1935	RottDD	7987	12,248	483–0	59–4	27–5	12.0
Taria (m)	1939	NedSM	10,354	15,172	525–4	64–7	29–7	13.0
Tibia (m)	1939	NedSM	10,356	15,147	525–4	64–7	29–7	13.0

NEDERLANDSCH INDISCHE TANKSTOOMBOOT MAATSCHAPPIJ

Marpessa (m)	1927	RottDD	7408	10,519	458–6	59–4	26–8	10.5
Phobos (m)	1926	NedSM	7412	10,564	458–6	59–5	26–8	10.5
Saidja (s2)	1939	RottDD	6671	8700	450–2	62–8	20–11	11.0
Saroena (s2)	1939	WiltnF	6671	8710	450–2	62–8	20–11	11.0
Semiramis	1921	SouthW	5792	8914	427–0	53–4	24–7	9.5

Funnel: Yellow with blue band bearing yellow emblem
Hull: Grey
Services: UK, NW Europe–Tenerife–Mediterranean–Egypt–Palestine–Red Sea
Notes: * Sold Koninklijke Nederlandsche SM, 1939; ** sold Compagnie Côtière de l'Annam, Saigon, 1939, renamed *Tranninh* (French flag); † sold Koninklijke Nederlandsche SM, 1939, for delivery 1940 and to be renamed *Jupiter*; †† sold Germany 1939, renamed *Salzburg*

MIDDELANDSCHE ZEEVAART COMPAGNIE NV, (Emzetco Line),
Calandstraat 7, Rotterdam

Jonge Willem* (r/t,P3)								
	1939	Vuijk	1632	3035	304–5	42–3	18–7	11.0

MAATSCHAPPIJ STOOMSCHIP 'JONGE ELISABETH' NV

Jonge Elisabeth**	1928	SmitP	1463	2546	278–0	38–8	18–0	10.5

MAATSCHAPPIJ STOOMSCHIP 'JONGE JOHANNA' NV

Jonge Johanna†	1928	SmitP	1464	2546	278–0	38–8	18–0	10.5

MAATSCHAPPIJ STOOMSCHIP 'JONGE MARIA' NV

Jonge Anthony††	1922	DGroot	1756	3000	279.4	39–4	17.8	10.0
ex Slot Loevestein 24								

'MILLINGEN' NV, SCHEEPVAART MAATSCHAPPIJ
Willemskade 2, Rotterdam

Funnel: Black with blue M on white diamond on broad blue band bordered by narrow white bands
Hull: Black
Services: General tramping

Beursplein	1920	DeutsH	4368	7200	412–0	50–1	23–6	9.0
Emmaplein	1926	SmitP	5436	8700	375.5	52–3	26–3	10.0
Kerkplein	1921	Bartm2	5085	8340	413–0	52–2	25–2	10.0
ex Ramsay 30								
Oostplein	1921	CFCN	5059	8000	379.1	51–6	30.3	9.0
ex Luigi Accame 37, ex Monte Nero 29								
Westplein	1920	DeutsH	4370	7200	412–2	50–4	23–6	9.0
Willemsplein	1910	LithR	5489	9100	414.3	56–0	24–9	8.5
ex Morus 29, ex Valdura 26								

Note: Manager of this fleet was G A Spliethoff

'NEDERLAND', NV STOOMVAART MAATSCHAPPIJ
Het Scheepvaarthuis, Prins Hendrikkade 108–114, Amsterdam

Funnel: Yellow, black top
Hull: Black or grey, red boot-topping
Services: Amsterdam, Rotterdam, Southampton–Algiers–Genoa–Port Said–Suez–Colombo–Singapore–Batavia–Sabang–Sourabaya; Hamburg, Bremen, Antwerp–Netherlands East Indies; Batavia–Singapore–Calcutta–Colombo–New York–(Montreal –Quebec)–Halifax; Calcutta – Batavia–Makassar–Philippines–Los Angeles–San Francisco–Seattle –Vancouver; Hamburg, Rotterdam, Antwerp–Australia; round-the-world service

Passenger/general cargo vessels								
Christiaan Huygens (m2,P269/1,250/2,53/3)								
	1928	NedSM	16,287	11,236	570–0	68–10	30–3	17.0
Jan Pieterszoon Coen (s2,P200/1,166/2,46/3)								
	1915	NedSM	11,140	6782	521–7	60–8	26–5	15.0
Johan de Witt (s2,P197/1,120/2,36/3)								
	1920	NedSM	10,474	7762	523–0	59–2	28–11	16.0
lengthened 33								
Johan van Oldenbarnevelt (m2,P245/1,246/2,64/3,48/4)								
	1930	NedSM	19,429	10,955	609–2	74–9	27–11	17.0
Marnix van Sint Aldegonde (m2,370/1,281/2,64/3,60/4)								
	1930	NedSM	19,355	10,879	609–0	74–10	27–11	17.0
Oranje (m3,P687)	1939	NedSM	20,017	7056	656–5	83–6	28–10	21.0
General cargo vessels								
Bali (m,P28)	order	RottDD	9250	12,070	520–0	63–4	20–10	15.5
Bengkalis	1918	Fyenrd	6453	9470	438–0	54–9	27–5	12.0
Bintang (m)	1916	Fyenrd	6481	9124	438–0	54–9	27–5	12.5
conv steamer 25								
Celebes (m,P28)	bldg	NedSM	10,439	12,002	520–4	63–3	30–10	15.5
Enggano	1920	Sundld	5412	8886	438–0	55–0	25–8	12.0
Java (m,P38)	1939	Desch3	9250	11,927	520–4	63–3	30–11	15.5
Madoera (m)	1922	Forth	9382	13,335	523–0	60–6	30–3	14.5
lengthened, conv steamer 33								
Manoeran (m)	1922	Forth	9371	12,695	523–0	60–5	30–2	14.5
lengthened, conv steamer 33								
Mapia (m)	1923	Laing	9389	13,330	523–0	60–6	30–3	14.5
lengthened, conv steamer 34								
Moena	1923	Laing	9286	13,598	500–0	60–5	30–5	12.0
Poelau Bras (m,P52/1,–/d)								
	1929	Scheld	9278	10,911	517–0	61–4	29–1	14.5
Poelau Laut (m,P52/1,–/d)								
	1929	NedSM	9272	10,894	517–0	61–2	29–1	14.5
Poelau Roebiah (m,P52/1,–/d)								
	1928	RottDD	9251	10,914	517–0	61–2	29–1	14.5
Poelau Tello (m,P52/1, –/d)								
	1929	Scheld	9272	10,940	517–0	61–4	29–1	14.5
Salabangka	1920	Hamtn2	6586	8989	438–4	54–9	27–5	12.0
Salawati (m)	1920	Lithgw	6643	8947	438–4	54–8	27–5	12.0
conv steamer 31								
Saleier	1920	Lithgw	6562	9172	438–4	54–8	27–5	12.0
Saparoea (m)	1921	RottDD	6668	8931	438–4	54–9	27–4	12.0
conv steamer 31								
Simaloer	1921	NedSM	6533	9113	438–0	54–9	27–5	12.0
Singkep (st)	1922	NedSM	6607	9173	438–0	54–9	27–8	12.0
Soemba (st)	1924	Conrad	6718	9156	440–9	54–9	27–8	12.0
Sumatra (m,P28)	bldg	NedSM	10,439	12,064	520–0	63–4	30–11	15.5
Tabian (m,P21/1,–/d)								
	1930	NedSM	8151	10,388	490–0	62–2	29–0	14.5
Tabinta (m,P21/1,–/d)								
	1930	NedSM	8156	10,423	490–1	62–2	29–0	14.5
Tajandoen (m, P19/1,–/d)								
	1931	NedSM	8159	10,568	490–1	62–2	29–0	14.5
Talisse (m,P21/1,–/d)								
	1930	Caledn	8169	10,275	489–7	62–4	29–1	14.5
Tanimbar (m,P21/1,–/d)								
	1930	Caledn	8169	10,366	489–7	62–2	29–0	14.5

La Corona: Gadila *was completed at Kiel in April 1935. She is pictured here with the 'shell' emblem on her funnel which was adopted in Shell group vessels in 1945. She survived the war and her wartime service included a brief period in service with the Royal Netherlands Navy as an auxiliary MAC ship in 1944. She was returned to La Corona in 1945. Her postwar service lasted until 1958 when she was broken up (Alex Duncan)*

La Corona: Magdala *was completed by Van der Giessen at Krimpen in September 1931 and was fitted with two Werkspoor 6-cylinder oil engines of 4200bhp. The German U-boat* U758 *claimed a torpedo hit on the tanker west of Ireland on March 17 1943 when she was in convoy HX229.* Magdala *sailed from Reykjavik on January 15 1945 for Manchester in ballast and was not heard from again. It was at first suspected she had been sunk by an enemy submarine, but as no such reportings were later made, it was decided that her loss was due to unknown marine causes (Alex Duncan)*

La Corona: Malvina, *pictured postwar, was completed in January 1931 at the Fyenoord shipyard, and was fitted with two Werkspoor 12-cylinder oil engines of 4200bhp, which were standard in all vessels in this class. She served the Allies during the war, coming through the conflict unscathed, and was broken up in 1961 (Alex Duncan)*

La Corona: The motor tanker Taria, *pictured postwar, was completed at the Nederland shipyard at Amsterdam in October 1939. She served the Allies during the war, and was returned to La Corona in 1945. She was broken up at Hong Kong in 1961 (Alex Duncan)*

Nederland: Johan van Oldenbarnevelt *was launched on August 3 1929 and made her maiden voyage from Amsterdam to the Netherlands East Indies in May 1930, although this was delayed by three days as a result of a collision before she had reached the open sea. In 1939 she was chartered by Holland-Amerika for one round voyage Amsterdam–New York– Amsterdam, when she carried 634 US citizens returning home when war seemed imminent. She served as an Allied troopship during the war, retaining her Dutch crew and managed by Orient Steam Navigation Co. Postwar she was still trooping for a few months. Apart from her regular service, she carried emigrants to Australia and later to Canada up to 1958. She was then extensively rebuilt for round-the-world voyaging, but this service lasted only three years. In March 1963 she was delivered to Greece to become the cruise ship* Lakonia. *Her career was soon to come to a tragic end, for on December 22 1963 when on a cruise from Southampton, she was on fire about 200 miles northeast of Madeira; the fire spread rapidly and the vessel was gutted. She was taken in tow for Gibraltar but sank on December 29. She had on board 643 passengers and 385 crew, from which a total 128 lives were lost (EH Cole)*

Nederland: Poelau Bras *was built at the Vlissingen shipyard of De Schelde and completed in July 1929, and was fitted with a Sulzer 8-cylinder oil engine of 7040bhp. In peacetime she carried 52 passengers and 62 crew.* Poelau Bras *left Tjilatjap on February 28 1942 calling at Wijnkoops Bay, Java to pick up passengers. She sailed from there on March 6 and on March 7 was bombed and sunk by Japanese aircraft. Of the 160 passengers and 91 crew on board, 33 were killed and the remainder taken prisoner by the Japanese (De Schelde)*

Nederland: The motor vessel Talisse, *fitted with a Sulzer 8-cylinder oil engine of 7040bhp, was one of seven sisterships built during 1930–31 in Britain and the Netherlands and which were improved versions of the* Poelau Laut *class built in 1928–29. The 'T' class were slightly smaller but had the same general appearance. Each of the vessels in these classes carried a small number of first class passengers and when required were able to adapt spaces for the seasonal carriage of Hadj pilgrims from the Netherlands East Indies to Jeddah (for Mecca).* Talisse *carried a crew of 52 in peacetime conditions. She was one of five which survived the Second World War, and was sold to breakers at Kure in October 1961 (Alex Duncan)*

Holland-Amerika: Volendam *was delivered on October 12 1922 and made her maiden voyage from Rotterdam, Boulogne and Plymouth to New York. She also made winter cruises to the Caribbean, South America, Bermuda, and the Mediterranean. She made her last transatlantic voyage from Rotterdam to New York in April 1940, and soon aftrer was requisitioned by Britain for use as a troopship. She was converted for this role by Cammell, Laird. On August 30 1940, having been assigned to the child evacuation programme,* Volendam *was torpedoed by* U60 *200 miles west of the Bloody Foreland when evacuating children to Canada and a part of convoy OB205. There were over 900 persons on board, including 335 children and 271 adults, but miraculously only one life was lost from among the crew.* Volendam *was taken in tow and beach on the Isle of Bute, badly damaged. After refloating, she was repaired by Cammell, Laird, and while at the shipyard a second, unexploded, torpedo was found embedded in her hull. She re-entered service as a troopship, and during the war she carried over 100,000 troops. Following a partial refit at Schiedam in 1945 she continued trooping for Britain, and in the summer of 1946 carried Dutch troops to the Netherlands East Indies. She later was involved in Europe–Australia emigrant voyages, before going back to the Rotterdam–New York service. During 1949–51 she made several voyages from Rotterdam to Quebec on charter to the Netherlands government. In 1952* Volendam *was broken up at Hendrik-Ido-Ambacht (RW Jordan collection)*

Holland-Amerika: Blommersdijk *was completed in February 1922 by Van der Giessen, Krimpen. She was fitted with two Harland & Wolff DR geared turbines of 3000shp.* Blommersdijk *was the fourth of eight sisterships built for service from Rotterdam and northwest Europe to the US and Canada, and was the only one of the series to survive the Second World War. From May 1940 she was operated by the Ministry of Shipping, later Ministry of War Transport, and was operated mainly in African waters and the Mediterranean. In 1946 she reverted to North Atlantic service as* Blommersdyk. *She was sold to Italy in 1957 and renamed* Vivara, *and was broken up at Trieste in 1959–60 (Alex Duncan)*

Tarakan (m,P21/1,–/d)

1930	Fyenrd	8183	10,420	490–1	62–4	29–0	14.5

Tawali (m,P19/1,–/d)

1930	NedSM	8178	10,423	490–1	62–4	29–0	14.5

NEDERLANDSCHE-AMERIKAANSCHE STOOMVAART MAATSCHAPPIJ NV (Holland-Amerika Lijn),

Wilhelminakade, Postbus 486, Rotterdam

Funnel: Yellow with broad white band bordered by two narrow green bands
Hull: Black with gold band, red boot-topping
Services: Mail and passenger – Rotterdam–Boulogne–Plymouth–New York; Rotterdam–Antwerp –Boulogne–Bilbao–La Coruña–Havana–Vera Cruz–Tampico–New Orleans; Antwerp–New York (*Pennland, Westernland*, on Red Star Line passenger service); cargo – Rotterdam, Hamburg, Antwerp, UK, France–US and Canada W coast and E coast; Rotterdam, Hamburg, Antwerp, UK, France–Suez–British India; New York–Java

Passenger and passenger/general cargo vessels

Edam (st,P30/cab,60/3)	1921	Scheld	8871	11,563	466–0	58–2	30–3	13.0
Leerdam (st,P30/cab,60/3)	1921	NewWat	8815	11,563	466–0	58–2	30–3	13.0
Maasdam (st,P30/cab,60/3)	1921	Fyenrd	8812	11,563	466–0	58–2	30–3	13.0
Nieuw Amsterdam (st2,P556/cab,455/t,309/3)	1938	RottDD	36,287	10,265	758–6	88–4	31–6	20.5
Noordam (m2,P148/t)	1938	SmitP	10,726	10,150	501–7	64–5	31–8	16.0
Pennland (st3,P486/t)	1922	H&W,B	16,082	16,800	601–0	67–10	33–11	15.5
ex Pittsburgh 26								
Rotterdam* (s2,P540/1,643/t)	1908	H&W,B	24,149	14,140	668–0	77–5	33–0	16.0
Spaarndam (st,P30/cab,60/3)	1922	NewWat	8857	11,463	466–0	58–2	30–2	13.0
Statendam (st2,P?1654/cab,/t,/3)	1929	H&W,B	28,291	16,820	697–0	81–4	33–3	19.0
Veendam (st2,P262/1,430/2,480/t)	1923	H&WGw	15,450	13,290	576–1	67–4	32–5	15.0
Volendam (st2,P263/1,428/2,484/t)	1922	H&WGw	15,434	13,700	576–1	67–4	32–5	15.0
Westerdam (m2,P134/1)	bldg	WiltnF	12,149	10,150	518–5	66–4	31–3	16.0
Westernland (r/t3,P550/t)	1918	H&WGw	16,231	16,800	601–0	67–10	33–11	15.5
ex Regina 30								
Zaandam (m2,P148/t)	1938	WiltnF	10,909	10,150	501–8	64–5	31–8	17.0
laid down as Schiedam								
Zuiderdam (m2,P134/1)	bldg	WiltnF	12,150	10,150	518–5	66–4	31–3	16.0

General cargo vessels

Beemsterdijk (st)	1922	Fyenrd	6869	9852	416–6	54–4	30–2	12.0
Bilderdijk (st)	1922	Giessn	6856	9740	416–6	54–5	30–2	12.0
Binnendijk (st)	1921	DNoord	6873	9782	416–6	54–4	30–2	12.0
Blommersdijk (st)	1922	Giessn	6855	9700	416–5	54–4	30–2	12.0
Boschdijk (st)	1922	DNoord	6872	9852	416–6	54–4	30–2	12.0
Breedijk (st)	1922	Boele	6861	9822	416–6	54–4	30–2	12.0
Burgerdijk (st)	1921	Giessn	6853	9852	416–6	54–4	30–2	12.0
Damsterdijk (m2,P46/1)	1930	Wilton	10,155	12,534	509–2	64–9	30–10	14.5
Delftdijk (m2,P46/1)	1929	Wilton	10,220	12,480	509–2	64–9	30–10	14.5
Dinteldijk (m2,P30/1)	1922	H&WGw	9399	11,780	500–3	62–4	29–7	13.0
Drechtdijk (m2,P28/1)	1923	H&WGk	9338	11,800	500–2	62–4	29–7	13.0
Sloterdijk (m2,P12)	bldg	Odense	9340	11,780	492–7	62–4	31–0	15.5
Sommelsdijk (m2,P12)	1939	Odense	9227	11,780	492–7	62–4	31–0	15.5

Note: * LU 29.12.39, sold for BU at Hendrik-Ido-Ambacht

NEDERLANDSCHE KOLONIALE TANKVAART MAATSCHAPPIJ, NV

Gebouw Petrolea, Benoordenhoutscheweg, Postbus 64, The Hague; and Soengei Gerong, Palembang, Sumatra

Funnel: Black with emblem on white band
Hull: Black, red boot-topping
Trades: Far Eastern oil and petroleum
Note: This company was controlled by Standard Oil Co of New Jersey

Tankers

Benakat (s2)	1935	RottDD	4763	–	365.7	64–2	16-7	10.0
Djirak (s2)	1928	Palmer	3077	4325	336–9	55–2	14–8	10.0
ex Creole Jefe 33								

(*qv* in United States section)

Pendopo	1930	Giessn	5209	7150	385.8	56–1	22–3	10.0

Trades: Oil and petroleum
Note: This company was controlled by The Texas Co (*qv* in United States section)

NEDERLANDSCHE PACIFIC TANKVAART MAATSCHAPPIJ, NV

Korte Vijverberg 5,The Hague

Tanker

Nederland (m)	1937	WiltnF	8147	11,910	483–2	59–3	27–6	12.0

Funnel: Black with red band bearing vertical black band with three crosses (**X**) placed vertically and SM and MM vertically on red to left and right respectively
Services: Amsterdam, Rotterdam–Bilbao–Mediterranean–Casablanca

'NOORDZEE', NV STOOMVAART MAATSCHAPPIJ

Prins Hendrikkade 48, Postbus 401, Amsterdam

Boekelo	1930	Vuijk	2118	3480	293–6	42–9	18–4	9.5
Groenlo	1926	Boele	1984	3290	275.3	41–3	17–11	9.5
ex Helsinki 35, ex Groenlo 32								

Funnel: Blue with black top
Hull: Black, red boot-topping
Services: Hamburg, Amsterdam, Rotterdam (occasionally UK W coast ports)–Batavia–Macassar–Padang–Sourabaya–London–Amsterdam–Hamburg; Netherlands East Indies–New York

Note: This company was controlled by Alfred Holt & Co Ltd (*qv* in Great Britain section)

'OCEAAN', NEDERLANDSCHE STOOMVAART MAATSCHAPPIJ,

Prins Hendrikkade 159–160, Postbus 29, Amsterdam

Alcinous (m2,P8)	1925	Scott2	6189	8110	449–0	54–10	26–4	13.5
Jason (m)	order	CRDA2	6310	10,350	449.5	60–11	26–2	13.5
Laertes	1919	Taikoo	5825	7510	423.9	52–4	26–2	13.5
Melampus (st,P18)	1924	Palmer	5962	7848	449–6	54–11	26–5	13.5
Phrontis (m2,P2/1,6/2)	1925	Caledn	6181	8060	449–6	54–10	26–9	13.5
Polydorus (st,P8)	1924	Scott2	5922	7853	449–0	54–10	26–4	13.5
Polyphemus (m2,P–)	1930	Scott2	6269	7950	430.5	56–4	27–1	13.5

Funnel: Black with white over green bands
Trades: Oil and petroleum
Note: This company was controlled by Standard Oil Co of New Jersey (*qv* in United States section)

PETROLEUM INDUSTRIE MAATSCHAPPIJ NV,

Gebouw Petrolea, Benoordenhoutscheweg 7, Postbus 110, The Hague

Tankers

Amsterdam (m)	1922	ArmWh1	7329	11,215	455–0	57–6	27–7	10.0
Den Haag (m2)	1925	Krupp	8971	12,546	489–8	63–3	27–2	10.5
Rotterdam (m2)	1925	Krupp	8968	12,780	489–8	63–4	27–3	10.5

Funnel: Black (*Kedoe* had very narrow funnel)
Hull: Dove grey, white boot-topping
Services: Passenger and cargo – Rotterdam–Southampton–Lisbon –Tangiers–Gibraltar–Marseilles–Port Said–Suez–Colombo–Sabang–Belawan–Singapore–Batavia–Sourabaya; fast cargo – Rotterdam, Hamburg, Bremen–Netherlands East Indies–Marseilles–London–Bremen–Hamburg–Rotterdam; cargo – Antwerp, London–Genoa–Netherlands East Indies–Trieste–Barcelona–Havre–Liverpool–London–Antwerp; service in association with Silver Line Ltd (*qv* in Great Britain section) – Java–New York–San Francisco–Rangoon–Calcutta

RUYS & ZONEN, W, Veerhaven 7, Rotterdam

ROTTERDAMSCHE LLOYD NV

Passenger/general cargo vessels

Baloeran (m2,P236/1,280/2,70/3,48/4)	1930	Fyenrd	17,001	8436	574–0	70–5	28–4	18.0
Dempo (m2,P236/1,280/2,70/3,48/4)	1931	Scheld	17,024	8491	574–0	70–5	28–4	18.0
Indrapoera (m2,P141/1,184/2,68/3)	1925	Scheld	10,825	8115	507–11	60–3	28–10	17.0
lengthened 32, 34								
Sibajak (m2,P215/1,174/2,68/3)	1927	Scheld	12,226	8289	529–11	62–11	25–8	17.0
Slamat (st2,P411/1,2,3)	1924	Scheld	11,636	8370	529–11	62–0	26–0	17.0
laid down as Papandajan; lengthened 31								
Willem Ruys (m2,P344/1,320/2,131/3,74/4)	bldg	Scheld	21,119	7238	631–2	82–0	29–2	21.0

General cargo/passenger vessels

Bantam (m2,P12)	1939	Scheld	9312	12,048	515–4	62–9	30–10	16.0
Bengalen (m,P12)	1932	Scheld	6933	9330	453–0	55–10	28–2	13.5
Blitar (r/t)	1923	Fyenrd	7065	9910	446.2	54–4	28–0	13.0
Brastagi (m2,P12)	1937	Scheld	9246	11,700	513–2	62–10	28–1	16.0
Buitenzorg	1916	Scheld	7073	10,297	445.7	54–0	28–0	12.5
Djambi (m,P6)	1919	Fyenrd	6983	9825	445.6	54–4	28–0	13.5
conv steamer 31								
Garoet (st)	1917	Scheld	7118	10,610	446.6	54–4	28–0	13.0
Japara (m2,P12)	1939	SmitP	9312	12,166	515–4	62–9	30–10	16.0
Kedoe (m2,P15)	1921	B&W	3684	6561	380–9	51–6	23–4	11.5

Oceaan: Alcinous *was completed in 1926 for this Netherlands subsidiary of Alfred Holt, Liverpool. Oceaan was founded in 1891 in conjunction with the Amsterdam firm of J B Meyer, and with facilities at Amsterdam and Batavia, enabled Alfred Holt to compete with the large Dutch companies trading to the Netherlands East Indies and south-east Asia.* Alcinous *had been built by Scotts at Greenock, and was fitted with two B&W 8-cylinder oil engines of 4800bhp. On August 27 1940 when in westbound convoy OB197, she was torpedoed by* U46 *and damaged. She survived the Second World War and was renamed* Phemius *in 1950 when transferred to the British flag and owned by Ocean Steamship Co. She was broken up at Hong Kong in 1957 (Alex Duncan)*

Ruys & Zn: Dempo *was launched on July 26 1930 and delivered on February 21 1931 for Rotterdam Lloyd's service from Rotterdam and Southampton to Lisbon, Tangier, Gibraltar, Marseilles, Port Said, Colombo, Sabang, Belawan, Singapore and Batavia. She was fitted with two De Schelde/Sulzer 10-cylinder oil engines of 13,000bhp and achieved 18.5 knots on trials. In 1941* Dempo *was taken over for service as an Allied troopship and converted at Liverpool in March 1941 with accommodation for 2000 troops. In March 1944 she was at the Allied landings at Salerno. On March 17 1944 when in convoy SNF17, on passage from Naples (sailed March 15) to Oran, in ballast, she was torpedoed by* U371. *She sank over one hour later but without loss of life. Before attacking* Dempo, U371 *had torpedoed and sunk the US steamer* Maiden Creek *from the same convoy (De Schelde)*

Ruys & Zn: Willem Ruys *was ordered in August 1938 from De Schelde at Vlissingen. Her keel was laid on January 21 1939, and although quite well advanced, her construction was halted upon the German occupation. Work eventually restarted, but was deliberately slow and was hampered by sabotage by the Dutch resistance movement.* Willem Ruys *was launched on July 1 1946, and delivered on November 21 1947. On that day Rotterdam Lloyd received from Queen Wilhelmina the Royal prefix in recognition of the company's wartime role in service with the Allies. After several years of postwar service, which included a round-the-world service during 1959–64, she was sold to Italy in 1964 and renamed* Achille Lauro. *An eventful career under the Italian flag, which included fires on board, collisions, hijacking by terrorists, and the insolvency of her owner, came to an end on November 30 1994 when she was on fire off the Horn off Africa. She sank on December 2 (EH Cole)*

Ruys & Zn: Weltevreden *was launched on January 23 and ran trials on June 4 1937. When Holland was occupied in May 1940,* Weltevreden *was on voyage from Rotterdam to the Netherlands East Indies and Japan. She later went to Sydney and from then until the end of the war was on charter at various times to the US War Shipping Administration and the Ministry of War Transport. In June 1943 she was converted for use as a troop transport with accommodation for 1400 troops. She was in service in the Pacific until the end of the war, and on February 13 1946 was returned to Rotterdam Lloyd. She resumed her peacetime service in 1947. In February 1963* Weltevreden *was sold to Van Heyghen Frères for breaking up in Belgium (RW Jordan collection)*

Ruys & Zn: Kota Gedé *was delivered September 19 1928 by Fyenoord, Rotterdam, and was fitted with a Fyenoord/MAN 7-cylinder oil engine of 5200bhp. She had accommodation for 26 passengers. She came under Allied control in May 1940, and in 1943 was converted for use as a troop transport. In her postwar refit for commercial service, her passenger accommodation was reduced to 20 cabin class, but there was space for 129 passengers in steerage type accommodation. The latter was useful for postwar repatriation work, but was discontinued in 1948. In August 1958* Kota Gedé *arrived at Hong Kong to be broken up (RW Jordan collection)*

Ruys & Zn: Kota Radja *was launched on June 25 and was delivered on October 15 1927 by De Schelde, Vlissingen, as the first in a series of eight similar vessels built for the company. She sailed from Rotterdam on November 5 on her maiden voyage to Batavia. She was fitted with a Sulzer 8-cylinder oil engine of 5200bhp could carry 28 cabin passengers and over 2000 Hadj pilgrims in steerage accommodation. On February 24 1942 she was bombed by Japanese aircraft off the harbour at Sourabaya, and during February 25–26 was burnt out and abandoned.* Kota Radja *was scuttled in the Westervaartwater by RNN personnel to prevent explosions in the munitions cargo on board (De Schelde)*

Van Nievelt: The motor vessel Alkaid *was completed in July 1937 by Deutsche Werft at Hamburg. She survived the Second World War in Allied service and in 1964 was sold to Greece and renamed* Agios Nicolaos III. *She arrived at Bilbao in April 1965 to be broken up (Alex Duncan)*

Kertosono (m,P12)	1923	Scheld	9289	13,560	470.5	62–9	30–0	15.5
lengthened, conv steamer 35								
Kota Agoeng (m,P20/–,1300/d)	1930	Fyenrd	7355	9760	464–6	60–10	26–9	14.0
Kota Baroe (m,P30)	1928	Scheld	7281	9540	464–6	60–10	26–9	14.0
Kota Gedé (m,P26)	1928	Fyenrd	7323	9560	464–6	60–10	26–9	14.0
Kota Inten (m,P18,2000/d)	1927	Fyenrd	7206	9540	464–6	60–10	26–8	14.0
Kota Nopan (m,P20)	1931	Scheld	7322	9410	464–6	60–10	26–9	14.0
Kota Pinang (m,P20/–,2000/d)	1931	NedSM	7277	9620	464–6	60–10	26–9	14.0
Kota Radja (m,P28/–,2000/d)	1927	Scheld	7177	9580	464–6	60–10	26–7	14.0
Kota Tjandi (m,P20)	1930	Wilton	7295	9615	464–6	60–10	26–9	14.0
Modjokerto (m)	1922	GrayXX	7080	10,490	480.1	57–4	28–5	15.5
lengthened, conv steamer 34								
Palembang (r/t)	1921	Bonn&M	7070	10,255	445.8	54–4	28–0	13.5
Siantar (m)	1921	GrayXX	8667	11,225	471.3	57–5	29–6	15.5
lengthened, conv steamer 34								
Sitoebondo (st)	1916	Bonn&M	7049	10,350	444.0	54–4	28–0	12.5
Soekaboemi (st)	1923	Bonn&M	7051	10,210	445.8	54–4	28–0	13.5
Tapanoeli (st)	1924	DeMaas	7034	10,045	446.0	54–4	28–0	12.5
Tosari (m,P6,–/d)	1919	Bonn&M	7029	9665	445.8	54–4	28–0	13.5
conv steamer 31								
Weltevreden (m2,P12)	1937	SmitP	9245	11,600	513–3	62–10	28–1	16.0

NV STOOMVAART MAATSCHAPPIJ 'ROTTERDAM'

Ameland (r/t)	1930	RottDD	4537	7800	387.0	53–3	24–4	12.0
Marken (m)	1937	SmitP	5719	8910	450–9	55–4	24–4	13.5
launched as Tysa								

UITTENBOGAART, F W, Wijnhaven 103, Postbus 1205, Rotterdam

Services:: General tramping

NV STOOMSCHIP 'HANNAH'

Parklaan	1911	ThmpsJ	3807	6710	352.5	50–11	22–9	9.0
ex Rönnskär 37, ex Caldy Light 34, ex Arabier 22, ex Manningtry 16								

VAN NIEVELT, GOUDRIAAN & CO'S STOOMVAART MAATSCHAPPIJ, NV, Veerhaven 2, Rotterdam

Funnel: Yellow with white five-pointed star on blue band
Hull: Black with white band or grey, red boot-topping
Services: Hamburg, Rotterdam–Montevideo–Buenos Aires and other South American ports

Albireo* (P10)	1920	NewWat	4427	7863	385–4	50–1	23–10	10.5
Albireo (m,P34/1)	order	NedDok	7368	9500	476–10	60–2	25–10	13.0
Alchiba (P6)	1920	NewWat	4427	7863	385–4	50–4	23–10	10.5
Alcor (P4)	1920	RottDD	3526	6173	373–6	49–8	21–10	10.0
Alcyone (P12)	1921	Kuy&R	4534	7830	389–0	52–1	25–5	10.5
Aldabi (m,P42/1)	order	NedDok	7183	9468	476–10	60–2	25–10	13.0
Aldebaran (P2)	1920	Bremer	7891	12,255	493–9	60–6	27–10	12.0
ex Crefeld 20								
Alderamin (P2)	1920	Bremer	7886	12,255	493–9	60–6	27–10	12.0
Algenib (m,P4)	1937	DeutsH	5483	9300	451–6	58–9	24–1	12.0
Algol (m,P42/1)	bldg	NedSM	7289	9468	476–10	60–2	25–10	13.0
Algorab (st,P12)	1922	DeutsH	4938	8940	414–10	54–4	26–3	11.0
Alhena (P12)	1922	DeutsH	4930	8690	414–10	54–4	26–3	11.0
Alioth (m,P4)	1937	DeutsH	5483	9300	451–3	58–9	24–0	12.0
Alkaid (m,P4)	1937	DeutsH	5483	9300	451–3	58–9	24–0	12.0
Alphacca (P24/1)	1928	GraySd	5497	9200	423–8	56–2	26–1	12.0
Alphard (m,P4)	1937	DeutsH	5483	9300	451–3	58–9	24–0	12.0
Alpherat (P24/1)	1928	GraySd	5498	9200	423–8	56–3	26–1	12.0
Altair (m,P34/1)	order	NedSM	7258	9500	476–10	60–2	25–10	13.0
Aludra (P12)	1922	DeutsH	4930	8690	415–9	54–4	26–3	10.0
laid down as Odenwald								
Alwaki (P12)	1922	Kuy&R	4533	7830	389–0	52–3	25–5	10.5
Mirach†	1917	RottDD	3530	6367	373–6	49–11	21–7	10.0
Sirrah‡	1917	RottDD	3531	6424	373–6	49–11	21–7	10.0

Notes: * Sold Germany 1939, renamed *Hans Schmidt*; †, ‡ sold Greece 1939, renamed *Cygnet* and *Halcyon* respectively

Funnel: Black with white VO monogram
Hull: Black, red boot-topping
Trades: Oil and petroleum

VAN OMMEREN'S SCHEEPVAARTBEDRIJF, NV PHS,
Westerlaan 10, Postbus 845, Rotterdam

Tankers

NV MAATSCHAPPIJ MOTORSCHIP BARENDRECHT								
Barendrecht (m)	1938	Odense	9385	14,630	501–0	65–7	28–1	12.0
NV MAATSCHAPPIJ MOTORSCHIP DORDRECHT								
Dordrecht (m)	1928	Giessn	4402	5870	351.1	50–2	22–2	11.5
NV MAATSCHAPPIJ MOTORSCHIP KATENDRECHT								
Katendrecht (m)	1925	Fyenrd	5099	7440	402.1	53–4	22–5	10.5
lengthened 31								
NV MAATSCHAPPIJ MOTORSCHIP LOOSDRECHT								
Loosdrecht* (m)	1936	Odense	9314	14,620	510–2	65–4	27–11	12.0
NV MAATSCHAPPIJ MOTORSCHIP MIJDRECHT								
Mijdrecht (m)	1931	RottDD	7493	11,040	456–5	58–10	27–3	12.0
NV MAATSCHAPPIJ MOTORSCHIP MOORDRECHT								
Moordrecht (m)	1930	RottDD	7493	11,040	456–5	58–9	27–3	12.0
NV MAATSCHAPPIJ MOTORSCHIP PAPENDRECHT								
Papendrecht (m)	bldg	RottDD	10,746	15,597	514–4	73–4	28–4	12.5
NV MAATSCHAPPIJ MOTORSCHIP PENDRECHT								
Pendrecht (m)	1939	RottDD	10,746	15,597	514–4	73–2	28–4	12.0
NV MAATSCHAPPIJ MOTORSCHIP SLIEDRECHT								
Sliedrecht (m)	1924	RottDD	5133	7315	402.1	53–3	22–5	10.5
lengthened 31								
NV MAATSCHAPPIJ MOTORSCHIP WOENSDRECHT								
Woensdrecht (m)	1926	Fyenrd	4668	6840	370.0	53–4	23–0	10.5

Note: * Sold France 1939, renamed *Franche-Comté*

Funnel: Black with blue band bearing blue U on white diamond
Hull: Black, red boot-topping
Services: Cargo (limited passenger accommodation) – Bremen, Rotterdam, Antwerp–Savannah–Charleston

VAN UDEN'S SCHEEPVAART EN AGENTUUR MAATSCHAPPIJ, NV GEBR,
Veerhaven 14–15, Postbus 1123, Rotterdam

Lekhaven	1921	Dobson	4802	7788	371–9	52–1	25–3	10.0
NV SCHEEPVAART MAATSCHAPPIJ NOORZEE								
Veerhaven	1930	GraySd	5291	9260	421.3	54–5	25–2	11.0
NV MAATSCHAPPIJ STOOMSCHIP DELFSHAVEN								
Delfshaven	1930	GraySd	5281	9260	421.2	54–4	25–2	11.0
NV MAATSCHAPPIJ STOOMSCHIP JOBSHAVEN								
Jobshaven	1916	RottDD	3528	6365	372–8	49–11	21–7	9.0
NV MAATSCHAPPIJ STOOMSCHIP KEILEHAVEN								
Keilehaven	1919	Giessn	2967	5150	338–10	47–4	20–6	9.5
NV MAATSCHAPPIJ STOOMSCHIP MAASHAVEN								
Maashaven	1907	Bonn&M	2630	4450	316–6	44–8	19–10	8.5
NV MAATSCHAPPIJ STOOMSCHIP PARKHAVEN								
Parkhaven	1920	Dobson	4803	7790	371–9	52–0	25–3	10.0
NV MAATSCHAPPIJ STOOMSCHIP WAALHAVEN								
Waalhaven	1916	RottDD	3552	6370	372–8	49–11	21–7	9.5
NV MAATSCHAPPIJ STOOMSCHIP YSELHAVEN								
Yselhaven	1921	Dobson	4802	7810	371–9	52–0	25–3	10.0

Funnel: Black, orange band
Hull: Black, pink boot-topping
Services: Holland Afrika Lijn – Hamburg, Amsterdam, Rotterdam, Antwerp–Cape Town–Port Elizabeth–East London–Durban–Lourenço Marques–Beira–British E Africa–Suez–NW Europe; Hamburg, Amsterdam, Antwerp–Port Said–Port Sudan–Mombasa–Tanga–Zanzibar–Dar-es-Salaam–Mozambique–Beira–South Africa–NW Europe; Holland-Oost-Azië Lijn – Antwerp, Hamburg, Amsterdam, Rotterdam–Genoa–Port Said–Colombo–Singapore–Manila–Hong Kong–Shanghai–Dairen–Japan (Jaffa, Marseilles, on return); Holland-Australië Lijn – Bremen, Hamburg, Rotterdam, Antwerp–Port Said–Fremantle–Adelaide–Melbourne–

VEREENIGDE NEDERLANDSCHE SCHEEPVAART MAATSCHAPPIJ NV, (United Netherlands Navigation Co),
Stationsweg 137, The Hague

HOLLAND AFRIKA LIJN NV DIRECTIE-EN-AGENTUUR MAATSCHAPPIJ

Passenger/general cargo vessels

Bloemfontein (m2,P96/cab,21/st)								
	1934	NedSM	10,081	10,565	488–8	63–3	30–10	16.0
Boschfontein (m,P112)								
	1928	SmitP	7139	8302	472–5	59–7	26–8	15.5
ex Nieuwkerk 34; lengthened, conv steamer 34								
Elandsfontein (m2,P106/1,14/t)								
	bldg	Schich	10,574	10,300	527–11	62–10	30–2	17.0
launched as Rietfontein								
Jagersfontein (m2,P96/cab,21/st)								
	1934	NedSM	10,083	10,515	488–8	63–3	30–10	16.0
Klipfontein (m2,P106/1,14/t)								
	1939	SmitP	10,544	9933	527–4	62–11	30–3	17.0
Oranjefontein (m2,P106/1,14/t)								
	bldg	SmitP	10,547	9798	527–4	62–11	30–3	17.0
General cargo vessels								
Heemskerk	1919	Neptnl	6516	9518	438.0	57–3	25–7	10.5
ex Witram 21								

Van Ommeren: The motor tanker Barendrecht *was launched on May 21 and completed in July 1938 at Odense. She was fitted with a B&W 7-cylinder oil engine of 3800bhp.* Barendrecht *survived the Second World War under Allied control and managed from her owner's London office. In 1955 she was sold out of the fleet to become the Italian-owned* Humilitas, *and changed name later the same year to* Ariel, *also under Italian flag. In 1958 she was sold to a Liberian company and renamed* Gem. *As* Gem *she broke in two during a gale on March 8 1962 in 33 33N 75 18W. Three days later she was taken in tow for Jacksonville, found to be beyond economical repair, and was broken up there during 1962–63 (Alex Duncan)*

A Veder: The steamer Prins Willem Van Oranje, *a 'boilers on deck' type, was employed on the Oranje Line service between northwest Europe and the Canadian Great Lakes. She survived the Second World War, and to make way for a newer vessel to be given the same name, she was renamed* Prins Philips Willem *in 1952. In 1958 she was sold to Germany and renamed* Auguste Peters. *She was sold the following year to India and after more changes of owner under Indian registration was broken up in 1966 (Alex Duncan)*

VNSM: Amstelkerk *was completed by Nüscke & Co at Stettin in 1929 and was fitted with two Escher Wyss double reduction geared turbines of 3300shp. She was originally fitted with accommodation for 168 passengers, but postwar this was reduced to 70 in cabin class. She survived the war in Allied service and was broken up in 1953 (RW Jordan collection)*

VNSM: Oranjefontein *was under construction at Rotterdam when the Second World War started, having been ordered for her owner's service from Amsterdam and Southampton to South and East Africa. She was launched on March 21 1940 and upon completion was taken over by Germany and renamed* Pionier. *On April 30 1944 she struck a mine east of Rixhöft, and was taken to Kiel. She was found intact at Kiel in May 1944 when Allied forces entered the port, and she was taken to Newcastle for refit as a troopship for intended service in the Pacific area, but this did not materialise. On July 12 1945 she was officially returned to VNSM and renamed* Oranjefontein, *repaired by September 12 and made a voyage to Sydney, arriving there in mid November. Her first voyage to South and East Africa was made in April–May 1946, and her last voyage was in May–June 1967. She was broken up at Bilbao in 1967 (RW Jordan collection)*

Sydney–Brisbane (Verdon, Dunkirk, on return); Holland-Britisch Indië Lijn – Bremen, Hamburg, Rotterdam, Antwerp–Port Said–Kathiawar–Colombo–Madras–Calcutta; Bremen, Hamburg, Rotterdam, Antwerp–Port Said–Karachi–Bombay; Holland-West Afrika Lijn (jointly with Hollandsche SM NV – *qv*) – Hamburg, Amsterdam, Bordeaux–Las Palmas–Dakar–Freetown–Monrovia–P Bouet–Takoradi–Cape Coast–Saltpond–Winneba–Accra–Lome–Cotonou–Lagos–Port Harcourt–Calabar–Duala–Kribi–Santa Isabel (Havre, not Bordeaux, on return)

Meliskerk	1919	Blohm	6045	8629	465–9	58–3	24–9	11.5
ex Cesario 21, ex DADG 76 21								
Nijkerk (P14/cab)	1915	Blohm	5766	9471	435–6	56–4	26–2	11.0
ex Cassio 21, ex Pangani 21								
Randfontein (P33/cab)	1920	GrkDY	5653	8408	409.0	53–10	26–4	10.0
ex Staur 21								
Springfontein (P30–39)	1921	Lithgw	6406	9498	423.3	56–0	26–6	11.0

HOLLAND-OOST-AZIË LIJN NV DIRECTIE-EN-AGENTUUR MAATSCHAPPIJ

General cargo vessels

Abbekerk (m2,P–)	1939	Schich	7906	11,614	522–4	63–3	30–0	17.0
Amerskerk (m2,P–)	order	NedSM	7900	11,600	522–0	63–3	30–0	17.0
Arendskerk (m2,P–)	1938	Schich	7906	11,614	522–4	63–2	30–0	17.0
Gaasterkerk (st,P–)	1922	NewWat	8679	10,090	508–0	58–2	26–11	14.5
ex Gaasterdijk 31, lengthened 32								
Grootekerk (st,P–)	1923	NewWat	8685	10,090	508–0	58–2	27–0	14.5
ex Grootendijk 31, lengthened 32								
Meerkerk (r/t,P–)	1916	Bremer	7995	–	508.6	60–10	27–6	12.0
ex Tamora 21, ex Nienburg 21; lengthened 34								
Serooskerk (st,P12)	1922	NewWat	8456	10,370	503–0	60–5	29–5	12.0
ex Gemma 31, lengthened 33								
Zuiderkerk (st,P12)	1922	NewWat	8424	10,625	503–0	60–5	29–4	12.0
ex Zosma 31, lengthened 33								

HOLLAND-AUSTRALIË LIJN NV DIRECTIE-EN-AGENTUUR MAATSCHAPPIJ

General cargo vessels

Aagtekerk (m2,P11)	1934	NedSM	6811	9114	493–0	60–3	28–5	16.0
Almkerk (m2,P11)	1934	NedSM	6810	9114	493–0	60–3	28–5	16.0

Note: Also vessels under 1000gt on E Africa coast feeder services

HOLLAND-BRITISCH-INDIË LIJN NV DIRECTIE-EN-AGENTUUR MAATSCHAPPIJ

Note: This company was jointly owned by (*qv*) Stoomv Maats Nederland NV, Koninklijke Nederlandsche SM NV, Java–China–Japan Lijn NV, Koninklijke Paketv Maats NV, Nederlansche-Amerikanische SM, Rotterdamsche Lloyd NV (under W Ruys & Zn), SM De Maas NV (a Phs Van Ommeren SB NV subsidiary), and Van Nievelt, Goudriaan & Co

General cargo vessels

Hoogkerk	1911	Flensb	5132	8815	410.0	54–9	26–0	11.0
ex St Augustine Abbey 21, ex Atto 20								
Streefkerk (P6/cab)	1921	RottDD	6185	9741	437–5	55–5	26–6	11.5
laid down as Katendrecht								

HOLLAND-WEST AFRIKA LIJN NV

Passenger/general cargo vessels

Amstelkerk (st,P168/cab)	1929	Nüscke	4457	5955	383–9	53–2	23–6	12.5
Maaskerk (st,P168/cab)	1929	Nüscke	4452	5955	383–10	53–2	23–6	12.5

VINKE & CO,

Gelderschekade 10, Postbus 485, Amsterdam, and Leuvehaven 52–54, Rotterdam

Funnel: Hillegersberg – yellow with red over white over red bands separated from black top by yellow band; Houtvaart – yellow with black H on white diamond on broad green band separated from black top by narrow yellow band; Oostzee – yellow with red over black over red bands separated from black top by yellow band
Hull: Hillegersberg – black red boot-topping; Houtvaart – grey or black, red boot-topping; Oostzee – black with gold band, red boot-topping
Services: Argentina–NW Europe; general tramping; Hillegersberg, Oostzee – general tramping

STOOMBOOT MAATSCHAPPIJ HILLEGERSBERG NV

Larenberg (m)	order	Giessn	3713	7700	390–5	53–3	23–4	11.0
Soesterberg	1927	AwpEng	1890	3190	290–0	40–2	17–9	10.0
Trompenberg	1919	Vuijk	1995	3265	280.5	40–1	18–6	9.5
Zypenberg	1930	AyrDk	4973	8850	406.2	53–8	24–4	9.5
ex Charterhurst 35								

NV HOUTVAART

Amstel	1925	Vuijk	2115	3500	293–0	42–9	18–4	11.0
Berkel	1930	Vuijk	2130	3500	293–0	42–9	18–4	11.0
Gouwe	1927	Vuijk	2119	3500	293–0	42–9	18–4	11.0
Linge	1928	Vuijk	2114	3500	293–0	42–8	18–4	11.0
Maas	1920	Vuijk	1966	3250	281.5	40–4	18–6	10.5
Mark	1930	Vuijk	1514	2425	244.1	38–11	16–7	10.5
Merwede (m,P8)	bldg	Vuijk	5355	9440	458–7	59–4	24–9	12.0
Rijn	1916	Vuijk	1969	3260	281.3	40–4	18–6	9.5
Schie	1922	Vuijk	1967	3250	281.5	40–4	18–6	10.5
Vecht	1917	Vuijk	1695	3300	281.3	40–2	18–6	9.5
ex Graakallen 18								
Yssel (m)	1937	Vuijk	2262	3520	306–2	43–8	18–5	11.5

STOOMVAART MAATSCHAPPIJ OOSTZEE NV

Aalsum (st)	1922	Vuijk	5418	9045	420–9	56–3	25–8	10.5
Britsum	1929	Giessn	5255	9437	421.1	56–3	25–5	10.5
Bussum	1917	Vuijk	3636	5950	360.0	48–3	20–11	9.5

Farmsum	1929	Vuijk	5237	9450	420.0	56–0	25–7	10.5
Hilversum	1920	Vuijk	3717	6276	359.9	48–4	22–3	9.5
Ittersum	1938	Doxfrd	5199	9435	455–4	57–1	25–0	11.0
Leersum*	1916	Vuijk	3648	5950	360.0	48–4	20–11	9.5
Loppersum	1930	Rhead3	4691	8119	409–7	54–3	23–9	10.0
ex Harpalyce 37								
Ootmarsum	1920	Vuijk	3628	6275	360.2	48–3	22–3	9.5
Peursum (m)	bldg	Giessn	3710	7700	390–5	53–2	23–4	11.0
Rossum	1928	Vuijk	2118	3480	292–11	42–9	18–4	11.0
Winsum	1921	AwpEng	3224	5250	332.0	48–2	20–7	9.5
Wolsum (st)	1921	Vuijk	3668	6275	359.9	48–4	22–3	12.0

Note: * Sold Germany 1939, renamed *Henning Oldendorff*

'VRACHTVAART', NV MAATSCHAPPIJ, Westerkade 2, Rotterdam

Funnel: Black with white T on broad red band
Hull: Grey
Services: NW Europe–R Plate; general tramping

Tamo (m,P12)	order	SmitP	5340	8785	451–0	59–0	24–6	13.0
Tara	1929	SmitP	4760	8666	406.0	54–1	24–8	11.5
Tela	1911	GrayX	3777	6290	350.2	50–1	21–6	9.0
ex Hollinside 29, ex Robert Coverdale 17								
Tiba (m,P12)	1938	SmitP	5239	9558	455–11	59–4	24–4	13.0
Tourliani* (st)	1919	Bretgn	2486	3542	292.5	43–8	19.6	9.5
ex Marne 36								
Towa	1930	SmitP	5419	8984	420.3	55–2	24–4	11.5
Tuva (m)	1935	SmitP	4652	7825	390–5	53–2	25–0	12.5
Tysa (m,P12)	1938	SmitP	5327	9376	455–11	59–4	24–4	13.0

Note: * Sold Emanuele N Vintiadis, Genoa, 1939
Note: This company was controlled by Steenkolen-Handelsvereeniging NV

ZEETRANSPORT NV, MAATSCHAPPIJ, (Oranje Lijn),
Parklaan 28, Postbus 1246, Rotterdam

Funnel: Black or yellow with blue diamond on orange band
Hull: Grey, red boot-topping
Services: NW Europe–Great Lakes (Oranje Lijn)

Prins Willem III (m,P12)	1939	DeMwde	1524	2800	258–0	41–10	18–0	12.5
Prins Willem IV (m,P12)	bldg	DeMwde	1535	2800	258–0	42–1	18–0	12.5
Prins Willem V (m,P12)	order	DeMwde	1535	2800	258–0	42–1	18–0	12.5

Note: Also *Prins Frederik Hendrik* (built 1936/1288gt), *Prins Maurits* (36/1287), *Prins Willem van Oranje* (38/1303), *Prins Willem II* (38/1304) on ocean voyages
Note: This fleet was managed by Anthony Veder NV

ZUID HOLLANDSCHE, SCHEEPVAART MAATSCHAPPIJ NV,
Calandstraat 11, Postbus 349, Rotterdam

Funnel: Black with diagonal white stripe on green band
Services: General tramping

Driebergen (st)	1923	NewWat	5231	9515	402.3	58–4	26.5	9.5
Eibergen	1914	Pgill2	4801	8250	399–0	52–1	27.2	9.0
Kelbergen	1914	Pgill2	4823	8250	399–0	52–1	25–0	9.0

Note: This company was controlled by Furness Scheepvaart & Agentuur Maatschappij NV

Norway

AABY, E B, Tollbodgaten 28, Oslo

Funnel: Black with white A on red band
Hull: Grey or black, red boot-topping
Services: Mediterranean trades, general tramping; oil and petroleum trades

E B AABY'S REDERI-A/S

General cargo vessels								
Dicto (m)	1939	Göta	5263	9470	442–9	56–10	26–0	14.0
Iron Baron	1911	LithR	3231	5500	331.3	49–1	20–7	9.0
ex Kilbaha 20, ex Emerald Wings 18								
Tento (m2)	1921	Akers	4917	7550	376–10	51–6	25–10	9.0
ex America 36								
Victo*	1906	ThmpR2	3655	6170	346.5	50–10	22.9	8.5
ex Skogstad 27								
Tankers								
Drafn (m2)	1931	CRDA	8205	12,500	483–9	60–2	28–0	12.5
Svolder** (m)	1939	Laing	9472	14,833	503–10	68–4	28–2	12.0

Note: * Sold Dampsk-A/S Esito (Bj Ruud-Petersen) 1939;** sold Sweden 1939, renamed *Atlantides*
Note: Also short-sea vessels

AARSETH & CO A/S, ELLING, Aalesund

Services: General tramping

REDERI A/S BJØRKHAUG

Bjørkhaug	1919	Meyer	2058	3200	293–0	41–5	19.3	8.5
ex Stad Zaandam 38								

Aaby: Dicto *was completed in January 1939 and fitted with a Götaverken 6-cylinder oil engine of 5300bhp. She was one of a standard type built by Götaverken, of about 9500dwt on a draught of 26ft, and with high fuel economy.* Dicto *managed to take refuge in a Swedish port about the time of the German occupation of Norway and was laid up at Gothenburg effectively under Allied control. She survived the Second World War and in 1964 was sold to Greece and renamed* Onisilos. *In 1970 she was broken up at Shanghai (Alex Duncan)*

Sigval Bergensen dy: The twin-screw motor tanker Charles Racine *was completed at Odense in August 1937. She was torpedoed and sunk by the Italian submarine* Finzi *when on voyage from Bowling and River Clyde for Baytown in ballast. Her 41 crew were all saved (Bergesen dy Group archives)*

Bergenske: The twin-screw passenger vessel Venus *was was delivered on April 29 1931 for the Bergen–Newcastle service, with berths for 201 first and 76 second class passengers. She was fitted with two B&W 10-cylinder oil engines of 12,400bhp, and attained over 20 knots on trials. In September 1939 she was laid up, and was seized by Germany in September 1940 following the occupation of Norway.* Venus *was taken over by the Kriegsmarine on March 16 1941 and at the Neptunwerft at Rostock was converted for war purposes. On May 8 1941* Venus *was commissioned as a target ship for the 26 U-boat flotilla at Pillau. On March 20 1945 she was bombed by Allied aircraft and sunk at Hamburg, but later raised, and rebuilt at the Helsingör shipyard at a cost of £800,000. She emerged with accommodation for 425 passengers and resumed the North Sea service from May 12 1948. She also made winter cruises to Madeira and Tenerife.* Venus *was withdrawn from service in October 1968 and sold to be broken up at Faslane (EH Cole)*

AASS, H RICH, Stortingsgaten 20, Oslo

Trades: Oil and petroleum

D/S A/S SENITA

Tanker

Solna*	1918	SHWR	5550	8325	415–0	52–4	25–7	10.5
ex Granlund 30, ex Corbis 28, ex War Ranee 20								

Note: * Sold Greek navy 1939, renamed *Argo*

AMLIE & CO A/S, RICHARD, Haugesund

Funnel: Black with houseflag
Hull: Grey, red boot-topping
Services: General tramping, including frequent voyages to E coast US and Canada and West Indies

DAMPSK-A/S VESTLAND

Polarland	1923	Laxe	1591	2350	257–10	37–11	16–6	9.5
Sneland I	1922	Nüscke	1791	3000	280–10	42–3	17–10	9.0
ex Ingeborg 25								
Vestland	1916	Dtroit	1934	3100	261–0	43–10	17–9	9.0

ANDERSEN & CO'S EFTERFOLGER, A/S A O, Tollbodgaten 28, Oslo

Funnel: Yellow with markings
Hull: Grey
Services: Oil and petroleum trades

A O ANDERSEN SHIPPING CO A/S

Tankers

Beduin (m)	1936	Göta	8136	12,350	473–0	59–2	27–8	12.0
Buccaneer (m)	1927	NewWat	6222	9525	403.4	55–2	26–9	12.0
ex Duivendrecht 38								

ANDERSEN, HERLOF, Kristiansand

Services: General tramping

HERLOF ANDERSENS REDERI-A/S

Listo	1918	PtArth	1998	3375	261–0	43–9	20–4	9.5
ex Colmar 29, ex War Osiris 20								

ANDERSEN, ONESIMUS, Nedre Langgate 20, Tønsberg

Funnel: Grey
Hull: Grey
Services: Whaling
Note: * This company, controlled by Chr Salvesen & Co (*qv* in Great Britain section), also owned smaller vessels

A/S SEVILLA*

Whale factory vessel

Strombus	1900	ArmWh1	6549	8600	426–0	52–1	27–5	9.5
conv tanker 26								

ANDERSEN, THOMAS, Postboks 64, Arendal

Trades: Oil and petroleum

A/S RANELLA

Tanker

Ranella (m)	1912	SHWR	5590	7550	406.4	51–4	26–2	9.5

BACHKE & CO, Fjordgaten 17, Trondheim

Funnel: Black with white B on red band
Hull: Black, red boot-topping
Services: Scandinavia, NW Europe, UK–New York–Philadelphia; general tramping
Note: Also *Hilda* (built 1925/1237gt), *Inger* (30/1409) and short-sea vessels

A/S ELDRID								
Eldrid	1915	Nyland	1712	2700	265.1	40–3	17–6	9.0
A/S HERDIS								
Gunvor (r/t)	1935	Trondh	1942	3415	277.7	43–2	18–11	10.5

BANG, JØRGEN, Kristiansand S

Funnel: Yellow with red and white red and white band quartered diagonally with JB in blue on white quarters
Hull: Grey
Trades: Oil and petroleum

A/S ATHENE

Tankers

Athene (m)	1928	ArmWh1	4681	7100	359–2	53–6	24–2	10.5
Jenny (m)	1928	SHWR	4706	7100	359–2	53–6	24–3	10.5

BECH, ALEXANDER, Tollbodgaten 4, Oslo

Funnel: Black with blue B on white diamond on red band
Hull: Grey
Trades: Oil and petroleum

BECH'S REDERI-A/S

Tanker

Elise (m)	1931	ArmWh2	7910	11,447	475–0	59–10	25–11	11.0

Braathen: The tanker Bralanta *was completed by Kockums in September 1936 and was fitted with a Kockums 7-cylinder oil engine of 3800bhp. During the war she was under Allied control. She continued to serve her Norwegian owners until the early 1960s and was broken up during 1962–63 (Braathen archives)*

Brøvig: The motor tanker Erling Brøvig *was completed in December 1937 by Bremer Vulkan. She was torpedoed by* U510 *and badly damaged on April 22 1944 when in convoy PA69 off Majdaha. She arrived at Massowah on September 16 1944 in tow and was laid up. She was repaired, and re-enterd service as the Norwegian-owned* Bramora *in 1946. She was sold to China in 1960 and eventually broken up (Photograph courtesy Torbjorn Larsson-Fedde)*

T Dahl: The motor vessel Thor I *was completed at Sandefjord in 1938 for service in the Pacific. She was fitted with a Sulzer 6-cylinder oil engine of 1500bhp, and had accommodation for 12 passengers. After Allied service during the war she resumed Pacific service, mainly between US and Canadian ports and the Philippines and Pacific islands. In 1953* Thor I *was sold within Norway and renamed* Marstenen, *and after two more name changes became the Greek-owned* Fani *in 1963. On September 1 1969 she had a fire while repairing at Piræus, and was towed out of port for beaching on Salamis Island. The vessel was refloated the same month and taken to Eleusis for breaking up (Alex Duncan)*

Ditlev-Simonsen: The twin-screw motor tanker Velma *was completed by Götaverken in August 1930. Postwar she served her Norwegian owners until 1956 when she was sold to a Liberian company and renamed* Valmar. *She was later transferred to Venezuela and was broken up during 1961–62 (Ditlev-Simonsen archives)*

BERG, ODD, Karl Johansgaten 1, Oslo

Funnel: Black with solid black B on white disc
Hull: Black, red or grey boot-topping
Trades: Oil and petroleum

Note: * Sold France 1939, renamed *Picardie*

Tankers								
ODD BERGS TANKREDERI-A/S								
Koll (m2)	1930	DeutsH	10,044	15,080	505–4	66–0	37.3	11.0
Kollgrim* (m)	1936	Eriksb	8263	12,650	486–8	61–1	26–10	12.5
Kollskegg (m)	bldg	Eriksb	9858	15,000	518–5	65–4	28–7	13.0
A/S KOLLBJØRG								
Kollbjørg (m)	1937	Eriksb	8259	12,670	486–8	61–1	26–10	12.5

BERG, THORVALD, Tønsberg

Funnel: Yellow with white diamond on blue band
Trades: Oil and petroleum

A/S TANKTRANSPORT								
Tankers								
Marina (m)	1935	DeutsH	9898	14,823	510–8	66–1	28–5	12.0
Meline	1918	Laing	7019	10,924	440–4	57–0	26–0	10.0
Montana (m)	bldg	Göta	10,170	15,530	515–2	64–5	29–8	13.0
Morgenen (m)	1930	SHWR	7093	11,448	456–0	58–10	27–0	11.5

BERGENSKE DAMPSKIBSSELSKAB, A/S DET, Postboks 215, Bergen

Funnel: Black with three narrow white bands
Hull: Black or grey, red or green boot-topping; cruising vessels – white, red or green boot-topping
Services: Scandinavia, NW Europe–Canada; Bergen–Newcastle (passenger); cruising
Note: * *Brant County* operated on County Line (*qv*) services; ** *Cometa, Crux, Rigel* and (ordered for) *Cometa*, operated on Den Norske Syd-Amerika Linje (*qv*) services; † sold Sweden 1939, renamed *Bohus*
Note: Also the general cargo vessels *Castor* (20/1683), *Keret* (27/1718), *Pollux* (21/1676), *Severoles* (22/1757) and *Vaga* (24/1615) on some ocean voyages, and a fleet of short-sea coastal passenger and general cargo vessels

Cruising vessels								
Meteor (s2,P200/oc)	1904	Blohm	3718	1500	367–6	44–4	17–9	12.0
Stella Polaris (m2,P171/1)	1927	Göta	5020	1900	416–1	50–8	17–11	16.0
Passenger vessels								
Vega (m2,P217/1,248/2)	1938	CRDA5	7287	1500	445–0	58–0	20–0	20.0
Venus (m2,P185/1,78/2)	1931	Helsgr	5406	2200	420–6	54–2	20–0	19.5
General cargo vessels								
Brant County*	1915	Neptnl	5001	7875	419.4	54–2	24–10	12.0
ex Lennep 20, launched as Mulhausen								
Cometa** (m2)	1921	B&W	3794	6403	382–0	51–6	23–4	12.0
Cometa** (m2,P12)	bldg	Helsgr	5125	7630	460–4	57–0	25–6	16.0
Crux** (m2)	1923	B&W	3828	6850	382–0	51–6	23–5	12.0
Rigel** (m2)	1924	B&W	3828	6850	382–0	51–6	23–3	12.0

BERGESEN, SIGVAL, Postboks 44, Stavanger

Funnel: Black with black anchor on white band
Hull: Black
Trades: Oil and petroleum

Tankers								
SKIBS-A/S DALFONN								
Barfonn (m2)	1931	Göta	9739	14,800	494–10	64–2	28–11	11.0
Dalfonn (m2)	1928	Eriksb	9860	14,410	491–0	64–4	28–4	10.5
Krossfonn (m2)	1935	Odense	9323	14,400	496–7	65–0	28–0	12.0
President Herrenschmidt (m2)	1932	Kockum	9103	13,860	496–9	63–0	28–1	11.5
Solfonn (m)	1939	DeutsH	9925	14,825	510–8	66–1	28–5	12.5
Storfonn (m)	bldg	Göta	10,173	15,355	515–2	64–5	29–8	13.0
SKIBS-A/S RINGFONN								
Kaldfonn (m)	1936	DeutsH	9931	14,770	510–8	66–1	28–4	12.0

BERGESEN DY & CO, SIGVAL, Postboks 187, Stavanger

Funnel: White with black top having diagonal light green stripe and houseflag
Hull: Grey
Trades: Oil and petroleum

SKIBS-A/S SNEFONN								
Tankers								
Anders Jahre (m)	1939	Bremer	9970	14,900	510–8	66–1	28–4	12.0
Charles Racine (m2)	1937	Odense	9957	15,540	512–6	65–11	28–7	12.0
Président de Vogüe (m2)	1935	Odense	9320	14,290	495–10	65–0	28–0	12.0

Godager: Norseman, *pictured here as* Selandia, *was the first ocean-going motor ship. She was built by Burmeister & Wain for the East Asiatic Co of Denmark and completed as* Selandia *in January 1912. She was fitted with two B&W 8-cylinder diesel engines of 2500ihp.* Selandia *was purchased by Odd Godager, who took delivery on November 18 1936, registered in Panama and renamed* Norseman. *In November 1938 she was on voyage from Novorossisk to Oslo with a cargo of grain when she was stopped in the Mediterranean by Spanish nationalist warships. She was able to proceed after a long delay, only to suffer leaks in heavy weather in the Bay of Biscay. After repairing at Brest she eventually arrived at Oslo where a fire broke out in one of the holds. This caused considerable damage and the opportunity was taken to repair the vessel and reduce the passenger berths to 12. When ready for service there was no work available and the ship was laid up at Oslo. In October 1940 she was sold to Finland-Amerika Linjen and renamed* Tornator. *She stranded on January 26 1942 at Omaisaki when on voyage from China to Japan with a cargo of salt. On January 30 she broke in two and became a total loss (East Asiatic Co archives)*

Holter-Sorensen: The motor vessel Ivaran, *completed in 1938, was in Allied service during the Second World War. She was sold to Germany in 1955 and renamed* Kelkheim *and was broken up at Hong Kong in 1963 (Alex Duncan)*

Jebsen: The steamer Garnes, *which survived the Second World War under Allied control, became a war causes loss in 1947. On March 24 she struck a mine north of Terschelling.* Garnes *was taken in tow but sank in 53 26N 05 02E. She was on voyage from Antwerp to Emden in ballast (AJ Management AS)*

BERGH & HELLAND, (Harald Eie), Postboks 25, Bergen

Funnel: Black with white band
Services: General tramping

EIE'S REDERI A/S								
Olaf Bergh	1921	FurnH	5811	8950	400–0	53–1	26–0	10.5
ex Rigi 29								
A/S D/S KORSFJORD								
Korsfjord	1913	Bergen	1620	2440	255–0	37–8	16–9	9.0

BING, JENS, Hieronymus Heyerdahlsgaten 1, Oslo

Funnel: Very thin
Hull: Black
Services: General tramping
Note: * Sold Skips-A/S Rena (T Sommerfelt and O Pedersen) 1939

A/S BING & PEDERSEN'S REDERI								
Rena* (m2,P6/1)	1924	Odense	5242	8035	395–5	50–2	25–8	10.0
ex Fördefjord 37, ex Emma Mærsk 26								

BIØRNSTAD & CO, BIØRN, Stortingsgaten 8, Oslo

Funnel: Yellow with black B, black top; fruit carriers – yellow
Hull: Grey, red boot-topping; fruit carriers – white
Services: W coast North America–UK and NW Europe (Fruit Express Line); general tramping; oil and petroleum trades
Note: * Operated for Skibs-A/S Fruit Express Line (*qv* also under Sigurd Herlofsen & Co A/S)

Fruit carriers*								
SKIBS-A/S SEATTLE								
Pacific Express (m,P12)	bldg	Kockum	3401	4200	387–2	52–2	23–6	16.0
Washington Express (m2,P12)	1933	Göta	3643	3160	351–10	47–2	21–3	15.5
Tankers								
Beauregard (m)	order	Kockum	8539	13,510	496–4	62–2	27–2	13.5
DAMPSK-A/S AVENIR								
Beau (m)	1938	Kockum	9475	15,020	523–5	63–1	28–5	13.0
SKIBS-A/S BEAUFORT								
Beaufort	1929	Curle	5053	8550	388.8	52–10	25–6	11.0
SKIBS-A/S BEAULIEU								
Beaulieu (m)	1930	ArmWh2	6114	9431	408–0	55–1	26–10	10.5
SKIBS-A/S BEAUMONT								
Beaumont (m)	1929	Odense	5702	8600	411–0	55–2	25–9	11.0

BOE & CO, OLAF, Arendal

Funnel: Black
Trades: Oil and petroleum

Tanker								
SKIBS-A/S TRUMA								
Chr Th Boe (m2)	1930	Göta	6192	9568	421–10	55–4	26–3	10.5

BOE & PEDERSEN, Kirkegaten 14–18, Oslo

Funnel: Yellow with green band bordered by two white bands
Hull: Grey
Services: General tramping

SKIBS-A/S GAUSDAL								
Gausdal (m2)	1930	Odense	4795	8460	407–3	54–4	25–3	11.0
ex Høegh Trader 36, ex Guldborg 33								
A/S VESTERHAV								
Hallingdal (m2)	1929	B&W	3180	5550	334–5	50–0	20–5	10.5

BORGE, HANS, Stenmalveien 2, Tønsberg

Funnel: Yellow with white B on green band
Hull: Grey, red boot-topping
Services: General tramping

BORGES REDERI-A/S								
Wilford	1921	Nyland	2158	4065	300–0	44–1	19–1	9.0
ex Rio Rimac 36, ex Nauru Chief 36, ex Nyland 21								
Woolgar	1914	SHWR	3060	5466	350.0	47–1	22–1	9.0
Wyvern	1929	SHWRSd	4007	6750	376–0	50–8	22–5	9.5
ex Hopecrag 38								

BORTHEN & CO A/S, HARRY, Kirkegaten 20, Oslo

Funnel: Yellow with blue B on white diamond on blue band
Hull: Grey, red boot-topping
Trades: Oil and petroleum

Tankers								
SKIBS-A/S MOTORTANK								
Nina Borthen (m)	1930	ArmWh2	6123	9430	408–0	55–1	26–10	11.0
A/S OLJEFART II								
Elsa (m)	1928	Curle	5381	8500	400–0	52–9	25–6	11.0

Funnel: Yellow with house flag
Hull: Grey
Services: General tramping; oil and petroleum trades

BRAATHEN, LUDVIG G, Rådhusplassen, Oslo

General cargo vessel								
A/S BRAGANZA								
Braganza (m,P10)	1924	Doxfrd	6327	9640	436–8	58–0	27–2	11.5
ex Pacific Trader 38								
Tankers								
A/S BRACONDA								
Braconda (m)	bldg	Kockum	10,203	16,050	533–1	63–2	29–6	14.0
A/S BRAGANZA								
Brarena (m2)	1923	Denny2	6996	10,361	440–0	56–11	26–2	10.5
ex Scottish Borderer 38								
A/S BRALANTA								
Bralanta (m)	1936	Kockum	9608	15,030	523–5	63–1	26–5	13.0
A/S BRAMORA								
Bramora (m2)	1928	Eriksb	6361	9560	423–0	55–4	28–5	12.0
REDERI-A/S FREIKOLL								
Brajara (m)	1934	Göta	8116	12,262	473–0	59–2	27–8	12.0

Funnel: Black with blue B on white diamond on red band
Hull: Grey
Services: NW Europe–Canada, US, West Indies; general tramping; oil and petroleum trades

BRØVIG, TH, Farsund

General cargo vessels								
Balla (m2)	1923	Hill	2565	4740	314–0	43–6	22–8	10.0
ex Gresham 37, ex Margretian 28								
Bennestvet (r/t)	1937	Moss	2438	4100	316–0	47–8	19–2	11.5
Bertha Brøvig (r/t)	1938	Moss	2415	4060	316–0	47–5	19–0	12.0
Cate B	1920	Prstm1	4285	8100	377–6	51–8	24–10	9.5
ex Unden 38								
PARTREDERIET DEA								
Dea	1911	ThmpR2	2418	4175	299.4	44–6	19–2	9.5
ex Sangstad 23								
REDERISLSK GEZINA								
Gezina	1917	Dtroit	1828	2800	261–0	44–0	17–9	9.5
ex Lake Erie 20, launched as War Beaver								
PARTREDERIET LILLEMOR								
Lillemor	1935	Fredst	1570	2435	254–0	40–1	16–6	10.0
ex Margit R 36								
Tankers								
TH BRØVIG								
G C Brøvig (m2)	1930	Göta	9718	14,660	494–8	64–2	28–8	11.5
Ketty Brøvig	1918	Laing	7031	10,940	440–0	57–0	26–0	10.0
ex Montana 37								
PARTREDERIET BRØVIGTANK								
Andrea Brøvig (m)	1939	Göta	10,173	15,300	515–2	64–0	29–8	13.5
Erling Brøvig (m)	1937	Bremer	9970	14,820	510–8	66–1	28–4	13.0

Note: Also general cargo vessels *Ciss* (built 1925/1159gt, owner Th Brøvig), and (owner Partrederiet Lillemor), *Lillgunvor* (30/1305) and *Kirsten B* (30/1184) mainly on voyages NW Europe–North America–West Indies

Funnel: Black with black 'B&T' on white band
Services: General tramping

BRUMMENÆS & TORGERSEN, Strandgaten 156, Haugesund

A/S BRITANNIC								
Equatore* (m2)	1912	B&W	4953	7400	386–0	53–2	24–3	10.5
ex Clelia C 25, ex Fratelli Bandiera 23, ex Christian X 15, ex Fionia 12								
Ruth I	1900	SH1	3531	5800	330.0	48–0	23–0	7.0
ex Ruth 31								
A/S LIV								
Liv	1896	Ropnr1	3068	4850	322.2	41–6	23–0	7.0
A/S VENBORG								
Salonica	1912	WoodS2	2694	4800	324.0	46–6	19.8	8.0

Note: * BU Stavanger 1939

Funnel: Black with houseflag on red band
Hull: Black with white band
Services: Whaling
Note: This firm, which was associated with Anders Jahre (*qv*), also owned whalers

BRUUN & VON DER LIPPE, Tønsberg

Whale factory vessel								
Pelagos (s2)	1901	H&W,B	12,084	13,200	516–0	63–4	35–8	11.5
ex Athenic 28; conv passenger/general cargo 28								

BRUUSGAARD, KARL, Torvet 10, Drammen

Funnel: Black with black B on white band bordered by red over black bands above and black over red bands below
Services: General tramping; oil and petroleum trades

General cargo vessels								
A/S BRUUSGAARD								
Marita	1919	Shangh	1931	3100	279–7	42–2	17–9	10.0
A/S MABELLA								
Mabella	1926	Schich	1513	2324	271–6	40–1	15–10	10.0
Marosa	1925	Schich	1513	2324	271–6	40–1	15–10	10.0
Marpesia	1930	Austin	1958	3225	286–7	42–4	18–2	10.5
Tanker								
REDERI-A/S NORSK TRANSATLANTIC								
Minister Wedel (m)	1930	Doxfrd	6833	10,645	432–2	58–0	27–5	11.0

BRUUSGAARD, KIØSTERUD & CO, Drammen

Funnel: Black with band of red, white and blue vertical stripes
Hull: Black with white band, red boot-topping
Services: China coast services; general tramping, oil and petroleum trades

BRUUSGAARD, KIØSTERUDS SKIBS-A/S								
Passenger/general cargo vessel								
Hai Hing (m2,P1500/d)	1929	Göta	2561	3080	295–0	45–1	18–6	14.0
Hai Lee (m2,P10/1,26/2,1200/d)	1934	Akers	3616	4300	349–6	49–0	22–6	15.0
General cargo vessels								
Halldor	1925	Schich	1515	2350	271–6	40–1	15–10	10.0
Hektor (r/t)	1921	HK&Wh	5243	8150	412–0	52–2	25–3	9.5
Helios (P–/d)	1925	Fredst	1922	3200	290–10	42–1	18–7	10.0
Hellas (P–/d)	1925	Fredst	1921	3200	290–10	42–1	18–7	10.0
Hellen (r/t)	1921	HK&Wh	5289	8200	412–0	52–2	25–3	9.5
Hermelin (m,P10)	bldg	HK&Wh	1683	2620	291–2	43–1	17–9	12.5
Hermion (m,P5/1)	1937	Bremer	5202	8500	449–4	55–10	25–2	13.5
Hermod	1925	Schich	1515	2350	271–6	40–1	18–6	10.0
Hiram	1926	Fredst	1931	3200	290–10	42–1	18–7	10.0
Tanker								
Hamlet (m2)	1934	Göta	6578	9960	422–0	55–3	26–8	11.0
ex Abu 37, ex Eidsvold 34								

Note: Also vessels under 1500gt

BRUUSGAARD, KJELL, Tollbodgaten 27, Oslo

Services: General tramping

A/S PAVO								
Primo	1930	SmithM	1840	3110	265.4	43–3	18–0	10.5

BRUUSGAARD, MARTIN, AND HALFDAN BODTKER-NÆSS JR, Sjøfartsbygningen, Kongensgaten 6, Oslo

Funnel: Black with white 'BB' on red band
Hull: Black
Services: General tramping

A/S NEPTUN								
Betty*	1919	Yoshi	2439	4050	290.1	41–0	21–0	9.0
ex Hundvaagø 23, ex Kaihei Maru 19								
SKIBS-A/S ORION								
Bjerka	1916	Dtroit	1893	3100	261–0	43–10	17–10	9.5
ex Levisa 29, launched as Clinchfield								

Note: * Sold A/S Nesjar (Eilert Lund) 1939

BRUUSGAARD, SIGURD, Drammen

Funnel: Black with blue B on white band bordered by blue and red bands both above and below
Services: General tramping

A/S ACADIA								
Acadia (m,P–)	1938	Flensb	5002	8700	430–8	55–8	25–5	12.5

BUGGE, IVER, Larvik

Funnel: Black with green band bearing white disc and blue B
Hull: Grey, red boot-topping
Trades: Oil and petroleum

SKIBS-A/S NANSET								
Tankers								
Salsaas (m)	bldg	Göta	8200	12,600	483–10	59–5	27–11	12.5
Skaraas (m)	1936	Göta	9826	14,600	506–8	64–6	28–6	12.0
Skotaas (m2)	1931	Caledn	8190	11,400	469–6	59–3	26–0	11.0
Storaas (m2)	1929	Göta	7886	11,000	459–6	59–3	25–10	11.5

BUGGE MED FIERE, JORGEN O, Mandal

Services: General tramping

Halse	1910	Sundld	2136	3600	290.1	42–1	19–0	8.0
ex Quernstad 21, ex Signe 14								

BUGGE, N R, Tønsberg

Funnel: Black with blue and white diagonally halved band between two narrow red bands
Hull: Black
Services: Whaling
Note: Also whalers
Note: Associated with Hector Whaling Ltd (*qv* in Great Britain section)

A/S HEKTOR
Tanker

Ronald	1920	Duncan	6322	10,135	422.0	56–0	27–0	10.0

BUGGE, THORLEIF, Tønsberg

Services: General tramping

A/S FAGERHEIM

Fagerheim (r/t)	1938	Kaldns	1590	2440	258–0	42–2	18–2	10.5

CHRISTENSEN, CHR, Sjøfartsbygningen, Kongensgaten 6, Oslo

Funnel: Black with gold 'lion' on red square bordered in white
Hull: Black
Services: General tramping

A/S CHR CHRISTENSEN

Toran	1918	ThmpR2	3318		340.7	48–6	21.9	9.0

CHRISTENSEN, JACOB, Foreningsgaten 1, Postboks 162, Bergen

Funnel: Yellow, black top
Services: General tramping

A/S D/S MATHILDA

August	1911	GrayX	5254	9275	410.0	54–0	28.9	8.0
ex York County 30, ex August 29								
Jacob Christensen	1920	Blumr2	3594	6250	368–6	48–9	22–6	9.0
Mathilda	1920	Blumr2	3650	6275	368–6	48–10	22–6	9.0

COUNTY LINE, (Inter-Continental Transport Services Ltd), Bergen

Funnel: Red with white band, black top
Hull: Black
Services: Hamburg, Antwerp, Rotterdam, Dunkirk, Havre–Quebec–Montreal (St John NB winter)

This line operated on charter vessels owned by shareholder companies: A/S Det Bergenske D/S (*qv*) – *Brant County*; Westfal-Larsen & Co A/S (*qv*) – *Evanger*; D/S A/S Songa (*qv* under K W Hansen) – *Grey County*; A/S J Ludwig Mowinckels Rederi (*qv*) – *Hada County*

DAHL, A/S THOR, Sandefjord

Funnel: Grey with blue fish on broad white band between two narrow red bands
Hull: Black with white band, red boot-topping
Services: General tramping; oil and petroleum trades; whaling
Note: See also American Whaling Co Inc in United States section

BRYDE & DAHL'S HVALFSLSK A/S								
General cargo vessel								
Thor I (m)	1938	Framns	2502	4057	327–0	46–8	19–0	12.5
Tankers								
Thorøy	1893	ArmMit	2671	4000	293.8	39–5	23–4	9.0
ex Velløy 25, ex Kremlin 22, ex Snowflake 13								
Thorshavet (m)	1938	DeutsH	11,015	16,150	528–0	69–2	28–5	13.0
Thorshavn (m)	1930	Laing	6869	11,040	448–6	57–3	27–3	11.5
Thorsheimer (m)	1935	DeutsH	9955	14,305	510–8	66–1	28–5	13.0
Thorshov (m)	1935	Bremer	9955	14,305	510–8	66–1	28–5	13.0
Whale factory vessel								
Thorshammer	1914	Doxfrd	12,215	16,050	539–2	66–6	30–10	10.0
ex San Nazario 28; conv tanker 28								
A/S ODD								
Tanker								
Thorshøvdi (m)	1938	DeutsH	9944	14,710	510–9	66–1	28–4	13.0
Whale factory vessel								
Solglimt (s2)	1900	Blohm	12,246	15,100	571–0	62–1	31–10	11.0
ex Stockholm 29, ex Potsdam 15; conv passenger/general cargo 29								
A/S ØRNEN								
Whale factory vessel								
Ole Wegger	1914	SHWR	12,201	16,500	527.1	66–9	30–11	10.0
ex San Lorenzo 28; conv tanker 28								
SKIBS-A/S THORSHOLM								
Fruit carriers								
Scebeli (m,P12)	1937	B&W	3025	2250	336–0	45–10	19–0	15.5
Thorstrand (m)	1938	Framns	3041	2357	334–2	46–3	19–0	15.5
Tanker								
Thorsholm (m)	1937	DeutsH	9937	14,800	510–8	65–7	28–5	13.0

Knut Knutsen: Vibran *was completed in March 1935 and was the prototype of several fruit carriers built at the Helsingör shipyard. She was fitted with a B&W 9-cylinder oil engine of 4400ihp and had 150,600 cubic feet of refrigerated cargo space.* Vibran *left Cardiff on September 18 1942 for Halifax and on September 24 was torpedoed and sunk by* U582. *There were no survivors (RW Jordan collection)*

Knut Knutsen: The motor vessel Elisabeth Bakke *was completed by Götaverken in March 1937 and was in service between northwest Europe and the Pacific coast of Canada and the US. She was under Allied control during the Second World War and resumed her regular service in 1945. In 1970 she was sold to Mesa Industri-og Skipservice AS, of Norway, and renamed* Elisabeth, *and on June 30 1971 laid up at Sandefjord. In 1973 she was sold to other Norwegian owners and renamed* Bigra, *but without further trading was sold to breakers at Bilbao where she arrived in March 1974 (RW Jordan collection)*

Knut Knutsen: Anna Knudsen *was completed by Götaverken in December 1931 and was typical of the many tankers built at that shipyard during the late 1920s and early 30s. She was fitted with two Götaverken 6-cylinder oil engines of 3450bhp.* Anna Knudsen *survived the Second World War in Allied service. In postwar years her trading was mainly from Aruba and Curaçao to northwest Europe and Norway, although she did make occasional voyages from the Persian Gulf.* Anna Knudsen *was broken up at Inverkeithing in 1960 (Knutsen Shipping/Skyfotos)*

Lorentzen: The motor tanker Caledonia *was completed by Deutsche Werft, Hamburg, in 1936 and was an early example of a large series of sisterships built at this yard for non-German owners during the mid to late 1930s. She was torpedoed by* U96 *and sunk on April 28 1941 when on voyage from Aruba to the River Clyde with 13,745 tons of diesel oil and fuel oil. Of her crew of 35 and 2 gunners, 12 crew were lost (Lorentzen archives)*

Funnel: Yellow with red CD on white disc bordered by blue ring superimposed on red and blue bands
Services: General tramping

DANN, CLEMETH, Eilert Sundtsgaten 34/1, Oslo

DANN'S SKIBS-A/S

Danio (m)	1924	Hamtn2	3496	6050	354–6	50–0	21–11	10.0
ex Baron Dalmeny 37								

Trades: Oil and petroleum

DANNEVIG & CO, T, Kirkegaten 14–18, Oslo

A/S LABOREMUS
Tankers

Leiv Eiriksson (m)	1936	Bremer	9952	14,725	510–9	66–1	28–5	12.0
Lincoln Ellsworth (m2)	1927	Göta	5580	8340	395–6	55–3	26–2	10.5

Funnel: Yellow with houseflag on broad red band separated from black top by narrow yellow band
Hull: Grey, red boot-topping
Services: General tramping; oil and petroleum trades

DITLEV-SIMONSEN & CO, HALFDAN,
Sjøfartsbygningen, Kongensgaten 6, Oslo

General cargo vessel
SKIBS-A/S NORDHEIM

Vingnes (m)	bldg	Göta	5201	9370	442–9	56–10	25–11	13.5

Tankers
SKIBS-A/S NORDHEIM

Velma (m2)	1930	Göta	9720	14,780	495–0	64–2	28–11	11.5
Vilja (m)	1927	Kockum	6672	9680	426–8	56–2	26–5	10.5
SKIBS-A/S OSTHEIM								
Vav (m2)	1931	Eriksb	6415	9835	422–6	55–4	26–5	11.5
SKIBS-A/S SYDHEIM								
Vanja (m2)	1929	Göta	6198	9580	422–7	55–4	26–5	11.5
SKIBS-A/S VAARHEIM								
Vera (m2)	1934	Eriksb	6485	9800	422–7	55–3	26–5	11.5
A/S VESTHEIM								
Vivi (m2)	1932	Akers	6546	9815	423–0	56–3	26–5	11.5

Funnel: Yellow with houseflag on broad red band separated from black top by yellow band
Hull: Grey, red boot-topping
Services: General tramping

DITLEV-SIMONSEN JNR, OLAF,
Sjøfartsbygningen 266, Kongensgaten 6, Oslo

A/S SKAGERAK

Kattegat (m)	1936	B&W	4245	8370	401–11	55–2	26–5	12.0
Skagerak (m)	1936	B&W	4244	8370	401–11	55–2	26–5	12.0
Vito (m)	1937	Göta	5181	9140	442–9	56–10	25–7	13.5

Funnel: Yellow with houseflag on broad red band separated from black top by yellow band
Hull: Grey, red boot-topping
Services: General tramping

DITLEV-SIMONSEN & CO, SVERRE,
Sjøfartsbygningen, Kongensgaten 6, Oslo

A/S EIDSIVA

Eidsvold (m)	1934	Göta	4184	8330	397–0	55–3	24–6	12.0
A/S EIDSIVA OG SKIBS-A/S NORDHEIM								
Vinni (m)	1937	Göta	5181	9140	442–9	56–10	25–7	13.5

Services: General tramping

Note: Also *Brush* (built 1939/1320gt)

EINERSEN, K TH, Sjøfartsbygningen 545–7, Kongensgaten 6, Oslo

SKIBS-A/S GRØM

Bestum	1919	Domnn	2215	3630	261–0	43–11	21–0	9.0
ex Hessa 34								
SKIBS-A/S MANITOWOC								
Bestik	1920	Hill	2684	4300	324–8	44–4	20–2	9.5
ex Bestik 2 35, ex Annik 33								
Blink	1920	Hill	2701	4350	324–8	44–4	20–2	9.5
ex Arlette 33								

Services: General tramping, including voyages to US and Canada E coast and West Indies
Note: Also *Inga I* (built 1921/1304gt)

ELIASSEN, JOHAN, Tornøgaarden, Christiesgaten, Bergen

A/S D/S JAN

Jan	1921	VanD1	1946	3180	281–0	42–1	18–3	9.0
ex Torsol 36, ex Albert Sauber 26, ex Targis 22, ex Ledaal 22								

ENDRESEN, EDVIN, Stavanger

Services: General tramping

SKIBS-A/S SAPHIR								
Saphir	1905	SHWR	4306	7100	375.5	51–0	22–9	9.0
ex Christian Børs 39								

ERICHSEN, LEIF, Torvalmenning 4, Postboks 34, Bergen

Funnel: Yellow with houseflag; Forto – black with white F on green band
Hull: Black
Services: General tramping

LEIF ERICHSENS REDERI-A/S								
Herma (m)	1924	ArmWh1	2406	3296	302–10	45–4	18–8	11.5
ex Beldisa 37, ex Beldis 36								
Lenda (m)	1924	SHWR	4005	6550	370–0	51–4	22–3	10.0
ex Lenfield 37								
D/S A/S FORTO								
Erica	1919	Laxe	1593	2400	257–10	37–11	16–6	9.0
ex Kvernaas 28, ex Kaparika 27								

Note: Also vessels under 1500gt

EVENSEN, EIVIND, Radhusgaten 23, Postboks 686, Oslo

Funnel: Yellow with yellow E on blue oval, narrow black top
Trades: Oil and petroleum

Tankers								
TANKREDERIET GEFION A/S								
Gefion (m)	1938	Kockum	9475	14,925	523–5	63–1	28–3	13.0
SKIBS-A/S GYLFE								
Gylfe (m)	1930	ArmWh2	6129	9430	408–0	55–1	26–10	10.5

EVENSEN, N CHR, Hieronymus Heyerdahlsgaten 1, Oslo

Funnel: Yellow with yellow E on blue oval, narrow black top
Hull: Grey or black
Trades: Oil and petroleum

Tankers								
SKIBS-A/S FERM								
Ferm (m)	1933	Göta	6593	9860	422–0	55–2	26–9	12.0
SKIBS-A/S LAMPAS								
Fenris (m)	1936	Göta	9804	14,700	506–8	64–6	28–6	12.5
DAMPSK-A/S STOKKE								
Fenja (m)	1939	Göta	8268	12,620	483–9	59–5	27–10	14.0
Lampas*	1916	Craig2	5055	8300	383–4	51–5	27–5	10.0
ex Laurelleaf 22								

Note: * Sold Greece 1939, renamed *Loida* (Panamanian flag)

FARSJØ & CO, J T, Sjøfartsbygningen, Kongensgate 6, Oslo

Funnel: Yellow with houseflag
Services: General tramping
Note: Also *Askepot* (built 1937/1312gt), *Askot* (38/1323) occasionally engaged on ocean voyages

REDERI-A/S ALADDIN								
Askeladden	1920	Forth	2496	4150	296.9	43–7	19–9	9.0
Askild	1918	Schuyt	1930	3150	269.5	42–3	18.2	8.5
ex Bockenheim 24, ex Karpin 20, ex Megrez 20								

FEARNLEY & EGER, Sjøfartsbygningen, Postboks 355, Oslo

Funnel: Black with blue Maltese cross on white square on broad red band
Hull: Black, red boot-topping with white dividing line
Services: E Norway–La Pallice–Bordeaux; E Norway, W Sweden–Nantes–Pasajes–Bilbao; Norway–US, US Gulf ports, Far East; general tramping; oil and petroleum trades

DAMPSKIBSINTERESSENSKABET GARONNE								
General cargo vessels								
Asturias*	1912	Sørlan	1829	3050	277–2	42–1	17–7	9.0
ex Ærø 15								
Fernlane (m)	1927	B&W	4310	7735	400–0	53–10	24–11	12.0
Fernplant (m,P12)	1939	B&W	5274	8800	440–8	56–5	25–7	14.0
Graziella	1917	OsbGr1	2137	3500	296–0	43–4	19–0	8.5
ex Keighley 20								
Navarra	1921	OsbGr2	2118	3500	296–0	43–4	19–0	8.5
Oria	1920	OsbGr2	2127	3540	296–0	43–8	19–1	8.5
Tolosa	1930	SmithM	1974	3270	270.7	43–0	18.7	12.0
Tanker								
Garonne (m2)	1931	B&W	7113	11,000	442–6	58–10	26–8	11.5
A/S GLITTRE								
General cargo vessels								
Fernbank (m)	1924	DeutsH	4333	7890	395–8	53–4	25–2	11.5
Fernbrook (m2)	1932	B&W	4633	8450	407–5	55–3	25–8	13.0
Ferncliff (m)	1924	DeutsH	4333	7890	395–8	53–5	25–2	11.5
Ferndale (m)	1925	DeutsH	4302	7890	395–8	53–5	25–2	11.5
Fernglen (m)	1936	Göta	5205	9140	441–0	56–9	25–7	13.5
Ferngulf (m,P12)	order	B&W	5295	8800	440–6	56–5	25–7	14.0
Fernhill (m)	1926	Kockum	4116	7705	397–10	54–0	24–0	12.0

Fernmoor (m2)	1928	B&W	4268	7880	400–0	53–10	24–11	12.0
Fernwood (m2)	1930	Nakskv	4695	8300	406–0	55–2	25–6	12.0
Tanker								
Ferncastle (m)	1936	DeutsH	9940	14,790	510–8	66–1	28–4	12.5
SKIBS-A/S MARINE								
Tanker								
Ferncourt** (m)	1938	DeutsR	9918	14,780	510–8	66–1	28–4	12.5

Note: Also *Aragon* (built 1936/1416gt), *Biscaya* (39/1323), *Charente* (35/1282)
Note: * Sold Finland 1939; ** manager Fearnley & Astrup

FOSTENES, LARS, Haugesund

Funnel: Black, white F
Hull: White
Services: Fruit trades

LARS FOSTENES REDERI-A/S

Fruit carrier								
Olaf Fostenes (m,P12)	1936	Helsgr	2994	2930	336–0	45–10	20–3	15.0

GABRIELSEN, GABRIEL, Farsund

Funnel: Orange with black top and houseflag
Hull: Black
Services: General tramping

SKIBS-A/S BORGHOLM

Borgfred	1920	SHWRSd	2183	3560	295–4	41–5	19–6	9.0
ex Winroth 34, ex Rønnes 32, ex Krosfond 31								

GERRARD, E, AND H I RAMSLAND, Kristiansand

Services: General tramping

Note: * Sold Rederi-A/S Hauk (Bucha Godager & Co) 1939, renamed *Polyana*

SKIBS-A/S SKJOLDHEIM

Skjoldheim*	1919	Collwd	2267	3975	261–0	43–8	22–6	9.5
ex Emperor of Halifax 29, ex Canadian Signaller 25								

GERRARD JNR, JOH, Kristiansand

Funnel: Yellow with houseflag
Services: General tramping

Note: * Sold Höyrylaiva O/Y Usko (manager J Nurminen O/Y), Finland, 1939, renamed *Usko*

SKIBS-A/S GERMA								
Germa (r/t)	1920	H&W,B	5282	7750	413–0	51–10	25–4	10.5
ex Adderstone 37, ex Boswell 34								
SKIBS-A/S SONGDAL								
Songdal*	1917	Lindhm	1868	3140	277–0	42–9	18–1	8.5
ex Mongolia 27, ex Anten 19								

GILL-JOHANNESSEN, L, Engensgaten 7, Oslo

Funnel: Black with houseflag on red band
Services: General tramping; oil and petroleum trades

A/S BILL

General cargo vessel								
Bill (r/t,P12)	1938	Moss	2445	4020	316–0	47–9	19–2	11.5
Tankers								
Beth (m)	1930	Doxfrd	6852	10,475	432–2	58–0	27–5	11.0
Brali (m)	bldg	Göta	8479	13,450	496–4	62–1	27–2	12.5

GJERDING, PER, Bergen

Funnel: Yellow with diamond emblem containing G
Hull: Black
Trades: Oil and petroleum

A/S BINTA

Tankers								
Alfred Olsen (m2)	1934	Hamtn4	8817	14,050	492–4	63–4	28–5	12.0
ex Valverda 37								
Binta (m)	1928	ArmWh1	5873	9328	406–0	55–1	25–0	10.5
Bisca (m)	1930	ArmWh2	6089	9449	408–0	55–2	26–10	10.5

GJERPEN, HANS, Tollbodgaten 4, Oslo

Funnel: Black with white G on red over green bands
Services: General tramping

Note: Also vessels under 1500gt

DAMPSK-A/S GUDVIN

Gudvin	1918	Sørlan	1931	3050	277–7	42–1	17–7	8.5
ex Sørland 33								
Gudvor	1928	SHWRSd	2289	3720	293.1	44–1	18–6	9.0
ex St Therese 37								

GJERULDSEN, G A, Havstad, per Arendal

Services: General tramping

SKIBS-A/S GEIRULV

Løvaas	1917	Trondh	1891	3130	273–6	42–0	17–9	8.5
ex Røisheim 23								

GODAGER & CO, BUCHA,
Sjøfartsbygningen, Kongensgaten 6, PO Box 807, Oslo

Services: General tramping

REDERI-A/S HAUK

Polyana 1919 Collwd 2267 3975 261–0 43–8 22–6 9.5
ex Skjoldheim 39, ex Emperor of Halifax 29, ex Canadian Signaller 25

GODAGER, ODD, Sjøfartsbygningen, Kongensgaten 6, Oslo

Funnel: Black with houseflag
Services: General tramping

REDERI-A/S NORSE KING

Norse King 1920 Duthie 5701 8593 423–8 54–2 24–1 10.5
ex West Mahwah 37

REDERI-A/S NORSE LADY

Norse Lady (m) 1919 Merril 3489 5510 346–6 48–4 22–7 9.5
ex Samoan 37, ex Silverspruce 36, ex Ashbee 27; conv steamer 23

NORSEMAN STEAMSHIP CO INC, Panama (Panamanian flag)

Norseman (m2,P–) 1912 B&W 4950 6232 386–0 53–2 24–3 11.0
ex Selandia 36

GOGSTAD & CO, C T, Sjøfartsbygningen, Kongensgaten 6, Oslo

Funnel: Black with white five-pointed star
Hull: Black with white band
Services: General tramping, mainly to and from E coast N America and West Indies; fruit trades

DAMPSK-A/S LALY

Lago 1929 Doxfrd 2552 4135 306–7 47–1 19–3 10.0
ex Vinnie 34
Leif (m) 1937 LindVv 1582 2900 297–0 42–1 19–3 11.5
Leka 1922 White 1599 2560 255–10 40–4 16–11 10.0
ex Hitherwood 26
Lido 1930 Nyland 1918 3150 283–4 42–11 18–0 10.0
Loke 1915 Craig2 2421 4200 295.4 45–2 19–6 9.0
ex Claymont 28, ex Porthcawl 20

Note: Also *Lutz* (built 1933/1416gt)

GORRISSEN & CO A/S, Prinsensgaten 26a, Postboks 710, Oslo

Funnel: Black with red over white over blue over white over red bands
Services: In US E coast and Gulf of Mexico and West Indies

SKIBS-A/S KARAIBIEN

Austvangen 1930 IntDzg 2420 3450 305–11 45–8 17–11 10.5
Dalvangen 1931 IntDzg 2412 3450 305–11 45–6 18–0 10.5
Lindvangen 1931 IntDzg 2412 3450 305–11 45–6 18–0 10.5
Nordvangen 1929 IntDzg 2400 3445 305–11 45–6 17–11 10.5
Sørvangen 1930 IntDzg 2400 3445 305–11 45–6 17–11 10.5
Vestvangen 1930 IntDzg 2420 3450 305–11 45–6 18–0 10.5

GRAN, JOHAN, Olaf Kyrresgaten 9, Postboks 515, Bergen

Funnel: Yellow, black top
Hull: Grey
Services: General tramping

JOHAN GRAN'S REDERI-A/S

Eastern Star 1920 Nthmbl 5659 8800 413–6 53–0 26–3 10.0
ex Mabuhay III 38, ex Eir 37, ex Camilla Gilbert 28, launched as War Lodge

GRANN, HANS FR, Trudvangveien 2a, Oslo

Services: General tramping

DAMPKS-A/S IRIS

Grado 1918 Finch 3082 5020 342–0 47–4 21–8 10.5
ex Louis Mercier 37, ex Andreas Gerakis 27, ex Thermidor 26, ex Abergallus 24, ex War Forest 20

GRUNDTVIG, OTTO, Fjordgaten 19, Trondheim

Services: General tramping

SKIBS-A/S NEA

Nea 1921 Trondh 1877 3050 273–6 42–3 17–9 9.5
ex Ragnvald Jarl 36

GUNDERSEN & CO, CHRISTIAN, Sjøfartsbygningen, Kongensgaten 6, Oslo

Funnel: Yellow
Hull: White, red boot-topping
Services: Fruit trades

Fruit carriers

A/S CASTILLO

Duala (m2,P12) 1938 Göta 1800 2120 320–0 40–5 17–10 15.0

A/S SAMA

Sama (m2,P12) 1937 LindVv 1799 2110 320–0 40–5 17–10 15.0

A/S TITCHFIELD								
Gundersen (m2)	1927	Göta	1841	2400	280–0	37–8	20–6	14.0

Funnel: Black with black H on white band
Hull: Black with white band, red boot-topping
Services: General tramping; oil and petroleum trades
Note: Also short-sea vessels

HAALAND, CHRISTIAN, Haugesund

General cargo vessels								
DAMPSK-A/S ALASKA								
Alaska	1918	Coughl	5681	8169	426–6	54–5	24–2	10.5
ex Peel County 33, ex Alaska 30								
A/S ATLAS								
Nyhaug (m2)	1925	Nakskv	4044	6585	366–1	51–6	22–9	12.0
Nyhorn (m2,P8/1)	1929	B&W	4494	7895	395–0	53–8	25–3	12.0
D/S A/S IDAHO								
Ida Bakke (m,P12/1)	1938	Göta	5455	8490	453–2	58–10	25–7	16.0
Tankers								
D/S A/S IDAHO								
Nyholm (m2)	1927	Odense	5843	8660	402–2	55–2	25–9	11.0
Nyholt (m2)	1931	Odense	8087	12,350	481–9	60–4	27–8	11.5

Services: General tramping

HAALAND & CO A/S, JOHN K, Henrik Ibsensgate 15, Haugesund

DAMPSK-A/S ASLAUG								
Utsire	1917	Moorel	4441	6900	390–0	52–4	22–10	10.0
ex Elias Kræmmer 31, ex Capto 28								
DAMPSK-A/S FOLD								
Sydfold	1918	SmitP	2434	4000	287.1	45–3	20.6	9.0
DAMPSK-A/S KARMØY								
Karmøy	1921	Forth	2498	4150	295.7	43–8	19–9	9.5

Funnel: Yellow with emblem of three blue diamonds, narrow black top
Hull: Black
Trades: Oil and petroleum

HALLE & PETERSON, Skippergaten 22, Oslo

Tankers								
DAMPSK-A/S BALTIMORE								
Britamer (m)	1939	Curle	9976	15,235	515–0	66–11	28–4	13.0
Frontenac	1928	SHWR	7350	11,560	456–0	58–5	27–5	11.0
SKIBS-A/S MARATHON								
Marathon	1930	SHWR	7208	11,560	455–10	58–5	27–5	11.0

Funnel:
Hull: Black
Services: General tramping

HAMRE, INGRID A, Stabekk, per Oslo

A/S I A HAMRES REDERI								
Ingrid	1920	McDoug	2606	4145	261–0	43–8	24–4	9.5
ex Haiti 36, ex Great Falls 20, laid down as Lake Flomaton								

Funnel: Black with white band
Trades: Oil and petroleum

HANNEVIG A/S, CHRISTOFFER, Borre, per Horten

Tankers								
SKIBS-A/S DEODATA								
Deodata (m2)	1897	Laport	3295	–	324.8	45–6	24.1	7.5
ex Quevilly 26								
SKIBS-A/S IRANIA								
Irania (m)	1929	Blythw	2186	3227	287–1	44–2	18–4	9.0
SKIBS-A/S MEXICO								
Mexico (m2)	1920	Nakskv	3017	4500	317–3	44–2	23–10	9.0

Funnel: Black with emblem on white band
Hull: Grey
Trades: Oil and petroleum

HANSEN, JOHS, Arendal

JOHS HANSENS TANKREDERI-A/S								
Tanker								
Ole Jacob (m)	1939	Göta	8306	12,600	483–10	59–5	27–11	13.0

Funnel: Black with five-pointed white star
Services: General tramping
Note: Also *Dokka* (built 1925/1168gt)

HANSEN, KLAUS WIESE, Olav Kyrresgatan 9, Bergen

D/S A/S SONGA								
Grey County	1918	Earles	5194	8250	412–0	52–3	25–3	11.0
ex Turkistan 25, ex War Lark 19								

Lundegaard: The motor vessel Norbryn *was purchased from British owners in 1937, having then previously traded under the name* Pacific Commerce. *She was completed by Doxford in February 1922 as* Dominion Miller *for Furness, Withy, and in 1925 had been renamed* Pacific Commerce. *She was sold in 1936 to owners in Swansea and remained with them for under one year without changing name. She survived the Second World War and was broken up at Grimstad in 1959 (Photograph courtesy Torbjørn Larsson-Fedde, Farsund)*

Mosvold: The fruit carrier Moshill *was under construction in 1939, and completed the following year. She was fitted with a Sulzer 7-cylinder oil engine of 3870bhp and had 178,000 cubic feet of fruit carrying space. In 1940 she was taken over by the Kriegsmarine following the occupation of Norway, and was recovered in May 1945.* Moshill *served with Mosvold until 1958 when sold to Italy and renamed* Eritrea. *She became the Taiwan-flagged* Chen Tai *in 1965 and was broken up at Kaohsiung in 1969 (Photograph courtesy Torbjørn Larsson-Fedde, Farsund)*

Ludwig Mowinckels: The motor tanker Fosna *was completed by Caledon in 1930. During the Second World War she was under British control and managed by British Tanker Co.* Fosna *was sold out of the Mowinckels fleet in 1951 and became the Italian-owned* Marinella. *She was broken up during 1959–60 (J Ludwig Mowinckels)*

Note: See also under County Line

Lorentz W Hansen	1920	Hill	1918	3000	270.0	42–2	18–0	9.5

Funnel: Black with blue MH on white band
Services: General tramping

HANSEN, MATHIAS, Bellevue 4, Kristiansand

A/S FIDELIO

Fidelio	1930	Burntd	1843	3140	265.8	43–0	18.0	10.5

A/S FIDO

Fido	1918	AmSBLo	1857	2900	260–3	43–8	17–11	9.0
ex Lake Benton 29, launched as War Gull								

Funnel: Yellow with black TH monogram, black top
Hull: Black, red boot-topping
Services: General tramping

HANSEN, THORVALD, Kirkegatan 6B, Oslo

D/S A/S BJØRN

Elg (m)	1930	Göta	4014	7080	370–0	51–2	23–8	10.0
Tyr (m)	1926	Göta	4265	6870	370–0	51–4	23–8	10.0

Funnel: Yellow with red five-pointed star, black top
Services: General tramping

Note: Also *Hafnia* (built 1920/1316gt), *Hertha* (17/1365), *Skulda* (10/1105), *Svinta* (16/1267), *Vesla* (13/1108)

HANSEN, WILLIAM, (M Johansen), Tornøegaarden, Christiesgaten, Bergen

DAMPSK-A/S SEKSTANT

Sekstant	1920	Bergen	1626	2450	255–0	37–9	16–9	9.0
ex Nordstrand 22								

SKIBS-A/S WILLIAM HANSENS REDERI

Bauta	1919	NovaSc	1657	2725	269–4	38–3	17–6	8.5
ex Canadian Sealer 25								
Evviva	1921	Laxe	1597	2350	257–10	37–11	16–6	8.5
ex Edvard Greig 22								
Gyda	1920	Laxe	1591	2350	257–10	37–11	16–6	8.5
ex Gijonés 26								
Huldra	bldg	Nyland	2112	3150	275.0			12.0
Thyra	1920	NovaSc	1655	2700	269–4	38–3	17–6	8.5
ex Canadian Miner 24								

Funnel: Black with white H on red diamond on blue band
Hull: Grey
Trades: Oil and petroleum

HANSEN-TANGEN, H E, Hanneviken, Kristiansand S

Tankers

HANSEN-TANGENS REDERI-A/S

Regina (m2)	1937	B&W	9545	14,900	501–1	65–6	28–5	12.0

A/S HANSEN-TANGENS REDERI II

Evina (m)	1930	ArmWhl	6121	9430	408–0	55–1	26–10	11.0

A/S SAGONA

Sagona (m2)	1929	Giessn	7554	11,000	486–6	59–3	27–3	10.5
ex Lion 31								

Funnel: Yellow with blue cross (+) on white band between two narrow red bands separated from black top by broad yellow band
Hull: Black, red boot-topping
Trades: Oil and petroleum

HANSSEN & CO, BERNHARD, Flekkefjord

Tankers

SKIBS-A/S ARAMIS

Aramis (m2)	1931	B&W	7984	11,525	472–6	59–9	26–0	11.5

SKIBS-AS ATHOS

Athos (m2)	1937	B&W	8267	12,750	489–2	61–4	27–0	12.0

Funnel: Yellow with red and white houseflag
Services: NW Europe–E coast US, Canada–Great Lakes; general tramping
Note: * Sold H Reksten 1939, renamed *Vespasian*

HENRIKSEN, DAGFINN, AND HAAKON KIERULF, Rosenkrantzgaten 19, Postboks 993, Oslo

D/S A/S HENRIKSEN & KIERULF

Betta** (r/t)	1935	Porsgr	1570	2424	254–8	37–11	17–1	11.0
Bonde (r/t)	1936	Porsgr	1570	2425	254–8	37–11	17–1	11.0
Brott (r/t)	1937	Porsgr	1583	2425	254–8	37–11	17–1	11.0

Funnel: Black with red H on white diamond on blue band; fruit carriers – yellow
Hull: Black or grey, red boot-topping; fruit carriers – white, green boot-topping

HERLOFSON & CO A/S, SIGURD, Stortingsgaten 12, Oslo

Fruit carriers*

SKIBS-A/S EKSPRESS

Oregon Express (m2,P12)	1933	Odense	3642	3150	351–10	47–3	21–3	15.5

Company / Vessel	Built	Builder	GRT	DWT	Length	Beam	Draught	Speed
SKIBS-A/S PANAMA								
Panama Express (m,P12)	bldg	Örsnd2	4288	4200	376–7	51–2	23–8	16.0
SKIBS-A/S VICTORIA								
British Columbia Express (m2,P12)	1936	Göta	3339	3150	381–7	50–4	23–6	15.5
A/S WENOKA								
California Express (m2,P12)	1934	Göta	3649	3150	351–10	47–2	21–3	15.5
General cargo vessels								
SKIBS-A/S HERSTEIN								
Herdis (m)	order	Örsnd2	4928	9350	439.9	57–4	25.2	13.5
Herstein (m)	1939	B&W	5100	9030	440–8	56–5	25–7	14.0
Tankers								
SKIBS-A/S HERBJØRN								
Herbrand (m2) *ex Mosvold 37*	1935	B&W	9108	14,750	487–8	64–5	28–2	12.0
SKIBS-A/S JOLUND								
Herborg (m2)	1931	B&W	7892	12,405	475–8	59–9	25–11	11.5
SKIBS-A/S TANKEXPRESS								
Tankexpress (m) *ex Petrofina 39*	1937	Göta	10,095	15,200	513–0	64–5	29–6	13.5

Services: W coast North America–UK–NW Europe–Norway (Fruit Express Line); general tramping; oil and petroleum trades

Note: * Operated for Skibs-A/S Fruit Express Line (*qv* also under B Biørnstad & Co)

HØEGH & CO A/S, LEIF, Radhusplassen, Oslo

Funnel: White with houseflag on blue over white over blue bands near top
Hull: Grey, red boot-topping
Services: General tramping; Silver-Java-Pacific Line in association with Silver Line (*qv* in Great Britain section); oil and petroleum trades

Company / Vessel	Built	Builder	GRT	DWT	Length	Beam	Draught	Speed
General cargo vessels								
AKTIESELSKAPENE ABACO, ARUBA, ASTREA & NORUEGA								
Høegh Merchant (m)	1934	B&W	4858	8575	408–0	54–4	25–4	12.5
Høegh Silvercrest (m,P12/1)	1938	B&W	5480	9275	459–6	58–5	25–8	14.0
Høegh Silverdawn (m)	bldg	B&W	7715	10,550	465–6	58–5	26–10	15.0
Høegh Silverlight (m,P10/1)	1936	DeutsR	5197	8425	424–0	55–7	25–5	13.0
Høegh Silvermann (m)	order	B&W	7706	10,550	465–6	58–5	26–10	15.0
Høegh Silverstar (m,P12/1)	1938	B&W	5415	9275	459–6	58–5	25–8	14.0
Høegh Trader (m)	bldg	B&W	7715	10,550	465–6	58–4	26–10	15.0
Høegh Transporter (m,P4)	1935	Kockum	4914	9015	415–0	54–10	25–11	12.5
SKIBS-A/S ARIZONA								
Høegh Silvercloud (m,P5/1)	1939	Flensb	5287	8290	430–8	55–9	25–5	13.0
Tankers								
SKIBS-A/S ABACO								
Pan Europe (m	1931	SHWR	9468	15,320	508–10	65–6	29–0	10.5
AKTIESELSKAPENE ABACO, ARUBA, ASTREA & NORUEGA								
Høegh Giant (m)	1937	DeutsH	10,990	16,008	528–4	69–3	29–1	12.5
SKIBS-A/S ARCADIA								
Alexandra Høegh (m)	1935	Eriksb	8248	12,600	486–0	61–1	26–10	12.0
SKIBS-A/S ARUBA								
Pan Aruba (m)	1931	SHWR	9231	14,930	508–10	65–6	28–7	10.5
SKIBS-A/S ASTREA								
Pan Scandia (m)	1931	SHWR	9816	15,820	491.3	67–0	29–0	10.5
A/S ATLANTICA								
Høegh Hood (m)	1936	Odense	9351	14,640	501–0	65–8	28–0	12.0
A/S ATLANTICA & SKIBS-A/S ARNSTEIN*								
Høegh Scout (m)	1939	DeutsR	9924	14,600	510–8	66–1	28–0	12.5
SKIBS-A/S NORUEGA								
South Africa (m2)	1930	SHWR	9234	14,838	508–10	65–5	28–7	10.5
MARITIME TRADING LTD,** Oslo (Panamanian flag)								
Ohio (m) *ex Le Havre 39*	1938	DeutsH	10,191	16,060	528–5	69–2	29–2	12.5
Shabonee (m) *ex Laurel 34*	1930	Blythw	9716	14,970	500–0	65–6	28–6	12.0

Note: * *qv* under P Holm; ** until 1939 styled Compania Maritima Escandinavia Inc

Services: General tramping

HOGH-HERVIG, KR, Haugesund

DAMPSK-A/S SNAR

Snar 1920 Eltrgm 3176 5520 341–0 48–0 21–4 9.5
ex Grong 33, ex Fageraas 27

Funnel: Hoegh Carrier – black with houseflag and white zig-zag band near top
Services: General tramping; oil and petroleum trades
Note: * *qv* under Leif Høegh & Co A/S

HOLM, PER, Grensen 15vi, Oslo

SKIBS-A/S ARNSTEIN*

General cargo vessel
Høegh Carrier (m) 1935 B&W 4906 8675 406–0 54–4 25–5 13.0
Tanker
Pan Norway (m) 1931 SHWR 9231 15,300 508–10 65–6 28–7 10.5

Funnel: Black with blue H on white diamond on red band between two narrow blue bands
Services: General tramping

HOLTA, A/S, O & H, (H H Holta), Skien

A/S HAVILDE

Haalegg (st) 1922 Hølens 1758 2850 260.3 41–2 18–0 8.5
ex Fagervik 34
Haarfagre 1918 PuseyW 2478 3800 311–11 44–0 19–1 9.5
ex Belgica 32, ex Yzerhandel 28, ex Carabinier 26, ex Aurora 20, launched as War Compass

A/S HERDEBRED

Herleik 1914 G&G5 1893 3200 279.0 40–3 17–10 9.0
ex Mai 31, ex Wigmore 26, ex Venice 22

Services: General tramping
Note: * Sold Latvia 1939, renamed *Hercogs Jekabs*; ** sold Japan 1939, renamed *Tamaki Maru*; † sold Germany 1939, renamed *Iris*

HOLTA, THORALF, Akre, Borgestad, per Porsgrunn

REDERI-A/S HENNESEID

Aakre* (m) 1926 Kockum 4138 7800 397–10 54–0 24–0 11.0
ex Childar 35
Binna** 1917 BethU2 7815 11,650 410.9 56–2 30–6 10.5
ex Bessa 37
Bjønn 1921 Schich 5509 10,420 398.9 55–11 27–11 10.0
ex Bolivia 35
Helle 1918 PuseyW 2467 3800 311–11 44–0 19–0 9.5
ex Ganda 32, ex Marconier 29, ex Piqua 20, launched as War Nurse
Herøy† (r/t) 1921 Örsndl 3323 5000 321–0 44–10 24–0 9.5
ex Adour 34

Funnel: Black with white C on red band (some funnels very narrow)
Hull: Grey
Services: New York, Philadelphia, Baltimore, Hampton Roads–Rio de Janeiro–Rosario–Santos–Buenos Aires (Ivaran Lines); NW Europe–USA; NW Europe–South America; Baltimore–New York–Los Angeles–Kobe–Yokohama; general tramping

HOLTER-SØRENSEN, S, Tollbodgaten 11, Oslo

General cargo vessels

A/S BESCO

Besholt (m,P12) 1936 Kockum 4977 9015 419–2 54–10 25–11 13.0

SKIBS-A/S IGADI

Sørholt (m,P12) 1939 Kockum 4801 9180 426–0 55–8 26–4 13.0
Tercero (m2,P–) 1926 B&W 4415 7885 382–5 53–9 24–1 12.0
ex Sud Cubano 30, ex Tercero 29

A/S IVARANS REDERI

Buenos Aires (m2) 1928 B&W 4640 8330 397–1 53–10 26–0 11.0
ex Argentino 39, ex Sud Atlantico 31
Ivaran (m,P12) 1938 Kockum 4955 9015 419–6 54–10 25–11 13.0
Montevideo (m2) 1928 B&W 4639 8330 397–1 53–10 26–0 11.0
ex Uruguayo 39, ex Sud Pacifico 32
Primero (m2,P–) 1925 B&W 4414 7930 382–5 53–9 24–1 12.0
ex Sud Argentino 31, ex Primero 29
Reinholt (m,P12) 1939 Kockum 4801 9180 426–0 55–8 26–4 13.0
Santos (m2) 1928 B&W 4639 8330 397–1 53–10 25–11 11.0
ex Paraguayo 39, ex Sud Africano 32

Tankers

SKIBS-A/S HOLTER-SØRENSENS TANKREDERI

Katy (m) 1931 Doxfrd 6826 10,575 432–2 58–0 27–5 11.0

SKIBS-A/S LISE

Lise (m) 1931 Doxfrd 6826 10,575 432–2 58–0 27–5 11.0

HVIDE, JOHAN, Tornøgaarden, Christiesgaten, Bergen

HVIDE'S REDERI-A/S
Lynghaug 1919 WallSY 2829 4588 320.0 44–2 21–5 10.0
ex Canadian Trooper 32

Services: General tramping

HVISTENDAHL, YNGVAR, Tønsberg

General cargo vessels
Matros* (m2) 1915 H&WGw 4349 6690 381–10 50–1 23–7 10.0
ex Olymp 38, ex Falstria 36
SKIBS-A/S SKYTTEREN
Mim (m,P5/1) 1938 Flensb 4996 8700 432–6 55–9 25–5 13.0
Whale factory vessel
HVALFSLSK FINNHVAL A/S
Skytteren (s2) 1901 H&W,B 12,358 16,000 565–0 63–4 33–3 12.0
ex Suevic 28; conv passenger/general cargo 28; rebuilt 17 as Suevic

Funnel: Yellow, blue and white emblem, black top
Hull: Black with white band, or grey, red boot-topping
Services: General tramping; whaling

Note: * Under Panamanian flag

JACOBSEN, BERTRAND, Postboks 46, Arendal

SKIBS-A/S REMONSTRANT
Torungen 1931 Trondh 1948 3200 276.3 43–1 18–11 10.0

Services: Tramping, mainly E coast Canada and US and West Indies

JACOBSEN & SALVESEN, Prinsensgaten 3B, Oslo

DAMPSK-A/S VARD
Hird (m) 1924 Curle 4950 9171 411.9 55–5 25–7 10.5
ex Hoperange 37, ex Swanley 32

Hull: Black
Services: General tramping

JAHRE, ANDERS, Sandefjord

Fruit carriers
Jasmin (m,P12) bldg Framns 2956 2300 334–2 45–10 18–10 16.0
ANDERS JAHRE'S REDERI-A/S
Rose* (m,P12) 1938 Örsnd2 3063 2250 334–2 45–10 18–10 16.0
SKIBS-A/S ROSE
Jamaica (m,P12) 1936 B&W 3015 2600 336–0 45–10 19–0 16.0
ex Giuba 38
Tankers
SKIBS-A/S JAGUAR
Jaguar** (m2) 1928 Göta 9721 13,500 493–10 64–2 28–5 12.0
ex Nike 38
SKIBS-A/S JARIS
Aristophanes (m2) bldg Göta 10,224 15,360 515–10 64–5 29–8 15.0
SKIBS-A/S NORAVIND
Noravind (m2) 1930 Göta 8235 12,500 469–0 59–4 27–4 12.0
ex Nordanvik 34; shortened 35
SKIBS-A/S VIGRID
Jaspis (m) 1930 ThmpsJ 6094 9550 413.1 56–3 26–0 11.5
ex Vigdis 39
Whale factory vessels
HVALFSLSK KOSMOS A/S
Kosmos 1929 Work28 17,801 24,120 554.1 77–2 35–1 12.0
HVALFSLSK KOSMOS II A/S
Kosmos II 1931 Work28 16,966 25,410 553.4 77–2 34–6 12.5

Funnel: Black with houseflag on red band; fruit carriers – black with white band
Hull: Grey, green boot-topping
Services: Fruit trades; oil and petroleum trades; whaling

Note: * Sold Germany 1939, renamed *Alstertor*; ** broke in two, abandoned, Jan 17 1939, new forepart fitted, renamed *Janko* (Panamanian flag) 1939
Note: Also a fleet of whalers
Note: This firm was associated with Bruun & Von der Lippe (*qv*)

JAKHELLN, ALF, Radhusgaten 23, Oslo

General cargo vessels
SKIBS-A/S LAPLATA
Tropic Star (m) 1926 Denny2 5088 8455 415–0 52–3 25–0 12.5
ex Ashburton 37, ex Yomah 27
SKIBS-A/S TROPIC
Tropic Sea* (m2) 1920 Nakskv 5781 8750 406–10 53–2 27–2 10.5
ex Indien 38
Tanker
SKIBS-A/S VARILD
Attila (m) 1930 ArmWh2 7913 12,300 476–0 59–10 25–9 11.5

Funnel: Yellow with houseflag
Hull: Grey
Services: General tramping; oil and petroleum trades

Note: * Sold Chr Ostberg 1939

Funnel: Black with broad white band containing black zig-zag band
Hull: Black
Services: General tramping, mainly NW Europe to Mediterranean and North America

JEBSEN JR, KR, Torvalmenning 8, Bergen

A/S KRISTIAN JEBSENS REDERI

Garnes	1930	Bergen	1559	2545	250.6	39–4	17–0	10.0
Vigsnes	1930	Bergen	1599	2335	257–7	37–9	16–8	10.0
D/S A/S NOR								
Korsnes (r/t)	1936	Rosenb	1736	2550	271–8	41–2	16–9	10.5
Telnes (r/t)	1936	Rosenb	1694	2550	271–8	41–2	16–9	10.5

Funnel: Black with white cross (+) on red band
Trades: Oil and petroleum

JEBSEN, WILH & PAUL, Bergen

Tankers

A/R ATLANTIC

Sveve (m)	1930	SHWR	6313	10,350	435–0	57–6	26–5	11.5
A/R SELJAN								
Atlantic (m)	1925	ArmWh1	7342	11,072	455–0	57–6	27–6	10.0
Sildra (m)	1927	Schich	7313	11,170	458–0	57–5	26–6	11.0

Funnel: Black or yellow with houseflag
Hull: Black, red boot-topping
Trades: Oil and petroleum

Note: * Sold Italy 1939, renamed *Antonia C*

JENSEN, JØRGEN P, Hisøy, per Arendal

Tankers

A/S JENSENS REDERI I

Gundine*	1921	BethSP	6025	8272	427–9	53–4	24–7	9.5
ex Emile Deutsch de la Meurthe 30								
A/S JENSENS REDERI II								
Marit	1918	GrayX	5563	8400	412–0	52–4	25–7	10.5
ex Crenatula 30, ex War Subadar 21								
Marit II	1922	ArmWh1	7417	10,958	455–0	57–4	27–6	12.0
ex Scottish Strath 37								
A/S JENSENS REDERI III								
Petter (m2)	1935	B&W	9109	14,750	487–9	64–5	28–0	12.0
Petter II	1922	ArmWh1	7417	10,958	455–0	57–5	27–6	12.0
ex Scottish Castle 37								
A/S MYTILUS								
Mytilus	1916	SHWR	5693	8450	412.0	53–6	24–8	9.5

Funnel: Yellow with houseflag
Services: Fruit trades – mainly West Indies–USA–Canada

Note: Also *Port Antonio* (A/S Gulftrade, built 1913/1266gt)

JENSEN & CO, L HARBOE, Hieronymus Heyerdahlsgaten 1, Oslo

D/S A/S BANANFART

Fruit carriers

Cadmus	1926	B&W,K	1855	2515	281–0	39–3	20–9	12.0
Harboe Jensen (m2)	1929	Göta	1862	2400	282–0	37–9	20–9	13.5

Trades: Oil and petroleum

JENSSEN, VICTOR, Karl Johansgaten 1, Oslo

VICTOR JENSSENS REDERI-A/S

Tankers

Soli	1915	BethHH	5834	8396	426–0	53–5	24–7	9.5
ex Silver Shell 30								
Willy	1916	BethHH	5832	8396	426–0	53–5	24–7	9.5
ex Gold Shell 29								

Services: General tramping

JOHANNESEN & FALCK PEDERSEN, Ovre Slotsgaten 8, Oslo

SKIBS-A/S DON

Don	1924	AwpEng	2010	3170	278.7	40–3	17–9	9.5
ex Dunston 29								

Funnel: Black with blue J on white band with yellow over blue bands above and blue over yellow bands below
Services: General tramping
Note: Also smaller vessels

JOHANNESEN, J M, Farsund

J M JOHANNESEN'S REDERI-A/S

Finse	1916	Bergen	1618	2400	255–0	37–8	16–7	9.0
ex Snar 26								
Maurita	1925	Bergen	1569	2350	257–7	37–8	16–8	9.0

JOHNSEN, FINN, Lodin Leppsgaten 2, Bergen

Funnel: Black with blue and white emblem on red band
Hull:
Services: General tramping

A/S FINN JOHNSENS REDERI

Aun	1930	SmithM	1908	3175	280–0	43–0	19–4	10.0

JØRGENSEN, J C, Grimstad

Services: General tramping

JØRGENSENS REDERI-A/S

Eli (m)	1931	Eriksb	4332	7870	396–6	54–3	24–1	12.0

KLÆR & CO A/S, HANS, Drammen

Services: Mainly in Far East

SKIBS-A/S FJELD

Graciosa	1917	Clyde	1773	3295	265.2	42–3	19–5	8.5
ex Edfou 29, ex Rabymere 25								

KJØDE A/S, JACOB, Postboks 519, Fredtun, Bergen

Funnel: Black with white K on blue band
Hull: Black with white band, red boot-topping
Services: General tramping; oil and petroleum trades

A/S INGER

General cargo vessels								
Cissy	1920	Framns	2166	3900	289.5	44–2	19.4	8.5
Elin K (m)	1936	Bremer	5214	8500	434–5	55–10	25–2	13.0
Felix	1907	Dobson	2047	3500	290.4	42–0	19–0	7.5
Ingeren	1911	Dixon2	6118	8630	405.0	54–2	24–6	8.0
ex Berwindvale 24; conv tanker								
Ingerfem	1912	Doxfrd	3978	7000	370.5	51–2	22.7	8.0
ex Øvre 31, ex Athamas 16								
Ingerfire	1905	Short2	3835	6100	359–5	49–8	22–1	7.5
ex Alexandra 24								
Ingerseks	1913	Dixon2	4970	8200	392–8	52–6	24–5	9.0
ex Wascana 34								
Ingerto	1920	UnionS	3089	4700	318.6	46–2	20–7	9.5
ex John R Gibbons 24								
Ingertre	1921	Burntd	2462	4300	311–0	43–9	20–2	9.5
ex Julianne I 38, ex Løvstakken 33								
Ingria (m2)	1931	B&W	4391	7680	393–2	54–3	24–0	11.0
Kaprino	1907	Sundld	3249	5280	306.6	47–0	21–0	8.5
ex Ocland 18								
Tanker								
Arne Kjøde (m)	1938	DeutsH	11,019	16,150	528–0	69–3	29–2	13.0

Note: Also short-sea vessels

KLAVENESS & CO A/S, A F, Postboks 108, Lysaker, Oslo

Funnel: Black with white K on red band
Hull: Grey with blue band, red boot-topping, or black, red boot-topping; tankers – grey, red boot-topping
Services: Cargo – Portland–San Francisco–Los Angeles–Manila–Kobe–Yokohama–Hong Kong–Saigon–Singapore; New York–Far East; Far East–Europe; Oslo–US Gulf ports; UK–US; general tramping, oil and petroleum trades

General cargo vessels								
SKIBS-A/S GOODWILL								
Roseville (m2,P12/1)	1930	Odense	5745	9265	445–5	58–6	25–9	13.5
DAMPSK-A/S INTERNATIONAL								
Fingal	1923	Moss	2137	3450	276.1	43–9	18–8	9.5
Stirlingville (m,P1)	1935	Doxfrd	4995	9215	427–9	54–3	25–6	10.5
ex Stirling 36								
SKIBS-A/S MANDEVILLE								
Corneville (m2)	1930	B&W	4544	8311	407–5	55–2	29–8	13.0
Pleasantville (m2)	1929	B&W	4349	8311	407–5	55–2	29–8	13.0
SKIBS-A/S SANGSTAD								
Sangstad (m)	1925	DeutsH	4297	7850	395–8	53–5	25–3	11.0
SKIBS-A/S SILJESTAD								
Siljestad (m,P–)	1927	B&W	4301	7870	394–0	53–10	24–8	11.5
Slemmestad (m,P4)	1928	B&W	4258	7870	394–0	53–10	24–7	11.5
SKIBS-A/S SJØSTAD								
Bonneville (m)	1929	Odense	4665	8400	407–3	54–2	25–4	11.5
Bronxville (m)	1929	Odense	4663	8423	407–3	54–2	25–4	11.5
SKIBS-A/S SKOGSTAD								
Somerville (m2,P8)	1929	B&W	4265	7840	399–1	53–8	24–10	13.0
SKIBS-A/S SKRAMSTAD								
Skramstad (m)	1925	DeutsH	4300	7850	395–8	53–5	25–3	11.0
SKIBS-A/S SNESTAD								
Snestad (m)	1926	Kockum	4114	7710	397–10	54–0	24–0	11.0

SKIBS-A/S SOMMERSTAD

Granville (m2,P12/1) 1930 Odense 5745 9149 445–5 58–6 25–6 13.5

SKIBS-A/S STEINSTAD

Steinstad 1912 ThmpR2 2477 4175 300.5 44–6 19–2 9.0

Tankers

SKIBS-A/S GOLDEN WEST

Sir Karl Knudsen* (m2) 1928 Nakskv 7747 11,180 467–6 59–2 26–0 11.5

Teddy (m) 1930 Laing 6748 11,100 448–6 57–3 27–3 11.5

ex Thorsholm 36

DAMPSK-A/S INTERNATIONAL

Sir Osborn Holmden** (m2) 1928 B&W 9153 14,386 488–6 64–5 28–2 11.5

SKIBS-A/S SOLSTAD

Solstad (m) 1927 Odense 5952 8565 411–6 53–9 26–7 11.0

Stigstad (m) 1927 Kockum 5964 8590 401–2 55–3 27–0 11.0

SKIBS-A/S SOMMERSTAD

Sommerstad (m) 1926 Lindhm 5923 8670 394–0 55–1 25–2 10.5

Storstad (m2) 1926 Blythw 8998 13,460 500–0 62–3 27–8 11.0

UNIVERSAL SHIPPING CO A/S

Seirstad (m) 1937 DeutsH 9916 14,800 510–8 66–1 28–4 12.0

Stiklestad (m) 1938 Odense 9349 14,580 501–1 65–8 28–1 12.0

Note: * Sold Germany 1939, renamed *Charlotte Schliemann*; ** sold Trans-Ocean Shipping & Chartering Co Ltd, Panama, 1939, renamed *H G Wagon* (Panamanian flag), resold France 1939, renamed *Vendée*

KLEPPE, P, Bygdø Allè 51B Oslo

Funnel: Yellow with white K superimposed on blue over green bands
Services: General tramping

Hallfried 1918 BethWi 2848 5025 322–0 48–3 20–5 10.5

ex Fairfield 39, ex Catherine Weems 28, ex Garibaldi 25, launched as Pilón

SKIBS-A/S HALLBJØRG

Hallbjørg 1919 CanVic 2850 4560 320.0 44–4 21–6 10.0

ex Thuhaug 36, ex Canadian Voyageur 30

KLOSTER, LAURITZ, Tollbodgaten 25B, Oslo

Funnel: Yellow with LK monogram, black top; *Austvard*, *Sørvard* had no noticeable funnel
Hull: Grey
Services: General tramping

KLOSTERS REDERI-A/S

Austvard (m2) 1925 B&W 3677 7150 384–0 51–6 23–5 10.5

Heimvard (m,P5/1,5/2) 1930 Kockum 4851 8800 414–9 54–10 25–10 12.5

Lidvard (m,P8/1,5/2) 1939 Kockum 4785 9300 426–6 55–8 26–4 13.5

Nordvard (m) 1925 Kockum 4111 7705 397–10 54–0 24–0 12.0

Sørvard (m2) 1925 B&W 3673 7150 384–0 51–6 23–5 10.5

Vestvard (m) 1925 Neptnl 4319 7608 402–0 53–0 23.5 10.5

KNUDSEN, E D, Kirkegaten 14–18, Oslo

Funnel: Black with white anchor on blue band with narrow red over white bands above and white over red bands below
Services: General tramping

DAMPSK-A/S AKABAHRA

Akabahra 1929 Porsgr 1524 2375 244.7 37–11 18.3 10.0

ex Ørnefjell 37

KNUDSEN, GUNNAR, Borgestad, per Porsgrunn

Funnel: Black, white band (some funnels very narrow)
Hull: Light grey, red boot-topping
Services: General tramping

A/S BORGESTAD

Bidevind (m,P5/1) 1938 Flensb 4956 8600 432–6 55–9 25–5 13.0

Borgestad (m2) 1925 B&W 3924 6750 364–1 51–5 22–11 10.5

Brand (m2) 1927 Göta 4819 8880 395–3 54–9 24–8 11.0

Bratland (m) 1939 Lübecl 4965 8250 432–5 55–8 25–5 13.0

Brønnøy (m2,P4/1) 1926 Göta 4792 8482 395–3 54–8 24–8 11.0

Brynje (m2,P8/1) 1926 B&W 3916 6978 364–1 51–5 22–11 10.5

Chr Knudsen (m2,P–) 1925 B&W 4904 8490 396–0 54–9 24–4 11.0

Sønnavind (m,P5/1) 1935 Bremer 4965 8720 432–6 55–8 25–6 12.5

KNUTSEN, OLUF SKJELBRED, Kristiansand

Services: General tramping
Note: * Sold Reederij 'Oost Borneo' NV, Batavia, 1939, renamed *Loa-Koeloe* (Netherlands flag)
Note: Also smaller vessels

DAMPSK-A/S HEDRUM

Atna* 1930 Fredst 1846 3050 265.3 42–1 19–0 9.5

Ludwig Mowinckels: Para *was completed at the Rijkee shipyard in Rotterdam in 1921. She survived the Second World War and in 1956 was sold out of the fleet to become the Italian-flagged* San Nicolosio. *She was broken up in 1961 (J Ludwig Mowinckels)*

Fred Olsen: Black Watch *was launched on June 2 1938 and completed in January 1939 by Akers for the Oslo–Kristiansand–Newcastle passenger service. She was fitted with two Akers/B&W 9-cylinder oil engines of 7000ihp, which gave a speed in excess of 19 knots on trials and 18 knots in service. In September 1939 she was laid up at Oslo, and fell into German hands with the occupation of Norway in 1940.* Black Watch *was taken over by the Kriegsmarine and on August 28 commissioned as a U-boat crew accommodation vessel at Kirkenes. In a similar role she was at Hammerfest in 1943, and on May 4 1945 at the U-boat base at Kilbotn, near Harstad, was attacked and sunk by Avenger and Wildcat aircraft from the escort carriers* Queen, Searcher *and* Trumpeter *(from Operation 'Judgement' task force) (Fred Olsen archives)*

KNUTSEN O A S, KNUT, Strandgaten 161, Postboks 87 and 97, Haugesund

Funnel: Black with two red bands
Hull: Black or black with white band, red boot-topping
Services: Cargo – Scandinavia and NW Europe–S Pacific (Den Skandenaviske Syd-Pacific Linje); N Pacific–S Pacific; N Pacific ports–UK, NW Europe, Scandinavia; general tramping; oil and petroleum trades

Fruit carrier								
Vibran (m2,P12)	1935	Helsgr	2993	3050	336–0	45–10	20–3	15.0
General cargo vessels								
DAMPKS-A/S GOLDEN GATE								
Margrethe Bakke (m,P10/1)	1938	Göta	5478	8460	453–2	58–10	25–7	16.0
SKIBS-A/S HILDA KNUDSEN								
Emma Bakke (m2,P6)	1929	Kockum	4721	8215	414–6	54–9	25–9	12.5
ex Sveadrott 37								
Knut Bakke (m,P12/1)	order	Göta	5869	8570	474–11	58–9	25–9	15.5
Sofie Bakke (m,P12/1)	1938	Göta	5461	8440	453–2	58–10	25–7	16.0
DAMPSK-A/S JEANETTE SKINNER								
Elisabeth Bakke (m,P10/1)	1937	Göta	5450	8450	453–3	58–10	25–6	16.0
John Bakke (m2,P12/1)	1929	Göta	4718	8380	407–8	54–8	25–7	12.0
Olav Bakke (m,P12/1)	order	Göta	5879	8570	474–11	58–9	25–8	15.5
DAMPSK-A/S JOHN BAKKE								
Vinland (m2,P12/1)	1924	B&W	4436	7400	381–3	53–8	23–3	11.5
DAMPSK-A/S LISBETH								
Lisbeth	1922	Bergen	2732	4450	314–9	47–3	20–10	10.0
SKIBS-A/S MARIE BAKKE								
Marie Bakke (m2,P12/1)	1926	Odense	4307	8125	392–3	52–6	25–0	11.5
Martin Bakke (m,P10/1)	1936	Göta	5484	8500	453–2	58–10	25–6	16.0
SKIBS-A/S PACIFIC								
Geisha (m2,P12/1)	1921	NedSM	5113	7800	375.8	51–5	26–5	11.0
Indra (m2,P12/1)	1923	NedSM	5041	7750	375.8	51–5	26–5	11.0
Tosca (m2,P12/1)	1920	NedSM	5128	7800	375.0	51–2	26–5	11.0
SKIBS-A/S SAMUEL BAKKE								
Samuel Bakke (m2,P12/1)	1929	Göta	4719	8230	407–7	54–8	25–7	12.0
Tankers								
K J Knudsen (m)	bldg	Göta	10,500	16,600	539–0	66–0	29–6	14.0
SKIBS-A/S HILDA KNUDSEN								
Hilda Knudsen (m2)	1928	Nakskv	9178	14,100	489–0	64–6	28–4	12.0
John Knudsen (m2)	1934	Göta	9071	14,260	489–8	64–5	28–4	12.5
DAMPSK-A/S JEANETTE SKINNER								
Anna Knudsen (m2)	1931	Göta	9057	14,260	489–7	64–5	28–4	12.5
Eli Knudsen (m2)	1925	Blythw	9026	13,480	470.0	62–2	26–9	11.0
ex O A Knudsen 37								
Ida Knudsen (m2)	1925	Nakskv	8913	14,030	485–0	62–1	27–11	12.0
DAMPSK-A/S KEY WEST								
Suderholm	1917	SeatCD	4908	7000	381.4	53–3	23–9	9.5
ex Key West 30; conv general cargo 30								
SKIBS-A/S MARIE BAKKE								
O A Knudsen (m)	1938	DeutsH	11,007	16,150	528–0	69–3	29–2	13.0
SKIBS-A/S SAMUEL BAKKE								
Kaia Knudsen (m2)	1931	Blohm	9063	14,240	489–7	64–5	28–4	12.5
Whale factory vessel								
HVALF-A/S SUDERØY								
Suderøy I	1913	ArmWhl	7562	11,300	457–0	57–6	24–9	10.5
ex Balto 25, ex Kim 16; conv general cargo 29								

Note: Also short-sea vessels and a fleet of whalers

KONOW, MAGNUS, Radhusgaten 23, Oslo

Funnel: Yellow, separated from black top by yellow over red over blue bands
Trades: Oil and petroleum

SKIBS-A/S ABU								
Tanker								
Iselin (m)	1939	Kockum	9493	15,075	525–5	62–9	28–4	14.0

KRAG, JØRGEN, Radhusgaten 22, Oslo

Services: Whaling

HVALFSLSK BLAAHVAL A/S*

Whale factory vessel

C A Larsen	1913	SHWR	13,246	17,250	540.8	66–8	32–5	11.0
ex San Gregorio 26; conv tanker 26								

Note: * Controlled since 1936 by Hamburger Walfang-Kontor GmbH (*qv* in Germany section)

KRAGERØ SALTKOMPANI A/S,
Kragerø, and c/o (manager) Thv Johnsen Jr, Grev Wedels Plass 4, Oslo

Services: General tramping

REDERI-A/S SALT

Salt*	1918	Dtroit	1854	3660	261–0	43–10	21–1	9.5
ex Rondo 38, ex Strand 35, ex Panaghis Vergottis 25, ex Lake Weston 19, launched as War Swift								

Note: * Sold Finland 1939, renamed *Solbritt*

KRØGER, JOHS, Bogen, per Tønsberg

Funnel: Black with yellow outline triangle on white disc on broad blue band
Services: General tramping

DAMPSK-A/S ARDENT

Ardent	1917	Sørlan	1804	2990	277–7	42–1	17–9	9.0
ex Ørja 28, ex Boloma 25, ex Sonja 21								

KROGSTADS SHIPPING AGENCIES LTD, A/S, (Karl Krogstad),
Tollbodgaten 4, Oslo

Services: General tramping

REDERI-A/S NIDAROS

Belize	1919	Manito	2153	3245	261–0	43–9	20–2	9.5
ex Cornore 36, ex Cornucopia 29								
Frank Seamans	1928	Prstm2	4271	7100	352.0	60–0	22.2	10.0
Nidardal	1918	Dtroit	2368	3600	261–0	43–10	21–10	9.5
ex Lake Gorin 37								
Nidarland	1919	Standf	6076	9414	412–0	53–2	26–7	10.5
ex Wisconsin 39, ex Wawalona 28								
Nidaros	1918	Dtroit	2353	3660	261–0	43–10	21–1	9.5
ex Lake Benbow 37								

Note: Also *Nidareid* (built 1924/1321gt)

KUBON, WILLY, Bergen

Funnel: Red, black top, separated by white band
Services: General tramping

DAMPSK-A/S FLINT

Flint 2	1918	Coughl	5614	8550	427–0	54–3	24–2	11.0
ex Elgin County 31, ex Flint 2 30, ex Atlantis 28, ex Sierra Quemada 24, ex War Camp 19								

KUHNLE, HALFDAN, Bergen

Funnel: Black, three white bands
Hull: Black
Services: General tramping; oil and petroleum trades

H KUHNLES REDERI-A/S

General cargo vessels

Nordnes (m)	1932	Göta	4059	8200	407–1	55–3	24–10	11.5
ex Aurora 36								
Norne (m)	1930	Eriksb	3971	6850	365–7	50–10	23–3	11.0
Tanker								
Norden (m)	1931	DeutsH	8440	11,620	465.2	59–9	27–4	11.5

KUHNLE & SON, S M, Christiesgaten 5–7, Bergen

Funnel: Black with blue five-pointed star on white band between two narrow red bands
Services: General tramping

DAMPSK-A/S SVERRE

Arna (m)	1929	Eriksb	4325	7800	396–6	54–4	23–11	12.0

LANGE, EINAR, Tollbodgaten 4, Oslo

Services: General tramping

A/S OLYMP

Gunda	1919	McDoug	2241	3465	261–0	43–9	22.2	9.5
ex Chantier 29								

REDERI-A/S SKRIM

Skrim	1917	Lindhm	1902	3140	277–0	42–10	18–1	9.0
ex Dagali 35, ex Textil 22, ex Viken 19								

Fred Olsen: The passenger vessel Bretagne *was completed in 1937 by Akers and was equipped with an Akers/B&W 9-cylinder oil engine of 3500bhp. She fell into German hands upon the occupation of Norway in 1940, and in May 1945 was returned to Fred Olsen for service between Oslo and Newcastle as a replacement for war losses. In 1958 she was sold to Hellenic Mediterranean Lines of Greece and renamed* Massalia, *for service in the Mediterranean. In April 1967 she was withdrawn from service and laid up at Piræus. She was sold in 1974 to be broken up (Fred Olsen archives)*

Fred Olsen: Breñas *was one of four specially-designed fruit carriers completed in the early 1930s, and was mainly employed in service between the Canary Islands and London. Breñas was torpedoed, shelled, and sunk by* U108 *on August 7 1942 when on voyage from Ascension and Maranham for Trinidad and New York with 3044 tons of general cargo. She had a crew of 34, from which one was lost and the master made a prisoner of war (RW Jordan collection)*

Fred Olsen: Laurits Swenson *was completed at Odense in January 1930, and was fitted with two B&W 6-cylinder oil engines of 4300bhp. She was one of five vessels in service for Fred Olsen from Vancouver, Puget Sound, Portland, San Francisco and San Pedro via Panama to Liverpool, London, Hull and Oslo. These vessels were known as the 'Great Americans' class. With the outbreak of war in September 1939 the service was gradually run down, and during the conflict* Laurits Swenson *was managed from New York by the local office of Norske Amerikalinje. She continued in Fred Olsen service until 1963 when she was broken up in Hong Kong (RW Jordan collection)*

LANGFELDT & CO, A I, Markensgaten 10, Kristiansand

Funnel: Yellow with houseflag, narrow black top
Services: General tramping; oil and petroleum trades

General cargo vessels								
A/S HELGØY								
Sirehei	1907	ThmpsJ	3888	6628	346.1	49–8	23–4	8.0
ex Bratsberg 35								
Siremalm	1906	Rodger	2468	4290	313.6	43–10	19–9	8.0
ex Senta 39, ex Ottawa 35, ex Craigisla 10								
SKIBS-A/S ODDERØ								
Sirehav*	1917	BethU2	3785	5959	340.0	48–3	22–7	9.0
ex Regulus 38								
Sirenes	1913	Doxfrd	4341	8600	389.8	54–1	24–7	8.5
ex Hesperos 31								
Tanker								
A/S NORSK RUTEFART								
Madrono	1917	Palmer	5894	8607	407.5	52–5	25–0	9.5

Note: * Sold O L Lokke 1939, renamed *Senta*

LODDING, TRYGVE, Sjøfartsbygningen, Kongensgaten 6, Oslo

Funnel: Black with black L on white disc on red band
Trades: Oil and petroleum

Tankers								
SKIBS-A/S NORDHAV								
Nordhav	1919	Laing	5574	8440	412–0	52–4	25–1	10.5
ex Capsa 27, ex War Khan 21								
SKIBS-A/S OSTHAV								
Osthav (m)	1931	DeutsH	8417	11,500	465.2	59–9	27–5	11.5
SKIBS-A/S SYDHAV								
Sydhav (m)	1929	SHWR	7587	12,020	464–10	61–0	27–0	11.5
Vesthav (m)	order	Kockum	10,298	16,450	534–0	63–3	29–11	13.5

LØKKE, OLE L, Hølen, per Oslo

Services: General tramping

SKIBS-A/S SENTA								
Senta*	1906	Rodger	2468	4290	313.6	43–10	19–9	8.0
ex Ottawa 35, ex Craigisla 10								
Senta	1917	BethU2	3785	5959	354–6	48–3	22–7	9.0
ex Sirehav 39, ex Regulus 38								

Note: * Sold A I Langfeldt 1939, renamed *Siremalm*

LORENTZEN, ØIVIND, Frithjof Nansens Plass 5, Oslo

Funnel: Yellow
Hull: Grey
Services: N Brazil–New York (Northern Pan America Line A/S); general tramping

A/S SOBRAL								
Rio Branco (m,P8)	1925	Krupp	3210	4575	317–0	47–8	21–4	10.0
ex Boca Raton 36, ex Marie Horn 35								
Rio Negro* (m,P8)	1925	Krupp	3376	4556	317–0	47–8	21–4	8.0
ex Hindhead 36, ex Consul Horn 36								
Rio Novo	1937	Prstm2	2490	4500	325–0	47–0	20–8	11.0
Rio Pardo** (m,P8)	1925	Krupp	3133	4556	317–0	47–9	21–4	10.0
ex Pine Court 37, ex Henry Horn 34								
Rio Verde (m,P8)	1924	Krupp	3223	4550	317–0	47–9	21–4	10.0
ex Shoreham 37, ex Therese Horn 34								

Note: *, ** Sold Poland 1939, renamed *Morska Wola* and *Stalowa Wola*, respectively

LORENTZENS REDERI CO, Hieronymous Heyerdahlsgaten 1, Oslo

Funnel: Yellow with white L superimposed on red over blue bands
Trades: Oil and petroleum

LORENTZENS SKIBS-A/S								
Tankers								
Caledonia (m)	1936	DeutsH	9892	14,825	510–8	66–1	28–4	12.5
James Stove (m2)	1931	Caledn	8215	11,420	469–6	59–2	26–0	11.5
ex Bralanta 35								
Scotia (m)	1939	Bremer	9972	14,800	510–9	66–1	28–5	13.0

LUND, EILERT, Bergen

Funnel: Yellow with houseflag
Services: General tramping

A/S NESJAR								
Betty	1919	Yoshi	2439	4050	290.1	41–0	21–0	9.0
ex Hundvaagø 23, ex Kaihei Maru 19								
Gunny	1920	Eltrgm	2362	4110	290.4	44–0	20–0	9.0
Marianne	1920	VanD2	1915	–	265.4	42–2	18.6	8.0
Torny (st)	1918	PuseyW	2424	3800	311–11	44–0	19–0	9.5
ex Marshall 27, launched as War Crater								

LUNDEGAARD & SONNER, (A, T & M Lundegaard), Farsund

Funnel: Black with black L&S on white band
Hull: Black
Services: General tramping

Note: * Sold Germany 1939, renamed *Karibisches Meer*

General cargo vessels								
DAMPSK-A/S CAROLVORE								
Aust	1920	Ropnr1	5630	8475	390.0	52–6	25–11	10.0
ex Lasta 39, ex Danybryn 38, ex Nailsea Manor 37, ex Nailsea Court 36, ex H H Asquith 32								
Vest	1920	Brtrm2	5074	8271	413–1	52–2	25–2	10.0
ex Galeb 39, ex Cefnbryn 36, ex Ardenhall 36, ex Silverbirch 24, ex Stonewall 22								
SKIBS-A/S LUNDEGAARD								
Bordvik	1920	Bergen	1624	2370	255–0	37–9	16–9	8.5
ex Dageid 29, ex Hufterø 20								
Spurt	1918	GLakeE	2061	3360	261–10	43–9	19–10	9.0
ex Craincreek 29								
SKIBS-A/S VIKING								
Norbryn (m)	1922	Doxfrd	5089	9005	433–0	54–0	25–7	10.5
ex Pacific Commerce 37, ex Dominion Miller 26								
Tanker								
Mendocino*	1917	Laing	6864	10,360	424.1	57–0	26–0	10.0

LYKKE, PER T, Fjordgaten 23–25, Trondheim

Funnel: Black with white L on red diamond
Services: General tramping

SKIBS-A/S EINVIK								
Einvik	1918	Polson	2000	3330	261–0	43–5	20–2	9.5
ex Rendal 34, ex Femund 28, ex Cormount 24, ex War Taurus 20								
LYKKES REDERI-A/S								
Ila (r/t)	1939	Porsgr	1583	2425	254–8	37–11	17–1	11.0

MARCUSSEN, SAM, Sjøfartsbygningen, Kongensgaten 6, Oslo

Funnel: Black, two white bands
Hull: Grey
Trades: Oil and petroleum

A/S I M A								
Tanker								
Ima (m)	1930	Doxfrd	6842	10,550	432–2	58–0	26–0	11.0

MARTENS, HARALD GRIEG, Torvalmenning 10, Postboks 183, Bergen

Services: General tramping

Note: Also *Blaafjeld I* (built 1918/1146gt), *Fanefjeld* (21/1355), *Jernfjeld* (17/1369) on ocean voyages

A/S D/S STORFJELD								
Snefjeld	1901	SmitJ	1644	2700	270.0	37–8	17–8	8.5
ex Ottoland 15, ex Maasstad 09								
Storfjeld	1899	SmitJ	2199	3650	293.0	42–10	19.9	8.0
ex Dordrecht 15								

MATHESEN, EYVIND, Kirkegaten 14–18, Oslo

Funnel: Yellow, black top, black band
Hull: Grey, red boot-topping
Trades: Oil and petroleum

A/S TANK								
Tankers								
James Hawson (m)	1930	ArmWh2	6074	9448	408–0	55–1	26–10	10.5
ex Kim 35								
Trondheim (m)	1939	Eriksb	8258	12,648	486–4	61–1	26–10	12.0

MATHIESEN, ARTHUR H, Grev Wedels Plass 4, Oslo

Funnel: Yellow with white band, blue cross (**x**) with red rectangle in centre containing white M
Trades: Oil and petroleum

Tankers								
REDERI-A/S DAMP								
Liss	1921	FurnH	5932	9817	413–6	53–0	28–7	9.5
REDERI-A/S MASCOT								
Barbro (m)	1934	Göta	6325	9900	422–0	55–2	26–10	11.5
Belinda (m)	1939	Göta	8325	12,670	483–10	59–6	27–9	12.5
Bianca (m)	1926	Göta	5688	8300	395–0	55–2	26–2	10.0
Britta (m2)	1934	Helsgr	6214	8870	421–4	54–9	25–9	11.5

MEIDELL, ANTON, Smaastrandgaten 1, Postboks 58, Bergen

Services: General tramping

A/S D/S FJELD								
Fjeld	1916	OsakaO	2960	5100	314–11	44–0	23–2	9.0
ex Tela 36, ex Totai Maru 20								
Fjord	1914	TyneIr	4032	7085	355.3	50–10	22–10	9.0
ex Orla 37								

MELSOM & MELSOM, Nanset, per Larvik

Funnel: Yellow with black top and blue M on white diamond on red band
Hull: Black
Services: Oil and petroleum trades; whaling

HVALFANGERSLSK GLOBUS A/S

Whale factory vessel

Lancing	1898	Connl	7866	10,000	470.0	57–2	27–0	10.0

ex Flackwell 25, ex Calanda 22, ex Omsk 21, ex Rio Tiete 15, x Knight Errant 14; conv tanker 25

HVALFANGERSLSK POLARIS A/S

Tankers

Polarsol (m)	1939	Curle	10,022	15,140	519–4	66–1	28–4	12.0
Polartank (m)	1930	Curle	6536	10,353	436–6	58–6	26–6	11.0

Whale factory vessel

N T Nielsen-Alonso (s2)	1900	Connl	9348	12,250	481.7	57–2	31–5	10.0

ex Polcevera 26, ex Custodian 23; conv general cargo 26

Note: Also a fleet of whalers

MEYER, P, Kirkegaten 14–18, Oslo

Funnel: Grey with white M superimposed on red over grey over red bands
Hull: Light grey, red boot-topping
Services: UK, NW Europe, Scandinavia–E coast Canada, Great Lakes; general tramping; oil and petroleum trades

General cargo vessels

A/S HAVBØR

Havbør (m)	1930	SHWR	7614	12,400	471–2	59–6	26–0	12.0

A/S HAVTOR

Havtor	1930	Porsgr	1524	2375	254–8	37–11	17–3	10.5

Tankers

A/S HAVKONG

Havkong (m)	1936	Kockum	9666	15,075	519–0	63–1	28–5	12.5

A/S HAVPRINS

Havprins (m)	1935	Kockum	8066	12,585	481–1	59–10	27–4	12.0

P MEYERS TANKREDERI-A/S

Havfru (m2)	1931	Kockum	7923	12,450	480–6	59–9	27–4	12.0

Note: Also general cargo vessel *Havmøy* (built 1937/1342gt)

MITHASSEL, REINH, Sjøfartsbygningen, Kongensgaten 6, Oslo

Funnel: Black with white M on black band between two narrow white bands
Services: General tramping

A/S MALMFART

Varangberg	1915	GLakeA	2482	4725	282.8	43–8	24–4	9.0

ex Varangfjell 39, ex Jotunfjell 39, ex Morris Adler 16; lengthened 34

Varangmalm	1919	Vuijk	3618	5940	360.6	48–4	20–10	9.0

ex Hadjipateras 36, ex Oued Beht 34, ex Zwarte Zee 28

MOHN, ALF, Nobelsgate 3, Oslo

Funnel: Yellow with houseflag
Hull: Light grey, red boot-topping
Services: General tramping

D/S A/S ØSTLANDET

Lionel (m2)	1926	Odense	5653	8825	388–0	52–6	26–7	11.5

MOLTZAU & CHRISTENSEN, Hieronymus Heyerdahlsgaten 1, Oslo

Funnel: Grey with white M on dark red band
Hull: Grey
Services: General tramping; oil and petroleum trades

MOLTZAU'S TANKREDERI A/S

Fruit carrier

Prinsdal* (m,P12)	1939	B&W	2988	2413	337–1	45–10	19–5	15.5

General cargo vessel

Brattdal (m)	1935	Bremer	4968	8570	432–6	55–7	25–5	12.5

Tankers

Glomdal (m)	bldg	Örsnd2	3856	5865	367–10	47–6	22–3	12.0
Kongsdal (m)	1937	Bremer	9959	14,890	510–9	65–9	28–5	12.0
Maridal (m2)	1934	Eriksb	6479	9800	422–6	55–4	26–9	11.5
Slemdal (m2)	1931	Odense	7374	10,700	445–6	60–2	26–0	11.5

Note: * Sold Germany 1939 before completion, renamed *Ahrensburg*

MØRLAND, ARNT J, Postboks 1, Arendal

Funnel: Black with large white M
Hull: Black, red boot-topping
Services: General tramping; oil and petroleum trades

A/S AGDESIDENS REDERI

General cargo vessel

Ravnaas (m)	1931	Eriksb	4019	6850	365–7	50–10	23–3	10.5

Tanker

Vardaas (m2)	1931	DeutsK	8176	11,725	485–0	59–6	26–0	11.5

MØRLANDS REDERI-A/S

General cargo vessels

Kvernaas	1918	Fredst	1819	3060	277–6	42–1	18–0	9.0

ex Ferro 29, ex Eidshorn 27, ex Ingrid Brodin 21

Takstaas	1916	Sørlan	1830	3050	277–7	42–1	17–7	8.0
ex Stokke 27, ex Standford 17								
MØRLANDS TANKREDERI-A/S								
Tanker								
Fjordaas (m2)	1931	DeutsK	7361	11,010	440–3	60–0	27–3	11.5

Funnel: Black with yellow EM monogram on red disc on yellow band
Hull: Black
Services: General tramping

MORTENSEN A/S, ERLING, Kongensgaten 7, Postboks 551, Oslo

A/S ALMORA								
Almora	1905	Murdo1	2433	4000	299.3	44–6	19–3	8.5
ex Caballero 22, ex Toften 20, ex O H Wiens 18								

Funnel: Black with black M on white diamond on red band; fruit carriers – yellow with white circles on red band
Hull: Fruit carriers, white; tankers, black
Services: Fruit – Florida –Rotterdam/ London/Liverpool; oil and petroleum trades

Note: * Sold Germany 1939, renamed *Tine Asmussen*

MOSVOLD, MARTIN, Postboks 10, Farsund

Fruit carriers								
Mosdale (m,P12)	1939	B&W	3022	2450	336–4	45–8	19–4	16.0
Moshill (m,P12)	bldg	Framns	2959	2750	334–2	46–2	21–0	15.5
Mosstrand (m)	order	Kaldns	3549	3800	343.0	48–9		15.5
Mostun (m,P12)	1938	Eriksb	2713	4306	314.4	50–4	24–2	15.5
A/S MOSVOLD SHIPPING CO								
Mosfruit (m,P12)	1938	Eriksb	2714	4300	314.4	50–4	24–2	15.5
Tankers								
MARTIN MOSVOLD								
Torborg	1921	BethSP	6042	8270	427–6	53–3	25–7	10.0
ex Henry Deutsch de la Meurthe 30								
A/S MOSVOLD SHIPPING CO								
Mosli (m)	1935	Eriksb	8291	12,800	493–6	61–1	27–2	12.0
Radix*	1919	Doxfrd	6795	10,040	429–4	55–4	28–2	10.0
ex Linerton 21; conv general cargo 21								
A/S MOSVOLDS REDERI I								
Acasta	1918	Laing	5229	8000	412–8	52–5	25–3	10.0
ex War Matron 19								
A/S MOSVOLDS REDERI II								
Litiopa	1917	Brtrm2	5356	8000	412–6	52–5	24–11	10.0
ex Dockleaf 20, ex Oleary 17								

Funnel: Yellow with black top separated by red, white, blue, and white over red bands
Hull: Black or grey, red boot-topping
Services: General tramping; oil and petroleum trades

Note: Hada County operated on County Line (*qv*) services; *Norma, Para, Salta,* operated on Den Norske Syd-Amerika Linje (*qv*) services

MOWINCKELS REDERI, A/S J LUDWIG, Postboks 196, Bergen

General cargo vessels								
Goya (m)	order	Akers	5230	8500	463–3	57–0	25–5	14.0
Hada County	1921	Craig2	4853	8030	386.0	53–0	24–10	12.0
ex Hada 28, ex Nordkyn 25								
Heina (m)	1925	B&W,K	4028	7625	389–4	52–2	24–9	10.0
Hørda	1920	GrayWH	4301	7616	380.1	53–6	23–0	10.0
Lista	1920	Dobson	3671	6685	370–0	52–1	23–6	10.0
ex Rio Grande 25								
Molda (m)	1937	Desch3	5137	8425	449–4	55–10	25–2	13.0
Norma (m2)	1930	Akers	4487	7835	406–0	54–8	24–3	12.0
Ogna (m)	1939	Bremer	4998	8700	430–9	55–8	25–6	13.0
Para (m2)	1921	Rijkee	3986	6420	390–0	51–4	22–10	10.5
ex Sao Paulo 21								
Ronda (m)	1937	Desch3	5136	8425	449–4	55–10	25–2	13.0
Rygja	1920	Blumr2	3535	6247	369–9	48–9	22–6	9.0
Salta (m2)	1920	SmitK	3907	6350	375.8	51–6	22–10	10.5
ex Salerno 21								
Sygna	1907	Dixon2	3881	7400	360.1	52–1	23–9	9.5
Troma (m)	1937	Doxfrd	5029	9240	439–2	54–5	25–6	11.0
launched as Rodsley								
Tankers								
Egda (m)	bldg	Odense	10,047	15,700	522–6	66–2	28–7	13.0
Fosna (m2)	1930	Caledn	8202	12,310	468–6	59–2	27–4	11.0
Grena (m)	1934	Göta	8117	12,300	473–0	59–2	27–8	12.0
Strinda (m)	1937	DeutsH	10,973	16,008	528–1	69–2	29–1	13.0
Vinga (m)	1927	Schich	7321	10,990	458–0	57–5	26–6	11.0

Pedersen: The motor vessel Dagfred *was completed by Akers at Oslo in 1930, and was fitted with two Akers 6-cylinder oil engines of 3100bhp. She was shelled and sunk by two Japanese cruisers off India on April 6 1942 when on voyage from Sandheads to Madras in ballast*
(J P Pedersen)

Einar Rasmussen: The motor tanker Polycastle, *built by Eriksbergs, Gothenburg, was launched on February 16 and completed in April 1939. She was under Allied control during 1940–45 and remained with these Norwegian owners for her entire career, being broken up in 1962–63*
(Einar Rasmussen)

NIELSEN & CO A/S, CHR, Larvik

Funnel: Black with black N on broad blue band bordered by two narrow yellow bands
Hull: Grey
Services: Oil and petroleum trades; whaling
Note: Also whalers each of about 200gt

HVALFANGERSELSKABET NORGE A/S

Tanker

Solheim (m2)	1934	Nakskv	8070	12,400	477–11	59–9	27–5	12.0

NILSON, ROB, & ARILD NYQUIST, Lille Strandgate 1, Postboks 161, Oslo

Services: General tramping
Note: Also smaller vessels

SKIBS-A/S AKERSHUS

Fagersten	1921	Eltrgm	2342	4110	290.4	44–0	20–0	9.0
ex Frithjof 1 27								

NILSSEN & SØNNER, Karl Johansgaten 8, Oslo

Services: General tramping

A/S BRAA								
Braa	1908	MéditH	2214	3600	291.0	44–0	18–6	7.5
ex Tosca 16, ex Evanger 16, ex Loiret 12								
A/S BRASK								
Brask	1911	Doxfrd	4079	7100	350.8	51–1	23–0	8.0
ex Bogen 25, ex Orangemead 23, ex Orangemoor 20								

NORDBO JR, TH, Haugesund

Funnel: Black with red over white, blue, white, red bands
Hull: Black
Services: General tramping

D/S A/S FALKEID

H C Flood	1917	Bergen	1907	3062	266.9	42–1	18.0	8.0

NORDENFJELDSKE D/S, A/S DET, Trondheim

Funnel: Black with broad red band between two narrow white bands
Hull: Black, red boot-topping, with white dividing line
Services: Norway, NW Europe, UK–Mediterranean
Note: This company was associated with Kristian Hansen O/Y (*qv* in Finland section)
Note: Also *Roald Jarl* (built 1913/1405gt), *Torfinn Jarl* (22/1481) and several short-sea and coastal vessels

Bruse Jarl (P2/1)	1923	Trondh	1890	2960	273–6	42–2	17–9	10.5
Einar Jarl	1921	Sørlan	1858	2985	277–7	42–1	17–7	10.5
Orm Jarl	1922	Fredst	1850	2960	278–0	42–1	17–7	10.5
Rolf Jarl (P2/1)	1920	Trondh	1917	3000	273–6	42–1	17–9	10.5
Svein Jarl	1919	Trondh	1908	2950	273–6	42–1	17–9	10.0
Tore Jarl (P2/1)	1920	Fredst	1514	2470	254–10	39–4	17–3	10.0

NORSKE AMERIKALINJE, A/S DEN, Jernbanetorvet 2, Oslo

Funnel: Yellow with red, white, blue, white, over red bands
Hull: Silver grey, red boot-topping with white dividing line
Services: Passenger and cargo – Stavanger, Bergen–New York; Oslo, Stavanger, Kristiansand, Bergen–New York–Portland ME–(Montreal summer)

Passenger vessels								
Bergensfjord (r/t2,P90/cab,155/t,500/3)								
	1913	Cammel	11,015	7300	530–0	61–2	25–2	17.5
Oslofjord (m2,P150/cab,300/t,400/3)								
	1938	Desch3	18,673	7600	588–0	73–5	43.4	19.5
Stavangerfjord (r/t2,P147/cab,207/t,820/3)								
	1918	Cammel	13,156	7500	553–0	64–2	27–3	17.5
General cargo vessels								
Drammensfjord	1920	CanVic	5339	8307	413–1	52–4	25–2	11.0
ex Tatjana 25								
Idefjord (P6)	1921	CanVic	4287	6307	375–0	49–10	24–1	13.5
Kongsfjord (m2)	1937	Eriksb	4000	7465	424–0	55–2	24–0	14.5
Kristianiafjord (st,P6)	1921	Napr&M	6759	9050	437–0	55–10	26–7	12.0
Norefjord (P12)	1920	WoodS2	3082	5450	331.7	46–8	23–3	11.0
ex Norefos 21								
Randsfjord (m2)	1937	Eriksb	3999	7465	424–0	55–4	24–0	14.5
Skiensfjord (P6)	1922	Napr&M	5922	7714	410–0	53–2	25–6	13.0
Tanafjord (P6)	1921	Napr&M	5922	7714	410–0	53–2	25–6	13.0
Tønsbergfjord (m2)	1930	Göta	3156	5770	362–0	50–2	23–5	14.0
Topdalsfjord (P6)	1921	CanVic	4271	6310	375–0	49–9	24–1	13.5
Trondhjemsfjord (st)	1921	Napr&M	6753	9050	437–0	55–10	26–7	12.0
Tyrifjord	1919	WoodS2	3080	5450	342–0	46–9	21–8	11.0
ex Ramfos 21, launched as War Dene								

NORSKE SYD-AMERIKA LINJE, DEN, Lille Strandgate 5, PO Box 316, Oslo

Den Norske Syd-Amerika Linje was owned by A/S Det Bergenske Dampskibsselskab (*qv*), A/S J Ludwig Mowinckels Rederi (*qv*), and Fred Olsen & Co (*qv*). See footnotes under those company entries for vessels operating on this service in 1939

Funnel: Yellow with houseflag – white SAL on red ground
Hull: Black or grey
Services: Norway–E coast South America

ODFJELL, A/S REDERIET, Minde per Bergen

SKIBS-A/S GABON								
Gabon (m2)	1931	Örsndl	4651	8600	408–6	54–8	25–7	11.0
ex Rose 38, ex Sunnanvik 34								
DAMPSK-A/S HASSEL								
Cypria (m2)	1931	B&W	4366	7650	393–2	54–2	24–0	11.5
SKIBS-A/S NYE KRISTIANBORG								
Estrella (m2)	1920	Rijkee	3888	6700	390–0	51–6	22–10	10.5
ex Athene 21								
Gran (m,P–)	1938	Burntd	4140	7700	395–4	53–10	24–6	13.0
SKIBS-A/S SELJE								
Selje	1930	Palmer	6698	12,200	448.3	59–2	27–0	10.0
A/S STORLI								
Birk	1920	Duncan	3664	7400	359.8	52–1	23.6	9.5

Funnel: Black, white band
Hull: Black, white band
Services: General tramping

Note: Also smaller vessels

ODLAND, JACOB, Postboks 23, Haugesund

DAMPSK-A/S PRODUCE								
Anna Odland (m)	1939	Bremer	4998	8700	430–9	55–6	25–6	13.5
Profit	1918	Laxe	1608	2450	257–10	37–11	16–6	9.0
ex Utsire 26								
Prominent (P–)	1918	HK&Wh	2232	3030	281–6	40–1	18–11	9.5
Pronto (P–)	1920	Zeelnd	2201	2935	285–0	41–4	19–1	8.5
ex Lombardia 23								
Prosper (P–)	1917	HK&Wh	2232	3030	281–6	40–1	18–11	9.5
Proteus	1902	Crown2	1679	2775	260.0	36–10	18–7	7.5

Funnel: Grey with black O on red and yellow diagonally halved houseflag, narrow black top
Hull: Grey, red boot-topping
Services: General tramping; vessels operate mainly in Far East

Note: Also *Produce* (built 1905/1171gt), *Promise* (20/1291)

OLSEN A/S, BRØDRENE, (A Gowart Olsen), Stavanger

A/S D/S LEDAAL								
General cargo vessels								
Ledaal	1899	Blyth	3076	5100	322–10	47–0	21–0	8.0
ex Skudefjord 34, ex Skogland 30, ex Polcarne 13, ex Everingham 11								
SKIBS-A/S SOLVANG								
Henrik Ibsen	1906	Dixon2	4671	7650	383.9	52–10	23–2	8.0
Tankers								
SKIBS-A/S SOLVANG								
Kongsgaard (m)	1937	Kockum	9467	15,000	523–5	63–1	28–5	13.0
Kongsstein (m)	order	Kockum	10,342	16,250	534–0	63–3	29–6	13.5
STAVANGER TANKREDERI A/S, Nedre Strandgaten 3, Stavanger								
Senator* (m2)	1934	Göta	6589	9850	422–0	55–2	26–6	11.0

Funnel: Yellow with houseflag, black top
Hull: Grey
Services: General tramping; oil and petroleum trades

Note: * Sold France 1939, renamed *Touraine*

OLSEN, CARL, Kolbjørnsvik, per Arendal

Tankers								
Balaklava (m2)	1929	Göta	7941	11,840	459–6	59–2	27–1	11.0
CARL OLSENS TANKREDERI-A/S								
Buccinum*	1910	Dixon2	5237	8075	405.0	54–2	24–0	8.5
ex Berwindmoor 17								

Trades: Oil and petroleum

Note: * Oil carried in cylindrical tanks

OLSEN & CO, FRED, Fred Olsensgaten 2, Oslo

Passenger/general cargo vessels								
A/S GANGER ROLF								
Black Prince (m2,P185/1,65/2)	1939	Akers	5039	5500	385–9	53–4	18–6	18.0
Black Watch (m2,P181/1,65/2)	1938	Akers	5035	5500	385–9	53–4	18–6	18.0
Bretagne (m,P88/1,26/2,34/3)	1937	Akers	3285	2150	315–1	46–2	18–1	13.0

Funnel: Yellow with houseflag, or yellow with houseflag on red band
Hull: Grey, green boot-topping, or black, red boot-topping
Services: Passenger and cargo – Norway–UK, NW Europe; Norway–Canary Islands; Scandinavia–Panama–San Diego–Los Angeles–San Francisco–Portland–Tacoma–Seattle–Victoria–Vancouver; Norway–Spain–Portugal–

France–Italy–N Africa–Levant–Black Sea ports

General cargo vessels								
A/S BONHEUR								
Abraham Lincoln (m2,P10/1)	1929	Odense	5740	9475	461–2	56–2	26–9	13.5
Bravo I	1908	Fredst	1585	2150	241.4	36–1	19–0	8.5
ex Barfond 24, ex Bravo 16								
San José*	1920	WoodS2	1995	3100	302.6	42–2	17.9	10.0
A/S BORGA								
Borga (m2)	1923	Akers	4821	7250	362.4	51–5	31.9	12.5
Knute Nelson (m2,P10/1)	1926	Odense	5749	9460	461–2	56–2	26–8	13.5
A/S GANGER ROLF								
Bajamar** (m2,P–)	1931	Akers	2757	3900	343–9	48–2	22–7	14.5
Bañaderos** (m2,P–)	1930	Akers	2728	3920	343–9	48–2	22–1	14.5
Benjamin Franklin (m2,P10/1)	1927	PenhtS	7034	9900	470–4	59–6	26–7	13.5
Betancuria** (m2,P12)	1933	Akers	2696	3315	357–4	48–7	21–11	16.0
Bolivar (m2)	bldg	Akers	5230	7500	445.2	57–4	24.1	14.5
Borgland*** (m2)	1918	Akers	3636	6450	362.0	51–6	31.0	11.5
Bra-Kar*** (m2)	1928	Akers	3778	6875	382–0	51–10	23–10	12.0
Breñas** (m2,P12)	1933	Akers	2687	3315	357–4	48–9	21–10	16.0
Burgos*** (st)	1920	Nyland	3219	4700	310.7	45–2	27.7	11.0
ex Brabant 26								
Laurits Swenson (m2,P10/1)	1930	Odense	5725	9500	459–5	56–2	26–9	13.5
DEN NORSKE MIDDELHAVSLINJE A/S								
Baalbek (m,P–)	1937	Akers	2160	3210	330–0	44–4	19–11	13.0
Baghdad (m,P–)	1936	Akers	2161	3200	330–0	44–4	19–11	13.0
Balkis (m,P–)	1939	Akers	2161	3190	330–0	44–4	19–11	13.0
Bayard (m,P–)	1936	Akers	2160	3215	330–0	44–4	19–11	13.0
Bosphorus (m)	1934	Akers	2111	3200	335–0	44–2	20–0	13.0
Braga (m)	1938	Lindhm	1671	2740	297–3	42–4	19–3	13.5
San Andres (m)	1921	SmitK	1975	3000	315–0	42–2	19–3	10.5
San Miguel (m)	1920	SmitK	2380	3000	298–0	39–10	19–1	10.5
Sardinia (m)	1921	SmitK	1975	3000	315–0	42–2	19–3	10.5
Solferino	1918	Nyland	2580	3600	300.0	40–0	24–0	11.0
Tanker								
A/S BORGA								
Borgny (m)	1929	Aalb3	3015	4100	305.4	50–2	17–2	10.0

Note: * Sold Argonaut Shipping Co Ltd (manager Eugene Eugenides), Greece, 1939, renamed *Argo*; ** large fruit-carrying capacity; *** operated on Den Norske Syd-Amerika Linje (*qv*) services
Note: Den Norkse Middelhavslinje A/S also owned *Segovia* (built 1922/1387gt), *Sevilla* (21/1383) and *Stromboli* (02/1376), and the group also owned many short-sea vessels, and others under 1500gt

OLSEN, KORNELIUS, Stavanger

Funnel: Yellow with red K inside white O on white band, bordered by narrow blue bands, separated from black top by yellow band
Services: Fruit trades; oil and petroleum trades
Note: Also general cargo vessels *Gansfjord* (built 1913/1087gt), *Lysefjord* (15/1091), *Stavangeren* (03/1003)

SKIBS-A/S BYFJORD								
Fruit carrier								
Anderson (P4)	1925	Bergen	1694	2200	255.1	35–8	22.3	13.5
A/S M/S HIDLEFJORD								
Tanker								
Hidlefjord (m2)	1928	B&W	7639	11,750	470–8	59–2	25–8	11.5

OLSEN AND I HYSING OLSEN, O GROLLE, Nygaten 7, Postboks 225, Bergen

Funnel: Black with white disc
Services: General tramping

O GROLLE OLSEN & I HYSING OLSENS REDERI-A/S								
Bur	1917	Ropnr2	4344	7100	360.0	52–2	23–2	9.0
ex Sedbergh 20								
Gro	1917	ThmpsJ	4211	7064	352.2	50–11	23–7	9.0
ex Tenterden 20								

OLSEN & UGELSTAD, Tollbodgaten 4, Oslo

Funnel: Black with white OU monogram intersecting two narrow white bands, or yellow with OU monogram interesecting two narrow white bands all on broad black band
Hull: Grey, red boot-topping
Services: UK, NW Europe–E coast Canada–Great Lakes; general tramping; oil and petroleum

General cargo vessels								
A/S LUKSEFJELL								
Haukefjell	1921	Forth	2495	4120	295.8	43–8	19–9	9.5
Makefjell	1932	Porsgr	1567	2413	254–8	37–9	17–1	10.5
Varangfjell*	1915	GLakeA	2482	4725	282.8	43–8	24–4	9.0
ex Jotunfjell 34, ex Morris Adler 16; lengthened 34								
A/S RUDOLF								
Glitrefjell (r/t)	1934	Porsgr	1568	2410	254–8	37–11	17–1	11.0

Tankers
A/S DOVREFJELL
Dovrefjell (m) bldg Eriksb 9862 14,750 518–5 65–4 28–7 13.5
Fagerfjell (m) 1935 Kockum 8072 12,560 482–0 59–10 27–4 12.5
Jotunfjell (m) 1937 Eriksb 8264 12,690 486–7 61–1 26–9 13.0
A/S FALKEFJELL
Falkefjell (m2) 1931 Kockum 7927 12,450 482–0 59–9 27–4 12.0
A/S FILEFJELL
Filefjell (m) 1930 SHWR 7616 12,400 471–2 59–6 26–0 12.0
Vardefjell (m) bldg Eriksb 8316 12,900 486–4 61–1 26–9 13.5

trades
Note: Also, operating mainly to E coast Canada and Great Lakes – general cargo vessels *Svanefjell* (built 1936/1371gt), *Tindefjell* (36/1337) both owned by A/S Falkefjell; *Carmelfjell* (35/1334), *Ørnefjell* (37/1334), Ravnefjell (38/1339), owned by A/S Luksefjell; *Harpefjell* (39.1333), *Rutenfjell* (35/1334), *Taborfjell* (38/1339), owned by A/S Rudolf
Note: * Sold R Mithassel 1939, renamed *Varangberg*

ONSTAD SHIPPING A/S, (Haakon S Onstad), Frithjof Nansens Plass 6, Oslo

Funnel: Yellow with red and gold shield on blue band
Hull: Black
Trades: Oil and petroleum

Tankers
SKIBS-A/S ALSE
Albert L Ellsworth (m)
1937 Göta 8309 12,500 483–10 59–2 27–7 12.5
SKIBS-A/S CANADA
Britamsea (m) 1939 Göta 8238 12,630 483–10 59–5 27–10 12.5

OPPEN, WILLY, & ODD SØRENSEN, Ovre Slotsgaten 7v, Oslo

Funnel: Black with two blue stars on white rectangle on red band
Hull: Dark grey, red boot-topping
Trades: Oil and petroleum

OPPEN & SØRENSEN'S TANKREDERI-A/S
Tanker
William Strachan (m)
1931 Work28 6157 9945 422–0 55–2 27–0 11.0

ØRVIG, OLAF, Postboks 525, Bergen

Funnel: Black with white stylised Maltese cross
Services: General tramping

ØRVIGS DAMPSK-A/S
Christian Krohg 1917 Gusto 1992 3300 269.2 42–2 18–0 9.0
Lyder Sagen 1918 OsakaO 3944 6500 357–6 49–10 23–8 10.0
ex Laval County 31, ex Storborg 25, ex Meichu Maru 19

OSTBERG, CHR, Kongensgaten 16, Oslo

Funnel: Black with black O on blue band
Hull: Grey
Services: General tramping

REDERIET BESSEGGEN A/S
Rita (m2) 1922 Burger 1753 2700 250.5 40–11 17–0 9.5
ex Zulia 35, ex Karibia 28, ex Romø 28, ex Dordrecht 25
REDERIET VINDEGGEN A/S
Tropic Sea (m2) 1920 Nakskv 5781 8750 406–10 53–2 27–2 10.5
ex Indien 38
Vindeggen* 1921 ArmWh1 3124 5050 330.8 46–11 22–0 10.5

Note: * Sold Germany 1939, renamed *Olga Traber*

ØSTERVOLD, HENRIK, Kong Oscarsgate 62, Bergen

Services: General tramping

D/S NEPTUN A/S
Cetus 1920 Murdo2 2614 3550 325–6 43–10 18–9 9.0
ex Moto 36
Libra 1917 Murdo2 1536 2200 256.9 36–7 16–4 8.5
ex Grangewood 36, ex Grangetown 21

Note: Also short-sea vessels

ØSTLANDSKE PETROLEUMS COMPAGNI A/S,
Prinsensgaten 3A, Postboks 359, Oslo

Funnel: Yellow, black top, separated by white band bearing red OPC emblem
Hull: Black
Trades: Oil and petroleum
Note: These companies were associated with Standard Oil Co of New Jersey (*qv* in United States section)
Trades: Oil and petroleum, mainly US Gulf and West Indies

Tankers
Haakon Hauan (m)
1935 Akers 6582 9850 423–0 56–4 27–6 11.0
A/S VESTLANDSKE PETROLEUMS COMPAGNI
Tiger 1921 Fairfd 3941 5049 351.0 47–0 23–0 9.0

OWREN, SIGURD, Prinsensgaten 12, Oslo

Note: Also smaller tankers

D/S MARINA A/S
Tanker
Moira (r/t) 1935 SHWR 1560 2460 259–0 42–1 16–10 11.0

PEDERSEN & SON, JOHN P, Sjøfartsbygningen 428–36, Kongensgaten 6, Oslo

Funnel: Yellow with white diamond on red band, separated from black top by narrow yellow band
Hull: Grey, red boot-topping
Services: General cargo and fruit trade to and from US and West Indies; W coast US and Canada–Australia; general tramping, oil and petroleum trades

A/S OCEAN								
General cargo vessels								
Dagfred (m2)	1930	Akers	4434	8280	385.2	54–10	25–0	12.0
Dagrun (m)	1928	Kockum	4562	8310	400–0	54–0	25–3	10.5
Tankers								
Dageid (m2)	1932	Akers	6361	9770	423–0	56–2	26–5	11.0
Daghild (m2)	1927	B&W	9272	14,495	488–6	64–2	25–3	11.0

PEHRSON & WESSEL, Drammen

Funnel: Black with black P&W on white diamond on red band bordered by narrow blue bands
Services: General tramping
Note: Also *Hildür I* (built 1919/1497gt), *Kronprins Olav* (08/1138)

A/S D/S DRAFN								
William Blumer	1920	Blumr2	3604	6250	369–9	48–9	22–6	9.0
J H WESSELS KULFORRETNING A/S								
Janna	1919	Albina	2197	3701	289.7	44–1	21–6	9.0
ex Sveigen 36, ex Glendola 29								

POULSEN, FINN, Prinsensgaten 12, Oslo

Trades: Oil and petroleum
Note: * Sold A I Langfeldt & Co 1939

SKIBS-A/S MADRONO								
Tanker								
Madrono*	1917	Palmer	5894	8607	407.5	52–5	25–0	9.5

PREBENSEN, J W, Redernes Hus, Oslo

Funnel: Black with blue P on white band bordered by two red bands
Trades: Oil and petroleum

PREBENSENS TANKREDERI-A/S								
Tanker								
Credo (m2)	1916	GöteM	5069	7210	367–4	55–2	24–7	9.0
ex Hamlet 37, laid down as Varjag								

PREBENSEN & BLAKSTAD, (Alex Prebensen and Arne Blakstad), Risør

Funnel: Black with blue P&B on white diamond on blue band
Hull: Grey, red boot-topping
Trades: Oil and petroleum

SKIBS-A/S GARM								
General cargo vessel								
Akera	1918	Conn2	5248	7874	412–0	52–4	25–1	10.5
ex War Singer 19; conv tanker 38								
Tanker								
Arthur W Sewall	1926	ArmWh1	6030	9444	352.1	60–0	33.0	10.5
SKIBS-A/S PREBA								
Tankers								
Alar (m)	1939	Laing	9430	14,660	503–10	68–10	28–2	12.5
Astrell (m2)	1925	Caledn	7595	11,730	476–0	59–2	27–3	11.0
ex Athelchief 38								

RAFEN & LEONNECHEN, Tønsberg

Funnel: Black with blue disc on white diamond on red rectangle (houseflag)
Hull: Black with white band, red boot-topping
Trades: Oil and petroleum
Note: * Sold Great Britain 1939, renamed *Athelchief*

Tankers								
SKIBS-A/S HAVSTEN								
Havsten (m)	1930	Curle	6161	10,040	437–0	58–6	26–6	11.0
SKIBS-A/S LEIESTEN								
Leiesten (m)	1930	ArmWh2	6118	9311	408–0	55–1	26–10	11.0
TØNSBERG TANK A/S								
Solsten (m)	1929	Curle	5379	8375	400–0	52–9	25–6	10.5
TØNSBERGS REDERI-A/S								
Buesten (m)	1927	Curle	5187	8100	400–0	52–9	25–6	10.5
Kongsten* (m)	1939	Curle	10,000	15,140	519–4	66–8	28–5	12.0
Storsten (m)	1926	Curle	5343	8100	400–0	52–9	25–6	10.5

RASMUSSEN, EINAR, Kristiansand

Funnel: Black with emblem on blue band
Hull: Grey
Trades: Oil and petroleum

Tankers								
KRISTIANSANDS TANKREDERI-A/S								
Polykarp (m2)	1931	Eriksb	6405	9765	422–7	55–4	26–9	12.0
ex Fanny Høegh 36								
A/S KRISTIANSANDS TANKREDERI II								
Polycastle (m)	1939	Eriksb	8267	12,820	486–3	61–1	26–9	13.0

RASMUSSEN & CO, JOHAN, (Johan Rasmussen and Torger Moe), Sandefjord

General cargo vessels								
VIKING CORP, Panama (Panamanian flag)								
Nordal	1939	Fredst	3845	7200	383–4	57–4	22–3	11.5
Nortun	bldg	Fredst	3663	7200	383–4	57–4	22–3	11.5
Tankers								
HVALF-A/S VESTFOLD								
Norfold (m)	1930	Curle	6370	10,335	436–6	58–6	26–7	11.0
TANKER CORP, Panama** (Panamanian flag)								
Norbris (m)	1930	SHWR	7619	12,460	471–2	59–6	27–8	11.5
Nore*** (m)	1930	SHWR	7619	12,478	471–2	59–6	27–7	11.0
Norlys (m)	1936	DeutsH	9892	14,800	510–8	66–1	28–5	12.0
Norness (m)	1939	DeutsH	9577	14,863	510–7	65–9	28–4	12.0
Norvik (m)	1938	DeutsH	9555	14,800	510–7	65–9	28–4	12.0
Norvinn (m)	1930	Curle	6322	10,476	436–6	58–8	26–6	11.0
Whale factory vessels								
HVALF-A/S ROSSHAVET								
Sir James Clark Ross (m2)	1930	FurnH	14,362	21,828	554–0	74–4	33–10	11.0
VESTFOLD CORP, Panama* (Panamanian flag)								
Vestfold (s2)	1931	FurnH	14,547	21,800	554–1	74–4	33–8	11.0

Funnel: Yellow with two narrow black bands
Hull: Tankers, general cargo vessel – light grey, red boot-topping; whalers –black with white band, red boot-topping
Services: Oil and petroleum trades; general tramping; whaling

Note: * Vestfold Corp was a subsidiary of Vestfold Whaling Co Ltd, London EC2, a UK associate company of Johan Rasmussen & Co; ** Tanker Corp was a subsidiary of Viking Tanker Co Ltd, London EC2, a UK associate company of Johan Rasmussen & Co; *** sold France 1939, renamed *Limousin*

RASMUSSEN, KAARE K, Hjertnespromenaden 9, Sandefjord

K K RASMUSSENS REDERI-A/S								
K G Meldahl	1938	Fredst	3799	7260	383–4	57–4	22–3	11.0

Funnel: Yellow, red or blue band, white R
Hull: Grey
Services: General tramping

REIM, CHR, J, Porsgrunn

A/S FRANK								
Dixie (r/t)	1937	Porsgr	1571	2425	254–8	37–11	17–1	11.0
Frisco (r/t)	1939	Porsgr	1582	2425	254–8	37–11	17–1	11.0

Funnel: Black with green band bordered by two narrow white bands
Hull: Black
Services: General tramping

REKSTEN, HILMAR, Fjøsanger, per Bergen

Vespasian (r/t)	1935	Porsgr	1570	2424	254–8	37–11	17–1	11.0
ex Betta 39								
REDERI-A/S HADRIAN								
Hadrian	1919	Bergen	1620	2450	255–0	37–9	16–0	9.0
ex Nyhavn 33								
REDERI-A/S NERVA								
Nerva	1924	Curle	1564	2500	250.6	39–10	17–6	10.5
ex Gwentgate 35, ex Forestgate 26								
A/S REDERIET TITANIAN								
Titanian (m)	1924	SHWR	4880	8669	413–4	53–6	25–2	10.0
ex Iossifoglu 27								

Funnel: Black with broad white band containing two narow blue bands
Hull: Grey
Services: NW Europe–Great Lakes (summer) (*Hadrian, Nerva, Octavian, Vespasian*); general tramping

Note: Also *Octavian* (built 1938/1345gt) owned by A/S Rederiet Julian, *Trajan* (15/1347) owned by Skibs-A/S Trajan, and short-sea vessels

RINGDAL, OLAV, Tollbodgaten 28, Oslo

SKIBS-A/S GDYNIA								
Vigilant (m2)	1923	DeutsH	4765	7568	416–0	54–3	25–8	10.0
ex Talisman 37								
Vigrid (m2)	1923	DeutsH	4765	7568	416–0	54–3	25–7	10.0
ex Titania 37								
RINGDALS REDERI-A/S								
Ringar (m)	1921	Rosenb	5013	9700	428–9	54–6	26–1	10.0
ex Handicap 37								
SKIBS-A/S RINGULV								
Ringulv	1903	Napr&M	5153	7820	390.0	52–0	24–4	9.0
ex Norskehavet 37, ex Sigrun 29, ex Lyngenfjord 24, ex Keramiai 15; conv fish factory 37, conv general cargo 29								
SKIBS-A/S RINGWOOD								
Ringwood (m2)	1926	ArmWhl	7203	10,282	427–10	67–1	26–6	10.5
ex Beljeanne 37								

Funnel: Black with houseflag
Hull: Black or grey
Services: General tramping

Funnel: Yellow with two red bands
Hull: Grey
Services: General tramping; oil and petroleum trades

RØD, REIDAR, Tønsberg

SKIBS-A/S OILTANK 3

General cargo vessel								
Bernhard (m)	1924	Sørlan	3563	5963	343–1	50–1	22–6	10.5
ex Innaren 37								
Tanker								
Belita (m)	1933	Göta	6323	9840	422–0	55–3	26–9	11.5

Funnel: Black with red and white emblem
Hull: Black, red boot-topping
Services: General tramping

RØED & CO, HJALMAR, (Finn Christensen), Tønsberg

A/S MAUD								
Maud (m)	1930	B&W	3189	5550	340–9	50–0	20–6	11.0
A/S ULABRAND								
L A Christensen (m)	1925	DeutsH	4362	7890	395–8	53–4	25–3	11.0

Services: General tramping

RØGENÆS, FIN, Haugesund

SKIBS-A/S BRATSBERG

Ada	1921	BrownG	2456	4165	290.2	44–0	20–8	9.0

Funnel: Black with white R on red band
Hull: Black, red boot-topping
Services: General tramping

RØGENÆS, NIELS, Haugesund

A/S THEOLOGOS

Anna Sofie	1919	TyneIr	3100	5050	342–0	46–8	21–8	10.0
ex War Cove 20								
Fjordheim (r/t)	1930	SHWRSd	4115	6700	374.8	51–6	21–7	11.0
Skogheim	1919	Sørlan	2669	–	300.4	47–1	20.9	9.0

Funnel: Yellow with emblem
Hull: Grey
Trades: Oil and petroleum

RØNNEBERG, GEORG, & JENS FR GALTUNG, Moss

A/S ASPLUND

Tanker								
Realf (m)	1937	Kockum	8083	12,500	485–0	59–10	27–5	12.0

Services: General tramping

RUUD-PEDERSEN, BJARNE, Skippergaten 14, Oslo

DAMPSK-A/S ESITO

Victo	1906	ThmpR2	3655	6170	346.5	50–10	22.9	8.5
ex Skogstad 27								

Funnel: Black with red S on white band
Services: General tramping
Note: * Started by Newcastle Shipbuilding Co Ltd, completed Forth Ship building & Engineering Co (1921) Ltd
Notes: Also *Hild* (built 1919/1356gt) and short-sea vessels

SALVESEN, JACOB, Farsund

A/S SALVESEN								
Spind	1917	Austin	2129	3490	285.0	43–5	18.9	8.75
ex Homledal 35, ex Haslemere 20								
A/S SKIBSFART								
Far	1921	Forth*	2475	4120	295.5	43–9	19–9	9.5
ex Ravnefjell 37								

Funnel: Black with white K
Hull: Black
Services: General tramping; oil and petroleum trades

SAMUELSEN, ERLING H, Karl Johansgaten 1, Oslo

ERLING H SAMUELSENS REDERI-A/S

General cargo vessels								
Helgøy (m2)	1920	B&W	5614	9520	444–4	55–2	26–7	13.0
ex Theodore Roosevelt 36								
Soløy (m)	1929	Kockum	4402	8250	400–0	54–0	25–3	11.0
Tankers								
Innerøy (m)	1936	Eriksb	8260	12,675	486–0	61–1	26–10	12.0
New Zealand (m2)	1930	Curle	9311	13,500	484.3	65–6	28–7	11.5

Salvesen: The small steamer Hild, *which was completed at the 'De Maas' shipyard at Slikkerveer in 1919, quite often made ocean voyages, and was wrecked on September 17 1940 at Petite Valley, Quebec, when on voyage from Liverpool to Petite Valley and Gaspe in ballast (Photograph courtesy Torbjørn Larsson-Fedde, Farsund)*

Chr Smith: The twin-screw heavy-lift vessel Belpareil, *completed by Armstrong, Whitworth in July 1926, was fitted with two Armstrong, Whitworth 4-cylinder oil engines of 2750bhp. Her three heavy lift derricks had a capacity of 100 tons and she was suitable for carrying railway locomotives and coaches and small vessels such as tugs and barges. Following wartime service under Allied control, she remained under the Norwegian flag until 1965, when sold to a Panamanian company and renamed* New Zealand Venture. *In 1970 she was sold to Yugoslavia and renamed* Buga, *and was broken up in Yugoslavia in 1984. Her original engines were replaced in April 1950 by two Bremer Vulkan/MAN 4-cylinder oil engines of 3500bhp (Belships Co)*

Tønnevold: The tanker Thorhild, *completed by Götaverken in August 1935, was fitted with two Götaverken 6-cylinder oil engines of 7000ihp, and was among the largest tankers built at that shipyard prewar. She survived the Second World War and in 1954 was sold to Norwegian owner Einar Rasmussen and renamed* Polyrover. *She was broken up in 1959 (O T Tønnevold archives)*

Funnel: Black with white S on blue diamond on white band
Hull: Black
Services: General tramping

SAMUELSEN, JENS, Sunde, Farsund

SKIBS-A/S NOVASLI

Novasli	1920	ThmpR2	3204	5500	354–0	48–0	20–9	9.0
ex Maplewood 29, ex Ronalee 22								

Funnel: Black with white S on blue diamond on white band
Hull: Black
Services: General tramping

SAMUELSEN, VICTOR, Sunde, Farsund

SKIBS-A/S SUNDE

Løvland	1907	Short2	2389	4050	295.0	45–0	19.6	10.0
Løvstad	1921	Clyde	3246	5500	333–0	47–2	22–4	8.75
ex Georgios Mantacas 38, launched as Georgios								

Funnel: Black with black S on red band between narrow white bands
Services: General tramping
Note: Also *Grana* (built 1920/1297gt), *Silja* (19/1259)

SANDAAS, K, Kragerø

Eika (r/t)	1939	Langsd	1503	2620	254–10	38–8	17.2	11.0

Services: General tramping

SANNES, ERLING, Bodø

D/S A/S SYDFART

Banan	1913	Nyland	1581	1900	250.0	34–9	18–10	11.0
ex Edward M Raphel 36, ex Banan 36								

Services: General tramping

SCHAGE, VICTOR L, Radhusgaten 25, Oslo

A/S DUX

Dux	1934	Trondh	1590	2480	254–9	40–3	16–10	10.5

Funnel: Black with red over white, blue, white, red bands
Services: General tramping

SCOTT-HANSEN, OYVIND, Hieronymus Heyerdahlsgaten 1, Oslo

SCOTT-HANSENS REDERI-A/S

Nandi	1920	ArsnLo	1999	3050	281–6	39–8	19–10	9.5
ex Alba 37, ex Alga 37, ex Député Josselin de Rohan 36								

Funnel: Yellow with blue and white houseflag, black top
Services: General tramping

SIMONSEN & ASTRUP, Kirkegaten 14–18, Oslo

SKIBS-A/S MIRVA

Spero	1919	Asaki	3619	5453	330.5	46–2	23–0	9.5
ex Pacifico 34, ex Taigi Maru 20								

Funnel: Yellow with black S on white diamond bordered in blue and red
Services: General tramping; oil and petroleum trades

Note: * Sold Estonia 1939, renamed *Neme*; ** sold Finland 1939, renamed *Karl-Erik*

SKAUGEN, I M, Frithjof Nansens Plass 6, Oslo

DAMPSK-A/S EIKLAND

General cargo vessels								
Erland*	1914	OsbGr1	1914	3350	279.3	42–0	18.4	8.5
ex Vedamore 28, ex Wingate 22								
Sophocles (m)	1939	Göta	5184	9200	442–9	56–6	26–0	14.0
Tankers								
Alcides (m)	1930	Curle	7634	11,520	460.5	59–6	26–0	11.0
Pericles (m)	1936	Göta	8324	12,500	481–0	59–3	27–11	12.0
Salamis (m)	1939	Göta	8286	12,570	483–10	59–5	27–11	12.5

SALAMIS A/S

General cargo vessel								
Salamis**	1923	Trondh	1945	3100	265.8	42–2	18–0	9.5
ex Oddvar 37								

Funnel: Black with houseflag
Hull: Black, red boot-topping
Services: General tramping; oil and petroleum trades

SKJELBRED, O A T, (Kr Knudsen), Kristiansand

SKJELBREDS REDERI-A/S

General cargo vessels								
Benwood	1910	Craig2	3931	6900	344.9	51–4	23–1	9.0
Concordia (m)	bldg	B&W	5154	9000	440–8	56–5	25–6	13.0

Skjelbred (m) 1937 B&W 5096 8800 440–9 56–0 25–6 13.5
Truth* 1910 ThmpsJ 3655 6131 356.0 50–6 21–5 9.0
ex Ariadne Christine 20
Tanker
Egerø (m) 1929 SHWR 7590 12,100 464–0 61–0 27–0 11.0

Note: * Sold Panama 1939, renamed *Vahva*

SKOGLAND A/S, VALDEMAR, Salhusveien 125, Postboks 19, Haugesund

Funnel: Black with red (five) and white (four) alternating bands
Hull: Grey, red boot-topping
Services: General tramping

D/S A/S ANGLO
Carrier 1921 Seine 3105 4740 313.6 46–3 20–2 9.5
ex Capitaine Bonelli 36
ANGLO STEAMSHIP CORP, Panama (Panamanian flag)
Anglo 1905 ThmpsJ 2978 4770 327–0 46–6 21–2 7.5
ex Anana 37, ex Nordamerika 35
Basra (m) 1915 RottDD 3196 5452 331.2 48–0 24.5 8.25
ex Wieringen 38, ex Turbinia 24, laid down as Urk; conv steamer 24
D/S A/S CARRIER
Mammy 1911 B&W 1656 2004 266–6 35–9 18–2 8.0
ex Mandeville 35
D/S A/S NOTOS
Notos 1898 Irvin1 2713 4800 324.0 46–0 20.5 7.5
ex Knut Jarl 33, ex Laura Mærsk 08, ex Laura 06
D/S A/S TRANSPORT
Boreas 1920 BritAm 2801 4400 333–7 43–11 25–1 9.0
ex Canadian Squatter 34

SMEDVIG, PEDER, Postboks 210, Stavanger

Funnel: Yellow with red five-pointed star on white band
Hull: Black
Services: General tramping; oil and petroleum trades

General cargo vessels
SMEDVIG'S REDERI-A/S
Favorit 1920 PuseyW 2826 4350 315–0 44–2 21–3 10.0
ex Ionier 29, ex Fishers Island 20
D/S A/S VENI
Veni 1901 Pgill1 3006 4880 324.1 47–1 20–6 7.75
ex Tonbridge 19
Tanker
SMEDVIG'S TANKREDERI-A/S
Glittre (m2) 1928 Göta 6409 9500 421–10 55–4 26–3 12.0

Note: Also short-sea vessels

SMITH, CHRISTEN, Hieronymus Heyerdahlsgaten 1, Oslo

Funnel: Grey
Hull: Grey, red boot-topping
Services: Specialising in carriage of heavy loads, such as small craft, locomotives, etc, worldwide

SKIBS-A/S BELSHIPS CO LTD
Belmoira (m) 1928 ArmWh1 3214 4518 349–0 49–2 19–9 11.0
Belnor (m) 1926 ArmWh1 2871 3940 328–9 46–2 19–10 10.0
Belpamela (m) 1928 ArmWh1 3215 4518 349–0 49–2 19–9 11.0
Belpareil (m2) 1926 ArmWh1 7203 10,282 427–10 68–8 24–6 11.0
Belray (m) 1926 ArmWh1 2888 4094 328–9 46–5 19–8 10.0

SOMMERFELDT, T, & O PEDERSEN

Services: General tramping

SKIPS-A/S RENA
Rena (m2) 1924 Odense 5242 8035 395–5 50–2 25–8 10.0
ex Fördefjord 37, ex Emma Mærsk 26

SØRENSEN & SØNNER, C H, Arendal

Funnel: Black with white S on broad blue band bordered by narrow red over white bands above and narrow white over red bands below
Hull: Light grey, red boot-topping
Services: Fruit trades; general tramping; oil and petroleum trades

General cargo vessels
William Blumer* 1920 Blumr2 3604 6250 369–9 48–9 22–6 9.0
SKIBS-A/S VELOX
Velox (m2) 1922 Kockum 3831 7000 381–6 51–6 23–4 10.5
ex Sveajarl 36, ex Arator 22

A/S VIVA
Viva 1938 Fredst 3798 7260 383–4 57–4 22–8 11.0
Fruit carriers
A/S VIATOR
Viator** (m) 1938 Örsnd2 3053 2255 336–5 45–8 18–11 16.0
Viator (m) bldg B&W 3035 2900 336–4 47–3 20–5 16.0

H Virik: The tanker Sandar *was completed by Burmeister & Wain at Copenhagen in December 1928, and was fitted with two B&W 6-cylinder oil engines of 3200bhp. In 1940* Sandar *came under Admiralty control, and on May 2 1942 when on voyage from Trinidad to Gibraltar with 11,500 tons of fuel oil, she was torpedoed and sunk by* U66 *(Alex Duncan)*

Wallem: The steamer Solviken *photographed in May 1935, was laid down by Burmeister & Wain for Russian owners as* Aleut, *but completed for the East Asiatic Co, Denmark, as* St Lucia. *She was transferred to Russia in 1910 and renamed* Aleut, *and in 1912* Toula. *In March 1920 she was under the control of the White Russian administration in the Crimea, but with the fall of the Crimea in November that year was transferred to Russian interests based in Paris. In February 1923 she was sold to Wallem and renamed* Solviken, *and in 1940 following a change of beneficial owner was renamed* Capella *under the Panamanian flag. In December 1941 she was seized off Saigon by the Japanese, and in August 1942 renamed* Minami Maru. *In April 1944 she was torpedoed and sunk by the US submarine* Flying Fish *when moored off Kita Daito-Jima (Wallem & Co)*

Tanker
SKIBS-A/S AINO

Aino (m)	1932	ArmWh2	6126	9430	408–0	55–1	26–8	11.0
ex Ashmore 34								

Note: * Sold A/S D/S Drafn (Pehrson & Wessel) 1939; ** sold Germany 1939, renamed *Angelburg*

SØRENSEN & CO, O B, Arendal

Funnel: Yellow with black top and emblem between two bands
Hull: Black
Trades: Oil and petroleum
Note: * Managing director of this company was S H Smith Sørensen (*qv* below)

DAMPSK-A/S ORA*
Tanker

Ora (m)	1938	Kockum	9537	14,985	523–11	63–1	28–5	13.0

SØRENSEN, S H SMITH, Tromøy, per Arendal

Funnel: Yellow with black top and emblem between two bands
Hull: Black
Trades: Oil and petroleum

Tankers
A/S HERON

Heron*	1919	Lithgw	5540	8300	412–0	52–3	25–1	10.5
ex Chiton 26, ex War Shikari 21								
Heron (m)	bldg	Kockum	8484	13,524	496–3	62–2	27–2	13.5
SMITH SØRENSENS TANKREDERI-A/S								
O B Sørensen (m2)	1931	Kockum	7919	12,500	480–11	59–8	27–4	12.5
Orion (m)	1936	Kockum	8064	12,500	481–8	59–10	27–4	12.5

Note: * Sold Germany 1939, renamed *Rekum*
Note: See also under O B Sørensen & Co

STAMER, CLAUS, Bergen

Services: General tramping

STAMERS REDERI-A/S

Heimgar (m)	1921	Örsnd2	2978	4565	316–3	44–1	20–9	10.5
ex Sparreholm 36, ex Sulina 27								

STANG, J B, Jernbanetorvet 2, Oslo

Funnel: Black with white cross on blue rectangle on red band
Hull: Black or grey
Services: General tramping

Note: Also vessels under 1500gt

A/S STANDARD

Stanja	1915	Nyland	1845	3015	276–1	42–1	17–5	10.0
Star	1922	Ardrsn	1531	2500	255.2	39–6	18–0	10.0
ex Troldfos 23								

STAUBO & CO, HELMER, Sjøfartsbygningen, Kongensgaten 6, Oslo

Funnel: Yellow with blue diamond on white band bordered by narrow red bands
Hull: Fruit carriers – white, red boot-topping; general cargo vessel and tanker – grey
Services: Fruit trades, usually chartered to US companies; general tramping; oil and petroleum trades

A/S HAV
Fruit carriers

Crawford Ellis (P–)	1930	SHWR	2161	3200	280.8	40–0	18–11	15.5
Hvoslef (P–)	1927	SHWR	1630	2140	255.1	35–6	20–0	15.0
A/S HAV & A/S HAVTANK								
General cargo vessel								
Hav (m)	1939	SHWR	5062	9530	432–5	57–6	26–1	13.0
Tanker								
John P Pedersen (m)	1930	SHWR	6128	9960	435–0	58–6	25–9	11.5

STENERSEN, JOHAN, Hieronymus Heyerdahlsgaten 1, Oslo

Funnel: Yellow with red W
Hull: Grey, dark red boot-topping
Trades: Oil and petroleum

Tankers

Kathrine Stenersen (m)								
	order	Kockum	10,300	16,250	534–0	63–2	29–6	13.5
STENERSENS TANKREDERI-A/S								
Ragnhild Stenersen (m)								
	order	Göta	11,163	17,300	540–0	66–5	29–11	13.5
WAAGES TANKREDERI-A/S								
Rigmor (m2)	1931	Göta	6305	9610	422–0	55–4	26–5	12.0
WAAGES TANKREDERI II A/S								
Sysla (m2)	1932	Göta	6367	9670	422–0	55–4	26–5	12.0

STEPHANSEN & TORGERSEN, Radhusgaten 25, Oslo

Trades: Oil and petroleum

SKIBS-A/S DIESELTANK
Tanker

Strix (m2)	1930	Göta	6219	9700	422–0	55–4	26–5	12.0

Funnel: Black with white S on broad red band between two narrow white bands
Services: General tramping

STØLT-NIELSEN & SONNER A/S, B, Haugesund

A/S D/S FACTO								
Facto	1921	Larvik	1522	2500	244.8	39–6	17–1	9.5
ex Octo 21								
Pluto	1918	Laxe	1598	2400	267–10	37–11	16–6	9.5
ex Röver 22								

Services: Whaling

STOREN, FINN, Kragerø

HVALF-A/S LABOR								
Whale oil factory								
Labor	1904	LithR	4479	6225	360.0	49–0	24–0	8.5
ex Roald Amundsen 37, ex Cape Breton 22; conv general cargo 22								

Funnel: Black
Hull: Black
Services: General tramping
Note: Also *Bravore* (built 1916/1458gt), *Ellavore* (25/1302)

STRAY & SON, GUNSTEIN, Farsund

A/S VORE								
Annavore	1921	Murdo2	3324	5500	333.1	49–0	22.4	9.0

Funnel: Yellow with houseflag
Services: General tramping; oil and petroleum trades

STRAY, MARCUS CHR, Postboks 110, Tollbodgaten 10, Kristiansand

General cargo vessels								
A/S ALFA								
Astra	1919	Staten	2164	3570	276–6	42–2	20–11	9.5
ex York Harbor 29, launched as George Harbor, laid down as War Tramp								
A/S ANATINA								
Anatina (m)	1939	Örsnd2	4986	9501	453–9	57–5	25–7	14.0
Tanker								
A/S ALIDA								
Arena (m2)	1927	Göta	6392	9427	422–0	55–4	26–5	11.0
ex Svolder 37								

Funnel: Yellow with blue AS monogram on white disc on blue band containing five white five-pointed stars, black top
Services: Tramping, vessels operated in Far East
Note: Also *Dukat* (built 1920/1350gt), *Ngow Hock* (20/1329)

SVEEN, ARNE, Postboks 25, Hvalstad, per Oslo

A/S ARNE SVEENS REDERI								
Mui Hock	1936	Nyland	2144	3600	295–0	44–2	19–0	10.5

Funnel: Black with red star on white disc on green band
Hull: White, red boot-topping
Trades: Oil and petroleum

Note: This company was controlled by The Texas Co (*qv* in United States section), and its vessels managed by Haakon Chr Mathiesen, Stortingsgaten 30, Oslo

TEXAS CO (NORWAY) A/S, THE, Kongensgaten 15, Oslo

Tankers								
America (m2)	bldg	DeutsH	10,047	14,300	522–0	67–4	27–6	13.0
Brasil (m2)	1935	Nakskv	8130	12,400	477–0	59–9	27–5	12.0
Britannia (m2)	1939	DeutsH	9977	14,270	523–2	67–5	27–8	13.0
Europe (m)	1934	Odense	8371	12,835	485–11	62–4	27–0	12.0
Gallia (m2)	1939	DeutsH	9968	14,250	522–0	67–5	27–8	13.0
Germania (m2)	1939	DeutsH	9977	14,560	522–0	67–4	27–8	13.0
Italia (m2)	1939	DeutsH	9900	14,560	522–0	67–5	27–8	13.0
North America (m2)	1939	DeutsH	9789	14,300	522–0	67–4	27–6	13.0
Nueva Andalucia (m2)	bldg	DeutsH	10,044	14,150	525–0	67–4	27–6	13.0
Nueva Granada (m2)	1937	DeutsH	9968	14,150	522–0	67–5	27–8	13.0
Skandinavia (m2)	bldg	DeutsH	10,044	14,300	523–2	67–0	27–6	13.0
Solitaire (m2)	1920	Texas	3160	4750	315.4	43–8	23–3	9.5
South America (m2)	1931	Nakskv	6246	9640	417–9	55–2	26–8	10.5
ex Borneo 33, ex Henrik Ameln 32								

Funnel: Yellow with houseflag, black top
Services: General tramping

THORVIK, M, Lille Strandgate 1, Oslo

DAMPSK-A/S TRULS								
Bris	1938	Trondh	2027	3400	302–9	44–2	19–0	11.0
Kari	1920	Hill	1925	3000	270.0	42–3	18–0	9.5
ex Leif 37, ex Bygdø 25								
Sarpen	1912	Fredst	1864	3050	275–11	42–0	17–7	8.5

TØNNNEVOLD & CO A/S, O T, Grimstad

Funnel: Yellow with white T on red band
Hull: Grey
Trades: Oil and petroleum

Tankers								
TØNNEVOLDS REDERI-A/S								
Thelma (m)	1937	Göta	8297	12,800	483–0	59–2	27–11	12.5
Thordis (m2)	1931	Caledn	8210	11,410	469–6	59–2	26–0	12.0
TØNNEVOLDS TANKREDERI-A/S								
Thorhild (m2)	1935	Göta	10,316	15,625	512–8	64–0	29–8	12.0

TØNSBERG HVALFANGERSELSKAP A/S, Tønsberg

Funnel: Black with green band
Services: Whaling

Whale factory vessel								
Orwell	1905	Conn2	7920	11,500	470.0	58.0	27–0	11.0
ex Knight Templar 25; conv general cargo 25								

Note: Also a fleet of whalers

TORGERSEN & CO A/S, HANS H, Tønsberg

Funnel: Black with blue and white houseflag
Trades: Oil and petroleum

Tankers								
BULLS TANKREDERI-A/S								
Peik (m)	1930	ArmWh2	6099	10,020	409–2	55–1	26–9	10.5
SKIBS-A/S OILTANK								
Bello (m)	1930	SHWR	6125	9830	435–0	58–6	25–9	12.0

TORGERSEN, T B, Kongensgaten 15, Oslo

Services: Vessels operated in Far East

SKIBS-A/S PASAT								
Pasat	1932	SHWR	1920	2500	266.2	40–0	19–4	12.0
ex Grande Terre 39, ex Anatolian 33								
SKIBS-A/S THULE								
Fu Yang	1921	NSWGov	3359	6229	341–1	47–11	24–0	9.0
ex Mione 37, ex Maranoa 35, ex Eromanga 26								
Sheng Hwa	1920	Coughl	5492	8368	413–0	52–5	25–4	10.5
ex Mitwo 38, ex Prospector 35, ex Canadian Prospector 34								
Ven-koh	1920	Coughl	5752	8692	427–0	54–1	24–2	10.5
ex City of Vancouver 36								

Note: Also smaller vessels

TORKILDSEN, KARL, Ovre Alle 5, Trondheim

Services: General tramping

SKIBS-A/S TAUTRA								
Tautra	1920	OsbGr2	1749	2512	258.0	39–9	17–2	9.0
ex St Joseph 37, ex S B Lund 28								
SKIBS-A/S TROLLA								
Trolla	1923	Laxe	1598	2400	267–10	37–11	16–6	9.0
ex Ringaas 28								

TORKILDSEN, VILHELM, Kong Oscarsgate 62, Postboks 38, Bergen

Funnel: Yellow with three narrow red bands, black top
Services: General tramping
Note: Also *Fana* (built 1939/1345gt)

SKIBS-A/S VILHELM TORKILDSENS REDERI								
Marstenen	1915	Fredst	1832	3050	275–11	42–1	17–7	10.0
launched as Viv								

TSCHUDI & EITZEN, Kirkegaten 2, Postboks 428, Oslo

Funnel: Black with diagonally halved white and blue shield
Hull: Grey or black, red boot-topping
Services: General tramping; oil and petroleum trades

General cargo vessels								
SKIBS-A/S AVANTI								
Arosa (m)	1924	McMlln	5043	8000	400.0	53–3	24–2	9.5
ex Wind 38, ex Elmworth 37								
Maloja (m2)	1930	Fredst	6400	9400	386.6	60–2	25–2	11.5
ex Danwood 36								
HENRY TSCHUDIS TANKREDERI-A/S								
Silvaplana (m)	1938	Kockum	4793	9325	409–9	55–9	25.5	13.5
Tankers								
SKIBS-A/S AVANTI								
Turicum (m2)	1928	Giessn	7824	10,885	451–10	59–2	27–6	12.0
SKIBS-A/S NAVALIS								
B P Newton (m)	bldg	Kockum	10,324	16,000	534–0	63–2	29–6	13.5
Basilea (m)	1936	Kockum	9612	14,930	524–4	63–1	28–3	13.0

HENRY TSCHUDIS TANKREDERI-A/S

Glarona (m2)	1928	Göta	9912	13,550	493–10	64–2	28–5	11.5

UGELSTAD, ROLF, Tollbodgaten 4, Oslo

Services: General tramping

A/S GRANLI

Granli	1934	Nyland	1577	2255	258–0	39–3	17.4	11.0
ex Siredal 38								

UGELSTAD, S, Klingenberggaten 5, Oslo

Funnel: Black with white flag bearing blue U
Hull: Grey
Services: General tramping; oil and petroleum trades

S UGELSTADS REDERI-A/S

General cargo vessel								
Vigør (r/t)	1935	Langsd	1518	2620	254–10	38–8	17.2	11.0
Tankers								
Solør (m)	1938	Eriksb	8262	12,775	486–4	61–1	26–10	12.0
Svenør (m)	1931	SHWR	7616	11,410	460.5	59–6	34.1	11.0

UGLAND, JOHAN M, Grimstad

Funnel: Yellow, black top
Trades: Oil and petroleum

A/S UGLANDS REDERI

Tankers								
Evita (m2)	1927	Göta	6346	9575	422–5	55–4	26–1	10.5
ex Dagland 36								
Lisita (m)	bldg	Kockum	8484	13,525	496–4	62–2	27–2	13.0
Sarita	1914	Craig2	5824	8300	412.0	53–4	24–7	9.0
ex Melania 30								

URSIN-SMITH, ROLF, Frithjof Nansens Plass 4, Oslo

Services: General tramping

D/S A/S RAMØ

Ramø	1921	Eltrgm	2334	4065	290.4	44–0	20–0	9.0
ex Speed 33, ex Asborg 31								

VIRIK, HALDOR, Sandefjord

Funnel: Yellow with houseflag, narrow black top
Hull: Light grey, red boot-topping
Trades: Oil and petroleum

VIRIKS REDERI-A/S

Tankers								
Sandar (m2)	1928	B&W	7624	11,150	470–6	59–2	25–8	11.5
Sandefjord (m2)	1929	Göta	8038	11,020	459–6	59–2	25–10	11.5
ex Herbjørn 37								

WAAGE, HAGB, Sjøfartsbygningen, Kongensgaten 6, Oslo

Funnel: Red with yellow W
Hull: Grey, dark red boot-topping
Trades: Oil and petroleum

REDERI-A/S RUTH

Tankers								
Raila (m2)	1926	Göta	5551	8370	395–5	55–4	25–2	11.5
Raila (m)	bldg	Göta	8200	12,600	483–10	59–5	27–11	12.5
Ranja (m2)	1928	Göta	6355	9515	422–0	55–4	26–2	11.5
Ruth (m2)	1932	Göta	5486	8230	395–5	55–2	25–2	12.0

WALLEM, HAAKON J, Postboks 6, Bergen

Funnel: Yellow with blue band bordered by white bands and red bands
Hull: Black or grey
Services: General tramping; Far Eastern trading

WALLEM & CO A/S

Breiviken	1911	Dobson	2669	4600	313.0	46–6	20–0	8.5
ex Kronstad 31								
Dah Pu (P–)	1922	HwldtK	1974	3200	270.7	38–11	21.0	9.0
ex Clara Jebsen 36								
Daviken (P–)	1926	Hamtn2	2922	3500	305–0	45–8	18–8	10.0
Erviken	1921	Doxfrd	6595	10,800	420.0	54–0	28–4	11.0
Goviken	1917	SeatCD	4854	7544	396–9	53–1	23–9	10.5
ex Golden Gate 36								
Inviken	1925	Nüscke	4171	6500	346.4	50–10	23–0	10.5
ex Lu Hsing 37, ex Elaine L-D 35								
Kronviken	1904	GrayX	2363	3525	291.9	42–8	18–7	8.0
ex Domburg 22, ex Delta 20								

Westfal-Larsen: The motor vessel Hardanger *was completed by Lithgows in 1924. She was under Allied control during the Second World War and in 1953 was sold to Norwegian owner August Kjerland and renamed* Hop. *She was broken up in Belgium in 1958 (Alex Duncan)*

W Wilhelmsen: The motor vessel Taronga *was delivered by the Odense shipyard on May 5 1934, and was fitted with a B&W 7-cylinder oil engine of 9650bhp, and carried 12 passengers. On August 15 1940 she was seized by Germany, transferred to the Kriegsmarine, and renamed* Sperrbrecher 15. *She was recovered at Hamburg in May 1945 badly damaged. The hull was reconditioned by Beliard Crighton & Co, Antwerp, and the machinery by Burmeister & Wain, Copenhagen, and in August 1948* Taronga *was able to re-enter service. In October 1961 she was sold to breakers at Izumi-Ohtsu, near Osaka (Wilh Wilhelmsen)*

H M Wrangell: The twin-screw motor vessel Minerva *was completed in 1930. She was fitted with two B&W 6-cylinder oil engines of 2150bhp. She survived the Second World War and in 1955 was sold to Germany and renamed* Solveig Rickertsen. *She was broken up during 1960–61 (Alex Duncan)*

Morviken (m)	1938	Örsnd2	5008	9500	453–9	57–5	25–7	14.0
Norviken (P–)	1925	Hamtn2	2924	3500	305–0	45–9	18–9	10.0
Sandviken (P–)	1926	Hamtn2	2916	3500	305–0	45–8	18–8	10.0
Solviken (P–)	1910	B&W	2398	3100	292–0	41–4	19–2	8.5
ex Toula 23, ex Aleut 12, ex St Lucia 10, launched as Aleut								
Solviken	bldg	Fredst	3502	5000	351.1			12.0
Storviken	1917	SeatCD	4836	7500	396–9	53–2	23–9	10.5
Utviken	order	Fredst	3502	5000	351.1			12.0

WALLEM & CO,

Hongkong & Shanghai Bank Bldg, Postbox 40, Victoria, Hong Kong (Panamanian flag)

Bolivar	1919	Dtroit	2606	4100	261–0	43–8	26.1	9.5
ex Hwa Dah 38, ex Bolivar 37, ex Lake Fackler 23								
Foch	1905	Napr&M	2894	3650	314.1	41–11	20–0	7.5
ex Ha-Ven 37, ex Maréchal Foch 36, ex Buda II 19								
Gran	1919	Teikku	2049	3425	270.0	39–0	20–0	9.0
ex Ming-Shan 37, ex Gran 33, ex Kamiji Maru 20								
Kaiapoi	1906	OsbGr1	2003	3360	279.2	40–1	17–11	9.0
ex Holywood 06								
Needwood	1904	OsbGr1	2042	3363	279.5	40–1	18–0	9.0
ex Kaituna 37, ex Needwood 05								
Nord	1904	Sundld	3193	2100	314.0	46–6	20–3	8.0
ex Hai Shang 37, ex Nord 32								
Norse Carrier	1913	BethFR	3365	5465	348.7	45–1	23–0	8.0
ex Peh Shan 37, ex Frieda 37								
Norse Trader	1912	ThmpR2	3507	6232	352.7	50–10	21–5	8.5
ex Fotis 37								
San Antonio	1912	Koch	3451	6100	361.4	50–8	21–6	9.0
ex Nea Tyhi 39, ex Maid of Syra 31, ex Horncap 21								

Note: See also Wallem & Co Ltd in Great Britain section

WESTFAL-LARSEN & CO, A/S, Olav Kyrresgate 11, Postbox 192, Bergen

Funnel: Yellow with narrow black top and two narrow black bands; *Brimanger, Heranger, Hindanger, Villanger*, had no noticeable funnel
Hull: General cargo vessels – grey or black, red boot-topping; tankers – black, red boot-topping
Services: Scandinavia, NW Europe, UK–W coast US and Canada; W coast US and Canada–W coast South America–E coast South America (via Magellan Strait outwards and Panama Canal inwards); general tramping; oil and petroleum trades

General cargo vessels

Berganger (m,P12)	1932	NedSM	6826	9824	486–0	61–2	26–10	16.0
Brändanger (m2,P12)	1926	B&W	4624	8550	396–7	53–10	25–4	12.5
Brimanger (m2,P12)	1929	ArmWh1	4883	8370	415–0	54–6	25–7	13.0
Evanger	1920	Irvin3	3869	7280	377–0	52–3	23–11	10.0
Falkanger (m)	bldg	Nakskv	5349	8400	426–3	56–8	25–1	13.0
Grenanger (m,P12)	1939	Qurnro	5393	8600	408.1	55–11	25–5	13.0
Hardanger	1924	Lithgw	4000	7336	388–0	52–4	23–10	10.5
Heranger (m2,P12)	1930	B&W	4877	8380	415–0	54–10	25–6	13.0
Hindanger (m2,P12)	1929	ArmWh1	4885	8204	415–0	54–9	25–6	13.0
Høyanger (m2,P12)	1926	B&W	4624	8550	396–7	53–10	25–4	11.0
Leikanger	1923	Lithgw	4003	7336	388–0	52–4	23–10	10.5
Moldanger (m,P12)	1933	NedSM	6827	9762	486–0	61–2	26–10	16.0
Porsanger	1918	CanVic	4267	7365	393–6	49–3	24–3	10.5
Ravnanger	1919	Giessn	3371	5570	335.6	48–2	22.9	10.5
Risanger	1921	Pgill2	5455	8590	380.4	52–4	32.1	11.0
ex Labelle County 34, ex Tananger 29, ex Hufterö 24, ex Hiskö 21								
Samnanger	1918	CanVic	4276	7365	393–6	49–2	24–3	10.5
Siranger (m,P12)	1939	Qurnro	5393	8600	408.1	55–11	25–5	13.0
Taranger (m2)	1930	B&W	4873	8380	415–0	54–10	25–6	13.0
Torvanger	1920	Doxfrd	6568	10,750	420.1	54–0	34.4	10.5
Trondanger (m,P12)	1932	NedSM	6826	9774	486–0	61–2	26–10	16.0
Villanger (m2,P12)	1929	ArmWh1	4884	8215	415–0	54–8	25–6	13.0

Tankers

Davanger	1922	Hamtn2	7102	11,090	425.0	56–10	33.0	10.0
Eidanger (m)	1938	Laing	9432	14,615	503–10	68–4	28–2	13.0
Finnanger (m2)	1928	NedSM	9551	13,595	474.4	64–6	27–6	11.0
Hallanger (m2)	1928	NedSM	9551	13,582	474.4	64–6	27–6	11.0
Langanger (m2)	1930	Duncan	9215	14,510	493–6	64–4	28–9	12.0
Malmanger	1920	Laing	7078	10,925	440–4	57–0	27–0	10.0
Nordanger (m2)	1925	NedSM	9297	13,162	484–5	60–2	27–6	11.0
Orkanger (m)	1928	Seine	8030	11,610	458.0	59–10	34.8	11.0
Sandanger (m)	1938	Laing	9432	14,615	503–10	68–4	28–2	13.0
Spinanger (m)	1927	Schich	7429	11,070	458–0	57–5	26–6	11.0
Storanger (m2)	1930	Duncan	9223	14,505	493–6	64–6	28–9	12.0
Varanger (m2)	1925	NedSM	9305	14,092	484–5	60–3	27–6	11.0

SKIBS-A/S HOSANGER

General cargo vessels

Hosanger	1911	Bergen	1591	2450	255–0	37–9	16–0	9.5
Kaupanger	1930	Bergen	1584	2333	257–7	37–8	16–8	10.0

WIEL & AMUNDSEN A/S, Halden

Romulus (P7/1)	1921	ThmpsR	3708	6984	360–0	50–0	24–3	10.0

Funnel: Yellow with two black bands
Services: General tramping, mainly Far East and Pacific

WILHELMSEN, ANDERS, Oslo

A/S AWILCO

Segundo (m2)	1925	B&W	4414	7910	383–2	53–9	24–1	12.0
ex Sud Uruguayo 30, ex Segundo 28								

Funnel: Yellow with white W on red and blue halved diamond on yellow band bordered by narrow red bands
Services: General tramping

WILHELMSEN, WILH, Tollbodgaten 20, Oslo, and Orsnæs, Per Tønsberg

Funnel: Black with two blue bands
Hull: Black with white band, red boot-topping
Services: Norway–US E coast and Gulf of Mexico ports; US Gulf–NW Europe; Scandinavia–South Africa–E Africa; Scandinavia, NW Europe–British India–Ceylon–Burma–Java–Straits Settlements/–China–Japan/Australia–New Zealand; New York–Brazil–R Plate ports; New York, Norfolk, Los Angeles–Philippines–China–Japan

General cargo vessels

Cubano (r/t)	1921	ThmpsJ	5810	8470	410–0	53–4	25–11	12.0
Rinda	1917	Laing	6030	9430	405.3	53–6	27–2	12.0
ex Appleby 20, launched as Sjoa								
Simla	1917	Laing	6031	9430	405.3	53–6	27–2	12.0
ex Glastonbury 20, launched as Simla								
Tabor (m,P12)	1936	Akers	4768	7610	428–11	55–4	25–6	13.5
Tai-Ping (m2,P12)	1929	Kockum	7019	9860	481–0	60–8	27–8	14.5
Tai Ping Yang (m2,P10)	1929	DeutsK	7025	9886	481–1	60–7	27–8	14.5
Tai-Shan (m2,P8)	1929	Kockum	6962	9860	481–0	60–7	27–7	14.5
Tai Yang (m2,P8)	1929	DeutsK	7084	7886	481–0	60–7	27–8	14.5
Tai Yin (m2,P8)	1929	DeutsK	7077	9886	481–0	60–7	27–8	14.5
Taiwan (m2,P12)	1924	DeutsH	5500	9219	441–11	55–2	26–6	11.5
Talabot (m,P12)	1936	Göta	6798	10,740	498–0	62–4	27–8	16.5
Talisman (m2,P12)	1937	Kockum	6701	10,100	498–0	62–4	27–8	16.5
Talleyrand (m2,P12)	1927	DeutsK	6732	10,140	481–0	60–8	27–8	14.5
Tamerlane (m,P12)	1936	Kockum	6778	10,750	498–8	62–4	27–7	16.5
Tamesis (m2,P12)	1939	Schich	7256	10,450	518–0	63–5	27–6	15.0
Tampa (m,P8)	1923	DeutsH	4694	7019	370–11	51–2	25–7	12.0
Tana (P6)	1921	Palmer	5535	8153	396–0	52–2	26–10	11.0
Tancred (m2,P8)	1925	DeutsH	6094	9900	442.6	58–2	26–5	13.5
Tarifa (m2,P12)	1936	Schich	7229	10,850	517–11	63–4	27–7	16.0
Tarn (m2,P12)	1933	NedSM	6850	10,225	498–5	61–2	27–7	16.0
Taronga (m,P12)	1934	Odense	7003	10,550	505–7	61–4	27–7	16.0
Tatra (m,P12)	1936	Schich	4766	7580	428–11	55–6	25–5	14.5
Taurus (m,P12)	1935	Akers	4767	7610	428–11	55–4	25–6	13.5
Temeraire (m2,P12)	1927	PenhtS	6465	9553	471–10	60–2	26–7	14.5
Templar (m2,P12)	1929	DeutsK	6728	10,146	481–10	60–7	27–8	14.5
Teneriffa (m2,P10)	1922	B&W	5655	9615	444–4	55–2	26–9	11.5
Tennessee (m2,P10)	1922	B&W	5667	9615	444–4	55–2	26–8	11.5
Thalatta (m2,P10)	1922	B&W	5671	9615	444–4	55–2	26–8	11.5
Thermopylæ (m2,P12)	1930	B&W	6655	10,566	481–0	60–8	27–8	15.0
Thode Fagelund (r/t,P8)	1920	Laing	5757	7789	395.0	53–4	25–11	12.0
Tigre (m2,P7)	1926	Normnd	5498	8662	432–7	54–6	26–6	12.0
Tijuca (m2,P7)	1926	Normnd	5498	8662	432–7	54–6	26–5	12.0
Tiradentes (m2,P10)	1922	DeutsH	4961	8557	415–9	54–3	26–6	11.0
Tirranna (m2,P12)	1938	Schich	7230	10,850	517–9	63–4	27–8	16.0
Titania (m2,P12)	1937	Kockum	6704	10,090	498–0	62–4	27–8	16.5
Toledo (m,P8)	1926	Odense	4563	7109	394–5	52–2	24–3	12.0
Topeka (m2)	1925	DeutsK	4991	6385	383–6	51–2	23–0	10.5
Toronto (m2,P10)	1928	Normnd	5018	6608	397–6	52–2	24–10	12.5
Torrens (m2,P12)	1939	Kockum	6692	10,300	498–6	62–5	27–8	16.0
Tortugas (m,P12)	1923	DeutsH	4697	7019	370–11	51–2	25–7	12.0
Toulouse (m2,P10)	1934	DeutsK	7027	10,720	490–4	60–8	27–7	15.5
Touraine (m2,P12)	1925	Odense	5811	9651	456–4	56–2	26–7	13.0
Tourcoing (m2,P12)	1924	Odense	5798	9651	456–4	56–2	26–7	13.0
Trafalgar (m,P12)	1938	NedSM	5542	8690	455–0	57–4	25–11	15.0
Trianon (m2,P12)	1926	Odense	5805	9651	456–4	56–3	26–7	13.0
Tricolor (m2,P12)	1933	NedSM	6850	10,225	498–5	61–1	27–7	16.0
Triton (m2,P12)	1930	Kockum	6607	10,260	481–0	60–8	27–8	14.5
Troja (m2,P11)	1930	B&W	6649	10,706	481–4	60–7	27–8	14.5
Troubadour (r/t,P4)	1920	ThmpsJ	5808	7697	410–0	53–4	24–3	12.0
Tudor (m2,P12)	1930	Kockum	6607	10,260	481–0	60–8	27–8	14.5
Tugela (r/t,P8)	1921	Palmer	5559	8168	396–0	52–2	26–9	12.0
Tulane (m,P12)	bldg	Akers	5485	8300	452–3	57–4	25–9	15.0
Tungsha (m2,P12)	1924	DeutsH	5506	9230	441–11	55–2	26–6	11.5

Note: * Sold Germany 24.12.39, renamed *Nordmeer*

Tankers								
Mantilla*	1916	ArmWh1	5671	8667	420–0	52–2	25–3	10.0
Mirlo	1922	ArmWh1	7455	11,334	455–0	57–6	26–5	10.5

Services: General tramping

WILKENS & CO, A/S H TH, Storgaten 4, Fredrikstad

SKIBS-A/S KARLANDER

Karlander	1914	Nyland	1843	3015	276–0	42–1	17–5	8.0
ex Visna 29, ex Frolund 14								

Funnel: Black with white W on black band between two narrow white bands
Hull: Grey, red boot-topping
Services: Tramping, mainly Far East; oil and petroleum trades

WRANGELL & CO, A/S H M, Haugesund

SKIBS A/S CORONA

General cargo vessels								
Augvald	1920	McMlln	4811	8600	400.4	52–8	25–1	10.0
ex Torrey 23								
Corona	1920	SmithM	3264	5500	344–6	48–0	21–3	10.0
Fram	1907	TyneIr	2930	4750	313.0	47–0	19–11	9.0
Haraldsvang	1920	Craig2	3112	5010	325.3	48–0	20–8	9.5
ex Thomas Haaland 26								
Haugarland	1911	ArmWh1	6049	10,880	440.0	58–1	24–6	9.5
ex Sandefjord 19								
Karmt (m)	1938	Blythw	4991	8990	431–6	56–1	24–8	11.0
Minerva (m2)	1930	B&W	5883	9545	422–0	56–2	25–5	11.0
Tonjer	1920	SmithM	3268	5500	344–6	47–10	21–2	10.0
Unita	1906	Dobson	3586	6150	338.1	48–0	23–2	10.0
Tankers								
Gard (m)	1938	Eriksb	8259	12,800	486–4	61–1	26–10	13.0
Noreg (m2)	1931	B&W	7605	12,130	470–8	59–2	27–1	11.5

Palestine

Services: General tramping

PURVIS, NOÉL W, First Avenue House, High Holborn, London WC1

PALESTINE TRANSPORT & SHIPPING CO LTD (Palestine flag)

Haifa Trader	1903	Rhead2	3074	5325	322–11	47–1	23.7	8.0
ex Tregothnan 39								

Panama

Services: Tramping, mainly US/West Indies

BEHNKE, OTTO, 350 Wyoming Ave, South Orange NJ, USA

Ada	1922	Dijvdk	2589	4200	299.2	45–4	19–0	9.0
ex Heinrich Podeus 34, ex Witte Zee 27								

Services: General tramping

Note: This company was reported associated with Connell & Grace Ltd (*qv* in Great Britain section)

COMPAÑÍA DE VAPORES LTDA,
c/o P Wigham-Richardson & Co Ltd, London EC3

Vahva	1910	ThmpsJ	3655	6131	356.0	50–6	21–5	9.0
ex Truth 39, ex Ariadne Christine 20								

Peru

Funnel: Yellow with houseflag, black top
Hull: Black
Services: Covering W coast South America, R Plate region, and West Indies

COMPAÑÍA PERUANA DE VAPORES Y DIQUE DE CALLAO,
Plaza Indepencia, Casilla 208, Callao

Apurimac	1898	ThmpsJ	5361	7090	382.0	48–3	24–0	9.0
ex Paita 20, ex Anubis 20, ex Luciana 00								
Mantaro (s2)	1911	Normnd	4617	3970	360.0	46–0	22–0	9.0
Pérené	1905	HwldtK	2155	3030	284.1	39–1	18–0	9.0

ex Marie 20								
Urubamba (s2)	1911	ProvPB	4744	3970	381.2	45–11	22–0	11.0

Operator for
GOVERNMENT OF PERU

Marañon	1922	Krupp	3369	3780	305–0	47–0	20–1	8.5
ex Schleswig 37, ex Askania 36, ex Nord Schleswig 30								
Ucayali	1917	BethHH	2768	4561	299.2	45–3	22–2	8.5
ex Neti 37, ex T A D Jones 37, ex C A Snider 28, ex Olean 19								

Note: This company was controlled by the Government of Peru

Poland

GDYNIA-AMERIKA LINJE ZEGLUGOWE SPÓLKA AKCYJNA, (Gdynia-America Shipping Lines Ltd), Ulica Nabrzezna, PO Box 46, Gdynia

Funnel: Yellow with red band with shield in centre
Hull: Black with white band or white with black band, red boot-topping
Services: Passenger and cargo – Gdynia–Copenhagen–Halifax–New York; Constanta–Istanbul–Jaffa–Haifa–Piræus; Gdynia–Rio de Janeiro–Buenos Aires; Gdynia–Mexico

Passenger/general cargo vessels

Batory (m2,P280/1,75/int,415/3)	1936	CRDA2	14,287	3300	525–8	70–10	24–10	18.0
Chrobry (m2,P44/1,250/2,804/3)	1939	Nakskv	11,442	7200	509–11	66–9	22–8	17.0
Kosciuszko (s2P110/cab,180/t,500/3)	1915	Curle	6852	3398	440.0	53–5	24–4	13.5
ex Lituània 30, ex Czaritza 21								
Pilsudski (m2,P280/1,75/int,415/3)	1935	CRDA2	14,294	3300	525–8	70–10	24–10	18.0
Pulaski (s2,P110/cab,180/t,500/3)	1912	Curle	6345	6000	442–0	53–2	24–5	14.0
ex Estonia 30, ex Czar 21								
Sobieski (m2,P70/1,270/2,600/3)	1939	SHWR	11,030	7200	511–2	67–4	22–8	17.0
General cargo vessels								
Bielsko (m,P10)	bldg	IntDzg	4740	6178	436–5	55–2	24–9	14.0
Lódz (m,P10)	bldg	IntDzg	4737	6178	436–5	55–2	24–9	14.0
Morska Wola (m,P8)	1925	Krupp	3376	4556	317–0	47–8	21–4	10.0
ex Rio Negro 39, ex Hindhead 36, ex Consul Horn 36								
Stalowa Wola (m,P8)	1925	Krupp	3133	4556	317–0	47–9	21–4	10.0
ex Rio Pardo 39, ex Pine Court 37, ex Henry Horn 34								

'ZEGLUGA PÓLSKA' SPÓLKA AKCYNJA, Ulica Waszyngtona 55, Gdynia

Funnel: Black with white Z (Z with line through middle)
Hull: Black, red boot-topping
Services: Baltic and NW Europe–Levant–Palestine (jointly with Svenska Orient Linien – *qv* under Axel Broström & Son in Sweden section); several services inter-Baltic and Baltic–NW Europe/UK; general tramping

Katowice	1925	Caen	1995	2820	270.5	39–11	18–1	9.5
ex Vendemiaire 26								
Kraków	1926	Caen	2108	2850	277–6	39–9	18–4	9.5
ex Frimaire 26								
Lechistan (m,P6)	1929	Eriksb	1865	3240	305–2	43–0	18–9	11.0
ex Hemland 36								
Lewant (m,P6)	1930	Eriksb	1942	3240	305–2	43–0	18–9	11.0
ex Blåland 35								
Poznan	1926	Caen	2038	2952	277–6	39–9	18–1	9.5
ex Nivôse 26								
Torun	1926	Caen	2018	2952	277–6	39–9	18–1	9.5
ex Brumaire 26								
Wilno	1926	Caen	2018	3030	276–3	39–9	18–1	9.5
ex Pluviôse 26								
Wisla	1928	Craig2	3106	5125	336–4	48–0	20–8	9.5

Portugal

BENSAUDE & COMPANHIA LTDA, Rua Nova do Almada 11, Lisbon

Funnel: Yellow, black top
Hull: Black, red boot-topping with white dividing line
Services: Lisbon–Madeira–Azores

Manager for
EMPRESA INSULANA DE NAVEGAÇÃO,
Passenger/general cargo vessels

Carvalho Araujo (P78/1,78/2,78/3)	1930	CRDA1	4560	3600	370–2	50–2	23–9	14.0
Lima (P–)	1907	Irvin4	3881	3070	367–6	45–1	24–6	12.0
ex Westerwald 16								

Note: Also vessels under 1000gt

Gdynia-America: The twin-screw liner Batory *was delivered by CRDA, Monfalcone, on April 3 1936, and was, together with her sistership* Pilsudski, *paid for by way of a barter agreement in exchange for Polish coal to the value of £3m. Her regular service was from Gdynia and Copenhagen to New York, and she made winter cruises from New York to the Caribbean. Fitted with two CRDA/Sulzer 9-cylinder oil engines of 13,600bhp, she had accommodation for 280 first and 415 third class passengers, with another 75 berths interchangeable between the two classes. There was a crew of 250. For cruising her passenger complement was limited to 400. In September 1939* Batory *left Poland with many Polish patriots on board and made for Sweden, and then to Canada and the US, where she was at first laid up but then enlisted as an Allied troopship. Her service included taking troops to Norway in April 1940. During the war her manager was Lamport & Holt. After some early postwar problems concerning transfer back to Polish control she was returned to Gdynia-America in April 1946, and resumed commercial service from Gdynia to New York, following a refit which resulted in her passenger accommodation being increased to 450 first and 450 tourist class. Her postwar career saw many changes to her service areas, and in 1971 after two years as a floating hotel in Gdynia, she was sold to breakers at Hong Kong (EH Cole)*

Bensaude: Carvalho Araujo *was completed at the Triestino shipyard, Monfalcone, in March 1930, and was fitted with two Kincaid triple expansion engines of 3660ihp. When on voyage from the Azores to Germany in December 1939 she was stopped by British warships and 25 German nationals of military age were taken off, and in a similar incident in February 1940 she was stopped by French warships and two Germans were removed. During the war she made several voyages from Lisbon to the US.* Carvalho Araujo *survived the war and was broken up at Lisbon in 1972 (Alex Duncan)*

Cia Colonial: Colonial *was completed at Kiel in August 1908 for Hamburg-Amerika as* Ypiranga. *She was surrendered to the Shipping Controller on April 2 1919 and placed under the management of White Star. She was put to immediate use on troop repatriation duty, and from the spring of 1920 to the end of 1921 was laid up at Hull awaiting refit. Sold to Anchor Line in January 1921, she was renamed* Assyria, *and in October 1929 was sold to Portugal, being renamed* Colonial, *for service between Lisbon, Angola and Mozambique. In 1939 she was rebuilt and a modern funnel was fitted. The following year she commenced voyaging to South America, although due to wartime conditions these were infrequent. In September 1950 she was sold to be broken up at Dalmuir, and was renamed* Bisco 9 *for the delivery voyage in tow of the tug* Turmoil. *On September 17 in a gale, the tow line parted and the vessel stranded near Campbeltown. The skeleton crew of 17 were rescued. The wreck was broken up in situ (Alex Duncan)*

Cia Nacional: Quanza *was launched at Hamburg on June 1 1929 as* Portugal, *but was renamed while fitting-out and delivered on September 5. She was intended for service between Lisbon and the Portuguese African colonies but in 1931 made five voyages to Brazil. In December 1940 she made one voyage to Brazil but appears to have been inactive for most of the years of the conflict. Postwar service was again to Africa.* Quanza *was broken up at Castellon, Spain, in 1969 (Blohm & Voss)*

Sociedade Geral: The 1914-built Amarante *was the former Hamburg-Amerika vessel* Württemberg. *She took refuge at Lisbon in August 1914 and was laid up. She was seized by Portugal on February 23 1916 but did not change name until 1921. She survived the Second World War, during which she was largely inactive, and in 1955 was sold to become the Costa Rica-flagged* Veronica. *In June 1959 she arrived at Osaka to be broken up (RW Jordan collection)*

Sociedade Geral: Among the several fomer German steamers owned by this company was Inhambane, *completed in August 1912 for Deutsch Australische as* Essen. *She took refuge at Delagoa Bay in August 1914.* Essen *was seized by Portugal on February 23 1916 and transferred to Transportes Maritimos do Estado, a government organisation formed to take over the 71 German and Austrian vessels interned in Portuguese and colonial ports during the First World War. She was sold to Sociedade Geral in 1924, and was on their services from northwest Europe and Portugal to both Africa and Brazil.* Inhambane *survived the Second World War and became surplus in July 1953 when she was laid up at Lisbon. Sold in 1955 to become the Costa Rica-flagged* Vassiliki, *she was broken up at Hong Kong in 1959 (RW Jordan collection)*

Funnel: Yellow, with white band bordered by two narrow green bands
Hull: Grey, red boot-topping
Services: Lisbon–Angola; Lisbon–Mozambique; Lisbon–NW Europe

COMPANHIA COLONIAL DE NAVEGAÇÃO,

Rua do Instituto Virgilio Machado 14, Lisbon

Passenger/general cargo vessels								
Colonial (s2,P109/1,81/2,239/3)								
	1908	Krupp	8309	7700	449.8	52–1	25–3	12.5
ex Assyria 29, ex Ypiranga 21								
Joào Belo (P–)	1905	Blohm	6365	7680	411.6	50–9	26–5	10.0
ex City of Genoa 28, ex Windhuk 21, ex Gertrud Woermann 07								
Mouzinho (s2,P109/1,96/2,505/3)								
	1907	Krupp	8374	8200	448.3	55–2	25–11	12.5
ex Maria Cristina 31, ex Corcovado 27, ex Guglielmo Peirce 22, ex Corcovado 20, ex Sueh 20, ex Corcovado 14								
General cargo vessels								
Cassequel (P–)	1901	GrayX	4784	7240	384.5	52–1	23–0	10.0
ex Pangim 17, ex Numantia 16								
Ganda (P–)	1907	Flensb	4333	6770	387.8	51–0	23–11	9.0
ex City of Milan 30, ex Plauen 21								
Guiné (s2,P–)	1905	Dixon2	2648	3200	300.0	42–0	23–2	12.0
ex San Miguel 30								
Lobito	1906	Eider1	2720	4200	295.1	43–11	15–0	9.5
ex Porto Alexandre 24, ex Ingbert 16, ex Thora Menzell 13								
Malange	1904	Neptn1	3155	5090	314–0	45–4	22–0	9.5
ex Carlo Pisacane 29, ex Algier 16, ex Hornfels 08								
Pungue (P9/2)	1900	Irvin4	3993	6356	351–9	47–2	24–7	8.5
ex Morocco 30								

Note: Also vessels under 1500gt

Funnel: White, black top
Hull: Black, red boot-topping
Services: Azores–UK–NW Europe

COMPANHIA DE NAVEGAÇÃO CARREGADORES AÇOREANOS,

Ponta Delgada, St Michael's, Azores

Corte Real (P–)	1922	Vuijk	2044	3250	293–0	40–2	20–6	9.5
ex Peursum 34								
Gonçalo Velho	1913	Murdo2	1595	2670	265.5	38–8	18–8	8.5
ex Balboa 28, ex Linmere 23								
Pero de Alenquer	1913	Neptn1	2593	4450	343–3	46–1	20–2	9.0
ex Coimbra 25, ex Antares 16								
San Miguel	1931	SHWRSd	2112	3480	302–2	42–0	19–4	8.5
Villa Franca	1906	Seebk1	2043	3100	263.4	37–6	19–0	9.0
ex Esposende 24, ex Arkadia 16								

Funnel: Black
Hull: Black with white band
Services: Passenger and cargo – mainly Lisbon–E Africa

COMPANHIA NACIONAL DE NAVEGAÇÃO, Rua do Comércio 85, Lisbon

Passenger/general cargo vessels								
Angola (s2,P–)	1912	Cockll	7884	6036	439.5	55–9	25–1	13.0
ex Albertville 22								
Lourenço Marques (s2,P128/1,93/2,80/3)								
	1905	Blohm	6298	7050	420.0	50–2	26–6	13.0
ex Admiral 16								
Nyassa (s2,P–)	1906	Teckl	8980	9400	478–0	57–11	30–1	14.0
ex Trás-os-Montes 24, ex Bülow 16								
Quanza (s2,P111/1,120/2,98/3)								
	1929	Blohm	6636	6230	438–2	52–7	24–11	13.5
launched as Portugal								
General cargo vessels								
Cabo Verde	1908	Neptn1	4696	6760	353.2	50–2	23–7	8.0
ex Sao Thiago 24, ex Santa Barbara 16								
Congo	1905	Flensb	3110	5000	307.7	45–4	22–6	8.0
Cubango (P–)	1903	Flensb	5820	8350	425.0	53–0	25–5	11.0
ex Goa 24, ex Lichtenfels 16								
S Thomé (m, P6)	1938	Doxfrd	5237	9050	440–11	55–6	25–6	12.5

Note: Also vessels under 2000gt

Funnel: Black with blue SG on broad white band between two narrow red bands
Hull: Black, red boot-topping
Services: Lisbon–Portuguese Guinea; Lisbon–Angola; Lisbon–Brazil–Uruguay–Argentina

SOCIEDADE GERAL DE COMÉRCIO, INDUSTRIA E TRANSPORTES LTDA, Rua do Comércio 49, Lisbon

Amarante	1914	Bremer	7896	12,595	481–2	58–0	27–0	11.0
ex Württemberg 21								
Cunene	1911	Flensb	5875	9500	450.0	58–0	25–6	12.0
ex Adelaide 16								
Gaza	1914	Neptn1	6037	7800	400.0	53–11	25–2	12.5
ex Hof 16								

Inhambane	1912	Teckl	6051	9619	450.8	57–2	25–2	12.5
ex Essen 16								
Luso	1912	Neptn1	6207	10,125	459.9	58–1	25–6	12.5
ex Machico 25, ex Colmar 16								
Maria Amelia	1913	Neptn1	1766	2956	302–1	41–1	18–1	10.0
ex Gaia 24, ex Girgenti 16								
Maria Cristina	1920	SmithM	3265	5500	344–6	48–0	21–3	9.5
ex Maria Christina 22, ex Urd 22								
Mello	1915	Blyth	4020	6253	384–11	51–0	22–8	9.5
ex Graziella 22, ex Hebburn 19								
Mirandella	1906	Bremer	5179	8000	409.3	52–9	26–0	14.0
ex Fernão Veloso 25, ex Khalif 16								
Pinhel	1915	Ropnr2	3186	5874	335.5	48–2	22–6	9.0
ex Nelda 22, ex Ellawood 19								
Saudades	1913	Flensb	4758	6436	381–1	51–1	22–8	12.0
ex Peniche 25, ex Phoenicia 16								

Note: Also *Africa Ocidental* (built 1938/1268gt), *Alferrarede* (05/1452), *Costeiro Terceiro* (bldg/1213)

Romania

NAVIGATION & COAL TRADE CO LTD,

Billiter Bldgs, 22 Billiter St, London EC3

Funnel: A Vlasov – black with white V
Hull: Black, red boot-topping
Services: General tramping
Note: See A Vlasov also in Greece section under Société Commerciale et d'Armement SA and in Italy section under Società Trasporti Marittimi SA (SITMAR) and see Navigation & Coal Trade Co Ltd also in Great Britain section

Manager and/or agent for

ALEXANDRE VLASOV, Strada Academiei 47, Bucharest, Romania; and Via del Conservatorio 15, Milan, Italy

Oltul	1920	RDuck2	4328	7520	396–8	51–0	24–1	10.0
ex Dansborg 33								
Prahova	1922	ArmWh1	3609	6425	360.6	51–0	21–9	10.0
Siretul	1912	GrayX	3638	6600	360.0	51–0	22–2	10.0
ex Baharistan 14								

SERVICIUL MARITIM ROMÂN, (Romanian State Maritime Service),

Ministerul Aerului si Marinei, Bulevardul Tache Jonescu 1–3, Bucharest

Funnel: White, black top
Hull: Black or white, red boot-topping
Services: Passenger – Constanta–Piræus–Alexandria; Galatz–Port Said–Marseilles; Romania–Black Sea ports; Galatz–Constanta–Mediterranean ports; Black Sea ports–Levant; Romania–Mediterranean ports–Antwerp–London–Rotterdam–Hamburg

Passenger/general cargo vessels								
Alba Julia (r/t,P60/1,250/3)	1922	Marine	5701	7840	423–7	53–11	23–5	10.5
ex Carl Legien 33								
Ardeal (r/t,P60/1,250/3)	1922	Marine	5695	7840	423–7	53–11	23–5	10.5
ex Emil Kirdorff 32								
Basarabia (m2,P80/1,100/2,230/3)	1938	B&W	6672	1675	432–8	57–8	18–8	22.5
Dacia (s2,P–)	1907	LoireS	3419	1500	356.9	42–1	18–0	14.5
Peles (r/t,P60/1,250/3)	1922	Marine	5708	7840	423–7	53–11	23–5	10.5
ex Adolf von Baeyer 23								
Regele Carol I (s2,P–)	1898	Fairfd	2369	1400	350.0	42–0	18.5	11.5
România (s2,P–)	1904	LoireS	3152	1500	356.9	42–1	18–0	14.5
Suceava (r/t,P60/1,250/3)	1923	Marine	6876	7840	423–7	53–11	23–5	10.5
ex Albert Vögler 33								
Transilvania (m2,P80/1,100/2,230/3)	1938	B&W	6672	1675	432–8	57–8	18–8	22.5
General cargo vessels								
Balcic (m,P16)	bldg	CNR4	3495	5500	380–6	50–10	21–6	13.0
Bucegi	1913	G&G3	4501	7220	388–4	52–2	23–2	8.5
Bucuresti	1897	Napier	2499	3700	300.0	39–9	22.1	8.0
Carpati	1913	G&G3	4336	7220	388–4	52–2	23–2	8.5
laid down as Strathken								
Cavarna (m,P16)	1939	CNR4	3495	5500	380–8	50–10	21–6	13.0
Mangalia (m,P16)	1939	CNR4	3495	5500	380–8	50–11	21–6	13.0
Oituz	1905	Neptn1	2686	4215	291.3	44–0	23.7	8.5
ex Leros 21, ex Hornsund 20								
Sulina (m,P16)	1939	CNR4	3495	5500	380–8	50–10	21–6	13.0

SM Román: The 1923-built Peles *was fitted with a Marinewerft triple expansion engine and low pressure turbine which gave 3000ihp and a maximum speed of 13 knots. She was formerly named* Adolf von Baeyer, *owned until 1926 by Hugo Stinnes, and from November 1926 by Hamburg-Amerika. She was sold to Romania in 1933, together with three sisterships.* Peles *was torpedoed and sunk on August 14 1941 by the Russian submarine* SC-216 *near Cape Emine. A previous attack by* SC-211 *had failed (RW Jordan collection)*

SM Román: Transilvania *was completed in June 1938 by Burmeister & Wain for service from Constanta to Istanbul, Piræus, Genoa and Alexandria. Fitted with two B&W 12-cylinder oil engines of 11,500bhp, she attained 22.5 knots on trials, and with a service speed of over 20 knots* Transilvania *and her sistership* Basarabia *were for many years the fastest ships in Mediterranean service. Postwar she resumed this service for the successor company NAVROM. While repairing at Galatz she capsized on September 23 1979 and became a constructive total loss*
(RW Jordan collection)

SIMATU, GEORGE, (master of *Jiul*), Berlescu 13, Braila

Services: General tramping

EUGENIA AND CONSTANCE SIMATU

Jiul	1913	Prstm1	3127	5680	345.0	48–0	21.1	10.0
ex Ecaterini Matsouki 14								

STEAUA ROMANA SOCIETATE ANONIMA PENTRU INDUSTRIA PETROLEULUI, Bulevardul Carol I 17, Casuta Postala 120, Bucharest

Funnel: Black with emblem on white band
Hull: Black, red boot-topping
Trades: Oil and petroleum

Tankers

Campina	1912	FrerJ	3032	4250	298.2	44–2	24.7	8.5
ex Principele Barbu Stirbei 39, ex Artur von Gwinner 22								
Oltenia	1928	ArmWh1	6394	10,120	423.7	55–4	26–10	10.0
Steaua Romana	1914	VSE1	5311	8150	406–10	53–0	24–3	9.0
ex Emil Georg von Stauss 22, laid down as Olex								

VLASSOPULO BROS, (Theodore Vlassopulos), Creechurch House, 37–45 Creechurch Lane, London EC3

Funnel: Black with B on band
Hull: Black
Services: General tramping

Manager and/or agent for
SPIRIDION N VLASSOPOL, Strada Golesti 12, Braila, Romania

Inginer N Vlassopol	1911	G&G3	3610	6250	348.5	50–2	21–9	9.0
ex Loyal Devonian 32, ex Panayiotis 19, ex Essex Abbey 16								
Moldova	1911	Rickmr	4083	6500	367.1	47–8	24–4	9.0
ex Ithaki 39, ex Anne 22, ex Aenne Rickmers 15; conv seaplane carrier 17, conv general cargo 15								

Spain

ALTOS HORNOS DE VIZCAYA, SOCIEDAD ANÓNIMA, Alameda de Recalde 27, Ap 116, Bilbao

Funnel: Black with white shield bearing AHV on red band
Hull: Black, red boot-topping
Services: NW Europe and Mediterranean trades

Conde de Zubiria (st)	1918	EspB	3256	4790	314.0	48–1	20–1	9.0
Fernando L de Ybarra	1919	EspB	3308	4500	314.0	48–1	20–2	9.0
Marques de Chavarri (st)	1918	EspB	3256	4790	314.0	48–1	20–1	9.0
Marques de Urquijo	1894	Short1	2567	3790	300–5	40–1	20–0	7.5
ex Carlos 17, ex Benhead 12, ex Cyranom 04, ex Whitburn 99								
Victor de Chavarri	1919	EspB	3308	4500	314.0	48–1	20–2	9.0

ALVAREZ, S EN C, ANGEL, Ap 31, Aviles

Funnel: Black with houseflag
Hull: Black
Services: General tramping

Gayarre	1920	Ech&L	3276	5650	341–2	48–0	23–3	9.0
ex Arichachu 39								

ASTIGARRAGA, HIJOS DE, Calle Bertendona 4, Bilbao

Funnel: Black with HA monogram on white band between narrow white over blue bands above and narrow blue over white bands below
Hull: Black, red boot-topping
Services: General tramping UK/NW Europe/Mediterranean/W Africa

COMPAÑÍA NAVIERA BACHI

Bachi	1920	Blyth	3091	5200	342–0	46–9	21–9	9.5
ex Bologna 38, ex Bachi 37, launched as War Obelisk								
Bartolo	1918	Prstm1	3124	5150	342–0	46–10	21–9	9.5
ex Algorta 25, ex War Zephyr 20								
Juan de Astigarraga	1919	Napr&M	3561	6000	343.4	49–1	22–0	9.5
Kauldi	1922	Blyth	3153	5200	342–0	46–8	21–9	9.5
ex Perugia 39, ex Kauldi 37, ex Prado 22								
Manuchu	1921	Hamtn2	3118	5450	342–0	48–11	20–6	10.0
ex Aras 39, ex Manuchu 37								
Tom	1919	Blumr1	3056	5090	342–0	46–10	21–9	9.5
ex Cramond 21, launched as War Moon								

ASTORQUI, VIUDA DE FELIPE, Alameda de Urquijo 44, Bilbao

Services: General tramping

Maria Victoria	1920	Camp2	3619	6800	348.6	49–11	23–0	9.5
ex Potenza 39, ex Maria Victoria 37, ex Gydavore 30, ex Oceania 27								

Funnel: Black with red AM monogram on white band
Services: General tramping

AUXILIAR MARÍTIMA SOCIEDADE ANÓNIMA, Gran Via 31, Bilbao

Galdames	1918	Nervn	3337	5140	337–11	47–1	20–9	9.5
ex Aldam 38, ex Galdames 38								

Funnel: Yellow with ornamental AS monogram in red
Hull: Black, red boot-topping with white dividing line
Services: Spain–Hamburg – Rotterdam–Antwerp; Spain – Montevideo–Buenos Aires; Spain–Glasgow–Liverpool–Swansea

AZNAR SA, NAVIERA, Astarloa 9, Ap 13, Bilbao

Andutz-Mendi	1929	GrayWH	1808	2884	319–7	39–0	18–0	10.0
to be renamed Monte Buitre								
Ariaga-Mendi	1921	Dobson	5535	9230	411–0	53–0	25–7	10.5
ex Delfshaven 22; to be renamed Monte Oiz								
Aritz-Mendi	1920	Eusk	5754	8650	415–0	53–6	25–2	10.0
to be renamed Monte Navajo								
Artiba-Mendi	1921	Eusk	2543	3576	310–8	44–1	19–5	10.0
to be renamed Monte Espadán								
Ayala-Mendi (m,P–)	1929	Eusk	2955	3939	352–0	45–7	18–10	10.5
ex Elise 38, ex Ayala-Mendi 37; to be renamed Monte Ayala								
Eretza-Mendi	1909	GrayX	4153	6725	377–0	50–4	22–9	8.0
to be renamed Monte Jata								
Monte Abril (m,P–)	1930	Eusk	2955	3939	352–0	45–7	18–10	10.5
ex Artza-Mendi 39								
Monte Albertia (m,P–)	1929	Eusk	2955	3939	352–0	45–7	18–10	10.5
ex Axpe-Mendi 39								
Monte Almanzor (m,P–)	1929	Eusk	2955	3939	352–0	45–7	18–10	10.5
ex Aya-Mendi 39								
Monte Altube (m,P–)	1929	Eusk	2955	3939	352–0	45–7	18–10	10.5
ex Altube-Mendi 39								
Monte Anboto (m,P–)	1929	Eusk	2955	3939	352–0	45–7	18–10	10.5
ex Anboto-Mendi 39								
Monte Aralar (m,P–)	1930	Eusk	2955	3939	352–0	45–7	18–10	10.5
ex Araya-Mendi 39								
Monte Arnabal (m,P–)	1929	Eusk	2955	3939	352–0	45–7	19–3	10.5
ex Arnabal-Mendi 39								
Monte Banderas	1929	GrayWH	1597	2670	289–2	39–0	17–7	12.0
ex Atxuri-Mendi 39, ex Hidalgo 38, ex Atxuri-Mendi 37								
Monte Bizcargui	1929	GrayWH	1597	2670	289–4	39–0	17–7	12.0
ex Alona-Mendi 39								
Monte Bustelo	1928	GrayWH	1597	2670	289–4	39–0	17–7	12.0
ex Aralar-Mendi 39								
Monte Castelo	1921	Eusk	3222	5371	351–1	46–8	22–3	10.0
ex Arnotegi-Mendi 39								
Monte Contés	1898	Dixon2	2516	3599	299–10	42–1	19–10	7.5
ex Andraka-Mendi 39, ex Plencia 17								
Monte Coroña	1922	Eusk	2571	4202	311–7	44–2	21–2	10.0
ex Araitz-Mendi 39								
Monte Facho	1910	Eusk	2934	4890	320.0	46–8	20–1	8.0
ex Bizkargi-Mendi 39								
Monte Faro	1915	Eusk	2661	3930	311–11	44–2	21–2	8.5
ex Arate-Mendi 39, ex Ellen 38, ex Arate-Mendi 37, ex Rio Navia 35, ex Mar del Norte 28								
Monte Galera	1921	Eusk	3222	4958	351–1	46–8	20–5	10.0
ex Siena 39, ex Artxanda-Mendi 37								
Monte Gorbea (m)	1923	Eusk	3720	5668	345.8	48–9	23–2	10.0
ex Arantza-Mendi 39, ex Lecce 38, ex Arantza-Mendi 37								
Monte Gurugu	1921	Hill	3554	5680	325.0	48–0	23–2	9.5
ex Artea-Mendi 39								
Monte Iciar	1922	Ropnrl	3274	6250	351–1	48–8	23–1	10.5
ex Aizkarai-Mendi 39, ex Erica 38, ex Blanca 37, ex Aizkarai-Mendi 36								
Monte Igueldo	1921	Ropnrl	3453	6035	351–1	48–6	23–1	10.5
ex Arinda-Mendi 39								
Monte Inchorta	1920	Ropnrl	3350	6035	351–1	48–9	23–1	10.5
ex Alu-Mendi 39								
Monte Isabela	1921	Ropnrl	3615	6035	351–1	48–9	23–0	10.5
ex Atxeri-Mendi 39								
Monte Javalon	1914	Eusk	4313	6990	365.0	50–2	22–8	10.0
ex Unbe-Mendi 39								
Monte Moncayo	1913	Eusk	4291	6990	365.0	50–2	22–8	10.0
ex Gorbea-Mendi 39								

Monte Monjuich	1922	deKlop	4904	7165	367–6	50–4	22–11	9.0
ex Ardantza-Mendi 39, ex Maraglo 22								
Monte Mulhacen	1916	Eusk	4648	7438	397–4	50–2	22–11	9.5
ex Igotz-Mendi 39								
Monte Naranco	1920	Eusk	5754	8670	413–5	53–6	25–2	10.0
ex Arno-Mendi 39								
Monte Negro	1919	H&WGw	5263	8260	412–8	52–4	25–3	10.5
ex Astoi-Mendi 39, ex Highmead 22, ex Cromarty 20, ex War Jasmine 19								
Monte Nuria	1917	Eusk	5717	8540	416–8	53–6	25–2	9.5
ex Artagan-Mendi 39								
Monte Orduña	1922	Dobson	5529	9180	411–0	53–0	25–7	9.5
ex Agire-Mendi 39, ex Schiehaven 22								
Monte Saja	1921	FurnH	5989	9251	413–0	53–1	26–3	10.0
ex Altobizkar-Mendi 39								
Monte Serantes	1921	FurnH	5914	9251	413–0	53–0	26–3	10.0
ex Abodi-Mendi 39								
Monte Sollube	1921	FurnH	5914	9250	413–0	53–1	26–2	10.0
ex Arola-Mendi 39								
Monte Teide	1922	Rhead3	6202	9868	415–0	53–5	28–0	10.0
ex Aizkori-Mendi 39, ex Altuna-Mendi 37								
Upo-Mendi	1911	Eusk	4193	6605	365–4	49–11	21–7	10.0
to be renamed Monte Jarindo								

Note: Name changed from Compañia Naviera Sota y Aznar May 1939

CANDINA, ANTONIO, Plaza Circular 4, Bilbao

Services: General tramping

COMPAÑÍA NAVIERA BIDASOA

Candina	1897	TyneIr	2587	4310	328–1	43–4	19–6	8.0
ex Francisca Uravain 28, ex Petingaudet 21, ex Gloxinia 16								
Ulia	1896	RDuck1	2434	3960	310–0	43–2	19–0	8.0
ex Castillo Morella 39, ex Ulia 38, ex Yandiola 30, ex Swanley 00								

COMPAÑÍA ANÓNIMA MARÍTIMA UNION, Gran Via 12, Bilbao

Funnel: Black
Hull: Black, red boot-topping, some with white dividing line
Services: General tramping – Mediterranean/NW Europe/UK/Baltic/Kara Sea/W Africa

Apolo	1900	Napr&M	4320	6918	388–6	50–0	23–4	8.0
El Neptuno	1925	Dobson	3569	6862	371–4	50–0	23–11	9.0
ex Chatton 34								
El Saturno	1921	Burntd	3458	6200	371–5	48–7	22–3	8.5
ex Guipuzcoa 35, ex Bergsdalen 29								
Eolo	1929	Nthmb1	4409	7675	403–0	54–6	22–8	10.0
ex Statira 36, ex Tynemouth 32								
Hercules	1900	Cragg1	4144	6900	360.0	48–1	24–6	7.5
Indauchu	1920	Ropnr1	3126	5050	342–8	46–8	21–11	9.0
ex Sulmona 39, ex Indauchu –, ex Monkton 29								
Jupiter	1900	LithR	4833	8000	398–0	52–2	24–2	7.5
ex Arezzo 38, ex Jupiter 37								
Marte	1900	Lderry	3714	5950	371–0	46–2	23–3	8.0

COMPAÑÍA ARRENDATARIA DEL MONOPOLIO DE PETROLEOS SOCIEDAD ANÓNIMA, Torija 9, Ap 318, Madrid, and Conde de Trenor 5, Ap 312, Valencia

Funnel: Black with red diamond on white band
Hull: Black, red boot-topping, white dividing line
Trades: Oil and petroleum

Tankers

Badalona* (m2)	1922	SHWR	4202	6400	365.0	49–0	23–11	10.0
Campanil (m2)	order	UnionN	8392	10,800	487–0	62–0	27–3	13.5
Campante (m)	order	EspC	8452	10,762	488–0	62–0	27–3	13.5
Campas (m2)	1932	Ech&L	6276	8400	420–6	57–5	25–2	12.5
Campeche (m2)	1933	EspC	6382	8267	419–9	57–10	25–2	12.5
Campeón** (m)	order	UnionN	8458	10,760	487–2	62–5	27–3	13.5
Campero (m2)	1934	Ech&L	6382	8267	419–9	57–10	25–2	12.5
Campilo (m2)	bldg	UnionN	3971	4576	342–8	53–8	19–6	12.0
Campiz (m2)	order	EspC	8467	10,800	488–10	62–4	27–2	13.5
Campoamor (m2)	1931	Eusk	7873	10,600	471–1	59–0	26–10	12.5
Campomanes (m2)	1932	EspC	6276	8270	419–9	57–11	25–2	12.5
Campuzano (m2)	1932	UnionN	6320	8400	421–4	57–5	25–1	12.5
Elcano	1918	VickB2	5199	7900	412–0	52–5	25–3	10.0
ex War Master 20								

Aznar: Monte Nuria *was completed in 1917 as* Artagan-Mendi *for Sota y Aznar. She was renamed* Monte Nuria *in 1939 when Aznar was formed following the breaking up of the partnership of Sota and Aznar at the end of the Spanish Civil War. The whole fleet was renamed with 'Monte' names during 1939–40. She survived the Second World War and was broken up at Bilbao in 1963 (RW Jordan collection)*

CAM Union: El Neptuno *was completed as* Chatton *by W Dobson at Newcastle in October 1925 for local trampship owner T Pratt & Co. She was sold to Spain in 1934 and renamed* El Neptuno. *She was broken up at Aviles in 1966 (Alex Duncan)*

Campsa: The twin-screw tanker Campoamor *was completed at Bilbao in February 1931 for this Spanish oil company. She was fitted with two MAN 7-cylinder oil engines of 3200bhp. She was in service until 1969 when she was broken up (Photograph courtesy CLH SA)*

Gumersindo Junquera: Maruja y Aurora *was completed by Russell & Co in March 1905 as the British-owned* River Clyde. *She was sold to the Admiralty in 1915 for use as a landing ship, and had holes cut in her side to facilitate the rapid disembarkation of troops. On April 29, with 2000 troops on board,* River Clyde *was run aground off Gallipoli near the Turkish fort of Sidul Bahr, and with the aid of lighters was able to land troops of the 29th Division as part of assaults to overcome the Turkish-held positions. She was temporarily abandoned and plundered by the Turks, but later towed off. In February 1920 when lying at Malta she was sold to Spain, renamed* Angela, *and taken to Bilbao for extensive repairs. She became* Maruja y Aurora *in 1929, and was broken up at Aviles in 1966 (Alex Duncan)*

José Calvo Sotelo (m2)								
	order	Eusk	8452	10,800	487–3	62–4	27–3	13.5
Remedios (m2)	1921	ArmWhl	4461	6791	383–11	48–6	25–3	10.0
ex Conde de Churruca 30								
Saustan	1928	Duncan	5586	9375	419–3	54–1	24–3	11.0
ex Vallejo 37								
Zorroza	1921	Eusk	4598	5955	374–0	50–2	23–8	9.5
ex Artza-Mendi 30								

Note: * Also traded as *Sirius* during Spanish Civil War; ** planned construction suspended

COMPAÑÍA CANTABRICA DI NAVEGACIÓN, Gordoniz 10, Ap 150, Bilbao

Funnel: Black with white band
Trades: Oil and petroleum

Tanker (cylindrical tanks)

Gobeo	1921	Duncan	3346	–	341–0	47–10	21–6	9.5

COMPAÑÍA ESPAÑOLA DE NAVEGACÍON MARÍTIMA SOCIEDADE ANÓNIMA, Paseo de Colón 24, Barcelona

Services: Spain–US, Gulf of Mexico ports (both vessels laid up 1939)

Motomar (m2,P–)	1921	Göta	5724	8240	393–8	53–11	25–1	11.0
ex Cabo Tortosa 32, ex Hemland 26								
Navemar (P–)	1921	ArmWhl	5473	8900	407.1	53–10	26–10	9.0
ex Cabo Mayor 32, ex Frogner 27								

COMPAÑÍA NAVIERA AMAYA SOCIEDADE ANÓNIMA, Barroeta Aldamar 2–1°, Bilbao

Services: General tramping

C DE ZABALA

Josiña	1921	Tidew	3314	4800	343–3	46–10	21–9	10.0
ex Canadian Forester 29								
Manu	1921	Tidew	3267	4950	343–3	46–6	21–8	10.0
ex Marion 38, ex Manu 37, ex Canadian Fisher 29								

COMPAÑÍA NAVIERA AMAYA, Panama (Panamanian flag)

Cocle*	1918	Dobson	2958	5050	342–0	48–0	20–8	9.5
ex America 37, ex Vera Cruz 36, ex Santi 36, ex Hercule 25, ex War Glen 20								

Note: * Managed since 1937 by Alex Davaris, Piræus, Greece

COMPAÑÍA NAVIERA MUNDACA SOCIEDADE ANÓNIMA, Gran Via 12, Bilbao

Services: General tramping

Atalaya	1921	Ech&L	3309	5630	341–2	48–0	23–3	9.0
Bizkaya	1923	GirndH	4579	6850	377–0	48–11	23–2	10.5
ex Padova 39, ex Bizkaya 39, ex Vizcaya, ex Joseph Magne 29								

COMPAÑÍA NAVIERA VASCONGADA, Plaza de España 3, Bilbao

Funnel: Black with red N and blue V monogram on broad white band
Hull: Black
Services: UK, NW Europe and Mediterranean trades

Arraiz	1925	NewWat	4524	7500	385–2	56–4	22–8	9.0
ex Queenswood 32								
Banderas	1899	Pgill1	2140	3560	286.0	42–11	18–0	8.5
Cobetas	1914	LithR	3945	6630	367–6	49–6	24–4	9.0
ex Guadalquivir 26, ex Adelina 20								
Cristina	1920	Krupp	2421	3750	288–8	44–2	19–5	9.0
ex Land Scout 22, ex Betzdorf 21								
Miraflores	1919	Irvin1	3209	5150	323–2	46–11	21–9	9.5
ex Salazar 27, ex War Sirocco 19								
Sabina	1920	Krupp	2421	3750	288–8	44–3	19–5	9.0
ex Air Scout 22, ex Weilburg 21								
Serantes	1922	Schuyt	3518	6200	373–6	50–4	21–8	9.0
ex Kayeson 29								

COMPAÑÍA TRASATLÁNTICA, Ap 14, Plaza Medinaceli, Barcelona

Funnel: Black
Hull: Black, red boot-topping and white dividing line
Services: Passenger, mail, cargo – Spain, Portugal–South America; Bilbao–New York–Havana; Spain–Canary Is–Central America; Spain–W coast South America

Passenger/general cargo vessels

Antonio Lopez (P105/1,40/2,976/3)								
	1891	Denny1	6044	6096	430.0	50–1	25–2	11.0
ex Ruahine 00								
Argentina (r/t4,P152/1,144/2,1205/3)								
	1913	SHWR	10,137	6406	498–0	61–4	25–0	12.5
ex Reina Victoria Eugenia 31								
Buenos Aires (P901/1,48/2,836/3)								
	1887	Denny1	5205	5910	410.6	48–2	25–4	11.0

Habana (st2,P245/1,82/2,1072/3)
1923 EspB 10,551 10,370 500–0 60–8 29–11 17.0
ex Alfonso XIII 31
Juan Sebastian Elcano* (st2,P155/1,82/2,350/3)
1928 EspB 9965 6200 483–0 55–11 24–2 16.5
Magallanes (st2,P155/1,82/2,350/3)
1928 EspC 9689 5925 483–0 56–0 26–0 16.5
Manuel Arnús (st2,P149/1)
1923 EspC 7578 6410 435.0 56–0 24–5 13.0
Manuel Calvo (P112/1,36/2,930/3)
1892 ArmMit 5617 6900 435–11 48–0 26–4 13.0
ex H H Meier 01, ex Lucania 92
Marques de Comillas (st2,P155/1,82/2,350/3)
1928 EspF 9922 6245 483–0 55–11 25–10 16.5
Montevideo (P91/1,48/2,708/3)
1889 Dennyl 5205 5674 410.5 48–3 26–1 11.0
launched as Monte Video
Uruguay (r/t3,P160/1,148/2,951/3)
1913 Dennyl 10,348 6442 499–0 61–4 25–0 14.5
ex Infanta Isabel de Borbon 31

Note: * Seized Odessa by USSR 1939, transferred Soviet navy, renamed *Volga*

DE LA TORRE Y ALONSO, J M, Calle Elcano 18, Ap 252, Bilbao

Funnel: Black with white over black over red bands
Services: General tramping Spain/Mediterranean/NW Europe/UK
Note: * Sold Urquijo y Aldecoa 1939, renamed *Mar Tirreno*

COMPAÑÍA VASCO-ASTURIANA DE NAV

Luchana 1908 Irvinl 3000 5323 336–7 47–0 21–1 8.5
ex Oquendo 22, ex Tuscany 13

DE LOS COBOS, VIUDA DE LUIS CASO, Calle de la Cámara, Aviles

Funnel: Yellow with VA monogram, black top
Hull: Black, red boot-topping
Services: General tramping

COMPAÑÍA DE NAVEGACIÓN VASCO-ASTURIANA

Antonio de Satrustegui
1920 WallSY 3289 4950 343–3 46–6 21–9 10.0
ex Mari-Dolores 34, ex Tenax 30, ex Canadian Raider 29
José Tartiere 1920 McDoug 2289 3000 261–1 43–7 20–10 9.5
ex Tomasin 28, ex Josefa 28
Santiago Lopez 1903 Irvinl 2319 4100 300–2 44–4 18–8 8.0
ex Oceanic 08

DE NAVAS ESCUDER, JOSÉ, Paseo de Gracia 18, Bilbao

Services: General tramping

Albareda 1903 LithR 3925 6818 345.2 49–11 24–3 8.0
ex Gante 39, ex Udondo 38, ex Guardiaro 27, ex Black Prince 23, ex Provan 04
Antequera 1894 Pgill1 2810 4376 310.0 42–11 20–8 8.0
ex Erandio 39, ex Begoña No 6 23, ex Onton 20, ex Wilderspool 99
Argentona 1902 Irvinl 3552 6333 340.0 47–4 23–11 7.5
ex Urkiola-Mendi 38, ex Azalea 09

DE PINILLOS, MIGUEL MARTINEZ, Plaza Generalísimo Franco 6, Ap 47, Cadiz

Funnel: Black with red cross (+) on broad white band
Hull: White
Services: Fruit trades, general tramping

Fruit carriers

Darro (m) 1931 Eusk 2610 2190 306–1 42–4 18–1 13.0
ex Lealtad 39, ex Darro 37
Ebro (m) 1928 Eusk 2522 2200 306–0 42–2 18–0 13.0
ex Aniene 39, ex Ebro 37
Sil (m) 1928 Eusk 2522 2200 306–5 42–2 18–1 13.0
Turia (m) 1931 Eusk 2610 2160 306–1 42–1 18–1 13.0

Note: Also vessels under 1500gt

GARCIA FERNANDEZ, FRANCISCO, Wad-Ras 3, Ap 38, Santander

Funnel: Black with white and red halved disc on red over white bands
Hull: Black
Services: General tramping

Rita Garcia 1922 ThmpR2 3708 7150 359–2 50–0 24–1 9.5
ex Eider 38, ex Rita Garcia 36, ex Ellaston 30

GUIPUZCOANA, COMPAÑÍA NAVIERA, Gran Via 31, Bilbao, and San Sebastian

Services: General tramping Mediterranean/N Spain/UK/NW Europe

Galea 1918 Nervn 3333 4900 338–9 47–1 20–9 9.5
Iciar 1922 GirndB 4584 6750 377–0 40–6 23–3 10.0

ex Capitaine le Masne 30
Urumea 1913 Blumrl 3250 5320 341–0 48–0 21–1 8.5
ex San Salvador 28, ex Fairhaven 19
Zurriola 1899 ThmpRl 1866 2950 286–5 39–7 17–8 8.0
ex Begoña No 3 24, ex Matienzo 18

JUNQUERA BLANCO, GUMERSINDO, Felipe Menendez 6, Ap 176, Gijón

Funnel: Black with houseflag on white band
Hull: Black
Services: General tramping

GUMERSINDO JUNQUERA BLANCO Y VICENTE FIGAREDO
Maruja y Aurora 1905 LithR 3913 6988 358–4 49–11 23–6 8.5
ex Angela 29, ex River Clyde 20

MENCHACA, ANTONIO, Gran Via 34, Bilbao

Services: General tramping

Cilurnum 1919 Dixon2 3077 5080 343–0 48–2 21–8 10.0
ex Brescia 38, ex Cilurnum 37, launched as War Swell
Uribitarte 1922 Burntd 3456 6140 331–7 48–8 22–2 9.5
ex Cosenza 39, ex Uribitarte 37

MUMBRÚ, DOMINGO, Via Layetana 12, Barcelona

Services: General tramping

Norte 1893 Ropnrl 2825 4960 321–3 41–6 23–3 8.0
ex Alcazer 23, ex Eva 12
Sud 1894 Irvin4 2949 314.0 39–11 21–11 8.0
ex M Arnus –, ex Josefa Raich –, ex M Arnus 19, ex Temiya Maru 16, ex Saint Jerome 02

NAVAJAS, ALEJANDRO, Calle Aguirre 12, Bilbao

Services: General tramping

COMPAÑÍA GENERAL DE NAV
El Condado 1920 Hamtn2 3031 5555 343–6 48–11 20–7 9.5
El Montecillo 1920 DunlpB 3031 5555 343–6 48–11 20–7 9.5

PERO-SANZ Y ZORRILLA, TOMAS, Colon de Larreategui 5, Bilbao

Services: General tramping

JOSÉ AGUSTIN DE MUTIOZABAL
Achuri 1894 GrayX 2734 4140 315–11 43–0 20–1 8.0
ex Rafael 29, ex Garton 12
Sendeja 1921 Harkes 2647 4464 319–0 42–3 21–10 9.5
ex Pedrosa 33

RAMOS, HIJO DE RAMON A, Paseo de Colón 19, Barcelona

Services: General tramping

Nuria R 1893 GrayX 2733 3872 290.0 38–1 21–7 8.0
ex Maria Elisa 30, ex Rufina 29, ex Algorteño 22, ex Roumania 97
Ramon Alonso R 1898 McMlln 4017 6324 380–0 46–4 23–7 8.0
ex Balmes 28, ex José Gallart 11, ex Montclair 02

Note: Also vesssels under 2000gt

REAL SOCORRO, MARQUÉS DEL, Calle Navarra 5, Bilbao

Services: General tramping

Delfina 1919 TyneIr 3037 5080 331.2 46–10 21–9 9.0
ex Itxas-Gane 38, ex Delfina 36, Hallside 29
Sebastian 1920 Blumr2 3024 5174 346–0 46–10 21–9 9.0
ex Itxas-Alde 38, ex Sebastian 36, ex Azteca –, ex Sebastian –, ex Daybeam 29

ROMANI Y MIGUEL, SOCIEDAD ANÓNIMA, Muelle 15, Grao de Valencia

Services: General tramping

BANCO DE VALENCIA (registered owner), Alfredo Calderon 11, Valencia
Rita Sister 1900 Austin 2845 4882 333–10 46–11 20–8 8.0
ex Nuria 24, ex Almirall Lluis de Requesens 18, ex Asuarca 15, ex Agnes 13

Services: General tramping

RUEDA, DOMINGO, Nuñez de Balboa 12, Madrid

COMPAÑÍA DE VAPOR CARMEN SOCIEDAD LTDA

Ship	Year	Builder	GRT	DWT	Length	Beam	Draught	Speed
Nuestra Señora del Carmen	1895	Doxfrd	3482	5608	340.0	45–7	22–0	8.0
ex Begoña No 4 27, ex Diciembre 18								

Services: General tramping

SOCIEDAD METALÚRGICA DURO FELGUERA, Ap 51, Gijón

Ship	Year	Builder	GRT	DWT	Length	Beam	Draught	Speed
Ciaño	1901	Nthmbl	4264	7450	370–11	47–11	25–0	8.0
ex Vircov 39, ex Ciaño 37, ex Vicen 34, ex Pura Rasilla 29, ex Craonne 24, ex Turnwell 15, ex Queen Alexandra 13								
Valentin Ruiz Senen	1902	Craggl	3827	5540	339–11	42–2	23–6	8.0
ex Margari 27, ex Maria 20, ex Agenoria 20								

Services: Spanish ports–Mediterranean ports; most vessels laid up during Spanish Civil War

Note: The above vessels were seized by Nationalist forces during the Spanish Civil War

Note: Also several smaller vessels

SPAIN, NATIONALIST GOVERNMENT OF, Burgos

CERENCIA DE BUQUES MERCANTES PARA SERVICIOS OFICIALES

Ship	Year	Builder	GRT	DWT	Length	Beam	Draught	Speed
Castillo Ampudia	1912	Rijkee	3209	5315	357–7	48–5	21–4	9.0
ex Katayama 39, ex Jason 34, ex Charon 12								
Castillo Andrade	1914	RDuck2	3457	6000	380.5	48–0	22–7	8.5
ex Vigo 39, ex François 38, ex Pagasitikos 37, ex Sicily 33								
Castillo Bellver	1923	ThmpsJ	4713	6624	378–2	52–10	23–0	9.5
ex Lensovet 39, ex Kazan 35, ex Age 35								
Castillo la Mota	1916	WoodS2	2677	3859	320.8	43–0	19–2	9.0
ex Hordena 39, ex Horden 37								
Castillo Fuensaldana	1910	GrayX	3705	6180	362–0	50–2	21–5	8.0
ex Everards 39, ex Ronturn 33, ex Camerata 28								
Castillo Madrigal	1920	Sundld	4528	8287	390.0	54–0	24–4	10.0
ex Nicolaou Eleni 39, ex Eleni Nicolaou 37, ex Diadem 34								
Castillo Maqueda (m)	1931	61Komm	2152	3199	284–0	39–8	21–3	10.0
ex Skvortsov Stepanov 39								
Castillo Mombeltran	1904	Rickmr	3667	5980	370–8	45–0	23–11	8.0
ex Ellinico Vouno 39, ex Angelos L 37, ex Cape Point 27, ex Stambul 21, ex Maria Rickmers 12								
Castillo Montiel	1913	RDuck2	4792	8533	406–10	40–10	24–9	8.5
ex Farnham 39, ex Putney 36, ex Neotsfield 33, ex Trischen 19, Dartwen 17								
Castillo Montjuich (st)	1919	FurnH	6581	10,146	428–0	55–10	28–2	11.0
ex African Mariner 39, ex Bois-Soleil 37, ex Scheldemonde 28, Wolhanndel 28, ex Andalusier 25, ex War Vigour 20								
Castillo Olite	1921	RottDD	3545	6020	373–0	49–10	22–3	10.0
ex Postyschev 38, ex Zwartewater 35, ex Zaandijk 30								
Castillo Oropesa	1917	Doxfrd	6600	9380	434–6	54–0	28–4	9.5
ex Victoria 38, ex Ekaterini Nicolaou 38, ex General Church 32								
Castillo Peñafiel	1918	DeNrd2	2485	4217	296–4	45–4	20–0	8.0
ex Smidovitch 38, ex Noord 35								
Castillo Simancas	1907	Conn2	4937	8100	400.0	52–0	24–10	8.5
ex Coruña 39, ex Sydney 38, ex Polymnia 37, ex Kintyre 29, ex Wyncote 24, ex Den of Ruthven 15								
Castillo Villafranca (m)	1932	61Komm	2081	3194	284–0	39–8	21–3	10.0
ex Tsurupa 39								
Max Hoelts (m)	1930	Sevrny	3972	5950	361–3	48–10	21–9	11.0

Funnel: Black with white anchor
Hull: Black, red boot-topping, with white dividing line
Services: Barcelona–Galveston; Barcelona–UK–NW Europe; Mediterranean–Cuba–Central America

URQUIJO Y ALDECOA LTDA, Gran Via 1, Ap 170, Bilbao

COMPAÑÍA MARÍTIMA DEL NERVION

Ship	Year	Builder	GRT	DWT	Length	Beam	Draught	Speed
Mar Blanco	1920	EspB	5152	6700	371–8	48–1	26–8	10.0
Mar Cantabrico (m2,P12)	1930	Eusk	6632	7595	421–5	54–2	25–11	12.5
Mar Caribe	1920	EspB	5152	6700	371–8	48–1	26–8	10.0
Mar Negro (m2,P12)	1930	Eusk	6632	7595	421–5	54–2	25–11	12.5
Mar Rojo	1917	Nervn	3640	5050	336–2	47–1	20–9	9.5
Mar Tirreno	1908	Irvin1	3000	5323	336–7	47–0	21–1	8.5
ex Luchana 39, ex Oquendo 22, ex Tuscany 13								

FRANCISCO ALDECOA URIARTE

Ship	Year	Builder	GRT	DWT	Length	Beam	Draught	Speed
Aldecoa	1922	EspB	6089	8524	379–6	49–11	18–4	10.0

Menchaca: Cilurnum *was launched by Sir Raylton Dixon & Co in October 1919 as the standard War 'C' type* War Swell, *and following purchase while fitting out was delivered to Spain as* Cilurnum *in December 1919. The 'C' type was one of the most numerous of the First World War standard ship with 86 being completed and a further two orders cancelled. They were a scaled-down version of the 'A' and 'B' types.* Cilurnum *was fitted with a Richardsons, Westgarth triple expansion engine of 2200ihp. She was broken up at Santander in 1971 (Alex Duncan)*

Trasatlantica: Habana *was completed in August 1923 as* Alfonso XIII *(as pictured here) for service from Bilbao to Cuba and Mexico, later extended to New York. Her completion had been delayed due to heavy damage caused by a fire while fitting-out. She was fitted with Española/Parsons single reduction geared turbines of 9200shp. She was laid up at Bordeaux during most of the Spanish Civil War, and on June 26 1939 was transferred to Bilbao, where she was damaged by fire, which resulted in rebuilding with the loss of most of her passenger accommodation. Following a limited number of transatlantic voyages during the hositilities it was decided that passenger accommodation should be re-installed due to heavy demand for passages, and this was completed during a refit at Brooklyn in 1946–47.* Habana *was withdrawn from service in 1960 and sold to breakers at Vigo, but breaking was not started and in 1962 she was sold for conversion to a fish factory ship under the name* Galicia. *She was broken up in 1978 (RW Jordan collection)*

Services: General tramping

VELASCO MARTIN, JOAQUIN, Calle Felipe Menendez 8, Ap 62, Gijón

Mina Piquera	1900	BethMS	3754	5495	331.5	47–2	23–0	8.0
ex Cabo Santa Maria 31, ex Segundo 24, ex Pleiades 22								

Funnel: Black with with emblem of two white **X**s joined in the centre by a horizontal white line
Hull: White or black, red boot-topping
Services: Italy–France–Spain–Portugal–US–Brazil–Uruguay–Argentina

YBARRA & COMPAÑÍA, S EN C, Calle Menéndez Pelayo 2, Ap 15, Seville

Passenger/general cargo vessels								
Cabo Quilates* (m,P76/3)								
	1927	Eusk	6629	7500	414–0	53–2	23–6	12.5
Cabo San Agustin** (m2,P12/2,500/3)								
	1931	EspB	12,589	9900	498–7	63–4	25–4	16.0
Cabo San Antonio (m2,P12/2,500/3)								
	1930	EspB	12,275	9880	498–7	63–4	25–4	16.0
General cargo vessels								
Cabo Cervera	1912	Eusk	2164	3690	273–11	38–11	21–9	8.0
ex Rachen 39, ex Cabo Cervera 37								
Cabo Creux***	1919	Nervn	3717	4800	325–7	47–1	21–0	8.5
ex Kardin 39, ex Cabo Creux 37								
Cabo Espartel	1920	Ech&L	4282	6536	330.1	48–0	26–6	9.5
ex Sparire 39, ex Cabo Espartel 37								
Cabo Huertas	1922	EspB	2776	4067	292–6	42–0	22–6	10.0
ex Tausend 39, ex Cabo Huertas 38								
Cabo La Plata	1908	EspB	2002	3290	265.1	38–8	21–2	8.0
ex Plaustra 39, ex Cabo la Plata 37								
Cabo Menor	1912	G&G5	2043	3607	265–1	38–6	21–6	8.0
Cabo Ortegal	1919	Nervn	3660	4882	338–9	47–1	21–1	9.5
ex Libero 39, ex Aketz 37, ex Cabo Ortegal 37								
Cabo Prior	1917	Eusk	3367	4643	331–2	44–0	22–1	9.0
ex Rio Tajo 35, ex Mar Tirreno 28								
Cabo Quintres	1916	Eusk	2905	4097	306.0	44–3	21–0	8.5
ex Baurdo 39, ex Cabo Quintres 37, ex Mouro 29								
Cabo Razo	1926	Eusk	2879	4063	317–10	43–3	23–1	10.0
ex Raggio 39, ex Cabo Razo 37								
Cabo Roche	1922	EspB	2776	4097	292–7	42–6	22–5	10.0
ex Gadofu 39, ex Cabo Roche 37								
Cabo Sacratif	1909	Eusk	2174	3457	273–11	38–8	21–5	8.5
ex Zafra 39, ex Cabo Sacratif 38								
Cabo Silleiro	1915	Eusk	2896	4132	318–11	47–5	20–10	9.5
ex Roosile 39, ex Anzora 37, ex Cabo Silleiro 37, ex Rio Miño 35, ex Mar Mediterraneo 28								
Cabo Villano	1920	Ech&L	4282	6523	341.2	47–11	25–9	10.0
ex Waltraud 38, ex Contra 37, ex Fermia 36, ex Cabo Villano 36								
YBARRA Y COMPAÑÍA, S EN C AND NAVIERA AZNAR SA (*qv*)								
Cabo San Sebastian	1921	Ech&L	2661	3720	299–11	44–0	19–6	9.5
ex Rio Segre 39, ex Santamaña 28								

Note: * Sequestrated by Republican Government 1936, renamed *Ibai*, seized by USSR 1939, renamed *Dvina*; ** sequestrated by Republican Government 1936, seized by USSR 1939, renamed *Dnepr*; *** sunk Valencia 1.2.39

Services: General tramping

ZABALA, GOITA Y COMPAÑÍA, Calle de Buenos Aires, Ap 84, Bilbao

COMPAÑÍA NAVIERA ANÓNIMA BASOA, SA

Iñake	1888	GrayX	2292	3500	290.0	38–2	21–1	7.5
ex Arantzazu 35, ex Horacio 17, ex Evelyn 05								

Sweden

ABRAHAMSEN, S, Sveavågen 34–36, Stockholm

REDERI-A/B IRIS

Lestris	1898	Rodger	2629	4310	314–4	44–2	19–8	9.0
ex Lao 20, ex Hyllos 15, ex Craigneuk 07								

Funnel: Black with white band
Hull: Black
Services: General tramping
Note: This firm also owned short-sea vessels and vessels under Finnish flag – see S Abrahamsen in Finland section

BANCK, CHRISTER, Villa Blasut, Själlandsgatan, Helsingborg

C A Banck	1913	Sørlan	1825	2950	275–0	42–1	17–7	9.5
ex Kapolna 28, ex Gogsjø 19, ex Libra 15								

BARTHEN, IVAR, Nybrokajen 7vii, Stockholm

REDERI-A/B SUECIA

Sårimner	1909	Doxfrd	2409	3800	302–0	43–7	18–11	8.5
ex Inland 34								

Funnel: Black with white B on blue five-pointed star on white band
Services: General tramping

BERGLUND, C A, Fiskhamnen, Gothenburg

REDERI-A/B MAJVIKEN

Ella	1908	Craig2	2102	3550	281.0	43–10	18–0	9.5
ex Norburn 29								

Services: General tramping

Note: This firm also controlled vessels under the Finnish flag – see I Barthen in Finland section

BÖRJESSON, ALLAN, Hamntorget 5, Helsingborg

REDERI-A/B ALFA								
Mona	1902	GrayX	2352	3350	279.6	42–8	18–10	8.5
ex Bratland 27, ex Wermland 11								
REDERI-A/B ATOS								
Ariel (st)	1920	Baltca	1768	3100	301–9	40–2	19–1	9.0
ex Öresund 27, ex Danemark 26								
Atos	1902	Helsgr	2160	3500	302–3	42–8	18–7	8.0
ex Uppland 24, ex Marie 17								
Hildur	1906	Kockum	2119	3350	279.8	43–9	18–3	8.0
ex Colombia 25, ex Brei 22, ex Nord 15								
REDERI-A/B SIGYN								
Sigyn	1897	Camp1	1973	3200	280.2	40–6	18–10	9.0
Siljan	1920	TyneIr	3060	5150	328.0	46–10	21–8	9.0
ex Pilton 38								
Sixten	1912	Sundld	2119	3640	287.1	42–1	19–4	8.0
ex Sydhavet 32, ex Böklund 30, ex Svartfond 29, ex Petra 18								

Funnel: Black with yellow B on black disc superimposed on blue over white over blue bands all on broad white band
Services: General tramping

Funnel: Black with blue emblem on yellow band
Services: General tramping

Note: Also smaller vessels

BRODIN, ERIK O, Regeringsgatan 45, Postfack 1214, Stockholm

Lena	bldg	Fredst	1938	3340	315–4	44–2	18–9	11.5
REDERI-A/B BUR								
Bur	1919	Shangh	1954	2985	279–7	42–2	17–9	10.0
ex Risvær 22								
REDERI-A/B DISA								
Anita (m)	1938	LindVv	2543	3750	331–4	44–8	18–8	12.5
Astri (m)	1937	LindVv	2536	3760	331–4	44–7	18–8	12.5
Disa	1918	Shangh	1959	2980	279–7	42–4	17–10	10.0
ex Solvær 22								
Lali	order	Fredst	1931	3340	315–4	44–1	18–9	11.5
REDERI-A/B KARE								
O A Brodin	1921	Brodin	2119	2990	266.1	42–10	18–0	10.5
ex Erato 35, ex O A Brodin 22								

Funnel: Yellow with three narrow blue bands with blue disc superimposed on middle band
Hull: Grey, red boot-topping
Services: General tramping

Note: Also vessels under 1500gt

BROSTRÖM & SON, AXEL, Broströmia, Pakhusplatsen 6, Gothenburg

Manager and/or agent for

ANGBATS-A/B FERM								
General cargo vessel								
Falsterbo (m,P10)	1925	Eriksb	4104	6750	365–7	50–8	23–2	12.5
A/B SVENSKA AMERIKA LINIEN								
Passenger vessels								
Drottningholm (st3,P532/cab,854/t)	1905	Steph1	11,285	8450	538–5	60–0	32–0	16.5
ex Virginian 20								
Gripsholm (m2,P700)	1925	ArmWh1	18,815	9957	574–6	74–5	29–0	16.5
Kungsholm (m2,P209/cab,395/t,970/3)	1928	Blohm	21,256	9340	609–2	78–2	29–1	17.0
Stockholm (m3,P1350;640cr)	order	CRDA2	30,390	7255	678–3	83–2	35.4	19.0
A/B SVENSKA AMERIKA–MEXIKO LINIEN								
Blankaholm (m,P4)	1930	Eriksb	2901	5065	349–5	46–11	21–8	12.5
Braheholm (P4)	1920	Coughl	5610	8674	427–0	54–1	24–4	11.0
Danaholm (m,P12)	1939	Helsgr	3643	5935	428–6	53–2	23–5	16.0

Funnel: Yellow with blue and red bands bearing white AB; Ferm – black with three red and two bands bearing white F; SAL, SAML, SOK – yellow with blue disc bearing three yellow crowns
Hull: Black or white, red boot-topping; SAL – white, red boot-topping; SAML, SOK – black or white, red boot-topping
Services: SAL – Gothenburg–New York–Halifax; SAML – Scandinavia–Canada–US E coast–US Gulf ports–Cuba–Mexico; SOK – Scandinavia–British India–Ceylon; Scandinavia–Red Sea ports–Straits Settlements–Philippines–China–Japan; SOL – Gothenburg–Near East; Gothenburg–UK; general tramping

Broström/SAML: The motor vessel Vasaholm *was completed by Götaverken in January 1930, and was fitted with a Götaverken/B&W 6-cylinder oil engine of 2150bhp. With her full-funnel appearance she resembled more a steamer than a motor vessel. In 1944 she was employed as a Swedish Red Cross relief ship in the Mediterranean, a duty undertaken by many Swedish ships.* Vasaholm *survived the war and in 1954 changed hands within Sweden and was renamed* Victoria. *A Greek company purchased her in 1965 and she was renamed* Stavros, *and a further sale in 1967 saw her trading as the Greek-owned* Priamos. *She was broken up in 1973 (Alex Duncan)*

Broström/SOK: Bali *was on order from Öresunds at the end of 1939, and was completed in December 1941. She was fitted with two Götaverken 6-cylinder oil engines with a total 7900bhp.* Bali *survived the war and was in service with Broström until 1968 when she was sold to Cyprus and renamed* Alma. *She was broken up at Kaohsiung in 1979 (RW Jordan collection)*

Joh Gorthon: Herma Gorthon, *a boilers on deck type with a quadruple expansion engine of 2300ihp, was built at Fredrikstad, Norway, and completed in December 1936. During the Second World War she did not suffer any war damage, but on December 12 1943 ran aground at Negrillos Reef, Colombia. She refloated on January 10 1944, and on April 15 was declared a constructive total loss. In October 1944 she was resold by her insurers to Gorthon, repaired, and re-entered service. She was sold within Sweden in April 1951 and renamed* Stellatus. *Her career came to an end on March 3 1959 when she ran aground in Freswick Bay, 2.5 miles south of Duncansby Head, when on voyage from Turku to Ellesmere Port with woodpulp. She was abandoned by her crew and on March 10 broke in two and became a total loss (Gorthon Lines)*

Kexholm (m)	1937	Eriksb	3777	6780	397–0	52–2	23–7	13.5
Korsholm (m,P4)	1925	Göta	2685	5100	339–8	45–8	21–4	10.5
Lagaholm (m,P4)	1929	Eriksb	2858	5155	348–6	46–11	21–7	11.0
Ragnhildsholm (m,P4)	1929	Eriksb	2858	5155	348–5	46–11	21–7	11.0
Rydboholm (m)	1933	Göta	3201	5430	387–7	49–2	21–8	13.0
Stegeholm (m,P12)	1939	LindVv	4571	7350	455–7	57–2	23–11	15.0
Stureholm (m2)	1919	Göta	4600	7880	408.7	54–0	23–7	11.5
Svaneholm (m,P2)	1930	Eriksb	2921	5065	349–6	47–0	21–8	12.5
Trolleholm (m2)	1922	Kockum	5084	7535	381–4	51–4	24–9	11.5
Tunaholm (m,P8)	1938	Göta	3460	6060	428–6	53–2	23–3	15.0
Uddeholm (m)	1934	Eriksb	3606	6820	371–0	52–2	23–6	13.0
Vasaholm (m,P8)	1930	Göta	4209	7345	411–7	52–8	23–11	12.0
A/B SVENSKA OSTASIATISKA KOMPANIET (Swedish East Asiatic Co Ltd)								
General cargo vessels								
Agra (m2,P2)	1925	Göta	4569	7905	408–10	52–8	25–2	12.0
Bali (m2)	order	Örsnd2	6584	10,100	477–10	64–2	27–4	16.0
Canton (m2,P10)	1922	Örsnd2	5783	9370	440–0	56–2	26–3	13.0
Ceylon	1911	Leslie	5235	9165	441–3	53–11	25–10	12.0
Delhi (m2,P2)	1925	LindMo	4592	7845	409–1	52–7	25–2	12.0
Formosa (m2)	1921	B&W	5559	10,860	442–6	55–1	26–10	14.0
Japan (r/t)	1911	Leslie	5230	9165	441–3	54–1	25–5	12.0
Mindoro (m2)	order	Göta	6532	10,040	477–10	64–2	27–4	16.0
Nagara (m2,P6)	1929	Göta	6589	10,320	455–10	57–0	27–5	14.0
Nanking (m2)	1924	Göta	5957	9830	443–9	56–1	26–10	12.0
Ningpo (m2,P12)	1938	Eriksb	6089	10,100	461.8	62–3	27–6	15.5
Peiping (m2,P6)	1931	Göta	6393	10,320	455–10	57–0	27–6	14.0
Shantung (m2,P6)	1929	Göta	6598	10,400	455–10	57–0	27–6	14.0
Sumatra	1914	Earles	5352	9360	442–10	53–10	26–0	12.0
Tamara (m2,P6)	1931	Göta	6393	10,330	455–11	57–0	27–6	14.0
Tonghai (m2)	bldg	Göta	6543	10,040	477–10	64–2	27–4	16.0
ÅNGFARTYGS-A/B TIRFING								
General cargo vessels								
Atland	1910	Doxfrd	5349	8030	388.9	52–5	24–2	9.5
Hemland (m)	bldg	Kockum	4767	8850	452–2	58–2	25–1	13.0
Nyland	1909	Doxfrd	3526	5650	326.9	48–8	21–1	8.5
Sydland	1920	Doxfrd	5136	9390	434–11	54–1	25–7	10.0
Ore carriers								
Amerikaland (m2)	1925	DeutsH	15,337	22,780	571–8	72–2	34–0	11.0
Malmland (m)	order	Eriksb	8673	12,620	491–6	61–0	26–9	12.0
Svealand (m2)	1925	DeutsH	15,339	22,780	571–7	72–2	34–0	11.0
SVENSKA ORIENT LINIEN*								
General cargo vessels								
Bardaland (m,P2)	1936	Göta	2588	4575	370–10	50–2	21–6	14.5
Birkaland (m,P2)	1935	Eriksb	2658	4760	370–4	50–2	21–6	14.5
Boreland (m,P2)	1938	Eriksb	2613	4680	370–4	50–2	21–6	14.5
Brageland (m,P2)	1937	Eriksb	2602	4680	370–4	50–2	21–6	14.5
Gotland (m)	1929	Eriksb	1874	3240	305–2	43–0	18–9	12.0
Lappland** *ex Benares 34*	1920	FurnH	5762	9190	413–8	52–4	26–2	10.0
Sagoland (m2)	1939	Eriksb	3243	5105	406–6	54–8	22–6	15.0
Skogaland (m2)	order	Eriksb	3244	5075	406–6	54–9	22–6	15.0
Sunnanland (m2)	bldg	Eriksb	3240	5110	406–6	54–9	22–6	15.0
Vasaland (m,P12)	1934	Eriksb	2712	4770	364–6	48–8	21–6	14.0
Vikingland (m,P12)	1932	Eriksb	2629	4275	355–7	46–8	21–8	14.0
Vingaland (m,P12)	1935	Eriksb	2720	4755	364–6	48–8	21–6	14.0

Note: * Vessels listed here were owned by Tirfing and operated on Svenska Orient Linien services, which also see under 'Zegluga Pólska' Spólka Akcynja in Poland section; **Sold Greece 1939, renamed *Pegasus*
Note: Also vessels under 1500gt

BRUNKMAN, RAGNAR, Kungsgatan 8, Helsingborg

Funnel: White with blue B, black top
Services: General tramping
Note: Also short-sea vessels

REDERI-A/B BRUBOR

Graculus *ex Bifrost 29*	1923	Boeles	1967	3140	265.9	42–1	18–2	9.5

DE CHAMPS, ARNOLD, Kungsgatan 7, Stockholm

Funnel: Blue, black top
Services: NW Europe–London–Mediterranean (1939)
Note: Also short-sea vessel *Ethel* (built 1882/1511gt)

REDERI-A/B MONARK

Monark (r/t)	1938	LindVv	1786	–	307–10	43–2	19–1	11.0

Funnel: Blue with white Maltese cross
Services: General tramping

FANGES & PAHLSSON'S REDERIER, Kungsgatan 8, Helsingborg

REDERI-A/B ÆOLUS								
Kattegatt	1903	GrayX	2138	3550	290.0	42–1	18–9	8.0
ex John Lundwall 32, ex Elizabeth Harrison 24, ex Madame Enterprise 21, ex Alicia 18								
REDERI-A/B AMFITRITE								
Triton	1908	Irvin1	1869	3200	279.2	40–1	18–0	8.5
ex Patria 36, ex Phyllis Seed 24, ex Westmore 22, ex Portinglis 22								
REDERI-A/B ORVAR								
Orvar	1908	NordsE	1633	2700	281–4	39–7	17–2	9.0
ex Klosterfos 28, ex Hilde Podeus 12								

Services: General tramping

GALEEN, IVAR H, Engelsbraktsgatan 12, Gothenburg

REDERI-A/B ERLING								
Miramar	1938	Helsbg	1555	2460	267–11	38–2	17–0	11.0

Services: General tramping

GLÜCKSMAN, LEOPOLD,
c/o A/B Glücksmans Metallaffår, Kungsgatan 1, Gothenburg

REDERI-A/B RUTH								
Ruth	1912	Laing	4229	5824	344.5	46–8	23–4	10.0
ex Mexicano 35								

Funnel: White with blue disc bearing yellow monogram, black top
Hull: Grey, red boot-topping
Services: General tramping; timber trades
Note: Also vessels engaged in Baltic/NW Europe/UK trade

GORTHON, JOH, (Joh and Stig Gorthon), Järnvågsgatan 1, Helsingborg

REDEREI-A/B ACTIV								
Alida Gorthon	1902	GrayX	2370	3850	302.4	43–3	18–11	8.5
ex Karlsvik 34, ex Alida 19, ex Atheniana 13, ex Athinaia 11, ex Atheniana 09								
Carl Gorthon	1939	Fredst	1811	3415	300–0	43–11	18–11	12.0
Convallaria	1921	Versch	1996	3250	280.4	40–2	18–5	9.5
Tilia Gorthon	1930	Fredst	1776	3400	273–5	42–2	19–5	10.5
REDEREI-A/B GEFION								
Ada Gorthon	1917	Boeles	2399	3950	292.0	44–0	19.9	9.0
ex H Unér 22, ex Vettern 19, ex Signe 18								
Ivan Gorthon	1935	Aalb3	1799	3450	298–6	43–6	19–2	11.0
Ragna Gorthon (r/t)	1935	Aalb3	1844	3425	298–0	43–7	19–2	11.0
Stig Gorthon	1924	NewWat	2262	3750	304–1	44–11	18–7	10.0
ex Elva Seed 29								
REDERI-A/B GYLFE								
Frans Gorthon	1937	Fredst	1768	3450	315–4	44–2	18–9	11.5
Herma Gorthon	1936	Fredst	1768	3380	315–0	44–2	18–9	11.5
Maria Gorthon	1930	Örsnd2	1572	2910	275–0	40–6	17–9	10.0
Oscar Gorthon	1939	Fredst	1811	3415	300–0	44–0	18–11	12.0

Funnel: Black with yellow GO emblem on blue band (some had very small funnels)
Hull: Grey, red boot-topping
Services: Mainly ore; some tramping

GRÄNGESBERG-OXELÖSUND, TRAFIKAKTIEBOLAGET,
Gustaf Adolfs Torg 18, Postfack 1189 and 1190, Stockholm

Abisko	1913	Göta	3130	4900	336.8	46–11	20–6	9.0
Boden (r/t)	1914	ThmpsJ	4292	7480	399–8	53–9	23–9	10.0
C F Liljevalch	1920	Göta	5514	8470	394.4	52–2	25–7	10.0
Erik Frisell (m)	1926	Göta	5025	7425	410–0	52–8	24–4	10.5
Grängesberg (r/t)	1921	NewWat	5448	7380	399–0	50–1	24–11	10.0
Kalix	1913	Dixon2	2817	5015	325–0	46–5	22–0	9.5
Kiruna	1921	Göta	5513	8470	398–1	53–2	25–7	10.0
Laponia (m2)	1922	Göta	5659	8855	399–0	53–8	26–3	10.5
Luleå (m2)	1922	Göta	5659	8855	399–0	53–5	26–3	10.5
Luossa (m2)	1923	Göta	5623	8820	399–0	53–5	26–2	10.5
Mertainen	1907	Hamtn2	4665	7194	385–5	52–2	23–0	10.0
ex Strathlyon 15								
Murjek (m)	1925	Göta	5024	7425	410–0	52–8	24–4	11.0
Narvik (r/t)	1914	ThmpsJ	4281	7480	399–8	53–9	23–9	10.0
Nuolja (m2)	1923	Göta	6864	10,480	421–0	55–1	28–7	10.5
Oxelösund (m2)	1923	Göta	5653	8820	399–0	53–8	26–2	10.5
Pajala (m2)	1924	Göta	6865	10,480	429–2	55–1	28–6	10.5
Polcirkeln	1907	Lindhm	1927	3355	291.6	39–11	18–4	9.0
Porjus	1906	Austin	3006	4725	318–7	46–6	19–9	9.5
ex Hampshire 12								
Sarek (m)	order	Göta	5415	8980	442–10	56–9	25–11	12.0

Sir Ernest Cassel	1910	Leslie	7738	10,780	454.4	60–4	25–9	10.0
ex Ernest 22, ex Sir Ernest Cassel 21								
Stråssa (m2)	1922	Göta	5650	8855	399–0	53–5	26–3	10.5
Svartön	1906	ThmpR2	2469	3970	299–0	44–6	19–2	9.5
ex Cedargrove 12								
Torne	1913	Lindhm	3867	6100	359.5	50–2	21–6	9.5
Vollrath Tham (m)	1909	Leslie	5806	8000	387.1	56–6	24–3	10.0
conv steamer 25								

HALL, F L, Rekekroken, Jonstorp

Services: General tramping

REDERI-A/B JONSTORP

Leonardia	1906	Blyth	1706	2600	258.9	37–0	18–0	8.0
ex Sheaf Field 23								

HILLERSTRÖM, OTTO, Kungsgatan 2, Helsingborg

Funnel: Yellow with houseflag
Hull: Black or grey, red boot-topping
Services: General tramping

REDERIET BELOS

Eros	1898	Craggl	2146	3550	292.0	43–2	18–1	8.0
ex Vessman 21, ex Enon 19, ex Biarritz 13, ex Royal Exchange 11								

REDERI-A/B HELSINGBORG

Belos	1929	ThmpR2	2830	5300	333–0	46–7	22–4	10.0
Consul Corfitzon	1912	Dixon2	2870	5200	336–8	46–11	21–2	9.0
ex Mikelis 27, ex Atlantis 23, ex Fullerton 23								
Consul Olsson*	1905	SHWR	2721	4650	324–6	46–6	19–9	8.0
ex Gracefield 25								
Milos	1898	Blyth	3058	5150	325.1	47–0	20–11	7.5
ex Brynmead 22, ex Izaston 20, ex William Broadley 12								

Note: * Sold K M Kallström 1939, renamed *Korsö*
Note: Also the smaller *Vera* (built 1904/1341gt)

HÖGBERG, ERIK, Birger Jarlsgatan 4, Stockholm

Funnel: Fredrika – black with white F on black shield on white band
Services: General tramping

REDERI-A/B FREDRIKA

Dorotea	1918	Lindhm	1814	3308	277–0	42–6	18–11	9.0
ex Adolf Bratt 37, ex Adolf 24								
Gudmundrå	1921	Örsnd2	1772	3300	287–0	41–2	19–11	9.0
Orania	1919	Lindhm	1874	3140	277–0	42–9	18–11	9.0

REDERI-A/B MANHEM

Fredhem	1923	Koch	2752	3790	300–2	42–7	19–0	9.5
ex Grekland 31, ex Heinz Horn 28								

Note: Also short-sea vessels

JOHNSON, AXEL AXELSON, (Johnson Line), Stureplan 3, Postfack 7196, Stockholm

Funnel: Black with blue J on yellow star on blue band between two narrow yellow bands
Hull: Light grey, red boot-topping
Services: Sweden–Brazil–R Plate; Sweden, Antwerp–Colombia–Panama–Central America–W coast North America; Sweden, NW Europe–W coast South America

REDERI-A/B NORDSTJERNAN

General cargo vessels

Annie Johnson (m2,P22/1,28/3)	1925	Göta	4917	7310	409–0	52–7	25–2	13.0
Argentina (m2,P12/1)	1935	Göta	5300	7060	440–0	55–11	25–3	15.5
Axel Johnson (m2,P22/1,28/3)	1925	Göta	4919	7310	409–0	52–7	25–2	13.0
Balboa (m2,P12/1,10/3)	1919	Göta	5554	9460	440–0	56–2	26–1	12.0
Brasil (m2,P12/1)	1935	Göta	5301	7060	440–0	55–11	25–3	15.5
Buenos Aires (m2,P12/1,10/3)	1920	Göta	5653	9440	439–8	56–2	26–3	12.0
Canada (m2,P12/1,10/3)	1921	Göta	5558	9460	439–8	56–2	26–2	12.0
Chile (m2,P12/1)	1937	Göta	5305	7060	440–1	55–11	25–3	15.5
Colombia (m2,P12/1)	1937	Göta	5305	7060	440–1	55–11	25–3	15.5
Ecuador (m2,P12/1)	bldg	Göta	6980	7400	440–1	55–11	26–3	15.5
Kronprinsessan Margareta (m2,P10/1)	1914	B&W	3774	6550	375–10	51–5	23–4	10.5
Lima (m2,P12/1)	1918	B&W	3805	6530	384–0	51–6	23–5	11.0
Margaret Johnson (m2,P22/1,28/3)	1928	Göta	5210	7470	425–7	54–1	25–3	13.5

Johnson: The motor vessel Nordstjernan *was one of a large series of similar ships built for this owner during the 1930s. She was completed in August 1935 and was fitted with two Götaverken 8-cylinder oil engines of 5300bhp. During the Second World War she spent much of the time laid up and the rest of the time sailing in safe-conduct traffic.* Nordstjernan *was sold to Greece in 1968 and renamed* Frances. *She was broken up at Kaohsiung in 1969 (RW Jordan collection)*

Källström: Malmen, *built at Dordrecht in November 1919 for the Transatlantic company, was sold to K M Kallström in 1936 and renamed* Ljusterö. *She survived the Second World War, during which she made many voyages between Germany and Sweden, and arrived at Ystad, Sweden, in November 1959, to be broken up (Alex Duncan)*

Svea: Hedrun *was completed at Landskrona in September 1920 as* Hjalmar Blomberg *and renamed* Hedrun *in 1921. She was torpedoed and sunk by* U48 *on August 16 1940 when on voyage from Swansea to Newport, Rhode Island, with 3009 tons of coal (Alex Duncan)*

Nordstjernan (m2,P12/1)	1935	Göta	5301	7060	440–1	56–0	25–3	15.5
Pacific (m2,P12/1)	1914	B&W	3730	6550	380–0	51–6	23–4	10.5
Pedro Christophersen (m2,P12/1)	1913	B&W	3731	6550	377–0	51–8	23–4	10.5
Peru (m2,P12/1)	1938	Göta	6022	6910	440–1	55–11	25–3	13.5
San Francisco (m2,P12/1)	1915	B&W	3705	6550	376–4	51–2	23–4	10.5
Santos (m2,P10/1)	1925	Kockum	3877	6680	367–0	51–6	23–4	12.0
Suecia (m2,P12/1)	1912	B&W	3726	6550	375–10	51–8	23–4	10.5
Uruguay (m2,P12/1)	1935	Göta	5301	7060	440–0	55–11	25–3	15.5
Valparaiso (m2,P12/1)	1917	B&W	3671	6530	367–0	51–5	23–5	10.5
Venezuela (m2,P12/1)	1939	Göta	6991	9200	440–0	55–11	26–2	15.5
Tankers								
Janus (m)	1939	Örsnd2	9965	15,100	510–10	65–10	28–6	13.0
Oceanus (m)	bldg	Göta	10,217	15,380	515–2	64–4	29–8	14.0
Silenus (m)	bldg	Caledn	8410	12,200	483–2	59–5	27–11	13.0
Sinus (m)	order	Göta	8377	12,620	483–6	59–4	27–11	13.0

JONASSON, MAURITZ, Långgatan 14, Postfack 10, Råå

Funnel: Black with blue J on yellow band
Services: General tramping

REDERI-A/B A TH JONASSON

Anna	1924	HwldtK	1573	2090	249–8	37–2	15–9	9.5
John	1918	Blyth	3435	5150	341–6	46–8	22–3	9.5
ex Danybryn 37, ex Sheaf Lance 36, laid down as War Haven								
Theodor	1919	Schuyt	1934	3005	280–0	42–2	17–11	8.5
ex Byna 27								

RÅÅ REDERI-A/B

Mauritz	1917	Bergen	1622	2300	255–6	37–10	18–4	8.0
ex Lukseffjell 30, ex Storøy 25, ex Rigel 22, ex Jomfruland 19								

KÄLLSTRÖM, K M, Västra Trädgårdsgatan 4, Stockholm

Funnel: Black with blue emblem on white band
Services: General tramping

REDERI-A/B REX

Dalarö	1911	Prstm1	3927	6260	347.2	50–9	21–7	8.5
ex Siljan 30, ex Vard 15								
Korsö	1905	SHWR	2721	4650	324–6	46–6	19–9	8.0
ex Consul Olsson 39, ex Gracefield 25								
Ljusterö	1919	Dordr	3653	6400	352.5	51–3	22–2	8.5
ex Malmen 36								
Rådmansö (P8)	1914	ThmpsJ	4325	7790	398–8	53–8	23–9	10.5
ex Nordic 38								
Tynningö (P8)	1914	ThmpsJ	4315	7791	398–8	53–9	23–9	10.5
ex Sydic 38								

Note: Also vessels engaged in Baltic/NW Europe/UK trade

MYRSTEN, G, Sturegatan 6, Stockholm

Funnel: Yellow
Hull: Black, red boot-topping
Services: General tramping

REDERI-A/B VOLO

Dalhem (m)	1931	Eriksb	3088	5645	345–6	48–11	21–9	12.5

NORDSTRÖM & THULIN, (P G Thulin), Skeppsbron 34, Stockholm

Funnel: Yellow with white N&T on blue band
Services: General tramping

REDERI-A/B ROSLAGEN

Roslagen	1925	LindMo	1864	3150	262.0	42–9	18–0	11.0

NORRTHON, CARL, Höganäs

Funnel: Höganäs – black with black H on white band
Services: General tramping

REDERI-A/B HÖGANÄS

Norita	1924	Larvik	1512	2500	242.7	39–5	17–0	9.5
ex Harpefjell 35, ex Gorm 34, ex Snefond 30								
Norruna (st)	1919	Fredst	2640	4700	311–0	47–2	20–10	9.0
ex Astur 25, ex Aquila 20								

Note: Also smaller vessels

Services: Oil and petroleum

Note: This company also managed a fleet of Baltic traders

OLSON & WRIGHT AKTIBOLAGET, (Reinhold Weylandt),
Skeppsbron 44, Stockholm

Manager for

REDERI-A/B GOTTFRID

Tanker

Oljaren (m2)	1922	Göta	5469	8194	389.7	54–11	25–2	11.0

Trades: Oil and petroleum

PETTERSON, J, Gothenburg

REDERI-A/B ZENIT

Tanker

Bellona (m)	bldg	Göta	11,267	16,400	540–4	66–2	29–7	13.0

Funnel: Black with band of blue and white diagonal stripes
Hull: Black, red boot-topping
Trades: Oil and petroleum

Note: Also small tankers

REUTER, HAKON A, Hertzia, Packhusplatsen 2, Gothenburg

REDERI-A/B REUT

Tanker

Gustaf E Reuter (m2)	1928	Eriksb	6294	9550	422–8	55–1	26–1	10.5

Funnel: Yellow with green band
Hull: Black or white
Services: Fruit trades, NW Europe–W coast US, Canada, general tramping

Note: * Sold France 1939, renamed *Sinfra*

SALÉN, SVEN, Frihamnen, Stockholm

REDERI-A/B JAMAICA								
Korshamn (m2)	1920	H&WGw	6683	9075	420–9	54–3	27–0	11.0
ex Vigeo 39, ex Ionopolis 37, ex Glenluce 36								
Sandhamn* (m2,P4)	1929	Akers	4476	8230	385.3	54–10	25–0	12.0
ex Fernglen 34								
Sven Salén (m)	order	Eriksb	4892	9060	432–3	56–7	25–9	14.0
REDERI-A/B PULP								
General cargo vessels								
Christer Salén (m)	order	Eriksb	4928	9100	432–3	56–7	25–9	14.0
Dagmar Salén (m,P8)	1937	Örsnd2	4995	9500	453–8	57–2	25–7	14.0
Fruit carrier								
Sandhamn (m,P4)	order	Örsnd2	3134	3090	351–0	47–1	20–1	15.5

Trades: Oil and petroleum

SCHONMEYER, C L, Stockholm

Tanker

Atlantides (m)	1939	Laing	9472	14,833	503–10	68–4	28–2	12.5
ex Svolder 39								

Funnel: Black with yellow S on blue band
Services: General tramping

Note: Also *Frode* (built 1898/1635gt) on short-sea voyages

SELANDER, HILMER, Arsenalsgatan 4, Stockholm

REDERI-A/B FRODE

Senta	1905	SmitJ	1760	2505	251.3	37–10	16.3	7.5
ex Acacia 36, ex Sallingsund 27, ex Danery 26, ex Roma 16								
Trio	1922	Svndbg	1739	2430	261–0	38–2	16–9	8.5
ex Inge Mærsk 38								

Funnel: Black with yellow K on blue disc on white band
Services: General tramping
Note: Also *Hedda* (built 1920/1498gt)

SJÖSTEN, AXEL, Strandgatan 15, Höganäs

REDERI-A/B KULLABERG

Hedera	1900	GrayX	2294	3831	312–9	43–4	19–0	8.0
ex Baltia 35, ex Varna 26, ex Daland 18, ex Helsingborg 17								

Trades: Oil and petroleum

SOOT-TISELL, T, Kungsbacka

Tanker

Pan Gothia (m2)	1931	Göta	10,398	15,550	508–6	64–2	29–1	11.5

SVEA, STOCKHOLMS REDERIAKTIEBOLAGET, Skeppsbron 28, Stockholm

General cargo vessels								
Fenris (m,P10/1)	bldg	Finnb	1921	3375	322–4	44–2	18–10	13.0
Hedrun (st,P2)	1920	Örsnd2	2325	4400	323–0	44–11	21–0	9.5
ex Hjalmar Blomberg 21								
Thule	1930	Fredst	1778	3465	273–5	42–1	19–5	11.0
ex C G Thulin 34								
Vidar	1907	Murdol	2140	3500	285.3	42–1	19–2	9.5
Tankers								
Sveaborg (m2)	1931	Blohm	9076	14,240	489–7	64–5	28–4	11.0
Sveaborg (m)	order	Kockum	8673	13,500	496–4	62–1	27–2	12.5
Sveadrott (m)	1938	Kockum	10,019	15,310	523–5	63–0	28–6	13.5
Sveajarl (m)	order	Kockum	10,200	16,050	533–1	63–3	29–6	13.0
REDERI-A/B SATURNUS								
Tanker								
Saturnus (m)	bldg	Nakskv	9965	15,320	510–2	65–9	29–1	13.5

Funnel: Black with broad white band bearing black S
Hull: Light grey, red boot-topping
Services: Sweden–NW Europe – Mediterranean; proposed service Gothenburg–Oslo–Colombia–Ecuador–Chile; general tramping

Note: This company, managed by Emanuel Högberg, owned *Fidra* (built 1939/1483gt), *Freja* (38/1497), and a large fleet of short-sea vessels

SVENSKA LLOYD, REDERIAKTIEBOLAGET, Skeppsbron 5–6, Gothenburg

Passenger vessels								
Britannia (st,P177/1,42/3,68/stge)	1929	SHWR	4295	2210	376–4	50–3	20–4	16.5
Patricia (P112/1,80/2,52/3)	1926	SHWR	3994	2950	352–3	47–6	20–1	14.0
ex Patris II 35								
Saga (m,P160/1,80/2,100/3,60/4)	bldg	LindVv	6687	2150	420–10	55–4	18–11	17.5
Suecia (st,P177/1,42/3,68/stge)	1929	SHWR	4295	2210	376–4	50–1	20–4	16.5
General cargo vessels								
Algeria	1921	Oskar	1543	2650	286–0	41–2	17–8	10.0
Camelia (m,P–)	order	LindVv	1715	2920	297–0	42–3	19–3	13.0
Gdynia (m,P10)	1934	Kockum	1553	2665	293–6	41–2	17–11	12.5
Gothia (m,P–)	1937	Eriksb	1550	2745	296–4	41–2	17–11	12.5
Græcia	1911	Blumrl	2929	5265	331.0	47–6	20–8	8.5
ex Marietta N 16								
Industria (m,P–)	1939	LindVv	1688	2700	296–8	42–1	19–3	13.0
Liguria	1914	Lindhm	1691	3315	283–0	43–0	18–6	10.0
Masilia	1917	Oskar	1527	2680	285–6	41–1	17–10	10.0
Scandinavia (m,P–)	1937	Eriksb	1551	2745	296–0	41–2	17–11	12.5
Scania (m,P10)	1934	Kockum	1549	2715	293–6	41–4	17–11	12.5
Scotia	1919	Lindhm	1874	3250	277–0	42–9	18–11	9.5
Sicilia (m,P10)	1934	Kockum	1552	2715	293–5	41–1	17–11	12.5
Valencia	1925	Örsnd2	1514	2860	285–5	41–1	17–10	10.0
Venezia (m,P–)	1938	LindVv	1593	2940	296–6	42–2	19–3	13.0

Funnel: Black with yellow star on blue disc on white band; white base with yellow star on blue disc, black top
Hull: Black or light grey, red boot-topping
Services: Passenger – Gothenburg–Tilbury; Gothenburg–Newcastle; Gothenburg–Leith; Sweden–Portugal–Mediterranean–W Africa; fruit service – Sicily–Gdynia

Note: Also *Andalusia* (built 1916/1284gt), *Bernicia* (20/1451), *Bothnia* (19/1488), *Calabria* (16/1270), *Caledonia* (13/1209), *Canadia* (20/1379), *Dahlia* (07/1078), *Gallia* (26/1419), *Hispania* (12/1242), *Iberia* (03/1410), *Ivernia* (21/1452), *Mansuria* (13/1083) and *Tunisia* (38/1351), which traded from the Baltic and NW Europe to the Mediterranean and/or W Africa and several vessels under 1500gt in Baltic/NW Europe/UK services

THORE, J A, Arild

REDERI-A/B ARILD								
Mongolia	1909	Pgill2	2323	3500	286–0	43–4	18–3	8.0
ex Clayton 27, ex Pelica 20								
Scania	1901	OsbGrl	1999	3000	275.0	40–2	17–9	7.5
ex Saltburn 24, ex Norman 14								

Funnel: Black with white band
Services: General tramping

THORE, NILS M, Jonstorp, and Drottninggatan 50, Helsingborg

REDERI-A/B ALLIANS								
Balticia	1905	Craigl	1966	3260	280.3	42–3	17–10	8.0
ex Lord Erskine 26, ex Eric Petersen 20, ex Dwina 12, ex Kara Sea 06								
REDERI-A/B VIRGINIA								
Virginia	1907	StephR	2791	4750	318.0	46–8	19–10	8.0
ex Gustavsholm 29, ex Oscar Trapp 19, ex Marina 13								

Services: General tramping

TRANSATLANTIC, REDERIAKTIEBOLAGET, Södra Hamngatan 17, Gothenburg

General cargo vessels								
Anten (P6)	1920	Doxfrd	5234	9325	433–9	53–10	25–7	11.0

Funnel: Yellow with blue top, or black with white T (some had very narrow funnel)
Hull: Silver grey, red boot-topping
Services: Scandinavia–South Africa,

Svenska Lloyd: Saga *was laid down at the Lindholmen shipyard on November 9 1939. She was launched on October 10 1940, and following was laid up at Gothenburg. She was not delivered to Svenska Lloyd until May 9 1946 after fitting-out by Götaverken. As completed she had accommodation for 408 passengers in three classes and could carry 14 cars.* Saga *was fitted with four Götaverken 8-cylinder oil engines of 8600bhp, and attained 18.5 knots on trials. She left Gothenburg on May 23 1946 on her maiden voyage to London. She was sold out o the fleet in 1956 and became CGT's* Ville de Bordeaux. *In 1964 she was sold to Bulgaria and renamed* Nessebar, *and was broken up at Split, Yugoslavia, during 1976 (RW Jordan collection)*

Svenska Lloyd: Scandinavia *was completed by Eriksbergs in November 1937, and was fitted with a Götaverken 7-cylinder oil engine of 1400bhp.* Scandinavia *was stopped by* U510 *on July 9 1943 when on voyage from Philadelphia and Curaçao to Rio de Janeiro and Montevideo with a general cargo which included paper, machinery and steel. The master of* Scandinavia *was ordered on board* U510 *with the ship's papers. An order was given for* Scandinavia *to be abandoned within 30 minutes and the vessel was sunk (Alex Duncan)*

Transatlantic: Eknaren *was completed by Doxford, Sunderland, in September 1922. She was fitted with a Doxford 4-cylinder oil engine of 2500bhp. On July 7 1942 she was torpedoed and sunk by the Japanese submarine* I-16 *when on voyage from Suez to Table Bay and New York, in ballast. Some survivors were picked up by* Mundra, *but some of these were lost when that vessel was sunk five days later. The captain and four others were picked up by a whaler (Krister Bång)*

Boren (P8)	1921	LindMo	4585	8320	393–8	54–3	24–2	11.0
Bullaren (m2,P12)	1918	Göta	5750	9347	436–10	56–2	26–3	12.0
Eknaren (m,P6)	1922	Doxfrd	5293	9053	433–10	54–0	25–7	12.0
Glimmaren (m2,P2/1)	1939	Eriksb	3173	6170	380–8	51–8	23–8	14.5
Goonawarra (m2,P12/1)	1937	Göta	4861	7560	438–6	56–8	26–2	16.0
Gullmaren (m2,P12/1)	1938	Eriksb	3397	5945	380–8	51–8	23–8	14.5
Hallaren (m)	1929	Eriksb	2792	5188	340–4	45–9	21–5	12.0
Hammaren (m2,P20/1)	1930	Göta	3299	5898	361–10	50–1	23–6	13.0
Hjelmaren (m)	1922	Göta	2382	4660	321–0	45–9	22–7	11.5
Kaaparen (m2,P20/1)	1930	Göta	3393	5460	379–0	50–1	23–6	14.5
ex Larviksfjord 33								
Kanangoora (m2,P12/1)	1938	Göta	4850	7560	437–10	58–8	26–2	16.0
Klipparen (m2,P12/1)	1935	Göta	3581	5970	387–7	50–1	23–5	14.5
Kolsnaren (m,P12)	1923	Göta	2382	4730	316–0	45–6	21–7	12.0
Mälaren (m)	1927	Göta	2744	5218	340–4	45–9	21–5	11.5
Remmaren (m2)	bldg	LindVv	3777	6160	425–9	53–3	23–3	15.0
Roxen (P8)	1921	LindMo	4585	8320	393–8	54–3	24–2	10.5
Temnaren (m2,P2/1)	1939	LindVv	3142	6030	381–1	51–7	23–9	14.5
Tisnaren (m2,P12)	1918	Göta	5788	9347	441–9	56–3	26–3	12.5
Tolken (P6)	1922	LindMo	4521	8347	394–10	54–1	24–2	10.5
Vaalaren (m2,P11)	1936	Eriksb	3403	5940	381–0	51–9	23–9	14.5
Vingaren (m2,P2/1)	1936	Eriksb	3147	6135	380–8	51–8	23–9	14.5
Yngaren (m,P6)	1921	Doxfrd	5293	9053	433–10	54–0	25–7	11.5

Australia, E coast North America; W coast North America–Australia; South Africa–Australia; oil and petroleum trades

REDERI-A/B TANKOIL

Tanker

W R Lundgren (m)	1938	Göta	8408	12,590	483–8	59–1	27–10	13.0

REDERI-A/B TRANS-EX

General cargo vessel

Mongabarra (m,P12/1)	order	Eriks	5029	9160	432–2	56–9	25–9	14.0

REDERI-A/B TRANSMARK

Tankers

Balaklava* (m2)	1929	Göta	8036	11,840	459–6	59–2	27–1	11.0
Bera (m)	1939	Göta	11,236	16,540	540–3	66–4	29–7	14.0
Kalmia (m2)	1931	Caledn	8187	12,316	468–6	58–7	27–5	11.5

REDERI-A/B TRANSOCEAN

Tanker

Cleopatra (m)	1933	Göta	6687	10,170	433–0	55–4	26–11	11.5

REDERI-A/B TRANSOIL

Tankers

Nike (m)	1939	Göta	8454	12,550	483–10	59–2	27–10	12.5
Pegasus (m)	1930	Doxfrd	9749	14,913	497–4	65–0	28–10	11.0

REDERI-A/B TRANSPACIFIC

General cargo vessels

Kookaburra (m,P4)	1939	Eriksb	4913	9190	432–2	56–8	25–9	14.5
Mirrabooka (m2,P24/1)	1928	Göta	5819	9244	457–0	57–1	26–10	14.5
Parrakoola (m2,P20/1)	1928	Göta	5841	9244	457–0	57–1	26–10	15.0
Yarrawonga (m,P4/1)	order	Eriksb	4893	9200	432–2	56–9	25–10	14.5
ordered as Rigoletto								

Note: * Sold Norway 1939

TRANSMARIN, AKTIEBOLAGET, Kungsgatan 2, Helsingborg

Funnel: Black with yellow T
Hull: Grey, red boot-topping
Services: Scandinavia, NW Europe–Mediterranean, West Africa, E coast North America, E coast South America; general tramping

Etna	1918	Fredst	2615	4680	311–4	47–2	20–10	10.0
ex Arcturus 21								
Flora	1930	Fredst	1770	3465	273–5	42–2	19–5	10.5
Gudrun	1924	Fredst	1501	2850	265–8	40–2	18–0	10.0
Gunda	1930	Fredst	1770	3465	273–5	42–3	19–5	10.5
Hera	1935	Örsndl	1526	2950	274–6	40–5	18–9	10.0
Inger	1932	Örsndl	1564	3110	275–0	40–6	18–9	9.5
Irene	1937	Helsbg	1518	2460	267–11	38–3	16–8	10.0
Magna	1929	Fredst	1780	3330	273–6	42–1	18–10	9.5

Transatlantic: Kookaburra *was completed by Eriksbergs in March 1939 and left Gothenburg on March 30 on her maiden voyage to Los Angeles. She was in service with Transatlantic until 1958 when she was sold and renamed* Lilian. *She was sold to Germany in 1961 and renamed* Minerva. *On January 14 1964 she sailed from Hamburg in tow for Gothenburg, and was later broken up (Krister Bång)*

Transatlantic: Vaalaren, *completed by Eriksbergs in 1936, was fitted with two Eriksbergs 6-cylinder oil engines of 5100ihp. On April 4 1943,* Vaalaren *was a part of eastbound convoy HX231 which was attacked by U-boats. As darkness fell,* Vaalaren *and two other vessels broke from the convoy. The two others rejoined the convoy the following day, but in the meantime* Vaalaren *had been torpedoed and sunk by* U229 *with the loss of her entire crew (Krister Bång)*

Transatlantic: Nike *was completed by Götaverken in July 1939 for Rederi-A/B Transoil. She was fitted with a Götaverken 8-cylinder oil engine of 5100ihp. She was laid up at Stockholm for most of the Second World War. In 1955 she was sold within Sweden, converted to an ore/oil carrier, and renamed* Hasselö. *In 1967 she was sold to German breakers, but resold to Cyprus and renamed* Hassel. *She was broken up at Shanghai in 1968 (Krister Bång)*

Sonja	1923	Helsbg	1828	2890	283–6	40–2	17–2	9.5
Sonja (P2/1)	order	Helsbg	1588	2950	295–7	41–5	18–5	10.0
Thyra	1925	Fredst	1798	3077	278–0	42–1	17–9	9.5
Torsa	1934	Örsndl	1513	2950	274–6	40–5	18–9	10.0
Ulla	1920	Fredst	1842	2960	278–0	42–1	18–0	9.5
ex Alcor 21								
Wanja	1919	Fredst	2668	4475	311–6	47–2	20–10	10.0
ex Esther Elina 26, ex Aldebaran 21								

Note: This company, managed by Sven Redig, also owned vessels under 1500gt and short-sea vessels

TRAPP, J R, Hertzia, Packhusplatsen 2, Postfack 34, Gothenburg

Funnel: Grey with emblem, black top
Services: General tramping

REDERI-A/B BIFROST

Agne	1917	Craig2	2470	4160	295–0	45–5	19–5	9.0
ex Ukside 31, ex Maindy Forest 21, ex Firtree 19								
Bohus	1922	Ouse	1757	2450	262.5	40–0	17–0	9.0
ex Severoles 39, ex Terne 23								

Note: Also short-sea vessels

TRELLEBORGS ÅNGFARTYGS NYA AKTIEBOLAG, Trelleborg

Funnel: Black with black T on white band
Hull: Grey, red boot-topping
Trades: Oil and petroleum
Note: * Operated by Compagnie des Produits Chimiques et Raffineries de Berre, France
Note: This company, managed by Jarl Malmros, also owned *Aasne* (built 1931/1574gt), *Gunborg* (30/1574), *Isa* (36/1589) and short-sea vessels

Tankers

Capella (m2)	1930	Eriksb	9720	14,640	491–0	64–2	28–4	11.0
Castor (m2)	1928	Kockum	8945	13,440	486–9	61–10	27–3	11.0
Falsterbohus (m)	order	Kockum	10,232	16,250	513–0	66–1	29–10	13.0
Malmöhus (m)	order	Kockum	10,232	16,250	513–0	66–1	29–10	13.0
Pollux (m2)	1928	Kockum	8971	13,465	486–9	61–11	27–3	11.0
Procyon (m2)	1933	Kockum	8982	13,625	489–6	64–11	28–5	11.5
Saint Gobain* (m)	1936	DeutsH	10,290	14,735	510–9	66–1	28–5	12.5
ex Regulus 39								

WALLER, PER, Våstra Hamngatan 18, Gothenburg

Funnel: Yellow, black top
Hull: Silver grey, red boot-topping
Services: Tramping; oil and petroleum trades

REDERI-A/B CASTELLA

Tanker

Carina (m2)	1931	Göta	6405	9920	423–10	55–2	26–7	11.5

REDERI-A/B CONCORDIA

General cargo vessel

Bellona	1917	GöteN	5895	8810	409–8	53–9	24–11	9.5
ex Skagern 39								

Tankers

Abadan (m2)	1928	Göta	6308	9620	422–0	55–4	26–1	11.0
Juno (m)	order	Göta	8422	12,500	483–6	59–4	27–11	13.0

REDERI-A/B UNDA

General cargo vessel

Trione	1931	LindMo	1610	2737	278–2	40–4	17–8	10.0

Note: Also short-sea vessels

WINCK, CARL W, Järnvägsgatan 7, Helsingborg

Funnel: Black with white W
Services: General tramping

REDERI-A/B WALHALL

I W Winck	1929	Fredst	1514	2750	259.6	40–2	17–9	10.5
Osric	1919	Limham	1550	2300	251.7	38–0	17–0	9.5
ex Motala Ström 22, ex Rymmen 19								

Note: Also smaller vessels in Baltic/White Sea/NW Europe/UK trade

Switzerland

ANDRÉ & COMPAGNIE, Avenue Secretan 27, Lausanne

Funnel: Black with green band
Hull: Grey, red boot-topping
Services: General tramping

Manager for

DEMARAUX & PASCHE (Panamanian flag)

St Cergue	1937	GrayWH	4260	7590	395–6	53–2	23–10	10.0
ex Felldene 39								

Services: General tramping

Note: See also Neptun Sea Navigation Co Ltd in Hungary section

SOCIÉTÉ ANONYME MARITIME ET COMMERCIALE,
66 Rue du Stand, Geneva

Under Panamanian flag

Adria	1919	GLakeE	2450	4150	261–10	43–9	24–3	9.5
ex Cottonwood 37								
Atlas	1919	Downey	4810	7827	386.8	52–2	24–0	10.5
ex Pan American 38, ex Willpolo 33, ex Yaphank 19								

Turkey

Funnel: Red with black top separated by five-pointed blue star on broad white band
Hull: Black
Trades: Oil and petroleum

CATSELL & CO LTD, S, (Selman Catsell), 36 Camomile St, London EC3

Manager for

PAVIL DIACON ZADEH, Persembepazar, 1ci kat, Arslan Han 1, Galata, Istanbul, Turkey (Panamanian flag)

Tanker

Beme	1904	ArmWh1	3039		309.5	41–6	23–4	8.0

Funnel: Yellow with red star and crescent and crossed anchor emblem on broad white band, separated from black top by narrow yellow band
Hull: Black or white
Services: Passenger and cargo in Mediterranean

Note: This nationalised company, controlled by Denizbank (Maritime Bank) since 1938, also owned smaller vessels

DENIZBANK DENIZYOLLARI ISLETMESI MÜDÜRLÜGÜ,
Denizbank, Galata, Istanbul

Passenger/general cargo vessels

Aksu (P68/1,30/2)	1909	LloydA	3905	3850	368–5	44–3	21–9	10.0
ex Campidoglio 34, ex Leopolis 32								
Ankara (P68/1,41/1,24/3,30/4)	1906	Scheld	4765	4545	406–1	47–1	20–1	13.0
ex Angora 30, ex Rindjani 26								
Cumhuriyet (P–)	1894	Denny1	4179	4700	371.2	45–1	27.5	10.5
ex Djumhouriet 28, ex Queen Olga –								
Dogu (r/t2,P65/1,46/2,38/t,480/3)	order	Blohm	6133	5000	399–7	52–8	21–9	16.0
Ege (P77/1,50/2,30/3)	1908	Scheld	5275	4940	413–10	49–2	24–0	13.0
ex Tabanan 30								
Egemen (r/t2,P65/1,46/2,38/t,480/3)	bldg	Blohm	6133	5000	399–7	52–8	21–9	16.0
Etrüsk (r/t2,P390)	1938	Neptn2	2992	2300	325–4	43–8	18–7	15.0
Günesyu (P68/1,30/2)	1908	LloydA	3845	3805	368–10	44–2	21–8	11.0
ex Bulgaria 34, ex Graz 31								
Izmir (P–)	1907	Scheld	4875	4625	406–1	47–1	20–1	13.0
ex Kawi 27								
Kades (r/t2,P390)	1939	Neptn2	2990	2300	325–4	43–8	18–7	15.0
Karadeniz (P64/1,38/2,24/3,30/4)	1905	Scheld	4731	4625	406–1	47–1	20–1	13.0
ex Wilis 24								
Salon (r/t2,P390)	1939	Neptn2	3161	2300	325–4	43–8	19–0	15.0
Savas (r/t2,P65/1,46/2,38/t,480/3)	bldg	Blohm	6133	5000	399–7	52–8	21–9	16.0
Tari	1908	Irvin4	4026	4775	367–10	45–1	24–5	10.5
ex Tadla 34, ex Frankenwald 20								
Tirhan (r/t2,P390)	1938	Neptn2	2990	2260	325–4	43–8	19–0	15.0

Services: Turkey–NW Europe–UK; Mediterranean trades; general tramping

Note: In 1939 this firm changed its name from Muhip Ozyigit

SOSYETESILEP, TURK ANONIM SIRKETI,
3ci kat, Denizbank Han, Posta Kutusu 1453, Karaköy, Galata, Istanbul

Bakir	1921	GrkDY	4584	7250	391–0	52–4	23–7	9.0
ex Glenardle 38, ex Nordkyn II 23								
Demir	1925	Rhead3	3709	6388	363–3	49–2	23–4	9.0
ex Eastpool 38, ex Eastville 37								
Krom	1927	Napr&M	3359	5777	340.2	48–9	21–6	10.0
ex Braddovey 38, laid down as Bradtamar								

Catsell & Co: Beme, *completed by Armstrong Whitworth in May 1904, was shelled and damaged by the Italian submarine* Capitano Tarantini *on July 11 1940 when on voyage from Haifa to Istanbul in ballast.* Beme *was abandoned by her crew and she was seen afloat on July 12, but is believed to have sunk the same day (RW Jordan collection)*

Denizcilik Bankasi: Launching of Dogu *at the Blohm & Voss shipyard, Hamburg, on March 15 1939, for Turkish State Lines. She was completed on August 31 but not delivered to Turkey.* Dogu *was taken over by Germany in 1940 and renamed* Luderitzbucht. *When serving as target ship for the 26 U-boat flotilla, Pillau, she was reported torpedoed off the port on January 26 1944, and was towed in. Postwar she was taken over by the Allies, firstly as the British-flag* Empire Ock, *then the Russian* Petr Veliki, *the Polish* Jagiello, *before reverting to Russia as* Petr Veliky *in 1949 for service in the Black Sea. She arrived at Castellon, Spain, in November 1973, to be broken up (Blohm & Voss)*

Sovtorgflot: Kim *was completed by the Severney Shipbuilding Yard at Leningrad in 1932, and was fitted with a Russki 6-cylinder oil engine. She continued to make ocean voyages up to the 1970s, when she was broken up.* Kim *is pictured here on May 10 1944 (Canadian Forces, Ottawa)*

Sovtorgflot: Lozovski *had been built in 1903 by Irvine at West Hartlepool and for most of her time under the Russian ensign, since 1923, had been based at Vladivostok. She is pictured here on May 3 1944 when on voyage from Seattle to Vladivostok.* Lozovski *survived the Second World War but dropped out of deep sea voyaging by 1949 (Canadian Forces, Ottawa)*

Union of Soviet Socialist Republics

Funnel: Black or white with red band bearing yellow hammer and sickle emblem
Hull: Black, grey or white, red or green boot-topping
Services: Leningrad–Baltic ports–London; Leningrad–UK, –NW Europe, –Mediterranean, –US; trans-Pacific; Black sea services; worldwide general cargo; oil and petroleum trades, mainly from Black Sea
Note: The vessels listed below are known to have undertaken regular service passenger voyages or ocean voyages in 1938–39

SOVTORGFLOT, Moscow

Passenger vessels								
Abkhaziya (m2,P450)	1927	Baltic	4727	1600	363–0	51–0	19–0	13.0
Adzharistan (m2,P450)	1927	Baltic	4727	1600	363–0	51–0	19–0	13.0
ex Adzharia								
Andrei Zhdanov (m,P328/1,24/2,240/3)	1928	Sevrny	3870	2800	341–3	48–0	18–8	12.5
ex Aleksey Rikov 37								
Armeniya (m2,P450)	1928	Baltic	4727	1600	363–0	51–0	19–0	13.5
Cooperatzia (m,P28/1,24/2,240/3)	1929	Sevrny	3767	2350	341–3	48–0	18–8	12.0
Dnepr (m2,P12/1,500/3)	1931	EspB	12,589	9900	498–7	63–4	25–4	16.0
ex Cabo San Agustin 39								
Gruziya (m2,P450)	1928	Krupp	4857	1520	380–2	51–1	19–0	13.0
Ilich (P–)	1895	Denny1	4166	7900	390.0	45–0	27.5	10.5
ex Veche 18, ex Emperor Nicholas II 18								
Josif Stalin (te2,P48/1,164/2,296/3)	1939	NedSM	7500	2640	445–1	60–2	20–10	15.0
Krim (m2,P450)	1928	Krupp	4867	1520	380–2	51–1	19–0	13.0
Mariya Ulyanova (m,P38/1,24/2,240/3)	1928	Sevrny	3870	2350	341–3	48–0	18–8	12.5
ex Jan Rudzutak 37								
Neva (s2,P250/1,250/2)	1914	Workmn	8489	5380	468–0	57–10	25–6	14.0
ex Essequibo 35								
Sibir (m,P28/1,24/2,240/3)	1929	Sevrny	3767	2350	341–3	48–0	18–8	12.0
Smolni (m,P28/1,24/2,240/3)	1929	Sevrny	3767	2269	341–3	48–0	18–8	12.0
Sovet (P–)	1903	Caledn	2763	3000	292.3	40–6	19–8	9.0
ex Imperitriza Alexandra 18, ex Wologda 10								
Svanetia (m2,P244)	1937	Helsgr	4125	3300	335–1	47–10	24.4	16.0
Transbalt (s2,P300/2)	1899	Blohm	11,439	13,100	501–4	62–4	24–11	11.0
ex Riga 19, ex Belgravia 05								
Ukraina (m2,P450)	1928	Baltic	4727	1600	363–0	51–0	19–0	13.0
Ural (m,P28/1,24/2,240/3)	1929	Sevrny	3767	2350	341–3	48–0	18–8	12.0
ex Feliks Dzerzhinsky 37								
Volga (st2,P155/1,82/2,350/3)	1928	EspBlb	9965	6200	483–0	55–11	24–2	16.0
ex Juan Sebastian Elcano 39								
Vyacheslav Molotov (te2,P48/1,164/2,296/3)	bldg	NedSM	7974	2643	445–1	60–2	20–10	15.0
General cargo vessels								
A Andreev (m)	1936	NedSM	2850	3635	301–10	49–0	19–8	11.5
Alma Ata	1920	Burger	3611	6550	373–0	50–4	22–3	10.0
ex Chubar 38, ex Dijkwater 35, ex Maasdijk 30								
Amur	1923	FurnH	2917	3900	306.3	45–1	19–4	9.5
ex Japix 33, ex Eldon 28								
Anadir (P–)	1930	Baltic	3554	5300	314.7	46–1	21–0	10.0
Anatoli Serov	1926	SmithM	2922	3650	310.0	44–8	20–2	10.0
ex Garthorpe 39, ex John Holt 37								
Angarstroi	1927	H&WGk	4761	8978	412.1	55–1	25–3	10.0
ex Grantleyhall 32								
Arktika	1936	FurnH	2920	4050	337–11	48–0	19–7	10.5
Ashkabad	1917	H&WGw	5284	8050	412–4	52–4	25–3	10.0
ex Dneprostroi 39, ex Kutais 35, ex Mistley Hall 34, ex Aldersgate 26, ex Milazzo 24, ex War Hostage 19								
Astrakhan (P–)	1912	Nevsky	2692	2000	286.0	40–8	22–0	10.0
Belomorcanal	1936	FurnH	2920	4050	337–11	48–5	19–7	10.5
Belorussiya	1936	FurnH	2920	4050	337–11	48–5	19–7	10.5
Beresina	1928	Blumr2	3087	5050	342–0	46–10	21–8	10.5
ex Bracondale 34, ex Seatonia 27, ex War Highway 19								
Bolshoi Shantar	1923	Flendr	3018	5400	337.7	48–2	21.1	10.0
ex Neidenfels 35								

Buryat	1919	AmSBCl	2599	4200	261–0	43–8	24–4	9.0
ex Lake Farley 32								
Chapaev	1915	RottDD	3566	6020	345.8	48–10	21–7	10.0
ex Vitebsk 35, ex Thuban 34								
Chapaev	1919	AmSBCl	2638	4200	261–0	43–7	24–4	9.0
ex Commercial Navigator 38, ex Lake Farber 28								
Chavicha	1923	Flendr	3021	5400	337.7	48–2	22–0	10.0
ex Hohenfels 35								
Chelyuskinets (m)	1936	Sevrny	5115	7460	397–9	53–2	24–6	11.0
Chernyshevski	1919	RottDD	3588	6050	373–0	49–11	21–7	9.0
ex Pokrovski 38, ex Hagno 35								
Chukcha	1920	Dtroit	2606	4200	261–0	44–7	24–4	9.0
ex Lake Fandon 30								
Dalstroi	1918	Scheld	6948	11,470	447.5	62–10	27–6	11.0
ex Yagoda 39, ex Almelo 35								
Dejnev (P–)	1937	Marti	3578	3325	334.6	49–3	22–3	12.0
Dekabrist (s2)	1903	VickB3	7363		475.8	54–1	32.6	10.0
ex Anadyr 22, ex Franche-Comté 18								
Dikson	1936	FurnH	2920	4050	337–11	48–5	19–7	10.5
Dimitrov	1920	RottDD	3689	6020	373–0	49–10	21–7	10.0
ex Haarlem 34								
Djurma	1921	NewWat	6908	9960	418–7	58–4	28–1	11.0
ex Brielle 35								
Dnepr	1914	Clyde	3071	3000	304.3	44–9	18–0	10.0
ex Miltonstar 27, ex Brodhurst 20, launched as Yula								
Dneprostroi	1918	Standd	4756	7850	395–9	52–0	23–8	10.5
ex Dallas 30								
Dvinoles (m)	1932	MartiL	3946	5950	361–3	51–6	21–9	10.0
Erivan (P–)	1913	Nevsky	2692	2000	286.1	40–8	22–0	10.0
Eskimos (P–)	1919	Ishkwa	3108	4950	305.1	43–8	22–0	8.0
ex Eastern Belle 29								
Feliks Djerzhinsky (s2)								
	1926	SHWR	9180	11,985	488.8	59–0	29–3	12.0
ex Nikolai Ejov 37, ex Dominia 37; conv cable vessel 37								
Friedrich Engels (m)	1930	Sevrny	3972	5950	361–3	51–7	21–9	11.0
Igarka	1936	FurnH	2920	4050	337–11	48–5	19–7	10.5
Ilmen	1923	FrerJ	2369	4000	295.2	42–6	20–0	9.0
ex Athena 33, ex Irma Kimme 25								
Indigirka	1920	Manito	2689	4200	261–10	43–11	24–4	9.0
ex Commercial Quaker 38, ex Malsah 28, ex Ripon 26								
Iskra	1928	Baltic	2513	3500	283.8	43–0	19–0	10.0
Itelmen (P–)	1918	OsakaI	4385	6600	357–6	49–11	23–8	10.5
ex Eastport 30								
Ivan Papanin (m)	1933	Sevrny	3974	5700	361–3	51–6	21–9	11.0
ex Nikolai Ejov 39, ex Karl Lepin 38, ex Murmanles 33								
Jana	1923	FurnH	3059	3900	306.3	45–1	19–4	9.5
ex Melita 33, ex Throckley 28								
Jean Jaurés (m)	1931	Sevrny	3972	5950	361–3	48–9	21–9	11.0
Kaganovich	1920	Gusto	3663	6363	373–0	50–6	21–7	10.0
ex Molenwater 35, ex Ellewoutsdijk 30								
Kalinin (m)	1924	Schich	4156	6300	348.8	48–7	23–0	10.0
ex Karin 27								
Kamchadal	1919	AmSBLo	2598	4150	261–0	43–8	24–4	9.0
ex Lake Fansdale 30								
Kamchatneft-Razvedka								
	1920	Toledo	2559	4170	261–0	43–7	24–5	9.0
ex Commercial Alabaman 38, ex Commercial Mariner 31, ex Rushville 27								
Kamenets-Podolsk	1915	Bartm2	5117	7700	400.0	52–5	24–10	10.0
Karl Liebknecht	1900	HwldtK	3341	5200	346.5	46–7	21–10	8.0
ex Pallada 22								
Karl Marx	1899	HwldtK	3505	5400	346.5	46–8	21–10	8.0
ex Diana 18								
Kashirstroi	1918	ToddDD	4907	7500	395–9	53–1	23–9	10.0
ex Chebaulip 30, launched as Tacoma, laid down as War Artist								
Kazakhstan (r/t)	1938	Loire	3039	4000	326.3	48–1	20–0	12.0
Khabarovsk (P–)	1932	Baltic	3553	5300	314.7	46–1	22–0	9.5
Kharkov	1914	Bremer	6689	11,390	472.1	59–1	26–10	12.0
ex Anhalt 32, ex Aya-Mendi 25, ex Anhalt 21								
Kiev	1916	Flensb	5823	9400	449.3	58–2	25–3	11.0
ex Remscheid 32, ex Cambrian Queen 28, ex Maritime 22, ex Waldenburg 21								
Kim (m)	1932	Sevrny	5114	7540	397–8	53–2	24–8	11.0
Kingisepp	1933	Baltic	2325	3500	300–0	43–3	19–0	10.0
Klara Zetkin (m)	1934	MartiL	3974	5950	361–3	51–6	21–9	10.0

Klim Voroshilov (m)								
	1933	Baltic	5460	8500	405.0	54–4	24.8	11.0
Kola	1906	Flensb	2654	4300	291.3	44–0	21–0	8.0
ex Amantea 32, ex Galata 30, ex Spartivento 23, ex Ilmenau 21								
Kolkhosnik	1925	Rhead3	3880	6400	364.2	50–8	21–7	9.5
ex Rockcliffe 35								
Kollektivizatzia (m)	1934	61Komm	3925	5950	361–3	51–6	21–9	10.0
Komiles (m)	1932	MartiL	3962	5950	361–3	51–6	21–9	10.0
Komsomolsk	1936	FurnH	2920	4050	337–11	48–2	19–7	10.5
Kosarev (m)	1935	NedSM	2850	3635	301–10	49–0	19–8	11.5
Kotlin	1921	Thorny	2545	4250	298.7	44–7	20–4	8.5
ex Aldebaran 35, ex Sir James Bell 33								
Krasnoarmeets	1919	Domnn	2200	3630	261–0	43–8	20–2	9.0
ex Certo 35, ex Saga 20, ex General Williams 10								
Krasny Oktyabr	1911	Irvine	3295	5350	324.8	46–11	21–1	8.5
ex Veerhaven 24, ex Zevenbergen 15								
Krasny Partizan	1927	Baltic	2418	3500	289–0	43–0	19–0	9.5
ex Gregori Zinoviev 33								
Krasny Profintern	1902	Craggl	4648	7000	332.5	48–0	24–0	9.5
ex Argun 18, ex Alexei Trapani 04, ex Hafis 03								
Krechet (P–)	1899	Gourly	2282		281.3	38–2	19–5	8.0
ex Polaris 18								
Kuban (m)	1931	MartiL	3113	4000	337–5	48–7	21–2	12.5
Kulu	1918	NedSM	6492	9440	438–0	54–8	27–10	10.5
ex Batoe 35								
Kura	1919	McDoug	2324	3300	261–0	43–5	22–11	9.5
ex Siredal 33, ex Stein 33, ex Cerosco 29								
Kursk (P–)	1911	SHWR	5801	8700	407.4	51–1	26–0	10.0
Kuzbass	1914	TyneIr	3109	5350	342–0	48–0	20–6	8.5
ex David Dawson 35, ex Crandon 33, ex Havenside 27, ex Gardenia 23								
Kuznets Lesov (m)	1933	MartiL	3974	5950	361–3	51–8	21–9	10.0
ex Severoles 33								
Kuznetskstroi	1936	B&W	2981	4250	341–5	48–1	20–0	12.0
Lieutenant Schmidt								
	1913	Neptn1	2493	2500	297.3	40–2	15.7	9.5
ex Alfa 18, ex Frascati 15								
Litvinov (m)	1937	Sevrny	5114	7540	397–8	53–4	24–8	11.0
Lozovski	1903	Irvine	3011	5000	324.2	47–0	21–0	7.5
ex Merkur 23, ex San Pietro 22, ex Peter Berg 20, ex Vera 06								
Manich	1920	Irvine	3122	5100	342–0	46–10	21–9	10.0
ex Mary Walton 34, ex Heathside 33, ex Portscatho 21								
Maxim Gorky (m)	1932	MartiL	3974	5950	361–3	51–6	21–9	10.0
ex Exportles 33								
Memel (m)	1934	DeutsH	3183	4600	358.8	50–2	21–0	12.5
ex Cairo 35								
Menjinsky	1919	Gusto	3683	6363	372–9	50–4	21–7	10.0
ex Oudewater 35, ex Kinderdijk 30								
Michurin (m2)	1923	FurnH	3908	6100	383–8	52–2	23–3	10.0
ex Genrich Yagoda 37, ex Eñukidse 35, ex Castilian Prince 33, ex Sycamore 25								
Mikoyan	1929	Baltic	2332	3500	300–0	43–2	19–0	10.0
Minsk	1918	Flensb	5949	9320	451.4	58–3	25–3	9.5
ex Murla 32, ex Baron Ogilvy 24, ex Forst 21								
Molotov	1929	Baltic	2332	3500	300–0	43–1	19–0	10.0
Mongol	1919	Dtroit	2606	4200	261–0	43–4	24–2	9.0
ex Lake Fablus 30								
Neva (m)	1930	MartiL	3113	4010	337–5	48–7	21–2	12.0
Nevastroi	1918	ToddDD	4837	7500	395–9	53–0	23–9	10.0
ex Bellingham 30, launched as War Herald								
Okhotsk	1912	FrerJ	3367	5250	342.8	48–1	22–0	9.0
ex Henner 32, ex Wigbert 20, ex Sperrbrecher 8 18, ex Sperrbrecher 1 18, ex Sperrbrecher 8 17, ex Wigbert 17								
Orochon (P–)	1917	Uraga	4584	6610	350.9	51–4	20–1	9.5
ex Eastern Cross 30, ex Kirishima Maru No 6 19								
Pamyat Lenina	1910	B&W	2372	3109	295–3	41–4	18–11	8.0
ex Kishinev –, ex Jakut –								
Pavlin Vinogradov	1929	SmitP	2864	4700	310.6	45–11	21–0	10.0
ex Chapaev 35, ex Tiba 35								
Perekop	1922	Forth	2493	4150	295.7	43–8	20.6	9.5
ex Dampen 35								
Petrovski	1921	Gusto	3771	6680	372–11	50–4	22–6	10.0
ex Minnewater 35, ex Ysseldijk 30								
Revolutsioner	1936	FurnH	2920	4050	337–11	48–2	19–7	10.5
Rion (m)	1931	MartiL	3113	4000	337–5	48–7	21–2	12.5

Rodina	1922	Lobith	4441	7550	385.0	50–4	24–8	10.5
ex Alkaid 33, ex Tenbergen 28								
S A Levanevski	bldg	USSR	3640	4034	341–3	50–10	22–10	12.0
Sahalinneft	1919	GLakeE	2674	4250	261–10	43–10	24–4	9.0
ex Commercial Orleanian 38, ex City of Albany 29, ex Lake Elmhurst 26								
Sakhalin (P–)	1930	Baltic	3554	2800	314.7	46–2	22–0	9.5
Samoied	1919	Toledo	2560	4100	261–0	43–7	24–4	9.0
ex Lake Festina 30								
Saratov (P–)	1932	Baltic	3559	2800	314.7	46–2	22–0	9.5
Selenga	1919	Finch	2492	4100	303.0	43–0	19–10	9.5
ex Neath Abbey 34, ex Bellas 21, ex War Apple 19								
Sergei Kirov	1925	Blyth	4146	6480	370.2	51–2	22–0	11.0
ex Hebburn 31								
Sergei Lazo (P–)	1909	Clyde	2975	3562	295.6	42–0	18–11	8.0
ex Hua-Shan 29, ex South Africa 16								
Sever (P–)	1930	Baltic	3554	2800	314.7	46–1	22–0	9.5
Sevzaples (m)	1932	MartiL	3974	5950	361–3	51–7	21–9	10.0
Shaturstroi	1918	ToddDD	4905	7500	395–9	53–4	23–9	10.5
ex Puget Sound 30, launched as War Guide								
Shchors	1921	Gusto	3770	6680	373–0	50–4	22–5	11.0
ex Galgewater 35, ex Vechtdijk 30								
Shchors	1921	Manito	2690	4050	261–10	43–11	24–4	9.0
ex Commercial Floridian 37, ex Osceola 29, ex Lake Haresti 26								
Sima	1923	Flendr	3048	5400	337.7	48–2	22–0	10.0
ex Tannenfels 35								
Simféropol (P–)	1912	Nevsky	2696	2200	286.0	40–8	19–0	8.5
Skala	1920	H&W,B	6600	10,500	412.6	55–10	28–0	10.0
ex Maine 32, launched as War Riddle								
Smolensk (P–)	1931	Baltic	3559	2800	314.7	46–1	22–0	9.5
Stalingrad (P–)	1931	Baltic	3559	2800	314.7	46–1	22–0	9.5
Stary Bolshevik (m)	1933	Sevrny	3974	5950	361–3	51–7	21–9	10.0
Sverdlovsk (P–)	1931	Baltic	3559	2800	314.7	46–1	22–0	9.5
Svirstroi	1919	Standd	4769	7400	395–9	52–0	23–8	9.5
ex Aledo 30								
Taiganos	1920	Fergsn	2630	4400	300.5	43–7	21–0	9.0
ex Okhta, ex Carronpark 33, ex Ellen Stub 21								
Tashkent	1906	SHWR	5552	9030	424.5	53–2	26–0	7.5
ex Holger 32								
Tbilisi	1912	Flensb	7169	11,900	470.5	60–10	26–4	10.5
ex Tiflis 37, ex Pfalz 33, ex Ramses 20								
Terek	1918	Staten	2189	3535	276–6	42–0	20–10	9.0
ex Sirehav 33, ex Sagn 33, ex Mariners Harbor 29, launched as War Post								
Theodor Nette (P–)	1912	Nevsky	2619	2470	286.1	40–8	19–0	10.0
ex Soria 25, ex Tver 21								
Timlat	1921	Hill	2699	4330	324–8	44–0	20–3	9.0
ex Ijora 35, ex Mountpark 33								
Tobolsk (P–)	1912	Nevsky	2663	2200	286.1	40–8	19–0	10.0
Tomsk (P–)	1913	Nevsky	2693	2200	286.0	40–7	19–0	10.0
Tovarisch Krasin	1927	Baltic	2414	3500	289–0	43–0	19–0	9.0
Tungus	1920	GLakeA	2607	4250	261–10	43–7	24–2	9.0
ex Lake Elva 29								
Turkmen	1919	AmSBCl	2599	4150	261–0	43–7	24–4	9.0
ex Lake Ferrona 30								
Turksib (st)	1922	Vuijk	3160	5596	325.9	48–5	22–5	12.0
ex Hardenburg 35								
Udarnik	1920	Duncan	3110	5350	341–0	48–0	21–8	9.5
ex Georgii 35, ex Antonios Yannoulatos 28								
Uellen (Wellen)	1913	Doxfrd	5135	8900	434–0	54–1	25–6	10.5
ex Nürnberg 32, ex Kosmo 28, ex Nordmark 20								
Uralmash	1936	B&W	2975	4250	341–5	48–1	20–0	12.0
Uzbekistan (r/t)	1937	Loire	3039	4000	328.1	47–11	20–0	12.0
Vatslav Vorovsky	1912	Short	4793	7920	361.5	52–0	24–11	9.0
ex Maskinonge 23								
Vladimir Mayakovsky (m)	1930	Sevrny	3972	5950	361–3	48–8	21–9	11.0
ex Bela Khun 37								
Volga (m)	1931	MartiL	3113	4010	337–5	48–7	21–2	12.5
Volga (m)	1936	NedSM	2847	3635	301–10	49–0	19–8	11.5
ex Kosarev 38								
Volgoles (m)	1932	MartiL	3946	5950	361–3	51–8	21–9	10.0
Volkhovstroi	1918	Standd	4943	7900	395–9	52–0	23–8	9.0
ex Galesburg 30								

Voroshilov (m2)	1924	FurnH	3908	6100	383–7	52–2	23–1	11.0
ex Brazilian Prince 33, ex Tramore 25								
Vtoraya Pyatiletka (m)								
	1933	Sevrny	3974	5950	361–3	51–7	21–9	10.0
ex Lesbel								
Yakut	1919	GLakeE	2694	4050	261–10	43–7	24–2	9.0
ex Lake Elmsford 32								
Ziryanin	1919	AmSBLo	2593	4050	261–0	43–7	24–2	9.0
ex Lake Favonia 30								
Tankers								
Apsheron (m)	1923	Göta	3781	5420	323–0	49–1	23–8	10.0
ex Apsheronneft 34, ex Zoroaster 23								
Azerbaidjan (m2)	1932	AMarti	6114	8425	435–2	54–6	22–4	12.0
Batumi (m)	1932	Odense	6236	9800	424–1	54–8	27–1	12.0
ex Batum 39, ex Batumsky Soviet 34, ex Bente Mærsk 32								
Donbass (m2)	1935	MartiN	7661	11,450	446.0	56–1	26–0	12.0
Emba (m	1929	MartiN	7886	10,400	437.9	58–6	27–0	11.5
ex Embaneft 34								
Grozny (m2)	1916	Poutlv	4964	6625	487.0	49–10	26.9	12.0
ex Grozneft 34, ex cruiser Admiral Spiridov; conv cruiser 26								
Josif Stalin (m2)	1932	MartiN	7745	10,800	445.8	56–1	26–6	12.0
ex Ural								
Kreml (m2)	1932	MartiN	7661	10,800	446.1	56–1	26–0	12.0
ex Soyuz Vodnikov SSSR 38								
Moskva (m2)	1931	61Komm	6086	8550	429–0	54–6	26–0	12.0
ex Mossoviet 34								
Sakhalin (m2)	1931	MartiN	6085	8425	422–1	54–7	26–0	11.0
Sergo (m2)	1930	MartiN	7956	11,460	446.1	56–1	26–0	10.5
ex Soyuz Gornorabotchikh SSSR 34								
Sovetskaya Neft (m2)								
	1929	Caen	8228	12,400	477–4	57–0	29–2	12.0
ex Baku 34, ex Sovetskaya Neft 34								
Tuapse (m)	1931	SHWR	6320	10,350	420.5	57–4	26–5	11.0
ex Stanislav Kossior 38, ex Germanic 31								
Valerian Kuibishev (m2)								
	1914	TyneIr	4629	7900	374.4	51–2	23–6	8.5
ex Surahany 35, ex Surakhanneft 34, ex Elbrus 33								
Varlaam Avanesov (m2)								
	1932	Göta	6557	9600	422–0	55–0	26–9	11.5
ex Eidsvold 32								
Vayant Kuturie (m2)	1934	MartiN	7596	11,460	446.1	56–1	26–0	12.0
ex Nikolai Janson 39, ex Soyuz Metallistov SSSR 34								
Training ship								
Svir (s2)	1919	Scheld	9922	4352	500–0	57–4	25–9	13.5
ex Patria 35								

United States of America

ALCOA STEAMSHIP CO INC, (Aluminum Line), New York

Funnel: Grey with blue band separated from black top by narrow grey band
Hull: Silver grey (aluminium), red boot-topping
Services: New Orleans–West Indies–Guianas–Venezuela–N Colombia; New York–Caribbean

Note: See footnote at United States Maritime Commission entry

Alcoa Patriot (st,P12)								
	order	BethSF	6759	9780	417–9	60–1	28–5	14.0
Alcoa Pennant (st,P12)								
	order	ConsSt	6679	9367	417–9	60–1	27–6	14.0
Alcoa Pilgrim (st,P12)								
	order	BethSF	6759	9780	417–9	60–1	27–6	14.0
Alcoa Pioneer (st,P12)								
	order	BethSF	6759	9780	417–9	60–1	27–6	14.0
Alcoa Polaris (st,P12)								
	order	ConsSt	6679	9319	417–9	60–1	27–6	14.0
Alcoa Puritan (st,P12)								
	order	BethSF	6759	9780	417–9	60–1	27–6	14.0

ALL AMERICA CABLES & RADIO INC, 67 Broad St, New York

Funnel: Yellow
Services: Cable laying and maintenance
Note: This company was associated with Commercial Pacific Cable Co (*qv*)

Cable vessels								
All America (s2)	1921	SHWR	1819	2327	293–0	37–0	20–6	12.5
Edouard Jéramec (s2)								
	1914	MéditH	2316	–	289.2	41–2	23.7	11.5

AMERICAN COAST LINE INC, New York

Hull: Black, red boot-topping

Eastern Trader (st)	1920	AISB	5117	7800	401–0	54–2	24–5	12.0
ex Erica Reed 39, ex Conness Peak 38								

AMERICAN EXPORT LINES INC, Cunard Bldg, 25 Broadway, New York

Funnel: Black with blue E on broad white band between two narrow red bands
Hull: Black, red boot-topping with white dividing line
Services: Philadelphia, Baltimore, New York/–Malta–Alexandria–Jaffa–Haifa–Beirut; /–Piræus–Salonica–Constantinople–Constanta; /–N Africa–Mediterranean ports; US–India (service operated from Dec 1939)

Passenger/general cargo vessels								
Excalibur (st,P147/1)	1930	NYSB3	9359	9500	474–0	61–8	27–11	16.0
Excambion (st,P147/1)	1931	NYSB3	9359	9500	474–0	61–8	27–11	16.0
Exeter (st,P147/1)	1931	NYSB3	9360	9500	474–0	61–8	27–11	16.0
Exochorda (st,P147/1)	1931	NYSB3	9359	9500	475–4	61–8	27–11	16.0
General cargo vessels								
Examelia (st,P12)	1920	AISB	4981	7800	401–0	54–2	24–5	12.0
ex Coeur d'Alene 28								
Examiner (st,P12)	1919	AISB	4909	7800	401–0	54–2	24–5	12.0
ex Sinsinawa 28, laid down as Cinnebar								
Examiner (st,P12/1)	order	BethQu	6736	9902	473–1	66–3	27–10	16.0
Excello (st)	1919	AISB	4990	7800	401–0	54–2	24–5	12.0
ex Luxpalile 28, laid down as Shavano								
Exchange (st,P12/1)	bldg	BethQu	6736	9514	473–1	66–3	27–2	16.0
Exchequer (st,P12/1)	order	Ingall	7898	12,920	492–0	69–8	29–5	16.0
Exchester (st,P12)	1920	AISB	4964	7800	401–0	54–2	24–5	12.0
ex Winona 28								
Exchester (st,P12/1)	bldg	Ingall	7939	12,919	492–0	69–8	29–5	16.0
Executive (st,P12)	1920	AISB	4978	7800	401–0	54–2	24–5	12.0
ex Carenco 29								
Executor (st,P12/1)	bldg	BethQu	6736	9382	473–1	66–5	27–10	16.0
Exemplar (st,P12/1)	bldg	BethQu	6736	9902	473–1	66–5	27–10	16.0
Exermont (st)	1920	AISB	4969	7800	401–0	54–2	24–5	12.0
ex Clontarf 28								
Exhibitor (st,P12)	1919	AISB	4959	7800	401–0	54–2	24–5	12.0
ex Saucon 29								
Exhibitor (st,P12/1)	bldg	BethQu	6736	9902	473–1	66–5	27–1	16.0
Exilona (st,P12)	1919	AISB	4971	7800	401–0	54–2	24–5	12.0
ex Exchange 39, ex Blair 28, laid down as Scitico								
Exiria (st)	1919	AISB	4999	7800	401–0	54–2	24–5	12.0
ex Corson 28, laid down as Shawangunk								
Exminster (st,P12)	1919	AISB	4985	7800	401–0	54–2	24–5	12.0
ex Saugus 28								
Exmoor (st,P12)	1919	AISB	4999	7800	401–0	54–2	24–5	12.0
ex Nobles 28, laid down as Shetucket								
Exmouth (st,P12)	1920	AISB	4979	7800	401–0	54–2	24–5	12.0
ex Blue Triangle 28, laid down as Colosse								
Explorer (st,P12/1)	1939	BethQu	6736	9518	473–1	66–5	27–2	16.0
Exporter (st,P12/1)	1939	BethQu	6736	9518	473–1	66–5	27–2	16.0
Express (st,P12)	1919	AISB	4969	7800	401–0	54–2	24–5	12.0
ex Hog Island 28								
Express (st,P12/1)	bldg	BethQu	6736	9518	473–1	66–5	27–2	16.0
Extavia (st,P12)	1919	AISB	4986	7800	401–0	54–2	24–5	12.0
ex City of St Joseph 28, laid down as Cloverdale								

AMERICAN FOREIGN STEAMSHIP CORP,
Maritime Exchange Bldg, 80 Broad St, New York

Funnel: Black with broad red band between two narrow white bands
Hull: Black
Services: New York–Baltimore–New Orleans–Los Angeles–Everett–Seattle–Tacoma

American Oriole	1920	YokoU	5169	8650	399.9	54–9	24–8	11.5
ex Eastern Glen 33								
American Robin (st)	1919	AISB	5172	7498	401–0	54–2	24–5	12.0
ex Magmeric 37, laid down as Clearfield								

American Export: Excalibur *was the first of four sisterships, known as the 'Four Aces', completed in 1930–31 for Export Steamship Co, which changed its name to American Export Lines in August 1936.* Excalibur *made her maiden voyage on a new service from New York to the Mediterranean in January 1931. Each of the vessels was fitted with three steam turbines of 8000shp. In December 1941 she was taken over by the US Navy, and converted to the transport* Joseph Hewes. *In October 1942 she joined the Allied task force which was assigned to land in Morocco in the invasion of North Africa. The force arrived off Fedala and landed its troops with little resistance from the French garrison. After the troops on board* Joseph Hewes *had all landed she was torpedoed by* U173 *and sank about one hour later (RW Jordan collection)*

American Export: Exchequer *was a C-3 type and the first of a batch ordered in 1939 from Ingalls Shipbuilding Co. She was to be the first all-welded dry cargo ship built in the US. She was completed in October 1940 and soon afterwards taken over by the US Navy for conversion to the seaplane tender* Pocomoke *(AV 9). In March 1946 she went into Reserve.* Pocomoke *was stricken in June 1961, sold six months later, and during 1962 was broken up in the US (Ingalls Shipbuilding Co)*

American-Hawaiian: Nevadan *was completed in July 1912 as* Bochum *for Deutsch-Australische. She put into Manila on August 23 1914 after serving for a short time as a naval collier and was laid up. She was seized there on April 6 1917 when the US entered the First World War, and under the control of the US Shipping Board was renamed* Montpelier, *later serving as a USN transport. She was purchased by American-Hawaiian in 1927.* Nevadan *was one of the many US vessels which were transferred to the Soviet Union on bareboat charter in 1943. She raised the Soviet flag in 1943 as* Jan Tomp, *and was returned to the US in 1944, reverted to her previous name. She came under the control of the US War Shipping Administration and was chartered to the US Army Transportation Corps as a spare parts ship. In 1946 she was laid up and was broken up in 1948–49 at San Francisco (Canadian Forces, Ottawa)*

Liberty Glo (st)	1919	AISB	4979	7498	401–0	54–2	24–5	12.0
laid down as Scooba								
Wildwood (st)	1919	AISB	5043	7498	401–0	54–2	24–5	12.0
laid down as Clito								

AMERICAN-HAWAIIAN STEAMSHIP CO, (The Panama Canal Line),
215 Market St, San Francisco, and 90 Broad St, New York

Funnel: Yellow with broad blue band
Hull: Black, red boot-topping
Services: Boston, Philadelphia, New York–Jacksonville–Los Angeles–San Diego–San Francisco–Alameda–Oakland–Tacoma–Seattle–Coos Bay; Vancouver, Victoria BC–Hawaii–Australia–Far East

Alabaman (P–)	1921	Kiangn	7004	10,289	442–11	55–3	28–2	11.5
ex Diana Dollar 36, ex Cathay 22								
Alaskan	1918	BethSP	5364	9050	415.0	53–9	29–7	12.0
ex Wheaton 28, laid down as War Jupiter								
American	1916	Cramp	4846	8100	420–6	53–11	28–5	12.0
ex Santa Barbara 25								
Arizonan	1920	SunSB	5815	10,425	450–0	57–6	28–2	11.5
ex Willhilo 29, ex Conshohocken 20								
Arkansan (P–)	1921	Kiangn	6997	10,292	442–11	55–2	28–2	11.5
ex Margaret Dollar 36, ex Celestial 22								
Californian (m2)	1922	MerchC	5908	10,250	445.1	59–10	26–8	12.0
Canadian	1920	Duthie	5802	8541	423–10	54–3	24–0	11.5
ex Golden West 37, ex West Ivan 28								
Carolinian (P–)	1921	Kiangn	6997	10,252	442–11	55–2	28–2	11.5
ex Melville Dollar 36, ex Oriental 22								
Coloradan	1920	OsakaO	6557	10,649	414.7	55–9	27–7	11.5
ex Willboro 37, ex Eastern Admiral 26								
Columbian	1913	Cramp	4954	7900	420–6	53–11	28–5	11.5
ex Santa Clara 25								
Dakotan	1912	BethMS	5220	8900	429–0	53–8	29–5	12.0
Delawarean	1920	BethSW	5705	8515	427–0	54–2	24–6	11.5
ex Golden Coast 38, ex West Nivaria 28								
Floridian (P–)	1921	Kiangn	6999	10,322	442–11	52–2	28–2	11.5
ex Stuart Dollar 36, ex Mandarin 22								
Georgian	1920	SunSB	5825	10,425	450–0	57–9	28–2	12.0
Hawaiian	1919	Cramp	6264	9460	420–6	53–11	28–5	11.5
ex Santa Malta 25								
Honolulan	1921	LosAng	7493	10,970	430.7	54–4	28–11	11.5
ex Golden Hind 37, ex West Faralon 28								
Illinoian	1918	OsakaO	6473	10,695	415.1	55–9	27–7	11.5
ex Isthmian 39, ex Willkeno 37, ex Eastern Light 26								
Indianan	1919	Ames	5582	8884	423–0	54–2	25–9	11.5
ex Willhilo 37, ex Golden Rod 34, ex West Islip 28								
Iowan	1914	BethMS	5165	8900	429–0	53–8	29–6	12.0
Kansan	1918	Cramp	4870	8100	420–6	53–9	28–5	11.5
ex Santa Olivia 25								
Kentuckian	1910	BethMS	5200	8825	429–0	53–9	29–6	12.0
Louisianan	1919	Duthie	5484	8543	423–10	54–4	24–0	11.5
ex Golden Fleece 37, ex Dewey								
Mexican (s2)	1907	BethU1	7061	11,800	472.3	57–3	31–5	12.0
Minnesotan	1912	BethMS	5202	8900	429–0	53–9	29–6	12.0
Missourian (m2)	1922	MerchC	5908	10,250	445.1	59–10	26–8	12.0
Montanan	1917	Cramp	4897	8100	420–6	53–11	28–5	11.5
ex Santa Paula 25								
Nebraskan	1912	Bremer	6572	10,860	471.1	59–2	26–11	12.0
ex Kermit 27, ex Appeles 20, ex Elsass 17								
Nevadan	1912	Neptn1	4734	10,340	460.0	57–11	26–11	12.0
ex Montpelier 27, ex Bochum 17								
Ohioan	1920	Standf	6078	9400	412–0	53–3	26–7	11.5
ex Willsolo 37, ex Golden Wall 34, ex Pawlet 26								
Oklahoman	1920	WPipe	5508	8584	427–0	54–0	24–6	11.5
ex Golden Harvest 37, ex West Calera 27								
Oregonian	1917	Cramp	4862	8100	420–6	53–11	28–5	11.5
ex Santa Rosa 25								
Panaman	1913	BethMS	5195	8900	429–0	53–9	29–6	12.0
Pennsylvanian	1913	BethMS	5191	8900	429–0	53–9	29–6	12.0
ex Scranton 19, ex Pennsylvanian 18								
Puerto Rican	1919	Standf	6076	9400	412–3	53–3	26–7	11.5
ex Golden Tide 37, ex Montague 28								
Tennessean	1919	Skinnr	6379	9720	415–11	54–10	26–7	11.5
ex Golden Star 37, ex Elk Ridge 29								
Texan (s2)	1902	NYSB1	7005	12,225	471.0	57–3	31–6	12.0
Utahan	1919	Skinnr	7031	10,230	423.9	54–2	28–0	12.0
ex Golden Peak 37, ex Crosskeys 28								

Virginian (s2) 1903 BethMS 7895 11,207 492.0 58–4 29–0 12.0
ex Maine 07
Washingtonian (P–) 1920 OsakaO 6617 10,661 415.1 55–9 27–7 11.5
ex Willzipo 37, ex Eastern Mariner 26

Funnel: Yellow with company insignia (white ring bearing company name and houseflag in centre), black top
Hull: Black with white band, red boot-topping
Services: Seattle, Puget Sound ports, Victoria–Yokohama–Kobe–Osaka–Shanghai–Hong Kong–Taku Bar–Dairen–Tsingtao–Chefoo–Amoy–Cebu–Iloilo–Zamboanga–Davao (passenger service discontinued 1937, President vessels laid up 1936–38)

Note: * Sold Philippines 1939, renamed *President Quezon*
Note: This company was controlled by American President Lines Inc (*qv*); see also footnote at United States Maritime Commission entry

AMERICAN MAIL LINE LTD, 759 White Henry Stuart Bldg, Seattle WA

China Mail (m,P12/1)
order SunSBD 6586 10,120 474–1 63–2 27–6 15.0
Island Mail (m,P12/1)
order SunSBD 6586 10,120 474–1 63–2 27–6 15.0
Japan Mail (m,P12/1)
order SunSBD 6586 10,120 474–1 63–2 27–6 15.0
President Grant (st2)
1921 BethSP 14,119 11,440 535–2 72–2 30–7 18.0
ex Pine Tree State 22; conv passenger/general cargo 37–38
President Jackson (st2)
1921 NNews 14,123 11,440 535–2 72–2 30–7 18.0
ex Silver State 22; conv passenger/general cargo 37–38
President Jefferson (st2)
1921 NYSB1 14,174 11,442 535–2 72–2 30–7 18.0
ex Wenatchee 22, originally building as C M Schwab, later as Beaver State, laid down as Canonicut; conv passenger/general cargo 38
President McKinley (st2)
1921 NYSB1 14,127 11,440 535–2 72–2 30–7 18.0
ex Keystone State 22; conv passenger/general cargo 37–38
President Madison* (st2)
1921 NYSB1 14,187 11,440 535–2 72–2 30–7 18.0
ex Bay State 22; conv passenger/general cargo 37

Trades: Oil and petroleum, mainly US Gulf–US E coast

AMERICAN MINERAL SPIRITS CO, 155 East 44th St, New York

General cargo vessels
Trento (m) – IntPas 4670 6889 385–10 52–2 22–0 10.0
at Mobile unfinished, launched 1920
Trieste (m) – IntPas 4670 6889 385–10 52–2 22–0 10.0
at Mobile unfinished, launched 1920

AMSCO NAVIGATION CO INC
Tanker
Amsco 1938 IntPas 4627 6900 385–10 52–2 22–7 11.0
ex Torino 38; conv steamer when incomplete 38; launched 1920

Funnel: Black with white eagle and four white stars emblem on broad red band
Hull: Black with thin red band, red boot-topping
Services: New York–Havana–Cristobal–Balboa–Los Angeles–San Francisco–Honolulu–Yokohama–Kobe–Shanghai–Hong Kong–Manila–Singapore–Penang–Colombo–Port Said–Alexandria–Naples–Genoa–Marseilles–Boston–New York; also trans-Pacific service

AMERICAN PRESIDENT LINES LTD, 311 California St, San Francisco CA, and 29 Broadway, New York

Passenger/general cargo vessels
President Adams (s2,P140)
1921 NYSB1 10,544 12,484 522–8 62–2 32–4 14.0
ex Centennial State 22, laid down as Idas
President Adams (st,P96/1)
order NNews 9255 10500 491–10 69–6 27–6 16.0
President Cleveland (st2,P934)
1921 NNews 12,568 11,081 535–2 71–11 30–7 18.0
ex Golden State 22
President Coolidge (te2,P440/1,170/2,378/3)
1931 NNews 21,936 17,300 654–3 81–5 32–0 21.0
President Fillmore (s2,P194/1,66/t)
1904 NYSB1 15,575 12,267 615–8 65–4 33–6 16.0
ex Mongolia 29, laid down as Minnelora
President Garfield (s2,P149/1)
1921 NYSB1 10,501 12,284 522–8 62–2 32–4 14.0
ex Blue Hen State 22, laid down as Idman
President Garfield (st,P96/1)
order NNews 9255 10,500 491–10 69–6 27–6 16.0
President Harrison (s2,P140/1)
1921 NYSB1 10,509 12,284 522–8 62–2 32–4 14.0
ex Wolverine State 22, laid down as Jakin
President Hayes (s2,P140/1)
1920 NYSB1 10,533 12,862 522–8 62–2 32–4 14.0
ex Creole State 22, laid down as Iassus

American Mail: China Mail *was laid down in 1941 at the Sun Shipbuilding yard as* Japan Mail, *and her intended name changed promptly after the attack on Pearl Harbor. She was completed in February 1942 as* China Mail. *Her only substantial contact with the enemy occurred on March 15 1944 during a German air raid on the port of Naples. She was damaged by several near misses, but was soon repaired. She had arrived from Philadelphia with a cargo of war supplies.* China Mail *was in service until 1959, when she was transferred to Marad and laid up. In February 1962 she arrived at Portland, Oregon, to be broken up (RW Jordan collection)*

American President: Pictured in her former livery with Dollar Steamship Lines, President Garfield *was one of a series of standard type transports completed after the First World War. She was built by New York Shipbuilding Corp, being launched as* Blue Hen State *on February 23 1921. Like her sisters,* Blue Hen State *was fitted with two triple expansion engines of 7000ihp. She was assigned to United States Mail Line, delivered on June 21 in the same year, and laid up until March 1922. She was transferred to United States Lines in August 1921. In May 1922 she was renamed* President Garfield, *and in August 1923 was sold to Dollar Line for its round-the-world service.* President Garfield *was transferred to American President Lines in 1938, was renamed* President Madison *in 1940 and continued the round-the-world service. This was soon curtailed and the vessel was taken over by the US Navy. After service as the transport* Kenmore *and hospital ship* Refuge, *she was transferred to the USMC in 1946, renamed* President Madison, *and laid up at Olympia, Washington. She was broken up in 1948 (RW Jordan collection)*

American South African: Launched on October 19 1929 and making her maiden voyage in February 1930, City of New York *was the first new ship and the first passenger ship to be built for this company, the predecessor of Farrell Lines. She was built for service from New York to Cape Town, Lourenço Marques and Beira. On March 29 1942* City of New York *was on voyage from Cape Town and Trinidad to New York when she was torpedoed twice by* U160 *40 miles east of Cape Hatteras. From among 83 crew, 9 armed guards and 41 passengers, 16 crew, 1 guard and 7 passengers were lost (RW Jordan collection)*

President Hayes (st,P96/1)	order	NNews	9255	10,500	491–10	69–6	27–6	16.0
President Jackson (st,P96/1)	bldg	NNews	9273	10,500	491–10	69–6	27–6	16.0
President Johnson (s2,195/1,66/t)	1904	NYSB1	15,543	12,267	615–8	65–4	33–6	16.0
ex Manchuria 29, laid down as Minnekahda								
President Lincoln (st2,P934)	1921	NYSB1	12,594	11,081	535–2	71–11	30–7	18.0
ex Hoosier State 22								
President Monroe (s2,P140/1)	1920	NYSB1	10,533	12,862	522–8	62–2	32–4	14.0
ex Panhandle State 22, laid down as Icaria								
President Monroe (st,P96/1)	order	NNews	9255	10,482	491–10	69–8	27–6	16.0
President Pierce (st2,P934)	1921	BethSP	12,579	11,758	535–2	71–11	30–7	18.0
ex Hawkeye State 22, laid down as Berrien								
President Polk (st2,P140/1)	1921	NYSB1	10,508	12,284	522–8	62–2	32–4	14.0
ex Granite State 22, laid down as Jadwin								
President Polk (st,P96/1)	order	NNews	9255	10,480	491–10	69–8	27–6	16.0
President Taft (st2,P280/1,194/t)	1921	BethSP	12,562	11,758	535–2	71–11	30–7	18.0
ex Buckeye State 22, laid down as Bertice								
President van Buren (s2,P140/1)	1920	NYSB1	10,533	12,862	522–8	62–2	32–4	14.0
ex Old North State 22, laid down as Woodbury								
President van Buren (st,P96/1)	order	NNews	9255	10,500	491–10	69–8	27–6	16.0
President Wilson (st2,P280/1,194/t)	1921	NYSB1	12,597	11,081	535–2	71–11	30–7	18.0
ex Empire State 22								

Note: American President Lines Inc was controller of American Mail Line Ltd (*qv*)

PRESIDENT TERMINAL STEAMSHIP CO LTD

Ruth Alexander (s2)	1913	VulcSt	8135	3300	457–0	56–2	23–7	13.0
ex Callao 22, ex Sierra Cordoba 17								

Services: US E coast–US Gulf ports

AMERICAN RANGE LINES INC,

860 Drexel Bldg, 5th and Chestnut Streets, Philadelphia PA

COLABEE STEAMSHIP CO, 110 West 10th St, Wilmington DE

Colabee	1920	AtlC	5519	8550	431–5	54–0	24–2	10.5
ex Pagasset 37								

MARSODAK STEAMSHIP CO, 110 West 10th St, Wilmington DE

Marsodak (st)	1919	SubmBC	3279	6036	335–6	46–2	22–2	9.5
laid down as Tripp, ordered as Absolona								

PLOW CITY STEAMSHIP CO, 110 West 10th St, Wilmington DE

Plow City (st)	1920	SubmBC	3282	6036	335–6	46–2	22–2	9.5
ex The Plow City 20, laid down as Yapam								

SUWIED STEAMSHIP CO, 110 West 10th St, Wilmington DE

Suwied (st)	1919	SubmBC	3249	6036	335–6	46–2	22–2	9.5
laid down as Sterling Steel Bridge, ordered as Yukpa								

Funnel: Yellow with houseflag
Hull: Black, red boot-topping with white dividing line
Services: ASAL – New York, New Orleans–Cape Town, Durban, Beira, Mombasa; Argonaut – mainly cargo services in Pacific

AMERICAN SOUTH AFRICAN LINE INC, 26 Beaver St, New York

Passenger/general cargo vessel

City of New York (m2,P75/1)	1930	SunSBD	8272	9308	471–0	61–10	26–0	14.0

General cargo vessels

Challenger (m,P12)	1918	BethAl	7667	10,100	410.0	56–0	29–9	11.0
conv steamer 24								
Chincha*	1912	ThmpsJ	6348	9650	403.0	52–4	24–0	10.5
West Cawthon	1919	BethSW	5612	8576	427–0	54–4	24–6	11.5
West Isleta	1919	Ames	5680	8822	423–0	54–2	25–9	11.0

ARGONAUT LINE INC

Atlantic	1919	BethSW	5524	8600	427–0	54–0	24–6	11.5
ex West Catanace 24								
Charles H Cramp	1920	Cramp	6220	9450	420–6	53–11	28–5	12.0
Henry S Grove	1920	Cramp	6220	9450	420–6	53–11	28–5	12.0

Lancaster	1918	SunSB	7516	10,000	450–0	57–9	26–1	11.0
launched as War Trojan								
Pacific (st)	1915	BethU1	6034	9350	418–0	56–2	25–5	11.0
Sagadahoc	1918	Texas	6275	9950	420.5	54–2	26–8	11.0

Note: * Sold Yugoslavia 1939, renamed *Milena*

AMERICAN SUGAR TRANSIT CORPORATION, 120 Wall St, New York

Services: West Indies–US E coast ports; Mexico–US E coast ports; oil and petroleum trades

General cargo vessels								
Defacto	1919	Downey	4800	7300	386.8	52–2	24–0	10.5
ex Northern Star 23, ex Waterbury 19								
Domino	1919	BethWi	3170	5177	327.2	46–2	21–2	10.5
ex Delco 22								
Tanker								
Dixiano	1921	Staten	4323	6678	360.0	50–2	24–0	9.5

AMERICAN TRADING & PRODUCTION CORPORATION, 900–910 American Bldg, Baltimore MD

Funnel: Black with houseflag
Hull: Black, red boot-topping
Trades: Oil and petroleum

Tanker								
American Trader	1923	SunSB	8862	12,882	480.5	66–0	28–2	10.0
ex Pennsylvania Sun 38								

AMERICAN TRADING & SHIPPING CO, San Francisco

Services: San Francisco, Los Angeles and other US W coast ports–Honolulu–Canton Is–Australia; /–Midway Is–Philippines

Admiral Chase (st)	1920	SubmBC	3285	5350	335–6	46–2	22–2	9.5
ex Sutransco 29, laid down as Glenora, ordered as Tomahegan								
Admiral Wiley (st)	1920	SubmBC	3514	5350	335–6	46–2	22–2	9.5
ex Surichco 30, laid down as Jelcaw, ordered as Nehumkee								
Admiral Y S Williams (st)	1920	SubmBC	3252	5350	335–6	46–2	22–2	9.5
ex Sunewco 34, laid down as Piston								

Note: This company was owned by John N Raymond

AMERICAN WHALING CO INC, 19–21 Dover Green, Dover DE, and 39 Water St, New York

Services: Whaling

Note: This company, associated with A/S Thor Dahl (*qv* in Norway section), also owned a fleet of whalers

Whale factory vessel								
Frango	1917	Chestr	6400	9075	401.9	54–4	26–6	9.5
ex Golaa 27; conv tanker 27								

ATLANTIC GULF & WEST INDIES STEAMSHIP LINES, (Agwilines), Pier 13, East Riover, Foot of Wall St, New York

Funnel: Clyde-Mallory – black with red five-pointed star and narrow blue bands above and below, all on broad white band; NY&C – black with white five-pointed star on black band bordered by two white bands; NY&PR – black with white band bordered by two yellow bands
Hull: Black or grey, red boot-topping
Services: Passenger – New York–Charleston, Jacksonville, Miami, Galveston; New York–Havana–Vera Cruz; New York–Guantanamo–Manzanillo–Cienfuegos; cargo – Boston, New York–Key West, Tampa, New Orleans, Jacksonville; New York–Tampico; New York–Philadelphia–Havana–Progreso–Vera Cruz–Tampico–Puerto Mexico

Operated by
NEW YORK & CUBA MAIL STEAMSHIP CO

Passenger vessel								
Yucatan (s2,P200/1,75/2)	1907	Cramp	6678	5500	430–0	50–3	24–0	16.0
ex Havana 35, ex Comfort 27, ex Havana 17								

AGWILINES INC

Operated by
CLYDE-MALLORY LINES

Passenger vessels								
Brazos (P–)	1899	NNews	4497	3460	405–9	48–4	22–6	15.0
ex El Rio 25								
General cargo vessels								
Agwidale	1918	NNews	4763	7210	385–0	53–1	24–2	12.0
Alamo	1919	GLakeA	2676	4070	261–10	43–9	24–3	9.5
ex Lake Elon 25								
Colorado	1920	Manito	2689	4125	261–4	43–11	24–2	9.0
ex Lake Galisteo 24								
Henry R Mallory	1916	NNews	6063	5950	440–2	54–6	24–0	13.0
conv passenger/general cargo 36								
Medina	1914	NNews	5426	4800	420–8	54–4	24–0	15.0
Norfolk	1916	GLakeE	2453	2535	261–0	43–6	19–0	9.0
Oneida	1919	Dtroit	2664	4092	261–4	43–8	24–4	9.5
ex Lake Gilboa 23								

Osage	1919	AmSBCl	2649	4080	261–4	43–8	24–4	9.5
ex Lake Fannin 23								
Ozark	1919	Manito	2689	4288	261–4	43–11	24–6	9.5
ex Lake Savus 24								
Pawnee	1907	BethHH	1907	1960	250.5	40–0	17–0	12.0

Operated by Clyde-Mallory Lines for

CHEROKEE–SEMINOLE STEAMSHIP CORP

Passenger vessels

Algonquin (st,P421/1,25/st)	1926	NNews	5945	2785	402–2	55–0	18–1	15.0
Cherokee (st,P421/1,25/st)	1925	NNews	5896	2740	402–2	55–0	18–1	15.0
Seminole (st,P421/1,25/st)	1925	NNews	5896	2740	402–2	55–0	18–1	15.0

Operated by Clyde-Mallory Lines for

NEW YORK & MIAMI STEAMSHIP CORP

Passenger vessels

Iroquois (st2,P640/1,114/st)	1927	NNews	6209	3040	409–4	62–2	20–7	18.0
Shawnee (st2,P640/1,114/st)	1927	NNews	6209	3040	409–4	62–2	20–7	18.0

Operated by

NEW YORK & PORTO RICO STEAMSHIP CO

Passenger vessel

San Jacinto (s2,[P80/1,50/2])	1903	Delwre	6069	5305	404–0	53–0	22–0	14.0

General cargo vessels

Comerio	1910	GrayX	3349	4874	361–9	46–6	20–7	9.0
ex Guantanamo 27, ex Registan 11								
Corozal	1911	NNews	3110	4700	347–6	46–10	20–1	10.0
Isabela	1911	NNews	3110	4700	347–6	46–10	20–1	10.0
Mariana	1915	NNews	3110	4700	347–6	46–10	20–1	10.0
Montoso	1911	NNews	3110	4700	347–6	46–10	20–1	10.0
Ponce	1899	BethHH	3506	3200	335–0	42–0	21–7	12.0
conv passenger/general cargo 37								
San Juan	1900	BethHH	3512	3200	335–0	42–0	21–7	12.0
conv passenger/general cargo 37								

Operated by New York & Porto Rico Steamship Co for

COAMO STEAMSHIP CORP

Passenger vessels

Borinquen (st,P222/1,50/2)	1931	BethQu	7114	4646	429–0	59–10	24–8	16.5
Coamo (st,P271/1,90/2)	1925	NNews	7057	5164	429–2	59–6	25–8	16.5

NEW YORK & CUBA MAIL STEAMSHIP CO

Passenger/general cargo vessels

Mexico (st,P139/1,24/t)	1932	NNews	5236	4660	404–5	57–6	23–8	18.0
ex Colombia 38								
Oriente (te2,P430/1,100/t)	1930	NNews	11,520	6909	508–0	70–11	39.0	19.0
Orizaba (st2,P204/1,100/3)	1918	Cramp	6938	4300	444–0	60–0	24–6	17.0
Siboney (st2,P201/1,100/3)	1918	Cramp	6938	4300	444–0	60–0	24–6	17.0
launched as Oriente								

General cargo vessels

Agwimonte (st,P12)	order	Fed1	6679	7815	417–9	60–0	27–6	14.0
laid down as Cape Mendocino								
Agwiprince	order	ConsSt	6750	7815	417–9	60–0	27–6	14.0
Agwistar	1919	NNews	4661	7410	385–0	53–2	24–2	10.0
Panuco	1917	SeatCD	3570	4970	351.0	47–11	22–2	10.0

Operated by New York & Porto Rico Steamship Co

PUERTO RICO NAVIGATION CO

Monterey (st,P139/1,24/t)	1932	NNews	5236	4660	404–5	57–10	23–8	17.0
ex Puerto Rico 39, ex Haiti 38								

Note: See also footnote at United States Maritime Commission entry

Atlantic Refining: Pictured here at a US west coast oil terminal, J W Van Dyke *(left) and* E J Henry *were completed in 1938 and 1939 respectively, by Sun Shipbuilding. Both survived the Second World War, and in 1960* J W Van Dyke *was sold within the US and renamed* Montauk. *In 1962 at Bilbao she was converted into a bulk carrier and in 1965 was cut in two and joined to part of another vessel. The 410 feet forward section of* Montauk *was joined to the 119 feet stern section of the turbo-electric tanker* Satucket, *which had been completed in 1944. The forward section of* Satucket *was broken up. The grafting was done at Newport News, and the major net results were that* Montauk *now had an increased deadweight tonnage and steam turbines of 7700shp six years younger than her previous turbo-electric machinery of 6040shp. She was sold again in 1965 and renamed* Rambam *under the US flag and in 1973 was registered in Panama as* Sampan. *She was broken up at Kaohsiung in 1974.* E J Henry *had a less complicated career. In 1960 she was sold and renamed* Henry *under the US flag, changed to Panamanian flag in 1968 and in 1971 was broken up at Vinaroz, Spain (ARCO archives, Los Angeles)*

Atlantic Gulf: Pictured on trials is the C1 type steamer Agwimonte, *which was launched for US Maritime Commission as* Cape Mendocino. *On May 28 1943* Agwimonte *sailed from Cape Town for Durban and Suez in convoy CD20, which comprised 14 merchant vessels and 4 escorts. She was torpedoed by* U177 *on the same day. Her crew of 69 abandoned the vessel and after about an hour since the first torpedo struck,* Agwimonte *was torpedoed again and sank within 10 minutes. All the crew were picked up by South African vessels (RW Jordan collection)*

A H Bull: Emilia *was a standard War type laid down by Bethlehem at Sparrow's Point as* War Mercury *for British account, but completed for the United States Shipping Board in June 1918 as* Cape Romain. *Following several years service as* Emilia, *she was sold in 1951 to Honduras-flag owners and was renamed* Isabel. *In 1953 she changed hands again and was renamed* Rosalind *under Panamanian registry. On February 2 1956 she signalled that she was in distress and the following day was abandoned and foundered in 33 21N 27 50E when on voyage from Split to Dammam with a cargo of cement (RW Jordan collection)*

Funnel: Base of black and white vertical bands, black top and white over black bands, company insignia on white band; *Brunswick, Permian* – no funnel
Hull: Black, red boot-topping
Trades: Oil and petroleum
Note: Also tankers under 1000gt

ATLANTIC REFINING CO, 260 South Broad St, Philadelphia PA

Tankers

Albert Hill	1917	BethU1	7115	10,267	452–0	56–0	27–4	10.0
ex J W Van Dyke 24								
Bessemer (me)	1919	PuseyG	4762	7077	364.9	51–0	26–0	9.5
conv steamer 27								
Bohemian Club	1921	Moore	6906	10,645	438–5	57–2	27–1	10.0
E H Blum (te)	order	SunSBD	11,615	19,200	543–10	70–3	30–4	13.0
E J Henry (te)	1939	SunSBD	11,615	19,200	543–10	70–3	30–4	13.0
Edwin R Cox (me)	1918	PuseyG	4928	7100	364.9	51–0	26–0	9.5
conv steamer 24								
Francis E Powell (st)	1922	Baltmr	7096	10,256	450–0	59–2	26–7	11.0
ex Macy Willis 23								
H C Folger	1916	BethU1	7086	10,267	452–0	56–0	27–3	10.0
Hahira	1920	BethSP	6855	10,238	453–0	56–2	27–1	10.0
Herbert L Pratt (st)	1918	BethAl	7118	10,122	453–9	56–0	27–2	11.0
J C Donnell	1918	NNews	9783	14,970	516–6	68–2	28–7	10.5
J E O'Neil (st)	1918	BethAl	7070	10,122	453–9	56–0	27–2	11.0
J W Van Dyke (te)	1938	SunSBD	11,652	19,200	543–10	70–2	30–4	13.0
Point Breeze (me)	1918	Penns	4756	7095	364.9	51–0	26–0	9.5
ex John M Connelly 26; conv steamer 27								
Robert C Tuttle (te)	bldg	SunSBD	11,615	19,200	543–10	70–2	30–4	13.0
Robert H Colley (te)	1938	SunSBD	11,651	18,105	543–10	70–2	30–4	13.0
Sharon (me)	1918	PuseyG	4762	7077	364.9	51–0	26–0	9.5
conv steamer 27								
Tustem	1921	Moore	6906	10,645	438–5	57–2	27–1	10.5
W C Yeager (te)	order	SunSBD	11,615	19,200	543–10	70–2	30–4	13.0
W D Anderson	1921	Moore	10,227	17,430	500.0	71–2	29–7	10.5
ex Tamiahua 36								
W M Burton (st)	1918	BethAl	7094	10,122	452–0	56–0	27–2	11.0
W M Irish (st)	1918	BethAl	7123	10,122	452–0	56–0	27–2	11.0
ATLANTIC OIL SHIPPING CO (Panamanian flag)								
Brunswick (me)	1928	Scott2	8890	14,180	483–2	63–4	28–2	10.5
Permian (me)	1931	Scott2	8890	14,180	483–2	63–3	28–1	10.5
Winkler (me)	1930	Scott2	6907	11,062	421.2	58–3	27–7	10.5

Funnel: Black with black BL on white band between two narrow red bands
Hull: Black
Trades: Oil and petroleum
Note: This company controlled BL Shipping Co Ltd (*qv* in Great Britain section)

BL SHIPPING CO INC, Graybar Bldg, 420 Lexington Ave, New York

Tankers

BERNUTH, LEMBCKE CO INC								
O M Bernuth (st)	1938	SunSBD	7972	12,950	459–6	65–4	28–8	13.0
TRIMOUNTAIN STEAMSHIP CORP								
Trimountain	1919	BethQu	6389	9910	416.9	56–2	26–6	10.0

Funnel: Black with white B on red five-pointed star superimposed on four blue bands separated by three white bands
Hull: Black, red boot-topping
Services: New York, New Orleans, Port Arthur–W Africa; jointly with Dodwell-Castle Line (J Chambers & Co, *qv* in Great Britain section)

BARBER STEAMSHIP LINES INC,
923–943 Whitehall Bldg, 17 Battery Place, New York

AMERICAN-WEST AFRICAN LINE INC

Cathlamat	1919	Ames	5869	8900	423–0	54–2	25–9	10.5
Otho	1920	ToddDD	4839	7500	395–9	53–1	23–9	10.5
West Humhaw (st)	1918	Skinnr	5527	8600	424–0	54–2	24–0	10.5
West Irmo	1919	Ames	5775	8900	423–0	54–2	25–9	10.5
West Kebar	1920	LBeach	5620	8550	427–0	54–2	24–2	10.5
West Lashaway (st)	1918	Skinnr	5637	8578	424–0	54–2	24–0	10.5
Zarembo	1919	ToddDD	4957	7500	395–9	53–1	23–9	10.5

Services: US E coast coal trades

BERWIND-WHITE COAL MINING CO, 1 Broadway, New York

WILMORE STEAMSHIP CO,
c/o Staples Coal Co, Suite 1035, 80 Federal St, Boston MA

Berwindglen	1929	BethQu	4411	–	350.5	50–2	28.3	11.5
Berwindvale (st)	1929	BethQu	4411	–	350.5	50–2	28.3	11.5

BETHLEHEM STEEL CORPORATION,
2600 Terminal Tower Bldg, Cleveland OH

Funnel: Calmar – Black with white C on broad blue band bordered by two narrow white bands; Ore – grey with white O on grey band between two narrow white bands
Hull: Calmar – black with CALMAR LINE in white, red boot-topping; Ore – grey, red boot-topping
Services: Calmar – cargo and passenger, US Atlantic–US Pacific; Ore – ore trades, US Atlantic ports/US Pacific ports/West Indies

CALMAR STEAMSHIP CORP, Cunard Bldg, 25 Broadway, New York

Alamar (st)	1916	Unionl	5689	9650	399.7	56–2	27–0	10.0
ex Eurana 29								
Calmar	1920	Mtsuil	5787	9157	385.0	51–0	27–1	9.5
ex Albert Jeffress 27, ex Eastern Importer 22								
Flomar	1919	Columb	5551	8350	423–10	54–2	24–1	10.0
ex Corvus 29								
Kenmar (st)	1919	Skinnr	6844	10,295	424–0	54–2	24–0	11.0
ex Elmsport 38								
Losmar	1919	NWStl	5549	8600	423–10	54–2	24–0	10.5
ex Clauseus 29								
Marymar (st)	1919	Skinnr	6847	10,300	424–0	54–2	24–0	11.0
ex Colorado Springs 38								
Massmar	1920	Kwsaki	5828	9157	385.0	51–2	27–1	9.5
ex James B Duke 27, ex Eastern Cloud 22								
Oakmar	1920	Mtsuil	5766	9200	385.0	51–0	27–1	9.5
ex William Campion 27, ex Eastern Exporter 22								
Oremar (st)	1919	Skinnr	6854	10,305	424–0	54–2	24–0	11.0
ex Edgehill 39								
Pennmar	1920	Kwsaki	5868	9517	385.3	51–2	27–1	9.5
ex George Allen 27, ex Eastern Ocean 23								
Portmar	1919	NWStl	5551	8600	423–10	54–2	24–0	10.5
ex Centaurus 29								
Texmar	1919	BethSW	5505	8500	427–0	54–4	24–6	10.0
ex Edgar Bowling 27, ex West Cavanal 22								
Vermar	1919	Columb	5568	8350	423–10	54–2	24–0	10.0
ex Circinus 29								
Yorkmar	1919	Ames	5612	9216	423–0	54–2	25–9	10.0
ex William Perkins 27, ex West Islay 22								

ORE STEAMSHIP CORP, Cunard Bldg, 25 Broadway, New York

Ore carriers

Bethore (s2)	1922	BethSP	8257	22,320	550.3	72–2	34–0	10.5
Chilore (st2)	1922	BethAl	8310	22,200	549.6	72–3	34–0	10.5
Cubore (m)	1920	BethQu	7051	11,200	450.6	57–2	29–0	9.5
conv steamer 24								
Firmore (st)	1918	BethSP	7117	12,355	449.1	57–2	29–0	9.5
Lebore (st2)	1923	BethSF	8289	22,410	549.6	72–3	34–0	10.5
Mangore	1918	BethSP	4066	6060	357.3	50–4	24.5	8.5
Marore (st2)	1922	BethSP	8215	22,980	550.3	72–3	34–0	10.5
Santore	1918	BethSP	7117	12,230	449.1	57–2	29–0	9.5
Steelore (st2)	1922	BethSP	8215	22,980	550.3	72–2	34–0	10.5

Note: Companies in the Bethlehem Steel group also owned smaller vessels, and a large fleet operating on the Great Lakes

BLACK DIAMOND LINES INC, 39 Broadway, New York

Funnel: Yellow base separated from black top by yellow band bearing black elongated diamond over narrow black band
Services: Mail, passenger and cargo – Norfolk, New York–Antwerp; New York, Boston, Philadelphia, Baltimore, Norfolk–Rotterdam–Antwerp

Black Condor (st)	1921	MerchH	5358	8750	400.7	54–2	25–8	12.0
ex Ala 35								
Black Eagle (st,P–)	1920	AISB	5060	7997	401–0	54–2	24–6	13.0
ex Tomalva 32, laid down as Carlecay								
Black Falcon (st,P–)	1918	AISB	5049	7997	401–0	54–2	24–4	13.0
ex Sac City 32								
Black Gull (st,P–)	1919	AISB	5029	7997	400–4	54–2	24–9	13.0
ex City of Alton 32, laid down as Claybourne								
Black Hawk (st,P–)	1919	AISB	4988	7997	401–0	54–2	24–6	13.0
ex Saco 32								
Black Heron (st,P–)	1918	AISB	4926	7997	401–0	54–2	24–6	13.0
ex Sacandaga 32								
Black Osprey (st)	1918	Skinnr	5589	8567	424–0	54–1	24–1	13.0
ex West Arrow 35								
Black Tern (st)	1919	AISB	5032	7997	401–0	54–2	24–6	13.0
ex Coahoma County 32, laid down as Clauston								

BULL & CO INC, A H, Bull Steamships Line Bldg, 115 Broad St, New York, and Pier 5, Pratt St, Baltimore MD

Funnel: Black with blue B on broad white band between two narrow red bands
Hull: Black or white, red boot-topping
Services: New York–Baltimore–Jacksonville–San Juan; US E coast services

A H BULL STEAMSHIP CO INC

Angelina (st)	1934	NNews	4772	7500	411–0	55–4	24–6	13.0
Arlyn	1919	PuseyG	3304	5141	321.7	50–0	20–6	9.5
ex Castle Wood 25								

Barbara (P43)	1913	Cramp	4637	6520	398–0	50–2	23–6	10.5
ex Santa Cruz 30								
Beatrice	1917	BethSP	3451	5163	327.2	46–2	21–2	9.5
Carolyn	1912	NNews	3209	5025	328–2	46–0	21–3	9.5
Catherine (P–)	1918	Manito	2286	2855	261–0	43–9	20–2	9.0
ex Lake Greenwood 20, launched as War Mist								
Clare	1915	BethMS	3372	5146	327.2	46–2	21–2	9.5
Cornelia	1916	BethSP	3129	4644	327.7	46–9	21–11	11.5
Dorothy	1918	BethSP	4647	7350	391–9	52–4	24-0	10.5
ex Cape Henry 30, launched as War Dolphin								
Edith	1915	BethMS	3382	5146	327.2	45–3	21–2	9.5
Elizabeth	1918	Standd	4727	6150	395–9	52–0	23–8	10.5
ex Floridian 36, ex Muscatine 28								
Ellenor	1920	BethWi	3483	5175	328.0	46–2	21–5	10.0
ex Mason City 22								
Emilia	1918	BethSP	4719	7350	391–9	52–4	24–0	10.5
ex Cape Romain 29, launched as War Mercury								
Evelyn	1912	NNews	3141	5025	328–2	46–1	21–3	9.5
Georgeanna	1916	BethHH	2089	2400	242.2	39–0	17–4	9.5
ex Georgeanna Weems 32								
Helen	1916	BethSP	3129	4412	327.7	46–9	21–11	11.5
Hilton	1918	Standd	4741	6150	395–9	52–0	23–8	10.5
ex Georgian 36, ex Ice King 28, launched as Passaic, laid down as War Unit								
Irene	1919	BethWi	3482	5175	328.0	46–3	21–5	11.0
ex Bethnor 22								
Jean	1918	BethSP	4902	7350	391–9	52–4	24–0	10.5
ex Kosciuszko 29, ex Cape Lookout 19, launched as War Shark								
Lillian	1922	BethWi	3482	5175	328.0	46–3	21–5	11.0
ex Maddequet 22								
Mae (st)	1918	Skinnr	5607	8192	424–0	54–2	24–0	11.5
ex West Eldara 36								
Manuela (st)	1934	NNews	4772	7500	411–0	55–4	24–6	13.0
Margaret	1916	BethMS	3352	5163	327.2	46–2	21–2	9.5
Marina (st,P8/1)	order	PuseyW	6750	7815	417–9	60–2	27–4	14.0
Marjory	1919	McDoug	2323	3610	261–0	43–8	22–11	9.5
ex Marjory Weems 31, ex Chamberino 28								
Mary (st)	1920	AISB	5104	7800	401–0	54–2	24–5	12.0
ex Cody 39, laid down as Cassimir								
Millinocket	1910	BethMS	3274	4739	317.3	44–2	22–4	9.5
Rosario	1920	BethWi	4659	7350	391–9	52–4	24–0	10.5
ex Natirar 32								
BALTIMORE INSULAR LINE INC, Pier 5, Pratt St, Baltimore MD								
Delfina	1919	Hanlon	3480	5210	320.7	46–0	22–1	9.5
Delisle	1919	Hanlon	3478	5210	320.7	46–0	22–1	9.5
Governor John Lind	1918	Hanlon	3431	5017	319–10	46–0	23–0	9.5
Major Wheeler	1918	Hanlon	3431	5040	319–10	46–0	23–0	9.5

Funnel: Black
Trades: Oil and petroleum

CARGILL INC, Albany, NY

Tanker

Carlantic (m)	order	Cargll	7400	12,600	409.9	60–1	28–6	14.0

Funnel: Black with white emblem
Hull: Black, red boot-topping
Trades: Oil and petroleum

CITIES SERVICE OIL CO, 60 Wall St, New York

Tankers

Cities Service Boston	1921	BethSP	9348	14,300	468.3	62–9	29–6	10.5
ex Agwipond 30								
Cities Service Denver	1921	BethSP	9316	14,300	468.3	62–9	29–6	10.5
ex Agwilake 29								
Cities Service Empire	1918	BethSP	8103	12,650	464.7	60–2	27–5	10.5
ex Ampetco 28								
Cities Service Fuel (st)	1916	BethFR	5343	8700	389.0	54–9	25–11	9.0
ex Sucrosa 26								
Cities Service Kansas (st)	1920	Baltmr	7641	10,950	450–0	59–2	26–7	10.5
ex Cecil County 30								

Cities Service Koolmotor								
	1918	BethAl	6762	10,820	453–9	56–0	27–2	10.0
ex Shreveport 29, ex W S Rheem 21								
Cities Service Missouri (st)								
	1920	Baltmr	7506	10,950	450–0	59–2	26–7	10.5
ex Clement Smith 30								
Cities Service Ohio (m)								
	1921	Baltmr	7245	10,950	450–0	59–2	26–7	10.5
ex Herman Falk 29, ex Tuxpanoil 27; conv steamer 27								
Cities Service Oklahoma (st)								
	1920	Baltmr	7529	10,950	450–0	59–2	26–7	10.5
ex Hampton Roads 30								
Cities Service Toledo	1918	BethWi	8192	12,650	465.2	60–0	27–5	10.5
ex J A Bostwick 29								
Hadnot	1919	BethQu	6257	9850	416.9	56–2	26–6	10.0
Hagood	1919	BethSP	6866	10,910	453–9	56–2	27–1	10.0
Halo	1920	BethAl	6986	10,750	453–9	56–0	27–1	10.0
Watertown	1919	BethQu	6372	9850	416.9	56–2	26–6	10.0

COLOMBIAN STEAMSHIP CO INC,
25th floor, Whitehall Bldg, 17 Battery Place, New York

Martinique* (P–)	1920	Toledo	2559	4190	261–0	43–7	24–5	9.5
ex Pulwico 22, ex Pulaski 21, laid down as Lake Fine								

Funnel: Yellow, black top
Hull: Grey, red boot-topping
Services: Cargo and passenger – New York–West Indies–Central America–Canal Zone, via Haiti and Jamaica
Note: * Sold Brazil 1939, renamed *Salineiro*

COMMERCIAL PACIFIC CABLE CO, 67 Broad St, New York

Cable vessels								
Dickenson	1923	SunSB	831	–	174.3	30–2	15–2	11.0
Restorer (s2)	1903	ArmWh1	3180	2600	358.4	44–0	24–6	14.5

Funnel: Yellow
Services: Pacific area cable laying and maintenance
Note: This company was associated with All America Cables & Radio Inc (*qv*) and Commercial Cable Co Ltd (*qv* in Great Britain section)

COMMERCIAL SOLVENTS CORPORATION, 230 Park Avenue, New York

Services: Molasses carriage

COMMERCIAL MOLASSES CORP

Tankers								
Castana (st)	1920	AISB	5030	8100	401–0	54–2	24–5	11.5
conv general cargo 21								
Comol Rico (st)	1919	AISB	5034	8000	401–0	54–2	24–5	11.5
ex Kishacoquillas 39, laid down as Sebethe; conv general cargo 20								
Under Panamanian flag								
Comol Cuba (st)	1919	AISB	5036	8000	401–0	54–2	24–5	12.0
ex Dora 38, ex Inspector 27, launched as Red Jacket; conv general cargo 21								

CONTINENTAL OIL CO,
Drawer 1267, Ponca City OK, and 100 West 10th St, Wilmington DE

Trades: Oil and petroleum

CONTINENTAL STEAMSHIP CO INC,
Postbox 1637, Baltimore MD and 60 East 42 St, New York

Tankers								
Garnet Hulings	1920	Moore2	7036	10,625	438–5	57–0	27–1	10.0
ex Salina 28								
W W Bruce	1918	SunSB	6728	11,380	445–5	59–2	26–9	10.0
ex Sabine Sun 29								

COSMOPOLITAN SHIPPING CO INC,
42 Broadway, New York, and Pier 1, Hoboken, NJ

Operators of								
AMERICA–FRANCE LINE								
Collamer (st)	1920	AISB	5112	8015	401–0	54–2	24–5	12.0
Independence Hall (st)								
	1920	AISB	5050	8000	401–0	54–2	24–5	12.0
launched as Conconnully								
Pipestone County (st)	1919	AISB	5102	8000	401–0	54–2	24–5	12.0
Schodack (st)	1919	AISB	5041	8000	401–0	54–2	24–5	12.0

Funnel: A–FL – black with blue AFL on broad white band between two narrow red bands
Services: A–FL – Philadelphia, Baltimore, New York, Boston–Havre, Dunkirk, Antwerp, London; New York–Bordeaux

Note: America–France Line and its vessels were owned by United States Maritime Commission (*qv*)

Funnel: Yellow with white over blue bands
Hull: Grey, red boot-topping
Services: Philippine–W coast North America
Note: Also smaller vessels on local services

DE LA RAMA Y CIA, HIJOS DE I,
53 I de la Rama St, Iloilo, Panay Island, Philippines

DE LA RAMA STEAMSHIP CO INC

Doña Aniceta (m,P12/1)	bldg	CRDA5	5011	8560	439–5	55–8	25–9	14.0
Doña Aurora (m,P12/1)	1939	CRDA5	5011	8560	439–5	55–9	25–9	14.0
Doña Nati (m,P12/1)	1939	CRDA5	5011	8560	439–5	55–8	25–9	14.0

Services: Fisheries

DEEP SEA FISHERIES INC, 34 Davis St, San Francisco CA

Tanker

Manatawny (st)	1920	AISB	5030	8118	401–0	54–2	24–5	11.0

laid down as Casagrande; conv general cargo 21

Trades: Oil and petroleum
Note: * Sold Aztec Petroleum Trading Corp, Dover DE, 1939, renamed *Aztec*

EASTERN STATES PETROLEUM CO INC,
International Bldg, 630 5th Avenue, New York

Tanker

R W McIlvain* (m2)	1916	Baltmr	3262	5090	306–0	47–2	23–0	9.0

ex Los Alamos 32, ex Bramell Point 23

Funnel: Black with red CM monogram on white band
Services: Eastern region oil and petroleum trades

FERNANDEZ HERMANOS INC,
Calle Juan Luna 109, Postbox 805, Manila, Philippines

COMPAÑÍA MARÍTIMA

Tanker

Mindanao	1918	BrownJ	5236	7995	412–8	52–4	25–3	10.0

ex Anatina 38, ex War Hermit 19

Services: Philadelphia, New York–Buenos Aires; US E coast
Note: Also vessels operating on US E coast, the Great Lakes and inland waterways

FORD MOTOR CO, 3674 Schaefer Rd, Dearborn MI

East Indian (m2)	1918	Uraga	8159	11,650	461–8	58–0	28–8	11.5

ex Beikoku Maru 25; conv steamer 26

Services: Sulphur transportation – Port Sulphur–New York, Baltimore and other US E coast ports (vessel laid up Freeport 1939)

FREEPORT SULPHUR CO, Chanin Bldg, 122 East 42 St, New York

Sulphur carrier

Freeport Sulphur No 5	1920	Fed1	4127	6700	363–6	52–6	22–4	11.0

Services: US, Gulf of Mexico, West Indies
Note: Also smaller vessels

GARCIA, LISARDO, Puerto Cortes, Honduras; and Postbox 534, Port Arthur TX

Under Honduras flag

Jupiter (m2)	1917	Manito	2063	2800	250.5	43–6	20–2	8.5
ex Ormidale 38, ex Astmahco III 22, ex Lake Mohonk 19, ex Motor I 18								
Neptuno	1919	Albina	2220	3580	289.0	44–2	19–1	9.0
ex Munisla 37, ex Glorieta 20								

Funnel: Green base separated from black top by white band
Hull: Black, red boot-topping
Services: Passenger and cargo – New York–Havana (eastbound)–Colombia–Panama–El Salvador–Guatemala, Mexico–California; New York–Havana (northbound) –Panama–Colombia–Ecuador–Peru–Chile; cargo – Puget Sound, San Francisco–W coast ports–Chile

GRACE & CO, W R,
7 Hanover Sq, New York and Oceanic Bldg, 2 Pine St, San Francisco CA

GRACE LINE INC, 10 Hanover Sq, New York

Passenger/general cargo vessels

Santa Barbara (m2,P157/1)	1928	FurnH	7858	6723	486–0	64–0	25–1	16.0
Santa Clara (te2,P170/1)	1930	NYSB3	8183	7300	505–0	64–0	25–0	16.5
Santa Elena (st2,P225/1,65/t)	1933	Fed2	9135	7525	508–0	72–3	25–11	19.0
Santa Inez (m2,P75/1,42/t)	1929	B&W	4576	4480	386–0	53–3	21–10	14.0

Grace Line: Santa Paula *was launched on June 11 1932 and made her maiden voyage from New York to Seattle in January 1933. She was placed on the South America service in 1938 and in November 1941 was taken over as a troopship. She returned to peacetime passenger service on May 2 1947.* Santa Paula *was laid up at New York in June 1958. She was sold to Typaldos Lines of Greece in 1961 and renamed* Acropolis, *but was laid up at Perama in 1968 after her owners went into bankruptcy. She was broken up in 1977 (RW Jordan collection)*

Gulf Oil: Gulfwax *was built by Sun Shipbuilding Co at Chester, Pennsylvania, and completed in October 1921, being one of a large group of similar tankers built from about the end of the First World War. She is pictured here in wartime livery in the Pacific. Gulfwax was broken up in 1953 (Canadian Forces, Ottawa)*

Lykes Bros SS Co: Almeria Lykes *was completed in July 1940 and is pictured here in neutral colours before the US came into the war. In 1941–42 she transferred to the British flag and under the ownership of the Ministry of War Transport was named* Empire Condor. *Returning to the US flag in 1942 as* Almeria Lykes, *she only lasted a few more weeks and in August was torpedoed and sunk by an E-boat off Tunisia while in the Operation 'Pedestal' convoy to Malta (Lykes Bros SS Co)*

Mississippi Shipping Co: The steamer Delorleans, *was ordered in December 1938 for the service from New Orleans to Brazil and Argentina. Launched on February 17 1940, she was delivered in August 1940. Taken over by the US Navy in June 1941, she was converted by Alabama Dry Dock at Mobile into the transport* Crescent City. *In February 1945 she was converted at Pearl Harbor into a temporary hospital ship and four years later went into reserve and was laid up at San Francisco. In 1971 she was acquired by the California Maritime Academy and became the training ship* Golden Bear *(RW Jordan collection)*

Santa Isabel* (P108/1,165/t)								
	1915	NedSM	5641	5750	396–0	48–9	24–11	12.5
ex Venezuela 31								
Santa Lucia (st2,P225/1,65/t)								
	1933	Fed2	9135	7525	508–0	72–3	25–11	19.0
Santa Maria (m2,P157/1)								
	1928	FurnH	7857	6800	486–0	64–0	25–1	16.0
Santa Paula (st2,P225/1,65/t)								
	1932	Fed2	9135	7290	508–0	72–2	25–11	19.0
Santa Rita (m2,P75/1,42/t)								
	1929	B&W	4576	4480	386–0	53–1	21–10	13.0
Santa Rosa (st2,P225/1,65/t)								
	1932	Fed2	9135	7290	508–0	72–2	25–11	19.0
General cargo vessels								
Cacique	1918	BethEl	2718	4125	300.0	45–2	21–4	11.0
ex Nosa Chief 35, ex Garfield 29								
Capac	1919	Duthie	5586	8500	423–0	54–2	24–0	10.5
ex Deuel 26								
Charcas	1919	BethSW	5555	8600	427–0	54–3	24–1	10.5
ex West Inskip 26								
Chipana	1920	Mobile	3280	5191	336–5	46–2	23–0	10.5
ex Nosa Prince 35, ex Oklahoma City 29								
Condor	1920	ToddDD	4747	7600	395–9	53–1	23–8	10.5
ex Rotarian 27								
Coya	1919	ToddDD	4954	7600	395–9	53–1	23–8	10.5
ex Orcus 24								
Curaca	1920	Mobile	3280	5171	336–5	46–2	23–0	10.5
ex Nosa Queen 35, ex Atlanta of Texas 29								
Cuzco	1919	LBeach	5496	8550	427–0	54–3	24–0	11.0
ex West Kasson 26								
Falcón	1919	PuseyW	2966	4425	315–0	44–2	21–3	10.0
ex Rock Island 26, launched as War Shield								
Lara	1919	PuseyW	2967	4425	315–0	44–2	21–3	10.0
ex Moline 25, launched as War Dart								
Santa Ana (st)	bldg	NNews	8095	9758	459–3	63–2	26–10	16.0
Santa Elisa (st)	order	Fed2	8380	9020	459–3	63–2	25–9	16.0
Santa Rita (st)	order	Fed2	8380	9020	459–3	63–2	25–9	16.0
Santa Teresa (st)	bldg	NNews	8095	9758	459–3	63–0	26–10	16.0
Tachirá	1920	McDoug	2325	3360	261–0	43–8	22–11	9.5
ex Elizabeth R 22, ex Antonio 22								

Note: * BU Baltimore 1939

GULF OIL CORPORATION,

Whitehall Bldg, 17 Battery Place, New York, and Gulf Bldg, Pittsburgh PA

Funnel: Yellow with black top separated by white G on red band
Hull: Black, red boot-topping
Trades: Oil and petroleum

Tankers								
Gulf of Mexico	1917	NYSB1	7807	13,550	485–0	62–8	28–1	11.0
Gulf of Venezuela (m)								
	1919	Moore2	6910	10,520	438–5	57–0	27–1	10.5
ex Miskianza 25; conv steamer 25								
Gulfbelle (st)	1936	SunSBD	7104	11,402	441–8	64–2	27–9	12.5
Gulfbird (m)	1928	FurnH	10,208	16,420	511.7	69–6	28–5	11.0
Gulfbreeze	1922	NYSB1	6651	10,480	436–4	56–6	25–10	11.0
ex Eurana 26								
Gulfcoast (st)	1937	BethSP	7140	11,426	442–1	64–2	27–9	12.5
Gulfcrest (m2)	1926	NYSB2	8916	14,875	460.4	65–3	29–8	11.0
Gulfdawn (st)	1936	SunSBD	7096	11,402	441–9	64–0	27–9	12.5
Gulfdisc (st)	1938	BethSP	7141	11,426	442–1	64–2	27–9	12.5
Gulfgem	1920	SunSB	6917	11,280	445–5	59–2	26–8	11.0
ex Agwisun 29								
Gulfhawk (m)	1928	FurnH	10,208	16,420	511.7	69–6	28–5	11.0
Gulfking	1921	UnionB	6561	10,600	419.5	56–5	26–11	11.0
Gulfland	1918	NYSB1	5277	7790	406–0	51–2	24–7	10.5
Gulfmaid	1917	NYSB1	5225	7790	406–0	51–2	24–7	10.5
Gulfoil	1912	NYSB1	5189	7790	406–6	51–2	24–7	10.0
Gulfpenn	1921	SunSB	8862	13,840	480.5	66–0	28–1	11.0
ex Agwihavre 29								
Gulfpoint	1920	BethSP	6972	10,910	453–0	56–2	27–1	10.5
ex Hahatonka 23								
Gulfpride (m2)	1927	Fed2	12,510	20,040	543–11	74–4	30–7	11.0
Gulfprince	1921	UnionB	6561	10,600	419.5	56–5	25–9	10.5
Gulfqueen	1919	NYSB1	6599	10,500	436–4	56–6	25–6	10.5
Gulfstar	1920	SunSB	6969	11,250	445–5	59–2	26–5	11.0

Gulfstate	1920	BethAl	6882	10,735	453–9	56–0	26–0	10.5
ex Halway 23								
Gulftide (st)	1937	BethSP	7140	11,426	442–1	64–2	27–9	12.5
Gulftrade	1920	SunSB	6776	11,250	445–5	59–2	26–5	10.5
Gulfwave (st)	1938	BethSP	7140	11,426	442–1	64–2	27–9	12.5
Gulfwax	1921	SunSB	8862	13,840	480.5	66–0	28–1	11.0
ex Agwimex 29								
Gulfwing (m)	1928	FurnH	10,208	16,420	511.7	69–6	28–5	11.0

Note: Also tankers under 2500gt and others owned by a Venezuelan subsidiary company

HILLCONE STEAMSHIP CO LTD, 311 California St, San Francisco CA

Funnel: Black with white band
Hull: Black
Trades: Oil and petroleum

Tankers

Brandywine (st)	1919	PuseyG	4931	7582	364.9	51–0	26–0	11.0
Edwin B de Golia (st)	1917	Baltmr	3322	5210	306–0	47–2	23–0	10.0
ex William Isom 32								
J J Coney	1920	Terry	5168	7437	391.9	51–0	25–1	10.0
ex W D Anderson 35, ex Pearldon 23								

HYMAN-MICHAELS CO, 122 South Michigan Ave, Chicago, IL

Services: Vessel at Norfolk VA laid up for sale 1939

Bellflower (st)	1919	Fed1	6085	9808	411–6	55–0	27–2	12.0

INTERNATIONAL FREIGHTING CORPORATION INC, 17 Battery Place, New York

Funnel: White or black with emblem on yellow band
Hull: Irénée Du Pont – grey with IFC LINES, red boot-topping
Services: Oil and petroleum trades; general tramping

General cargo vessel								
Irénée Du Pont (st)	order	NNews	6125		439.0	63–4	26–6	15.0
Tanker								
Lammot Du Pont	1914	NofIre	5102	8550	405.0	52–0	26–2	10.0
ex San Francisco 33, ex Saint Francis 19, ex San Francisco 18								

Manager for
CUBA DISTILLING CO INC, 60 East 42nd St, New York

Carrabulle (st)	1920	AISB	5030	7800	401–0	54–2	24–5	11.5
conv general cargo 21								
Cassimir (st)	1920	AISB	5030	7800	401–0	54–2	24–5	11.5
laid down as Chenoa; conv general cargo 21								
Catahoula (st)	1920	AISB	5030	7800	401–0	54–2	24–5	11.5
conv general cargo 21								

ISTHMIAN STEAMSHIP CO, Cunard Bldg, 25 Broadway, New York

Funnel: Yellow
Hull: Grey, red boot-topping
Services: US–NW Europe; Vancouver–San Francisco–Panama–London–Liverpool–Avonmouth; New York/Boston/Baltimore/New Orleans–Manila–Saigon–Singapore–Batavia–Calcutta; E coast US–Gulf ports–W coast US, Canada; Baltimore–Honolulu; Gulf ports–Calcutta–Persian Gulf

Anniston City (st,P–)	1921	Chick	5686	9370	442–0	56–2	25–10	11.0
Atlanta City (st,P–)	1921	Chick	5686	9700	441–11	56–2	25–10	11.0
Birmingham City (P–)	1920	Chick	6194	9400	411–6	55–0	27–3	11.0
Chattanooga City (st,P–)	1921	Chick	5687	9370	442–0	56–2	25–10	11.0
Chickasaw City (P–)	1920	Chick	6196	9400	411–6	55–0	27–3	11.0
Ensley City (P–)	1920	Chick	6157	9430	411–6	55–0	27–3	11.0
Fairfield City (st,P–)	1921	Chick	5686	9370	442–0	56–2	25–10	11.0
Knoxville City (st,P–)	1921	Chick	5686	9370	442–0	56–2	25–10	11.0
Memphis City (st,P–)	1921	Chick	5686	9200	442–0	56–2	25–10	11.0
Mobile City (P–)	1920	Chick	6157	9430	411–6	55–0	27–3	11.0
Montgomery City (st,P–)	1920	Chick	5686	9200	411–6	56–4	25–10	11.0
Selma City (st,P–)	1921	Chick	5686	9370	442–0	56–2	25–10	11.0
Steel Age (st,P–)	1920	Fed1	6188	9500	411–6	55–0	27–3	11.0
Steel Engineer (st,P–)	1920	Fed1	5686	9200	442–0	56–2	25–10	11.0
Steel Exporter (st,P–)	1920	Fed1	5687	9200	442–0	56–2	25–10	11.0
Steel Inventor (st,P–)	1920	Fed1	5686	9200	442–0	56–2	25–10	11.0
Steel Mariner (st,P–)	1920	Fed1	5686	9200	441–11	56–2	25–11	11.0
Steel Navigator (st,P–)	1921	Fed1	5719	9200	442–0	56–2	25–10	11.0
Steel Ranger (st,P–)	1920	Fed1	5686	9200	442–0	56–2	25–10	11.0
Steel Scientist (st,P–)	1921	Fed1	5688	9200	442–0	56–2	25–10	11.0
Steel Seafarer (st,P–)	1921	Fed1	5719	9200	442–0	56–2	25–10	11.0
Steel Trader (st,P–)	1920	Fed1	5686	9200	442–0	56–2	25–10	11.0
Steel Traveler (st,P–)	1922	Fed1	7056	9750	442–0	56–2	25–10	11.0
Steel Voyager (st,P–)	1920	Fed1	6198	9500	411–6	55–0	27–3	11.0
Steel Worker (st,P–)	1920	Fed1	5687	9200	442–0	56–2	25–10	11.0

Note: Isthmian Steamship Co was a subsidiary of United States Steel Corporation

Steelmaker (st,P–)	1920	Fed1	6176	9756	411–6	55–0	27–3	11.0
Tuscaloosa City (st,P–)	1920	Chick	5686	9200	442–0	56–2	25–10	11.0

Trades: Oil and petroleum

Note: This company was a subsidiary of Spencer Kellogg & Sons Inc, Edgewater NJ

KELLOGG STEAMSHIP CORP, 75 West St, New York

Tankers

Elizabeth Kellogg	1920	Terry	5189	7899	391.9	51–0	25–1	10.5
ex Darden 29								
Gertrude Kellogg	1920	Terry	5159	8125	391.9	51–0	25–1	10.5
ex Gladysbe 29								
Ruth Kellogg (st)	1920	AISB	5037	8125	401–0	54–2	24–5	11.5
ex Vaba 29, ex Freeport 29, ex Vaba 29, laid down as Calaumet; conv general cargo 21								
Spencer Kellogg	1919	BethWi	5307	7965	391.0	51–4	25–2	10.5
ex Romulus 29								

Funnel: White with blue top separated by white over blue bands
Trades: Oil and petroleum

KERR STEAMSHIP CO INC, Whitehall Bldg, 17 Battery Place, New York 4

MARITIME TRADING LTD, Panama (Panamanian flag)

Tanker

Alfred Clegg (m)	bldg	B&W	9428	14,590	516–6	65–7	27–11	12.5

Services: Alaska cannery services Seattle–Alaska (vessels at Seattle from Aug–Sept 1938)

LIBBY, MCNEILL & LIBBY, 88 Hamlin St, PO Box 1902, Seattle WA

Passenger/general cargo vessels

David W Branch (P186/1,144/st)	1915	Scheld	5544	5750	396–0	48–9	25–0	13.0
ex Santa Olivia 37, ex Ecuador 31								
General W C Gorgas (P93)	1902	Neptn1	4636	5200	386–0	45–4	24–6	9.5
ex Prinz Sigismund 17								
Otsego (P99)	1902	Reiher	4638	5200	385–0	45–4	24–6	9.5
ex Prinz Eitel Friedrich 17								

Funnel: Black with white L on broad white band between two narrow white bands
Hull: Black with LUCKENBACH LINE in white amidships, red boot-topping
Services: US E coast–US W coast; US Gulf ports–US W coast

LUCKENBACH STEAMSHIP CO INC,
120 Wall St, New York, and Pier 135, Foot of 35th St, Brooklyn, NY

Andrea F Luckenbach (st2)	1919	BethQu	10,652	14,251	496.0	68–2	29–0	12.5
Dorothy Luckenbach (st2,P–)	1919	SunSB	6370	9600	448.9	60–2	27–5	13.5
ex Edellyn 22								
Edgar F Luckenbach	1916	NNews	6002	10,470	442–0	57–4	28–2	11.5
Edward Luckenbach (st)	1916	BethFR	7916	12,250	436.6	57–3	31–7	13.5
F J Luckenbach (st2)	1917	BethFR	7821	11,552	446.0	56–1	30–6	12.5
Florence Luckenbach	1910	Steph2	5049	8360	415–5	52–3	24–3	10.0
ex Damara 15								
Harry Luckenbach (st,P–)	1919	SunSB	6355	9800	448.9	60–2	27–4	13.5
ex Sol Navis 20								
Horace Luckenbach (s2,P–)	1919	Asano	6475	11,043	461–8	58–0	27–0	12.5
ex Eastern Trader 23								
J L Luckenbach (st2,P–)	1919	SunSB	6369	9590	448.9	60–2	27–4	13.5
ex South Bend 22								
Jacob Luckenbach	1918	SunSB	5817	10,380	450–0	57–8	28–1	12.0
ex Radnor 30, laid down as War Indian								
Julia Luckenbach (st)	1917	BethFR	5950	9980	436.6	57–2	27–10	13.5
K I Luckenbach (st2)	1918	BethQu	5887	9485	446.0	56–1	27–0	12.5
Katrina Luckenbach (st2)	1918	BethQu	5854	9425	446.0	56–1	27–0	12.5
Lena Luckenbach (r/t)	1920	Harim1	5238	8930	425.0	53–8	25–8	10.0
ex Eastern Soldier 22								
Lewis Luckenbach (st2)	1919	BethQu	10,653	14,197	496.0	68–0	29–0	12.5

Lillian Luckenbach (st2,P–)	1919	SunSB	6369	9590	448.9	60–2	27–4	13.5
ex Marica 22								
Mathew Luckenbach	1918	SunSB	5821	10,775	450–0	57–9	26–1	12.0
ex Kelvinia 29, ex Deerfield 26								
Paul Luckenbach	1913	Bremer	6606	11,050	471.1	59–2	26–11	12.5
ex Poznan 22, ex Suwanee 20, ex Mark 17								
Robert Luckenbach (s2,P–)	1919	Asano	6461	11,043	461–8	58–0	27–6	12.5
ex Eastern Merchant 22								
Susan V Luckenbach (r/t)	1918	SunSB	5781	9725	450–0	57–9	26–1	12.5
ex Neponset 29								
Walter A Luckenbach (st2)	1918	SeatCD	8077	11,284	469–3	56–1	30–6	13.5
William Luckenbach (P16)	1913	Bremer	6938	10,654	471.7	59–2	26–11	13.0
ex Rappahannock 34, ex Pommern 17								

LUDWIG, DANIEL K, International Bldg, 630 Fifth Avenue, New York

Funnel: Black
Hull: Black, red boot-topping
Trades: Oil and petroleum

Tankers

AMERICAN PETROLEUM TRANSPORT CORP

Caliche (m)	1918	Penns	4767	7095	364.9	51–0	26–0	11.0
ex Chestnut Hill 28; conv steamer 28								

NATIONAL BULK CARRIERS INC

Bulkoil (st)	order	Weldng	8071	13,080	456–6	59–2	29–7	14.0
Invincible* (te)	1918	BethAl	7592	11,721	458–0	56–0	28–7	11.5
launched as War Rock								
Pan-Carolina (st)	1919	PuseyG	7762	12,980	456–0	60–2	29–10	12.0
ex Bulkoil 38, ex Daniel Webster 36; conv general cargo 37								
Pan-Delaware (st)	1918	BethAl	8128	13,266	472–1	56–1	31–1	12.0
ex Defiance 38, launched as War Ocean; conv general cargo and mv 38, conv steamer, lengthened 29								
Pan-Georgia (st)	1919	PuseyG	8197	12,980	456–6	60–2	29–10	12.0
ex Andrew Jackson 38, launched as War March; conv general cargo 38								
Pan-Massachusetts (st)	1919	BethAl	8202	10,670	472–0	56–0	28–7	11.5
ex Triumph 38, launched as War Cape; conv general cargo and mv 38, conv steamer, lengthened 29								
Pan-Pennsylvania (m2)	bldg	Alabam	7294	13,000	432–10	56–2	28–8	14.0
Pan-Virginia (st)	1919	PuseyG	8143	12,980	456–5	60–0	29–10	12.0
ex John Adams 38; conv general cargo 38								
Virginia (st)	order	Weldng	10,731	18,900	501.2	70–0	31–0	14.0
William C McTarnahan (m2)	order	Alabam	7306	13,000	432–10	56–2	28–8	14.0

PHOENIX STEAMSHIP CORP

Phoenix	1918	Chester	5731	9310	400.8	54–4	26–6	11.0

TANKERS OCEANIC CORP, Delaware Trust Bldg, Wilmington DE

Chiloil	1920	BethWi	5228	7950	391.6	51–2	25–1	11.0
ex Kehuku 26								

Note: * Intended 1938–39 conversion to tanker
Note: Also smaller vessels

LYKES BROS STEAMSHIP CO INC,
925 Whitney Central Bank Bldg, New Orleans

Funnel: Black with broad white beand bearing white L in blue diamond *Hull:* Black with LYKES LINES in white, red boot-topping
Services: US Gulf ports–Mexico–Puerto Rico–West Indies–Canal Zone; US Gulf ports–UK–NW Europe; US Gulf ports–Mediterranean

Adabelle Lykes (st,P8/1)	order	PuseyW	6750	7815	417–9	60–2	27–4	14.0
Almeria Lykes	1920	GLakeE	2637	4278	261–10	43–10	19–9	9.5
ex Lake Slavi 22								
Almeria Lykes (st,P12/1)	bldg	Fed2	7821	12,830	492–0	69–7	29–2	16.0
American Press (st)	1920	AISB	5131	7880	400–4	54–2	24–9	12.0
laid down as Comiskey								
Aquarius	1920	Standf	6094	9599	412–0	53–2	26–7	11.0
Cardonia (st)	1920	AISB	5104	8000	400–4	54–2	24–5	12.0
Chester Valley (st)	1919	AISB	5078	8030	400–4	54–2	24–5	12.0
laid down as Cleghorn								
City of Joliet	1920	Fullr2	6167	9841	411–9	55–1	27–3	11.5
City of Omaha	1920	Fullr2	6124	9841	411–9	55–1	27–3	11.5
Cranford	1920	Fullr2	6096	9841	411–9	55–1	27–3	11.5
Cripple Creek	1919	Skinnr	6320	9707	415–11	54–11	26–7	11.0

Dryden*	1919	SunSB	5836	10,405	450–0	57–8	26–1	11.0
Duquesne (st)	1919	Fed1	6262	9848	411–6	55–0	27–2	11.0
Edgehill** (st)	1919	Skinnr	6854	10,305	424–0	54–2	27–0	11.5
Effingham	1919	Skinnr	6421	9694	415–11	54–10	26–7	11.0
Eglantine	1919	Skinnr	6312	9703	415–11	54–10	26–7	11.0
Endicott	1919	Skinnr	6319	9704	415–11	54–11	26–7	11.0
Ethan Allen	1920	PuseyG	7777	12,648	455–0	60–2	28–5	11.5
Fred Morris (st,P8/1)								
	order	Fed2	6656	9290	417–9	60–0	27–6	14.0
Frederick Lykes (st,P12/1)								
	bldg	Fed2	7773	12,902	492–0	69–7	29–2	15.5
ordered as Sea Hound								
Genevieve Lykes	1919	Manito	2659	4050	261–10	43–11	24–2	9.5
ex Lake Gadsden 24								
Hanover††	1919	SunSB	7466	10,405	450–0	57–9	26–1	11.0
Howell Lykes (st,P12/1)								
	bldg	Fed2	7821	12,828	492–0	69–7	29–2	16.0
Hybert	1920	Fullr1	6120	9841	411–9	55–0	27–3	11.5
James Lykes (st,P8/1)								
	order	BethSP	6760	9271	417–9	60–0	27–7	14.0
James McKay (st.P8/1)								
	order	BethSP	6760	9271	417–9	60–0	27–7	14.0
John Lykes (st,P8/1)								
	order	Fed2	6829	9429	417–9	60–0	27–7	14.0
Joseph Lykes (st,P8/1)								
	bldg	Fed2	6829	9290	417–9	60–0	27–6	14.0
Liberator	1918	BethSF	7720	11,713	410.0	56–0	30–6	11.0
Lipscomb Lykes (st,P12/1)								
	order	BethSP	6760	9270	417–9	60–0	27–7	14.0
Margaret Lykes	1919	Mobile	3537	5130	335–5	46–2	23–1	11.0
ex Moshico 28								
Meanticut (st)	1921	PacC	6061	9373	416–0	53–0	27–6	12.0
Narbo (st)	1920	Moore2	6085	9402	416–0	53–0	27–6	12.0
Nashaba (st)	1921	PacC	6062	9349	416–0	53–0	27–6	12.0
Nemaha	1920	Fullr1	6501	9841	411–9	55–1	27–3	11.5
Nishmaha	1919	Standf	6076	9412	412–0	53–2	26–7	10.5
Oakman	1920	VirgAl	6081	9455	417–0	53–2	26–6	10.5
ex Clemence C Morse 26, ex Boshbish 20								
Oakwood	1920	VirgAl	6071	9455	417–0	53–2	26–6	10.5
ex Colin H Livingstone 24								
Patrick Henry	1920	PuseyG	7743	12,648	455–0	60–2	28–5	11.0
Reuben Tipton (st,P8/1)								
	order	Fed2	6829	9290	417–9	60–2	27–7	14.0
Ruth Lykes	1919	Chicgo	2612	4145	261–0	43–8	24–4	9.5
ex Southlands 27, ex Lake Gera 22								
Scottsburg	1919	NYSB1	7771	12,249	419.4	56–6	31–6	11.5
Solon Turman (st,P8/1)								
	order	BethSP	6763	9290	417–9	60–0	27–6	14.0
Stella Lykes	1919	McDoug	2609	4145	261–0	43–9	24–4	9.5
ex Lake Flagstaff 26								
Stella Lykes (st,P8/1)								
	order	Staten	6750	7815	417–9	60–0	27–6	14.0
Syros	1920	Fullr1	6191	9841	411–9	55–1	27–3	11.0
Thompson Lykes (st,P12/1)								
	order	BethSP	6763	9271	417–9	60–2	27–7	14.0
Tillie Lykes	1920	McDoug	2572	4145	261–0	43–9	24–4	9.5
ex Lake Florian 22								
Tripp (st)	1919	NWStl	5703	8546	423–10	54–2	24–0	11.5
Velma Lykes	1920	McDoug	2572	4145	261–0	43–9	24–4	9.5
ex Southseas 27, ex Lake Flournoy 22								
Volunteer (st)	1918	BethAl	7717	11,850	410.0	56–0	30–6	12.0
Waban	1919	Standf	6038	9428	412–0	53–2	26–7	11.0
West Chatala (st)	1919	NWStl	6187	8426	423–10	54–2	24–0	11.5
West Cobalt (st)	1918	Columb	6055	8624	423–10	54–2	24–1	11.5
West Cohas (st)	1918	Skinnr	5647	8554	424–0	54–2	24–0	11.5
West Ekonk (st)	1918	Skinnr	5630	8554	424–0	54–2	24–0	11.5
West Gambo (st)	1918	Skinnr	5579	8554	424–0	54–2	24–0	11.5
West Harshaw (st)	1919	Columb	5756	8624	423–10	54–2	24–1	11.5
West Hobomac (st)	1918	Skinnr	5755	8604	424–0	54–2	24–0	11.5
West Quechee (st)	1919	Columb	5711	8624	423–10	54–3	24–1	11.5
West Tacook (st)	1919	NWStl	6176	8593	423–10	54–2	24–0	11.5
Western Queen (st)	1918	Skinnr	5853	8614	424–0	54–2	24–0	11.5
Winston Salem	1920	Fullr2	6223	9841	411–9	55–1	27–3	11.0

Moore & McCormack: Mormacdove, *launched in 1939, was taken over by the US Navy in 1941 and renamed* Alchiba *(AK 23) for use as a cargo carrier. In 1943 she was reclassified as an attack cargo ship (AKA 6). In 1946 she was transferred to the USMC, and in 1948 passed to Netherlands owners and renamed* Tjipanas; *she was sold again in 1967, and six years later broken up at Whampoa (RW Jordan collection)*

Moore & McCormack: Scanstates *was one of the well-known 'Hog Islanders', the numerous series of standard ships built by American International Shipbuilding Corp at Hog Island, Pennsylvania, at the end of the First World War. In 1931, together with three sisterships, she was purchased by Moore & McCormack and refitted with passenger accommodation for operation on a new service from New York to Scandinavian and Baltic ports which commenced in 1932. In November 1939* Scanstates *was sold, with several other US vessels, to Brazil, and was delivered in 1940, being renamed* Cantuaria. *She survived the Second World War and was broken up in 1958 (Alex Duncan)*

North Negros Sugar: Nonsuco, *registered in Manila, was completed in June 1938 by Doxford at Sunderland and was fitted with two Doxford 4-cylinder oil engines with a total 3600bhp. She survived the Second World War, and following its independence was transferred to the Philippines flag in 1948. She was sold within the Philippines in 1962 and renamed* Sirius, *and was broken up in 1971 (RW Jordan collection)*

Zoella Lykes (st,P8/1)	bldg	Fed2	6829	9307	417–9	60–2	27–7	14.0

LYKES COASTWISE LINE INC, Cotton Exchange Bldg, Houston TX

Jolee (st)	1920	AISB	4994	8000	400–4	54–2	24–5	12.0
laid down as Cardington								
Labette (st)	1919	AISB	4989	8000	400–4	54–2	24–5	12.0
laid down as Shoccoree								
Liberty Bell (st)	1920	AISB	5107	8015	400–4	54–2	24–5	12.0
Quistconck (st)	1918	AISB	5144	7825	401–0	54–2	24–9	12.0
laid down as Red Jacket								

TAMPA INTEROCEAN STEAMSHIP CO, (Gulf West Mediterranean Line), 917 Whitney National Bank Bldg, New Orleans LA

Carlton (st)	1920	AISB	5127	7800	401–0	54–2	24–5	12.0
Cody† (st)	1920	AISB	5104	7800	401–0	54–2	24–5	12.0
laid down as Cassimir								
Jomar (st)	1920	AISB	5104	7800	401–0	54–2	24–5	12.0
laid down as Comerant								
Lafcomo (st)	1919	AISB	5028	7800	401–0	54–2	24–5	12.0
laid down as Shivwits								
Ogontz‡ (st)	1919	AISB	5028	7800	401–0	54–2	24–5	12.0
laid down as Scatacook								
Prusa (st)	1919	AISB	5113	7800	401–0	54–2	24–5	12.0
Sahale (st)	1919	AISB	5028	7800	401–0	54–2	24–5	12.0
Sapinero (st)	1919	AISB	5106	7800	401–0	54–2	24–5	12.0

Note: * Sold Waterman SS Corp 1939, renamed *Lafayette*; ** sold Calmar SS Corp (*qv* under Bethlehem Steel Corp) 1939, renamed *Oremar*; † sold A H Bull & Co Inc 1939, renamed *Mary*; ‡ sold N Bez 1939, converted for fisheries service †† sold Greece 1939, renamed *Adamastos*

MADRIGAL & CO, 8 Muelle de Banco Nacional, PO Box 254, Manila, Philippines

Funnel: Red, black top
Services: General tramping, mainly East and Pacific areas

Don José (s2)	1920	Teckl	10,893	13,300	544–6	65–8	30–1	11.5
ex Chief Capilano 37, ex Robert Moller 31, ex Kurland 19								
Sagoland	1913	Earles	5334	9930	430.2	54–2	25–3	9.5
Susana	1914	CRDA1	5929	9303	401.4	51–10	27–2	10.0
ex Stanley Dollar 36, ex Warszawa 23, ex Erny 19								
Under Honduras flag								
Paz	1914	Sundld	4260	7260	375–3	50–9	23–6	8.0
ex Iron Monarch 37, ex Koolonga 17								

Note: Also smaller vessels on local services

MALLORY & CO INC, C D, Bowling Green Bldg, 11 Broadway, New York

Funnel: Black with houseflag
Services: E coast US ports to Pacific, US Gulf ports and West Indies; oil and petroleum trades

General cargo vessels

C D MALLORY CORP

Malamton	1918	NYSB1	4553	8597	362.3	51–3	32.2	10.0
ex Missoula 35, ex M J Scanlon 25								
Malang	1920	Fuji	3734	6500	344.8	50–1	24–0	10.0
ex Eastern Leader 29								
Malantic	1929	Nthmb2	3837	6600	370.3	51–10	22–10	9.5
ex Themoni 37, ex Burnhope 33								
Malchace (st)	1920	Merril	3516	5800	333.8	48–0	23–0	10.0
ex Chickamauga								
Mallard	1917	BethU2	3804	6000	354–6	48–3	22–7	10.0
ex American Cardinal 36, ex Dicto 33								
Mallemak (st)	1919	Merril	3516	5800	333.8	48–0	23–0	10.0
ex Wekika 29								
Malton	1923	Napr&M	2972	5620	332.6	48–4	20–8	9.5
ex Baron Glenconner 33								
Maltran (st)	1920	Merril	3513	5800	333.8	48–0	23–0	10.0
ex Carolinas 27, ex Pinellas 22								

Tankers

ARDMORE STEAMSHIP CO INC, Dover DE

Ardmore	1913	Neptn1	7035	10,900	449.6	59–8	26–0	9.5
ex Delphin 14								
Matinicock	1914	HwldtK	6769	11,200	459.1	60–0	25–0	9.5
ex Leda 15								
Muskogee	1913	Schich	7034	10,250	451.0	58–0	31.3	9.5
ex Triton 14								

C D MALLORY CORP

Malacca	1919	Baltmr	7051	10,250	450–0	59–2	26–7	10.0
ex Bethelridge 25								

MALSTON CO INC, Dover DE

Dillwyn	1919	BethAl	6913	10,700	453–9	56–0	27–1	11.0
Durango	1920	BethAl	6986	10,700	453–9	56–0	27–1	11.0
Halsey	1920	BethAl	7088	10,700	453–9	56–0	27–1	11.0

Hoxbar	1919	BethSP	6958	11,370	454–0	56–3	27–7	11.0
Hugoton	1919	BethSP	6943	11,370	454–0	56–3	27–7	11.0
Imlay	1919	Moore2	6779	10,600	437–11	57–0	27–0	11.0
Mevania	1920	Moore2	6886	10,600	437–11	57–0	27–0	11.0
SEMINOLE STEAMSHIP CORP, Dover DE								
Malabar	1914	NNews	8465	11,980	474–6	60–0	26–1	9.5
ex John D Rockefeller 24								
Malay	1921	NWBrdg	8207	12,020	482–1	60–2	26–8	10.5
ex Swiftwind 33								
SWIFTARROW STEAMSHIP CO, 1 Exchange Place, Jersey City NJ								
Swiftarrow	1921	NWBrdg	8207	12,020	482–1	60–3	26–8	10.5
SWIFTLIGHT STEAMSHIP CO, 1 Exchange Place, Jersey City NJ								
Swiftlight	1921	NWBrdg	8207	12,020	482–1	60–3	26–9	10.5
SWIFTSCOUT STEAMSHIP CO, 1 Exchange Place, Jersey City NJ								
Swiftscout	1921	NWBrdg	8207	12,020	482–1	60–3	26–8	10.5
SWIFTSURE STEAMSHIP CO, 1 Exchange Place, Jersey City NJ								
Swiftsure	1921	NWBrdg	8207	12,020	482–1	60–3	26–10	10.5

MATSON NAVIGATION CO, Matson Bldg, 215 Market St, San Francisco CA

Funnel: Yellow with blue M, blue top
Hull: Black or dark brown, red boot-topping with white dividing line
Services: San Francisco–Hawaii; San Francisco–Portland–Seattle–British Columbia ports–Hawaii; W coast US–Vancouver; Hawaii inter-island

Passenger vessels								
Lurline (st2,P700)	1932	BethQu	18,009	11,176	631–6	79–4	28–4	22–0
Matsonia (st2,P600)	1927	Cramp	17,226	7650	582–0	83–2	29–0	22.0
ex Malolo 37								
Yale (st3,P465/1)	1906	Delwre	3818	1000	407–0	61–4	19–0	20.0
Out of commission								
General cargo vessels								
Coquina	1919	Manito	2140	3200	261–0	43–9	20–4	9.5
Corrales	1918	Manito	2146	3330	261–0	43–8	20–4	9.5
Diamond Head	1919	LosAng	5603	8300	423–2	54–0	24–0	12.0
ex West Erral 28								
Ewa (st)	1919	Skinnr	7001	10,300	424–0	54–2	24–0	12.0
ex Tacoma 37, ex Eldridge 28								
Hamakua	1919	Skinnr	6406	9695	415–11	54–10	26–7	11.5
ex Olympia 37, ex City of Spokane 28								
Honomu	1919	Skinnr	6999	10,243	424–0	54–2	24–0	12.0
ex Grays Harbor 37, ex Edmore 28								
Kahuku (st)	1920	PacC	6062	10,215	416–6	53–0	27–6	11.5
ex Shelton 37, ex Cuprum 28								
Kailua	1919	LosAng	5356	8366	423–2	54–5	24–0	12.0
ex Golden Bear 37, ex West Cajoot 27								
Kaimoku	1919	Skinnr	6367	9747	415–6	54–11	26–7	11.5
ex Golden Horn 38, ex Crisfield 27								
Kainalu	1920	Moore2	6047	9060	416–6	52–7	27–6	11.5
ex General M H Sherman 38, ex Mursa 28								
Kalani (st)	1918	Skinnr	5506	8257	424–0	54–2	24–0	12.0
ex Helen Whittier 38, ex West Lianga 29								
Kohala	1919	Duthie	5833	8541	423–0	54–2	24–4	11.5
ex Golden Cross 38, ex West Henshaw 27								
Lahaina	1920	WPipe	5645	8614	427–0	54–2	27.2	11.5
ex Golden State 37, ex West Carmona 27								
Lihue	1919	Skinnr	7001	10,243	424–0	54–2	24–0	12.0
ex Seattle 37, ex Wheatland Montana 28								
Liloa (st)	1918	Skinnr	5523	8198	424–0	54–2	24–0	12.0
ex Constance Chandler 38, ex West Hosokie 27								
Mahimahi	1921	LosAng	7350	10,970	430.7	54–4	28–11	11.0
ex Golden Dragon 38, ex West Chopaka 27								
Mahukona	1919	GLakeE	2512	4200	261–10	43–8	23–6	9.5
ex Coverun 22								
Makawao (st)	1921	SubmBC	3253	5350	335–6	46–2	22–2	9.5
ex Sujerseyco 28, ordered as Dearing								
Makena	1919	GLakeA	2729	4200	261–10	43–6	23–6	9.5
ex Cowboy 22								
Makiki	1917	Texas	5924	8198	402.0	54–2	27–0	10.0
ex Woonsocket 23, ex Rhode Island 18								
Makua (st)	1920	SubmBC	3275	5350	335–6	46–2	22–2	9.5
ex Suholco 28, laid down as Tustem, ordered as Onata								
Malama (st)	1919	SubmBC	3275	5350	335–6	46–2	22–2	9.5
ex Milwaukee Bridge 27, laid down as Ontonagon								
Maliko	1918	BethSP	6847	10,325	415.0	53–8	29–7	12.5
ex Cape May 25, laid down as War Saturn								

Mana (st)	1920	SubmBC	3283	5350	335–6	46–2	22–2	9.5
ex Moravia Bridge 26, ordered as Missanco								
Manini (st)	1920	SubmBC	3253	5350	335–6	46–2	22–2	9.5
ex Susherico 28, ordered as Nugunket								
Manoa	1913	NNews	6806	8500	446–2	54–0	26–6	13.5
Manukai (st,P6)	1921	Moore2	9547	14,440	498–0	62–2	31–6	13.5
Manulani (st,P6)	1921	Moore2	9556	14,440	498–0	62–2	31–6	13.5
Mapele (st)	1920	SubmBC	3297	5350	335–6	46–2	22–2	9.5
ex Mala 36, ex Pittsburgh Bridge 27, laid down as Archbold Bridge, ordered as Tashmoo								
Maui* (st2,P12)	1917	BethU2	9940	9950	501–0	58–0	30–6	16.0
Mauna Ala	1918	Texas	6256	9947	420.5	54–2	26–7	11.0
ex Canibas 23								
Mauna Kea	1919	PacC	6064	9042	416–6	53–0	27–6	11.5
ex Golden River 34, ex Diablo 30								
Mauna Loa	1919	LosAng	5436	8102	423–2	54–5	24–0	12.0
ex Golden Eagle 34, ex West Conob 27								
Maunalei (st)	1921	MerchC	7159	10,517	457–0	57–2	28–9	12.5
ex Mount Clinton 25; conv passenger/general cargo 23								
Maunawili (st)	1921	MerchC	7409	10,517	457–0	57–2	28–9	12.5
ex Mount Carroll 25; conv passenger/general cargo 23								
Mokihana	1921	LosAng	7460	10,970	430.7	54–4	28–11	11.0
ex Golden Sun 38, ex West Prospect 27								
Olopana	1920	Standf	6069	9400	412–0	53–2	26–7	11.0
ex Golden Mountain 38, ex Bearport 27								
Onomea	1917	Skinnr	5520	8480	424–0	54–1	24–0	11.0
ex Marian Otis Chandler 38, ex West Haven 29, launched as War Flame								
Waimea	1920	BethSW	5670	8550	427–0	54–4	25–3	10.5
ex Golden Cloud 38, ex West Sequana 27								
Waipio (st)	1919	Skinnr	5548	8500	424–0	54–2	24–0	11.0
ex Golden Kauri 39, ex West Elcajon 27								
Wilhelmina	1909	NNews	6725	7000	451–0	54–1	26–2	14.0
Out of commission								
Molasses tanker								
Makaweli	1919	GLakeA	2630	4200	261–10	43–6	23–6	9.5
ex Cowee 22								

Note: * Chartered Panama Pacific Line for Intercoastal cargo service
Note: Matson Navigation Co also controlled Inter-Island Navigation Co Ltd, Honolulu, which owned vessels operating in the Hawaiian islands area

OCEANIC STEAMSHIP CO

Passenger vessels

Mariposa (st2,P475/1,229/cab)	1931	BethQu	18,017	11,295	638–0	79–4	28–4	21.0
Monterey (st2,P471/1,229/cab)	1932	BethQu	18,017	11,295	638–0	79–4	28–4	21.0

MISSISSIPPI SHIPPING CO INC, (Delta Line),

PO Box 316, Board of Trade Bldg, New Orleans LA

Funnel: Yellow with yellow Greek 'delta' on green disc, separated from black top by green over yellow over green bands
Hull: Black or grey, red boot-topping
Services: New Orleans/Port Arthur/Mobile/Gulfport/Pensacola/Tampa–Pernambuco–Rio de Janeiro–Santos–Montevideo–Buenos Aires

Clearwater (st)	1920	AISB	4970	7825	401–0	54–2	24–9	12.0
Delalba (st)	1919	AISB	5101	7825	400–4	54–2	24–9	12.0
ex Saugerties 35								
Delargentino (st,P67/1)	bldg	BethSP	7922	8602	491–0	65–8	25–8	16.5
Delbrasil (st,P67/1)	bldg	BethSP	7922	8602	491–0	65–8	25–9	16.5
Delmar (st)	1920	AISB	5107	7825	400–4	54–2	24–9	12.0
ex Bibbco 35, laid down as Manatawny								
Delmundo (st,P38/1)	1919	AISB	5032	7104	400–4	54–2	24–9	13.0
ex Casey 32, laid down as Clarcona								
Delnorte (st,P28/1)	1919	AISB	4982	7104	400–4	54–2	24–9	13.0
ex Schoodic 32								
Delorleans (st,P67/1)	bldg	BethSP	7922	8602	491–0	65–8	25–8	16.5
Delplata (st)	1920	AISB	5127	7825	400–4	54–2	24–9	12.0
ex Lorraine Cross 36								
Delrio (st,P–)	1919	AISB	5052	7825	400–4	54–2	24–9	12.0
ex Afel 36								
Delsud (st,P28/1)	1919	AISB	4982	7104	400–4	54–2	24–9	13.0
ex Salvastion Lass 31, laid down as Shawan								
Delvalle (st,P38/1)	1919	AISB	5032	7104	401–0	54–2	24–9	13.0
ex Clavarack 32								

MOORE & McCORMACK CO INC, 5 Broadway, New York

Funnel: Yellow with black top separated by green band bearing red M on white disc
Hull: Black or grey
Services: US–NW Europe, Baltic ports ('Scans' – New York–Copenhagen–Stockholm–Gdynia–Helsinki–Leningrad); US coastal

MOORE-MCCORMACK LINES INC (American Scantic Line)

Mormacdale (m,P8/1)	order	Penns	6750	8015	417–9	60–2	27–4	14.0
Mormacmail (m,P12/1)	bldg	SunSBD	7886	11,735	492–0	69–2	27–3	16.0
Mormacpenn (st,P12/1)	bldg	SunSBD	7898	11,735	492–0	69–2	27–3	16.0
laid down as Sea Swallow								
Mormacport (st,P12)	1919	AISB	4942	7650	401–0	54–2	24–5	13.0
ex City of Fairbury 38, laid down as Sheshequin								
Mormacsea (st,P16/3)	1919	AISB	4955	7650	401–0	54–2	24–5	13.0
ex Cliffwood 38								
Mormacstar (st,P12)	1919	AISB	4941	7650	401–0	54–2	24–5	13.0
ex Minnequa 38, laid down as Shinnecock								
Mormacsun (st)	1920	AISB	4996	7650	401–0	54–2	24–5	12.0
ex Argosy 38, laid down as Casanova								
Mormacsun (st,P12/1)	order	Moore3	7898	12,609	492–0	69–2	29–2	16.0
Mormactide (st,P12)	1919	AISB	4951	7650	401–0	54–2	24–5	13.0
ex Sagaporack 38								
Mormactide (st,P12/1)	order	Ingall	7898	12,609	492–0	69–7	29–5	16.0
Mormacyork (I) (m,P12/1)	order	Fed2	7796	12,296	492–0	69–7	29–1	16.0
Mormacyork (II) (st,P12/1)	order	Fed2	7898	12,600	492–0	69–7	29–1	16.0
Scanmail (st,P74/1)	1919	AISB	5152	7140	401–0	54–2	24–5	13.0
ex Chickasaw 32								
Scanpenn (st,P74/1)	1919	AISB	5152	7140	401–0	54–2	24–5	13.0
ex Bird City 32, laid down as Shepaug								
Scanstates (st,P74/1)	1919	AISB	5163	7140	401–0	54–2	24–5	13.0
ex Saguache 32								
Scanyork (st,P74/1)	1919	AISB	5163	7140	401–0	54–2	24–5	13.0
ex Schenectady 32								
Southerner (st,P12)	1919	AISB	5083	8168	401–0	54–2	24–5	13.0
ex Exton 36, ex Sangamon 28								
Southfolk (st,P12)	1919	AISB	4925	7825	401–0	54–2	26–6	13.0
ex Scantic 36								
Southland (st,P12)	1919	AISB	5052	8000	401–0	54–2	24–5	13.0
ex Excellency 36, ex Liberty Land 28, laid down as Sebewa								
Southlure (st,P12)	1920	AISB	4986	7650	401–0	54–2	24–5	13.0
ex Carplaka 36								

Note: Moore & McCormack Co Inc also controlled Mooremack Gulf Lines Inc which owned coastal vessels, and was associated with Mooremack South American Line Inc (*qv* below)

MOOREMACK SOUTH AMERICAN LINE INC, 5 Broadway, New York

Funnel: Black with blue diamond on yellow band
Hull: Black
Services: ARL – New York, Baltimore–Barbados–Rio de Janeiro–Pernambuco–Montevideo–Santos–Buenos Aires

Operator of
AMERICAN REPUBLICS LINE
Passenger/general cargo vessels

Argentina (te2,P380/1,350/t)	1929	NNews	20,614	17,810	613–1	80–4	34–4	18.0
ex Pennsylvania 38								
Brazil (te2,P380/1,350/t)	1928	NNews	20,614	17,810	613–1	80–4	34–4	18.0
ex Virginia 38								
Pan America* (st2,P260/1,170/3)	1922	BethSP	13,712	11,600	535–2	72–2	30–6	17.0
launched as Palmetto State								
Rio de Janeiro (m,P216)	order	SunSBD	12,500		492–0	69–9	24–2	17.5
Rio de La Plata (m,P216)	order	SunSBD	12,500		492–0	69–9	24–2	17.5
Rio Hudson (m,P216)	bldg	SunSBD	12,500		492–0	69–9	24–2	17.5

Name	Built	Builder	GRT	DWT	Length	Beam	Draught	Speed
Rio Parana (m,P216)	bldg	SunSBD	12,500		492–0	69–9	24–2	17.5
Uruguay (te2,P380/1,350/t)	1928	NNews	20,183	17,250	601–1	80–4	34–4	18.0
ex California 38								
Western World** (st2,P260/1,170/3)	1922	BethSP	13,712	11,600	535–2	72–2	30–6	17.0
launched as Nutmeg State								
General cargo vessels								
Donald McKay (m,P12/1)	1939	SunSBD	6400	9758	459–0	63–0	25–9	15.5
Mormacdove (m,P12/1)	1939	SunSBD	6343	9758	459–1	63–2	27–9	15.5
Mormacgull (m,P12/1)	1939	SunSBD	6531	9758	459–0	63–2	27–9	15.5
Mormachawk (m,P12/1)	1939	SunSBD	6523	9758	459–0	63–2	27–8	15.5
Mormacland (m,P12/1)	bldg	SunSBD	7900	9902	492–0	69–2	27–3	16.0
ordered as Archer								
Mormaclark (m,P12/1)	1939	SunSBD	6525	9758	459–0	63–2	27–9	15.5
Mormacmar	1920	LosAng	5453	8366	423–0	54–2	24–0	12.0
ex Culberson 38								
Mormacrey	1919	LosAng	5946	8368	423–0	54–5	24–0	12.0
ex West Calumb 38								
Mormacrio	1919	LosAng	5940	8366	423–0	54–5	24–0	12.0
ex West Selene 38								
Mormacstar (m,P70)	bldg	Moore3	7773	12,327	492–1	69–7	29–1	16.0
ordered as Sea Star								
Mormacsul	1920	LosAng	5481	8366	423–0	54–5	24–0	12.0
ex The Angeles 38								
Mormacwren (m,P12/1)	1939	SunSBD	6281	9758	459–0	63–2	27–9	15.5

Note: *, ** Transferred US War Department 1939, renamed *Hunter Liggett* and *Leonard Wood*, respectively
Note: American Republics Line and vessels operating on it were owned by United States Maritime Commission (*qv*), and Mooremack South American Line Inc was associated with Moore & McCormack Co Inc (*qv* above)
Note: See also footnote at United States Maritime Commission entry

MYSTIC STEAMSHIP CO, 250 Stuart St, Boston MA

Funnel: Black with red M on broad white band
Hull: Black, red boot-topping
Services: Occasional general tramping, but mainly US coastal (E coast)

Name	Built	Builder	GRT	DWT	Length	Beam	Draught	Speed
A L Kent	1920	Bath	6030	9500	394.1	55–1	27–0	10.5
Felix Taussig	1917	NNews	5965	9500	410–3	55–1	27–1	10.0
Glen White	1918	NYSB1	5438	8686	368.6	55–2	27–0	10.0
James L Richards	1916	NNews	4282	7250	375–0	49–2	23–9	10.5
ex Munalbro 36								
Kopperston	1919	Standd	5191	7388	395–9	52–0	23–8	10.5
ex Bannack 37								
Sewall's Point	1918	NYSB1	5432	8743	368.6	55–2	27–0	10.0
William A McKenney	1916	NNews	6153	9500	410–3	55–1	27–1	10.0
William N Page	1918	NYSB1	5438	8684	368.6	55–2	27–0	10.0
Winding Gulf	1918	NYSB1	5438	8686	368.6	55–2	27–5	10.0

Note: Also vessels engaged in E coast US voyages

NORTH NEGROS SUGAR CO INC, 3rd floor, Chaco Bldg, Manila, Philippines

Funnel: Yellow with white circle
Hull: Black with white band, red boot-topping
Services: General tramping

Name	Built	Builder	GRT	DWT	Length	Beam	Draught	Speed
Nonsuco (m)	1938	Doxfrd	5212	9217	439–0	56–1	25–6	12.5

OLYMPIC STEAMSHIP CO LTD, 311 California St, San Francisco CA

Funnel: Black with Olympic emblem on broad blue band between two narrow white bands
Trades: Oil and petroleum

Name	Built	Builder	GRT	DWT	Length	Beam	Draught	Speed
Tanker								
Olympic	1907	Rhead2	5335	8340	370.0	50–1	27–2	9.0
ex Dayton 25, ex Harport 14								

PACIFIC ATLANTIC STEAMSHIP CO, 810 Porter Bldg, Portland OR

Funnel: Black with swastika type emblem on broad red band
Hull: States – black, red boot-topping
Services: PA and CEL – US E coast–US W coast; States – Seattle, Tacoma, Astoria, Portland–Dairen–Shanghai–Yokohama–Nagasaki–Osaka–Philippines

Name	Built	Builder	GRT	DWT	Length	Beam	Draught	Speed
Jefferson Myers	1920	BethSF	7582	11,724	457–6	56–0	28–8	10.5
ex Hannawa 28								
Peter Kerr	1920	OsakaO	6476	10,616	415.0	55–9	27–7	11.0
ex Eastern Sailor 22								
San Angelo	1918	Ames	5605	8541	423–2	54–2	25–9	11.0
ex Willanglo 29, ex Westmead 27, launched as War Dido								
San Anselmo	1920	Ames	5758	8855	423–2	54–2	25–9	11.0
ex Oran 29, ex West Jester 26								

Pacific Atlantic: Built at San Pedro in 1919, San Clemente *was transferred in 1943 to the Soviet Union and renamed* Tobol *(pictured here). She was involved in trans-Pacific voyages in the early postwar period, and was based at Petropavlovsk. She was later laid up and her fate uncertain (Canadian Forces, Ottawa)*

Pennsylvania Shipping: Antietam *was completed in 1919 and one of a large series of similar tankers. On January 30 1946, when on voyage from New York to Blaye, France, the vessel was about to take on a pilot in the Gironde River when she was struck by a mine on the starboard side by way of the engine room. The stern had settled on the bottom within a few minutes. One crewman was lost in the blast and four were injured. The survivors were rescued by a French pilot boat (Alex Duncan)*

San Bernardino	1920	Ames	5751	8826	423–2	54–2	25–9	11.0
ex Oriole 29, ex West Jappa 26								
San Clemente	1919	LosAng	5493	8366	423–2	54–5	24–0	12.0
ex West Mingo 29								
San Felipe	1919	Ames	5913	8645	423–2	54–2	25–9	11.0
ex Willwelo 29, ex Western Glen 27, launched as War Juno								
San Gabriel	1920	Downey	4943	7814	386.8	52–2	24–0	11.0
ex Georgian 29, ex Clarksburg 22								
San Lucas	1919	OsakaO	6517	10,500	415.1	55–8	27–9	11.0
ex Eastern Knight 29								
San Marcos	1919	Ames	5758	8764	423–2	54–2	25–9	11.0
ex Myrtle 29, ex West Jena 26								
San Rafael	1919	LosAng	5402	8366	423–2	54–5	24–0	12.0
ex West Montop 30								
San Simeon	1919	LBeach	5561	8556	427–0	54–4	24–2	11.0
ex West Katan 30								
San Vincente	1920	LBeach	5597	8556	427–0	54–4	24–2	11.0
ex West Keats 29								
CALIFORNIA EASTERN LINE INC								
Maine	1920	BethSW	5435	8564	427–0	54–4	24–6	11.0
ex Pacific Pine 37, ex West Norranus 26								
Vermont	1919	Duthie	5670	8527	423–8	54–2	24–1	10.5
ex Pacific Hemlock 37, ex West Helix 28								
STATES STEAMSHIP CO								
California	1920	LosAng	5441	8366	423–0	54–5	24–0	12.0
ex West Hixton 28								
Illinois	1920	LosAng	5447	8394	423–0	54–0	24–0	12.0
ex Las Vegas 28								
Kentucky	1921	LosAng	5446	8600	423–0	54–2	24–0	12.0
ex West O'Rowa 28								
Michigan (st)	1919	Columb	5594	8625	423–10	54–2	24–1	12.5
ex West Hartland 28								
Texas (st)	1919	Columb	5638	8625	423–10	54–2	24–1	12.5
ex West Harts 29								
Washington	1919	BethSW	5564	8542	427–0	54–4	24–6	11.0
ex West Cayote 28								

Note: See also footnote at United States Maritime Commission entry

PACIFIC NORTHWEST ORIENTAL LINE

Services: New York, Baltimore, Hampton Roads–Rio de Janeiro–Buenos Aires; Baltimore, New York, Boston–UK, NW Europe
Note: Puget Sound Orient Line and the above vessels were owned by United States Maritime Commission (*qv*)

Operator of
PUGET SOUND ORIENT LINE

Capillo (st)	1920	AISB	5135	8000	401–0	54–2	24–5	11.5
Coldbrook (st)	1919	AISB	5104	8015	401–0	54–2	24–5	11.5
Collingsworth (st)	1920	AISB	5101	8015	401–0	54–2	24–5	11.5
Satartia (st)	1919	AISB	4994	8000	401–0	54–2	24–5	11.5

PACIFIC STEAMSHIP LINES LTD INC, (The Admiral Line),

112 Market St, San Francisco, CA, Stuart Bldg, Seattle WA, and 21 West St, New York

Funnel: Yellow with Admiral Line emblem, black top
Hull: Black, red boot-topping
Services: Most of the vessels listed below were laid up at San Francisco in 1939, but some did voyage San Francisco and other W coast US port–Honolulu–Guam–Manila

Passenger/general cargo vessels								
Emma Alexander (s2,P253)								
	1913	NYSB1	7793	3200	442–0	54–11	25–9	16.0
ex Nanking 23, ex Congress 18								
H F Alexander (st3,P648/1)								
	1914	Cramp	8357	3800	524–0	63–1	21–9	22.0
ex USS Columbia 22, ex Great Northern 21								
General cargo vessels								
Admiral Chase* (st)								
	1920	SubmBC	3285	5350	335–6	46–2	22–2	9.5
ex Sutransco 29, laid down as Glenora, ordered as Tomahegan								
Admiral Wiley* (st)								
	1920	SubmBC	3514	5350	335–6	46–2	22–2	9.5
ex Surichco 30, laid down as Jelcaw, ordered as Nehumkee								
PACIFIC LIGHTERAGE CORP								
Admiral Halstead (st)								
	1921	SubmBC	3289	5350	335–6	46–2	22–2	9.5
ex Suwordenco 30, laid down as Quinney								
PORTLAND CALIFORNIA STEAMSHIP CO								
Admiral Cole (st)	1920	SubmBC	3285	5350	335–6	46–2	22–2	9.5
ex Surailco 31, laid down as Beargrove								

Admiral Day (st) 1920 SubmBC 3285 5350 335–6 46–2 22–2 9.5
ex Sutermco 32, laid down as Natirar, ordered as Pemetic
Admiral Gove (st) 1920 SubmBC 3513 5350 335–6 46–2 22–2 9.5
ex Surico 32, laid down as Oronoke
Admiral Laws (st) 1921 SubmBC 3268 5350 335–6 46–2 22–2 9.5
ex Sunugentco 31, laid down as Kaboka
Admiral Nulton (st)
1920 SubmBC 3267 5350 335–6 46–2 22–2 9.5
ex Suscolanco 30, laid down as Neskett
Admiral Senn (st) 1920 SubmBC 3260 5350 335–6 46–2 22–2 9.5
ex Sulanierco 32, laid down as Nebelow
Admiral Wood (st) 1920 SubmBC 3285 5350 335–6 46–2 22–2 9.5
ex Sugillenco 32, laid down as Tamara, ordered as Desha
Admiral Y S Williams* (st)
1920 SubmBC 3252 5350 335–6 46–2 22–2 9.5
ex Sunewco 34, laid down as Piston

Note: * Sold American Trading & Shipping Co Sept 1939

PANAMA RAIL ROAD CO INC, 24 State St, New York

Funnel: Yellow, two silver bands
Hull: Grey
Services: New York–Panama Canal

Operated by
PANAMA RAIL ROAD STEAMSHIP LINE
Passenger/general cargo vessels
Ancon (s2,P130/1,52/st)
1902 BethMS 9640 11,980 505–0 58–0 29–6 12.5
ex Shawmut 09
Ancon (st2,P202) 1939 BethQu 10,241 6800 493–7 64–3 26–3 16.0
Cristobal (s2,P130/1,52/st)
1902 BethMS 9604 12,380 505–0 58–0 29–6 12.5
ex Tremont 09
Cristobal (st2,P202) 1939 BethQu 10,241 6800 493–6 64–1 26–3 16.0
Panama (st2,P202) 1939 BethQu 10,241 6800 493–7 64–3 26–3 16.0
General cargo vessels
Buenaventura 1919 McDoug 2609 4145 261–0 43–9 24–4 9.5
ex Lake Flattery 23
Guayaquil 1919 AmSBLo 2592 4155 261–0 43–8 24–4 9.5
ex Lake Fanquier 25

PENINSULAR & OCCIDENTAL STEAMSHIP CO,
Postbox 846, Jacksonville FL

Funnel: Black with houseflag
Hull: Black, red boot-topping
Services: Passenger – Tampa–Key West–Havana

Passenger vessel
Florida (st2,P612/1,130/2)
1931 NNews 4945 2350 387–8 56–5 20–2 19.5

Note: Also *Cuba* (built 1921/2472gt)

PENNSYLVANIA SHIPPING CO, 260 South Broad St, Philadelphia PA

Hull: Grey
Trades: Oil and petroleum

Tankers
CHAS KURZ & CO INC, 119 South 4th St, Philadelphia PA
Beta (st) 1917 Chestr 5665 9300 400.8 54–4 26–6 11.0
ex Hisko 25
Camden 1921 NYSB1 6653 10,500 436–4 56–6 25–10 10.0
Elwood 1918 SunSB 7098 11,367 445–4 59–3 26–8 10.0
ex D J Moran 36, ex Chester Sun 29
Naeco 1918 BethWi 5373 8649 428–0 53–5 25–7 10.0
ex Charles M Everest 33
Olney 1920 Moore2 7294 10,683 438–5 57–0 27–1 10.0
ex Walter Miller 35, ex Stockton 28
PACO TANKERS INC
Antietam 1919 BethSP 6972 10,871 453–0 56–3 27–1 10.0
Baldbutte 1919 BethQu 6295 9853 416.9 56–2 26–6 10.0
Baldhill 1919 BethQu 6413 9853 416.8 56–1 26–6 10.0
Chas Kurz (st) 1918 Chestr 5731 9310 400.8 54–4 26–6 11.0
ex Tracy Brothers 33, ex Avondale 25
Chilbar 1919 BethWi 5030 7920 391.8 51–4 25–1 10.0
ex Cabrille 27
Dannedaike (st) 1919 Baltmr 4310 6340 340.1 49–3 24–1 9.5
Dilworth 1919 BethAl 7045 10,671 453–9 56–1 27–3 10.0
Hagan 1919 BethQu 6401 9853 416.9 56–3 26–6 10.0
Meton 1920 Moore2 7027 10,674 438–5 57–0 27–1 10.0

Roosevelt: American Banker *had been laid down as the 'Hog Islander'* Shohola, *was building as* Mount Michael, *and was launched as the transport* Cantigny *on October 27 1919. She was renamed* American Banker *in 1924, when assigned to American Merchant Lines as a cargo ship. She was then refitted to carry passengers and as such made her first voyage from New York to London in May–June 1926.* American Banker *was sold to United States Lines in 1931, and when the Neutrality Act came into force she was transferred to the newly-formed Société Maritime Anversoise, of Antwerp, in 1940, and renamed* Ville d'Anvers. *She was sold in 1946 becoming* City of Athens, *in 1947 and renamed* Protea, *and to Arosa Line in 1951 and renamed* Arosa Kulm. *She was rebuilt at Bremerhaven for emigrant service. Her owners were bankrupt by the end of 1958, and* Arosa Kulm *was broken up at Bruges in 1959*

Roosevelt: Pictured here as African Comet, *the United States Lines vessel* American Banker *was ordered on October 9 1939. Her keel was laid on July 1 1940, and it was intended she be completed for the North Atlantic service with accommodation for 12 passengers. Restrictions which banned US vessels voyaging in war zones, brought about the sale of the contract to American South African Line in September 1940 and the vessel was launched as* African Comet *on June 28 1941. She was converted for the New York–South Africa service and was to have accommodation for 116 passengers and to carry a crew of 122. She was delivered on December 3 1941, but was already earmarked for use by the US Navy. As the transport* Arthur Middleton *she could carry 1400 troops and carry 27 landing craft. In January 1943 she suffered grounding damage in the Aleutians, but this was soon repaired. During her service in the Pacific she was at the landings at Saipan, Lingayen Gulf and Leyte, among others. She was in reserve in 1946, transferred to the Marad Reserve, James River, in 1959, and was broken up at Brownsville in 1973 (Ingalls Shipbuilding)*

Paco	1920	Terry	5187	7895	391.9	51–2	25–1	10.0
ex E J Nicklos 37, ex Dartford 29								
Thermo	1920	Fed1	4487	6688	355.0	52–8	23–0	9.5
ex Freeport Sulphur No 6 29								

PETROLEUM NAVIGATION CO, Petroleum Bldg, Postbox 1321, Houston TX

Tankers

Papoose	1921	BethSW	5939	8960	412.0	53–4	25–8	10.0
ex Silvanus 27								
Pueblo (st)	1920	Baltmr	4469	6420	340.1	49–2	24–1	10.5
ex City of Freeport 27								
Republic	1920	BethWi	5287	7940	391.8	51–4	25–1	10.0
ex Liberty Minquas 26								

Trades: Oil and petroleum

Note: Also smaller vessels

PHILIPPINE MAIL LINE LTD, Manila, Philippines

General cargo/passenger vessel

President Quezon (st2,P934)								
	1921	NYSB	14,124	11,440	535–2	72–2	30–7	18.0
ex President Madison 39, ex Bay State 22								

POPE & TALBOT LUMBER CO, Sheldon Bldg, 461 Market St, San Francisco CA

MCCORMICK STEAMSHIP CO								
Absaroka	1918	Skinnr	5698	8584	424–0	54–2	24–6	10.5
Brookings	1919	GLakeA	2327	4200	261–6	43–8	24–3	9.5
ex Cowiche 22								
Charles L Wheeler Jr								
	1918	Albina	2205	3760	289.0	44–1	19–1	9.0
ex Point Judith 29								
Charles R McCormick								
	1920	Standf	6027	9400	412–0	53–2	26–7	10.5
ex Apus 23								
Forbes Hauptmann	1919	Ames	5674	8614	423–0	54–2	25–9	10.5
ex Western Ally 29, launched as War Hector								
Hamlin F McCormick								
	1919	PuseyG	3317	5166	335–4	50–0	21–0	9.5
ex Castle Point 23								
Munami	1919	Bufflo	2594	4050	261–0	43–8	24–4	9.5
ex Lake Fernando 26								
Peter Helms	1920	Mobile	3326	5206	335–6	46–2	23–1	9.5
ex Hutchinson 29								
Point San Pablo	1920	Mobile	3280	5000	335–6	46–2	23–1	9.5
ex Minooka 29								
Point San Pedro	1920	Mobile	3280	4620	335–6	46–2	23–1	9.5
ex Houston 29								
Sidney M Hauptmann								
	1920	Standf	6027	9400	412–0	53–2	26–7	10.5
ex Argus 23								
West Cape	1918	Ames	5661	8615	423–0	54–2	25–9	10.5
PACIFIC ARGENTINE BRAZIL LINE INC								
Hollywood	1920	BethSW	5498	8545	427–0	54–4	24–8	11.0
West Cactus	1919	WPipe	5581	8584	427–0	54–0	24–6	10.5
West Camargo	1920	WPipe	5804	8584	427–0	54–2	24–6	10.5
West Ira	1919	Ames	5681	8834	423–0	54–2	25–9	10.5
West Ivis	1919	Ames	5666	8834	423–0	54–2	25–9	10.5
West Nilus	1920	BethSW	5495	8573	427–0	54–4	24–8	10.5
West Notus	1920	BethSW	5496	8583	427–0	54–4	24–8	10.5
West Portal (st)	1920	MerchH	5333	8804	400.7	54–2	25–8	12.0
ex Emergency Aid 39								
PORTLAND STEAMSHIP CO,								
McCormick Terminal, 618 NW Front Avenue, Portland OR								
Ernest H Meyer	1918	Albina	2186	3760	289.2	44–2	19–1	9.5
ex Point Lobos 29								
Nabesna	1919	Toledo	2451	4050	261–0	43–8	24–4	9.5
ex Lake Filbert 23								
SILVERADO STEAMSHIP CO								
Silverado	1918	LBeach	2298	3200	245.6	42–0	20–10	9.5

Funnel: McCormick – black with white band bearing red M on white disc on centre of blue five-pointed star; PABL – black with emblem on white band
Hull: Black, red boot-topping
Services: Pacific lumber trades; US E coast–US W coast; PABL – Vancouver, Seattle, San Francisco, Los Angeles–Trinidad, Brazil, Buenos Aires

SILVERADO STEAMSHIP CO & WALLINGFORD STEAMSHIP CO

West Planter	1919	McDoug	2609	4050	261–0	43–8	24–4	9.5
ex Texas Planter 35, ex Lake Flatonia 32								
West Shipper	1920	Chicgo	2592	4050	261–0	43–8	24–4	9.5
ex Texas Shipper 35, ex Lake Giddings 32								
WALLINGFORD STEAMSHIP CO								
Wallingford	1919	LBeach	2256	3200	245.6	42–1	20–10	9.5

Funnel: Yellow with houseflag, black top
Services: New York and other US E coast ports–US Gulf ports; US Gulf ports–US W coast ports

PRUDENTIAL STEAMSHIP CORPORATION, 17 State St, New York

Eastern Guide	1919	YokoDk	3704	6558	344–10	50–0	24–0	10.0
POSTAL STEAMSHIP CORP								
Eastern Glade	1920	YokoU	5057	8600	400.0	54–6	25–9	10.0

Funnel: Blue with blue 'Pure' emblem on white band
Hull: Black
Trades: Oil and petroleum

PURE OIL CO, Graybar Bldg, 420 Lexington Avenue, New York, and Pure Oil Bldg, 35 East Wacker Drive, Chicago IL

Tankers

W C Fairbanks	1917	Cramp	6353	11,150	446–4	58–2	27–0	9.5
ex Harold Walker 35								
W E Hutton	1920	BethAl	7076	10,078	453–9	56–0	27–3	10.0
ex Portola Plumas 22								
W F Burdell	1920	BethAl	7044	10,100	453–9	56–0	27–3	10.0
ex City of Alameda 22								
W W Mills	1921	MerchC	6817	10,184	424.4	58–2	26–6	10.0
ex Puente 22								

Funnel: Black with blue R on yellow band
Hull: Black, red boot-topping
Trades: Oil and petroleum

RICHFIELD OIL CORPORATION,
Richfield Bldg, 555 South Flower St, Los Angeles CA

Tankers

Agwiworld	1921	SunSB	6771	10,600	445–5	59–2	26–8	10.5
Huguenot	1919	BethSP	6964	10,250	453–0	56–2	27–1	10.0
Kekoskee	1920	BethWi	5193	7900	391.8	51–4	25–1	10.0
Larry Doheny	1921	SunSB	7038	10,570	445–0	59–4	26–8	10.5
ex Foldenfjord 28								
Pat Doheny	1921	SunSB	7053	10,570	445–0	59–2	26–8	10.5
ex Sunoco 27								
Topila	1913	NNews	5125	7900	395–0	59–1	23–0	9.0
Torres	1917	NNews	4943	8300	395–0	59–1	23–0	9.0

Funnel: Baltimore – Yellow wih black top separated by yellow over black bands; APL – black with green AP monogram on white band between two narrow green bands; USL – red with white band and blue top
Hull: Baltimore, APL – black, red boot-topping; USL – black, red boot-topping with white dividing line
Services: Baltimore – New York–Havana–Panama–Los Angeles–San Francisco; APL – New York, Los Angeles–Manila–China–Japan–Hong Kong; New York–Australia; Philadelphia, Baltimore, New York–Aden–Karachi–Calcutta; USL – New York–Queenstown–Havre–Southampton–Hamburg; New York–London; New York–Manchester–Liverpool–Glasgow–Belfast

ROOSEVELT STEAMSHIP CO INC, 1 Broadway New York

BALTIMORE MAIL STEAMSHIP CO,* 650 Baltimore Trust Bldg, Baltimore MD

Passenger/general cargo vessels

City of Baltimore (st,P81/t)								
	1919	BethAl	8378	7553	506–0	56–0	28–8	16.0
ex Steadfast 31; lengthened 31								
City of Los Angeles (st,P81/t)								
	1918	BethAl	8378	7553	506–0	56–0	28–8	16.0
ex City of Havre 38, ex Victorious 31, launched as War Haven; lengthened 31								
City of Newport News (st,P81/t)								
	1919	BethAl	8378	7553	506–0	56–0	28–8	16.0
ex Archer 31, launched as War Wave; lengthened 31								
City of Norfolk (st,P81/t)								
	1918	BethAl	8378	7553	506–0	56–0	28–8	16.0
ex Independence 31, launched as War Harbour; lengthened 31								
City of San Francisco (st,P81/t)								
	1919	BethAl	8378	7553	506–0	56–0	28–8	16.0
ex City of Hamburg 38, ex Eclipse 31, launched as War Surf; lengthened 31								

UNITED STATES LINES CO**

Passenger vessels

America (st2,P543/1,418/cab,241/t, as designed)								
	bldg	NNews	33,961	13,061	723–0	93–3	33–5	20.0
Manhattan (st2,P582/cab,461/t,196/3)								
	1932	NYSB3	24,289	13,250	705–0	86–4	30–0	20.5
Washington (st2,P582/cab,461/t,196/3)								
	1933	NYSB3	24,289	13,250	705–0	86–4	30–0	20.5

Roosevelt: President Roosevelt *was a standard transport completed in 1921 as* Peninsula State *for the US Shipping Board. She was assigned to United States Lines and made her maiden voyage from New York to Bremen in February 1922 as* Peninsula State. *She was renamed* President Pierce *briefly in 1922, and by the end of July had been renamed* President Roosevelt. *She served as a transport for most of the Second World War and was broken up in 1948 (RW Jordan collection)*

Roosevelt: City of Dalhart *was completed in 1921 by Oscar Daniels Co, at Tampa, Florida, and was converted from steam propulsion to a motor vessel in 1927. She was operated by the WSA during the Second World War, and was broken up in 1947 (Alex Duncan)*

Passenger/general cargo vessels

American Banker (st,P78/t)
1920 AISB 7430 8000 448–0 58–2 28–0 16.0
ex Cantigny 24, building as Mount Michael, laid down as Shohola

American Banker (st,P12/1)
order Ingall 10,812 6800 489–0 69–0 28–6 16.0

American Farmer (st,P78/t)
1920 AISB 7430 8000 448–0 58–2 28–0 16.0
ex Ourcq 24, laid down as Sisseton

American Farmer (st,P12/1)
order Ingall 10,812 6800 489–0 69–0 28–6 16.0

American Importer (st,P78/t)
1920 AISB 7590 8000 448–0 58–2 28–0 16.0
ex Somme 24, building as Mount Black, laid down as Siskowit

American Merchant (st,P78/1)
1921 AISB 7430 8000 448–0 58–2 28–0 16.0
ex Aisne 24, laid down as Sisladobsis

American Merchant (st,P12/1)
order Ingall 10,812 6800 489–0 69–0 28–6 16.0

American Shipper (st,P78/t)
1921 AISB 7430 8000 448–0 58–2 28–0 16.0
ex Tours 24, laid down as Skanawono

American Shipper (st,P12/1)
order Ingall 10,812 6800 489–0 69–0 28–6 16.0

American Trader (st,P78/t)
1920 AISB 7430 8000 448–0 58–2 28–0 16.0
ex Marne 24, laid down as Sitkum

American Traveler (st,P120/t)
1920 AISB 7555 8000 448–0 58–2 28–0 16.0
ex Cambrai 31, building as Mount Wolf, laid down as Shohokin

President Harding (st2,P201/cab,236/3)
1921 NYSB1 13,869 11,758 535–2 72–2 30–6 18.0
ex President Taft 22, ex Lone Star State 22

President Roosevelt (st2,P201/cab,236/3)
1921 NYSB1 13,869 11,758 535–2 72–2 30–6 18.0
ex President Pierce 22, ex Peninsula State 22

AMERICAN PIONEER LINE***

General cargo vessels

American Builder (m,P8/1)
order WPipe 6834 7815 417–9 60–2 27–4 14.0

American Leader (m,P8/1)
order WPipe 6750 7815 417–9 60–2 27–4 14.0

American Manufacturer (m,P8/1)
order WPipe 6902 7815 417–11 60–11 27–4 14.0

American Packer (m,P8/1)
order WPipe 6802 7815 417–9 60–2 27–4 14.0

American Press (m,P8/1)
order WPipe 6841 7815 417–9 60–2 27–4 14.0

City of Dalhart (m) 1921 Daniel 5878 9185 401.9 54–2 27–0 12.0
conv steamer 27

City of Elwood (m)1921 DoultW 6197 9116 411–6 55–0 27–2 13.0
conv steamer 29

City of Rayville (m)1920 Daniel 5883 9050 401.9 54–2 27–0 12.0
conv steamer 27

Crown City (m) 1920 LosAng 5428 8006 423–0 54–5 24–0 12.0
conv steamer 27

Jeff Davis (m) 1921 DoultW 6174 9183 411–6 55–0 27–2 13.0
conv steamer 29

New Orleans† (m) 1920 DoultW 6172 9084 411–6 55–0 27–2 13.0
conv steamer 29

Nightingale (st,P12/1)
1939 NNews 8223 9503 459–2 63–2 25–11 15.5

Potter (m) 1920 DoultW 6174 900 411–6 55–0 27–2 13.0
conv steamer 29

Red Jacket (st,P12/1) 1939 Fed2 7194 9748 459–2 63–2 27–8 15.5

Sawokla† (m) 1920 Daniel 5882 9105 401.9 54–2 27–0 12.0
conv steamer 27

Shooting Star (st,P12/1)
bldg Tampa 8200 8900 459–2 63–2 27–8 15.5

Tampa (m) 1920 Daniel 5959 9120 401.9 54–2 27–0 12.0
conv steamer 26

Unicoi† (m) 1920 Daniel 5873 9155 401.9 54–2 27–0 12.0
conv steamer 26

Note: Roosevelt Steamship Co Inc was associated with International Mercantile Marine Co
Note: * Operated from 1938 by United States Lines Co (*qv*); ** United States Lines Co was jointly owned by Dawson and Roosevelt–International Mercantile Marine Co interests; *** Roosevelt Steamship Co Inc was operator of

Ward† (m)	1921	DoultW	6167	9009	411–6	55–0	27–2	13.0
conv steamer 29								
Wichita (m)	1921	DoultW	6174	9147	411–6	55–0	27–2	13.0
conv steamer 29								
Yomachichi (m)	1919	Daniel	5868	9235	402.1	54–0	27–0	12.0
conv steamer 27								

American Pioneer Line – the line and its vessels were owned by United States Maritime Commission (*qv*); † sold American Export Lines Inc (*qv*) Dec 1939, for delivery 1940

SABINE TRANSPORTATION CO INC,

c/o Munger T Ball, Postbox 1500, Port Arthur TX

Funnel: Red with emblem, black top
Hull: Black, red boot-topping
Trades: Oil and petroleum

Tankers

A S Hansen	1915	NYSB1	5189	7790	406–6	51–2	24–7	9.5
ex Gulfcoast 36								
C B Watson	1920	BethSW	5607	8550	428–1	54–4	25–1	10.5
ex Mary Luckenbach 36								
H M Fredrichsen	1914	NYSB1	5189	7790	406–6	51–2	24–7	9.5
ex Gulfstream 36								
Henry M Dawes	1916	BethHH	4710	7900	406–4	51–4	25–0	9.5
ex Oscar D Bennett 32, ex George E Paddleford 20								
L L Abshire	1917	Cramp	6353	11,150	446–4	58–3	27–0	10.5
ex William Green 36								
Munger T Ball	1920	Terry	5104	7890	391.9	51–2	25–1	10.5
ex Chilsco 35, ex Lilmae 27								
R P Smith	1916	Cramp	6226	11,150	446–4	58–2	27–0	10.5
ex J M Danziger 36								
R W McIlvain* (m2)	1916	Baltmr	3262	5200	306–0	47–2	23–1	9.0
ex Los Alamos 32, ex Bramell Point 23								
Rawleigh Warner	1912	NYSB1	3664	5082	321.7	46–3	23–0	9.0
ex Rayo 28								

Note: * Sold Eastern States Petroleum Co Inc 1939

SEAS SHIPPING CO INC, (Robin Line), 39 Corlandet St, New York

Funnel: Black with emblem; Santa – red, black top
Hull: Black, red boot-topping, white dividing line
Services: Seas – New York, Baltimore–Cape Town/Mombasa range; Santa – US–West Indies

Greylock	1921	LosAng	7460	10,900	430.7	54–4	28–11	11.0
ex West Greylock 23								
Robin Adair (st)	1920	Skinnr	6895	10,400	424.8	55–2	28–0	12.0
Robin Doncaster (st,P12/1)	order	BethSP	7101	9970	479–8	66–6	27–0	19.0
Robin Goodfellow (st)	1920	Skinnr	6885	10,400	424.8	55–2	28–0	12.0
Robin Gray (st)	1920	Skinnr	6896	10,400	424.8	55–2	28–0	12.0
Robin Hood (st)	1919	Skinnr	6887	10,400	424.8	55–2	28–0	12.0
Robin Kettering (st,P12/1)	order	BethSP	7101	9970	479–8	66–6	27–0	19.0
Robin Locksley (st,P12/1)	order	BethSP	7101	9970	479–8	66–3	27–0	19.0
Robin Sherwood (st,P12/1)	order	BethSP	7101	9970	479–8	66–3	27–0	19.0
Robin Tuxford (st,P12/1)	order	BethSP	7101	9970	479–8	66–6	27–0	19.0
Robin Wentley (st,P12/1)	order	BethSP	7101	9970	479–8	66–6	27–0	19.0
FAIRFIELD STEAMSHIP CORP								
Maine	1917	Texas	6032	9532	420.0	54–2	27–0	10.0
QUINNIPIAC SHIPPING CORP								
Fairfield*	1918	BethWi	2848	5025	322–0	48–3	20–5	9.5
ex Catherine Weems 28, ex Garibaldi 25, launched as Pilón								
SANTA STEAMSHIP CORP (American & Cuban Steamship Line Inc)								
Santa Isabel	1920	Toledo	2647	4165	261–0	43–8	24–5	9.5

Note: * Sold Norway 1939, renamed *Hallfried*

SEATRAIN LINES INC,

39 Broadway, New York, and Whitney National Bank Bldg, New Orleans LA

Funnel: Yellow with houseflag, black top
Hull: Black
Services: Carriage of railway cars New York–Havana; New York–Havana–New Orleans

Railway car carriers

Seatrain Havana (st)	1932	SunSBD	8061	11,531	478–0	63–8	27–2	16.0
Seatrain New Jersey (st)	bldg	SunSBD	8108	11,683	483–0	64–1	27–2	16.0
Seatrain New Orleans	1928	SHWR	7633	9078	470–1	62–2	25–9	13.0
ex Seatrain 32; lengthened 38								

Seas Shipping Co: The steamer Greylock *was completed by Los Angeles Shipbuilding, San Pedro, in 1921 as* West Greylock *for US Shipping Board. When on voyage from Murmansk to the US in convoy RA52 and 600 miles northeast of Iceland, she was torpedoed by* U255 *on February 3 1943. The torpedo struck between Nos 5 and 6 holds, blowing a large hole below the waterline and locking the steering gear. The ship was abandoned after 15 minutes, and the crew of 45 and 25 gunners were picked up by the escort trawler HMS* Lady Madeleine. *A British escort vessel later shelled and sank* Greylock *(Alex Duncan)*

Socony-Vacuum: Daylight *was completed by Sun Shipbuilding, at Chester, in June 1931. She is pictured here in September 1942 in wartime livery and armed fore and aft. In 1947 she was sold within the US and renamed* Seabird, *at first under US flag, later transferring to Panama. She was broken up in 1961–62 (Mobil Oil Co)*

Standard Oil California: W H Berg *survived the Second World War. In 1963 she was sold within the US and renamed* Point Bonita, *and was broken up during 1963–64 (Chevron archives)*

Seatrain New York (st)	1932	SunSBD	8061	11,610	477–3	64–1	27–2	16.0
Seatrain Texas (st)	bldg	SunSBD	8108	11,683	483–0	63–11	27–2	16.0

SEEKONK CORPORATION, 111 Sutter St, San Francisco CA

Hull: Black
Services: General tramping

Willmoto (m)	1919	AISB	4999	7825	401–0	54–2	24–9	11.5
ex Seekonk 29; conv steamer 23								

SHEPARD STEAMSHIP CO,
40 Central St, Postbox 992, Boston MA, and 205 East 42nd St, New York

Funnel: Yellow with red S on white band between two narrow blue bands
Services: Boston–New York–Philadelphia–Panama–San Francisco–Seattle–Tacoma–Everett

Harpoon (st)	1920	Groton	5964	9400	402.6	53–0	33.2	12.0
ex Hopatcong 31								
Sage Brush (st)	1919	NWStl	5565	8625	423–10	54–2	24–0	12.0
ex West Cherow 29								
Sea Thrush (st)	1920	MerchH	5447	8750	400.7	54–2	25–8	12.0
ex Exilona 37, ex Delanson 28								
Timber Rush (st)	1919	Columb	5542	8625	423–10	54–2	24–1	12.0
ex Explorer 33, ex City of Eureka 28								
Wind Rush (st)	1918	Columb	5586	8800	423–10	54–2	24–1	12.0
ex Westbrook 29								

SINCLAIR REFINING CO, 39 Corlandet St, New York

SINCLAIR NAVIGATION CO, International Bldg, 630 Fifth Avenue, New York

Funnel: Red with Sinclair emblem on white band, green top
Hull: Black, red boot-topping
Trades: Oil and petroleum, particularly US and Gulf of Mexico

Tankers								
Albert E Watts	1921	BethWi	7137	11,398	445–0	59–2	26–10	10.5
E R Kemp	1921	BethWi	4887	7435	391–6	53–2	24–0	10.0
E W Sinclair	1921	BethWi	4887	7435	391–6	53–2	24–0	10.0
Eugene V R Thayer	1920	BethWi	7138	11,398	445–0	59–2	26–10	10.5
Harry F Sinclair Jr (st)	1931	BethQu	6151	9275	416.5	57–1	26–6	12.0
J Fletcher Farrell	1921	BethQu	7061	11,398	445–0	59–3	26–10	10.5
Joseph M Cudahy	1921	SunSB	6950	11,350	445–0	59–2	26–8	10.5
Samuel L Fuller	1921	SunSB	6950	11,350	445–0	59–2	26–8	10.5
Virginia Sinclair (st)	1930	BethQu	6151	9275	416.5	57–1	26–6	12.0
Wm Boyce Thompson	1921	BethQu	7061	11,398	445–0	59–4	26–10	10.5

SOCONY-VACUUM OIL CO INC, 26 Broadway, New York

Funnel: Black with white S
Hull: Black, red boot-topping
Trades: Oil and petroleum

Tankers								
Acme	1916	BethU1	6878	10,100	452–0	56–0	26–10	10.5
Algonquin	1920	BethAl	7229	10,250	453–9	56–0	25–10	11.0
Altair	1920	SunSB	6933	10,600	445–5	59–3	26–9	10.5
ex Agwimoon 27								
Argon	1920	BethSP	6952	10,750	453–0	56–2	27–1	10.5
Ario	1920	BethSP	6952	10,750	453–0	56–2	27–1	10.5
Astral	1916	BethU1	7542	11,950	439.5	58–0	29–2	10.0
Atlas	1916	Cramp	7058	11,200	446–0	58–2	27–0	10.0
ex Sunoil 27								
Aurora (m)	1920	Baltmr	7050	10,250	450–0	59–2	26–7	10.5
ex Miller County 27, conv steamer 23								
Birkenhead	1921	Moore2	6960	10,700	438–5	57–2	27–4	11.0
Brilliant (m)	1930	SunSBD	9132	14,350	500–1	66–0	28–11	11.5
Broad Arrow	1918	NYSB1	7718	13,400	485–0	62–9	28–0	10.5
Caddo (te)	order	BethSP	10,173	15,850	501–6	68–3	29–11	14.0
Calusa (te)	order	BethSP	10,172	15,850	501–6	68–3	29–11	14.0
Catawba (te)	order	BethSP	10,170	15,850	501–6	68–3	29–11	14.0
China Arrow	1920	BethQu	8403	12,500	468.3	62–9	28–1	10.5
Colina (te)	order	BethSP	10,200	15,850	501–6	68–3	29–11	14.0
Comet	1930	SunSBD	9154	14,363	500–1	66–0	28–11	11.5
Conastoga (te)	order	BethSP	10,200	15,850	501–6	68–3	29–11	14.0
Corsicana (te)	order	BethSP	10,200	15,850	501–6	68–3	29–11	14.0
Daylight (m)	1931	SunSBD	9180	14,606	500–1	66–0	29–0	11.5
Dixie Arrow	1921	NYSB1	8046	13,400	485–3	62–9	28–1	10.5
Eagle	1917	BethU1	6003	9950	410.0	56–0	28–9	10.0
ex Peerless 19, ex Eagle 18								

Emidio	1921	BethSF	6912	10,250	453–0	56–2	27–3	10.5
ex Hammac 23								
Gargoyle	1921	Moore2	7003	10,700	438–6	57–2	27–4	10.5
India Arrow	1921	BethQu	8327	13,350	485–3	62–9	28–2	10.5
Japan Arrow	1920	BethQu	8327	13,350	485–3	62–9	28–1	10.5
Java Arrow	1921	BethQu	8327	13,350	485–3	62–8	28–1	10.5
Lebec	1921	BethAl	6893	10,750	453–4	56–3	27–3	10.5
ex Hamer 22								
Liebre	1921	UnionC	7057	10,250	452–0	56–0	27–3	10.5
Magnolia (st)	1935	NYSB3	9511	14,900	500–1	66–0	30–0	13.5
Mobilfuel (st)	1939	BethSP	10,221	16,550	501–9	68–4	29–11	14.0
Mobilgas (st)	1937	SunSBD	9860	15,515	501–8	68–4	29–11	13.5
Mobiloil (st)	1937	SunSBD	9860	15,515	501–8	68–4	29–11	13.5
Mobilube (st)	1939	BethSP	10,222	16,550	501–9	68–4	29–11	13.5
Mojave	1921	BethAl	6900	10,750	453–4	56–2	27–3	10.5
ex Hambro 22								
Olean	1919	Cramp	7118	11,200	446–0	58–3	27–1	10.0
ex Alameda 24								
Paulsboro	1916	BethU1	6699	10,750	435.0	56–0	26–10	10.0
Rochester	1920	BethSP	6836	10,750	453–4	56–2	27–0	10.5
Royal Arrow	1916	NYSB1	7794	13,400	485–0	62–8	28–1	10.0
Socony-Vacuum (st)	1935	NYSB3	9511	14,900	500–1	66–0	30–0	13.5
Standard Arrow	1916	NYSB1	7794	13,400	485–10	62–9	28–0	10.0
Sylvan Arrow	1918	NYSB1	7797	13,400	485–0	62–9	28–1	10.0
Tejon	1920	Moore2	7034	10,700	438–5	57–0	27–4	10.5
ex City of Reno 23								
Tiger	1917	BethU1	5992	9950	410.0	56–0	28–9	10.0
Vacuum	1920	Moore2	7020	10,700	438–5	57–0	27–4	10.5
Yankee Arrow	1921	NYSB1	8046	13,400	485–3	62–9	28–1	10.5
Yorba Linda	1921	BethAl	6900	10,750	453–4	56–0	27–1	10.5

Note: Socony-Vacuum Oil Co Inc, a subsidiary of Socony-Vacuum Corp, also owned tankers under 2500gt

SOUTH ATLANTIC STEAMSHIP CO INC,
9th floor, Savannah Bank & Trust Co Bldg, Bryan and Bull Streets, Savannah GA, and 7 West 10th St, Wilmington DE

Funnel: Yellow with blue band bordered by two white bands, all separated from black top by broader yellow band
Hull: Black, red boot-topping
Services: Savannah, Charleston, Jacksonville–Brest–Liverpool; Savannah–Plymouth–Antwerp–Hamburg; Jacksonville–London – Rotterdam–Hamburg–Antwerp; Savannah, Jacksonville –Liverpool–Manchester–Hamburg

Fluor Spar (st)	1919	AISB	5055	7498	400–4	54–2	24–5	12.0
laid down as Shandaken								
Saccarappa (st)	1918	AISB	4965	7498	400–4	54–2	24–5	12.0
Schoharie (st)	1919	AISB	4971	8080	401–0	54–2	24–5	12.0
Shickshinny (st)	1919	AISB	5103	7178	400–4	54–2	24–5	12.0
Sundance (st)	1919	AISB	5035	7498	400–4	54–2	24–5	12.0
laid down as Cockspur								
Tulsa (st)	1919	AISB	5083	7866	401–0	54–2	24–9	12.0
laid down as Zetella								

SOUTHGATE-NELSON CORPORATION, Southgate Pier, Norfolk VA

Funnel: Yellow with blue diamond, black top; AHRL – black with orange band
Services: Philadelphia, Baltimore, Norfolk, Boston–London, Southampton, Leith, Dundee; Norfolk, Baltimore, Boston, Portland–London, Hull, Middlesbrough

Operators of
AMERICAN HAMPTON ROADS LINE, YANKEE LINE, ORIOLE LINES

Artigas (st)	1920	AISB	5161	8000	401–0	54–2	24–5	12.0
laid down as Mindoka								
Capulin (st)	1920	AISB	4977	8000	401–0	54–2	24–5	12.0
Challenge (st)	1939	Fed2	6085	9758	459–0	63–2	25–9	15.5
City of Flint (st)	1920	AISB	4963	8015	401–0	54–2	24–5	12.0
laid down as Collingdale								
Coelleda (st)	1920	AISB	4986	8015	401–0	54–2	24–5	11.5
Cold Harbor (st)	1920	AISB	5010	8015	401–0	54–2	24–5	12.0
Lehigh (st)	1919	AISB	4983	8000	401–0	54–2	24–5	12.0
laid down as Senatobia								
Liberty (st)	1918	Fed1	6211	9748	411–6	55–0	27–2	12.0
McKeesport (st)	1919	Fed1	6198	9808	411–6	55–0	27–2	12.0
Quaker City (st)	1920	AISB	4961	8015	401–0	54–2	24–5	12.0
laid down as Clematis								
Sarcoxie (st)	1919	AISB	5116	8000	401–0	54–2	24–5	12.0
Vincent (st)	1919	Fed1	6210	9808	411–6	55–0	27–2	12.0
West Cusseta (m)	1921	LosAng	5428	8006	423–0	54–2	24–0	12.0
conv steamer 27								

Note: These lines and vessels were owned by United States Maritime Commission (*qv*)

STANDARD FRUIT & STEAMSHIP CORP, (Vaccaro Line),

American Bank & Trust Co Bldg, 200 Carondelet St, Postbox 830, New Orleans LA, and 21 West St, New York

Funnel: Black with red V on white band between two narrow blue bands
Hull: White, red boot-topping
Services: Fruit – Caribbean, Central America–mainly New Orleans, New York, Philadelphia

Fruit carriers

SEABOARD STEAMSHIP CORP (Honduras flag)

Ceiba (P12)	1911	SHWR	1698	2734	309.6	39–2	17–10	12.5
lengthened 15								
Morazan (P12)	1908	Scott2	2984	2900	300.3	45–3	20–11	11.0
ex Manco 21								
Virginia (P–)	1904	Cockll	1636	2000	265.0	36–0	18–6	11.0
ex Minadora 23, ex Rousslane 21								
Yoro (P12)	1911	SHWR	1697	2723	309.3	39–3	17–10	12.5
lengthened 15								
STANDARD FRUIT & STEAMSHIP CO (Honduras flag)								
Oradell (st)	1924	SHWR	1645	2200	264–10	35–8	20–0	13.0
Oriskany (st)	1924	SHWR	1644	2200	264–10	35–8	19–11	13.0
STANDARD NAVIGATION CORP (Honduras flag)								
Amapala (P76/1)	1924	SHWR	4148	3504	365–0	50–2	20–5	15.0
Atlántida (P76/1)	1924	Workmn	4191	3380	365–0	50–4	20–4	15.0
Cefalu (P90/1)	1930	Workmn	5221	4325	396–0	53–5	23–10	16.0
Contessa (P90/1)	1930	Curle	5512	4450	396–0	53–8	23–10	16.0
Gatun (P12/1)	1925	Workmn	3362	2900	328–0	45–2	20–2	14.0
Granada (P12/1)	1925	SHWR	3332	2843	328–0	45–2	20–2	14.0
Tegucigalpa (P40/1)	1897	HallR	2928	4215	330.1	41–3	22–4	10.0
ex Ingeli 13								
Wawa (P12)	1925	SHWR	1650	2320	255.2	38–2	17–6	11.5
Tanker								
Under United States flag								
Caloria	1906	ArmWh1	4095	6030	370.4	51–0	24–3	10.0
ex Chatham 15								

Note: This company also managed vessels of under 1500gt
Note: See also in Great Britain section

STANDARD OIL CO OF CALIFORNIA, (Soccal),

Standard Oil Bldg, 225 Bush St, San Francisco CA

Funnel: Black with white S
Hull: Black, red boot-topping
Trades: Oil and petroleum

Tankers

Captain A F Lucas	1904	Trigg	4188	5882	360.0	50–1	23–0	8.0
D G Scofield	1916	BethU1	8640	12,333	439.5	58–1	29–2	9.5
District of Columbia (st)	1921	Baltmr	7162	10,945	450–0	59–2	26–7	11.0
F H Hillman (s2)	1921	BethAl	10,837	16,036	500.0	68–3	29–0	11.0
H D Collier (st)	1938	SunSBD	8298	12,700	441.1	65–4	29–0	13.5
H M Storey (s2)	1921	BethAl	10,763	16,036	500.0	68–3	29–0	11.0
H T Harper (m)	1921	Moore2	3803	4935	329.9	46–2	23–0	10.0
J A Moffett	1915	BethU1	6199	8872	419.4	54–2	25–9	9.0
J C Fitzsimmons	1918	Ames	6716	10,006	421.4	57–4	25–0	10.0
ex Montrolite 25								
K R Kingsbury	1921	BethAl	8761	12,049	440.0	58–2	30–0	10.5
M E Lombardi (st)	bldg	SunSBD	5325	7692	396–9	57–3	24–9	13.5
R J Hanna	1921	Moore2	6905	10,670	438–0	57–2	27–3	11.0
Richmond	1913	BethFR	6192	9105	419.4	54–3	26–0	11.0
S C T Todd	1920	Moore2	7024	10,509	438–0	57–3	27–3	11.0
W H Berg (st)	1938	SunSBD	8298	12,700	444.1	65–4	29–0	13.5
W S Miller	1920	BethAl	6984	10,713	453–9	56–0	27–3	11.0
W S Rheem (s2)	1922	BethAl	10,872	16,036	500.0	68–2	29–0	11.0
FOREIGN TANKSHIP CORP (Panamanian flag)								
Bahrein	1921	UnionC	7095	10,899	452–0	56–2	27–3	11.0
ex R J Hanna 35								
California Standard (m2)	1929	Krupp	11,179	17,172	513.5	68–1	29–10	12.0

Note: See also Balboa Transport Corp under The Texas Co
Note: This company also owned smaller vessels

STANDARD OIL CO, (INDIANA),

910 South Michigan Avenue, Postbox 5910A, Chicago IL, and Whiting IN

Funnel: Black with emblem
Hull: Black, red boot-topping
Trades: Oil and petroleum

PAN AMERICAN PETROLEUM & TRANSPORT CO,

Lee Circle Bldg, New Orleans LA and Chanin Bldg, 122 East 42nd St, New York

Tankers

Pan-American (st)	1936	SunSBD	9862	15,515	501–7	68–4	30–0	13.5
Pan-Amoco (st)	1936	SunSBD	9862	15,515	501–7	68–4	30–0	13.5

Standard Oil New Jersey: Esso Aruba *was completed in July 1931 by Swan, Hunter & Wigham Richardson. On August 23 1942 she sailed from Güiria, Venezuela, for New York, via Trinidad, in the 25-ship convoy TAW15. Aware of an attack by several U-boats, the escorts made a cordon around the convoy, but* U511 *succeeded in getting through and torpedoed* Esso Aruba *about 120 miles from Guantánamo, Cuba. Although badly damaged, and in danger of breaking in two, the tanker arrived at Guantánamo on August 28. She was repaired at Galveston and re-entered service in February 1943.* Esso Aruba *survived the Second World War and was sold to Panama in 1953 (World Ship Photo Library)*

Standard Oil New Jersey: G Harrison Smith, *fitted with two De Laval double reduction geared steam turbines of 4400shp, was completed in October 1930 by Federal Shipbuilding. She survived the Second World War and was transferred to the British flag in 1950 as* Esso Belfast. *Her transfer was one of those made to fill gaps while two new buildings of the* Esso Oxford *class were under construction. She was broken up at La Seyne in 1958 (World Ship Photo Library)*

Standard Oil New Jersey: Esso Bolivar *was built by Krupp Germaniawerft, and completed in July 1937. She survived the Second World War and was transferred in 1950 to Panamanian registry, and in 1953 to Germany, both still within the Standard Oil group fleet.* Esso Bolivar *was broken up in 1960–61 (World Ship Photo Library)*

Standard Oil New Jersey: The twin-screw tanker Fred W Weller *was completed in December 1917 by Bethlehem Shipbuilding at San Francisco. She survived the Second World War and was broken up in 1948 (World Ship Photo Library)*

Pan-Florida (st)	1936	Fed2	7237	12,937	445–0	66–10	28–0	13.5
Pan-Maine (st)	1936	Fed2	7237	12,937	445–0	66–10	28–0	13.5
Pan-Maryland (st)	1938	Fed2	7701	13,108	450–0	66–8	28–2	13.5
Pan-New York (st)	1938	Fed2	7701	13,038	450–0	66–10	28–2	13.5
Pan-Rhode Island (st)	order	Fed2	7742	13,064	450–0	66–10	28–2	13.5

Note: Standard Oil Co, Indiana, group companies also owned tankers operating on the Great Lakes, and other inland waters including the Mississippi and Ohio rivers

STANDARD OIL CO OF NEW JERSEY,

Room 2300, 30 Rockefeller Plaza, New York

Funnel: Black with white band and 'Standard' emblem; PTC – black with white band and PTC emblem
Hull: Black or dark grey, red boot-topping
Trades: Oil and petroleum

Tankers

A C Bedford (s2)	1918	BethSF	9485	15,775	516–6	68–0	28–6	11.0
Allan Jackson	1921	BethAl	6635	11,010	453–9	56–0	27–3	10.5
ex Crampton Anderson 30								
Beacon (s2)	1921	NNews	10,388	16,150	516–6	68–2	28–6	11.5
ex Agwistone 30								
Beaconhill	1919	BethSP	6941	11,030	452–0	56–2	27–1	10.5
ex Hoven 26								
Beaconlight	1920	BethAl	6926	10,720	453–9	56–0	27–3	10.5
ex Richconcal 23								
Beaconoil	1919	BethAl	6893	10,670	453–9	56–0	27–3	10.5
ex Devolente 23								
Benjamin Brewster	1917	BethHH	5950	8595	411.6	53–5	25–6	10.0
C A Canfield	1913	ArmWh1	6161	10,320	405.0	55–0	27–0	9.5
C J Barkdull	1917	BethU1	6773	11,175	452–0	56–0	27–4	10.0
ex Frederic Ewing 31, ex Wilhelm Jebsen 21								
Cerro Azul	1921	SunSB	9059	13,860	480.5	66–0	28–2	10.5
Cerro Ebano	1921	SunSB	8880	13,860	480.5	66–0	28–2	10.5
Charles G Black (s2)	1921	BethSP	14,305	22,135	550.3	72–2	43.7	11.5
ex G Harrison Smith 26								
Charles Pratt (s2)	1916	NNews	8982	15,955	516–6	68–0	28–6	10.0
Chester O Swain	1921	Standf	8146	12,477	463.2	60–2	27–3	10.5
ex Albertolite 28								
Christy Payne	1921	Standf	8156	12,477	463.3	60–2	27–3	10.5
ex Calgarolite 28								
Cimarron (st2)	1939	SunSBD	11,335	18,300	553–0	75–0	31–7	18.0
Dean Emery	1919	SunSB	6664	11,310	445–5	59–3	26–9	10.5
ex Sunshine 22								
E G Seubert	1918	NYSB1	9181	13,640	485–0	62–9	29–6	10.0
ex F H Wickett 30, ex E L Doheny Third 25								
E J Sadler (s2)	1921	Fed1	9639	16,030	516–5	68–0	28–11	11.5
ex Vancolite 26								
E M Clark (s2)	1921	Fed1	9647	16,030	516–5	68–1	28–11	11.5
ex Victolite 26								
E T Bedford (m2)	1921	Fed1	9563	15,655	516–5	68–1	28–11	11.5
conv steamer 26								
Edward L Doheny	1913	SHWR	5871	9970	415.0	54–0	26–10	9.5
Elisha Walker	1920	SunSB	7007	11,365	445–5	59–3	26–9	10.5
Esso Albany (st2)	bldg	BethSP	11,316	18,300	553–0	75–0	31–7	18.0
Esso Annapolis (st2)	bldg	BethSP	11,316	18,300	553–0	75–0	31–7	18.0
Esso Aruba	1931	SHWR	8773	15,145	484.2	65–6	28–8	11.0
ex Pan Boliver 36								
Esso Augusta (m)	bldg	SunSBD	11,237	17,950	547–3	70–2	30–4	13.0
Esso Baltimore (st)	1938	BethSP	7949	12,960	463–0	64–2	28–6	14.0
Esso Baton Rouge (st)	1938	BethSP	7989	12,950	463–0	64–2	28–6	14.0
Esso Bayonne (st)	1937	Fed2	7689	13,045	450–0	66–10	28–1	14.0
Esso Baytown (st)	1937	SunSBD	7991	13,045	462–4	65–4	28–8	14.0
Esso Bayway (st)	1937	Fed2	7699	13,045	450–0	66–10	28–1	14.0
Esso Boston (st)	1938	Fed2	7699	13,090	450–0	66–10	28–1	14.0
Esso Charleston (st)	1938	BethSP	7949	12,960	463–0	64–3	28–6	14.0
Esso Columbia (st2)	1939	NNews	11,335	18,300	553–0	75–0	31–7	18.0
Esso Concord (st)	bldg	Fed2	7698	13,080	450–0	66–8	28–0	14.0
Esso Houston (st)	1938	Fed2	7699	13,085	450–0	66–8	28–0	14.0
Esso Little Rock (m)	order	SunSBD	11,237	17,950	547–3	70–3	30–4	18.0
Esso Montpelier (st)	bldg	Fed2	7698	13,085	450–0	66–8	28–0	14.0
Esso Nashville (st)	bldg	BethSP	7943	12,960	463–0	64–3	28–6	14.0
Esso New Orleans (st2)	1939	SunSBD	11,340	18,300	553–0	75–0	31–7	18.0
Esso Raleigh (st2)	bldg	NNews	11,316	18,300	553–0	75–0	31–7	18.0
Esso Richmond (st2)	bldg	NNews	11,316	18,300	553–0	75–0	31–7	18.0

Esso Trenton (st2)	1939	Fed2	11,325	18,414	553–0	75–4	31–7	18.0
Esso Williamsburg (m)	order	SunSBD	11,237	17,950	547–3	70–2	30–4	18.0
F Q Barstow (s2)	1917	NNews	9003	15,955	516–6	68–3	28–6	11.0
F W Abrams	1920	NYSB1	9310	14,492	485–0	62–9	29–6	10.5
ex Nora 34								
Franklin K Lane	1920	BethAl	6589	11,010	453–9	56–0	27–11	10.5
Fred W Weller (s2)	1917	BethSF	9485	16,075	516–6	68–0	28–8	11.0
Frederic R Kellogg	1917	Moore1	7127	11,050	438–5	57–0	27–4	10.5
G Harrison Smith (st)	1930	Fed2	11,752	20,615	544–0	74–5	30–7	11.0
Geo H Jones	1919	SunSB	6914	11,205	445–5	59–2	26–9	10.5
George W Barnes	1918	BethQu	6214	9750	416.8	56–1	26–6	10.0
Glenpool	1913	Krupp	5444	8370	400.0	53–2	27–0	9.0
ex Hagen 14								
H H Rogers (s2)	1916	NNews	8807	15,955	516–6	68–1	28–6	10.0
H M Flagler	1918	NNews	8208	12,430	477–9	60–0	27–3	10.0
I C White	1920	SunSB	7052	11,365	445–5	59–3	26–9	10.5
J A Moffett Jr (m2)	1921	Fed1	9788	15,620	516–6	68–1	28–11	11.5
conv steamer 28								
James Magee (s2)	1917	BethSP	9859	15,650	516–6	68–2	28–6	11.0
John D Archbold (s2)	1921	NNews	12,590	22,600	572–6	75–4	31–8	11.5
John Worthington	1920	Standf	8166	12,500	462.4	60–3	27–3	10.5
Joseph Seep	1920	SunSB	7088	11,120	445–5	59–3	26–9	10.0
L J Drake	1918	Ames	6693	9845	419.6	57–3	25–0	10.0
Livingston Roe	1921	Standf	8151	12,500	462.4	60–2	27–3	10.5
M F Elliott	1921	Moore2	6940	10,450	438–5	57–0	27–4	10.5
Norman Bridge	1913	SHWR	4323	6875	365.4	50–4	22–10	9.0
Paul H Harwood (st)	1918	BethSF	6610	10,840	454–9	56–0	27–2	10.5
R G Stewart	1917	NYSB1	9229	13,640	485–0	62–9	29–6	10.0
ex R W Stewart 31, ex Edward L Doheny Junior 25								
R P Resor (st)	1936	Fed2	7451	12,914	435.0	66–10	30–0	13.5
R W Gallagher (st)	1938	BethSP	7989	12,950	463–0	64–2	28–6	14.0
S B Hunt	1919	SunSB	6840	11,205	445–5	59–2	26–9	10.0
Standard	1914	HwldtK	9724	18,075	523.8	68–9	29–4	9.0
ex Jupiter 15								
T C McCobb (st)	1936	Fed2	7452	12,914	435.0	66–10	30–0	13.5
Thomas H Wheeler	1921	Moore2	6950	10,450	438–5	57–0	27–4	10.5
Vistula (m2)	1920	HwldtK	8537	13,725	498.6	64–1	28–0	10.5
conv steamer 26								
W C Teagle (s2)	1917	BethSP	9552	16,080	516–7	68–3	28–6	10.5
W H Libby	1921	Standf	7992	12,495	462.4	60–2	27–3	10.5
W L Steed	1918	BethQu	6182	9750	416.8	56–1	26–6	10.0
W S Farish (st)	1930	Fed2	11,787	20,615	544–0	74–0	30–7	12.0
Wallace E Pratt (st)	1937	SunSBD	7991	13,055	462–4	65–4	28–8	14.0
Walter Jennings (s2)	1921	Fed1	9564	16,030	516–5	68–1	28–11	11.5
Wm G Warden (s2)	1917	NNews	9114	15,955	516–6	68–2	28–6	11.5
Wm Rockefeller (s2)	1921	NNews	14,054	22,390	572–6	75–4	31–8	11.5
KEYSTONE TANKSHIP CORP, 260 South Broad St, Philadelphia PA								
Markay (st2)	1939	Fed2	11,355	18,300	553–0	75–0	38.9	18.0
Seakay (st2)	1939	SunSBD	11,355	18,300	553–0	75–0	38.9	18.0
PANAMA TRANSPORT CO, Panama (Panamanian flag)								
Baltic (m2)	1920	NordsE	8805	13,580	525–0	64–0	26–11	10.5
conv steamer 26								
C O Stillman (m2)	1928	Bremer	13,006	24,000	584–10	75–8	33–11	11.0
Calliope (m2)	1926	HwldtK	8426	13,070	490–0	63–2	27–4	11.0
Clio (m2)	1926	VulcSt	8580	12,660	489–6	63–2	27–2	11.0
D L Harper (m2)	1933	DeutsH	11,210	18,025	542–0	70–4	30–6	12.0
Esso Balboa (m)	1939	DeutsH	9554	14,750	510–8	66–0	28–4	12.0
Esso Bolivar (m)	1937	Krupp	10,389	15,256	506–6	70–1	30–0	12.0
Esso Copenhagen (m2)	1939	B&W	9245	15,000	501–1	65–5	28–5	12.5
F H Bedford Jnr (m2)	1930	FurnH	10,844	17,460	542–6	70–3	30–4	12.0
F J Wolfe (m2)	1932	Bremer	11,244	17,920	542–0	70–5	30–5	12.0
Franz Klasen (m2)	1932	DeutsH	11,194	18,070	542–0	70–4	30–6	12.0
George G Henry	1917	BethU1	6265	10,840	452–0	56–0	27–4	10.0
Geo W McKnight (m2)	1933	Krupp	11,231	18,025	542–0	70–3	30–5	12.0
Hanseat (m)	1929	Desch4	7932	11,915	461–6	64–3	28–6	10.5

Harry G Seidel (m2)								
	1930	Krupp	10,354	17,420	530–0	68–1	30–1	12.0
Heinrich v Reidemann (m2)								
	1930	Bremer	11,020	17,650	542–0	70–3	30–6	12.0
J A Mowinckel (m2)								
	1930	CRDA2	11,147	17,755	542–0	70–5	30–8	12.0
J H Senior (m2)	1931	NordsE	11,065	17,620	542–0	70–4	30–6	12.0
James J Maguire (m)	1939	CRDA2	10,525	15,000	506–8	70–0	29–11	13.0
Josiah Macy (m)	1917	Skinnr	6401	9750	419.4	57–3	26–1	10.0
conv steamer 25								
Leda (m2)	1925	HwldtK	8546	12,915	490–0	63–3	27–3	11.0
Motocarline (m2)	1925	Krupp	8600	12,350	489–8	63–2	27–2	11.0
Niobe	1915	Seebkl	7352	11,745	494–9	62–4	25–9	9.5
Orville Harden (m2)								
	1933	CRDA2	11,191	17,990	542–0	70–5	30–5	12.0
Penelope (m2)	1925	HwldtK	8436	12,915	490–0	63–3	27–3	11.0
Persephone (m2)	1925	Krupp	8426	12,815	489–8	63–3	27–2	11.0
Peter Hurll (m2)	1930	Palmer	10,871	17,585	542–4	70–3	30–5	11.0
Phoebus (m2)	1923	HwldtK	8863	13,360	498.9	64–1	26–10	11.0
Prometheus (m2)	1923	HwldtK	8890	13,270	499.0	64–1	26–10	11.0
Svithiod (m)	1917	Skinnr	6550	9650	441–10	57–2	26–1	10.5
ex S V Harkness 25; rebuilt 34, conv steamer 25								
T J Williams	1921	Daniel	8212	12,555	481–0	60–2	27–8	10.5
Thalia (m2)	1926	HwldtK	8329	13,100	490–0	63–3	27–4	11.0
Victor Ross (m2)	1933	Bremer	11,188	17,930	542–0	70–4	30–5	12.0

Note: See also Anglo-American Oil Co Ltd and Imperial Oil Shipping Co Ltd in Great Britain section, Standard American Petroleum Co SA in Belgium section, Det Danske Petroleums A/S in Denmark section, Standard Française des Pétroles in France section, Baltisch-Amerikanische Petroleums Import GmbH and Waried Tankschiff Rhederei GmbH in Germany section, 'La Columbia' Soc Mar per Trasporto di Petrolio e Derivati in Italy section, Nederlandsche Koloniale Tankv Maats NV and Petroleum Industrie Maats NV in Netherlands section, and Ostlandske Petroleums Compagnie A/S in Norway section

SUDDEN & CHRISTENSON,

Floor 7, Alaska Commercial Bldg, 310 Sansome St, San Francisco CA

Services: Everett–Seattle–San Francisco–Los Angeles–Baltimore–Boston–New York

Catherine G Sudden*								
	1908	NNews	2052	3508	295–9	43–0	17.3	8.5
ex Thorbjörg 22, ex George W Fenwick 16								
CHRISTENSON STEAMSHIP CO								
Charles Christenson								
	1919	Duthie	5630	8560	423–0	54–2	24–1	10.0
ex West Hepburn 26								
Edwin Christenson	1918	NWStl	5670	8600	423–10	54–2	23–11	10.0
ex West Wind 26								
Jane Christenson	1918	Duthie	5667	8560	423–8	54–2	24–0	10.0
ex Westboro 27, launched as War Moon								

Note: * Sold Greece 1939, renamed *Hellenic Trader*

SUN OIL COMPANY, 1608 Walnut St, Philadelphia 3

Funnel: Black
Hull: Grey, red boot-topping
Trades: Oil and petroleum

Tankers								
Atlantic Sun*	1920	SunSB	6735	11,260	445–5	59–2	26–7	10.5
Bidwell (m)	1920	Baltmr	6837	10,790	450–0	59–2	26–7	10.5
conv steamer 23								
Delaware Sun	1922	SunSB	8964	14,136	480.5	66–0	28–2	10.5
J N Pew	1921	SunSB	9033	13,282	480.5	66–0	28–2	10.5
Pennsylvania Sun (m)								
	1938	SunSBD	11,373	17,878	543–7	70–3	30–4	15.0
Sun (m)	1928	SunSBD	9002	14,586	497–0	66–0	28–7	12.0
Sunoil (m)	1927	SunSBD	9005	14,549	497–0	66–0	28–7	12.0
Texas Sun (m)	1937	SunSBD	9900	15,780	535–2	66–0	29–8	15.0
MOTOR TANKSHIP CORP								
America Sun (m)	bldg	SunSBD	11,355	17,955	547–2	70–3	30–4	15.0
Atlantic Sun (m)	order	SunSBD	11,355	17,955	547–2	70–3	30–4	15.0
Chester Sun (m)	1930	SunSBD	9097	14,584	497–10	66–0	28–7	11.5
Eastern Sun (m)	1930	SunSBD	9100	14,521	497–10	66–0	28–8	11.5
Mercury Sun (m)	1932	SunSBD	8893	14,791	497–10	66–0	28–9	11.5
Northern Sun (m)	1931	SunSBD	8865	14,677	497–10	66–0	28–11	11.5
Pacific Sun (m)	1929	SunSBD	9097	14,540	497–10	66–0	28–7	11.5
Southern Sun (m)	1931	SunSBD	8893	14,828	497–10	66–0	28–9	11.5
Western Sun (m)	1930	SunSBD	9100	14,521	497–10	66–0	28–7	11.5

Note: * Sold Italy 1939, renamed *Giorgio Fassio*
Note: Also tankers under 2000gt

SWAYNE & HOYT INC, Matson Bldg, 215 Market St, San Francisco CA

Funnel: Gulf Pacific – yellow with white band bordered by two narrow blue bands
Services: New Orleans, Mobile, Tampa, Panama City FL–

GULF PACIFIC MAIL LINE LTD*								
Point Ancha	1919	ToddDD	4727	7634	395–9	53–1	23–9	11.0
ex Delight 31								

Los Angeles–San Francisco–Seattle –Tacoma

Point Judith	1919	ToddDD	4810	7634	395–9	53–1	23–9	11.0
ex Remus 34								
Point Lobos	1919	ToddDD	4802	7634	395–9	53–1	23–9	11.0
ex Ossining 33								

SWAYNE & HOYT LTD (Gulf Pacific Line)

Point Arena	1917	Standd	4673	7867	395–9	52–0	23–8	10.5
ex Democracy 37, ex Jupiter 18								
Point Bonita	1918	SeatCD	4782	7711	395–9	53–3	23–9	10.5
ex Sacramento 37								
Point Brava	1919	Downey	4834	7829	386.8	52–2	24–0	10.5
ex Manhattan Island 30, ex Osakis 23								
Point Caleta	1919	Downey	4823	7829	386.8	52–0	24–0	10.5
ex Dio 30								
Point Chico	1918	Downey	4905	7829	386.8	52–0	24–0	10.5
ex Abron 30								
Point Clear	1920	ToddDD	4839	7600	395–9	53–1	23–9	11.0
ex S A Perkins 33, ex Pallas 25								
Point Estero	1920	ToddDD	4743	7971	395–9	53–1	23–9	10.5
ex Nelson Traveler 36, ex Commercial Traveler 29, ex Red Hook 22								
Point Palmas	1919	Downey	4869	7829	386.8	52–2	24–0	10.5
ex Sabotawan 30								
Point Salinas	1919	Downey	4886	7829	386.8	52–2	24–0	10.5
ex Dochet 30								
Point Vincente	1920	ToddDD	4744	7971	395–9	53–1	23–9	11.0
ex Charles Nelson 36, ex Commercial Spirit 29, ex Hoboken 22								

Note: * Managed by Swayne & Hoyt Ltd (*qv*)

WESTERN TRANSPORT CO

Eldorado	1918	LBeach	2180	3200	245.6	42–0	20–10	9.0

SWORD STEAMSHIP LINE INC, 76 Beaver St, New York

Funnel: Black with SWORD in white on white-bordered red diamond
Hull: Black, red boot-topping
Services: New York–New Orleans; New York, Hampton Roads, Norfolk, Wilmington NC–Boca Grande; between E coast US ports

Dixie Sword (st)	1919	SubmBC	3283	5350	335–6	46–2	22–2	9.5
ex Florida 37, ex Point Fermin 34, ex Continental Bridge 26, laid down as Stanley, ordered as Anquam								
Eastern Sword	1920	Uraga	3785	5620	330.3	46–1	23–8	10.0
Golden Sword	1918	BethAl	4078	5881	341.0	48–2	22–7	10.0
ex Delecto 36, ex Redondo 23								
Northern Sword	1918	BethWi	2648	4360	312–0	45–0	22.6	9.5
ex Norma 32								
Silver Sword	1919	Downey	4937	7817	386.8	52–2	24–0	10.0
ex New Britain 34								
Western Sword	1920	ToddDD	4794	7684	395–9	53–1	23–9	10.5
ex Biboco 33, ex St Anthony 28								

TEXAS COMPANY, THE, (Texaco),
135 East 42nd St, New York, and 7 West 10th St, Wilmington DE

Funnel: Black with red star on white disc on green band
Hull: Black, red boot-topping
Trades: Oil and petroleum

Tankers

Arizona	1919	BethWi	5174	7755	391.8	51–3	25–1	10.0
ex Galena 29, ex Salem County 23								
Aryan	1919	Texas	6452	10,026	416.8	56–1	26–9	10.0
Australia (m2)	1928	SunSBD	11,628	18,686	509.7	70–4	32–2	11.0
ex Mary Ellen O'Neil 29								
California (s2)	1921	NNews	10,388	16,100	516–6	68–1	28–7	10.5
ex Helen Vinmont 30, ex Agwismith 27								
Connecticut (st)	1938	BethSP	8684	12,785	490–6	64–5	28–0	13.0
Derbyline	1919	BethAl	6917	10,686	453–9	56–0	27–3	10.0
Dirigo	1919	Texas	6418	10,038	416.8	56–1	26–9	10.0
Dungannon	1920	BethAl	6928	10,736	453–9	56–0	27–3	10.0
Florida (m)	1937	SunSBD	8562	12,382	490–6	65–4	28–0	13.0
Harvester	1920	Texas	6416	9940	416.8	56–1	26–9	10.0
Illinois	1921	Texas	6448	9859	416.8	56–1	26–9	10.0
Lightburne	1919	Texas	6429	9950	416.8	56–1	26–10	10.0
Louisiana (m)	1937	SunSBD	8569	12,380	490–6	65–4	28–0	13.0
Nevada	1919	BethSP	6915	11,061	453–0	56–2	27–1	10.0
New Jersey	1921	Texas	6414	9847	416.8	56–1	26–9	10.0
New York	1916	BethFR	6401	9830	416.8	56–1	26–7	10.0
Occidental	1920	Texas	6403	10,038	416.8	56–1	26–10	10.0
Ohio (st)	bldg	SunSBD	9265	14,100	513–10	68–4	28–6	16.0
Oklahoma (st)	bldg	SunSBD	9265	14,100	513–10	68–4	28–6	16.0
Oregon	1919	Moore2	7017	10,767	438–5	57–0	27–2	10.0
ex Emma H Coppage 29, ex Cape Cod 26, ex Quabbin 23								

Union Oil Co: Los Angeles *was completed in April 1916 by Union Iron Works, San Francisco. In 1941* Los Angeles *was sold the Mexican national oil company Pemex and renamed* Toteco. *She was broken up during 1971–72 (Union Oil Co)*

Union Oil Co: La Purisima, *built by Southwestern Shipbuilding Co, San Pedro, pictured on trials on October 15 1921. In 1943 she was transferred to the Soviet Union on bareboat charter and renamed* Taganrog. *She transferred back to the US the following year under the WSA and reverted to her original name.* La Purisima *was broken up in 1948 (Union Oil Co)*

Union Oil Co: Utacarbon *was built by Bethlehem Shipbuilding Corp, Alameda, California, and completed in 1920. She was transferred on bareboat charter to the Soviet Union in 1943 and renamed* Varlaam Avanesov, *and in 1945 went back to the US flag as the WSA's* Utacarbon. *She was at Pearl Harbor in June 1945 and it was intended that she be renamed* Yucca, *but this did not materialise and* Utacarbon *was broken up in 1946 (Union Oil Co)*

Pennsylvania	1917	BethFR	6390	9830	416.8	56–1	26–7	9.5
Reaper	1920	Texas	6407	9940	416.8	56–1	26–9	10.0
Rhode Island (m)	1937	SunSBD	8562	12,382	490–6	65–4	28–0	13.0
Roanoke	1920	Texas	6425	10,038	416.8	56–1	26–9	10.0
Shenandoah	1919	Texas	6414	10,026	416.8	56–1	26–9	10.0
Texas	1916	BethFR	6368	9830	416.8	56–1	26–7	9.5
Virginia	1917	BethFR	6390	9830	416.8	56–1	26–7	9.5
Washington	1920	Moore2	7030	10,620	438–5	57–2	27–1	10.0
ex Helen Olmsted 29, ex Cape Ann 26, ex Sapulpa 23								

Note: * Balboa Transport Corp was jointly owned by Standard Oil Co of California (*qv*) and The Texas Co
Note: See also Texas Co (Norway) A/S in Norway section and NV Nederlandsche Pacific Tankvaart Maatschappij in Netherlands section

BALBOA TRANSPORT CORP,* Panama (Panamanian flag)

China (m2)	1938	Krupp	10,781	17,432	530–0	68–1	30–3	12.5
El Segundo	1912	NYSB1	3664	5082	321.7	46–2	23–0	9.0

TIDE WATER ASSOCIATED OIL CO, Whitehall Bldg, 17 Battery Place, New York

Funnel: Black with two orange bands
Hull: Black, red boot-topping
Trades: Oil and petroleum, Pacific area

Tankers

ASSOCIATED DIVISION,
Associated Bldg, 79 New Montgomery St, San Francisco CA

Associated (st)	1938	SunSBD	8407	12,750	462–4	65–4	28–8	13.5
Frank G Drum	1921	BethAl	7048	10,749	453–9	56–2	27–4	10.5
Mericos H Whittier	1919	BethSP	6972	9938	453–0	56–2	27–1	10.5
ex Hulaco 23								
Paul Shoup	1921	MerchC	6817	10,515	424.4	58–2	25–6	10.5
ex Playa 22								
Solana	1921	NYSB1	6703	10,026	435–10	56–6	26–11	10.5

TIDE WATER DIVISION

Axtell J Byles	1927	SunSBD	8955	14,362	497–0	66–0	28–7	11.0
Byron D Benson	1922	Daniel	7953	12,536	481–0	60–2	27–7	10.5
David McKelvy	1921	SunSB	6821	11,277	445–5	59–2	26–9	10.5
Edward L Shea	1924	NYSB1	6746	10,544	436–4	56–8	25–10	10.5
ex Priscilla 27								
Robert E Hopkins	1921	MerchC	6625	10,833	424.4	58–2	26–7	10.5
Samuel Q Brown	1921	MerchC	6625	10,833	424.4	58–2	26–7	10.5
Tide Penn	1920	Baltmr	7198	9954	450–0	59–3	26–7	10.5
ex Betterton 38								
Tide Water (m)	1930	SunSBD	8886	14,704	498–3	66–0	28–11	11.5
Tide Water Associated (m)	1930	SunSBD	8906	14,704	498–3	66–0	28–11	11.5
Tulsagas	1921	Baltmr	7110	9954	450–0	59–2	26–7	10.5
William F Humphrey	1921	BethQu	7983	13,478	468.3	62–9	29–6	10.5
ex Axtell J Byles 27, ex Agwibay 26								

Note: Also tankers under 4000gt

UNION OIL CO OF CALIFORNIA,
1102 Union Oil Bldg, 617 West 7th St, Los Angeles CA

Funnel: Black with white U
Hull: Black, red boot-topping
Services: Pacific oil and petroleum trades

Tankers

A C Rubel (st)	order	BethSP	8187	12,920	463–1	64–2	28–5	14.0
Cathwood	1920	BethAl	7071	10,749	453–9	56–0	29–0	10.0
Deroche	1919	BethAl	7059	10,749	453–9	56–0	29–0	10.0
L P St Clair (st)	1939	BethSP	8066	12,945	463–1	64–2	28–6	14.0
La Brea	1916	BethU1	6666	10,676	452–0	56–2	26–9	10.0
La Placentia	1921	BethSW	8272	12,304	440.0	58–2	30–6	10.0
La Purisima	1921	BethSW	5092	7924	392.3	51–2	27–6	10.5
Los Angeles	1916	BethU1	6752	10,676	452–0	56–2	26–10	10.0
Montebello	1921	BethSW	8272	12,304	440.4	58–2	31–0	10.0
Paul M Gregg (st)	order	BethSP	8187	12,849	463–1	64–2	28–5	14.0
Santa Maria	1922	Duncan	8432	12,957	460.0	60–3	28–8	10.5
Utacarbon	1920	BethAl	6878	10,749	453–9	56–0	27–1	10.0
Victor H Kelly (st)	bldg	BethSP	8186	12,920	463–1	64–2	28–6	14.0
Warwick (st)	1921	Baltmr	4469	6346	340.1	49–2	24–1	10.0

Note: Also coastal vessels

UNION SULPHUR CO INC, Frasch Bldg, 33 Rector St, New York

Funnel: Yellow with red 'devil' emblem, black top
Services: Sulphur transportation

Henry D Whiton (st2)	1921	Nburgh	4548	7230	370–10	51–7	25–5	11.5
Herman F Whiton	1919	NWStl	5557	8523	409.8	54–2	24–0	11.0
ex J R Gordon 29								
Herman Frasch (st2)	1920	Nburgh	4494	7304	370–10	51–8	25–4	11.5
W R Keever	1920	Nburgh	5350	8434	400.5	54–3	25–0	10.5
ex Exanthia 34, ex Half Moon 28								

Union Oil Co: Warwick *was completed at Baltimore in 1921 and throughout her career under the US flag was voyaging on the Pacific coast of the US and Canada. In 1940, she was one of several US vessels sold to Brazil, and was renamed* Santa Maria *owned by Navebras of Rio de Janeiro. From 1940 until she was broken up in 1952,* Santa Maria *was voyaging mainly from Venezuela to Brazilian oil terminals (Union Oil Co)*

United Fruit: Platano *was originally delivered in 1930 to Unifruitco under the British flag, but soon after transferred to Panamanian flag. She survived the Second World War, transferred to Honduras flag in 1947, and was sold out of the fleet in 1965. Under the name* El Toro *she was broken up soon after (Alex Duncan)*

USMC: The first C1-B type motorship Cape Alava *was also the first ship launched by the Seattle Tacoma Shipbuilding Corp, on August 1 1940. Upon entry into service in April 1941,* Cape Alava *was operated by American Mail Line. As designed there was accommodation for 8 passengers in C1 type ships, but variations up to 12 were common. Crew in the C1-B was normally 41. In 1948* Cape Alava *was sold to Union Steamship Co of New Zealand and renamed* Wairimu, *in 1966 she became the Chinese-owned* Ta Tung, *in 1969* Ta Tzong, *and was broken up in 1970 at Kaohsiung (World Ship Photo Library)*

Funnel: Yellow with black top separated by red band bearing white diamond or yellow with black top
Hull: White, red boot-topping (some smaller vessels have black hull); *Francis R Hart* – black, red boot-topping
Services: Fruit – West Indies and Central America–New Orleans/Galveston/Mobile/Baltimore/Philadelphia/New York; New York–Boston–West Indies; bulk sugar from West Indies to US ports

UNITED FRUIT CO, 1 Federal St, Boston MA and Pier 3, North River, New York

BALBOA SHIPPING CO INC, Balboa, Canal Zone (Panamanian flag)

Fruit carriers								
Darien (te,P24)	1924	Cammel	4299	3318	384–0	48–1	22–6	13.0
ex La Marea 30; conv mv, lengthened 30								
La Playa (me,P24)	1923	Cammel	3682	3238	352–7	48–1	23–8	12.0
Macabí	1921	Workmn	2802	3920	310–6	47–2	20–3	10.0
Maraví	1921	Workmn	2802	4020	310–6	47–2	20–4	10.0
Mayarí	1921	Workmn	2802	4020	310–6	47–2	20–4	10.0
Musa (te,P16)	1930	Workmn	5663	5520	434–0	56–4	25–9	15.5
Platano (te,P16)	1930	Cammel	5949	5420	433–6	56–2	25–10	15.5
San Benito (te,P12)	1921	Workmn	3724	3140	336–0	46–4	23–9	12.0
San Blas (P12)	1920	Workmn	3628	3325	336–0	46–4	23–9	12.0
San Bruno (P12)	1920	Workmn	3627	3325	336–0	46–4	23–8	12.0
San Gil (P12)	1920	Workmn	3627	3325	336–0	46–4	23–9	12.0
San Pablo (P4)	1915	Workmn	3305	3056	315.2	44–2	22–10	12.0

MAYAN STEAMSHIP CORP, Tela, Honduras (Honduras flag)

Fruit carriers								
Argual	1927	Cammel	2690	2615	314–6	44–3	20–6	12.5
Baja California	1914	ThmpR2	1648	2592	265.8	38–6	18–0	10.5
Castilla (P12/1)	1927	Workmn	3910	2600	356–0	48–0	20–3	14.0
Iriona (P10/1)	1927	Workmn	3910	2600	356–0	48–0	20–3	14.0
launched as Ciudad de Pasto, laid down as Iriona								
Orotava	1927	Steph2	2711	3470	314–0	44–2	20–4	12.5
Sinaloa	1915	ThmpR2	1648	2592	265.0	38–6	18–0	10.5
Tela (P12/1)	1927	Workmn	3901	2600	356–0	48–0	20–3	14.0
Telde	1927	Steph2	2726	2615	314–0	44–2	20–6	12.5
Tanker								
Francis R Hart (st)	1938	Bremer	7623	11,135	473–1	60–4	27–0	12.0

MUNARGO LINE CO

Passenger/fruit carrier								
Munargo (st,P190)	1921	NYSB	6336	4785	432–4	57–10	24–3	15.0

UNITED FRUIT STEAMSHIP CORP

Passenger/fruit carriers								
Toloa (s2,P131)	1917	Workmn	6495	5285	450–0	54–4	26–0	12.5
Ulua (s2,P131)	1917	Workmn	6495	5285	450–0	54–4	26–0	12.5
Fruit carriers								
Abangarez (P12)	1909	Workmn	6539	4550	394–0	50–4	24–6	12.5
Atenas (P12)	1909	Workmn	4639	4550	394–0	50–4	24–6	12.5
Calamares (s2)	1913	Workmn	7233	6057	486–5	55–4	27–4	14.5
Carrillo (P12)	1911	Workmn	4593	4227	394–0	50–4	24–10	12.5
launched as La Señora								
Cartago (P12)	1908	Workmn	4732	4660	394–0	49–10	23–0	12.5
ex General Lee 37, ex Cartago 32								
Choluteca (s2,P25)	1921	Nburgh	2494	2093	301.3	42–4	16–7	13.5
Comayagua (s2,P25)	1921	Nburgh	2494	2093	301.3	42–4	16–7	13.5
Coppename (P12)	1908	Workmn	3289	3350	339.5	42–8	23–4	12.5
Esparta	1904	Workmn	3366	1956	330.6	44–6	21–6	12.0
Heredia (P12)	1908	Workmn	4732	4660	394–0	50–5	23–0	12.0
ex General Pershing 37, ex Heredia 32								
La Perla (P24)	1925	Cammel	3793	3180	352–7	48–1	23–9	13.0
Metapan (P12)	1909	Workmn	4736	4550	394–0	50–4	24–6	12.0
Olancho (s2,P25)	1921	Nburgh	2494	2093	301.3	42–4	16–7	13.5
Parismina (P12)	1908	Workmn	4732	4660	394–0	50–4	23–0	12.0
ex General Sherman 37, ex Parismina 32								
Pastores (s2)	1912	Workmn	7242	6100	486–5	55–4	27–4	14.5
Sagua (P30)	1914	SHWR	3299	3386	331.1	45–2	21–1	11.0
ex Cuyamapa 35, ex Sagua 23, ex Van der Duyn 17								
San José (P12)	1904	Workmn	3358	3686	330.0	44–8	21–6	12.0
San Mateo (P4)	1915	Workmn	3289	3056	315.2	44–2	22–10	12.5
Santa Marta (P12)	1909	Workmn	4736	4550	394–0	50–4	24–6	12.5
Sixaola (P12)	1911	Workmn	4693	4364	394–0	50–4	24–10	12.5
Tanamo (P30)	1914	SHWR	3212	3390	331.2	45–2	21–1	11.0
ex Lempira 34, ex Tanamo 23, ex Van Hogendorp 17								
Tivives (P12)	1911	Workmn	4596	4227	394–6	50–4	24–10	12.5
Turrialba (P12)	1909	Workmn	4539	4550	394–6	50–4	24–6	12.0
Zacapa (P12)	1909	Workmn	4489	4550	394–6	50–4	24–6	12.5

UNITED MAIL STEAMSHIP CO

Passenger/fruit carriers								
Antigua (te2,P99/1)	1932	BethQu	6983	4420	447–10	60–4	25–3	17.5

Chiriqui (te2,P99/1)								
	1932	NNews	6964	4610	446–9	60–0	25–3	17.5
Jamaica (te2,P99/1)								
	1933	NNews	6968	4280	446–9	60–3	25–3	17.5
ex Peten 37, launched as Segovia								
Quirigua (te2,P99/1)								
	1932	BethQu	6983	4420	447–10	60–4	25–4	17.5
Talamanca (te2,P99/1)								
	1931	NNews	6963	4280	446–9	60–2	25–3	17.5
Veragua (te2,P99/1)								
	1932	BethQu	6983	4420	447–10	60–4	25–3	17.5

Note: Also vessels under 1500gt
Note: United Fruit Co controlled Elders & Fyffes Ltd (*qv* in Great Britain section), and had an interest in 'Union' Handels und Schiffahrts GmbH (*qv* in Germany section)

UNITED STATES MARITIME COMMISSION,

Department of Commerce Bldg, Washington DC

Funnel: Various
Hull: Black or grey
Services: See footnotes regarding services operated for USMC; (R) – in Reserve Fleet, laid up as at 31 Dec 1939

Passenger and passenger/general cargo vessels								
America (s2,P835/cab,516/t)(R)								
	1905	H&W,B	21,329	12,560	687–0	74–4	31–0	17.0
ex Amerika 17								
American Legion (st2,P260/1,170/3)								
	1921	NYSB1	13,736	10,840	535–2	72–2	30–7	18.0
building as Gopher State, laid down as Koda								
Artemis (s2,P–) (R)								
	1902	H&W,B	8414	11,925	500.5	58–4	30–3	12.0
ex Bohemia 17, ex Iowa 13								
Courageous (me,P–) (R)								
	1918	BethAl	7573	10,680	472–1	56–0	31–1	14.0
launched as War Sea; conv steamer, lengthened 28								
George Washington (s2,P573/cab,442/t,1485/3) (R)								
	1908	VulcSt	23,788	12,464	722–0	78–3	33–0	16.0
Monticello (s2,P–) (R)								
	1902	VulcSt	19,361	8700	706–6	72–4	29–0	16.0
ex Agamemnon 29, ex Kaiser Wilhelm II 17								
Mount Vernon (s2,P742/1,326/2,740/3) (R)								
	1906	VulcSt	18,372	8300	706–6	72–2	29–0	16.0
ex Kronprinzessin Cecilie 17								
Southern Cross (st2,P260/1,170/3)								
	1921	NYSB1	13,789	10,840	535–2	72–2	30–7	18.0
launched as Sea Girt, building as Badger State, laid down as Manmasco								
General cargo vessels								
Abercos (R)	1920	Standf	6076	9414	412–0	53–3	26–7	11.5
laid down as Weepuiset								
Algic (st) (R)	1920	MerchH	5496	8727	400.7	54–2	25–8	12.0
Anacortes (R)	1918	ToddDD	4889	7503	395–9	53–1	23–9	11.5
launched as War Comrade								
Arcturus	1920	Standf	6094	9400	412–0	53–2	26–7	11.5
Ashland County	1919	AmSBLo	2592	4100	261–0	43–8	24–4	9.5
Askawake (st)	1919	SeatNP	6148	9492	416–6	53–1	27–6	12.0
Bakersfield (R)	1919	BethSW	5545	8542	427–0	54–4	24–6	11.0
Bangu (R)	1919	ToddDD	4782	7699	395–9	53–1	23–9	11.5
ex Orphis 28								
Barreado (R)	1919	SeatCD	4781	7624	380.5	53–1	23–9	11.0
ex Gaffney 28								
Bayou Chico (st) (R)	1920	Pensac	5401	8534	418–0	54–2	25–5	12.0
Bellemina (st) (R)	1919	Fed1	6085	9786	411–6	55–2	27–2	12.0
Bellhaven (st) (R)	1919	Fed1	6098	9808	411–6	55–0	27–2	12.0
Bensalem (st) (R)	1919	MerchH	5513	8756	400.7	54–2	25–8	12.0
Berury (R)	1919	ToddDD	4924	7631	395–9	53–1	23–9	11.5
ex Olen 28								
Braddock (st) (R)	1919	Fed1	6629	9848	411–6	55–0	27–2	12.0
Brave Cœur (R)	1919	Skinnr	6458	9702	415–11	54–2	26–7	11.0
Brush (st) (R)	1919	AISB	5114	7825	400–4	54–2	25–0	12.0
ex Schroon 24								
Cape Alava (m,P12/1)								
	order	Tacoma	6797	7815	417–9	60–2	27–6	14.0
Cape Ann (st,P12/1)								
	order	Staten	6797	7815	417–9	60–2	27–6	14.0
Cape Clear (m,P12/1)								
	order	Tacoma	6797	7815	417–9	60–2	27–6	14.0
Cape Cod (st,P12)	order	Staten	6750	7815	417–9	60–2	27–6	14.0
Cape Douglas (m,P12/1)								
	order	Tacoma	6797	7815	417–9	60–2	27–6	14.0

Cape Fairweather (m,P12/1)	order	Tacoma	6797	7815	417–9	60–2	27–6	14.0
Cape Flattery (m,P12/1)	order	Tacoma	6797	7815	417–9	60–2	27–6	14.0
Cape Lookout (m,P12/1)	order	Penns	6750	8015	417–9	60–0	27–6	14.0
Cape May (st,P12/1)	order	Staten	6797	7815	417–9	60–2	27–6	14.0
Cape Mendocino (st,P12/1)	order	ConsSt	6750	7815	417–9	60–0	27–6	14.0
Cape Neddick (m,P12/1)	order	Staten	6750	7815	417–9	60–2	27–6	14.0
Cape San Martin (st,P12)	order	BethSF	6250	7815	417–9	60–0	27–6	14.0
Cape (unnamed) (st,P12/1)	order	ConsSt	6750	7815	417–9	60–0	27–6	14.0
Chepadoa (st)	1919	SeatNP	6035	9507	416–6	53–1	27–6	12.0
City of Weatherford (st) (R)	1920	Pensac	5401	8572	418–0	54–2	25–5	12.0
Clairton (st) (R)	1919	Fed1	6080	9808	411–6	55–0	27–2	12.0
Coaxet (R)	1919	Standf	6038	9341	412–0	53–2	26–7	11.0
Cockaponset (st) (R)	1919	PacC	5995	9627	416–6	53–0	27–6	12.0
Coelleda (st) (R)	1920	AISB	4986	8015	400–4	54–2	25–0	12.0
Cokesit	1919	Standf	6176	9600	412–0	53–0	26–7	11.0
Comet (st)	bldg	Fed2	6085	9758	459–0	63–2	25–9	15.5
Coronado (st)	1918	Moore1	5989	9400	416–0	53–0	26–6	12.0
Cotati (st) (R)	1919	Moore2	5963	8408	416–6	53–0	26–6	12.0
Courageous (me)	1918	BethAl	7573	11,700	458–0	56–0	28–7	11.5
launched as War Sea; conv steamer 28								
Culberson	1920	LosAng	5453	8350	423–2	54–2	24–0	11.0
Davenport (st) (R)	1920	MerchH	5491	8727	400.7	54–2	25–8	12.0
Deer Lodge (st) (R)	1919	NWStl	6187	8516	423–10	54–2	23–11	12.0
Eastern Planet	1920	Kwsaki	5815	9150	384.8	51–2	27–1	9.5
Eastern Queen	1918	Kwsaki	5834	9150	385.0	51–0	27–1	9.5
ex Tofuku Maru 19								
Eastern Shore	1918	Harim1	6731	11,054	425.0	53–8	28–7	9.5
Edenton (st) (R)	1918	Skinnr	6958	10,076	424–0	54–2	25–9	12.0
Edgefield (st) (R)	1918	Skinnr	6990	10,041	424–0	54–2	25–9	12.0
Edgemont (st) (R)	1919	Skinnr	6865	10,038	424–0	54–2	25–9	12.0
Edgemoor* (st) (R)	1919	Skinnr	7038	10,360	424–0	54–2	25–9	12.0
Editor (R)	1919	Skinnr	6326	9698	415–11	54–10	26–7	11.0
Eelbeck (R)	1919	Skinnr	6318	9693	415–11	54–10	26–7	11.0
Effna (R)	1919	Skinnr	6461	9696	415–11	54–10	26–7	11.0
Egremont (R)	1919	Skinnr	6864	9958	424–0	54–2	24–0	11.0
Eldena (st) (R)	1919	Skinnr	6900	10,315	424–0	54–2	25–9	12.0
Flying Cloud (st)	1939	Fed2	6085	9758	459–2	63–2	27–8	15.5
Flying Fish (st)	bldg	Fed2	6085	9758	459–2	63–2	27–8	15.5
Galveston (m) (R)	1921	DoultW	6173	9217	411–6	55–0	27–2	13.0
conv steamer 29								
George Peirce (st) (R)	1920	MerchC	5462	8747	400.7	54–2	25–8	12.0
Guimba (st) (R)	1919	Moore2	6100	8370	416–6	53–0	26–6	12.0
Higho (R)	1920	ToddDD	4828	7630	395–9	53–1	23–9	10.0
Hoxie (R)	1918	BethSP	4623	7461	377.0	52–0	29.5	10.5
Jacob Ruppert (R)	1920	WPipe	5645	8584	427–0	54–0	24–6	10.5
ex Pacific Fir 38, ex West Cahokia 25								
Jadden (R)	1919	Skinnr	6869	9958	424–0	54–2	24–0	11.0
Jalapa (st) (R)	1920	Moore2	6085	9407	416–6	53–0	26–6	12.0
Janelew (st) (R)	1920	Moore2	6085	9415	416–6	53–0	26–6	12.0
Kisnop (R)	1919	AtlC	5874	8630	427–0	54–2	24–1	11.0
Lake Elsah	1919	GLakeA	2674	4070	261–10	43–9	24–3	9.5
Lake Fernalda	1919	AmSBCl	2595	4100	261–0	43–8	24–4	9.5
Lake Flagon	1919	McDoug	2609	4145	261–0	43–9	24–4	9.5
Lake Freeland	1919	AmSBLo	3069	5250	323–0	43–7	23–1	9.5
lengthened 29								
Lake Frugality	1919	AmSBLo	3069	5250	323–0	43–7	23–1	9.5
lengthened 29								
Lightning (st)	1939	Fed2	7194	9758	459–2	63–2	25–9	15.5
Lorain (st) (R)	1919	Fed1	6213	9676	411–6	55–0	27–2	12.0
Ludington (st,P–)	1920	PuseyG	8266	12,850	439.6	60–2	24–0	12.0
Manatee (R)	1920	Daniel	5948	9569	402.1	54–0	27–0	11.0
Mercer (st) (R)	1919	Fed1	6219	9653	411–6	55–0	27–2	12.0

USMC: Sea Witch *was built by Tampa Shipbuilding and completed in February 1940. In December 1942 she entered the service of the US War Shipping Administration, having been converted at San Francisco into a transport capable of carrying 1567 troops. After the war she was laid up by the USMC, and after several changes of owner and name ended her days under the People's Republic of China flag as* Hong Qi 149
(RW Jordan collection)

Waterman SS Corp: De Soto *was completed by Columbia River Shipbuilding Corp, Portland, Oregon, in 1919, and was purchased by Pan-Atlantic in 1938. In 1943 she was sold to the Soviet Union and renamed* Luga *(pictured here). She made a few postwar trans-Pacific voyages and was apparently laid up at Vladivostok. Her fate is uncertain (Canadian Forces, Ottawa)*

Mercer Victory (st) (R)	1919	MerchH	5500	8756	400.7	54–2	25–8	12.0
Monasses (st) (R)	1919	Moore2	5983	8409	416–6	53–0	26–6	12.0
Monroe (st) (R)	1920	Nburgh	5628	8822	400.5	54–2	25–0	12.0
Mosella (st) (R)	1920	Moore2	6034	9467	416–6	53–0	26–6	12.0
Mount Evans (st) (R)	1919	Columb	6267	8624	423–10	54–2	24–1	12.0
Narcissus (st) (R)	1920	Moore2	6085	9435	416–6	53–0	26–6	12.0
New Windsor (st) (R)	1919	Nburgh	5590	8822	400.5	54–2	30.0	12.0
Nightingale (st)	1939	NNews	6085	9758	459–0	63–2	25–9	15.5
Nipmuc	1919	AtlC	5969	8630	427–0	54–2	24–1	11.0
Nockum (st) (R)	1919	Moore2	6024	8409	416–6	53–0	26–6	12.0
Oldham (m) (R)	1921	DoultW	6173	8983	411–6	55–0	27–2	13.0
conv steamer 29								
Orani (st)	1919	SeatNP	6040	9507	416–6	53–1	27–6	12.0
Oskawa (st) (R)	1918	Moore2	6100	8370	416–6	53–0	27–6	12.0
Ozette (st)	1919	SeatNP	6078	9519	416–6	53–0	27–6	12.0
Pacific Oak (R)	1919	Duthie	5622	8570	423–8	54–2	24–1	11.0
ex West Hembrie 29								
Pacific Redwood (R)	1918	Ames	5683	8682	423–2	54–2	24–1	12.0
ex Westmount 28								
Pacific Spruce	1920	WPipe	5509	8575	427–0	54–2	24–6	11.0
ex West Canon 27								
Polybius (st) (R)	1919	Skinnr	7041	10,290	424–0	54–2	24–0	12.0
Poughkeepsie (st) (R)	1919	Nburgh	5588	8822	400.5	54–2	30.0	12.0
Provincetown (st)	1920	Groton	6216	9375	402.6	53–0	33.2	12.0
Red Jacket (st)	1939	Fed2	6085	9748	459–0	62–2	25–9	15.5
Rockport (st)	1920	Pensac	5401	7600	418–0	54–2	25–5	12.0
Salaam (st) (R)	1920	MerchH	5991	8727	400.7	54–2	25–8	12.0
Sea Arrow (st,P12/1)	bldg	Moore3	7773	12,327	492–0	69–7	29–2	16.0
Sea Fox (st,P12/1)	bldg	Fed2	7773	12,768	492–0	69–7	29–1	16.0
Sea Panther (I) (st,P12/1)	bldg	Fed2	7773	12,902	492–0	69–7	29–2	16.0
Sea Panther (II)(st,P12/1)	order	Moore3	7773	12,340	492–1	69–7	29–1	16.0
Sea Star (st,P12/1)	bldg	Moore3	7773	12,327	492–1	69–7	29–1	16.0
Sea Witch (m,P12/1)	bldg	Tampa	6021	9274	459–3	63–6	27–8	15.5
Seattle Spirit (R)	1919	Duthie	5627	8553	423–8	54–2	24–1	11.0
Seminole (m) (R)	1920	Daniel	5867	9152	402.0	54–0	27–0	12.0
conv steamer 27								
Shooting Star (m,P12/1)	bldg	Tampa	6085	9758	459–3	63–6	25–9	15.5
Siletz (st) (R)	1919	Columb	5757	8610	423–10	54–2	24–1	12.0
Springfield	1920	AtlC	5641	8550	427–0	54–2	24–1	11.0
Stag Hound (st)	1939	NNews	6085	9758	459–3	63–2	25–9	15.5
Stanley (R)	1919	Skinnr	6463	9704	415–11	54–10	26–7	11.0
Surprise (m,P12/1)	order	Tampa	6022	9758	459–0	63–6	25–9	15.5
Sweepstakes (m,P12/1)	order	Tampa	6085	9758	459–0	63–6	25–9	15.5
The Angeles	1920	LosAng	5481	8350	423–2	54–5	24–0	11.0
Tolosa (R)	1920	AtlC	5527	8550	427–0	54–2	24–1	11.0
Waukau (st) (R)	1919	MerchH	6126	8888	400.7	54–2	25–8	12.0
Waukegan (st) (R)	1919	Fed1	6209	9789	411–6	55–0	27–2	12.0
West Amargosa (R)	1919	LosAng	5462	8366	423–2	54–5	24–0	11.0
West Caddoa (R)	1919	WPipe	5641	8584	427–0	54–0	24–6	11.0
West Calumb	1919	LosAng	5946	8350	423–2	54–5	24–0	11.0
West Campgaw (R)	1920	Duthie	5565	8591	423–8	54–2	24–1	11.0
West Celeron (st) (R)	1919	NWStl	5763	8782	423–10	54–2	23–11	12.0
West Celina (st) (R)	1919	NWStl	6187	8677	423–10	54–2	23–11	12.0
West Cheswald (st) (R)	1919	NWStl	5711	8587	423–10	54–2	23–11	12.0
West Chetac (R)	1919	BethSW	5627	8554	427–0	54–4	24–6	11.0
West Compo (st)	1919	NWStl	5700	8635	423–10	54–2	23–11	12.0
West Corum (st) (R)	1919	Columb	5795	8635	423–10	54–2	24–1	12.0
West Cressey (st) (R)	1918	Skinnr	5596	8595	424–0	54–2	24–0	12.0

West Durfee (st) (R)	1918	Skinnr	5522	8592	424–0	54–2	24–0	12.0
West Elcasco (st) (R)	1918	Skinnr	5766	8568	424–0	54–2	24–0	12.0
West Gotomska (st) (R)	1918	Skinnr	5728	8586	424–0	54–2	24–0	12.0
West Grama (m) (R)	1918	LosAng	5326	8028	423–0	54–4	24–0	11.5
conv steamer 27								
West Hardaway (st) (R)	1919	Columb	5702	8624	423–10	54–2	24–1	12.0
West Hartley (st)	1919	Columb	5757	8619	423–10	54–2	24–1	12.0
West Hematite (R)	1919	Duthie	5621	8556	423–8	54–2	24–1	11.0
West Honaker (m) (R)	1920	LosAng	5428	8006	423–0	54–2	24–0	11.5
conv steamer 27								
West Imboden (st) (R)	1919	Columb	5751	8624	423–10	54–2	24–1	12.0
West Jaffrey (st) (R)	1919	NWStl	5663	8533	423–10	54–2	24–0	12.0
West Kedron (R)	1920	LBeach	5620	8565	427–0	54–2	24–2	11.0
West Keene (R)	1919	LBeach	5600	8541	427–0	54–4	24–2	11.0
West Loquassuck (st)	1918	Skinnr	5644	8578	424–0	54–2	24–0	12.0
West Maximus (st) (R)	1919	Skinnr	5561	8595	424–0	54–2	24–0	12.0
West Modus (st) (R)	1919	NWStl	5690	8677	423–10	54–2	23–11	12.0
West Neris (R)	1919	BethSW	5588	8542	427–0	54–4	24–6	11.0
West Nohno (st) (R)	1919	NWStl	5769	8580	423–10	54–2	23–11	12.0
West Pocasset (st) (R)	1919	NWStl	5707	8553	423–10	54–2	23–11	12.0
West Raritans (st) (R)	1919	NWStl	5703	8544	423–10	54–2	23–11	12.0
West Saginaw (st) (R)	1919	NWStl	6187	8582	423–8	54–2	24–0	12.0
West Segovia (st) (R)	1919	NWStl	5701	8627	423–9	54–2	24–1	12.0
West Selene	1919	LosAng	5940	8400	423–0	54–4	24–0	11.0
West Totant (st) (R)	1919	Columb	5628	8649	423–10	54–2	24–1	12.0
West Wauna (st) (R)	1918	NWStl	5735	8521	423–10	54–2	23–11	12.0
West Zeda (st) (R)	1918	NWStl	5658	8500	423–10	54–2	23–11	12.0
Western Chief (st) (R)	1918	NWStl	5759	8800	423–10	54–2	23–11	12.0
Western City (st) (R)	1918	Columb	5828	8680	423–10	54–2	24–1	12.0
launched as War Arrow								
Western Hero (st)	1918	Skinnr	5611	8571	424–0	54–1	24–1	12.0
Western Maid (st) (R)	1918	NWStl	5760	8594	423–10	54–2	23–11	12.0
Western Ocean (st) (R)	1918	NWStl	5760	8800	423–10	54–2	24–0	12.0
Western Plains (st)	1918	Columb	5688	8842	423–10	54–2	24–1	12.0
Western Wave (st)	1918	NWStl	5832	8800	423–10	54–2	23–11	12.0
Westpool (R)	1918	Duthie	5724	8622	423–8	54–2	24–1	11.0
Westport (R)	1918	Ames	5665	8452	423–0	54–2	25–9	11.0
William Penn (m2) (R)	1921	PuseyG	7615	12,358	455–0	60–2	28–5	12.0
Willimantic (R)	1918	ToddDD	4857	7615	395–9	53–0	23–9	10.5
Wilscox (m) (R)	1919	Daniel	5861	9169	401.9	54–2	27–0	12.0
conv steamer 27								
Winona County (st) (R)	1919	Fed1	6049	9808	411–6	55–0	27–2	12.0
Yapalaga (st) (R)	1920	MerchH	5976	8727	400.7	54–2	25–8	12.0

Note: * Converted to training ship, renamed *American Seaman*
Note: Of the above vessels, *Cape Ann, Cape May*, were completed 1941 for Alcoa SS Co Inc (*qv*) as *Alcoa Prospector, Alcoa Pathfinder* respectively; *Cape Alava, Cape Fairweather, Cape Flattery*, were allocated to American Mail Line Ltd (*qv*) for operation; *Cape Clear, Cape Douglas*, were completed 1941 for States SS Co Inc (*qv* under Pacific Atlantic SS Co), as *Oregon, Idaho* respectively; *Cape Lookout* was completed 1941 as *Fomalhaut* for US Navy; *Cape Mendocino* and *Cape* (unnamed) were completed 1941 for New York & Cuba Mail SS Co (Atlantic Gulf & West Indies SS Lines) (*qv*) as *Agwimonte, Agwiprince* respectively; *Cape San Martin* was completed 1941 as *Santa Cruz* for American Mail Line Ltd (*qv*); *Sea Panther* (I) was completed 1940 as *Doctor Lykes* for Lykes Bros SS Co inc (*qv*)
Note: See USMC also under Cosmopolitan Shipping Co Inc, Mooremack South American Line Inc, Pacific Northwest Oriental Line, Roosevelt SS Co Inc, Southgate-Nelson Corp

WATERMAN STEAMSHIP CORPORATION, (Mobile Oceanic Line),
13th floor Merchants' National Bank Bldg, Mobile AL

Afoundria (st,P16)	1919	AISB	5010	7999	400–4	54–2	24–5	13.0
laid down as Haddix								
Antinous (st)	1920	Standf	6034	9648	412–0	53–3	26–7	13.0
Arizpa (st)	1920	MerchH	5437	8804	400.7	54–3	25–8	13.0
Azalea City (st)	1920	MerchH	5588	8800	400.7	54–2	25–8	13.0
ex Excelsior 37, ex Waterbury 29								
Bellingham (P–)	1920	LosAng	5345	8996	423–2	54–5	24–0	12.0
ex West Himrod								

Funnel: Waterman – Yellow with W on white diamond on blue band, narrow black top; MOL – MOL instead of W; Pan-Atlantic – P-A instead of W
Hull: Black, red boot-topping
Services: US Gulf ports–Puerto Rico–Haiti–Dominica–Cuba–Mexico; US Gulf ports–NW Europe

Bienville (st)	1921	MerchH	5491	8800	400.7	54–3	25–8	13.0
ex Exarch 37, ex Naamhok 28								
City of Alma (st)	1920	MerchH	5446	8804	400.7	54–3	25–8	13.0
Gateway City (st)	1920	MerchH	5432	8804	400.7	54–3	25–8	13.0
Hastings (st)	1920	Pensac	5401	8690	418–0	54–2	25–5	13.0
Iberville (st)	1919	Chestr	5685	8820	400.7	54–2	25–8	12.0
ex Munmystic 37, ex Mystic 29								
Ipswich (st)	1919	Chestr	5671	8820	400.7	54–2	25–8	12.0
Jean Lafitte	1919	Ames	5773	9442	423–2	54–2	25–9	12.0
ex Everett 38, ex West Ison 28								
Kofresi (st,P16)	1920	AISB	4934	7999	400–4	54–2	24–5	13.0
ex Kenowis 39								
Lafayette	1919	SunSB	5836	10,405	434.3	57–8	27–0	11.5
Maiden Creek (st,P12)								
	1919	AISB	5031	7984	400–4	54–2	24–5	13.0
laid down as Sebewaing								
Pan Gulf (st)	1918	Duthie	5599	8594	423–8	54–2	24–1	11.0
ex Barbara Cates 38, launched as War Topaz								
Topa Topa (P–)	1920	LosAng	5356	8366	423–3	54–5	24–0	12.0
Wacosta (st)	1920	MerchH	5432	8804	400.7	54–2	25–8	13.0
Warrior	1920	PuseyG	7551	12,650	455–0	60–2	28–5	12.0
ex John Jay 37								
West Kyska (st)	1918	NWStl	5552	8480	423–10	54–2	24–0	12.0
West Madaket (st)	1918	Skinnr	5565	8573	424–0	54–2	24–0	12.0
Yaka (st)	1920	MerchH	5432	8804	400.7	54–2	25–8	13.0
PAN-ATLANTIC STEAMSHIP CORP								
De Soto	1919	Columb	5591	8635	423–10	54–3	24–1	11.5
ex Pan Atlantic 38, ex Dorothy Cahill 38, ex West Wauneke 29								
Pan Atlantic	1920	LBeach	5411	8582	427–0	54–5	24–2	11.0
ex Desoto 38, ex Eleanor Christenson 38, ex Vinita 25								
Pan Kraft	1919	WPipe	5644	8584	427–0	54–2	24–6	11.0
ex New York 37, ex West Kader 27								
Pan Royal	1918	BethSW	5627	8600	427–0	54–4	24–6	11.0
ex Exford 33, ex West Carnifax 28								
Panama City	1920	ToddDD	4846	7667	395–9	53–1	23–9	11.0
ex Exbrook 33, ex Ossa 28								

Services: Whaling

WESTERN OPERATING CORPORATION,
100 West 10th St, Wilmington DE, and 26 Broadway, New York

Whale factory vessel

Ulysses	1915	BethMS	12,395	–	514.0	65–3	36.5	10.0
conv tanker 37; conv general cargo 30								

Funnel: Blue with tree emblem in yellow
Hull: Black, red boot-topping
Services: Lumber trades W coast US–E coast US

WEYERHAEUSER TIMBER CO, Post Office Drawer 629, Newark NJ

WEYERHAEUSER STEAMSHIP CO

Hanley	1920	BethSF	7583	11,700	457–6	56–0	28–8	12.0
Heffron	1919	BethAl	7611	11,700	457–6	56–0	28–8	12.0
Hegira	1919	BethAl	7588	11,700	457–6	56–0	28–8	12.0
Pennsylvania	1920	BethSW	5595	8560	427–0	54–4	24–6	11.0
ex West Nomentum 28								
Pomona	1920	BethSF	7583	11,725	457–11	56–0	28–8	12.0
Winona (st)	1919	Fed1	6197	9861	411–6	55–0	27–2	12.0
ex Exporter 37, ex The Lambs 28								

Services: General tramping

Notes: * Sold American Coast Line 1939, renamed *Eastern Trader*; ** sold Norway 1939, renamed *Nidarland*

WISCONSIN STEAMSHIP CO INC, 165 Broadway, New York

Erica Reed* (st)	1920	AISB	5117	7800	400–4	54–2	24–5	12.0
ex Conness Peak 38								
Wisconsin**	1919	Standf	6076	9414	412–0	53–0	26–7	10.5
ex Wawalona 28								

Uruguay

ADMINISTRACIÓN NACIONAL DE PUERTOS – MONTE VIDEO, Calle Juan Carlos Gomez y Calle 25 de Agosto, Montevideo

Presidente Terra	1912	GrayX	3646	6600	360.0	51–0	22–2	8.5
ex Michalis 37, ex Oakfield 33								

Funnel: Black with white ANP on black disc bordered by red circle
Services: Montevideo–NW Europe–UK

COMPAÑÍA URUGUAYA DE NAVEGACIÓN LTDA, Calle Piedras 351, esquina Solis, Montevideo, Uruguay

Parana	1915	TyneIr	3286	4876	349–7	46–11	21–2	10.0
ex Gaboon 33								

Funnel: Yellow, black top
Services: Uruguay–Argentina –Brazil
Note: This company, which also operated River Plate services, was controlled by Compañía Argentina de Nav Mihanovich Ltda (*qv* in Argentina section), to whose ownership and Argentinean flag *Parana* was transferred in 1939

Yugoslavia

'ALCESU' PAROBRODARSKO DRUSTVO S O J, Orebic, and Post pretinac 163, Susak

Services: General tramping

Bosiljka	1896	Curle	3009	4700	322.0	42–4	22–7	7.0
ex Falco 35, ex Bia 21, ex Augusta 18, ex Polycarp 12								
Karmen	1896	Dixon1	2541	3700	312.2	42–9	20–0	8.0
ex Edoardo 32, ex Gianni 32, ex Algeria 25, ex Algerie 25, ex Minneburg 08								
PAROBRODARSKO DRUSTVO JUGOLEVANT S O J								
Vido	1906	HwldtK	1919	3700	294–11	42–1	19–9	8.5
ex Aarö 39, ex Børglum 28, ex Secalia 10								

ATLANTSKA PLOVIDBA DD, (Atlantic Navigation Co Ltd), Strossmayerova ulica 17, Susak

Funnel: Black with white R on blue band
Services: General tramping

Senga	1913	Duncan	5140	8270	418–4	53–0	24–2	9.5
ex Lasta 36, ex Naana 35, ex Manchurian Prince 33, ex Ardgair 18								
Slava	1911	Doxfrd	4512	7510	369.5	50–0	23–7	9.0
ex Wynacre 31, ex Tafna 26								
Sloga	1913	GrayX	4316	7260	365.2	50–10	23–3	8.5
ex Brynymor 32, ex Pensilva 31								
Sréca	1918	Workmn	5355	8170	412–11	52–4	25–3	10.5
ex Eglantier 39, ex War Beetle 19								
JADRAN BRODARSKO DRUSTVO S O J								
Lucijana	1928	Burntd	4067	7750	380–11	51–5	24–0	10.0
ex Offham 37, ex Pentyne 33								

Note: This company was associated with Jugoslavenska Plovidba dd (*qv* below)

BABAROVIC, ANT, Post pretinac 57, Susak

Services: General tramping

Milena	1912	ThmpsJ	6348	9650	403.0	52–4	28–8	11.0
ex Chincha 39								
Princ Pavle	1918	Short2	5263	8302	413–6	52–5	25–4	10.5
ex Valparaiso 35, ex Coquimbo 32, ex Nevesinje 29, ex Savannah 27, ex Grecian Prince 24, ex War Hind 19								
LEVANT DD								
Kotor	1904	GrayX	3678	6100	339.6	48–0	22–4	8.0
ex Eurymedon 39, ex Stylianos 35, ex Sverre 27								

Note: Also *Anton* (built 1919/1480gt), *Ivan* (14/1275)

BANAZ & RUSKO, Dubrovnik 2

Services: General tramping

PLOVIDBA RAD								
Rad	1910	Irvin3	4201	7600	370.3	51–5	23–9	9.5
ex Thistletor 30								

DUBROVACKA PLOVIDBA ACKIONARSKO DRUSTVO, (Ragusa Steam Navigation Co Ltd), Placa Kralja Petra, Dubrovnik

Funnel: Yellow, narrow black top
Hull: Passenger vessels – white, red boot-topping; cargo vessels – black, red boot-topping with white dividing line

Bosanka	1905	Nthmb1	3456	6184	351–3	46–10	22–8	8.0
Dubac	1901	Blumr1	2819	4850	319.7	46–1	20–3	8.0

Services: Dubrovnik–Bari–Greece–Anatolia–Egypt–Syria–Asia Minor; worldwide general tramping

Note: Also vessels under 2000gt and others operated on local services

Dubravka	1905	Rhead2	3798	6428	347.0	49–2	22–8	8.25
ex Maria Immaculata 22								
Dubrovnik	1938	Lithgw	5156	9150	448–6	56–2	24–9	10.5
Durmitor	1913	LithR	5638	9467	436–9	56–0	31–0	10.5
ex Plutarch 31								
Federiko Glavic	1923	Workmn	5283	9830	432–7	54–8	25–2	10.0
Nikola Pàsic	1927	Hamtn2	4753	8194	390.6	52–0	24–0	10.0
Princ Andrej	1930	Lithgw	5041	9420	432–0	55–0	25–0	10.0
Srebreno	1901	Rhead2	3304	5800	331.0	47–1	22–4	8.0
ex Leopoldina 22								
Sveti Vlaho	1928	Lithgw	5965	9800	439–6	56–0	25–5	9.5

FERIC, BRODARSTVO, Split

Funnel: Black, four blue bands
Hull: Black
Services: General tramping

Note: Also vessels under 1000gt

Sveti Duje	1902	LithR	3624	5960	339.2	46–0	23–4	8.0
ex Monte Maggiore 30, ex Chlumecky 22								
Vicko Feric	1911	Nthmb1	4173	7560	370.2	51–0	23–7	8.5
ex Ante Topic 39, ex Oreland 31								

GRGIC, PAROBRODARSKO DRUSTVO, S O J, Sinjska ulica 7, Split

Services: General tramping

Talas	1895	GrayX	2480	3976	304.0	44–0	20.7	7.0
ex Fina 32, ex Fina Saglimbene 26, ex Hocking 25, ex Grönland 16, ex Ameland 15, ex Parklands 99								

JUGOSLAVENSKA KOMERCIJALNA PLOVIDBA DD, Susak

Funnel: Black with white diamond on blue band
Hull: Black
Services: General tramping

Perast	1911	Short2	3871	6663	355.5	51–0	22–1	8.0
ex Anderton 30, ex Coquetmede 26, ex Thornhill 19								

JUGOSLAVENSKA OCEANSKA PLOVIDBA DD, (Yugoslavian Ocean Navigation Co), Strossmayerova ulica 6, Sisak

Services: General tramping

Drava	1919	RottDD	3505	6364	375–0	49–11	21–6	9.0
ex Essex Druid 38, ex Kediri 24								
Velebit	1911	ArmWh1	4153	7280	378.2	52–4	22–8	8.5
ex Atlantica 33, ex Gróf Khuen Hédervàry 24								

JUGOSLAVENSKA PLOVIDBA DD, (Yugoslavian Navigation Co), Strossmayerova ulica 17, Susak

Funnel: Black
Hull: Black
Services: General tramping

Note: *, ** Sold Norway 1939, renamed *Vest* and *Aust* respectively; *** sold Greece 1939, renamed *Rio Grande*
Note: This company was associated with Atlantska Plovidba dd (*qv* above) and Ambrose, Davies & Matthews Ltd (*qv* in Great Britain section)

Galeb*	1920	Brtrm2	5074	8250	413–1	52–3	25–2	10.0
ex Cefnybryn 36, ex Ardenhall 36, ex Silverbirch 24, ex Stonewall 22								
Labud	1918	Hamtn2	5334	8750	419–0	52–8	24–6	9.5
ex Ezra 34, ex Apsleyhall 32, ex Silverash 25, ex Ardgowan 22								
Lasta**	1920	Ropnr3	5630	8475	390.0	52–6	25–11	10.5
ex Danybryn 38, ex Nailsea Manor 37, ex Nailsea Court 36, ex H H Asquith 32								
Orao	1919	GrkDY	5135	8250	412–6	52–4	25–3	10.5
ex Ger-y-Bryn 38, ex Beechpark 37								
Sokol***	1919	Lithgw	5695	9450	437–7	56–0	25–5	10.0
ex Nile 33								

JUGOSLAVENSKI LLOYD ACKIONARSKO DRUSTVO, Gunduliceva ulica 3, Post pretinac 80, Zagreb

Funnel: Pale blue, black top
Hull: Black, red boot-topping
Services: Passenger and cargo – Yugoslavian ports–Buenos Aires, Rosario, Santa Fé, Bahia Blanca, Montevideo; passenger vessels – Trieste–Dubrovnik–Piraeus–Haifa–Alexandria (summer), cruising (winter)

Passenger vessels								
Kraljica Marija (s2,P365/t)								
	1906	Workmn	10,196	7810	532–5	61–4	27–2	13.0
ex Araguaya 30								
Princesa Olga (s2,P206/1,28/2,64/3)								
	1915	Workmn	8480	5400	467–0	57–9	25–6	13.8
ex Ebro 35								
General cargo vessels								
Aleksandar I	1927	Lithgw	5948	9750	439–6	56–0	25–5	11.0
Avala	1929	Doxfrd	6378	10,760	440–2	58–3	26–5	10.0
Carica Milica	1928	Doxfrd	6371	9950	440–2	56–1	25–7	10.0
Istok	1913	LithR	5904	9670	438–0	56–0	25–4	9.0
ex Mongolian Prince 28, ex Verdala 17								

Jugoslavenska Plovidba: Labud *was completed in July 1918 for British owners, and after four name changes became* Labud *in 1934. On June 19 1940 she was torpedoed by* U32 *and sunk in the North Atlantic when on voyage from Table Bay to Liverpool with a cargo of maize (R Sherlock)*

Jugoslavenski Lloyd: The steamer Aleksandar 1 *was completed for these owners in May 1927 by Lithgows at Port Glasgow. She survived the Second World War, and with the reorganisation of Yugoslav shipping in 1946 was transferred to Jugoslavenska Slobodna Plovidba of Rijeka and renamed* Biokovo. *She gave several years' postwar service, before being broken up at Split in 1964 (Alex Duncan)*

Jugoslavenski Lloyd: Completed by Doxford at Sunderland in February 1928, Carica Milica *was an early war loss, having struck a mine, laid by* U19, *and sunk in the North Sea. She was on voyage from Newcastle to Dubrovnik with a cargo of coal (Alex Duncan)*

A Topic: Olga Topic *entered service in May 1918 as* Trevose *for Hain Steamship Co. She was sold to Yugoslavia in 1935. Serving the Allied cause apparently without coming to any harm, she was released to Yugoslavia after the ceasefire and was one of many Yugoslavian vessels which were transferred in 1946 to the newly-formed state-controlled shipping entities. Her new owners were Jugoslavenska Slobodna Plovidba, of Rijeka, under whose flag she remained in service for just under four years as* Kosmaj. *Early in 1950 she left Rosario for Rotterdam with a cargo of linseed. On February 25 she had a fire and was abandoned southeast of St Paul Rocks, but was taken in tow for Fortaleza. The fire was extinguished, but broke out again and the vessel was gutted. In April 1950 she was settled by insurers as a constructive total loss (Alex Duncan)*

Oceania: The steamer Dinara *was completed at the Wilton shipyard in Rotterdam in August 1917 and when purchased by Yugoslavia in 1936.* Dinara *was the fifth name to be held by the vessel. In 1946 she was transferred to the newly-formed Jugoslavenska Linijska Plovidba and was renamed* Split. *She remained under the Yugoslavian flag until broken up during 1961–62 (RW Jordan collection)*

Dubrovacka: Pictured postwar, Durmitor *put in several years' service before being broken up at Split in 1963. She had been completed in 1913 by Russell & Co, Port Glasgow, as* Plutarch *for Lamport & Holt. In 1931 she was sold to Yugoslavia and renamed* Durmitor. *On October 21 1940 she was captured by the German auxiliary cruiser* Atlantis *in the Sunda Strait. Four months later, in February 1941, she was retaken at Mogadishu by the cruiser HMS* Shropshire. *As* Radwinter *she was transferred to the Ministry of War Transport, and having come through the rest of the war unscathed, was returned to Yugoslavia in 1946 and reverted to* Durmitor *(Alex Duncan)*

Ivo Racic	1907	Rhead2	3718	6560	350.4	49–1	23–0	8.0
ex Dan 24, ex Gerolamo Ulloa 24, ex Dan 17								
Izgled	1911	Dobson	4338	7770	395–0	53–4	23–2	8.5
ex Auguszta Föherczegnö 22								
Marija Petrinovic	1918	Nthmbl	5684	8900	412–10	53–0	26–3	10.0
ex Efstathios 24, ex War Citadel 20								
Marija Racic*	1911	ArmWhl	4211	7280	378.1	52–4	22–8	8.5
ex Atlantica 22								
Nemanja	1918	Brtrm2	5226	8220	412–9	52–3	25–3	10.5
ex Hoosac 26, ex Trojan Prince 24, ex War Perch 19								
Njegos	1908	McMlln	4387	7510	375.3	52–0	24–2	8.0
ex Norman Isles 26, ex Suruga 24								
Preradovic	1907	Bremer	5341	8750	420.5	54–6	25–7	9.0
ex Riol 21								
Tomislav	1928	Duncan	5387	8725	403.0	52–5	24–6	10.0
Trepca	1930	AyrDk	5042	8920	407.0	53–8	24–4	10.0
Triglav	1929	Doxfrd	6363	10,760	440–2	58–2	26–5	10.0
Vidovdan	1906	SHWR	5586	9450	435–9	55–4	25–1	8.0
ex Braunfels 24								
Vojvoda Putnik	1916	Nthmbl	5876	9450	400.0	52–0	28–5	9.5
ex Blossom Heath 22, ex Kerry Range 19								
Zrinski	1920	Nthmbl	5635	8850	412–9	53–0	26–3	9.0
ex Erle 27, launched as War Chateau								

Note: * Sold Great Britain 1939, renamed *Marcrest*

KVARNER BRODARSKO DD, Set aliste Prestolnsl Petra 27, Susak

Services: General tramping

Dinaric	1919	DunlpB	2555	3950	313–0	42–11	19–10	9.5
ex Coatsworth 39, launched as War Lemon								

MAROVIC, G J, Via della Borsa 2, Casella Postale 104, Trieste, Italy

Services: General tramping

PAROBRODARSKO DRUSTVO MAROVIC S O J,
Jelacicev 3, Susak, Yugoslavia

Neti	1900	Pgill1	2908	4875	324.0	47–1	20–6	7.0
ex Jela Topic 39, ex Olga Topic 35, ex Ben Corlic 28, ex Frank Parish 22								

Note: Also *Pavia* (built 1895/1419gt), *Petar* (10/1806)

MATKOVIC, BRODARSKO PODUZECE EUGEN, Split

Services: General tramping

Ante Matkovic (st)	1920	Bretgn	2710	3800	302–0	43–4	20–0	10.0
ex Mossi 34								
Ivo Matkovic (st)	1920	Bretgn	2527	3800	302–0	43–4	20–0	10.0
ex La Rochefoucauld 34								
Lina Matkovic	1914	Nüscke	2317	3400	304–0	41–6	17–10	9.0
ex Emile Delmas 36, ex Arucas 21								
Ljubica Matkovic (st)	1919	SubmBC	3252	5350	335–6	46–3	22–2	9.5
ex Phyllis Soto 38, ex Chetopa 37								
Nikolina Matkovic (m2)	1918	LBeach	3898	5625	340.5	48–0	24.7	10.0
ex Carriso 37, ex Magunkook 23; conv steamer 23								

Note: Also *Niko Matkovic* (built 1906/1425gt)

OCEANIA, BRODARSKO ACKIONARSKO DRUSTVO, (Oceania Shipping Co Ltd), Susak

Funnel: Black with white O on red band
Hull: Black with white band, red boot-topping
Services: Adriatic–Marseilles – Morocco–Canary Islands; Adriatic–Egypt; Adriatic–Spain –Morocco; Adriatic–London; general tramping

Bor	1910	Doxfrd	3518	6500	360.2	50–4	21–1	8.5
ex Izrada 35, ex Poldennis 21, ex Izrada 15								
Dinara	1917	Wilton	3156	5530	337–4	47–2	21–8	9.0
ex Ruurlo 36, ex Uuras 35, ex Ruurlo 32, ex Eigen Hulp II 19								
Dunav	1912	Dobson	4307	7780	390–7	53–4	23–8	8.5
ex Izabran 36, ex Polish Monarch 22, ex Polmont 16, ex Karpat 15								
Kostrena	1902	Napr&M	2562	4400	314.0	44–0	19–11	8.5
Plavnik	1922	SMvJS	2733	3780	342–9	45–2	19–0	9.0
ex Matignon 36, ex Schleswig-Holstein 28								
Sava	1910	CRDA1	3403	5125	330.2	46–4	21–1	9.0
ex Nereide 24								
Sud	1901	Rodger	2520	4420	314.4	44–0	20–0	7.5
Susak	1927	Rhead3	3839	6560	388.8	52–6	21–7	9.0
ex Hazelwood 38; lengthened 34								

Timok	1924	Wilton	3117	5636	341–1	47–0	21–11	9.5
ex Emmy L-D 33, ex Oisterwijk 24								
Vid	1910	Doxfrd	3547	6500	360.5	50–4	21–0	8.5
ex Istina 35								

Note: Also *Una* (built 1904/1397gt) and *Vis* (21/1772)

Services: General tramping

PETRINOVIC & CO LTD, 160 Gresham St, Bishopsgate, London EC2

Manager for
FRANO PETRINOVIC, Split, Yugoslavia

Balkan	1911	GrayX	4125	7580	396–4	53–6	24–10	9.0
ex Epsilon 38, ex Madras City 33, ex Langholm 19								
Supetar	1909	GrayX	3748	6380	346.4	50.8	23.1	8.5
ex Maria N Roussou 35, ex Caterino 21								

Funnel: Black with blue six-pointed star on red band
Hull: Black
Services: Mediterranean, UK and R Plate trades; general tramping

PREKOMORSKA PLOVIDBA DD, (Overseas Navigation Co Ltd), Gunduliceva ulica 3, Zagreb

Korana	1929	Duncan	5407	8700	403.0	52–5	24–6	10.0
Kupa	1917	Rhead3	4382	8150	412–0	52–1	24–2	9.5
ex Trewidden 37								
Lika*	1919	SHWR	5278	9290	412–6	52–5	25–3	10.0
ex Kobac 38, ex Cefn-y-Bryn 38, ex Dacre Castle 37								
Recina	1930	GraySd	4732	8750	413–6	54–2	24–10	10.0
ex Lady Plymouth 32								
Zvir	1926	Clyde	5607	8750	403–11	54–0	25–7	9.5

Note: * Sold Great Britain 1939, renamed *Milcrest*

Services: General tramping

SLOBODNA PLOVIDBA DRUSTVO S O J, Dubrovnik

Duba	1910	ThmpsJ	4115	7200	351.7	51–0	23–3	8.5
ex Collingham 30								

Funnel: Black with red cross on white rectangle
Hull: Black with white band, red boot-topping
Services: General tramping

TOPIC, ANT, Via San Nicolo 7, Casella Postale 63, Trieste, Italy, and Susak

SLOBODNA PLOVIDBA TOPIC DD, Susak, Yugoslavia

Ante Topic*	1911	Nthmb1	4173	7560	370.2	51–0	23–7	8.5
ex Oreland 31								
Ivan Topic	1920	Rhead3	4943	8030	401–3	53–7	24–6	10.0
ex Ronda 37								
Jela Topic**	1900	Pgill1	2908	4875	324.0	47–1	20–6	7.0
ex Olga Topic 35, ex Ben Corlic 28, ex Frank Parish 22								
Jurko Topic	1919	Hendn2	5160	8270	412–10	52–4	25–4	10.5
ex Trematon 37, launched as War Lily								
Olga Topic	1918	Rhead3	4375	8150	413–0	52–1	24–2	10.5
ex Trevose 35								
Serafin Topic	1913	Rhead3	4259	7908	369.9	51–1	24–2	9.0
ex Wien 33, ex Trevilley 32								

ILIRIJA DD ZA BRODARSTVO, (Ilirija Navigation Co Ltd), Zagreb, Yugoslavia

Rosina Topic	1913	Rhead3	4299	7913	369.9	51–1	24–2	9.0
ex Trevider 33								

Note: * Sold Brodarstvo Feric 1939, renamed *Vicko Feric*; ** sold G J Marovic 1939, renamed *Neti*

Services: General tramping

ZETSKA PLOVIDBA ACKIONARSKO DRUSTVO, Cetinje

Boka	1920	CanVic	5399	8400	413–1	52–5	25–4	10.5
ex Canadian Planter 36								

Note: Also vessels operated on local services

Losses

Losses 1.1.1939–31.12.1945 through marine hazard
Losses 3.9.1939–31.12.1945 through Second World War causes, including Axis states' vessels ceded to or prizes of Allied nations
Losses through Spanish Civil War causes 1939
Vessels scuttled for war purposes
Vessels sunk as breakwaters Mulberry Harbour, Normandy
Vessels sunk postwar with surplus war materials
Vessels lost postwar through striking mines
Changes of name, flag, role, and disposals 1939–45

Listed in this section are the hundreds of Second World War ocean-going vessel losses, and many of the changes of name, flag, role and disposals which occurred.
These include vessels lost by either marine causes or by war causes from January 1 1939 to December 31 1945. A few vessels lost in 1939 by Spanish Civil War causes are also listed.
Vessels scuttled as blockships are listed separately from war losses, except those which were scuttled by retreating forces, such as in French ports from July 1944.
Vessels sunk as breakwaters in Mulberry Harbour, Normandy, are listed, as are the many vessels scuttled postwar with surplus war materials, such as poison gas shells, and also vessels which were lost postwar as a result of striking mines.
To avoid numerous cross-references vessels are usually listed by the name under which they were in service in 1939, followed, where applicable, with dates and changes which occurred prior to loss.
Changes of name, flag, role, and disposals which occurred during the war years are listed.
Where appropriate, details of changes occurring up to the late 1940s are also shown, for example where troopships had such service extended well beyond the war years.

Explanatory notes

Dates of losses: Dates quoted are generally consistent with Lloyd's wartime publications and are therefore based on Greenwich Mean Time (GMT).
Positions of losses: There has been much variation in published official sources, many entries in which have been proven erroneous. Positions quoted here are extracted from official sources thought to be accurate.
Fatalities, numbers survived, etc: There is also much variation in published official sources. Most figures quoted are extracted from Lloyd's and US Coast Guard wartime publications for Allied and neutral vessels and usually accurate sources for enemy vessels.

The following abbreviations are used in these sections

Vessels

abv	armed boarding vessel
a/c	aircraft
accom	accommodation (ship)
Adm	Admiralty
amc	Armed merchant cruiser
ar	arrived
aux	auxiliary
BC RAF	Bomber Command, Royal Air Force
BU	broken up
CC RAF	Coastal Command, Royal Air Force
commd	commissioned
conv	conversion/converted
CTL	constructive total loss
est	estimated
FAA	Fleet Air Arm
fl	flotilla
GMSA	German Minesweeping Administration
HMAS	His Majesty's Australian Ship
HMCS	His Majesty's Canadian Ship
HMNZS	His Majesty's New Zealand Ship
HMS	His Majesty's Ship
IJN	Imperial Japanese Navy
IN	Italian Navy
(ind)	sailing independently (not in convoy)
KM	Kriegsmarine
LSH	Landing ship headquarters
LSI	Landing ship infantry
Lt	Light (lighthouse)
LU	laid up
LV	Light vessel

MN	Marine National (French navy)
MoS	Ministry of Shipping
MoT	Ministry of Transport (succeeded MoWT in April 1946)
MoWT	Ministry of War Transport (although the May 1941 successor of Ministry of Shipping and Ministry of Transport, MoWT is used largely)
NEI	Netherlands East Indies
obv	Ocean boarding vessel
Opn	Operation
RAF	Royal Air Force
RAN	Royal Australian Navy
RCN	Royal Canadian Navy
reconv	reconverted
req	requisitioned
RIN	Royal Indian Navy
RN	Royal Navy
RNN	Royal Netherlands Navy
SAAF	South African Air Force
sd	sailed
Sq	Squadron
subm	submarine
TAF	Tactical Air Force
TL	total loss
transf	transferred
USAAF	United States Army Air Force
USCG	United States Coast Guard
USMC	United States Maritime Commission
USN	United States Navy
USS	United States Ship
VTS	Verwundetentransport schiff
WSA	United States War Shipping Administration
WT	Wireless transmission

Flags

Arg	Argentina
Bel	Belgium
Br	Great Britain
Brz	Brazil
Bul	Bulgaria
Can	Canada
Chl	Chile
Chn	China
CR	Costa Rica
Cub	Cuba
Cze	Czechoslovakia
Dmk	Denmark
Dom	Dominican Republic
Egy	Egypt
Eir	Eire (Republic of Ireland)
Est	Estonia
Fin	Finland
Fra	France
Ger	Germany
Gre	Greece
Hon	Honduras
Ind	India
Ita	Italy
Jpn	Japan
Lat	Latvia
Leb	Lebanon
Lit	Lithuania
Mex	Mexico
Ne	Netherlands
NF	Newfoundland (British)
Nor	Norway
Pal	Palestine
Pan	Panama
Per	Peru
Phi	Philippines (US)
Pol	Poland
Por	Portugal
Rom	Romania
Rus	Russia (Union of Soviet Socialist Republics)

SA	South Africa
Spn	Spain
Swe	Sweden
Swi	Switzerland
Tha	Thailand
Tur	Turkey
Uru	Uruguay
US	United States of America
VFr	Vichy France
Yug	Yugoslavia

Convoys
Convoy numbers are quoted in many cases, and in others vessels lost while sailing independently are shown – (ind)

Personnel

†	preceded by number – number of fatalities in or following casualty/loss, includes crew, gunners, guards, passengers
intnd	interned
pow	prisoner(s) of war
reptr	repatriated
surv	survivors

Argentina

Loss through war causes
Uruguay 27.5.40 Torpedoed by *U37* 43 40N 12 16W, sunk by explosive charge (15†, 13 surv)

Belgium

Losses through marine hazard
Ampetco 18.9.44 Collision with *Punta Gorda* 5m off Cape San Roman, on fire; towed St Nicholas; 4.45 sunk as torpedo target off Curaçao
Astrida 19.3.45 In distress in heavy weather 75m SE of Port Elizabeth; foundered in tow 34 35S 26 50E (–†, 29 surv)
Brabo 14.3.42 Collision with *Poznan* (*qv*) off Blyth; towed Shields harbour, aground; TL; 49–50 wreck salved, partly BU *in situ*
Flandres 12.2.40 Collision with *Kabolo* (*qv*), sank, 0.5m S of Goodwin Fork buoy, 51 12 51N 01 27 21E
Kabinda 8.12.39 Ashore E of W Goodwin buoy 51 15 03N 01 29 17E, broke in two; TL
Louis Sheid 7.12.39 Stranded near Salcombe, refloated, stranded again at Leas Foot beach, Thurlestone, 50 15 48N 03 52 12W (46 surv); broke in two, TL
Mobeka 19.1.42 Ashore Carskey Bay, Mull of Kintyre; TL

Losses through war causes
Albertville 11.6.40 Bombed by German aircraft, sunk, Havre roads (to evacuate British and French troops)
Alex van Opstal 15.9.39 Struck mine (laid 8.9.39 by *U26*), sunk, 0.5m E of Shambles LV
Antverpia 19.5.40 Bombed by German aircraft Boulogne roads; 21.5.40 beached (0†); 23.5.40 set on fire by incendiary bombs
Anvers 13.11.40 Bombed by German aircraft, sunk, 57 43N 01 49W (1†, 36 surv)

Baudouinville 6.40 Seized Bordeaux by Germans; 28.10.41 commd KM hospital ship *Lindau* (Ger); 1.1.43 accom ship Nantes; 10.8.44 scuttled Nantes by Germans; 46 raised; 47–48 BU Boom
Brabant 14.5.42 Torpedoed by *U155*, sunk, 11 32N 62 43W (3†, 30 surv)
Bruges 9.7.40 Shelled by aux cruiser *Thor*, sunk, 10 59N 23 54W (some crew pow)
Bruxelles 8.6.42 Torpedoed, shelled (in convoy TA5) by *U502*, sunk, 11 05N 66 41W (1†, 47 surv)

Carlier 11.11.43 Bombed (in convoy KMS31) by German Do217, He111 and Ju88 aircraft, sunk, 36 13N 00 05W (72†, 19 surv)

Egypte 15.8.41 Seized by French; 41 (Fra); 6.44 lost by war causes
Elisabeth van Belgie 10.9.42 Torpedoed (in convoy ON127) by *U96*, sunk, 51 30N 28 25W (1†, 49 surv)

Emile Francqui 16.12.42 Torpedoed (in convoy ON153) by *U664*, sunk, 50 58N 24 42W (46†, 41 surv)
Escaut 21.6.40 Adm charter, store carrier; 3.8.41 torpedoed by German aircraft, sunk, 232° 17.3 cables from South Beacon Ships Head, Attika Bay, Suez (3†)

Félicien Cattier 40 Keel laid; 10.5.40 seized by Germans, towed Rotterdam for completion as KM base ship *Füsilier* (Ger); 10.1.43 commd; 8.43 U-boat target ship; 9.44 transport; 20.11.44 shelled by Russian artillery, partially submerged, 55 52N 21 01E (287†; 5.12.44 wreck torpedoed by *U475*
Florida 40 Building Hoboken; 10.5.40 seized by Germans; completed for KM as U-boat target vessel; 2.4.45 bombed by Russian aircraft, on fire, sunk, 54 06N 11 07E (4†); wreck allocated Belgium; 52 raised, sold

Gand 10.5.41 Torpedoed, shelled (in convoy OB318) by *U556*, sunk, 57 54N 37 34W (1†, 43 surv)
Gandia 22.1.42 Torpedoed (convoy ON54 straggler) by *U135*, sunk, 42 45N 53W (66†, 22 surv)

Hainaut 6.7.42 Torpedoed (in convoy QS15) by *U130*, sunk, 49 13N 66 49W (1†, 42 surv); sunk 49 12N 66 55W

Indier 3.4.41 Torpedoed (in convoy SC26) by *U74*, sunk, 58 12N 27 40W (42†, 4 surv)

Jean Jadot 20.1.43 Torpedoed by *U453*, sunk, off Cape Ténès (6†, 397 surv, incl 323 army pers)
Josephine Charlotte 16.1.40 Struck mine (laid by German destroyer of 1 DD Fl), sunk, 51 28 12N 01 27 12E (4†); wreck dispersed

Kabalo 15.10.40 Torpedoed (dispersed from convoy OB223) by subm *Comandante Cappellini* (Ita), sunk, 31 59N 31 21W (1†, 42 surv)
Kasongo 26.2.41 Torpedoed (in convoy OB290) by *U47*, sunk, 55 40N 14 20W (6†)

Leopold II 23.12.41 Struck mine 52 53 48N 02 05 20E (35†, 6 surv); sunk 205° 0.5m from No 56 Buoy, off R Ouse
Leopoldville 5.40 MoWT, troopship; 24.12.44 torpedoed (in convoy WEP3, for Cherbourg) by *U486*, sunk, 49 48 08N 01 46 19W (819†, 1555 surv)
Liège 6.40 Seized by Germans; 40 (Ger); 13.3.43 shelled by British light surface craft, sunk, off Terschelling
Limbourg 29.3.41 Torpedoed (in convoy HX115) by *U48* 61 18N 22 05W (–†, 2 surv); blew up, sunk, 61 11N 22 25W
Lubrafol 42 (Pan); 9.5.42 torpedoed by *U564*, on fire 26 26N 80W (13†, 31 surv); 11.5.42 drifting on fire, sunk; 54 wreck sold for BU
Luxembourg 21.6.40 Torpedoed by *U38*, sunk, 47 25N 04 55W (0†)

Macedonier 12.12.40 Torpedoed (in convoy HX92) by *U96*, sunk, 57 52N 08 42W (4†, 37 surv)
Mercier 9.6.41 Torpedoed by *U204*, sunk, 48 30N 41 30W (7†, 61 surv)
Moanda 28.3.43 Torpedoed (in convoy RS3) by *U167*, sunk, 24 44N 16 48W (29†, 27 surv)
Moero 6.40 Seized Bordeaux by Germans; 8.8.40 KM, Seelöwe transport *H16*; 8.42 transport, Norway; 22.9.44 torpedoed by Russian aircraft, sunk, 57 26N 20 18E (582†)
Mokambo 1.5.43 Torpedoed (in convoy TS37) by *U515* 07 40N 14 05W, taken in tow (0†, 58 surv); 2.5.43 sank Freetown harbour

Olympier 30.1.41 Bombed by German aircraft 250m SW of Ireland; 31.1.41 attacked again, sunk, 56 04N 11W (8†, 19 surv)
Ostende 17.1.43 Struck mine Loch Lathaich, Mull; beached, on fire, ammunition cargo blew up (2†, 46 surv)

Persier 11.2.45 Torpedoed (in convoy BTC65) by *U1017* 340° 4m from Eddystone (20†); attempted to take in tow; 11–12.2.45 sunk Bigbury Bay, 50 17N 03 58 09W
Piriapolis 11.6.40 Bombed by German aircraft, sunk, 237° 5.25m from Antifer Light, Havre (–†), during evacuation of British forces from France
Portugal 20.1.41 Torpedoed by subm *Marcello* (Ita), sunk, about 50N 19W (0 surv)
President Francqui 28.12.42 Torpedoed (convoy ONS154 straggler) by *U225*, damaged, 43 23N 27 14W; 29.12.42 torpedoed by *U336*, sunk (5†, 1 pow, 43 surv)

Roumanie 22.9.42 Torpedoed (convoy SC100 straggler) by *U617*, sunk, 58 10N 28 20W (42†, 1 surv/pow)

Sunk Mulberry Harbour, Normandy
Belgique 44 Adm; 8.6.44 sunk as breakwater Gooseberry 4, off Juno Beach, Courseulles

Changes of name, flag, role, disposals, etc
Alex van Opstal 41 Seized by Germans; KM, V-ship base *Kannonier*; 6.8.43 U-boat target ship; 5.45 recovered Copenhagen, returned; 45 *Alex van Opstal* (Bel)
Armand Grisar 41 Seized by Germans; 41 *Grenadier* (Ger); 9.9.44 scuttled Antwerp, raised, repaired; 46 *Armand Grisar* (Bel)
Atlantier 40 Seized by Germans while building; 18.5.41 KM, transport; 28.7.43 U-boat target ship *Askari*; 1.9.43–5.45 U-boat trials/target ship; 28.6.45 (Br); 46 *Atlantier* (Bel)
Belgian Gulf 42 (Pan)
Elisabethville 40–46 Allied troopship; 46 returned; 30.5.47 MoT, *Empire Bure* (Br)
Espagne 40 Seized by Germans; 41 (Ger); 5.45 at Lübeck, returned; 45 (Bel)
Esso Belgium 40 (Pan); 45 (Bel)
Good Gulf 42 (Pan)
Gouverneur Galopin 40 Seized by Germans while building; 41 *Musketier* (Ger); 9.9.44 scuttled Antwerp by Belgians to prevent destruction by retreating Germans; 45 raised; 46 *Gouverneur Galopin* (Bel)
Lys 40 (Ger); 45 (Bel)
Mar del Plata 6.40 Seized Bordeaux by Germans; 8.40 KM, Seelöwe transport *H15*; 7.1.42 VTS, ambulance carrier; 1.45 refugee transport; 5.45 struck mine off Århus, damaged, repaired; 45 *Mar del Plata* (Bel)
Prince de Liege 8.40–10.5.44 MoWT (Br); 45 returned
Prinses Maria-Pia 10.10.40–4.46 MoWT charter; 1.11.44 Adm service; 4.46 returned
Thysville 40–9.45 Allied troopship

Brazil

Losses through marine hazard
Atalaia 25.5.41 In distress in storm, lost rudder 39 07N 01 10W (0 surv); no further reports
Ayuruoca 10.6.45 Collision with *General Fleischer* (Nor), sank, 40 12 30N 73 46 30W
Siqueira Campos 25.8.43 Collision with *Cuyabá* (*qv*) 4m off Caponga, beached; TL

Losses through war causes
Alegrete 1.6.42 Torpedoed, shelled, by *U156*, sunk, 13 40N 61 30W (0†, 64 surv)
Bagé 1.8.43 Torpedoed, shelled (convoy TJ2 straggler), by *U185*, sunk, 11 29S 36 58W (48†, 87 surv); 1.8.43 sunk
Barbacena 28.7.42 Torpedoed by *U155*, sunk, 13 10N 56W (6†, 56 surv)
Cabedello 25.2.42 Torpedoed by subm *Leonardo da Vinci* (Ita), sunk, 16N 42 30W (0 surv)
Campos 23.10.43 Torpedoed by *U170*, sunk, 24 07N 45 50W (16†, 52 surv)
Lagés 27.9.42 Torpedoed (in convoy) by *U514* 00 13N 47 47W (3†, 46 surv); sunk 00 12N 47 55W
Parnahyba 1.5.42 Torpedoed by *U162*, sunk, 10 12N 57 16W (4†, 71 surv)

Bulgaria

Loss through marine hazard
Knyaguinya Maria Louisa 30.5.41 Bombed by British aircraft, on fire, blew up, Piræus harbour entrance (–†)

Losses through war causes
Balkan 23.12.43 Torpedoed by subm HMS *Sportsman* 39 44N 25 16E; sunk off Mudros
Bourgas 45 Reported sunk at Thessaloniki; 3.48 BU *in situ*
Chipka 16.9.41 Struck mine (laid 15.9.41 by subm *L-4* (Rus)), sunk, 43 17N 28 05E (0†); 7.52 refloated; refitted for re-entry into service
Rodina 19.9.41 Struck mine, sunk, 42 23N 27 48E
Tsar Ferdinand 26.4.41 KM charter, transport; 3.9.44 hospital ship; 2.10.44 torpedoed (in convoy) by subm *Curie* (Fra) 39 20N 23 20E; sunk 19m NW of Skiathos
Varna 20.8.43 Torpedoed by subm *D-4* (Rus), sunk, 45 13N 32 35E (32†, 0 surv)

Chile

Loss through marine hazard
Antofagasta 25.7.45 Ashore Punta Tucapel, Gulf of Lebu, sunk

Changes of name, flag, etc
Aconcagua 10.8.43 US, transport (US); 48 *Giresun* (Tur)
Copiapó 10.8.43 US, transport (US); 48 *Ordu* (Tur)
Imperial 10.8.43 US, transport (US); 48 *Trabzon* (Tur)
Tarapacà 41 *Aviles* (Chl)

Denmark

When Germany occupied Denmark in April 1940, its fleet positioned outside home waters or the Baltic Sea, was transferred largely to British registration or was operated by the Danish Ship Operating Corporation (DSOC), based New York. Many vessels operated by DSOC were registered in Panama. A German–Danish agreement of May 15 1940 generally made Danish vessels in home waters available for German-controlled trade. In this list such vessels are annotated '40 German control'; except where stated, such vessels resumed normal service for their Danish owners following the liberation in 1945.

Losses through marine hazard

Aarø 40 MoWT (Br); 6.10.44 dragged anchor off N France, collision with *Yewdale* (Br), TL
Alsia 9.5.39 On fire 20m S of Barberyn Light, Ceylon, drifted ashore about 2m N of Galle; TL
Anna Mærsk 40 USMC, *Lookout* (Pan); 12.12.44 struck wreck, sunk, off Vlissingen
Bonita 40 German control; 14.10.41 collision with *Bojan* (Swe), sank, SE of Trelleborg (21† 4 surv)
Broholm 40 LU New York; 8.41 USMC, *Hindoo* (Pan); 9.9.44 collision with *Australia Star* (*qv*), sank, 11N 77 57W (0†)
Ebro 11.5.40 MoWT (Br); 8.3.42 stranded Strathbeg Bay, 2m N of Rattray Head LH; TL
Emilie Mærsk 40 German control; 14.1.41 aground off Borkum (0†); TL
Frode 11.4.40 At Norfolk VA, LU; 11.8.41 seized by US; 8.10.41 USMC, *Omaha* (Pan); 27.2.44 stranded Egret Reef, 7m E of Monkhouse Point, near Cooktown, badly damaged; 6.3.44 refloated, taken Cairns; 8.2.45 condemned; later cut down to bilges at Stockton, Hunter R, NSW; remains sank in mud following heavy weather
Herta Mærsk 40 USMC, *Montrose* (Pan); 6.7.42 stranded in fog 60 57N 45 40W; TL
Inga 40 German control; 27.4.42 lost South Horns Reef
Kalø 40 MoWT (Br); 24.9.41 collision with *Fishpool* (*qv*), sank, 19 08N 39 13E
Lily 25.4.40 Sd Kirkwall for Århus; missing (0 surv)
Manø 40 MoWT (Br); 21.8.44 wrecked Geirfuglasker, SW of Reykjanes
Nordhavet 24.9.45 Struck submerged object, sank, 46 47N 54 08W
Normandiet 40 German control; 1.8.43 collision with *Maasburg* (*qv*), broke in two, sank, R Elbe; 48 wreck dispersed
Oregon 1.7.40 Captured by RN; 40 MoWT, *Oregon I* (Br); 4.1.45 ashore Wilson's Point, near Bangor NI, broke in two; 10.45 both parts refloated, BU
Panama 15.4.40 MoWT (Br); 11.4.45 engines disabled in heavy weather, ballast shifted, capsized, sank, 44 30N 33 30W (45†, 5 surv)
Paris 15.2.41 Collision with *Selvik* (Nor) off Scarborough, beached off Boggle Hole, Robin Hood's Bay; 25.2.41 back broken; TL
Sejrø 40 German control; 41 *Poul Carl* (Dmk); 9.1.42 rammed while at anchor, sank, The Sound (0†)
Sonja Mærsk 10.5.40 MoWT (Br); 5.6.42 stranded in fog off Ketch Harbour NS in 44 29N 63 32W; sank
Stockholm 40 German control; 10.11.44 sprung leak, sank, Baltic Sea
Svanhild 40 German control; 8.11.44 collision with *Fortuna* (Ger), sank, Baltic (0†)

Losses through war causes

Aase 15.2.40 Torpedoed by *U37*, sunk, 49 17N 08 15W (15†, 1 surv)
Afrika 5.40 MoWT (Br); 7.2.43 torpedoed (in convoy SC118) by *U402*, sunk, 55 16N 26 31W (23†, 37 surv)
Agnete 40 German control; 16.3.43 torpedoed (in convoy) by *MTB88*, *MTB93* (Br), sunk, NE of Terschelling
Agnete Mærsk 5.40 MoWT (Br); 24.3.41 shelled (dispersed from convoy OG56) by subm *Veniero* (Ita), sunk, 49N 22 55W (28†, 0 surv)
Alfa 21.6.40 Torpedoed by subm HMS *H44*, sunk, 12m NW of Eierland Lt (Texel) (4†)
Algier 21.3.40 Torpedoed by *U38*, sunk, 60 17N 02 49W (5†, 20 surv)
Almena 6.40 Req by VFr; 40 *St Philippe* (Fra); 41 *Bengasi* (Ger); 11.11.42 torpedoed by subm HMS *Turbulent* 39 10N 09 39E; sunk
Alssund 41 USMC, *Bold Venture* (Pan); 16.10.41 torpedoed (in convoy SC48) by *U432*, sunk, 57N 30W (17†, 17 surv)
Amerika 5.40 MoWT (Br); 22.4.43 torpedoed (in convoy HX234) by *U306*, sunk, 57 30N 42 50W (86†, 44 surv)
Anglo Mærsk 40 MoWT (Br); 26.10.42 torpedoed (convoy SL125 straggler) by *U509*, damaged, 27 50N 22 15W; 27.10.42 torpedoed by *U604*, sunk, 27 15N 18 50W (0†, 37 surv)
Argentina 17.3.40 Torpedoed by *U38*, sunk, W of Shetlands (33†, 0 surv)
Arnold Mærsk 10.4.40 Req by MoS, transf France; 6.40 seized Bayonne by VFr; 40 *Ste Irène* (Fra); 41 German control; 22.5.43 ashore Grune aux Dardes, Nantes; TL
Astra 5.40 MoWT, *Astra II* (Br); 29.8.40 torpedoed (in convoy AO204) by *U100*, sunk, 56 09N 12 14W (5†, 21 surv)
Australian Reefer 10.4.40 LU New York; 30.6.41 req by US; 41 USMC, *Pontiac* (Pan); 11.5.42 USN, storeship USS *Pontiac* (AF 20); 30.1.45 sunk in heavy weather 44 17N 63 09W; 17.2.45 raised, repaired; 20.5.45 decomm; 21.5.45 USMC (US); 30.8.45 LU James River; 48 LU Baltimore

Australien 12.6.40 Ar Dakar, seized by VFr; 40 *St Adolphe* (Fra); 9.41 *Cuma* (Ger); 2–3.3.42 bombed by RAF Wellington bombers from Malta, exploded, sunk, Palermo; 46–48 wreck BU

Betta 6.40 Seized Dakar by VFr; 40 *Saint Albert* (Fra); 25.11.42 seized Marseilles by Germans; 42 (Ger); 18.2.43 in gale struck mole, entrance Valencia harbour, submerged; 46 wreck BU *in situ*
Bintang 5.40 MoWT (Br); 22.2.42 bombed by aircraft, sunk, 31 50N 26 01E (12†, 30 surv)
Birgit 6.40 Seized by VFr; 40 *St Etienne* (Fra); 41 *Birgit* (Ger); 12.6.43 bombed by Russian aircraft, sunk, Crimea
Birgitte 5.40 MoWT (Br); 19.11.42 torpedoed by E-boat (of German 5 MTB fl), sunk, 118° 5.5m from Eddystone Light (10†, 13 surv)
Boringia 5.40 MoWT (Br); 7.10.42 torpedoed by *U159*, sunk, 35 09S 16 32E (32†, 33 surv on *Clan Mactavish* (*qv*), sunk after picking up surv)
Britta 25.3.40 Torpedoed by *U47*, sunk, 59 45N 04 30W (13†, 5 surv)
Brosund 12.11.40 Req at Baltimore by US; 41 USMC, *Crusader* (Pan); 14.11.41 torpedoed (convoy SC53 straggler) by *U561*, sunk, 49 30N 37 15W (0 surv)

Canada 3.11.39 Struck mine (laid 10.39 by German destroyer), 2nm E of Holmpton, Spurn Head; 4.11.39 sunk 53 42 24N 00 07 06E; wreck dispersed
Canadian Reefer 18.1.40 Torpedoed by *U44*, sunk, 25m NE of Cape Villano (0†)
Caroline Mærsk 40 USMC, *Ben Brush* (Pan); 12.4.42 shelled by subm *Pietro Calvi* (Ita), on fire, sunk, 04 32S 35 03W (1†, 34 surv)
Chastine Mærsk 13.2.40 Torpedoed by *U25*, sunk, 61 30N 02E
Chile 5.40 MoWT (Br); 7.6.42 torpedoed by subm *Leonardo da Vinci* (Ita), sunk, 04 17N 13 48W (5†, 39 surv)
Chilean Reefer 22.4.40 MoWT (Br); 16.3.41 shelled (ind) by *Gneisenau*, on fire, sunk, 46 13N 44 45W (9†, 3 pow, 27 surv)
Chr J Kampmann 40 MoWT (Br); 3.11.42 torpedoed (in convoy TAG18) by *U160*, sunk, 12 06N 62 42W (19†, 8 surv)
Christiansborg 21.3.40 Torpedoed by *U38*, broke in two, 60 17N 02 49W (6†, – surv); forepart sunk 60 15N 02 40W; afterpart shelled by HM ship, sunk
Columbia 41 USMC, *Sir Huon* (Pan); 30.8.42 torpedoed by *U66*, sunk, 10 52N 54W (0†, 46 surv)
Cornelia Mærsk 40 German control; 5.1.42 sunk by British aircraft off Hook of Holland (0†)

Dagmar 4.5.40 MoWT (Br); 9.6.41 bombed (in convoy HG53) by German FW aircraft, sunk, 50 29 40N 02 00 30W (3†, 15 surv)
Danmark (8391gt) 5.40 MoWT (Br); 30.7.42 torpedoed, shelled, by *U130*, sunk, 07N 24 19W (–†)
Danmark (10,517gt) 12.1.40 Torpedoed by *U23* 58 59N 02 53W, broke in two, ashore; 21.1.40 afterpart sank, forepart refloated, taken Inverkeithing; storage hulk

Edv Nissen 5.40 MoWT (Br); 30.5.40 sunk by British to block Dunkirk harbour entrance
Eleonora Mærsk 40 MoWT (Br); 17.5.41 bombed by German aircraft, on fire, Suda Bay, Crete (20†, 7 pow, 17 surv); salved; 23.10.48–3.51 at Skaramanga (Gre); 51 reported sold Germany
Elie 40 German control; 24.11.44 struck mine, sunk, near Stolpmünde
Else 4.40 MoWT (Br); 23.4.40 seized by VFr, *Saint Blaise* (Fra); 8.11.42 badly damaged by US aircraft during Allied landings Casablanca; 18.12.45 abandoned; 51 wreck BU *in situ*
Erik Boye 5.40 MoWT (Br); 15.6.40 torpedoed (in convoy HX48) by *U38*, sunk, 50 37N 08 44W (0†, 22 surv)
Erna 26.6.40 MoWT, *Erna III* (Br); 25.9.41 torpedoed (ind) by *U562*, sunk, 51 45N 35 15W (0 surv)
Estrid 5.40 Seized by VFr; 40 *Saint Guillaume* (Fra); 41 *Sturla* (Ita); 12.7.42 torpedoed by MTB and FAA aircraft, sunk, off Mersa Matruh
Europa 40 MoWT (Br); 3.5.41 bombed by German aircraft in dock Liverpool, burnt out, beached (0†, 45 surv); CTL; 46 BU New Ferry, R Mersey

Flynderborg 22.8.40 MoWT (Br); 3.11.41 torpedoed (in convoy SC52) by *U202*, sunk, 51 21N 51 45W (3†, 21 surv)
Fredensborg 27.1.40 Torpedoed by *U20*, sunk, 58 25N 01 53W (20†, 0 surv)
Frida 4.40 Ar Talcahuano, LU; 16.2.41 seized by Chile; 2.41 *Rapel* (Chl); 15.4.44 struck rock in Guia Narrows, Magellan Strait, in 50 45S 74 25W, beached; TL

Gerd 5.40 Seized by VFr, *Saint Raymond* (Fra); 41 *Gerd* (Ger); 22.2.43 bombed by British aircraft, sunk, 37 45N 11 37E
Gerda 9.4.40 Captured Bergen by Germans; 8.5.40 struck mine, reached port damaged; 41 *Mitra* (Nor); 44 seized by Germans; 5.45 (Nor)
Gerda Toft 4.40 Seized by VFr, *Saint Alain* (Fra); 40 *Gertrud* (Ger); 1.6.44 bombed by British aircraft NW of Heraklion, towed into port; 2.6.44 again bombed, explosion, sunk (–†)
Gorm 14.5.40 Struck mine, sunk, 020° 1.3m from S Mole Lt, Zeebrugge (0†)

Grete 15.4.40 LU Valencia; 11.2.43 torpedoed by subm HMS *Torbay*, sunk, off Cape Oropesa (0†)
Gustav Diederichsen 24.4.40 Seized Dairen by Japanese; 10.41 *Teikyu Maru* (Jpn); 2.9.42 torpedoed by subm USS *Guardfish*, sunk, 42 08N 141 15E

Hanne 28.12.39 Struck mine (laid 22.12.39 by *U22*), broke in two, sunk, 096° 7 cables from Blyth E Lt (15†)
Hans Broge 40 German control; 15.6.41 bombed by British aircraft, sunk, 15nm WSW of Texel; raised by KM, target hulk
Helene 10.4.40 Captured by patrol boat *P24* (Fra); 5.40 taken over by MN for conv to amc (Fra); 9.7.40 seized La Pallice by Germans; 8.10.40 KM, Seelöwe transport *H9* (Ger); 41 (Dmk); 26.9.41 *Hilma* (Dmk); 9.7.42 *Hilma Lau* (Dmk); 12.10.44 torpedoed by subm *Lembit* (Rus); 13.10.44 sunk 55 20N 15 20E (4†)
Helga 40 LU Talcahuano; 16.2.41 seized by Chile; 2.41 *Choapa* (Chl); 21.9.44 collision with tankers *Voco* (*qv*) and *Empire Garrick* (Br), sunk, 40 16N 73 47W
Henning Mærsk (10,106gt) 5.40 Seized by Germans while building; 40 KM, aux supply ship *Hydra* (Ger); 5.45 at Kiel, damaged; 26.4.46 *Empire Taganax* (Br); 47 *Busen Star* (Br)
Herdis 42 Seized by Brazil; 42 *Chuiloide* (Brz); 7.8.44 collision with *Tiete* (Brz), sunk, 28 05S 48 30W
Hulda Mærsk 40 USMC, *Chant* (Pan); 15–16.6.42 attacked (in Opn 'Harpoon' convoy WS19Z) by German aircraft, sunk, 36 25N 11 40E (4†, 81 surv)

Ingeborg S 6.40 Seized by VFr, *Ste Martine* (Fra); 42 *Ingeborg S* (Ger); 29.10.43 torpedoed by subm HMS *Unsparing*, sunk, 36 33N 25 54E
Inger Toft 40 MoWT (Br); 16.3.45 torpedoed (in convoy RU156) by *U722*, sunk, 57 25 30N 06 52W (0†, 30 surv)
Irene Maria 40 MoWT (Br); 28.11.40 torpedoed by *U95*, sunk, N Atlantic (25†, 0 surv)

Jane Mærsk 40 *Ambo* (Ne); 40 RNN, aux *TAN 8* (Ne); 2.3.42 scuttled by own crew, Sourabaya; 42 salved by Japanese; 42 *Teikai Maru* (Jpn); 30.12.44 sunk (in convoy) by USAAF aircraft 17 18N 119 25E
Jessie Mærsk 40 MoWT (Br); 7.10.42 torpedoed (in convoy) by E-boat (Ger), sunk, 53 06N 01 24 30E (20†, 9 surv); wreck dispersed
Johanne Justesen 40 MoWT (Br); 15.2.42 torpedoed by subm *I-65* (Jpn), sunk, 09 04N 75 58E (1†, 58 surv)
Johannes Mærsk 6.40 Req by VFr; 40 *Sainte Giselle* (Fra); 40 German control; 42 *Johanna* (Ger); 8.44 disappeared Black Sea (believed torpedoed, sunk, shortly after sd Istanbul 10.8.44); postwar in service as *Marshal Tolbukhin* (Rus)
Jonna 4.40 LU New York; 2.8.41 USMC, *Pillory* (Pan); 5.6.44 torpedoed by *U539*, broke in two, sunk, 18 26N 67 17W (25†, 22 surv)
Jytte 19.12.39 Struck mine (laid by German destroyer), sunk, 18m E of Souter Point (10†, 8 surv)

Kai 4.40 German control; 11.7.41 struck mine, sunk, between Rotterdam and Århus
Kejserinde Dagmar 40 German control; 2.4.44 lost on voyage Copenhagen–Bremen
Kirsten 4.40 German control; 19.8.40 struck mine, sunk, Little Belt
Kjøbenhavn 4.40 German control; 20.2.43 struck mine, sunk, near Borkum
Knut 40 MoWT (Br); 23.12.42 struck mine, sunk, SE 0.5 E magnetic 10m from Bardsey Island (0†, 23 surv)

Lars Kruse 40 MoWT (Br); 2.12.43 attacked by German aircraft, caught fire; blew up following explosion on ammunition ship, at Bari (19†, 14 surv)
Leise Mærsk 40 MoWT (Br); 23.11.40 torpedoed (in convoy SC11) by *U100*, sunk, 55 30N 11W (17†, 7 surv)
Lexa Mærsk 40 USMC, *Buchanan* (Pan); 12.11.42 torpedoed by *U224*, sunk, 52 06N 25 54W (0†, 73 surv)
Lifland 40 MoWT (Br); 28.9.42 torpedoed (convoy SC101 straggler) by *U160*, sunk, 56 40N 30 30W (32†, 0 surv)
London 40 MoWT, *London II* (Br); 21.3.41 bombed by German aircraft, sunk, 51 23 38N 04 19 59W
Lotta 40 LU Talcahuano; 16.2.41 seized by Chile; 2.41 *Tolten* (Chl); 13.3.42 torpedoed by *U404*, sunk, 40 10N 73 50W (25†, 2 surv)
Lundby 41 *Pink Star* (Pan); 19.9.41 torpedoed (in convoy SC44) by *U552*, sunk, 61 36N 35 07W (11†, 23 surv)

Maja 40 German control; 31.1.41 struck mine, sunk, 3m NW of Elbe 11 LV (0†)
Malaya 40 MoWT, *Malaya II* (Br); 26.6.41 torpedoed (in convoy HX133) by *U564*, sunk, 59 56N 30 35W (39†, 6 surv)
Margit 40 MoWT (Br); 7.2.44 torpedoed (in convoy RA56) by *U985*, sunk, 61 30N 10 30W (30†, 0 surv)
Maria Toft 5.40 Sunk Dunkirk; raised by Germans; 40 German control; 16.3.43 torpedoed (in convoy) by *MTB88*, *MTB93* (Br), sunk, off Terschelling
Marie Mærsk 40 MoWT (Br); 12.4.41 bombed by enemy aircraft, sunk, Salamis Bay;

27.4.41 captured upon German occupation; 3.42 raised, towed Trieste (Ger); 2.45 bombed by aircraft, damaged, Zaule Bay, Trieste; returned; 47 repaired; 48 *Luisa* (Ita)
Marna 40 LU New York; 2.8.41 USMC, *Azra* (Pan); 15.11.42 collision with destroyer HMCS *Saguenay*, damaged by loose depth charge, sank, 12m S of Cape Race (1†)
Martin Goldschmidt 14.2.40 Torpedoed by *U53*, sunk, 55 53N 12 37W (15†, 5 surv)
Maryland 15.2.40 Torpedoed by *U50*, sunk, 57 09N 12W (32†, 0 surv)
Michael Jebsen 40 MoWT (Br); 14.8.42 torpedoed (in convoy TAW12) by *U598*, sunk, 21 45N 76 10W (7†, 40 surv)
Muinam 6.40 Req by VFr; 40 *St Rene* (Fra); 41 *San Marco* (Ita); 9.11.41 shelled (in convoy) by RN Force K warships, sunk, 37 08N 18 09E

Nevada 4.40 LU Santos; 26.2.42 seized by Brazil; 42 *Apaloide* (Brz); 22.11.42 torpedoed (in convoy BRN3) by *U163*, sunk, 13 11N 54 39W (5†, 51 surv)
Nicoline Mærsk 6.40 Seized Marseilles by Germans; 40 *Saint Felix* (Fra); 41 *Nicoline Mærsk* (Ger); 24.12.43 found near Tortosa by destroyer *Le Fantasque* (Fra), ran aground near San Carlos de la Rapita, Spain; TL
Niel Mærsk 40 USMC, *Johnstown* (Pan); 5.6.42 torpedoed by subm *I-20* (Jpn), sunk, 13 12S 42 06E (2†, 42 surv)
Nora 22.1.40 Delivered; 2.8.41 USMC, *Halma* (Pan); 3.6.43 struck mine (laid 1.6.43 by *U119*), sunk, 44 17N 62 23W (0†, 42 surv)
Nordbo 18.4.40 Ar Kobe; 3.42 seized by Japanese; 42 *Teibo Maru* (Jpn); 25.9.42 torpedoed by subm USS *Sargo*, sunk, 10 31N 109 31E
Norden 7.42 USMC, *Firethorn* (Pan); 7.10.42 torpedoed by *U172*, sunk, 34 10S 17 07E (12†, 49 surv)
Nordhval 9.41 USMC, *Donerail* (Pan); 9.12.41 torpedoed by subm *I-10* (Jpn), sunk, 08N 152W (32†, 8 surv)
Nordvest 7.42 USMC, *Alan-A-Dale* (Pan); 23.12.44 sunk by German midget subm 51 21 36N 03 47 18E (0†, 65 surv)

Olga S 6.40 MoWT (Br); 6.4.41 bombed by German aircraft, sunk, 55 48N 09 45W (1†, 30 surv)
Oluf Mærsk 40 German control; 30.11.41 attacked by British aircraft, sunk, W of Borkum (0†)
Olympia 41 USMC, *Snark* (Pan); 24.2.42 struck mine near Amedee Lt; beached, broke in two amidships; TL
Oslo 40 German control; 28.9.44 struck mine, sunk, off Swinemünde
Otto Petersen 40 German control; 12.1.45 struck mine, beached, off Svelvik; TL
Ove Toft 3.12.39 Torpedoed by *U31*, sunk, 55 36N 00 46W (6†)

Pacific 40 MoWT (Br); 45 sold (Br)
Paula 4.40 LU New York; 2.8.41 USMC, *Montana* (Pan); 11.9.41 torpedoed (in convoy SC42) by *U105*, sunk, 63 40N 35 50W (26†)
Peru 40 MoWT (Br); 12.11.41 torpedoed by *U126*, sunk, 01 30N 13 20W (0†, 45 surv)
Peter Mærsk 40 MoWT (Br); 7.12.42 torpedoed by *U185*, sunk, 39 47N 41W (67†, 0 surv)

Rigmor 40 MoWT (Br); 20.2.41 attacked by German aircraft, sunk, 49 40N 04 51W (0†, 20 surv)
Robert 40 MoWT (Br); 3.1.42 struck mine 52 17 30N 02E (0†, 18 surv); 4.1.42 sunk
Rosenborg (1997gt) 40 MoWT (Br); 24.4.43 torpedoed (convoy RU71 straggler) by *U386*, sunk, 61N 15W (28†, 2 surv)

Sally Mærsk 40 MoWT (Br); 10.9.41 torpedoed (in convoy SC42) by *U81* 61 38N 40 40W (0†, 34 surv); abandoned, sunk 61 40N 40 30W
Samsø 40 MoWT (Br); 1.5.41 torpedoed by *U103*, sunk, 08 35N 16 17W (1†, 19 surv)
Sessa 4.40 LU New York; 2.8.41 USMC, *Longtaker* (Pan); 17.8.41 torpedoed (ind) by *U38*, sunk, 61 26N 30 50W (24†, 3 surv)
Siam 4.40 MoWT, *Siam II* (Br); 30.9.42 torpedoed by *U506*, sunk, 03 25N 15 46W (0†, 39 surv)
Sicilien 4.40 LU New York; 30.3.41 req by US; 12.7.41 USMC (US); 23.7.41 US Army transport; 8.6.42 torpedoed by *U172*, sunk, 17 30N 71 29W (46†, 31 surv)
Skagerak 40 MoWT (Br); 24.8.41 struck mine 51 58 08N 01 16 06E, broke in two (18†, 9 surv); sunk 148° 6.2 cables from Collimer Point, River Orwell; wreck dispersed
Stella 6.40 Seized by VFr, *Saint Sauveur* (Fra); 6.5.43 sunk by aircraft Reggio di Calabria; 9.43 salved; 44 *Capo Faro* (Ita)
Stjerneborg 12.5.40 Seized by Netherlands, at NEI; 40 *Koenjit* (Ne); 12.5.42 torpedoed by *U156*, sunk, 15 30N 52 40W (0†, 37 surv)
Storaa 6.40 MoWT (Br); 7.40 seized Port Lyautey by VFr; 11.41 scuttled there; 1.43 raised, repaired; 3.11.43 torpedoed (in convoy) by E-boat *S138* off Hastings near C1 Buoy, 50 43 39N 00 37 18E (21†, 15 surv)
Susan Mærsk 5.40 MoWT (Br); 13.6.41 torpedoed by *U553*, sunk, N of Azores (24†, 0 surv)

Tacoma 40 MoWT (Br); 25.6.40 seized Dakar by VFr; 24.9.40 struck by shells during attack on battleship *Richelieu* (Fra) at Dakar, beached (6†, 24 repatr)
Tanja 40 LU New York; 2.8.41 USMC, *Alcedo* (Pan); 28.2.45 torpedoed (in convoy

VR155) by *U1022*, sunk, 64 07N 23 17W (3†)
Tasmania 40 MoWT (Br); 30.10.42 torpedoed (in convoy SL125) by *U659*, damaged, 36 06N 16 59W; torpedoed by *U103*, sunk (2†, 88 surv, incl 44 surv from *Hopecastle – qv*)
Tekla 21.1.40 Torpedoed by *U22*, sunk, 58 18N 02 25W (9†, 9 surv)
Tennessee 1.6.40 MoWT (Br); 22.9.42 torpedoed (convoy SC100 straggler) by *U617*, sunk, 58 40N 33 41W (15†, 20 surv)

Venus 40 German control; 7.8.41 struck mine, sunk, off Schleimünde

Losses through war causes
Viborg 40 German control; 28.1.45 torpedoed by subm *K-51* (Rus), sunk, when anchored off Rügenwalde LH in 54 26N 16 20E
Viola 6.40 Seized by VFr, *Saint Denis* (Fra); 9.12.41 torpedoed by *U652*, sunk, off Balearic Islands

Lost postwar through striking mine
Marianne 28.5.46 Struck mine, sunk, off Stevns, The Sound

Changes of name, flag, sold, disposals, etc
Aase Mærsk 40 MoWT (Br); 46 (Dmk)
Absalon 40 German control
African Reefer 16.4.40 LU Funchal; 23.8.41 LU New York; 23.8.41 USMC, *Roamer* (Pan); 11.41 US Army transport; 22.7.422 USN (AF-19); 7.5.46 decomm; 14.6.46 USMC; 14.6.46 *African Reefer* (Dmk)
Alabama 40 German control; 44 LU Stockholm
Alice 40 German control
American Reefer 40 LU Argentina; 29.12.41 sold; 42 *Rio San Juan* (Arg)
Anna 10.4.40 MoWT (Br); 5.40 (Fra); 8.40 German prize at Bordeaux; 40 (Ger); 9.41 (Dmk); 2.11.42 *Anna Lau* (Dmk)
Annam 9.4.40 In port Rotterdam; 5.40 German control; by 44 LU Copenhagen
Anne 40 German control
Arizona 13.4.40 LU Vitoria, Brazil; 26.2.42 seized by Brazil; 1.3.42 *Gavealoide* (Brz);27.8.45 *Arizona* (Dmk)
Asbjorn 40 Canadian govt (Can); 46 returned
Asia 40 German control; LU Copenhagen
Aslaug 40 German control
Astoria 40 Australian govt (Aus); 45 (Dmk)
Astrid 40 German control; 17.9.42 struck mine 15nm SE of Hals Lt, Ålborg Bay (0†); 43 salved
Belgien 5.40 MoWT (Br); 7.7.40 seized Casablanca by VFr; 11.42 scuttled Port Lyautey; 43 salved; 43 MoWT (Br); 45 (Dmk)
Bente Mærsk 4.40–45 MoWT (Br); 45 (Dmk)
Betty Mærsk 40 German control; 45 retuned
Birte 40 German control
Brasilien 40 German control; 44 LU Stockholm
Brazilian Reefer 40 LU Bahia Blanca; 29.12.41 sold; 42 *Rio Mendoza* (Arg)
Bretagne 42 *Rio Iguazu* (Arg)
Brynhild 5.40–45 MoWT (Br); 45 (Dmk)
California 24.4.40 Ar Pernambuco, LU; 26.2.42 seized by Brazil; 1.3.42 *Pirailoide* (Brz); 28.11.45 *California* (Dmk)
Carmen 40 German control; 26.9.41 *Katja* (Dmk); 9.7.42 *Katja Lau* (Dmk); 5.45 Danish control
Caroline Mærsk 41 Seized by Germans while building; 41 *Polarstern* (Ger); 45 *Caroline Mærsk* (Dmk)
Chr Sass 41 *Colonia* (Uru); 46 *Chr Sass* (Dmk)
Clara 40 Seized by Germans; 40 (Ger); 45 (Dmk)
Cyril 5.40 MoWT (Br); 11.6.40 seized Casablanca by VFr; 11.42 scuttled Port Lyautey; 1.43 raised; 45 (Dmk)
Delaware 5.40 German control; 7.7.41 attacked by British aircraft, damaged, off The Hague; 11.2.45 LU Troense; 5.45 at Copenhagen; recovered, resumed service
E M Dalgas 41 DSOC, *War Admiral* (Pan); 46 *E M Dalgas* (Dmk)
Edouard Suenson 40 German control; 44 LU Sweden; 45 resumed service
Elisabeth Mærsk 40 German control; 5.45 at Umeå, returned
Emma Mærsk 41 DSOC, *Salvator* (Pan); 46 *Emma Mærsk* (Dmk)
Erria 40 MoWT (Br); 45 (Dmk)
Falstria 40 German control
Fanø 40 MoWT (Br); 45 (Dmk)
Fionia 40 German control; LU Copenhagen; 5.45 returned
Frederiksborg 40 German control; 5.45 returned
Georgia 4.40 LU New York; 12.7.41 req by USMC; 26.9.41 *Aristides* (Pan); 22.9.45 US Reserve Fleet (US); 14.6.46 *Georgia* (Dmk)
Gertrude Mærsk 41 *Cavalcade* (Pan); 45 *Gertrude Mærsk* (Dmk)
Grete Mærsk 41 USMC, *Cricamola* (Pan); 41 troop transport *Pennant* (US); 46 *Grete Mærsk* (Dmk)

Gudrun 40 German control; 5.45 at Copenhagen, returned
Gudrun Mærsk 40–46 MoWT (Br); 46 (Dmk)
Hanne 40 German control; 5.10.43 struck mine, sunk, near Drogden (5†); raised, repaired; 45 *Hanne Skou* (Dmk)
Hans Mærsk 40 German control; 45 returned
Harriet 40 German control; 18.10.41 *Hedda* (Ger); 18.9.42 *Hedda Lau* (Dmk); 5.45 at Nykøbing; Danish control
Heinrich Jessen 40–42 MoWT (Br); 28.5.42–4.46 RIN, depot ship *Barracuda*; 46 *Heinrich Jessen* (Dmk)
Henry Tegner 40 German control; 45 returned
Hilde 2.6.40 Seized Casablanca by VFr, *St Benoit* (Fra); 11.42 scuttled Port Lyautey; 43 refloated, repaired; 45 *Hilde* (Dmk)
India 40 German control; LU Copenhagen
Indian Reefer 40 LU Buenos Aires; 29.12.41 sold; 42 *Rio Gallegos* (Arg); 2.1.46 *Indian Reefer* (Dmk)
Inge Mærsk 4.40 Req by South Africa (SA regn); 46 (Dmk)
Inger 40 German control; 6.6.42 *Inger Lau* (Dmk)
Irland 42 *Tumbes* (Per)
Ivar 40 German control; 5.45 at Copenhagen, returned
Jakob Mærsk 40 German control; 5.45 Danish control
Java 40 German control; LU Nakskov; 5.45 Danish control
Jenny 1.10.40 Sold; 10.40 *Jørgen* (Dmk)
Johanne 40 German control; 5.12.41 *Jelva* (Dmk); 9.7.42 *Jelva Lau* (Dmk); 5.45 Danish control
Jutlandia 40 German control; LU Nakskov; 5.45 returned
Jutta 4.40 LU Portland ME; 41 USMC, *Kingman* (Pan); 4.2.46 *Jutta Dan* (Dmk)
Karla 40 German control; 28.2.41 sold; 45 rebuilt as cable ship
Katrine Mærsk 8.42 *Campana* (Spn)
Kentucky 40 German control; LU Copenhagen; 5.45 returned
Kina 40 MoWT, *Kina II* (Br); 45 *Kina* (Dmk)
Kirsten Mærsk 6.6.40 MoWT (Br); 11.6.45 (Dmk); 10.47 *Finnborg* (Fin)
Knud Rasmussen 40 *Toltec* (Hon)
Korea 40 German control; LU Copenhagen; 5.45 returned
Laila 40 LU Talcahuano; 12.5.41 seized by Chile; 5.41 *Maule* (Chl); 26.1.46 *Laila Dan* (Dmk)
Lalandia 40 German control; LU Copenhagen; 5.45 returned
Laura 4.40 LU Montevideo; 9.9.41 seized by Uruguay; 13.2.42 WSA, *Rocha* (US); 27.12.45 returned; 16.3.46 *Laura Dan* (Dmk)
Laura Mærsk 41 USMC, *Day Star* (US); 46 *Laura Mærsk* (Dmk)
Lica Mærsk 40 German control; 5.45 returned
Lilian 10.4.40 MoWT (Br); 5.40 (Fra); 21.8.40 MoWT, *Lilian I* (Br); 11.10.45 *Lilian* (Dmk)
Linda 4.40 LU Las Palmas; 10.43–11.45 Danish govt service; 8.1.46 *Linda Dan* (Dmk)
Lotte 40 German control; 3.45 *Lotte Skou* (Dmk)
Louisiana 40 German control; LU Copenhagen; 5.45 returned
Marchen Mærsk 12.41 USMC, *Caldera* (Pan); 41 *Perida* (US); 46 *Marchen Mærsk* (Dmk)
Margrete 40 German control; LU Sweden, then Copenhagen; 5.45 returned
Maria 40 LU New York; 2.8.41 USMC, *Uranus* (Pan); 11.8.41 USN stores ship (AF-14); 8.5.46 decomm; 9.5.46 USMC; 5.46 *Maria Dan* (Dmk)
Marocco 40 German control; LU Copenhagen; 5.45 returned
Martin Carl 40 German control; 5.45 returned
Mathilde Mærsk 28.9.42 *Irish Ash* (Eir)
Meonia 6.40 Seized by VFr, *Ste Edith* (Fra); 45 *Meonia* (Dmk)
Mette 40 German control; 3.45 *Mette Skou* (Dmk); 5.45 at Elsinore; Danish control
Nancy 9.4.40 Seized by RN, taken Kirkwall; 5.40 *Saint Thomas* (Fra); 22.6.40 interned Lisbon; 40 *Nancy* (Dmk); 12.3.43 sold (Swi); 20.7.43 (Dmk); 23.11.43 MoWT (Br); 29.4.44 (Dmk); 11.9.45 returned owners; 8.1.46 *Nancy Lau* (Dmk)
Nerma 40 German control; 9.7.42 *Nerma Lau* (Dmk); 5.45 Danish control
Niobe 40 German control; 11.3.42 *Ninna* (Dmk); 5.11.42 *Ninna Lau* (Dmk)
Nordborg 40 German control; 5.45 returned
Nordfarer 40 German control; 40–45 LU Nakskov; 5.45 returned
Nordkap 40 German control; 40–45 LU Nakskov; 5.45 returned
Nordkyn 40 German control; LU Nakskov; 9.45 delivered
Nordlys 9.4.40 Intercepted by RN vessels; 7.6.40 MoWT (Br); 3.11.45 (Dmk); 24.4.46 *Karla Dan* (Dmk)
Nordpol 7.42 USMC, *Manuel* (Pan); 7.46 *Nordpol* (Dmk)
Orion 40 German control; LU Copenhagen
Orneborg 40 German control
P Madsen 39 *Signe* (Est); 40 *Florida* (Hon)
P N Damm 41 *Spokane* (Hon); 17.3.44 Red Cross ship *Caritas II* (Swi); 2.6.45 *Spokane* (Hon); 46 *P N Damm* (Dmk)
Peter Lassen 40 *Aztec* (Hon)
Ragnhild 41 DSOC, *Leonatus* (Pan); 46 *Ragnhild* (Dmk)
Randa 6.40 Canadian govt (Can); 4.12 45 returned (Dmk)
Rikke 40 German control; 7.8.44 struck mine S of Amager (0†); towed Copenhagen;

9.9.44 at Elsinore, repairing; 45 *Rikke Skou* (Dmk)
Rita Mærsk 41 USMC, *Lawrin* (Pan); 41 *Pegasus* (Pan); 42 *Lawrin* (US); 46 *Rita Mærsk* (Dmk)
Robert Mærsk 6.40–46 MoWT (Br); 46 (Dmk)
Selandia 6.40 MoWT (Br), Allied troopship; 45 (Dmk)
Selma 40 LU Talcahuano; 12.5.41 seized by Chile; 41 *Elqui* (Chl); 26.1.46 *Selma Dan* (Dmk)
Silkeborg 40 German control; 5.45 returned at Copenhagen
Skodsborg 40 German control; 5.45 returned
Slesvig 40 MoWT (Br); 45 (Dmk)
Søborg 10.7.40 MoWT (Br); 13.9.45 (Dmk)
Stensby 40 MoWT (Br); 45 (Dmk)
Store Nordiske 40 MoWT (Br); 45 (Dmk)
Svend Pii 40 German control; 5.45 returned
Texas 40 German control; LU Copenhagen; 5.45 returned
Thyra S 40 MoWT (Br); 45 (Dmk)
Tovelil 40 MoWT (Br); 45 (Dmk)
Trein Mærsk 40 Launched; 40 German control; LU Copenhagen, then Holbæk; 5.45 returned
Tunis 27.1.41 USMC, *Aquila* (Pan); 45 (US); 10.45 *Bonanza* (Pan); 25.6.46 *Tunis* (Dmk)
Uffe 40 German control; LU Copenhagen; 5.45 returned
Ulla 4.40 MoWT (Br); 12.10.45 (Dmk)
Uranienborg 9.4.40 Seized near Aden; 17.4.40 British prize; 8.5.40 MoWT (Br); 14.9.45 (Dmk)
Virginia 40 German control; LU Copenhagen; 5.45 returned
Vitus Bering 40 *Maya* (Hon)
Westralia 24.4.40–4.3.46 MoWT (Br); 3.46 (Dmk)
Wilh Colding 40 German control; 5.45 returned

Egypt

Losses through marine hazard
Memphis 28.2.41 Engines disabled in heavy weather 56 40N 10 20W, foundered (0 surv; † incl 29 surv from *Benjamin Franklin – qv*)
Rod-el-Farag 14.4.44 On fire following *Fort Stikine* explosion Bombay (–†); burnt out, TL; sunk for use as jetty
Star of Ramleh 5.40 MoWT, *Empire Lotus* (Br); 12.4.42 engine room flooded in heavy weather, foundered, 44 06N 62 07W (0†)

Losses through war causes
Angele Mabro 6.7.40 Torpedoed by *U30*, sunk, WSW of Brest (0 surv)
Georges Mabro 28.9.40 Torpedoed by *U37*, sunk, 52N 19W (0 surv)
Kawsar 11.4.42 Bombed by enemy aircraft 31 34N 31 14E (2†); towed Port Said, CTL; 46 BU
Khedive Ismail 2.40 MoWT (Br); 29.2.40 military stores ship; 4.41 troopship; 12.2.44 torpedoed (in convoy KR8) by subm *I-27* (Jpn), sunk, 00 57N 72 16E (137†, 46 surv; troops 1134†, 190 surv)
Mohamed Ali el-Kebir 3.40 MoWT, military store ship (Br); 7.8.40 torpedoed (in convoy HX61) by *U38*, sunk, 55 22N 13 18W (120†, 740 surv)
Radames 20.5.41 Torpedoed by *U103* 06N 12W (1†); sunk
Samir 17.8.42 Torpedoed (in convoy PG6) by *U658*, sunk, 18 30N 75 20W
Sesostris 30.1.41 Torpedoed (in convoy SC19) by *U106*, sunk, 56N 15 23W (0 surv)
Star of Luxor 10.12.41 Torpedoed (in convoy SC57) by *U130*, sunk, 56 57N 16 35W (4†, 52 surv)
Star of Suez 15.12.42 Torpedoed by *U159*, sunk, 00 42S 29 34W (2†, 40 surv)
Zamzam 17.4.41 Shelled by aux cruiser *Atlantis* (*c*24†, 320 surv), badly damaged, sunk by bombs, 27 41S 08 08W

Change of name, flag, role, disposals
Al Rawdah 40 MoWT (Br); 5.3.40–26.3.46 military/RN service (43–46 hospital ship); 46 refit; 46 (Egy)
El Nil 6.42 MoWT (Br); 42–43 diplomatic mission ship; 6.43 Hospital Ship No 53; then troopship; 47 (Egy)

Estonia

Loss through marine hazard
Neme 22.3.40 Damaged by ice, abandoned, sank, 58 53 05N 18 52E

Losses through war causes
Eestirand 6.41 Seized Danzig by USSR; 26.8.41 bombed by German aircraft, beached, CTL
Hildur 40 USSR control; 22.6.41 seized Stettin by Germans; 41 *Rimage* (Ger); 17.3.45 bombed by RAF aircraft, sunk, Ålesund
Kolga 4.7.40 Bombed (in convoy OA178) by German Ju87 aircraft, sunk, 50 13N 02W (1†, 29 surv)
Lake Lucerne 41 USSR control; 28.8.41 sunk by German Ju88 aircraft off Koppelbucht
Merisaar 12.7.40 Stopped by *U99*, prize, directed to French port; 15.7.40 bombed by German aircraft, sunk, off Queenstown (0†)
Peet 6.40 Seized Baltic by USSR; 10.8.41 captured by Germans in Finnish waters; 41 *Frauenburg* (Ger); 7.11.41 struck mine, sunk, 57 26N 21 20E
Sigrid 40 Seized by Germans; 40 *Detlef* (Ger); 4.45 bombed by RAF aircraft, sunk, Kiel; 48 raised, BU
Vapper 6.7.40 Torpedoed by *U34*, sunk, 49 30N 09 15W (1†, 32 surv)

Sunk Mulberry Harbour, Normandy
Lake Hallwil 41 MoWT, *Signe* (Br); 41 *Ingman* (Br); 9.6.44 sunk as breakwater, Gooseberry 3, Gold Beach, Arromanches; 45 raised, BU Newport Mon (ar 12.8.45)

Changes of name, flag, role, disposals
Elna 40 MoWT, *Elna II* (Br); 42 (Rus)
Kadri 41 *Nordlicht* (Ger); 4– *Nordsturm* (Ger); 5.45 at Brunsbüttel; 46 (Rus)
Koidula 42 *Uhlenhorst* (Ger); 5.45 at Bremerhaven; 45 returned; 48 *Dabaibe* (Pan)
Kuressaar 41 *Merida* (Hon)
Liina 45 (Rus)
Osmussaar 41 (Rus)
Otto 3.10.41 *Irish Willow* (Eir); 6.5.46 *Veraguas* (Pan)
Piret 12.1.42 *Irish Alder* (Eir); 7.8.46 *Trebol* (Pan)
Sulev 40 MoWT (Br); 45 sold (Br)

Finland

Losses through marine hazard
Bore VIII 28.2.41 Foundered Hubertgat
Delaware 27.12.41 Req by USMC, *Puchero* (Pan); 7.9.42 aground Herrero Point, 19 18N 87 27W; TL; 43 wreck BU
Equator 6.12.41 Stranded near Luleå, refloated, sprang leak, sank 65 20 07N 22 15E (0†)
Garryvale 30.1.39 Stranded 2m SE of South Gare, R Tees; refloated, BU
Margareta (1860gt) 26.3.44 Collision with *Ligur* (Swe) while at anchor between Moen and Gedser, sank
Wiides 40 German control; 15.1.44 wrecked Rotesand
Wirma 13.3.41 Lost off German North Sea coast
Wirta 24.1.41 Aground Skerjafjord, Iceland; TL
Yildum 6.41 Seized by GB; 41 MoWT (Br); 1.1.44 collision with *Odysseus* (*qv*), sunk, 48 44N 59 13W

Losses through war causes
Agnes 40 German control; 1.11.42 torpedoed by subm *SC-406* (Rus), sunk, 12m N of Rixhöft
Anja 9.39 Interned Baltimore; 27.12.41 USMC, *Scapa Flow* (Pan); 14.11.42 torpedoed by *U134*, sunk, 12N 30W (33†, 27 surv)
Argo 16.6.42 Torpedoed by subm *SC-317* (Rus), sunk, 59 21N 20 14E
Astrid Thordén 6.44 Seized Stockholm by Sweden; 3.1.45 USSR; 47 *Gribojedov* (Rus)
Atlanta 3.1.45 Ceded USSR; 46 *Vilnus* (Rus)

Betty H 26.10.43 Torpedoed by subm *SC-307* (Rus), sunk, 59 54N 19 54E
Bore X 3.1.45 Ceded USSR; 46 *Marshal Govorov* (Rus)
Britannic 41 German control; 6.9.42 struck mine, on fire, sunk, Ålborg Bay

Carolina Thordén 8.41 MoWT (Br); 26.3.41 bombed by German aircraft entrance Thorshavn Bay, on fire, beached 62 11 20N 07 00 10W, burnt out; (1†, 68 surv) 8.10.41 refloated, towed Kirkwall, CTL; 17.10.41 (Br); 10.4.42 sunk as blockship Water Sound, Scapa Flow, 58 50 30N 02 54 04W; 49 wreck refloated
Carolus 41 Seized by GB; 41 MoWT (Br); 9.10.42 torpedoed by *U69*, sunk, 48 47N 68 10 30W (11†, 19 surv)

Dagmar 40 MoWT, *Dagmar I* (Br); 9.2.41 bombed by German aircraft, sunk, 35 42N 14 38W
Daphne 3.4.41 Torpedoed (ind) by *U76*, sunk, 60N 20W (18†, few surv)
Diana 44 (Swe); 5.3.44 bombed by RAF aircraft, sunk, off Schiermonnikoog (2†)
Edit H 41 Seized by Germans; 41 (Ger); 19.9.44 struck mine, towed Copenhagen by Germans; CTL; 5.45 at Nordhavn, Copenhagen; 10.48 ar shipbreaker's yard, Copenhagen, for BU
Elle 27.8.40 Torpedoed (ind) by *U101*, sunk, 57 43N 12 18W (2†, 27 surv)

Fidra 27.12.41 USMC, *Tambour* (Pan); 26.9.42 torpedoed by *U175*, sunk, 08 50N 59 50W (8†, 24 surv)

Hogland 21.8.41 Torpedoed by subm *Rubis* (Fra), sunk, 58 28N 05 47E (8†)

Ingrid Thordén 7.44 Confiscated Stockholm by Sweden; 3.1.45 ceded USSR; 46 *Narva* (Rus)

Jäämeri (ex *Charterhague*) 26.4.44 Struck mine, sunk, off German Baltic coast
Josefina Thordén 41 MoWT (Br); 6.4.43 struck mine 232° 4.5m from Sunk Head Buoy, Thames estuary, beached (15†, 40 surv); broke in two, sunk 51 47 18N 01 28 42E; forepart salved, BU
Jussi H 41 German control; 12.9.42 torpedoed by subm *S-13* (Rus), sunk, 60 21N 18E

Kastelholm 6.6.41 Struck mine, sunk, 63 06N 34 19W (1†, 37 surv)
Killoran 10.8.40 Stopped by aux cruiser *Widder*, sunk by time bombs, 32 30N 34W (0†)
Kronoborg 3.1.45 USSR; 45 *Kronstadt* (Rus)
Kurikka 12.41 USMC, *Chenango* (Pan); 20.4.42 torpedoed by *U84*, sunk, 36 25N 74 55W (36†, 1 surv)

Lawhill 39–5.40 LU Rothesay Bay; 7.41 seized East London; 4.42 (SA); 46 sold; 47 derelict at Lourenço Marques

Margareta 9.6.40 Torpedoed by *U46*, sunk, 45N 14 30W (5†, 20 surv)
Margarita 40 Seized Gibraltar by GB; 40 MoWT (Br); 27.9.41 torpedoed by *U201*, broke in two, sunk, 50 15N 17 27W (0†, 34 surv)
Marisa Thordén 12.41 USMC, *Bushranger* (Pan); 31.5.42 torpedoed by *U107*, sunk, 18 15N 81 25W (17†, 26 surv)
Martti-Ragnar 9.4.40 Detained Bergen by Germans; 4.40 seized by Germans; 40 *Herrenwyk* (Ger); 4.5.42 struck mine, sunk, Kiel Bay
Mercator 1.12.39 Torpedoed by *U31*, sunk, 57 25N 01 35W (1†)
Modesta 41 MoWT (Br); 25.4.42 torpedoed by *U108*, sunk, 33 40N 63 10W (19†)

Nagu 2.43 Seized by USSR; 3.1.45 (Rus); 46 *Petrozavodsk* (Rus)

Olivebank 8.9.39 Struck mine, sunk, 55 53N 05 07E (14†)
Olovsborg 12.41 Seized by Brazil; 42 *Lesteloide* (Brz); 48 Brazilian navy training ship
Orient 21.7.44 Torpedoed (in German convoy) by British aircraft, sunk, S of Heligoland
Orion 46 To USSR, reparations; 46 *Valdai* (Rus)

Pamir 41 Seized as prize, Wellington NZ; 51 (Ger)
Pandia 41 USMC, *Desert Light* (Pan); 16.4.42 torpedoed by *U572*, sunk, 35 35N 72 48W (1†, 30 surv)
Penang 8.12.40 Torpedoed by *U140*, sunk, NW of Tory Island
Pluto 28.6.41 Torpedoed by *U146*, sunk, about 59 39N 08 20W (12†, 18 surv);
Pohjanmaa 41 German control; 45 to USSR, reparations; 46 *Pulkovo* (Rus)

Rosenborg 41 MoWT (Br); 8.6.42 shelled by *U504*, sunk, 18 47N 85 05W (4†, 23 surv)

Sarmatia 18.6.40 Torpedoed by *U28*, sunk, 49 04N 12 05W (0†, 23 surv)
Sirius 41 German control; 3.1.45 to USSR, reparations; 46 *Pechenga* (Rus)
Snabb 3.6.40 Torpedoed by *U37*, sunk, 300m off Cape Finisterre (1†)

Tauri 41 German control; 12.9.41 attacked by British aircraft, sunk, off Bergen
Tilda 42 *Annette Fritzen* (Ger), chartered by Japan; 26.7.45 struck mine, sunk, off Pusan

Virgo 40 (Swe); 13.1.43 struck mine, sunk, near Borkum Lt (1†, 26 surv)

Wiiri 17.7.40 Bombed by enemy aircraft, abandoned, sunk, 30m off Malta (0†, 26 surv)
Wilja 17.2.40 Torpedoed by *U48*, sunk, 49N 06 33W (0†, 27 surv)
Wipunen 27.12.41 Seized Norfolk VA by US; 41 USMC, *Granville* (Pan); 17.3.43 torpedoed (in convoy SC122) by *U338*, sunk, 52 50N 30 35W (12†, 35 surv)
Wirma 40 *Rainier* (Fin); 14.3.41 sunk NE of Norderney Lt (–†)

Sunk Mulberry Harbour, Normandy
Winha 7.12.41 Seized by GB; 42 MoWT (Br); 44 Adm; 8.6.44 sunk as breakwater, Gooseberry 3, Gold Beach, Arromanches

Changes of name, flag, role, disposals, etc
Aagot 41 USMC, *Potomac* (Pan); 47 *Aagot* (Fin)
Advance 6.12.41 Seized Philadelphia by US; 41 USMC, *Trojan* (Pan); 44 MoWT, *Trojan III* (Br); 47 *Advance* (Fin)
Airisto 40 German control; 41 *Inga* (Fin); 44 LU Malmo
Angra 42 *Mercator* (Fin); 43 (Ger); 5.45 captured Copenhagen by Allies; 45 *Empire Crouch* (Br); 46 *Mercator* (Fin)
Archibald Russell 9.39 At Hull; 39 MoS food store (Br); 48 returned; 49 BU
Aurora 42 USMC, *Rosemount* (Pan); 47 *Aurora* (Pan); 9.48 (Fin)
Björneborg 45 *Maria* (Fin)
Brita Thordén 41 MoWT (Br); 47 (Fin)
Ericus 41 Seized by GB; 41 Canadian govt (Can); not returned
Ester Thordén 41 MoWT (Br); 46 (Fin)
Ferrum 42 *Eva* (Swe)
Flora H 40–44 German control; 9.10.44 at Oskarshamn; 47 Rosa H (Swe)
Greta Thordén 1.45 To be handed over to USSR; 3.45 refused; remained under Finnish flag
Hammarland 42 *Karlshamn* (Swe)
Herakles 42 Seized by Germans; 8.43 damaged by aircraft attack Åbo; 5.45 recovered, repaired
Hulda Thordén 9.44 Detained Oskarshamn; 45 released, returned
Karin 43 Seized by Germans; 44 *Ursa* (Ger); 26.4.45 scuttled Bremen; 45 raised, beached, repaired; 47 *Margareta* (Fin)
Karin Thordén 3.1.45 To be handed over to USSR; refused, returned owner
Karl-Erik 3.1.45 To be handed over to USSR; refused, returned owner; 47 *Strelma* (Rus)
Koura 41 *Caribe* (Cub)
Kuurtanes 12.41 USMC, *Arc Light* (Pan); 44 MoWT (Br); 47 *Kuurtanes* (Fin)
Mathilda Thordén 12.41 USMC, *Amazon* (Pan); 41 *Thunderer* (Pan); 46 *Mathilda Thordén* (Fin)
Maud Thordén 12.7.44 Reported confiscated in Sweden; 3.1.45 to be handed over to USSR; refused; 45 returned owners
Moshulu 10.4.40 Ar Farsund, captured by Germans; 5.45 at Narvik; 45 returned
Oddvar II 41 Seized by GB; 41 MoWT (Br); 46 (Fin)
Passat 39 LU Mariehman; 44 grain store, Stockholm; 45 returned; 6.45 at Mariehamn
Peggy Thordén 3.1.45 To be handed over to USSR; refused, returned owners
Pommern 39 LU Mariehman; 44 grain store, Stockholm; 45 returned; 6.45 at Mariehamn
Saimaa 42 *Yemassee* (Ger); USMC (Pan); 47 *Saimaa* (Fin)
Siggy 41 *Hondu* (Hon); 42 *Random* (NF)
Solbritt 17.6.41 Seized Kirkwall by GB; 41 MoWT (Br); 46 (Fin)
Veli Ragner 3.1.45 To be handed over to USSR; 3.45 refused, returned owner
Vicia 20.4.42 *Irish Spruce* (Eir)
Vienti 10.43 Sunk Bremen, salved, seized by Germans; 44 *Kommerzienratsieg* (Ger); 45 *Vienti* (Fin)
Viking 39 LU Mariehamn; 44 grain store Stockholm; 45 released
Wiima 41 *Avenir* (Fin)
Winterhude 39 At Stavanger, grain store; 44 (Ger); 10.45 coal hulk, Hamburg; 49 BU
Wisa 44 *Alden* (Fin)
Yrsa 45 To be handed over to USSR; refused, returned owner
Zephyr 41 German prize; 41 (Ger); 45 (Fin)

France

Losses through marine hazard
Alaska 15.11.39 Collision with *Dotterel* (Br), sank, 12m SE of Owers LV, 50 30 17N 00 30 35W (0 surv)
Asni 9.9.39 Ashore Itu Abi Island, Spratley archipelago; TL
Cabourg 20.1.39 Sd Ghent for Nantes; 22.1.39 sighted 18m N of Triagoz LH; missing (0 surv)
Cambraisien 9.11.42 Wrecked in heavy weather on voyage Sfax–Marseilles
Casamance 40 MoWT (Br); 17.2.41 stranded 500 metres S of Skinningrove, 54 34 30N 00 54W, broke in two; TL
Champenois 18.4.41 Stranded 20m SW of Casablanca, TL
Châteauroux 2.11.44 Stranded near Dingle Jetty, R Mersey, badly damaged; refloated, BU
Dahomey 17.11.42 Stranded off Bouznika, 48km N of Casablanca during Allied landings, set on fire, burnt out; TL; wreck sold
Divatte 28.10.41 Ashore Ras el Koran, near Bizerta; sank; 46 raised, BU
Enseigne Maurice Préchac 26.5.42 Sprang leak; 27.5.42 sank, 37 55N 23 40W
Gallois 6.40 MoWT (Br); 6.8.41 wrecked 52 54 30N 01 43 30E
Kervégan 40 MoWT (Br); 8.2.41 sd Halifax for Loch Ewe; 9.2.41 distress signals from 43 40N 61 33W; wreckage washed up Nova Scotia, untraced (0 surv)
Lamoricière 6.40 Taken over by VFr; 9.1.42 leaking, foundered, in severe gale 3m N of Minorca (277†)
Loire 12.11.39 Sd Oran for Dunkirk; untraced; wreckage drifted ashore near Malaga
Montauban 9.1.40 Ashore in gale Saltscar Rocks, Redcar, 54 37 45N 01 02 27W; 15.1.40 broke up
Nevada 6.40 MoWT, *Nevada II* (Br); 19.7.42 aground in sea mist 4m W of Cairns of Coll, W Scotland, 56 41 25N 06 29 35W; TL

Normandie 9.39 LU New York; 12.41 req by US; 12.12.41 USMC; 16.12.41 USN, USS *Lafayette* (AP-53); 9.2.42 on fire New York harbour, listed, settled on side (1†); 43 refloated, LU; 10.46 sold breakers; 46–47 BU Newark NJ
Paris 18.4.39 On fire Havre, heeled over, settled on bottom (2†); abandoned, TL; 47 BU *in situ*
Patria 40 Sold (Fra); 15.8.40 req at Haifa by GB; 10.40 MoWT (Br); 25.11.40 explosion, capsized, sank, Haifa harbour (279†) (bomb planted by 'Haganah' to prevent vessel taking illegal immigrants to Mauritius); 52 wreck BU
Picardie 1.2.40 Struck submerged object, broke in two, 39N 39 30W; forepart sank, afterpart towed to Oran, where later badly damaged by gunfire
Pierre Loti 4.11.40 Seized Sydney; 41 MoWT (Br); 12.12.42 aground on sandbank, Laval Bank, Gabon estuary, in 00 47N 09 18E; 4.11.43 abandoned, TL
Saint Prosper 6.3.39 Sd Algiers for Marseilles; WT 8.3.39, missing
Sainte Maxime 6.40 Seized Bordeaux by Germans; 5.8.40 KM, Seelöwe transport *H3* (Fra); 11.40 returned CGT; 8.11.42 seized Casablanca by Allies; 14.1.44 collision with *Wendell Phillips* (US), sank, off Cap Bon
Sunik 27.7.39 Collision with *Grängesberg* (*qv*) about 25m S of Fowey, on fire, capsized; 31.7.39 sank 49 55N 04 30W (10†, 24 surv)
Ville de Tamatave 41 MoWT (Br); 24.1.43 rudder broken in gale, sinking, 50 17N 40 55W (88†, 0 surv)

Losses through war causes
Aden 27.5.40 Bombed by German aircraft, sunk, Dunkirk
Aïn-el-Turk 31.5.40 Bombed by German aircraft, sunk, Dunkirk
Albi 26.10.40 Intercepted by RN warships, set on fire, scuttled (voyage Dakar–Libreville) (0†)
Algérie 42 *Aquila* (Ita); 1.4.43 sunk (in convoy) near Cape Zebib, near Bizerta; 51 wreck upperworks BU
Alice Robert 41 Seized by Germans; 41 KM, aux minelayer *SG11*; 2.6.44 torpedoed by subm HMS *Ultor*, sunk, 42 30N 09 07E
Alsacien 24.1.40 Torpedoed (in French convoy 56KS) by *U44*, sunk, 38N 09 55W (4†)
Alsina 13.11.42 Bombed by aircraft Bougie; 43 raised; 53 BU
Amienois 22.6.40 Attacked by German aircraft, sunk, off Verdon
Anadyr 40 Seized Gibraltar by GB; 6.40 MoWT (Br); 6.5.44 torpedoed by *U129*, sunk, 10 55S 27 30W (6†, 47 surv)
André Moyrand 26.4.41 Torpedoed (ind) by *U110*, sunk, WNW of Achill Head
Ange Schiaffino 6.40 (Ger); 8.40 KM, Seelöwe transport *H25*; 22.9.41 *Blankenese* (Ger); 22.4.42 torpedoed by subm *M-173* (Rus), sunk, 70 32 02N 30 47E
Aramis 6.9.39 MN, amc; 1.8.40 decomm; 4.42 captured Saigon by Japanese; 42 *Teia Maru* (Jpn); 18.8.44 torpedoed (in convoy) by subm USS *Rasher*, sunk, 18 09N 119 56E
Arica 6.40 Taken over by VFr; 42 seized by GB; 42 MoWT (Br); 6.11.42 torpedoed (in convoy TRIN24) by *U160* 10 58N 60 52W (12†, 55 surv); broke in two, sunk
Arijon 22.11.39 Torpedoed (in convoy 14BS) by *U43*, sunk, 45 40N 04 50W (–†)
Arizona 1.12.42 Seized Marseilles by Germans; 17.4.44 sunk by Allied aircraft Palermo; 22.10.46 refloated; grounded while in tow, TL
Artésien 42 Seized by Italy; 42 *Chieti* (Ita); 29.2.44 torpedoed by subm HMS *Uproar*, sunk, 43 02N 05 19E
Asie 40 Taken over by VFr; 13.3.43 seized Marseilles by Germans; 4.5.43 transf Italy, *Rossano* (Ita); 9.43 seized by Germans; 10.5.44 attacked by Allied aircraft, on fire, capsized, Genoa; 46 BU
Astrée 42 Seized by Germans; 42 *Siena* (Ger); 1.5.44 torpedoed by subm HMS *Untiring*, sunk, Port Vendres
Aurigny 40 Interned Buenos Aires; 22.12.41 on fire, repaired; 42 sold Argentina, *General San Martin* (Arg)
Aurillac 6.40 MoWT (Br); 15.4.41 torpedoed by subm *Enrico Tazzoli* (Ita), sunk, 37 09N 18 42W (1†, 40 surv)
Auvergne 40 German control; 11.42 req by Italian navy; 21.12.42 *Potenza* (Ita); 20.8.44 scuttled Port Saint Louis Rhône; 47 raised, BU
Aveyron 10.7.41 *Capo Pino* (Ita); 43 *Petrella* (Ger); 8.2.44 torpedoed by subm HMS *Sportsman*, sunk, 35 34N 24 18E (2647†, 691 surv)
Azrou 42 *Terni* (Ita); 16.6.43 torpedoed by subm HMS *Unison*, sunk, off Augusta

Bamako 9.4.43 Torpedoed by *U515*, sunk, 14 57N 17 15W (17†)
Baoulé 31.10.39 Torpedoed (in French convoy 20K) by *U25*, sunk, 43 48N 09 08W (13†)
Beauce 42 Seized by Italians, *Proserpina* (Ita); 9.10.42 torpedoed by subm HMS *Traveller*, sunk, 35 45N 23 13E
Beaumanoir 40 MoWT (Br); 2.6.41 bombed by German aircraft 3m E of Robin Hood's Bay; taken in tow, again bombed, sunk, 180° 8 cables from 19 buoy, Robin Hood's Bay (0†, 30 surv)
Bélain d'Esnambuc 11.42 Escaped from N Africa during Allied landings, ar Marseilles; 16.12.42 seized Marseilles by Germans, conv to aux minelayer *Pommern* (SG2); 43 *SG12*; 5.10.43 struck Italian mine, sunk, 1.5m S of San Remo
Belle Isle 42 Seized by Germans, accom ship; 5.1.43 U-boat depot ship; 6.7.43 experimental ship; 24.11.43 attacked by USAAF aircraft, on fire, Toulon docks; 13.3.44

again bombed, TL; 45 BU
Benty 2.43 Sunk Naples by war causes; 47 salved, BU Naples
Bernardin de St Pierre 41 Seized by Japanese; 42 *Teibi Maru* (Jpn); 10.10.43 torpedoed by subm USS *Bonefish*, sunk, 14 44N 110 19E
Biscarosse 21.6.40 Scuttled Havre; raised, BU
Bonifacio 3.12.42 Seized Marseilles by Germans; transf Italy, *Campo Basso* (Ita); 4.5.43 shelled by destroyer HMS *Nubian* 8m E of Kelibia, sunk
Bougainville 10.4.42 Taken over Indo-China by Japanese; 42 *Teifu Maru* (Jpn); 21.1.45 attacked by USN carrier-based aircraft, sunk, 22 37N 121 15E
Bougaroni 42 Seized by Italians; 42 *Modena* (Ita); 22.3.43 bombed by Allied aircraft, sunk, near Palermo; raised; 15.1.45 at Palermo; 48 BU Palermo
Bourges 40 German control; 20.8.44 scuttled Port Saint Louis de Rhône; 25.12.44 raised, BU
Brazza 28.5.40 Shelled by *U37*, sunk, 42 43N 11W
Brestois 12.42 Seized by Italians; 43 *Vercelli* (Ita); 30.1.43 bombed by RAF aircraft 30m off Cap Bon, taken in tow, sunk, 1.5m off Cape Farina
Bretagne 14.10.39 Torpedoed (in convoy KJF3) by *U45* 50 20N 12 45W, shelled, sunk (7†)
Brumaire 20.6.40 Bombed by German aircraft, sunk, 47 14N 03 16W

Calédonien 11.42 (Ger); 42 *Spoleto* (Ita); 31.1.43 attacked by USAAF B17 aircraft Bizerta, blew up
Calvados 41 *Tourquennois* (Fra); 43 *Ferrara* (Ita); 8.44 sunk by aircraft Genoa; 47 raised, repaired
Cambronne 6.40 Seized Bordeaux by Germans; 3.8.40 KM, Seelöwe transport *H13*; 11.8.41 Channel Islands transport; 10.1.42 Baltic transport; 11.3.45 attacked by Allied aircraft, damaged, in floating dry dock sunk at Hamburg; refloated, ship put ashore, partly submerged; 10.50 salved; 51 BU Hamburg
Cap Blanc 40 Seized by Germans; KM, supply vessel *Felix 1* (Ger); 27.6.44 torpedoed by subm HMS *Ultor*, sunk, 43 38N 07 19E
Cap Guir 6.40 Seized Bordeaux by Germans; 6.40 (Ger); 5.8.40 KM, Seelöwe transport *H11*; 31.8.41 KMD, Stettin; 31.10.41 returned; 16.4.45 torpedoed by aircraft, sunk, 56 12N 17 44E (756†)
Cap Padaran 6.40 Seized by VFr; 40 (Fra); 2.11.41 captured S of Durban by RN; 41 MoWT (Br), troopship; 9.12.43 torpedoed (in convoy HA11) by *U596*, 39 15N 17 30E; taken in tow, line parted, back broken, sank (5†, 190 surv)
Cap Varella 10.4.42 Seized Yokohama by Japanese; 42 *Teika Maru* (Jpn); 7.5.45 struck mine (laid by subm USS *Finback*), sunk, 34 06N 130 47E
Capitaine Augustin 17.3.40 Struck mine, sunk, 51 29 48N 01 24 54E (2†, 28 surv); wreck dispersed
Capitaine Damiani 40 (Ger); 40 KM, supply vessel *Tempo 1* (Ger); 22.8.44 scuttled Marseilles; 4.46 raised; 6.7.46 stricken, BU
Capitaine Edmond Laborie 21.10.39 Struck mine (laid 17.10.39 by *U19*), sunk, 53 19 08N 00 38 03E; wreck dispersed
Capitaine Le Bastard 6.40 Seized Nantes by Germans; 40 (Ger); 8.40 KM, Seelöwe transport *R3N*; 9.40 *A3N*; 20.11.40 High Command, Antwerp; 1.41 *Signal* (Ger); 4.11.44 bombed by Allied aircraft, sunk, Hamburg; raised, CTL
Capitaine Le Diabat 21.12.42 Seized Marseilles by Germans; 14.7.43 bombed by Allied aircraft, sunk, off Montecristo Is
Capitaine Luigi 12.1.44 Struck German mine, sunk, off Marseilles port entrance
Capitaine Maurice Eugene 18.6.40 Scuttled (with damage) Brest
Caraibe 39–40 MN, aux patrol vessel *P-6*; 9.12.42 seized by Germans; 14.3.43 sunk by Allied carrier aircraft 10m N of Marittima, Italy
Carbet 6.40 Taken over by VFr; 11.1.43 seized Marseilles by Germans; 4.43 sunk off Piombino
Carimaré 7.40 *Verona* (Ita); 23.1.43 torpedoed by British aircraft, sunk, NNW of Ustica
Champagne 40 (Ger); 40 KM, *Trapez 1*; 24.9.43 torpedoed by subm *Dzik* (Pol) then subm HMS *Ultor*, 11nm NE of Bastia, stranded S of Bastia; 27.9.43 torpedoed by subm HMS *Uproar*, TL
Champlain 17.6.40 Struck mine off entrance to La Pallice, heeled over, resting on bottom (11†, 370 surv); 21.6.40 torpedoed by *U65*; 63–64 BU *in situ*
Charles L-D 40 MoWT (Br); 9.12.42 torpedoed (convoy HX217 straggler) by *U553*, sunk, 59 02N 30 45W (36†, 12 surv)
Château Palmer 6.40 Seized by Germans; 8.40 Seelöwe transport *H18*; 13.6.41 *Château Palmer* (Ger); 27.8.41 *Walter Ohlrogge* (Ger); 21.1.42 struck mine, sunk, off Sovgaar, Norway
Château Yquem 40 German control; 27.7.43 torpedoed by subm HMS *Usurper*, sunk, 42 04N 08 20E
Chella 2.6.40 Bombed by aircraft, on fire, Marseilles; towed out, shelled by coastal batteries, sunk to NW of port in shallow water; postwar raised
Chenonceaux 5.40 Troopship; 40 taken over by VFr; 43 seized Marseilles by Germans; 22.8.44 scuttled Marseilles; 4.48 refloated, BU Toulon
Colleville 40 (Ger); 43 *Randazzo* (Ita); 43 (Ger); 22.8.44 scuttled Marseilles; 47 raised, BU
Commissaire Ramel 7.40 Seized by Australians; 40 MoWT (Br), troopship; 19.9.40 shelled by aux cruiser *Atlantis*, on fire, sunk, 28 25S 74 23E (3†, 63 surv)
Condé 40 Req KM, accom ship (Fra); 8.7.44 seized Nice by Germans; 7.8.44 bombed by Allied aircraft, on fire, sunk, Nice; 28.12.44 refloated; 45 coal hulk Marseilles; 9.5.47

sold La Seyne breakers

Congo 3.12.42 Seized Marseilles by Germans; 12.42 transf Italy, *Frosinone* (Ita); 2.12.43 bombed by German aircraft, blew up, sunk, Bari; raised BU

Cornouaille 40 German control; 5.8.40 Seelöwe transport *H1*; 31.8.41 KMD Oslo; 12.11.44 shelled (in German convoy KS357) by cruisers HMS *Bellona*, *Kent*, sunk, SE of Egersund

Criton 9.5.41 Captured by amc HMS *Cilicia*, taken Freetown; 5.41 MoWT control; 21.6.41 stopped (convoy straggler), shelled, by VFr cruiser, sunk, 7m S of 09 06N 13 40W (10†, 24 surv)

Cuba 6.40 Taken over by VFr; 31.10.40 captured by RN; 12.40 MoWT (Br), troopship; 6.4.45 torpedoed (in convoy VWP16) by *U1195*, sunk, 50 36 50N 00 57W (1†, 264 surv); wreck dispersed

D'Artagnan 10.40 Taken over by VFr; 10.41 on fire Shanghai; TL; 42 taken over by Japanese; 42 IJN troopship *Teiko Maru* (Jpn); 22.2.44 torpedoed by subm USS *Puffer*, sunk, 03 03N 109 16E

D'Entrecasteaux 1.7.41 Captured by cruiser HMS *Dunedin*; 41 MoWT (Br); 7.11.42 torpedoed by *U154*, sunk, 15 30N 57W (3†, 64 surv)

Dalila 18.6.40 Sunk Cherbourg; 14.10.40 raised, repaired (Ger); 12.3.43 torpedoed by British MTB, sunk, off Gravelines

Dalny 25.12.42 Seized Marseilles by Germans; 42 (Ger); 10–11.1.43 torpedoed by subm HMS *Tribune* near San Remo, damaged, beached; 4.6.43 torpedoed by subm *Arethuse* (Fra), further damaged, 41 08N 09 32E; 45 wreck BU

Daphné 40 MoWT, *Daphne II* (Br); 18.3.41 torpedoed by E-boat *S102* near 59 buoy, off R Humber (0†, 28 surv); taken in tow, beached 53 31 59N 00 03 10E, broke in two, TL

De La Salle 8.40 KM, Seelöwe transport *H17;* 28.10.41 returned; 9.7.43 torpedoed (in convoy) by *U508*, sunk, 05 50N 02 22E (10†, 239 surv)

Dioné 40 MoWT, *Dione II* (Br); 3.2.41 attacked (convoy SC20 straggler) by German FW200 Kondor aircraft, damaged, 55 40N 14 23W; 4.2.41 torpedoed by *U93*, sunk, 55 50N 10 30W (27†, 1 surv)

Djurdjura 40 Seized Falmouth by GB; 41 MoWT (Br); 13.6.41 torpedoed (in convoy SL75) by subm *Brin* (Ita), sunk, 38 53N 23 11W (33†, 5 surv)

Douaisien 29.5.40 Struck mine, sunk, off Dunkirk (3†, *c*1250 surv)

Dunkerquois 8.40 KM, Seelöwe transport *H6*; 19.9.40 leaking, ashore, off Havre; 12.40 bombed by British aircraft, sunk; 3.44 raised; 45 BU

Dupleix 3.8.41 Intercepted by patrol vessel *Bellatrix* (Ne), taken Tandjong Priok; 41 *Boero* (Ne); 25.2.42 torpedoed by subm *I-58* (Jpn), sunk, S of Sunda Strait (0†, 70 surv)

Elima 40 Captured by Germans; 20.2.44 collision off Trondheim, beached, broke up; 23.2.44 sunk

Emile Miguet 12.10.39 Shelled (French convoy KJ2 straggler) by *U48*, on fire, abandoned, sunk, 50 15N 14 50W (2†)

Explorateur Grandidier 21.8.44 Scuttled to block Mirabeau dock, Marseilles; 48 wreck BU

Felix-Henri 42 Seized by Germans; 42 KM, aux escort *SG10*; 28.8.43 torpedoed by subm HMS *Sickle*, sunk, 42 26N 09 50E

Firuz 40 KM, supply vessel *Friedrike* (*Tempo 2*) (Ger); 28.8.44 scuttled as blockship entrance to Constanta; raised, to USSR, *Volganeft* (Rus)

Flandre 6.40 Seized Marseilles by Germans; 5.8.40 KM, Seelöwe transport *H9*; 13.9.40 struck by magnetic mine abeam Terre Negre, R Gironde (–†); 14.9.40 beached to prevent sinking; wreck broke up

Floride 1.12.39 Struck by magnetic mine off Dunkirk; beached near Dunkirk at Malo-les-Bains; broke in two, TL

Fort de Souville 12.42 Seized by Italians; 43 *Benivento* (Ita); 1.4.43 torpedoed by MTB 210° 3m off Cani Is, beached Ras Zebib, TL

Fort de Vaux 29.11.43 Torpedoed by *U68*, sunk, 06 32N 12 20W (0†, 61 surv)

Fort Lamy 7.40 Seized Falmouth by GB; 40 MoWT (Br); 8.3.43 torpedoed (convoy SC121 straggler) by *U527*, sunk, 58 30N 31W (46†, 3 surv)

Fort Médine 7.40 Seized Falmouth by GB; 9.40 MoWT (Br); 20.2.41 struck mine 51 33 30N 03 56 30W, broke in two, both sections sank (1†, 46 surv)

Fort Richepanse 18.2.41 Captured by RN, taken Gibraltar; 41 MoWT (Br); 3.9.41 attacked by German aircraft 52 46N 23W, damaged; torpedoed by *U567*, sunk, 52 15N 21 10W (41†, 22 surv)

Foucauld 20.6.40 Bombed by German aircraft La Pallice, badly damaged; wreck sank in shallow water, back broken

Frimaire 15.6.42 Torpedoed by *U68*, sunk, 11 50N 73 40W (0 surv)

Gazcon 40 MoWT (Br); 1.9.42 torpedoed by subm *I-29* (Jpn), sunk, 13 01N 50 30E (12†, 37 surv)

Général Metzinger 5.40 Troopship; 11.6.40 bombed by German aircraft, sunk, Havre roads; 50 refloated, BU *in situ*

Gonneville 28.12.42 seized by Germans; 43 transf Italy, *Castelvetrano* (Ita); 43 seized Civitavecchia by Germans, *Gonneville* (Ger); 20.8.44 sunk as blockship Marseilles; 44–46 BU *in situ*

Grandlieu 24.6.40 Seized Nantes by Germans, 8.40 KM, Seelöwe transport *H23* (Ger); 4.41 transport; 20.6.44 scuttled by Germans at entrance Transatlantique dock, Cherbourg; 8.46 wreck removed
Gravelines 40 MoWT (Br); 31.5.41 torpedoed (convoy HX127 straggler) by *U147* 56N 11 13W (11†, 25 surv); broke in two, afterpart shelled, sunk; forepart towed R Clyde (ar 3.6.41), beached Kames Bay, CTL; 42 BU Rothesay
Guilvinec 19.2.41 Torpedoed by subm HMS *Tigris*, sunk, 44 48N 03 01W
Guyane 4.12.42 Seized Marseilles by Germans; 12.42 transf Italy, *Acqui* (Ita); 9.43 scuttled Spezia, raised by Germans, KM minelayer *Niedersachsen*; 15.2.44 torpedoed by subm HMS *Upstart*, sunk, 43 03N 05 54E

Henri Estier 7.3.43 Bombed by British aircraft, sunk, NNE of Zembra Is, Tunisia
Henri Mory 7.40 Seized Swansea by GB; 40 MoWT (Br); 26.4.41 torpedoed by *U110*, sunk, 330m WNW of Blaskets (28†, 4 surv)
Henry Desprez 41 KM, *Trapez 4* (Ger); 3.6.43 torpedoed by subm HMS *Unruffled* 39 13N 16 01E; 4.6.43 sunk

Iméréthie II 22.8.44 Scuttled by Germans S entrance Marseilles harbour; 25.10.44 raised, BU
Ipanema 17.11.42 Seized Marseilles by Germans; transf Italy, *Villarosa* (Ita); 19.9.43 sunk by Allied aircraft at Naples; wreck abandoned; 6.45 refloated, repaired; 6.47 *Taurinia* (Ita)

Jean et Jacques 8.40 Req by Germans, Seelöwe transport *H12*; 3.3.42 torpedoed by British MTB, sunk, off Cap Blanc Nez (8†)
Jean Labourde 22.8.44 Scuttled Martigues (Marseilles) by Germans; 46 raised, towed La Seyne; BU Savona

Kakoulima 43 *Aversa* (Ita); 19.10.43 torpedoed by subm HMS *Ultor*, sunk, off Rapallo
Khai Dinh 41 Seized Indo-China by Japanese; 22.11.42 attacked by USAAF aircraft, sunk, 20 58N 106 40E
Kilissi 41 (Ger); 12.3.44 bombed by Allied aircraft, sunk, off R Ebro
Kindia 10.4.42 Seized Indo-China by Japanese; 42 *Teikin Maru* (Jpn); 27.7.43 struck mine, sunk, 19 57N 109 05E
Kita 41 KM, aux minelayer *Brandenburg* (Ger); 21.9.43 torpedoed by subm HMS *Unseen*, sunk, SW of Leghorn

Languedoc 40 MoWT (Br); 17.10.40 torpedoed (in convoy SC7) by *U48*, abandoned, 59 10N 17 52W (0†, 41 surv); 18.10.40 sunk 59 14N 17 51W
Le Rhin 24.9.40 Commd RN as decoy ship HMS *Fidelity*; 29.12.42 torpedoed (convoy ONS154 straggler) by *U435*, sunk, 43 23N 27 07W (0 surv – incl 42 surv from *Empire Shackleton* (Br), sunk 28.12.42))
Lillois 42 German control; 28.3.43 torpedoed by subm HMS *Torbay*, sunk, off Cape Scalea, Italy
Linois 14.12.42 Seized by Italians, *Orvieto* (Ita); 9.43 seized Genoa by Germans; 22.8.44 scuttled by Germans N entrance Marseilles harbour; 45 refloated, BU
Lipari 8.11.42 Struck by Allied shells during landings Casablanca, on fire, broke in two, sank
Lorient 40 MoWT (Br); 5.5.43 torpedoed (convoy ONS5 straggler) by *U125*, sunk, 54N 44W
Lorraine 8.11.42 Scuttled Oran
Louis Charles Schiaffino 25.2.41 Attacked by aircraft, sunk, E of Collo
Louisiane 13.10.39 Torpedoed (in convoy OA17) by *U48*, damaged, 3m off Cap de la Hève (1†); shelled, sunk, 50 14N 15 05W
Lyon 6.40 Seized by Germans while building Rouen; 42 completed as *Johannisberger* (Ger); 16.3.43 torpedoed by subm *M-104* (Rus) off Kirkenes, aground (0 surv); TL

Madali 6.40 Seized Bordeaux by Germans; 40 (Ger); 5.8.40 KM, Seelöwe transport *H7;* 25.6.41 Channel Islands transport; 27.9.43 torpedoed by *MTB202* (Ne) and *MTB204*, *MTB231* (Br), sunk, 50 22 03N 01 04 02E (52†)
Marcel Schiaffino 6.40 Seized Nantes by Germans; 7.8.40 KM, Seelöwe transport *H24*; 17.5.41 *Dockenhuden* (Ger); 10.3.42–4.6.42 troop transport; 30.3.45–8.4.45 bombed by Allied aircraft, sunk, Hamburg; 48 raised, repaired; 15.3.50 *Clare Grammerstorf* (Ger)
Maréchal Lyautey 22.8.44 Scuttled Marseilles by Germans; 47–48 wreck BU
Marie Dawn 40 MoWT (Br); 2.11.41 bombed by German aircraft 210° 4m from 59A Buoy, Humber estuary, abandoned; 3.11.41 sunk 2m SW of H2 Buoy, Humber estuary (0†, 28 surv)
Marie José 29.5.40 Torpedoed, shelled, by *U37*, sunk, 40m NW of Vigo, near Salvors Is
Mariette Pacha 22.8.44 Scuttled Marseilles; 48 wreck BU
Martinière 9.39 Req by French govt; 6.40 bombed by German aircraft, on fire, badly damaged, Lorient; 41 conv to aac battery by Germans; 45 retaken; 45 MN, hulk; 55 BU St Nazaire
Massilia 42 German control, accom ship; 22.8.44 scuttled Marseilles by Germans; post-war raised, BU
Massis 2.5.41 Seized by Italians; 41 IN, *Saturno* (Ita); 20.1.43 bombed by British aircraft 37 16N 10 28E; taken in tow, sunk
Maurice Delmas 12.42 Seized by Italians, *Modica* (Ita); 15.2.43 bombed by Allied aircraft, sunk, Naples; 3.47 raised, repaired; 47 *Modica* (Ita)

Mecanicien Principal Carvin 21.6.40 Attacked by German aircraft, sunk, Verdon
Medjerda 40 MoWT (Br); 18.3.41 torpedoed (in convoy SL68) by *U105*, sunk, 17N 21W (54†)
Meknès 24.7.40 Torpedoed by E-boat *S27*, sunk, 50 04 10N 02 14 30W (383†, 898 surv)
Melpomène 40 MoWT (Br); 6.3.42 torpedoed by subm *Giuseppe Finzi* (Ita), sunk, 23 35N 62 39W (0†, 49 surv)
Mendoza 18.2.42 Captured by amc HMS *Asturias*; 42 MoWT (Br), troopship; 1.11.42 captured by *U178*, torpedoed, sunk, 29 20S 32 14E (23†, 383 surv)
Menhir Bras 11.42 Found sunk at Oran; 11.43 refloated, not repaired; 10.50 towed Spezia for BU
Mexique 9.39 MN, aux cruiser X22; 4.40 troopship; 19.6.40 struck by magnetic mine, sunk, Verdon harbour entrance (0†, 178 surv); TL
Min 8.12.42 Seized Bizerta by Germans; 12.42 transf Italy, *Conegliano* (Ita); 6.6.43 attacked by aircraft, sunk, Olbia (–†); 5.3.49 refloated, sank in deep water
Mitidja 8.11.42 Bombed by Allied aircraft, sunk, Oran
Monique 12.6.40 Lost by enemy action 'off France' on voyage Haifa–Havre (4 pow)
Monique Schiaffino 30.5.40 Attacked by German aircraft, sunk, Dunkirk
Monselet 20.9.41 Bombed by RAF aircraft, sunk, Gulf of Gabes, Tunisia
Mont Agel 9.43 Bombed Bastia; 47 wreck BU
Mont Viso 2.11.43 Torpedoed (in convoy KMS30) by *U593* 36 45N 01 55E, sunk
Montesquieu 12.42 Seized by Italians, *Enna* (Ita); 30.5.43 attacked by British aircraft, sunk, Naples; 47 raised, BU Naples
Moron 8.11.42 Scuttled Bizerta entrance channel
Mostaganem 18.1.42 Seized Bizerta by Italians; 18.4.43 attacked by aircraft, damaged, Levanzo; 19.4.43 sunk
Myson 7.40 Seized Falmouth by GB; 23.8.40 MoWT (Br); 15.3.41 captured (in convoy) by *Gneisenau*; 16.3.41 sunk 42N 43W (0†, 43 pow)

Nicole Schiaffino 40 Seized by Germans; 5.8.40 KM, Seelöwe transport *H5*; 2.4.41 KMD Stettin; 22.10.41 transport, Norway; 15.3.42 aground Finsnes; submerged, TL
Normand 29.6.44 Scuttled Cherbourg; 11.47 raised, beached Mieilles Bay, TL

Ophelie 20.5.40 Bombed by German aircraft, sunk, Boulogne roads, 251° 4265 yards from Dique Carnot North Lt
Oued Sebou II 42 Seized by Italians; 42 *Pistoia* (Ita); 24.1.43 torpedoed by British aircraft, sunk, NNW of Ustica

Pallas 40 Seized by Germans; 41 KM, supply vessel *Tempo 3* (Ger); 27.6.44 torpedoed by subm HMS *Ultor*, sunk, 43 34N 07 15E
Pavon 20.5.40 Bombed by German aircraft, on fire, stranded near Calais; TL
Penerf 7.40 Taken over by VFr; 14.4.43 torpedoed by subm HMS *Ultor*, sunk, 43 32N 07 12E (20†, 11 surv)
Penthièvre 7.40 Taken over by VFr; 4.8.40 KM, Seelöwe transport *H2*; 29.6.41 Channel Islands transport; 2.3.43 shelled by Dover long-range batteries, sunk, off Calais (22†)
Perros Guirec 40 German control; 31.8.44 scuttled Rouen by Germans; 5.45 at Rouen sunk; wreck dispersed *in situ* after 6.45
Phénix 40 MoWT (Br); 24.12.41 struck mine, sunk, Haifa harbour
Phryné 24.9.39 Struck mine (laid 4.9.39 by *U13*), sunk, 3.5m from Aldeburgh LV, 52 09 26N 01 42 52E (–†)
Pierre L-D 41 *Persee* (Fra); 31.3.42 captured Saigon by Japanese; *Teihoku Maru* (Jpn); 11.8.45 torpedoed by subm USS *Jallao*, sunk, 38 03N 133 13E
Platon 42 Seized by Germans; 22.8.44 scuttled Marseilles; 1.7.45 raised; 23.9.45 ar La Ciotat in tow; 18.12.47 condemned, BU
Pluviôse 40 Seized by Germans; 40 KM, *Bitonto* (*Tempo 4*) (Ger); 8.44 scuttled Marseilles; raised BU
Poitiers 16.9.40 Intercepted on voyage Dakar–Tabou by RN warship, set on fire by own crew to prevent capture, shelled, sunk
Porthos 8.11.42 Bombed during Allied landings Casablanca, capsized; wreck driven on rocks in gale; 7.6.45 refloated, BU in port
Portrieux 22.5.40 Attacked by German aircraft, sunk, near Gravelines (–†, 10 surv); wreck BU
Président Doumer 19.7.40 MoWT (Br), troopship; 30.10.42 torpedoed (in convoy SL125) by *U604*, sunk, 35 08N 16 44W (260†, 85 surv)
Président Sergent 8.7.40 Seized Bermuda by GB; 40 MoWT (Br); 18.11.42 torpedoed (in convoy ONS144) by *U624*, sunk, 54 07N 38 26W (20†, 39 surv)

Rhuys 19.11.39 Struck mine (laid by German destroyer), sunk, 6.8m E of Humber LV, 53 30 48N 00 23 07E (16†, 17 surv); 10.46 wreck dispersed
Rose Schiaffino 1.41 Seized Gibraltar by GB; 41 MoWT (Br); 28.10.41 torpedoed (ind) by *U105* E of White Bay, Newfoundland (41†, 0 surv)
Roubaisien 8.11.42 Sunk by French naval authorities in channel at Bizerta; 12.47 refloated; 25.3.48 ar Algiers in tow; 50 BU
Rouennaise 25.4.43 Struck mine (laid 10.4.43 by *U455*) 34 04N 07 23W, wrecked (16†, 39 surv)
Roussillon 41 KM, *Trapez 5* (Ger); 22.7.44 bombed, aground 3km W of Gênes; raised;

11.1.46 sunk Multedo, W of Genoa

Saint Ambroise 12.42 Seized Marseilles by Italians; 42 *Nuoro* (Ita); 31.3.43 torpedoed by British aircraft, sunk, off Cap Bon
Saint Basile 14.6.44 Torpedoed by *U547*, sunk, 05 03N 09 14W (6†, 58 surv)
Saint Camille 26.5.40 Struck by magnetic mine, sunk, Dunkirk roads
Saint Clair 7.40 MoWT, *Saint Clair II* (Br); 23.9.41 torpedoed (in convoy SL87) by *U67*, sunk, 30 25N 23 35W (13†, 34 surv)
Saint Cyrille 22.8.44 Scuttled by Germans N entrance Marseilles harbour; 48 raised, BU
Saint Didier 4.7.41 Torpedoed by 829 Sq Albacore aircraft, damaged, off Anatolia; later sunk by British aircraft in port at Antalya, Turkey (when under Turkish flag)
Saint Enogat 7.40 Seized Plymouth by GB; 40 MoWT (Br); 19.8.44 torpedoed (in convoy ETC72) by *U413*, sunk, 50 16 24N 00 50W (0†, 34 surv)
Saint Firmin 6.40 Seized Nantes by Germans; 8.8.40 KM, Seelöwe transport *H14*; 19.6.41 *Gotenhafen* (Ger); 11.3.45 attacked by Allied aircraft, bradly damaged, Dock 72 Hamburg; 2.6.45 at Hamburg, sunk; 28.1.51 raised; BU
Saint Louis 1.3.44 Torpedoed (in convoy) by *U66*, sunk, 05 23N 00 09W (85†, 49 surv)
Saint Malo 8.40 Seized Halifax; 8.40 Canadian govt (Can); 12.10.40 torpedoed (convoy HX77 straggler) by *U101*, sunk, 57 58N 16 32W (28†, 16 surv)
St Nazaire 23.9.43 Torpedoed by subm HMS *Sibyl*, sunk, 44 13N 09 13E
Saint Octave 5.40 Scuttled Dunkirk; 18.8.41 raised by Germans; 41 *Ilse Fritzen* (Ger); 25.1.45 bombed by British aircraft, sunk, near Askeroll, Eidsfjord
San Antonio 5.40 Taken over by VFr; 21.12.42 (Ger); 5.5.43 bombed by Allied aircraft, sunk, off Cape St Vito, near Taranto
San Diego 24.6.40 Taken over by VFr; 21.12.42 (Ger); 6.4.43 bombed by British aircraft, sunk, on way to Bizerta
San Francisco 24.6.40 Taken over by VFr; 21.12.42 (Ger); 14.7.43 bombed by British aircraft, sunk, 35m W of Cape Corso, Corsica
Saumur 43 (Ger); 21.5.44 torpedoed by subm HMS *Upstart*, sunk, 0.5m E of Port Vendres
Senneville 42 (Ger); 8.44 scuttled Marseilles; 47–48 salved; part BU *in situ*; part towed Savona for BU
Shéhérazade 41 (Pan); 1.6.42 torpedoed, shelled, by *U158*, sunk, 28 41N 91 20W (1†, 58 surv)
Si-Kiang 14.12.41 Detained Manila by US; 12.41 USMC (US); 24.12.41 bombed by Japanese aircraft, on fire, burnt out, Marivales harbour, Bataan (10†)
Sinaia 40 German control; 11.42 seized Marseilles by Germans; 43 hospital ship; 22.8.44 scuttled Marseilles by Germans; 9.12.46 refloated, TL; 53 wreck BU
Sinfra 12.42 German control; KM, transport; 19.10.43 sunk during USAAF, RAF, air attack, N of Crete (1998†, 566 surv)
Solon 17.7.40 Seized Swansea by GB; 40 MoWT, *Solon II* (Br); 3.12.42 torpedoed by *U508*, sunk, 07 45N 56 30W (75†, 8 surv)
Sphinx 39 MN, hospital ship; 6.40 seized Marseilles by Italians; 40 *Subiaco* (Ita); 5.1.44 attacked by Allied aircraft, sunk, Genoa; 45–46 raised, BU
Strabon 40 German control; 18.10.43 seized Etang de Berre by Germans; 5.2.44 scuttled Toulon; 2.6.45 raised; 12.47 condemned, BU
Surville 6.11.43 Struck mine 8m SE of Cap Bon; beached 228° 1.03m from Ras el Mustafa Lt (–†); TL
Syrie 11.6.40 Attacked by German aircraft, sunk, off Cap la Hève

Theophile Gautier 40 Taken over by VFr; 4.10.41 torpedoed by subm HMS *Talisman*, sunk, 37 45N 24 35E (20†)
Thésée 40 German control; 11.42 *Pinerola* (Ita); 30.12.43 scuttled off Naples; 46 raised, BU Bagnoli
Tlemcen 18.12.42 Seized by Germans; 43 *Partinico* (Ita); 11.5.43 bombed by Allied aircraft, sunk, Catania
Tourny 25.1.40 Torpedoed (French convoy 56KS straggler) by *U44*, sunk, 38 09N 09 55W (8†)

Vermont 15.10.39 Captured by *U37* 48 01N 17 22W, sunk by explosive charges and shelling (2†)
Victor Schœlcher 9.39–15.10.40, 27.11.41–42 (VFr) amc *Bougainville* (Fra); 5.5.42 torpedoed by RN aircraft, sunk, Diego Suarez
Ville de Metz 4.8.40 Seized Bordeaux by Germans; 4.8.40 KM, Seelöwe transport *H4*; 22.5.41 *Othmarschen* (Ger); 3.3.42 transport, Norway; 1.2.43 torpedoed by subm *L-20* (Rus), sunk, 71 07 02N 27 29 09E (4†)
Ville de Rouen 40 Captured by RN; 40 MoWT (Br); 28.12.42 torpedoed (in convoy ONS154) by *U225*, damaged, 43 25N 27 15W; 29.12.42 torpedoed by *U662*, sunk (0†, 71 surv)
Ville de Verdun 42 Captured by Japanese, *Teison Maru* (Jpn), transport; 14.10.42 torpedoed by subm USS *Finback*, sunk, 25 22N 121 15E
Ville du Havre 6.40 Taken over by VFr; 8.11.42 torpedoed by subm USS *Herring*, sunk, 33 34N 07 52W
Villiers 42 *Parma* (Ita); 30.1.43 bombed, torpedoed, by Allied aircraft, sunk, off La Goulette
Vulcain 6.40 MoWT (Br); 23.5.41 torpedoed by *U38*, sunk, 09 20N 15 35W (7†)

Winnipeg 40 Taken over by VFr; 6.41 captured by RN; 41 (Br); 42 MoWT, *Winnipeg II*

(Br); 22.10.42 torpedoed (in convoy ON139) by *U443*, sunk, 49 51N 27 58W (0†, 192 surv)
Wyoming 15.3.43 Torpedoed (in convoy UGS6) by *U524*, sunk, 40 18N 28 56W (0†, 127 surv)

Yalou 12.12.42 Seized Marseilles by Germans; 42 transf Italy; 12.42 *Rovereto* (Ita); 6.4.43 bombed (in convoy) by British aircraft, exploded, on fire, Cape Zebib, 5m N of Bizerta (–†)

Scuttled for war purposes
Tabarka 6.40 MoS (Br); 18.5.41 sunk as blockship Kirk Sound, Scapa Flow, 58 53 20N 02 53 50W; wreck raised; 27.7.44 removed to Burra Sound, sunk near *Inverlane* (*qv*)

Sunk Mulberry Harbour, Normandy
Forbin 6.40 Seized Gibraltar by GB; 7.40 MoWT (Br); 44 Adm; 8.6.44 sunk as breakwater, Gooseberry 5, Sword Beach, Ouistreham; gutted by fire; raised postwar, BU
Formigny 9.12.40 Captured off Lisbon by armed trawler *Alouette*; 41 MoWT (Br); 9.6.44 sunk as breakwater, Gooseberry 5, Sword Beach, Ouistreham; raised, BU

Lost postwar through striking mine
Prosper Schiaffino 8(10).11.45 Struck unswept mine off Porquerolles, sunk (5†, 25 surv)

Changes of name, flag, role, disposals, etc
Albert le Borgne 7.40 MoWT (Br); 43 army training ship; 3.46 condemned; 47 BU Boom
André Lebon 6.5.43 Seized Toulon by Germans; 5.43 accom ship, Toulon; 31.1.44 returned; 11.3.44 bombed, sunk, Toulon; 5.5.45 raised, repaired; 19.10.46 returned commercial service
Ango 6.40 Seized Bordeaux by Germans; 6.8.40 KM, Seelöwe transport *H21*; 24.5.41 *Lokstedt* (Ger); 2.44 transport, Norway; 3.7.44 accom ship, Altafjord; 5.45 at Mosjøen; 45 *Ango* (Fra); 5.48 BU Ghent
Aragaz 45 *Monchique* (Por)
Arago 9.39–8.40 MN, auxiliary *X82*; 46 MN, salvage vessel
Athos II 11.42 Allied troopship; 3.43 WSA control; 3.46 returned France; 3.48 returned owner

Banfora 12.4.41 Captured off Mauritania by RN vessels; 42 MoWT (Br), troopship; 46 (Fra)
Bangkok 2.11.41 Captured off South Africa by RN vessels; 42 MoWT, *Bangkok II* (Br); 45 *Bangkok* (Fra)
Barfleur 9.39 MN, amc *X-19* (Fra); 7.40 Allied control; 47 returned

Campana 40 LU Buenos Aires; 28.7.43 seized by Argentina, *Rio Jachal* (Arg); 46 *Campana* (Fra)
Canada 40 MN, hospital ship *X45*; 12.42 Allied service; 47 returned
Cantal 10.1.41 Captured by obv HMS *Maron;* 41 MoWT (Br); 45 (Fra)
Cap des Palmes 39 MN, amc; 9.11.40 seized off Libreville by *Commandant Domine* (FFr); 40–42 amc (FFr); 42 MoWT (Br); 45 (Fra)
Cap el Hank 6.40 MoWT (Br); 46 (Fra)
Cap Hadid 40 Seized by Germans; 41 KM, *Python* (Ger); conv to *Sperrbrecher 122*; 25.9.41 commd; 25.8.44 scuttled St Nazaire; 6.46 raised; repaired; *Cap Hadid* (Fra)
Cap Saint Jacques 6.40 Detained Suez; 4.10.40 seized by GB; 15.11.40 MoWT (Br), personnel ship; 4.45 RN hospital ship No 57; 4.46 (Fra)
Cap Sim 40 KM (Ger); 25.9.41 commd as *Sperrbrecher 121*; 5.9.44 decomm; 45 *Cap Sim* (Fra)
Cap Tafelneh 6.40 Sunk Dunkirk; salved by Germans, *Carl Arp* (Ger); 5.45 at Hamburg; 45 *Empire Chelmer* (Br); 45 *Cap Tafelneh* (Fra)
Cap Tourane 40 MoWT (Br); 45 (Fra)
Champollion 40 LU Algiers; 12.42 Allied troopship; 46 returned
Chantilly 5.40 Troopship; 1.1.41 captured by RN near Tres Forcas; 26.1.41 MoWT (Br); 3.44–19.11.45 Hospital Ship No 63; 45 (Fra)
Charles Plumier 3.9.39 MN, amc *X-11*; 22.10.40 decomm; 22.11.40 captured off Gibraltar by destroyer HMS *Faulknor*; 40 MoWT (Br); 5.41 RN, obv HMS *Largs*; 8.42–12.45 RN service, landing ship; 12.45 French govt, *Charles Plumier* (Fra); 48 returned owner
Chef Mécanicien Armand Blanc 43 Seized by Italians; 43 *Lercara* (Ita); 28.5.43 bombed by USAAF aircraft, sunk, Leghorn; 46 raised; 46 (Fra)
Circe 40 MoWT, *Circe II* (Br); 45 *Circe* (Fra)
Colombie 11.11.39–7.9.40 MN, amc; 40 taken over by VFr; 12.42 seized Bone by US; 10.43 US troopship; 4.45 hospital ship *Aleda E Lutz* (US); 11.4.46 *Colombie* (Fra)
Commandant Dorise 2.11.41 Captured off South Africa by RN; 41 MoWT (Br); 5.44 returned (Fra)

Danaé 40 MoWT, *Danae II* (Br); 45 *Danaé* (Fra)
De Grasse 7.40 Scuttled Bordeaux; raised by Germans; 8.40 (Ger), depot/accom ship for Italian subms, Bordeaux; 25.8.44 scuttled by Germans; 30.8.45 raised, repaired, returned (Fra); 6.47 returned to service
Desirade 18.6.40 Captured off St Helena by amc HMS *Pretoria Castle*; 40 MoWT (Br); 45 (Fra)
Djenne 40 German control; 43 *Freigeleit* (Ger); 22.8.44 damaged by quayside explosions, sprang leak, capsized, Marseilles; 26.8.46 refloated, repaired; 7.8.48 re-entered

service as *Djenne* (Fra)

Edea 40 German control; 45 returned
Egeé 40 MoWT (Br); 45 (Fra)
Eridan 19.1.43–20.5.46 MoWT (Br), troopship; 5.46 (Fra)
Esperance 25.10.40 Seized off Djibouti by RN; 1.11.40–14.8.45 MoWT (Br); 3.45 returned
Ésterel 9.39–2.11.40 MN, amc *X-21* (Fra); 9.2.42 seized Marseilles by Germans; 42 (Ita); 9.43 (Ger); 5.47 (Fra)

Felix Roussel 7.40 GB govt control; 11.40 MoWT (Br), troopship; 16.4.46 (Fra)
Formose 28.7.43 Seized Buenos Aires by Argentina; 43 *Rio Tunuyan* (Arg); 46 *Formose* (Fra)
Fort de France 11.42 Seized Marseilles by Germans (Ger); 42 *Belluno* (Ita); 5.3.43 forced ashore during evacuation of Tunisia; refloated; 45 *Fort de France* (Fra)
Fort de Troyon 8.40 Seized Douala by GB; 40 MoWT (Br); 45 (Fra)
Fort Royal 6.2.42 Seized New York by US, US control; 5.11.45 returned
Franche-Comté 40 MoWT (Br); (45) (Fra)

Hortensia Bertin 41 *Nicaragua* (Pan); 46 *Greater Shanghai* (Chn)

Île de France 40 Allied control; 10.3.41 completed conv to troopship; 22.9.45 French troopship; 3.2.46 returned CGT
Indiana 9.11.42 Req as New Orleans by US; 42 USMC (Pan); 3.45 returned (Fra)
Indochinois 18.10.40 Captured by RN cruiser; 40 MoWT (Br); 45 (Fra)

Jean L-D 45 *Betelgeuse* (Fra)

Katiola 43 *Rio Lujan* (Arg); 46 *Katiola* (Fra)
Kerguelen 40 MN, troopship; 6.40 Seized Bordeaux by Germans; 40 *Winrich von Kniprode* (Ger); 6.8.40 KM, Seelöwe transport *H6*; 16.10.41 transport, Norway; 4.1.45 accom ship; 1.45 VTS; 5.45 at Kiel; 3.11.45 *Kerguelen* (Fra)
Kolente 40 (Ger); 25.9.41 commd KM *Sperrbrecher 20*; 11.8.44 scuttled Nantes; raised, repaired; 47 *Saint Michel* (Fra)
Koutoubia 9.39–5.9.40 MN, amc; 11.42 attacked by Axis aircraft, sunk, Bona; 44 refloated; 23.8.46 resumed service

La Saône 40 Seized by Germans while building Dunkirk; 40 KM, aux supply vessel *Rheinpfalz* (Ger); 6.44 scuttled incomplete at slipway, builder's yard; repaired; 48 completed; 23.4.49 *La Saône* (Fra)
La Seine 40 Seized by Germans while building Dunkirk; 40 KM, aux supply vessel *Stormarn* (Ger); 6.44 scuttled incomplete at slipway, builder's yard; repaired; 29.1.49 *La Seine* (Fra)
Leconte de Lisle 10.4.42 Seized Indo-China by Japanese; 42 *Teiritu Maru* (Jpn); 28.7.45 struck US mine, sunk, 35 32N 135 20E; 18.8.48 raised, repaired Maizuru; 12.50 *Leconte de Lisle* (Fra)
Leopold L-D 41 *Aldebaran* (Fra)
Lieutenant de la Tour 40 Taken over by VFr; 44 returned
Lieutenant Robert Mory 18.7.40 MoWT (Br); 6.7.45 (Fra)
Lieutenant St Loubert Bie 18.5.41 Stopped off St Helena by RN; 29.5.41 British prize; 41 MoWT (Br); 9.5.45 (Fra)

Malgache 40 (Ger); 8.40 KM, Seelöwe transport *H28*; 5.45 at Flensburg; 45 (Fra)
Maréchal Joffre 12.12.41 Req Manila by US; transport; 42 *Rochambeau* (US); 45 *Maréchal Joffre* (Fra)
Maréchal Pétain 6.44 Launched; 8.44 scuttled Port de Bouc by Germans; 8.46 refloated; repaired; 49 completed as *Marsellaise* (Fra)
Marguerite Finaly 41 KM, *Trapez 5* (Ger); 27.6.44 scuttled as blockship NW entrance Marseilles; 7.46 raised; repaired; 48 *Esso Provence* (Fra)
Marigot 40 MN, aux patrol vessel *P-1*; 45 returned
Marrakech 26.12.42–19.8.43 MoWT (Br); 7.43 military store ship; 45 (Fra)
Maurienne 7.40 MoWT (Br); 45 (Fra)
Meduana 40 Seized Bordeaux by Germans; 6.8.40 KM, Seelöwe transport *H20* (Ger); 16.10.40 transport, Norway; 1.45 VTS; 5.45 recovered Kiel, damaged; 11.45 returned; 48 re-entered service as *Kerguelen* (Fra)
Merope 43 *Potrero del Llano II* (Mex)
Mont Everest 11.42 Taken over New Orleans by US; 45 returned

Palmyre 6.40 Seized by Germans while building; 40 *Vierlanden* (Ger); 10.8.44 scuttled Nantes; 10.44 raised, repaired; 5.46 *Palmyre* (Fra)
Pasteur 8.40 Allied troopship; 6.45 returned

Quercy 4.9.39–15.11.40 MN, amc *X-20* (Fra); 47 returned

Rémois 43 *Lanusei* (Ita); 22.3.43 bomb damage at Palermo; 48-50 reconditioned

Taranto; 50 *Rémois* (Fra)

Sagittaire 41 Taken over by VFr; 7.43 (Fra)
Saint Gobain 40 German control; 45 returned
Saint Palais 21.6.40 Scuttled Brest; 8.41 salved by Germans; 41 *Adolf Winter* (Ger); 5.45 taken over Bilbao; 46 returned, *Saint Palais* (Fra)
Saintonge 40 MoWT (Br); 45 (Fra)
Salomé 7.6.40 Sunk Dunkirk while completing; salved, towed Rotterdam; 40 *Breisgau* (Ger); 27.9.44 scuttled as blockship Waalhaven, Rotterdam; 12.1.46 returned France; 24.6.46 raised; 16.1.47–11.6.48 repaired; 12.6.48 *Salomé* (Fra)
San José 12.42 Seized Marseilles by Germans; ..... sunk in Allied aircraft attack; 46 raised; 50 re-entered service
San Mateo 24.6.40 Seized Nantes by Germans; 40 (Ger); 8.40 KM, Seelöwe transport *H27*; 42 KM, accom ship, then landing flotilla ship; 5.45 at Hamburg, damaged; 29.6.45 returned; 7.45 *San Mateo* (Fra)
San Pedro 6.40 Taken over by VFr; 8.44 scuttled Marseilles; raised, badly damaged; 48 returned
Sèvre 40 Seized by Germans; 22.8.40 KM, Seelöwe transport *H21*; 8.4.41 (Ger); 31.8.41 KMD Oslo; 5.45 recovered badly damaged Hamburg; 46 returned, BU France
Shapur 40 German control; 28.8.44 scuttled R Gironde
Sontay 40–45 MoWT (Br), troopship; 45 (Fra)

Tamara 42 *Niger* (Ger); 45 *Tamara* (Fra)
Theodora 40 *Heide* (Ger); 46 *Theodora* (Fra)
Tombouctou 8.9.40 Seized Pointe Noire; 40 MoWT (Br); 45 (Fra)

Vendée 40 KM, supply ship *Hermann von Salza* (Ger); 22.3.43 bombed by Allied aircraft, damaged, St Nazaire, repaired; 30.9.44 scuttled St Nazaire by Germans; 4.1.47 raised, repaired; 5.47 *Vendée* (Fra)
Vendémiaire 40 Seized by Germans; 41 KM, *Tempo 7* (Ger); 44 scuttled; 12.44 raised; repaired; (Fra)
Ville d'Amiens 18.9.40 Seized Papeete by FFr; 40 MoWT (Br); 9.44 (Fra)
Ville de Reims 24.6.40 Seized St Nazaire by Germans; 8.40 KM, Seelöwe transport *H22*; 24.5.41 *Harvesthude* (Ger); 10.3.43 KMD Oslo, transport; 5.45 repairing Fredrikstad; 6.45 returned; 8.46 *Ville de Reims* (Fra)
Ville de Strasbourg 3.41 Captured; 41 MoWT (Br), troopship; 9.45 (Fra)

Wisconsin 12.41 Seized by US, transf USN; 12.41 (Pan); 13.11.45 (Fra)

Yang-Tsé 40 German prize; 9.8.40 KM, Seelöwe transport *H19* (Ger); 23.5.41 *Marko Brunner* (Ger); 5.45 found damaged Korsor; 45 repaired; 9.45 returned, *Yang-Tse* (Fra)
Yolande Bertin 41 *Honduras* (Pan); 7.41–1.46 MoWT charter; 47 *Foo Hsiang* (Chn)

Germany

Losses through marine hazard
Adalia 8.39 KM; 11.39 returned; 8.40 KM, Seelöwe transport *RO39*, later *O10*; 7.12.40 collision with *Mendoza* (*qv*), sprung leak, sunk, Vlissingen roads
Bahia Blanca 9.1.40 Struck iceberg Denmark Strait; 11.1.40 sunk 66 09N 26 20W
Barmbek 24.4.44 Broke in two 62 00 25N 05 10 01E; forepart sank, afterpart towed to Måløy, beached; 49 recovered, taken Flensburg, rebuilt; *Kate Grammerstorf* (Ger)
Casablanca 13.8.40 KM, Seelöwe transport *A50*; 8.1.41 returned; 25.11.43 lost in storm N Baltic (2 surv)
Elise Schulte 10.1.42 Stranded off Tromsø; 11.1.42 sank
Eschersheim 13.3.40 Abandoned in sinking condition 2m S of Hirtshals, Denmark; sank near Rubjaerg Lt (8†)
Europa 15.3.44 Collision, sank, near Stavanger
Frankenwald 6.1.40 Struck uncharted rock off Bratholm, near Bergen; TL
Gerrit Fritzen 25.11.39 Wrecked E coast of Schiermonnikoog Is
Gillhausen 26.9.41 Stranded near Kirkenes; TL
Gratia 7.1.40 Stranded off Borkum, broke in two; sank in storm
Helgoland 3.11.39 Passed near St Thomas after breaking out of Puerto Colombia and eluding US destroyers; ar St Nazaire; 23.1.42 stranded off Bogskar, abandoned; TL
Herta Engeline Fritzen 26.10.41 Wrecked Hook of Holland
João Pessõa 7.6.42 Struck rock 2m from San Sebastian, Spain; 8.6.42 sank
Johann Schulte (5334gt) 1.1.40 Wrecked S of Kya LH, near Rørvik, Norway
Jürgen Fritzen 21.4.40 Stranded 1.5m E of Landsort
Kelkheim 28.2.44 Collision, stranded, later sank, S of Rautingen
Köln 26.6.40 Stranded Argusgrund, Stockholm; 27.6.40 broke in two, sunk
Kurt Hartwig Siemers 11.2.43 Stranded Nidingen; TL
Kythera 40 *Gerda Ferdinand* (Ger); 28.11.41 stranded Argusgrund, Stockholm; TL
Lahneck 6.3.42 Collision with *Treuenfels* (*qv*), taken in tow, sunk, 58 04 04N 08 04 04E;

46 raised, BU
Marion Traber 14.10.39 Wrecked off Havringe
Monsun 17.12.42 Stranded off Rørvik, Norway; TL
Natal 7.1.44 Stranded off Makkaur, N Norway; TL
Orizaba 25.1.40 Stranded Skjervøy, N Norway; TL
Ostland 9.11.42 Ashore between Havringe and Arkobadan; TL
Savona 5.5.41 KM, transport; 28.6.42 struck wreck off Benghazi, beached off Sidi Buciedo; TL
Sivas 9.2.45 Stranded Askevold; 6.45 at Måløy; CTL, BU Grimstad
Tanger 25.12.39 Collision with *Vulkan* (Ger), sunk, off Brunsbüttelkoog
Troyburg 21.8.41 Wrecked off Farsund
Vegesack 7.9.39 Wrecked Jæren (near Stavanger)
Walküre 20.12.42 Stranded Hjelmbodan, W of Haftenssund, Norway; TL
Walter L-M Russ 45 GB; 45 to be renamed *Empire Concourse* (Br); 15.7.45 stranded Grassholm Is, sank

Losses through war causes
Aachen 40 KM, transport; 9.4.40 sunk by British destroyers, Narvik; 51 raised, repaired, *Oakhill* (Br)
Achaia 20.4.41 KM, transport; 17.3.42 bombed by British carrier aircraft, took evasive course, struck mine, sunk, 25m E of Tripoli
Adana 12.1.41 KM, transport; 16.4.41 shelled (in convoy) by destroyer HMS *Jervis*, sunk, off Kerkennah Islands
Adele Traber 5.45 In Kiel Canal; 24.7.45 GB, *Empire Oykell* (Br); 46 *Bruse* (Nor)
Adolf Binder 20.5.45 At Trondheim; 45 (Bel); 47 *Astrida* (Bel)
Adolf Leonhardt 8.12.39 Found by cruiser HMS *Shropshire* off Angola; scuttled to avoid capture
Adolph Woermann 21.11.39 Sighted by British steamer, found by cruiser HMS *Neptune*, scuttled to avoid capture near Ascension Is
Adria 5.45 At Kiel; 4.6.45 GB, *Empire Tageos* (Br); 46 *Kazbek* (Rus); 47 *Karpaty* (Pol)
Ægina 15.1.41 KM, Sonnenblume transport; 16.4.41 shelled (in convoy) by Force K destroyer HMS *Janus* and others, sunk, off Kerkennah Islands
Aegir 4.5.43 Struck mine, sunk, N of Juist
Afrika 10.4.40 Sunk by artillery off Ulvik, Norway
Ahrensburg 12.39 KM, U-boat target ship, Wesermunde; 9.5.40 transf Gotenhafen; 43 transf Memel; 21.5.44 transf Norway; 1.10.44 transf Danzig; 45 (Nor); 46 *Asnes* (Nor); 46 *Thornes* (Nor); 47 *Mona Lisa* (Nor)
Ajax 8.40 KM, Seelöwe transport *A44*; 7.12.40 returned; 29.3.43 torpedoed (in convoy) by subm *S-101* (Rus), sunk, 70 49.5N 29 30E (2†)
Akka 5.45 At Flensburg; 10.10.45 GB, *Empire Calder* (Br); 47 *Isgo* (Br)
Albert Janus 14.1.40 Scuttled off Vigo
Albert Jensen 9.4.45 Bombed by Russian aircraft, sunk, off Hela; raised, *Professor Popov* (Rus)
Alicante 22.10.40 KM, transport; 30.5.41 burnt out following explosion Piræus harbour on munitions transport *Knyaguinya Maria Louisa* (*qv*)
Aller 43 *Sofala* (Por)
Alster 18.3.40 KM, troop transport for Weserubung; 10.4.40 captured N of Bodø by destroyer HMS *Icarus*; 40 MoWT, *Empire Endurance* (Br); 20.4.41 torpedoed by *U73*, sunk, 53 05N 23 14W (70†, 24 surv)
Alstertor 39 KM, supply ship/blockade runner; 23.6.41 found by obv HMS *Marsdale* and 4 destroyers, scuttled 41 12N 13 10W to avoid capture
Alsterufer 39 KM, supply ship; 27.12.43 hit by rockets from Liberator aircraft of 311 Sq (Cze), on fire, NW of Cape Finisterre; scuttled 46 40N 19 30W
Altenfels 4.6.43 Torpedoed by *MTB620*, *626*, sunk, S of Bergen
Altona 10.4.40 Torpedoed by destroyers HMS *Havock*, *Hunter*, *Hardy*, sunk, off Narvik
Amasis 40 Blockade runner; 9.4.40 torpedoed by subm HMS *Sunfish*, sunk, 58 13N 11 13E
Amerika 21.2.42 Struck mine; 22.2.42 sunk E of Terschelling
Ammerland 40 KM, escort vessel; 12.10.43 torpedoed (in convoy) by subm *S-55* (Rus), Porsangerfjord
Ammon 39 KM; 21.6.39 escort vessel; 41 gunnery school ship; 22.10.44 transport; 17.1.45 bombed, and 31.3.45 bombed, aground, partly submerged, Hamburg; 48 raised, BU Rosyth
Anatolia 42 *Santa Fé* (Arg); 43 *Rio Carcarana* (Arg)
Andros 9.8.40 KM, transport; 45 refugee transport; 3.3.45 attacked by aircraft Swinemünde, badly damaged; 12.3.45 bombed by Allied aircraft, sunk, Swinemünde
Angelburg 25.9.39–5.45 KM, U-boat target ship, Wesermünde; 9.5.40 transf Memel; 16.6.44 reefer; 4.6.45 VTS; 5.45 Allied prize; 25.9.45 GB, *Empire Wharfe* (Br); 47 *Zent* (Br)
Anhalt 27.12.41 Sunk by destroyers HMS *Chiddingford* and *Offa*, off Vaagsøy
Anita L-M Russ 27.12.41 Driven on beach at Måløy Sound by destroyers HMS *Onslow* and *Oribi*
Ankara 40 KM, transport; 18.1.43 struck mine (laid 17.1.43 by subm HMS *Rorqual*), sunk, 5m NE of Cani Is, Bizerta
Anneliese Essberger 40 KM, supply ship; blockade runner; 21.11.42 found by cruiser USS *Milwaukee*, scuttled 400m E of St Pauls Rocks
Annelis Christophersen 5.45 At Flensburg; 45 *Empire Concern* (Br); 46 *Laknes* (Nor); 27.11.46 wrecked Ronglevaer, Norway

Antares 5.3.40 KM, transport; 10.4.40 torpedoed by subm HMS *Sunfish*, sunk, 58 11N 11 17E (*c*500†)
Antarktis 10.8.44 Scuttled Coueron, R Loire, upon German evacuation; 46 part raised; 48 BU; part BU *in situ*
Antilla 10.5.40 Scuttled Aruba to avoid seizure by Netherlands authorities; salvage abandoned
Antiochia 23.11.39 Scuttled SE of Iceland to avoid capture by RN vessels
Antje Fritzen 21.9.43 Torpedoed by *TKA-15* (Rus), sunk, off Fischer peninsula
Antonio Delfino 17.4.40 KM, accom ship, Kiel; 1.2.44 U-boat depot, Gotenhafen; 3.45 VTS; 5.45 captured by British forces; 1.10.45 MoT (Br); 45 *Empire Halladale* (Br)
Apollo 12.8.40 KM, Seelöwe transport *O1*; 30.11.40 returned; 5.45 at Flensburg; 24.6.45 GB, *Empire Taff* (Br); 47 *Alhama* (Br)
Arauca 19.12.39 Put into Port Everglades to avoid RN warships; 30.3.41 seized by US; 12.41 USN, *Sting* (US); 42 refrigerated store USS *Saturn* (AK-49)
Arcturus 22.10.39 KM, transport; 1.5.41 torpedoed (in convoy) by subm HMS *Upholder*, sunk, 34 38N 11 39E
Arkadia 29.4.41 KM, transport; 28.4.43 struck mine, sunk, 10m NE of Constanta; 46 raised; 46 USSR
Arta 21.1.41 KM, transport; 16.4.41 reported (in convoy) by Force K destroyer HMS *Janus* off Kerkennah Is, run aground; 26.4.41 shelled by subm HMS *Upholder*, on fire; TL
Arucas 3.3.40 Found by cruiser HMS *York* E of Iceland; scuttled to avoid capture
Asien 7.4.44 Torpedoed by subm HMS *Unshaken*, sunk, 58 07N 13 05E
Asuncion 23.5.42 Struck mine (laid 8.4.42 by subm *K-1* (Rus)), sunk, 70 17N 21 21E
Athen 40 KM; 30.7.40 commd *Sperrbrecher 2*; 11.42 returned; 5.45 at Neustad Bay; 16.3.46 *General Brusilov* (Rus); 47 *Warynski* (Pol)
Atlas 12.12.41 KM, Sonnenblume transport; 13.4.42 torpedoed by subm HMS *Thrasher*, sunk, 31 42N 19 07E
Augsburg 40 KM, blockade runner 'Vreeburgh'; 41 *Teiryu Maru* (Jpn); 19.7.44 torpedoed by subm USS *Guardfish*, sunk, 20 07N 118 20E
August Bolten 16.8.40 KM, Seelöwe transport *H50*; 4.7.42 returned; 20.11.44 attacked by Allied MTB, stranded, sunk, Korsfjord
August Leonhardt 7.3.40 KM, Weserübung transport; 11.4.40 torpedoed by subm HMS *Sealion*, sunk, 56 30N 11 30E
August Thyssen 18.1.40 Struck mine, sunk, E of Understen Lt, Stockholm

Babitonga 4.9.39 KM, aux cruiser supply ship; 21.6.41 found by cruiser HMS *London*, scuttled 02 05S 27 42W to avoid capture
Baden 39 KM, supply vessel; 26.12.40 found by cruiser HMS *Berwick* 43N 27 45W, scuttled to avoid capture, abandoned, shelled, sunk
Bahia 9.4.40 KM, Seelöwe transport *A13*; 24.11.41 torpedoed by subm HMS *Seawolf*, beached, off Verberg; 7.12.41 submerged; 42 raised, repaired; 22.4.44 torpedoed by subm *Ula* (Nor), sunk, 58 07N 06 27E
Bahia Camarones 9.39 KM; 2.10.39 commd *Sperrbrecher I*; 30.7.40 returned; 5.6.41 KM, transport; 11.1.45 shelled by cruisers HMS *Bellona*, *Norfolk*, destroyers HMS *Onslow*, *Orwell*, *Onslaught*, damaged; 12.1.45 stranded 58 22.8N 06 02.8E; wreck BU
Bahia Castillo 40 KM, transport; 21.5.40 returned; 1.8.40 torpedoed (in convoy) by subm HMS *Narwhal* 57 05N 11 35E; towed Kiel, BU
Bahia Laura 22.8.40 KM, Seelöwe transport *RO43*; 41 returned; 25.5.41 transport, Norway; 30.8.41 torpedoed (in troop convoy) by subm HMS *Trident*, sunk, 70 35N 21 45E (450†)
Baldur 17.2.40 Ordered to stop by destroyer HMS *Ivanhoe*, scuttled, off Lister
Barcelona 17.4.41 KM, transport; 29.10.41 bombed by British aircraft, sunk, Ålesund roads
Bärenfels 8.3.40 KM, Weserübung transport; 10.5.42 transport; 14.4.44 sunk by limpet mine (attached by subm *X24*, towed by subm HMS *Sceptre*) off Takseraag, Norway; 47 raised, BU
Barmbek 8.8.40 KM Seelöwe transport *O13*; 25.3.41 transport, Norway; 8.9.41 returned; 24.4.44 disabled 62 00 25N 05 10 01E; towed Måløy; 45 towed Flensburg; 49 sold
Belgrad 15.8.40 Commd KM *Sperrbrecher 3*; 26.8.44 scuttled Bordeaux 44 50N 00 34W; 9.7.47 raised, repaired; 51 *Nicole Schiaffino* (Fra)
Belgrano 21.3.40 KM, Seelöwe transport A6; 5.12.40 returned; 17.1.41 comm conv to *Sperrbreacher 11*; 17.5.41 commd; 4.1.45 struck mine off Flensburg, badly damaged; 46 repaired, served with GMSA as *Sperrbrecher 11 Belgrano*; 20.9.47 GB; 47–48 BU Inverkeithing
Berlin 23.8.39 KM, hospital ship *A*, Baltic; 44 accom ship, Gotenhafen; 30.1.45 struck mine (dropped 1.45 by RAF aircraft) off Swinemünde, taken in tow for Kiel; 1.2.45 sunk 56 02 36N 14 19E; 49 raised; 3.9.51–2.5.57 repaired, rebuilt, *Admiral Nakhimov* (Rus)
Bertha Fisser 20.11.39 Attempted scuttling SW of Iceland to avoid capture when stopped by amc HMS *Chitral* (0†); shelled by *Chitral*, on fire; 21.11.39 drifted ashore Iceland
Bertram Rickmers 30.3.41 Found Strait of Perim by destroyer HMS *Kandahar*, scuttled to avoid capture
Bessel 6.5.45 Surrendered Vigo; 45 *Empire Coniston* (Br); 12.47 *Birgitte Skou* (Dmk)
Birkenau 24.8.40 KM, Seelöwe transport *A32*; returned; 13.2.44 transport; 5.45 at Århus; 2.9.46 transf Denmark; 8.12.47 *Else Skou* (Dmk)

Birkenfels 13.8.40 KM, Seelöwe transport *H32*; 18.12.40 torpedoed by British MTBs, sunk, Schelde estuary 51 25N 03 28.5E; 41 wreck dispersed by explosives; 10.66 wreck cleared
Biskaya 10.39 Stopped, captured, N Atlantic by Northern Patrol vessels; 40 MoWT, *Empire Unity* (Br); 47 *Stordale* (Br)
Bitterfeld 10.5.40 Seized Padang by Netherlands; 40 *Mariso* (Ne); 20.3.43 torpedoed by *U518*, sunk, 13 20S 37 25W (2†, 2 pow, 107 surv)
Böchum 9.4.40 KM, transport, Norway; 8.40 Seelöwe transport *A8*; 22.5.42 returned; 5.45 at Stavanger; 45 GB; 28.2.46 *General Chernakhovsky* (Rus)
Bockenheim 1.1.41 Commd KM *Sperrbrecher 14*; 26.8.44 scuttled off Bordeaux; raised; 49 BU
Bolheim 10.12.39 Torpedoed in error by subm *S-1* (Rus), sunk, 61 26N 21 04E
Bollwerk 12.41 Seized by Brazil; 12.41 *Norteloide* (Brz); 28.10.45 explosion in cargo, on fire, off Cabo Sao Thome, taken in tow; 31.10.45 tow abandoned off Macahe; 1.11.45 drifted ashore Lagoa Feia, between Sao Thome and Macahe; TL
Boltenhagen 12.8.42 Torpedoed by subm HMS *Sturgeon*, sunk, 59 08N 06 25E
Boltenhof 13.12.44 Bombed by Allied aircraft, sunk, Swinemünde; 46 raised; 46 *Kuznarenko* (Rus); 47 *Kalisz* (Pol)
Borbeck 9.3.45 Attacked by Russian aircraft, on fire; torpedoed by subm *SC-303* (Rus), sunk, 55 03N 20 45E
Borkum 18.11.39 Captured by RN warships; 23.11.39 torpedoed by *U33* 59 30 02N 02 50W; 25.11.39 abandoned, drifted ashore Papa Sound; 18.8.40 refloated, towed Rosyth, BU
Brage 6.5.40 Struck mine, sunk, Kiel Bay
Brake (5347gt) 20.11.41 KM, transport, Baltic; 28.5.42 VTS; 5.45 at Bremerhaven; 6.45 US prize; 7.9.45 (Br); 46 (US); 49 BU Chester PA
Brake (9925gt) 42 IJN; 12.3.44 tound Indian Ocean by cruiser HMS *Newcastle*, destroyers HMS *Roebuck* and *Quadrant*, and escort carrier HMS *Battler*; shelled by *Roebuck*, sunk, 32S 72E (surv on *U168*)
Braunfels 9.39 Interned Mormugao; 8.3.43 scuttled (on fire) by own crew at Mormugao, burnt out, aground; 3.43 Portuguese govt; BU *in situ*
Bremen 18.6.40 KM, accom ship, Bremerhaven; intended Seelöwe special transport; 16.3.42 deliberately set on fire, burnt out, Bremerhaven; beyond repair, stripped to waterline; 52–53 remains of wreck BU
Bremerhaven (1615gt) 40 *Teiun Maru* (Jpn); 1.1.42 struck mine, sunk, 16 05N 120 20E
Bremerhaven (5355gt) 15.5.42 KM, transport, Baltic; 44 VTS; 31.10.44 bombed by Russian aircraft, on fire, sunk, 55 03 48N 18 24 30E (410†)
Brigitte 5.45 At Hamburg; 45 *Empire Soar* (Br); 47 *Preveza* (Gre)
Buenos Aires 1.5.40 Torpedoed (in convoy) by subm HMS *Narwhal*, sunk, 57 05N 11 35E (30†)
Bugsee 18.6.44 Bombed by Allied aircraft, sunk, Hamburg
Bukarest 40 KM, floating workshop; 5.45 at Kiel; 7.6.45 *Empire Ettrick* (Br); 7.46 *Bremnes* (Nor); 47 *Clio* (Nor)
Burgenland 40 KM, blockade runner; 5.1.44 sighted by US flying-boat from Natal; found by cruiser USS *Omaha*, destroyer USS *Jouett*, scuttled 05S 25W to avoid capture

Cairo 10.5.42 Commd KM, aux cruiser *Stier* (Schiff 23, Raider 'J'); 27.9.42 encountered in bad weather *Stephen Hopkins* (US 'Liberty' ship), exchanged gunfire, *Stephen Hopkins* sunk; *Stier* badly damaged, abandoned, sunk, 24 44S 21 50W (4†)
Campinas 7.3.40 KM, transport; 10.5.40 struck mine, sank, off Drogden, Copenhagen
Cap Arcona 29.11.40 KM, accom ship, Gotenhafen; 1.45 refugee transport; 3.5.45 bombed by 2nd TAF Typhoons, on fire, capsized, off Neustadt (5594†); drifted ashore 54 04N 10 50E; 49 wreck BU
Cap Norte 3.9.39 At Pernambuco; 9.10.39 captured off Iceland by cruiser HMS *Belfast*; 40 MoWT, *Empire Trooper* (Br)
Capri 5.45 At Kiel; 45 MoWT, *Empire Galaxy* (Br); 46 *Nadezhda Krupskaya* (Rus)
Caribia 1.8.40 KM, accom ship, Mürwik; 5.45 captured Flensburg by British forces; 45 (Br); 7.45 (US); 6.46 USSR; 15.7.46 *Ilyich* (Rus)
Carl Fritzen 3.9.39 Stopped by cruiser HMS *Ajax* between Rio Grande do Sul and R Plate; scuttled to avoid capture
Carl Jüngst 5.45 At Kiel; 45 MoWT, *Empire Durant* (Br); 46 *Tambov* (Rus)
Carl Vinnen 26.8.39 Ar Carthagena; 21.10.45 still there, LU
Cassel 10.5.40 Seized Sourabaya by Netherlands, *Mendenau* (Ne); 9.8.42 torpedoed by *U752*, sunk, 04 45N 18W (69†, 16 surv/pow)
Castellon 22.10.40 KM, transport; 2.10.41 torpedoed (in convoy) by subm HMS *Perseus*, sunk, 32 30N 19 09E
Catania 4.4.44 KM, transport; 20.8.45 *Empire Neath* (Br); 46 *Meridian* (Rus); 47 *Ekvator* (Rus)
Ceuta 13.8.40 KM, Seelöwe transport *A29*; 4.6.42 returned; 28.3.43 bombed by Allied aircraft, sunk, Rotterdam; 43 raised, repaired; 17.2.44 KM, transport, Norway; 5.45 at Kiel; 24.10.45 GB, *Empire Camel* (Br)
Charlotte Cords 5.45 At Travemünde; 45 GB, *Empire Connah* (Br); 46 *Nikolai Baumann* (Rus)
Charlotte Schliemann 39 KM, U-boat supply vessel; 12.2.44 found by destroyer HMS *Relentless*, scuttled 23 23S 74 37E to avoid capture (surv on *U532*)
Chemnitz 29.9.39 Captured 38 05N 30 40W by subm *Poncelot* (Fra), taken Casablanca;

40 *Saint Bertrand* (Fra); 6.40–45 MoWT charter
Chios 23.9.44 Struck mine; 24.9.44 sunk off Brunsbüttelkoog
Christel Vinnen 29.3.44 Torpedoed by British aircraft, sunk, NW of Borkum
Christoph v Doornum 3.9.39 Seized Botwood; 30.10.39 MoS, *Empire Commerce* (Br); 9.6.40 struck mine 220° 5 cables from NE Spit Buoy, Margate roads (2†, 35 surv); beached 261° 19 cables from NE Spit Buoy; 11.6.40 refloated, towed towards London; 12.6.40 beached 51 26 30N 10 24E; BU
Clara L-M Russ 27.11.41 Sunk by British aircraft Lübeck; 42 raised, repaired; 14.12.44 sunk Libau; 12.44 raised, repaired; 5.45 at Lübeck; 16.5.47 *Ioannis Marketos* (Gre)
Cläre Hugo Stinnes 1 9.4.40 Captured by Norway, taken Ulvik; later sunk; 40 raised by Germans; 27.9.44 in convoy struck mine (laid 27.9.44 by subm *Rubis* (Fra)), sunk, 58 45N 05 24E
Claus Horn 39 *Claus* (Ger); 39 KM, U-boat tender *Neisse*; 45 GMSA; 46 Kiel Univ accom ship; 47 *Topusko* (Yug)
Claus Rickmers 4.5.40 KM, troop transport; 8.40 Seelöwe transport *A10*; 20.11.40 returned; 22.6.41 sunk Windau, raised, repaired; 30.4.47 *Empire Carron* (Br); 47 *Andrian* (Gre)
Coburg 4.3.41 Found by cruisers HMAS *Canberra*, HMNZS *Leander*, SE of Seychelles, scuttled to avoid capture
Columbus 19.12.39 Found by destroyer HMS *Hyperion*, E of Norfolk VA; scuttled 38 01N 65 41W to avoid capture (2†)
Constantia 5.45 At Lübeck-Travemünde; 47 GB; 48 BU Rosyth
Consul Horn 1.6.40 KM, accom ship *Consul*, Gotenhafen; 27.6.40 returned; 41 KM, *Sperrbrecher 27*; 20.7.42 struck mine, sunk, NE of Borkum
Cordillera 20.4.40 KM, accom ship, KM Werft, Wilhelmshaven; then flak school Swinemünde; 45 refugee transport; 12.3.45 bombed by 8th USAAF B17s, B24s, sunk, Swinemünde; 7.6.49 raised by USSR, repaired Warnemünde; 3.52 *Russ* (Rus)
Cordoba 19.8.40 KM, Seelöwe transport *H42*; 11.9.40 struck mine off Havre, damaged; LU Havre; 8.44 scuttled Havre as blockship; raised postwar, BU
Corrientes 9.39 Interned Las Palmas; 9.42 sold Spain; 44 *Monte Moncayo* (Spn)
Crefeld 4.4.41 Scuttled Massowah; wreck BU *in situ*
Cronshagen 24.4.40 Struck mine, sunk, S of Drogden Lt
Curityba 7.3 40 KM, Weserübung transport; 10.4.40 shelled by coastal battery, sunk, Oslofjord; 4.6.40 raised, repaired; 9.8.40 Seelöwe transport *A42*; 29.4.42 torpedoed by subm *M-171* (Rus), sunk, 70 07.5N 30 34E

Dalbek 16.8.40 KM, Seelöwe transport *A33*; 9.12.40 returned; 5.45 at Rendsburg; 5.45 GB; 31.8.45 *Empire Weaver* (Br); 46 *Cherniakov* (Rus)
Delos 12.4.40 KM, transport; 11.7.42 bombed by British aircraft, on fire, Tobruk; grounded to assist firefighting; 30.7.42 TL; 50 raised, BU Savona
Der Deutsche 40 KM, transport; 18.2.41 accom ship, Danzig; 3.4.41 U-boat depot, Gotenhafen; 12.7.44 troop transport; 2.2.45 VTS, refugee transport; 3.5.45 bombed off Fehmarn LV, put ashore, CTL; 47 salvaged; 47 USSR; repaired; 9.6.50 *Asia* (Rus)
Derindje 13.4.40 KM, transport; 28.8.44 scuttled Bordeaux as blockship; 45 raised, taken Finland; 47 *Derindje* (Fin); 50 BU Inverkeithing
Deutschland 17.12.40 KM, accom ship; 16.12.41 U-boat depot, Gotenhafen; 43 transf Danzig; 45 refugee transport; 3.5.45 bombed by Typhoons of 2nd TAF, on fire, capsized, sunk off Neustadt, Lübeck Bay 54 03N 10 48E (–†); 48 raised; BU
Diana 42 *Ria de Cormes* (Spn)
Dieter Hugo Stinnes 12 16.2.45 Struck mine (dropped 1–2.45 by RAF aircraft), sunk, NE of Swinemünde
Donau (9035gt) 20.9.39 KM, troop transport; 11.7.40 Seelöwe transport *A2*; 40 accom ship; 18.8.42 transport; 17.1.45 internal explosion or explosion caused by limpet mine, beached, broke in two, stern section sunk, 12m S of Droeback (–†); 49 raised; 52 BU
Donau (2931gt) 30.8.41 Torpedoed (in troop convoy) by subm HMS *Trident*, sunk, 70 35N21 45E (*c*250†)
Dora Fritzen 8.40 KM, Seelöwe transport *R5N*; 9.40 *R2N*; 6.1.45 torpedoed by Norwegian MTBs, sunk, 62 30N 04 59 02E
Dortmund 43 Taken over by Portugal; 25.5.43 *Lugela* (Por)
Drachenfels 10.39 Interned Mormugao; 9.3.43 scuttled (on fire) by own crew Mormugao to avoid seizure by Portuguese; 3.43 Portuguese govt; 12.48 sold; salved; 12.50 beached, BU
Drau 43 Completed; 43 KM, *Sperrbrecher 33*; 5.45 at Copenhagen; 45 GMSA; 47 (US); 48 *Sunni* (Nor)
Dresden 40 KM, U-boat supply vessel (Schiff 171)/blockade runner; 25.8.44 scuttled Bordeaux; 9.45 raised, repaired; 46 *Doba* (Fra)
Duisburg 22.10.40 KM, Sonnenblume transport; 9.11.41 shelled (in Italy–N Africa convoy) by vessels of RN Force K, sunk, 37 08N 18 09E
Düsseldorf 12.39 Captured N of Antofagasta, off Caldera, by cruiser HMS *Despatch*; 40 MoWT, *Poland* (Br); 40 *Empire Confidence* (Br); 46 *Star of El Nil* (Egy)

Eberstein 41 Sold (Ger); 41 KM, torpedo school ship; 5.45 at Lübeck; 28.8.47 GB, BU
Edmund Hugo Stinnes 4 24.3.40 Torpedoed by subm HMS *Truant*, sunk, 56 42N 08 04E
Ehrenfels 9.39 Interned Mormugao; 9.3.43 scuttled by own crew Mormugao to prevent

seizure by Portuguese; 50 salved, BU
Eifel 17.2.45 Bombed by Allied aircraft, sunk, off Libau
Eilbek 18.11.39 Captured; 40 MoWT, *Empire Scout* (Br); 46 *Kellwyn* (Br)
Eisenach 13.3.41 Scuttled Punta Arenas; 11.41 raised; 42 *Oceanica* (CR); 43 *Ultramarino* (Por)
Elbe 39 KM, supply ship/blockade runner; 6.6.41 torpedoed by 5 aircraft from carrier HMS *Eagle*, sunk, 900nm NW of Cape Verde Is (2†)
Elisabeth Bornhofen 4.10.44 Bombed by British aircraft, sunk, Bergen roads (5 surv)
Elisabeth Hendrik Fisser 18.10.43 Struck mine, sunk, 6m off Dubrovnik
Ellen Larsen 24.2.45 Struck mine (dropped 1–2.45 by RAF aircraft) off Warnemünde, stranded; TL
Elsa Essberger 40 KM, U-boat supply vessel/blockade runner; 25.8.44 scuttled Lagrange, R Gironde, as blockship
Else Hugo Stinnes 15 41 KM, salvage vessel; 4.5.45 torpedoed by 18 Group RAF Mosquito aircraft, sunk, off Arø; raised, repaired; 45 US; 47 *Ruhr* (Ger)
Emily Sauber 28.4.45 Torpedoed by TKAs from Neufahrwasser, sunk, off Hela; raised; *Kielce* (Pol)
Emmy Friederich 39 KM, supply vessel; 23.10.39 stopped by cruiser HMS *Caradoc*, scuttled to avoid capture, W of Tampico in Yucatan Channel
Ems 2.6.40 Commd KM, aux cruiser *Komet* (Schiff 45; Raider 'B'); 14.10.42 torpedoed by *MTB 236* (Br), sunk, 49 44N 01 32W (0 surv)
Emshörn 21.12.41 Torpedoed by subm *M-174* (Rus), sunk, 70 04N 30 32E
Emsland 20.1.44 Torpedoed (in convoy) by British aircraft off Stadlandet, damaged, beached near Eervik; 5.2.44 wreck torpedoed by subm HMS *Satyr*, badly damaged
Emsstrom 16.2.45 Bombed by Russian aircraft, sunk, off Memel
Entrerios 13.3.40 KM, transport; 4.8.40 Seelöwe transport *H43*; 20.7.42 returned; 14.1.44 torpedoed by British aircraft, sunk, off Lister (40†, 0 surv)
Erfurt 40 KM, transport; 20.3.44 struck mine, sunk, off Fehmarn; raised; 15.10.44 torpedoed, sunk, off Libau
Erika Fritzen 26.2.45 Struck mine (dropped 2–3.45 by RAF aircraft), sunk, 54 23N 11 59E
Erika Hendrik Fisser 25.11.42 Bombed by British aircraft, sunk, 5m S of Kristiansand (46†, 4 surv)
Erlangen 25.7.41 Found off Uruguay by cruiser HMS *Newcastle*, scuttled to avoid capture
Ermland 42 KM, *Weserland* (Ger); blockade runner; 3.1.44 shelled by destroyer USS *Somers*, sunk, 17S 21W (–†, 134 surv)
Erna Oldendorff 9.9.44 Bombed by Allied aircraft, sunk, off St Nazaire; 14.4.49 wreck dispersed
Ernst Brockelmann 5.45 At Flensburg; 45 MoWT, *Empire Concession* (Br); 47 *Brazen Head* (Br)
Ernst Hugo Stinnes 11 4.5.45 Torpedoed by Mosquito aircraft of 18 Group RAF, sunk, off Årø; raised, repaired; 47 *Rhein* (Ger)
Ernst L-M Russ 18.10.44 KM, troop transport; 5.45 at Flensburg; 23.6.45 *Empire Roding* (Br); 1.9.46 US; 47 *Eastport* (US)
Esmeralda 25.6.44 Delivered; 5.45 surrendered Kiel; 12.6.45 *Empire Wye* (Br); 47 *Eastern Saga* (Br)
España 4.9.39 KM, troop transport; 9.3.41 Weserübung transport; 3.6.42 returned; 5.45 GB prize at Sandefjord; 10.5.46 *General Bagration* (Rus)
Essen 10.5.40 Seized Sourabaya by Netherlands; 40 *Terkoelei* (Ne); 17.3.43 torpedoed (in convoy HX229) by *U631*, sunk, 51 45N 32 26W (36†, 61 surv)
Esso Hamburg 39 KM, U-boat supply ship; 4.6.41 found by cruiser HMS *London*, destroyer HMS *Brilliant*, scuttled to avoid capture 07 35N 31 25W
Este 10.5.40 Seized Curaçao by Netherlands; 40 *Suriname* (Ne); 13.9.42 torpedoed (in convoy TAG5) by *U558*, sunk, 12 07N 63 32W (13†, 69 surv)
Euler 40 KM, supply ship; 14.10.40 struck mine, sunk, 47 11 50N 02 18 40W; raised, BU
Eurofeld 11.39 Req KM; 17.9.44 scuttled Charpentier Channel, St Nazaire; 50 raised, BU
Europa 10.39 KM, accom ship, Wesermünde; 18.6.40 intended Seelöwe special transport; 42 intended conversion to carrier; 12.42 project abandoned; 22.12.42 intended troop transport; 5.45 US; 25.8.45 USN, transport AP 177; 8.6.46 sold France; 47 *Liberté* (Fra)

Felix Heumann 3.3.41 Sunk by RN destroyers in Lofotens raid (Opn 'Claymore'); 47 raised; 49 *Bygdøy* (Nor)
Feodosia 9.8.40 KM, Seelöwe transport *RO44*; 5.8.42 returned; 4.4.45 bombed by British aircraft, exploded, sunk, Skagerrak
Florianopolis 28.6.44 Bombed (in convoy) by Russian Il-2 aircraft, sunk, near Kirkenes; 45 raised, BU UK
Florida 21.3.40 KM, transport; 14.4.40 torpedoed by subm HMS *Snapper*, sunk, 57 59N 10 51E
Flottbek 8.11.41 Struck mine (laid 27.10.41 by subm *K-1* (Rus)), sunk, 70 56N 25 43E
Fortuna 2.8.43 Bombed by British aircraft, sunk, off Texel
Franken 10.5.40 Seized Padang by Netherlands; 40 *Wangi Wangi* (Ne); 25.5.41 torpedoed by *U103*, sunk, 05 24N 12W (1†, 92 surv)
Frankfurt 4.8.41 Found N Atlantic by obv HMS *Cavina*, scuttled to avoid capture
Franz Jürgen 9.4.45 Bombed by RAF BC aircraft, sunk, Kiel
Frauenfels 4.4.41 Scuttled Massowah, salved; 13.11.42 MoWT, *Empire Niger* (Br); 48 *Belapur* (Br)

Freienfels 18.11.40 KM, Sonnenblume transport; 19.12.40 struck mine, sunk, off Leghorn
Frida Horn 40 *Frida* (Ger); 5.45 GB; 25.2.46 *Bogdan Khmelnitzki* (Rus)
Friderun 10.5.40 Seized NEI by Netherlands; 40 *Meroendoeng* (Ne); 3.3.42 sunk at Tandjong Priok
Friedenau 8.4.40 KM, Weserübung transport; 10.4.40 torpedoed by subm HMS *Triton*, sunk, 57 50N 11 23E
Friedrich Breme 40 KM, supply ship for *Bismarck*; 12.6.41 found by cruiser HMS *Sheffield*, scuttled to avoid capture 44 44N 22 20W (4†)
Frielinghaus 10–13.4.40 Sunk Narvik during invasion of Norway; raised, repaired; 41 KM, *Sperrbrecher 65*; later *Sperrbrecher 165*; 28.6.42 struck mine, sunk, off Frisian Islands
Friesenland 39 KM, aircraft catapult ship; 10.9.44 torpedoed by Russian aircraft off Billefjord, beached; 10.44 recovered, repaired; 4.46 GB, for RAF use
Friesland 1.4.41 Scuttled off Paita, Peru, in 04 56S 81 09W to avoid capture
Fulda 40 *Teikai Maru* (Jpn); 30.12.44 bombed by USAAF aircraft, sunk, 17 18N 119 25E

Galilea 2.3.41 KM, transport; 23.1.43 torpedoed by subm HMS *Unseen*, sunk, off Tripoli
Gedania 40 KM, supply ship; 4.6.41 captured by obv HMS *Marsdale* 43 38N 29 15W; 8.41 MoWT, *Empire Garden* (Br); 10.47 *Southern Garden* (Br)
Geierfels 18.11.40 KM, Sonnenblume transport; 19.12.40 struck mine, sunk, off Leghorn
General Artigas 10.39 KM, accom ship, Hamburg; 25.7.43 bombed by RAF BC aircraft, on fire, Kuhwärder Hafen, Hamburg; burnt out, capsized; 45–46 raised, BU Hamburg
General Osorio 10.4.40 KM, accom ship, Kiel; 31.12.43 transf Flensburg; 24.7.44 bombed by RAF BC aircraft Howaldtswerke shipyard, Kiel, afterpart burnt out, partially submerged; 2.10.44 refloated; 29.3.45 returned owner, temp repaired; 9.4.45 bombed by RAF BC aircraft, badly damaged, burnt out, Kiel; 29.8.47 refloated; 47–48 BU Inverkeithing
General San Martin 22.1.40 KM, U-boat depot, Königsberg; 15.1.41 transf Kiel; 1.10.41 transf Königsberg; 25.1.45 VTS; 4.4.45 hospital ship; 5.45 at Copenhagen; 26.6.45 seized, prize; 8.10.45 (Br); 46 *Empire Deben* (Br); 49 BU Newport
Genua 40 KM, netlayer *Netzleger VI*; 14.10.40 attacked by RN destroyers, sunk, off Egersund; raised; 45 GMSA; 1.11.47 (US)
Georg L-M Russ 12.8.42 Torpedoed by subm HMS *Unshaken*, sunk, 58 42.1N 05 27.7E
Gera 4.4.41 Scuttled Massowah; 42 raised, repaired; 42 MoWT, *Empire Indus* (Br); 47 *Bosveld* (Br/SA); 48 *Pan Ocean* (Pan)
Germania 15.12.42 Found W of Cape Finisterre by British destroyer, scuttled to avoid capture
Ginnheim 5.45 At Brunsbüttel; 45 *Empire Ouse* (Br); 47 *Eindhoven* (Ne); 47 *Parkhaven* (Ne)
Gloria 21.10.39 Captured SE of Iceland by cruiser HMS *Sheffield*; 40 MoWT, *Empire Conveyor* (Br); 20.6.40 torpedoed by *U122*, sunk, 56 16N 08 10W (13†, 38 surv)
Glücksburg 26.12.39 Scuttled off Cape St Vincent
Gneisenau 1.40 KM, accom ship; 22.4.40 troop transport, Norway; 22.12.41 accom ship, Tollerort; 5.42 planned conv to carrier *Jade*; 25.11.42 plan abandoned; 29.3.43 accom ship, Swinemünde; 2.5.43 struck mine 54 38N 12 25 01E, put ashore, abandoned, capsized; 12.7.50 refloated; BU Denmark
Godfried Bueren 18.1.41 Struck mine, sunk, 20m E of Limfjorden, Denmark
Goldenfels 19.12.39 Commd KM, aux cruiser *Atlantis* (Schiff 16, Raider 'C'); 23.11.41 intercepted by cruiser HMS *Devonshire*, scuttled to avoid capture, 04 12S 18 42W (8†, surv resc by *U126*)
Gonzenheim 19.10.39 Scuttled S of Iceland to avoid capture by warships of Northern Patrol
Goslar 10.5.40 Scuttled off Paramaribo
Gottingen 44 Completed; 23.2.45 torpedoed by subm *SC-309* (Rus), sunk, 56 18N 20 16E
Gravenstein 27.3.45 Scuttled Gotenhafen as blockship
Greifswald 5.45 Seized in builder's yard Lübeck; 48 *Empire Ely* (Br)

Halle 16.10.39 Found W of Dakar by cruiser *Duguay-Trouin* (Fra), scuttled to avoid capture
Hamburg 1.1.40 KM, U-boat depot, Kiel; 1.10.41 transf Danzig; 6.43 transf Gotenhafen; 45 refugee transport; 7.3.45 struck mine (dropped by RAF aircraft), sunk, 54 30N 13 42 12E; 50 raised, repaired; conv to whale factory vessel *Yuri Dolgoruky* (Rus)
Hamburg (fish factory) 3.3.41 Sunk by destroyer HMS *Offa*, Vaagsfjord, during commando raid on Lofoten Is (Opn 'Claymore')
Hameln 1.4.41 Seized by Mexico; 41 *Oaxaca* (Mex); 26.7.42 torpedoed by *U171*, sunk, 28 23N 96 08W (6†, 39 surv)
Hamm 6.3.40 KM, Weserübung transport; 18.4.40 torpedoed by subm HMS *Seawolf*, sunk, 58 09N 10 32E (1†)
Hammonia 42 *Nordfahrt* (Ger); 10.2.45 struck mine, sunk, Kiel Bay; 46 raised, *Clara Blumenfeld* (Ger)
Hanau 6.3.40 KM, Weserübung transport; 8.8.40 Seelöwe transport *H46*; 25.4.42 returned; 30.1.44 struck mine, sunk, 54 31.2N 10 28E
Hanna Cords 4.45 Scuttled as blockship Stettin
Hannah Böge 9.9.39 Captured off Kirkwall; 39 *Crown Arun* (Br) – *qv*
Hannover 7–8.3.40 Captured Mona Passage by destroyer HMCS *Assiniboine*, and prevented from scuttling by boarding party from cruiser HMS *Dunedin*; 40 *Sinbad* (Br); 40 MoWT, *Empire Audacity* (Br); 40 RN, conv to carrier HMS *Audacity*; 23.12.41 torpedoed by *U67*, sunk, 43 55N 19 50W
Hans Arp 8.12.41 KM, transport; 16.11.42 torpedoed by subm HMS *Safari*, sunk, 30

28N 18 48E
Hans Bornhofen 13.2.44 Torpedoed by subm HMS *Taku*, sunk, 59 09N 05 24E
Hans Christophersen 21.7.41 Struck mine, sunk, off Texel
Hans Leonhardt 14.8.40 KM, Seelöwe transport *A47*; 41 returned; 24.5.41 Blaufuchs (Blue Fox); 8.42 transport, Norway; 25.9.42 returned; 1.6.44 torpedoed by Barracuda aircraft from carriers HMS *Furious*, *Victorious*; ammunition cargo exploded, sunk, SE of Kvam Is, near Stadlandet
Hans Rickmers 17.4.40 KM, troop transport; 8.40 Seelöwe transport *A11*; 41 returned; 22.5.41 transport, Norway; 17.10.42 returned; 30.11.42 struck mine off Petsamo, beached; destroyed by Russian artillery
Hans Schmidt 24.1.43 Struck mine, sunk, off Pola
Hansa 26.9.40 KM, accom ship for *Tirpitz*; 2.12.40 U-boat depot, Gotenhafen; 1.45 refugee transport; 6.3.45 struck mine (dropped by RAF aircraft) off Gedser LV; taken in tow for Warnemünde, sunk; 12.49 raised, repaired Antwerp and Warnemünde; 50 USSR; 55 *Sovetsky Sojus* (Rus)
Hansestadt Lübeck 5.45 At Tommernes; 45 *Saltnes* (Nor)
Havelland 22.12.43 Torpedoed by US subm, damaged, off Kobe, towed in; 44 IJN, subm tender *Tatsumiya Maru* (Jpn); 30.7.45 sunk by USN carrier-based aircraft 35 33N 135 31E
Havenstein 26.4.41 *Teisho Maru* (Jpn); 12.10.44 bombed by USN carrier-based aircraft, sunk, 22 37N 120 16E
Heddernheim 21.3.40 Torpedoed by subm HMS *Ursula*, sunk, 57 48N 10 53E
Heidelberg 2.3.40 Found by cruiser HMS *Dunedin*, scuttled to avoid capture off Windward Passage
Heimdal 19.9.40 Struck mine off Terschelling, sunk
Heinrich Arp 5.45 At Hamburg; 45 *Empire Connemara* (Br); 45 *Liza Chaikina* (Rus)
Heinrich Schmidt 5.45 At Rendsburg; 45 GB, *Empire Constable* (Br); 46 *Dimitri Laptev* (Rus)
Heinrich Schulte 28.1.44 Torpedoed by subm *S-56* (Rus), sunk, 70 08N 28 14E
Heinz Horn 24.11.39 KM, U-boat tender, Wesermünde; 15.1.41 transf Memel; 18–19.12.44 bombed by RAF aircraft, stranded, Gotenhafen; 45–46 accom ship, GMSA Kiel; 29.6.46 GB; 10.7.46 *Betuwe* (Ne); 47 *Livarden* (Nor)
Helene 22.5.40 Struck mine, sunk, off Hubertgat
Helga Böge 40 *Helga Ina* (Ger); 5.45 at Wesermünde; 46 *Kertch* (Rus); 47 *Kutno* (Pol)
Helga Ferdinand 8.11.44 Bombed by British aircraft, sunk, off Midtgulen
Helga L-M Russ 8.40 KM, Seelöwe transport *RO38*; 5.45 at Oslo; 21.9.45 *Hesnes* (Nor); 47 *Rita* (Nor)
Helios (3821gt) 39 Interned Spain; 43 *Ria de Vigo* (Spn)
Helios (2883gt) 8.40 KM, Seelöwe transport; 40 gunnery training ship; 5.45 at Flensburg, badly damaged by bombing; 2.5.48 GB, BU Sunderland
Henning Oldendorff 17.11.39 Captured in 63N 10 13W by HMS *Colombo*; 40 MoWT, *Empire Industry* (Br); 16.3.41 shelled, sunk (in convoy) by *Gneisenau* 43 28N 45 24W (0†, 38 pow)
Henry Horn 10.5.40 Captured off Curaçao; 9.40 (Ne); 40 *Bonaire* (Ne)
Heraklea 28.12.40 KM, transport; 28.3.41 torpedoed (in convoy) by subm HMS *Utmost*, sunk, 35 40N 11 19E
Hercules 20.8.40 KM, Seelöwe transport *A35*; 9.12.40 returned; 3.4.41 KM, transport, Norway; 15.6.42 returned; 5.45 at Copenhagen; 20.6.45 *Empire Dovey* (Br); 46 *Kirovograd* (Rus)
Herman Sauber 40 KM, netlayer *Netzleger II*; 46 (Rus)
Hermonthis 39 KM, supply ship/blockade runner; 1.4.41 found 250nm S of Callao by aux cruiser HMCS *Prince Henry*, scuttled to avoid capture
Hestia 8.40 KM, Seelöwe transport *A20*; 40 gunnery training ship; 5.45 at Copenhagen; 21.6.45 GB; 45 *Margaret* (Ne); 46 *Kishiniv* (Rus)
Hindenburg 8.40 KM, Seelöwe transport *A40*; 2.12.40 returned; 17.11.42 struck mine (laid 2.11.42 by subm *L-3* (Rus)) off Utö (many Russian pow†); taken in tow by *V305*; 19.11.42 sunk in tow
Hochsee 15.7.44 Lost off Steinort
Hödur 20.4.42 Torpedoed by subm HMS *Trident*, sunk, 64 38N 10 49E
Hohenfels 25.8.41 Seized Bandar Shapur (Opn 'Countenance') by RN; 41 *Empire Kamal* (Br); 44 *Van Ruisdael* (Ne); 47 *Ridderkerk* (Ne)
Huascaran 40 KM, repair ship; 5.45 at Trondheim; 14.11.45 GB; 7.2.48 *Beaverbrae* (Br)
Huelva 24.4.45 Torpedoed by Russian aircraft, sunk, 8m from Libau
Hundseck 40 Interned Spain; 21.9.42 to Spain; 43 *Ria de Pontevedra* (Spn); 47 *Monte Betayo* (Spn)
Iberia 17.6.40 KM, accom ship, Gotenhafen; 45 transf Kiel; 5.45 at Kiel; 9.6.45 (Br); 18.2.46 (Rus); 15.4.47 *Pobeda* (Rus)
Ida Blumenthal 45 Interned Karlskrona; 46 *Krymov* (Rus)
Idarwald 5.12.40 Found S of Cuba by cruiser HMS *Diomede*, set on fire to avoid capture; 9.12.40 sunk
Iller 9.10.44 Bombed by Russian aircraft, sunk, off Mantu, Ösel Island
Ilona Siemers 5.45 at Lübeck, damaged; 45 GB, *Empire Teme* (Br); 46 *Aivazovsky* (Rus)
Ilse L-M Russ 5.45 At Kiel; 45 GB, *Empire Conqueror* (Br); 46 *Ekornes* (Nor)
Ina Lotte Blumenthal 5.45 At Kiel; 47 *Elefsis* (Gre)

Inge Christophersen 9.10.44 Bombed by Russian aircraft, sunk, off Mantu, Ösel Island
Ingo 22.10.40 KM, transport; 27.1.41 attacked (in convoy) by FAA Swordfish of 830 NAS, sunk, 34 27N 11 48E
Ingrid Horn 40 KM, *Hilfssperrbrecher B*; *Sperrbrecher B*; 41 *Sperrbrecher 25*; 41 target ship; 25.7.44 bombed by RAF aircraft, sunk, Kiel (3†); raised, BU
Inn 5.9.39 Sunk off Para, Brazil
Ionia 6.4.40 KM, Weserübung troop transport; 11.4.40 torpedoed by subm HMS *Triad*, 58 30N 10 35E; 12.4.40 capsized, sunk
Iris 17.3.45 Reported torpedoed by British subm, sunk, off Ålesund; 12.47 sold salvors
Irmtraut Cords 3.5.45 Bombed by Typhoons of 2nd TAF, exploded (munitions cargo), sunk, Kiel Bay (–†)
Isar 10.7.39 KM, troop transport; 11.7.40 Seelöwe transport *A1*; 7.8.42 transport; 9.42 transport, Norway; 5.45 at Moss; 19.8.47 *Stanroyal* (Br)
Iserlohn 2.41 KM, Sonnenblume transport; 16.4.41 shelled (in convoy) by Force K destroyers HMS *Janus*, *Jervis*, *Mohawk*, *Nubian* off Kerkennah Islands
Itauri 6.3.40 KM, Weserübung transport; 8.40 Seelöwe transport *A12*; 10.7.42 returned; 26.4.44 bombed by Allied carrier-based aircraft, W of Fugløya Røssoskjørnvarde, aground; TL
Ithaka 4.5.41 KM, transport; 10.11.41 torpedoed by subm HMS *Proteus*, sunk, 2m SW of Milos (469†)

Jacobus Fritzen 14.10.42 Struck mine, sunk, N of Cap Arkona
Jan Wellem 39 KM, base ship; 13.4.40 sunk by British destroyers at Narvik; 7–8.40 raised, largely burnt out; partly repaired; by 45, had been scuttled 54 22 12N 10 11 33E; 45 (Br); 46 at Kiel; 47–48 BU Blyth
Jersbek 14.8.40 KM, Seelöwe transport *H37*; 19.6.42 returned; 28.3.45 struck mine (laid by RAF aircraft) 54 40 48N 19 53E, stranded
Johann Blumenthal 40 KM, collier; 18.9.40 bombed by RAF Blenheim aircraft, sunk, Cherbourg roads; wreck dispersed
Johann Wessels 17.9.41 Attacked by British aircraft, sunk, NW of Juist
Johannes Molkenbuhr 4.9.39 Found off Orkney Islands by destroyers HMS *Jersey*, *Jervis*, scuttled to avoid capture
Julius Hugo Stinnes 27 10.9.41 Struck mine, sunk, off Kolberg
Juno 24.3.45 Bombed by British aircraft, sunk, Wilhelmshaven

Kamerun 5.45 At Trondheim; 12.11.45 GB; 47 *Goya* (Nor)
Kandelfels 39 KM; 6.2.40 comm aux cruiser *Pinguin* (Schiff 33, Raider 'F'); 8.5.41 engaged by cruiser HMS *Cornwall*, direct hit on mines on board, sunk, 03 30N 57 48E (341† + pow; 87 surv)
Karibisches Meer 9.39 KM, *Ölschiff 1*; 24.8.44 scuttled off Rouen-Sahours as blockship; 20.4.46 refloated; 15.8.46 beached Hénouville for BU
Karnak 40 KM, *Hermes* (Ger); blockade runner; 10.7.41 found off St Paul's Rocks by amc HMS *Canton*, scuttled to avoid capture (–pow)
Karpfanger 16.8.40 KM, Seelöwe transport *A27*; 1.6.41 Blaufuchs transport; 26.1.42 returned; 17.9.42 torpedoed by British aircraft, sunk, off Egersund 58 41.8N 05 30E
Käte Grammerstorf 22.5.41 Struck mine, sunk, 12m S of Heligoland
Katharina Dorothea Fritzen 4.6.42 Struck mine, sunk, near Langeoog
Kattegat 40 KM, *Olschiff 2*; 9.4.40 sunk by British destroyer 58 26N 17 25E; 7.40 raised, repaired; 5.45 at Sandefjord; 45 GB, *Empire Tegebaya* (Br); 6.9.46 *Sandar* (Nor)
Kellerwald 6.3.40 KM, Weserübung transport; 8.40 Seelöwe transport *A14*; 25.4.40 returned; 14.3.42 struck mine, sunk, Heligoland Bight
Kiel 13.8.40 KM, Seelöwe transport *H30*; 26.11.40 returned; 22.11.44 bombed by British aircraft, on fire, sunk, off Kladesholm, Sweden
Klaus Fritzen 4.5.42 Bombed by RAF aircraft, sunk, off Brimanger
Klaus Howaldt 8.40 KM, Seelöwe transport *H29*; 5.42 returned; 13.5.43 in poor visibility torpedoed by Hampden aircraft of 455 Sq RAF, sunk, 58 03 45N 06 39 15E(8†)
Klaus Schoke 5.12.40 Scuttled off Azores
Kommodore Johnsen 5.45 At Flensburg; 45 USSR (Rus); 49 *Sedov* (Rus)
Königsberg *39* KM, supply ship; 16.6.40 found by French aux cruiser, scuttled 41 36N 10 37W to avoid capture
Königsberg-Preussen 1.2.41 Struck mine, sunk, off Cuxhaven
Konsul Carl Fisser 3.5.42 Torpedoed by aircraft of 608 Sq RAF off Ålesund; 30.9.57 salved, sunk in deeper water
Konsul Hendrik Fisser 22.11.39 Captured N waters by GB; 40 MoWT, *Empire Soldier* (Br); 16.9.42 collision with *F J Wolfe* (*qv*), sunk, 47 35N 51 44W
Konsul Schulte 5.2.42 Torpedoed by subm *SC-421* (Rus), sunk, 70 54N 26 02E
Kreta 15.8.40 KM, transport; 4.40 sunk Oslofjord; 22.5.40 raised; 5.45 at Flensburg; 15.3.46 USSR, *Yalta* (Rus)
Kulmerland 40 KM, supply ship; 40 *Tokyo Maru* (–); 23.9.43 bombed by aircraft, badly damaged, Nantes; 8.44 scuttled Nantes by Germans; 45 salved; 50 BU Briton Ferry
Kurmark 10.39 KM; 9.12.39 commd aux cruiser *Orion* (Schiff 36, Raider 'A'); 42 training ship; 12.1.44 gunnery school ship *Hektor* (Ger); 30.4.45–4.5.45 bombed by Russian aircraft N of Swinemünde 53 57N 14 17E; 4.5.45 foundered (50†); raised; 52 BU Poland

Kybfels 22.10.40 KM, Sonnenblume transport; 21.5.41 struck mine (laid 21.5.41 by minelayer HMS *Abdiel*), sunk, E of Cape Dukato, Ithaka
Kyphissia 17.5.43 Torpedoed by British aircraft, sunk, off Den Helder

La Coruña 13.3.40 Found by amc HMS *Maloja*, set on fire to avoid capture 63N 10 20W (0†, 60 surv); shelled by *Maloja*, sunk
La Plata 23.6.42 KM, transport; 4.4.43 attacked by US aircraft off Bodø, on fire, aground near Rodøy, 66 39N 13 06E; 26.4.44 wreck further damaged in aircraft attack; afterpart salved, BU Stavanger; 49 forepart BU *in situ*
Lahn 7.9.42 *San Martin* (Arg); 43 *Rio Parana* (Arg)
Larache 43 *Ria de Camarinas* (Spn)
Larissa 13.4.41 KM, transport; 1.5.41 struck mine, sunk, off Trikkeri Channel, Gulf of Velos
Las Palmas 7.8.40 KM, Seelöwe transport *RO41*; 30.5.41 Blaufuchs transport; 6.6.42 returned; 5.45 captured Flensburg by British forces; 19.6.45 *Empire Kennet* (Br); 46 *Brest* (Rus)
Lasbek 4.8.40 KM, Seelöwe transport *A38*; 31.1.41 returned; 26.4.44 sunk by British carrier-based aircraft off Bergen
Lauterfels 22.7.39 KM, auxiliary; 24.8.40 Seelöwe troop transport *RO46*; 7.10.42 struck mine, sunk, 53 34N 05 05E
Lech 40 KM, blockade runner; 28.5.41 intercepted S Atlantic by RN warships, scuttled to avoid capture
Leesee 25.4.43 Bombed by Allied aircraft, sunk, off Makkar, N Norway
Leipzig 1.4.41 Attempted scuttling Callao; on fire; towed N end of harbour, beached, TL
Leuna 44 Bombed by Allied aircraft, Hamburg; 5.45 at Trondheim; 21.6.46 *Kozma Minin* (Rus); 47 *Pulaski* (Pol)
Levante 10.7.39 KM, troop transport; 5.45 at Oslo; 3.10.45 GB, *Empire Kent* (Br); 47 *Oakmore* (Br)
Leverkusen 22.10.40 KM, Sonnenblume transport; 1.5.41 torpedoed (in convoy) by subm HMS *Upholder*, sunk, 34 38N 11 39E (–†)
Lichtenfels 4.4.41 Scuttled Massowah; 50 wreck BU *in situ*
Liebenfels 4.4.41 Scuttled Massowah; 30.9.42 seized as prize; salved, repaired India; 42 MoWT, *Empire Nile* (Br); 47 *Alipur* (Br)
Lindenfels 10.5.40 Seized Sabang by Netherlands; 40 *Mangkalihat* (Ne); 1.8.43 torpedoed (in convoy BC2) by *U198* 25 11S 34 06E, taken in tow, abandoned, reboarded (18†, 84 surv); 4.8.43 sunk 25 44S 33 32E
Linz 43 Completed; KM, aux minelayer; 45 *Empire Wansbeck* (Br)
Lipari 1.12.43 Reported LU Carthagena; 24.7.45 *Empire Garston* (Br); 46 *Arnhem* (Ne); 47 *Orion* (Ne)
Lippe 7.3.44 Torpedoed by subm HMS *Sceptre* 64 32N 10 38E, damaged, beached; 8.3.44 broke in two, TL
Lisboa 10.11.42 KM, Sonnenblume transport; 31.1.43 torpedoed by subm HMS *Unruffled*, sunk, 4m N of Susa
Livadia 5.8.40 KM, Seelöwe transport *O4*; 4.10.43 shelled by Dover long-range battery, sunk, 51 01N 01 51 03E (5†)
Livorno 26.4.41 KM, transport; 11.9.41 torpedoed by subm HMS *Thunderbolt*, sunk, 31 58N 19 23E
Lorenz L-M Russ 13.11.43 Bombed by Allied aircraft, sunk, Piræus; 48 raised, *Pontresina* (Pan)
Lotte Leonhardt 7.9.39 KM; 17.11.39 returned; 16.8.40 Seelöwe transport *O11*; 7.12.40 returned; 26.4.44 bombed, sunk, E of Fuglø, S of Bodø
Lübeck 18.1.40 *Frankenstein* (Ger); 4.41 bombed by British aircraft, sunk, off Florø
Luise Bornhofen 30.11.39 Interned Fayal; 7.12.43 *Sete Cidades* (Por)
Luise Leonhardt 12.8.40 KM, Seelöwe transport *A46*; 28.11.40 returned; 5.45 at Kiel, damaged; 5.3.46 *Magnitogorsk* (Rus)
Lüneburg 15.9.39 Commd KM *Sperrbrecher IX*; 40 *Sperrbrecher 9*; 1.7.44 scuttled Brest upon German evacuation; 46 raised; 48 BU
Luvsee 23.9.41 Torpedoed by subm HMS *Triumph*, sunk, 6m NE of Sibenik

Macedonia 28.10.42 KM, transport; 13.12.42 torpedoed by subm HMS *Umbra* 5m N of Sousa, Tunis; stranded, TL
Maceio 2.9.39 Interned Bahia; 24.9.41 *Suloide* (Brz); 26.3.43 struck submerged wreck of *W E Hutton* (*qv*), sunk, 34 30N 76 54W
Madrid 40 KM, accom ship; 15.2.41 U-boat depot; 9.12.41 bombed by British aircraft, sunk, Den Helder (12†)
Magdalena Vinnen 5.45 At Copenhagen; 45 *Empire Ribble* (Br); 45 *Oosterbeek* (Ne)
Magdeburg 5.10.39 Commd KM, *Sperrbrecher VI*; 40 *Sperrbrecher 6*; 13.8.44 attacked by RAF aircraft at Royan; on fire Royan roads 45 37N 01 01W (8†); 14.8.44 sunk; raised, BU
Main 4.10.39 KM, troop transport; 18.3.40 Weserübung transport; 9.4.40 sunk by destroyer *Draug* (Nor) off Haugesund
Malaga 5.45 At Copenhagen; 13.5.45 KM, accom ship; 23.5.47 *Vis* (Yug)
Marburg 40 KM, transport; 22.5.41 struck mine (laid 21.5.41 by minelayer HMS *Abdeil*), sunk, NE of Cape Dukato, Ithaka
Margarethe Cords 17.3.45 Torpedoed by subm *K-53* (Rus), sunk, 54 38N 15 28E (–†)
Marie Ferdinand 10.1.43 Struck mine off Steinort, near Libau; stranded, TL
Marie Leonhardt 5.3.40 KM, Weserübung transport; 8.40 Seelöwe transport *O15*;

22.6.42 returned; 13.2.46 *Skotnes* (Nor); 47 *Sabac* (Yug)

Marienfels 25.8.41 Seized Bandar Shapur (Opn 'Countenance') by RN; 23.9.41 MoWT, *Empire Rani* (Br); 10.48 LU; 5.50 *Karachi* (Ita)

Maritza 1.41 KM, transport; 24.11.41 shelled, torpedoed, by Force K cruiser HMS *Penelope* and destroyer HMS *Lively*, sunk, 100m W of Crete (0 surv)

Mars 13.8.40 KM, Seelöwe transport *A36*; 15.12.40 returned; 13.5.42 transport, Norway; 5.45 at Copenhagen; 1–20.6.45 hospital ship; 23.7.45 GB, *Empire Forth* (Br); 46 *Ekvator* (Rus)

Martha Hendrik Fisser 11.4.40 Sunk by British destroyer during invasion of Norway, Narvik

Masuren 5.45 At Copenhagen; 45 *Empire Annan* (Br); 50 *Thomas N Epiphaniades* (Gre)

Mathias Stinnes 45 *Empire Teviot* (Br); 46 *Akademik Krilov* (Rus)

Max Albrecht 3.9.39 Interned Ferrol; 22.7.45 taken over by Allies; 27.7.45 GB; 11.10.45 MoWT, *Empire Tagralia* (Br); 47 *Repton* (Br)

Mecklenburg 12.11.39 Scuttled off Iceland

Melilla 22.2.43 Struck mine, sunk, off Ijmuiden

Memel 7.40 (Rus)

Memphis 5.45 Seized in damaged condition Eckernförde; 46 Greece

Mendoza 7.3.40 KM, Weserübung transport; 4.8.40 Seelöwe transport *A28*; 7.8.42 returned; 9.4.45 bombed by Russian aircraft, sunk, off Pillau

Menes 22.10.40 KM, Sonnenblume transport; 3.12.42 struck mine, sunk, 7m E of Cani Is, Tunisia

Messina 5.45 At Travemünde; 45 *Empire Cherwell* (Br); 46 *Polus* (Rus)

Milos 20.10.44 Struck mine, sunk, 58 13.8N 06 17.8E

Milwaukee 7.3.40 KM, accom ship, Kiel; 5.45 captured Kiel; 9.5.45 GB, *Empire Waveney* (Br); 1.3.46 on fire Liverpool; 3.3.46 partly submerged; 4.5.46 refloated; 47 BU Dalmuir

Mimi Horn 28.3.40 Intercepted Denmark Strait by amc HMS *Transylvania*, scuttled to avoid capture

Minden 24.9.39 Scuttled S of Iceland

Mittelmeer 5.45 At Brunsbüttel; 4.6.45 *Empire Tagealand* (Br); 46 *Pamir* (Rus)

Moltkefels 8.3.40 KM, transport; 8.40 Seelöwe transport *A3*; 8.42 transport, Norway; 10.4.45 bombed by Russian aircraft, damaged, off Hela; on fire, aground; 11.4.45 beached, TL

Moni Rickmers 10.5.40 Seized Sabang by Netherlands; 40 *Salando* (Ne); 40–46 MoWT charter

Monserrate 39 KM, supply ship; 1.4.41 scuttled Callao; 41 taken over by Peru, raised, repaired; 41 Peruvian navy, *Callao* (Per)

Monte Olivia 4.1.40 KM, support ship for *Nürnberg*, *Walter Kophamel*, Kiel; 41 accom ship, Gotenhafen; 23.5.44 transf Hamburg; 15.2.45 hospital ship; 3.4.45 bombed by 8th USAAF aircraft, burnt out, while repairing Kiel; 12.6.46 raised; 48 BU

Monte Rosa 11.1.40 KM, accom ship, Kiel; 42 transport; 10.43–4.44 workshop vessel for *Tirpitz*; 44 VTS; 15.1.45 hospital ship; 5.45 at Copenhagen; 1.8.45 prize; 18.11.45 (Br); 46 *Empire Windrush* (Br)

Monte Sarmiento 21.12.39 KM, support ship for *Prinz Eugen*, Kiel; 30.7.40 accom ship, Kiel; 26.2.42 bombed by RAF BC aircraft (38†), Kiel, burnt out; 43 raised, BU Hamburg

Montevideo 20.11.39 Sequestrated Rio Grande; LU; 27.1.42 *Brasiloide* (Brz); 18.2.43 torpedoed by *U518*, broke in two, sunk, 12 38S 37 57W (0†, 40 surv)

Morea 12.2.40 Captured by HMS *Hasty* 41 50N 15 22W; 19.4.40 MoWT, *Empire Seaman* (Br); 4.12.40 sunk as blockship East Weddel Sound, Orkney, 58 52 17N 02 54 33W

Mosel 41 *Taisui Maru* (Jpn); 1.3.45 struck mine, sunk, off Shimonoseki

Muansa 9.39 KM, aux; 6.3.40 Weserübung transport; 5.8.40 Seelöwe transport *RO36*; 4.8.42 returned; 1.1.43 torpedoed by subm *L-20* (Rus), sunk, 70 52 48N 29 27E (1†)

Mülheim-Ruhr 5.45 At Kristiansand S; 46 *Falkenes* (Nor); 47 *Brynje* (Nor)

München 40 KM, supply ship; 1.4.41 broke out from Callao; found 200nm W of Callao by aux cruiser HMCS *Prince Henry*; 2.4.41 on fire (scuttling), shelled, sunk, by cruiser *Almirante Grau* (Per)

Munsterland 40 KM, blockade runner; 43 U-boat supply vessel *Walkenreid*; 20–21.1.44 aground in fog W of Cap Blanc Nez, shelled by Dover long-range batteries (59†); TL

Mur 42 Commd KM *Sperrbrecher 32*; 44 *München* (Ger); 5.45 at St Nazaire; 45 *Île d'Oleron* (Fra)

Natal 9.4.41 KM, troop transport; 13.8.40 Seelöwe transport *O14*; 26.10.42 returned; 7.1.44 struck mine off Makkar, ran ashore, Altafjord (1†); 8.1.44 hull broken, TL

Naumburg 10.5.40 Seized Sourabaya by Netherlands; 40 *Kentar* (Ne); 1.8.42 torpedoed by *U155*, sunk, 11 52N 57 30W (3†, 76 surv)

Neckar 4.10.39 KM, commd *Sperrbrecher VIII*; 40 *Sperrbrecher 8*; 26.8.44 bombed by Allied aircraft, badly damaged, Deschimag SY, Brest, while refitting; 28.8.44 scuttled Brest; 46 refloated, BU

Neidenfels 7.3.40 KM, Weserübung transport; 8.40 Seelöwe transport *A4*; 29.5.41 Blaufuchs transport; 7.41 transport, Norway; 5.45 captured by British forces Eckernförde; 7.6.45 GB, *Empire Dee* (Br); 5.46 *Admiral Ushakov* (Rus)

Neptun (7250gt) 39 KM; 5.45 at Flensburg; 7.7.45 GB; 45 *Thule* (Br)

Neptun (1594gt) 5.45 At Flensburg, damaged – repaired; 48 *Ioannis Nomikos* (Gre)

Nestor 8.40 KM, Seelöwe transport *H35*; 10.41 Commd KM *Sperrbrecher 21*; 14.6.43 struck mine, sunk, R Gironde 45 39N 01 22W (2†)

Neuenfels 10.4.40 Scuttled by own crew at Narvik after torpedo attack by British destroyers
Neumark 12.9.39 Commd KM, aux cruiser *Widder* (Schiff 21; Raider 'D'); 5.45 at Trondheim; 14.11.45 GB; 47 *Ulysses* (Gre)
New York 1.6.40 KM, support ship for *Bismarck*, Gotenhafen; 28.12.40 accom ship, Kiel; 1.45 refugee transport; 3.4.45 bombed by Allied aircraft, capsized, Kiel; 48 raised; BU Dalmuir
Nienburg 42 *Belgrano* (Arg); 43 *Rio Jaramento* (Arg)
Njassa 9.8.39 KM, accom ship, KM Werft, Kiel; 42 transf Wilhelmshaven; 30.3.45 bombed by Allied aircraft, on fire, sunk, Wilhelmshaven; 45 raised; 46 BU *in situ*
Norburg 40 KM, transport; 10.9.41 torpedoed by subm HMS *Torbay*, damaged; 10.11.41 torpedoed by subm *Glafkos* (Gre), badly damaged; 24.11.41 torpedoed by subm HMS *Triumph*, sunk, Heraklion harbour; 42 raised; proposed conv Trieste to Sperrbrecher; 5.45 aground at Trieste, CTL
Nord Atlantic 43 Interned El Ferrol; 6.5.45 GB; 5.45 MoWT; 11.48 *Southern Atlantic* (Br)
Nordcoke 42 *Nordlicht* (Ger); 45 *Empire Conwear* (Br); 46 *Armavir* (Rus); 47 *Kolno* (Pol)
Nordenham 1.5.42 KM, accom ship, Stettin; 10.44 VTS transport; 7.12.44 torpedoed by subm *SC-309* (Rus) 57 24N 22E; beached near Hangö; 9.12.44 sunk
Norderney (3667gt) 15.8.41 Found NE of Amazon estuary by cruiser HMS *Despatch* and amc HMS *Pretoria Castle*; scuttled to avoid capture
Norderney (1487gt) 5.45 At Copenhagen; 45 *Alert* (Br)
Nordmark 10.5.40 Seized Batavia by Netherlands, *Mandalika* (Ne); 18.3.41 torpedoed (in convoy SL68) by *U105* 18 16N 21 26W (3†, 59 surv); 19.3.41 abandoned, sunk
Nordmeer 40 KM; 26.8.44 scuttled Gironde; 2.45 raised; 47 *Artvine* (Fra)
Nürnberg 40 KM, mine carrier *MRS12*; 5.45 seized Copenhagen; 45 GMSA; 13.12.47 *Dundalk Bay* (Br)

Oakland 16.9.39 Commd KM *Sperrbrecher IV*; 40 *Sperrbrecher 4*; 27.8.44 bombed by Allied aircraft Brest, badly damaged; 31.8.44 scuttled; 47 raised, repaired; 50 *Alain L-D* (Fra)
Ockenfels 19.2.43 Struck mine, sunk, N of Vlieland
Oceana 21.12.39 KM, accom ship, Hamburg; 9.4.41 transf Gotenhafen; 5.45 at Flensburg; 22.6.45 *Empire Tarne* (Br); 46 *Sibir* (Rus)
Odenwald 39 KM, blockade runner; 6.11.41 captured by cruiser USS *Omaha* and destroyer USS *Somers* on the line 27 44W; 42 USMC, *Willmoto* (US); 42 *Blenheim* (US); BU
Oder 24.3.41 Scuttled Straits of Perim to avoid capture by sloop HMS *Shoreham*
Odin 9.5.44 Underwater explosion, sunk, outside Narvik harbour
Oldenburg (2312gt) 40 KM (*Schiff 35*); 14.4.40 torpedoed by subm HMS *Sunfish*, sunk, 57 50N 11 15E
Oldenburg (8537gt) 15.8.40 KM, Seelöwe transport *H36*; 10.7.42 returned; 28.12.43 torpedoed by subm HMS *Seadog*, sunk, 62 13N 05 08E
Oldenburg (4798gt) 7.4.45 Bombed by RAF aircraft, sunk, Vadheim, Sognefjord
Olga Traber 5.45 At Kiel; 45 *Empire Orwell* (Br); 46 *Poltava* (Rus)
Olinda 3.9.39 Stopped by cruiser HMS *Ajax*, scuttled to avoid capture, shelled by *Ajax*, sunk, 33 50S 53 30W
Oliva 1.4.41 Scuttled Massowah to avoid capture by British forces; 51 BU *in situ*
Orinoco 1.4.41 Seized Vera Cruz by Mexico; 41 *Puebla* (Mex); 11.42 USN, transport USS *Puebla*; 46 *Puebla* (Mex); 47 *Olympia II* (Arg); 47 *Juan de Garay* (Arg)
Orotava 39 *Robert Mohring* (Ger); 5.6.40 KM, accom ship, Swinemünde; 7.8.40 Seelöwe transport *O7*; 28.6.41 VTS, Baltic; 5.11.41 transport; 42 U-boat depot ship; 44 VTS; 7.3.45 at scene of sinking of *Z28*, attacked by Russian aircraft off Sassnitz-Fährbett 1, sunk (353†); 45 raised, BU
Oslebshausen 2.9.41 Torpedoed by British aircraft, sunk, off Obrestad
Osnabrück 40 KM, mine transporter *MRS11*; 11.6.42 struck mine, sunk, N of Reval (84†); raised, repaired; 12.2.45 struck mine off Swinemünde (–†), beached; 26.2.45 wreck decomm
Osorno 40 KM, blockade runner *Burnau* (Ger); 25.8.44 scuttled Gironde estuary; raised, BU
Ostmark (1281gt) 40 KM, catapult vessel for flying boats; 24.9.40 torpedoed by subm HMS *Tuna*, sunk, 47 01N 03 02W
Ostmark (8730gt) 40 Keel laid; 5.45 incomplete hull seized Kiel by British forces; 48 *Skaugum* (Nor)
Ostpreussen 22.8.41 Torpedoed by subm HMS *Trident*, sunk, 70 12N 21 05E
Otto Leonhardt 2.5.42 Torpedoed by subm HMS *Proteus* 38 39N 20 22E, badly damaged; beached, used as training target for frogmen; 3.45 at Venice, sunk; 12.45 raised, (Br); 9.47 *Albatros* (Ita)

Padua 40 KM, barrage training ship; 5.45 at Flensburg; 9.1.46 *Kruzenstern* (Rus)
Palacia 41 USSR, *Khasan* (Rus); 22.6.41 seized German Baltic port by Germans, *Palatia* (Ger); 21.10.42 bombed by British aircraft near Lindesnes; 22.10.42 sunk
Palermo 31.12.44 Bombed by British aircraft, sunk, Flekkefjord; 46 raised; 47 *Nina* (Nor)
Palime 25.4.40 Torpedoed by subm HMS *Trident* 57 30N 06 10E, badly damaged; struck mine, beached off Jaederensrev; 5.6.40 struck by mine laid by subm HMS *Narwhal*, damaged beyond repair; TL
Panther 40 KM, U-boat target ship *Salzburg*; 5.45 in Kiel Canal; 45 *Empire Mole* (Br);

47 *Reventazon* (Br)
Parana 12.11.39 Scuttled Denmark Strait when found by cruiser HMS *Newcastle* (0†)
Paranagua 21.3.40 KM, transport; 8.40 Seelöwe transport *A7*; 28.11.40 transport; 5.12.40 struck mine, sunk, 52 55.2N 04 40.9E
Pasajes 7.9.40 KM, transport; 20.2.41 returned; 11.1.45 stranded, sunk, 58 05N 08 15E; raised; 5.45 GB; 5.11.45 *Empire Rhondda* (Br); 14.2.46 *Henri Barbusse* (Rus)
Passat 9.42 Attacked by British aircraft, damaged, Pauillac; 11.8.44 scuttled Nantes; raised, BU
Patria 11.1.41 KM, accom ship, Flensburg; 1.7.45 GB, *Empire Welland* (Br); 46 USSR, *Rossia* (Rus)
Patricia 10.5.40 Seized Aruba by Netherlands; 40 *Aruba* (Ne); 46 *Haarlem* (Ne)
Paul Harneit 40 KM; 5.45 at Brunsbüttel; 2.6.45 *Empire Tagalam* (Br); 47 *Tagalam* (US)
Pauline Friederich 7.12.41 Seized by US; 12.41 USMC, *Ormondale* (Pan); 48 BU
Pelikan 40 KM; 5.45 At Brunsbüttel; 45 GB; 11.3.46 *Empire Alde* (Br); 47 *Pacuare* (Br)
Pernambuco 13.3.40 KM, transport; 8.40 Seelöwe transport *H44*; 40 transport; 5.45 at Kiel; 5.9.45 *Empire Dart* (Br); 46 *Krasnodar* (Rus)
Peter Vith 5.45 At Flensburg; 45 *Empire Constitution* (Br); 46 *Grannes* (Nor); 46 *Selnes* (Nor)
Petropolis 28.9.39 Commd KM *Sperrbrecher XI*; *Sperrbrecher 11*; 4.8.40 decomm, returned; 29.7.44/29.4.45 bombed, badly damaged, Hamburg; 5.45 beached Juelssand, R Elbe; 29.5.45 TL in gale 52 35 44N 9 36 51E; 46 BU
Phoenicia 5.45 Scuttled Kiel; raised, repaired; 21.2.46 *Admiral Senyavin* (Rus)
Phrygia 16.11.40 Scuttled off Tampico when US destroyers nearby were mistaken for British
Pionier 2.9.40 Torpedoed by subm HMS *Sturgeon*, sunk, 57 58N 10 45E (–†)
Planet 40 KM, accom ship; 14.4.40 sunk by British warships Narvik; 8.10.40 raised, repaired; 2.2.45 struck mine, sunk, near Swinemünde
Plus 41 *Bilbao* (Ger); 16.6.42 struck mine, sunk, off Borkum
Pollux 5.45 At Namsos, damaged; 47 GB, BU
Pomona 3.9.39 Seized at London; 39 MoWT, *Empire Merchant* (Br); 16.8.40 torpedoed by *U100* 55 21N 13 40W; sunk, 55 23N 13 24W (7†, 48 surv)
Pompeji 5.45 At Kiel; 45 *Empire Blackwater* (Br); 49 *Krusaa* (Dmk)
Pontos 5.45 At Flensburg; 45 GB; 21.7.45 *Empire Mowddach* (Br); 47 *Nicoya* (Br)
Porta 5.45 At Bremerhaven; 46 *Walcheren* (Ne); 50 *Adolf Vinnen* (Ger)
Portland 13.3.43 Scuttled 06 12N 21 45W to prevent capture by cruiser *Georges Leygues* (FFr)
Porto 43 *Ria de el Ferrol* (Spn)
Porto Alegre 21.3.40 KM, transport; 8.40 Seelöwe transport *A9*; 22.3.43 returned; 21.2.45 bombed by British aircraft, damaged, Skagerrak; 12.3.45 sank in tow
Poseidon (5864gt) 22.10.39 Scuttled W of Ireland to avoid capture by Northern Patrol warship
Poseidon (3911gt) 5.45 At Oslo; 47 (Gre)
Possehl 5.45 At Lübeck; 45 *Empire Exe* (Br); 46 *Hermoupolis* (Gre)
Potsdam 22.2.40 KM, accom ship for Seelöwe; 21.7.41 returned; 7.3.42 troop transport, Norway; 5.42 intended conv to aux carrier *Elbe*; 2.2.43 work stopped; conv to accom ship; 17.7.44 accom ship, Gotenhafen; 45 *Empire Jewel* (Br); 20.6.46 *Empire Fowey* (Br)
Pretoria 29.11.39 KM,U-boat depot ship; 12.40 accom ship, Pillau; 22.2.45 hospital ship; 5.45 seized Copenhagen by British forces; 1.10.45 *Empire Doon* (Br); 49 *Empire Orwell* (Br)
Preussen 25.2.41 KM, Sonnenblume transport; 22.7.41 torpedoed (in convoy) by British Blenheim aircraft, sunk, off Pantellaria (190†)
Priwall 41 To Chile, converted to cadet training ship mv *Lautaro* (Chl); 18.2.45 off Peru, burnt (20†)
Procida 2.41 KM, transport; 24.11.41 shelled by Force K cruiser HMS *Penelope*, destroyer HMS *Lively*, sunk, 100m W of Crete
Python 39 KM, U-boat supply ship; 1.12.41 intercepted by cruiser HMS *Dorsetshire* 27 53S 03 55W when fuelling *UA*, *U68*; U-boats submerged and salvo from *Dorsetshire* hit *Python* which blew up (0†)

R C Rickmers 41 *Teifuku Maru* (Jpn); 22.12.42 torpedoed by subm USS *Trigger* 34 52N 139 49E, stranded off Shiba; TL
Rabat 13.8.40 KM, Seelöwe transport *R47*; 10.5.42 returned; 4.10.43 attacked by Dauntless and Avenger aircraft from British and US carriers including USS *Ranger*, sunk, Bodø roads
Radbod 6.12.44 Bombed by British aircraft, sunk, Ålesund
Ramses KM, blockade runner; 28.11.42 scuttled Indian Ocean to avoid capture by cruisers *Jacob van Heemskerck* (Ne) and HMAS *Adelaide* and Australian corvettes
Rauenfels 7.3.40 KM, Weserübung transport; 10.4.40 shelled by destroyer HMS *Havock*, sunk, Westfjord, Narvik, during invasion of Norway
Regensburg KM, supply ship; blockade runner; 30.3.43 found by cruiser HMS *Glasgow* in Denmark Strait, W of Iceland; scuttled by crew to avoid capture (–†, 6 surv on *Glasgow*)
Reichenfels 21.6.42 Torpedoed by RAF Beaufort aircraft off Kerkennah Is, explosion in war materiel cargo, abandoned, sunk
Reimar-Edzard Fritzen 27.12.41 Driven on beach Måløy Sound by destroyers HMS *Onslow*, *Oribi*
Reinbek 10.12.39 Torpedoed by subm *SC-322* (Rus), sunk, 59 42N 24 26E
Reinhart L-M Russ 5.45 At Strander Bay; 47 *Reias* (Nor)

Rekum 40 KM; 20.3.44 shelled by Dover long-range batteries, sunk, off Boulogne (8†)
Rendsburg 10.5.40 Seized Batavia by Netherlands; 40 *Toendjoek* (Ne); 2.3.42 sunk as blockship Tandjung Priok; 8.12.42 raised by Japanese; 43 *Tango Maru* (Jpn); 25.12.44 torpedoed by subm USS *Rasher*, sunk, 07 46S 115 09E
Rhakotis 40 KM, blockade runner; 1.1.43 shelled by cruiser HMS *Scylla*, scuttled 45 01N 10 50W to avoid capture (0†, 155 surv)
Rhein 11.12.40 Scuttled Florida Strait to avoid capture by gunboat *Van Kinsbergen* (Ne)
Rheingold 25.10.39 Captured SW of Iceland by cruiser HMS *Delhi*; 40 MoWT, *Empire Mariner* (Br); 12.7.46 *St Ina* (Br)
Rheinhausen 7.2.44 Torpedoed by subm HMS *Taku*, sunk, 59 07N 05 37E
Rheinland (6622gt) 10.5.40 Seized Padang by Netherlands, *Berhala* (Ne); 23.5.41 torpedoed (in convoy OB318) by *U38*, sunk, 09 50N 17 10W (3†, 59 surv)
Rheinland (2570gt) 5.45 At Brunsbüttel; 45 *Empire Ure* (Br); 47 *Amberstone* (Br)
Rio de Janeiro 7.3.40 KM, troop transport; 6.4.40 Weserübung transport; 8.4.40 torpedoed by subm *Orzel* (Pol), sunk, 58 08N 08 29E (26†, + *c*125troops†, *c*150 surv)
Rio Grande 3.9.39 KM, raider supply ship; blockade runner; 4.1.44 shelled by cruiser USS *Omaha* and destroyer USS *Jouett*, sunk, 06 40S 25 39W (–†, 1 surv)
Robert Bornhofen 30.8.39 KM; 10.39 commd *Sperrbrecher C*; 17.5.40 *Sperrbrecher A*; 41 target ship; 12.9.42 struck mine (laid 6.8.42 by subm *K-1* (Rus)), sunk, 70 43N 25 58E (0†)
Robert Ley 25.9.39 KM, hospital ship *A*; 22.11.39 commd; 40 accom ship; 40 U-boat tender, Gotenhafen; 42 accom ship; 29.7.44 VTS; 9.9.44 U-boat depot ship; 1.45 refugee transport; 24.3.45 bombed by Allied aircraft, on fire, badly damaged, Hamburg (–†); 46 salved; 47 BU Inverkeithing
Robert Sauber 5.45 At Flensburg; 23.6.45 *Empire Wensum* (Br); 47 *Bruce M* (Br)
Roda 8.3.40 KM, Weserübung transport; 9.4.40 sunk Stavanger by torpedo boat *Sleipner* (Nor), during German invasion of Norway; 3.12.53 raised, sank in tow; 56 raised, BU Hamburg
Rolandseck 23.8.40 KM, Seelöwe transport *A30*; 15.9.40 bombed by RAF aircraft, sunk, Antwerp; raised, repaired; 29.3.41 Blaufuchs transport; 18.5.42 returned; 12.2.45 bombed by Allied aircraft, sunk, off Skagen
Rostock 11.2.40 Captured N Atlantic by sloop *Elan* (Fra); *40 St Maurice* (Fra); 40 seized by Germans, *Rostock* (Ger); 20.5.41 commd KM *Sperrbrecher 19*; 44 hospital ship, Rostock; 16.9.44 captured off Lorient by *MTB696*, *MTB713* (Fra); 45 *St Maurice* (Fra)
Rotenfels 16.8.40 KM, Seelöwe transport *A21*; 6.1.42 returned; 5.45 prize Oslo, damaged; 2.10.46 *Alcyone Hope* (Br)
Rudolf Albrecht 5.45 At Kiel; 6.45 *Empire Taginda* (Br); 47 *Basingstream* (Br)
Ruhr 22.10.40 KM, Sonnenblume transport; 22.1.43 bombed, torpedoed, by Allied aircraft, sunk, 30m NW Cap Bon

Saar 30.7.40 Commd KM *Sperrbrecher 1*; 26.8.44 bombed by Allied aircraft, sunk, Brest
Saarland 30.9.40 *Teiyo Maru* (Jpn); 3.3.43 attacked (in convoy) by USAAF and RAAF aircraft, sunk, 07 15S 148 30E
Sabine Howaldt 11.5.44 Struck mine, sunk, off Borkum
Sachsen 39 Interned Vigo; 12.40 reached Germany; 4.10.43 attacked by aircraft from carrier USS *Ranger*, sunk, off Bodø; 49 raised, BU
St Louis 6.2.40 KM, U-boat depot, Kiel; 30.8.44 bombed by RAF aircraft, on fire, badly damaged, beached, Kiel; 16.2.45 returned; 5.45 at Hamburg, damaged; 46 hospital/refugee hostel ship, Hamburg; 50 BU Bremerhaven
Salzburg 1.10.42 Torpedoed by subm *M-118* (Rus), sunk, 45 54 05N 30 19 05E (c2000†)
Samos 40 KM, transport; 17.4.41 torpedoed by subm HMS *Truant*, sunk, off Benghazi
Santa Cruz 15.3.40 Commd KM, aux cruiser *Thor* (Schiff 10, Raider 'E'); 30.11.42 on fire following explosion on *Uckermark*, TL, Yokohama (13†)
Santa Fé 25.10.39 Captured by destroyers *Le Fantastique*, *Le Terrible* (Fra), taken Dakar; 40 *Saint André* (Fra); 6.40 recaptured by Germans; 40 *Santa Fé* (Ger); 6.7.42 KM, Sonnenblume transport; blockade runner; 7.11.43 Black Sea Command; 23.11.43 torpedoed (while escorted) by subm *D-4* (Rus), sunk, 45 05N 33 16E (20†)
Santos 13.3.40 KM, transport; 20.8.40 Seelöwe transport *H41*; 5.9.41 returned; 10.8.44 bombed by British aircraft, sunk, off Wangerooge, Heligoland Bight
São Päulo 8.3.40 KM, Weserübung transport; 9.4.40 struck mine; 10.4.40 sunk 60 30N 05 10E
Sardinien 5.45 At Bergen; 46 *Losinj* (Yug)
Sauerland 11.9.39 Commd KM *Sperrbrecher VII*; 40 *Sperrbrecher 7*; 12.8.44 torpedoed by cruiser HMS *Diadem*, bombed by RAF aircraft, on fire, engine disabled; torpedoed by destroyer *Piorun* (Pol), sunk, 46 03.6N 01 41.8W
Scharnhorst 2.42 IJN, conv Kure to carrier *Shinyo*; 15.12.43 commd; 17.11.44 torpedoed by subm USS *Spadefish*, sunk, 33 02N 123 33E (–†)
Scheer 10.5.40 Seized Makassar by Netherlands; 40 *Mangkai* (Ne); 16.3.41 shelled by *Scharnhorst*, sunk, 43 15N 43 05W (36†, 9 pow)
Schiffbek 18.8.40 KM, Seelöwe transport *A31*; 9.12.40 returned; 6.11.44 struck mine, sunk, 56 32.2N 20 54.7E (10†)
Schleswig-Holstein 40 KM, gunnery training ship; 45 *Herkules* (Ger); 15.3.46 *Ochakov* (Rus); 48 *Kolobrzeg* (Pol)
Schürbek 31.12.40 Commd KM *Sperrbrecher 18* (Schiff 40); 12.3.45 bombed by USAAF

aircraft, badly damaged, Hamburg, CTL; 5.45 at Hamburg; 45 GB; 48–49 BU

Schwaben 19.8.40 KM, Seelöwe transport *A24*; 13.12.40 transport, Norway; 4.10.44 damaged by bombing, Bergen; 5.45 at Bergen, repairing; 31.5.47 *Bosna* (Yug)

Schwaneck 9.39 KM, anti-subm vessel (Schiff 43); 18.8.40 Seelöwe transport *A19*; 6.1.41 returned, *Schwaneck* (Ger); 17.11.41 struck mine, sunk, Oder estuary off Stettin

Schwanheim 4.10.39 Commd KM *Sperrbrecher V*; 40 *Sperrbrecher 5*; 13.8.44 bombed by RAF aircraft, on fire, Royan roads; 14.8.44 explosions in afterpart, sunk, 45 37N 01 02W (13†)

Schwarzes Meer 25.8.44 Scuttled by Germans off Bordeaux; 2.3.45 raised, BU

Seattle 9.4.40 Shelled, sunk, off Kristiansand

Sebu 5.45 At Trondheim, damaged; 46 *Matros Shelesniak* (Rus)

Sesostris (3987gt) 1.4.41 Set on fire by own crew, Puerto Cabello; heavily damaged, towed out, abandoned on Isla Larga, off Puerto Cabello; TL

Sevilla 43 *Ria de Ares* (Spn)

Sierra Cordoba 29.3.40 KM, accom ship, Kiel; 1.10.41 U-boat depot ship; 15.2.44 accom ship, Hamburg; 4.8.44 bombed Hamburg, partly burnt out; 24.9.44 minesweeper depot ship, Hamburg; 45 (Br), British minesweeper depot ship, Hamburg; 13.1.46 damaged by fire; 18.1.48 stranded off Fanø 55 50N 07 33E on way to England

Simon von Utrecht 8.8.40 KM, Seelöwe transport *RO42*; 12.8.42 returned; 5.45 at Kristiansand; 21.1.46 (Gre)

Sizilien 4.5.43 Bombed by RAF aircraft, sunk, off Terschelling

Skagerrak 39 KM, *Olschiff 3*; 14.4.40 sunk by cruiser HMS *Suffolk* 64 05N 08E

Sofia 40 KM, accom ship; 41 E-boat support ship; 5.42–1.43 rebuilt Århus; 1.7.43 E-boat support ship, Swinemünde; 7.3.45 struck mine 0.5nm N of Swinemünde mole, forepart aground (0†); 45 salved; 11.2.46 *Nadir* (Rus)

Soneck 10.5.40 Seized Padang by Netherlands; 40 *Karsik* (Ne)

Sophie Rickmers 10.5.40 Scuttled Sabang roads; TL

Sparta 40 KM, *Sperrbrecher 123*; 5.45 found Oneglia, sunk; 20.5.46 salved; 47 repaired Genoa, *Sparta* (Ita)

Spezia 2.41 KM, transport; 22.12.41 struck drifting mine (laid by Italian cruiser off Tripoli), sunk, 32 26N 15 01E

Spree 27.11.44 Bombed, torpedoed, by aircraft from carrier HMS *Implacable*, badly damaged, when anchored off Mosjøen; salved; 5.45 at Stavanger; 46 *Hedel* (Ne)

Spreewald 40 KM, supply ship/blockade runner; 31.1.42 torpedoed in error by *U333*, sunk, 45 12N 24 50W (–†, + 23 pow †; 24 crew, 58 Br pow surv)

Stadt Emden 13.6.43 Bombed by RAF aircraft, sunk, S of Den Helder

Stahleck 5.45 British prize Kiel; 46 *Aardenburgh* (Ne); 47 *Danae* (Ne)

Stassfurt 10.5.40 Seized Tjilatjap by Netherlands; 40 *Langkoeas* (Ne); 2.1.42 torpedoed by subm *I-58* (Jpn), sunk, N of Bawean (91†, 3 surv)

Steiermark 9.10.40 Commd KM; 12.40 aux cruiser *Kormoran* (Schiff 41, Raider 'G'); 19.11.41 engaged by cruiser HMAS *Sydney* about 170nm W of Shark Bay, Western Australia; shelled, on fire; 20.11.41 abandoned, sunk, 26 34S 111E (76†)

Steinbek 9.12.41 Torpedoed in error by *U134*, sunk, 71 09N 29 25E

Steuben 3.6.40 KM, accom ship, Danzig; 1.3.44 support ship, Danzig; 31.7.44 VTS; 22.12.44 support ship, Baltic; 45 refugee transport; 10.2.45 torpedoed by subm *S-13* (Rus), sunk, 55 09N 16 37E (3608†, 659 surv)

Stolzenfels 28.9.39 Commd KM *Sperrbrecher XII*; 7.40 *Sperrbrecher 12*; 5.3.41 struck mine, sunk, off Schiermonnikoog

Sturmfels 25.8.41 Seized Bandar Shapur (Opn 'Countenance') by RN; 41 MoWT, *Empire Kumari* (Br); 26.8.42 torpedoed by *U375* 31 58N 34 21E (3†, 89 surv); towed Haifa Bay, sank off breakwater; 6.52 BU commenced *in situ*

Stuttgart 23.8.39 Commd KM, hospital ship *C*; 9.10.43 bombed by USAAF aircraft, on fire, Gotenhafen (*c*100†); towed out of port, shelled, sunk

Sudmeer 14.10.44 Torpedoed by Russian aircraft, sunk, 70 03N 25 18E during German evacuation of Lyngenfjord

Süllberg 19.11.42 KM, Sonnenblume transport; 9.12.42 torpedoed by subm HMS *Umbra*, sunk, 36 14N 10 32E

Tacoma 39 KM, supply ship for *Admiral Graf Spee*; 39 interned Montevideo; 40 (Uru)

Tanganjika 39 KM, accom ship, Kiel; 42 transf Wilhelmshaven; 4.11.43 bombed by 8th USAAF B17 aircraft Wilhelmshaven, burnt out, CTL; 47 BU Dover (arr 20.8.47)

Tannenfels 40 KM, aux cruiser supply ship/blockade runner; 25.8.44 scuttled R Gironde

Telde 16.8.40 KM, Seelöwe transport *A26*; 5.45 at Copenhagen; 23.6.45 *Empire Helmsdale* (Br); 48 *Sea Trader* (US)

Tenerife (4996gt) 21.11.39 Scuttled 62 55N 20W to avoid capture by cruiser HMS *Newcastle* (0†)

Tenerife (2436gt) 6.8.40 KM, Seelöwe transport *RO26*; 6.12.40 returned; 5.45 at Travemünde; 29.7.46 *Baalbek* (Fra)

Thalatta 5.45 At Kiel; 15.7.45 GB; 45 *Empire Tegaya* (Br); 47 *Artist* (Pan)

Theresia L-M Russ 18–19.12.44 Bombed by RAF aircraft, sunk, Gotenhafen; raised; 45 *Empire Concrete* (Br); 46 *Velsen* (Ne); 47 *Cronenburgh* (Ne)

Thessalia 11.11.42 Bombed by RAF aircraft, sunk, 20m SW of Benghazi

Thetis 24–30.3.45 Bombed by Allied aircraft, sunk, Egersund; 47 raised; 47 *Strømsøy* (Nor)

Thielbek 40 *Ingrid Traber* (Ger); 17.7.45 *Empire Condover* (Br); 46 *Fornes* (Nor)

Thor 2.3.44 Torpedoed by subm HMS *Venturer*, sunk, 62 10N 05 05E
Tijuca 8.3.40 KM, transport; 4.8.40 Seelöwe transport *H43*; 42 transport; 5.7.42 returned; 5.45 prize, with mine damage, at Århus; 10.1.46 GB; 46 (Dmk); 47 *Marie Skou* (Dmk)
Tilly L-M Russ 1.3.41 KM, transport; 11.6.41 torpedoed by subm HMS *Taku*, ammunition cargo exploded, sunk, Benghazi roads
Tine Asmussen 1.4.41 Seized by Mexico; 41 *Juan Casiano* (Mex); 19.10.44 foundered in heavy weather 90m off Savannah (21†)
Tinos 5.6.41 KM, transport; 25.11.41 bombed by RAF aircraft, sunk, Benghazi; 23.5.42 raised; 6.7.42 again bombed, explosion in munitions cargo, sunk
Tirpitz 22.7.41 KM, Sonnenblume transport; 23.7.41 struck mine, sunk, off San Remo
Togo 41 KM, conv to aux cruiser; 12.42 *Coronel* (Schiff 14); 44 night fighter direction ship; 5.45 at Kiel; 13.8.45 GB; 15.1.46 US; 47 *Svalbard* (Nor)
Trapani 24.4.41 KM, transport; 17.10.43 shelled by destroyers *Miaoulis* (Gre) and HMS *Hursley*, Kalymnos harbour; 10.11.43 torpedoed by subm HMS *Simoom*, sunk, Kalymnos harbour
Trautenfels 11.12.42 Struck mine, sunk, N of Borkum
Travemünde 13.8.45 At Lübeck; 47 *Bojana* (Rus)
Treuenfels 17.8.40 KM, Seelöwe transport *A22*; 12.12.40 returned; 11.6.45 British prize Århus; 45 *Empire Garry* (Br); 46 *Vergray* (Br)
Trifels 14.11.39 Captured by aux cruiser *Koutoubia* (Fra) off Azores; 40 *Ste Louise* (Fra); 40 retaken by Germans; 40 *Trifels* (Ger); blockade runner; 9.9.41 sunk off Calais
Troja 29.2.40 Intercepted off Aruba by cruiser HMS *Despatch*, scuttled to avoid capture
Tübingen 6.3.40 KM, Weserübung transport; 13.8.40 Seelöwe transport *RO39*; 3.8.42 returned; 24.4.45 bombed by RAF CC aircraft, sunk, Kattegat
Tucuman 8.3.40 KM, Weserübung transport; 8.40 Seelöwe transport *A43*; 31.5.41 Blaufuchs transport; 29.7.42 returned; 17.4.45 bombed by Allied aircraft, sunk, 54 21N 10 20E

Ubena 24.11.39 KM, U-boat depot ship, Kiel, then Pillau; 2.2.45 VTS; 17.7.45 GB, *Empire Ken* (Br)
Uckermark 14.2.41 After leaving Kismayu, found by RN vessels; attempted scuttling to avoid capture; sunk in tow
Uhenfels 39 Blockade runner; 5.11.39 spotted by aircraft from carrier HMS *Eagle*, captured off Freetown by destroyer HMS *Hereward*; 40 MoWT, *Empire Ability* (Br); 27.6.41 torpedoed (in convoy SL76) by *U69*, sunk, 23 50N 21 10W (2†, 104 surv)
Ulanga 5.45 At Oslo; 46 *Stornes* (Nor); 47 *Taranger* (Nor)
Ulm 39 KM, aux minelayer; 41 Schiff 11; 25.8.42 shelled by destroyers HMS *Marne*, *Martin*, *Onslaught*, sunk, 210m N of North Cape
Unitas 18.12.44 Bombed, sunk, Gotenhafen (25†); raised; 5.45 at Flensburg; 21.6.45 GB, *Empire Victory* (Br); 50 *Abraham Larsen* (Br)
Ursula Rickmers 41 *Teisen Maru* (Jpn); 3.5.44 torpedoed by subm USS *Flasher*, sunk, 12 54N 114 07E
Uruguay 6.3.40 Found 67 05N 16 12W by cruiser HMS *Berwick*, scuttled to avoid capture (0†)
Urundi 29.3.40 KM, transport; 8.40 Seelöwe transport *A18*; 15.11.43 target ship, torpedo school, Travemünde; 12.3.45 VTS; 5.45 at Copenhagen; 19.6.45 GB; 45 *Kalamai* (Gre); 46 *Empire Thames* (Br); 48 *Valparaiso* (Pan)
Usambara 17.10.39 accom ship, Mürwik; 15.2.40 U-boat support ship; 1.7.41 transf Stettin; 11.4.44 bombed, on fire, Stettin; repaired; 20.3.45 bombed again, several direct hits; 31.3.45 wreck scuttled E of Kranichwerder
Usaramo 9.39 At Vigo; 2.10.40 KM; 22–29.10.40 Italian subm depot ship, Bordeaux; 25.8.44 sunk as blockship off Lagrange, R Gironde
Ussukuma 5.12.39 Found off Corrientes by cruisers HMS *Ajax* and *Cumberland*, scuttled to avoid capture

Vale 9.4.45 Bombed by Russian aircraft, sunk, off Pillau; 45 raised; 45 *Pamyat Ilisha* (Rus)
Valencia 1.2.44 Bombed by RAF aircraft, badly damaged, beached off Stadlandet; 48 *Skottland* (Nor)
Vancouver 10.5.40 Seized Curaçao by Netherlands; 40 *Curaçao* (Ne); 46 *Duivendijk* (Ne)
Vaterland (bldg) 24.8.40 Launched; 25–26.7.43 bombed by RAF and USAAF aircraft, on fire, badly damaged, Blohm & Voss shipyard, Hamburg; beyond repair; 5.45 wreck surrendered; 48 BU
Victoria 41 Launched; 44 bombed, badly damaged while still building; LU Hamburg; 5.45 surrendered; allocated Yugoslavia; 47–49 repaired; 49 *Makedonija* (Yug)
Vigo 28.9.39 Commd KM *Sperrbrecher X*; 1.7.40 *Sperrbrecher 10*; 6.3.43 struck mine 53 49.2N 06 32E (1†); 7.3.43 sunk 53 59N 07 09.5E
Vogesen 6.5.40 Struck mine (laid 4.5.40 by subm HMS *Seal*), sunk, off Vinga Lt
Vogtland 10.5.40 Seized Batavia by Netherlands; 40 *Berakit* (Ne); 7.5.43 torpedoed, shelled, by subm *I-27* (Jpn), sunk, 03 04N 75 20E (3†, 1 pow, 76 surv)

Wachtfels 41 KM, Sonnenblume transport; 7.8.42 torpedoed by subm HMS *Proteus*, sunk, 36 55N 24 10E (5†)
Wadai 6.11.39 KM, torpedo school accom ship; 1.6.43 target ship; 26.6.45 GB, *Empire Yare* (Br); 46 *Gogol* (Rus)
Wagogo 5.43 *Bailundo* (Por)

Wahehe 21.2.40 Captured off Iceland by cruiser HMS *Manchester* and destroyer HMS *Kimberley*; 40 MoWT, *Empire Citizen* (Br); 3.2.41 torpedoed (in convoy OB279) by *U107*, sunk, 58 12N 23 22W (78†, 5 surv)
Wakama 13.2.40 Found by cruiser HMS *Dorsetshire*, scuttled 22 35 07S 41 39 05W to avoid capture
Waldtraut Horn 41 Commd KM *Sperrbrecher 24*; 22.11.42 decomm; 45 GMSA; 17.1.46 *Kushka* (Rus)
Walter Rau 40 KM, depot ship, Gotenhafen; 21.11.45 GB; 12.45 Norway; 46 *Kosmos IV* (Nor)
Wameru 43 *Huambo* (Por)
Wandsbek 6.3.40 KM, Weserübung transport; 14.8.40 Seelöwe transport *H40*; 18.10.40 returned; 21.7.41 bombed by RAF aircraft, sunk Narvik; 29.3.43 raised, taken Helsingør, repaired; 4.8.45 GB, *Empire Medway* (Br); 46 *Aleksandr Pushkin* (Rus)
Wangoni 21.6.40 KM, accom ship, Gotenhafen; 15.9.41 transf Swinemünde; 12.3.45 VTS; 5.45 at Rendsburg; 19.3.46 *Chukotka* (Rus)
Wartenfels 4.5.42 Scuttled Diego Suarez; salved; 24.11.42–9.8.46 MoWT, *Empire Tugela* (Br); 8.46 sold (Br); 47 *Chitpur* (Br)
Wasgenwald 10.5.40 Seized Sabang by Netherlands; 40 *Sembilangen* (Ne); 13.3.43 torpedoed (in convoy OS44) by *U107*, sunk, 42 45N 13 31W (86†, 1 surv)
Watussi 2.12.39 Reported off South Africa by SAAF aircraft; found by cruiser HMS *Sussex*, and battlecruiser HMS *Renown*, scuttled to avoid capture 80m S of Cape Point
Weissenfels 25.8.41 Set on fire, scuttled, Bandar Shapur, to avoid capture intact by British forces (Opn 'Countenance'); salved, BU
Weissesee 17.1.45 Bombed by Allied aircraft, sunk, Hamburg; 49 raised, BU
Welheim 28.11.44 Torpedoed (in convoy) by *MTB627*, *MTB717* (Br), beached, near Stavenaes
Werdenfels 10.5.40 Seized Sabang by Netherlands; 40 *Balingkar* (Ne); 18.8.42 torpedoed (in convoy SL118) by *U214*, sunk, 41 34N 19 49W (2†, 91 surv)
Werner Vinnen 24.5.44 Sunk off Vogelsand
Weser 40 KM, supply ship; 25.9.40 captured by cruiser HMS *Orion*, aux cruiser HMCS *Prince Robert*, off Manzanillo; 19.11.40 MoWT, *Vancouver Island* (Br); 15.10.41 torpedoed (ind) by *U558*, sunk, 53 37N 25 37W (105†, 0 surv)
Wesermünde 9.39 Interned Port Limon; 41 US prize; 42 *Chirripo* (Hon); 46 (Br)
Westfalen 8.9.44 Struck mine, sunk, off Stora Polsan, Gothenburg (carrying *c*200 German personnel and 50 pow (Nor); 200+† (incl 45 pow), 78 surv (incl 5 pow))
Westsee 30.11.42 Struck mine, shelled by Russian shore batteries on Fischer peninsula, on fire, partially submerged, at entrance to Petsamo
Widar 18.3.41 Torpedoed by British aircraft, sunk, Hubertgat
Wiegand 5.3.40 KM, Weserübung transport; 10.8.40 Seelöwe transport *R31*; 27.6.42 returned; 8.5.45 at Kiel; 14.3.46 *Mikhail Frunze* (Rus)
Wigbert 6.3.40 KM, troop transport; 10.4.40 torpedoed by subm HMS *Triton*, sunk, 57 50N 11 23E
Wikinger 8.5.45 At Kiel; 7.8.45 *Empire Venture* (Br); 46 *Slava* (Rus)
Wildenfels 25.8.41 Seized Bandar Shapur by RN (Opn 'Countenance'); 41 MoWT, *Empire Raja* (Br); 49 *Lansdowne* (Br)
Wilhelm A Reidemann 2.8.44 Bombed by Allied aircraft, burnt out, Nantes; 11.8.44 wreck scuttled Nantes; 1.5.45 raised; 47 BU
Wilhelm Gustloff 22.9.39 KM, hospital ship *D*; 20.11.40 U-boat base accom ship; 5.43 accom ship; 45 refugee transport; 30.1.45 torpedoed 28nm NNE of Leba by subm *S-13* (Rus) 55 08 04N 17 39 05E, sunk (figures vary from 5100† to 5384† and 654 surv to 904 surv); wreck in 55 07N 17 42E BU
Wilhelm Traber 4.7.45 *Empire Wandle* (Br); 24.9.46 USMC; 47 *Yankee Dawn* (US)
Windhuk 12.41 Seized by Brazil; 42 USN, troop transport USS *Lejeune* (US); 48 LU
Winnetou 8.39 KM, supply vessel; 4.42 *Teikon Maru* (Jpn); 12.8.44 torpedoed by subm USS *Puffer*, sunk, 13 17N 120 07E
Wittekind 40 KM, collier; 14.1.44 torpedoed by RAF aircraft, sunk, off Lister (29†)
Wolfgang L-M Russ 4.5.45 Struck mine, sunk, SE of Århus; 5.55 wreck raised, BU
Wolfram 6.3.40 KM Weserübung transport; 13.8.40 Seelöwe transport *O5*; 17.11.40 returned; 10.2.42 torpedoed by British aircraft, sunk, N of Vlieland
Wolfsburg 2.3.40 Found 67 30N 22 47W by cruiser HMS *Berwick*, scuttled to avoid capture
Wuppertal 10.5.40 Seized Padang by Netherlands; 40 *Noesaniwi* (Ne); 8.7.46 *Kertosono* (Ne)

Yalova 41 KM, transport; 28.9.41 torpedoed by subm HMS *Tetrarch* 37 04N 24 02E; 29.9.41 again torpedoed S of Agios Georgios, beached (9†); 3.10.41 torpedoed by subm HMS *Talisman*, sunk

Sunk postwar with surplus war materials

Bernlef 5.45 Seized Copenhagen; prize; 14.8.45 explosion in munitions cargo, sank, 56 10 01N 12 07 01E (German flag when lost, munitions were for jettisoning)
Dessau 5.9.39 KM, auxiliary; 10.11.39 returned; 5.3.40 KM, troop transport; 10.8.40 Seelöwe transport *RO32*; 42 returned; 10.4.42 transport, France; 20.4.42 returned; 24.8.44 torpedoed (in convoy W127) by subm *S-15* (Rus), damaged, Tanafjord; 46 (Br); 17.5.46 sunk North Sea with gas shells
Dora Oldendorff 5.2.47 Scuttled 47 40N 09 22W with poison gas shells
Duburg 5.45 At Kristiansand; 45 (Br); 4.10.45 scuttled North Sea with surplus shells

Edith Howaldt 45 (Br); 17.11.45 Scuttled North Sea with poison gas shells
Eider 40 KM, transport; 41 *Sperrbrecher 36*; 42 target ship; 12.4.45 bombed by Allied aircraft, exploded, capsized, Wilhelmshaven; 46 (Br); 15.10.46 scuttled North Sea with poison gas shells
Falkenfels 6.8.40 KM, Seelöwe transport *H48*; 24.2.41 returned; 5.45 at Kiel with bomb damage; 45 (Br); 16.3.46 sunk Skagerrak with poison gas shells
Fechenheim 4.40 KM, Seelöwe transport *H31*; 12.2.43 torpedoed by subm *K-3* (Rus), sunk, Batsfjord; 16.3.43 raised; 23.1.44 towed Germany; 46 (Br); 13.6.46 sunk off Arendal with poison gas shells
Freiburg 40 KM, torpedo school ship; 4.5.45 bombed by Allied aircraft, on fire, beached, Eckernförde, burnt out; 46 (Br); 13.7.46 scuttled Skagerrak with poison gas shells
Gertrud Fritzen 2.5.45 Attacked by Allied aircraft, damaged, Travemünde; later partially submerged Lübeck, CTL; refloated; 13.7.46 scuttled Skaw with poison gas shells
H C Horn 9.39 *Heinrich* (Ger); 13.12.39 KM, minesweeper depot; 15.3.43 *Sperrbrecher 27*; 2.5.45 bombed, badly damaged, R Trave; 26.5.45 GB; 7.46 scuttled Skagerrak with poison gas shells
Hagen 3.9.39 Seized Cape Town by South Africa; 40 MoS; 40 *Ixia* (Br); 42 MoWT *Empire Success* (Br); 22.8.48 sunk 47 16 30N 09 24W with poison gas shells
Harm Fritzen 12.2.44 Torpedoed by subm HMS *Taku*, badly damaged, beached off Stavanger; 48 (Br); 1.3.48 scuttled 47 55N 08 58W with poison gas shells
Jantje Fritzen 5.45 Seized as prize Fredrikstad; 17.11.45 scuttled Skagerrak with shells
Karl Leonhardt 30.9.39–2.40 KM, *Sperrbrecher II*; 7.40 returned; 8.5.45 at Hamburg; 45 (Br); 16.3.46 scuttled Skagerrak with poison gas shells
Kersten Miles 39 Interned Las Palmas; 5.45 British prize; 6.5.45 *Empire Lark* (Br); 27.7.47 scuttled 47 55N 08 25W with chemical ammunition
Monte Pascoal 11.1.40 KM, accom ship, Wilhelmshaven; 3.2.44 bombed by 8th USAAF aircraft, burnt out, sunk; 12.5.44 raised; 5.45 (Br); 31.12.46 scuttled Skagerrak with poison gas ammunition and other surplus war materials
Olga Siemers 45 (Br); 17.10.45 scuttled Skagerrak with poison gas shells
Patagonia 15.12.42 KM, transport; 14.5.44 bombed by Russian aircraft, badly damaged, Kirkenes; 5.45 found by British forces damaged at Brunsbüttelkoog; 45 (Br); 4.10.45 scuttled Skagerrak with poison gas shells
Rhön 5.45 At Hamburg, damaged; 46 (Br); 8.9.46 scuttled 25m S of Arendal with poison gas shells
Rosario 8.3.40 KM, transport; 4.8.40 Seelöwe transport *H45*; 10.7.44 transport, Norway; 9.4.45 attacked by Allied aircraft, damaged, Hamburg; 5.45 at Hamburg; 23.5.45 GB; 46 allocated Denmark, repaired; 47 sold; 48 *Albertina* (Fin); 50 *Kotka* (Fin); 23.7.56 scuttled N Atlantic with poison gas shells
Schwabenland 40 KM; 24.3.44 torpedoed by subm HMS *Terrapin*, stranded off Egersund; 6.44 refloated; 7.2.45 hulk Oslofjord; 5.45 at Oslo; 46 (Br); 31.12.46 scuttled Skagerrak with poison gas shells
Sesostris (2013gt) 5.45 Seized Kiel; British prize; 17.11.45 scuttled North Sea with chemical ammunition
Tagila 45 (Br); 17.11.45 scuttled Skagerrak with poison gas shells
Theda Fritzen 5.45 At Århus; 45 (Br); 17.11.45 scuttled Skagerrak with poison gas shells
Triton 45 (Br); 4.10.45 scuttled off Jutland with surplus ammunition

Returned to owners postwar
Arion 19.8.40 KM, Seelöwe transport *RO48*; 27.11.40 returned; 11.3.45 bombed Hamburg, beached Blankenese; hull broken; 47–48 forepart raised, repaired, rebuilt; re-entered service, *Arion* (Ger)
Emma Sauber 17.1.45 Bombed by Allied aircraft, sunk, Hamburg; raised; 49 rebuilt, re-entered service
Emsriff 29.7.44 Bombed by Allied aircraft, partially submerged, Hamburg; 47 refloated; 50 repaired, re-entered service
Franz-Jürgen 3.4.45 Bombed by RAF aircraft, sunk, Kiel; 5.49 raised, repaired; returned owner
Frigga 3.45 Bombed by Allied aircraft Schulau; 49 raised, rebuilt for previous owner
Goldbek 5.1.40 *Thielbek* (Ger); 16.8.40 KM, Seelöwe transport *H39*; 12.8.42 returned; 3.5.45 bombed by Typhoons of 2nd TAF, sunk, Neustadt Bay (*c*3000†); 1.50 raised, repaired; *Reinbek* (Ger)
Hein Hoyer 9.4.40 Sunk off Narvik; 52–53 salved, repaired, re-entered service
Henry Böge 40 *Henry John* (Ger); 18.6.44 bombed by Allied aircraft, sunk, Hamburg; 8.46 raised, *Henry Böge* (Ger)
Hermann Fritzen 4.11.44 Bombed by 8th USAAF aircraft, sunk, at Hamburg; raised, returned
Hermod 25.7.43 Bombed by Allied aircraft, sunk, Hamburg; raised; 50 re-entered service
Minerva 9.40 Commd KM *Sperrbrecher 13*; 5.45 at Copenhagen; 45 GMSA; 29.4.48 US; 13.5.48 returned owner
Stettiner Greif 6.11.44 Bombed by Allied aircraft, sunk, Hamburg; raised, repaired
Vesta 19.8.44 Bombed by Allied aircraft, sunk, Bremen; raised, rebuilt for owner
Zeus 4.8.40 Commd KM *Sperrbrecher 11*; 22.10.40 decomm; 41 *Sperrbrecher 22*; 8.5.45 at Århus; 29.4.48 US; 14.5.48 *Zeus* (Ger)

Great Britain, Dominions and Colonies

Losses through marine hazard

Aberhill 6.8.41 Ashore Haisboro' Sands, back broken, 52 54 30N 01 43 30E; TL
Alcora 30.10.40 Ashore in storm 2m N of Rattray Head in 57 37 45N 01 44W, broken in two (0†); 11.40 declared TL
Anthea 8.12.40 Collision with *Maasdam* (*qv*), abandoned, 48 44N 46 37W; sunk
Antonio 43 Sold (Br); 28.3.45 collision with *Fort Moose* (Br) off Milford Haven, badly damaged; 31.3.45 capsized, sank, 5m off St Ann's Head
Ardangorm 4.1.40 Stranded in thick fog Gwineas Rock, W of Mevagissey, abandoned, broke in two 50 14 42N 04 45 36W; part salvaged
Argos Hill 7.8.45 On fire 41 35N 54 54W, abandoned (1†, 40 surv); towed St John's Nfl, CTL; 9.47 ar Sydney NS to be BU
Ashbury 8.1.45 Ashore in heavy weather and fog, near Black Rocks, Talmine Skerries, entrance to Kyle of Tongue; sank 58 32 30N 04 24 10W (0 surv)
Asian 26.12.43 Collision with *Harmatris* (*qv*), sunk, 07 45N 77 40E (–†, 14 surv)
Athelduchess 20.8.43 Ashore Southern Rocks, The Smalls; broke in two, CTL; afterpart salved, joined to new forepart 12.47
Atlantic Scout 8.1.40 Stranded 2m NE of Cap Gris Nez; 9.1.40 refloated, beached Boulogne, TL; 49 wreck dispersed by explosives

Bangalore 20.7.41 Collision with *Richmond Castle* (*qv*) 01 30N 41 54W, damaged; 21.7.41 shelled by escort, sunk, 00 59N 43W
Baroda 14.4.44 On fire following explosion on *Fort Stikine* (Br), Bombay docks (–†); burnt out, removed from dock, beached Green Island; 12.44 sold for BU
Baron Ardrossan 30.12.40 Aground SE corner of Sanday Island; back broken, TL
Baron Minto 30.10.40 Ashore Strathbeg Bay, near Rattray Head, in 57 35 15N 01 50W; 11.11.40–5.41 damaged during aircraft attacks; 9.5.41 declared TL
Barrister 4.1.43 Aground Inishark Is, Galway; broke in two, TL
Beaverhill 24.11.44 Stranded Hillyards Reef, St John NB, broke in two; 11.12.46 stern part towed St John, sank at berth, refloated, towed out to sea, sunk
Beltinge 6.1.40 Ashore in dense fog near Sables d'Olonne; TL
Bencleuch 11.12.41 On fire (?sabotage) SE of Cape Farewell; 12.12.41 sank 53 10N 38W
Bereby 24.9.41 Ashore Ringfad Point, Co Down, due to LH light extinguished; TL
Blairatholl 26.11.42 Collision with *John Bakke* (*qv*), sank, 51 25N 48 30W
Blairnevis 13.2.45 Collision with frigate HMCS *Orkney* in 53 38N 04 38W, beached Taylor Bank, R Mersey; TL
Boardale 30.4.40 Aground Aasen Fjord, near Narvik, abandoned; 1.5.40 swept from rocks, sank
Bodnant 30.12.40 Collision (in convoy) with *City of Bedford* (*qv*), sank, 60 03N 23 01W (0†)
Brynymor 14.3.42 Collision with *Empire Hawksbill* (*qv*), sank, off Bishop's Rock, near Milford Haven

Cairnglen 22.10.40 Ashore in fog Frenchman's Bay, 2m S of R Tyne entrance, TL; 19.1.41 broke in two during gale
Cambria 8.11.45 Collision with *Almirante Rodriguez Luis* (Uru), sunk, when entering Montevideo; CTL
Cape Clear 21.8.44 Collision with *Henry Dearborn* (US), sank, 28 21N 33 11 30E (0†)
Cape Horn 28.3.42 Explosion in cargo, on fire, sank, E of Ascension Island (0†)
Cape St George 5.8.40 Collision with *Grodno* (Pol), damaged, 42 35N 20W; 6.8.40 sank 12 15N 19 31W
Castilian 12.2.43 Ashore in fog East Platters, near Skerries LH, Anglesey; TL
Castlemoor 16.2.40 Sd Halifax for R Tees; 25.2.40 last seen by *Merchant Royal* (*qv*) about 800m W of Ushant; missing
Chancellor 2.12.39 Collision (in convoy) with *Athelchief* (*qv*) about 70m from Halifax NS, taken in tow, sank (0†, 42 surv)
Cheldale 17.2.40 Collision with *Greystoke Castle* (*qv*), sank, 24m E of Durban (16†)
City of Bedford 30.12.40 Collision (in convoy) with *Bodnant* (*qv*), sank, 60 03N 23 01W (48†)
City of Hankow 18.12.42 Ashore South Point, 4m N of Saldhanha Bay
City of Marseilles 21.1.43 Ashore 1m off Batticaloa, Ceylon; TL
City of Pittsburg 11.1.42 Ashore outside Alexandria harbour, broke back; TL
Clan Macfarlane 17.7.40 Collision with *Ganges* (*qv*), sank, 12 38N 55 31E (41†, 47 surv)
Clan Macindoe 15.4.43 On fire Alexandria; 27.4.43 beached, partly submerged, back broken, burnt out, TL
Clan Macnab 17.3.41 Collision (in convoy SL68) with tanker *Strix* (*qv*), badly damaged, 17 13N 21 22W; 18.3.41 sank
Clan Stuart 11.3.40 Collision with *Orlock Head* (Br), sank, 18m SE of Start Point
Clare Lilley 17.3.42 Ashore near Portuguese Cove, Halifax harbour entrance; broke in two, TL
Clearpool 4.6.44 Ashore Skitter Sands, R Humber; back broken, TL
Comorin 5.9.39 Req as amc HMS *Comorin*; 6.4.41 on fire in heavy weather off Sierra

Leone (20†, 455 surv); 7.4.41 shelled, sunk, by destroyer HMS *Lincoln*
Coryton 16.2.41 Attacked (in convoy) by German aircraft, damaged; struck rocks near Farne Is, beached Ross Links, near Budle Bay, Bamburgh; TL

Deerpool 12.11.39 Stranded near Spurn Point, R Humber; TL; 48 wreck dispersed
Defoe 24.9.42 Explosion, bow blown off, on fire, abandoned 52 11N 19 32W; 26.9.42 wreck drifting 51N 18 10W, not recovered
Delphinula 18.5.43 Ashore near Alexandria, explosion, on fire, gutted; TL
Dundrum Castle 2.4.43 Explosion, on fire, Red Sea; abandoned, sank, 14 37N 42 23E
Dunedin Star 29.11.42 Struck submerged object 18 12S 11 42E; 30.11.42 beached 18 13S 11 55E, abandoned; TL

El Hind 14.4.44 Badly damaged following *Fort Stikine* explosion Bombay Docks (–†); TL
Eldonpark 7.2.40 Ashore Helwick Shoal, Port Eynon, South Wales; broke in two, TL
Elisabeth Lensen 42 *Elisabeth Dal* (Br); 3.8.44 collision with tanker *Jacksonville* (US) R Mersey, beached; TL, BU
Empress of Russia 11.40 Troopship; 8.9.45 on fire while refitting Barrow, sank; refloated, CTL; 46 BU Barrow
English Trader 26.10.41 Ashore in NNE gale Hammond Knoll, 24m from Great Yarmouth, in 52 52 57N 01 54 18E (5†, 44 surv); TL

Farndale 31.3.40 Ar Takoradi on fire; 1.4.40 beached, gutted; CTL
Floristan 19.1.42 Ashore Kilchiaran Bay reef, W coast of Islay, 55 48 08N 06 28 15W; TL

Garthbrattan 5.11.40 Collision, sunk, 51 03N 19 35W
Gladys Moller 7.11.42 Aground Baker Rocks about 60m S of Trincomalee, Ceylon; 11.11.42 abandoned; TL
Gleneden 25.1.40 Struck rock, beached, 0.5m SE of Puffin Island, Anglesey; TL
Golconda 24.2.40 Aground Karnaphuli R, near Chittagong; TL
Graig 5.5.40 Stranded near Egg Island NS, broken in two; both parts refloated, BU Halifax
Gypsum Prince 4.3.42 Collision with tanker *Voco* (*qv*), sunk, 3.5m off Lewes, Delaware

Hannington Court 13.7.41 On fire; 19.7.41 shelled by cruiser HMS *Dragon*, sunk, 34 46 05S 19 23 07E (danger to navigation)
Highcliffe 6.2.40 Ashore Forewick Holm, Shetlands, 60 19 08N 01 39 35W; 10.2.40 declared CTL
Homeside 8.1.41 Sd Freetown; 28.1.41 in WT 43 52N 18 40W – leaking heavily; missing

Incemore 16.9.40 Wrecked Heath Point, E side of Anticosti Island, Gulf of St Lawrence
Ionic Star 17.10.39 Ashore near Bar LV, R Mersey, about 1m W of Formby Point, TL

Jalapadma 14.4.44 Badly damaged following *Fort Stikine* explosion Bombay Docks (–†); broken in two; BU
Jamaica Planter 27.12.44 Collision with tanker *Wellesley* (US), sank, 51 21 45N 03 14 22W (0†)
Jenny Moller 4.1.43 Damaged in gale leaving Benghazi harbour, beached; TL
Jessmore 19.2.41 Collision with *Baron Haig* (*qv*) 54N 16 56W; taken in tow; 21.2.41 sank
Joyous 14.4.40 Collision (in convoy KM472) with tanker *Ingeniero Luis A Huergo* (Arg), sunk, off Parana R

Kalewa 1.8.42 Collision with *Boringia* (*qv*), sank, 30 16S 13 38E (0†)
Kingyuan 14.4.44 Destroyed following *Fort Stikine* explosion Bombay Docks (–†)
Kufra 24.6.40 Collision with *San Diego* (*qv*), sunk, 44 11N 02W

Lindenbank 9.5.39 Stranded Arena Island, Sulu Sea; 10.5.39 refloated, sank
Lisbon 30.10.40 Ashore 1m E of Rattray Head, 57 37 10N 01 47W; TL

Magician 14.4.44 Ashore Craig Ewen Point, 2m N of Peterhead (in convoy); TL in 57 31 30N 01 48W
Mahratta 6.10.39 Aground Fork Spit, Goodwin Sands; broke in two 51 14 45N 01 30 05E, abandoned; TL
Maindy Hill 39 Adm req; 9.3.40 collision with *St Rosario* (*qv*), sunk, 74° true 6.5 cables from Heugh Lt, off Hartlepool
Manchester Regiment 4.12.39 Collision (in convoy) with *Oropesa* (*qv*), sank, 150m SW of Cape Race (9†, 63 surv)
Maria de Larrinaga 24.1.39 Sd Houston, Texas; 8.2.39 WT in distress 42 15N 46 50W; missing
Matakana 1.5.40 Ashore in heavy weather Plana Cay, Bahamas; TL
Mervyn 1.11.39 Collision with *Langleeford* (*qv*), sank, 10m SE of Smalls Lt
Middleton 18.2.42 Collision with *Tungsha* (*qv*), sank, 55 07 30N 05 27W
Milcrest 7.10.42 Collision with *Empire Lightning* (Br), sank, 43 53N 62 25W
Miriam 2.2.44 Stranded in fog off Cape Otranto; TL

Nigaristan 24.9.41 Fire in bunkers (in convoy HX150), abandoned 57 55N 27 32W (0†); sunk

Orungal 21.11.40 Stranded off Barwon Head, Victoria; 13.12.40 explosion, badly damaged; TL
Ovington Court 26.11.40 Dragged anchor, drifted ashore Durban Beach, TL

Parthenia 29.11.40 Collision (in convoy) with *Robert F Hand* (*qv*), sank, about 7m SW of Sanda Lt, near Mull of Kintyre, 55 10N 05 40 30W
Pegu 24.11.39 Aground Crosby Channel, R Mersey, broke in two; TL
Politician 4.2.41 Struck rock, ashore badly damaged, Eriskay Sound, Outer Hebrides; refloated, beached; abandoned as TL
Polo 17.1.43 Explosion in hold, on fire, abandoned, Bougie; 18.1.43 towed out; 19.1.43 burnt out, shelled, sunk (0†)
Port Bowen 18.7.39 Ashore Castleshore Beach, 1m N of Wanganui, New Zealand; TL; BU *in situ*
Port Napier 40 Sold Adm when building; conv to minelayer HMS *Port Napier*; 26.11.40 dragged anchor during gale, aground, Kyle of Lochalsh, 57 15 59N 05 41 21W; 27.11.40 while lightening, fire in engine room, fire spread, abandoned by crew, explosions among mines on board (0†), TL; 44 part salvage commenced

Ridley 9.11.40 On fire, abandoned; sank 20 08N 29 36W
Rockpool 1.2.41 Aground Little Cumbrae Is, Firth of Clyde, abandoned; CTL; 41 salved, to MoWT, *Empire Trent* (Br); 46 *General George Brink* (SA); 47 *Africana* (Pan)
Rossington Court 13.3.40 Collision with *Athelviking* (*qv*), sank, about 600m E of Halifax NS
Rothesay Castle 4.1.40 Aground on rocks, Sanaig Point, Isle of Islay, 55 53 13N 06 21 44W (0†); back broken, TL

Santhia 40 Troopship; 6–24.11.43 on fire Hooghly R, Calcutta, capsized; TL; 4.11.45 righted, BU
Sea Glory 5.7.40 Sd Fowey for Philadelphia; untraced (31†, 0 surv)
Sea Rambler 10.2.40 Hatches stove in, abandoned in heavy weather, foundered 47 16N 41 18W
Simonburn 30.10.40 Stranded between Rattray Head and Fraserburgh, drifted off, sank
Socony 9.1.41 Collision (in convoy) with *Tongariro* (*qv*), sank, 51 03N 41 32W
South Wales 26.9.41 Ashore 6m W of Point Amour, Belle Isle Strait; TL
Stanforth 17.8.45 Ashore Grundkallegrund, E of Grasso; broke in two, TL
Stanwood 5.12.39 Fire in cargo, put in Falmouth, towed Falmouth Roads; 7.12.39 beached; 10.12.39 holds flooded, sank off Trefusis Point, 50 10 15N 05 02 18W (1†); 49 wreck demolished
Sui Sang 29.4.42 On fire while loading oil Abadan; TL
Svend Foyn 19.3.43 Struck iceberg 58 05N 44 15W; 21.3.43 sank
Szechuen 42 Adm service; 27.11.42 explosion (probably sabotage), sank, off Port Said

Takliwa 40 Troopship; 14.10.45 stranded in heavy weather, on fire, burnt out, Great Parsons Point, Nicobar Is; TL
Temple Bar 8.4.39 Struck rock off Carroll Is, 20m S of Cape Flattery, near Seattle, sank
Thala 8.2.41 Stranded on rocks Hartimeal, South Uist; broken in two; 13.2.41 declared TL
Trevorian 28.11.43 Collision with *Oli Garda* (trawler), sank, North Sea
Trongate 11.4.42 Fire in cargo (included explosives) off Halifax NS, sunk by Allied warships

Ulmus 18.1.39 On fire 36 14N 06 58W, abandoned; towed Gibraltar, CTL

Verbormilia 6.2.40 Ashore in fog 1m W of Fast Castle Point, above Berwick, 55 56 10N 01 14 30W

Waikouaiti 28.11.39 Wrecked near Dog Is, Foveaux Strait, off Bluff
Warkworth 10.10.41 Collision (in convoy) with *Selvistan* (*qv*) 58 24N 22 28W, abandoned, sank (13†)
Wilston 22.1.39 Drove ashore in heavy weather at Wicca Cove, St Ives, 5m NE of Pendeen (30†, 0 surv); TL
Winga 2.6.40 Collision with *Jernland* (Nor), sank, 5m E of West Hartlepool, 54 42 54N 01 02 06W (14†)

Zitella 6.2.40 Ashore in fog Bodan Bay, 2m S of Peterhead, 57 28 15N 01 46 30W; 10.2.40 broke in two, TL

Losses through war causes
Abosso 29.10.42 Torpedoed by *U575*, sunk, 48 30N 28 50W (340†, 31 surv)
Accra 26.7.40 Torpedoed (in convoy OB188) by *U34*, sunk, 55 40N 16 28W (24†, 475 surv)
Adda 8.6.41 Torpedoed by *U107* 08 30N 14 39W (12†, 402 surv); sunk
Adelaide Star 9.4.40 Seized at B&W shipyard, Copenhagen, by Germans; 28.8.40 KM; 19.11.40 U-boat target ship *Seeburg* (Ger); 4.12.44 torpedoed by subm *SC-407* (Rus), sunk, 54 39N 18 39E (0†); 52 raised, repaired, *Jastarnia* (Pol)
Adellen 22.2.42 Torpedoed (in convoy ONS67) by *U155*, sunk, 49 20N 38 15W (36†, 12 surv)
Aelybryn 11.3.43 Torpedoed by *U160*, sunk, 28 30S 34E (8†, 32 surv)

Aeneas 39 Troopship; 2.7.40 bombed (in convoy) by German aircraft 21m SE of Start Point, on fire; 4.7.40 abandoned, sunk 45° 11m Portland Bill (21†, 122 surv)
Afric Star 29.1.41 Captured by aux cruiser *Kormoran* 08 44N 24 38W, shelled, torpedoed, sunk (1†, 73 pow)
Agapenor 11.10.42 Torpedoed by *U87*, sunk, 06 53N 15 23W (7†, 88 surv)
Agnita 22.3.41 Sunk by aux cruiser *Kormoran* 03 20N 23 48W (39 pow)
Aguila 19.8.41 Torpedoed (in convoy OG71) by *U201*, sunk, 49 23N 17 56W (157†, 10 surv)
Ahamo 8.4.41 Struck mine, sunk, 53 22N 00 59E (14†, 38 surv)
Ainderby 10.6.41 Torpedoed by *U552*, sunk, 55 30N 12 10W (12†, 27 surv)
Aircrest 30.6.42 Torpedoed by German aircraft 31 49N 34 34E (0†, 45 surv); sunk 31 50N 34 39E
Akenside 22.9.39 Torpedoed by *U7*, sunk, 60 07N 04 37E (0†)
Albionic 11.9.40 Torpedoed by *U99*, sunk, SSE of Rockall (25†, 0 surv)
Albuera 24.6.40 Torpedoed by E-boat *S36*, sunk, 2m SW of Lydd Light Float, 50 43 16N 00 48 05E (7†, 28 surv)
Alderpool 3.4.41 Torpedoed (in convoy SC26) by *U46*, sunk, 58 21N 27 59W (0†, 41 surv)
Aldersdale 4–5.7.42 Attacked (in convoy PQ17) by German Ju88 aircraft of KG30, damaged, abandoned; 7.7.42 shelled, torpedoed, by *U457*, broke in two, sunk (0†)
Aldington Court 31.10.42 Torpedoed by *U172*, sunk, 30 20S 02 10W (34†, 10 surv)
Alert 24.2.45 Sunk 51 20 36N 01 36 48E (49†, 0 surv); presumed torpedoed by U-boat or midget subm or possibly fouled mine
Alfred Jones 1.6.41 Torpedoed (dispersed from SL convoy) by *U107*, sunk, 08N 15W (2†, 33 surv)
Alhama 24.10.41 Torpedoed (in convoy HG75) by *U564*, sunk, 35 42N 10 58W (0†, 33 surv)
Alice Marie 24.11.40 Struck mine, aground, 255° 8 cables from Knob LV, Barrow Deep, Thames estuary (0†, 20 surv); 25.11.40 back broken, TL
Alipore 30.9.42 Torpedoed (ind), shelled, by *U516*, sunk, 07 09N 54 23W (10†, 73 surv)
Allende 17.3.42 Torpedoed by *U68*, sunk, 04N 07 44W (5†, 33 pow)
Alma Dawson 24.11.40 Struck British mine, sunk, 55 32N 06 44W (0†, 35 surv)
Almeda Star 17.1.41 Torpedoed by *U96* 58 16N 13 40W; sunk 58 40N 13 38W (360†, 0 surv)
Almenara 20.9.43 Struck mine, sunk, 20–25m SSE of Taranto (41†, 43 surv)
Alnmoor 15.2.41 Torpedoed (convoy SC21 straggler) by *U123*, sunk, 55N 13W (0 surv)
Aloe 5.4.43 Torpedoed by *U182*, sunk, 32 37S 37 50E (0†, 1 pow, 48 surv)
Alpera 22.5.43 Bombed by German aircraft, sunk, 300° 15m from Cape St Vincent (0†, 35 surv)
Alva 19.8.41 Torpedoed (in convoy OG71) by *U201*, sunk, 48 48N 17 46W (1†, 24 resc by *Clonlara* – 15† when *Clonlara* sunk 22.8.41)
Amakura 25.8.42 Torpedoed (convoy TAW15 straggler) by *U558*, sunk, 17 46N 75 52W (13†, 31 surv)
Amicus 19.12.40 Torpedoed (dispersed from convoy SC15) by subm *Alpino Bagnolini* (Ita), sunk, 54 10N 15 50W (37†, 0 surv)
Ampleforth 18.8.40 Torpedoed (ind) by *U101*, sunk, 56 10N 10 40W (9†, 28 surv)
Anadara 26.2.42 Torpedoed (strayed from convoy ONS67) by *U558*, sunk, 43 45N 42 15W (62†, 0 surv)
Analock 8.12.41 Seized Yokohama by Japanese (Japanese charter); 42 *Rozan Maru* (Jpn); 21.9.44 sunk (in convoy) by USN carrier-based aircraft 14 35N 120 55E
Anchises 27.2.41 Bombed by German FW200 Kondor aircraft 55 14N 13 17W; 28.2.41 again bombed, sunk (16†, 169 surv)
Andalucia Star 6.10.42 Torpedoed (ind) by *U107*, sunk, 06 38N 15 46W (4†, 242 surv)
Andalusian 17.3.41 Torpedoed (in convoy SL68) by *U106*, sunk, 14 33N 21 06W (0†, 42 surv)
Andania 9.39 RN; 11.39 amc HMS *Andania*; 16.6.40 torpedoed by *UA*, sunk, 62 36N 15 09W (0†)
Anglo Canadian 25.6.42 Torpedoed by *U153*, sunk, 25 12N 55 31W (1†, 49 surv)
Anglo Peruvian 23.2.41 Torpedoed (in convoy OB288) by *U96*, sunk, 59 30N 21W (29†, 17 surv)
Anglo Saxon 21.8.40 Sunk by aux cruiser *Widder* 26 10N 34 09W (39†, 2 surv)
Anking 41 RN base ship, Malta; 42 base ship Batavia; 3.3.42 shelled by Japanese cruisers, sunk, 11 30S 109 03E (3†)
Anselm 40 Troopship; 5.7.41 torpedoed by *U96*, sunk, 44 25N 28 35W (258†, 1058 surv)
Anshun 6.9.42 Sunk by Japanese warship Milne Bay, New Guinea; 46 salved; 47 *Culcairn* (Br)
Antigone 11.5.43 Torpedoed (in convoy SC129) by *U402*, sunk, 40 30N 32 30W (3†, 43 surv)
Antiope 27.10.41 Bombed by German aircraft 53 10 45N 01 06E; sunk 53 13 12N 01 08 18E (1†, 46 surv); wreck dispersed
Apapa 15.11.40 Bombed (in convoy) by German FW200 Kondor aircraft, sunk, 54 34N 16 47W (24†, 229 surv)
Appalachee 1.12.40 Torpedoed (in convoy HX90) by *U101*, sunk, 54 30N 20W (7†, 32 surv)
Arabistan 11.8.42 Shelled by aux cruiser *Michel*, sunk, 11 30S 26W (65†, 2 pow/surv)
Araby 27.12.40 Struck mine, sunk, 93° 9 cables from Nore LV, Thames estuary (6†, 37 surv)
Aracataca 29.11.40 Torpedoed by *U101*, sunk, 57 08N 20 50W (36†)
Arakaka 40 Weather obs vessel; 23.6.41 torpedoed (ind) by *U77*, sunk, 47N 40W (34†, 0 surv)
Arandora Star 2.7.40 Torpedoed by *U47*, 55 20N 10 33W (847†, 761 surv); sunk 56 30N 10 38W
Araybank 3.5.41 Bombed by German aircraft Suda Bay, Crete; 16.5.41 again bombed,

on fire (0†); 31.5.41 wreck seized by Germans, taken Trieste; 47 repaired; 48 *Napoli* (Ita)
Ardanbhan 27.12.40 Torpedoed (in convoy OB263) by *U38* with subm *Enrico Tazzoli* (Ita), sunk, 59 16N 20 27W (40†, 0 surv)
Ardenvohr 10.6.42 Torpedoed (in convoy) by *U68*, sunk, 12 45N 80 20W (1†, 64 surv, incl 17 surv from *Velma Lykes* – *qv*)
Ardeola 9.11.42 Captured off Bizerta by VFr torpedo boats; 8.12.42 seized by Germans; 1.43 transf Italy, *Aderno* (Ita); 23.7.43 torpedoed by subm HMS *Torbay*, sunk, 42 04N 11 47E
Ariadne Moller 12.12.41 Scuttled Hong Kong to avoid capture by Japanese; 25.12.41 wreck seized by Japanese; 42 raised, *Chikuzan Maru* (Jpn); 12.7.43 sunk by USAAF aircraft 20 52N 106 41E
Arinia 19.12.40 Struck mine, on fire (60†, 1 surv); 21.12.40 broke in two, sunk, 113° 1.5 cables from Nore LV, Thames estuary, 51 29 08N 00 51 03E
Ariosto 24.10.41 Torpedoed (in convoy HG75) by *U564*, sunk, 36 20N 10 50W (6†, 42 surv)
Arkleside 16.9.39 Shelled by *U33*, sunk, 48N 09 30W (0†)
Arletta 5.8.42 Torpedoed by *U458*, sunk, 44 44N 55 22W (34†, 5 surv)
Arlington Court 16.11.39 Torpedoed (in convoy SL7) by *U43*, sunk, 48 14N 11 42W (12†, 22 surv)
Armanistan 3.2.40 Torpedoed (in convoy OG16) by *U25*, sunk, 38 15N 11 15W (0†)
Artemisia 14.3.41 Bombed by German aircraft 52 53N 01 39E (2†, 46 surv); sunk 52 50 45N 01 38 30E; 45 wreck dispersed
Arthur F Corwin 13.2.41 Torpedoed (in convoy HX106) by *U103*, damaged, became straggler, 60 25N 17 11W; 13.2.41 torpedoed by *U96*, on fire, sunk (46†, 0 surv)
Ashantian 21.4.43 Torpedoed (in convoy ONS3) by *U415*, sunk, 55 46N 45 14W (16†, 44 surv)
Ashby 30.11.41 Torpedoed (in convoy WS13) by *U43*, sunk, 36 54N 29 51W (17†, 33 surv)
Ashlea 7.10.39 Sunk by *Admiral Graf Spee* 09S 03W (0†)
Ashworth 13.10.42 Torpedoed (in convoy SC104) by *U221*, sunk, 53 05N 44 06W (49†, 0 surv)
Aska 40 Troopship; 16.9.40 bombed by German aircraft 55 15N 05 55W, on fire, abandoned (30†, 514 surv); 17.9.40 ashore off Cara House, Cara Is, on rocks amidships; CTL
Assyrian 18.10.40 Torpedoed (in convoy SC7) by *U101* 57 12N 10 43W (17†, 31 surv); 19.10.40 sunk
Astronomer 1.6.40 Torpedoed by *U58* 58 04N 02 12W (4†, 100 surv); 2.6.40 sunk 58 02N 02 07 30W
Athelbeach 7.3.41 Torpedoed (in convoy OB293) by *U47*, damaged, 60 30N 13 30W; shelled, torpedoed, by *U99*, abandoned, sunk (7†, 36 surv)
Athelcrest 25.8.40 Torpedoed (in convoy HX65A) by *U48*, damaged, 58 24N 11 25W (30†, 6 surv); wreck sunk by HM ship
Athelcrown 22.1.42 Torpedoed by *U82*, sunk, 45 06N 40 56W (4†, 46 surv)
Athelduke 16.4.45 Torpedoed (in convoy FS1784) by *U1274*, sunk, 55 38 50N 01 30 30W (1†, 46 surv)
Athelempress 29.4.42 Torpedoed, shelled, by *U16* 13 21N 56 15W (3†, 47 surv); 30.4.42 sunk
Athelfoam 15.3.41 Shelled (dispersed from convoy) by *Scharnhorst* 42N 43 25W, sunk (2†, 45 pow)
Athelking 9.9.40 Shelled by aux cruiser *Atlantis* 21 48S 67 40E (4†, 36 pow); sunk 22S 67 30E
Athelknight 27.5.42 Torpedoed, shelled, by *U172*, on fire, sunk, 27 50N 46W (5†, 47 surv)
Athellaird 2.7.40 Torpedoed by *U29* 47 24N 16 49W (0†, 42 surv); 3.7.40 sunk
Athelmonarch 15.6.43 Torpedoed by *U97*, sunk, 32 20N 34 39E (0†, 51 surv)
Athelprincess 23.2.43 Torpedoed (in convoy UC1) by *U522*, sunk, 32 02N 24 38W (1†, 50 surv)
Athelqueen 15.3.42 Torpedoed, shelled, by subm *Enrico Tazzoli* (Ita), sunk, 26 50N 75 40W (3†, 46 surv)
Athelstane 9.4.42 Bombed by Japanese carrier-based aircraft, sunk, 07 30N 81 56E (0†)
Athelsultan 22.9.42 Torpedoed (in convoy SC100) by *U617*, sunk, 58 24N 33 38W (50†, 8 surv)
Atheltemplar 14.9.42 Torpedoed (in convoy PQ18) by *U457*, on fire, abandoned, 76 10N 18E (3†, 58 surv); wreck shelled by minesweeper HMS *Harrier*, sunk
Athelviking 14.1.45 Torpedoed (in convoy BX141) by *U1232* 44 20N 63 24W (4†, 47 surv); sunk 44 21N 63 30W
Athenia 3.9.39 Torpedoed by *U30*, shelled, listed; 4.9.39 sunk 56 42N 14 05W (112†, 1290 surv)
Athenic 4.4.41 Torpedoed (in convoy SC26) probably by *U73* 58 32N 20 13W (0†, 40 surv); 5.4.41 sunk
Auckland Star 28.7.40 Torpedoed (in convoy) by *U99*, sunk, 52 17N 12 32W (0†, 74 surv)
Auditor 4.7.41 Torpedoed by *U123*, sunk, 25 53N 28 23W (1†, 70 surv)
Auretta 26.2.45 In convoy, struck mine (laid 22–23.2.45 by German E-boat) 51 24 06N 02 49 04E (2†, 47 surv); sunk 51 24 12N 02 48E
Auris 28.6.41 Torpedoed by subm *Leonardo Da Vinci* (Ita), 34 27N 11 57W; 29.6.41 again torpedoed, sunk (32†, 27 surv)
Australind 14.8.41 Shelled by aux cruiser *Komet*, sunk, 04 13S 91 03W (3†, 42 pow)
Autolycus 6.4.42 Shelled (in convoy) by Japanese cruiser, sunk, 19 40N 86 50E (18†, 82 surv)
Automedon 11.11.40 Shelled, captured, by aux cruiser *Atlantis*, sunk 04 18N 89 20E (8†, 97 pow)
Avelona Star 30.6.40 Torpedoed by *U43*, damaged, 46 46N 12 17W (– surv on *Beignon*

(*qv*); 3† when *Beignon* lost); 1.7.40 sunk 46 59N 11 39W
Aviemore 16.9.39 Torpedoed (in convoy OB4) by *U31*, sunk, 49 11N 13 38W (23†)
Avila Star 5.7.42 Torpedoed by *U201*, sunk, 38 04N 22 46W (62†, 134 surv)
Avoceta 25.9.41 Torpedoed (in convoy HG73) by *U203*, sunk, 47 57N 24 05W (123†, 36 surv)
Awatea 9.41 Troopship; 11.11.42 bombed by German aircraft during Opn 'Torch', on fire, abandoned, 1m N of Bougie breakwater, Algeria (0†, 228 surv); 12.11.42 sunk near Cap Carbon
Aylesbury 9.7.40 Torpedoed by *U43*, sunk, 48 39N 13 33W (0†, 35 surv)
Aymeric 17.5.43 Torpedoed (in convoy ONS7) by *U657*, sunk, 59 42N 41 39W (53†, 24 surv)

Bahadur 7.4.42 Shelled, torpedoed, by subm *I-6* (Jpn), sunk, 19 44N 68 28E (0†, 86 surv)
Balmoralwood 14.6.40 Torpedoed (convoy HX48 straggler) by *U47*, sunk, 50 19N 10 28W (0†, 41 surv)
Balmore 11.11.40 Bombed by aircraft, sunk, 52N 17W (27†, 0 surv)
Baltistan 27.2.41 Torpedoed (in convoy OB290) by subm *Michele Bianchi* (Ita), sunk, 51 52N 19 55W (51†, 18 surv)
Baluchistan 8.3.42 Torpedoed, shelled, by *U68*, sunk, 04 13N 08 32W (3†, 63 surv)
Balzac 22.6.41 Shelled by aux cruiser *Atlantis*, sunk, 12S 29W (approx) (3†, 45 pow)
Bancrest 30.1.40 Bombed by German aircraft, sunk, 58 53N 01 52W (1†, 35 surv)
Bandar Shahpur 30.4.43 Torpedoed (in convoy TS37) by *U515*, sunk, 07 15N 13 49W (1†, 69 surv)
Banffshire 29.9.42 Torpedoed by *U532*, sunk, 09 26N 71 20E (1†, 99 surv)
Bankura 21.4.41 Bombed by aircraft at Tobruk (0†, 84 surv); further damaged by aircraft, TL; 50 raised, BU Tobruk
Barbara Marie 12.6.40 Torpedoed by *U46*, sunk, 44 16N 13 54W (32†, 5 surv)
Barn Hill 20.3.40 Bombed by German Do17 aircraft 3m SSW of Beachy Head (3†); 21.3.40 towed in, beached Langney Point; 26.3.40 back broken, TL in 50 47 38N 00 20 33E
Barnby 22.5.41 Torpedoed (ind) by *U111*, sunk, 60 30N 34 12W (2†, 43 surv)
Baron Ailsa 17.2.43 Struck mine, sunk, 53 17 04N 01 11 30E (2†, 34 surv)
Baron Blythswood 20.9.40 Torpedoed (in convoy HX72) by *U99*, sunk, 56N 23W (34†, 0 surv)
Baron Carnegie 11.6.41 Torpedoed by German aircraft 51 55N 05 34W (25†, 14 surv); taken in tow; sunk 52 04N 05 01 30W
Baron Cochrane 28.12.42 Torpedoed (convoy ONS154 straggler) by *U406*, damaged, 43 23N 27 14W; torpedoed by *U123*, sunk (2†, 42 surv)
Baron Dechmont 3.1.43 Torpedoed by *U507*, sunk, 03 11S 38 41W (7†, 1 pow later †, 36 surv)
Baron Erskine 6.1.42 Torpedoed (ind) by *U701*, sunk, 59 15N 18 30W (40†)
Baron Jedburgh 10.3.45 Torpedoed (dispersed from convoy FS1753) by *U532*, sunk, 10 02S 25W (1†, 58 surv)
Baron Kelvin 19.10.41 Torpedoed (ind) by *U206*, sunk, 100° 14m from Tarifa Point (26†, 16 surv)
Baron Kinnaird 7.3.43 Torpedoed (convoy ONS169 straggler) by *U653*, sunk, 53 15N 43 50W (42†, 0 surv)
Baron Loudoun 19.6.40 Torpedoed (in convoy HGF34) by *U48*, sunk, 45N 11 21W (3†, 30 surv)
Baron Lovat 6.6.41 Torpedoed (in convoy OG63) by subm *Guglielmo Marconi* (Ita), sunk, 35 30N 11 30W (0†, 35 surv)
Baron Nairn 7.6.41 Torpedoed (ind) by *U108*, sunk, 47 36N 39 02W (1†, 39 surv)
Baron Newlands 16.3.42 Torpedoed (in convoy) by *U68*, sunk, 04 35N 08 32W (18†, 20 surv)
Baron Ogilvy 29.9.42 Torpedoed by *U125*, sunk, 02 30N 14 30W (8†, 32 surv)
Baron Pentland 10.9.41 Torpedoed (in convoy SC42) by *U652* 61 15N 41 05W (2†, 39 surv), broke back, abandoned; 19.9.41 wreck torpedoed by *U372*, sunk
Baron Saltoun 12.6.40 Struck mine, sunk, Cherbourg outer roads (1†, 32 surv)
Baron Semple 2.11.43 Torpedoed by *U848*, sunk, 05S 21W (62†, 0 surv)
Baron Vernon 30.10.42 Torpedoed (in convoy SL125) by *U604*, sunk, 36 06N 16 59W (0†, 44 surv)
Barrdale 17.5.42 Torpedoed (ind) by *U156*, sunk, 15 15N 52 27W (1†, 52 surv)
Barrhill 28.6.41 Bombed by German aircraft, sunk, 52 50N 01 46E (5†, 35 surv)
Barrwhin 29.10.42 Torpedoed (in convoy HX212) by *U436*, sunk, 55 02N 22 45W (24†, 90 surv)
Bassa 29.9.40 Torpedoed (ind) by *U32*, sunk, 54N 21W (51†, 0 surv)
Bassano 9.1.41 Torpedoed by *U105*, sunk, 57 57N 17 42W (1†, 56 surv)
Batna 12.5.42 Torpedoed (in convoy ONS92) by *U94*, 52 09N 33 56W (1†, 42 surv); 13.5.42 sunk
Beacon Grange 27.4.41 Torpedoed by *U552*, sunk, 62 05N 16 26W (2†, 80 surv)
Beatus 18.10.40 Torpedoed (in convoy SC7) by *U46*, sunk, 57 31N 13 10W (0†, 37 surv)
Beaverbrae 25.3.41 Bombed (ind) by German FW200 Kondor aircraft 60 12N 09W (0†, 84 surv); 26.3.41 on fire, sunk, 60 01N 09 46W
Beaverburn 5.2.40 Torpedoed (in convoy OB84) by *U41*, sunk, 49 20N 10 07W (1†)
Beaverdale 2.4.41 Shelled, torpedoed (in convoy SC26), by *U48*, sunk, 60 50N 29 19W (21†, 58 surv)
Beaverford 5.11.40 Shelled (in convoy HX84) by *Admiral Scheer*, sunk, 52 26N 32 34W (77†, 0 surv)
Beechwood 26.8.42 Torpedoed by *U130*, sunk, 05 30N 14 04W (1†, 1 pow, 40 surv)

Behar 24.11.40 Struck mine 51 42 19N 05 07 27W; beached 230° 4.5 cables from Great Castle Head Lower Lt (0†, 71 surv); TL

Beignon 1.7.40 Torpedoed (in convoy SL38) by *U30*, sunk, 47 20N 10 30W (3†, + 3 surv from *Avelona Star* (*qv*)†, 30 surv)

Belcrest 14.2.41 Torpedoed (convoy SC21 straggler) by subm *Michele Bianchi* (Ita) 54N 21W (36†, 0 surv)

Belgravian 5.8.41 Torpedoed (in convoy SL81) by *U372* 53 03N 15 54W (2†, 48 surv); 6.8.41 sunk

Benalbanach 7.1.43 Torpedoed (carrying military personnel/stores) by enemy aircraft, blew up, sunk, 37 07N 04 38E (410†, 62 surv)

Benarty 10.9.40 Captured by aux cruiser *Atlantis*, abandoned, sunk by time bombs 18 40S 70 54E (0†, 49 surv)

Benavon 12.9.40 Shelled by aux cruiser *Pinguin*, sunk, 25 20S 52 17E (24†, 25 surv pow)

Bencruachan 5.7.41 Struck mine, sunk, 297° 9.8 cables from Mex High Lt (off Alexandria) (3†, 48 surv); 50–51 wreck BU

Benlawers 6.10.40 Torpedoed by *U123*, sunk, 53 20N 26 10W (24†, 27 surv)

Benlomond 23.11.42 Torpedoed by *U172*, sunk, 00 30N 38 45W (est) (55†, 1 surv)

Benmacdhui 21.12.41 Struck mine, sunk, 53 40N 00 30E (2†, 58 surv); wreck dispersed

Benmohr 5.3.42 Torpedoed by *U505*, sunk, 06 05N 14 15W (0†, 56 surv)

Bennevis 9.12.41 Captured by Japanese off Hong Kong; 42 *Gyokuyo Maru* (Jpn); 14.11.44 torpedoed by subm USS *Spadefish*, sunk, 31 04N 123 56E

Benvenue 15.5.41 Torpedoed by *U105*, sunk, 04 27N 18 25W (2†, 56 surv)

Benvorlich 19.3.41 Sunk by German FW200 Kondor aircraft 54 48N 13 10W (20†, 32 surv)

Benvrackie 13.5.41 Torpedoed by *U105*, sunk, 00 49N 20 15W (13†, + 15 surv from *Lassell* (*qv*)†, 47 surv)

Benwyvis 21.3.41 Torpedoed (in convoy SL68) by *U105*, sunk, 20N 26W (32†, 22 surv)

Berwickshire 20.8.44 Torpedoed (in convoy DN68) by *U861*, sunk, 30 58S 38 50E (8†, 94 surv)

Bhima 20.2.42 Torpedoed by subm *I-65* (Jpn), sunk, 07 47N 73 31E (0†, 70 surv)

Bhutan 14.6.42 Bombed (in Opn 'Harpoon' convoy) by German Ju88 aircraft of LG1 from Crete, sunk, 34N 23 40E (6†, 202 surv)

Bibury 2.9.40 Torpedoed (dispersed from convoy OB205) by *U46*, sunk, 12N 25W (36†, 0 surv)

Biddlestone 40 *Llancarvan* (Br); 30.5.43 bombed by enemy aircraft, sunk, 160° 2m from Cape St Vincent (0†, 49 surv)

Biela 14.2.42 Torpedoed by *U98*, sunk, 42 55N 45 40W (49†, 0 surv)

Birchbank 11.11.43 Torpedoed (in convoy KMS31) by German aircraft, sunk, 36 13N 00 06W (2†, 65 surv)

Birtley 15.9.41 Struck mine 53 06N 01 16E, back broken; 16.9.41 abandoned, sunk, 53 03 31N 10 17 11E (3†, 29 surv); 7–12.43 wreck dispersed

Blackheath 10.1.45 Torpedoed (in convoy) by *U870* 35 49N 06 03W (0†, 52 surv); aground 2m S of Cape Spartel, broke in two, TL

Blairangus 21.9.40 Torpedoed (in convoy HX72) by *U48*, sunk, 55 18N 22 21W (7†, 27 surv)

Blairbeg 40 *Fellside* (Br); 17.7.40 torpedoed by *U43*, sunk, 56 09N 12 30W (0†)

Blairlogie 11.9.39 Torpedoed, shelled, by *U30*; abandoned, sunk, 54 59N 15 08W (0†)

Blairmore 24.8.40 Torpedoed (in convoy SC1) by *U37* 56N 27 30W (5†, 30 surv); 25.8.40 sunk

Blythmoor 10.4.40 Sunk by British destroyers Narvik (6†, 30 interned Sweden, 7 surv); 53 salved, BU Stavanger

Bolton Castle 5.7.42 Bombed (in convoy PQ17) by German Ju88 aircraft, on fire, sunk, 76 40N 36 30E (0†, 58 surv)

Boma 5.8.40 Torpedoed (in convoy OB193) by *U56* 55 44N 08 04W (3†, 50 surv); 6.8.40 sunk

Bonheur 15.10.40 Torpedoed (in convoy OB228) by *U138* 57 10N 08 36W (0†); sunk 57 14N 08 20W

Bonnington Court 19.1.40 Bombed by German aircraft, sunk, 275° 9.5 cables from Sunk LV, Thames estuary (2†, 35 surv)

Borodino 26.9.39 Sold Adm; 27.5.40 sunk as blockship Zeebrugge

Bosnia 5.9.39 Torpedoed, shelled, by *U47*, sunk, 45 29N 09 45W (1†)

Botavon 2.5.42 Torpedoed by German aircraft of I/KG26 while anchored (dispersed from convoy PQ15) 73 02N 19 46E (21†, 52 surv); 3.5.42 sunk by RN escort

Botusk 31.1.41 Struck mine, sunk, 6m NE of Rona Is, 57 37N 05 57 30W (4†, 34 surv)

Botwey 26.7.41 Torpedoed (in convoy OS1) by *U141* 55 42N 09 53W (0†, 53 surv); sunk

Boulderpool 7.3.41 Torpedoed by E-boat *S61* (3 MTB fl), broke in two, forepart sunk 52 58 13N 01 28 40E, stern part grounded Scroby Sand, 52 37 58N 01 47 52E (0†); wreck dispersed

Box Hill 31.12.39 Struck mine (field laid by German destroyers) 53 32 05N 00 24E (20†); sunk 53 32 24N 00 25 06E; 52 wreck dispersed

Bradford City 1.11.41 Torpedoed by *U68*, sunk, 22 59N 09 49E (0†, 44 surv)

Bradfyne 22.11.40 Torpedoed (in convoy SC11) by *U100*, sunk, 55 04N 12 18W (39†, 4 surv)

Bradglen 19.9.41 Struck mine (in convoy) 228° 2m from B3 Buoy, Barrow Deep, Thames estuary (8†, 61 surv); sunk 51 31 02N 01 03 24E

Brambleleaf 9.6.42 Torpedoed (in convoy AT49) by *U559*, damaged (13†); towed Alexandria, repaired, hulked; 15.9.44 suddenly sank at stern; TL

Bramwell 40 *Glendinning* (Br); 5.7.44 torpedoed (in convoy) by *U953*, sunk, 50 32 30N 00 22W (4†, 29 surv)
Brandon 8.12.39 Torpedoed (in convoy OB48) by *U48*, sunk, 50 28N 08 26W (9†)
Breconshire 39 Adm, store carrier HMS *Breconshire*; 23–27.3.42 attacked (in convoy) by German Ju87 and Ju88 aircraft at Malta; 27.3.42 sunk off Malta; 50 wreck raised, towed Genoa; 54 BU Trieste
Bretwalda 18.12.42 Torpedoed (convoy MKS3Y straggler) by *U563*, sunk, 44 35N 16 28W (1†, 55 surv)
Brighton 6.5.40 Struck mine, sunk, 51 03 06N 02 08 40E (0†, 34 surv)
Bristol City 5.5.43 Torpedoed (in convoy ONS5) by *U358*, sunk, 54N 43 55W (15†, 29 surv)
Britannia 40 Troopship; 25.3.41 shelled by aux cruiser *Thor* 07 24N 24 03W, abandoned, sunk (249†, 233 surv)
Britannic 9.2.40 Bombed (in convoy HG53) by German FW200 Kondor aircraft, sunk, 35 42N 14 38W (1†, 36 surv)
British Advocate 20.2.41 Captured W of Seychelles by *Admiral Scheer*, prize; taken Bordeaux; 41 *Nordstern* (Ger); 23–24.7.44 bombed by Allied aircraft, sunk, Donges pier; 17.8.47 raised, BU
British Ardour 5.4.43 Torpedoed (in convoy HX231) by *U706*, sunk, 58 08N 33 04W (0†, 54 surv)
British Captain 2.12.41 Struck mine near No 54C buoy; sunk 52 13 10N 01 54 41E (1†, 53 surv)
British Chivalry 22.2.44 Torpedoed by subm *I-37* (Jpn), sunk, 00 50S 68E (20†, 29 surv)
British Colony 13.5.42 Torpedoed by *U162*, damaged, 13 12N 58 10W (4†, 40 surv); sunk
British Commander 27.8.40 Shelled, torpedoed, by aux cruiser *Pinguin*, sunk, 29 37S 45 50E (0†, 46 pow)
British Consul 19.8.42 Torpedoed (in convoy TAW(S)) by *U564*, sunk, 11 58N 62 38W (2†, 42 surv)
British Corporal 42 MoWT, *Empire Corporal* (Br); 14.8.42 torpedoed (in convoy TAW12) by *U598*, sunk, 21 45N 76 10W (6†, 49 surv)
British Councillor 2.2.40 Torpedoed (in convoy AN8442) by E-boat or struck mine, damaged, 53 48N 00 34E; 3.2.40 torpedoed by *U620*, sunk, 53 44 42N 00 24 05E (38†, 15 surv)
British Dominion 10.1.43 Torpedoed (in convoy TM1) by *U522*, damaged, 30 30N 19 55W; torpedoed by *U620*, sunk (38†, 15 surv)
British Emperor 7.5.41 Sunk by aux cruiser *Pinguin* 08 30N 56 25E (45 pow, 8 surv)
British Endeavour 22.2.40 Torpedoed (in convoy OGF19) by *U50*, broke in two, sunk, 42 11N 11 35W (5†, 33 surv)
British Fame 12.8.40 Torpedoed (dispersed from convoy OB193) by subm *Alessandro Malaspina* (Ita), sunk, 37 44N 22 56W (3†, 1 pow, 45 surv)
British Fortune 31.10.41 Bombed (in convoy) by German aircraft 265° 1m from Aldeburgh Lt Buoy (8†, 40 surv); sunk 270° 2.9m from Aldeburgh Lt Buoy
British Freedom 14.1.45 Torpedoed (in convoy BX141) by *U1232*, sunk, 44 27 30N 63 27 30W (1†, 56 surv)
British General 6.10.40 Torpedoed by *U37* 51 42N 24 03W (47†, 0 surv); 7.10.40 sunk 51 42N 24 50W
British Grenadier 22.5.41 Torpedoed by *U103* 06 15N 12 59W (0†, 46 surv); sunk 06 20N 12 50W
British Gunner 24.2.41 Torpedoed (in convoy OB289) by *U97* 61 09N 12 04W (3†, 44 surv); abandoned, sunk, 61 16N 12 20W
British Influence 14.9.39 Stopped by *U129*, abandoned, torpedoed, shelled, sunk, 50 20N 13 30W
British Inventor 13.6.40 Struck mine 230° 5m from St Alban's Head, beached 2m from White Nose; 30.6.40 broke in two (0†, 44 surv); forepart in 50 35 03N 02 18 05W, dispersed, afterpart BU
British Liberty 6.1.40 Struck mine (on Allied minefield) 2m NE of Dyck LV (24†); sank
British Loyalty 5.5.42 Attacked by midget subm from subm *I-20* (Jpn), damaged, sunk 37° 5 cables from Antsirana LH; 20.12.42 refloated, taken Addu Atoll; 10.43 storage hulk; 9.3.44 torpedoed by *U183* from outside port, badly damaged (0†); 15.1.46 scuttled 00 38 12S 73 07 24E
British Mariner 20.10.41 Torpedoed by *U126* 07 43N 14 20W (3†, 46 surv); towed Freetown; CTL; 41 MoWT, hulk Freetown; scuttled postwar
British Monarch 19.6.40 Torpedoed (in convoy HGF34) by *U48*, sunk, 45N 11 21W (40†, 0 surv)
British Motorist 19.2.42 Bombed by Japanese aircraft, sunk, Port Darwin (2†, 59 surv)
British Officer 1.12.40 Struck mine, about 0.5m E of North Pier Light, R Tyne (5†, 42 surv); beached just inside Tyne Pier on S side of channel, broke in two; TL; forepart refloated, BU; afterpart in 55 00 40N 01 23 25W
British Petrol 13.6.40 Shelled by aux cruiser *Widder*; 14.6.40 sunk 18N 54 30W (2†, 44 pow)
British Premier 24.12.40 Torpedoed *U65*, sunk, 06 20N 13 20W (32†, 13 surv)
British Prince 26.9.41 Bombed by German aircraft, sunk, 53 51 40N 00 25 22E (0†, 38 surv)
British Progress 4.11.43 Torpedoed (in convoy FN1170E) by E-boats (2 MTB fl) 52 55N 02E (2†, 51 surv); towed R Tyne; 44 BU Rosyth
British Prudence 23.3.41 Torpedoed by *U754*, sunk, 45 28N 56 13W (3†, 47 surv)
British Reliance 2.4.41 Torpedoed (in convoy SC26) by *U46* 58 21N 28 30W (0†); sunk

58 25N 28 21W
British Resource 14.3.42 Torpedoed by *U124* 36 04N 65 38W, on fire; 15.3.42 sunk (46†, 5 surv)
British Science 18.4.41 Torpedoed by aircraft, on fire, abandoned, sunk, 36 06N 24E (0†, 47 surv)
British Security 20.5.41 Torpedoed (in convoy HX126) by *U556*, on fire, 57 28N 41 07W (53†, 0 surv); 23.5.41 still burning, sunk 57 14N 39 23W
British Sergeant 9.4.42 Bombed by Japanese carrier-based aircraft, sunk, 08 01N 81 38E (0†, 59 surv)
British Splendour 7.4.42 Torpedoed by *U552*, sunk, 35 07N 75 19W (12†, 41 surv)
British Strength 15.3.41 Shelled (in convoy) by *Scharnhorst* and *Gneisenau*, sunk, 42N 43W (2†, – pow)
British Triumph 13.2.40 Struck mine 53 06 30N 01 25E (4†); sunk 53 01 36N 01 30 18E; wreck dispersed
British Trust 1.5.43 Torpedoed by German aircraft, sunk, 32 40N 19 53E (10†, 59 surv)
British Union 18.1.41 Shelled by aux cruiser *Kormoran*, sunk, 26 34N 30 58W (1†, 8 surv, 36 pow)
British Venture 24.6.43 Torpedoed by subm *I-27* (Jpn), sunk, 25 13N 58 02E (42†, 19 surv)
British Vigilance 3.1.43 Torpedoed (in convoy TM1) by *U514* 20 58N 44 40E (27†, 26 surv); abandoned, drifted; 24.1.43 torpedoed by *U105*, sunk
British Viscount 3.4.41 Torpedoed (in convoy SC26) by *U73* 58 12N 27 40W, on fire, abandoned (28†, 20 surv); sunk 58 18N 27 50W
British Workman 3.5.42 Torpedoed (convoy ON89 straggler – engine trouble) by *U455*, sunk, 44 07N 51 53W (7†, 46 surv)
British Yeoman 14.7.42 Torpedoed by *U201* 26 42N 24 20W, on fire (43†, 10 surv); 15.7.42 shelled by *U201*, sunk
Brittany 29.10.42 Torpedoed (in convoy SL125) by *U509*, sunk, 33 29N 18 32W (14†, 44 surv)
Brockley Hill 24.6.41 Torpedoed (in convoy HX133) by *U651*, on fire, sunk, 56 13N 37 21W (0†, 42 surv)
Bronte 27.10.39 Torpedoed (in convoy HX5A) by *U34*, damaged, 49 48N 10 52W, taken in tow; 30.10.39 sunk by destroyers HMS *Walpole* and *Whirlwind* 50 07N 10 36W (0†)
Brookwood 23.8.40 Torpedoed, shelled, by *U37* 54 40N 27 57W, on fire (1†, 36 surv); 24.8.40 exploded, sunk
Broompark 25.7.42 Torpedoed (in convoy ON113) by *U552* 49 02N 40 26W (4†, 45 surv), taken in tow by *Cherokee* (*qv*); 1.8.42 sunk 47 42N 51 55W
Browning 12.11.42 Torpedoed (in convoy KMS2) by *U595*, abandoned, on fire, exploded, sunk, 35 53N 00 33W (1†, 60 surv)
Bruyère 23.9.42 Torpedoed by *U125*, sunk, 04 55N 17 16W (0†, 51 surv)
Bullmouth 29.10.42 Torpedoed (in convoy SL125) by *U409*, damaged; dropped behind convoy; torpedoed by *U659*, sunk, 33 20N 18 25W (50†, 5 surv)
Bulysses 10.9.41 Torpedoed (in convoy SC42) by *U82* 62 22N 38 22W; abandoned, sunk (4†, 50 surv)
Burdwan 15.6.42 Bombed (in Opn 'Harpoon' convoy) by German Ju87 and Ju88 aircraft of StG3, damaged by near miss, 35m S of Pantellaria Is; abandoned, sunk by escorts (3†, 122 surv)

Cadillac 1.3.41 Torpedoed (in convoy HX109) by *U552* 59 44N 11 16W, on fire (35†, 7 surv); 2.3.41 sunk
Cairndale 30.5.41 Torpedoed by subm *Guglielmo Marconi* (Ita), sunk, 35 19N 08 33E (4†)
Cairnmona 30.10.39 Torpedoed (in convoy HX5B) by *U13*, sunk, 57 38N 01 45W (3†)
Cairnross 17.1.40 Struck mine (laid 6.1.40 by *U30*), sunk, 276° 7–8m from Bar LV, R Mersey (0†)
Calabria 8.12.40 Torpedoed (ind) by *U103*, sunk, 52 43N 18 07W (472†, 0 surv)
Calchas 21.4.41 Torpedoed by *U107*, sunk, 23 50N 27W (32†, 82 surv)
Calderon 2.5.42 Bombed by enemy aircraft, on fire, sunk, 31 05 30N 29 07E (0†)
Caledonia 30.8.39 Req as amc HMS *Scotstoun*; 13.6.40 torpedoed by *U25*, sunk, 57N 09 57W (6†, about 345 surv)
Caledonian Monarch 12.1.42 Torpedoed (from scattered convoy SC63) by *U333*, sunk, 57N 26W (41†)
Calgarolite 9.5.42 Shelled, torpedoed, by *U125*, sunk, 19 24N 82 30W (0†, 45 surv)
California 25.8.39 Req as amc HMS *California*; 1.4.42 troopship; 11.7.43 bombed (in convoy) by German FW200 Kondor aircraft of KG40, on fire, badly damaged, 41 15N 15 24W (72†, 695 surv); 12.7.43 sunk by escort destroyer HMS *Douglas*
California Star 4.3.43 Torpedoed by *U515*, sunk, 42 32N 37 20W (49†, 1 pow, 24 surv)
Cambridge 7.11.40 Struck mine (laid by aux cruiser *Pinguin*) 6m E of Wilson's Promontory, Bass Strait (1†, 55 surv); 8.11.40 sunk
Camerata 8.5.43 Attacked by Italian assault craft, sunk, Gibraltar; CTL; 50 repaired, *Campo Grande* (Spn)
Camito 6.8.40 Req as obv HMS *Camito*; 26.9.40 commd; 6.5.41 torpedoed by *U97* 50 34N 21 40W; sunk 50 15N 21 16W
Canadian Cruiser 21.2.41 Sunk by *Admiral Scheer* 06 36S 47 18E (0†, 34 pow)
Canadian Star 18.3.43 Torpedoed (in convoy HX229) by *U221*, sunk, 53 24N 28 34W (29†, 59 surv)

Canadolite 25.3.41 Captured by aux cruiser *Kormoran* 05N 33W (0†); 41 prize, *Sudetenland* (Ger); 13–14.8.44 bombed by RAF aircraft, sunk, Brest; raised, BU
Canford Chine 10.2.41 Torpedoed (convoy OG52 straggler) by *U52*, sunk, SSW of Rockall (35†, 0 surv)
Canonesa 21.9.40 Torpedoed (in convoy HX72) by *U100* 54 55N 18 25W (1†, 62 surv); 22.9.40 sunk
Cape Corso 2.5.42 Torpedoed (in convoy PQ15) by German aircraft, sunk, 73 02N 19 46E (50†, 6 surv)
Cape Horn 28.3.42 Blew up, sunk, E of Ascension Is, following fire believed caused by delayed action incendiary in cargo (4†)
Cape Howe 15.9.39 Commd decoy Q-ship HMS *Cape Howe* (*Prunella*); 21.6.40 torpedoed by *U28*, sunk, S of Iceland (–†, 13 surv)
Cape Nelson 23.2.41 Torpedoed (in convoy OB288) by *U95*, sunk, 59 30N 21W (4†, 33 surv)
Cape of Good Hope 11.5.42 Torpedoed, shelled, by *U502*, sunk, 22 48N 58 43W (0†, 37 surv)
Cape Race 10.8.42 Torpedoed (in convoy SC94) by *U660*, sunk, 56 45N 22 50W (0†, 63 surv)
Cape Rodney 5.8.41 Torpedoed (in convoy SL81) by *U75* 53 26N 15 40W; 7.8.41 taken in tow 52 11N 14 42W; 9.8.41 sunk 52 44N 11 41W (0†, 39 surv)
Cape St Andrew 13.11.40 Torpedoed by *U137* 55 14N 10 29W (15†, 53 surv); taken in tow, sunk
Cape Verde 9.7.42 Torpedoed by *U203*, sunk, 11 32N 60 17W (2†, 40 surv)
Cape York 26.8.40 Torpedoed (in convoy HX65A) by German He115 aircraft 45° 10m from Kinnaird Head, on fire; 27.8.40 abandoned, taken in tow, sunk 57 42N 01 33 05W
Caprella 19.10.40 Torpedoed (in convoy HX79) by *U100* 56 37N 17 15W (1†, 52 surv); 22.10.40 located 56 28N 17 53W, submerged vertically, bow showing 50ft above water
Capulet 28.4.41 Torpedoed (in convoy HX121) by *U552* 60 10N 17W (9†, 35 surv), on fire, back broken, abandoned; 2.5.41 torpedoed by *U201*, sunk
Carare 28.5.40 Struck mine, sunk, 51 17 30N 03 44W (10†, 116 surv)
Cardita 31.12.41 Torpedoed by *U87* 59 18N 12 50W; 3.1.42 foundered 59 42N 11 58W (27†, 33 surv)
Carinthia 8.39 Adm; 1.40 amc HMS *Carinthia*; 6.6.40 torpedoed by *U46* (4†) SE of Iceland; 7.6.40 sunk 53 13N 10 40W
Carlton 20.12.40 Shelled, torpedoed (in convoy OB260), by subm *Pietro Calvi* (Ita), sunk, 55 18N 18 49W (31†, 4 surv)
Caroni River 20.1.40 Struck mine (laid 20.1.40 by *U34*), sunk, 56 06 08N 05 01 08W (0†)
Carperby 1.3.42 Torpedoed (ind) by *U588*, sunk, 39 57N 55 40W (47†, 0 surv)
Carsbreck 24.10.41 Torpedoed (in convoy HG75) by *U564*, sunk, 36 20N 10 50W (23†, 19 surv)
Casanare 3.11.40 Torpedoed by *U99* 53 58N 14 13W (9†, 55 surv); sunk 55 57N 14 15W (see also *Laurentic*)
Caspia 16.4.42 Torpedoed by *U81*, sunk, 10m S of Beirut (26†, 11 surv)
Cathay 25.8.39 Req as amc HMS *Cathay*; 5.2.42 troopship; 11.11.42 bombed (during Opn 'Torch' landings) by German aircraft at Bougie (1†, 284 surv); 12.11.42 delayed action bomb exploded, stern blown off, sunk 36 44 35N 05 06 41E
Cavallo 23.4.41 Attacked by aircraft Nauplia, Greece; 23–25.4.41 attacked again, on fire, sunk (0†, 40 surv)
Cedarbank 21.4.40 Torpedoed by *U26*, sunk, 62 49N 04 10E (0 surv)
Cedrington Court 7.1.40 Struck mine (laid by German 1 DD fl destroyer) 51 22N 01 35E; sunk 51 23 02N 01 35 49E (15†); wreck dispersed
Celtic Star 29.3.43 Torpedoed by subm *Giuseppe Finzi* (Ita), sunk, 04 16N 17 44W (2†, 1 pow, 63 surv)
Centaur 27.4.40 Requisitioned; 4.40 hospital ship; 17.4.42 RAN service; 5.42 returned; 13.5.43 torpedoed by subm *I-174* (Jpn), sunk, 27 17S 154 05E (299†, 63 surv)
Ceramic 2.40 Troopship; 6.12.42 torpedoed by *U515*, sunk, 40 30N 40 20W (656†, 1 surv)
Cerinthus 9.11.42 Torpedoed by *U128* 12 27N 27 45W; 10.11.42 torpedoed again, abandoned, shelled, sunk (20†, 19 surv)
Cervantes 27.9.41 Torpedoed (convoy HG73) by *U124*, sunk, 48 37N 20 01W (8†, 32 surv)
Chagres 9.2.40 Struck mine (laid 9.1.40 by *U30*), sunk, 270° 5.5m from Bar LV, R Mersey (2†)
Chakdina 8.39 abv HMS *Chakdina*; 5.12.41 sunk by Italian aircraft 32 11N 24 30E (18†)
Chakla 8.39 abv HMS *Chakla*; 29.4.41 sunk by aircraft Tobruk harbour; 50 afterpart salved, BU Savona
Chama 23.3.41 Torpedoed (in convoy OG56) by *U97*, sunk, 49 35N 19 13W (58†, 0 surv)
Chantala 39 abv HMS *Chantala*; 7.12.41 struck mine, sunk, Tobruk
Charlbury 29.5.42 Shelled, torpedoed, by subm *Barbarigo* (Ita), 06 22S 29 44W (2†, 40 surv)
Chaucer 29.7.41 Intercepted, shelled, by aux cruiser *Orion* 16 46N 38 01W (0†, 48 pow)
Chelsea 30.8.40 Torpedoed (in convoy HX66A) by *U32*, sunk, 59 45N 04W (24†, 11 surv)
Cheyenne 15.9.39 Torpedoed, shelled, by *U53* 50 20N 13 30W, damaged; wreck sunk by HM destroyer
Chilka 11.3.42 Shelled by subm *I-2* (Jpn), sunk, 00 23S 95 41E (5†, 114 pow, 7 surv)
Chinese Prince 12.6.41 Torpedoed by *U552*, sunk, 56 12N 14 18W (45†, 18 surv)
Chulmleigh 5.11.42 Damaged in attack by German Ju88 aircraft, stranded on ice off South Cape, Spitsbergen (9 surv); 16.11.42 while stranded torpedoed by *U625*; TL
Cingalese Prince 20.9.41 Torpedoed by *U111*, sunk, 02S 25 30W (56†, 17 surv)

Circe Shell 40 Adm service; 21.2.42 torpoedoed by *U161*, sunk, 10 59N 62 05W (1†, 57 surv)
Ciscar 19.8.41 Torpedoed, shelled (in convoy OG71) by *U204*, sunk, 49 10N 17 40W (13†, 26 surv; 5 surv on *Cervantes* (*qv*) – 2† when *Cervantes* sunk)
City of Adelaide 30.3.44 Shelled, torpedoed, by subm *I-8* (Jpn), sunk, 12 01S 80 27E (0†, 90 surv)
City of Athens 8.10.42 Torpedoed by *U179*, sunk, 33 40S 17 03E (1†, 90 surv)
City of Bagdad 11.7.40 Shelled, captured, by aux cruiser *Atlantis*, sunk by explosives 00 16S 90E (4†, 81 pow)
City of Baroda 2.4.43 Torpedoed (in convoy NC9) by *U509* 26 56S 15 21E (13†, 290 surv); grounded 27 20S 15 06E, broke in two; TL
City of Bath 2.12.42 Torpedoed by *U508*, sunk, 09 29N 59 30W (6†, 76 surv)
City of Benares 17.9.40 Torpedoed (in convoy OB213) by *U48*, sunk, 56 48N 21 15W (258†, 160 surv)
City of Birmingham 16.8.40 Struck mine, sunk, 53 32 25N 00 15 26E (0†, 80 surv)
City of Bombay 13.12.42 Torpedoed, shelled, by *U159*, sunk, 02 43S 29 06W (20†, 130 surv)
City of Brisbane 2.8.40 Bombed by German aircraft, on fire, off S Longsand Buoy, Thames estuary, ashore 51 32 30N 01 23 30E (8†, 90 surv); 5.8.40 gutted, TL
City of Cairo 6.11.42 Torpedoed by *U68*, sunk, 23 30S 05 30W (104†, 192 surv)
City of Canton 16.7.43 Torpedoed by *U178* 13 52S 41 10E (7†, 1 pow, 84 surv); 17.7.43 sunk
City of Cardiff 28.8.42 Torpedoed (in convoy SL119) by *U566* 40 20N 16 02W (21†, 63 surv); 30.8.42 sunk
City of Christchurch 21.3.43 Bombed by German FW200 Kondor aircraft from Bordeaux 39 35N 12 46W (0†, 102 surv); 22.3.43 sunk 38 42N 10 14W
City of Corinth 17.11.42 Torpedoed by *U508* 10 55N 61 01W (11†, 76 surv); sunk 10 52 30N 61 03 30W
City of Guildford 27.3.43 Torpedoed by *U593*, sunk, 33N 22 50E (127†, 13 surv)
City of Johannesburg 23.10.42 Torpedoed by *U504*, sunk, 33 20S 29 30E (2†, 87 surv)
City of Karachi 13.4.41 Bombed by German aircraft, badly damaged, Volo (0†, 90 surv); 14.4.41 taken in tow, beached SW of Volo; 15.4.41 again bombed; TL
City of Kobe 19.12.39 In convoy FS56, struck mine (laid 17.12.39 by *U60*), sunk, 52 34 54N 01 59 30E (1†)
City of Manchester 28.2.42 Torpedoed, shelled, by subm *I-53* (Jpn), sunk, 08 16S 108 52E (3†, 6 pow, 128 surv)
City of Mandalay 17.10.39 Torpedoed (in convoy HG3) by *U46*, sunk, 44 57N 13 36W (7†)
City of Manila 19.8.42 Torpedoed (in convoy SL118) by *U406* 43 21N 18 20W, abandoned (1†, 49 surv); 20.8.42 reboarded, broke in two, abandoned, sunk
City of Melbourne 13.5.42 Torpedoed, shelled (ind), by *U156* 15N 54 40W (1†, 77 surv); broke in two, forepart sunk, afterpart shelled, sunk
City of Mobile 16.9.40 Bombed by German aircraft 54 18 30N 05 16 30W (0†, 76 surv); sunk 54 19N 05 16 15W
City of Nagpur 29.4.41 Torpedoed by *U75*, sunk, 52 30N 26W (16†, 462 surv)
City of Oran 2.8.43 Torpedoed (in convoy CB21) by *U196*, badly damaged, 13 45S 41 16E (0†, 96 surv); 3.8.43 shelled by RN rescue tug, sunk
City of Oxford 15.6.42 Torpedoed (in convoy HG84) by *U552*, sunk, 43 32N 18 12W (1†, 43 surv)
City of Perth 26.3.43 Torpedoed (in convoy KMS10) by *U431* 35 50N 01 41W; beached near Cape Fegalo (2†, 81 surv); TL
City of Pretoria 3.3.43 Torpedoed (in convoy UGS5) by *U172*, blew up, sunk, 42 39N 36 30W (145†, 0 surv)
City of Ripon 11.11.42 Torpedoed, shelled, by *U160*, sunk, 08 40N 59 20W (56†, 27 surv)
City of Roubaix 6.4.41 Bombed by German He111 aircraft, Piræus; 7.4.41 on fire following explosion on *Clan Fraser* (*qv*) (0†, 94 surv), exploded, broke in two; TL
City of Shanghai 10.5.41 Torpedoed, shelled, by *U103* 06 40N 27 50W (8†, 70 surv); 11.5.41 sunk
City of Simla 21.9.40 Torpedoed (in convoy OB216) by *U138*, 55 55N 08 20W (3†, 347 surv); sunk 55 59N 08 16W
City of Singapore 1.1.43 Torpedoed (in convoy TS37) by *U515*, sunk, 07 55N 14 16W (0†, 97 surv)
City of Venice 4.7.43 Torpedoed (in convoy KMS18B) by *U375*, on fire, sunk, 36 44N 01 31E (11†, 169 surv; troops †, – surv)
City of Wellington 21.8.42 Torpedoed by *U506*, sunk, 07 29N 14 40W (7†, 66 surv)
City of Winchester 9.5.41 Torpedoed by *U103*, sunk, 08 20N 26 14W (6†, 91 surv)
Clan Alpine 13.3.43 Torpedoed (in convoy OS44) by *U107* 42 45N 13 31W (26†, 68 surv); sunk by depth charges by escort sloop HMS *Scarborough*
Clan Buchanan 28.4.41 Sunk by aux cruiser *Pinguin* 05 24N 62 46E (121 pow on *Pinguin*; 107 pow† when *Pinguin* sunk)
Clan Campbell 23.3.42 Bombed, torpedoed (in convoy MW9A) by German aircraft 245° 8m from Filfola Island, near Malta (6†); abandoned, sunk by escort (10†, 59 surv)
Clan Chattan 14.2.42 Bombed (in convoy MW9A) by German Ju88 aircraft 35 01N 20 11E (0†, 358 surv, incl 230 troops); sunk by escort
Clan Chisholm 17.10.39 Torpedoed (in convoy HG3) by *U48*, sunk, 44 57N 13 40W (–†, 41 surv)

Clan Cumming 7.4.41 Damaged following explosion on *Clan Fraser* (*qv*), Piræus; 14.4.41 bombed by German aircraft, badly damaged; 15.4.41 struck by mine, sunk, 37 49N 23 38 30E (0†, 77 pow, 36 surv)

Clan Ferguson 12.8.42 Torpedoed (in Opn 'Pedestal' convoy WS21S) by German Ju88 aircraft, 20m N of Zembra Is, badly damaged; torpedoed by subm *Alagi* (Ita), sunk (18†, 96 pow)

Clan Fraser 6.4.41 Bombed by German He111 aircraft; 7.4.41 exploded, sunk, Piræus (7†, 6 pow, 95 surv)

Clan Macalister 29.5.40 Bombed by German Ju87 aircraft off No 6 buoy, Dunkirk east roads, on fire, abandoned (18†, 61 surv); sank 2m off La Penne

Clan Macarthur 11.8.43 Torpedoed by *U181*, sunk, 23S 53 11E (52†, 99 surv)

Clan Macdougall 31.5.41 Torpedoed by *U106*, sunk, 16 50N 25 10W (2†, 83 surv)

Clan Macfadyen 26.11.42 Torpedoed by *U508*, sunk, 08 57N 59 48W (82†, 10 surv)

Clan Mackinlay 6.11.40 Bombed by German aircraft 58 33N 02 53W (5†, 77 surv); abandoned 52° 4.75m from Noss Head, sunk 58 34 15N 02 56W

Clan Macnaughton 1.8.42 Torpedoed by *U155*, sunk, 11 54N 54 25W (5†, 81 surv)

Clan Macphee 16.8.40 Torpedoed (in convoy OB197) by *U30*, sunk, 57 30N 17 14W (67†, 41 surv rescued by *Kelet* – *qv*)

Clan Macpherson 1.5.43 Torpedoed (in convoy TS37) by *U515* 07 58N 14 14W (4†, 139 surv); sunk 08 04N 14 12W

Clan Macquarrie 13.6.42 Torpedoed, shelled, by subm *Leonardo Da Vinci* (Ita), sunk, 05 30N 23 30W (1†, 89 surv)

Clan Mactaggart 16.11.42 Torpedoed (in convoy MKS1X) by *U92*, sunk, 36 08N 07 23W (3†, 169 surv)

Clan Mactavish 8.10.42 Torpedoed by *U159*, sunk, 34 53S 16 45E (61† incl 7† from *Boringia* – *qv*; 74 surv)

Clan Macwhirter 26.8.42 Torpedoed (convoy SL119 straggler) by *U156*, sunk, 35 45N 18 45W (11†, 77 surv)

Clan Menzies 29.7.40 Torpedoed (ind) by *U99*, sunk, 54 10N 12W (6†, 88 surv)

Clan Monroe 29.7.40 Struck mine (laid by E-boat) 51 52N 01 48E; 31.7.40 taken in tow, beached Hollesley Bay, stranded, 224° 3.8m from Orfordness LH (13†, 66 surv)

Clan Morrison 24.2.40 Struck mine (in convoy), sunk, 53 07 15N 01 21 45E

Clan Ogilvy 20.3.41 Torpedoed (in convoy SL68) by *U105*, sunk, 20 04N 25 45W (61†, 21 surv)

Clan Ross 2.4.42 Torpedoed by subm *I-6* (Jpn), sunk, 15 55N 68 26E (11†, 75 surv)

Clan Skene 10.5.42 Torpedoed by *U333*, sunk, 31 43N 70 43W (9†, 73 surv)

Clarissa Radcliffe 9.3.43 Torpedoed (convoy SC122 straggler) by *U663*, sunk, 42N 62W (52†, 0 surv)

Clea 13.2.41 Torpedoed (convoy HX106 straggler) by *U96*, sunk, about 60 25N 17 10W (59†, 0 surv)

Clearton 1.7.40 Torpedoed by *U30* 47 53N 09 30W (8†, 26 surv); sunk 042° 240m from Smalls

Clement 30.9.39 Captured by *Admiral Graf Spee* 09 05S 34 05W (0†); sunk

Cliftonhall 12.6.42 Torpedoed by subm *I-20* (Jpn), sunk, 16 25S 40 10E (2†, 41 surv)

Clintonia 19.10.40 Torpedoed (in convoy SC7) by *U99*, damaged, 57 10N 11 20W; shelled by *U123*, sunk (1†, 34 surv)

Clytoneus 8.1.41 Bombed by German FW200 Kondor aircraft, sunk, 56 23N 15 28W (0†, 62 surv)

Coimbra 15.1.42 Torpedoed by *U123*, sunk, 40 25N 72 21W (36†, 10 surv)

Colonial 26.5.41 Torpedoed by *U107*, sunk, 09 13N 15 09W (0†, 93 surv)

Conch 1.12.40 Torpedoed (in convoy HX90) by *U47* 55 40N 19W (0†, 53 surv); 2.12.40 torpedoed by *U95*; 3.12.40 torpedoed by *U99*, sunk, 54 21N 19 30W

Confield 8.10.40 Torpedoed (convoy HX76 straggler) by *U58* 56 48N 10 17W; 9.10.40 abandoned, shelled, sunk, by HM ship (1†, 36 surv)

Congella 24.10.43 Torpedoed, shelled, by subm *I-10* (Jpn), sunk, 01 02N 71 14E (28†, 1 pow, 37 surv)

Congonian 18.11.40 Torpedoed by *U65*, sunk, 08 21N 16 12W (1†, 38 surv)

Contractor 7.8.43 Torpedoed (in convoy GTX5) by *U371*, sunk, 37 15N 07 21E (5†, 78 surv)

Conus 4.4.41 Torpedoed by *U97*, sunk, 56 14N 31 19W (59†, 0 surv)

Corabella 30.4.43 Torpedoed (in convoy TS37) by *U515*, sunk, 07 14N 13 48W (9†, 39 surv)

Coracero 17.3.43 Torpedoed (in convoy HX229) by *U384*, sunk, 51 04N 33 20W (6†, 51 surv)

Corbis 18.4.43 Torpedoed by *U180*, sunk, 34 56S 34 03E (50†, 10 surv)

Cordelia 3.2.43 Torpedoed (convoy HX224 straggler) by *U632*, sunk, 56 37N 22 58W (46†, 1 pow)

Corinaldo 29.10.42 Torpedoed (convoy SL125 straggler) by *U509* 33 20N 18 12W, damaged, abandoned (8†, 50 surv); 30.10.42 shelled by *U203*, sunk, 33 12N 18 24W

Corinthic 13.4.41 Torpedoed by *U124*, sunk, 08 10N 14 40W (1†, 39 surv)

Cornish City 29.7.43 Torpedoed by *U177*, sunk, 27 41S 52 25E (37†, 6 surv)

Cornwallis 3.12.44 Torpedoed by *U1230*, sunk, 43 59N 68 20W (43†, 5 surv)

Corrientes 26.9.40 Torpedoed (from convoy OB217) by *U32*, damaged; 28.9.40 abandoned, torpedoed, shelled, by *U37*, sunk, 53 47N 24 19W (0†)

Cortes 26.9.41 Torpedoed (in convoy HG73) by *U203*, sunk, 47 48N 23 45W (36†)

Cortona 11.7.42 Torpedoed (dispersed from convoy OS33) by *U116* and *U201*, damaged, 32 30N 24 47W; torpedoed by *U201*, sunk, 32 45N 24 45W (32†, 23 surv)

Coultarn 30.3.41 Torpedoed (in convoy OB302) by *U69*, sunk, 60 18N 29 28W (3†, 39 surv)
Counsellor 8.3.40 Struck mine (laid 7.3.40 by *U32*) 280° 6m from Bar LV, R Mersey; 9.3.40 sunk 53 37 44N 03 23 06W (0†)
Craftsman 9.4.41 Captured by aux cruiser *Kormoran* 00 32N 23 37W (6†, 43 pow); shelled, sunk
Cranfield 23.11.42 Torpedoed by subm *I-166* (Jpn), sunk, 08 26N 76 42E (9†, 67 surv)
Cree 21.11.40 Torpedoed by *U123*, sunk, 54 39N 18 50W (43†, 0 surv)
Creekirk 18.10.40 Torpedoed (in convoy SC7) by *U101*, sunk, 57 30N 11 10W (36†)
Creemuir 11.11.40 Torpedoed by aircraft, sunk, 10m SE of Aberdeen (27†, 13 surv)
Cressdene 16.3.42 Struck mine 52 08N 01 52E, taken in tow; 17.3.42 sunk 82° 2.3m from Sunk lightfloat (0†, 40 surv); wreck dispersed
Cressington Court 19.8.42 Torpedoed by *U510*, sunk, 07 58N 46W (8†, 35 surv – 1† when *Woensdrecht* (*qv*) sunk)
Crispin 8.40 obv HMS *Crispin*; 3.2.41 torpedoed by *U107* 56 38N 20 05W; 4.2.41 sunk
Cristales 12.5.42 Torpedoed (in convoy ONS92) by *U124* 52 55N 29 50W, damaged, abandoned (0†, 82 surv); shelled, sunk, by escort
Crown Arun 17.9.40 Torpedoed, shelled (convoy HX72 straggler) by *U99*, sunk, 58 02N 14 18W (0†, 25 surv)
Culebra 18.1.42 Shelled (ind) by *U123*, sunk, 40N 50W (est) (45†, 0 surv)
Cumberland 23.8.40 Torpedoed (in convoy OB202) by *U57*, damaged, 55 43N 07 33W (4†, 54 surv); 24.8.40 sunk 5° 8m from Inishtrahull
Cyclops 11.1.42 Torpedoed (ind) by *U123*, sunk, 41 51N 63 48W (87†, 93 surv)
Cymbeline 2.9.40 Sunk by aux cruiser *Widder* 28N 35W (7†, 26 pow, 3 surv)
Cyprian Prince 6.4.41 Bombed by German He111 aircraft, struck by parachute mine; 7.4.41 badly damaged by explosion on *Clan Fraser* (*qv*), Piræus (4†, 32 surv); beached near Salamis; wreck found at Peristeri, Salamis Is, postwar

Daghestan 25.3.40 Torpedoed by *U57*, sunk, 212° 9m from Copinsay LH, Orkneys (4†, 30 surv)
Dagomba 3.11.42 Torpedoed (in convoy TS23) by subm *Ammiraglio Cagni* (Ita), sunk, 02 29N 19W (10†, 23 surv)
Dahomian 1.4.44 Torpedoed by *U852*, sunk, 34 25S 18 19E (2†, 49 surv)
Daisy Moller 13.12.43 Torpedoed by subm *Ro-110* (Jpn), sunk, 16 21N 82 13E (55†, 14 surv)
Dakotian 21.11.40 Struck mine Dale Roads, Milford Haven (0†, 49 surv); back broken, sank 90° 5 cables from Dale Point in 51 42 12N 05 08 19W
Dalblair 28.8.40 Torpedoed (in convoy OA204) by *U100*, sunk, 56 06N 13 33W (24†, 18 surv)
Dalcairn 21.9.40 Torpedoed (in convoy HX72) by *U100*, sunk, 59N 19W (0†, 42 surv)
Dalcroy 2.11.42 Torpedoed (in convoy SC107) by *U402*, sunk, 52 30N 45 30W (0†, 49 surv)
Daleby 4.11.42 Torpedoed by *U89* 57 24N 35 54W (0†, 47 surv); 5.11.42 sunk
Dalemoor 15.1.45 Struck mine 53 23 06N 00 47 24E; sunk 53 22 06N 00 50E (0†, 56 surv)
Dalfram 4.8.43 Torpedoed by *U181*, sunk, 20 53S 56 43E (2†, 41 surv)
Dalhousie 9.8.42 Sunk by aux cruiser *Stier* 20 22S 24 40W (36 pow)
Dallas City 4.7.40 Bombed (in convoy OA178) by German Ju87 aircraft of StG2, on fire, 50 09N 02 01W; later sank following collision with *Flimston* (*qv*) (0†, 37 surv)
Dalryan 1.12.39 Struck mine (laid by German destroyer), sunk, 51 29 36N 01 21 36E; wreck dispersed
Dalveen 28.9.40 Bombed by German aircraft, sunk, 58 10N 02 19W (11†, 32 surv)
Darcoila 28.9.40 Torpedoed (in convoy OB217) by *U32*, sunk, North Atlantic (31†, 0 surv)
Dardanus 5.4.42 Attacked (in convoy) by Japanese aircraft, damaged, when in tow of *Gandara* (*qv*) 16 38N 82 30E; 6.4.42 again attacked by aircraft, then shelled by Japanese cruisers, sunk, 15 55N 82 05E (0†, 78 surv)
Darina 20.5.42 Torpedoed, shelled (in convoy ON93), by *U158*, sunk, 29 17N 54 25W (6†, 50 surv)
Darino 19.11.39 Torpedoed by *U41*, sunk, 44 12N 11 07W (19†)
Darkdale 22.10.41 Torpedoed by *U68*, explosion, sunk, 15 55 30S 05 43 15W (41†, 0 surv)
Darlington Court 20.5.41 Torpedoed (in convoy HX126) by *U556*, sunk, 57 28N 41 07W (25†, 12 surv)
Dartford 12.6.42 Torpedoed (in convoy ONS100) by *U124*, sunk, 49 19N 41 33W (30†, 17 surv)
Daru 15.9.41 Bombed (in convoy) by German aircraft, sunk, 51 56 30N 05 58W (0†, 56 surv)
Davisian 10.7.40 Captured by aux cruiser *Widder* 18N 54 30W (1†, 10 pow, 38 surv); sunk
Daydawn 21.11.40 Torpedoed (in convoy OB244) by *U103*, sunk, 56 30N 14 10W (2†, 36 surv)
Dayrose 14.1.42 Torpedoed by *U552*, broke in two, sunk, 46 32N 53W (38†, 4 surv)
Daytonian 13.3.42 Torpedoed, shelled, by subm *Enrico Tazzoli* (Ita), sunk, 26 33N 74 43W (1†, 58 surv)
Delambre 5.7.40 Shelled by aux cruiser *Thor*, sunk, 04S 26W (some crew pow)
Demeterton 16.3.41 Shelled (in convoy) by *Scharnhorst*, sunk, 46 30N 43 40W (0†, – pow)
Denpark 12.5.42 Torpedoed (in convoy SL109) by *U128*, sunk, 22 28N 28 10W (21†, 25 surv)
Deptford 13.12.39 Torpedoed (ind) by *U109*, sunk, 0.24m NNW of Honningsvaagstadt (30†, 5 surv)
Derrymore 13.2.42 Torpedoed by subm *I-25* (Jpn), sunk, 05 18S 106 20E (9†, 236 surv)
Derrynane 12.2.41 Shelled (in convoy SLS64) by *Admiral Hipper* 37 12N 21 20W, blew up (36†, 0 surv)

Designer 9.7.41 Torpedoed (ind) by *U98*, sunk, 42 59N 31 40W (68†, 10 surv)
Deslock 8.12.41 Seized Yokohama by Japanese (on Japanese charter); 42 *Uzan Maru* (Jpn); 2.5.42 torpedoed by subm USS *Trout*, sunk, 33 26N 135 52E
Deucalion 12.8.42 Bombed (in Opn 'Pedestal' convoy) by German and Italian aircraft, damaged, 37 56N 08 40E; 12.8.42 torpedoed by aircraft 270° 5m from Cani Rocks, on fire, sunk (1†, 152 surv)
Devis 5.7.43 Torpedoed (in convoy KMS18B) by *U593*, sunk, 37 01N 04 10E (0†, 53 surv; 52 troops †, 237 troops surv)
Devon 19.8.41 Captured by aux cruiser *Komet* 05S 91W (approx); crew and passengers taken off, sunk by time bombs (0†, 144 taken off)
Diala 15.1.42 Torpedoed (in convoy ON52) by *U553* 44 50N 46 50W, abandoned; 19.3.42 seen afloat in 47N 37W (57†, 8 surv); no further reports (attempts to tow unsuccessful)
Dido 18.6.40 Abandoned Brest, seized by Germans; 40 *Dorpat* (Ger); 11.4.43 struck mine Århus roads; 12.5.43 salved, repaired; 45 KM, trials vessel; 3.5.45 attacked by Allied aircraft, sunk, near Svendborg; 45 salved, *Leila* (Fin)
Diplomat 27.11.40 Torpedoed (convoy HX88 straggler) by *U104*, sunk, 55 45N 11 57W (14†, 39 surv)
Director 14.7.44 Torpedoed by *U198*, sunk, 24 30S 35 44E (1†, 71 surv)
Discina 3.9.39 Seized by Germans while building; 39 *Posidonia* (Ger); 20.1.40 req by KM, *Stedingen*; 8.4.40 torpedoed by subm HMS *Trident*, sunk, 48 57N 10 28E; 6.40 salved; 5.45 as *Ossag III*, at Hamburg, wrecked; TL
Dixcove 24.9.41 Torpedoed (in convoy SL 87) by *U107*, sunk, 31 12N 23 41W (1†, 52 surv)
Dolius 5.5.43 Torpedoed (in convoy ONS5) by *U638*, sunk, 54N 43 35W (4†, 68 surv)
Domala 40 MoWT, *Empire Attendant* (Br); 15.7.42 torpedoed (in convoy OS33) by *U582*, sunk, 23 48N 21 51W (59†, 0 surv)
Domingo de Larrinaga 31.7.40 Sunk by aux cruiser *Pinguin* 05 26S 18 06W (8†, 30 pow)
Donax 22.10.42 Torpedoed (in convoy ON139) by *U443* 49 51N 27 58W; 29.10.42 abandoned (0†, 63 surv); sunk 48 04N 24 41W
Donovania 21.7.42 Torpedoed (ind) by *U160*, sunk, 10 56N 61 10W (5†, 51 surv)
Doric Star 2.12.39 Captured by *Admiral Graf Spee*, shelled, sunk, 19 15S 05 05E (0†)
Dorington Court 24.11.42 Torpedoed by *U181* 27 14S 34 25E (4†, 42 surv); abandoned, shelled, sunk
Dorsanum 3.9.39 Seized while building; completed for KM, *Ossag II* (Ger); 40 USSR, *Feolent* (N2) (Rus); 9.41 struck mine, sunk, Gulf of Bothnia
Dorset 13.8.42 Bombed (in Opn 'Pedestal' convoy WS21S) by German Ju88 and Ju87 aircraft, 36 12N 12 49E (0†, 101 surv); 14.8.42 sunk 25m NW of Linosa Is
Doryssa 25.4.43 Torpedoed, shelled, by subm *Leonardo Da Vinci* (Ita), sunk, 37 03S 24 03E (53†, 11 surv)
Dosinia 26.10.40 Struck mine, near Q1 Black Buoy, Queens Channel, R Mersey (0†, 56 surv); back broken, beached 1370 yards from Q1 Black Buoy; wreck dispersed
Draco 11.4.41 Bombed by aircraft at Tobruk, beached (1†, 30 surv); 21.4.41 again bombed, CTL; 7.48 refloated, BU Valencia
Dromore Castle 12.12.41 Struck mine (in convoy), sunk, 53 29 08N 00 52E (0†, 55 surv)
Duchess of Atholl 10.10.42 Torpedoed (in convoy WS17) by *U178*, sunk, 07 03S 11 12W (5†, 826 surv)
Duchess of York 11.7.43 Bombed by German FW200 Kondor aircraft of KG40, on fire (34†, 854 surv); torpedoed by escort, sunk, 48 18N 15 24W
Duffield 8.4.41 Attacked (in convoy OG57) by *U107* 31 13N 23 40W; 9.4.41 torpedoed, sunk, 31 13N 23 24W (25†, 27 surv)
Dulwich 9.6.40 Beached and set on fire off Villequier, R Seine; salved by Germans, prize; 41 *Holtenau* (Ger); 17.10.42 struck mine, sunk, NE of Calais
Dumana 9.39 Air Ministry charter, base ship; 42 flying-boat mother ship; 25.12.43 torpedoed by *U515*, sunk, 04 27N 06 58W (31†, 138 surv)
Dumfries 23.12.44 Torpedoed (in convoy MUS71) by *U772*, sunk, 50 22 48N 01 42 36W (0†, 69 surv)
Dumra 5.6.43 Torpedoed by *U198*, sunk, 28 15S 33 20E (26†, 1 pow, 66 surv)
Dunaff Head 7.3.41 Torpedoed (in convoy OB293) by *UA*, sunk, 60 33N 18 50W (5†, 39 surv)
Dunbar Castle 9.1.40 When in convoy struck mine (laid by destroyer of German 1 DD fl) 51 23N 01 34E (9†); sunk 51 22 08N 01 36 02E; 59 wreck dispersed
Dunkwa 6.5.41 Torpedoed by *U103*, sunk, 08 43N 17 13W (8†, 39 surv)
Dunstan 6.4.40 Bombed by aircraft, sunk, 59 09N 08 22W (2†, 46 surv)
Dunvegan Castle 7.9.39 Req as amc HMS *Dunvegan Castle*; 27.8.40 torpedoed by *U46* W of Aran Islands; 28.8.40 sunk 54 54N 11W (27†, 254 surv)
Duquesa 18.12.40 Shelled, captured, by *Admiral Scheer* 00 57N 22 42W (0†, 99 pow); 18.2.41 sunk after use as stores ship
Durham Castle 39 Adm stores ship; 26.1.40 struck mine (laid 22.1.40 by *U57*), sunk, off Cromarty while in tow for Scapa Flow for use as base ship

Earlspark 12.6.40 Torpedoed by *U101*, sunk, 42 26N 11 33W (7†, 31 surv)
East Wales 16.12.42 Torpedoed by *U159*, sunk, 00 24N 31 27W (17†, 28 surv)
Eastlea 30.3.41 Torpedoed (in convoy HX115) by *U48*, sunk, 60N 18 10W (34†, 0 surv)
Eastmoor 31.3.42 Torpedoed by *U71*, sunk, 37 33N 68 18W (16†, 36 surv)

Edencrag 14.12.42 Torpedoed (in convoy TE9) by *U443*, sunk, 35 49N 01 25W (13†, 13 surv)
Edward Blyden 22.9.41 Torpedoed (in convoy SL87) by *U103*, sunk, 27 36N 24 29W (0†, 62 surv)
Edwy R Brown 18.2.41 Torpedoed (convoy HX107 straggler) by *U103*, sunk, 61N 18W (48†, 0 surv)
Egyptian 6.3.43 Torpedoed (in convoy SC121) by *U230*, sunk, 56 25N 37 38W (44†, 3 surv)
El Argentino 26.7.43 Bombed by German FW200 Kondor aircraft, sunk, 39 50N 13 36W (4†, 100 surv)
El Grillo 10.2.44 Bombed by German FW200 Kondor aircraft of I/KG40, sunk, Seidisfjord, Iceland (0†, 49 surv)
El Madina 40 Troopship; 16.3.44 torpedoed by subm *Ro-111* (Jpn), sunk, 20 54N 89 36E (53†, 79 surv; 364 troops †, 797 surv)
El Oso 11.1.40 From convoy HX14B, struck mine (laid 6.1.40 by *U30*), sunk, 280° 6m from Bar LV, R Mersey
Elba 40 *Aldergrove* (Br); 23.8.41 torpedoed (in convoy OG71) by *U201*, sunk, 40 43N 11 39W (1†, 31 surv)
Elmbank 21.9.40 Torpedoed (in convoy HX72) by *U99*, shelled by *U47* and *U99*, on fire, 55 20N 22 30W; torpedoed again by *U99*, abandoned, sunk (1†, 55 surv)
Elmdale 1.11.42 Torpedoed (ind) by *U174*, sunk, 00 17 30N 34 55W (6†, 36 surv)
Elmdene 8.6.41 Torpedoed by *U103*, sunk, 08 16N 16 50W (0†, 36 surv)
Elstree Grange 3.5.41 During air raid, struck by landmine, badly damaged, in dock at Liverpool (5†, 49 surv); 7.41 beached R Mersey for BU
Elysia 5.6.42 Shelled by aux cruisers *Aikoku Maru*, *Hokoku Maru* (Jpn) 27 15S 36 24E, abandoned; 9.6.42 still afloat, torpedoed by Japanese I-class subm, sunk, 27 33S 37 05E
Embassage 27.8.41 Torpedoed (in convoy OS4) by *U557*, sunk, 54N 13W (39†, 3 surv)
Empire Merchant 16.8.40 Torpedoed (ind) by *U100* 55 21N 13 40W (7†, 47 surv); sunk 55 23N 13 24W
Empire Song 9.5.41 Struck mine (in convoy), on fire, explosion, sank, off Malta (18†, 128 surv)
Empire Star 23.10.42 Torpedoed (ind) by *U615*, sunk, 48 14N 26 22W (32†, 71 surv)
Empress of Asia 2.40 Troopship; 5.2.42 attacked by Japanese aircraft off Singapore, on fire, drifted ashore, sunk, 0.75m E Sultan Shoal LH, W of Keppel harbour (16†, 2772 surv); 4.3.60 salvage ops started
Empress of Britain 3.40 Troopship; 26.10.40 bombed by German FW200 Kondor aircraft of 2/KG40, on fire, 54 53N 10 49W; taken in tow by destroyer *Burza* (Pol); 28.10.40 torpedoed by *U32*, sunk, 55 16N 09 50W (45†, 568 surv)
Empress of Canada 29.11.39 Troopship; 13.3.43 torpedoed by subm *Leonardo da Vinci* (Ita) 01 13S 09 57W (392†, 1360 surv); 14.3.43 again torpedoed, sunk
Ena de Larrinaga 5.4.41 Torpedoed by *U105*, sunk, 01 10N 26W (5†, 38 surv)
Eocene 20.5.42 Torpedoed (in convoy AT46) by *U431*, sunk, 31 57N 25 11E; 21.5.41 sunk (0†, 42 surv)
Erinpura 40 Troopship; 1.5.43 bombed (in convoy) by German aircraft, sunk, 32 40N 19 53E (57†, 133 surv; 609 troops †, 416 surv)
Eskdene 8.4.41 Torpedoed (in convoy OG57) by *U107* 34 43N 24 21E (0†, 39 surv)
Esmond 9.5.41 Torpedoed (in convoy OB318) by *U110*, sunk, 60 28N 32 40W (0†, 50 surv); sunk 60 45N 33 02W
Essex Lance 16.10.43 Torpedoed (convoy ONS20 straggler) by *U426*, sunk, 57 53N 28W (0†, 52 surv)
Estrellano 9.2.41 Torpedoed (in convoy HG53) by *U37*, sunk, 35 53N 13 13W (6†, 21 surv)
Ethel Radcliffe 17.4.41 Torpedoed by E-boat near No 6 buoy, Great Yarmouth (0†, 40 surv); beached N of North Pier, Gorleston; later bombed; CTL
Etrib 14.6.42 Torpedoed (in convoy HG84) by *U552*, sunk, 43 18N 17 38W (4†, 36 surv)
Ettrick 15.11.42 Torpedoed (in convoy MK1) by *U155*, sunk, 36 13N 07 54W (24†, 225 surv)
Eulima 23.2.43 Torpedoed, shelled (convoy ON166 straggler) by *U186*, sunk, 46 48N 36 18W (63†, 0 surv)
Eumaeus 14.1.41 Shelled by subm *Comandante Cappellini* (Ita), on fire, sunk, 08 55N 15 03W (23†, 63 surv)
Euphorbia 14.12.40 Torpedoed by *U100*, sunk, WSW of Rockall (33†, 0 surv)
Eurylochus 29.1.41 Stopped by aux cruiser *Kormoran* 08 19N 25 01W; torpedoed, sunk (15†, 38 pow, 29 surv)
Eurymedon 25.9.40 Torpedoed (in convoy OB217) by *U29* 53 34N 20 23W (28†); 27.9.40 sunk 53 24N 18 37W (29†, 64 surv)
Everleigh 6.2.45 Topedoed (in convoy TBC60) by *U1017*, sunk, 50 29 22N 01 46 57W (6†, 43 surv)

Fabian 16.11.40 Torpedoed by *U65*, sunk, 02 49N 15 29W (6†, 33 surv)
Fanad Head 14.9.39 Torpedoed, shelled, by *U30*, sunk, 56 43N 15 21W
Faraday 26.3.41 Bombed by German aircraft 038° 3m from St Anne's Head (8†, 117

surv); 27.3.41 sunk West Dale Bay; broke in three, TL
Federlock 8.12.41 Seized China Sea by Japanese (Japanese charter) (1†); 42 *Fukuzan Maru* (Jpn); 9.1.45 sunk by USN carrier-based aircraft 22 37N 120 15E
Fidra 5.3.43 Torpedoed (in convoy XK2) by *U130*, sunk, 43 50N 14 50W (17†, 12 surv)
Filleigh 18.4.45 Torpedoed (in convoy TAM142) by *U245*, sunk, 51 19 30N 01 42E (5†, 49 surv)
Fintra 23.2.43 Torpedoed by *U371*, sunk, 36 57N 03 41E (5†, 30 surv)
Fiona 31.8.39 Adm, abv HMS *Fiona*; 18.4.41 attacked by enemy aircraft, sunk, off Sidi Barani, Egypt
Firby 11.9.39 Torpedoed, shelled, by *U48*, sunk, 59 40N 13 50W
Fiscus 18.10.40 Torpedoed (in convoy SC7) by *U99*, sunk, 57 29N 11 10W (38†, 1 surv)
Fishpool 26.7.43 Bombed by enemy aircraft, blew up, Syracuse, Sicily (28†, 25 surv); sunk 37 03 05N 15 17 10E; 49 wreck removed
Florian 20.1.41 Torpedoed (ind) by *U94*, sunk, N Atlantic (44†, 0 surv)
Forafric 24.12.41 Bombed by Japanese aircraft, sunk, 03 40N 121E (0†)
Fowberry Tower 12.5.41 Bombed by German aircraft, sunk, 227° 6.5 cables from Humber LV (6†, 39 surv); sunk 53 33 57N 00 21E; wreck dispersed
Foylebank 13.9.39 Req as aux anti-aircraft vessel HMS *Foylebank*; 3.40 commd; 4.7.40 bombed (in convoy OA178) by German Ju87 aircraft, sunk, Portland harbour; 49 bow section raised, BU Grays; 52 stern section raised, BU
Frances Massey 6.6.40 Torpedoed by *U48*, sunk, 55 33N 08 26W (34†, 1 surv)
Francol 3.3.42 Attacked by Japanese aircraft, shelled by Japanese cruisers and destroyers, sunk, 11 30S 109 03E (4†, 2 pow, 13 surv)
Frederick S Fales 21.9.40 Torpedoed (in convoy HX72) by *U100*, sunk, 55 30N 13 40W (20†, 28 surv)
Frederika Lensen 40 Sold (Br); 20.7.42 torpedoed (in QS convoy) by *U132* 49 22N 65 12W (4†, 43 surv); beached Grand Vallée Bay, broke back, TL
Fresno City 5.11.40 Shelled (in convoy HX84) by *Admiral Scheer* 51 47N 33 29W (1†); 6.11.40 sunk
Frumenton 4.3.42 Struck mine 170° 0.5m from 54E Buoy, off Orfordness (0†, 38 surv); taken in tow, broke back, sunk, 52 21N 01 58E; wreck dispersed
Fultala 7.4.42 Torpedoed by subm *I–3* (Jpn), sunk, 06 52N 76 54E (0†)

Gairsoppa 16.2.41 Torpedoed (convoy SL84 straggler) by *U101*, sunk, 300m SW of Galway Bay (84†, 1 surv)
Gandara 6.4.42 Sunk (in convoy) by Japanese destroyer 16 03N 82 20E (13†, 69 surv)
Ganges 6.4.42 Bombed by Japanese aircraft, on fire; shelled by Japanese destroyers and 2 cruisers, abandoned, sunk 17 48N 84 09E (15†, 64 surv)
Gardenia 12.3.40 Struck mine, sunk, 53 04 30N 01 33E (0†, 33 surv)
Garlinge 10.11.42 Torpedoed by *U81*, sunk, 21m N of Cape Ivi, Algeria (25†, 15 surv)
Garmula 23.7.42 Torpedoed by *U752*, sunk, 05 32N 14 45W (21†, 67 surv)
Gartavon 7.9.39 Shelled by *U47*, sunk, 47 04N 11 32W
Gemstone 4.6.42 Sunk by aux cruiser *Stier* 01 52N 26 38W (19†, 24 pow)
Ger-y-Bryn 5.3.43 Torpedoed (in convoy XK2) by *U130*, sunk, 43 50N 14 45W (0†, 46 surv)
Geraldine Mary 4.8.40 Torpedoed (in convoy HX60) by *U52* 56 58N 15 55W (3†, 48 surv); sunk 56 51N 15 51W
Germanic 29.3.41 Torpedoed (in convoy HX115) by *U48* 61 18N 22 05W (5†, 35 surv); sunk
Gharinda 5.5.43 Torpedoed (in convoy ONS5) by *U266*, sunk, 53 10N 44 40W (0†, 92 surv)
Glendene 8.10.42 Torpedoed by *U125*, sunk, 04 29N 17 41W (5†, 39 surv)
Glenlea 7.11.42 Torpedoed (convoy ON143 straggler) by *U566*, sunk, 50N 30W (44†, 1 pow, 3 surv)
Glenmoor 27.11.40 Torpedoed by *U103*, sunk, 54 35N 14 31W (31†, 2 surv)
Glenorchy 13.8.42 Attacked (in Opn 'Pedestal' convoy WS21S) by German Ju88 aircraft, damaged; torpedoed by MTB *Ms31* (Ita), sunk, 5m NW of Kelibia LH, Tunisia (7†, 74 pow)
Glenshiel 2.4.42 Torpedoed by subm *I-7* (Jpn), sunk, 00 48S 78 33E
Gloucester Castle 15.7.42 Shelled by aux cruiser *Michel*, sunk, 08S 01E (93†, 61 surv)
Gloucester City 16.7.42 Sunk by aux cruiser *Michel* 08S 01E (est)
Goalpara 15.4.41 Bombed by aircraft Eleusis Bay, Piræus (0†, 74 surv); on fire, beached, abandoned, TL; 11.45 wreck at Skaramanga
Goathland 25.8.40 Bombed, shelled, by German aircraft 50 21N 15 08W (0†, 36 surv); sunk 50 07N 14 50W
Gogovale 4.8.40 Torpedoed (in convoy HX60) by *U52*, sunk, 57 08N 16 26W (3†, 36 surv)
Gogra 2.4.43 Torpedoed (in convoy OS45) by *U124*, sunk, 41 02N 15 39W (82†, 8 surv)
Gold Shell 16.4.45 Struck mine (laid by E-boat 12–13.4.45) 51 21 36N 02 54 30E; sunk 51 21 09N 02 53 30E (35†, 29 surv)
Goodleigh 2.12.40 Torpedoed (in convoy HX90) by *U52*, sunk, 55 02N 18 45W (1†, 36 surv)
Goolistan 23.11.42 Torpedoed (in convoy QP15) by *U625*, sunk, 75 50N 16 45E (42†, 0 surv)
Gothic 12.9.40 Struck mine, sunk, 130° 7500 yds from Spurn Point (12†, 12 surv)
Gourko 21.5.40 Adm; 4.6.40 struck mine, sunk, Dunkirk
Gracefield 14.7.40 Sunk by aux cruiser *Thor* 13S 31W (crew pow)
Gracia 19.2.41 Bombed (in convoy OB287) by German FW200 Kondor aircraft, sunk, 59 39N 07 24W (0†, 48 surv)

Graigwen 9.10.40 Torpedoed (convoy SC6 straggler) by *U103* 58 11N 13 57W; 10.10.40 abandoned, torpedoed by *U123*, sunk (7†, 27 surv)
Grangepark 20.11.42 Torpedoed (in convoy KRS3) by *U262*, sunk, 35 55N 10 14W (3†, 66 surv)
Gray Ranger 22.9.42 Torpedoed (in convoy QP14) by *U435* 71 23N 11 03W (21 surv); sunk by escort
Grayburn 29.6.41 Torpedoed (in convoy HX133) by *U651*, sunk, 59 30N 18 07W (35†, 18 surv)
Gregalia 9.5.41 Torpedoed (in convoy OB318) by *U201*, sunk, 60 34N 32 37W (0†, 66 surv)
Grelhead 2.12.41 Torpedoed by *U562*, sunk, 2m from Punta Negri, Morocco (41†, 2 surv)
Grelrosa 28.1.41 Bombed (convoy straggler) by German FW200 Kondor aircraft, sunk, 55 12N 15 41W (5†, 31 surv)
Gretafield 14.2.40 Torpedoed (convoy HX18 straggler) by *U57* 58 27N 02 33W (11†, 30 surv); on fire, drifted ashore Dunbeath, near Wick, 58 14 15N 03 25 45W; 19.3.40 broke in two, TL
Gretavale 3.11.41 Torpedoed (in convoy SC52) by *U202*, sunk, 51 21N 51 45W (42†, 5 surv)
Guelma 17.7.41 Torpedoed by subm *Alessandro Malaspina* (Ita), sunk, 30 44N 17 33W (0†, 41 surv)
Guido 8.3.43 Torpedoed (convoy SC121 straggler) by *U526*, sunk, 58 08N 32 20W (10†, 35 surv)
Gypsum Empress 3.11.42 Torpedoed (in convoy TAG18) by *U160* 12 27N 64 04W (0†, 40 surv); sunk
Gypsum Queen 11.9.41 Torpedoed (in convoy SC42) by *U82*, damaged, 63 05N 37 50W; torpedoed by *U433*, sunk (10†, 26 surv)

Hadleigh 16.3.43 Torpedoed (in convoy ET14) by *U77* 36 10N 00 30W, abandoned; 17.3.43 reboarded, taken Mers el Kebir; 18.5.43 broke in two, beached about 8m from Oran; TL
Halizones 27.7.43 Bombed (in convoy OS52) by German FW200 Kondor aircraft 38 04N 12 59W (0†, 90 surv); 30.7.43 sunk in tow 37 22N 13 03W
Hamla 23.8.42 Torpedoed by *U506*, sunk, 04S 24W (est) (42†, 0 surv)
Hannah Moller 15.12.42 Bombed by aircraft, sunk, at Benghazi (0†, 55 surv)
Har Zion 31.8.40 Torpedoed (in convoy OB205) by *U38*, sunk, 56 20N 10W (35†, 1 surv)
Harbledown 4.4.41 Torpedoed (in convoy SC26) by *U94*, sunk, 58 30N 23W (16†)
Harborough 14.9.42 Shelled, torpedoed, by *U515*, sunk, 10 03N 60 20W (5†, 47 surv)
Harbury 5.5.43 Torpedoed (convoy ONS5 straggler) by *U628* 55 01N 42 59W (7†, 43 surv), damaged, abandoned; 5.5.43 torpedoed by *U264*, sunk
Harcalo 6.6.40 Struck mine 51 19N 01 32 25E (3†, 36 surv); beached 51 19 05N 01 30 02E, broke in two; wreck dispersed
Hardwicke Grange 12.6.42 Torpedoed, shelled, by *U129*, sunk, 24 45N 65 45W (3†, 78 surv)
Hardingham 8.6.40 Struck mine 51 34N 01 37 30E (2†, 36 surv); sank 51 59 05N 01 40 04E; wreck dispersed
Haresfield 9.9.42 Torpedoed by subm *I-29* (Jpn), sunk, 13 05N 54 35E (0†, 85 surv)
Harlesden 22.2.41 Shelled (dispersed from convoy) by *Gneisenau*, sunk, 47 12N 40 18W (7†, 34 pow)
Harlingen 5.8.41 Torpedoed (in convoy SL81) by *U75*, sunk, 53 26N 15 40W (2†, 42 surv)
Harmala 7.2.43 Torpedoed (in convoy SC118) by *U614*, sunk, 55 14N 26 37W (53†, 11 surv)
Harmodius 8.3.41 Torpedoed (in convoy SL67) by *U105*, sunk, 20 35N 20 40W (11†, 64 surv)
Harmonic 15.7.43 Torpedoed by *U172*, abandoned, sunk, 23S 33W (1†, 46 surv)
Harmonides 25.8.42 Torpedoed by subm *I-165* (Jpn), sunk, 01 47N 77 27E (14†, 71 surv)
Harpa 27.1.42 Struck British mine, sunk, off Singapore (35†, 5 surv)
Harpagon 19.4.42 Torpedoed by *U109*, sunk, 34 35N 65 50W (41†, 8 surv)
Harpagus 20.5.41 Torpedoed (in convoy HX126) by *U94*, sunk, 56 47N 40 55W (58†, incl 26 surv from *Norman Monarch* (*qv*), 18 surv)
Harpalion 13.4.42 Bombed (in convoy QP10) by German Ju88 aircraft 73 33N 27 19E, abandoned (0†, 70 surv); shelled by HM ship, sunk
Harpalyce 25.8.40 Torpedoed (in convoy HX65A) by *U124*, sunk, 58 52N 06 34W (37†, 10 surv)
Harpasa 5.4.42 Bombed by Japanese aircraft 19 19N 85 46E, abandoned (6†, 33 surv); sunk
Harpathian 8.4.41 Torpedoed (in convoy OG57) by *U107*, sunk, 32 22N 22 53W (4†, 39 surv)
Harperley 5.5.43 Torpedoed (in convoy ONS5) by *U264* 55N 42 58W (11†, 38 surv); sunk 55 03N 42 56W
Hartington 2.11.42 Torpedoed (in convoy SC107) by *U522* 52 30N 45 30W (24†, 23 surv), damaged; torpedoed by *U438* and by *U521*, sunk
Hartismere 8.7.42 Torpedoed, shelled, by subm *I-10* (Jpn), sunk, 18S 41 22E (0†, 47 surv)
Hartlebury 7.7.42 Torpedoed (dispersed from convoy PQ17) by *U355*, sunk, 72 30N 52E (38†, 18 surv)
Hatarana 18.8.42 Torpedoed (in convoy SL118) by *U214*, sunk, 41 07N 20 32W (0†, 108 surv)
Hatasu 2.10.41 Torpedoed by *U431*, sunk, 600m E of Cape Race (40†, 7 surv)
Hatimura 3.11.42 Torpedoed (in convoy SC107) by *U132* 55 38N 39 52W (4†, 86 surv), damaged; torpedoed by *U442*, sunk
Hatterlock 8.12.41 Seized Hakodate by Japanese; 42 *Renzan Maru* (Jpn); 1.1.43 torpedoed by subm USS *Porpoise*, sunk, 39 11N 141 44E
Hauraki 12.7.42 Captured by aux cruisers *Aikoku Maru*, *Hokoku Maru* 17 32S 80 25E;

prize, taken Singapore; *Teifu Maru* (Jpn); 11.43 transport *Hoki Maru* (Jpn); 17.2.44 bombed (in convoy) by USN carrier-based aircraft, sunk, 07 22N 151 45E
Havre 10.6.42 Torpedoed (in convoy AT49) by *U431*, on fire, sunk, about 50m W of Alexandria (20†, 25 surv)
Hawkinge 27.7.41 Torpedoed (in convoy OG69) by *U203*, sunk, 44 55N 17 44W (15†, 16 surv)
Hawnby 20.4.40 Struck mine, sunk, 51 32N 01 12 36E (0†, 39 surv)
Haxby 24.4.40 Sunk by aux cruiser *Orion* 31 30N 51 30W (17†, 24 pow – later rescued from *Tropic Sea* (*qv*) by subm HMS *Truant*)
Hazelside (4646gt) 24.9.39 Torpedoed, shelled, by *U31*, sunk, 51 17N 09 22W (11†)
Hazelside (5297gt) 28.10.41 Torpedoed by *U68*, sunk, 23 10S 01 36E (2†, 43 surv)
Hector 27.8.39 Req as amc HMS *Hector*; 5.4.42 bombed by Japanese carrier-based aircraft, on fire, Colombo harbour, sunk; 46 refloated, beached 5 cables from Uswetakeiyawa church, 5m N of Colombo; BU *in situ*
Hektoria 11.9.42 Torpedoed (in convoy ON127) by *U211* 48 55N 33 38W; 11.9.42 torpedoed by *U608*, sunk (1†, 86 surv)
Helen Moller 5.6.44 Torpedoed by *U183*, sunk, 04 28S 74 45E (4†, 69 surv)
Helena Margareta 8.4.41 Torpedoed (in convoy OG57) by *U107*, sunk, 33N 23 52W (27†, 9 surv)
Helenus 3.3.42 Torpedoed by *U68*, sunk, 06 01N 12 02W (5†, 81 surv)
Helka 25.5.41 Bombed by enemy aircraft, sunk, off Sollum (2†, 44 surv)
Helmspey 11.2.43 Torpedoed by *U516*, sunk, 34 22S 24 54 30E (4†, 42 surv)
Heminge 30.9.40 Torpedoed by *U37*, sunk, 53 26N 18 33W (1†, 25 surv)
Henry Stanley 6.12.42 Torpedoed by *U103* 40 35N 39 40W (64†, 1 pow); 7.12.42 torpedoed again, sunk
Henzada 24.7.43 Torpedoed by *U199*, sunk, 25 15S 44 08W (2†, 62 surv)
Herland 7.11.40 Struck mine, sunk, 51 29 10N 00 53 35E (18†, 19 surv)
Hermes 25.6.40 Seized Algiers by VFr; 40 *St Francois* (Fra); 12.42 *Alcamo* (Ita); 24.2.43 bombed by RAF aircraft; 25.2.43 sunk, 62m NNE of Marettimo
Heronspool 13.10.39 Shelled, torpedoed (convoy OB17 straggler), by *U48*, sunk, 50 13N 14 48W (0†)
Herport 14.3.41 Struck mine, sunk, 53 15 25N 01 05E (4†, 33 surv); wreck dispersed
Hertford 29.3.42 Torpedoed by *U571*, sunk, 40 50N 63 31W (4†, 57 surv)
Highland Patriot 1.10.40 Torpedoed by *U38*, sunk, 52 13N 19 04W (3†, 140 surv)
Hillfern 31.10.40 External explosion, believed not torpedo, sunk, 57 57N 02 25 30W (8†, 11 surv)
Hindpool 8.3.41 Torpedoed (in convoy SL67) by *U124*, sunk, 20 51N 20 32W (28†, 12 surv)
Hinsang 25.12.41 Scuttled Hong Kong to prevent capture by Japanese; salved by Japanese, *Kensei Maru* (Jpn); 12.1.45 sunk (in convoy) by USN carrier-based aircraft 11 10N 108 55E
Hoihow 2.7.43 Torpedoed by *U181*, sunk, 19 30S 55 30E (144†, 5 surv)
Hollinside 3.9.42 Torpedoed (in convoy) by *U107*, sunk, 112° 3m off Cape Sines (3†, 49 surv)
Holmbury 5.5.43 Torpedoed, shelled, by *U123*, sunk, 04 30N 10 20W (2†, 1 pow, 43 surv)
Holmelea 28.2.41 Shelled, torpedoed (convoy OB290 straggler), by *U47*, sunk, 54 24N 17 25W (28†, 11 surv)
Holmpark 24.10.42 Torpedoed by *U516*, sunk, 13 11N 47W (1†, 49 surv)
Holmside 19.7.41 Torpedoed by *U66*, sunk, 19N 21 30W (22†)
Holystone 15.2.41 Torpedoed by *U101*, sunk, W of Ireland (40†, 0 surv)
Homefield 2.4.41 Bombed by enemy aircraft, sunk, off Gavdo Island, Piræus
Hopecastle 28.10.42 Torpedoed (convoy SL125 straggler) by *U509*, damaged, 31 39N 19 23W (5†, 41 surv), abandoned 31 39N 19 35W; 29.10.42 torpedoed, shelled, by *U203*, sunk
Hopetarn 29.5.43 Torpedoed by *U198*, sunk, 30 50S 39 32E (7†, 1 pow, 36 surv)
Horn Shell 26.7.41 Torpedoed by subm *Barbarigo* (Ita), sunk, 33 23N 22 18W (17†, 40 surv)
Hosang 8.2.42 Aground Palembang; 13.2.42 abandoned; 14.2.42 captured by Japanese; refloated; 42 *Gyozan Maru* (Jpn); 21.11.44 torpedoed by subms USS *Flounder* and *Guavina*, sunk, 10 39N 115 05E
Housatonic 19.2.41 Bombed (in convoy OB287) by German FW200 Kondor aircraft 59 39N 07 24W (3†, 31 surv); 20.2.41 sunk
Houston City 21.10.40 Struck mine, sunk, 225° 0.5m of E Oaze light, Thames estuary; beached on sandbank 51 28 53N 01 00 12E (0†, 35 surv); submerged at hw; salved operations abandoned due to German aircraft attacks on wreck; TL
Humber Arm 8.7.40 Torpedoed (in convoy HX53) by *U99*, sunk, 50 36N 09 24W (0†, 43 surv)
Huntingdon 24.2.41 Torpedoed (in convoy OB288) by *U96*, sunk, 58 25N 20 23W (0†, 62 surv)
Huntsman 10.10.39 Captured by *Admiral Graf Spee* 08 30S 05 15W; 17.10.39 sunk by depth charges 16S 17W (0†)
Hurunui 14.10.40 Torpedoed (in convoy OB227) by *U93*, sunk, 58 58N 09 54W (2†, 73 surv)
Hylton 29.3.41 Torpedoed (in convoy HX115) by *U48* 60 02N 18 10W (0†, 36 surv); sunk

Iddesleigh 10.8.44 Torpedoed by German E-boat, damaged, off Sword Beach, Normandy (3†, 134 surv); taken in tow, beached 0.75m S of 90 Buoy, off Langrunè assault area, Normandy; 17.8.44 sunk by one-man torpedo while aground
Ilvington Court 26.8.40 Torpedoed by subm *Dandolo* (Ita), sunk, 37 14N 21 52W (0†, 39 surv)
Imperial Star 27.9.41 Torpedoed (in Opn 'Halbard' convoy) by Italian aircraft 37 31N 10 46E,

badly damaged; taken in tow; 28.9.41 slowly sinking, sunk by depth charges from HM ship
Inanda 9.9.40 Sunk in air raid London docks; salved, MoWT *Empire Explorer* (Br); 8.7.42 torpedoed by *U575*, shelled, abandoned, 11 40N 60 55W (3†, 68 surv); 9.7.42 sunk
Incomati 18.7.43 Torpedoed, shelled, by *U508*, sunk, 03 09N 04 15E (1†, 220 surv)
Indian Prince 11.11.43 Torpedoed (in convoy KMS31) by German aircraft, 36 10N 00 06W (1†, 60 surv); taken in tow, sank
Indora 6.4.42 Shelled by 3 Japanese cruisers, sunk, Bay of Bengal (2†, 81 surv)
Induna 30.3.42 Torpedoed (convoy PQ13 straggler) by *U376*, sunk, 70 55N 37 18E (31†, 19 surv)
Indus 20.7.42 Shelled by aux cruiser *Thor*, sunk, 26 44S 82 50E (23†, – pow)
Inverarder 24.2.42 Torpedoed (in convoy ONS67) by *U558*, sunk, 44 34N 42 37W (0†, 42 surv)
Inverdargle 16.1.40 Struck mine (laid 5.11.39 by *U33*) 51 16N 03 43 30W (45†, 0 surv); broke in two, stern section sunk 51 16 31N 03 47 15W, bow section sunk 1300 metres to NE
Inverilen 3.2.43 Torpedoed (in convoy HX224) by *U456* 56 35N 23 30W (31†, 16 surv); 4.2.43 abandoned, sunk 56 13N 20 35W
Inverlee 19.10.41 Torpedoed by *U204*, broke in two, sunk, 240° 30m from Cape Spartel (21†, 22 surv)
Inverliffey 11.9.39 Torpedoed by *U38* 48 14N 11 48W, damaged; shelled, sunk, 48 18N 11 24 30W
Inverness 9.7.41 Torpedoed (ind) by *U98*, broke in two, sunk, 42 46N 32 45W (6†, 36 surv)
Invershannon 20.9.40 Torpedoed (in convoy HX72) by *U99*, abandoned (16†, 31 surv); 21.9.40 bombs placed on board, sunk, 55 40N 22 04W
Inversuir 2.6.41 Torpedoed by *U48* 48 28N 28 20W; shelled, sunk, 48 30N 28 30W (0†, 45 surv)
Ionian 29.11.39 Struck mine (laid 22.11.39 by *U20*) 132° 1.5m from Newarp LV; abandoned 340° 4m from Newarp LV, sunk 52 45 15N 01 56 15E
Ixion 7.5.41 Torpedoed (in convoy OB318) by *U94* 61 29N 22 40W (0†, 105 surv); 8.5.41 sunk

Jalabala 11.10.43 Torpedoed by *U532*, sunk, 11 40N 75 19E (5†, 73 surv)
Jalapadma 14.4.41 Badly damaged following *Fort Stikine* explosion Bombay; TL; BU *in situ*
Jalapalaka 30.1.42 Shelled by subm *I-64* (Jpn), sunk, 13N 81 08E (13†, 54 surv)
Jalarajan 14.1.42 Torpedoed by subm *I-65* (Jpn) 00 12S 97E 4†, 74 surv); abandoned, shelled; 15.1.42 sunk
Jalatarang 30.1.42 Shelled, torpedoed, by subm *I-64* (Jpn), sunk, 12 59N 81E (38†, 11 surv)
Jamaica Pioneer 25.8.40 Torpedoed (ind) by *U100*, sunk, 57 05N 11 02W (2†, 66 surv)
Jamaica Progress 30.7.40 Torpedoed by *U99*, sunk, 56 26N 08 30W (7†, 47 surv)
Janeta 1.5.44 Torpedoed (in convoy RA59) by *U181*, sunk, 18 10S 20W (14†, 34 surv)
Javanese Prince 20.5.41 Torpedoed by *U138*, sunk, 59 46N 10 45W (2†, 58 surv)
Jeanne M 2.12.40 Torpedoed (in convoy OG46) by *U37*, sunk, 39 19N 13 54W (7†, 19 surv)
Jedmoor 16.9.41 Torpedoed (in convoy SC42) by *U98*, sunk, 59N 10W (31†, 36 surv)
Jersey 23.4.42 Struck mine (laid by *U561*), sunk, 249.5° 1.45m from West Beacon, Suez Bay (0†, 42 surv)
Jersey City 31.7.40 Torpedoed (in convoy OB191) by *U99*, sunk, 55 47N 09 18W (2†, 43 surv)
Jervis Bay 25.8.39 Req as amc HMS *Jervis Bay*; 5.11.40 shelled (when escorting convoy HX84) in engagement with *Admiral Scheer*, sunk, 52 26N 32 34W (190†, 65 surv)
Jevington Court 24.2.40 Struck mine, sunk, 161° 8.25m from Cromer Knoll LV (0†, 35 surv)
Jeypore 3.11.42 Torpedoed (in convoy SC107) by *U89*, sunk, 55 30N 40 16W (1†, 90 surv)
Jhelum 21.3.41 Torpedoed (from scattered convoy SL68) by *U105*, sunk, 21N 25W (8†, 46 surv)
Joan Moller 12.12.41 Scuttled Hong Kong; 25.12.41 wreck seized by Japanese; 42 salved, *Gyoyu Maru* (Jpn); 3.7.44 torpedoed by subm USS *Seahorse*, sunk, 19 28N 115 41E
John Holt 24.9.41 Torpedoed (in convoy SL87) by *U107*, sunk, 31 12N 23 32W (0†, 84 surv, 2 pow† on *U107* when sunk)
Jonathan Holt 24.2.41 Torpedoed (in convoy OB289) by *U97*, sunk, 61 10N 11 55W (52†, 3 surv)
Jose de Larrinaga 7.9.40 Torpedoed (in convoy SC2) by *U47*, sunk, 58 30N 16 10W (0 surv)
Jumna 25.12.40 Sunk by *Admiral Hipper* 44 51N 27 45W (108†, 0 surv)
Juna 18.4.41 Bombed, sunk, off Sidi Barrani
Jura 9.2.41 Bombed (in convoy HG53) by German FW200 Kondor aircraft, sunk, 35 42N 14 38W (17†, 8 surv)
Justitia 22.11.40 Torpedoed (in convoy SC11) by *U100* 55N 13 10W (13†, 26 surv); 23.11.40 sunk
Jutland 41 MoWT; 2.5.42 torpedoed (in convoy PQ15) by German aircraft of I/KG26, 73 02N 19 46E; 3.5.42 torpedoed by *U251*, sunk (1†, 62 surv)

Kafiristan 17.9.39 Torpedoed by *U53*, sunk, 50 16N 16 55W (6†)
Kaiping 2.1.42 Captured Manila by Japanese; 42 *Kaiho Maru* (Jpn); 27.4.45 struck US mine, sunk, 34N 130 50E
Kalgan 12.12.41 Seized Bangkok by Japanese; 42 *Nishi Maru* (Jpn); 13.11.44 bombed by USN carrier-based aircraft, sunk, Manila
Kantara 22.2.41 Shelled (from dispersed convoy) by *Scharnhorst* and *Gneisenau* 47 12N

40 13W (– pow)
Karanja 40 Troopship; 24.7.41 landing ship infantry HMS *Karanja*; 12.11.42 bombed by German aircraft, sunk, off Bougie (50†)
Kars 22.2.42 Torpedoed by *U96* 44 15N 63 25W, on fire; 25.2.42 abandoned (46†, 1 surv); broke in two; afterpart towed Halifax; 27.2.42 beached
Katha 2.4.43 Torpedoed (in convoy OS45) by *U124*, sunk, 41 02N 15 39W (6†, 63 surv)
Kavak 2.12.40 Torpedoed (in convoy HX90) by *U101*, sunk, 55 03N 18 04W (25†, 16 surv)
Kayeson 2.10.40 Torpedoed by *U32*, sunk, 51 12N 24 22W (38†, 0 surv)
Kaying 6.42 Adm, wireless station Siamese waters; 18.3.43 torpedoed (in convoy) by *U593* 32 59N 22 21E (9†, 72 surv); 19.3.43 foundered in heavy weather
Kellwyn 26.7.41 Torpedoed (in convoy OG69) by *U79*, sunk, 43N 17W (14†, 9 surv)
Kelso 8.8.42 Torpedoed (in convoy SC94) by *U176*, sunk, 56 30N 32 14W (3†, 42 surv)
Kelvinbank 9.3.43 Torpedoed (in convoy BT6) by *U510*, sunk, 07 24N 52 11W (28†, 31 surv)
Kemmendine 13.7.40 Shelled by aux cruiser *Atlantis* 04S 82E; on fire, abandoned, sunk by torpedo (82†, 65 surv)
Kenbane Head 5.11.40 Shelled (in convoy HX84) by *Admiral Scheer*, sunk, 52 26N 32 34W (23†, 22 surv)
Kennebec 8.9.39 Torpedoed, shelled, by *U34*, badly damaged, 49 18N 08 13W; 9.9.39 sunk by HM ship
Kensington Court 18.9.39 Shelled by *U32*, sunk, 50 31N 08 27W (0†)
Kiangsu 8.12.41 Captured off Amoy by Japanese; 42 *Kinmon Maru* (Jpn); 10.6.44 gutted by fire Singapore; TL
Kildale 3.11.40 Bombed by German aircraft, sunk, 57 45N 01 45W (2†, 35 surv)
King Alfred 4.8.40 Torpedoed (in convoy HX60) by *U52* 56 59N 17 38W, broke in two; bow sank, stern sunk by HM vessel (5†, 34 surv)
King Arthur 15.11.42 Torpedoed by *U67*, sunk, 10 30N 59 50W (0†, 40 surv)
King City 24.8.40 Torpedoed, shelled, by aux cruiser *Atlantis*, sunk, 17S 66E (6†, 37 surv)
King Edgar 2.3.45 Torpedoed (in convoy SC167) by *U1302* 52 05N 05 42W; taken in tow, sunk (4†, 42 surv)
King Edward 27.12.42 Torpedoed (in convoy ONS154) by *U356*, sunk, 47 25N 25 20W (23†, 25 surv)
King Egbert 12.12.39 Struck mine (minefield laid by destroyers *Erich Giese* and *Hans Lody*), sunk, 4m SW of Haisboro' LV, off Norfolk; wreck dispersed
King Frederick 19.7.44 Torpedoed by *U181*, sunk, 09 29N 71 45E (25†, 21 surv); wreck dispersed
King Gruffyd 14.9.39 Adm, decoy ship HMS *King Gruffyd* (RFA *Maunder*); 12.3.41–12.41 amc; 22.8.41 MoWT (Br); 17.3.43 torpedoed (in SC convoy) by *U338*, sunk, 51 55N 32 41W (22†, 25 surv)
King Idwal 23.11.40 Torpedoed (in convoy OB244) by *U123*, sunk, 56 44N 19 13W (12†, 28 surv)
King John 13.7.40 Sunk by aux cruiser *Widder* 20N 60W (0†, 5 pow, 28 surv)
King Lud 8.6.42 Torpedoed by subm *I-10* (Jpn), sunk, 20S 40E (39†, 0 surv)
King Malcolm 31.10.41 Torpedoed by *U374*, sunk, 47 40N 51 15W (38†, 0 surv)
King Robert 29.1.41 Torpedoed (in convoy SC19) by *U93*, sunk, 56N 15 23W (0†, 42 surv)
Kingsbury 17.3.43 Torpedoed (in convoy SC122) by *U338*, sunk, 51 55N 32 41W (4†, 44 surv)
Kingston Hill 7.6.41 Torpedoed by *U38*, sunk, 09 35N 29 40W (14†, 32 surv)
Kingswood 17.12.43 Torpedoed by *U515*, sunk, 05 57N 01 43E (0†, 48 surv)
Kinross 24.6.41 Torpedoed (in convoy OB336) by *U203*, sunk, 55 23N 38 49W (0†, 37 surv)
Kioto 15.9.42 Torpedoed by *U514*, sunk, 11 05N 60 46W (21†, 55 surv)
Kirkland 23.4.42 Torpedoed (in convoy TA36) by *U565*, sunk, 31 51N 26 37E (1†, 22 surv)
Kirkpool 10.4.42 Sunk by aux cruiser *Thor* 33S 07W (– pow, – surv)
Kirnwood 10.12.41 Torpedoed (in convoy SC57) by *U130*, sunk, 56 57N 16 35W (12†, 33 surv)
Kohinur 15.11.40 Torpedoed by *U65*, sunk, 04 24N 13 46W (48†, 1 pow, 34 surv)
Koolama 16.1.42 Requisitioned for war service; 20.2.42 bombed by Japanese aircraft, damaged (1†), to prevent sinking ran ashore 14 10S 127 20E; 21.2.42 again attacked, damaged further; 2.3.42 refloated; 3.3.42 again attacked, abandoned, sank by stern; 46 salved, refloated, CTL, towed away, scuttled
Koranton 27.3.41 Torpedoed by *U98*, sunk, 59N 27W (34†, 0 surv)
Kumasian 5.8.41 Torpedoed (in convoy SL81) by *U74*, damaged, 53 11N 15 38W; torpedoed by *U204*, sunk (1†, 50 surv)
Kumsang 30.9.42 Torpedoed by *U125*, sunk, 04 07N 13 40W (4†, 110 surv)
Kung Wo 18.1.41 Adm; 4.41 commd aux minelayer; 14.2.42 bombed by Japanese aircraft, sunk, 6m NW of Pompong Is
Kurdistan 10.12.41 Torpedoed (in convoy SC57) by *U130* 56 51N 16 36W; 11.12.41 sunk (10†, 43 surv)
Kwangtung 4.1.42 Torpedoed by subm *I-56* (Jpn), sunk, 09 12S 111 10E (48†, 50 surv)
Kyleglen 14.12.40 Torpedoed by *U100*, sunk, 58N 25W (36†, 0 surv)
Kyno 28.8.40 Torpedoed (in convoy HX66) by *U28*, sunk, 58 06N 14 34W (5†, 31 surv); sunk 58 06N 13 36W

La Carrière 24.2.42 Torpedoed by *U156* 16 53N 67 05W; 25.2.42 again torpedoed, sunk (15†, 26 surv)
La Cordillera 5.11.42 Torpedoed by *U163*, sunk, 12 02N 58 04W (3†, 38 surv)

La Estancia 19.10.40 Torpedoed (in convoy HX79) by *U47*, sunk, 57N 17W (1†, 33 surv)
La Paz 1.5.42 Torpedoed by *U109* 28 30N 80 10W, beached; sold US; 47 *Rubens* (Bel)
Lackenby 23.1.43 Torpedoed (ind) by *U624*, sunk, 55N 37 50W (39†, 0 surv)
Laconia 5.9.39 Req as amc HMS *Laconia*; 1.10.41 MoWT, troopship; 12.9.42 torpedoed by *U156*, sunk, 05 05S 11 38W (2279†, 975 surv)
Lady Drake 5.5.42 Torpedoed by *U106*, sunk, 35 43N 64 43W (12†, 240 surv)
Lady Glanely 2.12.40 Torpedoed (in convoy HX90) by *U101*, sunk, 55N 20W (33†, 0 surv)
Lady Hawkins 19.1.42 Torpedoed by *U66*, sunk, 35N 72 30W (251†, 71 surv)
Lady Somers 4.10.40 Req as obv HMS *Lady Somers*; 5.41 commd; 15.7.41 torpedoed by subm *Morosini* (Ita), sunk, 37 12N 20 32W (0†, 175 surv)
Lafian 24.9.41 Torpedoed (in convoy SL87) by *U107*, sunk, 31 12N 23 32W (0†, 46 surv)
Lagosian 28.3.43 Torpedoed (in convoy RS3) by *U159*, sunk, 25 35N 15 43W (7†, 39 surv)
Lahore 8.3.41 Torpedoed (in convoy SL67) by *U124*, on fire, 21 03N 20 38W (0†, 82 surv); 9.3.41 abandoned, sunk
Lancaster Castle 14.4.42 Bombed by German aircraft when anchored Murmansk roads, submerged (9†, 48 surv)
Lancastria 40 Troopship; 17.6.40 bombed by German aircraft, Charpentier roads, off St Nazaire, rolled over, capsized, sunk, 47 08 48N 02 20 18E (*c*3000†, 2477 surv); 51 wreck BU
Lancastrian Prince 11.4.43 Torpedoed (in convoy ON176) by *U404*, sunk, 50 18N 42 48W (45†, 0 surv)
Langleeford 14.2.40 Torpedoed by *U26*, sunk, 51 40N 12 40W (4†, 30 surv)
Langleegorse 23.1.41 Bombed by German FW200 Kondor aircraft, sunk, 53 19N 13 11W (37†, 0 surv)
Laplace 29.10.42 Torpedoed by *U159*, sunk, 40 33S 21 35E (0†, 63 surv)
Lapland 28.7.41 Torpedoed (in convoy OG69) by *U203*, sunk, 40 36N 15 30W (0†, 25 surv)
Larchbank 9.9.43 Torpedoed by subm *I-27* (Jpn), sunk, 07 38N 74E (46†, 30 surv)
Larpool 2.11.41 Torpedoed by *U208*, broke in two, sunk, 250m ESE of Cape Race (26†, 17 surv)
Lassell 30.4.41 Torpedoed by *U107*, sunk, 12 55N 28 56W (17†, 36 resc – 25 surv on *Benvrackie* (*qv*) – 15† when sunk)
Latymer 2.10.40 Bombed by German aircraft, on fire, sunk, 51 20N 10 30W (6†, 22 surv)
Laurentic 26.8.39 Req as amc HMS *Laurentic*; 3.11.40 torpedoed (while picking up surv from *Casanare – qv*) by *U99* 53 58N 14 13W (49†, 368 surv); 4.11.40 sunk (see also *Patroclus*)
Lavington Court 19.7.42 Torpedoed (in convoy OS34) by *U564* 42 38N 25 28W (6†, 39 surv); taken in tow; 1.8.42 foundered 49 40N 18 04W
Leana 7.7.43 Torpedoed, shelled, by *U198*, sunk, 25 06S 35 33E (2†, 1 pow, 65 surv)
Ledbury 24.10.40 Shelled (in convoy) by *U37*, sunk, 36 01N 07 22W
Leo Dawson 4.2.40 Torpedoed by *U37*, sunk, 60 10N 00 39W (35†, 0 surv)
Lerwick 13.1.42 Bombed by German aircraft 54 26N 00 24W (5†, 39 surv); sunk 54 26 18N 00 22 48W
Lesbian 23.6.40 Detained Beirut by French; badly damaged in aircraft attacks, in danger of sinking; 6.41 taken to deep water, scuttled
Lilian Moller 18.11.40 Torpedoed (dispersed from convoy SLS53) by subm *Maggiore Baracca* (Ita), sunk, 52 57N 18 05W (0 surv)
Limerick 25.4.43 Torpedoed (in convoy) by subm *I-177* (Jpn), sunk, 28 51S 153 54E (2†, 70 surv)
Linaria 24.2.41 Torpedoed (dispersed from convoy OB288) by *U96*, sunk, 59 30N 21W (31†, 0 surv)
Lindenhall 7.11.42 Torpedoed (in convoy TAG19) by *U508*, broke in two, sunk, 11 34N 63 26W (42†, 10 surv)
Lissa 21.9.41 Torpedoed (in convoy OG74) by *U201*, sunk, 47N 22W (26†, 0 surv)
Llanarth 27.6.40 Torpedoed by *U30* 47 39N 10 17W (0†, 35 surv); 28.6.40 sunk
Llanashe 17.2.43 Torpedoed by *U182*, sunk, 34S 28 30E (28†, 13 surv)
Llandaff Castle 40 Troopship; 30.11.42 torpedoed by *U177*, sunk, 27 20S 33 40E (3†, 310 surv)
Llandilo 2.11.42 Torpedoed by *U172*, sunk, 27 03S 02 59W (24†, 20 surv)
Llanfair 11.8.40 Torpedoed by *U38*, sunk, 54 48N 13 46W (3†, 29 surv)
Llanishen 23.8.40 Torpedoed (in convoy) by German He115 aircraft, sunk, 58 17N 02 27W (8†, 28 surv)
Llanover 12.5.42 Torpedoed (in convoy ONS92) by *U124*, damaged, 52 50N 29 04W (0†, 65 surv); sunk by HM ship
Llanwern 26.2.41 Bombed (in convoy OB290) by German FW200 Kondor aircraft, sunk, 54 07N 17 06W (27†, 12 surv)
Loch Don 1.4.42 Torpedoed by *U202*, sunk, 37 05N 61 40W (3†, 44 surv)
Loch Lomond 20.10.40 Torpedoed (convoy HX79 straggler) by *U100*, sunk, 56N 15 30W (1†, 40 surv)
Loch Maddy 21.2.40 Torpedoed by *U57* 070° 20m from Copinsay LH, Orkneys (4†, 35 surv); broke in two, afterpart beached Inganess Bay, part salved
Loch Ranza 3.2.42 Bombed by Japanese aircraft, on fire, 00 37 10N 104 14E; beached 00 36N 104 12E, explosion on board (7†, 2 pow, 41 surv); TL
Lochavon 14.10.39 Torpedoed (in convoy KJF3) by *U45*, sunk, 50 25N 13 10W
Lochgoil 6.10.39 Struck mine Bristol Channel, damaged; 40 MoWT, repaired, *Empire Rowan* (Br); 27.3.43 torpedoed by enemy aircraft, sunk, 37 16N 06 54E
Lochkatrine 3.8.42 Torpedoed (in convoy ON115) by *U553*, sunk, 45 52N 46 44W (9†, 81 surv)

Logician 14.5.41 Bombed by aircraft, Suda Bay, Crete; 16.5.41, 25.5.41 again bombed, sunk 303° 2m 2 cables from Kalani Prism (6†, 20 pow, 27 surv rescued)
Lord Strathcona 5.9.42 Torpedoed by *U513*, sunk, 47 35N 52 59W (0†, 44 surv)
Lornaston 8.3.45 Torpedoed (in convoy ONA289) by *U275*, sunk, 50 34 40N 00 03 20W (0†, 48 surv)
Louise Moller 13.11.42 Torpedoed by *U178*, broke in two, sunk, 30 50S 35 54E (11†, 48 surv)
Lowther Castle 27.5.42 Torpedoed (in convoy PQ16) by German aircraft (He111s or Ju88s) 60m ESE of Bear Is, on fire; 28.5.42 blew up, sunk (1†, 53 surv)
Lulworth Hill 19.3.43 Torpedoed by subm *Leonardo Da Vinci* (Ita), sunk, 10 10S 01E (36†, 1 pow, 2 surv)
Lumen 42 MoWT, *Empire Light* (Br); 7.3.43 torpedoed (convoy ON170 straggler) by *U638*, 53 57N 46 14E; 12.3.43 torpedoed by *U468*, sunk (45†, 5 surv)
Lunula 9.4.41 Struck by mine, sunk, Shell Haven Jetty (28†, 11 surv); CTL, BU Grays
Lurigethan 23.1.41 Bombed by German FW200 Kondor aircraft 53 46N 16W, abandoned (16†, 35 surv); 25.1.41 sunk
Lustrous 22.2.41 Sunk (from dispersed convoy) by *Scharnhorst* 47 12N 40 13W (0†, 37 pow)
Lylepark 11.6.42 Sunk by aux cruiser *Michel* 14S 10W (approx) (23†, 19 pow, 2 surv rescued)
Lynton Grange 28.12.42 Torpedoed (convoy ONS154 straggler) by *U406*, damaged, 43 23N 27 14W; torpedoed by *U628*, sunk (0†, 52 surv)

Mabriton 25.9.40 Torpedoed by *U32*, sunk, 56 12N 23W (12†, 25 surv)
Macdhui 17.6.42 Bombed by Japanese aircraft, Port Moresby; 18.6.42 again attacked (11†); on fire, drifted on to reef off Tatana Is, capsized, TL
Macgregor 27.2.42 Shelled by *U156*, sunk, 19 50N 69 40W (1†, 30 surv)
Maclaren 3.12.41 Struck mine, sunk, 51 21 21N 03 17 17W (3†, 28 surv); 1.7–31.12.43 wreck dispersed
Magdalena 18.9.40 Torpedoed by *U48*, sunk, 57 20N 20 16W (31†, 0 surv)
Magdapur 10.9.39 Struck mine (laid 4.9.39 by *U13*), sunk, 52 11N 01 43E (6†, 80 surv)
Mahanada 26.2.41 Torpedoed (in convoy OB290) by German FW200 Kondor aircraft 54 07N 17 06W, on fire, abandoned (3†, 91 surv); 27.2.41 sunk 245° 13m from 53 52N 16 26W
Mahronda 11.6.42 Torpedoed by subm *I-20* (Jpn), sunk, 14 37S 40 58E (1†, 156 surv)
Mahseer 18.10.41 Struck mine 51 40 32N 01 18 50E (0†, 97 surv); sunk 51 44 01N 01 23 07E; 50 wreck dispersed
Maidan 5.11.40 Shelled (in convoy HX84) by *Admiral Scheer*, blew up, sunk 52 26N 32 34W (90†, 0 surv)
Maimoa 20.11.40 Captured by aux cruiser *Pinguin*, sunk 31 50S 100 21E (0†, 87 pow)
Maja 15.1.45 Torpedoed by *U1055*, sunk, 53 40N 05 14W (25†, 40 surv)
Makalla 23.8.40 Bombed (in convoy) by German He115 aircraft 58 17N 02 27W, on fire (12†, 72 surv); 24.8.40 explosion, sank
Malabar 29.10.39 Torpedoed (in convoy HX5A) by *U34*, sunk, 49 57N 07 37W (5†, 70 surv)
Malakand 3.5.41 Bombed by German aircraft in dock Liverpool; partly deflated barrage balloon fell on deck; on fire; 4.5.41 abandoned, blew up, TL (1†, 75 surv)
Malda 6.4.42 Bombed by Japanese aircraft, shelled by Japanese cruisers, sunk, 19 45N 86 27E (25†, 154 surv)
Malvernian 24.8.40 Req as obv HMS *Malvernian*; 1.1.41 commd; 11.7.41 bombed by German aircraft 47 37N 19 07W, abandoned (–†, 57 landed); 19.7.41 floating 297° 190m from Cabo Prior, sunk
Mamari 7.9.39 Sold Adm, converted to dummy aircraft carrier *Hermes*; 2.6.41 struck wreck of *Ahamo* (*qv*) Wold Channel, aground off Cromer, 53 22 30N 01 00 02E; 4.6.41 torpedoed by E-boats, partially submerged, used for target practice, later blown up
Manaar 6.9.39 Stopped, shelled, torpedoed, by *U38*, sunk, 38 28N 10 50W (7†, 85 surv)
Manaquí 15.3.42 Torpedoed (in convoy) by *U504*, sunk, 17 15N 61W (41†, 0 surv)
Manchester Brigade 26.9.40 Torpedoed (in convoy) by *U137*, sunk, 54 53N 10 22W (58†, 4 surv)
Manchester Citizen 9.7.43 Torpedoed (in convoy) by *U508*, sunk, 05 50N 02 22E (15†, 52 surv)
Manchester Merchant 25.2.43 Torpedoed (in convoy ON166) by *U628*, sunk, 45 10N 43 23W (36†, 29 surv)
Mandasor 24.1.41 Shelled by aux cruiser *Atlantis* 04 18S 61E (5†, 76 pow); abandoned, sunk by bombs
Mangalore 24.11.39 Struck mine (laid by German destroyer), sunk, 288° 1.5m from Spurn Lt (0†, 77 surv)
Manipur 17.7.40 Torpedoed (in convoy HX55A) by *U57* 58 41N 05 14W (14†, 65 surv); sank about 6m NW of Cape Wrath
Manistee 14.9.40 Req as obv HMS *Manistee*; 12.40 commd; 23.2.41 torpedoed by *U107*, sunk, 58 13N 21 33W; 24.2.41 torpedoed again, sunk 58 55N 20 50W
Mansepool 24.2.41 Torpedoed (in convoy OB289) by *U97* 61 12N 12 36W, abandoned (2†, 39 surv); sunk 61 02N 12 05W
Marcella 13.3.43 Torpedoed (in convoy OS44) by *U107*, sunk, 42 45N 13 31W (44†, 0 surv)
Marconi 20.5.41 Torpedoed (in convoy HX126) by *U109*, sunk, 58N 41W (22†, 56 surv); 21.5.41 sunk
Marcrest 7.9.41 Bombed by German aircraft 090° 2m from Great Yarmouth (0†, 38 surv); taken in tow, sunk 0.75m NE of South Scroby buoy
Mardinian 9.9.40 Torpedoed (in convoy SC2) by *U28*, sunk, 56 37N 09W (6†, 31 surv)

Mareeba 26.6.41 Sunk by aux cruiser *Kormoran* 08 15N 88 06E (26†, 25 pow)
Margam Abbey 25.4.40 Struck mine, sunk, Thames estuary, 51 32 10N 01 08 31E (0†, 23 surv)
Margot 23.5.42 Shelled by *U588*, sunk, 39N 68W (1†, 44 surv)
Marietta E 4.3.43 Torpedoed (in convoy DN21) by *U160*, sunk, 31 49S 31 11E (5†, 41 surv)
Marina 17.9.40 Torpedoed by *U48* 56 46N 21 15W (2†, 34 surv); 18.9.40 sunk
Marion Moller 5.11.44 Torpedoed by subm *Ro-113* (Jpn), sunk, 10 40N 81 10E (0†, 71 surv)
Maritima 2.11.42 Torpedoed (in convoy SC107) by *U522*, sunk, 52 20N 45 40W (32†, 27 surv)
Marlene 4.4.41 Torpedoed by *U124*, sunk, 08 15N 14 19W (13†)
Maron 7.8.40 Req as obv HMS *Maron*; 7.4.42 decomm; 4.42 returned owner; 3.11.42 torpedoed (in convoy) by *U81*, sunk, 36 27N 00 58W (0†, 93 surv)
Marsa 43 Sold (Br); 21.11.43 bombed by German He177 aircraft 46 40N 18 18W; 22.11.43 last seen 46 35N 18 20W; no further reports (1†, 47 surv)
Marslew 23.2.41 Torpedoed (in convoy OB288) by *U95*, sunk, 59 18N 21 30W (13†, 23 surv)
Marton 8.5.41 Bombed by German aircraft, badly damaged, in dry dock Liverpool (0†), CTL; 27.7.41 beached Tranmere, BU
Mary Moller 8.12.41 Seized Wangpu R, N China by Japanese (2 pow); 42 *Kaiko Maru* (Jpn); 26.10.44 bombed by USAAF aircraft, sunk, 20 27N 111 49E
Mary Slessor 7.2.43 In convoy MKS7, struck mine (laid 1.2.43 by *U118*), sunk, 35 54N 05 59W (32†, 47 surv)
Marylyn 30.10.42 Torpedoed by *U174* 00 46S 32 42W (15†, 27 surv); 31.10.42 sunk
Mashobra 2.10.39 Adm, FAA base ship, Scapa Flow; 40 Adm; 25.5.40 bombed by German aircraft, beached Halstad badly damaged; destroyed by British forces
Matadian 20.3.44 Torpedoed by *U66*, sunk, 05 07N 04 47E (0†, 43 surv)
Matheran 19.10.40 Torpedoed (in convoy HX79) by *U38*, sunk, 57N 17W (7†, 74 surv)
Matina 24.10.40 Torpedoed by *U28* 57 30N 16 31W (68†, 0 surv); 29.10.40 wreck sunk by *U31*
Matra 13.11.39 Struck mine (laid by German destroyer) 1m E of Tongue LV (17†); beached Shingles Patch, 51 31 34N 01 17 32E; TL
Mattawin 2.6.42 Torpedoed by *U553*, sunk, 40 34N 66 34W (0†, 71 surv)
Medjerda 18.3.41 Torpedoed (in convoy SL68) by *U105*, sunk, 17N 21W (0 surv)
Medon 10.8.42 Shelled, torpedoed, by subm *Reginaldo Giuliani* (Ita), sunk, 09 26N 38 28W (0†, 64 surv)
Melbourne Star 2.4.43 Torpedoed (ind) by *U129*, sunk, 28 05N 57 30W (113†, 4 surv)
Melmore Head 28.12.42 Torpedoed (in convoy ONS154) by *U225*, sunk, 43 27N 27 15W (14†, 35 surv)
Melrose Abbey 27.12.42 Torpedoed (in convoy ONS154) by *U356*, sunk, 47 30N 24 30W (7†, 27 surv)
Memnon 11.3.41 Torpedoed by *U106*, sunk, 20 41N 21W (5†, 4 pow, 65 surv)
Menin Ridge 24.10.39 Torpedoed (in convoy) by *U37*, sunk, 36 01N 07 22W (20†)
Mentor 28.5.42 Torpedoed by *U106*, sunk, 24 11N 87 02W (4†, 81 surv)
Merchant 24.12.41 Struck mine 52 39 30N 02 00 56E; 25.12.41 abandoned, sunk 52 40N 02 04 30E (1†, 44 surv)
Meriones 25.1.41 Bombed by German aircraft, ran aground Haisboro' Sands (0†, 81 surv); 25–26.1.41 bombed again while ashore; TL
Mersington Court 15.4.40 Sunk Narvik (0†, 8 rescued, 28 interned Sweden); 52 refloated, put ashore, wreck sold and used as hulk in Belgium
Michael E 5.41 Adm, CAM vessel; 2.6.51 torpedoed (dispersed from convoy OB326) by *U108*, sunk, 48 50N 29W (4†, 47 surv)
Middlesex 10.1.41 Struck mine, sunk, 198° 0.8m from Flatholm Is (0†); wreck dispersed
Mill Hill 30.8.40 Torpedoed (in convoy HX66A) by *U32*, sunk, 58 48N 06 49W (34†, 0 surv)
Ming Sang 25.12.41 Scuttled Hong Kong; salved by Japanese; 42 *Bizan Maru* (Jpn); 18.6.45 (in convoy) struck US mine, sunk, 33 58N 130 44E; 48 raised, repaired
Modavia 27.2.43 Torpedoed (in convoy) by E-boat (of German 5 MTB fl), sunk, 090° 14m from Berry Head, Lyme Bay (0†, 54 surv)
Monarch 16.4.45 Torpedoed by *U2324*, sunk, 52 06 04N 01 50 19E (3†, 68 surv)
Montenol 21.5.42 Torpedoed (in convoy OS28) by *U159*, badly damaged, 36 41N 22 45W, abandoned (3†); shelled by HM ships, sunk
Montreal City 21.12.42 Torpedoed (convoy ONS152 straggler) by *U591*, sunk, 50 23N 38W (40†, 0 surv)
Montrolite 4.2.42 Torpedoed by *U109*, sunk, 35 14N 60 05W (28†, 20 surv)
Montrose 4.9.39 Req as amc HMS *Forfar*; 11.39 compl conv, Northern Patrol; 1.12.40 torpedoed by *U99* 54 23N 20 11W (173†, 21 surv); 2.12.40 sunk
Mopan 5.11.40 Shelled (ind) by *Admiral Scheer* 52 48N 32 15W (0†, 68 pow)
Mostyn 23.1.41 Bombed by German FW200 Kondor aircraft, sunk, 54 37N 15 35W (2†, 20 surv)
Mountpark 26.4.41 Bombed by German aircraft 56 17N 12 21W (6†, 35 surv); sunk 56 15N 12 09W
Muncaster Castle 30.3.42 Torpedoed by *U68*, sunk, 02 02N 12 02W (–†)
Mundra 6.7.42 Shelled, torpedoed, by subm *I-18* (Jpn), sunk, 28 45S 32 20E (45†, 155 surv)
Muneric 10.9.41 Torpedoed (in convoy SC42) by *U432*, sunk, 61 38N 40 40W (63†, 63 surv)
Munlock 8.12.41 Seized China Seas by Japanese; 42 *Rizan Maru* (Jpn); 25.9.44 torpedoed by subm USS *Searaven*, sunk, 49 36N 145 30E
Myrmidon 5.9.42 Torpedoed by *U506*, sunk, 00 45N 06 27W

Nagara 29.3.43 Torpedoed (in convoy SL126) by *U404* 46 50N 16 40W (0†, 97 surv), taken in tow; 4.4.43 sunk 47 52N 14 03W
Nagina 30.4.43 Torpedoed (in convoy TS37) by *U515*, sunk, 07 19N 13 50W (2†, 11 surv)
Nagpore 28.10.42 Torpedoed, shelled (in convoy SL125) by *U509*, then torpedoed, shelled, by *U203*, 31 30N 19 36W (2†, 79 surv), broke in two, sank
Nailsea Court 10.3.43 Torpedoed (in convoy SC121) by *U229*, sunk, 58 45N 21 57W (45†, 5 surv)
Nailsea Lass 24.2.41 Torpedoed (convoy SLS64 straggler) by *U48*, sunk, 60m SW of Fastnet (5†, 2 pow, 29 surv)
Nailsea Manor 10.10.41 Torpedoed by *U126*, sunk, 18 45N 21 18W (0†, 41 surv)
Nailsea Meadow 11.5.43 Torpedoed by *U196*, sunk, 32 04S 29 13E (2†, 44 surv)
Nailsea River 15.9.40 Torpedoed by German aircraft 4m E of Montrose (0†); sunk 56 41N 02 05W
Nalgora 2.1.41 Torpedoed, shelled, by *U65*, sunk, 22 24N 21 11W (0†, 105 surv)
Nalon 6.11.40 Bombed by German aircraft, sunk, 53 57N 15 31W (0†, 72 surv)
Nancy Moller 18.3.44 Torpedoed by subm *I-165* (Jpn), sunk, 02 14N 78 25E (32†, 1 pow, 32 surv)
Nankin 10.5.42 Shelled, captured by aux cruiser *Thor* 26 43S 89 56E, prize taken Yokohama; 42 *Leuthen* (Ger); 30.11.42 on fire following explosion on *Uckermark* at Yokohama; TL
Nanning 11.12.41 Scuttled Hong Kong; 25.12.41 wreck seized by Japanese; 42 salved, *Nannei Maru* (Jpn); 16.7.45 struck US mine, sunk, 33 56N 130 52E
Napier Star 18.12.40 Torpedoed by *U100*, sunk, 58 58N 23 13W (71†, 14 surv)
Naphtha Shipper 28.8.39 Arrested for debt while repairing Hamburg; 3.9.39 seized Hamburg by Germans; 40 *Altengamme* (Ger); 4.5.45 bombed by Russian aircraft, sunk, off Neu Mukran, Prerow Wiek; 50 raised, BU
Nardana 8.3.41 Torpedoed (in convoy SL67) by *U124*, sunk, 20 51N 20 32W (19†, 108 surv)
Nariva 17.3.43 Torpedoed (in convoy HX229) by *U600*, damaged, abandoned 50 40N 34 10W (0†, 94 surv); torpedoed by *U91*, sunk 50 54N 33 35W
Narkunda 40 Troopship; 14.11.42 bombed (in Opn 'Torch') by aircraft 36 52N 05 01E (31†); sunk 36 49 38N 05 00 44E
Narragansett 25.3.42 Torpedoed by *U105*, sunk, 34 46N 67 40W (49†, 0 surv)
Natia 8.10.40 Sunk by aux cruiser *Thor* 00 50N 32 24W (2†, 84 pow)
Navarino 4.7.42 Torpedoed (in convoy PQ17) by German He111 aircraft of I/KG26 75 57N 27 14E (15†); torpedoed by subm HMS *P-614*, sunk
Navasota 5.12.39 Torpedoed (in convoy OB46) by *U47*, sunk, 50 43N 10 16W (37†)
Nebraska 8.4.44 Torpedoed by *U843*, sunk, 11 55S 19 52W (2†, 66 surv)
Nellore 29.6.44 Torpedoed by subm *I-8* (Jpn), sunk, 07 51S 75 20E (79†, 11 pow, 119 surv)
Neptuna 19.2.41 Bombed by Japanese dive-bomber aircraft, Port Darwin (45†); sunk at quay
Neptunian 7.9.40 Torpedoed (in convoy SC2) by *U47*, sunk, 58 27N 17 27W (36†, 0 surv)
Nerissa 30.4.41 Torpedoed (ind) by *U552*, sunk, 55 57N 10 08W (207†, 80 surv)
Nestlea 18.11.40 Bombed, shelled, by German aircraft, sunk, 50 38N 10W (0†, 39 surv)
Neuralia 1.5.45 Struck Italian mine, sunk, 40 11N 17 44E (4†, 273 surv)
New Brunswick 21.5.42 Torpedoed (in convoy OS28) by *U159*, sunk, 36 53N 22 55W (3†, 59 surv)
New Columbia 31.10.43 Torpedoed by *U68*, sunk, 04 25N 05 03E (0†, 84 surv)
New Sevilla 20.9.40 Torpedoed (in convoy OB216) by *U138* 55 50N 07 30W, taken in tow; 21.9.40 sunk 55 48N 07 22W (2†, 283 surv)
New Toronto 5.11.42 Torpedoed by *U126*, sunk, 05 57N 02 30E (4†, 85 surv)
New Westminster City 3.4.42 Bombed by German aircraft at Murmansk (dispersed from convoy PQ13), on fire, beached, CTL (3†); 6.45 salved, repaired, returned GB, sold
Newbury 15.9.41 Torpedoed (convoy ON14 straggler) by *U94*, sunk, 54 39N 28 04W (45†, 0 surv)
Newfoundland 40 Hospital ship; 13.9.43 bombed by German aircraft, on fire, (21†, 294 surv); 14.9.43 shelled by destroyers USS *Mayo* and *Plunkett*, sunk, 40 14N 14 21E
Newton Ash 8.2.43 Torpedoed (in convoy SC108) by *U402*, sunk, 56 25N 22 26W (34†, 4 surv)
Newton Beech 5.10.39 Captured by *Graf Spee* 09 35S 06 30W; 8.10.39 sunk
Newton Pine 41 Sold (Br); 16.10.42 torpedoed (convoy ONS136 straggler) by *U410*, sunk, 55N 30W (47†, 0 surv)
Niagara 18.6.40 Struck mine (laid 6.40 by aux cruiser *Orion*), sunk, 35 53S 174 54E (0†)
Niceto de Larrinaga 22.9.41 Torpedoed (in convoy SL87) by *U103*, sunk, 27 32N 24 26W (3†, 48 surv)
Nicoya 12.5.42 Torpedoed by *U553* 49 19N 64 51W (6†, 79 surv); sunk 49 52N 65 02W
Nigerian 8.12.42 Torpedoed by *U508*, sunk, 09 17N 59W (5†, 4 pow, 52 surv)
Nirpura 3.3.43 Torpedoed (in convoy DN21) by *U160*, sunk, 32 47S 29 47E (32†, 93 surv)
Norah Moller 3.2.42 Bombed by Japanese aircraft of West Nangka Point, Banka Strait, on fire, engines damaged (57†, 70 surv); 4.2.42 sunk
Norfolk 18.6.41 Torpedoed by *U552*, sunk, 57 17N 11 14W (1†, 64 surv)
Norman Monarch 20.5.41 Torpedoed (in convoy HX126) by *U94*, sunk, 56 41N 40 52W (0†, 48 resc by *Harpagus – qv*)
Norman Prince 28.5.42 Torpedoed by *U156*, sunk, 14 40N 62 15W (16†, 33 surv)
North Britain 4.5.43 Torpedoed (convoy ONS5 straggler) by *U125*, sunk, 55 08N 42

43W (34†, 12 surv)
North Cornwall 15.4.40 Sunk Narvik (–†, 17 surv resc, 4 intnd Sweden); 5.53 raised, BU Stavanger
Northern Prince 3.4.41 Bombed (in convoy) by German aircraft, Antikithera Channel, Greece (3†, 107 surv); sunk 35 34N 23 23E
Northmoor 17.5.43 Torpedoed (in convoy LMD17) by *U198*, sunk, 28 27S 32 43E (12†, 25 surv)
Nottingham 7.11.41 Torpedoed (ind) by *U74*, sunk, 53 24N 31 51W (62†, 0 surv)
Nova Scotia 1.41 Troopship; 28.11.42 torpedoed (while transporting Italian internees) by *U177*, sunk, 28 30S 33E (112†, 62 resc; 650 pow†, 130 pow surv)
Nowshera 18.11.40 Sunk by aux cruiser *Pinguin* 30S 90E (0†, Euro crew pow)
Nurmahal 9.11.42 Torpedoed by *U154* 14 45N 55 45W (0 surv); 11.11.42 sunk

Oakbank 27.12.42 Torpedoed by *U507*, sunk, 00 46S 37 58W (25†, 2 pow, 38 surv)
Oakdene 6.5.41 Torpedoed by *U105*, sunk, 06 19N 27 55W (0†, 35 surv)
Oakgrove 9.1.40 Bombed by German aircraft, sunk, 107° 15m from Cromer Knoll LV (1†)
Observer 16.12.42 Torpedoed by *U176*, sunk, 05 30S 31W (66†, 15 surv)
Oilfield 28.4.41 Torpedoed (in convoy HX121) by *U96*, on fire, 60 05N 16W (47†, 8 surv); 29.4.41 broke in two, sunk, 60 06N 16 06W
Oilpioneer 8.6.40 Shelled by *Admiral Hipper*, torpedoed by German destroyer, sunk, 67 44N 03 52E (20†, – pow)
Oiltrader 29.3.41 Bombed by German aircraft 52 34 30N 02 01 30E (0†, 45 surv); sunk 325° 3.5m from No 5 buoy
Oleander 26.5.40 Damaged, beached, Harstad Bay; 8.6.40 badly damaged through aircraft attack near miss, sunk (0†, 39 surv)
Olivegrove 7.9.39 Torpedoed by *U33*, sunk, 49 05N 15 58W (0†)
Olna 18.5.41 Bombed by German aircraft, on fire, Suda Bay, Crete; beached, burnt out; 31.5.41 seized by Germans; 5.45 wreck at Skaramanga, BU
Opawa 6.2.42 Torpedoed, shelled, by *U106*, sunk, 38 21N 61 13W (56†, 15 surv)
Oporto 13.3.43 Torpedoed (in convoy OS44) by *U107*, sunk, 42 45N 13 31W (43†, 4 surv)
Orama 40 Troopship; 8.6.40 shelled by *Admiral Hipper*, torpedoed, sunk, 67 44N 03 52E (19†, 280 surv, some pow)
Orangemoor 31.5.40 Torpedoed by *U101*, sunk, 49 43N 03 23W (18†, 22 surv)
Orcades 39 Troopship; 10.10.42 torpedoed (in convoy) by *U172*, sunk, 35 51S 14 40E (48†, 1016 surv)
Oregon 10.8.42 Torpedoed (in convoy SC94) by *U660*, damaged, 57 05N 22 41W, straggling; torpedoed by *U438*, sunk (1†, 31 surv)
Orfor 14.12.42 Torpedoed by *U105*, sunk, 16N 50W (19†, 39 surv)
Orford 39 Troopship; 1.6.40 bombed by aircraft Marseilles, on fire, beached, burnt out (14†); 47 recovered, BU Savona
Orminster 40 Sold (Br); 25.8.44 torpedoed (conv FTM74 straggler) by *U480*, sunk, 50 07 48N 00 41 54W (6†, 57 surv)
Oronsay 39 Troopship; 9.10.42 torpedoed (in convoy) by subm *Archimede* (Ita), sunk, 04 29N 20 52W (5†, 26 pow, 413 surv)
Oropesa 9.39 Troopship; 16.1.41 torpedoed by *U96* 56 30N 11 46W (106†, 143 surv); sunk 56 30N 11 40W
Oswestry Grange 12.2.41 Shelled (in convoy SLS64) by *Admiral Hipper*, on fire, sunk, 37 10N 21 20W (5†, 37 surv)
Otaio 28.8.41 Torpedoed (in convoy OS4) by *U558*, sunk, 52 16N 17 50W (13†, 58 surv)
Otina 20.12.42 Torpedoed (ind) by *U621*, sunk, 47 40N 33 06W (60†, 0 surv)
Otterpool 20.6.40 Torpedoed (in convoy HGF34) by *U30*, sunk, 48 47N 07 50W (23†, 15 surv)
Ousebridge 29.7.40 Struck mine Queen's Channel, off Liverpool; ashore 5° 800ft from Q5 red buoy, Queen's Channel, bows blown off, back broken; TL
Ovatella 9.4.40 Seized Odense by Germans; KM *Weissenburg* (Ger); 23.11.43 bombed by RAF aircraft, sunk, 53 10N 04 50E

Pacific Grove 12.4.43 Torpedoed (in convoy HX232) by *U563*, sunk, 54 10N 30W (11†, 59 surv)
Pacific Pioneer 29.7.42 Torpedoed (in convoy ON113) by *U132*, sunk, 43 32N 60 38W (0†, 66 surv)
Pacific President 2.12.40 Torpedoed (in convoy HX90) by *U43*, sunk, 56 04N 18 45W (0 surv)
Pacific Ranger 12.10.40 Torpedoed (in convoy HX77) by *U59* 56 20N 11 43W (0†, 53 surv); sunk 56 20N 11 45W
Pacific Reliance 4.3.40 Torpedoed by *U29*, sunk, 50 23N 05 49W (0†, 53 surv)
Pacific Star 27.10.42 Torpedoed (in convoy SL125) by *U509* 29 16N 20 57W; 28.10.42 abandoned 29 21N 19 28W; 30.10.42 sunk (0†, 97 surv)
Palma 29.2.44 Torpedoed by *U183*, sunk, 05 51N 79 58E (7†, 50 surv)
Palmella 1.12.40 Torpedoed by *U37*, broke in two, sunk, 40 30N 13 30W (1†, 28 surv)
Pampas 42 Troopship; 26.3.42 (and later dates) bombed by German aircraft, sunk, Valletta (0†, 60 surv)
Parracombe 2.5.41 Bombed by Italian aircraft, sunk, 62° 8.5m from Cap Bon (30†, 18 pow)
Patella 19.4.42 Sunk by aux cruiser *Michel* 23S 20W (3†, 64 pow)
Patia 10.40 Req as obv/fighter catapult vessel HMS *Patia*; 4.11.40–16.4.41 conv; 3.41

aux fighter catapult vessel; 27.4.41 bombed by German aircraft near 20G buoy, Coquet Is, off Northumberland, sunk (39†, – surv)
Patroclus 12.9.39 Req as amc HMS *Patroclus*; 1.40 commd; 3.11.40 torpedoed (standing by to pick up surv from *Laurentic* – *qv*) by *U99* 53 48N 14 13W; 4.11.40 sunk 53 43N 14 41W (79†, 264 surv)
Pearlmoor 19.7.40 Torpedoed by *U62*, sunk, 55 23N 09 18W (13†, 26 surv)
Pecten 25.8.40 Torpedoed (convoy HX65 straggler) by *U57*, sunk, 56 22N 07 55W (49†, 8 surv)
Peder Bogen 23.3.42 Torpedoed by subm *Morosini* (Ita) 24 41N 57 44W; 24.3.42 shelled by *Morosini*, sunk (0†, 53 surv)
Pegasus 10.6.40 Detained Beirut by VFr; 13.7.41 attacked by British aircraft, sunk, alongside North Mole, Beirut harbour; TL
Peisander 17.5.42 Torpedoed by *U653*, sunk, 37 24N 65 38(0†, 64 surv)
Pelayo 14.6.42 Torpedoed (in convoy HG84) by *U552*, sunk, 43 18N 17 38W (16†, 31 surv)
Pennington Court 9.10.42 Torpedoed (ind) by *U254*, sunk, 58 18N 27 55W (0 surv)
Penolver 19.10.43 In convoy WB65, struck mine (laid 9.10.43 by *U220*), sunk, 47 19N 52 27W (27†, 14 surv)
Penrose 3.9.42 Torpedoed by *U107*, sunk, 112° 3m off Cape Sines (2†, 43 surv)
Pensilva 19.11.39 Torpedoed, shelled, by *U49*, sunk, 46 51N 11 36W
Perseus 16.1.44 Torpedoed by subm *I-165* (Jpn), sunk, 12N 80 14E (0†, 115 surv)
Peshawur 23.12.43 Torpedoed by subm *Ro-111* (Jpn), sunk, 11 11N 80 11E (0†, 137 surv)
Peterton 17.9.42 Torpedoed by *U109*, sunk, 18 45N 29 15W (9†, 1 pow, 33 surv)
Phemius 19.12.43 Torpedoed by *U515*, sunk, 05 01N 00 17W (23†, 1 pow, 92 surv)
Phenix 24.12.41 Struck mine, on fire, Haifa harbour (4†, 29 surv); 26.12.42 gutted, broke in two, TL; 42 wreck removed; 6.52 refloated; BU
Phidias 8.6.41 Torpedoed, shelled (in convoy) by *U46*, on fire, blew up, sunk, 48 25N 26 12W (8†, 43 surv)
Philipp M 24.2.44 Torpedoed (in convoy FS1371) by E-boat, sunk, 52 45N 02 12E (7†, 18 surv)
Piako 18.5.41 Torpedoed by *U107*, sunk, 07 52N 14 57W (10†, 63 surv)
Pikepool 22.11.40 Struck mine, sunk, 23m ESE of Smalls Light (17†, 15 surv)
Pinna 3.2.42 Bombed by Japanese aircraft 00 52S 104 19E; 4.2.42 again bombed, on fire, aground (20†, 25 pow, 7 surv); TL
Pinto 8.9.44 Torpedoed (in convoy HXF305) by *U482*, sunk, 55 27N 08 01W (21†, 41 surv)
Pizarro 31.1.41 Torpedoed by subm *Dandolo* (Ita), sunk, 49 30N 19 40W (23†, 6 surv)
Planter 16.11.40 Torpedoed (in HG convoy) by *U137*, sunk, 55 38N 08 28W (13†, 60 surv)
Pleiodon 15.2.42 Captured Singapore by Japanese; 42 *Nansei Maru* (Jpn); 18.8.44 torpedoed by subm USS *Ray*, sunk, 08 48N 116 58E
Plumleaf 26.3.42 (and later dates) Bombed by German and Italian aircraft, aground, Parlatorio Wharf, Malta; attacked again, sunk; 28.8.47 raised; BU Catania (ar 11.10.47)
Polycarp 2.6.40 Torpedoed by *U101*, sunk, 49 19N 05 35W (0†, 43 surv)
Polzella 17.1.40 Torpedoed by *U25*, sunk, 6–7m N of Muckle Flugga, Shetlands (36†, 0 surv)
Pomella 9.7.42 Torpedoed (in convoy) by E-boat *S67*, sunk, 50 19N 03W (6†, 53 surv)
Pontypridd 11.6.42 Torpedoed (in convoy ONS100) by *U569*, damaged, 49 50N 41 37W; torpedoed by *U94*, then again by *U569*, sunk (2†, 1 pow, 45 surv)
Ponzano 13.11.39 Struck by magnetic mine (minefield laid by German destroyer) 51 28 38N 01 25 20E; sunk 51 28 03N 01 27 06E; wreck dispersed
Port Auckland 17.3.43 Torpedoed (in convoy SC122) by *U305* 52 25N 30 15W; 18.3.43 torpedoed again by *U305*, back broken, sunk (8†, 100 surv)
Port Brisbane 21.11.40 Shelled by aux cruiser *Pinguin*, abandoned 29 22S 95 36E (1†, 61 pow, 29 surv); 22.11.40 sunk by bombs placed on board and torpedoed
Port Denison 26.9.40 Bombed by German aircraft 6m NE of Peterhead (16†, 67 surv); 27.9.40 sunk 260° 7m Rattray Head LH
Port Gisborne 11.10.40 Torpedoed (in convoy HX77) by *U48* 56 38N 16 40W; sunk 57 02N 17 24W (26†, 38 surv)
Port Hardy 28.4.41 Torpedoed (in convoy HX121) by *U96*, sunk, 60 14N 15 20W (1†, 97 surv)
Port Hobart 24.11.40 Captured by *Admiral Scheer*, shelled, sunk 24 44N 58 21W (0†, 73 pow)
Port Hunter 11.7.42 Torpedoed (dispersed from convoy OS33) by *U582*, sunk, 31N 24W (88†, 3 surv)
Port Montreal 10.6.42 Torpedoed by *U68*, sunk, 12 17N 80 20W (0†, 86 resc – incl 45 surv from *Tela* (*qv*), 2† when *Port Montreal* sunk)
Port Nicholson 16.6.42 Torpedoed (in convoy XB25) by *U87*, sunk, 42 11N 69 25W (4†, 83 surv)
Port Townsville 3.3.41 Bombed by German aircraft 51 57N 05 43W, abandoned 52 05N 05 24W; 4.3.41 sunk 52 06N 05 23W (2†, 74 surv)
Port Wellington 1.12.40 Shelled by aux cruiser *Pinguin* 32 10S 75E (2†, 82 resc, – pow); sunk by depth charges placed on board
Portsea 24.7.44 Struck mine, sunk, 43 28 25N 13 44 15E (25†, 4 surv)
Pozarica 20.6.40 Adm aux AA vessel; 29.1.43 torpedoed by German (while escorting convoy TE14) aircraft; towed to off Bougie; 1.2.43 beached; 13.2.43 capsized, sunk; 2.49 salvage commenced; 5.3.51 raised; 14.6.51 ar Savona for BU
Primrose Hill 29.10.42 Torpedoed by *UD5*, sunk, 18 58N 28 40W (3†, 46 surv)
Prince Rupert City 1.6.41 Bombed by German aircraft; 2.6.41 abandoned, sunk, 58 46N 04 41 30W (4†, 45 surv)

Protesilaus 21.1.40 Struck mine (laid 5.12.39 by *U28*) 51 31N 04 04W; towed in damaged, beached Swansea Bay; towed Greenock; 13.9.40 when in tow for Scapa Flow for sinking as blockship, sunk by gunfire 295° 4.9m from Skerryvore
Pukkastan 7.9.39 Torpedoed, shelled, by *U34*, sunk, 49 23N 07 49W
Putney Hill 26.6.42 Torpedoed, shelled, by *U203*, sunk, 24 20N 63 16W (3†, 35 surv)
Pyrrhus 17.2.40 Torpedoed (in convoy OG18) by *U37* 44 02N 10 18W (8†, 77 surv), broke in two, afterpart sank; 19.2.40 forepart sank

Quebec City 19.9.42 Torpedoed, shelled, by *U156*, sunk, 02 12S 17 36W (1†, 40 surv)
Queen Anne 10.2.43 Torpedoed (in convoy CA11) by *U509*, sunk, 34 53S 19 51E (5†, 39 surv)
Queen City 21.12.42 Torpedoed, shelled, by subm *Enrico Tazzoli* (Ita); crew taken off, shelled, sunk, 00 49S 41 34W (6†)
Queen Maud 5.5.41 Torpedoed by *U38*, sunk, 07 54N 16 41W (1†, 38 surv)
Queen Victoria 28.6.42 Torpedoed by subm *I-10* (Jpn), sunk, 21 15S 40 30E (48†, 0 surv)
Queensbury 6.6.41 Bombed by German aircraft 56 50N 02 07W (11†, 27 surv); shelled by trawler HMS *Sturton*, sunk 56 47 30N 02 09W
Quiloa 14.4.41 Bombed by aircraft Eleusis Bay, Piræus (0†, 97 surv); 15.4.41 beached; 19.4.41 abandoned; TL; 11.45 wreck at Skaramanga

Rabaul 14.5.41 Sunk by aux cruiser *Atlantis* 19 30S 04 30E (9†, 1 pow, 46 surv)
Rahmani 12.7.43 Torpedoed by subm *I-29* (Jpn), sunk, 14 52N 52 06E (20†, 286 surv)
Rajputana 4.9.39 Req as amc HMS *Rajputana*; 12.39 commd; 13.4.41 torpedoed by *U108*, sunk, 64 50N 27 25W (41†, 242 surv)
Ramillies 8.5.41 Torpedoed by *U97*, sunk, 48 05N 32 26W (29†, 12 surv)
Ramon de Larrinaga 41 MoWT, *Empire Mersey* (Br); 14.10.41 torpedoed (in convoy SC104) by *U618*, sunk, 54N 40 15W (16†, 39 surv)
Ramsay 9.6.42 Torpedoed (in convoy ONS100) by *U94*, sunk, 51 53N 34 59W (40†, 8 surv)
Ranee 40 Troopship; 5.2.41 struck mine Suez Canal, broke in two (9†, 70 surv); forepart taken Port Said; afterpart sank
Rangitane 27.11.40 Shelled, torpedoed, by aux cruisers *Komet* and *Orion*, sunk, 36 58S 175 22W (16†, 299 surv)
Rawalpindi 26.8.39 Req as amc HMS *Rawalpindi*; 23.11.39 shelled by *Scharnhorst* and *Gneisenau*, sunk, SE of Iceland (275†, 37 surv)
Rawnsley 8.5.41 Bombed by aircraft 34 56N 26 13E; 9.5.41 taken in tow; 12.5.41 again attacked by aircraft, on fire, sunk, 34 59N 25 46 26E
Reedpool 20.9.42 Torpedoed by *U515*, sunk, 08 58N 57 34W (6†, 1 pow, – surv)
Refast 26.1.42 Torpedoed (in convoy ON56) by *U582*, sunk, 42 41N 53 02W (10†, 33 surv)
Regent Lion 17.2.45 Torpedoed by *U300* 35 56N 05 45W, damaged; taken in tow, grounded La Perla rocks, 1m S of Carnero Point (3†, 40 surv); TL
Regent Tiger 8.9.39 Torpedoed by *U29*, on fire, 49 57N 15 34W; 10.9.39 sunk 49 48N 14 33W
Registan 13.9.40–11.41 obv HMS *Registan*; 28.9.42 torpedoed by *U332*, sunk, 12 37N 57 10W (16†, 40 surv)
Remuera 26.8.40 Torpedoed (in convoy HX65A) by German He115 aircraft, sunk, 57 50N 01 54W (0†, 94 surv)
Retriever 11.4.41 Bombed by enemy aircraft, sunk, 264° 1m from Aliki Rocks, off Phleva Is, Greece (–†)
Reynolds 31.10.42 Torpedoed by *U504*, sunk, 30S 35 10E (47†, 0 surv)
Rhexenor 3.2.43 Torpedoed, shelled, by *U217*, sunk, 24 59N 43 37W (3†, 2 pow on *U217*, 65 surv)
Richard de Larrinaga 12.5.41 Bombed by German aircraft 4 cables N of 20 R Buoy, off R Tyne; taken in tow, back broken, ashore Herd Sand (0†, 43 surv); TL
Richmond Castle 4.8.42 Torpedoed by *U176*, sunk, 50 25N 35 05W (14†, 50 surv)
Rio Azul 29.6.41 Torpedoed (in convoy SL76) by *U123*, sunk, 29N 25W (33†, 9 surv)
Rio Blanco 1.4.42 Torpedoed by *U160*, sunk, 35 16N 74 18W (19†, 21 surv)
Rio Claro 6.9.39 Torpedoed, shelled, by *U47*, sunk, 46 30N 12W
Rio Dorado 15.3.41 Shelled by *Gneisenau*, sunk,42N 43W (39†, 0 surv)
Ripley 40 Sold (Br); 12.12.41 torpedoed (in convoy) by *U161*, sunk, 00 35S 32 17W (0†, 41 surv)
River Afton 5.7.42 Torpedoed (dispersed from convoy PQ17) by *U703*, explosion, broke in two, sunk, 75 57N 43E (22†, 33 surv)
River Lugar 26.6.41 Torpedoed (in convoy SL76) by *U69*, sunk, 23 50N 21W (41†, 6 surv)
Riverton 24.4.40 Sunk Narvik during German invasion (33 intnd Sweden)
Robert L Holt 4.7.41 Shelled by *U69*, sunk, 24 15N 20W (0 surv)
Rodney Star 16.5.41 Torpedoed by *U105* 05 03N 19 02W (0†, 83 surv); sunk 05 08N 19 15W
Rohna 41 Troopship; 26.11.43 bombed (in convoy KMF26) by German He177 aircraft of II/KG40, on fire, sunk, 36 56N 05 20E (1149†, 1083 surv)
Romanby 22–23.4.40 Sunk alongside jetty Narvik, when jetty blown up (30 interned Sweden)
Ronwyn 18.6.40 Damaged by crew before abandoned off Rochefort; salved by Germans; 41 *Hochheimer* (Ger); 21.5.44 torpedoed by subm HMS *Sceptre*, sunk, 43 24N 03 30W
Rosalie Moller 8.10.41 Bombed by aircraft, sunk, Anchorage H Suez (2†); postwar raised, BU
Rose Castle 2.11.42 Torpedoed by *U518*, sunk, 47 36N 52 57 30W (Wabana Anchorage Nfl) (24†, 19 surv)

Roseburn 19.6.40 Torpedoed, shelled, by E-boats *S19*, *S26* 5m off Dungeness (0†, 30 surv); beached 247° 1.3m from Dungeness High Lt; TL
Rosewood 9.3.43 Torpedoed (in convoy SC121) by *U409* 58 37N 22 32W, broke in two (42†, 0 surv); 11.3.43 both sections sunk by USCG cutter *Bibb* 58 30N 20 31W
Ross 29.10.42 Torpedoed by *U159*, sunk, 38 51S 21 40E (1†, 39 surv)
Rothermere 20.5.41 Torpedoed (in convoy HX126) by *U98*, sunk, 57 48N 41 36W (22†, 34 surv)
Rothley 19.10.42 Torpedoed by *U332*, sunk, 13 34N 54 34W (2†, 40 surv)
Rotorua 9.39 Troopship; 11.12.40 torpedoed (in convoy HX92) by *U96* 58 56N 11 20W (21†, 139 surv); sunk 58 56N 11 08W
Rowallan Castle 14.2.42 Bombed (in convoy MW9B) by German Ju88 aircraft, damaged, 34 54N 19 40E (0†, 100 surv); taken in tow, sunk by HM escort vessel
Rowanbank 31.1.41 Sunk by German aircraft 57N 16 30W (68†, 0 surv)
Roxburgh Castle 22.2.43 Torpedoed by *U107*, sunk, 38 12N 26 22W (0†, 64 surv)
Roxby 7.11.42 Torpedoed (convoy ON143 straggler) by *U613*, sunk, 49 35N 30 32W (34†, 12 surv)
Royal Crown 15.3.41 Sunk (in convoy) by *Gneisenau* 42N 43W (0†, 39 pow)
Royal Sceptre 5.9.39 Shelled by *U48* 46 23N 14 59W (1†); abandoned, torpedoed, sunk
Royal Star 20.4.44 Torpedoed (in convoy) by German aircraft, sunk, 37 02N 03 41E (1†, 78 surv)
Royston Grange 25.11.39 Torpedoed (in convoy SL8B) by *U28*, sunk, 49 10N 09 16W
Ruckinge 19.12.41 Torpedoed by *U108*, damaged (2†, 39 surv); shelled by corvette HMS *Samphire*, sunk, 38 20N 17 15W
Runa 21.9.41 Torpedoed (in convoy OG74) by *U201*, sunk, 46 20N 22 23W (14†, 9 surv)
Runo 11.4.43 Torpedoed by *U593*, sunk, 32 15N 23 55E (16†, 21 surv)
Ruperra 19.10.40 Torpedoed (in convoy HX79) by *U46*, sunk, 57N 16W (30†, 7 surv)
Rupert de Larrinaga 14.7.41 Torpedoed by subm *Morosini* (Ita), sunk, 36 18N 21 11W (0†, 44 surv)
Rushpool 29.1.41 Torpedoed (in convoy SC19) by *U94*, sunk, 56 00N 15 42W (0†)
Rutland 30.10.40 Torpedoed (convoy HX82 straggler) by *U124*, sunk, 57 14N 16 00W (24†, 0 surv)

Sabor 7.3.43 Torpedoed by *U506*, sunk, 34 30S 23 10E (6†, 52 surv)
Sacramento Valley 6.6.41 Torpedoed by *U106*, sunk, 17 10N 30 10W (3†, 46 surv)
Sagaing 9.4.42 Attacked by Japanese carrier aircraft, on fire, abandoned, Trincomalee (2†, 136 surv); drifted into Malay Cove; 8.43 sunk deliberately for use as pier
Saganaga 5.9.42 Torpedoed by *U513*, sunk, when lying at anchor Wabana Nfl 47 35N 52 59W (30†, 14 surv); 24.8.43 sunk
Saint Agnes 14.9.40 Torpedoed, shelled (dispersed from convoy SLS46), by subm *Emo* (Ita), sunk, 41 27N 21 50W (0†, 64 surv)
Saint Anselm 30.6.41 Torpedoed, shelled, by *U66*, sunk, 31N 26W (34†, 33 surv)
Saint Dunstan 23.8.40 Torpedoed (in convoy OB202) by *U57*, damaged, 55 43N 08 10W; 25.8.40 abandoned; 26.8.40 taken in tow; 27.8.40 sunk 68° 4.75m from Pladda (14†, 49 surv)
St Elwyn 28.11.40 Torpedoed by *U103*, sunk, 55 30N 19 30W (29†, 11 surv)
St Essylt 4.7.43 Torpedoed (in convoy KMS18B) by *U375* 36 44N 01 31E, on fire (1†, 98 surv); 5.7.43 blew up, sunk
Saint Germain 17.11.40 Torpedoed (in HG convoy) by *U137* 55 40N 08 40W (0†, 18 surv); 18.11.40 sunk 55 20N 08 50W
St Glen 6.9.40 Bombed by German aircraft, sunk, 57 25N 01 38W (3†, 40 surv)
St Helena 12.4.41 Torpedoed by *U124*, sunk, 07 50N 14W (0†, 38 surv)
St Lindsay 14.6.41 Torpedoed, probably by *U751*, sunk, 51N 30W (43†, 0 surv)
St Margaret 27.2.43 Torpedoed (ind) by *U66*, sunk, 27 38N 43 23W (3†, 1 pow, 46 surv)
St Merriel 2.1.43 Bombed by German Ju88 aircraft, on fire, Bone harbour (6†, 52 surv), resting on bottom; 9.2.43 struck by bomb, broke in two; 12.12.48 refloated, towed Bona outer port, beached Grenovillere; 4.8.50 afterpart foundered in tow 44 05 20N 08 33 50E
St Quentin 8.12.41 Captured China Seas by Japanese (Japanese charter); 42 *Taizan Maru* (Jpn); 11.11.44 bombed by USN carrier-based aircraft, sunk, 10 50N 124 35E
St Usk 20.9.43 Torpedoed by *U161*, sunk, 16 30N 29 28W (0†, 1 pow, 46 surv)
Salmonpool 3.5.40 Seized by Germans Saudafjord (34 pow, 4 repatr); prize; 40 *Putzig* (Ger); 5.45 retaken Bremerhaven; MoT *Empire Salmonpool* (Br); 47 *Irene K* (Br)
Saltwick 21.10.43 Torpedoed by German aircraft, sunk, 36 55N 01 36E (1†, 51 surv)
Salvestria 27.7.40 Struck by acoustic mine 042° 2.8m from Inchkeith LH, Firth of Forth (10†, 47 surv); sunk 56 04 06N 03 04 48W
Salvus 4.4.41 Bombed by German aircraft, broke in two, sunk, 53 05N 01 27E (4†, 39 surv)
Samala 30.9.40 Torpedoed, shelled, by *U37*, sunk, 46N 33W (67†, 0 surv)
Sambre 27.7.40 Torpedoed (in convoy OB188) by *U34*, sunk, 56 37N 17 53W (0†, 48 surv)
San Alberto 9.12.39 Torpedoed (in convoy OB48) by *U48* (1†), broke in two; forepart sank 49 28N 09 51E, afterpart reboarded, abandoned in worsening weather; 11.12.39 shelled by escort HMS *Mackay*, sunk, 49 20N 09 45W
San Alvaro 23.2.44 Torpedoed (in convoy PA69) (1†) by *U510*, on fire 13 46N 48 55E, abandoned (1†, 52 surv); sunk by escort vessel 13 46N 48 55E
San Arcadio 31.1.42 Torpedoed, shelled, by *U107*, broke in two, bow on fire, sunk, 38

10N 63 50W (41†, 9 surv)
San Calisto 2.12.39 Struck mine (laid by German destroyer), sunk, 2.5m NNE of Tongue LV (6†); sunk 51 31 09N 01 25E; wreck dispersed
San Casimiro 15.3.41 Shelled, captured 39 58N 43 19W by *Gneisenau*; 20.3.41 set on fire by prize crew, spotted by aircraft from HMS *Ark Royal*, sunk by HMS *Renown* 45 12N 19 42W after crew picked up (3 pow, 38 surv)
San Conrado 1.4.41 Bombed, machine-gunned (in convoy), by German aircraft of KG27 325° 13m from the Smalls; on fire, abandoned; taken in tow, reboarded, again bombed, abandoned; 2.4.41 still on fire 170° 12m from Tuskar Rock, sunk
San Delfino 10.4.42 Torpedoed by *U203*, sunk, 35 35N 75 06W (28†, 21 surv)
San Demetrio 17.3.42 Torpedoed by *U404*, sunk, 37 03N 73 50W (19†, 34 surv)
San Emiliano 9.8.42 Torpedoed (in convoy E7) by *U155*, on fire, 07 22N 54 08W; broke in two, sunk (40†, 8 surv)
San Ernesto 15.6.43 Torpedoed by subm *I-37* (Jpn), back broken, again torpedoed, shelled, 09 18S 80 20E (4†, 46 surv); abandoned, drifted *c*2000m, grounded, listing, on Pulau Nias Is; 6.49 wreck rediscovered 01 15N 97 15E
San Fabian 28.8.42 Torpedoed by *U511*, sunk, 18 09N 74 38W (26†, 33 surv)
San Fernando 21.6.40 Torpedoed (in convoy HX49) by *U48* 50 20N 10 24W (0†, 49 surv); 22.6.40 taken in tow, sunk
San Florentino 1.10.41 Torpedoed (in convoy ON19) by *U94*, damaged, 52 50N 34 40W; 2.10.41 torpedoed 52 42N 34 51W (22†, 34 surv); shelled by USCG cutter *Campbell*, sunk
San Gerardo 31.3.42 Torpedoed by *U71*, sunk, 36N 67W (51†, 6 surv)
San Tiburcio 4.5.40 Struck mine (laid 9.2.40 by *U9*, broke in two, sunk, 330° 4m from Tarbet Ness (0†, 40 surv)
Sandsend 18.10.40 Torpedoed by *U48*, sunk, 58 15N 21 29W (5†, 34 surv)
Santa Clara Valley 23.4.41 Bombed by German aircraft, sunk, Nauplia Bay, Greece (7†, 90 surv); 21.10.52 wreck raised; 53 BU Trieste
Saranac 25.6.40 Torpedoed, shelled (in TA convoy), by *U51*, sunk, 48 24N 15 05W (4†, 40 surv)
Sarastone 29.10.41 Bombed by German aircraft, sunk, 37 05 10N 06 48 30W (1†, 28 surv)
Sardinian Prince 16.3.41 Shelled (in convoy) by *Scharnhorst* 44N 43W, sunk (0†, 44 pow)
Sarthe 8.10.42 Torpedoed by *U68*, sunk, 34 50S 18 40E (0†, 57 surv)
Saugor 27.8.41 Torpedoed (in convoy OS4) by *U557*, sunk, 53 36N 16 40W (59†, 23 surv)
Scalaria 19.10.42 Bombed, torpedoed, by aircraft, sunk, Ras Gharib, Red Sea (11†, 37 surv)
Scholar 21.9.40 Torpedoed (in convoy HX 72) by *U100*, damaged, 55 11N 17 58W; 23.9.40 taken in tow; 24.9.40 tow abandoned 54 38N 16 40W (0†, 45 surv)
Scientist 3.5.40 Captured by aux cruiser *Atlantis*, shelled, torpedoed, sunk 20S 04 30E (2†, 48 surv)
Scoresby 17.10.40 Torpedoed (in convoy SC7) by *U48*, sunk, 59 14N 17 51W (0†)
Scottish Chief 19.11.42 Torpedoed by *U177*, sunk, 30 39S 34 41E (36†, 12 surv)
Scottish Maiden 5.11.40 Torpedoed (in convoy HX83) by *U99*, sunk, 54 36N 14 23W (16†, 28 surv)
Scottish Minstrel 16.7.40 Torpedoed (in convoy HX55) by *U61*, damaged, 56 10 12N 10 20W (9†); 17.7.40 sunk
Scottish Monarch 1.6.41 Torpedoed by *U105*, sunk, 12 58N 27 20W (1†, 48 surv)
Scottish Prince 17.3.42 Torpedoed (in convoy) by *U68*, sunk, 04 10N 08W (1†, 37 surv)
Scottish Standard 21.2.41 Attacked (convoy OB287 straggler) by German FW200 Kondor aircraft 59 09N 16 18W, damaged; torpedoed by *U96*, sunk, 59 20N 16 12W (5†, 39 surv)
Scottish Star 20.2.42 Torpedoed by subm *Luigi Torelli* (Ita), sunk, 13 24N 49 36W (4†, 69 surv)
Scottish Trader 6.12.41 Torpedoed by *U131*, sunk, S of Iceland (43†, 0 surv)
Sea Glory 7.7.40 Torpedoed by *U99*, sunk, S of Fastnet (31†, 0 surv)
Sea Venture 20.10.39 Torpedoed, shelled, by *U34*, sunk, 60 50N 00 15E
Seaforth 18.2.41 Torpedoed by *U103*, sunk, 58 48N 18 17W (59†, 0 surv)
Sedgepool 19.10.40 Torpedoed (in convoy SC7) by *U123*, sunk, 57 20N 11 22W (3†, 36 surv)
Sellinge 6.9.43 Struck mine, sank, off Hurd Bank, Malta
Selvistan 5.5.43 Torpedoed (in convoy ONS5) by *U266*, sunk, 53 10N 44 40W (6†, 40 surv)
Serbino 21.10.41 Torpedoed (in convoy SL89) by *U82*, sunk, 51 10N 19 20W (14†, 51 surv)
Severn Leigh 23.8.40 Torpedoed by *U37*, sunk, 54 31N 25 41W (33†, 10 surv)
Shaftesbury 12.7.42 Torpedoed (dispersed from convoy OS33) by *U116*, sunk, 31 42N 25 30W (0†, 1 pow, 44 surv)
Shahjehan 6.7.43 Torpedoed (in convoy MWS36) by *U453* 33 01N 21 32E; 7.7.43 taken in tow, sunk 32 55N 21 10E (1†, 438 surv)
Shahristan 29.7.41 Torpedoed (in convoy OS1) by *U371* 35 19N 23 53W (65†, 73 surv); 30.7.41 sunk
Shakespear 5.1.41 Shelled by subm *Comandante Cappellini* (Ita), sunk, 18 05N 21 11W (20†, 22 surv)
Sheaf Crest 30.11.39 Struck mine (laid by German destroyer) 51 32 30N 01 25 48E (1†); sunk 51 32 05N 01 26 02E; wreck dispersed
Sheaf Field 28.10.40 Struck mine 2m SW of Sunk LV, on fire; beached 51 58 45N 01 27 15E (0†, 26 surv); settled, TL

Sheaf Mead 27.5.40 Torpedoed by *U37*, sunk, 43 48N 12 32W (31†, 5 surv)
Sheaf Mount 24.8.42 Torpedoed (in convoy ONS122) by *U605*, sunk, 48 55N 35 10W (31†, 27 surv)
Sheaf Water 7.10.42 Torpedoed by E-boat 53 06N 01 25E, taken in tow; 8.10.42 sunk 52 48 04N 01 37 02E (0†, 29 surv)
Shekatika 18.10.40 Torpedoed (convoy SC7 straggler) by *U123*, damaged, 57 12N 11 08; torpedoed by *U100*, damaged further; torpedoed again by *U123*, sunk (0†, 36 surv)
Shetland 23.6.43 Bombed (in convoy) by German aircraft, sunk, 180° 2.5m from Cape St Vincent (4†, 30 surv)
Shillong 4.4.43 Torpedoed (in convoy HX231) by *U635* 57 10N 35 30W (66†, 7 surv); 5.4.43 sunk
Shinai 28.12.41 Scuttled Kuching; 42 refloated by Japanese, towed Singapore; 42 *Shinai Maru* (Jpn); 16.9.44 sunk by USN land-based aircraft 04 07S 122 44E
Shinkuang 6.4.42 Shelled by 3 Japanese cruisers off Puri, Bay of Bengal (3†)
Shirak 19.10.40 Torpedoed (convoy HX79 straggler) by *U47*, on fire, stopped, 57N 16 35W; torpedoed by *U48*, sunk (0†)
Shirvan 10.11.44 Torpedoed by *U300* 64 08N 22 50W (18†, 27 surv); sunk 64 29N 23 04W
Shrewsbury 12.2.41 Shelled, torpedoed (in convoy SLS64) by *Admiral Hipper*, sunk, 36 46N 20 12W (20†, 19 surv)
Shropshire 10.39 amc HMS *Salopian*; 13.5.41 torpedoed by *U98*, sunk, 56 43N 38 57W (–†, 278 surv)
Shuntien 23.12.41 Torpedoed (in convoy TA5, carrying pow) by *U559*, sunk, 32 06N 24 46E (–†)
Siamese Prince 17.2.41 Torpedoed by *U69*, sunk, 59 53N 12 13W (67†, 0 surv)
Silksworth 6.4.42 Shelled by 3 Japanese cruisers off Puri, Bay of Bengal (0†, 57 surv)
Silveray 4.2.42 Torpedoed by *U751*, sunk, 43 54N 64 16W (8†, 50 surv)
Silverbeech 28.3.43 Torpedoed (in convoy RS3) by *U172*, sunk, 25 20N 15 55W (62†, 7 surv)
Silverbelle 22.9.41 Torpedoed (in convoy SL87) by *U68*, damaged, 25 45N 24W; 29.9.41 abandoned 26 30N 23 14W, sunk
Silvercedar 15.10.41 Torpedoed (in convoy SC48) by *U553*, sunk, 53 36N 30W (21†, 26 surv)
Silverfir 16.3.41 Shelled (in convoy) by *Gneisenau*, sunk, 42N 43W (1†, 40 pow)
Silverlaurel 18.12.44 Torpedoed (in convoy BTC10) by *U486*, sunk, 50 07 45N 04 39 05W (0†, 67 surv)
Silvermaple 26.2.44 Torpedoed by *U66*, sunk, 04 44N 03 20W (7†, 57 surv)
Silverpalm 9.6.41 Torpedoed by *U101*, sunk, 51N 26W (68†, 0 surv)
Silverpine 5.12.40 Torpedoed (convoy OB252 straggler) by subm *Argo* (Ita), sunk, 54 14N 18 08W (36†, 19 surv)
Silverwillow 30.10.42 Torpedoed (in convoy SL125) by *U409* 35 08N 16 44W; 5.11.42 abandoned 34 07N 14 39W; 11.11.42 foundered 37 24N 10 45W (5†, 62 surv)
Silveryew 30.5.41 Torpedoed by *U106*, sunk, 16 42N 25 29W (3†, 57 surv)
Simnia 15.3.41 Shelled (dispersed from convoy) by *Gneisenau*, sunk, 40 28N 43 30W (3†, 54 pow)
Sinkiang 6.4.42 Bombed by Japanese aircraft, sunk, 17 32N 82 50E (–†)
Sirdhana 13.11.39 Struck mine off Singapore, 148° 3.5m from Fort Canning Lt (20†); sunk 01 14 42N 103 52 36E; wreck demolished from 6.52
Sire 31.5.41 Torpedoed by *U107*, sunk, 08 50N 15 30W (3†, 46 surv)
Sirikishna 24.2.41 From dispersed convoy OB288, shelled, torpedoed, by *U96*, sunk, 58N 21W (37†, 0 surv)
Siris 12.7.42 Torpedoed, shelled (dispersed from convoy OS33), by *U201*, sunk, 31 20N 24 48W (3†, 52 surv)
Sitala 19.10.40 Torpedoed (in convoy HX79) by *U100* 150m SW of Rockall (1†, 43 surv); 20.10.40 abandoned, broke in two, sunk
Sithonia 13.7.42 Torpedoed (dispersed from convoy OS33) by *U201*, sunk, 29N 25W (7†, 46 surv)
Slavol 26.3.42 Torpedoed (in convoy) by *U205*, sunk, 32N 25 57E (36†, 20 surv)
Sneaton 14.10.39 Torpedoed, shelled, by *U48*, sunk, 49 05N 13 05W (1†)
Somali 26.3.41 Bombed (in convoy FN442) by German He111 aircraft 55 23 30N 01 21W, on fire, abandoned; 27.3.41 magazine exploded, sunk, 1m E of Snoop Point, Sunderland (1†, 78 surv)
Somersby 13.5.41 Torpedoed (convoy SC30 straggler) by *U111*, sunk, 60 39N 26 13W (0†, 43 surv)
Somerset 11.5.41 Bombed (in convoy) by German FW200 Kondor aircraft of I/KG40, settled, broke in two, afterpart sunk, 54 54N 16 20W (0†); forepart sunk by HMS *Alisma*
Somme 18..2.42 Torpedoed by *U108*, sunk, 35 30N 61 25W (48†, 0 surv)
Soochow 11.12.41 Scuttled Taikoo Dock, Hong Kong; 25.12.41 wreck seized by Japanese; 42 raised; 42 *Tozan Maru* (Jpn); 22.3.45 struck mine, sunk, off Moji
Soudan 15.5.42 In convoy struck mine (laid by *Doggerbank*), sunk, 36 10S 20 22E (0†, 100 surv)
Sourabaya 27.10.42 Torpedoed (in convoy HX212) by *U436*, sunk, 54 32N 31 02W (77†, 81 surv)
Southern Empress 13.10.42 Torpedoed (in convoy SC104) by *U221*, sunk, 53 40N 40 40W (48†, 77 surv)
Southern Princess 17.3.43 Torpedoed (in convoy HX229) by *U600*, on fire, sunk, 50 36N 34 30W (4†, 96 surv)

Speybank 31.1.41 Captured Indian Ocean by aux cruiser *Atlantis*, prize, sent Bordaeux; KM, aux minelayer *Doggerbank* (Schiff 53); 3.3.43 torpedoed in error by *U43*, sunk, 29 10N 34 10W (–†, 1 surv)

Spirila 12.2.42 Captured Singapore by Japanese; 8.45 scuttled by them; 4.53 wreck raised, BU

Springbank 11.39 Req as aux fighter catapult vessel HMS *Springbank*; 10.40 conv completed; 25.11.40 commd; 27.9.41 attacked (escort in convoy HG73) by German FW200 Kondor aircraft 49 05N 20 10W; torpedoed by *U201*, damaged (32†); sunk by corvette HMS *Jasmine*

Stanburn 29.1.40 Bombed (ind) by German aircraft, sunk, 10m SE by E 0.5 E of Flamborough Head (25†, 3 surv)

Stancliffe 12.4.40 Torpedoed by *U37*, sunk, 45m NE of Unst Is, Shetlands (22†, 16 surv)

Stangrant 13.10.40 Torpedoed (convoy HX77 straggler) by *U37*, sunk, 58 27N 12 36W (8†, 30 surv)

Stanhall 30.5.40 Torpedoed by *U101*, sunk, 48 59N 05 17W (1†, 36 surv)

Stanholme 25.12.39 Struck mine (laid 5.11.39 by *U33*), sunk, 51 20 10N 03 39W (13†, 13 surv)

Stanlake 14.4.43 Torpedoed by E-boat, sunk, 060° 12m from Lizard Head (0†, 24 surv)

Stanleigh 14.3.41 Bombed (in convoy) by German aircraft, sunk, 288° 12m from Bar LV, R Mersey (17†, 6 surv)

Stanmore 1.10.43 Torpedoed (in convoy MKS27) by *U223* 36 41N 01 10E, damaged (0†, 49 surv); 3.10.43 towed, beached Tenes, broke in two; 44 TL

Stanmount 24.12.41 Struck mine 52 39 22N 02 00 31E; sunk 52 39 40N 02 00 40E (0†, 41 surv)

Stanpark 20.1.41 Captured by *Admiral Scheer*, sunk by bombs and torpedoes 09 27S 03W (0†, 37 pow)

Starcross 20.5.41 Torpedoed (in convoy SL73) by subm *Otaria* (Ita), damaged, 51 45N 20 45W (0†, 40 surv); sunk by escort

Start Point 10.11.42 Torpedoed by *U128*, sunk, 13 12N 27 27W (2†, 2 pow on *U128*, 43 surv)

Statesman 17.5.41 Bombed by German FW200 Kondor aircraft, sunk, 56 44N 13 45W (1†, 50 surv)

Statira 3.8.40 Bombed by German aircraft 38m N of Stornoway, on fire; towed Stornoway, fire extinguished; towed Rothesay Bay, then Glasgow; CTL, BU Troon

Stentor 27.10.42 Torpedoed (in convoy SL125) by *U509*, sunk, 29 13N 20 53W (44†, 202 surv)

Stirlingshire 2.12.40 Torpedoed (in convoy HX90) by *U94* 55 36N 16 22W (0†, 74 surv); sunk

Stonegate 5.10.39 Shelled by *Deutschland*, sunk, 31 10N 54W

Stonepool 11.9.41 Torpedoed (in convoy SC42) by *U207*, sunk, 63 05N 37 50W (42†, 7 surv)

Stornest 13.10.42 Torpedoed (in convoy ONS136) by *U706* 54 25N 27 42W in heavy weather; 14.10.42 sunk (39†, 0 surv)

Stratford 26.9.40 Torpedoed (in convoy) by *U137* 55 01N 10 02W, on fire, abandoned (2†, 32 surv); sunk 54 50N 10 40W

Strathallan 4.2.40 Req MoWT, troopship; 21.12.42 torpedoed (in convoy KMF5) by *U562* (11†, 5101 surv); 22.12.42 taken in tow, sunk 36 01 08N 00 33 03W

Streonshalh 7.12.39 Sunk by *Admiral Graf Spee* 25 01S 27 50W (0†)

Subadar 13.2.42 Bombed by Japanese aircraft, on fire, S entrance to Banka Strait; abandoned, sunk (5†, 81 surv)

Sulaco 19.10.40 Torpedoed (in convoy OB229) by *U124*, sunk, 57 25N 25W (66†, 1 surv)

Sulairia 25.9.40 Torpedoed (in convoy OB217) by *U43*, sunk, 53 43N 20 10W (1†, 56 surv)

Sultan Star 14.2.40 Torpedoed by *U48*, sunk, 48 54N 10 03W (1†)

Surada 26.1.44 Torpedoed (in convoy) by *U188*, sunk, 13N 55 15E (0†, 103 surv)

Surat 6.5.41 Torpedoed by *U103* 08 23N 15 17W (3†); sunk 08 23N 15 13W

Surrey 10.6.42 Torpedoed by *U68*, sunk, 12 45N 80 20W (12†, 61 surv)

Sutlej 26.2.44 Torpedoed by subm *I-37* (Jpn), sunk, 08S 70E (50†, 23 surv)

Swainby 17.4.40 Torpedoed by *U13*, sunk, 065° 25m from Muckle Flugga, Shetlands (0†, 38 surv)

Swedru 16.4.41 Bombed by German FW200 Kondor aircraft (24†, 37 surv), on fire, badly damaged, 55 21N 12 50W, abandoned; 19.4.41 torpedoed by HM escort, sunk, 54 44N 11 02W

Swiftpool 5.8.41 Torpedoed (in convoy SL81) by *U372*, sunk, 53 02N 15 58W (42†, 2 surv)

Swinburne 26.2.41 Bombed (in convoy OB290) by German FW200 Kondor aircraft, sunk, 54N 16 58W (0†, 44 surv)

Sylvafield 15.8.40 Torpedoed (convoy HX62 straggler) by *U51*, sunk, 56 39N 11 16W (3†, 36 surv)

Sylvia de Larrinaga 14.8.42 Torpedoed by subm *Reginaldo Giuliani* (Ita), sunk, 10 49N 33 35W (3†, 50 surv)

Tabaristan 29.5.41 Torpedoed (ind) by *U38*, sunk, 06 32N 15 23W (21†, 39 surv)

Tacoma City 13.3.41 Struck mine 104° 2.5 cables from Rock Ferry Lt, R Mersey (4†, 41 surv); broke in two; TL

Tacoma Star 1.2.42 Torpedoed by *U109*, sunk, 37 33N 69 21W (85†, 0 surv)

Tafelberg 28.1.41 Struck mine, damaged, 51 21N 03 16W; 2.43 MoWT, 43 *Empire Heritage* (Br); 8.9.44 torpedoed (in convoy HXF305) by *U482*, sunk, 55 27N 08 01W

Tafna 24.10.39 Torpedoed by *U37*, sunk, 35 44N 07 23W (2†)

Tai Sang 24.1.42 In convoy struck Allied mine, sunk, 00 55N 103 35E (34†, 2 pow, 32 surv)
Tainui 39 Retrieved from breakers yard; 40 MoWT, *Empire Trader* (Br); 21.2.43 torpedoed (in convoy ON166) by *U92* 48 25N 30 10W (0†, 106 surv); 22.2.43 abandoned, shelled by escort HMS *Dauphin*; 23.2.43 last seen 47 40N 28 46W, presumed sunk
Tairoa 3.12.39 Shelled by *Admiral Graf Spee*, sunk 20 20S 03 05E (0†)
Taiyuan 15.2.42 Transf US forces for special service; 8.3.42 attacked by Japanese surface craft, sunk, 07 11 38S 112 45 21E (3 pow)
Taksang 6.4.42 Shelled (in convoy) by Japanese aircraft carrier, sunk, 17 52N 83 40E (15†, 107 surv)
Talamba 40 Hospital ship; 10.7.43 bombed by German aircraft 36 55N 15 14E (5†, 563 surv); 11.7.43 sunk
Talthybius 3.2.42 Bombed by Japanese aircraft Singapore, on fire; 12.2.42 abandoned, scuttled; 12.42 salved by Japanese; 43 *Taruyasu Maru* (Jpn); 30.6.45 struck mine, sunk, 37 07N 137 04E; salved, repaired Hong Kong; MoT, *Empire Evenlode* (Br); 49 BU Briton Ferry
Tanda 15.7.44 Torpedoed by *U181*, sunk, 13 26N 74 14E (19†, 197 surv)
Tantalus 26.12.41 Attacked by Japanese aircraft, on fire, abandoned, sunk, off Manila (45 pow, 23 landed Manila)
Tascalusa 10.7.40 Bombed by German aircraft, sunk by stern, alongside northern arm Falmouth harbour (0†); 29.8.40 refloated; 5.9.40 beached Mylor Flats; 11.40 sold for BU
Teddington 17.9.41 Torpedoed by E-boat *S51* 53 04N 01 34E, on fire, taken in tow; 18.9.41 ashore 52 55 48N 01 22 36E, back broken, TL (0†); 7.54 wreck dispersed
Teesbank 5.12.42 Torpedoed by *U128*, sunk, 03 33N 29 35W (1†, 1 pow, 60 surv)
Teiresias 17.6.40 Bombed by German aircraft 47 07N 02 23W, listing; 18.6.40 again attacked, abandoned 1m NW of wreck buoy off entrance to St Nazaire channel; CTL (1†, 70 surv)
Telena 29.5.40 Shelled by *U37*, on fire, abandoned, 42 25N 09 08W (18†, 18 surv); aground in shallow water; 17.8.40 ar Bilbao; seized by Spain; 41 *Gerona* (Spn)
Temple Mead 21.1.41 Bombed by German FW200 Kondor aircraft, sunk, 54 14N 14 30W (14†, 26 surv)
Temple Moat 23.2.41 Torpedoed (convoy OB288 straggler) by *U95*, sunk, 59 27N 20 20W (42†, 0 surv)
Terje Viken 7.3.41 Torpedoed (in convoy OB293) by *U47* and *U99*, damaged, 60N 12 50W; capsized, sunk (0†, 102 surv)
Terlings 21.7.40 Bombed by German aircraft, sunk, 10m SW of St Catherine's Point (10†, 17 surv)
Testbank 2.12.43 Attacked by German aircraft, blew up following explosion on nearby ammunition ship, Bari (70†, 4 surv)
Tewkesbury 21.5.41 Torpedoed by *U69*, sunk, 05 49N 24 09W (0†, 42 surv)
Thiara 27.7.40 Torpedoed (in convoy OB188) by *U34*, sunk, 56 37N 17 56W (25†, 36 surv)
Thirlby 23.1.42 Torpedoed by *U109*, sunk, 43 20N 66 15W (3†, 42 surv)
Thistlebrae 9.4.40 Seized Trondheim dry dock by Germans (33 pow, 6 repatr); prize; 27.8.40 Seelöwe transport *R6N*; 1.9.40 *Altkirch, R3N* (Ger); 5.1.44 *Inster* (Ger); 3.5.45 bombed by RAF 236 Sq Beaufighter, on fire, sunk, 54 30 42N 10 22 58E (560†); 53 wreck BU
Thistlegarth 15.10.40 Torpedoed (in convoy OB227) by *U103*, sunk, 58 43N 15W (30†, 9 surv)
Thistleglen 10.9.41 Torpedoed (in convoy SC42) by *U85* 62 14N 39 29W (3†, 46 surv); sunk 61 59N 39 46W
Thistlegorm 6.10.41 Bombed by German He111 aircraft of II/KG26, sank, Anchorage F, inner channel, Strait of Jubal, Gulf of Suez (9†)
Thomas Walton 7.12.39 Torpedoed by *U38*, sunk, 67 51 48N 14 28 30E (13†)
Thorland 12.4.40 Seized Sandefjord by Germans; prize, storage vessel; 5.45 retaken Tønsberg; 46 (Nor), used as food store, Oslo
Thornlea 2.9.40 Torpedoed (dispersed from convoy OB205) by *U46*, sunk, 55 14N 16 40W (3†, 34 surv)
Thornliebank 29.11.41 Torpedoed (in convoy OS12) by *U43*, sunk, 41 50 30N 29 48W (75†, 0 surv)
Thurso 15.6.42 Torpedoed (in convoy HG84) by *U552*, sunk, 43 41N 18 02W (13†, 29 surv)
Thursobank 22.3.42 Torpedoed by *U373*, sunk, 38 05N 68 30W (30†, 34 surv)
Thurston 4.3.40 Torpedoed by *U29*, sunk, 50 23N 05 49W (34†)
Tiberton 14.2.40 Torpedoed by *U23*, sunk, E of Orkneys (34†, 0 surv)
Tielbank 8.3.41 Torpedoed (in convoy SL67) by *U124*, sunk, 20 51N 20 32W (4†, 62 surv)
Tilawa 23.11.42 Torpedoed by subm *I-29* (Jpn), damaged, 07 36N 61 08E; abandoned, again attacked, sunk, 07 35N 61 06E (280†, 678 surv)
Tinhow 11.5.43 Torpedoed by *U181*, sunk, 25 15S 33 30E (75†, 132 surv)
Titan 4.9.40 Torpedoed (in convoy OA207) by *U47*, sunk, 58 14N 15 15W (6†, 89 surv)
Torinia 21.9.40 Torpedoed (in convoy HX72) by *U100*, sunk, 54 55N 18 17W (5†, 50 surv)
Toronto City 40 Weather obs vessel; 2.7.41 torpedoed by *U108*, sunk, 47 03N 30W (0 surv)
Tottenham 17.6.41 Captured by aux cruiser *Atlantis* 07 39S 19 12W, shelled, sunk (26 pow, 17 surv)
Toussika 30.6.40 Seized Casablanca by VFr; 40 *St Hugues* (Fra); 8.11.42 scuttled Port Lyautey as blockship
Tower Field 10.5.41 Bombed by German aircraft, damaged, off Outer Dowsing buoy;

41 MoWT, repaired, *Empire Tower* (Br); 5.3.43 torpedoed (in convoy XK2) by *U130*, sunk, 43 50N 14 46W (38†, 6 surv)

Tower Grange 18.11.42 Torpedoed by *U154*, sunk, 06 20N 49 10W (6†, 41 surv)

Towneley 7.1.40 Struck mine (laid by German destroyer of 1 DD Fl), sank, 1m ENE of NE Spit Buoy, off Margate

Trafalgar 24.5.41 Sunk by aux cruiser *Atlantis* 25S 01E (12†, 32 surv)

Transylvania 8.39 Req as amc HMS *Transylvania*; 10.8.40 torpedoed by *U56* (48†, 300+ surv); taken in tow, foundered 55 50N 08 03W

Traveller 26.1.42 Torpedoed by *U106*, exploded, sunk, 39 30N 64 20W (52†, 0 surv)

Trebartha 11.11.40 Bombed by German aircraft 4m SE of Aberdeen (4†), on fire, run ashore Cove Bay, Kincardineshire, 3m S of Aberdeen, 57 06 30N 02 03 30W; 15.11.40 broke in two, abandoned, TL

Trecarrell 4.6.41 Torpedoed by *U101*, sunk, 47 10N 31 04W (4†, 39 surv)

Tredinnick 25.3.42 Torpedoed by subm *Pietro Calvi* (Ita), sunk, 27 15N 49 15W (46†, 0 surv)

Trefusis 5.3.43 Torpedoed (in convoy XK2) by *U130*, sunk, 43 50N 14 46W (3†, 44 surv)

Tregarthen 6.6.41 Torpedoed by *U48*, sunk, 46 17N 36 20W (45†, 0 surv)

Tregenna 17.9.40 Torpedoed (in convoy HX71) by *U65*, sunk, 58 22N 15 42W (33†, 4 surv)

Trehata 8.8.42 Torpedoed (in convoy SC94) by *U176*, sunk, 56 30N 32 14W (31†, 24 surv)

Trekieve 4.11.42 Torpedoed by *U178*, sunk, 25 46S 33 48E (3†, 45 surv)

Trelawny 22.2.41 Shelled (from dispersed convoy) by *Gneisenau*, sunk, 47 12N 40 13W (1†, 39 pow)

Trelissick 23.6.41 Bombed by German aircraft 114° 3.5m from Sheringham Buoy, Cromer (2†, 40 surv); sunk 53 07 01N 01 24 09E; wreck dispersed

Treminnard 2.8.42 Torpedoed by *U160*, sunk, 10 40N 57 07W (0†, 47 surv)

Tremoda 27.8.41 Torpedoed (in convoy OS4) by *U557*, badly damaged, 53 42N 15 43W; 28.8.41 last seen 54 08N 15 28W (32†, 21 surv)

Trentbank 24.11.42 Torpedoed by aircraft 10m N of Cap Tenes, Algeria (2†, 75 surv); on fire, blew up, sunk

Trentino 8.5.41 Bombed by German aircraft, sunk, dock at Liverpool; 30.5.41 refloated, BU Liverpool

Tresillian 13.6.41 Torpedoed by *U77*, sunk, 44 40N 45 30W (0†, 46 surv)

Trevalgan 30.11.42 Torpedoed by *U508*, badly damaged; 2.12.42 abandoned, sunk, 09 40N 59 15W (0†, 43 surv)

Trevanion 22.10.39 Captured by *Admiral Graf Spee*, sunk by time bombs 19 40S 04 02E

Trevarrack 8.6.41 Torpedoed (in convoy) by *U46*, sunk, 48 46N 29 14W (44†, 0 surv)

Treverbyn 21.10.41 Torpedoed (in convoy SL89) by *U82*, sunk, 51 10N 19 20W (48†, 0 surv)

Trevethoe 11.3.41 Torpedoed by E-boat *S28*, sunk, 52 46 02N 01 56 09E (1†, 39 surv)

Trevilley 12.9.42 Torpedoed, shelled, by *U68*, sunk, 04 30S 07 50W (2†, 49 surv)

Trewellard 5.11.40 Shelled (in convoy HX84) by *Admiral Scheer*, sunk, 52 26N 32 34W (16†, 25 surv)

Treworlas 28.12.42 Torpedoed by *U124*, sunk, 10 52N 60 45W (38†, 10 surv)

Triadic 8.12.40 Sunk by aux cruisers *Komet* and *Orion*, off Nauru (1†, 11 pow, 57 surv)

Triaster 8.12.40 Sunk by aux cruisers *Komet* and *Orion*, off Nauru (15 pow, 59 surv)

Tribesman 1.12.40 Shelled by *Admiral Scheer*, sunk, 15N 35W (53†, 82 pow)

Tricula 3.8.42 Torpedoed by *U108*, sunk, 11 35N 56 51W (47†, 11 surv)

Trident 1.8.41 While at anchor, bombed by German aircraft 208° 4m from 20C Buoy, R Tyne (0†, 43 surv); 2.8.41 (0140) sunk

Triona 6.12.40 Sunk by aux cruisers *Komet* and *Orion*, 220m S of Nauru (4†, 60 pow)

Troilus 31.8.44 Torpedoed by *U859*, sunk, 14 10N 61 04E (6†, 95 surv)

Troutpool 20.7.40 Struck mine 54 40N 05 40W (11†, 21 surv); sunk 3° 8 cables from Bangor Pier Lt

Tucurinca 10.3.43 Torpedoed (in convoy HX228) by *U221*, sunk, 51N 30 10W (1†, 81 surv)

Tulagi 27.3.44 Torpedoed by *U532*, sunk, 11S 78 40E (47†, 7 surv)

Tunisia 4.8.41 Bombed (in convoy SL81) by German FW200 Kondor aircraft 53 53N 18 10W (38†, 5 surv); sunk 53 53N 19 02W

Turakina 20.8.40 Shelled by aux cruiser *Orion*, on fire, torpedoed, sunk, 38 27N 167 35E (36†, 73 surv)

Turbo 20.8.41 Torpedoed by aircraft, badly damaged, 32 08N 31 57E; ar Port Said; 4.4.42 when in tow in heavy weather, broke in two 25 16N 35 25E, forepart shelled, sunk, afterpart foundered

Tuscan Star 6.9.42 Torpedoed by *U109*, sunk, 01 34N 11 39W (52†, 62 surv)

Tweed 8.4.41 Torpedoed by *U124*, sunk, 07 43N 15 11W (3†, 28 surv)

Tymeric 23.11.40 Torpedoed (in convoy OB244) by *U123*, sunk, 57N 20 30W (72†, 3 surv)

Tynefield 5.10.41 Struck mine, broke in two, Km 153.3 Suez Canal (7†, 31 surv); stern section manned to 6.6.42, CTL; 54 raised, BU Savona

Uganda 19.10.40 Torpedoed (in convoy HX79) by *U38*, sunk, 56 37N 17 15W (0†, 40 surv)

Ulea 28.10.41 Torpedoed (in convoy HG75) by *U432* 41 17N 21 40W (19†, 9 surv); sunk 41 13N 21 38W

Ullapool 13.3.41 Struck by parachute mine, broke in two, sunk, 215° 1500ft from N end of Princes Landing Stage, Liverpool (15†, 23 surv); wreck demolished

Ulysses 11.4.42 Torpedoed by *U160*, sunk, 34 23N 75 35W (0†)

Umona 30.3.41 Torpedoed by *U124*, sunk, abt 90m SW of Freetown (100†, 3 surv)

Umtata 9.3.42 Torpedoed by *U161*, damaged, Port Castries; 7.7.42 while under tow St Lucia–Port Everglades, torpedoed by *U571*, sunk, 25 35N 80 02W (0†, 90 surv)
Umvuma 7.8.43 Torpedoed by *U181*, sunk, 20 18S 57 14E (22†, 87 surv)
Uniwaleco 7.3.42 Torpedoed by *U161*, broke in two, sunk, 13 23N 62 04W (13†, 38 surv)
Upwey Grange 8.8.40 Torpedoed by *U37*, sunk, 54 20N 15 28W (36†, 50 surv)
Urla 28.1.41 Torpedoed by subm *Luigi Torelli* (Ita), sunk, 54N 19 20W (0†, 42 surv)
Uskbridge 17.10.40 Torpedoed (in conv OB228) by *U93*, sunk, 60 40N 15 50W (2†, 27 surv)
Uskmouth 25.11.39 Torpedoed, shelled, by *U43*, sunk, 43 22N 11 27W (2†)
Uskport 40 *Waldinge* (Br); 19.11.41 torpedoed by E-boat *S41* near No 55A Buoy, Smith's Knoll; 20.11.41 sunk 52 55 54N 02 01 57E (1†, 31 surv); 49 wreck demolished
Uskside 1.8.43 Bombed by aircraft, sunk, Palermo (1†, 42 surv); 46 raised, *Teseo* (Ita)

Vaclite 30.1.40 Torpedoed (in convoy OA80G) by *U55*, sunk, 49 20N 07 04W (0†, 35 surv)
Vancouver 21.9.41 Struck mine 51 51N 01 31E, on fire (39†, 3 surv); broke in two, afterpart sunk 51 51 21N 01 32 18E; 1.10.41 forepart still burning 51 51 21N 01 32E
Vancouver City 14.9.39 Torpedoed by *U28*, sunk, 51 23N 07 03W (3†)
Vandyck 6.39 Troopship; 9.39 req as abv HMS *Vandyck*; 15.1.40 commd; 6.40 shelled by *Admiral Hipper* off Harstad; 10–11.6.40 bombed by German aircraft, sunk, off Narvik (7†, 161 pow)
Venetia 16.3.41 Torpedoed (in convoy HX112) by *U99*, sunk, 61N 12 36W (0†, 40 surv)
Vernon City 28.6.43 Torpedoed by *U172*, sunk, 04 20S 27 20W (0†, 52 surv)
Viceroy of India 12.11.40 Req as troopship; 11.11.42 torpedoed by *U407* 36 26N 00 25W (4†, 450 surv); abandoned by most crew, taken in tow by destroyer HMS *Boadicea*; sank 36 24N 00 35W
Victolite 10.2.42 Torpedoed by *U564*, sunk, 36 12N 67 14W (47†, 0 surv)
Victoria City 2.12.40 Torpedoed by *U140*, sunk, W of the North Channel (43†, 0 surv)
Viking Star 25.8.42 Torpedoed by *U130*, sunk, 06N 14W (33†, 36 surv)
Vimeira 11.8.42 Shelled, torpedoed, by *U109*, sunk, 10 03N 28 55W (23†, 1 pow, 21 surv)
Vinemoor 26.7.40 Torpedoed (in convoy OB188) by *U34* 55 43N 16 25W; 27.7.40 sunk 55 25N 16 05W
Virgilia 24.11.41 Torpedoed (in convoy FS54) by E-boat *S109* 3m NE of Hearty Knoll Buoy, off Great Yarmouth, on fire (23†, 22 surv); broke in two, wreck submerged 28° 2300 yds from Hearty Knoll Buoy
Vitorlock 7.12.41 Seized by Japanese in China Seas (Japanese charter); 42 *Wazan Maru* (Jpn); 26.4.44 torpedoed by subm USS *Sargo*, sunk, 33 30N 135 27E
Voltaire 6.39 Troopship; 27.10.39 req as amc HMS *Voltaire*; 4.4.41 shelled by aux cruiser *Thor*, on fire, sunk, 14 30N 40 30W (75†, 197 surv)
Volturno 23.6.43 Bombed (in convoy) by German aircraft 1.5m WNW of Cape St Vincent; 24.6.43 sunk (3†, 43 surv)
Voreda 30.1.40 Bombed by German aircraft 52 59N 01 59E, beached Winterton Shoal (0†); 5.2.40 sank

W B Walker 29.1.41 Torpedoed (in convoy SC19) by *U93* 56N 15 23W (4†, 43 surv), back broken; 13.2.41 afterpart sunk 58 15N 07 01W; 6.2.41 forepart shelled by HM ship, sunk
W Hendrik 3.12.40 Bombed by German aircraft, sunk, 56 26N 12 20W (5†, 30 surv)
Waimarama 13.8.42 Bombed (in Opn 'Pedestal' convoy WS21S) by German Ju88 aircraft, sunk, 36 25N 12E (83†, 21 surv)
Waiotira 26.12.40 Torpedoed by *U95*, damaged, 58 05N 17 10W (1†, 89 surv); 27.12.40 torpedoed by *U38*, sunk, 58 10N 16 56W
Wairangi 13.8.42 Attacked (in Opn 'Pedestal' convoy WS21S) by E-boats *S30* and *S36* (Ger) and MTBs *MAS54* and *MAS557* (Ita), torpedoed, sunk, 36 34N 11 15E (0†, 117 surv)
Waiwera 29.6.42 Torpedoed (ind) by *U754*, sunk, 45 49N 34 29W (8†, 97 surv)
Wallsend 2.12.42 Torpedoed by *U552*, sunk, 20 08N 25 50W (4†, 1 pow, 36 surv)
Wandby 19.10.40 Torpedoed (in convoy HX79) by *U46* and *U47*, damaged; 20.10.40 abandoned 56 45N 17 07W (0†, 34 surv); 21.10.40 sunk
Wanstead 21.4.43 Torpedoed (in convoy ON178) by *U415*, sunk, 55 46N 45 14W (1†, 48 surv)
War Diwan 16.12.44 Struck mine R Schelde (5†, 37 surv), broke in two, both parts sunk – afterpart 51 25 31N 03 27 21E, forepart 51 25 45N 03 29 37E; 4.5.52 forepart refloated, taken Vlissingen
War Mehtar 19.11.41 Torpedoed by E-boat *S104* 52 50N 02 08E (0†, 45 surv); 20.11.41 sunk 52 35 45N 02 09 30E
War Sirdar 1.3.42 Aground Sunda Strait, Java; 42 salved by Japanese; 43 *Honan Maru* (Jpn); 28.3.45 torpedoed by subm USS *Bluegill*, sunk, 12 39N 109 37E
Warfield 15.8.43 Bombed by German aircraft, sunk, 39 59N 12 58W (2†, 94 surv)
Warlaby 12.2.41 Shelled (in convoy SLS64) by *Admiral Hipper*, sunk, 37 12N 21 20W (36†, 3 surv)
Waroonga 5.4.43 Torpedoed (in convoy HX231) by *U630*, badly damaged, 57 10N 35 30W (17†, 115 surv); 6.4.43 sunk
Warwick Castle 9.39 Troopship; 14.11.42 torpedoed (in convoy MKF1) by *U413*, sunk, 39 16N 13 25W (63†, 365 surv)
Wayfarer 19.8.44 Torpedoed by *U862*, sunk, 14 30S 42 20E (est) (51†, 10 surv)
Waynegate 24.2.41 Torpedoed (dispersed from convoy OB288) by *U73*, sunk, 58 50N

21 47W (0†, 44 surv)
Waziristan 2.1.42 Torpedoed (detached from convoy PQ7A) by *U134* 74 09N 19 10E (47†, 0 surv); stranded in ice, attacked by German aircraft, sunk
Weirbank 27.7.42 Torpedoed by *U66*, sunk, 11 29N 58 51W (1†, 66 surv)
Welcombe 4.4.41 Torpedoed (in convoy SC26) by *U98*, sunk, 59 07N 23 42W (15†, 26 surv)
Wellfield 4.6.41 Torpedoed by *U48*, sunk, 48 34N 31 34W (8†, 33 surv)
Wellington Star 16.6.40 Torpedoed, shelled, by *U101*, sunk, 42 39N 17 01W (0†, 69 surv)
Wellpark 28.3.42 Shelled by aux cruiser *Thor*, sunk, 25S 10W (7†, 41 pow)
Welsh Prince 7.12.41 Struck mine 110° 5 cables from No 59 Buoy, off Spurn Head, abandoned; aground 53 23 40N 00 58 55E, broke in two (0†, 47 surv)
Wendover 16.7.40 Shelled by aux cruiser *Thor*, on fire, sunk, 23S 35W (4†, 37 pow)
Wentworth 5.5.43 Torpedoed (convoy ONS5 straggler) by *U358*, damaged, 53 59N 43 55W (5†, 42 surv); shelled by *U628*, sunk
West Wales 29.1.41 Torpedoed (convoy SC19 straggler) by *U94*, sunk, 56 05N 15 35W (16†, 21 surv)
Westbury 12.2.41 Shelled (in convoy SLS64) by *Admiral Hipper*, sunk, 37 10N 21 20W (5†, 33 surv)
Western Head 28.5.42 Torpedoed by *U107*, sunk, 19 57N 74 18W (24†, 6 surv)
Western Prince 14.12.40 Torpedoed by *U96*, sunk, 59 32N 17 47W (16†, 154 surv)
Westmoreland 1.6.42 Torpedoed, shelled, by *U566*, sunk, 35 55N 63 35W (3†, 65 surv)
Westpool 3.4.41 Torpedoed (in convoy SC26) by *U73*, sunk, 58 12N 27 40W (35†, 8 surv)
White Crest 24.2.42 Torpedoed (in convoy ON67, but lost contact 19.2.42 in heavy weather) by *U558*, sunk, 43 45N 42 15W (41†, 0 surv)
Whitford Point 20.10.40 Torpedoed (in convoy HX79) by *U47*, sunk, 56 38N 16W (37†, 2 surv)
Widestone 17.11.42 Torpedoed (in convoy ONS144) by *U184*, sunk, 54 30N 37 10W (42†, 0 surv)
Willamette Valley 9.39 Adm, decoy ship HMS *Willamette Valley* (RFA *Edgehill*); 29.6.40 torpedoed by *U51*; sunk 49 27N 15 25W
Willesden 1.4.42 Sunk by aux cruiser *Thor* 16 00S 16 00W (est) (5†, 42 pow)
William Wilberforce 9.1.43 Torpedoed by *U511*, sunk, 29 20N 26 53W (3†, 60 surv)
Willowbank 12.6.40 Torpedoed by *U46*, sunk, 44 16N 13 54W (0†, 51 surv)
Willowpool 10.12.39 Struck mine (laid 21.11.39 by *U20*) 3m E of Newarp LV; sunk 52 52 48N 01 51 12E
Winamac 31.8.42 Torpedoed by *U66*, sunk, 10 36N 54 34W (30†, 15 surv)
Windsor Castle 39 Troopship; 23.3.43 torpedoed (in convoy) by German aircraft 37 27N 00 54E (1†, 2988 surv); sunk 37 28N 01 10E
Windsorwood 25.6.40 Torpedoed (in convoy) by *U51*, sunk, 48 31N 14 50W (0†, 40 surv)
Winkfield 19.5.41 Struck mine 51 34 42N 01 09 56E (10†, 84 surv); sunk 51 34 02N 01 09 03E; wreck dispersed
Winkleigh 8.9.39 Torpedoed by *U48*, sunk, 48 06N 18 12W (0†)
Woodbury 17.7.40 Torpedoed by *U99*, sunk, 50 46N 13 56W (0†, 35 surv)
Wray Castle 3.5.41 Torpedoed by *U103*, sunk, 06 48N 13 55W (1†, 43 surv)
Wrotham 28.7.41 Torpedoed (in convoy OG69) by *U561*, sunk, 43N 17W (0†, 26 surv)
Wuchang 23.2.42 Sd Tjilatjap for Colombo; missing, presumed lost by war causes

Yarraville 21.6.40 Torpedoed (in French convoy 65X) by *U43*, on fire, sunk, 39 40N 11 34W (5†)
Yoma 17.6.43 Torpedoed (in convoy GTX2) by *U81*, sunk, 33 03N 22 04E (484†, 1361 surv)
Yorkmoor 28.5.42 Shelled by *U506*, sunk, 29 54 30N 72 25 30W (–†)
Yorkshire 17.10.39 Torpedoed (in convoy HG3) by *U46*, damaged, 44 52N 14 31W (58†, 220 surv); torpedoed by *U37*, sunk
Yorkwood 8.1.43 Torpedoed by *U507*, sunk, 04 10S 35 30W (1†, 1 pow, 46 surv)
Yu Sang 14.3.42 Taken over by USN; 9.4.42 bombed by Japanese aircraft, blew up, Mariveles harbour, Philippines (–†)

Zarian 28.12.42 Torpedoed (convoy ONS154 straggler) by *U406*, damaged, 43 23N 27 14W (4†, 49 surv); 29.12.42 torpedoed by *U591*, sunk
Zealand 28.6.42 Torpedoed by *U97*, sunk, 32 27N 34 43E (14†, 15 surv)
Zealandia 6.40 Troopship; 19.2.42 bombed by Japanese aircraft Port Darwin; on fire, blew up (3†)
Zealandic 17.1.41 Torpedoed by *U106*, sunk, 58 28 20N 20 43W (73†, 0 surv)
Zouave 17.3.43 Torpedoed (in convoy SC122) by *U305*, sunk, 52 25N 30 15W (13†, 30 surv)
Zurichmoor 24.5.42 Torpedoed by *U432*, sunk, 39 30N 66W (45†, 0 surv)

Losses through Spanish Civil War causes 1939
African Mariner 1.39 Abandoned Barcelona in damaged condition; taken over by Spain; 39 *Castillo Montjuich* (Spn)
Miocene 24.1.39 Attacked by insurgent aircraft, on fire, sunk, off Barcelona

Scuttled for war purposes
Atlantic Guide 9.39 Adm; 27.5.40 sunk as blockship Zeebrugge
Cape Ortegal 39 Sold breakers at Blyth ... but sold Adm, sunk as blockship, part of No

2 Barrier, Skerry Sound, Scapa Flow, 58 53N 02 53 48W; rolled over in gale, broke up
Emerald Wings 40 Adm; 5.7.40 ar Scapa Flow; sunk as blockship, part of Churchill Barrier, Skerry Sound, Scapa Flow
Florentino 22.9.39 Adm; 25.5.40 sunk as blockship Zeebrugge
Gambhira 39 Sold breakers at Blyth; but ... 5.11.39 Adm; 10.11.42 sunk as blockship, part of Churchill Barrier, Scapa Flow, 58 53 45N 02 54W; 43 raised, used as subm training target, sunk off Llandudno, North Wales
Inverlane 14.12.39 Struck mine 55 05N 01 07W; beached near Whitburn Steel, broke in two; forepart refloated, later beached Longhope; 20.5.44 refloated; 6.44 sunk as blockship Burra Sound, Orkney, 58 55 33N 03 18 41W
Lake Neuchatel 39 Adm; 10.39 sunk as blockship, part of No 1 Barrier, Kirk Sound, Scapa Flow; 6.48 raised, BU
Lycia 2.1.40 MoS; 20.10.40 Adm; 1.41 sunk as blockship, part of No 2 Barrier, Skerry Sound, Scapa Flow, 58 53 03N 02 53 57W
Martis 40 Adm; 6.40 sunk as blockship, part of No 3 Barrier, East Weddel Sound, Scapa Flow, 58 53 15N 02 54 49W
Minnie de Larrinaga 7–9.9.40 Bombed by aircraft, on fire, burnt out, in dock London; CTL; 41 Adm; 5.2.41 sunk as blockship Dover
Redstone 40 Adm; 2.5.40 sunk as blockship, part of No 1 Churchill Barrier, Kirk Sound, Scapa Flow, 58 54 35N 02 53 50W; 9.48 raised, BU Cairnryan
River Tyne 40 Adm; 10.6.40 sunk as blockship Dieppe
Transeas 1.40 Adm; 25.5.40 sunk as blockship Zeebrugge
Umvoti 40 Adm; 29.7.40 sunk as blockship Dover; 43 wreck removed, BU Folkestone
War Sepoy 19.7.40 Bombed by German aircraft, badly damaged, Dover; 21.7.40 back broken, CTL; 7.9.40 sunk as blockship Dover harbour western entrance; 64 wreck dispersed

Sunk Mulberry Harbour, Normandy
Alynbank 12.10.39 Adm, aux AA ship; 4.40 commd; 30.10.41 MoWT; 44 Adm; 9.6.44 sunk as breakwater Gooseberry 3, Gold Beach, Arromanches; 12.45 raised, BU Troon
Becheville 44 MoWT; 8.2.44 Adm; 9.6.44 sunk as breakwater Gooseberry 5, Sword Beach, Ouistreham
Bendoran 44 MoWT; 28.3.44 Adm; 9.6.44 sunk as breakwater Gooseberry 4, Juno Beach, Courseulles; 5.47 refloated, BU Blyth
Bosworth 10.7.44 Adm; 4.9.44 sunk as breakwater storm replacement; 5.49 raised, BU Dalmuir
Dover Hill 4.4.43 Bombed by German aircraft, damaged, Mishukov anchorage, Kola Inlet (from convoy JW53); 2.44 MoWT; 44 Adm; 9.6.44 sunk as breakwater Gooseberry 5, Sword Beach, Ouistreham
Elswick Park 10.2.44 Adm; 9.6.44 sunk as breakwater Gooseberry 3, Gold Beach, Arromanches; 47 raised, BU
Flowergate 41 Sold (Br); 7.2.44 Adm; 9.6.44 sunk as breakwater Gooseberry 3, Gold Beach, Arromanches; 46 refloated; 7.7.46 beached Mumbles; 46–47 BU Briton Ferry
Innerton 44. MoWT; 16.4.44 Adm; 9.6.44 sunk as breakwater Gooseberry 3, Gold Beach, Arromanches; salved, BU
Manchester Spinner 44 MoWT; 25.3.44 Adm; 9.6.44 sunk as breakwater Gooseberry 4, Juno Beach, Courseulles
Mariposa 44 MoWT; 27.3.44 Adm; 9.6.44 sunk as breakwater Gooseberry 4, Juno Beach, Courseulles
Panos 6.44 Sunk as breakwater Gooseberry 4, Juno Beach, Courseulles
Saltersgate 44 MoWT (Br); 11.2.44 Adm; 9.6.44 sunk as breakwater Gooseberry 3, Gold Beach, Arromanches; raised, BU
Stanwell 29.6.44 MoWT; 16.7.44 sunk as breakwater storm replacement, Arromanches; 46 raised; 47 BU
Vera Radcliffe 30.3.44 Adm; 30.6.44 sunk as breakwater Gooseberry 4, Juno Beach, Courseulles

Sunk postwar with surplus war materials
Botlea 15.9.39 Q-ship HMS Botlea (RFA *Lambridge*); 16.9.39 commd; 2.41 amc; 1.10.41 MoWT; 30.12.45 scuttled 55 30N 11W with poison gas shells
Clan Matheson 48 *Harmodius* (Br); 51 *Claire T* (Br); 55 *Empire Claire* (Br); 27.9.55 scuttled 56 30N 12W with surplus war materials
Egba 9.8.43 MoWT, *Empire Severn* (Br); 12.10.46 scuttled 58 18 30N 09 37E with poison gas shells
Gemlock 2.3.39 Aground 38 56N 121 07E, arranged TL; 29.7.39 refloated, towed Shanghai, repurchased, repaired; 45 damaged Mediterranean; 45 MoWT; 11.7.46 scuttled 31 44N 30 25E with defective surplus ammunition
Ixia 42 *Empire Success* (Br); 22.8.48 scuttled in Bay of Biscay
Leighton 28.8.46 Sold Glasgow breakers; but ... 9.8.47 scuttled 56 22N 09 27W with poison gas shells
Manitowoc 26.1.39 At Marseilles with damage sustained during Spanish hostilities; 11.1.40 on fire R Tyne; 40 MoWT, stores hulk; 5.9.47 scuttled N Atlantic with poison gas shells
Oligarch 14.4.46 Scuttled Red Sea, 27 30N 34 45E, with poison gas shells
Pengreep 25.6.40 Detained Casablanca by VFr; 40 *Ste Jacqueline* (Fra); 11.42 scuttled

Port Lyautey, Morocco; 1.43 refloated by Allies; 43 *Pengreep* (Br); 43 MoWT (Br); 43 *Empire Fal* (Br); 2.7.45 scuttled 58N 11W with chemical bombs loaded in Italy
Pentridge Hill 30.12.45 Scuttled 55 30N 11W with poison gas shells and surplus ammunition
Thorpebay 1.39 At Barcelona, damaged by aircraft attack during Spanish Civil War; 23.1.39 more such damage, taken Marseilles, then R Tyne; 11.1.40 on fire R Tyne; 40 MoWT; 40–41 storage hulk, Scapa Flow; 8.9.47 scuttled 47 47 03N 08 21W with poison gas shells
Wairuna 40 MoWT, store ship; 12.8.45 badly damaged by fire Greenock; 30.10.45 scuttled 55 30N 11W with 8342 tons phosgene gas bombs, gas shells, and explosives

Lost postwar through striking mine
Suiyang 27.3.46 Struck mine in Chao Phraya R, 4m above Paknam, beached; TL

Changes of name, flag, role, disposals, etc
Aba 9.9.39 RN, Hospital Ship No 34; 7.1.47 decomm, returned; 1.5.47 sold, *Matrona* (Br); 31.10.47 CTL; 48 BU Barrow
Acavus 43–45 MAC
Achilles 8.40 Adm, destroyer depot ship HMS *Blenheim*; 48 BU Barrow
Adula 43–45 MAC
Agamemnon 40 Aux minelayer HMS *Agamemnon*; 10.40 commd; 44–46 harbour service; 46 returned
Akbar 40 Troopship; 45 returned
Alaunia 25.8.39 Req as amc HMS *Alaunia*; 8.2.44 sold Adm; 9.45 completed conv to repair ship
Alca 2.40–45 RN, aux minelayer HMS *Alca*; 45 returned
Alcantara 25.9.39 Req as amc HMS *Alcantara*; 29.6.43 returned; 7.43 MoWT troopship
Alex 43 Sold; 45 *Noemi* (Br)
Alice Moller 46 *Ling Yung* (Chn)
Almanzora 39–40 Adm, accom ship; 40–45 troopship
Amarapoora 9.39 Hospital ship; 46 MoT, various uses
Amra 12.40 Hospital Ship No 41; 45 returned
Andes 9.39–45 Troopship; 46 returned; 1.48 commercial service
Anglo Indian 43 Sold (Br); 48 *Tacoma City* (Br)
Anglo Norse 7.41 MoWT, *Empire Norse* (Br); 6.46 *Anglo Norse* (Br)
Antenor 13.9.39 Req as amc HMS *Antenor*; 31.10.41 returned; 42 troopship
Antonia 9.39 Hired by Adm as repair ship; 24.3.42 sold Adm, *Wayland*; 48 BU Troon
Aorangi 9.40 Troopship; 7.44–46 accom ship; 4.46 returned
Aquitania 21.11.39 Req as troopship; 3.48 returned
Arawa 27.8.39 Req as amc HMS *Arawa*; 25.7.41 returned; 41–45 troopship and pow repatriation; 45 returned
Argyll 5.7.40 Seized Dakar by VFr; 41 *St Henri* (Fra); 43 recaptured; *Argyll* (Br)
Ariguani 41–43 CAM; 10.43 RN, obv HMS *Ariguani*; 43 MoWT; 46 returned
Aronda 41 Troopship; 45 returned
Arundel Castle 39 Troopship; 47 emigrant ship; 6.49 returned
Ascania 4.9.39 amc HMS *Ascania*; 29.10.42 returned; 42 troopship; 43 LSI(L); 12.47 returned
Ascanius 40 Troopship; 45 emigrant ship; 45 returned
Ashridge 13.3.42 Req by MoWT; 24.9.44 military stores carrier; 9.4.46 ammunition hulk; 46 MoT (Br); 11.46 (Pan); 48 BU Calcutta
Asiatic 43 MoWT, *Empire Torridge* (Br); 46 *Huntress* (Br)
Asturias 28.8.39 Req as amc HMS *Asturias*; 25.7.43 torpedoed by subm *Ammiraglio Cagni* (Ita), abandoned; LU; 30.5.44 MoWT
Athelviscount 21.3.42 Torpedoed by *U202*, damaged, 38 46N 55 44W; 42 MoWT, repaired, *Empire Viscount* (Br); 46 *Athelviscount* (Br)
Athlone Castle 40 Troopship; 46 returned
Atlantis 9.39–46 Hospital ship No 33; 44–46 hospital and repatriation ship
Atreus 11.39–45 RN, aux minelayer HMS *Atreus*; 45 returned
Aurania 30.8.39 Req Adm, amc HMS *Aurania*; 20.10.41 comm conv to repair ship; 1.12.42 *Artifex*
Ausonia 2.9.39 Req as amc HMS *Ausonia*; 27.3.42–44 conv to repair ship

Badjestan 46 *Ferriby* (Br)
Barpeta 40–41 Adm, store carrier; 10.42–8.45 landing ship; 45 returned
Bengloe 46 *Bethlehem* (Pal)
Blairspey 18–19.10.40 Torpedoed (in convoy SC7) by *U100* and *U101* ENE of Rockall, badly damaged; 42 MoWT, rebuilt, *Empire Spey* (Br); 46 *Blairspey* (Br)
Briarwood 45 *Gardenia* (Br)
Britannic 29.8.39 Req as troopship; 9.39 commd; 46 repatriation ship; 3.47 returned
British Diplomat 41 MoWT, *Empire Diplomat* (Br); 46 BU Dunston
Bulolo 22.9.39 Req as amc HMS *Bulolo*; 1.40 commd; 25.3.42 HQ ship; 4.12.46 returned
Burma 40 Troopship; 45 returned

Cairo City 40 MoWT; 6.3.40–45 RN – 3.40–2.41 guard ship, Port Tewfik; 2.41–12.45 personnel ship; 9.1.46 LU R Blackwater; 27.9.49 ar Blyth for BU

Cameronia 12.40 Troopship; 8.45 returned, LU
Canton 19.10.39 Req as amc HMS *Canton*; 10.4.44 MoWT, troopship; 28.9.47 returned
Cape Sable 19.9.39 Req as Q-ship HMS *Cape Sable* (RFA *Cyprus*); 3.41 commd; 41 amc; 11.3.42 MoWT; 29.4.46 returned
Cape St Francis 11.2.42–22.1.44 Government service; 44 coal hulk Trincomalee; 22.11.46 LU; 47–48 BU Bombay
Capetown Castle 40 Troopship; 46 returned
Carlo 14.9.39 Adm, ammunition hulk; 51 BU
Carnarvon Castle 8.9.39–11.43 amc HMS *Carnarvon Castle*; 29.11.43 returned; 1.44 MoWT, troopship; 3.47 returned
Carthage 7.9.39–10.43 amc HMS *Carthage*; 30.12.43 returned; 43 MoWT, troopship; 48 commercial service
Cathcart 10.46 *Tung Hai* (Chn)
Cavelier 11.46 *Nan Hai* (Chn)
Cavina 6.8.40 Req as obv HMS *Cavina*; 15.10.40 commd; 9.4.42 returned; 4.42–46 MoWT/MoT charter; 46 returned
Cemenco 40 *Bruce M* (Br)
Changte 27.8.39–43 RN store carrier; 43 returned
Charlton Hall 44 Sold (Br); 46 *St Elwyn* (Br)
Cheshire 29.8.39 Req as amc HMS *Cheshire*; 9.6.43 returned; 7.43 MoWT, troopship; 45 repatriation ship; 5.10.48 returned
Chitral 8.39 Adm; 10.39 amc HMS *Chitral*; 43 troopship; 48 commercial service
Christine Marie 47 *Costa Rica* (Pan)
Cilicia 31.8.39 Rq as amc HMS *Cilicia*; 15.10.39 commd; 16.2.44 returned; 3.44 MoWT, troopship; 16.12.44 commenced trooping; 46 returned
Circassia 14.10.39 Req as amc HMS *Circassia*; 5.3.42 returned; 3.42 MoWT, troopship; 43–45 LSI(L); 47 returned
City of Canterbury 40 Troopship; 46 returned
City of Durban 9.39 Decoy ship HMS *City of Durban* (RFA *Brutus*); 3.41–42 amc HMS *City of Durban*; 1.4.42 returned
City of Edinburgh 9.43 LSH HMS *Lothian*; 4.46 *City of Edinburgh* (Br)
City of London 11.39 Troopship; 1.46 returned; 46 BU Dalmuir
City of Paris 40 Troopship; 44 for conv to personnel ship; 9.45 accom ship; 46 troopship; 46 returned
City of Rangoon 25.1045 MoWT; 15.11.45 coal hulk Singapore; 47 *Oscar III* (Br)
Clan Brodie 10.40 Completed for Adm as a/c transport HMS *Athene*; 46 *Clan Brodie* (Br)
Clan Buchanan 22.11.41 Delivered Adm as a/c transport HMS *Engadine*; 6.7.45 to MoWT; 46 *Clan Buchanan* (Br)
Clan Colqhoun 47 *Ioannis Livanos* (Pan)
Clan Lamont 3.43 Troop transport; 43 Adm; 4.44 LSI HMS *Lamont*; 8.8.45–10.45 accom ship *Ardpatrick*; 46 troop transport; 2.48 returned, *Clan Lamont* (Br)
Clan Macbean 47 *Korthion* (Gre)
Clan Macinnes 47 *San George* (Br)
Clan Ranald 47 *Valletta City* (Br)
Clumberhall 6.46 *Ormos* (Br)
Corfu 14.9.39 Req as amc HMS *Corfu*; 25.11.39 commd; 17.2.44 MoWT, troopship; 31.7.47 returned; 2.49 commercial service
Corinthian 9.40 Req as obv HMS *Corinthian*; 16.11.40 commd; 12.8.43–10.44 conv to CW training; 45 returned
Corlock 4.42–5.45 *Adana* (Tur); 45 *Corlock* (Br); 47 *Nan Shan* (Chn)
Coronda 15.10.45 LU Firth of Clyde; 46 BU Ghent

Dalesman 14.5.41 Bombed by enemy aircraft, beached Suda Bay, Crete; 31.5.41 seized by Germans; 41 refloated; 42 *Pluto* (Ger); 45 MoWT *Empire Wily* (Br); 46 *Dalesman* (Br)
Derbyshire 14.10.39 Req as amc HMS *Derbyshire*; 19.2.42 returned; 2.42 MoWT, troopship; 43–45 LSI(L); 45 troopship; 11.46 returned
Desmoulea 31.1.41 Torpedoed by destroyer or E-boat 35 31N 02 34E; towed Crete, then Suez, where damaged in aircraft attack; towed Bombay; 42 MoWT, *Empire Thane* (Br); 11.43–1.47 storage hulk, Cochin; 47 *Desmoulea* (Br)
Dominion Monarch 8.40 Troopship; 46 returned; 12.48 commercial service
Dorsetshire 9.39 Hospital Ship No 23; 8.3.48 returned
Duchess of Bedford 29.8.39 Troopship; 47 returned; 48 *Empress of France* (Br)
Duchess of Richmond 14.2.40 Troopship; 46 returned; 47 *Empress of Canada* (Br)
Dunluce Castle 39 Sold for BU; 39 sold Adm, accom ship; 45 BU Inverkeithing
Dunnottar Castle 30.8.39 Req as amc HMS *Dunnottar Castle*; 27.7.42 returned; 42–3.48 MoWT/MoT, troopship; 3.48 returned
Duntroon 10.42 Troopship; 4.46 returned; 7.46 Adm charter; 3.49 returned
Durban Castle 9.39 Troopship; 42 LSI; 46 returned

E Sang 25.12.41 Scuttled Hong Kong to prevent capture by Japanese; salved
Eastern Prince 41 Troopship
Edinburgh Castle 8.39 Sold British govt; 1.40 Adm, accom/base ship, Freetown; 25.9.45 towed 60m to sea, shelled, sunk, by HM armed trawler *Cape Warwick* and

corvettes HMS *Portchester Castle* and HMS *Launceston Castle*
Egorlock 26.8.40–21.8.46 Req MoWT/MoT; 46 sold (Br); 47 *Inchona* (Br)
Egra 4.41 Troopship; 45 returned
Ekma 42 Troopship; 46 returned
Elizabeth Moller 44 MoWT charter; 47 BU India
Ellenga 41 Troopship; 45 returned
Empress of Australia 9.39–52 Troopship
Empress of Japan 11.39 Troopship; 16.10.42 *Empress of Scotland* (Br); 5.48 returned
Erica Moller 46 *Chong Lee* (Chn)
Erin 30.9.40 Adm; 1.41 obv HMS *Maplin*; then fighter catapult ship; 12.12.42 returned, *Erin* (Br)
Esperance Bay 13.9.39 Hired by Adm; 23.11.39 commd as amc HMS *Esperance Bay*; 12.11.41 returned; 11.41–45 troopship; 45 returned
Esturia 47 *Rina Corrado* (Ita)
Ethiopia 12.40 Troopship; 46 returned

Fairwater 45 *Sherborne* (Br)
Flaminian 44 MoWT, *Empire Flaminian* (Br); 47 sold, training ship; 50 BU Dover
Framlington Court 45 *Stancourt* (Br)
Frances Dawson 8.3.41 On fire Halifax, CTL; 41 MoWT, *Empire Tyne* (Br); 47 *Inchcrag* (Br)
Franconia 9.39 Troopship; 3.46 repatriation ship; 8.48 returned

Gambian 5.7.40 Seized Dakar by VFr; 41 *St Gabriel* (Fra); 43 *Gambian* (Br); 43 MoWT, *Empire Tweed* (Br); 46 *Gambian* (Br)
Georgic 11.3.40 Troopship; 14.7.44 bombed, on fire, CTL; 44 MoWT, troopship
Glenearn 15.10.39 Adm; 22.10.39–6.5.40 conv fleet supply ship; 2.7.40 comm conv to infantry assault ship; 13.12.40 commd; 18.7.46 decomm; 12.47 returned owner's regular service
Glengarry 5.40 Captured Copenhagen by Germans; KM, *Meersburg* (Ger); 42 KM aux cruiser *Hansa* (Ger); training ship; 4.5.45 recovered Kiel, *Empire Humber* (Br); 46 *Glengarry* (Br)
Glengyle 10.39 Adm; 19.10.39–6.4.40 conv fleet supply ship; 27.6.40–9.40 conv infantry assault ship; 10.9.40 commd; 6.44–4.45 conv LSI(L); 3.48 returned owner's regular service
Glenroy 39 Adm; 23.10.39–30.4.40 conv to fleet supply ship; 10.6.40–24.11.40 conv to infantry assault ship; 15.10.43–21.2.44 conv to LSI(L); 21.6.46 decomm; 27.5.48 returned owner's regular service
Greystoke Castle 43 Sold (Br); 46 *Freetown* (Br)
Gurna 40 Adm, aux mine carrier; 45 returned

Haitan 9.2.41 MoWT; 8.11.41–7.1.46 RN, depot ship Rangoon/Trincomalee; 8.6.46 LU, returned
Harpenden 11.9.40 Torpedoed by *U28*, damaged; 41 MoWT, *Empire Stour* (Br); 46 *Bharatjal* (Ind)
Haughton Hall 40 *Stanpark* (Br)
Helga Moller 47 *Lan Chow* (Chn)
Highland Brigade, *Highland Chieftain* 40 Troopship; 46 returned
Highland Monarch, *Highland Princess* 39 Troopship; 46 returned
Hilary 16.10.40–26.7.42 obv HMS *Hilary* (25.1.41 commd; 15.4.42 decomm); 7.42 returned; 3.43–3.46 landing ship; 3.46 returned
Hilda Moller 47 *Tang Shan* (Chn)
Hopemount 45 *Kelletia* (Br)

Ingola 40 *Tenax* (Br); 47 *Kwok Sing* (Chn)
Inkosi 9.9.40 Sunk during air raid London docks, salved; 41 MoWT, *Empire Chivalry* (Br); 46 *Planter* (Br)
Isabel Moller 43 *Trabzon* (Tur); 46 *Tripoli* (Leb)
Islami 40 Troopship

Jeannette Skinner 8.44 MoWT; 12.44 WSA (US); 45 BU Baltimore

Kanimbla 27.8.39 Req Adm; 10.39 commd amc HMS *Kanimbla*; 41 RAN; 31.5.43 decomm to conv to LSI(L); 43 LSI(L); 6.43 commd HMAS *Kanimbla*; 49 returned
Karoa 9.39 Troopship; 40 Hospital Ship No 60; 46 returned
Katie Moller 43 *Odemis* (Tur); 46 *Beyrouth* (Egy)
Katoomba 2.42 Troopship; 2.46 returned
Kenya 40 Adm, HMS *Hydra*; 23.7.41 landing ship; 10.41 *Keren*; 3.4.46 sold Adm; 46 MoT; 46 sold
Kiungchow 7.42 Adm, fuel transporter; 28.11.42 on fire while loading Tobruk, scuttled, sold; salved, later returned to commercial service
Kutsang 40 Troopship

Lady Nelson 10.39 Hired by RCN, abv (conv not completed); 5.43 commd as hospital ship; 46 decomm; 46 transport; 10.46 returned

Lady Rodney 6.42–11.45 Troopship; 45–46 transport duties; 46 returned
Langleebrook 41 Sold (Br); 46 *Akenside* (Br)
Laomedon 8.39–4.46 Adm, boom carrier; 4.46 returned
Largs Bay 41 Troopship; 47 returned
Laristan 15.1.42 Aground Tiree, refloated, CTL; 7.1.43 MoWT, *Empire Gulf* (Br); 7.46 *Laristan* (Br)
Letitia 9.9.39 Req Adm; 39 amc HMS *Letitia*; 7.6.41 returned; 6.41 MoWT troopship
Llandovery Castle 9.40–3.41 Conv to Hospital Ship No 39; 5.41 commd; 9.46 returned
Llangibby Castle 7.40 Troopship; 43 LSI; 45 troopship; 1.47 returned
Llanstephan Castle 44 Troopship; 45 LSI; 46 returned

Maloja 11.9.39–11.41 amc HMS *Maloja*; 6.11.41 returned; 11.41 MoWT troopship; 15.1.47 returned
Manchester City 39–45 Adm, ML base ship; 45 returned
Mandalay 45 BU
Manela 10.39 Flying-boat mother ship; 45 troopship; 45 mother ship; 46 returned; 46 BU
Manoora 14.10.39 RAN, amc HMAS *Manoora*; 30.9.42 decomm; 42–2.43 conv to LSI(L); 9.45–11.47 troop repatriation; 31.8.49 returned
Mantola 40–45 Troopship; 45 returned
Mariston 41 *English Monarch* (Br); 47 *Jalabala* (Ind)
Marklyn 42 MoWT, *Empire Usk* (Br); 46 *Heminge* (Br)
Marsdale 18.8.40–14.6.41 Adm, obv HMS *Marsdale* (16.10.40 commd); 6.41 returned
Mataroa 11.40 Conv to troopship; 47 returned
Maunganui 1.41–8.46 Hospital ship; 8.46 returned, LU Wellington; 47 *Cyrenia* (Pan)
Mauretania 6.3.40 Troopship; 8.46 returned
Menestheus 14.12.39 Aux minelayer HMS *Menestheus*; 42 RAN, HMAS *Mercedes*; 2.45 recreation vessel; 8.46 returned
Miralda 43–45 MAC
Monarch of Bermuda 11.39–46 Troopship; 1.47 returned
Monowai 23.10.39 Hired by Adm; 8.40 commd amc HMNZS *Monowai*; 18.6.43 returned; 6.43–2.44 conv to LSI; 44–9.46 troopship; 46–12.48 refit; 1.49 resumed service
Montcalm 25.8.39 Req as amc HMS *Wolfe*; 11.41 troopship; 1.42 sold Adm; 5.42 subm depot ship
Montclare 28.8.39 Req as amc HMS *Montclare*; 2.6.42 sold Adm, subm depot ship
Mooltan 9.9.39–20.1.41 amc HMS *Mooltan*; 20.1.41 returned; 41 MoWT troopship; 16.7.47 returned
Moreton Bay 27.8.39 amc HMS *Moreton Bay*; 20.8.41 returned; 9.41 MoWT troopship; 45 returned
Mourino 14.9.39 Sold Adm, ammunition hulk

Nela 45–46 BU Ghent
New Northland 40 Troopship; 40 MoWT (Br); 46 sold
Nils Moller 46 *Tien Loong* (Chn)
Noemijulia 40 (Pan); 17.6.41 *Irish Hazel* (Eir); 17.11.43 MoWT, *Empire Don* (Br); 5.9.45 *Irish Hazel* (Br)
North Star 11.3.40 Sold RCN, amc HMCS *Prince Henry*; 30.5.43 decomm; 44 LSI(M); 46 *Empire Parkeston* (Br)
Northumberland 40 Troopship; 42 returned

Oakfield 25.11.40 MoWT; 27.11.46 sold (Br)
Oilreliance 45 *Kellia* (Br)
Olwen 47 *Mushtari* (Br)
Olynthus 6.46 Sold
Orbita 41–45 Troopship; 46 emigrant service
Orduña 41–45 Troopship; 45–50 government trooping
Orion 9.39 Troopship; 46 returned
Ormiston 5.43 Conv to troopship; 2.44–8.7.46 troopship; 7.46 returned
Ormonde 39 Troopship; 46 returned
Orontes 40 Troopship; 47 returned
Otranto 39 Troopship; 11.42 assault ship; 46 returned
Oxfordshire 9.39 Hospital Ship No 6; 46–49 hospital, emigrant service, trooping

Pakeha 9.39 Sold Adm, conv to dummy battleship HMS *Revenge*; 6.41 MoWT, reconverted, *Empire Pakeha* (Br); 46 *Pakeha* (Br)
Palomares 8.40 Req Adm; 40 obv HMS *Palomares*; 12.42 conv fighter direction ship; 4.46 returned
Penrith Castle 43 Sold (Br); 46 *Fantee* (Br)
Philoctetes 8.40 Destroyer depot ship HMS *Philoctetes*; 48 BU Newport Mon
Polar Chief 41 MoWT (Br); 11.41 *Empire Chief* (Br); 8.46 *Polar Chief* (Br)
Port Quebec 40 Minelayer HMS *Port Quebec*; 43 aircraft repair ship; 1.1.45 sold Adm, *Deer Sound*; 20.12.47 sold, returned, *Port Quebec* (Br)
Pretoria Castle 2.10.39 Req Adm; 10.39–8.42 amc HMS *Pretoria Castle*; 42 sold Adm, conv to carrier; 45 resold original owner; 45–46 reconv; 46 *Warwick Castle* (Br)

Prince David 10.39 Sold RCN, amc HMCS *Prince David*; 1.5.43 comm conv to LSI(M); 46 *Charlton Monarch* (Br)
Prince Robert 10.39 Sold RCN, amc HMCS *Prince Robert*; 1.43–7.43 conv to AA ship; 10.12.45 decomm; 10.46 sold

Queen Elizabeth 40–2.46 Troopship; 46 returned
Queen Mary 40–46 Troopship; 46 returned
Queen of Bermuda 30.8.39–4.43 amc HMS *Queen of Bermuda*; 5.43 MoWT troopship; 47 returned

Raby Castle 43 Sold (Br); 45 *Stanhill* (Br)
Rajula 40 Troopship; 46 returned
Ranchi 27.8.39 Req Adm; 39–3.43 amc HMS *Ranchi*; 16.3.43 returned; 3.43 MoWT troopship; 18.7.47 returned
Rangitata 16.3.43 MoWT troopship; 5.45 repatriation/trooping; 48 returned
Rangitiki 12.40 Troopship; 4.45 repatriation/trooping; 47 returned
Ranpura 6.9.39 amc HMS *Ranpura*; 5.43–44 conv fleet repair ship; 8.12.44 sold Adm
Rapana 43–45 MAC
Ravelston 41 MoWT, *Empire Bond* (Br); 46 *Prenton* (Br)
Reaveley 43 *Begonia* (Br)
Registan 13.9.40 Req as obv HMS *Registan*; 11.41 returned
Reina del Pacifico 12.39–45 Troopship; 46 repatriation ship; 47 returned
Rimutaka 8–9.39 Hired by Adm for conv to amc; 9.39 returned, not suitable

Salween 41 Troopship; 46 returned
Samaria 40–48 Troopship and government service
San Tirso 45 *Kelliella* (Br)
Scythia 11.39–48 Troopship; 48 refugee carrier; 49 returned
Seringa 46 *Firoza* (Br)
Solen 2.42 Captured Singapore by Japanese; 42 *Shosei Maru* (Jpn); 6.11.45 recaptured Palembang; 45 *Solen* (Br)
Somersetshire 9.39 Hospital Ship No 25; 2.48 returned
Southern Prince 1.40 Adm; 5.6.40 commd, aux minelayer HMS *Southern Prince*; 10.44 accom ship; 45 returned; 1.4.47 sold; 47 *Anna C* (Ita)
Springfjord 5.40 Seized by Germans while building Trondheim; *Rudesheimer* (Ger); 5.45 British prize, Tønsberg; 46 *Empire Springfjord* (Br); 47 *Springfjord* (Br)
Staffordshire 4.40 Troopship; 11.48 returned
Stakesby 25.8.41 Torpedoed (in convoy HX65) by *U124*, damaged, 58 52N 06 34W; 1.42 raised, repaired; 43 MoWT, *Empire Derwent* (Br); 46 *Swan Point* (Br)
Stanland 15.9.39 Adm, ammunition hulk; 51 BU Milford Haven
Stirling Castle 40–46 Troopship; 46 returned
Strathaird 26.8.39 Troopship; 20.9.46 released
Stratheden 19.3.40 Troopship; 29.5.47 released
Strathmore 31.3.40 Troopship; 15.5.48 released
Strathnaver 7.1.40 Troopship; 10.48 released

Tairea 40 Hospital Ship No 35; 45 repatriation ship; 46 returned
Takoradian 5.7.40 Seized Dakar by VFr; 41 *St Paul* (Fra); 43 *Takoradian*; 43 MoWT, *Empire Swale* (Br); 46 *Takoradian* (Br)
Talma 41 Troopship; 46 returned
Tamaroa 11.40 Conv to troopship; 48 returned
Taroona 1.42 Troopship; 2.46–10.46 refit; 10.46 returned owner's service
Telemachus 1.42 Escort carrier HMS *Activity*; 4.46 *Breconshire* (Br)
Temple Pier 17.6.40 Seized Algiers by VFr; 41 *St Fernand* (Fra); 14.12.42 attacked by aircraft, damaged, Tunis; 43 *Temple Pier* (Br); 46 *Lake Geneva* (Br)
Teviotbank 9.39 Aux minelayer HMS *Teviotbank*; 8.44 returned
Thurland Castle 43 Sold (Br); 46 *Fulani* (Br)
Tolten 41 Sold (Br); 45 *St Merriel* (Br)
Tortuguero 41–42 Adm, obv HMS *Tortuguero*; 42 returned

Ulmus 46 *Alberto Gianpaolo* (Ita)

Varela 40 Troopship; 46 returned
Varsova 9.39 Troopship; 46 returned

Waimana 9.39 Adm, conv to dummy battleship HMS *Resolution*; 41 MoWT reconv to cargo vessel; 2.42 *Empire*
Waimana (Br); 46 *Waimana* (Br)
Waiotapu 46 *Victoria Peak* (Br)
Westralia 2.11.39 Adm; 17.1.40 commd amc HMAS *Westralia*; 42–43 accom ship; 12.42 comm conv to LSI; 31.5.43 LSI; 9.45–50 troopship; 27.3.51 returned
Winchester Castle 41 Troopship; 41 RN service; 42 troopship; 46 returned
Winifred Moller 46 *Tsze Yung* (Chn)

Worcestershire 17.9.39–43 amc HMS *Worcestershire*; 43–10.47 troopship; 10.47 returned

Yuen Sang 7.46 *Hai Hsia* (Chn)

Greece

Losses through marine hazard
Adamantios J Pithis 27.1.40 Wrecked Cam Rocks, off St Anne's Head, near Milford Haven
Adamas 8.2.43 Collision (in convoy), badly damaged; shelled by escort, sunk, 56 35N 22 23W
Aghia Eirini 5.12.40 Engine failure 52 21N 23 40W; 10.12.40 drifted on to rocks near Achill Head, Clewbay, Ireland
Anghyra 17.10.43 Ar San Francisco in tow following fire, badly damaged; 12.43 CTL; 5.44 sold; 5.6.44 ar Vancouver in tow, repaired; 44 *Spartan* (Pan)
Anna Mazaraki 24.5.42 Wrecked East Bar, Sable Is
Anthippi N Michalos 22.12.40 Collision with *Beaverdale* (*qv*), sank, 53 10N 05 03W
Avra 25.9.41 Collision with *Marvia* (*qv*), sank, E of Duncansby Head, 58 38N 02 55W (0†)
Axios 28.3.44 Ashore off Sandheads, CTL

Chelatros 3.11.41 Aground Brion Is, Magdalen Islands, Gulf of St Lawrence; TL

Dioni 8.11.40 Stranded, badly damaged, Sandy Haven Bay, near Milford Haven; refloated, BU
Dionyssios Stathatos 11.12.39 Lost rudder; 12.12.39 abandoned 58 31N 21 55W, sank

Elengo A Kydoniefs 12.4.39 Wrecked 2m N of Cape Verde
Emmy 25.5.42 Ashore Morien Bay, Cape Breton Is; TL
Eugenie S Embiricos 21.2.42 Broke adrift when in tow for R Clyde, stranded Leanish Point, Barra Is, Outer Hebrides, 56 58 03N 07 22W; sank
Evgena Cambani 28.11.40 In distress in heavy weather, abandoned, 46 53N 48 37W, presumed foundered (0 surv)
Evgenia Chandri 15.3.43 Collision with wreck of *Oslofjord* (*qv*) off R Tyne, beached Outer Herd Sands, S of R Tyne; TL

Flora 20.1.40 Sd Sunderland for Rosario; 22.1.40 reported The Downs; missing (25†)
Fotini Carras 7.6.39 Ashore South Bellona Reefs 21 25S 159 34E; back broken, sank

Georgios 14.12.39 Struck wreck of *Canada* (*qv*), sunk, 0.5m NE of Dimlington, 53 42 24N 00 11E (0†, 22 surv)
Gioannoulis Gounaris 2.5.40 Stranded near Foreland Point, North Devon, damaged; 8.7.40 refloated; BU Briton Ferry

Ioannis P Goulandris 1.12.42 Collision with *Intrepido* (Pan), sank, 40 15N 73 45W

Katina Bulgari 8.2.39 Collision with *Meanticut* (US), sunk, 5m S of Humber LV, 53 35 28N 00 31 20E; wreck dispersed

Marouko Pateras 3.11.41 Stranded in fog Double Is, Labrador; 5.11.41 refloated, sank 2m SW of Double Is
Michael J Goulandris 21.12.44 Wrecked South-West Reefs, 3.5m S of D'Entrecasteaux Point
Michalis (4680gt) 20.11.41 Ashore St Lawrence R 6m above Quebec, TL
Mount Ida 9.10.39 Ashore near Ower Bank, 32m E of Cromer, 53 07 30N 02 06 30E; back broken
Mount Othrys 6.1.45 Collision with *Erinna* (*qv*), badly damaged, on fire, off Hole Haven, R Thames; beached Mucking Flats; 16.3.45 broke in two; BU
Mount Pera 19.9.42 Ashore Dane Reef, off Inchaca, near Lourenço Marques; broke in two, afterpart sank, forepart beached; TL

Nestos 2.4.41 Aground East Hoyle Bank, 6m S of Bar LV, R Mersey; TL

Odysseus 17.1.45 Ashore Cape Sambro, 44 28N 63 33W, entrance to Ketch Harbour, near Halifax NS; TL

Pelinaion 16.1.40 Ashore off St David's Head, Bermuda; broke in two, TL
Phæax 7.12.40 Ashore near Nojimazaki, Japan; TL

Ronin 41 *Iran* (Pan); 14.4.44 badly damaged in *Fort Stikine* explosion Bombay docks; TL, wreck BU

Spyros 17.2.42 Ashore near Lawrencetown NS; broke in two, sank

Teti 10.42 Wrecked near Volo
Theoskepasti 43 *Cygnet* (Pan); 10.7.43 aground near Cape d'Or; refloated, making water,

beached Port Greville, W of Parrsboro; refloated, drydocked, declared CTL; repaired, resold previous owner
Tonis Chandris 10.1.40 Chased by U-boat in fog, struck reef 1.5m from shore off North Shetlands; abandoned as TL, 60 42 07N 00 48 54W
Turkia 17.5.41 Explosion, on fire, 2.5m from Zafarana LH, near Suez, sunk

Vassilios T 19.3.39 Struck rock, foundered near Point Stupisce, Vis Is, Adriatic

Losses through war causes
Adamandios Georgandis 19.6.40 Torpedoed by *U28*, sunk, 49 35N 11 15W (1†)
Adamantios 20.6.40 Bombed by German aircraft off Île de Re; 21.6.40 beached Île de Re (0†, 32 surv)
Adamastos 1.7.40 Shelled by *U29*, sunk, 46 20N 14 30W (0†, 25 surv)
Adelfotis 1.5.43 Torpedoed, shelled, by *U182*, sunk, 03 32S 21 33W (1†, 1 pow, 35 surv)
Aeas 7.9.42 Torpedoed (in convoy QS33) by *U165*, sunk, 49 10N 66 50W (2†, 29 surv)
Aegeon 11.4.41 Torpedoed by *U124*, sunk, 06 55N 15 38W (4†, 27 surv)
Aegeus 2.11.42 Torpedoed by *U177*, sunk, 32 30S 16E (0 surv)
Aenos 17.10.40 Torpedoed, shelled (convoy SC7 straggler) by *U38*, sunk, 59N 13W (4†, 25 surv)
Afroessa 27.8.40 Seized Dakar by VFr; 40 *Sahara* (Fra); 16.3.43 retaken Dakar; *Afroessa* (Br); 14.8.43 MoWT storage hulk Freetown, renamed *Woolworth* (Br); 52 dismantled
Aghios Georgios 4.2.41 Struck mine, sunk, between Km142 and Km143, Suez Canal (3†, 24 surv); wreck removed
Aghios Georgios IV 8.6.42 Shelled by subm *I-16* (Jpn), sunk, 16 12S 41E (7†, 24 surv)
Aghios Nicolaos 1.10.40 Shelled by subm *Baracca* (Ita), sunk, 40N 16 55W
Agios Markos 22.4.41 Bombed by enemy aircraft, sunk, Peristeri, Salamis Is
Aikaterini 29.1.41 Torpedoed (in convoy SC19) by *U93*, sunk, 56N 15 23W (0†, 30 surv)
Aikaterini T 23.1.44 Sd Louisburg, CBI for St John NB, untraced (0 surv)
Alexandros 14.9.40 Torpedoed (in convoy SC3) by *U48* 56 30N 16 30W (5†, 25 surv); 15.9.40 sunk 56 50N 15 04W
Aliakmon 11.11.41 Sd Loch Ewe (in convoy) for Sydney CB; 20.11.41 last seen when convoy dispersed in thick fog (0 surv)
Amarylis (Pan) 2.12.42 Torpedoed by *U181*, sunk, 28 14S 33 24E (29†, 8 surv)
Anastassia 18.12.40 Torpedoed (dispersed from convoy SC15) by subm *Veniero* (Ita); 20.12.40 sunk 54 24N 19 4W (18†, 10 pow)
Anastassios Pateras 6.7.42 Torpedoed (in convoy QS15) by *U132* 49 30N 66 30W (3†, 26 surv); sunk 49 12N 66 55W
Andreas 4.11.42 Torpedoed, shelled, by subm *Leonardo da Vinci* (Ita), sunk, 02S 30 30W (10†, 37 surv)
Anna Bulgari 25.6.41 Torpedoed (ind) by *U77*, sunk, 55N 38W (0 surv)
Annitsa 15.1.43 Torpedoed (in convoy) by *U617*, sunk, 33 04N 21 50E (1†, 33 surv)
Antonios Chandris 8.9.40 Intercepted by aux cruiser *Widder*, sunk 11 25N 34 10W (34 surv)
Antonis 6.1.41 Captured by aux cruiser *Kormoran*, sunk, 08 17N 23 32W (0†, 28 pow)
Antonis Georgandis 14.6.40 Shelled by *U101*, sunk, 42 45N 16 20W
Argo (ex *San José*) 29.11.42 Torpedoed by subm *Ammiraglio Cagni* (Ita), sunk, 34 53S 17 54E (18†, 18 surv)
Aris 12.10.39 Shelled by *U37*, sunk, 53 28N 14 30W (2†)
Aspasia 15.8.40 Torpedoed by *UA*, sunk, 35N 20W (0 surv)
Asteria 17.1.40 Struck mine (laid by destroyer of German 4th Destroyer fl), sunk, 334° 9.5m from Haisboro LV (14†, 11 surv); wreck dispersed
Athina Livanos 13.11.43 Torpedoed by subm *I-27* (Jpn), sunk, 12 23N 44E (11†, 25 surv)
Atlanticos 21.2.42 Struck mine, broke in two, 0.5m off B8 buoy, Barrow Deep, Thames estuary; sunk 2° 1.1m from B8 Buoy, 51 48 58N 01 30 37E
Atlas 6.9.40 Torpedoed by subm *Guglielmotti* (Ita), sunk, 15 50N 41 50E (0†)

Boris 3.6.43 Torpedoed by *U180*, sunk, 07 14S 18 41W (0†, 37 surv)

Calafatis 4.2.41 Bombed by enemy aircraft 56 27N 13 40W; sunk (18†, 13 surv)
Cape Corso 40 *Liberia* (Fra); 21.9.42 torpedoed (in convoy) by subm HMS *Unruffled*, sunk, 35 36N 11 09E
Carras 19.3.43 Torpedoed (convoy SC122 straggler) by *U666*, damaged; torpedoed by *U333*, sunk, 54 05N 24 19W
Chloe 6.5.42 Torpedoed, shelled, by subm *I-21* (Jpn), sunk, 22 59S 166 29E (0†, 35 surv)
Christos Markettos 8.6.42 Torpedoed by subm *I-20* (Jpn), sunk, 05 05S 40 53E (2†, 35 surv)
Clairy (Pan) 21.5.40 Attacked by German aircraft 8–9m off Boulogne, on fire; 22.5.40 abandoned, sunk
Cleanthis 3.12.42 Torpedoed, shelled, by *U181*, sunk, 24 29N 35 44E (12†, 22 surv)
Condylis 10.8.42 Torpedoed (in convoy SC94) by *U438* and *U660*, sunk, 57 03N 22 59W (9†, 26 surv)
Constantinos Louloudis 7.4.41 Bombed by German aircraft, sunk, Piræus; salved; 42 *Lüneburg* (Ger); 28.4.44 torpedoed by subm HMS *Sportsman*, sunk, 39 26N 25 07E
Corinthiakos 20.11.42 Torpedoed by *U181*, sunk, 25 42S 33 27E (11†, 21 surv)

Couloura-Xenos 2.4.41 Bombed by German aircraft, sunk, off Gavdo Island
Cygnet (Pan) 12.3.42 Shelled by subm *Enrico Tazzoli* (Ita), sunk, 24 05N 74 20W (30 surv)

Danapris 27.4.41 Bombed by German aircraft, sunk, Piræus; refloated, wrecked Chalkis
Delphin 9.10.40 Torpedoed (in convoy SC6) by *U103* 58 11N 13 57W; 10.10.40 sunk 57 46N 13 50W (0†)
Diamantis 3.10.39 Torpedoed by *U35*, sunk, 40m W of Skelligs (0†, 28 surv aboard *U35*)
Dimitrios G Thermiotis 18.1.42 Torpedoed (convoy SC63 straggler) by *U86*, sunk, 47 30N 52 20W (33†, 0 surv)
Dimitris 26.6.40 Shelled, by *U29*, sunk, 44 23N 11 41W (0†)
Dirphys 8.6.41 Torpedoed by *U108*, sunk, 47 44N 39 02W (6†, 19 surv)

Efploia 31.8.40 Torpedoed by *U101* 55 27N 13 17W, abandoned; 1.9.40 wreck shelled by HM warship, sunk, 55 43N 13 05W
Efthalia Mari 5.8.43 Torpedoed by *U177*, sunk, 24 21S 48 55E (1†, 42 surv)
Eirini Kyriakidou 13.6.41 Torpedoed (in convoy SL75) by subm *Brin* (Ita), sunk, 38 53N 23 11W (31†, 0 surv)
Ekatontarchos Dracoulis 20.1.40 Torpedoed by *U44*, sunk, 40 20N 10 07W (6†)
Elena R 22.11.39 Struck mine (laid 8.9.39 by *U26*), sunk, 2m S of Shambles LV, 50 30 12N 02 20 33W
Eleni Stathatou 28.1.40 Torpedoed, shelled, by *U34*, sunk, 200m W of Scilly Is (12†)
Ellin 17.2.40 Torpedoed by *U37*, sunk, 60m NW of Cape Finisterre (0†)
Ellinico 25.7.41 Torpedoed (ind) by *U108*, sunk, 55N 38W
Elpis 16.6.40 Torpedoed by *U46* (0†, 28 surv); 17.6.40 sunk 43 46N 14 06W
Embiricos Nicolaos 22.3.41 Bombed by enemy aircraft, sunk, 34 30N 24 45E (2†, 30 surv)
Epaminondas C Embiricos 15.2.44 Torpedoed, shelled, by *U168*, sunk, 01 30N 73E (4†, 2 pow, 36 surv)
Eugenie Livanos 7.12.42 Shelled by aux cruiser *Michel* 27 48S 53 58E, on fire, sunk (12†, 10 pow, 5 surv)
Evanthia 28.11.42 Torpedoed, shelled, by *U181*, sunk, 25 13S 34E (0†, 32 surv)
Evdoxia 15.7.40 Torpedoed by *U34*, sunk, 40m SW of Bull Rock, SW Ireland (1†, 22 surv)
Evgenia 16.5.40 Bombed by German aircraft 51 23N 03 07E; 18.5.40 sunk
Evoikos 6.4.41 Bombed by enemy aircraft, sunk, Piræus; refloated; 48 at Ambelaki for BU
Evros 17.10.41 Torpedoed (in convoy SC48) by *U432*, sunk, 57N 24 30W (30†, 2 surv)

Faneromini 23.10.43 Torpedoed by subm *I-37* (Jpn), sunk, 16 21S 40 04E (1†, 37 surv)
Frangoula B Gouldandri 29.6.40 Torpedoed by *U26*, sunk, 49 59N 11 24W (6†, 32 surv)

G S Livanos 20.7.42 Torpedoed by subm *I-11* (Jpn), sunk, 35S 151E (0†, 31 surv)
Galaxias 23.5.40 Bombed by aircraft, sunk, Dieppe (0†); 49–50 raised, BU
Garoufalia 11.12.39 Torpedoed by *U38*, sunk, 64 36N 10 42E (4†)
George J Goulandris 29.6.41 Torpedoed (convoy SL76 straggler) by *U66*, sunk, 29 05N 25 10W (0†, 28 surv)
Georgios Kyriakides 30.6.40 Torpedoed by *U47*, sunk, 50 25N 14 33W (0†, 30 surv)
Germaine 15.12.39 Torpedoed by *U48*, sunk, 51N 12 18W (0†)
Granicos 28.3.43 Torpedoed by subm *Finzi* (Ita), sunk, 02N 15 30W (30†, 1 pow, 1 surv)
Grigorios C II 20.2.41 Sunk by *Admiral Scheer* W of Seychelles (27 pow)

Halcyon (Pan) 5.2.42 Shelled by *U109* 34 20N 59 16W; 6.2.42 sunk (3†)
Hellenic Trader (Pan) 11.6.42 Shelled by subm *I-20* (Jpn), sunk, 14 37S 40 58E (9†, 33 surv)
Hollandia 27.4.41 Bombed by German aircraft, on fire, sunk, Hermion, near Nauplia Bay
Hydraios 6.7.43 Torpedoed by *U198*, sunk, 24 44S 35 12E (0†, 40 surv)

Ia 11.7.40 Torpedoed by *U99*, sunk, 51N 14W (3†, 27 surv)
Icarion 26.1.42 Torpedoed by *U754*, sunk, 46 02N 52 22W (9†, 20 surv)
Ioannis Fafalios 40 Adm collier; 5.9.44 torpedoed by *U861*, sunk, 04 20S 43 57E (8†, 20 surv)
Ioannis M Embiricos 5.2.41 Bombed by German aircraft 55 41N 12 26W ((0†); 6.2.41 sunk 55 50N 11 44W

Joannis 16.9.42 Torpedoed (in convoy SQ36) by *U165*, sunk, 49 10N 67 05W (0†, 32 surv)
Julia 27.5.41 Bombed by German aircraft, sunk, Suda Bay (0†); salved by Germans; 18.12.42 sunk Tripoli

Kalliopi 7.2.43 Torpedoed (in convoy SC118) by *U402*, sunk, 55 27N 26 08W (4†, 32 surv)
Kalliopi S 17.9.40 Bombed by German aircraft 11m SW of Tory Is, abandoned, drifted on rocks Sheephaven Bay, 10m E of Tory Is, broke in two, TL (0†)
Kalypso Vergotti 29.6.41 Torpedoed (convoy SL76 straggler) by *U66*, sunk, 29N 25W (0 surv)
Kapetan Stratis 22.1.41 Bombed by German FW200 Kondor aircraft, sunk, 54 34N 12 08W (28†, 0 surv)
Kassandra Louloudi 17.3.42 Torpedoed by *U124*, sunk, 35 05N 75 25W (0†, 25 surv)
Kastor 1.8.42 Torpedoed by subm *Enrico Tazzoli* (Ita), sunk, 11 06N 59 05W (4†, 31 surv)
Kate 28.1.41 Bombed by German aircraft, sunk, Salonica (2†)

Keramiai 30.1.40 Torpedoed (in convoy OA80G) by *U55*, sunk, 48 37N 07 45W (28 surv)
Kolchis 23.11.40 Torpedoed (in convoy OB244) by *U123*, sunk, (20+†, 0 surv)
Konistra 29.4.41 Bombed by enemy aircraft, sunk, Suda Bay, Crete
Konstantinos Hadjipateras 24.10.39 Struck mine (laid 17.10.39 by *U19*), sunk, 53 18 36N 00 36 57E (4†); 7.47 wreck dispersed
Korthion 14.4.42 Torpedoed by *U66*, sunk, 12 50N 60 30W (14†, 9 surv)
Kosti 7.40 Seized Copenhagen by Germans; 41 sold Finland; 41 *Arica* (Fin); 45 not returned
Koumoundoros 8.10.42 Torpedoed by *U68*, sunk, 34 10S 17 07E (5†, 26 surv)
Kyma (3959gt) 10.10.41 Struck mine 53 53N 00 21E (0†); 11.10.41 sunk 53 13 15N 00 24 27E; 48 wreck cleared
Kyma (3991gt) 24.5.40 Torpedoed by *U37*, sunk, 48 30N 09 30W (7†, 23 surv)
Kyriakoula 26.2.41 Bombed by German aircraft 55 02N 16 25W; not hit, but hull damaged by near misses; abandoned, sunk (0†, 28 surv)
Laconikos 7.5.43 Torpedoed (in convoy SL128) by *U89*, sunk, 41 40N 18 13W (23†, 11 surv)
Leonidas M 19.7.42 Torpedoed by *U332*, sunk, 37 01N 52 04W (0†, 29 surv, 2 pow)
Leonidas M Valmas 20.8.40 Torpedoed by *U46* 55 13N 10 38W, badly damaged; towed Greenock, beached; BU Kames Bay
Leonidas Z Cambanis 3.4.41 Torpedoed (in convoy SC26) by *U74*, sunk, 58 12N 27 40W (2†, 27 surv)
Lily 9.3.42 Torpedoed (in convoy ONS68) by *U587*, sunk, 43 32N 54 14W (3†, 29 surv)

Makis 11.6.40 Struck mine, sunk, 15m N of Pantellaria (0†)
Marathon 9.3.41 Sunk by *Scharnhorst* 21N 25W (0†, 38 pow)
Margit (Pan) 19.4.41 Bombed by German aircraft, sunk, Kalkara Creek, Malta
Mari Chandris 10.7.40 During attack by German aircraft Falmouth docks, set on fire by flames from *Tascalusa* (*qv*) (0†, 37 surv); badly damaged, BU
Maria 40 *Santa Margarita* (Pan); 2.7.40 shelled by *U29*, sunk, 47 10N 16 10W (3†, 36 surv; 21 surv picked up by *King John* (*qv*), of which 3† when *King John* sunk)
Maria Stathatou 26.4.41 Bombed by German aircraft, sunk, near Mylos
Marionga 23.5.41 Torpedoed by *U103*, sunk, 05 42N 10 29W (26†, 31 surv)
Maro Y 40 *Maro* (Gre); 14.1.42 torpedoed (in convoy ON55) by *U43*, sunk, 40N 50W
Maroussio Logotheti 9.7.40 Seized Diego Suarez by VFr; 40 *General Duquesne* (Fra); 1.5..42 recovered Mayotte by RN; 42 *Maroussio Logotheti* (Gre); 15.5.43 torpedoed by *U105*, sunk, 05 28N 14 28W (27†, 1 pow, 11 surv)
Mary Livanos 11.7.43 Torpedoed by *U178*, sunk, 15 40S 40 45E (8†, 28 surv)
Matronna 24.5.41 Bombed by German aircraft, sunk, Dale Roads, Milford Haven (0†, 28 surv); wreck dispersed
Max Wolf 9.6.40 Bombed by German aircraft, sunk, between Roque and Berville (2†); beached off Tancarville; wreck used as Luftwaffe target; 46–53 wreck BU
Meandros 16.1.41 Bombed by German aircraft 55 15N 11 40W (0†); abandoned 55 55N 12 24W, taken in tow; 20.1.41 shelled, sunk, by HM ship
Memas 16.4.41 Bombed by enemy aircraft, sunk, Chalkis (0†)
Mentor 7.3.41 Torpedoed by *U37*, sunk, 59 30N 25W (7†, 22 surv)
Meropi 15.2.42 Torpedoed by *U566*, sunk, 44 14N 62 41W (26†, 14 surv)
Michael Livanos 4.7.43 Torpedoed by *U178*, sunk, 22 52S 36 47 30E (2†, 39 surv)
Michalios 27.6.43 Torpedoed by *U81*, sunk, 3m W of Lattakia (1†)
Moscha L Goulandri 21.3.41 Bombed by enemy aircraft off Chalkis, damaged; 18.4.41 beached, bombed again; 51 raised, BU Trieste
Mount Athos 28.11.40 Torpedoed by *U103*, sunk, 54 30N 15 25W (19†)
Mount Helmos 24.11.42 Torpedoed, shelled, by *U181*, sunk, 26 38S 34 58E (1†, 34 surv)
Mount Hymettus 11.6.40 Shelled by *U101*, sunk, 42 13N 11 20W (0†, 24 surv)
Mount Kassion 8.8.42 Torpedoed (in convoy SC94) by *U176*, sunk, 56 30N 32 14W (0†, 54 surv)
Mount Kitheron 25.1.42 Torpedoed by *U754*, sunk, 47 32N 52 31W (12†, 24 surv)
Mount Lycabettus 17.3.42 Torpedoed by *U373*, sunk, 40 15N 61W (30†, 0 surv)
Mount Mycale 22.2.42 Torpedoed (convoy SC117 straggler) by *U413*, sunk, 52N 50 30W (0 surv)
Mount Myrto 14.6.40 Torpedoed, shelled, by *U38*, sunk, 50 03N 10 05W (4†, 20 surv)
Mount Olympus 14.5.42 Struck mine (laid 15.4.42 by *U561*) 31 20 48N 32 21 24E (3†, 27 surv), broke in three; sunk 31 19 45N 32 23 15E
Mount Parnes 12.5.42 Torpedoed (in convoy ONS92) by *U124*, sunk, 52 31N 29 20W (0†, 32 surv)
Mount Pelion 2.11.42 Torpedoed (in convoy SC107) by *U522*, sunk, 52 20N 45 40W (7†, 32 surv)
Mount Pindus 7.9.42 Torpedoed (in convoy QS33) by *U517*, sunk, 48 50N 63 46W (2†, 35 surv)
Mount Taurus 17.11.42 Torpedoed (in convoy ONS144) by *U264*, sunk, 54 30N 37 30W (2†, 38 surv)

Naftilos 15.7.40 Shelled by *U34*, sunk, 48 05N 10 25W (1†, 27 surv)
Neion 22.6.40 Torpedoed by *U38*, sunk, 47 09N 04 17W
Nellie 13.10.42 Torpedoed (in convoy SC104) by *U607* 53 41N 41 23W; 14.10.42

sunk (32†, 5 surv)
Nemea 16.1.41 Torpedoed by subm *Luigi Torelli* (Ita) 52 33N 24 13W, abandoned 52 57N 23 58W; 17.1.41 reboarded, sunk (17†, 14 surv)
Nicolaos D L 12.4.41 Shelled by aux cruiser *Kormoran* 01 54S 22 12W, sunk by explosive charge (0†, 35 pow)
Nicolaos Filinis 15.1.41 Torpedoed, shelled, by subm *Luigi Torelli* (Ita) 53N 24W; on fire, abandoned, sunk (3†, 26 surv)
Nicolaos M Embiricos 4.11.39 Struck British mine, sunk, 15m E of Dover, 51 13N 01 39E (1†)
Nicolaos Piangos 31.10.41 Bombed by German aircraft, on fire, 51 58 45N 01 37 30E; ashore, broke in two (8†, 27 surv); TL
Nicolaou Georgios 23.4.41 Bombed by German aircraft, on fire, back broken, sunk, Nauplia (0†)
Nicolaou Ourania 16.5.41 Bombed by German aircraft Suda Bay, beached; 31.5.41 seized by Germans, repaired; 42 *Nikolaus* (Ger); 21.9.43 torpedoed by subm *Dzik* (Pol), sunk, entrance to Bastia
Nicolaou Zografia 6.4.41 Attacked by German aircraft, sunk, 57 10N 12 30W (0†, 32 surv)
Nicolas Angelos 1.2.41 Torpedoed by *U48*, sunk, 59N 17W (0 surv)
Nicolas Pateras 24.6.41 Torpedoed (convoy OB336 straggler) by *U108*, sunk, 55N 38W (0 surv)
Nikoklis 14.7.41 Torpedoed by subm *Alessandro Malaspina* (Ita), sunk, 105m SW of Azores (17†, 11 surv)
Niritos 18.10.40 Torpedoed (in convoy SC7) by *U99*, sunk, about 4m from 57 14N 10 38W (1†, 27 surv)
Nitsa 2.12.43 Torpedoed by subm *I-27* (Jpn), 11 42N 45 32E (11†, 29 surv)
Nymphe 6.7.42 Torpedoed by subm *I-10* (Jpn), sunk, 15 48S 40 42E (1†, 40 surv)

Okeania 8.4.40 Struck mine, broke in two, sunk, 51 16 48N 02 03 12E (1†)
Olga E Embiricou 41 Adm, collier; 29.1.44 torpedoed by *U188*, sunk, 12 30N 50 10E (20†, 21 surv)
Oropos 21.12.42 Torpedoed (ind) by *U621*, sunk, 51N 37W (0 surv)

P Margaronis 9.3.40 Torpedoed by *U28*, sunk, 50N 06W (0 surv)
Pagasitikos 23.3.42 Captured by aux cruiser *Thor* 31S 11 35W; sunk (0†)
Panachrandos 16.1.40 Torpedoed by *U44*, sunk, 48 30N 09 10W (31†, 0 surv)
Panaghiotis Th Coumantaros 40 *Evgenia* (Gre); 15.5.40 attacked by German aircraft, damaged by near misses; abandoned; 18.5.40 scuttled Zeebrugge roads
Panam (Pan) 5.5.43 Torpedoed by *U129*, sunk, 34 11N 76 12W (3†, 48 surv)
Pancration 22.4.41 Torpedoed by German aircraft (during invasion of Greece), sunk, Milos
Pandias 13.6.41 Torpedoed by *U107*, sunk, 07 49N 23 28W (11†, 23 surv)
Pantelis 8.10.41 Torpedoed by *U172*, sunk, 34 20S 17 50E (28†, 5 surv)
Papalemos 28.5.41 Torpedoed by *U107*, sunk, 08 06N 16 18W (2†, 27 surv)
Paralos 6.12.39 Struck mine, sunk, 51 31 06N 01 25 05E (0†); wreck dispersed
Parthenon 3.11.42 Torpedoed (in convoy SC107) by *U442*, sunk, 53 30N 42 15W (6†, 23 surv)
Patrai 12.7.41 Bombed by aircraft, sunk, Port Said
Pegasus 15.9.41 Torpedoed (convoy ON14 straggler) by *U94* 54 40N 29 50W; 17.9.41 shelled, sunk 54 54N 30 32W (16†, 13 surv)
Peleus 13.3.44 Torpedoed by *U852*, sunk, 02S 10W (38†, 3 surv)
Perseus 12.2.41 Shelled (in convoy SLS64) by *Admiral Hipper*, sunk, 37 12N 21 20W (14†, 22 surv)
Petalli 7.4.41 Bombed by German aircraft Piræus and on fire following explosion on *Clan Fraser* (*qv*), towed out of harbour, scuttled
Pindos 4.8.40 Torpedoed (in convoy HX60) by *U58*, sunk, 55 22N 08 50W (3†, 29 surv)
Polyktor 6.2.43 Torpedoed (convoy SC118 straggler) by *U266*, sunk, 53 10N 30 34W (2 pow)
Popi S 24.4.41 Torpedoed by German aircraft (during German invasion of Greece), sunk, Milos
Possidon 8.9.40 Torpedoed (in convoy SC2) by *U47*, sunk, 56 43N 09 16W (17†)

Rinos 2.11.42 Torpedoed (in convoy SC107) by *U402*, sunk, 52 30N 45 30W (8†, 23 surv)
Rio Grande (Pan) 40 MoWT, *Empire Blanda* (Br); 18.2.41 torpedoed (convoy HX107 straggler) by *U69*, sunk, S of Iceland (40†, 0 surv)
Rokos 26.5.41 Bombed by German aircraft Suda Bay, Crete; 27.5.41 aground, TL
Rokos Vergottis 23.12.41 Struck mine off 55A buoy, S of Smith's Knoll, taken in tow; 24.12.41 aground 52 52 48N 02 12 12E, back broken; TL

Saronikos 7.12.42 Torpedoed by *U177*, sunk, 24 46S 35 30E (32†, 2 surv)
Stamatios G Embirocos 24.9.41 Sunk by aux cruiser *Kormoran*, 03 30N 70E (5†, 25 pow)
Stavros Coumantaros 40 *Kyriaki* (Gre); 24.4.41 bombed by German aircraft, sunk, Suda Bay, Crete (0†)
Styliani 6.4.41 Bombed by German aircraft Piræus, on fire; 7.4.41 sunk Kynosoura
Stylianos Chandris 22.12.41 Struck mine, sunk, 53 32 38N 01 31 04E (0†, 30 surv); 50 wreck dispersed

Teti Nomicou 19.4.41 Bombed by German aircraft, sunk, Chalkis
Thalia 18.10.40 Torpedoed (in convoy SC7) by *U99*, sunk, 57N 11 30W (22†, 4 surv)
Themoni 17.5.41 Bombed by German aircraft during invasion, blew up, sunk, Suda Bay, Crete

Theodoros T 27.8.40 Torpedoed, shelled, by *U37*, sunk, 50 10N 19 50W (0†)
Thetis A 14.7.40 Torpedoed by *U52*, sunk, 47 40N 13 20W (9†, 20 surv)
Thrasyvoulos 30.10.39 Torpedoed by *U37*, sunk, 49 25N 11 18W (23†)
Tuira (Pan) 19.8.40 Torpedoed by *UA* 54 46N 20 30W (2†); 20.8.40 sunk

Urania 40 MoWT (Br); 21.4.41 torpedoed by aircraft, sunk, off Tobruk; raised; 50 in use as temporary wharf

Vasilios A Polemis 22.1.42 Torpedoed (convoy ON53 straggler) by *U333*, sunk, 42 32N 52 38W (21†, 12 surv)
Victoria (4202gt) 30.10.40 Bombed by German aircraft 54 47N 13 32W; sunk 54 48N 13 28W (0†, 29 surv)
Victoria (6085gt) 21.11.40 Torpedoed (in convoy OB244) by *U103* 56 17N 14 12W (–†, 27 surv); abandoned 56 08 14 20W, sunk
Violando N Goulandris 10.6.40 Torpedoed by *U48*, sunk, 44 04N 12 30W (6†, 22 surv)
Virginia S 41 (Ita); 41 (Ger); 23.10.41 torpedoed by subm HMS *Truant*, sunk, 39 48N 19 06E

Yiannis 6.4.41 Seized Madagascar by VFr; 41 *Amiral Pierre* (Fra); 29.9.42 found by RN vessels and SAAF aircraft; 30.9.42 shelled, sunk, 26 04S 34 54E

Zannes Gounaris 9.10.40 Torpedoed (in convoy SC6) by *U103*, sunk, 58 11N 13 57W (1†)
Zannis L Cambanis 21.1.42 Struck mine, sunk, 01 15N 104 31E (2†)
Zeus 19.2.43 Torpedoed (in convoy ONS165) by *U403*, sunk, 49 28N 44 50W (0 surv)
Zinovia 11.6.40 Struck mine, sunk, 20m N of Pantellaria (2†)

Losses through war causes following capture/seizure by enemy
Adelfoi Chandris 17.7.40 Seized Dakar by VFr; 40 *St Marin* (Fra); 42 *Catania* (Ger); 4.8.43 sunk by Allied aircraft, Naples; 47 salved; 49 BU
Alba (Pan) 12.12.41 Seized Antwerp by Germans; 42 *Aquila* (Ger); 8.11.44 bombed by RAF aircraft, sunk, Midgulen, Norway
Aliki 19.6.40 Seized Dakar by VFr; 40 *Monaco* (Fra); 12.41 *Bologna* (Ita); 21.5.43 torpedoed by subm HMS *Unbroken*, sunk, 38 34N 15 44E
Athinai 28.10.40 Captured near Messina; 41 *Palermo* (Ita); 5.44 sunk of Tagliamento
Belgion 28.10.40 Seized Bordeaux by Germans; 23.10.41 prize; 41 *Scharlachberger* (Ger); 25.8.44 scuttled as blockship R Gironde; 45 raised; 46 BU Lagrange
Hellenic City 40 *Folozu* (Pan); 8.12.41 seized Shanghai by Japan; 2.42 *Eisho Maru* (Jpn); 29.5.43 torpedoed by subm USS *Tambor*, sunk, 17 35N 110 45E
Ioannis Chandris 14.4.41 Seized Antwerp by Germans; 41 *Johann Schulte* (Ger); 29.1.44 struck mine, sunk, N of Kiel
Karavados 12.41 Seized Chinese waters by Japanese; 41 *Tairiku Maru* (Jpn); 21.2.45 torpedoed by subm USS *Gato*, sunk, 35 24N 125 23E (–†)
Leontios Teryazos 28.10.40 Seized Bordeaux by Germans; 9.41 prize; 40 *Rastenburg* (Ger); 25.8.44 scuttled as blockship R Gironde; 45 BU
Mount Ithome 6.40 Detained Dakar by VFr; seized; 40 *Monrovia* (Fra); 42 *Venezia* (Ita); 14.7.43 bombed by British aircraft, on fire, sunk, Messina
Mount Prionas 7.40 Seized Dakar by VFr; 40 *Andorre* (Fra); 42 *Ancona* (Ita); 9.43 seized by Germans; sunk Savona as blockship; 46 BU
Olympos 41 German control; 7.10.43 sunk by RN vessels S of Levita
Omonia 20.10.39 Captured by Germans, taken Swinemünde; 40 seized, (Ger); *Ölsa* (Ger); 11.10.44 bombed by Russian aircraft, sunk, Kirkenes
Panaghis 12.41 Seized Shanghai by Japanese; later war loss
Perrakis L Cambanis 29.5.40 Bombed by German aircraft, sunk, Dieppe; 40 raised; 40 *Herta Engeline Fritzen* (Ger); KM Seelöwe transport *H26*; 5.45 at Brunsbüttel, sunk; 31.1.49 (Bel)
Petrakis Nomikos 17.4.41 Bombed by German aircraft, damaged, beached, Ambelaki; 42 salved; 43 *Wilhelmsburg* (Ger); 7.7.43 torpedoed by subm HMS *Rorqual*, sunk, 39 55N 25 50E (0†)
Tasis 27.6.40 Seized Dakar by VFr; 40 *Equateur* (Fra); 41 *Bari* (Ita); 1.8.43 bombed by Allied aircraft, Naples; beached in sinking condition; 3.49 salved, BU
Thermaikos 14.4.41 Seized Antwerp by Germans; prize; *Neukuhren* (Ger); 22.4.45 bombed by British aircraft Kattegat; beached 57 25 08N 10 35 20E; partly salved postwar
Valentini 8.12.41 Seized Yokohama by Japanese; 42 *Tai Maru* (Jpn); 24.9.42 torpedoed, sunk, off Omuda, Sakhalin Is

Losses through war causes following sale and change of flag
Andreas (Pan) 41 *Wakatu Maru* (Jpn); 16.12.43 attacked by Netherlands aircraft, sunk, 08 26S 126 48E
Aurora (Pan) 41 *Eizan Maru* (Jpn); 18.1.42 torpedoed by subm USS *Plunger*, sunk, 33 30N 135 00E (–†)
Carmar (Pan) 41 *Kaimei Maru* (Jpn); 4.9.42 torpedoed (in convoy) by subm USS *Guardfish*, 40 14N 141 51E
Erato 8.12.41 Seized Yokohama by Japanese; 42 *Urato Maru* (Jpn); 18.10.41 sunk (in convoy) by USN carrier-based aircraft 14 35N 120 55E

Illenao 40 *Syoto (Shoto) Maru* (Jpn); 31.8.43 torpedoed by subm USS *Seawolf*, sunk, 28 27N 128 03E
Miraflores 41 *Enzyu (Enju) Maru* (Jpn); 4.8.44 sunk by USN carrier-based aircraft 27 40N 141 48E
Mount Atlas 40 *Kuwayama Maru* (Jpn); 21.2.43 torpedoed by subm USS *Thresher*, sunk, off Macassar
Theodoros Coumantaros 40 *Kinkai Maru* (Jpn); 3.10.42 torpedoed by subm USS *Greenling*, sunk, 38 46N 142 02E

Sunk Mulberry Harbour, Normandy
Aghios Spyridon 44 (Br); 7.6.44 sunk as breakwater, Gooseberry 3, Gold Beach, Arromanches; 21.10.45 ar Briton Ferry (from Arromanches) for BU
Georgios P 44 Adm; 7.6.44 sunk as breakwater, Gooseberry 3, Gold Beach, Arromanches

Sunk postwar with surplus war materials
Marietta Nomikou 26.10.39 Stopped by German warship, taken Pillau; later at Hamburg, where seized 29.11.39; 40 *Drau* (Ger); 5.45 seized Flensburg by Allies; 45 (Br); 17.10.45 scuttled Skagerrak with chemical ammunition

Lost postwar through striking mine
Alexandra 20.3.47 Struck mine 53 31N 04 57E, badly damaged; 10.47 towed Zeebrugge for BU

Changes of name, flag, role, disposals, etc
Clairy 40 *Santa Lucia* (Pan)
Hadiotis 42 *Eiger* (Swi); 47 *Cristallina* (Swi)
Ioannis Carras 40 *Spyridon* (Gre); 15.4.41 seized Stavanger by Germans; 45 *Ekenes* (Ger); 41 *Komet* (Ger); 5.45 at Bremerhaven; 45 *Spyridon I* (Gre)
Ithakos 4.41 Seized Antwerp by Germans; 41 *Sigurd Faulbaum* (Ger); 5.45 at Kristiansand S; 45 *Ithakos* (Gre)
Keti Chandri 40 *Agios Vlasios* (Gre)
Marionga D Thermioti 47 *Antonios K* (Gre)
Moscha D Kydoniefs 46 *Varvassi* (Gre)
Nea Hellas 41 MoWT (Br), Allied troopship; 47 (Gre)
Takis 40 *Frederic* (Bel); 5.5.422 Red Cross ship *Caritas I* (Swi); 2.6.45 returned
Tassia 42 USMC, *Cockerel* (Pan); 47 returned
Vassilios Destounis 40 Bombed by German aircraft off Spain, taken Aviles; 9.4.41 *Irish Poplar* (Eir)
Yolanda 40 *Santa Helena* (Pan); 41 *Campechano* (Spn)

Hungary

Losses through war causes
Kelet 19.8.40 Torpedoed by *UA*, sunk, 50N 22W (0†, 33 surv)
Nyugat 41 (Pan); 13.4.41 intercepted 11 20S 123 40E by sloop *Kortenaer* (Ne); 41 Netherlands govt; 41 *Liran* (Pan); 2.3.42 scuttled Sourabaya by Netherlands navy personnel

Sunk Mulberry Harbour, Normandy
Csikos 40 (Pan); 42 *Vinriver* (Br); 42 *Vinlake* (Br); 44 MoWT; 9.6.44 sunk as breakwater, Gooseberry 3, Gold Beach, Arromanches; 46 refloated, ar Falmouth leaking badly, beached St Mawes; BU

Changes of name, flag, role, disposals
Csarda 40 (Pan); 42 MoWT, *Vinriver* (Br)
Szent Gellért 40 *Carola* (Pan)

Italy

Losses through marine hazard
Burma 6.40 Put in Cadiz, LU; 21.1.41 broke moorings, aground, Puerto Santa Maria, broke in two; both sections refloated, beached, BU
C Arrivabene 5.1.40 Ashore 2m S of Fedala, Morocco; BU
Lucia C 10.6.40 At Vigo; 8.9.43 at Gibraltar, Allied control; 9.4.45 explosion in munitions cargo Bari, aground (360†); salved, BU Taranto
Orazio 21.1.40 Explosion, on fire, abandoned, 42 33N 05 30E (106†, 539 surv) 24.1.40 sunk

Losses through marine hazard following change of flag

Alberta 10.6.40 At New York; 8.41 seized by US; 12.41 USMC (Pan); 42 *Ballot* (Pan); 2.1.43 grounded in fog Kildin Is; TL

Amelia Lauro 10.6.40 Seized Immingham by GB; 40 MoWT, *Empire Activity* (Br); 3.10.43 stranded, sank, 1.5m SE of Peckford Reef, Sir Charles Hamilton Sound Nfl

Drepanum 9.9.43 Seized Bordeaux by Germans; 43 (Ger); 20.11.43 collision with *Lippe* (*qv*), sunk, off Vinga LV, Gothenburg

Gabbiano 10.6.40 Seized Liverpool by GB; 40 MoWT, *Empire Energy* (Br); 4.11.41 ashore Big Brook, 11m W of Cape Norman, Belle Isle Strait NS; TL

Granatiere Padula 12.41 Req Shanghai by Japanese; 42 *Haryu Maru* (Jpn); 1.9.43 collision off Korea; 2.9.43 ashore; TL

Ida 8.9.43 Seized by Germans; 27.4.44 *Aalen* (Ger); 22.10.44 struck submerged wreck; 23.10.44 sank 54 38N 12 25E

Principessa Maria 6.40 Interned Buenos Aires; 25.8.41 taken over by Argentina; 41 *Rio de La Plata* (Arg); 18.8.44 on fire Acapulco; towed out, sank 1m off shore

San Leonardo 10.6.40 Interned USA; 12.41 USMC, *Reigh Count* (Pan); 5.6.43 collision in dense fog, sunk, 44 08N 63 13W (–†, 28 surv)

Losses through war causes

Absirtea 1.2.42 Torpedoed by subm HMS *Thunderbolt*, sunk, 37 50N 15 29E

Achille 24.10.41 Bombed by British aircraft, sunk, 38 26N 11 24E

Ada 6.42 Chartered to Japan; 42 *Ataka Maru* (Jpn); 23.8.43 torpedoed by subm USS *Paddle*, sunk, 34 37N 137 53E

Adria 12.2.41 Captured Red Sea by cruiser HMS *Ceres*; 5.41–9.42 MoWT (Br); 12.41 Adm service Bombay; 29.1.43–2.12.45 depot ship HMS *Gombroon*; 3.12.45–25.4.47 LU; 47 BU

Adriana 42 *Anna* (Ger); 13.10.44 bombed, sunk, off Volos

Adua 4.4.41 Scuttled Massowah; 51 BU *in situ*

Africana 8.9.43 Seized by Germans; 43 (Ger); 25.3.45 scuttled Danzig

Aida Lauro 12.41 Seized Pernambuco by Brazil; 42 *Vitorialoide* (Brz)

Alabama 43 USMC, *Osmond* (Pan); 45 *Quiros* (US); 46 BU

Alberto Fassio 26.7.43 Struck mine, sunk, Gulf of Patras

Alberto Treves 4.40 *Romolo Gessi* (Ita); 4.4.41 scuttled Massowah; 51 BU *in situ*

Alfredo Oriani 11.9.41 Bombed by British aircraft, damaged, 35 50N 20 30E; 13.9.41 sunk 35 05N 20 16E

Amba Alagi 20.12.41 Req by Japan; 12.41 *Aoki Maru* (Jpn); 13.11.44 bombed by US carrier-based aircraft, sunk, 14 35N 120 55E

Amsterdam 16.10.42 Torpedoed by British aircraft, damaged, ashore Ponte d'Homs; 20.1.43 abandoned

Andrea Gritti 3.9.41 Torpedoed by FAA Swordfish aircraft, sunk, 37 33N 16 26E

Anfora 9.3.43 Scuttled Mormugao, burnt out; 48 raised; 49 BU Bombau

Angelina Lauro 10.6.40 Seized Liverpool; 6.40 MoWT, *Empire Advocate* (Br); 45 BU Bo'ness

Antonia C 4.4.41 Scuttled Massowah; 51 BU

Antonietta Costa 2.10.40 Torpedoed by subm HMS *Regent* 41 21N 18 52E; beached, TL

Antonietta Lauro 25.4.41 Torpedoed by subm HMS *Upholder*, sunk, 34 57N 11 44E

Antonio Limoncelli 12.41 Seized by Brazil; 42 *Paranaloide* (Brz)

Antonio Locatelli 12.11.40 Shelled (in convoy) by British cruisers, sunk, 12m from Valona (0 surv)

Aquileja 24.5.40 Hospital ship; 9.43 seized Spezia by Germans; 6.10.43 KM commd hospital ship; 15.12.43 attacked by Allied aircraft, on fire, aground at quayside, Marseilles; 16.2.44 decomm, salvage started; 26.6.44 scuttled Marseilles; 44 raised, BU

Aquitania 25.7.43 Bombed by British aircraft, sunk, 41 34N 10 51E

Arabia 4.4.41 Scuttled Massowah alongside quay; 11.8.41 refloated; 11.41 *Arabia II* (Br); Adm, coal hulk; 29.8.43 wrecked

Ardor 10.9.43 Bombed by German aircraft, sunk, 5m N of Gulf of Kotor

Argentea 12.5.44 Attacked by Allied aircraft, sunk, Spezia; salved, BU

Ariosto 14.2.42 Torpedoed by subm HMS *P38* 63° 12m E of Cape Africa; 15.2.42 sunk (–†, incl 132 Allied pow†; – surv, incl 162 Allied pow)

Arlesiana 5–22.12.42, 1.2.43 Bombed by British aircraft Tunis, badly damaged; abandoned; 29.5.46 sold salvors; 31.10.46 refloated; 49 BU Dunston, R Tyne

Arno 40 IN, hospital ship; 10.9.42 torpedoed by British aircraft, sunk, 33 14N 23 23E (27†)

Asmara 39 IN, transport; 10.8.43 torpedoed by subm HMS *Unshaken* 3m E of Brindisi, beached; 11.8.43 capsized, sunk

Assunta di Gregori 19.4.42 Torpedoed by subm HMS *Umbra*, sunk, 34 55N 11 42E

Atlanta 10.6.40 At Las Palmas; 14.6.41 ar Bordeaux; 9.9.43 seized by Germans; 43 *Charlotte* (Ger); 11.1.45 shelled (in convoy) by RN warships, sunk, off Egersund

Augusta 12.41 Seized Bahia by Brazil; 42 *Minasloide* (Brz)

Augustus 7.7.42 IN; 42 conv to carrier *Sparviero* (Ita); 11.42 bombed, damaged; 9.43 seized by Germans; 25.9.44 scuttled Genoa as blockship; 12.46 wreck refloated; 47 BU Spezia

Bacicin Padre 40 Interned Puerto Cabello, Venezuela; 31.3.41 seized; 42 *Manzanares* (Ven); 42 USMC, *Swivel* (Pan); 43 *St Mary* (US); 44 *Clyde* (US); 45 *Swivel* (US); 49 abandoned, damaged

Bainsizza 15.10.41 Bombed, torpedoed, by British aircraft; 16.10.41 sunk 34 35N 12 12E
Barbarigo 15.7.41 Torpedoed by subm HMS *P33*, sunk, 36 27N 11 54E (0†)
Beatrice C 3.6.41 Bombed by British Martin Maryland aircraft, sunk, 20m NE of Kerkennah Islands
Beppe 19.10.42 Torpedoed by subm HMS *Unbending*, sunk, 35 45N 12 01E
Birmania 3.5.41 Blew up, sunk, Tripoli harbour
Bonzo 16.12.40 Torpedoed by subm HMS *Truant*, sunk, 38 28N 16 44E
Bosforo 31.3.42 Torpedoed by subm HMS *Proteus*, sunk, 36 54N 21 18E
Brenta 4.4.41 Scuttled Massowah; 51 salved, BU
Buccari 20.6.41 Struck mine, sunk, off Taranto
Burano 9.43 KM, (Ger); 26.8.44 scuttled Pauillac as blockship; 46 raised, BU
Butterfly 28.4.43 Sunk (in convoy) by British destroyer about 60nm NNE of Ushant

Caffaro 12.9.41 Bombed by British aircraft, sunk, 34 14N 11 54E
California 13.6.40 Req IN, conv to hospital ship; 11.8.41 torpedoed by RAF aircraft, sunk, Syracuse harbour (1†); 49 raised, BU
Campania 28.6.43 Bombed by Allied aircraft, sunk, Leghorn
Capacitas 30.6.41 Torpedoed by subm *O23* (Ne), sunk, 7m NW of San Vicenzo, S of Leghorn
Capitano A Cecchi 8.5.41 Shelled by British warships, including cruiser HMS *Ajax*, sunk, 31 51 15N 19 53 20E
Capitano Bottego 4.4.41 Scuttled Massowah; 51 salved, BU
Capo Alga 18.8.44 Scuttled nantes; 45 raised; 48 BU
Capo Arma 6.40 Italian govt; 29.5.42 torpedoed (in convoy) by subm HMS *Turbulent*, sunk, 33 07N 19 28E
Capo Faro 30.11.41 Bombed (in convoy) by British aircraft from Malta, sunk, 37 28N 19 20E
Capo Lena 42 KM, *Kapolena* (Ger); 43–8.44 converting to *Sperrbrecher 37*; 18.8.44 scuttled Charpentier channel, St Nazaire; 51 wreck BU
Capo Olmo 10.6.40 Seized Marseilles by French; to GB; 45 French govt; 46 *Koufra* (Fra)
Capo Orso 16.2.43 Bombed by British aircraft, sunk, 37 40N 12 07E
Capo Vado 12.11.40 Shelled (in convoy) by British cruisers, sunk, 315° 12m off Saseno
Capo Vita 9.3.41 Torpedoed (in convoy) by subm HMS *Utmost*, sunk, 36 10N 11 07E
Carducci 18.3.44 Scuttled Leghorn; 1.47 refloated; 48 BU
Carignano 9.9.43 *Teiyu Maru* (Jpn); 13.11.44 attacked by USN carrier-based aircraft, sunk, 14 35N 120 55E
Carlo del Greco 13.12.41 Torpedoed (in convoy) by subm HMS *Upright*, sunk, 40 10N 17 60E
Carlo Martinolich 9.1.41 Torpedoed by subm HMS *Parthian*, sunk, 38 28N 16 41E
Carnia 23.3.41 Torpedoed (in convoy) by subm *Triton* (Gre), sunk, 40 58N 18 27E
Casaregis 17.9.41 Req IN; 11.10.41 torpedoed by British aircraft, on fire, sunk, 34 02N 12 42E
Castelverde 14.12.42 Torpedoed (in convoy) by subm HMS *Unruffled*, sunk, 37 29N 10 46E
Caterina 18.10.41 Torpedoed by subm HMS *Ursula* 350° 62m N of Tripoli, taken in tow; 19.10.41 sunk
Caterina Madre 13.9.43 Struck mine, sunk, 330° 10m off S Andrea Is, near Gallipoli, Italy
Celeno 43 *Claudia* (Ger); 44 (Bul); 45 *Grozny* (Rus)
Cesco 15.8.43 Torpedoed by subm HMS *Unruly* off Brindisi, beached; 44 refloated, LU Naples (ar 29.6.44); 51 BU
Cesteriano (Pan) 27.2.44 Torpedoed by subm HMS *Universal* E of St Tropez, damaged; towed Toulon; 3.44 bombed by Allied aircraft, sunk, Toulon; 5.46 refloated, sunk again; 48 refloated; 1.49 towed Savona for BU
Clelia Campanella 4.4.41 Scuttled Massowah; 42 salved; 42 MoWT, *Empire Prize* (Br); 46 *Bankivia* (Br); 49 BU Hong Kong
Col di Lana 18.2.43 Torpedoed by British aircraft, sunk, 38 29N 12 49E
Colombo 8.4.41 Scuttled Massowah to avoid capture by British forces; 48 raised; 49–51 BU *in situ*
Colorado 8.41 Seized by US; 12.41 USMC, *Typhoon* (Pan); 44 *Villalobos* (US)
Comitas 21.12.39 Struck mine Wielingen fairway near buoy No 3, off Vlissingen, beached Rammekens; 21.1.40 abandoned as TL
Conte di Misurata 9.11.41 Shelled (in convoy) by vessels of RN Force K, sunk, 37 10N 18 10E
Conte di Savoia 11.9.43 Attacked by US fighter-bombers, on fire, heeled over, sunk, Malamocco, near Venice; 16.10.45 raised; 50 BU Monfalcone
Conte Rosso 3.12.40 Req IN, troop transport; 24.5.41 torpedoed by subm HMS *Upholder*, sunk, 36 57N 15 34E (1212†, 1680 trps surv)
Conte Verde 9.9.43 Scuttled Shanghai to avoid capture by Japanese; 43–44 salved; 44 *Kotobuki Maru* (Jpn); 8.5.45 sunk following US air raid 34 30N 126 30E (believed sunk by mine laid by aircraft); 1.49 refloated; 51 BU Japan
Cortellazzo 20.11.42 Found by Sunderland flying-boat of 10 Sq RAAF; 1.12.42 found by destroyers HMAS *Quickmatch* and HMS *Redoubt*; abandoned by crew, torpedoed, sunk, by *Redoubt*
Cuma 18.10.41 Struck mine, sunk, 37 02N 14 08E

Dalmatia L 41 German control; 25.1.42 torpedoed by subm HMS *Ultimatum* 37 45N 15 30E; 28.1.42 sunk in tow 1m from San Ranieri, Messina
Dandolo 8.10.42 Torpedoed by British aircraft, sunk, 21° 60m from Ras el Tin

Dea Mazzella 8.9.43 Seized Venice by Germans; 30.9.43 shelled by Yugoslav partisans S of Sebenik, abandoned, sunk
Delfin 14.12.42 Torpedoed by subm HMS *Taku*, sunk, 37 52N 24 06E
Delia 16.4.42 Torpedoed by subm HMS *Turbulent*, sunk, 3m off Villanova, near Brindisi
Duca Degli Abruzzi 25.5.42 Scuttled Diego Suarez
Duchesa D'Aosta 14.11.42 Captured Fernando Po by FFr; 43 MoWT, *Empire Yukon* (Br); 47 *Petconnie* (Br)
Duilio 9.43 Scuttled Trieste; raised by Germans; 44 (Ger); 10.7.44 bombed by Allied aircraft, sunk, Vallone di Zaule, near Trieste; 48 refloated, BU Trieste

Edda 19.1.43 Torpedoed by subm HMS *Unbroken*, sunk, 33 33N 11 20E
Emma 15.1.43 Torpedoed by subm HMS *Splendid* 40 37N 13 47E; 16.1.43 torpedoed again, sunk
Enrichetta 10.10.42 Torpedoed by subm HMS *Unison*, sunk, 37 11N 21 26E
Enrico Costa 26.6.41 Torpedoed by subm HMS *Utmost*, sunk, 38 07N 14 37E
Entella 11.4.43 Torpedoed (in convoy) by subm HMS *Safari*, beached off Torre Finocchia, Sardinia; 12.4.43 torpedoed again, sunk
Erice 14.5.43 Bombed by British aircraft, on fire, sunk, Civitavecchia
Eridano 4.12.41 Torpedoed by subm HMS *Trusty*, sunk, 280° 6m from Cape Dukato
Erminia Mazzella 13.2.41 Captured by cruiser HMS *Hawkins* off Kismayu; 41 *Impala* (Br); 41 *Agulhas* (SA)
Ernani 10.6.40 At Las Palmas; 40 taken over by Germany, *Sleipner II* (Ger); 28.6.41 torpedoed in error by *U103*, sunk, 27 52N 26 17W, while disguised as *Enggano* (Ne) attempting to break through to Bordeaux
Esperia 20.8.41 Torpedoed (in convoy) by subm HMS *Unique*, sunk, 33 03N 13 03E (31†)
Esquilino 8.6.40 Captured off Perim; 12.11.41 MoWT, *Empire Governor* (Br); 46 BU Dalmuir and Troon
Etiopia 16.9.42 Req IN; 13.11.42 bombed by British aircraft, on fire, sunk, Tobruk
Etruria 8.11.42 Req IN; 22.12. 42 torpedoed by British aircraft, sunk, 38 06N 11 33E
Ettore 8.9.43 Seized Leghorn by Germans; 18.2.44 bombed by Allied aircraft Leghorn, damaged, beached; 7.44 scuttled Leghorn as blockship; postwar, raised, BU
Eugenio C 10.6.40 At El Ferrol; 6.41 ar St Nazaire; 41 German control; 26.4.44 bombed by British aircraft, sunk, off Bodø
Euro 10.6.40 at Norfolk VA; 12.41 seized by US; 12.41 USMC, *Bateau* (Pan); 29.3.42 shelled (convoy PQ13 straggler) by destroyer *Z26* (Ger), sunk, 72N 33E (40†, 6 surv/pow)

Fabio Filzi 14.8.41 Req IN, auxiliary *R55*; 13.12.41 torpedoed (in convoy) by subm HMS *Upright*, sunk, 40 10N 17 60E
Favorita 23.11.42 Torpedoed by subm HMS *Splendid*, sunk, 39N 11 11E
Fede 8.12.41 Seized by Mexico; 41 *Poza Rica* (Mex)
Fedora 10.1.42 Torpedoed by subm HMS *Thrasher*, sunk, 38 59N 19 59E
Fella 30.3.41 Scuttled Punta Arenas; raised, BU
Fianona 12.6.41 Shelled, torpedoed, by subm *O24* (Ne), sunk, 43 08N 10 03E
Fidelitas 9.43 Seized Bordeaux by Germans; 43 (Ger); 27.11.44 bombed by Allied aircraft, sunk, near Ålesund
Firenze 24.12.40 Torpedoed by subm *Papanicolis* (Gre), sunk, 40 34N 19 02E
Florida II 31.5.41 Attacked by British aircraft, sunk, Sfax; 41 salved, towed Genoa; 9.43 seized by Germans; 18.8.44 attacked by Allied aircraft, sunk, Savona; raised, BU
Foscolo 15.5.40 Attacked in error by German aircraft 6m NE of Zeebrugge (0†); abandoned; 18.5.40 sunk
Franca Fassio 4.10.40 Torpedoed by subm HMS *Triton*, sunk, 97° 16m from Capo Noli
Francesco Barbaro 27.9.42 Torpedoed (in convoy) by subm HMS *Umbra*, sunk, 37 15N 19 55E
Francesco Crispi 19.4.43 Torpedoed (in convoy) by subm HMS *Saracen*, sunk, 42 46N 09 46E (800+†)
Franco Martelli 18.4.41 Torpedoed by subm HMS *Urge*, sunk, 46 31N 08 46W
Frisco 25.8.44 Scuttled as blockship Bourg, Bordeaux; 45 raised, BU
Fusijama 10.6.40 At Bangkok; 22.8.41 ar Kobe; 7.2.42 sd Kobe; 26.4.42 ar Bordeaux; 8.9.43 seized by Germans; 12.8.44 scuttled as blockship Bassens, R Gironde; 45 raised, BU France

Galilea 41 Hospital ship; 28.3.42 torpedoed by subm HMS *Proteus*, sunk, 39 04N 20 05E
Gianni M 11.5.41 Captured N of Las Palmas by obv HMS *Hilary*, taken Belfast by prize crew; 41 MoWT, *Empire Control* (Br); 48 *Kleinella* (Br)
Gino Allegri 31.5.42 Torpedoed (in convoy) by subm HMS *Taku*, damaged, 33 34N 18 30E; torpedod by subm HMS *Proteus*, sunk, 32 27N 18 54E
Giorgio 21.3.43 Torpedoed by subm HMS *Splendid* 38 05N 14 10E; taken in tow, sunk
Giorgio Fassio 8.12.41 Seized by Mexico; 41 *Panuco* (Mex)
Giorgio Ohlsen 14.2.40 Struck mine, sunk, 53 17N 01 10E (17†)
Giovanni Boccaccio 19.11.43 Torpedoed by subm HMS *Sickle*, beached Monemvassia; CTL
Giove 4.4.41 Scuttled Massowah; salved by British; 42 MoWT, *Empire Trophy* (Br); 47 BU
Giovinezza 18.5.41 Torpedoed by subm HMS *Tetrarch*, sunk, 31 55N 19 54E
Giulia 20.1.43 Sunk by chariots from subm HMS *Thunderbolt*, Tripoli
Giulio Cesare 11.9.44 Bombed by 16 Sq SAAF Beaufighters, capsized, Vallone di Zaule,

near Trieste; 48 refloated, BU Trieste
Giulio Giordani 17.11.42 Torpedoed by British aircraft, on fire, NE of Misurata; 18.11.42 torpedoed by subm HMS *Porpoise*, sunk, 32 58N 15 38E
Giuseppe Mazzini 2.3.41 Bombed, sunk, Dahlak Is, off Massowah; 51 BU *in situ*
Gloriastella 17.9.40 Torpedoed by British aircraft, sunk, during RN attack on Benghazi
Goffredo Mameli 9.43 Seized by Germans; 14.11.44 bombed by Allied aircraft, sunk off Trieste; 9.46 raised, BU
Gradisca 40 IN, hospital ship; 11.9.43 seized Piræus by Germans; 9.43 (Ger); 16.9.43 KM; 30.10.43 commd hospital ship; 28.10.44 captured Aegean by destroyer HMS *Kimberley*, taken Alexandria, then Algiers; 5.45 returned owners; 23.1.46 aground E coast of Gavdo Is; 9.7.47 refloated, LU; 50 BU Venice
Grazia 19.11.39 Struck mine, sunk, 10m NE of North Foreland (6†)

Hilda 25.8.41 Seized Bandar Shapur by RN (Opn 'Countenance'); 42 repair ship at Bombay
Himalaya 9.43 Seized by Germans; 43 (Ger); 12.8.44 sunk as blockship R Gironde; 45 raised, BU
Honestas 14.12.42 Torpedoed (in convoy) by subm HMS *Sahib*, sunk, 37 29N 10 46E
Honor 8.9.43 Seized Genoa by Germans; 12.9.44 scuttled San Remo; 47 raised, BU San Remo

India 10.6.41 Scuttled Assab alongside quay in main harbour; 49 refloated; 25.10.49 ar Massowah; BU
Integritas 16.2.41 Scuttled Kismayu
Iridio Mantovani 1.12.41 Torpedoed, bombed (in convoy), by British aircraft, sunk, 35 50N 12 50E (–†)
Isarco 5.9.41 Torpedoed by subm *O21* (Ne), sunk, 42 48N 09 58E
Ischia 28.2.43 Torpedoed by subm HMS *Torbay*, sunk, 1m off Portofino
Istria 27.8.42 Torpedoed by British aircraft, sunk, 33 33N 23 41E
Italia 43 Seized by Germans; 6.7.44 hit by rockets from Allied aircraft, internal explosion, on fire, heeled over, sunk, Arsa, Trieste; 50 refloated, BU
Italo Balbo 9.9.41 Torpedoed by subm *O24* (Ne) 42 47N 09 57E; 10.9.41 sunk
Ivorea 7.10.43 Bombed by German aircraft, sunk, Leros Is

Jole Fassio 31.3.41 Set on fire by crew Puerto Cabello; seized by Venezuela; 42 USMC, *Alcibiades* (Pan); 8.44 USN, *Andrew Doria* (IX-32); 46 USMC, *Alcibiades* (Pan); 49 BU
Juventus 16.2.41 Torpedoed by British Swordfish aircraft, sunk, 3m NE of Kuriat Is, Tunisia

Laconia 6.40 LU Newport News; 3.41 detained Newport News; 23.8.41 req by US; 8.41 USMC, *Elwood* (Pan); 8.45 LU Mobile; 23.12.48 (Ita); 49 BU Mobile
Laura C 3.7.41 Torpedoed by subm HMS *Upholder*, sunk, 37 54N 15 44E
Laura Corrado 30.3.41 Torpedoed, shelled, by subm HMS *Rorqual*, sunk, 38 45N 12 20E
Leonardo da Vinci 11.2.41 Captured Kismayu by British forces; 43 MoWT, hospital ship *Empire Clyde* (Br); 1.1.48 RN, hospital ship *Maine* (Br)
Leopardi 14.8.40 Struck mine (laid 14.8.40 by subm HMS *Rorqual*), sunk, 32 39N 21 03E
Lerici 15.8.42 Torpedoed by subm HMS *Porpoise*, sunk, 34 35N 21 32E
Liguria 40 Troopship; 22.1.41 bombed by British aircraft, on fire, capsized, sunk, Tobruk; 50 raised, BU Savona
Lina Campanella 9.43 (Ger); 23.5.44 attacked by Allied aircraft, damaged, Cherso; 5.45 taken over by Yugoslavia at Cherso; 8.45 at Split, used as storage vessel; 50 BU
Livenza 8.9.43 Seized by Germans; *Lisa* (Ger); 22.2.44 torpedoed by British aircraft, sunk, N of Heraklion
Loasso 26.6.40 Struck mine (laid 14.6.40 by subm HMS *Rorqual*), sunk, 3m off Gargano
Lombardia 40 Troopship; 4.8.43 bombed by Allied aircraft, on fire, burnt out, Naples; 46–47 raised; 47–48 BU Spezia
Lucania 12.2.42 Torpedoed by subm HMS *Una*, on fire, sunk, 39 20N 17 25E
Luciano 15.4.41 Attacked by British aircraft, sunk, Valona roads
Luigi 24.11.42 Torpedoed by British aircraft, sunk, 40 02N 17 20E

Madda 6.40 Chased by British warship near Tenerife, made for Spanish waters, beached; refloated, towed Santa Cruz; 45 *Monte Nafarrate* (Spn)
Maddalena G 5.3.42 Torpedoed by subm HMS *Torbay* inside Corfu harbour; 2.3.44 partly stripped by Germans; 1.3.45 sunk as blockship Venice; raised, BU
Maddalena Odero 17.7.41 Torpedoed by subm *O23* (Ne), badly damaged, S Tyrrhenian Sea; 18.7.41 bombed by British aircraft, sunk, off Lampedusa
Manzoni 22.3.43 Torpedoed by British aircraft, sunk, Tobruk; raised, BU
Mar Bianco 8.9.43 Seized Ancona by Germans; 43 (Ger); 7.12.43 bombed by Allied aircraft Zadar (Zara); sank to bottom; 2.2.44 wreck capsized
Marangona 10.12.40 Struck Italian mine, sunk, 36 13N 11 59E
Marco Foscarini 21.4.43 Torpedoed by subm HMS *Unison*, sunk, 37 48N 11 32E
Marco Polo 9.43 Seized Spezia by Germans; 12.5.44 scuttled Spezia by Germans as blockship; 49 wreck raised; 50 BU
Marghera 12.2.41 Scuttled Kismayu; BU *in situ*
Maria 9.11.41 Shelled (in convoy) by warships of RN Force K, sunk, 37 08N 18 09E
Maria Eugenia 17.9.40 Torpedoed by British aircraft, sunk, Benghazi; raised, BU

Mariarosa 29.2.40 Torpedoed by *U20*, sunk, 52 24 30N 01 59E (12†, 18 surv)
Marigola 22–23.9.41 Attacked by British aircraft, beached, 2m E of Kuriat; 1.11.41 shelled by subm HMS *Utmost*, on fire; TL
Marin Sanudo 3.3.42 Torpedoed by subm HMS *Uproar*, sunk, 35 18N 12 35E
Marina O 8.12.41 Seized by Mexico; 41 *Tabasco* (Mex)
Marte 29.12.42 Torpedoed by subm HMS *Turbulent*, sunk, 39 17N 09 41E
Marzocco 13.6.40 Attempted scuttling, ashore Ugie R, 1.5m N of near Peterhead; 21.6.40 abandoned, broke in two; taken in sections to Scapa Flow, used as blockship
Mauly 41 *Manfredo Campeiro* (Ita); 41 transport; 27.8.42 torpedoed by subm HMS *Umbra*, sunk, 35 39N 23 07E
Mediceo 9.43 Seized by Germans, (Ger); 31.1.45 bombed by British aircraft, sunk, off Tagliamento
Mira 15.5.43 Bombed by Allied aircraft, sunk, Civitavecchia; raised; 1.44 again sunk; 47 raised; 48 BU Savona
Mirella 1.3.40 Torpedoed by *U20*, sunk, 52 26 09N 02 05 02E (1†, 29 surv); 2.3.40 sunk; wreck dispersed
Monbaldo 10.6.40 Ar Parà; 24.7.41 ar Bordeaux; 9.43 (Ger); 24.3.45 sunk Stettin; raised; 45 USSR, *Kaliningrad* (Rus)
Moncalieri 13.2.41 Bombed by aircraft from HMS *Formidable*, damaged, Massowah; 4.4.41 scuttled; refloated by British, BU
Monfiore 10.6.40 At New Orleans; 12.41 seized by US; 42 USMC, *White Clover* (Pan); 45 *Leo Tolstoy* (Rus)
Monrosa 8.11.40 Req IN; 25.10.41 torpedoed by subm HMS *Triumph*, sunk, 37 41N 23 53E
Monstella 4.11.40 Req IN; 31.8.42 torpedoed by subm HMS *Rorqual* off Zante, beached Corfu roads; became target for both Allied and enemy aircraft; 47 raised, towed Corfu; 48 BU Piræus
Monte Piana 11.6.40 Beached Aden to avert attempted scuttling by crew; 15.7.40 refloated; 41 MoWT, *Empire Baron* (Br); 29.1.47 *Rubystone* (Br)
Montello 29.10.40 Req IN; 3.6.41 bombed (in convoy) by British Martin Maryland aircraft, sunk, 35 25N 11 57E
Morea 15.8.40 Torpedoed (missed), shelled, by subm HMS *Osiris* 50m W of Durazzo; 16.8.40 sunk

Nazario Sauro 6.4.41 Scuttled Dahlak Is, off Massowah; 48 raised, BU
Neptunia 30.5.41 IN, troopship; 18.9.41 torpedoed (in convoy) by subm HMS *Upholder*, sunk, 33 02N 14 42E (with *Oceania* (*qv*) total 384†)
Nicolo Odero 10.6.40 Seized Marseilles by French; 40 returned Italy; 24.1.41 req IN; 13.9.41 bombed by British aircraft 30m from Tripoli, on fire; beached 6m from Zuara; TL
Ninetto G 5.4.42 Torpedoed by subm HMS *Una* 37 05N 15 41E; sunk
Nino Padre 9.43 Seized Genoa by Germans; 11.4.44 attacked by Allied aircraft, sunk, Genoa
Ninuccia 28.1.42 Torpedoed by subm HMS *Thorn*, sunk, 43 30N 15 55E
Nirvo 24.5.43 Bombed by Allied aircraft, sunk, at Olbia; 46 salved, repaired
Nita 6.8.42 Torpedoed (in convoy) by British aircraft; 7.8.42 sunk 35 15N 12 17E; 54 wreck raised, BU
Norge 21.12.40 Torpedoed by British aircraft, sunk, 34 39N 10 48E
Numidia 9.43 Seized by Germans; 18.8.44 struck mine, sunk, off Parenzo

Oceania 26.5.41 IN, troopship; 18.9.41 torpedoed (in convoy) by subm HMS *Upholder* 33 02N 14 42E; taken in tow, again torpedoed, sunk (with *Neptunia* (*qv*) total 384†)
Ogaden 12.8.42 Torpedoed by subm HMS *Porpoise*, sunk, 9m NW of Ras el Tin (3 pow†, *c*200 pow surv)
Olimpia 9.9.43 Seized Trieste by Germans, (Ger); 14.10.43 shelled by RN destroyer, sunk, off Cattaro
Oreste 27.3.42 Struck mine, sunk, 13m SE of Cattaro

Palestina 40 *Eridania* (Ita); 8.7.40 Req IN; 11.9.43 under threat of German aircraft attack made for Zara, but captured, ordered Venice; 7.10.43 torpedoed by subm *Sokol* (Pol), sunk, off Cape Promontore
Pampano 12.41 Seized by Brazil; 42 *Rioloide* (Brz)
Paolina 27.8.42 Struck mine, sunk, 131° 6m from Cap Bon
Paolo 28.2.43 Attacked by Allied aircraft, on fire, sunk, Cagliari; salved; 13.5.43 again attacked; raised, BU
Pascoli 3.8.44 Torpedoed by subm *Curie* (Fra), damaged, La Ciotat; BU Marseilles
Pasubio 16.2.43 Torpedoed (in convoy) by subm HMS *Unrivalled*, sunk, 38 18N 16 29E
Pensilvania 13.2.41 Found off Mogadishu by RN vessels, sunk by bombs and gunfire
Perla 7.1.42 Torpedoed by British aircraft, sunk, 20m S of Pantellaria
Perseo 18.8.42 Torpedoed by subm HMS *Safari*, sunk, off Cape Carbonera
Petrarca 10.2.43 Torpedoed by subm HMS *Una*, damaged, 10m N of Cotrone, beached; 15.2.43 attacked by Allied aircraft; again torpedoed by *Una*, sunk, 39 16N 17 08E
Piave 10.6.41 Scuttled Assab alongside quay in main harbour; 50 refloated; 10.50 towed Massowah; 5.51 towed Italy, BU
Piemonte 17.11.42 Torpedoed by subm HMS *Umbra* 38 21N 15 28E, damaged, taken Messina, beached; 4.5.43 and 15.8.43 bombed by Allied aircraft, partly submerged, cap-

sized, sunk; 24.7.49 wreck raised, BU Spezia
Pietro Orseolo 6.10.40 At Kobe; 41 blockade runner; 24.12.41–23.2.42 Kobe–Bordeaux; 18.5.42 req IN; 1.10.42–2.12.42 Bordeaux–Kobe; 25.1.43–3.4.43 Kobe–Bordeaux; 8.9.43 German control; 18.12.43 torpedoed by British aircraft, sunk, Concarneau Bay
Pluto 40 Sold Portugal; 12.41 req by Japanese; 42 *Plutogo* (Ita); 24.6.45 bombed, sunk, 34 47N 126 25E
Po 21.11.40 Req IN; 14.3.41 hospital ship; 14.3.41 torpedoed by British aircraft, sunk, 40 22N 19 28E
Pollenzo 6.40 Interned Algeciras; 44 British prize at Gibraltar; 44 MoWT (Br); 45 sold for BU, but 46 *Alcantara* (Pan)
Portofino 6.11.42 Torpedoed by British aircraft, sunk, Benghazi
Poseidone 9.43 KM (Ger); 8.5.44 struck mine, sunk, near Punta Sabbioni, Venice; 45–46 raised, repaired; 53–54 BU
Pozzuoli 1.2.43 Torpedoed by subm HMS *Turbulent*, sunk, 60° 7m from Capo S Vito, Sicily
Premuda 11.11.40 Shelled (in convoy) by British cruisers, on fire, sunk, Strait of Taranto
Probitas 25.9.43 Bombed by German aircraft, sunk, voyage Santi Quaranta–Brindisi; 15.3.44 at Brindisi; CTL
Promoteo 4.4.41 Scuttled Massowah; CTL, BU
Provvidenza 22.9.40 Torpedoed by subm HMS *Truant*, sunk, 3.5m 150° from Punta Imperatore, Ischia
Pugliola 12.9.43 Struck mine, sunk, off Isola Sant' Andrea, near Gallipoli, Italy

Ramb I 9.6.40 Req IN, amc; 27.2.41 found by cruiser HMNZS *Leander*, shelled, exploded, sunk, 01N 68 30E (*c*150†, 100 surv)
Ramb II 9..4.40 Req IN, amc; 42 Japanese charter, *Calitea II* (Ita); 8.9.43 scuttled Kobe; raised and used by Japanese; 12.1.45 bombed by USAAF aircraft, sunk, Osaka
Ramb III 11.6.40 Req IN; 8.9.43 seized by Germans; KM, aux minesweeper *Kiebitz*; 5.11.43 bombed by Allied aircraft, sunk, Fiume; salved; 1.5.45 scuttled Trieste, salved; 50 *Galeb* (Yug)
Ramb IV 7.2.41 Req IN; 8.4.41 captured Red Sea by British warships; 41 MoWT, hospital ship (Br); 10.5.42 bombed by German aircraft 31 17N 29 23E, abandoned (165†, incl 155 hosp; 199 surv, incl 114 hosp); shelled by HM ship, sunk, 274° 12m from Ras el Tin
Rapido 15.6.44 Struck mine, sunk, 3m S of Grado
Recca 41 *Libertad* (Cub); 4.12.43 torpedoed by *U129*, sunk, 24 30N 74 32W (25†, 18 surv)
Recco 3.5.41 Intercepted by obv HMS *Hilary* 350m N of Azores, scuttled to prevent capture
Rex 9.9.43 Seized by Germans; 3.3.44 (Ger); 8–9.9.44 attacked by RAF Beaufighter aircraft and hit by 123 rockets in 48 hours, on fire, capsized, sunk, in shallow water off Capo d'Istria, Gulf of Muggia, S of Trieste; 8.47 raised; BU *in situ*
Rialto 5.10.41 Torpedoed by British aircraft, sunk, 80m from Misurata
Rina Corrado 9.11.41 Shelled (in convoy) by vessel of RN Force K, sunk, 37 08N 18 09E
Riv 6.4.41 Bombed by Allied aircraft Mediterranean, damaged, reached Tripoli; 30.8.41 bombed by British aircraft, sunk, Tripoli
Roma 10.40 IN, conv to carrier *Aquila* (Ita); 8.9.43 seized incomplete by Germans; 20.6.44 and 6.1.45 bombed by Allied aircraft, damaged, Genoa; 19.4.45 attacked by Italian one-man torpedoes, sunk at moorings, Genoa; 46 wreck refloated; 52 BU Spezia
Romolo 12.6.40 Found by amc HMAS *Manoora* 02 20S 163 45E; scuttled to avoid capture
Rosandra 14.6.43 Torpedoed by subm HMS *Tactician*, damaged, 40 14N 19 28E; beached, again torpedoed, TL
Rosario 10.3.43 Torpedoed by subm HMS *Trooper*, sunk, 4m NE of Punta Milazzo, Sicily
Rosolina Pilo 40 Transport; 18.8.42 torpedoed by subm HMS *United*, sunk, 50m S of Pantellaria

Sabaudia (ex *Stockholm*) 6.7.44 Bombed by British aircraft Trieste; on fire, aground; TL
Sabbia 4.7.43 Torpedoed by subm *Dolfijn* (Ne), badly damaged, 42 05N 11 47E; towed Civitavecchia, sank in port; CTL
Sagitta 9.11.41 Shelled (in convoy) by RN Force K vessels, sunk, 37 08N 18 09E
Salpi 9.2.42 Struck mine (laid 22.10.41 by subm HMS *Rorqual*), sunk, 100° 2m from Cape Ferrato
Salvatore 9.43 Seized by Germans; 43 *Sabine* (Ger); 1.6.44 bombed by British aircraft, sunk, off Crete
San Giovanni Battista 19.1.42 Torpedoed by British aircraft 33 47N 12 17E; 2.2.42 stranded 2m W of Tagiura after tow line broke; refloated, towed Tripoli; 19.1.43 scuttled Tripoli harbour entrance; refloated, BU
San Marco 1.6.41 Torpedoed by subm HMS *Clyde*, sunk, 5m E of Cape Carbonara, Sardinia
San Pietro 8.11.42 Sunk by British at Casablanca; salved, beached; later abandoned for BU
Sanandrea 30.8.42 Bombed by British aircraft, sunk, 39 49N 18 15E
Sangro 20.4.41 Captured N Atlantic by obv HMS *Camito*; 6.5.41 torpedoed by *U97*, sunk, 50 42N 21 22E
Sannio 10.4.41 Scuttled Assab; 3.50 salved; 51 BU Savona
Sant' Antioco 15.12.42 Torpedoed by subm HMS *Unruffled*, sunk, 37 32N 10 39E
Santa Maria 9.43 Seized by Germans; 10.44 attacked by Allied aircraft, damaged, Venice; scuttled as blockship Porto di Lido, Venice; refloated, BU

Santa Paola 9.43 Seized Venice by Germans; 43 (Ger); 20.3.44 scuttled by Germans to block entrance Porti di Lido, Venice; refloated, BU, postwar
Santagata 4.8.43 Bombed by Allied aircraft, sunk, Naples; wreck BU *in situ*
Sardegna 29.12.40 Torpedoed (in convoy) by subm *Proteus* (Gre), sunk, 40 31N 19 02E (0†)
Savoia 14.2.41 Captured by RN cruiser, taken Mombasa; 42 MoWT, *Empire Arun* (Br); 47 *Granlake* (Br)
Securitas 8.9.43 Seized Leghorn by Germans; 7.44 scuttled Leghorn; raised, CTL
Serenitas 5.7.40 Bombed by British aircraft, sunk, Tobruk; 51 raised, BU Savona
Sicilia 1.2.41 IN, hospital ship; 23.4.43 attacked by Allied aircraft, sunk; raised; 49 BU
Sileno 9.43 Sunk Naples by Germans; raised; 21.5.48 ar Savona for BU
Silvano 9.9.43 Seized Naples by Germans; later scuttled, raised; CTL, BU
Silvia Tripcovich 28.10.40 Req IN; 23.2.41 torpedoed (in convoy) by subm HMS *Upright*, sunk, 34 23N 11 49E (0 surv)
Sirio 29.11.42 Bombed by British aircraft, sunk, Tripoli
Snia Amba 4.11.40 Torpedoed by subm HMS *Tetrarch* 31 35N 19 20E; beached; 5.2.41 declared TL
Sniafiocco 40 *Sereno* (Ita); 20.7.40 torpedoed by British aircraft, sunk, Tobruk
Stella 14.8.41 Captured 25N 40W by RN vessels; 41 MoWT, *Empire Planet* (Br); 8.46 sold; 47 *Inchkeith* (Br)
Stelvio 8.12.41 Seized Tampico by Mexico; 41 *Ebano* (Mex)
Strombo 10.7.41 Torpedoed by subm HMS *Torbay*, Zea Canal, Greece, damaged; 22.8.41 explosion, sunk, Skaramanga Bay
Sumatra 8.12.41 Scuttled Phuket, Thailand
Superga 29.9.41 Torpedoed (in convoy) by subm *SC-211* (Rus) 43N 27 53E; ashore, broke in two; 30.9.41 both section torpedoed by *SC-211*; TL

Tagliamento 22.4.43 Torpedoed by subm HMS *Saracen*, sunk, 42 46N 09 46E
Tellaro 9.43 German control; 26.6.44 scuttled Leghorn port entrance by Germans; salved, BU
Tembien 21.9.40 Req IN; 27.2.42 torpedoed by subm HMS *Upholder*, sunk, 32 55N12 42E (–†, 78 pow†, 420 pow surv)
Teresa 10.6.40 At Rio de Janeiro; 12.41 seized by Brazil; 16.1.42 *Goiazloide* (Brz)
Teresa Odero 10.6.40 At Puerto Cabello; 30.11.42 scuttled; 44 *Quilmes* (Arg)
Tergestea 2.4.43 Torpedoed by subm *Katsonis* (Gre), sunk, off Gytheios
Tevere 5.40 IN, hospital ship; 17.2.41 struck mine off Tripoli, badly damaged; 17.1.43 towed out, stranded Tripoli harbour entrance; 20.1.43 scuttled Tripoli entrance as blockship upon German/Italian evacuation; 16.1.50 refloated; 50 BU Savona
Timavo 11.6.40 Overtaken by aircraft off Cape Vidal, 160m N of Durban; scuttled 27 49S 32 36E to avoid capture
Tina Primo 18.3.40 Struck mine, sunk, 51 20 43N 01 44 27E (1†, 36 surv)
Titania 19.10.42 Torpedoed (in convoy) by subm HMS *Unbroken*, damaged; 20.10.42 torpedoed by subm HMS *Safari*, sunk, 34 45N 12 31E
Todaro 6.40 Interned Santa Cruz; 18.6.41 ar Bordeaux; 7.41 KM charter; 8.9.43 seized Bordeaux by Germans; 14.8.44 scuttled R Gironde; 45 wreck raised, BU
Torcello 5.11.41 Torpedoed by subm *SC-214* (Rus), sunk, 42 55N 28 03E
Traviata 11.1.40 Struck mine (laid by destroyer of German 4 Destroyer fl), sunk, 135° 8m from Cromer Knoll LV (0†)
Trottiera 10.6.40 Interned Puerto Cabello; 31.3.41 scuttled by crew; 43 raised; 43 USMC, *Orissa* (Pan); USN, *Malvern*; 45 USMC, *Orissa* (Pan)
Trovatore 6.40 At Las Palmas; 44 *Cabo del Agua* (Spn)
Tuscania 10.6.40 At Tampico; 8.12.41 seized by Mexico; *Minatitlan* (Mex)

Ugo Bassi 31.7.40 Req IN; 28.6.41 torpedoed by subm HMS *Severn*, sunk, 40 07N 09 50E
Umbria 12.6.40 Scuttled 19 38N 37 17E to avoid capture by RN vessels; wreck raised, BU
Urania 4.4.41 Scuttled Massowah; 51 BU *in situ*
Utilitas 3.6.40 Req IN; 5.2.43 torpedoed by subm HMS *Turbulent*, sunk, outside Palermo

Valdirosa 9.43 Seized Leghorn by Germans; 7.44 scuttled Leghorn as blockship; 45 raised; BU
Valdivagna 9.1.41 Torpedoed by subm HMS *Pandora*, sunk, 39 15N 09 44E
Valentino Coda 14.6.43 Torpedoed by subm HMS *Unruly*, sunk, 38 52N 15 27E
Valsavoia 2.2.43 Torpedoed (in convoy) by subm HMS *Safari*, sunk, 40 35N 14 29E
Valverde 9.9.43 Sunk by German E-boats off Castellogncello
Veloce 2.12.42 Torpedoed by British aircraft, shelled by British warships, sunk, 20m S of Kerkennah Islands
Vesuvio 4.4.41 Scuttled Massowah; 4.53 refloated, towed Italy; BU
Vettor Pisani 24.7.42 Torpedoed by subm HMS *Unbeaten* 38 05N 20 12E; towed to Argostoli area; sunk by RAF torpedo aircraft and bombers
Victoria 40 Troopship; 23.1.42 torpedoed (in convoy) by FAA Swordfish and Albacore aircraft, sunk, 33 40N 17 45E
Viminale 3.1.43 Badly damaged by *Chariot XVI* Palermo; taken in tow for Taranto; 23.1.43 torpedoed by subm HMS *Unbending* 37 53N 15 43E; aground Port Salvo, Melito; refloated, 25.7.43 sunk by Allied warships 38 44N 15 50E while under tow

Virgilio 1.6.40 Req as transport; 18.3.41 hospital ship; 6.12.43 torpedoed by subm HMS *Uproar*, badly damaged, off Toulon; 6.44 scuttled Toulon
Volpi 8.12.41 Scuttled Phuket, Thailand

XXIII Marzo 4.4.41 Scuttled Massowah; raised, BU
XXIV Maggio 10.6.40 At Recife; 29.6.41–27.7.41 Recife–Royan; 8.9.43 captured Amsterdam by Germans; 22.9.44 sunk Amsterdam; raised, BU
XXI Aprile 17.2.43 Torpedoed by subm HMS *Splendid*, sunk, 38 13N 12 43E
XXVIII Ottobre 10.6.40 At Phuket, Thailand; 8.12.41 scuttled to prevent seizure

Zeffiro 20.5.41 Struck Italian mine, sunk, 6m from Cap Bon
Zena 10.10.41 Torpedoed by British aircraft, sunk, 34 52N 12 22E
Zenobia Martini 21.9.42 Req IN; 17.1.43 torpedoed by subm HMS *Unseen*, sunk, 33 56N 11 06E

Seized, change of flag, and lost through war causes
Ada O 10.6.40 At New Orleans; 41 seized by US; 8.41 USMC (US); 42 *Hermis* (Pan); 7.6.42 torpedoed by *U158* 23 08N 84 42W (1†, 50 surv); sunk
Adamello 41 Taken over by Uruguay; 41 *Montevideo* (Uru); 8.3.42 torpedoed by subm *Enrico Tazzoli* (Ita), sunk, 29 13N 69 35W (14†, 35 surv)
Americano 8.12.41 Seized by Mexico; 41 *Tuxpam* (Mex); 27.6.42 torpedoed, shelled, by *U129*, sunk, 20 15N 96 20W (8†, 31 surv)
Andrea 10.6.40 Seized Newcastle by GB; 40 MoWT, *Empire Adventure* (Br); 20.9.40 torpedoed (in convoy OB216) by *U138* off Islay, taken in tow; 23.9.40 sunk 55 11 30N "157" W (21†, 18 surv)
Arsa 10.6.40 At New York; 41 seized by US; 11.10.41 USMC, *Friar Rock* (Pan); 13.1.42 torpedoed by *U130* 45 30N 50 40W (6 surv); sunk 45 51N 50 52W
Auctoritas 12.41 Seized Rio de Janeiro by Brazil; 42 *Pelotasloide* (Brz); 4.7.43 torpedoed by *U590*, sunk, 00 24S 47 36W (5†, 39 surv)
Aussa 10.6.40 At New York; 8.41 seized by US; 20.10.41 USMC, *Africander* (Pan); 13.9.42 torpedoed (in convoy PQ18) by German aircraft, sunk, 76N 10E (0†)
Barbana G 10.6.40 Seized Leith by GB; 40 MoWT, *Empire Airman* (Br); 21.9.40 torpedoed (in convoy HX72) by *U100*, sunk, 54N 18W (33†, 4 surv)
Caboto 25.8.41 Captured Bandar Shapur by RN (Opn 'Countenance'); 41 MoWT, *Empire Kohinoor* (Br); 2.7.43 torpedoed by *U618*, damaged, 06 20N 16 30W; 3.7.43 torpedoed, sunk (6†, 82 surv)
Calabria 11.6.40 Seized Calcutta while drydocked; 21.6.40 MoWT (Br), intended name *Empire Inventor* not used; 8.12.40 torpedoed (convoy SL56 straggler) by *U103*, sunk, 52 43N 18 07W (360†, 0 surv)
Capo Noli 10.6.40 Seized St Lawrence estuary; 40 *Bic Island* (Br); 29.10.42 torpedoed (convoy HX212 straggler) by *U224*, sunk, 55 05N 23 27W (44†, 0 surv)
Cellina 10.6.40 Seized Gibraltar by GB; 40 MoWT, *Empire Sailor* (Br); 21.11.42 torpedoed (in convoy ON145) by *U518*, sunk, 43 53N 55 12W (22†, 36 surv)
Clara 8.40 Seized Savannah by US; 18.6.41 USMC, *Stone Street* (Pan); 13.9.42 torpedoed (convoy ON127 straggler – boiler trouble) by *U594*, sunk, 48 18N 39 43W (13†, 1 pow, 40 surv)
Dino 8.41 Seized Boston by US; 12.41 USMC, *Meridian* (Pan); 11.11.41 torpedoed (convoy SC53 straggler) by *U561*, sunk, N Atlantic
Elios 10.6.40 Seized Newcastle; 40 MoWT, *Empire Brigade* (Br); 19.10.40 torpedoed (in convoy SC7) by *U99*, sunk, 57 12N 10 43W (6†, 35 surv)
Euro 40 Seized by US; 41 USMC, *Bateau* (Pan); 29.3.42 shelled (convoy PQ13 straggler) by German destroyer *Z26*, sunk, 72N 33E (40†, 6 surv)
Fausto 9.41 Seized Montevideo by Uruguay; 41 *Maldonado* (Uru); 2.8.42 torpedoed, shelled, by *U510*, sunk, 28 20N 63 10W (0†, 49 surv)
Felce 10.6.40 Seized Haifa by GB; 41 MoWT, *Empire Defender* (Br); 15.11.41 torpedoed by Italian aircraft, sunk, 18m S of Galeta Is (4†, 65 pow)
Fortunstella 6.40 At Necochea; 25.8.41 to Argentina; 41 *Rio Tercero* (Arg); 22.6.42 torpedoed by *U202*, sunk, 39 15N 72 32W (5†, 37 surv)
Genoano 8.12.41 Seized Tampico by Mexico; 41 *Faja de Oro* (Mex); 21.5.42 torpedoed, shelled, by *U106*, sunk, 23 30N 84 24W (10†, 27 surv)
Gioacchino Lauro 10.6.40 Seized West Hartlepool by GB; 40 MoWT, *Empire Engineer* (Br); 4.2.41 torpedoed (SC20 straggler) by *U123*, sunk, 54N 35W (40†, 0 surv)
Guidonia 6.40 At Norfolk VA; 3.41 detained; 23.8.41 req by US; 9.41 USMC, *Plaudit* (Pan); 8.11.42 torpedoed, shelled, by *U181*, sunk, 36S 26 32E (3†, 47 surv)
Ida Z O 12.41 Seized Mobile by US; 12.41 USMC, *Macbeth* (Pan); 13.9.42 attacked (in convoy PQ18) by German aircraft, sunk, 76 05N 10E (0†)
Ircania 8.40 Seized Jacksonville by US; 41 USMC, *Raceland* (Pan); 28.3.42 attacked (in convoy PQ13) by German Ju88 aircraft, sunk, 72 40N 20 20E (33†, 13 surv)
Lucifero 10.6.40 At Tampico; 8.12.41 seized by Mexico; 41 *Potrero del Llano* (Mex); 14.5.42 torpedoed by *U564*, sunk, 25 35N 80 06W (13†, 22 surv)
Manon 13.2.41 Captured near Kismayu by RN vessels; 41 MoWT (Br); 7.10.42 torpedoed by subm *I-162* (Jpn), sunk, 15N 80 30E (8†, 74 surv)
Mincio 11.6.40 Stopped, sent Methil, seized; 40 MoWT, *Empire Fusilier* (Br); 9.2.42 torpedoed (ind) by *U85*, sunk, 44 45N 47 25W (9†, 38 surv)

Mongioia 10.6.40 At Houston; 41 seized by US; 41 USMC, *Exterminator* (Pan); 5.7.42 struck mine (in convoy) off Reykjavik (0†); temporarily repaired, proceeded St John's Nfl; 5.9.43 ar Hampton Roads; BU Philadelphia
Moscardin 10.6.40 Detained Newcastle; 27.6.40 seized by GB; 40 MoWT, *Empire Gunner* (Br); 7.9.41 bombed by German aircraft, 52 08N 05 18W (0†, 41 surv); 7.9.41 sunk 52 09N 05 16W
Mugnone 10.6.40 Seized Newcastle; 40 MoWT, *Empire Progress* (Br); 13.4.42 torpedoed by *U402*, sunk, 40 29N 52 35W (12†, 38 surv)
Pamia 10.6.40 Seized Liverpool by GB; 17.6.40 MoWT, *Empire Protector* (Br); 30.5.41 torpedoed by *U38*, sunk, 06N 14 25W (5†, 35 surv)
Pellice 10.6.40 Seized Newcastle by GB; 40 MoWT, *Empire Statesman* (Br); 11.12.40 torpedoed (ind) by *U94*, sunk, W of Ireland (32†, 0 surv)
Pietro Campanella 10.6.40 At Baltimore; 23.8.41 Req by US; 12.41 USMC, *Equipoise* (Pan); 27.3.42 torpedoed by *U160*, sunk, 36 36N 74 45W (40†, 13 surv)
Procida 10.6.40 Seized Cardiff by GB; 40 MoWT, *Empire Volunteer* (Br); 15.9.40 torpedoed (in convoy SC3) by *U48*, sunk, 56 43N 15 17W (6†, 33 surv)
San Giuseppe 12.41 Seized Norfolk VA by US; 42 USMC, *Aneroid* (Pan); 2.10.42 torpedoed by *U175*, sunk, 08 24N 59 12W (6†, 43 surv)
Santarosa 12.41 Seized Norfolk VA by US; 41 USMC; 42 *Ramapo* (Pan); 16.2.42 torpedoed by *U108*, sunk, 35 10N 65 50W (0 surv)
Sistiana 10.6.40 Seized Cape Town; 40 *Myrica* (Br); 41 MoWT, *Empire Union* (Br); 26.12.42 torpedoed (in convoy ONS154) by *U356*, sunk, 47 30N 24 30W (6†, 63 surv)
Vigor 8.12.41 Seized by Mexico; 12.41 *Amatlan* (Mex); 4.9.42 torpedoed by *U171*, sunk, 23 27N 97 30W (10†, 24 surv)
Villarperosa 41 Seized by US; 12.41 USMC; 42 *Colin* (Pan); 26.4.44 torpedoed (convoy SC157 straggler) by *U859*, sunk, 54 16N 31 58W (1†, 53 surv)

Seized, change of flag, sunk Mulberry Harbour, Normandy
Antonietta 41 Seized by US; 42 USMC, *Olambala* (Pan); 8.6.44 sunk as breakwater Gooseberry 2, Mulberry A, Omaha Beach, St Laurent
Belvedere 3.41 Detained Philadelphia by US; 6.6.41 seized; 10.41 USMC, *Audacious* (Pan); 8.6.44 sunk as breakwater Gooseberry 1, Arromanches
Carso 12.2.41 Scuttled Kismayu; salved, repaired; 43 MoWT, *Empire Tana* (Br); 9.6.44 sunk as breakwater Gooseberry 5, Ouistrehamn; 47 raised; while being towed from Arromanches to Strangford Lough, lost tow off Trevose Head 12.11.47, reclaimed; BU
Erica 10.6.40 Seized Liverpool; 6.40 MoWT, *Empire Defiance* (Br); 9.6.44 sunk as breakwater Gooseberry 5, Sword beach, Ouistreham; 51 raised, BU Antwerp (ar 15.9.51)
Liana 12.41 Seized Bahia by Brazil; 12.41 *Baialoide* (Brz); 44 WSA; 8.6.44 sunk as breakwater Gooseberry 2, Omaha Beach, St Laurent; 49 raised, BU Ghent
Verbania 10.6.40 Detained Port Said; 40 British prize at Haifa; 40 MoWT; 41 *Empire Tamar* (Br); 6.44 sunk as breakwater Gooseberry 5, Sword Beach, Ouistreham; 47 raised, towed Strangford Lough, BU

Lost postwar through striking mine
Maristella 6.40 Interned Argentina; 25.8.41 to Argentina; 41 *Rio Azul* (Arg); 46 *Maristella* (Ita); 3.8.48 struck mine off Borkum, damaged; 5.50 sold for BU Bruges
Santa Rita 28.2.43 Bombed by Allied aircraft, on fire, Cagliari; partially submerged following further attacks; 6.45 raised, returned owner to be repaired; 28.3.46 struck mine, sunk, 42 35N 10 10E

Changes of name, flag, role, disposals, etc
Aequitas 22.8.42 Seized Fortaleza; 42 *Recifeloide* (Brz)
Amabilitas 25.8.41 To Argentina; 41 *Rio Bermejo* (Arg)
Anteo 41 Seized by US; 41 USMC (Pan); 42 *Bostonian* (Pan); 47 *Anteo* (Ita)
Capo Rosa 6.40 At Buenos Aires; 25.8.41 to Argentina; 41 *Rio Dulce* (Arg)
Castelbianco 6.40 At San Lorenzo; 25.8.41 to Argentina; 41 *Rio Chubut* (Arg)
Caterina Gerolomich 6.40 LU Dublin; 19.6.43 *Irish Cedar* (Eir); 8.12.45 *Caterina Gerolimich* (Ita)
Cervino 25.8.41 To Argentina, *Rio Primero* (Arg); 46 *Cervino* (Ita)
Confidenza 12.41 Seized Jacksonville by US; 42 USMC, *Troubadour* (Pan); 47 *Confidenza* (Ita)
Conte Biancamano 10.6.40 LU Cristobal; 21.3.41 seized by US; 12.41 USN; 14.8.42 commd transport USS *Hermitage* (AP 54); 9.46 decomm, LU San Francisco; 18.8.47 *Conte Biancomano* (Ita)
Conte Grande 10.6.40 Interned Santos; 22.8.41 seized by Brazil; 10.3.42 sold US; 16.4.42 commd USS *Monticello* (AP 61); troopship *Monticello* (US); 23.7.47 *Conte Grande* (Ita)
Dante 25.8.41 To Argentina; 41 *Rio Segundo* (Arg); 46 *Dante* (Ita)
Dentice 6.40 Scuttled Maracaibo; 43 salved; 43 *Faireno* (US); 4.44 *Arayat* (US); 46 *Faireno* (Ita); 49 *Dentice* (Ita)
Edera 10.6.40 Interned Coruña; 24.12.43 taken over by Allies; 45 returned
Ercole 8.11.42 Req Italian govt; 20.7.44 struck mine, sunk, off Leghorn; 47 raised, repaired
Ernesto 42 German control; 45 returned

Gerarchia 22.5.45 Sd Bissao in tow for Lisbon (ar 17.6.45); 47 *Rosolino Pilo* (Ita)
Gianfranco 25.8.41 To Argentina; 42 *Rio Salado* (Arg)
Giuan 12.41 Seized Norfolk VA by US; 41 USMC, *Gallant Fox* (Pan); 45 (US); 14.9.45 LU James R
Ines Corrado 25.8.41 To Argentina; 42 *Rio Diamante* (Arg); 46 *Ines Corrado* (Ita)
Iris 25.6.43 Sunk by Allied aircraft Messina; 47–48 raised, repaired
Laura Lauro 12.41 Seized Ceara by Brazil; 42 *Cearaloide* (Brz)
Leme 6.40 At US port; 25.7.41 USMC; 12.41 MoWT, *Lowlander* (Br); 48 *Leme* (Ita)
Lucia C 24.9.43 Reported at Vigo; 9.43 Allied control; 5.45 released to Italian owner
Luigi Razza 18.4.43 Bombed by RAF aircraft, sunk, Porto Torres; 45 refloated, repaired; 46 *Antonino Strazzera* (Ita)
Mar Glauco 6.40 At Philadelphia; 12.41 seized by US; 12.41 USMC, *Mokatam* (Pan)
Mayan (Pan) 41 *Nino Claudio* (Ita); 47 *Valerio* (Ita)
Monte Santo 6.40 At Buenos Aires; 25.8.41 to Argentina; 41 *Rio Colorado* (Arg)
Olterra 10.6.40 At Algeciras; sunk in shallow water by British commandos; 41 IN midget subm base; 11.10.43 ar Gibraltar; 45 returned
Pagao 10.6.41 At Algeciras; scuttled by own crew; 44 new fore end; 45 *Zaragoza* (Spn)
Pelorum 10.6.40 At Necochea; 25.8.41 to Argentina; 41 *Rio Chico* (Arg); 46 *Pelorum* (Ita)
Principessa Giovanna 3.11.40 Transport; 12.42 conv to hospital ship; 2.43 commd as hospital ship; 1.44–23.12.46 Hospital Ship No 58 (Br); 30.12.46 (Ita); 47 *San Giorgio* (Ita)
R L Hague 45 *Splendor* (Ita)
Rapallo 10.6.40 At Cartagena, Colombia; 8.12.41 seized by Colombia; 12.41 transf US; 42 USMC, *Victorian* (Pan); 42 *Polonaise* (Pan); 44 *Manileno* (US); 47 *Rapallo* (Ita)
Remo 11.6.40 Seized Fremantle; 40 *Reynella* (Aus); 49 *Remo* (Ita)
Rubicone 8.9.43 Seized by Germans; 9.43 (Ger); 45 (Ita)
Saturnia 6.40 At New York; 12.41 seized by US; 42 USN, hospital ship USS *Frances Y Slanger* (US); 15.11.46 *Saturnia* (Ita)
Semien 10.6.40 At Dakar; 29.4.42 *Lugano* (Swi); Swiss safe conduct ship; 13.4.48 (Ita)
Tampico 3.11.41 Torpedoed by subm HMS *Proteus*, damaged, towed Venice; 8.9.43 seized Venice by Germans; 9.43 (Ger); 45 afloat Venice without main engine and only part of superstructure; 4.45 captured by Allies; 45 (Ita)
Tebro 10.6.40 At Santos; 12.41 seized by Brazil; 41 *Agreloide* (Brz); 49 *Tebro* (Ita)
Teseo 6.40 At Santa Fé; 25.8.41 to Argentina; 41 *Rio Corrientes* (Arg)
Toscana 1.44–6.12.45 Hospital ship No 59 (Br); 10.46 (Ita)
Tripolitania 6.4.41 Scuttled Massowah; raised; 3.43 MoWT; 3.43–31.10.46 store ship; 1.11.46–12.1.49 personnel ship; 1.49 returned owner
Valdarno 10.6.40 At Buenos Aires; 25.8.41 to Argentina; 41 *Rio Neuquen* (Arg)
Vittorio Veneto 6.40 At Bahia Blanca; 25.8.41 to Argentina; 41 *Rio Gualeguay* (Arg); 46 *Vittorio Veneto* (Ita)
Volodda 9.43 Scuttled Bari; 47 salved, repaired, returned to service
Voluntas 6.40 At Buenos Aires; 25.8.41 to Argentina; 41 *Rio Teuco* (Arg); 46 *Voluntas* (Ita)
Vulcania 43 Seized by US; troopship (US); 15.11.46 returned (Ita)

Japan

Losses through marine hazard

Ayaha Maru 10.5.40 Stranded 3m E of Meshima Lt, Goto Islands; sank
Bokuyo Maru 18.7.39 On fire in copper ore cargo, overheated, sank, Pacific Ocean
Gyoko Maru 23.2.44 Wrecked in 26 13N 127 40E
Haruna Maru 7.7.42 Wrecked near Surga Bay, in 34 36N 138 06E
Hokko Maru (4470gt) 23.3.44 Wrecked 35 42N 140 53E (Inubosaki, Honshu)
Izan Maru 24.10.39 Ashore off Oha, N Sakhalin; 24.1.41 refloated, towed Iloilo, abandoned, CTL
Karachi Maru 22.10.40 Stranded during heavy winds while anchored Esutoru, Sakhalin; engine room filled; TL
Kitahuku Maru 17.3.40 Stranded E of Kumishima, Ryukyu Is, 26 20N 126 56E; TL
Malacca Maru 4.5.39 Ashore near Wood Is, broke in two
Nansin Maru 31.3.43 Wrecked near Itozaki, Inland Sea, Japan, 34 13N 133 06E
Rikko Maru 6.3.45 Wrecked N Formosa

Losses through war causes

Note: In this listing submarines are US Navy unless otherwise specified and USAAF (United States Army Air Force) aircraft are land-based and US Navy (USN) aircraft are carrier-based unless otherwise specified

Aden Maru 43 Transport; 6.5.44 torpedoed (in Opn 'Take-Ichi'convoy) by subm *Gurnard*, sunk, 02 42N 124 10E
Africa Maru 20.10.42 Torpedoed (in convoy) by subm *Finback*, sunk, 24 26N 120 26E (–†)
Aikoku Maru 12.41 IJN, amc; 10.43 transport; 17.2.44 sunk by USN aircraft (Opn 'Hailstone') 07 22N 151 54E

Akagi Maru 12.41 IJN, amc; 42 transport; 17.2.44 sunk by USN aircraft 07 54N 151 25E
Akagisan Maru 7.12.44 Bombed (in convoy) by USAAF and USN land-based aircraft, sunk, 11 23N 124 18E
Akasisan Maru 3.3.44 Torpedoed by subm *Sandlance*, sunk, 45 52N 149 16E
Akatuki Maru 28.5.43 Torpedoed by subm *Saury*, sunk, 27 32N 126 08E
Akebono Maru 30.3.44 Sunk by USN aircaft (Opn 'Desecrate') 07 30N 134 30E
Aki Maru 43 IJN, transport; 26.7.44 torpedoed by subm *Crevalle*, sunk, 18 28N 117 59E
Akibasan Maru 30.1.44 Sunk by USN aircraft 08 42N 167 44E
Akita Maru 41 IJN, transport; 10.1.42 torpedoed by subm *O19* (Ne), sunk, 07 40N 102 50E
Akiura Maru 28.2.44 Torpedoed by subm *Balao*, sunk, 00 06N 132 53E (–†)
Alaska Maru 19.12.43 Sunk by USN land-based aircraft 02 37S 150 52E
Amagisan Maru 17.2.44 Sunk by USN aircraft (Opn 'Hailstone') 07 18N 151 53E
Anyo Maru 2.43 Sold (Jpn); 8.1.45 torpedoed by subm *Barb*, sunk, 24 54N 120 26E (–†)
Anzan Maru 16.3.44 Torpedoed by subm *Flying Fish*, sunk, 27 41N 128 41E
Aobasan Maru 30.12.44 Bombed (in convoy) by USAAF aircraft, sunk, 17 18N 119 25E
Arabia Maru 42 Transport; 18.10.44 torpedoed (in convoy) by subm *Bluegill*, sunk, 14 06N 119 40E (–†)
Aratama Maru 8.4.44 Torpedoed by subm *Seahorse*, sunk, 13 16N 144 45E
Argentina Maru 12.41 IJN, transport; 23.11.43 commd escort carrier *Kaiyo*; 24.7.45 bombed by USAAF and USN aircraft, damaged; 28–29.7.45 aground, capsized, 33 21N 131 32E (outside Beppu harbour); 46–48 BU *in situ*
Argun Maru 21.9.43 Torpedoed (in convoy) by subm *Trigger*, sunk, 26 27N 122 40E
Arima Maru 3.4.43 Torpedoed by subm *Haddock*, sunk, 10 26N 135E
Arizona Maru 42 IJN, transport; 14.11.42 sunk (during Guadalcanal evacuation) by USAAF, USN marine land-based and carrier-based aircraft 08 30S 158 45E
Asahisan Maru 24.7.44 Bombed by USAAF aircraft, sunk, 01 10N 127 54E
Asaka Maru 12.41 IJN, amc; 11.43 transport; 12.10.44 sunk by USN aircraft 23 30N 119 34E
Asakasan Maru 27.2.43 Bombed by USAAF aircraft, sunk, 15 53N 97 40E
Asakaze Maru 42 Transport; 5.12.43 sunk by USN aircraft (from TG50.3 carriers USS *Essex* and *Lexington*, raid on Kwajalein) 09 19N 167 25E (–†, few surv)
Asama Maru (4892gt) 42 Sold (Jpn); 26.1.43 torpedoed by subm *Wahoo*, sunk, 02 37N 139 14E
Asama Maru (16,975gt) 12.41 IJN, transport; 1.11.44 torpedoed by subm *Atule*, sunk, 20 09N 117 38E (–†)
Asosan Maru 42 IJN, transport; 1.5.44 torpedoed by subm *Bluegill*, sunk, 07 07N 129 56E
Asuka Maru 1.10.44 Torpedoed (in convoy) by subm *Seawolf*, sunk, 27 35N 127 30E
Atago Maru 28.11.44 Bombed by USAAF aircraft, sunk, 04 29N 114E
Atlantic Maru 30.3.44 Torpedoed by subm *Picuda*, sunk, 12 15N 145 42E (–†)
Atlas Maru 2.11.44 Torpedoed (in convoy) by subm *Pomfret*, sunk, 20 33N 121 32E
Atuta Maru 42 IJN, transport; 30.5.42 torpedoed by subm *Pompano*, sunk, 26 07N 129 06E
Atutasan Maru 16.12.41 Torpedoed by subm *Swordfish*, sunk 18 06N 109 44E
Awa Maru 5.3.43 Delivered; 43 IJN, transport; 1.4.45 torpedoed by subm *Queenfish*, sunk, 25 25N 120 07E
Awata Maru 1.42 IJN, amc; 10.43 transport; 22.10.43 torpedoed by subm *Grayback*, sunk, 26 48N 124 56E
Awazisan Maru 42 Jpn Army, transport; 8.12.41 sunk by RAAF aircraft 06 08N 102 16E
Ayatosan Maru 42 IJN, transport; 22.7.42 sunk by USAAF and RAAF aircraft 08 50S 148 50E
Azuma Maru 43 IJN, transport; 3.12.43 torpedoed by subm *Tinosa*, sunk, 06 29N 131 28E
Azumasan Maru 42 IJN, transport; 15.10.42 bombed (in convoy) by USAAF, USN marine land-based and USN carrier-based aircraft 09 25S 159 55E; beached, TL

Bandoeng (Bandon) Maru 17.12.42 Torpedoed by subm *Grouper*, sunk, 04 54S 154 17E
Bangkok Maru 12.41 IJN, amc; 20.5.43 torpedoed by subm *Pollack*, sunk, 05 47N 169 42E
Batavia Maru 12.6.44 Sunk (in convoy) by USN aircraft (from TG58.4) 17 32N 143 17E
Belgium Maru 18.12.44 Sunk (in convoy) by USN aircraft 14 35N 120 55E
Bengal Maru 24.3.44 Torpedoed by subm *Bowfin*, sunk, 05 27N 125 38E
Bordeaux Maru 42 IJN, transport; 1.2.42 sunk by US surface craft 09 28N 170 15E
Borneo Maru 8.10.42 Bombed by USAAF aircraft, sunk, 51 56N 177 27E
Boston Maru 42 IJN, transport; 16.11.42 torpedoed by subm *Seal*, sunk, 06 18N 135 20E
Brasil Maru 42 IJN, transport; 5.8.42 torpedoed by subm *Greenling*, sunk, 09 50N 158 38E (many †)
Brazil Maru 12.5.45 Struck mine, sunk, 34 40N 135 12E
Brisbane Maru 42 IJN, transport; 14.11.42 sunk (during Guadalcanal evacuation) by USAAF, USN marine land-based, and USN carrier-based aircraft 08 30S 158 45E (–†)
Buenos Aires Maru 42 IJN, hospital ship; 25.11.43 torpedoed, damaged, South China Sea, proceeded Japan; 27.11.43 sunk by USN aircraft 02 44S 149 15E
Burma Maru 12.6.42 Torpedoed by subm *Swordfish*, sunk, 10 08N 012 34E
Buyo Maru 42 IJN, transport; 26.1.43 torpedoed (in convoy) by subm *Wahoo*, sunk, 01 55N 139 14E

Calcutta Maru 1.5.42 Torpedoed by subm *Triton*, sunk, 28 07N 123 45E
Canberra Maru 42 IJN, transport; 14.11.42 sunk (during Guadalcanal evacuation) by USAAF, USN marine land-based, and carrier based-aircraft 08 30S 158 45E (–†)

Celebes Maru 15.11.44 Bombed by USN land-based aircraft, sunk, 13 17N 122 28E
Cheribon Maru 26.11.42 Bombed by USAAF aircraft, sunk, 52 45N 173 15E
Chicago Maru 15.10.43 Torpedoed by subm *Tullibee*, sunk, 24 35N 120 31E
Chile Maru 12.5.45 Bombed by USN land-based aircraft, sunk, 34 25N 129 40E
China Maru 21.9.44 Sunk (in convoy) by USN aircraft 14 35N 120 55E
Clyde Maru 29.1.45 Torpedoed by subm *Picuda*, sunk, 25 33N 120 54E
Columbia Maru 30.11.43 Torpedoed by subm *Gato*, sunk, 01 56N 147 23E

Daigen Maru No 3 26.2.44 Torpedoed by subm *Gato*, sunk, 00 55S 139 02E
Dainiti Maru 8.10.43 Torpedoed (in convoy) by subm *Gurnard*, sunk, 18 24N 119 09E
Dakar Maru 31.7.44 Torpedoed (in convoy) by subm *Steelhead*, sunk, 18 57N 120 50E
Delagoa Maru 2.11.43 Torpedoed (in convoy) by subm *Trigger*, sunk, 28 55N 134 43E
Durban Maru 21.8.44 Torpedoed by subm *Muskallunge*, sunk, 11 43N 109 17E

Ehime Maru 2.11.43 Torpedoed by subm *Halibut*, sunk, 28 18N 134 48E
Eihuku Maru 31.8.42 Torpedoed by subm *Growler*, sunk, 25 43N 122 38E
Eiyo Maru 20.2.45 Torpedoed by subm *Guava*, sunk, 11 17N 109E
England Maru 17.5.43 Torpedoed by subm *Grayback*, sunk, 01S 148 40E
Erie Maru 11.1.43 Torpedoed by subm *Sturgeon*, sunk, 32 56N 132 02E

Florida Maru 2.4.43 Bombed by USAAF aircraft, sunk, 02 40S 150 40E
France Maru 12.1.45 Sunk by USN aircraft 09 10N 107E

Ganges Maru 28.5.42 Torpedoed by subm *Salmon*, sunk, 09N 111E
Genoa Maru 11.6.43 Torpedoed by subm *Finback*, sunk, 07 36N 134 17E
Genyo Maru 42 IJN; 20.6.44 sunk by USN aircraft (from TF58 covering Opn 'Forager') 15 30N 133 55E
Getuyo Maru 40 *Mogamigawa Maru* (Jpn); 41 IJN, aux minelayer; 10.2.43 IJN, aircraft transport; 1.8.43 torpedoed by subm *Pogy*, sunk, 11 16N 153 34E
Ginyo Maru 16.12.43 Torpedoed by subm *Flying Fish*, sunk, 22 27N 120 08E
Glasgow Maru 22.8.43 Sunk Indian Ocean, cause unknown (–†)
Gokoku Maru 9.42 IJN, amc; 10.43 IJN, transport; 10.11.44 torpedoed by subm *Barb*, sunk, 33 23N 129 03E (–†)
Gosyu Maru 41 IJN, a/c transport; 10.43 IJN, transport; 30.3.44 sunk (in convoy) by USN aircraft (Opn 'Desecrate') 07 30N 134 30E
Goyo Maru 3.2.44 Torpedoed (in convoy) by subm *Tambor*, sunk, 29 11N 124 45E

Hague Maru 8.1.0.42 Torpedoed by subm *Drum*, sunk, 34 06N 136 22E
Hakkai Maru 42 IJN, salvage vessel; 17.1.44 sunk (in convoy) by USN land-based aircraft 04 13S 152 12E; 12.11.45 reported at Sourabaya
Hakodate Maru 16.7.42 Torpedoed by subm *Seadragon*, sunk, 12 55N 109 29E
Hakone Maru 27.11.43 Torpedoed by USAAF aircraft, sunk, 25 20N 120E
Hakonesan Maru 18.10.42 Torpedoed by subm *Greenling*, sunk, 38 46N 142 03E
Hakozake Maru 40 IJN, transport; 19.3.45 torpedoed by subm *Balao*, sunk, 33 09N 122 08E (–†)
Hakubasan Maru 28.7.44 Torpedoed by subm *Crevalle*, sunk, 16 18N 119 44E (–†)
Hakusan Maru 43 IJN, transport; 4.6.44 torpedoed by subm *Flier*, sunk, 22 55N 136 44E
Hakusika Maru 18.10.44 Torpedoed (in convoy) by subm *Bluegill*, sunk, 14 06N 119 40E
Hamburg Maru 2.11.44 Torpedoed (in convoy) by subm *Pomfret*, sunk, 20 20N 121 30N
Hankow Maru 2.9.43 Sunk (in convoy) by USAAF aircraft 03 35S 143 39E
Havana Maru 18.11.42 Bombed by USAAF aircraft, sunk, 06 48S 155 49E
Havre Maru (5652gt) 43 IJN, transport; 6.6.44 torpedoed (in convoy) by subm *Pintado*, sunk, 16 41N 142 43E
Hawaii Maru 43 Sold (Jpn); 2.12.44 torpedoed (in convoy) by subm *Sea Devil*, sunk, 30 51N 128 45E (–†)
Hayo Maru 41 IJN, transport; 22.12.41 torpedoed by subm *S-38*, sunk, 16 37N 120 17E
Heian Maru (11,614gt) 10.41 IJN, subm tender *XAS5*; 17.2.44 sunk by USN aircraft (Opn 'Hailstone') 07 23N 151 51E; wreck raised, towed Japan for BU
Heian Maru (5346gt) 13.11.44 Sunk by USN aircraft 14 35N 120 55E
Heiei Maru No 7 War loss (no details)
Heimei Maru 4.1.44 Bombed by USAAF aircraft, sunk, 10 10S 123 35E
Heiyo Maru 41 IJN, transport; 17.1.43 torpedoed by subm *Whale*, sunk, 10 13N 151 25E
Hie Maru 41 IJN, transport; 42 subm tender *XAS4*; 10.43 transport; 17.11.43 torpedoed by subm *Drum*, sunk, 01 48N 148 24E
Hikawa Maru 44 IJN, hospital ship; 8.45 surrendered
Himalaya Maru 2.12.43 Bombed by USAAF aircraft, sunk, 00 52S 148 50E
Hirokawa Maru 42 IJN, transport; 15.11.42 sunk by USAAF and USN land-based aircraft, and USN surface craft 09 20S 159 50E (–†)
Hitati Maru 14.2.43 Sunk by USN land-based aircraft 06 45S 155 50E
Hoeisan Maru 18.10.44 Sunk by USN aircraft 14 35N 120 50E
Hohuku Maru 21.9.44 Sunk by USN aircraft 15 25N 119 50E
Hokkai Maru 8.45 Bombed by Allied aircraft, sunk, off Sourabaya
Hokki Maru 27.9.44 Torpedoed by subm *Lapon*, sunk, 15 45N 117 48E

Hokko Maru (5347gt) 28.11.43 Torpedoed by subm *Raton*, sunk, 01 40N 141 45E
Hokoku Maru 12.41 IJN, amc; 42 transport; 11.11.42 in engagement with *Aikoku Maru* (*qv*) against minesweeper *Bengal* (Ind) and tanker *Ondina* (*qv*) (Ne), broke off engagement, on fire, explosion, sunk, 19 45S 92 40E (–†)
Hokuroku Maru 18.3.44 Torpedoed by subm *Lapon*, sunk, 19 22N 116 52E
Hokutai Maru 30.3.44 Sunk by USN aircraft 07 30N 134 30E
Holland Maru 17.10.42 Torpedoed by subm *Trigger*, sunk, 32 21N 132 04E
Horai Maru 42 IJN, transport; 1.3.42 attacked (with troops for Java landing) by USAAF, RAAF and Netherlands aircraft, and USN and Netherlands surface craft, sunk, 05 56S 106 12E; 10.12.46 raised; 12.12.46 towed in, beached Siglap; 48 towed Japan, BU
Hoyo Maru 17.2.44 Sunk by USN aircraft (Opn 'Hailstone') 07 23N 151 50E
Hukko Maru 17.5.44 Torpedoed by subm *Sandlace*, sunk, 14 55N 142 30E
Hukuyo Maru 6.12.44 Torpedoed (in convoy) by subm *Trepang*, sunk, 18 59N 121 05E
Husimi Maru 1.2.43 Torpedoed by subm *Tarpon*, sunk, 34 16N 138 17E
Huso Maru 43 Transport; 31.7.44 torpedoed (in convoy) by subm *Steelhead*, sunk, 18 57N 120 50E
Huzikawa Maru 41 IJN, aircraft transport; 1.44 transport; 17.2.44 sunk by USN aircraft (Opn 'Hailstone') 07 20N 151 53E
Huzisan Maru 17.2.44 Sunk by USN aircraft (Opn 'Hailstone') 07 23N 151 53E

India Maru 14.4.43 Bombed by USAAF aircraft, sunk, 03 25S 143 40E
Indus Maru 15.5.43 Torpedoed by subm *Gar*, sunk, 13 07N 121 49E
Isin Maru 41 *Nichiwa Maru* (Jpn); 17.5.44 torpedoed by subm *Tunny*, sunk, 14 45N 142 40E
Italy Maru 42 IJN, transport; 27.12.42 sunk by USAAF aircraft 04 15S 152 10E
Itukusima Maru 29.10.44 Sunk by USN land-based aircraft 06 45N 116 55E
Izumo Maru 40 IJN, while building; 5.42 completed as carrier *Hiyo*; 20.6.44 sunk by USN torpedo aircraft from carrier USS *Bellau Wood* (from TF58 covering Opn 'Forager'), on fire, explosion, sunk, 15 30N 133 50E (few surv)

Johore Maru 24.10.43 Torpedoed (in convoy) by subm *Silversides*, sunk, 02 05N 144 39E

Kagu Maru 42 IJN, transport; 4.11.44 torpedoed by subms *Bream*, *Guitarro*, *Ray*, sunk, 15 54N 119 45E
Kaisyo Maru 3.8.43 Torpedoed by subm *Finback*, sunk, 05 18S 111 52E
Kaizyo Maru 1.3.42 Torpedoed by subm *Grampus*, sunk, 04 52N 151 20E
Kamakura Maru 42 IJN, transport; 28.4.43 torpedoed by subm *Gudgeon*, sunk, 10 18N 121 44E
Kamikawa Maru 39 IJN, seaplane tender; 41 transport; 28.5.43 torpedoed by subm *Scamp*, sunk, 01 36S 150 24E (many †)
Kamikaze Maru 40 IJN, MTB depot ship; 30.3.44 sunk by USN aircraft (Opn 'Hailstone') 07 30N 134 30E
Kamo Maru 3.7.44 Torpedoed (in convoy) by subm *Tinosa*, sunk, off 32 24N 128 46E
Kamogawa Maru 41 IJN, a/c transport; 2.3.42 torpedoed by subm *Sailfish*, sunk, 32 55N 129 26E
Kano Maru 42 IJN, transport; 8.8.42 bombed by USAAF aircraft, shelled USN surface craft, sunk, 51 58N 177 33E (–†)
Kansai Maru 18.9.43 Torpedoed by subm *Scamp*, sunk, 25N 118 29E
Kanto Maru 41 IJN, transport; 20.7.42 aircraft transport; 11.9.42 torpedoed by subm *Saury*, sunk, 03 16S 118 29E
Kashiwara Maru 41 IJN; 6.42 completed as carrier *Junyo*; 8.45 surrendered; 45–47 Allied repatriation transport; 47 BU
Kasii Maru 10.11.44 Bombed by USAAF aircraft, sunk, 10 50N 124 35E
Kasima Maru 27.9.43 Torpedoed by subm *Bonefish*, sunk, 10 14N 109 45E (–†)
Kasuga Maru 40 IJN; 40–9.41 conv to escort carrier *Taiyo*; 15.9.41 commd; 18.8.44 torpedoed by subm *Rasher*, sunk, 18 16N 120 20E (–†)
Kasyu Maru 8.10.43 Torpedoed by subm *Guardfish*, sunk, 00 25S 146 22E
Katori Maru 41 IJN, transport; 23.12.41 torpedoed by subm *K-XIV* (Ne), sunk, 02 30N 110E
Katuragi Maru 41 IJN, a/c transport; 1.10.42 torpedoed by subm *Sturgeon*, sunk, 05 51S 153 18E
Keisyo Maru 42 IJN, transport; 12.10.43 bombed by USAAF aircraft, sunk, 04 13S 152 12E
Keiyo Maru 41 IJN, a/c transport; 1.44 transport; 12.6.44 sunk by USN aircraft and USN surface craft 15 14N 145 44E
Kenkon Maru 42 IJN, transport; 21.1.43 torpedoed by subm *Gato*, sunk, 06 12S 155 51E
Kenryu Maru 42 IJN, transport; 29.11.43 torpedoed by subm *Snapper*, sunk, 33 19N 139 34E
Kensyo Maru 17.2.44 Sunk by USN aircraft (Opn 'Hailstone') 07 18N 151 53E
Kenyo Maru (6470gt) 23.3.43 Torpedoed by subm *Whale*, sunk, 17 16N 144 56E
Kenyo Maru (10,022gt) 14.1.44 Torpedoed by subm *Guardfish*, sunk, 05 22N 141 27E
Kenzan Maru 25.11.43 Torpedoed by subm *Albacore*, sunk, 00 51N 145 46E
Kimikawa Maru 39 IJN, seaplane tender; 10.43 transport; 23.10.44 torpedoed by subm *Sawfish*, sunk, 18 58N 118 31E
Kinai Maru 42 IJN, transport; 10.5.43 torpedoed (in convoy) by subm *Plunger*, sunk, 14 29N 149E

Kinka Maru 13.11.44 Sunk (in convoy) by USN aircraft 14 35N 120 55E
Kinkasan Maru 1.10.43 Torpedoed (in convoy) by subm *Peto*, sunk, 04 01N 143 47E
Kinryo Maru 21.8.44 Torpedoed (in convoy) by subm *Haddo*, sunk, 13 23N 120 19E
Kinryu Maru 12.41 IJN, amc; 7.42 transport; 25.8.42 sunk by US marine land-based aircraft, sunk, 07 47S 160 13E
Kinugasa Maru 42 IJN, transport; 7.10.44 torpedoed by subms *Baya* and *Hawkbill*, sunk, 14 30N 115 48E
Kinugawa Maru 42 IJN, transport; 15.11.42 sunk (during Guadalcanal evacuation) by USAAF, USN marine land-based, and land-based aircraft and USN surface craft 09 20S 169 50E (–†)
Kirisima Maru 42 IJN, transport; 25.9.43 torpedoed by subm *Bowfin*, sunk, 09 44N 111 56E
Kiso Maru 22.11.43 Torpedoed (in convoy) by subm *Tinosa*, sunk, 07 09N 134 34E
Kitano Maru 27.3.42 Struck Japanese mine, sunk, 16 10N 120 24E
Kiyo Maru 4.1.44 Torpedoed by subm *Rasher*, sunk, 05 46N 108 36E
Kiyokawa Maru 39 IJN, seaplane tender; 4.43 transport; 24.5.45 struck mine, badly damaged, 32 44N 129 52E; 8.45 surrendered
Kiyosumi Maru 12.41 IJN, amc; 10.43 transport; 17.2.44 sunk by USN aircraft (Opn 'Hailstone') 07 23N 151 53E
Kizan Maru 27.9.43 Destroyed Singapore by British underground forces using explosives
Koan Maru 17.5.45 Struck mine, sunk, 34 38N 135 11E
Kogyo Maru 24.9.44 Sunk by USN aircraft 11 59N 120 02E
Kohuku Maru 1.6.42 Bombed by USAAF aircraft, sunk, 16 16N 98 18E
Koki Maru 4.7.43 Torpedoed (in convoy) by subm *Snook*, sunk, 28 40N 124 10E
Kokuyo Maru 42 IJN; 30.7.44 torpedoed by subm *Bonefish*, sunk, 06 03N 119 54E
Komaki Maru 41 IJN, transport; 18.4.42 bombed by USAAF aircraft, sunk, 04 12S 152 10E
Kongo Maru 12.41 IJN, amc; 42 transport; 10.3.42 sunk (in convoy) by USN aircraft 06 49S 147 02E
Konzan Maru 19.6.45 Torpedoed by subm *Bonefish*, sunk, 37 13N 137 18E
Koryu Maru 22.4.44 Bombed by USAAF aircraft, sunk, 10 19N 107 05E
Kosei Maru (8265gt) 7.4.43 Torpedoed by subm *Tunny*, sunk, 08 50N 147 06E
Kosei Maru (6668gt) 10.3.42 Struck Japanese mine, sunk, 16 05N 120 20E
Kosin Maru 22.1.44 Torpedoed by subm *Tinosa*, sunk, 07 22N 115 05E
Kotoku Maru 42 IJN, transport; 8.8.42 bombed by USAAF aircraft, sunk, 07 01N 147 07E
Koyu Maru 20.1.44 Torpedoed by subm *Gar*, sunk, 06 40N 134 17E
Kozan Maru 4.9.43 Torpedoed by subm *Sunfish*, sunk, 22 22N 120 04E
Kozui Maru 42 IJN, transport; 14.10.43 torpedoed by subm *Grayback*, sunk, 27 35N 127 27E
Kunikawa Maru 39 IJN, seaplane tender; 11.42–12.42 amc; 10.43 transport; 30.4.45 sunk by USAAF aircraft 01 15S 116 50E
Kurama Maru 9.2.42 Sunk East China Sea, cause unknown
Kuretake Maru 41 IJN, transport; 24.1.42 sunk (in Balikpapan invasion force convoy) by USN surface craft 00 10N 118 00E
Kurohime Maru 30.3.43 Torpedoed by subm *Tuna*, sunk, 00 22S 147 46E
Kurosio Maru 21.1.45 Sunk by USN aircraft 22 37N 120 15E: 46 salved; 47 *Yung Hao* (Chn)
Kusuyama Maru 8.2.43 Torpedoed by subm *Tunny*, sunk, 22 40N 119 12E
Kuwayama Maru 21.2.43 Torpedoed by subm *Thresher*, sunk, 07 53S 119 13E
Kyokko Maru 15.11.43 Torpedoed by subm *Crevalle*, sunk, 14 53N 119 54E
Kyokusei Maru 42 IJN, transport; 2.3.43 sunk (in convoy) by USAAF Flying Fortress aircraft 05 05S 148 28E (–†)
Kyokuto Maru 42 IJN; 21.9.44 sunk by USN aircraft 14 25N 120 55E
Kyokuyo Maru 13.11.43 Lost East China Sea
Kyusyu Maru 42 IJN, transport; 15.10.42 attacked (in convoy) by USAAF, USN marine land-based and USN land-based aircraft 09 25S 159 55E, beached; TL

La Plata Maru 41 *Kanzyu (Kanju) Maru* (Jpn); 43 IJN, transport; 1.45 sunk by USN aircraft Saigon harbour
Lima Maru 8.2.44 Torpedoed by subm *Snook*, sunk, 32 18N 129 20E
Lisbon Maru 42 IJN, transport; 1.10.42 torpedoed by subm *Grouper*, sunk, 29 57N 122 56E (on board 1800 British pow; few surv)
Liverpool Maru 4.7.43 Torpedoed (in convoy) by subm *Snook*, sunk, 28 40N 124 10E
London Maru 22.4.44 Bombed (in convoy) by USAAF aircraft, sunk, 10 19N 107 05E
Lyons Maru 41 IJN, a/c transport; 1.44 transport; 17.1.44 sunk by USN land-based aircraft 04 13S 152 12E

Macassar Maru 7.10.44 Torpedoed by subm *Aspro*, sunk, 17 54N 119 57E
Madras Maru 31.5.44 Torpedoed by subm *Barb*, sunk, 48 21N 151 19E
Maebasi Maru 30.9.43 Torpedoed by subm *Pogy*, sunk, 06 01N 139 08E
Malta Maru 10.2.44 Torpedoed (in convoy) by subm *Pogy*, sunk, 23 12N 121 30E
Manila Maru 42 Hospital ship; 25.11.44 torpedoed by subm *Mingo*, sunk, 05 30N 113 21E (–†)
Mantai Maru 16.7.44 Torpedoed by subm *Guardfish*, sunk, 18 20N 119 42E
Manzyu Maru 21.1.45 Sunk by USN aircraft 22 37N 120 15E
Matue Maru 17.4.44 Torpedoed by subm *Harder*, sunk, 09 22N 142 18E
Matumoto Maru 25.10.44 Torpdoed (in convoy) by subm *Tang*, sunk, 25 06N 119 31E

Meigen Maru 39 Req Japanese govt; 22.3.43 torpedoed by subm *Gudgeon*, sunk, 06 31S 112 47E
Meiten Maru 20.6.43 Torpedoed by subm *Tautog*, sunk, 15 57N 140 55E
Meiu Maru 20.1.43 Torpedoed (in convoy) by subm *Silversides*, sunk, 03 52N 153 56E
Mexico Maru 29.8.44 Torpedoed by subm *Jack*, sunk, 02 07N 122 28E (–†)
Milan Maru 6.9.43 Bombed by USAAF aircraft, sunk, 16 46N 96 10E
Mito Maru 16.4.44 Torpedoed (in convoy) by subm *Paddle*, sunk, 02 02S 127 20E
Mitu Maru 12.7.45 Struck mine, sunk, 33 38N 135 03E
Miyadono Maru 19.6.43 Torpedoed by subm *Growler*, sunk, 01 38N 148 14E
Mizuho Maru 21.9.44 Torpedoed by subm *Redfish*, sunk, 18 35N 120 39E (–†)
Momoyama Maru 13.3.43 Bombed by USAAF aircraft, sunk, 02 45S 143 20E
Montevideo Maru 42 IJN, transport; 1.7.42 torpedoed by subm *Sturgeon*, sunk, 18 37N 11929E
Montreal Maru 5.1.43 Bombed by USAAF aircraft, sunk, 52 40N 178 15E
Morioka Maru 4.3.42 Struck mine, sunk, 32 55N 129 26E
Muroran Maru 30.12.44 Sunk (in convoy) by USAAF aircraft 17 18N 119 25E
Muko Maru 13.11.43 Torpedoed by subm *Thresher*, sunk, 08 57N 152 36E
Myoko Maru 42 IJN, transport; 17.6.43 torpedoed by subm *Drum*, sunk, 02 03S 153 44E

Nagara Maru 42 IJN, transport; 14.11.42 sunk (during Guadalcanal evacuation) by USAAF, USN marine land-based and USN carrier-based aircraft 08 30S 158 45E (–†)
Nagato Maru 2.9.43 Bombed (in convoy) by USAAF aircraft, sunk, 03 35S 143 39E
Nagisan Maru 30.3.44 Sunk by USN carrier-based aircraft (Opn 'Desecrate') 07 30N 134 30E
Nagoya Maru 10.41 IJN, subm depot ship; 4.42 aircraft transport; 12.43 transport; 1.1.44 torpedoed by subm *Herring*, sunk, 32 10N 138 37E
Nako Maru 42 IJN, transport; 14.11.42 sunk (during Guadalcanal evacuation) by USAAF, USN marine land-based and USN carrier-based aircraft 08 30S 158 45E
Nana Maru 24.1.42 Sunk (in Balikpapan invasion force convoy) by Netherlands aircraft 00 10N 118E
Naniwa Maru 3.8.42 Torpedoed by subm *Gudgeon*, sunk, 07 37N 150 18E
Nankai Maru 42 IJN, transport; 12.9.44 torpedoed (in convoy) by subm *Sealion II*, sunk, 18 42N 114 30E
Nanman Maru 27.10.43 Torpedoed by subm *Flying Fish*, sunk, 12 34N 134 48E
Naples Maru 20.11.43 Sunk by USN land-based aircraft 03 22S 151 45E
Naruto Maru 42 IJN; 8.8.43 torpedoed by subm *Whale*, sunk, 24 12N 142 51E
Nasusan Maru 24.6.44 Torpedoed (in convoy) by subm *Tang*, sunk, 32 30N 129 35E
Natisan Maru 13.11.43 Torpedoed by subm *Trigger*, sunk, 32 57N 125 06E
Nippon Maru (tk) 42 IJN; 14.1.44 torpedoed by subm *Scamp*, sunk, 05 02N 140 43E
Nissan Maru 18.6.42 Bombed by USAAF aircraft, sunk, 51 58N 177 40E
Nissin Maru 6.5.44 Torpedoed by subm *Crevalle*, sunk, 07 17N 116 51E
Nissin Maru No 2 17.4.43 Sunk off Formosa (cause unknown) (–†)
Nissyo Maru (tk) 42 IJN; 25.2.44 torpedoed by subm *Hoe*, sunk, 05 55N 126 05E
Nissyu Maru 18.7.44 Torpedoed by subm *Cobia*, sunk, 28 43N 139 24E
Nitiai Maru 3.2.44 Bombed by USAAF and USN land-based aircraft, sunk, 03S 150 10E
Nitian Maru 8.9.44 Torpedoed (in convoy) by subm *Spadefish*, sunk, 24 46N 123 15E
Nitiei Maru 42 IJN; 6.1.45 torpedoed by subm *Besugo*, sunk, 06 57N 102 57E
Nitiho Maru 21.10.42 Torpedoed (in convoy) by subm *Guardfish*, sunk, 27 03N 122 42E
Nitii Maru 27.11.43 Bombed by USAAF aircraft, sunk, 02S 149 15E
Nitimei Maru 15.1.43 Bombed by USAAF aircraft, sunk, 13 30N 98 30E
Nitiran Maru 12.7.44 Torpedoed by subm *Piranha*, sunk, 18 33N 122 53E
Nitiren Maru 16.3.44 Torpedoed (in convoy) by subm *Tautog*, sunk, 42 25N 144 55E
Nitiryu Maru 7.1.43 Bombed by USAAF aircraft, sunk, 06 30S 149E
Nitiyo Maru 40 *Kumagawa Maru* (Jpn); 12.1.45 sunk by USN aircraft 10 20N 107 05E
Nitiyu Maru 43 IJN, transport; 3.3.43 torpedoed by subm *Halibut*, sunk, 10 22N 145 21E
Nitta Maru 9.41 IJN, troopship; 5.42–11.42 conv, and 25.11.42 commd as escort carrier *Chuyo*; 4.12.43 torpedoed by subm *Sailfish*, sunk, 32 37N 143 39E
Nittai Maru 3.3.44 Torpedoed by subm *Rasher*, sunk, 03 17N 123 55E
Norfolk Maru 21.8.44 Torpedoed (in convoy) by subm *Haddo*, sunk, 13 23N 120 19E
Norway Maru 21.9.44 Sunk by USN aircraft 14 35N 120 55E
Nosiro Maru 12.41 IJN, amc; 8.42 transport; 21.9.44 sunk by USN aircraft 14 35N 120 55E
Noto Maru 2.11.44 Bombed by USAAF aircraft, sunk, 10 30N 125E
Nozima Maru 42 IJN, ransport; 28.9.42 sunk by USAAF aircraft 51 58N 177 33E

Ogura Maru No 1 21.9.44 Sunk by USN aircraft 15 25N 119 50E
Ogura Maru No 2 16.9.44 Torpedoed by subm *Redfish*, sunk, 21 23N 121 17E
Ogura Maru No 3 23.2.44 Torpedoed by subm *Cod*, sunk, 03 53N 129 17E
Okitu Maru 26.1.44 Torpedoed by subm *Skipjack*, sunk, 09 22N 157 26E
Olympia Maru 24.9.44 Sunk (in convoy) by USN carrier-based aircraft 11 59N 120 02E
Omurosan Maru 22.12.44 Torpedoed (in convoy) by subm *Flasher*, sunk, 15 04N 109 06E
Onoe Maru 26.11.43 Torpedoed by subm *Raton*, sunk, 00 40N 148 14E
Oregon Maru 42 IJN, salvage vessel; 42 transport; 17.11.42 torpedoed by subm *Salmon*, sunk, 14 46N 119 44E

Oridono Maru 10.5.42 Struck Japanese mine, sunk, 07S 112 40E
Otowasan Maru 22.12.44 Torpedoed by subm *Flasher*, sunk, 15 04N 109 06E
Oyo Maru 20.10.44 Torpedoed (in convoy) by subm *Hammerhead*, sunk, 04 41N 113 22E

Pacific Maru 31.10.44 Torpedoed by subm *Guitarro*, sunk, 15 17N 119 49E
Penang Maru 9.4.43 Torpedoed (in convoy) by subm *Tautog*, sunk, 05 29S 123 02E

Rakuyo Maru 12.9.44 Torpedoed (in convoy, with 1350 pow) by subm *Sealion II*, sunk, 18 42N 114 30E (many †)
Reiyo Maru 17.2.44 Sunk by USN aircraft (Opn 'Hailstone') 07 25N 151 45E
Rio de Janeiro Maru 10.41 IJN, subm tender; 9.43 transport; 17.2.44 sunk by USN aircraft (Opn 'Hailstone') 07 20N 151 53E
Ryoka (Ryoga) Maru 15.2.44 Struck mine, sunk, 31 16N 121 45E
Ryoyo Maru 2.5.44 Torpedoed by subm *Tautog*, sunk, 48 04N 153 16E
Ryunan Maru 20.10.42 Torpedoed by subm *Drum*, sunk, 34 08N 136 46E
Ryusei Maru 25.2.44 Torpedoed by subm *Rasher*, sunk, 07 56S 115 14E
Ryuyo Maru 1.1.44 Torpedoed by subm *Puffer*, sunk, 08 24N 122 56E
Ryuzan Maru 30.7.43 Torpedoed by subm *Finback*, sunk, 06 31S 111 26E
Ryuzin Maru 13.4.42 Torpedoed by subm *Grayling*, sunk, 31 51N 132 50E

Sado Maru 42 IJN, transport; 14.11.42 sunk (in convoy) by USAAF, USN marine land-based and carrier-based aircraft 08 30S 158 45E
Sagami Maru 42 IJN, transport; 3.11.42 torpedoed by subm *Seawolf*, sunk, 07 02N 125 33E
Sagara Maru 40 IJN, seaplane tender; 12.42 transport; 23.6.43 torpedoed by subm *Harder*, sunk, 33 45N 138 10E
Saigon Maru 12.41 IJN, transport; 18.9.44 torpedoed by subm *Flasher*, sunk, 14 11N 12002E
Saiko Maru 40 *Hiburi Maru* (Jpn); torpedoed by subm *Herring*, sunk, 48N 153E
Sakito Maru 43 Army transport; 29.2.44 torpedoed by subm *Trout*, sunk, 22 40N 131 50E
Sakura Maru 42 IJN, transport; 1.3.42 sunk by USAAF aircraft 05 56S 106 12E
San Clemente Maru 42 IJN; 4.5.43 torpedoed by subm *Seal*, sunk, 06 54N 134 55E
San Francisco Maru 17.2.44 Sunk by USN aircraft (Opn 'Hailstone') 07 22N 151 54E
San Luis Maru 12.1.45 Sunk (in convoy) by USN aircraft 14 15N 109 10E
San Pedro Maru 25.6.44 Torpedoed by subm *Jack*, sunk, 16 07N 119 44E
San Ramon Maru 27.11.43 Torpedoed by subm *Seahorse*, sunk, 33 38N 129 05E
Santos Maru 10.41 IJN, subm tender; 3.43 transport; 25.11.44 torpedoed by subm *Atule*, sunk, 20 12N 121 51E (–†)
Sanuki Maru 39 IJN, seaplane tender; 8.42 transport; 28.1.45 torpedoed by subm *Spadefish*, sunk, 33 56N 123 06E
San-Yo Maru 39 IJN, seaplane tender; 4.43 transport; 26.5.44 torpedoed by subm *Cabrilla*, sunk, 02 48N 124 19E
Sasako Maru 42 IJN, transport; 15.10.42 attacked (in convoy) by USN carrier-based and marine land-based aircraft 09 25S 159 55E; beached, TL
Seattle Maru 16.7.44 Torpedoed by subm *Piranha*, sunk, 19 26N 120 18E (–†)
Seizan Maru 23.2.44 Sunk by USN carrier-based aircraft 15N 145 30E
Shanghai Maru 9.4.43 Torpedoed by subm *Grayling*, sunk, 13 11N 121 45E
Sikisan Maru 24.10.44 Torpedoed by subm *Drum*, sunk, 20 27N 118 31E
Shoryu Maru 4.5.44 Torpedoed by subm *Parche*, sunk, 20 48N 118 03E
Sinko Maru 42 IJN, transport; 18.10.44 sunk by USN aircraft 18 35N 121 40E
Sinkoku Maru 17.2.44 Sunk by USN aircraft (Opn 'Hailstone') 07 20N 151 40E
Sinno Maru 30.5.45 Struck mine N of Tsuruga Bay, badly damaged; BU
Sinsei Maru No 1 23.10.44 Torpedoed by subm *Snook*, sunk, 19 44N 118 25E
Siraha Maru 14.1.43 Torpedoed by subm *Searaven*, sunk, 09 12N 130 38E
Somedono Maru 20.1.43 Torpedoed (in convoy) by subm *Silversides*, sunk, 03 52N 153 56E
Soyo Maru 7.12.43 Torpedoed by subm *Pogy*, sunk, 14 04N 152 09E
Sugiyama Maru 14.11.44 Torpedoed (in convoy) by subm *Barbel*, sunk, in 15 14N 112 13E
Sumatra Maru 12.5.43 Torpedoed by subm *Gudgeon*, sunk, 12 43N 124 08E
Sunten Maru 17.11.44 Torpedoed by subm *Gunnel*, sunk, 16 56N 110 30E
Surabaya Maru 20.1.43 Torpedoed (in convoy) by subm *Silversides*, sunk, 03 52N 153 56E
Suwa Maru 41 IJN, transport; 28.3.43 torpedoed by subm *Tunny*, beached near Wake Is, 19 13N 166 34E; 5.4.43 torpedoed by subms *Seadragon* and *Finback*, TL
Sydney Maru (4105gt) 14.4.43 Bombed by USAAF aircraft, sunk, 04 10S 144 55E
Sydney Maru (5425gt) 28.11.43 Torpedoed (in convoy) by subm *Bowfin*, sunk, 12 46N 109 42E
Syogen Maru 4.8.44 Sunk by USN aircraft 27 40N 141 48E
Syohei Maru 10.5.44 Torpedoed by subm *Cod*, sunk, 15 38N 119 25E (–†)
Syoryu Maru 4.5.44 Torpedoed by subm *Parche*, sunk, 20 48N 118 03E
Syoyo Maru 21.9.43 Torpedoed (in convoy) by subm *Trigger*, sunk, 26 27N 122 40E
Syozin Maru 20.6.43 Torpedoed by subm *Seawolf*, sunk, 24 39N 118 52E
Syunko Maru (6781gt) 14.10.42 Torpedoed by subm *Skipjack*, sunk, 05 35N 144 25E
Syunko Maru (4027gt) 16.1.44 Sunk by USN land-based aircraft 02 30S 149 42E
Syunsei Maru 1.4.42 Torpedoed (in convoy) by subm HMS *Truant*, sunk, 05 42N 98 57E
Tacoma Maru 1.2.44 Torpedoed (in convoy) by subm *Hake*, sunk, 01 35N 128 58E

Taian Maru 8.10.43 Torpedoed (in convoy) by subm *Gurnard*, sunk, 18 24N 119 09E
Taibun Maru 30.8.43 Torpedoed by subm *Halibut*, sunk, 41 53N 141 10E
Taigen Maru 6.5.42 Torpedoed (in convoy) by subm *Triton*, sunk, 28 19N 123 38E
Taihei Maru 9.7.44 Torpedoed by subm *Sunfish*, sunk, 51 17N 155 34E
Taiyo Maru 8.5.42 Torpedoed by subm *Grenadier*, sunk, 30 45N 127 40E (780†, *c*220surv)
Taizin Maru 20.2.44 Torpedoed by subm *Pogy*, sunk, 24 12N 123 20E
Takao Maru 41 IJN, transport; 10.12.41 bombed (in Padan invasion force convoy) by USAAF aircraft (and US sabotage) 17 29N 120 26E, on fire, run ashore
Takaoka Maru 43 IJN, transport; 5.6.44 torpedoed (in convoy) by subm *Shark*, sunk, 1737N 140 32E
Taketoyo Maru 21.8.44 Torpedoed by subm *Ray*, sunk, 13 23N 120 19E
Tamagawa Maru 41 IJN, transport; 2.2.42 torpedoed by subm *Seadragon*, sunk, 17 16N 11948E
Tamahoko Maru 24.6.44 Torpedoed (in convoy) by subm *Tang*, sunk, 32 30N 129 35E
Tamaki Maru 40 *Nissyu Maru* (Jpn); 18.7.44 torpedoed by subm *Cobia*, sunk, 28 43N 13924E
Tamon Maru 2.5.43 Torpedoed by subm *Stingray*, sunk, 27 18N 121 38E
Tango Maru 13.11.43 Sunk by US aircraft East China Sea
Tasmania Maru 11.12.44 Bombed by USAAF and USN land-based aircraft, sunk, 1120N 124 10E
Tatekawa Maru 42 IJN; 24.5.44 torpedoed (during Opn 'A-Go') by subm *Gurnard*, sunk, 05 45N 125 45E
Tatibana Maru 9.10.44 Torpedoed by subm *Sawfish*, sunk, 19 33N 116 38E
Tatuha Maru 17.2.44 Sunk by USN aircraft (Opn 'Hailstone') 07 46N 150 27E
Tatukami Maru 24.1.42 Torpedoed (in Balikpapan invasion force convoy) by US destroyers of TF5, sunk, 00 10N 118E (–†)
Tatumiya Maru 43 IJN, transport; 30.7.45 sunk by USN aircraft 35 33N 135 31E; salved; 8.45 surrendered
Tatuno Maru 15.1.44 Torpedoed (in convoy) by subm *Thresher*, sunk, 19 45N 120 40E
Tatuta Maru 41 IJN, transport; 8.12.43 torpedoed by subm *Tarpon*, sunk, 33 45N 140 25E (0 surv)
Tatuwa Maru 10.5.45 Struck mine, sunk, 34 05N 132 27E
Tazan Maru 17.5.42 Torpedoed by subm *Skipjack*, sunk, 06 22N 108 36E
Tazima Maru 43 Transport; 6.5.44 torpedoed (in Opn 'Take-Ichi' convoy) by subm *Gurnard*, sunk, 02 42N 124 10E
Teiyo Maru 18.8.44 Torpedoed (in convoy) by subm *Rasher*, sunk, 18 09N 119 56E
Tensyo Maru 43 Transport; 11.11.44 sunk (in convoy) by USN aircraft (of TG38.1) 10 50N 124 35E (many †)
Tenyo Maru 10.3.42 Sunk (in convoy) by USN aircraft from carriers USS *Lexington* and *Yorktown*, sunk, 06 49S 147 02E
Terukawa Maru 21.12.43 Torpedoed by subm *Skate*, sunk, 09 50N 151 55E
Terukuni Maru 21.11.39 Struck mine, sunk, 51 50 04N 01 31 04E (Thames est) (0†, 206 surv); wreck dispersed
Thames Maru 25.7.43 Torpedoed by subm *Pompon*, sunk, 02 40N 148 26E
Tihuku Maru 16.1.43 Torpedoed by subm *Growler*, sunk, 04S 151 55E
Toa Maru (10,051gt) 42 IJN, transport; 25.11.43 torpedoed by subm *Searaven*, sunk, 08 20N 158E
Toa Maru (6732gt) 30.1.43 Sunk by USN marine land-based aircraft 07 50S 156 50E
Toba Maru 25.4.42 Torpedoed by subm *Spearfish*, sunk, 17 01N 120 15E
Toei Maru (10,023g) 18.1.43 Torpedoed by subm *Silversides*, sunk, 06 21N 150 23E
Toei Maru (4004g) 1.2.44 Torpedoed by subm *Seahorse*, sunk, 04 21N 143 16E
Toho Maru 42 IJN; 29.3.43 torpedoed by subm *Gudgeon*, sunk, one the line 118 18E
Tohuku Maru 24.12.43 Torpedoed by subm *Gurnard*, sunk, 33 58N 136 16E
Tokai Maru 26.1.43 Torpedoed by subm *Flying Fish* and *Snapper*, sunk, 13 27N 144 37E
Tokiwa Maru 19.6.43 Torpedoed by subm *Gunnel*, sunk, 32 31N 126 19E
Tokusima Maru 16.9.44 Torpedoed by subm *Picuda*, sunk, 21 15N 121 29E
Tokyo Maru 42 IJN, transport; 10.11.43 torpedoed by subm *Scamp*, sunk, 03 36N 150 34E
Tonan Maru 28.11.43 Torpedoed (in convoy) by subm *Bowfin*, sunk, 12 46N 109 42E
Tonan Maru No 2 22.8.44 Torpedoed by subm *Pintado*, sunk, 29 44N 125 22E
Tonan Maru No 3 17.2.44 Sunk by USN aircraft (Opn 'Hailstone') 07 23N 151 51E
Tone Maru 21.9.42 Torpedoed by subm *Grouper*, sunk, 31 18N 123 27E
Tosan Maru 26.7.44 Torpedoed by subm *Crevalle* and *Flasher*, sunk, 18 13N 117 50E
Tosei Maru 12.12.43 Torpedoed by subm *Tuna*, sunk, 02 44N 126 14E
Tottori Maru 15.5.45 Torpedoed by subm *Hammerhead*, sunk, 09 21N 102 25E
Toyama Maru 29.6.44 Torpedoed by subm *Sturgeon*, sunk, 27 41N 129 09E
Toyohasi Maru 4.6.42 Torpedoed by subm HMS *Trusty*, sunk, 07 30N 98 10E
Toyooka Maru 9.9.44 Torpedoed by subm *Queenfish*, sunk, 19 45N 120 56E
Turuga Maru 41 IJN, transport; 24.1.42 (in Balikpapan invasion force convoy) sunk/torpedoed by USN surface craft/subm *K-XVIII* (Ne), 00 10N 118E (–†)
Turusima Maru 30.6.44 Torpedoed by subm *Jack*, sunk, 14 25N 119 47E
Tusima Maru 22.8.44 Torpedoed by subm *Bowfin*, sunk, 29 32N 129 31E
Tuyama Maru 2.10.44 Torpedoed by subm *Pomfret*, sunk, 21N 121 46E
Tyoko Maru 21.10.42 Torpedoed by subm *Gudgeon*, sunk, 03 30S 150 30E

Ume Maru 2.11.43 Torpedoed by subm *Seahorse*, sunk, 28 37N 134 45E
Unyo Maru 41 *Kenun Maru* (Jpn); 24.10.42 torpedoed by subm *Nautilus*, sunk, 41 24N 141 50E (0†)
Ural Maru 42 IJN, transport; 27.9.44 torpedoed by subm *Flasher*, sunk, 15 40N 117 18E
Ussuri Maru 28.6.44 Bombed by USAAF aircraft, sunk, 23 14N 119 49E
Utide Maru 28.2.44 Torpedoed by subm *Sargo*, sunk, 08 57N 132 52E
Uyo Maru 40 *Sinanogawa Maru* (Jpn); 14.11.42 sunk (during Guadalcanal evacuation) by USAAF, USN carrier-based aircraft and USN marine land-based aircraft 08 30S 158 45E

Venice Maru 11.11.42 Torpedoed by subm *Haddock*, sunk, 35 36N 123 44E
Victoria Maru 2.6.44 Reported sunk

Wales Maru 24.5.44 Torpedoed by subm *Lapon*, sunk, 07 16N 109 04E

Yae Maru 1.4.42 Torpedoed (in convoy) by subm HMS *Truant*, sunk, 05 42N 98 57E
Yahiko Maru 11.1.44 Torpedoed by subm *Seawolf*, sunk, 27 10N 127 28E
Yamabiko Maru 43 IJN, repair ship; 43 transport; 10.1.44 torpedoed by subm *Steelhead*, sunk, 31 28N 137 44E
Yamabuki Maru 21.9.44 Sunk by USN aircraft 14 45N 120 12E
Yamagiku Maru 28.6.44 Torpedoed by subm *Pargo*, sunk, 06 50N 122 41E
Yamagiri Maru 17.2.44 Sunk by USN aircraft (Opn 'Hailstone') 07 23N 151 51E
Yamahagi Maru 12.10.44 Sunk (in convoy) by USN aircraft 22 37N 120 15E
Yamahuku Maru 42 IJN, transport; 29.11.43 torpedoed (in convoy) by subm *Snook*, sunk, 18 37N 139 45E
Yamahuzi Maru 20.10.42 Torpedoed (in convoy) by subm *Finback*, sunk, 24 26N 120 26E
Yamasimo Maru 43 IJN, salvage vessel; 23.2.44 torpedoed by subm *Tang*, sunk, 14 45N 144 32E
Yamaura Maru 42 IJN, transport; 15.11.42 sunk (during Guadalcanal evacuation) by USAAF, USN land-based and USN marine land-based aircraft and USN surface craft 09 20S 159 50E
Yamayuri Maru 42 IJN, transport; 24.1.44 sunk by USN aircraft 04 13S 152 11E (Bougainville)
Yamazato Maru 22.4.43 Torpedoed by subm (Ne), sunk, 03 28S 99 47E
Yamazuki Maru 42 IJN, transport; 15.11.42 sunk (during Guadalcanal evacuation) by USN land-based and marine land-based aircraft, sunk, 09 20S 159 50E (–†)
Yasukawa Maru 42 IJN, transport; 2.11.42 sunk by USAAF aircraft 08 41S 148 27E
Yasukuni Maru 10.41 IJN, subm tender; 43 transport; 31.1.44 torpedoed by subm *Trigger*, sunk, 09 21N 147 02E
Yawata Maru 11.41 IJN, troopship; 1.42–5.42 converted to escort carrier; 31.5.42 commd as *Unyo*; 16.9.44 torpedoed (in convoy) by subm *Barb*, sunk, 19 18N 116 26E (–†)
Yodogawa Maru 11.5.43 Torpedoed by subm *Grayback*, sunk, 00 47S 149 02E
Yokohama Maru 42 IJN, transport; 10.3.42 sunk (in convoy) by USAAF aircraft and USN carrier-based aircraft from *Lexington* and *Yorktown*, sunk, 07 01S 147 07E
Yoneyama Maru 1.7.43 Torpedoed by subm *Thresher*, sunk, 20N 119 32E
Yosida Maru No 1 43 Transport; 26.4.44 torpedoed (in Opn 'Take-Ichi' convoy) by subm *Jack*, sunk, 18 06N 119 47E
Yosida Maru No 3 24.8.44 Torpedoed (in convoy) by subm *Ronquil*, sunk, 25 13N 121 49E
Yosyu Maru 12.1.45 Sunk (in convoy) by USN aircraft 14 15N 109 10E
Yuri Maru 28.11.43 Torpedoed (in convoy) by subm *Raton*, sunk, 01 40N 141 45E
Yuzan Maru (6380g) 27.4.43 Torpedoed by subm *Scorpion*, sunk, 38 08N 143 03E
Yuzan Maru (6039g) 30.7.45 Torpedoed by subm *Sennet*, sunk, 42 36N 139 48E

Zenyo Maru 2.8.42 Torpedoed by subm *O23* (Ne), sunk, 05 36N 99 53E
Zinzan Maru 16.7.44 Torpedoed by subm *Guardfish*, sunk, 18 20N 119 42E
Zuiyo Maru 1.10.44 Torpedoed (in convoy) by subm *Cabrilla*, sunk, 16 15N 119 43E
Zyunyo Maru 18.9.44 Torpedoed by subm HMS *Tradewind*, sunk, 02 53S 101 10E (*c*6000†, *c*1000 surv)
Zyuyo Maru 8.3.44 Struck mine, sunk, 13 10N 100 50E

Vessels in service postwar
Kiyokawa Maru (6862gt)
Koei Maru (6774gt)
San Diego Maru

Note: The status of many Japanese vessels was not recorded in official sources at the end of the war

Latvia

Losses through war causes

Abgara 6.5.42 Torpedoed by *U108*, sunk, 20 45N 72 55W (0†, 34 surv)
Andrejs Kalnins 40 Seized by Germans; 41 *Stadt Riga* (Ger); 6.7.44 bombed by British aircraft, sunk, N of Norderney
Ciltvaira 19.1.42 Torpedoed by *U123* 35 25N 75 23W (2†, 29 surv); taken in tow, abandoned, sunk off Carolina
Everalda 29.6.42 Shelled, captured, by *U158*, scuttled by *U158* crew 31N 70W (0†, 2 pow, 34 surv)
Everasma 28.2.42 Torpedoed (in convoy TAW12) by subm *Leonardo da Vinci* (Ita), sunk, 17N 48W (–†, 15 surv)
Everelza 13.8.42 Torpedoed (in convoy TAW12) by *U600*, sunk, 19 55N 73 49W (23†, 14 surv)
Everene 25.1.40 Torpedoed by *U19*, sunk, 5m off Longstone, Farne Is (1†, 30 surv)
Everita 28.8.41 Struck mine on Juminda barrage, Gulf of Finland, sunk; 1.11.44 reported in Kronstadt area, under USSR control
Everoja 40 MoWT (Br); 3.11.41 torpedoed (in convoy SC52) by *U203* 077° 80m from Belle Isle (0†, 41 surv); 3.11.41 sunk 52 18N 53 05W
Gaisma 6.41 Reported sunk off Almenscrag; 21.7.41 wreckage found E of Gotland (0 surv)
Hercogs Jekabs 42 Seized by USSR; 42 *Sovetskaya Latvia* (Rus)
Johann Faulbaums 39 *Johann Faulbaum* (Ger); 15.5.44 bombed by Allied aircraft, sunk, off Kirkenes
Katvaldis 40 MoWT (Br); 24.8.42 torpedoed (in convoy ON122) by *U605*, sunk, 48 55N 35 10W (3†, 44 surv)
Konsuls P Dannebergs 41 *Braunau* (Ger); 5.45 at Hamburg; 46 *Konsul P Danneberg* (Rus)
Regent 14.6.42 Torpedoed by *U504*, sunk, 17 50N 84 10W (11†, 14 surv)
Sigurds Faulbaums 39 *Sigurd Faulbaum* (Ger); 40 (Bel); 23.5.40 torpedoed by *U9*, sunk, 51 29N 02 38E
Spidola 22.7.40 Transf Latvian state; 5.8.40 USSR; 30.6.41 seized Liepaja by Germans; 20.2.42 KM, *Rudau* (Ger); 5.45 at Egersund; 47 *Spidola* (Br)
Valdona 41 Seized by Germans, *Baltenland* (Ger); 27.12.44 torpedoed by subm *K-56* (Rus), sunk, 55 13N 16 57E

Captured/seized by enemy and lost through marine hazard

Everonika 41 *Irma* (Ger); 13.3.44 stranded Vetterbrae, sunk

Captured/seized by enemy and lost through war causes

Arija 40 Captured by Germans; 40 *Wartheland* (Ger); 12.12.44 bombed E end of Eidfjord, sunk; 50 raised, BU
Dole 40 Captured N of Kristiansand by Germans; prize; 42 *Anke* (Ger); 11.9.43 torpedoed by Allied MTB, sunk, off Kristiansand
Everiga 40 Seized Baltic by USSR, not renamed; 6.41 sunk Pernau as blockship; raised by Germans; 24.5.45 at Copenhagen; 45 ceded USSR
Everolanda 40 USSR control; 1.11.44 in Kronstadt area
Gundega 24.4.40 Captured by Germans; 40 *Weichselland* (Ger); 21.12.44 struck mine (laid 19.12.44 by subm *Rubis* (Fra)), sunk, 58 50N 05 29E
Rolfs Faulbaums 40 *Makki Faulbaum* (Ger); 11.2.44 (1219) torpedoed (in convoy) by subm HMS *Stubborn*, sunk, 24m WNW of Namsos
Tautmila 6.41 Seized by Germans, *Baltenland* (Ger); 16.10.41 torpedoed by subm *SC-323* (Rus), sunk, 57 42N 17 20E; raised, CTL

Changes of name, flag, role, disposals

Dagø 4.40 MoWT, *Dago II* (Br); 45 *Dagø* (Dmk)
Everagra 41 USMC (Pan); 46 (Hon)
Everest 40 *Kegums* (Lat); 12.41 WSA (Lat); 46 returned
Evertons 40 *Rotesand* (Ger); 5.45 repairing Wesermünde; 49 *Evertons* (Pan)
Kaupo 40 *Westpreussen* (Ger); 8.5.45 at Flensburg, damaged; 47 *Kaupo* (Br)
Lettonia 40 *Anita* (Pan); 24.4.41 *Calanda* (Swi); 12.11.46 *Storaa* (Dmk)
Rasma 10.7.41 Captured by German warship; 41 captured by USSR; 41 (Rus)
Vizma 45 *Runø* (Dmk)

Lithuania

Loss through marine hazard

Panevézys 13.11.39 Struck rock, sunk, 2m S of Revelstein Reef

Loss through war causes

Kaunas 17.11.39 Torpedoed by *U57*, sunk, 6.5m WNW of Noord-Hinder LV (1†)

Mexico

Losses through war causes
Minatitlan 30.4.41 Seized by Italians while building Genoa; 41 (Ita); 9.11.41 shelled by warships of RN Force K, sunk, 37 08N 18 09E
Panuco 30.4.41 Seized by Italians while building Genoa; 41 (Ita); 23.10.44 sunk Genoa as blockship; 4.48 sold salvors (dispersed, danger to navigation)
Pozarica 30.4.41 Seized by Italians while building Genoa; 21.8.42 attacked by Allied aircraft, badly damaged, 12m N of Paxos; 15.10.43 captured Adriatic by British warships; taken Bari; 44 returned to Italians; 45 transf IN
Tacona 30.4.41 Seized by Italians while completing Genoa

Netherlands

During the period of German occupation of the Netherlands, and in some cases beyond that period, Netherlands vessels not in German or Axis hands, came under the control of the Netherlands Ministry of Shipping, London, and most were under the management of British companies

Losses through marine hazard
Alhena 28.1.41 Aground Pladdy Rock, near South Rock, Co Down; TL
Alkmaar 16.2.40 Ashore Cima Is, Cape Verde Islands; TL
Buitenzorg 14.1.41 Struck rocks near Grey Is, Sound of Mull, sank 56 30 15N 05 44 28W (0†)
Cremer 5.9.43 Stranded St Bees Is, Great Barrier Reef, TL
Djambi 13.3.43 Collision with *Silverbeech* (*qv*), sank, 39N 10W (0†)
Driebergen 28.8.40 Collision with *Port Darwin* (*qv*), sunk, 55 25N 01 22W
Magdala 15.1.45 Sd Reykjavik for UK (0 surv); no U-boat claim
Meliskerk 8.1.43 Aground 0.5m off Port St John's, Cape Province; TL
Palembang 6.11.44 Struck submerged wreck outside Alexandria harbour, leaking; 7.11.44 abandoned; 15.11.44 sank; 50 BU *in situ*
Rozenburg 2.8.41 Collision with *Murena* (*qv*), sank, off Halifax NS
Van der Hagen 4.3.42 Burned out, sank, Tjilatjep
Soemba 5.1.41 Cargo shifted, capsized, sank, 45 52N 49 10W (34†, 24 surv)
Springfontein 26.2.41 Explosion, on fire, sank, Freetown
Stolwijk 7.12.40 Wrecked between Inishdovey and Inishborin, Co Donegal (10†, 18 surv)
Trompenberg 29.11.45 Stranded near Ulvo Is; refloated, taken in tow, tow broke, drifted on rocks; TL
Waalhaven 40 German control; 8.40 KM, Seelöwe transport *RO2*; 15.12.40 returned; 18.9.42 wrecked Pinngrund, off Ronnskar; 24.9.42 declared TL
Willemsplein 4.10.42 Ashore in St Mary's Bay, near Cape English NS; TL

Losses through marine hazard after change of flag
Peursum 41 Building Krimpen, seized by Germans; 5.11.41 *Eberstein* (Ger); 42 *Rauenthaler* (Ger); 8.9.43 collision with *Signal* (*qv*), sank, N of Trondheim
Yssel 8.40 KM, Seelöwe transport *RO21*; 12.4.41 KMD Rotterdam; 3.2.42 Channel Islands transport; 20.2.43 stranded in fog, sank, Pierres des Portes, off St Malo; 45 wreck BU

Losses through war causes
Aagtekerk 14.6.42 Bombed (in convoy WM11) by German Ju87 and Ju88 aircraft, on fire, 34 00N 23 40E (46†, 104 surv); grounded off Mingar Garab in 31 01 30N 24 39E; TL
Abbekerk 24.8.42 Torpedoed by *U604*, sunk, 52 05N 30 50W (2†, 62 surv)
Achilles 1.10.42 Torpedoed by *U202*, sunk, 09 06N 59 48W (1†, 35 surv)
Agamemnon 8.11.40 Bombed by German aircraft 220° 7 cables from SW Swin LV (2†, 27 surv); sunk 51 43 09N 01 24 09E; wreck dispersed by explosives
Alchiba 8.7.42 Torpedoed, shelled, by subm *I-10* (Jpn), sunk, 18 30S 41 40E (5†, 40 surv)
Alcyone 16.3.42 Struck mine (laid by *Doggerbank*), sunk, 25m off Cape Town (0†, 62 surv)
Alderamin 17.3.43 Torpedoed (in convoy SC122) by *U338*, sunk, 51 30N 34 55W (15†, 49 surv)
Alioth 10.6.42 Torpedoed, shelled, by subm *Leonardo da Vinci* (Ita) 00 08N 18 52W (8†, 28 surv); 11.6.42 sunk
Almkerk 16.3.41 Torpedoed (ind) by *U106*, sunk, 13 21N 20 25W (0†, 66 surv)
Alphacca 4.4.42 Torpedoed by *U505*, sunk, 01 50N 07 40W (15†, 57 surv)
Alpherat 21.12.43 Bombed by German aircraft, sunk, 36 16N 16 58E (0†, 89 surv)
Altair 40 Seized Amsterdam incomplete by Germans; 40 (Ger); 9.10.41 delivered as KM target ship; 4.4.43 torpedoed by British aircraft, sunk, 63 01N 07 02E
Aludra 14.5.40 Seized Rotterdam by Germans; 5.8.40 KM, Seelöwe transport *RO5;* 26.3.41 Blaufuchs transport; 31.8.41 KDM, Oslo; 8.42 transport, Norway; 29.4.43 torpedoed by British aircraft, sunk, 53 28N 04 01E

Alwaki 10.7.40 Torpedoed (in convoy A180) by *U61*, sunk, 10m NE of Cape Wrath
Amazone 6.5.42 Torpedoed by *U333*, sunk, 27 21 18N 80 04 30W (14†, 20 surv)
Ameland 18.2.40 Torpedoed by *U10*, sunk, 51 54N 03 01E (0†)
Amerskerk 41 Seized by Germans while building; 42 *Coburg* (Ger) (Schiff 49) 15.6.44 struck mine, sunk, N of Schiermonnikoog
Amor 11.3.40 Struck mine, sunk, 51 24N 02 09E (0†, 33 surv)
Amstel 17.11.45 Struck mine, sunk, 54 36 36N 10 49 30E
Amstelland 26.2.41 Bombed by German aircraft 54 12N 16W (1†, 44 surv); 28.2.41 taken in tow by tug *Ierse Zee*; abandoned 54 10N 14 38W, sunk
Amsterdam 16.4.42 Torpedoed by *U66*, sunk, 12N 62 45W (2†, 38 surv)
Arendskerk 15.1.40 Torpedoed by *U44*, broke in two, sunk, 46 55N 06 34E (0†)
Arundo 28.4.42 Torpedoed by *U136*, sunk, 40 10 30N 73 44W (6†, 37 surv)
Aurora 24.11.42 Attacked by enemy aircraf, sunk, Philippeville harbour (0†); 52 wreck sold; 53 raised; 10.11.53 sank off Cap de Fer when in tow for Italy

Baarn 11.7.43 Bombed by enemy aircraft (during Sicily landings) off Avola 36 55N 15 13E (0†, 72 surv); shelled by HM ship, sunk
Baloeran 9.5.40 Captured Rotterdam by Germans; 11.5.41 KM; 20.7.41–30.5.43 hospital ship *Strassburg*; 1.9.43 struck mine off Egmond aan Zee, beached 52 29 18N 04 32 23E, abandoned; 19.9.43 torpedoed by British MTBs, badly damaged, TL
Barentsz 12.41 Req Ne navy, repair ship; 6.3.42 bombed by Japanese aircraft, burnt out, sunk, Tjilatjap
Barneveld 20.1.41 Shelled, captured, by *Admiral Scheer* 07S 03E (0†, 100 pow); 21.1.41 sunk by explosives 09 27S 03W
Baud 40 Seized Rotterdam incomplete by Germans; 11.10.44 scuttled Maassluis
Beatrice 8.12.41 Seized Yokohama by Japanese; 42 *Biwa Maru* (Jpn); 1.11.42 sunk 03 54S 109 13E (marine causes)
Beemsterdijk 27.1.41 Struck by British mine when anchored, sunk, 51 17N 06 23W (39†, 3 surv)
Benakat 20.5.43 Torpedoed by *U197*, sunk, 06 05S 12 56W (0†, 44 surv)
Bengalen 2.3.42 Scuttled by RNN in Westervaartwater, Sourabaya, to prevent capture by Japanese
Bennekom 31.10.41 Torpedoed (in convoy OS10) by *U96*, sunk, 51 20N 23 40W (8†, 46 surv)
Berenice 21.6.40 Torpedoed by *U65*, sunk, 47 10N 03 35W (47†, 8 surv)
Beuersplein 26.2.41 Bombed by enemy aircraft 54 07N 17 06W, on fire, abandoned (21†, 13 surv); 27.2.41 sunk about 245° 13m from 53 52N 16 26W
Beverwijk 5.40 German control; 26.2.45 bombed by Allied aircraft, sunk, Hamburg; 5.45 abandoned; 1.54 wreck raised, BU Hamburg
Bilderdijk 19.10.40 Torpedoed (in convoy HX79) by *U47*, sunk, 56 35N 17 15W (0†, 39 surv)
Binnendijk 7.10.39 Struck mine (laid 8.9.39 by *U26*); 8.10.39 (1400) sunk 50 32 01N 02 20 01W (0†, 42 surv); wreck dispersed by explosives
Bintang 21.11.42 Torpedoed by *U160*, sunk, 11 40N 53 50W (22†, 51 surv)
Blitar 5.4.43 Torpedoed (in convoy HX231) by *U632* 57 45N 27 30W; 6.4.43 sunk (26†, 54 surv)
Bodegraven 2.7.44 Torpedoed by *U547*, sunk, 04 14N 11W (9†, 1 pow, 101 surv)
Boekelo 18.10.40 Torpedoed (convoy SC7 straggler) by *U100*, damaged, and *U123*, sunk, 56 40N 10 45W (0†, 25 surv)
Boschdijk 11.5.40 Bombed by German aircraft, badly damaged, Rotterdam; KM, target ship; 42 expended as target
Breda 23.12.40 While at anchor, bombed by German He111 aircraft 56 29 12N 05 25W; beached 56 28 33N 05 25W, drifted off, sunk (0†, 54 surv); 61 wreck dispersed
Breedijk 14.9.42 Torpedoed by *U68*, sunk, 05 08S 08 36W (2†, 3 pow, 47 surv)
Britsum 4.7.40 Bombed, torpedoed (in convoy OA178) by German Ju87 aircraft of StG2, on fire, off Selsey (9†); 5.7.40 beached 54 40 04N 00 47 06W; wreck used by RAF as bombing target
Burgerdijk 10.2.40 Stopped by *U48* 49 45N 06 30W, crew ordered to leave vessel, torpedoed, sunk (0†)
Bussum 23.11.40 Torpedoed (in convoy SC11) by *U100* 55 39N 08 58W (–†, 29 surv); 24.11.40 sunk 55 37N 08 42W

Calypso 40 Captured by Germans; 40 *Norma* (Ger); 27.12.41 sunk Vaagso
Ceres 13.3.43 Torpedoed (in convoy GAT49) by *U68*, sunk, 14 50N 71 46W (2†, 35 surv)
Colombia 40 RNN, subm depot ship; 27.2.43 torpedoed by *U516*, sunk, 33 36S 27 29E (8†)
Costa Rica 40 Allied troopship; 27.4.41 bombed by German aircraft after Crete evacuation, sunk, 35 54N 23 49E (0†)
Crijnssen 10.6.42 Torpedoed by *U504*, sunk, 18 14N 85 11W (1†, 92 surv)

Delfshaven 6.8.42 Torpedoed by *U572*, sunk, 07 24N 25 37W (1†, 38 surv)
Dempo 40 Allied troopship; 17.3.44 torpedoed (in convoy SNF17) by *U371*, abandoned, sunk, 37 08N 05 24E (0†)
Den Haag 15.2.40 Torpedoed by *U48*, sunk, 48 02N 08 26W
Deucalion 4.7.40 Bombed, shelled (in convoy OA178) by German Ju87 aircraft of StG2, sunk, 20m SSW of Portland, 50 11N 02 35W (27 surv)

Dinteldijk 5.40 Seized by Germany; attacked by Allied aircraft, forepart burned out Rotterdam; 23.9.44 sunk as blockship near Maassluis
Djirak 40 RNN aux *TAN3*; 9.1.42 shelled by subm *I-57* (Jpn), sunk, 07 15S 116 23E (0†)
Drechtdijk 5.40 Seized Rotterdam by Germans; 7.8.40 Seelöwe transport *RO13*; *Russelheim* (Ger); 12.2.41 accom ship, Baltic; 8.42 transport, Norway; 17.2.45 struck mine 1m E of Swinemünde; 18.2.45 beached, on fire, 53 56N 14 17E; TL; 12.3.45 wreck bombed; 24.12.45 wreck returned owner; 1.2.47 ar Ghent for BU

Eibergen 3.6.41 Torpedoed by *U75*, sunk, 48 02N 25 06W (4†, 35 surv)
Elusa 21.5.41 Torpedoed (in convoy HX126) by *U93*, on fire, 59N 38 05W (3†, 49 surv); 23.5.41 sunk 58 30N 38 10W
Emmaplein 31.1.41 Struck British mine, sunk, 6m NE of Rona Is (0†, 34 surv)
Enggano 1.3.42 Bombed by Japanese aircraft, on fire, sunk, 12S 109 21E (0†, 67 surv)
Eulota 11.3.40 Torpedoed by *U28*, sunk, 48 35N 08 22W (0†, 42 surv)

Farmsum 7.12.40 Torpedoed (convoy OB252 straggler) by *U99*, sunk, 52 11N 22 56W (16†)
Fauna 18.5.42 Torpedoed by *U558*, sunk, 22 10N 72 30W (2†, 27 surv)
Flensburg 40 MoWT; 8.10.42 torpedoed by *U201* 10 45N 46 48W (0†, 48 surv); 9.10.42 shelled, sunk

Gaasterkerk 8.10.42 Torpedoed by *U68*, sunk, 34 20S 18 10E (0†, 64 surv)
Garoet 19.6.44 Torpedoed by *U181*, sunk, 12 30S 64E (88†, 10 surv)
Genota 9.5.42 Captured 15S 75E by aux cruisers *Aikoku Maru* and *Hokoku Maru* (Jpn); 42 *Ose* (Jpn); 30.3.44 sunk by USN carrier-based aircraft 07 30N 134 30E
Groenlo 24.11.41 Torpedoed (in convoy FS54) by E-boat *S52*, sunk, 52 19 32N 01 59 12E (10†, 19 surv)
Grootekerk 24.2.41 Torpedoed by *U123*, sunk 56N 25W (52†, 0 surv)

Haulerwijk 30.9.40 Shelled by *U132* 53 44N 27 28 48W, abandoned, sunk (4†, 27 surv)
Hector 24.5.42 Torpedoed by *U103*, sunk, 19 50N 81 53W (2†, 29 surv)
Heemskerk 20.1.41 Bombed (convoy SL61 straggler) by German aircraft, on fire, damaged, W of Foynes (8†, 40 surv); 21.1.41 torpedoed by *U105*, sunk, 53 43N 16 07W

Irene 40 German control; 8.40 KM, Seelöwe transport *RO8*; 24.5.41 Channel Is transport; 7.8.44 scuttled as blockship St Malo outer harbour; 45 raised; 1.46 towed Amsterdam; 46 BU Henrik Ido Ambacht

Jagersfontein 26.6.42 Torpedoed by *U107*, sunk, 32 02N 54 53W (0†, 165 surv)
Jan Pieterszoon Coen 14.5.40 Scuttled as blockship Ijmuiden; wreck cleared during war
Jason 10.5.40 Seized by Italians; 40 *Sebastiano Veniero* (Ita); 41 (Ger); 15.12.41 torpedoed by subm HMS *Torbay*, beached, near Capo Methoni (–†; *c*200 pow†, *c*1800 pow surv); TL in heavy weather; salved by Germans; 42 *Kapitan Diederichsen* (Ger); 29.2.44 shelled (in convoy) by destroyer *Le Terrible* (Fra), sunk, near Isto

Kertosono 1.7.40 Captured 12 40N 31 22W by aux cruiser *Thor*, sent to Lorient; 29.4.42 German prize; 30.1.43 commd KM U-boat depot ship, Nantes; 23.9.43 bombed by Allied aircraft, burnt out, Nantes; 10.8.44 scuttled Nantes; 8.45 wreck raised; 5.46 ar St Nazaire; 47 BU
Kota Nopan 17.8.41 Captured 07 21S 20 45W by aux cruiser *Komet*; 16.11.41 ar R Gironde, *Karin* (Ger); later named *Passau* (Ger); 10.3.43 found by cruiser USS *Savannah* and destroyer USS *Eberle*, sunk, 07S 21W
Kota Pinang 14.5.40 Seized Rotterdam by Germans; 40 KM, *Klara* (Ger) (blockade runner); 3.10.41 found by cruiser HMS *Kenya*, shelled, scuttled 43 32N 24 06W (0†, 119+ surv picked up by *U129*)
Kota Radja 24.2.42 Bombed by Japanese aircraft, on fire, Sourabaya roads (0†); sunk by minelayer *Krakatau* (Ne) 07 10 52S 112 44 22E
Kota Tjandi 30.4.43 Torpedoed (in convoy TS37) by *U515*, sunk, 07 15N 13 49W (6†, 93 surv)

Laertes 3.5.42 Torpedoed by *U564*, sunk, 28 21N 80 23W (18†, 48 surv)
Le Maire 1.3.42 Sd Tjilatjap for Australia; 4.3.42 torpedoed by subm *I-7* (Jpn), sunk, 330° 250m from Cocos Islands
Leto 12.5.42 Torpedoed by *U553*, sunk, 49 32N 65 19W (12†, 41 surv)
Loa-Koeloe (ex *Atna*) 2.3.42 Scuttled Sourabaya

Maas 11.9.40 Torpedoed (in convoy OA210) by *U28*, sunk, 55 34N 15 56W (–†, 2 surv)
Maasburg 5.40 German control; 8.40 KM, Seelöwe transport *R4N*; 9.40 *R1N*; 4.12.40 returned; 1.3.44 struck mine 10m SSW of Kijkduin; bombed by RAF aircraft, sunk, off Zuiderhaaks
Maasdam 26.6.41 Torpedoed (in convoy HX133) by *U564*, sunk, 60N 30 35W (2†, 77 surv)
Madrono 4.7.42 Captured by aux cruiser *Thor*, Indian Ocean, prize, taken Japan; 42 *Rossbach* (Ger); 7.5.44 torpedoed by subm USS *Burrfish*, sunk, 33 14N 134 40E
Mamura 26.2.42 Torpedoed by *U504*, sunk, 29N 76W

Manvantara 13.2.42 Bombed by Japanese aircraft, sunk, S of Banka Strait (4†, 47 surv)
Marisa 16.5.41 Torpedoed by *U107*, sunk, 06 10N 18 09W (3†, 46 surv)
Mark 9.9.39 Struck mine, sunk, 56 45N 04 04E
Marken 10.9.41 Torpedoed by *U111*, sunk, 01 36N 36 55W (0†, 37 surv)
Marnix van Sint Aldegonde 40 Allied troopship; 6.11.43 torpedoed (in convoy KMF25A) by German aircraft 37 12N 06 16E, damaged, abandoned (0†, 3235 surv); taken in tow; 7.11.43 sunk 88° 6.25m from Cape Bougaroni Lt
Merope 27.4.43 Torpedoed by *U371*, sunk, 10m ENE of Cap Bengut (10†, 24 surv)
Merula 13.2.42 Bombed (in convoy) by Japanese aircraft Banka Strait; taken in tow by *Herborg* (*qv*), sunk (42†, 8 surv)
Modjokerto 1.3.42 Shelled by cruiser *Chikuma* (Jpn), badly damaged, 12 30S 106E; 1.3.42 torpedoed by subm *I-54* (Jpn) sunk 12 40S 106 40E (42†, 0 surv)
Moena 24.8.42 Torpedoed by *U162*, sunk, 13 25N 57 15W (4†, 83 surv)
Montferland 27.6.41 Attacked by German aircraft 52 47N 01 50E (0†, 43 surv); 28.6.41 sunk off No 8 Buoy, North Sea; wreck, in 52 37 15N 01 50 30E, dispersed by explosives
Moordrecht 20.6.40 Torpedoed (in convoy HX49) by *U48*, sunk, 43 34N 14 20W (25†, 4 surv)

Naaldwijk 14.5.40 Sunk Ijmuiden; raised by Germans; 43 *Hans Christophersen* (Ger); 24.12.43 struck mine, sunk, Gulf of Bothnia
Nieuw Zeeland 40 Allied troopship; 11.11.42 torpedoed by *U380*, sunk, 35 57N 03 58W (15†, 241 surv)

Oberon 27.6.41 Torpedoed (in convoy SL76) by *U123* 25 43N 22 47W (6†, 28 surv); 28.6.41 sunk
Ocana 25.3.42 Torpedoed by *U552*, damaged, 42 36N 65 25W (49†, 8 surv); 15.4.42 sunk by minesweeper HMS *Burlington* 43 24N 64 45W
Olivia 14.6.42 Shelled by aux cruiser *Thor*, sunk, 26S 77E (42†, 6 surv)
Ombilin 12.12.42 Torpedoed by subm *Enrico Tazzoli* (Ita), sunk, 07 25N 39 19W (2 pow, 79 surv)
Onoba 16.1.41 Bombed by German aircraft, sunk, 55 55N 12 24W (0†)
Oostplein 8.8.40 Captured, shelled, sunk by aux cruiser *Widder*, 200m SW of Azores (0†, crew pow)
Ootmarsum 23.11.40 Torpedoed (in convoy SC11) by *U100*, sunk, 55N 12W
Op ten Noort 41 RNN hospital ship; 28.2.42 captured SW of Bawean by Japanese subm; 3.3.42 seized as prize; 42 IJN, hospital ship *Teno Maru* (Jpn); 43 decomm; 10.44 reported war loss
Orion 5.40 Seized Rotterdam by Germans; 40 (Ger); 9.8.40 KM, Seelöwe transport *RO9*; 23.5.41 Blaufuchs transport; 7.6.43 returned (Ne); 18.3.45 torpedoed by Russian aircraft, sunk, off Scholpin
Oscilla 16.3.42 Torpedoed, shelled, by subm *Morosini* (Ita), sunk, 19 15N 60 25W (4†, 51 surv)

Pendopo 40 RNN, aux *TAN4*; 2.3.42 scuttled Sourabaya; 31.7.43 salved by IJN; 43 *Eiho Maru* (Jpn); 12.1.45 attacked (in convoy) by USN carrier-based aircraft, sunk, 11 10N 108 55E
Pendrecht 8.6.41 Torpedoed by *U48*, sunk, 45 18N 36 40W (0†, 36 surv)
Pennland 8.40 Allied troopship; 25.4.41 bombed by German dive-bomber aircraft off Bela Pouli, near San Giorgio Is, Gulf of Athens (4†, 347 surv); sunk by HM ship
Phobos 14.5.40 (Ger); 40 KM, *Thann*; 29.12.44 struck mine, sunk, off Darsser Ort
Poelau Bras 7.3.42 Bombed by Japanese aircraft, sunk, 10S 105E (33†, 118 pow)
Poelau Roebiah 6.7.43 Torpedoed by *U759*, sunk, 17 55N 76 30W (2†, 85 surv)
Poelau Tello 27.1.42 Bombed by Japanese aircraft Emmahaven (Padang); beached Koeniginnabaai; TL
Polydorus 27.11.42 Torpedoed by *U176*, sunk, 09 01N 25 38W (2†, 78 surv)
Polyphemus 26.5.42 Torpedoed by *U578*, sunk, 38 12N 63 22W (45†, 30 surv)
Poseidon 28.5.42 Torpedoed by *U155* or *U502*, sunk, 36N 71W (31†, 0 surv)
Prins Frederik Hendrik 8.3.41 Bombed by German aircraft, on fire, sunk, 52 20N 05 37W (8†, 16 surv)
Prins Willem II 8.4.41 Torpedoed (convoy HX117 straggler) by *U98*, sunk, 59 50N 24 25W (12†, 22 surv)
Prins Willem III 26.3.43 Torpedoed by German aircraft; 27.3.43 taken in tow by tug *Hengist* (Br), capsized, sunk, 37N 02 14E (11†)

Randwijk 5.40 Repairing Bolnes SY; 5.40 German control; 25.10.44 attacked by Allied aircraft, sunk, alongside quay, Hamburg; 4.47 refloated; 4.48 ar Antwerp for BU
Reggestroom 9.7.42 Torpedoed (in convoy) by E-boat, sunk, 50 19N 03W (0†, 47 surv)
Reyniersz 5.40 Seized by Germans while building; 42 Completed; 15.8.42 commd KM, *Sperrbrecher 23*; 5.45 at Århus; 18.5.45 struck mine, sunk, Kiel Bay; 51 salved; 52 BU
Rhea 17.11.41 Seized Algiers by French; 1.3.43 wrecked near Naples
Roggeveen 41 RNN, aux depot ship; 2.3.42 scuttled Sourabaya
Rotterdam 28.8.42 Torpedoed by *U511*, sunk, 18 09N 74 38W (10†, 41 surv)
Rotula 1.3.41 Bombed by German aircraft 52 20 30N 05 29W (16†, 32 surv); sunk by HM trawler 52 24N 05 24W

Salabangka 1.6.43 Torpedoed (in convoy CD20) by *U178* 31 08S 31 18E; taken in tow, sunk 31 09S 29 13E
Saleier 10.4.41 Torpedoed (dispersed from convoy OB306) by *U52*, sunk, 58 04N 30 48W (0†, 63 surv)
Saturnus 15.9.42 Torpedoed by *U517*, sunk, 48 49N 64 06W (1†, 35 surv)
Sawahloento 14.12.42 Torpedoed by *U177*, sunk, 31 02S 34E (51†, 19 surv)
Schie 24.6.41 Torpedoed (in convoy OB336) by *U203*, sunk, 55 23N 38 49W (0 surv)
Sembilan 17.4.43 Torpedoed by subm *Leonardo da Vinci* (Ita), sunk, 32 30S 35 10E (95†, 1 surv)
Semiramis 15.2.42 Scuttled Pladjoe; raised by Japanese; 43 *Kyoko Maru* (Jpn); 27.12.43 torpedoed by subm USS *Ray*, sunk, 05S 121 22E
Serooskerk 6.12.42 Torpedoed (dispersed from convoy ON149) by *U155*, sunk, 37N 38W (73†, 0 surv)
Siantar 2.3.42 Torpedoed, shelled, by subm *I-1* (Jpn), sunk, 21 20S 108 45E (21†, 40 surv)
Simaloer 2.3.41 Bombed by German aircraft 56 43N 10 49W; abandoned; 4.3.41 sunk 55 36N 09 46W (2†, 69 surv)
Simón Bolívar 18.11.39 Struck mines 51 49 30N 01 41E (84†); sunk 51 49 01N 01 36 05E; wreck dispersed
Sitoebondo 30.7.41 Torpedoed (in convoy OS1) by *U371*, sunk, 35 19N 23 53W (19†, 64 surv)
Slamat 14.9.40 Allied troopship; 27.4.41 bombed (on way to Crete in convoy) by German aircraft, on fire, sunk, 37 01N 23 10E (650†; of surv on rescue ships also sunk, crew – 189†, 9 surv; troops – 1195†, 5 surv)
Sliedrecht 16.11.39 Torpedoed by *U28*, sunk, about 200m S of Rockall (26†)
Soekaboemi 87.12.42 Torpedoed (in convoy ONS154) by *U356*, damaged, 47 25M 25 20W, became straggler; later torpedoed by *U441*, sunk (1†, 65 surv)
Soesterberg 18.10.41 Torpedoed (in convoy SC7) by *U101*, sunk, 57 12N 10 43W (6†)
Spaarndam 27.11.39 Struck magnetic mine (laid by German destroyer), sunk, 51 33 05N 01 24 22E (7†)
Spar 5.8.42 Torpedoed (in convoy SC94) by *U593*, sunk, 53 05N 43 38W (3†, 36 surv)
Stad Alkmaar 7.9.40 Torpedoed (in convoy FS273) by E-boat *S33*, sunk, 52 25 20N 02 02W (–†, 14 surv)
Stad Amsterdam 25.8.40 Torpedoed (convoy TAW15 straggler) by *U164*, sunk, 16 39N 73 15W (3†, 35 surv)
Stad Dordrecht 40 German control; 13.11.44 struck mine, sunk, Kiel Bay
Stad Leiden 40 Seized Rotterdam incomplete by Germans; 42 *Narvik* (Ger); 17.6.43 struck mine, sunk, North Sea
Stad Maastricht 23.12.40 Attacked (in convoy FN366) by E-boats (1st MTB flotilla), torpedoed, 52 35N 02 03E (0†); 25.12.40 taken in tow, sunk 51 42 09N 01 22 08E
Stad Schiedam 16.9.40 Explosion, sunk, 2 days out from Bermuda (12 surv) (believed caused by bomb placed in cargo)
Statendam 11.5.40 Bombed by German He111 aircraft, Rotterdam, burnt out; 8.40 BU Hendrik Ido Ambacht
Stella 11.5.40 Bombed by German aircraft, sunk, Vlissingen roads (–†)

Tajandoen 7.12.39 Torpedoed by *U47*, sunk, 49 07N 05 07W (6†)
Tanimbar 14.6.42 Attacked (in Opn 'Harpoon' convoy) by Italian Savoia S79s torpedo aircraft, sunk 37 50N 06 44E (23†, 65 surv)
Tapanoeli 17.3.41 Torpedoed (in convoy SL68) by *U106*, sunk, 15 42N 20 49W (0†)
Tara 21.2.40 Torpedoed by *U50*, sunk, 42 45N 10 25W (0†)
Tela 19.7.40 Sunk by aux cruiser *Thor* 14S 33W (33 pow)
Telamon 24.7.42 Torpedoed by *U160*, sunk, 09 15N 59 54W (23†, 14 surv)
Tjikandi 2.3.42 Scuttled 07 11 17S 112 43 18E (Sourabaya) upon Japanese invasion
Tjikarang 2.3.42 Scuttled 07 11 02S 112 43 07E (Sourabaya) upon Japanese invasion; wreck removed after war
Tjileboet 28.11.42 Torpedoed (in convoy) by *U161*, sunk, 05 34N 25 02W (0 surv)
Tjinegara 25.7.42 Torpedoed by subm *I-169* (Jpn), sunk, 23 10S 165E (0†)
Tjisalak 26.3.44 Torpedoed by subm *I-8* (Jpn), sunk, 02 30S 78 40E (93†, 5 pow, 5 surv)
Tjisaroea 4.3.42 Captured S of Lombok Is by Japanese; 8.42 *Chihaya Maru* (Jpn); 2.11.43 torpedoed by subm USS *Seahorse*, sunk, 29N 134E
Towa 11.12.40 Torpedoed (in convoy HX92) by *U96*, sunk, 55 50N 10 10W (18†, 19 surv)
Triton 1.6.42 Torpedoed, shelled, by *U558*, sunk, 26N 59 34W (6†, 30 surv)
Tuva 2.10.41 Torpedoed by *U575*, sunk, 54 16N 26 36W (1†, 34 surv)
Tysa 30.6.42 Torpedoed (in convoy) by subm *Morosini* (Ita) 25 33N 57 53W; shelled by escort, sunk (0†, 43 surv)

Ulysses 12.4.43 Torpedoed (in convoy HX232) by *U168*, damaged, and *U706*, sunk, 54 30N 30 30W (0†, 40 surv)

Van Cloon 7.2.42 Torpedoed by subm *I-55* (Jpn), sunk, S of Bawean Is; refloated by Japanese; 43 *Tatebe Maru* (Jpn); 12.1.45 sunk by USN carrier-based aircraft 14 15N 109 10E
Van der Hagen 4.3.42 Burned out Tjilatjap; salved and removed by Japanese; 43 *Harusei Maru* (Jpn); 30.6.45 sunk Maizuru Bay; refloated and recovered by owners postwar

Van Linschoten 39 Sold France, *Gouverneur Général A Varenne* (Fra); 42 captured by Japanese; 42 *Teiren Maru* (Jpn); 1.12.43 attacked by USAAF aircraft, sunk, 22 13N 114 05E
Van Neck 2.3.42 Scuttled Sourabaya; 6.44 refloated by Japanese; fate unknown
Van Overstraten 22.1.42 Shelled by subm *I-64* (Jpn), sunk, 01 40N 90 13E (0 surv)
Van Rees 9.1.42 Torpedoed by subm *I-56* (Jpn), 80m S of Tjilatjap (6†)
Van Rensselaer 12.5.40 Struck mine inside south pier Ijmuiden (5†); ashore, TL
Van Waerwijk 3.3.42 Scuttled Tandjong Priok; salved by Japanese; 43 *Harukiku Maru* (Jpn); 26.6.44 torpedoed by subm HMS *Truculent*, sunk, 03 15N 99 46E
Vecht 7.3.40 Torpedoed by *U14*, sunk, 51 45N 03 05E
Veerhaven 11.11.42 Shelled by subm *Leonardo da Vinci* (Ita) 03 51S 29 22W (0†, 45 surv); sunk 03 40S 30W
Vesta 5.40 Seized Rotterdam by Germans; 5.8.40 KM, Seelöwe transport *RO6*; 23.5.41 Blaufuchs transport; 29.8.42 *Käthe* (Ger); 21.5.43 *Vesta* (Ne) 14.5.44 bombed by British aircraft, sunk, E of Terschelling

Winterswijk 10.9.41 Torpedoed (in convoy SC42) by *U432*, sunk, 61 38N 40 40W (20†, 13 surv)
Woensdrecht 12.9.42 Torpedoed by *U515* 10 27N 60 17W; broke in two, forepart towed Trinidad, TL (0†, 38 surv; 1 surv from *Cressington Court* (*qv*) † when torpedoed)
Wolsum 5.40 Seized (Ger); 40 KM, Seelöwe transport *RO20*; 26.1.41 transport, Norway; 16.9.44 bombed by Russian aircraft, exploded (ammunition cargo), sunk, 69 44N 30 07E

Yselhaven 6.6.41 Torpedoed (dispersed from convoy OB238) by *U43*, sunk, 49 25N 40 54W (24†, 10 surv)

Zaandam 6.42 US transport; 2.11.42 torpedoed by *U174*, sunk, 01 17N 36 40W (132†, 166 surv)
Zaanland 16.3.43 Torpedoed (in convoy HX229) by *U758*, sunk, 50 38N 34 36W (0†, 53 surv)
Zonnewijk 5.40 German control; 40 (Ger); 8.40 KM, Seelöwe transport *R24*; 12.4.41 *RO24*; 14.11.43 Luftwaffe aux, Travemünde; 8.10.44 torpedoed by subm *SC-310* (Rus), sunk, 57 13 05N 21 13 03E (260†)
Zuiderdam 5.40 Captured incomplete by Germans; 28.8.40 attacked by RAF aircraft, sunk, Schiedam; 25.7.42 refloated, LU; 22.9.44 scuttled by Germans as blockship near Maassluis, Nieuwe Waterweg; 13.11.46 raised; 48 BU Ghent
Zuiderkerk 28.8.42 Torpedoed (in convoy SL119) by *U566*, badly damaged, 40 20N 16 02W (0†, 68 surv); 29.8.42 sunk by HMS escort

Sunk Mulberry Harbour, Normandy
Parkhaven 44 Adm; 8.6.44 sunk as breakwater Gooseberry 3, Gold Beach, Arromanches

Sunk postwar with surplus war materials
Bantam 28.3.43 Attacked by Japanese aircraft, beached, Oro Bay (0†, 72 surv); salved, towed Sydney; 24.9.46 towed 36m out to sea, sunk in 1200 fathoms, with 4000 tons poison gas shells and obsolete ammunition

Struck mine, sunk, postwar
Christiaan Huygens 40 Allied troopship; 26.8.45 struck mine, badly damaged, aground Steenbank 51 37N 03 17E (1†); 5.9.45 hull broken, TL
Mars 29.5.45 Struck mine, on fire, outside Patras (5†); sank 3m NW of Papas Lt, near Patras
Meerkerk 16.6.46 Struck mine, broke in two, sunk, near West Kapelle (12†)

Changes of name, flag, role, disposals, etc
Albireo 42 German, troopship *Wuri* (Ger); 17.8.42 struck mine, sunk, 56 53 30N 10 31 42E (65†); broke in two, sank; 43 afterpart raised, taken Copenhagen, then sunk by sabotage; part salved postwar; 46 *Madame Butterfly* (Swe); 49 *Alnati* (Ne)
Aldabi 7.8.41 Seized by Germans; 2.2.42 commd KM U-boat target ship *Wolta*; 11.10.44 troop transport; 5.45 Luftwaffe accom ship, Flensburg; 29.6.45 returned, *Aldabi* (Ne)
Aldebaran 5.40 German prize; 5.8.40 KM, Seelöwe ransport *RO3*; 26.3.41 Blaufuchs transport; 19.5.45 returned
Algol 27.10.41 KM; 15.2.44 KM commd *Sperrbrecher 29*; 5.45 recovered Wilhelmshaven with bomb damage; repaired Rotterdam; 47 *Alhena* (Ne)
Alkaid 5.40 German control; 5.8.40 KM, Seelöwe transport *RO11*; 2.4.41 Blaufuchs transport; 8.42 transport, Norway; 5.45 at Kiel, damaged; 6.12.45 returned

Bali 40 Seized while building; (Ger); 12.9.44 scuttled Dordrecht as blockship; 45 raised; 47 (Ne)
Bantam 42–45 WSA and MoWT charters; 45 returned
Bloemfontein 42–45 Allied troopship; 46 returned, rebuilt
Boissevain 40–46 Allied troopship; 46 returned

Borneo 40 Seized by Germans while building; 40 (Ger); 9.44 scuttled incomplete; 45 raised; 47 (Ne)
Brastagi 42 WSA charter; 7.42–16.10.45 MoWT charter; 10.45 returned

Celebes 5.40 German control; 5.8.41 seized by KM, V-ship base; 4.11.43 U-boat target ship; 9.44 transport, Baltic; 3.45 bombed, badly damaged, Hamburg; 45–46 repaired; 11.46 (Ne)
Coryda 40 KM, *Schlettstadt* (Ger); 44 (Br); 5.45 at St Nazaire; 45 (Ne); 46 *Coryda* (Ne)

Damsterdijk 7.8.40 Seized Rotterdam by Germans; KM, Seelöwe transport *RO12*; 41 *Mülhausen* (Ger); 9.7.41–20.10.42 various KM uses; 20.10.42–1.43 rebuilt; 13.3.43 U-boat target ship; 5.45 at Kiel, damaged by fire; 16.2.46 returned, rebuilt; 28.1.49 *Dalerdijk* (Ne)

Elandsfontein 4.40 Hull seized Danzig by Germans; 14.3.45 incomplete hull sunk Weichsel estuary by Russian artillery; salved, LU Danzig; 9.8.47 to Ne; 50 *Jagersfontein* (Ne)
Etrema 5.40 Seized by Germans; KM supply ship *Memelland* (Ger); 5.45 at Kiel; 46 *Etrema* (Ne)

Gadila 44 RNN, aux MAC ship; 45 returned
Gouwe 5.40 German control; 5.45 at Kiel; 45 returned

Indrapoera 9.40 Allied troopship; 7.3.46 returned

Japara 13.12.41–31.1.46 WSA charter; 31.1.46 returned
Johan de Witt, *Johan van Oldenbarnevelt* 40 Allied troopship; 46 returned
Jonge Johanna 40 *Jupiter* (Ne)
Jonge Willem 40 *Gordias* (Ne); 40 German control; 9.8.40 KM, Seelöwe transport *RO25*; 21.4.41 training ship, Rotterdam; 1.44 transport, Norway; 5.45 at Trondheim; 7.9.45 returned

Katendrecht 2.7.43 At New York; 31.7.43 with collision and weather damage; in port 22.11.44; 44 (US); 46–47 BU
Katwijk 40 RNN, aux minesweeper; 45 returned
Kerkplein 19.8.40 Seized Rotterdam by Germans; 8.40 KM, Seelöwe transport *RO23*; 31.8.41 KMD, Stettin; 5.45 at Kristiansand damaged; 8.45 (Ne); 21.9.45 returned; 7.47 *Ossendrecht* (Ne)
Kota Agoeng 11.3.42 WSA charter; 19.7.42–45 MoWT charter, troopship; 45 returned
Kota Baroe 42 Allied troopship; 8.42 WSA charter; 12.3.46–48 Netherlands govt troopship charter
Kota Gede 43 Allied troopship; 3.46 returned
Kota Inten 43 Allied troopship; 1.10.43–25.2.46 WSA charter; then trooping to NEI

Larenberg 41 Seized by Germans while building Krimpen; 41 *Alsterdamm* (Ger); 5.45 at Kiel; 45 *Larenberg* (Ne)
Loppersum 5.40 German control; 40 (Ger); 8.40 KM, Seelöwe transport *RO1*; 12.4.41 accom ship; 42 *VB3*; 22.10.44 troop transport, Baltic; 5.45 at Århus; 12.8.45 returned; 24.11.45 *Loppersum* (Ne)

Maashaven 40 *Zuiderburgh* (Ne)
Macoma 44 RNN, aux MAC ship; 45 returned
Melchior Treub 26.2.42 Req MoWT; 6.43 hospital ship No D6; 45 returned
Merwede 40 Seized while building by Germans; 12.1.41 completed as *Gotha* (Ger); 2.1.42 KM transport, Norway; 27.7.43 target ship, Mürwik; 21.8.43 transport, KMD Copenhagen; 28.10.45 returned, damaged; 1.5.46 *Merwede* (Ne)

Nieuw Amsterdam 40 Allied troopship; 46 returned
Nieuw Holland 9.8.40–23.2.46 MoWT charter, troopship; 2.46 returned
Noordam 4.42–46 US troopship; 46 returned
Noordwijk 40 German control; 8.40 KM, Seelöwe transport *RO10*; 4.12.40 returned; 5.45 recovered Kristiansand with stern damage, repaired; 17.12.45 re-entered service

Omala 40 Captured by Germans; 40 *Wörth* (Ger); 5.45 at Oslo; 14.2.46 *Omala* (Ne)
Ophir 25.2.42 Req MoWT; 9.42 hospital carrier; 9.44–12.5.46 hospital ship No D4; 5.46 returned
Oranje 7.41 Hospital ship
Oranjefontein 17.3.41 Seized Capelle by Germans; completed as Luftwaffe target ship; 21.10.42 KM target and support ship *Pionier* (Ger); 30.4.44 struck mine E of Rixhöft, taken Kiel; 7.2.45 U-boat depot, Hamburg; 12.7.45 returned damaged, repaired Newcastle; 9.45 *Oranjefontein* (Ne)
Orestes 40 German control; 40 (Ger); 8.8.40 KM, Seelöwe transport *RO6*; 23.5.41 Blaufuchs transport; 5.45 at Copenhagen; 10.8.45 (Ne)

Papendrecht 40 Req by Germans; 40 *Lothringen* (Ger); 15.6.41 captured by cruiser

HMS *Dunedin*, carrier HMS *Ark Royal* 19 49N 25 31W; 41 MoWT, *Empire Salvage* (Br); 16.5.45 *Papendrecht* (Ne)
Perna 40 KM, *Forbach* (Ger); 5.45 at Kiel; 31.7.45 collision, damaged, returned; repaired; 2.5.46 *Perna* (Ne)
Plancius 13.1.42–9.4.42 Req MoWT; 42 returned; 42 RNN, aux depot ship; 45 returned
Poelau Laut 10.42–11.45 US Army transport; 11.45 returned
Prins Willem IV 40 Seized incomplete by Germans; KM; 31.12.44 while conv to *Sperrbrecher 179*, bombed by Allied aircraft Hamburg; conv abandoned; 45 *Prins Willem IV* (Ne)
Prins Willem V 40 Seized incomplete by Germans; KM; 5.10.44 during conv to *Sperrbrecher 105*, scuttled Nieuwe Waterweg off Maassluis; 11.12.47 raised, repaired; 7.1.49 *Prins Willem V* (Ne)

Ruys 40 Allied troopship; 45 returned

Sibajak 40 MoWT charter, Allied troopship; 46 returned
Stuyvesant 41 RNN, aux depot ship; 45 returned
Sumatra 40 Seized by Germans while building; 43 completed; 5.45 at Kiel; 45 delivered

Tamo 40 Seized by Germans when building; 13.10.43 commd KM *Sperrbrecher 28*; 47 *Tamo* (Ne)
Tegelberg 40 MoWT charter, troopship; 45 returned

Veendam 11.5.40 Damaged, on fire, during German air raid Rotterdam; 5.40 (Ger); 21.6.41 barracks ship, Gotenhafen; 15.3.42 barracks ship, Hamburg; 4.11.44 bombed by 8th USAAF bombers, Hamburg; 4.45 further damage during aircraft attacks; 5.45 recovered Kiel; 45 (Ne); 45–47 repaired; 30.1.47 re-entered service
Volendam 40 Allied control; 41 troopship; 7.45 returned
Vredenburg 42 *Punta del Este* (Uru); 42 *Almirante Rodriguez Luis* (Uru)

Weltevreden 42–2.46 WSA and MoWT charters; 13.2.46 returned
Westerdam 40 Launched; 40–1.45 scuttled 3 times Nieuwe Waterweg by Netherlands resistance; 45 raised; 45–46 repaired; 24.6.46 delivered
Westernland 7.40 Allied troopship; 11.42 MoWT (Br); 11.42 Adm, destroyer depot ship; 45 decommd; 47 BU Blyth
Westplein 5.40 Seized by Germans; 5.8.40 KM, Seelöwe transport *RO22*; 12.4.41 transport, Baltic; 43 accom ship; 30.7.44 troop transport; 9.8.45 (Ne); 47 *Zwijndrecht* (Ne)

Norway

When Norway was occupied on 9 April 1940, Norwegian ships in waters controlled by the Allies were requisitioned by Royal Norwegian Government and managed by Nortraship, the Norwegian Shipping & Trade Mission

Losses through marine hazard
Anderson 10.2.42 Ashore on Eastern Head, near St Shots Nfl; TL
Anna Sofie 23.2.44 Ashore off Haugesund, explosion on board, sank
Askild 2.12.42 Ashore Chance Cove, near Cape Race; TL
Basra (Pan) 16.3.40 Collision with *Listo* (*qv*), sank, North Sea (0†)
Benwood 9.4.42 Collision with tanker *Robert C Tuttle* (*qv*) off NE Molasses Reef, Florida; beached, CTL
Bjorkhaug 16.7.43 Explosion, badly damaged, Algiers; sank, TL
Bolivar (Pan) 27.8.40 Foundered 16 42N 92 41E (0†)
Braganza 12.10.44 Explosion in engine room, on fire, abandoned, sank, 32 40S 48 30W
Bur 1.9.42 Stranded Valiant Rock, E Long Island Sound, sank; 3.10.43 refloated, BU Baltimore
Ciss 8.2.41 Stranded, carried in ice to Little Shag Rock, Scatari Is, NS; 9.2.41 sank
Graciosa 14.4.44 Badly damaged following *Fort Stikine* explosion Bombay docks (–†); TL
Hada County 6.12.41 Aground Grand Manan Is NB; TL
Havørn 19.7.42 Collision with *Radhurst* (*qv*), sank, 47 23 09N 70 27 07W
Hellas 4.1.43 Struck submerged object during storm, sank, Benghazi harbour; TL
Høegh Silvercrest 7.1.39 Wrecked Prieto Diaz, 20m N of San Bernardino Is, Philippines
Ingrid 19.1.42 Ashore in heavy weather Grean, Tiree, Hebrides, 56 32 04N 06 56W
Kaiapoi (Pan) 25.1.39 Struck rocks Wenchow Bay, sank 28 16N 121 38E
Kollbjorg 24.1.43 Broke in two 58 28N 41 34W; 25.1.43 survs rescued from stern part; both parts sank
Korsfjord 21.1.41 Collision with *Bandar Shahpour* (*qv*), sank, 60 40N 12 09W
Løvland 18.8.39 Wrecked Cape North, Cape Breton Is
Mim 1.11.39 Ashore in gale Reef Dyke, North Ronaldsay Is, 59 21N 02 22 16W; TL
Nerva 40 German control; 7.2.43 stranded N of Rorvik, sank
Nidardal 16.12.41 Foundered 56 07N 21W

Norse Trader 14.4.44 Badly damaged following *Fort Stikine* explosion Bombay docks (–†); TL; wreck BU
Orm Jarl 4.3.39 Wrecked R Schelde
Produce 3.4.40 Wrecked Paracel Islands
Santos 18.8.43 Collision in dense fog with *Theodore Dwight Weld* (US) and *J H Senior* (*qv*), sank, 44 12N 52 58W
Sofie Bakke 4.8.40 Collision with *Lima* (*qv*), sank, about 5m E of Buchanness
Storfjeld 11.12.39 Wrecked Seaton Rocks, near Blyth, 55 05 15N 01 28W
Tamesis 7.3.43 Collision (in convoy) with *Alcoa Guard* (*qv*), sunk, 35 07N 62 45W
Tennessee 25.5.40 Collision with *Baron Fairlie* (*qv*); later wrecked Roana Bay, Deer Ness, Kirkwall
Thyra 27.5.41 Collision with HM ship, sank, 52 25N 19 22W (4†, 20 surv)
Vestland 15.1.42 Ashore Hvalfjord, Iceland; 3.42 refloated; 21.10.42 sd Reykjavik in tow for R Tyne; 24.10.42 sank

Losses through war causes
Akabahra 7.1.43 Torpedoed by aircraft, sunk, 37 07N 04 38E (0†, 25 surv)
Albert L Ellsworth 41 Adm service (RFA); 8.1.43 torpedoed (in convoy TM1) by *U436*, damaged 27 59N 28 50W, straggling; 9.1.43 shelled by *U436*, sunk (0†, 42 surv)
Alcides 41 Adm service (RFA); 23.7.43 torpedoed by subm *I-10* (Jpn), sunk, 03S 68E (49†, 3 pow)
Alexandra Høegh 21.1.42 Torpedoed by *U130*, broke in two, sunk, 40 54N 66 03W (0†, 28 surv)
Alfred Olsen 9.5.41 Torpedoed, shelled, by subm *Enrico Tazzoli* (Ita) 02 59N 20 26W (0†, 34 surv); 10.5.41 sunk 03N 20 10W
Almora 5.40 German control; 6.5.44 torpedoed by aircraft from carriers HMS *Searcher* and *Furious*, sunk, off Hustadvika
Andrea Brøvig 41 Adm service (RFA); 23.6.42 torpedoed by *U128*, sunk, 12 10N 59 10W (0†, 38 surv)
Anglo (Pan) 9.4.40 Seized Bergen by Germans; 40 *Seefahrer* (Ger); 18.4.42 struck mine, sunk, NW of Juist
Annavore 21.12.41 Torpedoed by *U567*, sunk, 43 55N 19 50W (34†, 4 surv)
Aramis 16.7.42 Torpedoed by E-boat from aux cruiser *Michel*; 17.7.42 shelled by raider, sunk, 19S 06W (19†, 6 pow, 18 surv)
Arne Kjøde 12.11.39 Torpedoed by *U41* (5†); forepart sank 59 06N 06 55W, afterpart sank 59 20N 07 12W
Arthur W Sewall 7.8.42 Torpedoed, shelled, by *U109* 08 28N 34 21W; 8.8.42 sunk (0†, 36 surv)
Astrell 5.11.42 Torpedoed (in convoy TAG18) by *U129* 12 21N 69 21W; sunk by escort (0†, 42 surv)
Athene 10.6.42 Torpedoed (in convoy AT49) by *U559*, sunk, between Alexandria and Mersa Matruh (13†, 17 surv)
Augvald 2.3.41 Torpedoed (in convoy HX109) by *U147*, sunk, 150–200m NW of Loch Ewe (29†, 1 surv)
Aust 3.4.42 Attacked by aircraft from aux cruiser *Thor*, shelled by *Thor*, abandoned; sunk by bomb placed on board 20S 16W (0†, – pow)
Austvard 30.1.41 Bombed by German aircraft, sunk, 130m W of Galway Is (23†, 5 surv)

B P Newton 8.7.43 Torpedoed (in convoy TJ1) by *U510*, on fire, sunk, 05 50N 50 20W (23†, 24 surv)
Baghdad 30.5.42 Torpedoed by *U155*, sunk, 14 15N 54 30W (9†, 21 surv)
Balkis 10.4.42 Torpedoed, shelled, by subm *Pietro Calvi* (Ita), sunk, 02 30S 38W (8†, 27 surv)
Barbro 20.9.41 Torpedoed (in convoy SC44) by *U552*, sunk, 61 30N 35 11W (34†, 0 surv)
Barfonn 17.10.41 Topedoed (in convoy SC48) by *U432*, sunk, 56 58N 25 04W (14†, 26 surv)
Bayard 6.7.42 Torpedoed by *U67*, sunk, 29 35N 88 44W (11†, 21 surv)
Beaulieu 4.8.40 Captured by aux cruiser *Widder* 26 30N 48W (4†); sunk by bombs placed on board
Beduin 16.3.41 Torpedoed (in convoy HX112) by *U99*, broke in two; 61 20N 11 55W (4†, 30 surv); 19.3.41 forepart shelled by HM trawler, sunk, 61 02N 11 53W; 20.3.41 afterpart sunk 61 07N 10 50W
Belita 41 Adm service (RFA); 3.12.42 torpedoed, shelled, by subm *I-29* (Jpn), sunk, 11 29N 55E (0†, 30 surv)
Belize 19.1.42 Torpedoed by *U754*, sunk, 47 21N 58 08W (0 surv)
Bello 16.12.42 Torpedoed (in convoy ON153) by *U610*, sunk, 51 45N 23 50W (33†, 8 surv)
Belmoira 30.6.40 Torpedoed by *U26*, sunk, 48 15N 10 30W (0†)
Benjamin Franklin 19.2.41 Torpedoed by *U103*, sunk, 58 50N 16 30W (0†, 36 resc: 29† when *Memphis* (*qv*) lost, 7 surv)
Bennestvet 15.6.42 Torpedoed by *U172*, sunk, 10 47N 82 12W (12†, 13 surv)
Berganger 2.6.42 Torpedoed by *U578*, sunk, 39 22N 69 50W (4†, 40 surv)
Besholt 2.12.42 Torpedoed by *U174*, sunk, 03 20N 30 20W (14†, 28 surv)
Beth 41 Adm service (RFA); 18.5.42 torpedoed by *U162*, sunk, 11 48N 57 32W (†, 30 surv)
Bianca 15.3.41 Captured by *Gneisenau* 40N 43W, prize crew put on board (0t, 34 surv); 20.3.41 intercepted by RN warship 44 16N 19 21W, set on fire; fire extinguished

by boarding party, but sunk
Bidevind 1.5.42 Torpedoed by *U752*, sunk, 40 13N 73 46W (0†, 36 surv)
Bill 29.7.42 Torpedoed by *U155*, sunk, 11 58N 55 02W (1†, 1 pow, 22 surv)
Birk 5.40 German control; 15.2.42 struck mine (laid 29.10.41 by subm *K-23* (Rus)), sunk, off Kirkenes (26†)
Bjonn 5.40 German control; 9.12.41 bombed, sunk, Hustadvika
Blaafjeld I 4.5.40 Attacked by German aircraft, sunk, Namsos (0†)
Black Prince 5.40 Seized by Germans; 24.8.40 Luftwaffe accom ship; 31.3.41 KM, accom ship, KMD Oslo; 15.5.41 U-boat base ship, Danzig; 11.9.41 *Lofjord* (Ger); 14.12.41 on fire Danzig-Neufahrwasser (28†), burnt out; became Luftwaffe target hulk; 51 BU Antwerp
Black Watch 40 Seized by Germans; 28.8.40 KM, accom ship, U-boat base Kirkenes; 43 accom ship, Hammerfest; 4.5.45 bombed by aircraft from Allied task force including carriers HMS *Queen*, *Searcher* and *Trumpeter*, sunk, near Narvik
Blink 11.2.41 Torpedoed by *U108*, sunk, 35N 72 27W (24†, 6 surv)
Bonde 5.5.43 Torpedoed (in convoy ONS5) by *U266*, sunk, 53 28N 44 20W (14†, 12 surv)
Bonneville 10.3.43 Torpedoed (in convoy SC121) by *U405*, sunk, 58 45N 21 57W (36†, 7 surv)
Bordvik 3.3.42 Scuttled Sourabaya prior to Japanese invasion; 42 raised by Japanese; 43 *Manryu Maru* (Jpn); 16.4.45 torpedoed by subm USS *Sunfish*, sunk, 39 36N 142 05E
Borga 5.40 German control; 15.4.43 bombed by British aircraft, sunk, 25m E of Borkum
Borgestad 12.2.41 Shelled (in convoy SLS64) by *Admiral Hipper*, sunk, 37 12N 21 20W (31†, 0 surv)
Borgland 26.2.41 Torpedoed (in convoy OB290) by *U47* 55 45N 14 27W; abandoned 55 53N 13 33W, sunk (0†, 32 surv)
Borgny 40 German control; 4.10.41 torpedoed by *MTB 56* (Nor), sunk, Korsfjord (14†)
Bra-Kar 3.5.41 Hit by incendiary bombs, on fire, Canada Dock, Liverpool (0†, 34 surv); 7.5.41 still on fire, settled on bottom; 6.41 refloated, beached Tranmere; CTL, BU
Bramora 14.9.43 Torpedoed (convoy straggler) by subm *I-10* (Jpn), sunk, 06 10N 67 37E (0†)
Brand 11.5.43 Torpedoed (in convoy HX237) by *U603*, sunk, 47 19N 24 41W (3†, 40 surv)
Brandanger 11.10.40 Torpedoed (in convoy HX77) by *U48*, sunk, 57 10N 17 42W (6†, 24 surv)
Brant County 11.3.43 Torpedoed (in convoy HX228) by *U757*, exploded, sunk, 52 05N 27 35W (35†, 23 surv)
Brarena 10.6.40 Seized by Italians; 22.7.41 torpedoed (in convoy) by British Blenheim aircraft, sunk, off Pantellaria
Brask 15.1.41 Torpedoed by subm *Luigi Torelli* (Ita), sunk, 52 45N 23 59W (12†, 20 surv)
Bratland 20.4.40 Seized by Germans; 30.4.40 KM, Baltic transport *Warthe* (Ger); 8.40 Seelöwe transport *A5*; 22.9.40 transport, Norway; 18.12.44 bombed by Allied aircraft, sunk, Gotenhafen; 45 salved; 5.49 *Warta* (Pol)
Brattdal 13.4.41 Bombed by enemy aircraft Volos Bay, Greece; 14–17.4.41 more attacks; 17.4.41 sunk; 50–52 salved, repaired, sold
Bravore 22.4.40 Struck mine (laid 22.4.40), sunk, 51 18 30N 01 30 54E (18†); wreck dispersed
Breiviken 4.7.43 Torpedoed (convoy DN50 straggler) by *U178*, sunk, 21 50S 37 50E (3†, 33 surv)
Breñas 6.8.42 Torpedoed, shelled, by *U108* 08 38N 53 45W; sunk 10 20N 56 10W (1†, 1 pow, 32 surv)
Bris 21.4.42 Torpedoed by *U201*, sunk, 33 35N 69 38W (5†, 20 surv)
Britta 6.12.39 Torpedoed by *U47*, sunk, 45m SW of Longships Light (6†)
Bronxville 31.8.42 Torpedoed (in convoy SC97) by *U609*, sunk, 57 13N 33 40W (0†, 39 surv)
Brott 7.7.41 Seized Saffi by VFr; 41 *Ste Monique* (Fra); 5.43 sunk Bizerta as blockship
Bruse 22.11.40 Torpedoed (in convoy SC11) by *U100*, broke in two, 55 04N 12 15W; afterpart sunk, forepart taken in tow, BU Troon 41
Buccaneer 1.4.42 Intercepted by German warships, scuttled, 6–7m off Kaeringoen, N of Gothenburg (1†, 43 pow)
Buesten 9.4.41 Shelled by German He111 aircraft, on fire, sunk, 150° 4m from Berry Head, 50 21 07N 03 24 11W (28†, 7 surv)
Burgos 28.3.41 Struck mine, sunk, 53 18N 01 09E (0†, 33 surv)

Cadmus 1.7.42 Torpedoed by *U129*, sunk, 22 50N 92 30W (2†, 20 surv)
Caledonia 28.4.41 Torpedoed (in convoy HX121) by *U96*, sunk, 60 03N 16 16W (12†, 25 surv)
Carrier 19.1.45 Struck mine 53 22 58N 00 58 54E (0†, 33 surv), sunk 0.75m from No 12A buoy
Cate B 13.4.40 Sunk off Narvik; 54 refloated; 55 BU Stavanger
Charente 1.4.42 Intercepted by German patrol vessels, scuttled, 6–7m off Kaeringoen, N of Gothenburg (0†, 31 pow)
Charles Racine 10.3.42 Torpedoed by subm *Giuseppe Finzi* (Ita), sunk, 23 10N 60 28W (0†, 41 surv)
Chr Knudsen 10.4.42 Torpedoed by *U85*, sunk, off US E coast
Christian Krohg 10.6.41 Torpedoed (in convoy OB328) by *U108*, sunk, 45N 36 30W (23†, 0 surv)
Cometa 26.3.40 Torpedoed by *U38*, sunk, 60 06N 04 36W
Corneville 9.5.43 Torpedoed by *U515*, sunk, 04 50N 01 10W (0†, 41 surv)

Corona 5.2.43 Torpedoed (in convoy) by *U617* 32 11N 24 46E (0†, 103 surv); 6.2.43 ar Tobruk in tow, beached, damaged in storm; 24.2.43 abandoned; 17.10.47 sd in tow; 19.10.47 sank 20m N of Derna
Crux 25.6.40 Torpedoed by *UA* 36 52N 14W (0†, 30 surv); 26.6.40 sunk
Cubano 19.10.40 Torpedoed (in convoy OB229) by *U124* 57 55N 24 57W; 20.10.40 abandoned, sunk (2†, 29 surv)

Dagfred 6.4.42 Shelled by 2 Japanese cruisers, sunk, 16 15N 82 09E (0†, 40 surv)
Daghild 7.2.43 Torpedoed (in convoy SC118) by *U402*, damaged, 55 25N 26 12W (0†, 39 surv); 8.2.43 torpedoed by *U608*, sunk
Dah Pu 28.6.43 Torpedoed by subm *I-27* (Jpn), sunk, 339° 2.75 cables from outer leading lt, Muscat harbour (15†, 44 surv)
Davanger 11.10.40 Torpedoed (in convoy HX77) by *U48*, sunk, 57N 19 10W (17†, 12 surv)
Deodata 21.10.39 Struck mine (laid 17.10.39 by *U19*) 53 19 50N 00 38 21 50E (0†), sunk 53 21N 00 36 09E; wreck dispersed
Dixie 40 German control; 17.6.44 attacked by Russian IL-4 aircraft, sunk by parachute torpedo, S of Vardø
Dokka 17.10.40 Torpedoed (in convoy OB228) by *U93*, sunk, 60 46N 16 30W (10†, 7 surv)
Dukat 8.12.41 Captured off Hong Kong by Japanese; 17.1.42 *Amoy Maru* (Jpn); 19.8.43 stranded 38 52N 122 20E; TL

Eastern Star 7.5.41 Torpedoed (in convoy OB318) by *U94*, sunk, 61 29N 22 40W (0†)
Eidanger 24.2.42 Torpedoed (in convoy ONS67) by *U587*, damaged, 44 11N 43 25W; torpedoed by *U558*, sunk (0†, 39 surv)
Eidsvold 20.1.42 Torpedoed by subm *I-59* (Jpn), broke in two, when anchored off Christmas Is (0†, 31 surv); aground, TL
Eika 29.1.40 Torpedoed by *U51*, sunk, 43N 10 35W (14†, 2 surv)
Einar Jarl 17.3.41 Struck mine, sunk, 56 17 30N 02 18W (1†, 20 surv)
Einvik 5.9.41 Torpedoed, shelled (convoy SC41 straggler) by *U501*, sunk, 60 38N 31 18W (0†, 23 surv)
Eldrid 10.4.40 Damaged Narvik (0†); 5.5.40 scuttled by Germans
Eli 10.9.40 Bombed by German aircraft, sunk, 144° 12m from Skerryvore Lt (1†)
Eli Knudsen 22.6.40 Torpedoed (in convoy HX49) by *U32* 50 36N 08 44W (0†, 37 surv); 23.6.40 taken in tow, sunk 50 36N 07 51W
Elin K 16.3.43 Torpedoed (in convoy HX229) by *U603*, sunk, 50 38N 34 46W (0†, 40 surv)
Ellavore 11.6.40 Attacked by German aircraft, sunk, Havre (0†, 14 surv); 12.5.47 refloated; 48 BU
Elsa 6.4.42 Shelled by Japanese warships, sunk, 35m E of Cuttack (1†, 29 surv)
Else Marie 5.40 German control; 7.7.42 sunk by Russian aircraft near Vardo (13†)
Erling Brøvig 22.4.44 Torpedoed (in convoy PA69) by *U510*, badly damaged, off Majhada; 16.9.44 ar Massowah in tow, LU; repaired; 46 *Bramora* (Nor)
Erviken 16.10.41 Torpedoed (in convoy SC48) by *U558*, sunk, 56 10N 24 30W (26†, 12 surv; 2 on destroyer HMS *Broadwater* lost when that vessel sunk)

Fagerheim 14.1.40 Torpedoed by *U44*, sunk, 47 20N 06 16W (14†)
Fagersten 13.10.42 Torpedoed (in convoy SC104) by *U221*, sunk, 52 54N 43 55W (19†, 10 surv)
Fanefjeld 10.4.42 Torpedoed by *U252*, sunk, NW of Iceland (25†, 0 surv)
Favorit 16.4.41 Bombed by German aircraft, sunk, 60 06N 08 31W (0†, 29 surv)
Ferm 16.3.41 Torpedoed (in convoy HX112) by *U99*, on fire, abandoned, 60 42N 13 10W (0†, 35 surv); taken in tow; 21.3.41 sunk 61 30N 09 30W
Ferncastle 17.6.43 Torpedoed by aux cruiser *Michel*, sunk, 25S 97E (18†, 19 surv)
Ferndale 40 Seized by KM; 16.12.44 bombed by Allied aircraft, sunk, Kraakehellesund
Fernhill 7.8.43 Torpedoed by *U757*, sunk, 06 58N 19 15W (4†, 40 surv)
Fernlane 7.5.41 Torpedoed by subm *Enrico Tazzoli* (Ita), sunk, 10 02N 20 17W (0†, 35 surv)
Fidelio 9.11.42 Torpedoed by German E-boat, sunk 58° 1.6m from C3 Buoy, off Lowestoft (7†, 20 surv)
Filefjell 26.8.40 Captured 24S 51E by aux cruiser *Pinguin*; 27.8.40 sunk (32 pow)
Fingal 5.5.43 Torpedoed by subm *I-180* (Jpn), sunk, 30 35S 153 29E (12†, 19 surv)
Finnanger 41 Adm service (RFA); 24.2.42 torpedoed (in convoy ONS67) by *U558*, sunk, 43 45N 42 15W (0 surv)
Fjord 2.12.41 Torpedoed by *U557*, sunk, off Estepona Point, Spain (14†, 22 surv)
Fjordheim 2.9.44 Torpedoed (in convoy ONS251) by *U482*, sunk, 55 20N 09 58W (3†, 35 surv)
Foch (Pan) 8.12.41 Seized Yokohama by Japanese; 42 *Hoshi Maru* (Jpn); 25.7.45 struck mine, sunk, 34 35N 135 21E
Frank Seamans 7.5.42 Torpedoed by *U162*, sunk, 06 21N 55 38W (0†, 27 surv)
Frisco 12.1.42 Torpedoed by *U130*, sunk, 44 50N 60 20W (13†, 3 surv)

Germania 40 *India* (Nor); 11.9.43 sunk by aux cruiser *Michel* 20S 115W (0 surv)
Glitrefjell 16.12.39 Torpedoed by *U59*, sunk, 56 21N 00 38E (5†)
Glittre 23.2.43 Torpedoed (in convoy ON166) by *U628* 47 11N 35 35W; became straggler, torpedoed by *U603*, sunk (3†, 34 surv)
Goviken 29.6.42 Torpedoed by subm *I-20* (Jpn), sunk, 13 25S 41 13E (13†, 40 surv)

Goya 4.40 Seized by Germans when building; 6.1.42 completed for KM, transport (Ger); 1.8.43 U-boat target ship; 1.45 refugee transport; 16.4.45 torpedoed (in convoy) by subm *L-3* (Rus) 55 13.5N 18 20E (reports vary, but often quoted are 6220† or 6666†/7028†, 165/172/334 surv); 17.4.45 broke in two, sunk
Grado 11.5.43 Torpedoed (in convoy SC129) by *U402*, sunk, 40 30N 32 30W (0†, 36 surv)
Gran 22.2.40 Seized Casablanca by VFr; 40 *Ste Odette* (Fra); 41 KM, *Odysseus* (Ger), for conv to fighter direction ship; 28.12.42 torpedoed by subm HMS *Ursula*, sunk, 12m N of Marettimo
Gran (Pan) 9.12.41 Seized Bangkok by Japanese; Japanese prize; 42 *Sugi Maru No 5* (Jpn); 22.8.44 torpedoed by subm HMS *Statesman*, sunk, 11 40N 92 45E
Granli 16.3.41 Shelled by *Gneisenau*, sunk, 300m E of Newfoundland (0†, 18 pow)
Graziella 40 German control; 16.9.43 torpedoed by British aircraft, ashore near Egersund, TL
Grena 21.3.44 Torpedoed, shelled, by subm *I-27* (Jpn), sunk, 20 48N 59 38E (7†, 34 surv)
Grenanger 11.4.42 Torpedoed, shelled, by *U130*, sunk, 22 45N 57 13W (0†, 36 surv)
Gro 7.9.40 Torpedoed (in convoy SC2) by *U47*, broke in two, sunk, 58 30N 16 10W (11†, 21 surv)
Gunda 19.11.42 Torpedoed by *U181*, sunk, 25 40S 33 53E (38†, 8 surv)
Gundersen 1.7.42 Torpedoed, shelled, by *U129*, sunk, 23 33N 92 35W (1†, 22 surv)
Gunny 2.3.42 Torpedoed by *U126*, sunk, 27 09N 66 33W (14†, 12 surv)
Gunvor 15.6.42 Struck Allied mine, sunk, 25N 81 45W (2†, 20 surv)
Gyda 18.7.40 Torpedoed by *U58*, sunk, 56N 10W (11†, 9 surv)

H C Flood 15.12.39 Struck mine (laid 12–13.12.39 by German destroyer), sunk, 55 02N 01 12W
Hadrian 22.6.40 Seized Dakar by VFr; 40 *Ste Germaine* (Fra); 42 *Helga* (Ger); 11.5.44 bombed by Russian aircraft, sunk, off Sevastopol
Hai Hing 40 Allied troopship; 4.11.42 torpedoed by *U178*, sunk, 25 55S 33 10E (25†, 42 surv)
Hallanger 41 Adm service (RFA); 30.3.43 torpedoed (in convoy ET16) by *U596*, sunk, 36 52N 01 47E (0†, 40 surv)
Halldor 25.12.41 Captured Hong Kong by Japanese; 42 *Haruta Maru* (Jpn); 21.1.45 attacked by USAAF aircraft, sunk, 22 20N 114 10E; 51 wreck BU
Hallfried 31.10.43 Torpedoed (in convoy MKS28/SL138) by *U262*, sunk, 46 05N 20 26W (31†, 3 surv)
Hamlet 27.5.42 Torpedoed by *U753*, sunk, 28 32N 91 30W (0†, 36 surv)
Haraldsvang 25.12.41 Scuttled Hong Kong; 6.6.42 raised by Japanese; 42 *Toryu Maru* (Jpn); 17.5.44 sunk off Choshi
Harboe Jensen 15.1.43 Torpedoed (in convoy) by *U617*, sunk, 33 04N 21 50E (18†, 6 surv)
Haugarland 5.40 German control; 10.6.42 struck mine, sunk, off Terschelling
Haukefjell 40 Seized by Germans; 40 (Ger); 24.2.45 bombed by Allied aircraft, badly damaged, Hamburg; stern section beached, other parts dispersed
Hav 14.5.42 Struck mine (laid 15.4.42 by *U561*) off Port Said (2†, 32 surv); beached 31 17 57N 32 21 09E; abandoned, stripped, on fire; TL
Havbor 15.11.40 Torpedoed by *U65*, sunk, 04 24N 13 46W (19†, 4 surv)
Havsten 41 Adm service (RFA); 3.8.42 torpedoed, shelled, by *U160*, on fire (2†, 1 pow, 30 surv); 6.8.42 torpedoed by subm *Enrico Tazzoli* (Ita), sunk, 11 18N 54 45W
Havtor 12.6.41 Torpedoed, shelled, by *U79*, sunk, 63 35N 28 05W (6†, 14 surv)
Heina 11.2.42 Torpedoed (in convoy SC67) by *U591*, sunk, 56 10N 21 07W (0†, 30 surv)
Helios 8.12.41 Captured off Saigon by Japanese; 42 *Setsuzan Maru* (Jpn); 6.7.44 torpedoed by subm USS *Sealion*, sunk, 29 59N 122 53E
Helle 3.4.41 Torpedoed (in convoy SC26) by *U98*, sunk, 59N 24 30W (0†, 24 surv)
Hellen 21.12.41 Torpedoed by *U573* 35 41N 05 10W (0†, 41 surv); 22.12.41 sunk
Herborg 19.6.42 Captured 28S 90E by aux cruiser *Thor*, prize; sent Yokohama; 42 *Hohenfreiburg* (Ger); 26.2.43 intercepted by cruiser HMS *Sussex*, sunk, 41 48N 20 50W
Herleik 40 (Pan); 8.12.41 seized Bangkok by Japanese; 1.42 *Yulin Maru* (Jpn); 24.2.45 wrecked 13 48N 109 14E
Hermod 6.4.42 Shelled by Japanese warships, sunk, Bay of Bengal (0†)
Herstein 20.1.42 Bombed by Japanese aircraft Rabaul (1†, 34 surv); on fire, gutted, TL
Hidlefjord 1.4.41 Bombed (in convoy) by German aircraft of KG27, on fire, abandoned NW of Smalls (29†, 5 surv); 2.4.41 presumed sunk 170° 12m from Tuskar Rock
Hindanger 11.9.42 Torpedoed (in convoy ON127) by *U584* 49 32N 32 21W (1†, 40 surv); shelled, sunk, by HM ship
Hird 15.9.40 Torpedoed by *U65*, sunk, 58N 12 20W (0†)
Høegh Carrier 40 German control; 18.4.43 bombed by British aircraft, sunk, off Den Helder
Høegh Giant 3.6.42 Torpedoed, shelled, by *U126* 06 52N 42 43W; 4.6.42 again torpedoed, 07 32N 44 36W; sunk 07 17N 43 06W (0†, 39 surv)
Høegh Merchant 14.12.41 Torpedoed by subm *I-16* (Jpn), sunk, 29m from Cape Makapuu (0†, 40 surv)
Høegh Silverdawn 15.6.43 Sunk by aux cruiser *Michel* 25 40S 92E (36†, 22 surv)
Høegh Transporter 3.10.39 Struck British mine, sunk, entrance to Singapore, 152° 7.7 cables from Outer Shoal Beacon (1†)
Hørda 24.3.41 Torpedoed (from dispersed convoy OG56) by *U97*, sunk, 49N 23W (0 surv)
Hosanger 27.1.40 Torpedoed by *U20*, sunk, 58 25N 01 53W (17†, 1 surv)
Huldra 5.40 German control; 1.3.41 struck mine, sunk, at Hustadvika

Hvoslev 11.3.42 Torpedoed by *U94*, sunk, 38 27N 74 54W (6†, 14 surv)

Ida Knudsen 21.7.41 Torpedoed by subm *Luigi Torelli* (Ita), sunk, 34 34N 13 14W (5†)
Ila 15.10.41 Torpedoed (in convoy SC48) by *U553*, sunk, 53 34N 29 57W (14†, 7 surv)
Indra 26.11.42 Torpedoed by *UD3*, sunk, 02 10N 28 52W (0†, 39 surv)
Inga I 28.7.41 Torpedoed (in convoy OG69) by *U126*, sunk, 43 10N 17 30W (3†, 16 surv)
Inger 23.8.41 Torpedoed by *U143*, sunk, 58 58N 07 50W (9†, 14 surv)
Inger Elisabeth 15.9.42 Torpedoed (in convoy SQ36) by *U517*, sunk, 48 49N 64 06W (3†, 23 surv)
Ingerfem 30.12.42 Torpedoed (convoy ONS154 straggler) by *U631*, sunk, 59N 21W (40†, 1 surv)
Ingerfire 11.4.43 Torpedoed (in convoy ONS2) by *U571*, sunk, 51 29N 42 59W (8†, 28 surv)
Ingerseks 5.40 Seized by Germans; 40 (Ger); 22.4.45 stranded Resnefjord, off Trondheim; 23.4.45 bombed by British aircraft while aground; TL
Ingerto 40 German control; 2.9.41 captured Spitsbergen; 9.41 Allied control; 12.3.42 torpedoed, probably by *U578*, sunk, 29 45N 66 30W (0 surv)
Ingria 24.2.43 Torpedoed (in convoy ON166) by *U600* and *U628*, sunk, 45 12N 39 17W (0†, 37 surv)
Inneroy 22.1.42 Torpedoed (ind) by *U553*, sunk, 41 16N 60 32W (31†, 5 surv)
Italia 14.6.40 Torpedoed (in convoy HX48) by *U38*, on fire, 50 37N 08 44W (19†, 16 surv), sunk 50 41N 08 52W

Jacob Christensen 18.6.40 Engines damaged by own crew, abandoned, Rochefort; 18.6.40 captured by Germans; salved, repaired; 41 *Baldur* (Ger); 23.5.44 torpedoed by subm HMS *Sceptre*, sunk, off Castro Urdiales, Spain
Jamaica 7.3.43 Torpedoed by *U221*, sunk, 48N 23 30W
James Stove 16.6.40 Torpedoed by subm *Galileo Galilei* (Ita), sunk, 12 35N 45 03E (0†)
Janna 11.7.40 Torpedoed (convoy HX54 straggler) by *U34*, sunk, 50 34N 12 10W (25 surv)
Jasmin 40 *Bélain d'Esnambuc* (Fra); 16.12.42 seized Marseilles by Germans; KM, minelayer *Pommern* (Ger); 6.10.43 struck mine, sunk, off San Remo (few surv)
Jaspis 40 Seized by Germans (Ger); 28.2.45 bombed by Allied aircraft, badly damaged, Kiel; 45 repaired; 45 (Pan)
John Knudsen 40 German control; 40 KM, *Rouergue* (Ger); 9.10.44 sunk as blockship Salamis
John P Pedersen 40 Adm service (RFA); 20.5.41 torpedoed (in convoy HX126) by *U94*, sunk, 150m S of Greenland (22†, 16 surv)

K G Meldahl 10.11.42 Torpedoed by *U181*, sunk, 34 59S 29 45E (2†, 30 surv)
Kari 22.6.40 Seized Casablance by VFr; 40 *Ste Colette* (Fra); 43 *Kari* (Ger); 16.10.43 torpedoed by subm HMS *Torbay*, sunk, 36 59N 26 10E (–†; 180 troops †, *c*320 troops surv)
Karlander 14.5.41 Attacked by German aircraft, badly damaged, 55 38N 13 38W; wreck sunk by corvette HMS *Campanula* 55 36N 13 24W (0†, 26 surv)
Karmøy 40 German control; 28.10.44 sunk by British aircraft Lodingen (6†)
Karmt 18.4.45 Torpedoed (in convoy TAM142) by *U245*, sunk, 207° 2m from South Falls Buoy, off North Foreland (4†, 38 surv)
Kattegat (4245gt) 20.5.42 Captured by aux cruiser *Michel* 28 11S 11 30W (0†, – pow); sunk
Keret 22.8.40 Torpedoed by *U37*, sunk, 54 16N 23 08W (13†, 7 surv)
Ketty Brøvig 2.2.41 Captured 04 30S 50 50E by aux cruiser *Atlantis* (4 pow, 37 surv); used as supply ship; 4.3.41 found by cruisers HMS *Leander* and HMAS *Canberra*, scuttled to avoid capture 04 50S 56E
Knute Nelson 40 German control; 27.9.44 in convoy struck mine (laid 27.9.44 by subm *Rubis* (Fra)), sunk, 58 45N 05 24E
Koll 6.4.42 Torpedoed, shelled, by *U571*, sunk, 35N 68 24W (3†, 33 surv)
Kollbjorg 26.1.43 Broke back in storm, torpedoed (in convoy HX223) by *U607*, sunk, 58 40N 33 10W
Kollskegg 6.4.42 Torpedoed by *U754* 35 01N 68 49W; 7.4.42 again torpedoed, sunk, 35 20N 70 03W (4†, 38 surv)
Kongsfjord 17.5.40 Seized Oslo by Germans; 40 KM; 1.1.41 commd as *Sperrbrecher 15*; 24.4.41 decoy ship *Gonzenheim*, reconnaissance ship for *Bismarck*; 4.6.41 set on fire for intended scuttling when intercepted by RN warships including battleship HMS *Nelson* and carrier HMS *Victorious*; shelled by amc HMS *Esperance Bay*, torpedoed by cruiser HMS *Neptune*, sunk, 43 29N 24 04W
Kongsgaard 21.2.42 Torpedoed by *U502*, on fire, abandoned, 7m off North Point, Curaçao; sunk 7m W of North Point (38†, 8 surv)
Kosmos 26.9.40 Captured by aux cruiser *Thor* 00 26S 32 01W; boarded, sunk by explosive charges
Kosmos II 28.10.42 Torpedoed (convoy HX212 straggler) by *U606* 54 40N 29W; torpedoed by *U624*, sunk, 54 30N 29 55W (40†, 110 surv)
Kvernaas 17.2.40 Torpedoed by *U10*, sunk, 51 50N 03 19E (0†)

L A Christensen 10.6.42 Torpedoed by *U129*, sunk, 27 44N 63 54W (0†, 31 surv)
Lancing 7.4.42 Torpedoed by *U552*, sunk, 35 08N 75 22W (1†, 49 surv)
Langanger 22.6.40 Seized Oran; 40 German control; *Toni III*; 17.8.44 scuttled Port de

Bouc; 2.47 raised, repaired Marseilles; 50 *Neuchatel* (Swi)
Leiesten 23.1.42 Torpedoed (in convoy ON56) by *U82*, sunk, 45 27N 43 19W (6†, 23 surv)
Leif 28.2.42 Torpedoed by *U653*, sunk, 34 45N 69 20W (18†, 10 surv)
Leikanger 27.7.42 Torpedoed (in convoy FN20) by *U752*, sunk, 04N 18W (18†, 13 surv)
Leiv Eiriksson 40 Adm service (RFA); 27.6.42 torpedoed by *U126*, sunk, 13 18N 59 57W (2†, 42 surv)
Lenda 27.6.40 Torpedoed, shelled, by *U47* 50 12N 13 18W (1†, 25 surv); 28.6.40 sunk 50N 13 24W
Lincoln Ellsworth 6.4.41 Torpedoed by *U94*, sunk, 62 37N 27 06W (0†, 29 surv)
Lindvangen 23.9.42 Torpedoed by *U515*, sunk, 09 20N 60 10W (15†, 8 surv)
Lise 12.5.42 Torpedoed, shelled, by *U69*, sunk, 13 53N 68 20W (12†, 21 surv)
Listo 5.40 German control; 16.2.43 sunk Baltic
Litiopa 40 Adm service (RFA); 22.10.43 torpedoed (ind) by *U68*, shelled by 3 subms, sunk, 06 18N 11 55W (0†, 35 surv)
Liv 10.6.40 Seized Trapani by Italians; 18.4.43 bombed by British aircraft, damaged, Porto Torres; raised; 8.5.43 torpedoed by subm HMS *Safari*, sunk, Porto Torres roads; raised; 1.48 ar Spezia for BU
Lorentz W Hansen 14.10.39 Sunk by *Deutschland* 49 05N 43 44W (3†)
Lysefjord 1.4.43 Torpedoed by *U155*, sunk, 23 09N 83 24W (4†, 19 surv)

Mabella 13.3.42 Torpedoed, shelled, by subm *I-64* (Jpn), sunk, 14N 81 47E (6†)
Madrono 4.7.42 Captured by aux cruiser *Thor* 29 50S 70E; sent Japan; 42 *Rossbach* (Ger); 7.5.44 torpedoed by subm USS *Burrfish*, sunk, 33 14N 134 40E
Malmanger 40 Adm Service (RFA); 9.8.42 torpedoed by *U130*, sunk, 07 13N 26 30W (18†, 2 pow, 14 surv)
Maloja 8.11.42 Torpedoed, shelled, by *U128*, sunk, 11 25N 27W (2†, 39 surv)
Mantilla 40 Seized by Germans; KM, *Nordmeer* (Ger); 25.8.44 scuttled off Bassens, Gironde estuary as blockship; 28.2.45–25.3.45 raised; repaired; 2.48 *Artvine* (Fra)
Marianne 12.12.42 Torpedoed by German E-boat, sunk, 345° 2m from No 4 Buoy, Lowestoft (14†, 16 surv)
Marit 40 Adm service (RFA); 4.10.43 torpedoed (in convoy XT4) by *U596*, sunk, 32 57N 21 11E (2†, 52 surv)
Marstenen 30.8.40 Bombed by German aircraft, sunk, 58 23N 02 37W (0†)
Meteor 27.7.40 Seized Bergen by Germans; 7.5.40 KM, hospital ship; 42 *Rostock* (Ger); 28.5.42 *Meteor II* (Ger); 9.3.45 attacked by Russian aircraft, sunk, Pillau harbour (24†)
Mexico 6.3.41 Struck mine 51 53N 01 37E, sunk 51 55 04N 01 38 01E (10†, 23 surv); wreck dispersed
Minister Wedel 40 Adm service (RFA); 9.1.43 torpedoed (in convoy TM1) by *U575* 28 08N 28 20W (0†, 38 surv); shelled by escort, did not sink; sunk about 28 18N 27 20W
Mirlo 40 Adm service (RFA); 11.8.42 torpedoed by *U130*, sunk, 06 04N 26 53W (0†, 37 surv)
Moira 17.6.42 Torpedoed by *U158*, sunk, 25 35N 96 20W (1†, 18 surv)
Moldanger 27.6.42 Torpedoed by *U404*, sunk, 38 03N 70 52W (23†, 21 surv)
Morviken 27.8.40 Captured by aux cruiser *Pinguin*, sunk, 29S 51E (0†)
Mosfruit 30.6.42 Torpedoed, shelled (ind) by *U458*, sunk, 56 10N 23 20W (0†, 36 surv)
Mosstrand 41 Seized by Germans on completion; 29.1.43 bombed by British aircraft, sunk, 10m SW of Stavanger
Mostun 40 Seized by Germans; KM, victualling ship *Hartmut* (Ger); 1.10.44 struck mine, sunk, 56 51.5N 10 37.5E (2†)

N T Nielsen-Alonso 22.2.43 Torpedoed (in convoy ON166) by *U92* and *U753*, damaged, abandoned, 48N 31 24W (3†, 50 surv); sunk by escort destroyer *Burza* (Pol)
Navarra 6.4.40 Torpedoed by *U59*, sunk, 59N 04W (12†)
Needwood (Pan) 12.41 Seized Tsingtao by Japanese; 42 *Kaiyo Maru* (Jpn); 22.12.42 wrecked Inland Sea, Japan
Ngow Hock 8.12.41 Captured Camranh Bay by Japanese; 42 *Hokuzan Maru* (Jpn); 26.10.43 attacked by USAAF aircraft, sunk, 20 05N 110 25E
Nidarholm 12.2.40 Torpedoed by *U26* 50 10N 14 09W (0†, 25 surv); abandoned, broke in two, both parts sank
Nidarland 9.11.42 Torpedoed by *U67*, sunk, 11 41N 60 42W (1†, 34 surv)
Nidarnes 3.6.42 Torpedoed by *U158*, sunk, 21 17N 85 07W (13†, 11 surv)
Nina Borthen 6.10.40 Torpedoed by *U103*, sunk, 54N 26W (0 surv))
Nord(Pan) 21.1.42 Torpedoed by subm *I-66*, sunk, 15 28N 94 36E (0†)
Nordal (Pan) 25.6.42 Torpedoed by *U404*, sunk, 34 20N 75 40W (0†, 32 surv)
Nordhav 40 Seized Yokohama by Japanese; 41 *Daisin Maru* (Jpn); 23.9.43 torpedoed by subm USS *Harder*, sunk, 34 15N 137E
Nordvangen 20.2.42 Torpedoed by *U129*, sunk, 10 50N 60 54W (0 surv)
Nordvard 16.9.40 Captured 30S 60E by aux cruiser *Pinguin*; prize, sent France with pow; KM, target ship; 43 U-boat supply/depot ship; 28–29.12.44 attacked by British aircraft, sunk, Moss Sound (9†)
Norhauk 21.12.43 Struck mine, sunk, 51 50 03N 01 33 01E (11†, 30 surv); wreck dispersed
Norland 20.5.42 Torpedoed, shelled (in convoy ON93) by *U108*, sunk, 31 22N 55 47W (0†, 48 surv)
Norne 30.8.40 Torpedoed (in convoy HX66A) by *U32*, sunk, 58 48N 06 49W

Norness (Pan) 14.1.42 Torpedoed by *U123*, sunk, 40 28N 70 50W (1†, 40 surv)
Norse Carrier (Pan) 8.12.41 Seized Shanghai by Japanese; 42 *Sana Maru* (Jpn); 20.10.43 torpedoed by subm USS *Kingfish*, sunk, 12 36N 109 30E
Norse King 28.12.42 Torpedoed (convoy ONS154 straggler) by *U591*, damaged 43 27N 27 15W; 29.12.42 torpedoed by *U435*, sunk (35†, 0 surv)
North America 40 Seized by Germans; 40 *Egerland* (Ger); 5.6.41 found 07N 31W by cruiser HMS *London*, destroyer HMS *Brilliant*; torpedoed, sunk, by *Brilliant*
Nortun (Pan) 20.3.43 Torpedoed by *U516*, sunk, 27 35S 14 22E (10†, 37 surv)
Norvik 9.1.43 Torpedoed (in convoy TM1) by *U575*, sunk, 28 08N 28 20W (2†, 43 surv)
Norviken 9.4.42 Bombed by Japanese aircraft, on fire, 07 03N 79 58E (4†, 47 surv), abandoned, ran aground, E coast of Ceylon 07 05N; on fire, gutted, broke in two, TL
Novasli 2.3.45 Torpedoed (in convoy SC167) by *U1302* 52 04N 05 42W (0†, 37 surv); taken in tow, sunk
Nyholt 40 Adm service (RFA); 17.1.42 torpedoed, shelled (dispersed from convoy ON52), by *U87* 45 46N 54 18W (20†, 20 surv); 18.1.42 abandoned, shelled, sunk

O A Knudsen 5.3.42 Torpedoed, shelled, by *U128*, sunk, 26 17N 75 50W (1†, 39 surv)
Octavian 17.1.42 Torpedoed by *U203*, sunk, 45N 60W (0 surv)
Olaf Fostenes 18.9.42 Torpedoed (in convoy ON129) by *U380*, sunk, 44 56N 41 05W (0†, 36 surv)
Ole Jacob 10.11.40 Captured by aux cruiser *Atlantis* 06 30N 90 13 01E, prize; 40 *Benno* (Ger); 6.12.40 ar Kobe; 24.12.41 bombed, torpedoed, by British aircraft, sunk, off Puerto Carino, NW Spain (1†)
Ole Wegger 14.1.41 Captured 57 40S 05 45W by aux cruiser *Pinguin*, prize; sent Bordeaux; 41 KM, base ship; 26.8.44 scuttled Rouen-Sahurs as blockship; 8.45 raised; 47 BU Gothenburg
Oregon Express 23.9.43 Torpedoed (in convoy ON202) by *U238*, sunk, 53 40N 39 50W (8†, 37 surv)
Oria 24.6.41 Seized Casablanca by VFr; 41 *Ste Julienne* (Fra); 22.11.42 *Oria* (Ger); 12–13.2.44 wrecked off Cape Sunion, Aegean, when trying to avoid subm attack
Orion 40 (Ger); 11.3.45 bombed by Allied aircraft, sunk, Hamburg; 45 raised; 13.8.45 (Nor)
Orkanger 12.6.40 Torpedoed by subms *Nereide* and *Naiade* (Ita), sunk, 31 42N 28 50E (4†)
Orland 29.4.40 Attacked by German aircraft, sunk, off Midsund
Oslofjord 10.40 Allied troopship; 1.12.40 damaged by acoustic mine 220° 0.5m from T2 Buoy, off R Tyne, beached S of South Tyne Pier (1†); 21–22.1.41 capsized in bad weather, TL

Pan Norway 26.1.42 Shelled (ind) by *U123*, sunk, 35 56N 50 27W (0†, 41 resc by *Mount Etna*)
Pasat 40 *Koa Maru* (Jpn); 4.4.43 torpedoed by subm USS *Porpoise*, sunk, 13 11N 161 57E
Pericles 41 Adm service (RFA); 26.3.41 damaged by Italian 1-man torpedo-boat Suda Bay (0†, 31 surv); 11.4.41 sd Suda Bay in tow for Alexandria; 14.4.41 broke in two in heavy weather; both parts shelled, sunk, 35m NW of Alexandria
Pleasantville 8.6.42 Torpedoed by *U135*, sunk, 34N 68W (2†, 45 surv)
Pluto 23.1.40 Torpedoed by *U19*, sunk, 55 33 24N 01 28 30W (0†)
Polarland 4.1.45 Torpedoed (in convoy SH194) by *U1232*, sunk, 44 30N 63W (18†, 4 surv)
Polyana 25.4.41 Torpedoed (from dispersed convoy OG60) by *U103*, sunk, 24N 27W (0 surv)
Port Antonio 19.7.42 Torpedoed by *U129*, sunk, 23 39N 84W (13†, 11 surv)
President Herrenschmidt 22.6.40 Seized Oran by Germans; 40 *Toni II* (Ger); 22.3.43 torpedoed by subm HMS *Tribune* 39 14N 15 59E, towed Naples; 30.5.43 bombed by Allied aircraft, burnt out, Naples; 9.9.43 scuttled Naples; 46 raised, repaired; 48 *Vampa* (Ita)
Primero 25.10.42 Torpedoed (ind) by *U67*, sunk, 13 38N 53 55W (2†, 37 surv)
Profit 17.4.41 Struck mine, sunk, 51 47 27N 01 30 33E (12†, 5 surv); wreck dispersed
Prominent 2.3.42 Shelled by Japanese warship, on fire, sunk, S of Tjilatjap (–†, 3 surv)
Proteus 2.3.42 Scuttled Sourabaya

Randsfjord 22.6.40 Torpedoed (in convoy HX49) by *U30*, sunk, about 70m SSE of Queenstown (4†, 29 surv)
Ranella 12.6.41 Torpedoed (in convoy OG64) by *U553*, sunk, 43 39N 28W (0†, 29 surv)
Ranja 17.3.42 Torpedoed by *U71*, sunk, 38N 65 20W (34†, 0 surv)
Ravnaas 8.12.41 Bombed by Japanese aircraft, sunk, off Surigao, Philippines; 42 salved by Japanese; 42 *Ikutagawa Maru* (Jpn); 12.1.45 sunk by USN carrier-based aircraft 10 45 03N 106 43 29E
Ravnanger 11.11.40 Bombed by German aircraft 1–1.5m NE of No 20 Buoy, Tees Bay, sunk (1†, 26 surv)
Realf 30.11.39 Struck mine (laid by German destroyer) 53 554 38N 00 25 04E (1†); 1.12.39 sunk
Rigel 40 German control; 27.11.44 torpedoed, bombed, by aircraft from carrier HMS *Implacable*, sunk, off Mosjøen (of 2721 on board, incl 2248 Rus and Yug pow, 415 surv)
Rigmor 2.4.42 Bombed by German aircraft, sunk, 57 27N 03 21E (0†, 40 surv) attempting to escape from Sweden
Rinda 30.5.41 Torpedoed by *U38*, sunk, 06 52N 15 14W (13†, 18 surv)
Ringstad 24.1.42 Torpedoed (in convoy ONS55) by *U335*, sunk, 45 50N 51 04W (30†, 13 surv)
Ringulv 17.6.40 Interned Oran; seized by VFr; 41 *Ste Marguerite* (Fra); 11.42 KM,

Ringulv (Ger); 14.6.43 torpedoed by subm HMS *United*, sunk, 37 54N 15 42E
Ringwood 15.10.40 Sunk by aux cruiser *Orion* 02 18N 116 40E (European crew repatriated Norway)
Risanger 27.12.40 Torpedoed, shelled, by *U65*, sunk, 12 30N 21 30W (0†)
Ronda 13.9.39 Struck mine, sunk, 54 10N 04 34E (17†)
Ruth 40 Captured by Germans, *Thorn* (Ger); 2.4.41 shelled, torpedoed, by subm HMS *Tigris* 25m SW of Loire estuary; 3.4.41 sunk
Ruth I 6.4.44 Torpedoed (in convoy SC156) by *U302*, sunk, 45 05N 35 11W (3†, 36 surv)
Rygja 40 German control; 4.4.43 struck mine, sunk, off Skagen

Salonica 23.11.40 Torpedoed (in convoy SC11) by *U100*, sunk, 55 16N 12 14W (9†, 8 surv)
Sama 22.2.42 Torpedoed (in convoy ONS67) by *U155*, sunk, 49 30N 38 30W (20†, 18 surv)
Samnanger 21.12.40 Torpedoed, shelled, by *U99*, sunk, 08 26N 16 50W (0 surv)
Sandanger 12.5.43 Torpedoed (convoy HX237 straggler) by *U221*, sunk, 46N 21W (20†, 19 surv)
Sandar 40 Adm service (RFA); 2.5.42 torpedoed by *U66*, sunk, 11 42N 61 10W (2†, 25 surv)
Sandefjord 18.1.41 Captured 11S 02W by *Admiral Scheer*; 17.3.41 *Monsun* (Ger); 25.9.43 bombed, on fire, Nantes; 10.8.44 scuttled Nantes; 3.45 raised, repaired; 3.48 *Brière* (Fra)
Sangstad 18.2.40 Torpedoed by *U61*, sunk, 59 03N 01 08E (1†)
Saphir 10.4.40 Shelled during German invasion, sunk, Narvik; 57 refloated, BU
Sarita 14.7.40 Torpedoed by *UA*, sunk, 15 22N 26 23W (0†, 29 surv)
Scebeli 21.4.43 Torpedoed (in convoy ONS3) by *U191*, sunk, 56 07N 44 26W (2†, 39 surv)
Scotia 27.11.43 Torpedoed, shelled, by subm *I-37* (Jpn), sunk, 03S 69 03E (8†, 1 pow, 31 surv)
Segundo 27.8.41 Torpedoed (in convoy OS4) by *U557*, sunk, 53 36N 16 40W (7†, 27 surv)
Sekstant 4.5.40 Bombed by German aircraft at Kolvereid, N of Namsos (0†)
Selbo 28.11.42 Torpedoed by enemy aircraft, sunk, 15m from Cape Cavello, Algeria (11†, 17 surv)
Selje 40 German control; 15.5.42 bombed by British aircraft, sunk, off Frisian Islands
Senta 13.10.42 Torpedoed (in convoy SC104) by *U221*, sunk, 55N 44W (0 surv)
Sheng Hwa 7.12.41 Seized Japan by Japanese; 42 *Kazan Maru* (Jpn); recovered after war; 25.1.46 scuttled Malacca Strait
Sildra 40 Adm service (RFA); 19.8.41 torpedoed by subm *Enrico Tazzoli* (Ita), sunk, 05 30N 12 50W (0†, 40 surv)
Silja 10.2.40 Torpedoed by *U37*, sunk, 51 21N 11 32W (16†, 0 surv))
Siljestad 15.5.42 Torpedoed by *U156*, sunk, 15 20N 52 40W (2†, 31 surv)
Silvaplana 10.9.41 Captured by aux cruiser *Atlantis* 26 16S 164 25W, prize; 11.41 ar Bordeaux; 42 *Irene* (Ger) (blockade runner); 10.4.43 intercepted by minelayer HMS *Adventure*, scuttled to avoid capture 43 18N 14 26W
Simla 22.9.40 Torpedoed (in convoy HX72) by *U100*, sunk, 55 08N 17 40W (5†)
Siranger 24.10.43 Torpedoed by *U155*, sunk, 00 00– 38 45W (0†, 1pow)
Siremalm 27.9.41 Torpedoed (in convoy HG73) by *U201*, sunk, 49 05N 20 10W (27†, 0 surv)
Skjelbred 23.9.43 Torpedoed (in convoy ON202) by *U238*, sunk, 53 18N 40 24W (0†, 43 surv)
Skottland 17.5.42 Torpedoed by *U588*, sunk, 43 07N 67 18W (1†, 23 surv)
Skramstad 5.40 German control; 31.3.41 aux ship, KMD Oslo; 4.10.43 bombed by aircraft from carrier USS *Ranger*, Bødø, stranded, CTL; 46 salved, *Bertnes* (Nor); 48 BU
Skrim 6.12.40 Torpedoed by *U43*, sunk, in about 53N 21W (0 surv)
Skytteren 1.4.42 Intercepted by German patrol boats, scuttled, 6–7m off Kaeringoen, N of Gothenburg (18 interned) while escaping from Sweden
Slemdal 40 Adm service (RFA); 14.6.42 torpedoed (in convoy HG84) by *U552* 43 28N 17 35W (0†, 37 surv); 15.6.42 sunk
Snefjeld 19.10.40 Torpedoed (in convoy SC7) by *U99*, sunk, 57 28N 11 10W (0†)
Sneland I 7.5.45 Torpedoed by *U2336*, sunk, 56 09 36N 02 31 24W (7†, 22 surv)
Snestad 11.2.40 Torpedoed by *U53*, sunk, 58 40N 13 40W (2†)
Solferino 26.2.41 Bombed by German aircraft, on fire, abandoned, 55 02N 16 25W (3†, 29 surv); sunk
Solglimt 14.12.40 Captured 59S 03W by aux cruiser *Pinguin*; sent Bordeaux; 41 *Sonderburg* (Ger); 29.6.44 scuttled by Germans as blockship, Cherbourg; 1.47 wreck demolished with explosives
Solheim 22.3.41 Bombed by German aircraft 34 30N 24 10E (1†, 31 surv); 23.3.41 abandoned, sunk 34 30N 24 45E
Soli 5.4.42 Bombed by Japanese carrier aircraft, beached, Colombo; 4.1.52 refloated, BU Karachi
Solor 27.1.45 Torpedoed (in convoy HX322) by *U825*, broke in two, 52 35N 05 18W, beached Oxwich Bay (4†, 40 surv); forepart refloated, BU Briton Ferry; afterpart BU *in situ*
Soloy 24.6.41 Torpedoed (in convoy HX133) by *U203*, sunk, 54 39N 39 43W (0†, 29 surv)
Solviken 5.40 German control; 25–26.5.44 torpedoed by Russian aircraft, sunk, E of Nordkyn
Solviken 40 *Capella* (Pan); 8.12.41 seized off Saigon by Japanese; 8.42 *Minami Maru* (Jpn); 1.4.44 torpedoed by subm USS *Flying Fish*, sunk, moored 25 59N 131 19E
Sørholt 15.9.42 Torpedoed by *U515*, sunk, 10 45N 60W (7†, 31 surv)
South Africa 8.6.42 Torpedoed by *U128*, sunk, 12 47N 49 44W (6†, 36 surv)
South America 6.4.44 Torpedoed (in convoy SC156) by *U302*, sunk, 45 05N 35 11W

(0†, 42 surv)
Spind 23.8.41 Torpedoed (in convoy OG71) by *U564* and *U552*, on fire, shelled, sunk, 40 43N 11 39W (0†, 25 surv)
Steinstad 15.2.40 Torpedoed by *U26*, sunk, 75m W of Aran Is (13†)
Stigstad 21.2.43 Torpedoed (convoy ON166 straggler) by *U332* and *U603*, sunk, 49 26N 29 08W (3†, 34 surv)
Storaas 28.5.43 Torpedoed (in convoy CD20) by *U177*, sunk, 34 57S 19 33E (3†, 36 surv)
Storstad 7.10.40 Captured by aux cruiser *Pinguin* Indian Ocean, prize, sent Bordeaux (30 crew repatr Norway, 1 pow); KM, conv to minelayer *Passat*; 2.9.42 attacked by Allied aircraft, sunk, off St Nazaire, damaged; 49 BU
Storsten 1.4.42 Intercepted by German patrol boat 32m S of Kristiansand, scuttled, while attempting escape from Sweden
Storviken 1.10.43 Torpedoed by subm *I-10* (Jpn), sunk, 11 43N 48 07E (37†, 2 pow, 17 surv)
Strombus 26.10.40 Struck mine 51 33 48N 03 56 48W, broke in two (0†, 48 surv); forepart drifted off, capsized, sank; afterpart beached 51 34 33N 03 58 21W; 42 refloated, BU Briton Ferry
Svein Jarl 23.1.41 Torpedoed (detached from convoy) by *U69*, sunk, 59 30N 21W (0 surv)
Svenør 40 Adm service (RFA); 27.3.42 torpedoed, shelled, by *U105*, sunk, 35 35N 69 20W (8†, 29 surv)
Sveve 40 Adm service (RFA); 10.9.42 torpedoed by *U96* 51 28N 28 30W (0†, 39 surv); shelled by escorts, sunk
Svinta 20.3.40 Attacked by German aircraft, damaged, North Sea; 21.3.40 torpedoed by *U57*, sunk, Copinsay bearing 40° 4.75m (0†)
Sydfold 22.1.40 Torpedoed by *U61*, sunk, 58 40N 00 30W (5†, 19 surv)
Sydhav 6.3.42 Torpedoed by *U505*, sunk, 04 47N 14 57W (12†, 12 surv)
Sysla 40 Seized by Germans; 40 *Belchen* (Ger); 3.6.41 shelled by cruisers HMS *Aurora*, *Kenya*, sunk, Davis Strait (49 surv on *U93*)

Tabor 9.3.43 Torpedoed, shelled, by *U506*, sunk, 38 30S 23 10E (12†, 34 surv)
Taborfjell 30.4.42 Torpedoed by *U576*, sunk, 41 52N 67 43W (17†, 3 surv)
Tai Ping 28.5.40 Seized by Germans; KM, *Sperrbrecher 14*; 42 *Bockenheim* (Ger); 12.9.42 struck mine, sunk, Honningsvaag; raised; 26.8.44 scuttled off Bassens, Gironde estuary; 46 raised; 29.2.48 sd Bassens in tow for Pasajes for BU
Takstaas 28.9.39 Torpedoed by *U7* 16m off Bergen (0†); abandoned, taken in tow; 29.9.39 broke in two; afterpart towed in, sold
Talabot 26.3.42 Bombed by German aircraft Valletta; on fire, forward end submerged; 28.3.42 scuttled to prevent explosion; 3.49 refloated, towed out to deep water, scuttled
Talleyrand 1.8.40 Captured 31S 67E by aux cruiser *Atlantis*; 2.8.40 sunk by explosive charges
Tana 4.7.41 Seized Safi by VFr; 41 *Ste Simone* (Fra); 11.42 *Tana* (Ger); 24.5.43 attacked by Allied aircraft, damaged, Olbia, Sardinia; 10.12.46 foundered 41 20N 10 57E in tow for Genoa
Tancred 26.9.40 Torpedoed, shelled (in convoy OB217) by *U32*, sunk, 53 32N 24 35W (0†, 36 surv)
Tankexpress 40 Adm service (RFA); 25.7.42 torpedoed, shelled, by *U130*, sunk, 10 05N 26 31(0†, 39 surv)
Taranger 2.5.41 Torpedoed, shelled (ind) by *U95* 61 07N 25 20W; 3.5.41 sunk
Tarifa 7.3.44 Torpedoed by *U510*, sunk, 12 48N 58 44E (6†, 146 surv)
Taurus 6.6.41 Bombed by German aircraft, sunk, 56 47N 02 15W (0†, 35 surv)
Teddy 8.11.40 Taken as prize 05 35N 88 22E for refuelling aux cruiser *Atlantis*; 14.11.40 set on fire, sunk, Indian Ocean (32 crew landed Japan)
Telnes 19.1.40 Torpedoed by *U55*, sunk, NW of Orkneys (18†, 0 surv)
Teneriffa 26.2.41 Bombed by German aircraft, sunk, 51 06N 04 49W (0†, 37 surv)
Tento 40 German control; 6.5.44 struck mine, sunk, Kiel Bay; wreck blown up
Thelma 40 Adm service (RFA); 26.8.42 torpedoed, shelled, by *U162*, sunk, 13 20N 58 10W (2†, 31 surv)
Thermopylae 19.1.42 Bombed (in convoy) by German aircraft S of Crete, on fire; sunk by escort vessel 34 03N 24 10E (3†, 35 surv; 30 troops†, 306 troops surv)
Thode Fagelund 17.11.41 Torpedoed by subm *Le Héros* (VFr), sunk, 60m E of East London (0†, 35 surv)
Thorshavet 40 Adm service (RFA); 3.11.42 torpedoed (in convoy TAG18) by *U160*, sunk, 12 16N 64 06W (3†, 43 surv)
Thorsheimer 10.6.40 Seized Spezia by Italians; 42 (Ger); 21.2.43 bombed by British aircraft, sunk, 20m SW of Marettimo
Thorstrand 6.3.42 Torpedoed (in convoy UGS6) by *U172*, sunk, 41 23N 42 59W (4†, 43 surv)
Tindefjell 40 Seized by Germans; 23.4.41 commd KM, *Sperrbrecher 74*; 41 *Sperrbrecher 174*; 28.5.42 struck mine, sunk, W of Buoy 11W, W of Dunkirk
Tirranna 10.6.40 Captured by aux cruiser *Atlantis* 23S 69E, sent Bordeaux with pow; 21.9.40 torpedoed by subm HMS *Tuna*, sunk, 45 19N 01 20W (87†, 205 surv incl pow from other ships)
Tolosa 9.2.42 Torpedoed by *U108*, sunk, 34 40N 73 50W (22†, 0 surv)
Tønsbergfjord 6.3.42 Torpedoed by subm *Enrico Tazzoli* (Ita), sunk, 31 22N 68 05W (1†, 32 surv)
Topeka 40 German control; 4.10.43 bombed by Allied aircraft, on fire, N of

Sandnessjøen, aground; refloated, towed Stavanger, CTL; 27.11.45 sd Stavanger in tow for Gothenburg, broke adrift in storm, aground Jaeren, TL
Toran 4.8.40 Torpedoed by subm HMS *Sealion*, sunk, 58 17N 08 38E (3†, 27 surv)
Torny 8.5.42 Torpedoed by *U507*, sunk, 26 45N 86 40W (2†, 24 surv)
Tortugas 18.11.42 Torpedoed by *U67*, sunk, 13 24N 54 59W (2 pow, 36 surv)
Torungen 22.2.42 Torpedoed, shelled, by *U96*, sunk, 44N 63 30W (19†, 0 surv)
Torvanger 23.6.42 Torpedoed by *U84*, sunk, 39 40N 41 30W (4†, 33 surv)
Tosca 10.4.40 Torpedoed by *U37*, sunk, 62 52N 07 34W (2†, 32 surv)
Touraine 7.10.40 Torpedoed by *U59*, sunk, 55 12N 10 18W (0†)
Tourcoing 40 German control; 24.8.42 struck mine, sunk, off Swinemünde
Trafalgar 15.10.42 Torpedoed by *U129*, sunk, 25 15N 50W (0†, 43 surv)
Trajan 3.5.41 Bombed by German aircraft, sunk, 53 10 30N 01 13E (0†, 21 surv)
Triton 17.8.42 Torpedoed (in convoy SL118) by *U566*, sunk, 39 31N 22 43W (0†, 43 surv)
Trolla 24.8.42 Torpedoed (in convoy ONS122) by *U438*, sunk, 48 55N 35 10W (5†, 17 surv)
Trondhjemsfjord 40 German control; 27.4.43 sunk by British aircraft off Ryvingen Lt
Tropic Sea 18.5.40 Captured 28 48S 160 38W by aux cruiser *Orion*, prize, sent France with pow; 3.9.40 scuttled 46 30N 11 30W when intercepted by subm HMS *Truant* (Norwegian crew rescued by *Truant*)
Tudor 19.6.40 Torpedoed (in convoy HGF34) by *U48*, on fire, abandoned, sunk, 45 10N 11 50W (1†, 38 surv)
Tugela 4.40 Scuttled Oslo, raised by Germans; 40 German control; 41 (Ger); 28.4.43 scuttled Oslo by Norwegian resistance; raised; 24.3.45 struck mine, sunk, near Florø
Tyr 9.3.42 Torpedoed by *U96*, sunk, 43 40N 61 10W (13†, 18 surv)
Tyrifjord 40 German control; 19.9.44 attacked by Allied aircraft, on fire, near Stavenes Lt, S of Florø; beached at Askvoll, TL

Utviken 23.3.45 Struck mine, sunk, off Sjaellands Odde

Vaga 5.40 German control; 13.1.45 torpedoed by British aircraft, sunk, off Homborsund (5†)
Varangberg 25.9.41 Torpedoed (in convoy HG73) by *U203*, sunk, 47 50N 24 50W (21†, 6 surv)
Varanger 25.1.42 Torpedoed by *U130* 38 58N 74 06W (0†, 38 surv); sunk 39 10N 73 45W
Varangmalm 29.10.39 Struck mine, sunk, 53 50N 00 17E (1†); wreck dispersed
Vardaas 40 Adm service (RFA); 30.8.42 torpedoed, shelled, by *U564*, sunk, 11 35N 60 40W (0†, 41 surv)
Vega 18.3.41 Seized by Germans; 1.6.41 KM, U-boat target ship *Wega*; 4.5.45 bombed by Allied aircraft, sunk, off Staberhuk, Fehmarn (1†)
Ven-Koh 7.12.41 Seized Japan by Japanese; 42 *Meizan Maru* (Jpn); 27.8.43 torpedoed by subm USS *Grayling*, sunk, 13 13N 121 23E
Venus (2456gt) 40 German control; 7.8.41 struck mine, sunk, near Borkum
Vespasian 24.1.41 Torpedoed by *U123*, sunk, 55N 15W (18†, 0 surv)
Vestfold 17.1.43 Torpedoed (in convoy HX222) by *U268*, sunk, 61 25N 26 12W (19†, 56 surv)
Vestvard 27.9.40 Torpedoed by *U31*, sunk, 300m W of Ireland (1†, 28 surv)
Vibran 24.9.42 Torpedoed by *U582*, sunk, 42 45N 42 45W (0 surv)
Victo 8.11.41 Bombed by German aircraft, broke in two, 54 20N 00 17W (2†, 30 surv); 9.11.41 abandoned, sunk
Vigør 6.40 Seized Casablanca by VFr; 40 *Ste Marcelle* (Fra); 14.3.42 reported torpedoed by British subm, sunk, W Mediterranean (voyage Marseilles–Tunis)
Vigrid 24.6.41 Torpedoed (convoy HX133 straggler) by *U371*, sunk, 54 30N 41 30W (27†, 21 surv)
Vigsnes 43–45 MoWT charter; 23.1.45 torpedoed (in convoy MH1) by *U1172*, sunk, 53 32N 04 19W (0†, 25 surv)
Vilja 13.9.42 Torpedoed (in convoy TAG5) by *U558* 12 15N 63 52W (0†); 14.9.42 put back Trinidad; 15.1.43 ar New Orleans, declared CTL; 44 BU
Vinni 7.12.40 Sunk by aux cruisers *Orion* and *Komet* 5m S of Nauru (0†, 32 pow – landed)
Viva 9.2.44 Torpedoed by *U188*, sunk, 12 30N 57 50E (0†, 37 surv)

Wilford 6.6.42 Shelled by subm *I-18* (Jpn), sunk, 20 20S 36 47E (9†, 37 surv)
William Hansen 21.1.43 Torpedoed by *U754* 46 56N 52 47W; sunk 46 56N 52 37W (10†, 9 surv)
Woolgar 7.3.42 Bombed by Japanese aircraft, sunk, 150m SW of Tjilatjap (38†, 1 pow, 5 surv)

Sunk Mulberry Harbour, Normandy
Sirehei 44 Adm (Br); 6.44 sunk as breakwater, Gooseberry 3, Gold Beach, Arromanches

Struck mine, sunk, postwar
Garnes 24.3.47 Struck mine, sunk, off Terschelling
Ramø 21.4.46 Struck by mine, blew up, while alongside quay at Henningsvær, Lofoten Is (14†)

Changes of name, flag, role, disposals, etc
Ada 4.40 German control; 46 *Bessa* (Nor)
Aino 4.40 Seized by Germans; 40 KM, supply vessel *Diedenhofen* (Ger); 12.8.45 *Aino* (Nor)
America 41 Seized by Germans while building; 41 *Schiff X* (Ger); 14.6.41 launched; 43

Texaco (Ger); 1.10.46 *Amerika* (Nor)
Ardent 40–46 MoWT charter; 46 *Hai Chen* (Chn)
Attila 40 Seized by Germans; 40 KM, *Saarburg* (Ger); 5.45 at Oslo; 45 *Attila* (Nor)
August 40 *Dimitris* (Gre) – see under Greece, Losses through war causes
Beaumont 4.40 Seized Trondheim by Germans; 40 *Bromberg* (Ger); 45 recovered; 45 *Beaumont* (Nor)
Bergensfjord 15.4.40 LU New York; 11.40 req by MoWT, conv to troopship; 46 returned
Binta 40 *Cerro Azul* (Mex)
Bisca 40 *Tampico* (Mex)
Bosphorus 6.40 Seized Algiers by VFr; 40 *Ste Mathilde* (Fra); 11.42 recaptured, Allied control; 43 *Bosphorus* (Nor)
Brabant 4.40 German control; 5.45 at Copenhagen, returned
Brali 42–45 LU Malmö under Allied control
Bravo I 4–5.45 German control
Bretagne 31.3.41 KM, commd as accom ship, KMD Oslo; 43 transport; 5.45 at Arendal;45 returned
C A Larsen 8.40–45 KM, tanker depot ship, Norway; 45 returned; 45 *Antarctic* (Nor)
Cometa 17.7.41 Seized by Germans while building; 1.1.42 commd KM target ship; 16.6.45 (Nor)
Crawford Ellis 46 *Shahin* (Pan)
Credo 40 *Realf II* (Nor); LU Sweden; 47 *Ariete* (Ita)
Dicto 42 LU Gothenburg under Allied control
Dovrefjell 41–45 LU Gothenburg under Allied control
Duala 24.6.40 Seized Dakar by VFr; 40 *St Sabine* (Fra); 11.42 retaken by Allies; 42 *Duala* (Nor)
Evina 40 Seized by Germans; 40 *Zabern* (Ger); 8.5.45 at Kiel; 45 *Evina* (Nor)
Falkanger 4.40 Seized by Germans while building; completed as KM target ship *Wartheland*; 20.3.44 transport, KMD Danzig; 5.45 at Copenhagen; 14.6.45 returned, repaired; 45 *Falkanger* (Nor)
Felix 4.40 German control; 44 torpedoed, repaired Bergen; 5.45 at Namsos, returned
Ferngulf 5.40 Seized by Germans while building Copenhagen; 12.6.41 delivered as *Ostland* (Ger); 13.4.45 struck mine, badly damaged, off Anholt; 6.45 at Århus; 4.7.45 returned, repaired; 45 *Ferngulf* (Nor)
Fjeld 4.40 German control; 5.45 at Bergen, returned

Gabon 5.7.40 Seized Dakar by VFr; 40 (Fra); 45 (Nor)
Glomdal 42 (Swe)
Haalegg 8.10.40 Sunk Narvik; 6.44 salved; 45 *Bodø* (Nor)
Haarfagre 4.40 German control; 5.45 at Narvik, returned
Hai Lee 40 Allied troopship; 45 returned
Hallingdal 40–45 German control
Halse 4.40 German control; 5.45 at Kiel, returned
Hektor 4.40 German control; 5.45 at Sandefjord, returned
Herdis 41 LU Landskrona under Allied control; 45 returned
Heron 40–45 LU Malmö under Allied control
Høegh Silvercrest 40 Launched, seized by Germans; 41 *Kurland* (Ger); 42 KM, target ship; 5.45 recovered; 45 *Høegh Silvercrest* (Nor)
Høegh Silvermann 40 Seized by Germans; 41 launched; *Lappland* (Ger); 43 *Goslar* (Ger); 5.45 recovered Copenhagen; 45 *Høegh Silverbeam* (Nor); 8.46 recommissioned
Høegh Trader 40 Seized by Germans while building Copenhagen; 7.41 KM, delivered as target vessel *Kurland*; 5.45 recovered Kiel; 45 returned; 2.47 delivered as *Høegh Silvercrest* (Nor)
Ingeren 40 (Swe); 45 (Nor)
Irania 4.40 German control; war damaged; 5.45 at Fredrikstad, repairing; 45 *Elisabeth Mary* (Nor)
James Hawson 46 *Jajce* (Yug)
Jaspis 6.40 Seized Casablanca by VFr; 5.45 at Kiel, badly damaged; repaired, returned
Kaprino 4.40 German control; 6.5.45 at Oslo, damaged; repaired, returned
Katherine Stenersen 41 Launched; 45 completed as *Sysla* (Nor)
Kattegat (6031gt) 5.40 German control; 10.11.44 ar Sandefjord for repairs to aircraft attack damage; 5.45 at Sandefjord; returned owner
Kaupanger 4.40 German control; 5.45 at Bergen, returned
Kongsstein 29.10.43 Completed; LU Malmö under Allied control; 5.45 delivered
Korsnes 4.40 German control; KM, collier *Pregel*; 27.11.44 torpedoed by aircraft from carrier HMS *Implacable*, on fire, burnt out, sunk, near Rørvik; 8.45 raised, repaired Bergen; 47 *Patricia* (Nor)
Kronviken 46 *Lee Ming* (Chn)
Krossfonn 26.6.40 Captured by aux cruiser *Widder* near West Indies, prize, sent Brest; *Spichern* (Ger); 9.8.44 bombed by Allied aircraft, badly damaged, Brest; 31.8.44 scuttled Brest as blockship; 47 raised in two parts, repaired; 49 *Ringfjell* (Nor)
Lionel 40–3.42 LU Gothenburg; 4.42–5.45 LU Gothenburg under Allied control; 5.45 returned
Lisita 40 Completed; 40 LU Sweden under Allied control
Lovaas 4.40 German control; 5.45 at Oslo, returned

Mammy 45 *Ambica* (Br)
Marie Bakke 40–45 British manager; 45 returned
Matros (Pan); 40 *Norseland* (Pan); 12.12.41 *Saentis* (Swi)
Montana 40 Launched; 42 LU Gothenburg under Allied control; 5.45 released
Moshill 40 (Ger); 5.45 repairing at Bergen; 45 (Nor)
Mytilus 45 (Br)
Nandi 4.40 German control; 2.9.41 captured Spitsbergen by British forces; 45 returned
Nidareid 46 *Way Tung* (Chn)
Norseman (Pan) 41 *Tornator* (Fin); 26.1.42 stranded Omaisaki, between Nagoya and Yokohama; 30.1.42 broke in two, sank
Nyhaug 4.40 German control; *Holla* (Nor); 5.45 at Oslo; 45 *Norseman* (Nor)
Nyhorn 3.6.40 Seized Casablanca by VFr; 11.42 scuttled Port Lyautey; 43 refloated by Allies; 43 returned
Orion 4.40 German control; 41 (Ger); 5.45 at Kiel; 45 (Nor)
Pacific Express 40 Completed; LU Malmö under Allied control; 5.45 delivered
Pelagos 15.1.41 Captured 59S 00 30W by aux cruiser *Pinguin*; German depot ship; 24.10.44 sunk Kirkenes; 45 raised, repaired, reconstructed; 46 *Pelagos* (Nor)
Polykarp 15.3.41 Captured by *Gneisenau* 45 40N 23 26W; prize; 41 *Taifun* (Ger); 3.5.45 sunk by Allied aircraft off Kjelnør; 45 salved, returned; 45 *Polykarp* (Nor), repaired Gothenburg; 47 *Wilstar* (Nor)
Pronto 40 MoWT charter; 46 returned
Ragnhild Stenersen 19.5.41 Launched; 42 LU Sweden under Allied control; 45 *Kim* (Nor); 45 *San Antonio* (Arg)
Raila (8200gt) 40 Completed; 9.40 LU Gothenburg under Allied control; 5.45 delivered
Raila (5551gt) 40 *Sigrid Reuter* (Swe)
Realf II 40 LU Gothenburg under Allied control; 5.45 released
Regina 22.6.40 Seized Oran; 40 German control; 41 *Toni IV* (Ger); 45 *Regina* (Nor)
Ringar 4.40 German control; 5.45 at Tønsberg, returned
Roald Jarl 4.40 German control; 5.45 at Stavanger, returned
Ronald 40 *Mafuta* (Bel)
Salsaas 40 Completed; 42 LU Sweden under Allied control; 4.45 released
San Antonio (Pan) 46 *Hsin Kong* (Chn)
Shabonee (Pan) 40 *Dauphine* (Fra); 25.9.44 at Port de Bouc, damaged; recovered
Sigurd Jarl 4.40 German control; 45 returned
Sirenes 4.40 In Swedish waters, req (Swe); 44 released from req (Nor); 44–5.45 LU Sweden
Stanja 4.40–5.45 German control
Stavangerfjord 12.39 LU Oslo; 20.9.40 KM; 3.10.40 commd as barracks ship; 44 hospital ship; 20.9.44 VTS transport; 21.2.45 returned
Stella Polaris 30.11.40 KM, commd as support ship, Norway; 1.1.41 accom ship, Norway; 21.8.41 support ship; 5.3.42 barracks ship, Narvik; 45 returned
Stirlingville 40–45 MoWT charter; 45 returned
Storfonn 40 Completed; 40 LU Gothenburg under Allied control; 45 released
Svolder 4.40 German control; 5.45 returned
Sygna 14.8.41–23.10.45 MoWT charter; 10.45 returned
Taiwan 4.40 German control; 5.45 at Oslo, returned
Tampa 4.40 Seized by Germans; 5.45 recovered Horten, returned
Taronga 15.8.40 Seized by Germans; 2.42 commd KM, *Sperrbrecher 15*; 43 target ship; 5.45 recovered Hamburg, burnt out following bombing; 45 returned, repaired Antwerp; 8.48 returned to service as *Taronga* (Nor)
Templar 10.8.40 Seized by Germans; 23.11.40 commd KM, *Sperrbrecher 17*; 5.45 retaken, damaged, Kiel; 45 *Templar* (Nor)
Thorshøvdi 40 Adm service (RFA); 4.8.43 attacked by Italian assault craft, guided torpedo, sunk, Gibraltar; 45 at Gibraltar; 46 *Giert Torgersen* (Nor)
Tiger 4.40 German control; 5.45 at Tønsberg, returned
Trianon 4.40 German control; 5.45 at Oslo, returned
Tropic Star 47 *Anja* (Fin)
Tulane 40 Seized by Germans; 16.11.40 commd KM, *Sperrbrecher 16* (Ger); 10.8.44 bombed La Pallice; 11.8.44 sunk; 30.7.46 raised, returned, repaired; 2.49 *Tulane* (Nor)
Turicum 40 *Ill* (Ger); 5.45 at Brunsbüttel; 45 *Turicum* (Nor)
Velox 40–45 MoWT charter; 45 returned
Venus (5407gt) 40 German control; 16.3.41 seized by Germans; 41 (Ger); 8.5.41 commd KM U-boat target ship; 20.3.45, 15.4.45 bombed, sunk, Hamburg; 45 raised, returned, repaired; 3.5.48 re-entered service
Vest 40–45 MoWT charter; returned
Vesthav 41 Completed; 41 LU Malmö under Allied control; 45 released
Viator 6.40 German control while building Copenhagen; 17.6.41 KM transport (Nor); 27.10.41 seized by Germans; 26.8.42–11.5.43 KM, conv to V-Schiff; 11.5.43 commd as *Christian Sinding*; 1.9.43 U-boat target ship; 5.45 recovered Copenhagen; 25.8.45 returned; 45 *Viator* (Nor); 46 *Guinée* (Fra)
Villanger 40–45 MoWT charter; 45 returned
Vingnes 41 Completed; 41 LU Gothenburg under Allied control; 45 released
William Blumer 2.4.45 Attacked by British aircraft, sunk, Sandefjord; 46 raised; 48 returned service

Palestine

Change of name, flag
Haifa Trader 40 (Br); 28.7.41 *Irish Larch* (Eir)

Panama

Change of name, flag, and lost through war causes
Ada 40 *Songa* (Nor); 22.1.40 torpedoed by *U25*, sunk, 220m W of Scilly Isles (0†)

Change of name
Vahva 40 *Suerte* (Pan)

Poland

Loss through marine hazard
Wigry 15.1.42 Aground in heavy weather 64 05N 22W (–†, 2 surv); TL

Losses through war causes
Bielsko 1.9.39 Seized by Germans while building Danzig; 40 KM, completed as *Bonn* (hospital ship, Schiff 26); 17.9.41 commd as aux cruiser *Michel* (Schiff 28, Raider 'H'); 17.10.43 torpedoed by subm USS *Tarpon*, sunk, 33 39N 139 01E (290†, 116 surv)
Chrobry 9.39 Allied troopship; 14.5.40 bombed by German Ju87 aircraft of I/StG1, on fire, off Bodø; 15.5.40 abandoned, gutted, sunk 67 40N 13 50E (11†, 148 surv)
Pilsudski 9.39 Allied troopship; 26.11.39 struck mine (laid by destroyer of German 4 Destroyer fl), sunk, 53 15N 00 30E (10†)

Changes of name, flag, role, disposals, etc
Batory 39 MoWT (Br), troopship; 46 returned
Kosciuszko 40 Polish navy, *Gdynia* (Pol); 45 *Koscuiszko* (Br); 46 *Empire Helford* (Br); 50 BU Blyth
Lodz 1.9.39 Seized by Germans while building Danzig; 43 completed Helsingør; 10.11.43 *Minden* (Ger); 1.2.44 KM target vessel; 19.10.44 decomm; 5.45 at Nyborg; 11.7.45 MoWT (Br); 45 *Empire Nidd* (Br); 46 *Denis Davydov* (Rus); 47 *General Walter* (Pol)
Pulaski 39 MoWT charter, troopship; 46 *Empire Penryn* (Br)
Sobieski 9.39 Allied troopship; 47 returned
Torun 40 Seized by Germans; 40 *Hannes Freymann* (Ger); 5.45 at Brunsbüttel; 46 *Torun* (Pol)

Portugal

Losses through war causes
Cassequel 14.12.41 Torpedoed (ind) by *U108*, sunk, 35 08N 11 14W (0†, 57 surv)
Corte Real 12.10.41 Stopped by *U83*, searched, torpedoed, sunk, 80m W of Lisbon (0†, 36 surv)
Ganda 20.6.41 Torpedoed by *U123*, sunk, 34 10N 11 40W (5†, 61 surv)

Romania

Loss through marine hazard
Bucuresti 11.1.40 Disabled 40 13N 25 20E; ashore Samothraki, badly damaged; refloated, taken to Greek port; CTL, BU

Losses through war causes
Alba Julia 8.41 Req by Germans, transport; 18.8.44 bombed, sunk, in harbour; 45 raised; 47 USSR reparations; 47 *Nikolaev* (Rus)
Balcic 15.10.43 Attacked by German aircraft, sunk, Split; 15.8.47 raised, LU Split; 47 *Srem* (Yug)
Basarabia 48 USSR reparations, *Ukraina* (Rus)
Bucegi 6.40 Intercepted Mediterranean; taken Haifa; 40 MoWT (Br); 46 sold; 47

Petsamo (Fin)
Campina 40 (Ita); 30.12.41 torpedoed by subm HMS *Thorn*, sunk, 38 35N 10 27E
Carpati 41 German control; 11.10.42 torpedoed by subm *SC-216* (Rus), sunk, 44 57N 29 46E
Cavarna 41 VTS charter, transport; 2.12.41 struck Russian mine, sunk, 1nm E of Burgas
Dacia 45 Seized as prize by USSR
Inginer N Vlassopol 41 *Hampton Lodge* (Br); 20.1.43 bombed by enemy aircraft 36 44N 01 50E; 21.1.43 sunk
Jiul 31.5.41 During attack by British aircraft at Piræus, sunk in harbour following explosion on *Knyaguinya Maria Luisa* (*qv*)
Mangalia 41 *Pleiades* (US); 45 *Scepter* (US)
Oituz 1.9.44 Torpedoed by *U23*, sunk, Constanta harbour (vessel was previously damaged); TL
Oltenia 40 MoWT, *Oltenia II* (Br); 8.1.43 torpedoed (in convoy TM1) by *U436*, sunk, 27 59N 28 50W (17†, 43 surv)
Oltul 8.40 LU Pernambuco; 2.41 (Pan); 11.41 *Esmeralda* (Arg); 10.43 *Rio Deseado* (Arg)
Peles 14.8.41 Torpedoed (in convoy) by subm *SC-216* (Rus); 16.8.41 explosion, sunk, 42 46N 27 59E
Regele Carol 1 40 Req by Romanian navy, aux minelayer; 13.9.41 struck mine (laid by subm *L-4* or *L-5* (Rus)), sunk, 2m E of Cape Galata
Romania 42 Req by KM; 6.12.42 torpedo boat depot ship (1 S-boat fl); 3.43 seized Constanta by Germans; 3.11.43 KM aux minelayer; 12.5.44 bombed by Russian aircraft, munitions explosion, sunk, Black Sea
Siretul 41 *Omega* (Pan); 42 MoWT (Br); 46 (Pan)
Steaua Romana 10.40 Req by MoWT; 12.41 seized by GB; 12.41 MoWT (Br); 47 *Polar Maid* (Br)
Suceava 41 VTS charter, transport; 20.4.43 torpedoed by subm *S-33* (Rus) 44 12N 30 22E; sunk 44 52N 31 22E (28†); raised, not repaired; 46 BU
Sulina 5.41 VTS charter, transport; 29.5.42 torpedoed by subm *A-3* (Rus), sunk, 46 33N 30 56E

Change of name, flag, role
Ardeal 41 VTS charter, transport; 11.6.42 torpedoed 46 32 30N 30 56 30 by subm *A-5* (Rus), beached 46 33 42N 30 45 18E; 30.9.44 at Constanta; captured by Russians; 45 refloated, repaired; 48 returned Romania
Moldova 41 (Pan)
Prahova 5.3.41 *Tropicus* (Pan); 8.9.42 USMC, *Cloverbrook* (Pan); 22.2.47 *Tropicus* (Pan)

Spain

Losses through marine hazard
Arantzazu Mendi 9.5.39 Ashore near Kearney Point, Co Down; wreck BU
Cabo San Antonio 29.12.39 On fire 10 01N 21W, abandoned (5†); 31.12.39 wreck shelled by destroyer *Cassard* (Fra), sunk
Delfina 4.2.40 Ashore entrance bar on Guadalquivir R, between Chipiona and Bonanza; 6.2.40 sank
Fernando L de Ybarra 20.12.43 Stranded near Peniche, 40m N of Lisbon; sank
Hercules 9.3.40 Struck river bank, beached, near Km309, Parana R; broke in two, TL
Monte Aralar 2.1.41 Stranded at Bonanza; TL

Losses through Second World War causes
Badalona 13.12.41 Torpedoed by *U453*, sunk, 36 43N 03 30W (3†)
Banderas 18.2.40 Torpedoed by *U53*, sunk, 8m NW of Cabo Villano (22†, 7 surv)
Bartolo 6.3.43 Torpedoed by subm HMS *Taurus*, sunk, Duene, near Marseilles (8†, 22 surv)
Cabo Tortosa 18.9.40 Torpedoed by subm *Bagnolini* (Ita), sunk, 41 20N 09 16W (0†)
Cabo Villano 20.6.42 Reported torpedoed by subm, sunk, off Brazil
Castillo Montealegre 8.4.43 Torpedoed by *U123*, sunk, 09 46N 16 50W (12†, 29 surv)
Castillo Oropesa 8.11.41 Torpedoed in error by subm *Dandolo* (Ita), sunk, off Melilla in Spanish waters (0†)
Juan de Astigarraga 26.2.43 Torpedoed by subm HMS *Torbay*, sunk, 1m W of Cape Mele (4†, 22 surv)
Monte Gorbea 19.9.42 Torpedoed by *U512*, sunk, 14 55N 60W (52†, 66 surv)
Monte Igueldo 24.2.43 Torpedoed by subm *Barbarigo* (Ita), sunk, 04 46S 31 55W (1†, 34 surv)
Monte Moncayo 28.9.40 Struck mine, sunk, 22m from Capo Carbonara, Sardinia (4†)
Navemar 23.1.42 Torpedoed by subm *Barbarigo* (Ita), sunk, 36 48N 15 26W (2†, 34 surv)
Sabina 9.6.41 Struck mine, sunk, 36 05N 05 12W (0†)
Sebastian 30.10.43 Seized by GB, taken Gibraltar; 21.11.43 MoWT; 44 *Empire Tees* (Br); 50 *Tees* (Pan)

Losses through Spanish Civil War causes
Argentina 16–23.1.39 Bombed by Nationalist aircraft, on fire, sunk, Barcelona; 8.9.39

refloated, LU; 45 BU
Cabo San Agustin 39 Seized Feodosia by Russians; *Dnepr* (Rus) – *qv*; 10.41 sunk by German aircraft Black Sea
Ibai 39 Seized by Russians at Murmansk; *Dvina* (Rus)
Manuel Arnus 38 Interned Vera Cruz; 7.3.41 broke from moorings Vera Cruz, stranded on sand bank; 11.41 refloated, sold for use as target
Uruguay 37 Prison ship at Barcelona; 16–23.1.39 bombed by Nationalist aircraft; 23.1.39 sunk, Barcelona; 26–27.7.39 refloated; 40 BU

Changes of name, flag, role, disposals
Antonio Lopez 45 BU Bilbao
Castillo Andrade 8.1.44 On fire when leaving Vigo; 10.1.44 sunk near beach; 4.45 refloated, temporary repairs Vigo, then repaired Bilbao (ar 25.7.45, LU); raised, LU Bilbao; rebuilt; 48 *Antartico* (Spn)
Habana 39 LU Bilbao, later damaged by fire; 40–41 rebuilt as general cargo; 46–47 rebuilt, passenger accom re-installed
Manuel Calvo 10.39 Conv to general cargo
Montevideo 40 BU Spain
Saustan 41 *Castillo Campanario* (Spn); 43 *Campanario* (Spn)

Sweden

Losses through marine hazard
Atland 25.3.43 Collision (in convoy) with *Carso*, sank, 57 28N 01 40W (19†)
Bothnia 21.11.41 Sunk Brunsbüttel when at anchor; TL
Gudmundra 7.11.41 Aground near St Pierre Is, Nfl; TL
Kaaparen 14.6.42 Collision with *Tungsha* (Nor), sank, 3m off Halifax East LV
Shantung 25.12.41 On fire 59 50N 23 30W; 2.1.42 shelled, sunk, 62 28N 18 30W
Sumatra 12.11.39 Stranded near Moyapore Bar, R Hooghly, 30m below Calcutta; 13.11.39 sank
Wanja 15.10.39 Wrecked Burness, Orkey Islands

Losses through war causes
Abisko 11.4.43 Struck mine, sunk, near Borkum, 53 43N 06 01E(1†)
Ada Gorthon 22.6.42 Torpedoed by subm *SC-317* (Rus), sunk, 56 36 04N 16 46 08E (14†, 8 surv)
Agra 20.4.42 Torpedoed by *U654*, sunk, 34 40N 69 35W (6†, 33 surv)
Albania 23.10.39 Struck mine, sunk, 53 37 07N 00 20E (2†)
Algeria 18.1.43 Bombed (in German convoy) by British aircraft off Den Helder; taken in tow, abandoned, broke in two, sunk, 11m SW of Terschelling (2†, 19 surv)
Alida Gorthon 29.8.40 Torpedoed (convoy OA204 straggler) by *U100*, sunk, 59 09N 12 14W (11† + 18† surv from *Dalblair* – *qv*, 17 surv)
Amerikaland 3.2.42 Torpedoed by *U106*, sunk, 36 36N 74 10W (29†, 11 surv))
Andalusia 17.1.40 Sd Verdon for Gothenburg, missing; 21.1.40 believed torpedoed by *U55*, sunk, North Sea (21†, 0 surv)
Anna 3.6.42 Torpedoed (missed), shelled, by *U404*, sunk, 34 10N 68 22W (0†)
Anten 23.11.40 Torpedoed (in convoy OB244) by *U123* 56 57N 18 18W (1†, 32 surv); 25.11.40 sunk about 57 15N 17 40W
Argentina 6.7.42 Struck mine, sunk, 57 39N 07 10E (5†)
Atos 3.8.40 Torpedoed by *U57*, sunk, 56N 07W (1†, 27 surv)

Balticia 17.4.40 Stopped by German MTB, taken Haugesund; 13.5.40 seized Haugesund by Germans; 41 *Gotia* (Ger); 11.10.44 bombed by Russian aircraft, sunk, off Langfjord
Belgia 26.1.41 Bombed by German aircraft, sunk, near Sunk LV, Thames estuary
Bellona 40 *Lidingö* (Swe); 6.11.42 struck mine, sunk, 54 32 54N 11 19 05E (0†)
Blankaholm 18.8.42 Torpedoed (in convoy PG6/TAW13) by *U553*, sunk, 19 41N 76 50W (5†, 23 surv)
Boden 10.4.40 Shelled, sunk, Narvik roads; 6.53 refloated, BU Stavanger
Boren 41 *Skåne* (Swe); 6.3.42 shelled by subm *Finzi* (Ita), sunk, 20 50N 62 05W (36 surv)
Brageland 1.1.43 Torpedoed by *U164* 00 19N 37 35W (0†, 28 surv); sunk 00 19N 37 38W
Brasil 9.1.43 Struck mine, sunk, 58 48N 03 36E (0†, 42 surv)
Britt 4.10.39 Seized Rendsburg by Germans; 40 *Leba* (Ger); 44 KM; 45 MoWT, *Empire Conavon* (Br); 46 *Baltkon* (Br)
Buenos Aires 31.12.40 Bombed by German aircraft, on fire, Liverpool docks; CTL; engines removed; 42 *Demeter* (Br), used as stores vessel Scapa Flow
Bullaren 6.40 Transferred Bordeaux to Germans; 7.41 KM, Z-schiff *Tanga* (Ger); 6.42 target ship; 1.7.43 based Travemünde; 8.11.44 VTS; 20.12.44 bombed by Allied aircraft, badly damaged, Libau; 4.45 seized by GB, return to Sweden offered; 47 repaired for German owners

C F Liljevach 18.8.42 Torpedoed (in convoy) by subm *L-3* (Rus), sunk, 1m S of

Kungsgrund, Westervik approach (33†, 7 surv)
Calabria 22.6.41 Torpedoed (in convoy SL75) by *U141*, sunk, 280° 100m from Inishtrahull (3†, 21 surv)
Canton 9.8.40 Torpedoed by *U30*, sunk, 55 04N 11 21W (16†, 16 surv)
Castor 31.3.41 Torpedoed by *U46*, on fire, abandoned, 57 59N 32 08W; last seen 57 58N 30 31W (15†, 27 surv)
Convallaria 18.10.40 Torpedoed (in convoy SC7) by *U46* 57 22N 11 11W (0†); sunk 57 20N 10 40W

Dalarö 12.2.40 Torpedoed by *U53*, sunk, 56 44N 11 44W (1†)

Eknaren 1.7.42 Torpedoed by subm *I-16* (Jpn), sunk, 17 14S 39 42E
Erik Frisell 19.5.40 Shelled by *U37*, sunk, 57 25N 09 15W (0†, 34 surv)
Eros 9.4.40 At Bergen, German prize; 40 KM; 1.9.40 *Illkirch* (Ger); 6.45 at Narvik; 11.3.46 *Goplo* (Rus)
Etna 14.12.42 Stopped by *U217*, searched, abandoned, sunk, 17 50N 46 20W (0†, 27 surv)

Gallia 6.4.40 Seized Bergen by Germans; 12.40 prize; 41 *Deime* (Ger); 42 KM, netlayer *Netzleger XII*; 7.45 at Trondheim; 46 *Retiaire* (Fra)
Gothia 22.1.40 Torpedoed by *U51*, sunk, 57 46N 09 50W (12†, 12 surv)
Grängesberg 2.8.40 Seized Nantes by Germans; 40 (Ger); 8.40 KM, Seelöwe transport *H26*; 11.4.41 transport, *Grängesberg* (Ger); 21.9.42 *Argonaut* (Ger); 29.12.42 collision with *Ceuta* (Ger), sunk, off Kirkenes
Gunborg 18.10.40 Torpedoed (in convoy SC7) by *U46*, sunk, 57 14N 10 38W (0†, 23 surv)
Gunda 19.6.41 Bombed by aircraft 37 36 30N 09 53W; taken in tow, sunk, 269° 3.1m from Cap Sardao (0†, 21 surv)
Gustaf E Reuter 26.11.39 Torpedoed by *U48*, broke in two, 14m WNW from Fair Isle, 59 38N 02 03W (1†); 28.11.39 sunk by escort

Hammaren 22.8.42 Shelled, torpedoed (dispersed from convoy OS36), by *U507*, sunk, 13S 38 15W (5†, 26 surv)
Hedda 23.11.41 Struck mine, sunk, 53 35 47N 06 23 35E (0†)
Hedrun 16.8.40 Torpedoed by *U48*, sunk, 57 10N 16 37W (10†, 20 surv)

Industria 25.3.43 Torpedoed (in convoy) by *U518*, sunk, 11 40S 35 55W (1†, 3 pow, 22 surv)

Janus 20.10.40 Torpedoed (convoy HX79 straggler) by *U46*, sunk, 56 36N 15 03W (4†, 33 surv)
Japan 4.5.41 Torpedoed (dispersed from convoy OB310) by *U38*, sunk, 249m NW of Freetown (0†, 54 pow)

Kexholm 12.4.41 Bombed, shelled, by German aircraft, sunk, 59 50N 08 22W (0†, 35 surv)
Korshamn 17.3.41 Torpedoed (in convoy HX112) by *U99*, sunk, 61 09N 12 20W (26†, 11 surv)
Korsholm 13.4.42 Shelled by *U123*, blew up, sunk, 28 21N 80 22W (9†, 17 surv)

Lagaholm 1.3.40 Shelled by *U32*, on fire, 59 34N 05 10W (1†); 2.3.40 sunk 59 42N 05 35W
Liguria 29.3.41 Torpedoed (in convoy OB302) by *U46*, sunk, 59N 28W (19†, 10 surv)
Lima 12.9.42 Torpedoed by *U506*, sunk, 02 35N 11 22W (3†, 30 surv)
Luleå 11.7.42 Torpedoed by subm *S-7* (Rus), sunk, 57 39 15N 16 54 30E (1†, 33 surv)

Mertainen 16.4.40 Bombed by German aircraft, sunk, off Trondheim, during German invasion of Norway
Milos 11.3.43 Torpedoed (convoy SC121 straggler) by *U530*, sunk, 58N 15W (28†)
Monark 3.5.40 Seized Stavanger by Germans; 5.5.40 torpedoed by subm HMS *Severn*, sunk, 57 57N 06 13E (0†)
Mongolia 13.8.40 Struck mine, broke in two, sunk, 54 30N 10 30E
Murjek 5.3.41 Torpedoed (ind) by *U95*, sunk, WNW of Rockall (0 surv)

Nämdö 12.8.44 Struck mine, sunk, 53 51 11N 08 56 58E (4†, 23 surv)
Nanking 29.4.43 Torpedoed by *U123*, sunk 05 10N 11 10W (0†, 32 surv)
Narvik 29.4.43 Torpedoed by British aircraft, sunk, 53 27N 04 49E (0†, 38 surv)
Ningpo 25.12.41 Shelled by Japanese warships, on fire, Hong Kong; salved, repaired, by Japanese; 42 *Nippo Maru* (Jpn); 29.6.44 torpedoed by subm USS *Flasher*, sunk, 00 43N 105 31E
Norita 28.7.41 Torpedoed (in convoy OG69) by *U203*, sunk, 40 10N 15 30W (2†, 18 surv)
Nyland 28.9.39 Torpedoed by *U16*, sunk, 45m SW of Stavanger

O A Brodin 17.7.40 Torpedoed by *U57*, sunk, 59 22N 03 40W (3†, 21 surv)
Orania 11.2.40 Torpedoed by *U50*, sunk, about 60m NE of Shetlands (14†, 10 surv)

Pajala 18.1.40 Torpedoed by *U25*, sunk, 72° 10m from North Rona (0†)
Pegasus 23.7.43 Torpedoed by *U197*, sunk, 28 05S 37 40E (0†, 38 surv)

Peiping 9.9.42 Torpedoed by *U66*, sunk, 23 50N 50 10W (3†, 31 surv)

Remmaren 22.10.42 Struck mine, sunk, 58 29N 03 50E (0†, 37 surv)
Roxen 41 *Sigyn* (Swe) (4585gt); 9.8.42 struck mine, sunk, 52 55N 04 34W (0†)
Ruth 7.5.42 Bombed by British aircraft, badly damaged, off Vlieland, beached, CTL
Rydboholm 25.2.41 Torpedoed (in convoy OB290) by *U47*, bombed by German aircraft, sunk, 500m W of Ireland (–†, 28 surv)

Santos 24.2.40 Torpedoed (in convoy HN14) by *U63*, sunk, 59 17N 00 42W (31†, 12 surv)
Scandinavia 9.7.43 Stopped by *U510* 08 21N 48 30W (0†, 25 surv); torpedoed, sunk, 07 58N 48 06 05W

Scania (1999gt) 11.9.41 Torpedoed (in convoy SC42) by *U82*, damaged, 63 14N 37 12W; fell behind convoy, torpedoed by *U202*, sunk
Scania (1549gt) 13.12.42 Stopped by *U176*; sunk by explosive charge 01 36N 32 22W (0†, 25 surv)
Scotia 12.4.42 Struck mine, sunk, 52 27N 02 05 20E (1†, 25 surv)
Senta 12.6.42 Bombed by aircraft, sunk, off Borkum (0†, 18 surv)
Sicilia 27.5.43 Stopped by *U181*, abandoned, torpedoed, sunk, 24 31S 35 12E (0†)
Sigyn (1973gt) 1.8.40 Torpedoed by *U59*, sunk, 56 10N 09 25W (0†, 23 surv)
Silesia 25.9.39 Torpedoed by *U36*, sunk, 45m WNW of Ekkerøy (–†)
Siljan 26.9.40 Torpedoed by *U46*, sunk, 250m SW of Ireland (9†)
Sir Ernest Cassel 16.4.41 Sunk by aux cruiser *Thor* 32N 35W (0†)
Sonja 10.6.40 Struck mine, sunk, SE of Fiskholmens Lt (12†, 9 surv)
Stig Gorthon 5.7.41 Struck mine, sunk, off Borkum (0†, 25 surv)
Stockholm 10.3.40 Launched; 41 taken over by Italy; troop transport *Sabaudia* (Ita); 10.43 (Ger), accom ship, Trieste; 6.7.44 bombed by British aircraft, on fire, burnt out, aground, Muggia; 49 refloated, BU Muggia
Strassa 10.4.40 Damaged by bombing Narvik; 11.5.40 sunk, believed caused by internal explosion
Stureholm 12.12.40 Torpedoed (in convoy HX92) by *U96*, sunk, 57 50N 08 40W (0 surv)
Suecia 16.8.42 Torpedoed (convoy SC95 straggler) by *U596*, sunk, 55 43N 25 58W (12†. 37 surv)
Sumatra 42 Seized by Germans; 42 (Ger); 14.8.44 scuttled Gironde estuary; 45 raised
Svartön 3.1.40 Torpedoed (in convoy HN6) by *U58*, sunk, 57 48N 01 47W (20†, 11 surv)
Svea Jarl 9.1.43 Struck mine, sunk, 58 48N 03 36E (37†, 3 surv)
Sveaborg 10.4.40 Torpedoed by *U37*, sunk, 62 52N 07 34W (5†, 29 surv)

Thule 30.9.42 Reported torpedoed by subm, sunk, off Terschelling (9†, 13 surv)
Thyra 28.2.42 Struck mine near 54 Buoy, off Great Yarmouth (0†, 24 surv); taken in tow, sunk about 51 56N 01 37 54E
Tilia Gorthon 20.6.40 Torpedoed by *U38*, sunk, 48 32N 06 20W (10†, 11 surv)
Tisnaren 18.5.42 Torpedoed, shelled, by subm *Mano* (Ita), on fire, 03 38N 32 01W; 19.5.42 sunk 03N 33W (0†, 40 surv)
Tolken 12.5.42 Torpedoed (in convoy ONS92) by *U94*, sunk, 51 50N 33 35W (0†, 34 surv)
Torne 9–10.4.40 Shelled during British attack Narvik; 12.4.40 scuttled by Germans; 55 refloated, BU Stavanger
Trolleholm 25.3.41 Sunk by aux cruiser *Thor* S Atlantic (0†, – pow)
Tynningö 7.9.42 Struck mine, sunk, off Borkum (0†, 32 surv)

Uddeholm 6.7.42 Struck mine, sunk, 57 39N 07 10E (0†)

Vaalaren 5.4.43 Torpedoed (convoy HX231 straggler) by *U229*, sunk, 58N 34W (0 surv)
Valencia 25.10.42 Struck mine, sunk, 56 11 01N 12 16 06E (0†)
Valparaiso 31.12.40 Torpedoed (convoy HX97 straggler) by *U38*, sunk, 60 01N 23W (35†, + – passengers†)
Venezia 21.6.43 Torpedoed by *U513*, sunk, 25 50S 38 38W (0†, 27 surv)
Venezuela 17.4.41 Torpedoed (ind) by *U123*, sunk, 53N 18W (0 surv)
Vidar 19.7.43 Struck mine (0†), taken in tow, beached, Baltic; TL
Vingaland 8.11.40 Bombed by German FW200 Kondor aircraft, on fire, sunk, 55 41N 18 24W (6†, 19 surv)
Vollrath Tham 10.11.41 Struck mine (laid by British aircraft), sunk, 1.5m from Hubertgat (0†)

Yngaren 12.1.42 Torpedoed (convoy HX168 straggler) by *U43*, sunk, 57N 26W (38†, 2 surv)

Struck mine, sunk, postwar
Acacia 12.4.47 Struck mine, sunk, off Falsterbo

Changes of name, flag, role, disposals, etc
Abadan 42 *Leo* (Swe); 46 *Snipaas* (Nor)
Balaklava 40 *Trykon* (Swe)
Bardaland 43–44 Swedish Red Cross relief ship, Mediterranean

Barranduna 42–45 LU Gothenburg
Bellona 40 Completed; LU Gothenburg; 45 *K J Knudsen* (Nor)
Boreland 44 Swedish Red Cross relief ship, Mediterranean
Britannia 39–8.45 LU; 9.45–4.46 MoT charter
Capella 42 *Grisslehamn* (Swe); 46 *Atalanta* (Swe)
Dahlia 25.5.40 Seized Bergen by Germans; 12.40 prize; 41 *Johannes Willi* (Ger); 45 *Dahlia* (Swe)
Drottningholm 44 Repatriation ship
Fenris 1.44 Swedish Red Cross relief ship, Mediterranean
Formosa 9.44 Swedish Red Cross relief ship, Mediterranean
Gudrun 43 *Iris* (Swe)
Hallaren 43–44 Swedish Red Cross relief ship, Mediterranean
Hjelmaren 44 *Braila* (Swe)
I W Winck 40 (Pan); 42 *Isobel* (Swe); 46 *Lotus* (Nor)
Kalmia 43 sold; 45 sold
Kolsnaren 2.44 *Rigoletto* (Swe)
Kungsholm 42–48 *John Ericsson* (US)
Lena 44 *Lena Brodin* (Swe)
Malaren 1.5.40 MoWT charter; 42 *Salén* (Swe); 23.8.45 off charter
Miramar 30.12.41 Seized Saigon by Japanese; 4.43 released; recovered after war
Mongabarra 8.43–44 Swedish Red Cross relief ship, Mediterranean
Nagara 44 Swedish Red Cross relief ship, Mediterranean
Oljaren 41 *Rio* (Swe); 43 *Bern* (Swe)
Oxelosund 10.4.40 Attacked by aircraft, damaged, Narvik; 8.5.40 sunk Narvik harbour; 47 refloated, repaired Gothenburg; 40 *Laidaure* (Swe)
Patricia 40 Chartered, then sold, Swedish navy, destroyer depot ship
Pedro Christophersen 2.44 Swedish Red Cross relief ship, for Piræus
Pollux 44 *Nordanbris* (Swe)
Procyon · 42 *Sunnanbris* (Swe)
Roslagen 41 *Fogdö* (Swe)
Tamara 43–44 Swedish Red Cross relief ship, Mediterranean
Theodor 41 *Havsbris* (Swe); 47 *Holmy* (Swe)
Travancore 44 Swedish Red Cross relief ship, Mediterranean
Trione 42 *Lunaria* (Swe)
Ulla 41 *Nordia* (Swe)
Vasaholm 43–44 Swedish Red Cross relief ship, cargoes to Greece
Yarrawonga 43–44 Swedish Red Cross relief ship, Mediterranean

Switzerland

Loss through marine hazard
Atlas 3.11.45 Stranded Bougainville Reef; TL

Changes of name, flag, role, disposals, etc
St Cergue (Pan) 10.7.41 (Swi)

Turkey

Losses through war causes
Beme (Pan) 11.7.40 Shelled by subm *Capitano Tarantini* (Ita), sunk, 33 12N 33 38E (0†)
Dogu 31.8.39 Completed, but not delivered; 40 *Lüderitzbucht* (Ger); 25.2.41 KM, *Duala* (Ger); 5.3.41 KM; 28.6.41 commd U-boat depot, Pillau; 43 U-boat target ship, Pillau; 5.7.45 *Empire Ock* (Br), troopship; 49 *Petr Veliki* (Rus); 47 *Jagiello* (Pol; 49 *Petr Veliki* (Rus)
Egemen 20.12.39 Completed but not delivered; 5.3.41 *Swakopmund* (Ger); commd KM target ship Kiel; 1.6.41 U-boat depot, Pillau; 20.8.43 target ship; 3.5.45 sunk off Staberhuk, NE of Fehmarn (0†); 50 wreck BU
Krom 30.3.44 Believed struck mine, sunk, off Marmarice, Turkey
Salon 40 KM, *Windhuk* (Ger); 8.5.45 at Hamburg; 45 *Primorje* (Rus)
Savas 15.6.40 Completed but not delivered; 5.3.41 *Daressalam* (Ger); 25.8.41 commd KM U-boat depot and target ship; 1.1.42 based Memel; 16.7.44 E-boat depot; 16.9.44 bombed by Allied aircraft, burnt out, Blücherbrücke, Kiel; 45 at Kiel aground at stern; 45 refloated, taken Hamburg; accom ship, Hamburg; 47 (US); 53 BU Grays

USSR (Union of Soviet Socialist Republics)

Losses through marine hazard

Bolshoi Shantar 13.2.43 Wrecked Bering Is
Dvinoles 1–4.2.42 Collision with *Havprins* (*qv*), sank, 47 14N 50 44W (0†)
Ilich 23.6.44 Capsized, sunk, in US shipyard, Portland OR; wreck BU
Kolkhosnik 16.1.42 Stranded on Sambro Shoal, Maine; sank
Kuzbass 26.9.44 Ashore 64 24N 173 57E; TL
Pavlin Vinogradov 23.4.44 Explosion, sank, 53 12N 160 22W (33†, 9 surv)
Timlat 11.1.44 Damaged in heavy pack ice, sank, near Cape Shipunski (–†, 14 surv)
Turksib 21.11.42 Ashore Scotch Gap, Unimak Is, Alaska; TL
Uzbekistan 1.4.43 Wrecked 48 43N 125 03W
Vatslav Vorovski 3.4.41 Ashore Cape Disappointment WA, mouth of Columbia R; TL

Losses through war causes

Abkhaziya 10.6.42 Bombed by German Ju88 aircraft, sunk, southern bay, Sevastopol
Andrei Zhdanov 11.11.41 Struck mine, sunk, off Hangö
Angarstroi 24.4.42 Stopped by Japanese warship about 130m from Japan; proceeded Japan, released; 1.5.42 torpedoed by subm USS *Grenadier*, sunk, 32m off SW Kyushu (0†, 32 surv)
Armeniya 7.11.41 Bombed by German aircraft, sunk, off Yalta
Ashkabad 30.4.42 Torpedoed by *U402* 34 19N 76 31W; 3.5.42 shelled by US warship, sunk

Belorussia 3.3.44 Torpedoed by subm USS *Sandlance*, sunk, La Perouse Strait (2 surv)

Chapaev 8.1.42 Attacked by German aircraft, sunk, Feodosia

Dekabrist 4.11.42 Attacked by German Ju88 aircraft of I/KG30, sunk, 75 30N 27 10E
Dikson 5.10.43 Torpedoed by *U302*, sunk, 75 37N 89 10E (0†)
Dnepr 3.10.41 Bombed by German aircraft, sunk, off Anapa (–†)
Donbass 7.11.42 Bombed by German aircraft, sunk by destroyer *Z27* (German 5 Destroyer fl) 76 24N 41 30E

Emba 30.7.43 Torpedoed by *U24*, sunk, at quay Sukhumi harbour

Gruziya 13.6.42 Sunk by German aircraft off Sevastopol

Ilmen 17.2.43 Torpedoed (in convoy) by subm USS *Sawfish*, sunk, 30 56N 136 30E (7†, 32 surv)
Ivan Papanin 41 Badly damaged, beached, near Suursaari (26.5.41 sd Leningrad for Stettin, ar prev to 6.6.41)

Josif Stalin 3.12.41 Struck mine, Corbetha mine barrage, off Hangö (–†); aground, captured by Germans, towed in; CTL, BU

Kaganovich 22.6.41 Seized German Baltic port by Germans; 41 prize; 42 *Libau* (Ger); 18.10.42 torpedoed by subm *Uredd* (Nor), damaged, 67N 12 46E; beached, CTL
Kalinin c15.1.43 Sunk Tuapse; cause unknown (0 surv)
Kamenetz-Podolsk 30.8.41 Attacked by German aircraft, sunk, off Elkjotshan, Black Sea, 44 49N 36 06E
Kharkov 1.43 Captured Black Sea by Germans; *Boy Feddersen* (Ger); 10.8.43 attacked by Russian aircraft off Crimea, damaged, taken in tow for Sevastopol; 11.8.43 torpedoed by subm *D-4* (Rus), sunk, 44 58N 33 08E
Kiev 13.4.42 Torpedoed (in convoy QP10) by *U435*, sunk, 73 22N 28 48E
Kola 15.7.42 Struck mine, sunk, off Kertsch
Krasny Partizan 29.1.43 Torpedoed (ind) by *U255*, sunk, Barents Sea (0 surv)
Krasny Profintern 14.2.43 Torpedoed by *U19*, sunk, SW of Tuapse (1†)
Krechet 25.12.41 Bombed by Japanese aircraft, sunk, Hong Kong
Kreml 5.5.43 Torpedoed by *U9*, damaged, 22m S of Cape Koder; TL
Kuznetz Lesov 23.11.42 Torpedoed (in convoy QP15) by *U601*, sunk, 75 30N 08E

Lenin 11.8.41 Struck mine, sunk, off Sevastopol

Maria Ulyanova 26.8.41 Torpedoed by *U571*, damaged, N of Cape Teriberka; beached, declared TL; 31.12.42 reported anchored Kola Inlet
Mikoyan 3.10.42 Torpedoed by subm *I-162* (Jpn), sunk, 19 24N 85 24E (0†, 99 surv)

Perekop 18.12.41 Bombed by Japanese aircraft, sunk, near Senoa, Natuna Is, NEI (8†, 32 surv)
Petrovski 27.8.43 Torpedoed (in convoy) by *U354*, damaged, 75 15N 84 30E; 28.8.43

torpedoed, probably by *U302*, sunk

Rodina 5.7.42 Struck British mine (in convoy QP13) in bad weather, sunk, 66 34N 23 14W (0†, 25 surv)

Shchors (3770gt) 14.10.42 Struck mine (laid 13.10.42 by *U592*) off Yugor Strait, 178° 15m from Greben Lt Point, beached; CTL
Sergei Kirov 5.10.43 Torpedoed (in convoy VA18) by *U703*, sunk, 20m from Izvesty Island
Sergei Lazo 25.12.41 Bombed by Japanese aircraft, sunk, Hong Kong; refloated; 20.10.45 aground Tsun Wan
Sibir 41 Hospital ship; 19.8.41 bombed by German aircraft, sunk, Gulf of Finland (400†, 900 surv)
Simferopol 25.12.41 Bombed by Japanese aircraft, sunk, Hong Kong; refloated; 20.10.45 ashore Tsun Wan; 50 BU Hong Kong
Sovetskaya Neft 31.3.43 Torpedoed by *U24*, sunk, Gagry Bay, Black Sea
Stalingrad 13.9.42 Torpedoed (in convoy PQ18) by *U408* and *U589*, sunk, 75 52N 07 55E
Svanetia 17.4.42 Bombed by German aircraft, sunk, Sevastopol
Svirstroi 25.12.41 Bombed by Japanese aircraft, sunk, Hong Kong; 20.10.45 aground Tsun Wan, Hong Kong; 50 BU Hong Kong

Tbilisi 6.9.43 Struck mine (laid 28.8.43 by *U636*), sunk, off Enisei estuary, Kara Sea (0†)
Transbalt 13.6.45 Torpedoed in error by subm USS *Spadefish*, sunk, 45 42N 140 41E (0†, 99 surv)
Tuapse 4.7.42 Torpedoed by *U129*, sunk, 22 13N 86 06W (8†, 38 surv)

Ukraina 2.7.42 Bombed by German aircraft, sunk, Novorossisk

Valerian Kuibyshev 2.4.42 Torpedoed by German aircraft, sunk, 44 57N 36 58E
Varlaam Avanesov 19.12.41 Torpedoed by *U652*, sunk, 39 27N 26 05E
Volgoles 22.6.41 Seized at German Baltic port by Germans; 42 *Colmar* (Ger); 19.8.44 attacked by TKAs (Rus), sunk, off Vardø (0 surv)
Vtoraya Pyatiletka 29.8.41 Attacked by German Ju88 aircraft, sunk, near Suursaari

Changes of name, flag, sold, disposals
Dnestr 22.6.41 Seized German Baltic port; 41 prize; 41 *Pernau* (Ger); 45 *Dnestr* (Rus)
Magnitogorsk 22.6.41 Seized Danzig; 3.8.41 *Trostburg* (Ger); 21.12.44 bombed by Allied aircraft, damaged, Hamburg; 47 refloated; 50 repaired; *Magnitogorsk* (Rus)
Sakhalin 45 *Krasnoyarsk* (Rus)

United States of America

To effectively operate in wartime about three-quarters of US merchant vessels were requisitioned during February–April 1942 by the US War Shipping Administration, formed to take over the merchant shipping interests of the United States Maritime Commission. This arrangement came to an end in September 1946. Vessels excluded from the arrangement were those owned or operated by the US Navy, US Army and US Coast Guard and certain defence-orientated vessels. In these lists vessels indicted as owned by USMC were transferred to US WSA during February–April 1942, and had, where appropriate, reverted to USMC by September 1946.

Losses through marine hazard
Admiral Day 6.40 Sold (Br); 18.9.40 ashore NE corner Canton Island; TL
Admiral Wiley 13.6.40 Wrecked Kitava Island, off New Guinea
Almeria Lykes 40 *Almeria* (Ita); 20.5.40 struck rock N coast of Trinidad; TL
Altair 21.11.43 Collision with *Bostonian* (*qv*), badly damaged, on fire, off Delaware Bay (10†, 33 surv); CTL, BU

Brazos 13.1.42 Collision with escort carrier *Archer*, sank, 32 48N 74 20W

Cape Clear 8.41 Completed as *Oregon* (US); 10.12.41 collision with US government vessel, sank, 41 20N 70 02W
Cassimir 26.2.42 Collision with *Lara* (*qv*), sank, 33 56N 77 56W (0†)
Cities Service Boston 16.5.43 Aground Bass Point NSW, TL
Cities Service Denver 24.3.41 Explosion, on fire, about 80m off Beaufort NC; 26.3.41 sank
Coldbrook 3.6.42 Stranded 50 25N 146 20W, TL (0†)
Comet 41 USN, stores ship USS *Pollux* (AKS 2); 18.2.42 ashore in gale Laron Head, entrance St Lawrence harbour Nfl; broke up in heavy weather; TL
Crown City 31.8.42 Ashore Sledge Island Lt, near Nome, Alaska; TL

Dixie Sword 11.2.42 Aground 41 35N 69 59; 12.2.42 broke up; TL

Edgar F Luckenbach 21.7.39 Wrecked near New Orleans
Exminster 19.4.42 Collision with *Algic* (*qv*) while anchored 41 45N 70 28W, holed, submerged; salved, raised; towed Brooklyn, hulked; 46 BU

Gulfland 20.10.43 Collision, badly damaged, on fire, 26 57N 80 01W, stranded on reef, broke in two; afterpart salved, towed Jacksonville; forepart TL

Hollywood 29.11.45 Aground 45 28 30N 10 11 30W; TL

Independence Hall 7.3.42 Struck reef off Sable Is, broke in two; 8.3.42 both sections floated off, sank, 43 55N 59 55W

J E O'Neil 41 *Ponta Verde* (Brz); 23.4.41 ashore Straggler Island, entrance to Santiago, Chile; broke in three; TL
Julia Luckenbach 22.9.43 Collision with *British Resolution* (*qv*), sank, 34 33S 22 06E

Kenmar 10.12.45 Aground Proposti Lt, Gargons Heads, Gulf of Manfredonia

Lancaster 30.12.42 Ashore off Casablanca; 31.12.42 broke up, TL
Lightburne 10.2.39 Ashore Block Island, broke up; TL
Lillian 26.2.39 Collision in fog with *Wiegand* (*qv*) off Barnegat LV; 27.2.39 sank 40 01N 73 31W; wreck removed
Lillian Luckenbach 27.3.43 Collision (in convoy ON48) with *Cape Henlopen* (US), sank, 36 58N 75 25W (0†)
Lipscomb Lykes 18.1.43 Ashore Durand Reef, SE of Loyalty Islands, TL

Mahukona 40 *Santa Clara* (Brz); 15.3.41 in distress in severe weather 30 48N 68 42W; abandoned (0 surv)
Maiden Creek 31.12.42 Abandoned 39 36N 71W, foundered (–†)
Mapele 15.1.43 Stranded on rocks in snowstorm 55 25N 160 12W (2†); TL
Mauna Ala 10.12.41 Ashore 4m S of mouth of Columbia R, 45 30N 122 45W; TL
Munami 40 *Lisieux* (Fra); 27.11.40 abandoned 48 20N 47 15W; sank

Narbo 21.2.45 Stranded Old Providence Is, badly damaged; refloated, ar Mobile, sold for BU
Northern Sword 8.2.43 Collision (in convoy GZ21) with *Fisher Ames* (US), sunk, 10 28N 79 32W

Oklahoman 7.7.42 Stranded near Dassen Is, Cape of Good Hope; refloated, sank in tow 1.25m W of Robben Is
Oneida 4.5.43 Foundered 31 24N 75 20W

Pan Royal 11.2.43 Collision (in convoy UGS5) with *Evita* (*qv*) and *George Davis* (US), sunk, 36 40N 67 20W (8†)
Panuco 18.8.41 On fire at Pier 27, Brooklyn, badly damaged; CTL, BU
Point Vincente 26.3.39 Stranded Bona Is; refloated, dismantled Balboa, towed out to sea, sunk
President Adams 11.40 USMC (US); 1.41 *President Grant* (US); 3.42 troopship; 26.2.44 aground Ulna Reef, New Guinea, 11 07N 150 58E; 17.6.44 declared CTL
President Polk 40 USMC, troopship *President Taylor* (US); 14.2.42 stranded off Canton Is, abandoned (0†); destroyed by Japanese aircraft attack
President Quezon 27.1.40 Stranded off Tanega Shima, S Japan; sunk 30 16 25N 130 56 50E

San José 17.1.42 Collision with *Santa Elisa* (*qv*), sank, 39 14N 74 14W (0†)
San Juan 30.7.41 Collision, sank, 28 32N 33 03E (0†)
San Lucas 40 *R J Cullen* (Br); 15.1.42 wrecked 2m NE of Castlebay, Outer Hebrides, in 56 57 23N 07 25 18W
Southlure 39 Sold Brazil; 40 *Tirandantes* (Brz); 13.2.45 collision with *Albert P Rider* (US), sunk, off Guianas

Timber Rush 3.3.40 Wrecked about 85m S of Acapulco

Ulysses 40 Conv to tanker; 42 *San Blas* (Arg); 27.9.44 explosion, on fire, sank, La Plata; wreck BU

Walter Jennings 41 *Vandalia* (US); 9.10.45 stranded Naha harbour, Okinawa; TL
West Jaffrey 8.2.42 Ashore near Peases Is LH, NS, 43 36N 66 30W; TL

Transferred Ministry of Shipping/War Transport and became losses through marine hazard
Anacortes 40 MoWT (Br); 41 *Empire Mallard* (Br); 26.9.41 collision with *Empire Moon* (Br) in fog, sank, near Point Amour, Belle Isle Strait, NS
Coaxet 41 MoWT, *Empire Kingfisher* (Br); 18.1.42 struck submerged object 4m S of

Cape Sable; 19.1.42 sank while at anchor S of Bantam Rocks buoy; TL
Duquesne 41 MoWT, *Empire Kudu* (Br); 26.9.41 ashore 6m W of Point Amour, Belle Isle Strait; abandoned, TL
Edgefield 41 MoWT, *Empire Ibex* (Br); 1.7.43 collision with *Empire MacAlpine* (Br) 53 30N 36 25W; 2.7.43 abandoned; 3.7.43 sank 53 36N 36 16W
Harpoon 40 MoWT, *Empire Tarpon* (Br); 6.10.42 engine trouble, in distress 57 20N 15 09W; 13.10.42 taken in tow; 14.10.42 sprang leak, abandoned, sank 57 24N 07 45W
Tolosa 40 MoWT, *Empire Dorado* (Br); 20.11.41 collision with *Theomitor* (*qv*) 57 58N 20 38W, taken in tow; 22.11.42 sank
West Harshaw 40 MoWT, *Empire Oryx* (Br); 41 *Empire Robin* (Br); 42 *Ferdinand Bol* (Ne); 29.7.42 collision with *Norse King* (*qv*), sunk, 45 21N 59 28W

Losses through war causes
Admiral Laws 40 *Suriyothai Nawa* (Tha); 42 *Columbine* (SA); 16.6.44 torpedoed by *U198*, sunk, 32 44S 17 22E (23†, 29 surv)
Afoundria 5.5.42 Torpedoed by *U108* 19 59N 73 26W (0†); sunk 8m N of Cape St Nicholas Mole, NW Haiti
Agwimonte 28.5.43 torpedoed (in convoy CD20) by *U177*, sunk, 34 57S 19 33E (0†, 69 surv)
Alamar 27.5.42 Attacked (in convoy PQ16) by German Ju88 or He111 aircraft, on fire, abandoned, 100m SE of Bear Island (0†, 45 surv; 23† returning from Russia to US); sunk by subm HMS *Trident*
Alaskan 28.11.42 Torpedoed, shelled, by *U172*, sunk, 03 58N 26 19W (7†, 39 surv)
Alcoa Pilgrim 28.5.42 Torpedoed by *U502*, sunk, 16 28N 67 37W (31†, 9 surv)
Alcoa Puritan 6.5.42 Shelled, torpedoed, by *U507*, sunk, 28 35N 88 22W (0†, 54 surv)
Allan Jackson 18.1.42 Torpedoed by *U66*, on fire, broke in two, sunk, 35 57N 74 20W (22†, 13 surv)
Almeria Lykes 41 MoWT, *Empire Condor* (Br); 42 *Almeria Lykes* (US); 13.8.42 attacked (in Opn 'Pedestal' convoy WS21S) by E-boats *S30*, *S36* (Ger), and MTBs *MAS554*, *MAS557* (Ita), torpedoed, sunk, 36 40N 11 35E (0†, 94 surv)
Amapala (Hon) 14.5.42 Shelled by *U507* 26 40N 89 15W, damaged, taken in tow by USCG cutter; 16.5.42 sunk by USCG cutter
American 11.6.42 Torpedoed by *U504*, sunk, 17 58N 84 28W (4†, 34 surv)
American Farmer 2.40 *Ville de Liège* (Bel); 13.4.41 torpedoed by *U52*, sunk, 59 40N 29 50W (–†, 10 surv)
American Importer 2.40 *Ville de Gand* (Bel); 18.8.40 torpedoed by *U48*, sunk, 55 32N 16W (15†, 38 surv)
American Leader (6778gt) 10.9.42 Shelled, torpedoed, by aux cruiser *Michel*, sunk, 34 21S 2E (11†, 47 pow)
American Merchant 2.40 *Ville de Namur* (Bel); 19.6.40 torpedoed by *U52*, 46 25N 04 35W (25†, 54 surv)
American Shipper 2.40 *Ville de Mons* (Bel); 2.9.40 torpedoed by *U47*, sunk, 58 20N 12W (0†, 54 surv)
American Trader 2.40 *Ville de Hasselt* (Bel); 30.8.40 torpedoed by *U46* SW of Lewis (0†, 63 surv); 31.8.40 sunk 57 40N 09W
American Traveler 2.40 *Ville D'Arlon* (Bel); 2.12.40 torpedoed (in convoy HX90) by *U47*, sunk, N Atlantic
Andrea F Luckenbach 10.3.43 Torpedoed (in convoy HX228) by *U221*, sunk, 51 04N 29 40W (21†, 63 surv)
Angelina 17.10.42 Torpedoed (in convoy ON137) by *U618* 49 39N 30 20W (47†, 8 surv); 18.10.42 sunk
Antinous 23.9.42 Torpedoed (ind) by *U515*, sunk, 08 58N 50 33W; 24.9.42 torpedoed by *U512*, sunk in tow 09 22N 60 09W (0†, 47 surv)
Ario 15.3.42 Torpedoed, shelled, by *U158* 34 20N 76 39W (8†, 28 surv); abandoned 34 14N 76 27W; sunk
Arkansan 16.6.42 Torpedoed by *U126*, sunk, 12 07N 62 51W (4†, 36 surv)
Arlyn 28.8.42 Torpedoed (in convoy SG6S) by *U165*, damaged; torpedoed by *U517*, sunk, 51 53N 55 48W (9†, 45 surv)
Astral 2.12.41 Torpedoed by *U43*, sunk, 35 40N 24W (37†, 0 surv)
Atlantic Sun 17.2.43 Torpedoed (in convoy ONS65) by *U607*, broke in two, sunk, 51N 41W (65†, 1 pow)
Atlas 9.4.42 Torpedoed by *U552*, on fire, sunk, 34 27N 76 16W (2†, 32 surv)
Australia 16.3.42 Torpedoed by *U332*, on fire, 35 07N 75 22W (4†, 36 surv); stern resting on bottom, bows afloat; 20.3.42 sunk; 8.54 wreck sold for BU
Azalea City 16.2.42 Torpedoed, probably by *U432*, sunk, 38N 73W (38†, 0 surv)

Baja California (Hon) 19.7.42 Torpedoed by *U84*, sunk, 25 14N 82 27W (3†, 34 surv)
Barbara 7.3.42 Torpedoed by *U126*, on fire, sunk, 20 10N 73 05W (34†, 54 surv)
Barreado 40 *Ruth* (US); 29.6.42 torpedoed by *U153*, sunk, 21 44N 74 05W (35†, 4 surv)
Beaconlight 40 (Pan); 16.7.42 torpedoed by *U160*, sunk, 10 59N 61 05W; sunk by tug *Roode Zee* 10 58N 61 10W
Beatrice 24.5.42 Shelled by *U558*, on fire, 17 23N 76 53W (1†, 30 surv); 25.5.52 sunk
Bellingham 22.9.42 Torpedoed (in convoy QP14) by *U435*, sunk, 71 23N 11 03W (0†, 49 resc, and 26 surv from other vessels)

Benjamin Brewster 10.7.42 While at anchor, torpedoed by *U67*, sunk, 29 05N 90 05W (27†, 15 surv); 9.51 salved for BU
Bensalem 41 *Alcoa Carrier* (US); 26.5.42 torpedoed, shelled, by *U103*, sunk, 18 45N 79 50W (0†, 33 surv)
Bienville 6.4.42 Bombed by Japanese carrier-based aircraft, on fire, Bay of Bengal; shelled by Japanese heavy cruiser, sunk, 17 48N 84 09W (24†, 17 surv)
Birmingham City 9.1.43 Torpedoed (in convoy TB1) by *U124*, sunk, 07 12N 55 37W (10†, 46 surv)
Black Eagle 41 *Hoosier* (US); 9.7.42 attacked (in convoy PQ17) by German aircraft of KG30, damaged, abandoned; 10.7.42 unsuccessful attempt by corvette HMS *Poppy* to sink by shelling; torpedoed by *U376*, sunk, 69 45N 38 35E
Black Falcon 41 *Mary Luckenbach* (US); 13.9.42 attacked (in convoy PQ18) by German torpedo aircraft of KG30 76 05N 10E (65†, 0 surv); aircraft crashed into vessel, vessel blew up, sunk
Black Point 5.5.45 Torpedoed in fog by *U853*, sunk, 41 19 02N 71 25 01W (12†, 34 surv)
Brazos 19.1.42 Torpedoed by *U123*, sunk, 34 30N 75 30W
Brilliant 18.11.42 Torpedoed (in convoy SC109) by *U43*, N Atlantic (11†, 44 surv); 24.11.42 reached St John's Nfl; 20.1.43 broke in two, forepart sank, while in tow St John's–Halifax; 25.1.43 afterpart sank in tow 45 18N 55 12W
Broad Arrow 8.1.43 Torpedoed (in convoy TB1) by *U124*, on fire, sunk, 07 23N 55 48W (23†, 24 surv)
Buenaventura 40 *Caribsea* (US); 11.3.42 torpedoed by *U158*, sunk, 34 35N 76 18W (–†, 7 surv)
Byron D Benson 4.4.42 Torpedoed by *U552*, on fire, sunk, 36 08N 75 32W (9†, 28 surv); 7.4.42 sunk

C J Barkdull 40 (Pan); 10.1.42 torpedoed (convoy UGS3 straggler) by *U632*, sunk, W of Ireland
C O Stillman (Pan) 6.6.42 Torpedoed by *U68*, sunk, 17 33N 67 55W (30†, 12 surv)
Caddo 23.11.42 Torpedoed (ind) by *U518*, sunk, 42 45N 48 27W (52†, 6 surv, 2 pow)
California 13.8.42 Torpedoed, shelled, by subm *Reginaldo Giuliani* (Ita) 09 21N 34 35W, sunk 09 24N 33 02W (1†, 35 surv)
Camden 4.10.42 Torpedoed by subm *I-25* (Jpn) 43 43N 124 54W (1†, 47 surv), taken in tow; 10.10.42 on fire, sunk, 46 46 38N 124 31 15W
Capac 40 *Cardina* (Pan); 15.6.42 torpedoed, shelled, by subm *Archimede* (Ita), sunk, 04 45N 40 55W (0†, 34 surv)
Cape Ann 3.41 Completed as *Alcoa Prospector* (US); 5.7.43 torpedoed by subm *I-27* (Jpn) 24 21N 59 04E, damaged; towed Persian Gulf, temp repairs; 2.44 towed Karachi, then Bombay; 45 ret USMC damaged; sold; 50 BU Philadelphia
Cape May 1.41 Completed as *Alcoa Pathfinder* (US); 21.11.42 torpedoed (ind) by *U181*, sunk, 26 45S 33 10E (5†, 56 surv)
Capillo 8.12.41 Bombed by Japanese aircraft Manila Bay, on fire, abandoned, listed (0†, 41 surv); 11.12.41 sunk; TL
Cardonia 7.3.42 Shelled, on fire, torpedoed, by *U126*, sunk, 19 53N 73 27W (1†, 38 surv)
Carlton 5.7.42 Torpedoed (dispersed from convoy PQ17) by *U88*, on fire, sunk, 76 14N 24E (3†, 42 resc/pow)
Carolyn 3.42 Commd USN, Q-ship USS *Atik*; 27.3.42 torpedoed, shelled, by *U123* 36N 70W (47†, 0 surv); 30.3.42 sighted, presumed sunk same day
Carrabulle 26.5.42 Stopped, shelled, torpedoed, by *U106*, sunk, 26 18N 89 21W (22†, 18 surv)
Castilla (Hon) 6.6..42 Torpedoed by *U107*, sunk, 21 03N 83 30W (24†, 35 surv)
Catahoula 5.4.42 Torpedoed by *U154*, sunk, 19 16N 68 12W (7†, 38 surv)
Ceiba (Hon) 17.3.42 Torpedoed by *U124*, sunk, 35 43N 73 49W (44†, 6 surv)
Challenger 17.5.42 Torpedoed by *U155*, sunk, 12 11N 61 18W (8†, 63 surv)
Charles G Black 40 Conv to ore carrier *Venore* (US); 23.1.42 torpedoed by *U66*, on fire, sunk, 34 50N 75 20W (17†, 23 surv)
Charles Pratt 40 (Pan); 21.12.40 torpedoed by *U65*, sunk, 08 26N 16 50W (2†, 50 surv)
Chattanooga City 22.2.43 Torpedoed (in convoy ON166) by *U606*, sunk, 40 53N 34 32W (0†, 52 surv)
Cherokee 3.42 WSA transport; 16.6.42 torpedoed (in convoy XB25) by *U87*, sunk, 42 11N 69 25W (86†, 83 surv)
Chickasaw City 7.10.42 Torpedoed (in convoy) by *U172*, sunk, 34 05S 17 16E (7†, 43 resc; surv on board *Zaandam* (*qv*), 18† when *Zaandam* sunk)
Chilore 15.7.42 Torpedoed (in convoy KS520) by *U576*, damaged, 34 47N 75 22W; struck mine when approaching Cape Hatteras under escort; beached near Norfolk in 36 57N 76 00 44.5W (2†, 47 surv); 8.54 wreck sold for BU
China Arrow 5.2.42 Torpedoed, shelled, by *U103*, sunk, 37 44N 73 18W (0†, 37 surv)
Cities Service Empire 22.2.42 Torpedoed by *U128*, sunk, 28 25N 80 22W (12†, 38 surv)
Cities Service Missouri 13.3.43 Torpedoed (in convoy GAT49) by *U68*, sunk, 14 50N 76 46W (2†, 52 surv)
Cities Service Toledo 12.6.42 Torpedoed by *U158*, on fire, sunk, 29 02N 91 59W (15†, 31 surv)
City of Alma 2.6.42 Torpedoed by *U159*, sunk, 23N 62 30W (29†, 10 surv)
City of Atlanta 19.1.42 Torpedoed by *U123*, sunk, 35 42N 75 21W (44†, 3 surv)
City of Birmingham 30.6.42 Torpedoed by *U202*, sunk, 35 10N 70 53W (12†, 369 surv)

City of Flint 25.1.43 Torpedoed (convoy UGS4 straggler) by *U575*, sunk, 34 47N 31 30W (6†, 1 pow, 58 surv)
City of Joliet 27.5.42 Attacked 10 times (in convoy PQ16) by German Ju88 or He111 aircraft, leaking, abandoned; 28.5.42 sunk 73 41N 26 06E (0†, 48 surv)
City of Los Angeles 10.40 USN; 41 transport USS *George F Elliot* (AP 13); 8.8.42 attacked by Japanese aircraft, bombed, struck by crippled Japanese bomber, on fire, sunk, Tulagi
City of New York 29.3.42 Torpedoed by *U160*, sunk, 35 16N 74 25W (26†, 118 surv)
City of Rayville 8.11.40 Struck mine (laid by aux minelayer *Passat*), broke in two, sunk, 38 51S 143 39E (1†, 38 surv)
Clare 20.5.42 Torpedoed by *U103*, sunk, 21 35N 84 43W (0†, 43 surv)
Coamo 1.42 US Army transport; 2.12.42 torpedoed (ind) by *U604*, sunk, 150m off Ireland (186†, 0 surv)
Cold Harbor 40 (Pan); 15.6.42 torpedoed by *U502*, sunk, 11 40N 62 55W (9†, 42 surv)
Collamer 5.3.42 Torpedoed (in convoy HX178) by *U404*, sunk, 44 19N 63 09W (7†, 31 surv)
Collingsworth 9.1.43 Torpedoed (in convoy TB1) by *U124*, sunk, 07 12N 55 37W (11†, 55 surv)
Coloradan 9.10.42 Torpedoed (ind) by *U159*, sunk, 35 47S 14 34E (6†, 48 resc, 6† on *Zaandam* – *qv* – when sunk)
Comayagua (Hon) 14.5.42 Torpedoed by *U125*, sunk, 19N 81 37W (6†, 36 surv)
Comol Rico 4.4.42 Torpedoed by *U154*, sunk, 20 46N 66 46W (3†, 39 surv)
Connecticut 20.4.42 Torpedoed by torpedo boat *Esan* (LS-4) from aux cruiser *Michel*, on fire, sunk, 23S 20W (37†, 18 resc/pow)
Coppename 40 *Anna Maria Gualdi* (Ita); 1.12.42 internal explosion Palermo; TL
Cranford 30.7.42 Torpedoed by *U155*, sunk, 12 17N 55 11W (11†, 36 surv)
Cripple Creek 13.8.42 Torpedoed by *U752*, sunk, 04 55N 18 30W (1†, 51 surv)
Cuzco 40 *Carmona* (Pan); 18.7.42 torpedoed by *U160*, sunk, 10 58N 61 20W (4†, 31 surv)

Davenport 40 *Alcoa Shipper* (US); 30.5.42 torpedoed by *U404*, sunk, 37 49N 65 15W (7†, 25 surv)
David H Atwater 3.4.42 Shelled by *U552*, on fire, sunk, 37 57N 75 10W (24†, 3 surv)
David McKelvy 14.5.42 Torpedoed by *U506* 28 30N 89 55W; on fire, beached Louisiana coast (17†, 23 surv); CTL
Deer Lodge 17.2.43 Torpedoed (ind) by *U516*, sunk, 33 46S 26 58E (2†, 55 surv)
Delfina 5.6.42 Torpedoed by *U172*, sunk, 20 22N 67 07E (4†, 27 surv)
Delsisle 19.10.43 In convoy WB65, struck mine (laid 9.10.43 by *U220*), sunk, 47 19N 52 27W (0†, 39 surv)
Delmundo 13.8.42 Torpedoed (in convoy TAW12) by *U600*, sunk, 19 55N 73 49W (8†, 60 surv)
Delplata 20.2.42 Torpedoed by *U156* 14 55N 62 10W (0†, 52 surv); 21.2.42 shelled by US warship, sunk
Delvalle 12.4.42 Torpedoed by *U154*, sunk, 16 51N 72 25W (2†, 61 surv)
Dixie Arrow 26.3.42 Torpedoed by *U71*, broke in two, sunk, 34 53 30N 75 44 42W (11†, 22 surv)
Don José 2.1.42 Bombed by Japanese aircraft, on fire, while anchored off NE point of the North Harbour, Corregidor, 14 35N 120 55E, beached; recovered by Japanese, towed Hong Kong; damaged by US bombing, BU
Dona Aurora 25.12.42 Torpedoed by subm *Enrico Tazzoli* (Ita), sunk, 02 02S 35 17W (7†, 2 pow, 62 surv)

E J Sadler 22.6.42 Shelled by *U159*, on fire, 15 36N 67 52W (0†, 36 surv); sunk by explosive charges
E G Seubert 23.2.44 Torpedoed (in convoy PA69) by *U510*, sunk, 13 50N 48 49E (6†, 64 surv)
E M Clark 18.3.42 Torpedoed by *U124*, sunk, 35 07N 75 35W (1†, 40 surv)
East Indian 3.11.42 Torpedoed by *U181*, sunk, 37 23S 13 34E (56†, 17 surv)
Eastern Sword 4.5.42 Torpedoed by *U162*, sunk, 07 10N 57 58W (11†, 18 surv)
Edith 7.6.42 Torpedoed (ind) by *U159*, sunk, 14 33N 74 35W (2†, 29 surv)
Edward Luckenbach 1.7.42 Struck US mine, sunk, 24 56N 81 53W (1†, 53 surv)
Effingham 30.3.42 Torpedoed (convoy PQ13 straggler) by *U435*, sunk, 70 28N 35 44E (12†, 31 surv)
Eldena 8.7.43 Torpedoed (in convoy TJ1) by *U510*, sunk, 05 50N 50 20W (0†, 66 surv)
Eldorado 40 (Pan); 25.12.41 scuttled Hong Kong; 42 raised by Japanese; 3.43 *Gyoryu Maru* (Jpn); 13.5.45 struck US mine, sunk, 34 40N 135 10E; 1.47 beached at Kobe, BU
Elizabeth 20.5.42 Shelled, torpedoed, by *U103*, sunk, 21 41N 84 54W (6†, 36 surv)
Elizabeth Kellogg 23.11.43 Torpedoed by *U516*, on fire, sunk, 11 10N 80 42W (10†, 38 surv)
Emidio 20.12.41 Torpedoed, shelled, by subm *I-17* (Jpn), damaged, 40 33N 125W (5†, 31 surv); drifted on to rocks near Crescent City CA, in 40 34 30N 124 50W; wreck sold
Esparta 9.4.42 Torpedoed by *U123*, sunk, 30 46N 81 11W (1†, 39 surv)
Esso Baton Rouge 23.2.43 Torpedoed (in convoy UC1) by *U202*, sunk, 31 15N 27 22W (3†, 65 surv)
Esso Boston 12.4.42 Torpedoed, shelled, by *U130*, on fire, 21 42N 60W; beached Barbuda (0†, 37 surv); TL

Esso Copenhagen (Pan) 25.2.42 Torpedoed, shelled, by subm *Luigi Torelli* (Ita) 10 32N 53 20W (1†, 38 surv); 26.2.42 sunk
Esso Houston 13.5.42 Torpedoed by *U162*, sunk, 12 12N 57 25W (1†, 41 surv)
Esso Williamsburg 22.9.42 Torpedoed by *U211*, on fire, sunk, 53 12N 41W (60†, 0 surv)
Eugene V R Thayer 10.4.42 Shelled by subm *Pietro Calvi* (Ita), on fire, 02 35S 39 58W; ashore Gulf of Patos, floated off, sunk 02 36S 39 43W
Examelia 9.10.42 Torpedoed by *U68*, sunk, 34 52S 18 30E (11†, 40 resc; 26 surv† when *Zaandam* (*qv*) sunk)
Examiner 40 *Excello* (US); 13.11.42 torpedoed (ind) by *U181*, sunk, 32 23S 30 07E (2†, 49 surv)
Excalibur 1.42 USN, transport USS *Joseph Hewes*; 11.11.42 from convoy UGF1, Opn 'Torch', torpedoed by *U173*, sunk, Fedala roads (100† + troops †)
Excambion 1.42 USN, transport USS *John Penn*; 13.8.43 attacked by Japanese dive-bomber and torpedo-bomber aircraft, sunk, off Guadalcanal
Executive 5.3.43 Torpedoed (in convoy RA53) by *U255* 72 44N 11 27E; shelled by destroyer, sunk (9†, 53 surv)
Exeter 1.42 USN, transport USS *Edward Rutledge*; 12.11.42 from convoy UGF1, Opn 'Torch', torpedoed by *U130*, sunk, Fedala roads
Exhibitor 40 *Expositor* (US); 22.2.43 torpedoed (in convoy ON166) by *U606*, damaged; 23.2.43 torpedoed by *U303*, sunk, 47N 34 30W (6†, 54 surv)
Exmoor 40 *Robin Moor* (US); 21.5.41 stopped by *U69* 06 28N 25 54W, crew left vessel, torpedoed, shelled, sunk (0†, 46 surv)
Exmouth 31.7.44 Struck British mines (ind) S of Fife Ness, in 56 33N 01 37W, broke in two, sunk, 56 30 16N 02 36 30W (0†, 70 surv)
Express 30.6.42 Torpedoed by subm *I-10* (Jpn), sunk, 23 30S 37 30E (14†, 42 surv)
Extavia 41 *Exmoor* (US); 6.4.42 shelled (in convoy) by Japanese cruisers, sunk, 19 53N 86 30E (0†, 37 surv)

F W Abrams 11.6.42 Struck mine 34 57N 75 56W (0†, 36 surv); grounded 34 58N 75 48W; 15.6.42 sank; 8.54 wreck sold for BU
Fairfield City 5.7.42 Attacked (after dispersal from convoy PQ17) by German Ju88 aircraft, sunk, 74 40N 39 45E (8†, 34 surv)
Florence Luckenbach 29.1.42 Torpedoed, shelled, by subm *I-64* (Jpn), sunk, 12 55N 80 33E (0†, 38 surv)
Francis E Powell 27.1.42 Torpedoed by *U130*, sunk, 31 45N 74 53W (4†, 28 surv)
Frango 40 *Clifford* (US); 41 *Hakko Maru* (Jpn); 4.1.44 torpedoed by subm USS *Bluefish*, sunk, 07 10N 108 25E
Franklin K Lane 9.6.42 Torpedoed, shelled (in convoy TA5) by *U502*, damaged, 11 12N 66 39W (4†, 37 surv); shelled by destroyer HMS *Churchill*, sunk

Geo H Jones 41 (Br); 11.6.42 torpedoed by *U455*, sunk, 45 40N 22 40W (2†, 42 surv)
George Peirce 40 *La Salle* (US); 7.11.42 torpedoed (ind) by *U159*, sunk, 40S 21 30E (60†, 0 surv)
Greylock 3.2.43 Torpedoed (in convoy RA52) by *U255* 70 52N 00 21W (0†, 70 surv); shelled by HM escort, sunk
Guayaquil 40 *Caribstar* (US); 4.10.42 torpedoed by *U175*, sunk, 08 30N 59 37W (5†, 30 surv)
Gulfoil 17.5.42 Torpedoed by *U506*, sunk, 28 08N 89 46W (21†, 19 surv)
Gulfpenn 13.5.42 Torpedoed by *U506*, sunk, 28 29N 89 12W (13†, 25 surv)
Gulfprince 10.7.43 Torpedoed (in convoy LT22) by *U371* 37 13N 05 12E (1†, 62 surv); 12.7.43 ar Algiers; 3.45 LU Taranto; 20.2.48 sold Italy for BU
Gulfstate 3.4.43 Torpedoed (ind) by *U155*, sunk, 24 22N 80 27W (43†, 19 surv)
Gulftrade 10.3.42 Torpedoed by *U588*, on fire, broke in two, sunk, 40 05N 73 58W (19†, 16 surv)

H D Collier 13.3.44 Torpedoed, shelled, by subm *I-26* (Jpn) 21 30N 66 11E (44†, 26 surv), on fire; 16.3.44 sunk
H H Rogers 40 (Pan); 21.2.43 torpedoed (in convoy ONS167) by *U664* 50 13N 24 48W (0†, 73 surv); 22.2.43 sunk 50 30N 24 38W
H M Storey 17.5.43 Torpedoed, shelled (ind), by subm *I-25* (Jpn), sunk, 17 30S 173 02E (2†, 63 surv)
Hagan 11.6.42 Torpedoed (ind) by *U157*, sunk, 22N 77 30W (6†, 38 surv)
Hahira 3.11.42 Torpedoed (in convoy SC107) by *U521*, sunk, 54 15N 41 47W (3†, 52 surv); shelled, sunk, by escort
Halo 19.5.42 Torpedoed by *U506*, on fire, sunk, 28 42N 90 08W (39†, 3 surv)
Halsey 6.5.42 Torpedoed by *U333*, on fire, sunk, 27 14N 80 03W (0†, 32 surv)
Hanseat (Pan) 9.3.42 Torpedoed, shelled, by *U126*, sunk, 20 25N 74 07W (0†, 38 surv)
Harry G Seidel (Pan) 29.4.42 Torpedoed by *U66*, sunk, 11 50N 62 50W (2†, 48 surv)
Harry Luckenbach 17.3.43 Torpedoed (in convoy HX229) by *U91*, sunk, 50 38N 34 46W (80†, 0 surv)
Hastings 23.2.43 Torpedoed (in convoy ON166) by *U186*, sunk, 46 48N 36 24W (9†, 53 surv)
Heffron 5.7.42 Struck British mine in bad weather (in convoy QP13), sunk, 66 34N 23

14W (1†, 61 surv)
Heinrich v Reidemann (Pan) 17.4.42 Torpedoed by *U66*, sunk, 11 55N 63 47W (0†, 44 surv)
Henry R Mallory 7.42 US Army transport; 7.2.43 torpedoed (in convoy SC118) by *U402*, sunk, 55 30N 29 33W (272†, 220 surv)
Heredia 19.5.42 Torpedoed by *U506*, sunk, 28 53N 91 03W (36†, 26 surv)
Honolulan 22.7.42 Torpedoed by *U582*, sunk, 08 41N 22 12W (0†, 40 surv)
Honomu 5.7.42 Torpedoed (dispersed from convoy PQ17) by *U456*, sunk, 75 05N 38E(10†, 1 pow, 30 surv)
Hugoton 41 *Tamaulipas* (US); 10.4.42 torpedoed by *U552* 34 25N 76W, back broken, on fire (2†, 35 surv); sunk
Hybert 5.7.42 Struck British mine in bad weather (in convoy QP13), sunk, 66 34N 23 14W (0†, 50 + 26 surv from *Syros* (*qv*) surv)

I C White 40 (Pan); 27.9.41 torpedoed by *U66*, sunk, 10 26S 27 30 30W (3†, 31 surv)
Iberville 41 USMC, *Ironclad* (Pan); 43 *Marina Raskova* (Rus); 12.8.44 torpedoed (in convoy BD5) by *U365*, sunk, 72 30N 66E (many†, 50 surv)
Illinois 2.6.42 Torpedoed by *U172*, sunk, 24N 60W (32†, 6 surv)
India Arrow 4.2.42 Torpedoed, shelled, by *U103*, on fire, sunk, 38 48N 72 43W (26†, 12 surv)
Irénée Du Pont 17.3.43 Torpedoed (in convoy HX229) by *U600*, damaged, abandoned (34†, 50 surv); torpedoed by *U91*, sunk, 51 05N 33 55W
Isabela 19.5.42 Torpedoed, shelled, by *U751*, sunk, 18 24N 75 01W (3†, 34 surv)

J A Moffett Jr 8.7.42 Torpedoed, shelled, by *U57*, on fire, 24 45N 80 42W (1†, 42 surv); 10.42 towed Key West; 4.1.43 ar Galveston; BU
J N Pew 21.2.42 Torpedoed by *U67*, sunk, 12 40N 74W (33†, 3 surv)
Jacob Ruppert 41 *Cocle* (Pan); 12.5.42 torpedoed (in convoy ONS92) by *U94*, sunk, 52 37N 29 13W (4†, 38 surv)
James McGee 40 (Pan); 20.6.40 struck mine 208° 2.4m from Nash Point; sunk 2m SW of Nash Point (0†)
James McKay 8.12.42 Torpedoed (ind) by *U600*, sunk, 57 50N 23 10W (62†, 0 surv)
John Worthington 28.5.43 Torpedoed (in convoy BT14) by *U154*, damaged, 03 52S 36 48W (0†, 57 surv); reached Trinidad, then Galveston (ar 21.6.43); 44 BU
Joseph M Cudahy 4.5.42 Torpedoed by *U507* 25 57N 83 57W, on fire (27†, 10 surv); 7.5.42 in 24 57N 84 10W, gutted; shelled, sunk, by US warship
Joseph Seep 40 (Pan); 25.5.40 struck mine, sunk, Havre roads (0†)
Jupiter 41 *Bluefields* (Nic); 15.7.42 torpedoed by *U576*, sunk, 34 46N 75 22W

Kahuku 16.6.42 Torpedoed, shelled, by *U126*, sunk, 11 52N 63 07W (9†, 37 resc; 63 surv from *Cold Harbor* – *qv* – (3†) and *Scottsburg* – *qv* – (6†) on board)
Kaimoku 8.8.42 Torpedoed (in convoy SC94) by *U379*, sunk, 56 32N 32 13W (4†, 46 surv)
Kentucky (9308gt) 42 (Br); 15.6.42 attacked (in Opn 'Harpoon' convoy) by German Ju87 and Ju88 aircraft of StG3 36 37N 12 10E (0†, 59 surv); 16.6.42 shelled by escorts, sunk
Kentucky (5446gt) 18.9.42 Torpedoed (in convoy PQ18) by German aircraft 68 45N 43 30E (0†, 71 surv); ashore, TL
Knoxville City 2.6.42 Torpedoed by *U158*, sunk, 21 25N 83 47W (2†, 53 surv)

L J Drake 5.6.42 Torpedoed by *U68*, blew up, sunk, 17 30N 68 20W (41†, 0 surv)
La Brea 40 (Br); 24.8.40 torpedoed (convoy HX65 straggler) by *U48*, sunk, 57 24N 11 21W (2†, 31 surv)
Lahaina 11.12.41 Torpedoed, shelled, by subm *I-9* (Jpn) 27 35N 147 25W, on fire (4†, 30 surv); 12.12.41 capsized, sunk
Lammot du Pont 23.4.42 Torpedoed, shelled, by *U125*, sunk, 27 10N 57 10W (18†, 38 surv)
Larry Doheny 6.10.42 Torpedoed by subm *I-25* (Jpn), sunk, 41 30N 125 22W (6†, 40 surv)
Lebore 14.6.42 Torpedoed by *U172*, sunk, 12 53N 80 40W (1†, 94 resc, incl 49 surv from *Crijnssen* – *qv*)
Leda (Pan) 3.11.42 Torpedoed (in convoy TAG18) by *U160* 12 16N 64 06W; 5.11.42 sunk in tow 11 12N 62 18W (0†, 48 surv)
Lehigh 19.10.41 Torpedoed by *U126*, sunk, 08 26N 14 37W (0†, 44 surv)
Liberator 19.3.42 Torpedoed by *U332*, sunk, 35 14N 75 33W (5†, 30 surv)
Lihue 23.2.42 Torpedoed, shelled, by *U161* 14 30N 64 45W; 26.2.42 sunk while in tow of minesweeper USS *Partridge* for St Lucia (0†, 45 surv)
Losmar 24.9.42 Torpedoed by subm *I-165* (Jpn), sunk, 07 40N 75 15E (27†, 21 surv)
Louise Lykes 9.1.43 Torpedoed by *U384*, exploded, sunk, 58 55N 23 40W (83†, 0 surv)
Louisiana 17.8.42 Torpedoed by *U108*, sunk, 07 24N 51 33W (49†, 0 surv)

M F Elliott 3.6.42 Torpedoed by *U502*, abandoned, sunk, 11 58N 63 33W (13†, 32 surv)
Macabi 29.10.42 Struck British mine, sunk, entering Port of Spain in 10 01 30N 60 54 30W (0†)
Mae 17.9.42 Torpedoed, shelled, by *U515*, sunk, 08 03N 58 13W (1†, 42 surv)
Major Wheeler 6.2.42 Torpedoed by *U107*, sunk, E of Cape Hatteras (35†, 0 surv)
Malama 2.1.42 Ordered to stop, shelled, by seaplane from aux cruiser *Aikoku Maru*, bombed, on fire, abandoned, sunk, 26 39S 151 24W of Tahiti (0†, 38 pow)

Malantic 9.3.43 Torpedoed (in convoy SC121) by *U409*, sunk, 58 37N 22 32W (25†, 21 surv)
Malchace 9.4.42 Torpedoed by *U160*, sunk, 34 28N 75 56W (1†, 28 surv)
Maltran 5.7.43 Torpedoed (in convoy GTMO134) by *U759*, sunk, 18 11N 74 57W (0†, 35 surv)
Manatawny 41 Sold Philippines; 10.12.41 bombed by Japanese aircraft Manila; 11.12.41 sunk
Manini 18.12.41 Torpedoed by subm *I-75* (Jpn), sunk, 17 46N 157 03E (2†, 31 surv)
Manuela 24.6.42 Torpedoed (in convoy) by *U404* 34 20N 75 40W (2†, 41 surv); taken in tow; 25.6.42 sunk
Margaret 15.4.42 Torpedoed by *U571*, sunk, off E coast US (29†, 0 surv)
Mariana 5.3.42 Torpedoed by *U126*, sunk, 22 14N 71 23W (36†, 0 surv)
Marina 16.1.45 Struck mine (in convoy CU53) off Havre (0†, 101 surv); beached, refloated; towed US, CTL; BU Philadelphia
Marore 26.2.42 Torpedoed, shelled, by *U432*, sunk, 35 33N 74 58W (0†, 39 surv)
Marsodak 41 *Namarib* (US); 42 *Balladier* (US); 15.8.42 torpedoed (in convoy SC95) by *U705*, sunk, 55 23N 24 32W (13†, 32 surv)
Mary 3.3.42 Torpedoed by *U129*, sunk, 08 25N 52 50W (1†, 33 surv)
Massmar 5.7.42 Struck British mine in bad weather (in convoy QP13), sunk, 66 34N 23 14W (48†, incl 26† surv from *Alamar* (*qv*), 42 surv)
Mathew Luckenbach 19.3.43 Torpedoed (convoy HX 229 straggler) by *U527*, sunk, 54 23N 23 34W (0†, 68 surv); torpedoed by *U523*, sunk
Mauna Loa 19.2.42 Bombed by Japanese dive-bomber aircraft, sunk, Darwin (5†, 39 surv)
McKeesport 29.4.43 Torpedoed (in convoy ONS5) by *U258*, damaged, 61 22N 30 20W (1†, 67 surv); shelled by frigate HMS *Tay*, sunk
Mercer Victory 41 *Alcoa Rambler* (US); 15.12.42 torpedoed (ind) by *U174*, sunk, 03 51S 33 08W (1†, 54 surv)
Mercury Sun 18.5.42 Torpedoed by *U125*, on fire, sunk, 21 01N 84 26W (6†, 29 surv)
Metapan 1.10.43 Struck mine (in convoy UGS15), sunk, 37 22N 10 37E (0†, 73 surv)
Meton 5.11.42 Torpedoed (in convoy TAG18) by *U129*, sunk, 12 21N 69 21W (0†, 47 surv)
Michigan 20.4.43 Torpedoed (in convoy UGS7) by *U565*, sunk, 36 01N 01 25W (0†, 63 surv)
Millinocket 17.6.42 Torpedoed by *U129*, sunk, 23 12N 79 28W (11†, 24 surv)
Mindanao 10.2.42 Captured by Japanese after aircraft attack 14 30N 120 45E; 42 *Palembang Maru* (Jpn); 4.3.45 torpedoed by subm USS *Baya*, sunk, 12 52N 109 30E
Minotaur 9.1.43 Torpedoed (in convoy TB1) by *U124*, sunk, 07 12N 55 37W (6†, 46 surv)
Mobiloil 29.4.42 Torpedoed, shelled, by *U108* 25 35N 66 18W, broke in two (0†, 52 surv); sunk 26 30N 66W
Montanan 3.6.43 Torpedoed (ind) by subm *I-27* (Jpn), sunk, 17 54N 58 09E (8†, 57 surv)
Montebello 23.12.41 Torpedoed by subm *I-21* (Jpn), sunk, 4m off Cambria, CA in 35 35 30N 121 16 30W (0†, 38 surv)
Morazan 4.41 (Pan); 8.12.41 seized Shanghai by Japanese; 6.42 *Ekkai Maru* (Jpn); 24.9.44 bombed by USN carrier-based aircraft, sunk, 11 59N 120 02E
Mormacport 40 *Tamandare* (Brz); 26.7.42 torpedoed by *U66*, sunk, 11 34N 60 30W (4†, 48 surv)
Mormacsul 27.5.42 Bombed (in convoy PQ16) by German Ju88 or He111 aircraft 73N 20W (3†, 45 surv); 28.5.42 sunk
Mormacsun (4996gt) 40 *Gonçalves Dias* (Brz); 24.5.42 torpedoed by *U502*, sunk, 16 09N 70W (6†, 39 surv)
Munger T Ball 4.5.42 Torpedoed, shelled, by *U507*, on fire, sunk, 25 17N 83 57W (33†, 4 surv)
Muskogee 22.3.42 Torpedoed by *U123*, sunk, 28N 58W (34†, 0 surv)

Naeco 23.3.42 Torpedoed by *U124*, on fire, broke in two, sunk, 33 59N 76 40W (24†, 14 surv)
Narcissus 40 *Potlatch* (US); 27.6.42 torpedoed by *U153*, sunk, 19 20N 53 18W (8†, 47 surv)
Nashaba 26.2.45 Struck mine (in convoy TAM19), back broken, sunk, 51 22 03N 02 55 04E (1†, 68 surv)
Neptuno (Hon) 41 *Managua* (Hon); 16.6.42 torpedoed by *U67*, sunk, 24 05N 81 40W (0†, 25 surv)
New Jersey 28.5.42 Torpedoed, shelled, by *U103*, sunk, 81 30N 82 28W (0†, 42 surv)
New Windsor 40 *Alcoa Mariner* (US); 28.9.42 torpedoed by *U175*, sunk, 08 57N 60 08W (0†, 54 surv)

Oakmar 20.3.42 Torpedoed, shelled, by *U71*, sunk, 36 37N 68 46W (6†, 30 surv)
Ogontz 40 Fishing industry vessel; 19.5.42 torpedoed by *U103*, sunk, 23 30N 86 37W (19†, 22 surv)
Ohio 42 (Br); 12.8.42 torpedoed (Opn 'Pedestal' convoy WS21S) by subm *Axum* (Ita), 75m N of Cap Bon, then continuously attacked by aircraft, bombed, between Cap Bon and Malta, until ar Malta 15.8.42 (2†, 75 surv); CTL; 19.9.46 towed out, shelled by HM ship, sunk
Ohioan 8.5.42 Torpedoed by *U564*, sunk, 26 31N 79 58W (15†, 22 surv)
Oklahoma 28.3.45 Torpedoed (ind) by *U532*, on fire, sunk, 13 52N 41 17W (40†, 22 surv)
Olancho (Hon) 11.3.43 Torpedoed by *U183*, sunk, 22 08N 85 14W (3†, 43 surv)

Olopana 7.7.42 Torpedoed, shelled, (after dispersal from convoy PQ17) by *U255* 72 10N 51E (6†, 35 surv); 8.7.42 abandoned, sunk
Olympic (Pan) 22.1.42 Torpedoed by *U130*, sunk, 36 01N 75 30W (0 surv)
Oneida 13.7.42 Torpedoed by *U166*, sunk, 20 17N 74 06W (6†)
Oregon 28.2.42 Shelled by *U156*, sunk, 22 44N 67 52W (6†, 30 surv)
Oregonian 13.9.42 Torpedoed (in convoy PQ18) by German aircraft, sunk, 76N 09 30E (24†, 29 surv)
Otho 3.4.42 Torpedoed by *U754*, sunk, 36 35N 72 22W (31†, 22 surv)

Pan Atlantic 6.7.42 Attacked (after dispersal from convoy PQ17) by German dive-bomber aircraft of KG30, sunk, 69N 48E (26†, 23 surv)
Pan Kraft 5.7.42 Bombed (after dispersal from convoy PQ17) by German Ju88 aircraft (2†, 45 surv); 6.7.42 sunk by corvette HMS *Lotus* 76 50N 38E
Pan-Massachusetts 19.2.42 Torpedoed by *U128*, on fire, sunk, 28 27N 80 08W (22†, 18 surv)
Pan-New York 29.10.42 Torpedoed (in convoy HX212) by *U624*, sunk, 54 58N 23 56W (40†, 16 surv)
Papoose 19.3.42 Torpedoed by *U124*, sunk, 34 20N 76 35W (2†, 32 surv)
Parismina 18.11.42 Torpedoed (in convoy ON144) by *U624*, sunk, 54 07N 38 26W (22†, 41 surv)
Paul Luckenbach 22.9.42 Torpedoed by subm *I-29* (Jpn), sunk, 10 03N 63 42E (0†, 61 surv)
Paz 26.12.41 Bombed by Japanese aircraft, on fire, Manila; 2.1.42 captured Manila by Japanese; 42 *Hatsu Maru* (Jpn); 13.11.44 bombed by USN carrier-based aircraft, sunk, off Manila
Penelope (Pan) 14.3.42 Torpedoed by *U67*, sunk, 15N 64 20W (2†, 47 surv)
Pennmar 23.9.42 Torpedoed (convoy SC100 straggler) by *U432*, sunk, 58 12N 34 35W (3†, 61 surv)
Persephone (Pan) 25.5.42 Torpedoed by *U593* 39 44N 73 53W; sunk 46 15N 74 02 01W (9†, 28 surv)
Peter Kerr 5.7.42 Attacked (after dispersal from convoy PQ17) by German Ju88 aircraft of KG30, bombed, on fire, sunk, 74 30N 35E (0†, 49 surv)
Pipestone County 21.4.42 Torpedoed by *U576*, sunk, 37 43N 66 16W (0†, 45 surv)
Plow City 21.5.42 Torpedoed by *U588*, sunk, 39 08N 69 57W (1†, 30 surv)
Point Brava 40 *Alcoa Guide* (US); 17.4.42 shelled by *U123*, sunk, 35 34N 70 08W (7†, 27 surv)
Point Caleta 40 *Alcoa Cadet* (US); 21.6.42 struck mine, broke in two, sunk, 06° 8 cables from Mishuka Point (1†, 33 surv)
Point Judith 40 (Gre); 26.4.41 attacked by German aircraft, sunk, Kythnos Island (0†)
Polybius 27.6.42 Torpedoed by *U128*, sunk, 10 55N 57 46W (4†, 40 surv)
Portmar 16.6.43 Torpedoed (in convoy GP55) by subm *I-174* (Jpn), sunk, 30 59S 153 48E (2†, 65 surv)
Poughkeepsie 41 *Alcoa Partner* (US); 26.4.42 torpedoed by *U66*, sunk, 13 32N 67 57W (10†, 25 surv)
President Cleveland 7.41 US Army transport *Tasker H Bliss*; 8.42 USN, transport USS *Tasker H Bliss* (AP 42); 12.11.42 from Opn 'Torch' convoy UGF1, torpedoed by *U130*, on fire, sunk, during assault landing Fedala, Morocco
President Coolidge 7.41 US Army troopship; 25.10.42 struck US mine Espiritu Santo harbour entrance (3†, 338 surv + 5050 troops evac); ran on to reef, capsized, sank
President Harding 40 *Ville de Bruges* (Bel); 14.5.40 attacked by German aircraft N of R Schelde 10m below Antwerp (3†, 149 surv); on fire, beached, abandoned 51 18 36N 04 16 24E; 1.52 wreck removed
President Harrison 8.12.41 Captured 31 12N 121 30E by Japanese; 42 *Kachidoki Maru* (Jpn); 12.9.44 torpedoed by subm USS *Pampanito*, sunk, 19 18N 111 53E
President Pierce 7.41 US Army transport *Hugh L Scott*; 8.42 USN, transport USS *Hugh L Scott* (AP 43); 12.11.42 from convoy UGF1 Opn 'Torch', torpedoed by *U130*, sunk, off Fedala
President Polk 40 *President Taylor* (US); 12.41 WSA troopship; 14.2.42 stranded off Canton Island, abandoned (0†); 1.3.42 attacked by Japanese aircraft, destroyed, 02 30S 175W
President Van Buren 1.42 USN, transport USS *Thomas Stone* (AP 59); 7.11.42 torpedoed by *U205*, stern damaged, 37 31N 00 00E, when in tow (0†); 11.11.42 at Algiers; 25.11.42 bombed by enemy aircraft, aground; 42 APA 29; salvaged; 44 stricken, CTL; 47 BU *in situ*
Prusa 18.12.41 Torpedoed by subm *I-72* (Jpn), sunk, 16 45N 156W (8†, 26 surv)
Puerto Rican 9.3.43 Torpedoed (convoy RA53 straggler) by *U586*, sunk, 66 44N 10 41W (61†, 1 surv)

Quaker City 18.5.42 Torpedoed by *U156*, sunk, 14 55N 51 40W (11†, 29 surv)

R M Parker Jr 13.8.42 Torpedoed, shelled, by *U171*, sunk, 28 37N 90 48W (0†, 44 surv)
R P Resor 26.2.42 Torpedoed by *U578*, on fire, 40 06N 73 56W (47†, 2 surv); 29.2.42 sunk
R W Gallagher 13.7.42 Torpedoed by *U67*, sunk, 28 32N 90 59W (8†, 44 surv)
Rawleigh Warner 23.6.42 Torpedoed by *U67*, on fire, sunk, 28 53N 89 13W (33†, 0 surv)
Republic 22.1.42 Torpedoed by *U504* 27 05N 80 15W; 23.2.42 sunk 5m E of Hobe

Sound FL (5†, 29 surv)
Reuben Tipton 23.10.42 Torpedoed (ind) by *U129*, sunk, 14 33N 54 58W (3†, 49 surv)
Rio de Janeiro 41–42 Conv to escort carrier; 1.7.42 HMS *Dasher* (D37); 27.3.43 explosion in hangar, sunk, S of Cumbrae, Firth of Clyde (–†)
Rio Hudson 7.41 Delivered incomplete for conv to escort carrier; 41 sold RN; 26.12.41 commd as HMS *Avenger* (D41); 15.11.42 torpedoed by *U155*, sunk, 36 15N 07 45W
Robert E Hopkins 7.2.43 Torpedoed (in convoy SC118) by *U402*, sunk, 55 14N 26 39W (15†, 42 surv)
Robert H Colley 4.10.42 Torpedoed (in convoy HX209) by *U254* 59 06N 26 18W, broke in two (28†, 33 surv); 5.10.42 afterpart shelled by corvette HMS *Borage*, sunk, 58 44N 24 54W
Robin Goodfellow 25.7.44 Torpedoed by *U862*, sunk, 20 03S 14 21W (68†, 0 surv)
Robin Hood 15.4.42 Torpedoed by *U575*, broke in two, 38 45N 66 45W; sunk 38 39N 64 38W (14†, 26 surv)
Rochester 30.1.42 Torpedoed, shelled, by *U106*, sunk, 37 10N 73 58W (3†, 32 surv)
Rosario 21.2.43 Torpedoed (in convoy ON167) by *U664*, sunk, 50 30N 24 38W (33†, 30 surv)
Ruth Alexander 31.12.41 Bombed by Japanese aircraft, abandoned, 01N 119 10E (1†, 48 surv); 2.1.42 sunk
Ruth Lykes 16.5.42 Torpedoed, shelled, by *U103*, sunk, 16 37N 82 27W (6†, 26 surv)

Sagadahoc 3.12.41 Stopped by *U124*, torpedoed, sunk, 21 50S 07 50W (1†, 34 surv)
Sage Brush 41 *Keystone* (US); 13.3.43 torpedoed (in convoy UGS6) by *U173*, sunk, 37 59N 37 40W (2†, 71 surv)
Sagoland 10.12.41 Attacked by Japanese aircraft off Manila; 11.12.41 sunk
Salaam 40 *Andrew Jackson* (US); 13.7.42 torpedoed by *U84*, sunk, 23 32N 81 02W (3†, 46 surv)
Samuel Q Brown 23.5.42 Torpedoed by *U103*, on fire 20 15N 84 38W (2†, 53 surv); 25.5.42 shelled by destroyer USS *Goff*, sunk
San Anselmo 40 *A D Huff* (Br); 22.2.41 shelled by *Gneisenau*, sunk, 47 12N 40 13W (2†, 37 pow)
San Blas (Pan) 17.6.42 Torpedoed by *U158*, sunk, 25 26N 95 33W (33†, 14 surv)
San Gabriel 40 (Gre); 30.8.40 torpedoed by *U59*, damaged, 56 04N 09 52W (2†, 22 surv); 3.9.40 ar R Clyde in tow; beached Cardross, TL
San Gil (Pan) 3.2.42 Torpedoed, shelled, by *U103*, sunk, 38 05N 74 40W (2†, 40 surv)
San Jacinto 21.4.42 Torpedoed, shelled, by *U201*, sunk, 31 10N 70 45W (14†, 169 surv)
San Pablo 2.7.42 Torpedoed by *U161* at Limon harbour, Costa Rica; 9.1.43 refloated, towed Tampa; 25.9.43 USMC (US); 25.9.43 US Army bbc; sunk as target 150° 9.2km from Pensacola Pass
Santa Barbara 7.40 USN, transport USS *McCawley* (APA 4); 30.6.42 torpedoed by Japanese torpedo-bomber aircraft off Rendova Is (15†); abandoned, torpedoed in error by US PT boat, sunk
Santa Clara 2.42 WSA transport; 8.42 USN, transport USS *Susan B Anthony* (AP 72); 7.6.44 struck mine, sunk, off Omaha Beach, Normandy, in 49 33N 00 47W (0†, 2200 surv); wreck dispersed
Santa Elena 7.42 WSA transport; 6.11.43 torpedoed (in convoy KMF25A) by German aircraft 37 12N 06 16E (4†, 2163 surv); 7.11.43 taken in tow, sunk, off Philippeville
Santa Lucia 3.42 WSA transport; 7.42 USN, USS *Leedstown* (AP 73); 8.11.42 torpedoed by *U331*, abandoned; 8–9.11.42 bombed by German aircraft off Algiers (8†); 9.11.42 sunk
Santore 17.6.42 Struck mine (laid 12.6.42 by *U701*) (in convoy KS511), sunk, 36 53N 75 49W (3†, 43 surv); 8.54 wreck sold for BU
Sapinero 40 *Vineland* (Pan); 42 (Br); 20.4.42 torpedoed, shelled, by *U154*, sunk, 23 05N 72 20W (1†, 34 surv)
Sarcoxie 40 Sold (US); 7.7.42 torpedoed, shelled (dispersed from convoy PQ17), by *U255*, sunk, 71 20N 51E (0†, 40 surv)
Satartia 43 *Kola* (Rus); 17.2.43 torpedoed (in convoy) by subm USS *Sawfish*, sunk, 30 56N 136 30E (69†, 4 surv)
Sawokla 40 *Excellency* (US); 41 *Sawokla* (US); 29.11.42 shelled by aux cruiser *Michel*, on fire, sunk, 23S 80 54E (–†, 39 pow)
Scanmail 40 *Cayru* (Brz); 8.3.42 torpedoed by *U94*, broke in two, sunk, 39 10N 72 02W (60†, 32 surv)
Scanpenn 1.40 *Buarque* (Brz); 15.2.42 torpedoed by *U432*, sunk, 36 35N 75 20W (2†, 73 surv)
Scottsburg 15.6.42 Torpedoed by *U502*, sunk, 11 51N 62 56W (5†, 45 surv)
Sea Thrush 28.6.42 Torpedoed by *U505*, sunk, 22 38N 60 59W (0†, 66 surv)
Seattle Spirit 18.6.42 Torpedoed (in convoy ONS102) by *U124* 50 23N 42 25W (4†, 51 surv); shelled by corvette HMCS *Agassiz*, sunk
Selma City 6.4.42 Bombed by Japanese aircraft, on fire, 17 29N 83 32E (0†, 29 surv); 8.4.42 sunk 17 40N 84 30E
Sidney M Hauptman 40 *Raphael Semmes* (US); 28.6.42 torpedoed by *U332*, sunk, 29 30N 64 30W (19†, 18 surv)
Silver Sword 20.9.42 Torpedoed (in convoy QP14) by *U255*, damaged, 75 41N 03 12W

(1†, 60 surv); shelled by destroyer HMS *Worcester*, sunk
Sixaola 13.6.42 Torpedoed by *U159*, sunk, 09 54N 81 25W (29†, 178 surv)
Solon Turman 13.6.42 Torpedoed by *U159*, sunk, 10 45N 80 24W (1†, 52 surv)
Steel Age 6.3.42 Torpedoed by *U129*, sunk, 06 45N 53 15W (34†, 1 pow)
Steel Navigator 19.10.42 Torpedoed (in convoy ON137) by *U610*, sunk, 49 45N 31 20W (16†, 36 surv)
Steel Scientist 11.10.42 Torpedoed (ind) by *U514*, sunk, 05 48N 51 39W (1†, 46 surv)
Steel Seafarer 6.9.41 Bombed by German aircraft near Shadwan Island, Gulf of Suez, in 27 20N 34 15E (0†, 36 surv)
Steel Traveler 18.12.44 Struck mine (in convoy ATM16) 350° 1.5 cables from NF Buoy, R Schelde; broke in two, sunk 51 24 46N 03 20 21E (2†, 69 surv)
Steel Voyager 23.9.43 Torpedoed (in convoy ONS18/ON202) by *U952*, sunk, 53 34N 40 40W (0†, 66 surv)
Steel Worker 3.6.42 Struck by mine (mine dropped by German aircraft), broke in two, sunk, 45° 15 cables from Mishaynmpi, Murmansk Roads (0†, 38 surv)
Steelmaker 19.4.42 Torpedoed by U654, sunk, 33 72N 70 36W (1†, 47 surv)
Stella Lykes (6801gt) 27.7.42 Torpedoed by *U582*, sunk, 06 46N 25 05W (1†, 2 pow, 50 surv)
Stella Lykes (2322gt) 40 *Josephine* (Pan); 41 *Leslie* (US); 12.4.42 torpedoed by *U123*, sunk, 28 35N 80 19W (4†, 28 surv); 54 wreck sold for BU
Sunoil 5.4.43 Torpedoed (in convoy HX 231) by *U530*, sunk, 58 15N 34 14W (43†, 0 surv)
Susana 14.10.42 Torpedoed (in convoy SC104) by *U221*, sunk, 53 41N 41 23W (38†, 21 surv)
Suwied 7.6.42 Torpedoed (ind) by *U107*, sunk, 20 05N 84 48W (6†, 24 surv)
Swiftscout 18.4.45 Torpedoed by *U548*, back broken, sunk, 37 30N 73 03W (1†, 46 surv)
Swiftsure 8.10.42 Torpedoed by *U68*, sunk, 34 40S 18 25E (0†, 33 surv – 24† when *Zaandam* – *qv* – sunk)
Sylvan Arrow 41 (Pan); 20.5.42 torpedoed (in convoy OT1) by *U155* 11 22N 62 14W, abandoned (1†, 38 surv); 28.5.42 sunk 12 50N 67 32W
Syros 26.5.42 Torpedoed (in convoy PQ16) by *U703*, broke in two, sunk, 72 35N 05 30E (12†, 28 surv)

T C McCobb 31.3.42 Torpedoed by subm *Pietro Calvi* (Ita) 07 10N 45 20W (24†, 15 surv); 1.4.42 sunk
T J Williams 41 (Br); 19.9.41 torpedoed (in convoy SC44) by *U552*, sunk, 61 34N 35 11W (17†, 22 surv)
Tachirá 12.7.42 Torpedoed by *U129*, sunk, 18 15N 81 54W (5†, 34 surv)
Tela (Hon) 8.6.42 Torpedoed by *U504*, sunk, 18 15N 85 20W (13†, 43 surv on *Port Montreal* – *qv* – 2† when that vessel sunk)
Texan 12.3.42 Torpedoed by *U126*, sunk, 21 34N 76 28W (9†, 47 surv)
Thalia (Pan) 23.2.42 Torpedoed by *U502*, sunk, 13N 70 45W (1†, 40 surv)
Tiger 31.3.42 Torpedoed by *U754* 36 50N 75 49W (1†, 41 surv); 1.4.42 in tow; 2.4.42 140° 5.25m from Buoy 2CB, Chesapeake Bay; 54 wreck sold for BU
Tillie Lykes 18.6.42 Torpedoed by *U161*, sunk, 19N 85 20W (33†, 0 surv)
Tivives 21.10.43 Torpedoed (in convoy MKS28) by enemy aircraft, sunk, 36 55N 01 36E (2†, 78 surv)
Topa Topa 29.8.42 Torpedoed by *U66*, sunk, 10 16N 51 30W (25†, 35 surv)
Trieste 41 Completed; 41 *Paderewski* (Pol); 30.12.42 torpedoed, shelled, by *U214*, sunk, 10 52N 60 25W (3†, 38 surv)
Tuscaloosa City 4.5.42 Torpedoed by *U125*, sunk, 18 25N 81 31W (0†, 34 surv)

Velma Lykes 4.6.42 Torpedoed by *U158*, sunk, 21 21N 86 31W (15†, 17 surv on *Ardenvohr* – *qv*)
Victor Ross 40 (Br); 2.12.40 torpedoed (in convoy OB251) by *U43*, sunk, 56 04N 18 30W (44†, 0 surv)
Vincent 12.12.41 Shelled, on fire, torpedoed, by aux cruisers *Aikoku Maru* and *Hokoku Maru*, sunk, 25 41S 118 19W (0†, 36 surv /pow)
Virginia 13.5.42 Torpedoed by *U507*, on fire, 28 53N 89 29W (29†, 12 surv); 13.5.42 sunk
Virginia Sinclair 10.3.43 Torpedoed (in convoy KW123) by *U185*, sunk, 20 11 45N 74 04 45W (7†, 37 surv)

W C Teagle 40 (Pan); 40 (Br); 16.10.41 torpedoed (in convoy SC48) by *U558*, sunk, 57N 25W (40†, 1 surv: 9 surv picked up by destroyer HMS *Broadwater*, lost when that vessel sunk)
W D Anderson 22.2.42 Torpedoed by *U504*, exploded, on fire, sunk, 27 09N 80 15W (35†, 1 surv)
W E Hutton 19.3.42 Torpedoed by *U124*, on fire, sunk, 34 25N 76 50W (13†, 23 surv)
W L Steed 2.2.42 Torpedoed, shelled, by *U103*, sunk, 38 25N 73W (34†, 4 surv)
Wacosta 13.9.42 Torpedoed (in convoy PQ18) by German aircraft, sunk, 76 05N 10E (0†, 55 surv)
Warrior 1.7.42 Torpedoed by *U126*, sunk, 10 54N 61 02W (7†, 49 surv)
Washington 5.7.42 Attacked (dispersed from convoy PQ17) by German Ju88 aircraft 76 25N 33 41E (0†, 46 surv); 6.7.42 on fire, exploded, sunk

Washingtonian 6.4.42 Torpedoed by subm *I-5* (Jpn), on fire, sunk, 07 25N 73 05E (0†, 41 surv)
Wawa 4.41 (Pan); 11.12.41 scuttled Hong Kong to avoid capture by Japanese; raised; 5.43 *Awa Maru* (Jpn); 14.7.45 torpedoed by USN carrier-based aircraft, sunk, 40 56N 141 52E
West Campgaw 41 *Capira* (Pan); 31.8.42 torpedoed by *U609*, sunk, 57 13N 33 40W (5†, 49 surv)
West Celina 19.8.42 Torpedoed (in convoy TAW5) by *U162*, sunk, 11 45N 62 30W (1†, 43 surv)
West Chatala 40 *Île d'Ouessant* (Fra); 40 taken over by VFr; 8.11.42 during Opn 'Torch' shelled by USN carrier-based aircraft US large warships, sunk, Casablanca
West Chetac 24.9.42 Torpedoed by *U175*, sunk, 08 45N 57W (31†, 19 surv)
West Hardaway 15.6.42 Torpedoed by *U502*, sunk, 11 50N 62 15W (0†, 50 surv)
West Hematite 26.9.41 *Irish Pine* (Eir); 16.11.42 torpedoed by *U608*, sunk, 42 45N 58W (33†, 0 surv)
West Humhaw 8.11.44 Torpedoed (in convoy) by *U161*, sunk, 04 21N 02 42W (0†, 59 surv)
West Imboden 21.4.42 Torpedoed, shelled, by *U752*, sunk, 41 14N 65 55W (0†, 35 surv)
West Ira 21.6.42 Torpedoed by *U128*, sunk, 12 28N 57 05W (1†, 48 surv)
West Irmo 3.4.43 Torpedoed by *U505* 02 10N 05 35W (10†, 99 surv); 4.4.43 taken in tow, sunk, 02 17N 05 25W
West Ivis 26.1.42 Torpedoed by *U125*, broke in two, sunk, 16 30N 71 45W (45†, 0 surv)
West Kebar 29.10.42 Torpedoed (ind) by *U129*, sunk, 14 57N 53 37W (14†, 53 surv)
West Lashaway 30.8.42 Torpedoed by *U66*, sunk, 10 30N 55 10W (39†, 17 surv)
West Madaket 5.5.43 Torpedoed (in convoy ONS5) by *U584* 54 47N 45 12W (0†, 61 surv); sunk by escort corvette HMS *Pink* with depth charges
West Maximus 5.5.43 Torpedoed (in convoy ONS5) by *U264*, sunk, 55 10N 43W (5†, 57 surv)
West Neris 26.9.41 *Irish Oak* (Eir); 15.5.43 torpedoed by *U607*, sunk, 47 51N 25 53W (0†)
West Notus 1.6.42 Shelled by *U404* 34 10N 68 20W (4†, 36 surv); abandoned, reboarded, scuttled by explosive charge (by *U404*)
West Pocasset 41 *Chepo* (Pan); 14.1.42 torpedoed (in convoy ON55) by *U43*, sunk, 58 30N 19 40W (17†, 21 surv)
West Portal 5.2.43 Torpedoed (convoy SC118 straggler) by *U413*, sunk, 53N 35W (77†, 0 surv)
West Zeda 23.2.42 Torpedoed by *U129*, sunk, 09 13N 59 04W (0†, 35 surv)
West Tacook 40 *Île de Bréhat* (Fra); 40 German control; 11.2.44 sunk by Allied aircraft 350° 4m from Capri breakwater, Bay of Naples (6†, 42 surv)
Wichita 19.9.42 Torpedoed by *U516*, sunk, 15N 54W (50†, 0 surv)
William A McKenney 5.10.42 Torpedoed, shelled (ind), by *U175*, sunk, 08 35N 59 20W (1†, 34 surv)
William F Humphrey 16.7.42 Shelled by aux cruiser *Michel*, torpedoed by torpedo boat from *Michel*, sunk, 05 37S 00 56E (7†, 29 pow (4† later), 11 surv)
William Boyce Thompson 7.7.43 Torpedoed (in convoy BT18) by *U185*, sunk, 04 05S 35 58W
William Rockefeller 28.6.42 Torpedoed by *U701*, damaged, 35 07N 75 07W; again torpedoed by *U701*, exploded, sunk, 35 11N 75 07W (0†, 50 surv)
Willmoto 41 *Melvin H Baker* (US); 5.6.42 torpedoed by subm *I-10* (Jpn), sunk, 21 44S 36 38E (0†, 42 surv, incl 6 surv from *Bienville – qv*)
Winkler (Pan) 23.2.43 Torpedoed (in convoy ON166) by *U628*, damaged, fell behind; torpedoed by *U223*, sunk, 46 48N 36 18W (20†, 31 surv)

Yaka 18.11.42 Torpedoed (in convoy ONS144) by *U624*, damaged, 54 07N 38 26W; torpedoed by *U522*, sunk (0†, 52 surv)
Yorkmar 9.10.43 Torpedoed (from scattered convoy SC143) by *U645*, sunk, 56 38N 20 30W (13†, 54 surv)

Transferred Ministry of Shipping/War Transport and lost by war causes
American Oriole 40 MoWT, *Barberrys* (Br); 26.11.42 torpedoed by *U663*, sunk, 50 36N 47 10W (32†, 20 surv)
Amsco 40 MoWT, *Empire Otter* (Br); 16.2.41 struck British mine, sunk, 10m NE of Trevose Head (0†)
Bangu 41 MoWT, *Empire Antelope* (Br); 2.11.42 torpedoed (in convoy SC107) by *U402*, sunk, 52 26N 45 22W (0†, 50 surv)
Berury 41 MoWT (Br); 11.9.41 torpedoed (in convoy SC42) by *U207* 62 40N 38 50W (1†, 41 surv); shelled by HM ship, sunk
Black Condor 41 MoWT, *Empire Lapwing* (Br); 41 *Belgian Fighter* (Bel); 9.10.42 torpedoed (in convoy) by *U68*, sunk, 35S 18 30E (5†, 46 surv)
Black Heron 41 MoWT, *Empire Barracuda* (Br); 15.12.41 torpedoed (in convoy HG76) by *U77*, sunk, 35 30N 06 17W (13†, 39 surv)
Black Osprey 40 MoWT (Br); 18.2.41 torpedoed (convoy HX107 straggler) by *U96*, sunk, 61 13N 18 10W (25†, 11 surv)
Black Tern 41 MoWT, *Empire Hawk* (Br); 12.12.42 torpedoed by subm *Enrico Tazzoli* (Ita), sunk, 05 56N 39 50W (0†, 51 surv)
Braddock 41 MoWT, *Empire Redshank* (Br); 22.2.43 torpedoed (in convoy ON166) by

U606, badly damaged, 46 53N 34 32W (0†, 47 surv); sunk by escort corvette HMS *Trillium*

Brave Coeur 41 MoWT, *Empire Gull* (Br); 12.12.42 torpedoed by *U177*, sunk, 26S 35E (2†, 44 surv)

Californian 40 MoWT, *Empire Kite* (Br); 40 *Empire Seal* (Br); 19.2.42 torpedoed by *U96*, sunk, 43 14N 64 45W (1†, 56 surv)

Clairton 41 MoWT, *Empire Reindeer* (Br); 10.8.42 torpedoed (in convoy SC94) by *U660*, sunk, 57N 22 30W (0†, 64 surv)

Cockaponset 41 MoWT (Br); 20.5.41 torpedoed (in convoy HX126) by *U111*, sunk, 57 28N 41 07W (0†, 41 surv)

Cotati 42 MoWT, *Empire Avocet* (Br); 29.9.42 torpedoed by *U125*, sunk, 04 05N 13 23W (2†, 47 surv)

Coya 40 MoWT, *Empire Tiger* (Br); 27.2.41 last communication 62 05N 19 50W – foredeck awash (0 surv)

Defacto 18.3.40 MoWT, *Empire Caribou* (Br); 10.5.41 torpedoed (in convoy OB318) by *U556*, sunk, 59 28N 35 44W (29†, 13 surv)

Delawarean 40 MoWT, *Empire Hawksbill* (Br); 19.7.42 torpedoed (in convoy OS34) by *U564*, sunk, 42 29N 25 26W (46†, 0 surv)

Eastern Glade 23.8.40 MoWT, *Empire Jaguar* (Br); 8.12.40 torpedoed (ind) by *U103*, sunk, 51 34N 17 34W (37†, 0 surv)

Editor 41 MoWT, *Empire Dunlin* (Br); 42 *Norlom* (Nor); 2.12.43 bombed by German aircraft, sunk following explosion on ammunition ship, Bari harbour (7†, 36 surv); 11.46 refloated; 47 BU Bari

Effna 40 MoWT (Br); 28.2.41 torpedoed (ind) by *U108*, sunk, 61 30N 15 45W (33†, 0 surv)

Eglantine 40 MoWT, *Empire Buffalo* (Br); 6.5.42 torpedoed by *U125*, sunk, 19 14N 82 34W (13†, 29 surv)

Endicott 40 MoWT, *Empire Mermaid* (Br); 26.3.41 torpedoed by German aircraft 58 36N 10W; 27.3.41 abandoned; 28.3.41 sunk 57 33N 12 43W (23†, 18 surv)

Forbes Hauptmann 40 MoWT, *Empire Kittiwake* (Br); 42 *Norfalk* (Nor); 24.6.44 to GB for use as breakwater; 20.7.44 struck mine on way to Normandy for use as breakwater, sunk 49 39N 01 05 30W (0†, 40 surv)

Freeport Sulphur No 5 12.6.40 MoWT, *Empire Toucan* (Br); 29.6.40 torpedoed, shelled, by *U47*, 49 20N 13 52W (3†, 31 surv); bow blown off by torpedo, afterpark sank; 29.6.40 bow section sunk by destroyer

Kalani 40 MoWT, *Empire Cheetah* (Br); 41 *Hobbema* (Ne); 3.11.42 torpedoed by *U132*, sunk, 55 55N 37 20W (28†, 14 surv)

Kisnop 14.11.40 MoWT, *Empire Dabchick* (Br); 3.12.42 torpedoed (in convoy ONS146) by *U183*, sunk, 43N 58 17W (48†, 0 surv)

Liberty Bell 41 MoWT, *Empire Mahseer* (Br); 3.3.43 torpedoed (in convoy DN21) by *U160*, sunk, 32 01S 30 48E (18†, 36 surv)

Lorain 41 MoWT, *Empire Thrush* (Br); 14.4.42 torpedoed by *U203*, sunk, 35 08N 75 18W (0†, 55 surv)

Maine 40 MoWT, *Empire Lynx* (Br); 3.11.42 torpedoed (in convoy SC7) by *U132*, sunk, 55 20N 40 01W (0†, 43 surv)

Monasses 41 MoWT, *Empire Whimbrel* (Br); 11.4.43 torpedoed, abandoned, shelled, by *U181*, sunk, 02 31N 15 55W (0†, 53 surv)

Mosella 41 MoWT, *Empire Heron* (Br); 15.10.41 torpedoed (in convoy SC48) by *U568*, sunk, 54 55N 27 15W (42†, 1 surv)

Nockum 41 MoWT, *Empire Starling* (Br); 21.11.42 torpedoed by *U163*, sunk, 13 05N 56 20W (0†, 55 surv)

Oakman 41 MoWT, *Empire Impala* (Br); 11.3.43 torpedoed (convoy SC121 straggler) by *U591*, sunk, 58N 15W (0 surv)

Oakwood 40 MoWT, *Empire Moose* (Br); 29.8.40 torpedoed (convoy OA204 straggler) by *U100*, sunk, 56 06N 14W (0†, 36 surv)

Onomea 40 MoWT, *Empire Leopard* (Br); 2.11.42 torpedoed (in convoy SC107) by *U402*, sunk, 52 26N 45 25W (37†, 4 surv)

Oriskany 4.41 (Pan); 41 MoWT (Br); 24.2.45 torpedoed (in convoy BTC78) by *U480*, sunk, 50 04 36N 05 50 40W (26†, 0 surv)

Pacific 40 MoWT (Br); 1.3.41 torpedoed (in convoy HX109) by *U95*, sunk, 180m WSW of Sydero Is, Faroes (34†, 1 surv)

Point Ancha 40 *Macon* (Br); 24.7.41 torpedoed by subm *Barbarigo* (Ita), on fire, 32 48N 26 12W (29†, 21 surv); 25.7.41 sunk

Point Lobos 41 MoWT, *Empire Wagtail* (Br); 28.12.42 torpedoed (in convoy ONS154) by *U260*, sunk, 43 17N 27 22W (43†, 0 surv)

San Angelo 40 MoWT, *Empire Springbuck* (Br); 10.9.41 torpedoed (convoy SC42 straggler) by *U81*, sunk, 61 38N 40 40W (0 surv)

San Felipe 40 MoWT, *Empire Gemsbuck* (Br); 3.11.41 torpedoed (in convoy SC52) by *U203*, broke in two, sunk, 52 18N 53 05W (0†, 43 surv)

San Marcos 40 MoWT, *Empire Ocelot* (Br); 28.9.40 torpedoed, shelled, by *U32* 54 37N 21 30W; sunk 54 55N 22 06W (2†, 33 surv)

Stanley 41 MoWT, *Empire Pelican* (Br); 14.11.41 torpedoed by Italian aircraft, sunk, 10m SW of La Galeta Island (1†, 44 pow)

Waban 40 *Empire Sambar* (Br); 41 MoWT, *Empire Beaver* (Br); 21.12.43 struck mine, sunk, 51 50 03N 01 33 14E (11†, 25 surv)

West Amargosa 14.11.40 MoWT, *Empire Crossbill* (Br); 11.9.41 torpedoed (in convoy SC42) by *U82*, sunk, 63 14N 37 12W (49†, 0 surv)
West Caddoa 40 MoWT, *Empire Guillemot* (Br); 24.10.41 torpedoed by enemy aircraft, sunk, W of La Galeta Is (11†, 33 surv)
West Cawthorn 40 MoWT, *Empire Bison* (Br); 1.11.40 torpedoed (convoy HX82 straggler) by *U124*, sunk, 59 30N 17 40W (31†, 4 surv)
West Cobalt 40 MoWT, *Empire Miniver* (Br); 18.10.40 torpedoed (in convoy SC7) by *U99*, sunk, 56 40N 10 45W (3†, 35 surv)
West Ekonk 41 MoWT, *Empire Wildebeeste* (Br); 24.1.42 torpedoed by *U106*, sunk, 39 30N 59 64W (9†, 22 surv)
West Gambo 41 MoWT, *Empire Hartebeeste* (Br); 20.9.42 torpedoed (in convoy SC100) by *U596*, sunk, 56 20N 38 10W (0†, 46 surv)
West Hobomac 40 *Île de Batz* (Fra); 40 MoWT (Br); 17.3.42 torpedoed, shelled (in convoy) by *U68*, sunk, 04 04N 08 04W (4†, 40 surv)
West Isleta 40 MoWT, *Empire Merlin* (Br); 25.8.40 torpedoed (in convoy HX65A) by *U48*, sunk, 58 30N 10 15W (32†, 1 surv)
West Kedron 40 MoWT, *Empire Eland* (Br); 15.9.41 torpedoed (convoy ON14 straggler) by *U94*, sunk, 54N 28W (0 surv)
West Quechee 40 MoWT, *Empire Panther* (Br); 1.1.43 struck British mine 8m off Strumble Head; sunk 52 17N 05 19W (6†, 42 surv)
Western Chief 10.40 MoWT (Br); 14.3.41 torpedoed (convoy SC24 straggler) by subm *Emo* (Ita), sunk, 58 52N 21 13W (22†, 21 surv)
Western City 4.2.41 MoWT, *Empire Turnstone* (Br); 22.10.42 torpedoed (in convoy ONS136 – 10.10.42 engine trouble; 21.10.42 turned back) by *U621*, sunk, 54 40N 28W (46†, 0 surv)
Wilhelmina 40 MoWT (Br); 2.12.40 torpedoed (in convoy HX90) by *U94*, sunk, 55 55N15 20W (5†, 33 surv)
Willimantic 41 MoWT (Br); 24.6.42 shelled by *U156*, sunk, 25 55N 51 58W (6†, 1 pow, 31 surv)
Winona County 41 MoWT, *Empire Whale* (Br); 29.3.43 torpedoed (in convoy SL126) by *U662*, sunk, 46 44N 16 38W (47†, 10 surv)

Sunk Mulberry Harbour, Normandy
Artemis 40 MoWT, *Empire Bittern* (Br); 6.44 Adm; 23.7.44 sunk as breakwater storm replacement
Courageous 16.8.44 Sunk as breakwater storm replacement, Gooseberry 2, Mulberry A, Omaha Beach, St Laurent
Eelbeck 41 MoWT, *Empire Bunting* (Br); 9.6.44 sunk as breakwater, Gooseberry 4, Juno Beach, Courseulles
Express 40 *Exford* (US); 26.8.44 sunk as breakwater storm replacement, Gooseberry 1, Utah Beach, Vierville; 51 refloated; 1.12.51 stranded Vierville in tow for Antwerp; BU *in situ*
Galveston 8.6.44 Sunk as breakwater, Gooseberry 2, Mulberry A, Omaha Beach, St Laurent
Indianan 41 MoWT, *Empire Eagle* (Br); 42 *Norjerv* (Nor); 26.6.44 sunk as breakwater; raised, sank in tow to breakers
Jolee 41 MoWT, *Empire Flamingo* (Br); 2.44 Adm; 9.6.44 sunk as breakwater, Gooseberry 4, Juno Beach, Courseulles
Kentuckian 12.8.44 Sunk as breakwater storm replacement, Gooseberry 2, Omaha Beach, St Laurent
Kofresi 14.8.44 Sunk as breakwater storm replacement, Gooseberry 2, Omaha Beach, St Laurent
Lena Luckenbach 16.8.44 Sunk as breakwater, Gooseberry 2, Omaha Beach, St Laurent
Manatee 41 MoWT, *Empire Waterhen* (Br); 2.44 Adm; 9.6.44 sunk as breakwater, Gooseberry 4, Juno Beach, Courseulles; 6.48 raised, BU Penarth
Pennsylvanian 8.6..44 Sunk as breakwater, Gooseberry 2, Omaha Beach, St Laurent
Potter (Pan) 8.6.44 Sunk as breakwater Gooseberry 2, Mulberry A, Omaha Beach, St Laurent
Robin Gray 8.6.44 Sunk as breakwater, Gooseberry 2, Omaha Beach, St Laurent
Sahale 24.8.44 Sunk as breakwater storm replacement, Gooseberry 2, Omaha Beach, St Laurent
Schodack 40 *Alcoa Leader* (US); 13.8.44 sunk as breakwater storm replacement
Victory Sword 8.6.44 Sunk as breakwater, Gooseberry 1, Utah Beach, Vierville
West Cheswald 8.6.44 Sunk as breakwater, Gooseberry 1, Utah Beach, Vierville
West Grama 8.6.44 Sunk as breakwater, Gooseberry 2, Mulberry A, Omaha Beach, St Laurent
West Honaker 8.6.44 Sunk as breakwater, Gooseberry 1, Utah Beach, Vierville
West Nilus 8.6.44 Sunk as breakwater, Gooseberry 2, Omaha Beach, St Laurent
West Nohno 8.6.44 Sunk as breakwater, Gooseberry 1, Utah Beach, Vierville
West Totant 40 MoWT, *Empire Moorhen* (Br); 2.44 Adm; 9.6.44 sunk as breakwater, Gooseberry 4, Juno Beach, Courseulles; 7.47 raised, BU Troon
Wilscox 8.6.44 Sunk as breakwater, Gooseberry 2, Mulberry A, Omaha Beach, St Laurent

Lost postwar through striking mine
Antietam 30.1.46 Struck mine off Blaye, France, sunk (1†, 39 surv)
Sunk postwar with surplus war materials
Bellhaven 41 MoWT, *Empire Peacock* (Br); 25.8.46 scuttled 47 57N 08 33 24W with poison gas shells
Emma Alexander 41 MoWT, *Empire Woodlark* (Br); 41 troopship; 7.45 LU; 2.11.46

scuttled 59 00N 07 40W with poison gas shells
Sundance 41 *Alcoa Banner* (US); 24–25.1.45 attacked by German aircraft, badly damaged, Antwerp, CTL; 2.45 WSA; 25.5.46 scuttled North Sea with poison gas shells
West Cohas 8.40 MoWT, *Empire Simba* (Br); 11.9.45 scuttled 55 30N 11W with poison gas shells
Western Maid 40 MoWT, *Empire Cormorant* (Br); 23.8.44 Sea Transport Service; 1.10.45 scuttled 55 30N 11W with poison gas shells

Changes of name, flag, sold, change of role, etc
A S Hansen 45 US WSA; 46 BU Mobile
Abangarez 47 BU Oakland CA
Abercos 41 MoWT, *Empire Ptarmigan* (Br); 11.41 (Pan); 42 *Norelg* (Nor); 11.48 *New*
Acme 44 WSA; 44 USN, *Abarenda* (IX 131); 46 USMC, *Acme* (US)
Asia (Chn)
Admiral Chase 40 (Br)
Admiral Cole 46 *Ashkhabad* (Rus)
Admiral Gove 40 *Ramona* (Pan); 8.12.41 seized Shanghai by Japanese; 6.42 *Hitora Maru* (Jpn); 25.7.45 attacked by US aircraft, beached, on fire, Innoshima; 11.8.49 Japanese ordered to raise vessel; 50 salved, *Ramona* (Pan)
Admiral Senn 40 *Thepsatri Nawa* (Tha); 41 MoWT, *Empire Hamble* (Br); 50 BU India
Admiral Y S Williams 12.12.41 Scuttled Kowloon; 5.12.41 wreck seized Hong Kong by Japanese; raised; 43 *Tatsutama Maru* (Jpn); 45 recovered
Agwidale 46 *Wei Ming* (Chn)
Agwiprince 2.44 WSA transport; 3.46 USMC Reserve
Albert E Watts 41 *L V Stanford* (US)
Albert Hill 41 (Pan); 46 USMC (US); 47 BU Oakland CA
Alcoa Patriot 11.43 WSA transport; 46 returned
Alcoa Polaris 1.44 WSA transport; 3.46 returned
Algonquin 3.7.40 On fire, sank, New York; 40 raised; 2.1.42 WSA transport; 7.43 US Army hospital ship; 46 LU James R
America (21,329gt) 10.40–41 US Army accom ship *Edmund B Alexander*; 6.41 US Army transport; 5.49 LU Baltimore
America (33,961gt) 7.41–1.46 USN, transport USS *West Point* (AP 23); 1.46 *America* (US)
American Banker 40 *Ville d'Anvers* (Bel); 46 *City of Athens* (Hon)
American Banker 1.7.40 Keel laid; 9.40 sold (US); building as *African Comet* (US); 1.42–10.46 USN, transport USS *Arthur Middleton* (AP 55); 2.43 APA 25; 10.46 LU USN Reserve
American Builder 45 USMC
American Farmer 9.40 Sold (US); building as *African Planet* (US); 1.42 USN, completed as transport USS *George Clymer* (AP 57); 2.43 APA 27
American Legion 11.39 US Army transport; 8.41–3.46 USN, transport USS *American Legion* (APA 17); 4.47 LU Astoria OR; 48 BU Portland OR
American Manufacturer 45 USMC; 48 *Høegh Merchant* (Nor)
American Packer 45 USMC Reserve Hudson R
American Press 45 USMC
American Robin 45 *Perekop* (Rus)
American Shipper 9.40 Sold (US); building as *African Meteor* (US); 2.42 USN; 6.42 transport USS *Samuel Chase* (AP 56); 2.43 APA 26; 2.47 LU USN Reserve
Ancon (9640gt) 40 *Exancon* (US); 40 *Permanente* (US); 41–46 US Army transport; 46 *Tidewater* (Pan)
Ancon (10,241gt) 11.1.42 US Army transport; 7.42 USN, transport USS *Ancon* (AP 66); then AGC 4; 25.2.46 returned
Antigua 12.41 USN, stores ship USS *Antigua* (AF 17); 46 returned
Aquarius 45 *Timiriazev* (Rus)
Ardmore 46 *Yung Cheng* (Chn)
Argentina 1.42–46 WSA transport; 3.46 returned
Artigas 46 BU
Aryan 40 *Arkansas* (US)
Aurora 12.5.42 War damage, CTL; 42 USMC, *Jamestown* (US); 45 *Miriviles* (US)
Aztec 44 *Azteca* (Mex)

Bakersfield 41 *Chagres* (Pan)
Beaconhill 40 (Pan)
Beaconoil 40 (Pan)
Bellemina 41 MoWT, *Empire Magpie* (Br); 48 *Jui Hsin* (Chn)
Birkenhead 45 *Antona* (US)
Black Gull 40 *Nira Luckenbach* (US)
Black Hawk 41 *Green Mountain* (US); 47 *Ocean Wave* (US)
Borinquen 12.41–2.46 US Army transport; 2.46 returned
Brush 40 *Alcoa Master* (US)
Bulkoil 41 MoWT (Br); 42 (US)
Cacique 46 BU
Calamares 12.12.41 USN, stores ship USS *Calamares* (AF 18); 4.46 USMC; 5.46 LU

James R; 47 BU Baltimore
Caliche 43 *Donbass* (Rus)
Calliope (Pan) 46 *Ampetco* (Bel)
Calmar 45 *Samarkand* (Rus)
Calusa 42 USN, *Winooski* (AO 38); 46 *Calusa* (US); 47 *Samuel L Fuller* (US)
Canadian 41 *Hokusei Maru* (Jpn); no further details
Cape Alava 48 *Wairimu* (Br)
Cape Cod 2.44 WSA transport; 46 sold (US)
Cape Douglas 9.41 Completed as *Idaho* (US)
Cape Flattery 1.43 WSA transport; 4.46 USMC Reserve
Cape Lookout 5.41 Completed for USN as cargo ship USS *Fomalhaut* (AK 22); 43 AKA 5; 44 AK 22; 48 AE 20
Cape Neddick 1.44 WSA transport; 47 USMC
Cape San Martin 40 Completed as *Santa Cruz* (US); 11.43 WSA transport; 2.46 USMC Reserve
Capulin 43 *Illapel* (Chi); 47 *Capulin* (US), BU Wilmington DE
Carlantic 41 *Victoria* (Arg); 42 WSA, *Culpepper* (Pan)
Catawba 42 USN, completed as USS *Neosho* (AO 48); 46 *Catawba* (US); 47 *Tascalusa* (US)
Catherine 7.41 USN, store ship USS *Stratford*; later transport (AP 41); 46 *Catherine* (US)
Cerro Azul 40 *Esso Providence* (US)
Cerro Ebano 40 *Esso Dover* (US)
Challenge 10.40 USN, stores ship USS *Castor* (AKS 1)
Charcas 40 *Carreta* (Pan)
Charles Christenson 45 *Plekhanov* (Rus)
China Mail 41 MoWT, *Empire Peregrine* (Br); 42 *Ocean Mail* (US); 43 WSA transport; 46 returned
Chiriqui 6.41 USN, stores ship USS *Tarazed* (AF 13); 1.46 *Chiriqui* (US)
Choluteca 42 (Hon)
Cimarron 2.39 USN, USS *Cimarron* (AO 22)
City of Baltimore 10.40 USN; 41 transport USS *Heywood* (APA 6); 46 LU James R
City of Newport News 11.40 USN; 41 transport USS *Fuller* (AP 14); 43 APA 7; 3.46 LU Seattle
City of Norfolk 12.40 USN; 41 transport USS *Neville* (AP 16); 43 APA 9; 46 LU James R
City of San Francisco 11.40 USN; 41 transport USS *William P Biddle* (AP 15); 43 APA 8; 7.46 LU James R
City of Weatherford 40 *Ponce de Leon* (US); 43 *Sarazen* (US)
Clearwater 40 MoWT, *Empire Shearwater* (Br); 46 *St Jessica* (Br)
Coelleda 41 *Alcoa Trader* (US)
Colina 42 USN, completed as USS *Kankakee* (AO 39)
Columbian 45 *Kapitan Smirnov* (Rus)
Comerio 40 USMC, *Vittorin* (Pan); 41 *Grey Lag* (US)
Conastoga 42 USN, completed as USS *Lackawanna* (AO 40); 46 *Conastoga* (US); 47 *Tatarrax* (US)
Condor 40 MoWT, *Empire Elk* (Br); 42 *Norvarg* (Nor); 46 (Pan); 47 *Nan Chiang* (Chn)
Corozal 46 *Yung Hsing* (Chn)
Corsicana 42 USN, *Kennebec* (AO 36)
Cristobal (9406gt) 10.40 *Philippa* (US)
Cristobal (10,241gt) 11.1.42–6.46 US Army transport; 14.6.46 returned
Cuba 42 Troopship; 45 returned

Dakotan 43 *Ziryanin* (Rus)
Davenport 40 *Alcoa Shipper* (US)
David W Branch 9.41–3.46 US Army transport; 46 sold (US); 47 *Luxor* (Pan)
De Soto 43 *Luga* (Rus)
Dean Emery 40 (Pan)
Delalba 40 *Lone Star* (US); 47 *Ocean Trader* (Pan)
Delargentino 6.41 US Army transport *J W McAndrew*; 47 USMC; 49 *African Enterprise* (US)
Delbrasil 8.43 USN, transport USS *George F Elliot* (AP 105); 6.46 USMC, *Delbrasil* (US); 49 *African Endeavor* (US)
Delmar 45 *Delouro* (US)
Delorleans 6.41 USN; 10.41–9.48 transport USS *Crescent City* (AP 40); 2.43 APA 21; 48 USN Reserve; 9.48 stricken; 48 USMC Reserve, Suisun Bay
Derbyline 41 *Vermont* (US)
Diamond Head 6.46 *Shahrokh* (Pan); 46 *New China* (Chn)
Dillwyn 42 *Cacalilao* (US)
Dirigo 40 *Idaho* (US)
Donald McKay 1.41 USN, stores ship USS *Polaris* (AF 11); 46 *Donald McKay* (US)
Dungannon 41 *Massachusetts* (US)

E W Sinclair 41 *Daniel Pierce* (US); 43 *Shikellamy* (US); 46 *Daniel Pierce* (US)
Eastern Trader 40 MoWT, *Empire Razorbill* (Br); 47 *M Xilas* (Gre)
Edward L Doheny 45 USMC (US); 45 *YO 234* (US); 47 BU Baltimore
Edwin Christensen 1.46 *Shapur* (Pan); 47 *S Miguel Bay* (Pan)

Egremont 41 *Calobre* (Pan); 45 *Borodino* (Rus)
Elisha Walker 40 (Pan)
Esso Albany 9.40 USN; completed as USS *Sabine* (OA 25)
Esso Annapolis 6.41 USN, USS *Chemung* (OA 30)
Esso Columbia 40 USN; completed as USS *Salamonie* (OA 26)
Esso New Orleans 5.41 USN; 42 escort carrier USS *Chenango* (CVE 28)
Esso Raleigh 6.41 USN, USS *Guadalupe* (OA 32)
Esso Richmond 10.40 USN, USS *Kaskaskia* (OA 27)
Esso Trenton 10.40 USN, USS *Sangamon* (AO 28) 25.8.42 compl conv to escort carrier USS *Sangamon* (CVE 26); 47 *Sangamon* (Pan)
Ethan Allen 40 MoWT, *Empire Puma* (Br); 47 *Inchwells* (Br)
Evelyn 9.42 USN, Q-ship USS *Asterion* (AK 63); 1.44 USCG, weather ship (WAK 123); 46 BU Baltimore
Ewa 43 *Nogin* (Rus); 25.6.43 seized La Perouse Strait by Japanese, taken Otomaru; 14.8.43 ar Vladivostok
Excello 40 *Wolverine* (US)
Exchange 12.43 WSA transport; 2.46 returned
Exchequer 10.40 USN, seaplane tender USS *Pocomoke* (AV 9); 3.46 USN Reserve
Exchester (4961gt) 40 *Patricia Skakel* (Pan); 43 *Tubul* (Chl); 46 *Patricia Skakel* (US); 47 BU Wilmington DE
Exchester (7939gt) 40 *Mormacmoon* (US); 11.43 WSA transport; 1.46 returned
Executor 5.41 USN, cargo ship USS *Almaack* (AK 27); 41 AKA 10; 46 *Executor* (US)
Exemplar 41 MoWT, *Empire Widgeon* (Br); 42 *Exemplar* (US); 9.42 USN, transport USS *Dorothea L Dix* (AP 67); 4.46 *Exemplar* (US)
Exermont 40 *Ann Skakel* (Pan); 43 *Lebu* (Chl); 47 BU
Exilona 45 *Riga* (Rus)
Exiria 41 *Exchester* (US); 45 *Exmoor* (US)
Exochorda 10.40 USN, transport USS *Harry Lee* (APA 10); 46 *Exochorda* (US); 48 *Tarsus* (Tur)
Explorer 11.43 WSA transport; 1.46 returned
Exporter 7.41 USN, cargo ship USS *Hercules* (AK 41); 7.46 *Exporter* (US)

F Q Barstow 45 USMC (US); 46 BU Baltimore
Felix Taussig 46 *Georgie* (Pan)
Flomar 45 *Uzbekistan* (Rus); 45 *Flomar* (US)
Florida (3945gt) 1.42–3.46 US Army transport; 3.46 returned
Fluor Spar 46 *Fryxos II* (Pan)
Flying Cloud 41 *Santa Catalina* (US); 41 USN, cargo ship USS *Jupiter* (AKA 43); 45 aviation supply ship (AVS 8); 47 USN Reserve
Flying Fish 40 *Mormacswan* (US)
Fred Morris 3.41 USN, subm tender *Otus* (AS 20); 6.45 repair ship (ARG 20); 46 *Fred Morris* (US)
Frederic R Kellogg 44 WSA (US); 47 BU New Orleans

General W G Gorgas 11.41 US Army transport; 2.45 *Mikhail Lomonosov* (Rus)
George G Henry (Pan) 42 USN, USS *Victoria* (AO 46); 46 *George G Henry* (Pan)
Glenpool 45 USMC (US); 47 BU New Orleans
Guimba 41 MoWT, *Empire Merganser* (Br); 47 *Ketos* (Br)
Gulfbelle 44 *Poucou* (US); 45 (Pan)
Gulfqueen 44 *Artemis* (Uru)

H C Folger 41 *Reconcavo* (Brz)
H F Alexander 41 MoWT (Br); 42 US Army transport *George S Simonds* (US); 46 USMC, *H F Alexander* (US); 48 BU Baltimore
H M Flagler 40 (Pan)
H M Fredrichsen 45 WSA; 45 USMC; 47 BU New Orleans
Hamakua 45 *Kuibyshev* (Rus)
Harry F Sinclair 11.4.42 Torpedoed by *U203*, salved; 43 *Annibal* (US)
Harvester 40 *Mississippi* (US)
Herman F Whiton 45 *Tomsk* (Rus)
Higho 41 MoWT, *Empire Gazelle* (Br); 46 *Inchmay* (Br)
Hisko 44 WSA (US); 48 BU Baltimore
Horace Luckenbach 47 *Giovanna C* (Ita)
Howell Lykes 41 MoWT, *Empire Pintail* (Br); 42 *Howell Lykes* (US); 12.43 WSA transport; 2.46 returned
Hoxie 41 MoWT, *Empire Albatross* (Br); 42 *Belgian Fisherman* (Bel); 46 *Belgique* (Bel)
Huguenot 43 *Sovetskaya Neft* (Rus); 45 *Huguenot* (US), LU San Francisco

Invincible 41 MoWT, *Empire Porpoise* (Br); 46 *Chrysanthemum* (Br)
Iowan 43 *Tashkent* (Rus)
Ipswich 42 USMC, *Campfire* (US); 45 *Surkov* (Rus)
Iroquois 7.40 USN; 41 hospital ship USS *Solace* (AH 5); 46 LU Norfolk; 48 *Ankara* (Tur)
Island Mail 12.42 WSA transport; 2.46 returned

J A Moffett 46 *J H McEachern* (US)
J C Fitzsimmons 44 *Valerian Kuibishev* (Rus); 44 *J C Fitzsimmons* (US)
J Fletcher Farrell 43 *Josif Stalin* (Rus)
Jalapa 40 *Klamath* (US); 43 *Lunacharski* (Rus)
Jamaica 3.42 USN, stores ship USS *Ariel* (AF 22); 6.46 returned
Jane Christenson 43 *Stalingrad* (Rus); 44 *Jane Christenson* (US); 45 *Kharkov* (Rus)
Janelew 40 MoWT, *Empire Plover* (Br); 49 *Plover* (Pan)
Japan Mail 2.42 Completed as *China Mail* (US)
Java Arrow 6.5.42 War damage, CTL; 6.42 USMC; 43 *Kerry Patch* (US); 44 *Celtic* (US); 45 *Kerry Patch* (US)
John Lykes 12.43 WSA transport; 2.46 returned
Jomar 40 *Île de Re* (Fra); 42 USMC (Pan); 45 (Fra)

Kailua 43 *Viborg* (Rus)
Kainalu 40 MoWT, *Pachesham* (Br)
Kohala 45 *Petr Tchaikovsky* (Rus)

La Perla 42 USN, stores ship USS *Cygnus* (AF 23); 46 *La Perla* (US)
La Purisima 43 *Taganrog* (Rus); 44 *La Purisima* (US)
Labette 40 MoWT, *Empire Ortolan* (Br); 46 *Stanland* (Br)
Lafayette 45 *Novosibirsk* (Rus)
Lafcomo 40 *Île d'Aix* (Fra); 6.40 captured by Germans; 8.40 KM, Seelöwe transport *H18*; 1.4.41 Channel Islands transport; 45 *Île d'Aix* (Fra); 5.45 repairing at Bergen
Lightning 40 *Mormactern* (US); 41 USN, stores ship USS *Mercury* (AK 42); 45 AKS 20
Liloa 45 *Belorussia* (Rus)
Los Angeles 41 *Toteco* (US)
Louisianan 40 MoWT, *Empire Gannet* (Br); 46 *Arion* (Br)
Lurline 12.41–5.46 US Army transport; 5.46 returned

Maine 45 *Istra* (Rus)
Makawao 40 (Nic); 31.12.41 USMC; 42 (Hon); 46 BU
Malabar 45 *Yung Tsin* (Chn)
Mallard 41 *Larranaga* (US)
Mallemak 41 USMC, *Dunboyne* (US)
Malton 41 USMC, *Tintagel* (US); 46 BU Perth Amboy
Manhattan 6.41 USN, transport USS *Wakefield* (AP 21); 5.46 LU Hudson R; 47 USMC
Manoa 43 *Balkhash* (Rus)
Mariposa 12.41–8.46 USMC/WSA transport; 8.46 returned
Markay 40 USN, USS *Suwanee* (AO 33); 24.9.42 completed conv to escort carrier USS *Suwanee* (CVE 27)
Matinicock 46 *Yung Che* (Chn)
Maua 40 (Nic); 41 USMC; 42 (Hon); 43–44 (Brz); 47 BU
Maui 12.41 USMC/WSA; US Army transport; 1.46 USMC; 8.46 LU Olympia WA; 49 BU Portland OR
Maunawili 46 *Socrates* (Pan)
Meanticut 45 *Poltava* (Rus); 45 *Meanticut* (US)
Mercer 41 MoWT, *Empire Kangaroo* (Br); 46 *Parthenia* (Br)
Mexico 5.42–3.46 WSA transport; 12.46 *Istanbul* (Tur)
Missourian 40 MoWT, *Empire Swan* (Br); 42 *Belgian Freighter* (Bel); 46 *Capitaine Potie* (Bel)
Monterey (18,170gt) 12.41–9.46 WSA transport; 9.46 returned
Monterey (5236gt) 2.42–3.46 WSA transport; 48 *Adana* (Tur)
Mormacdove 41 USN, stores ship USS *Alchiba* (AK 23); 43 AKA 6; 46 USMC; 48 *Tjipanas* (Ne)
Mormacgull 41 USN, stores ship USS *Alcyone* (AK 24); 43 AKA 7; 46 USMC; 47 *Star Alcyone* (Pan)
Mormachawk 40 USN, stores ship USS *Arcturus* (AK 18); 43 AKA 1; 46 USMC; 47 *Star Arcturus* (Pan)
Mormacland 17.11.41 RN, escort carrier HMS *Archer* (D78); 45 MoWT, *Empire Lagan* (Br); 1.1.46 USMC, *Archer* (US); 48 *Anna Salén* (Swe)
Mormaclark 41 USN, stores ship USS *Betelgeuse* (AK 28); 43 AKA 11; 46 USMC; 47 *Star Betelgeuse* (Pan)
Mormacmail 3.41 USN, conv to escort carrier USS *Long Island* (AVG 1); 46 LU; 49 *Nelly* (Pan)
Mormacmar 10.45 *Belinsky* (Rus)
Mormacpenn 40 USN, subm tender USS *Griffin* (AS 13); 10.45 USN Reserve
Mormacrio 45 *Magadan* (US); 45 *Mormacrio* (US)
Mormacsea 40 *Commandante Pessõa* (Brz)
Mormacstar 40 *Barroso* (Brz)
Mormacsun (7898gt) 9.42 USN, transport USS *Florence Nightingale* (AP 70); 46 *Mormacsun* (US)
Mormactide (4951gt) 40 *Midosi* (Brz)
Mormactide (7998gt) 9.42 USN, transport USS *Lyon* (AP 71); 5.46 USMC; 46

Mormactide (US)
Mormacwren 41 USN, stores ship USS *Algorab* (AK 25); 43 AKA 8; 46 USMC; 47 *Kamran* (US); 48 *Mongala* (Bel)
Mormacyork (I) 40 USN, subm tender USS *Pelias* (AS 14); 9.46 USN Reserve
Mormacyork (II) 11.9.42 USN, transport USS *Anne Arundel* (AP 76); 46 *Mormacyork* (US)
Munargo 25.3.41 US Army transport; 6.41–7.43 USN, transport USS *Munargo* (AP 20); 10.43 US Army hospital ship; 3.44 *Thistle*; 11.48 LU Astoria

Nabesna 40 *Angouléme* (Fra)
Nebraskan 43 *Sukhona* (Rus); 44 *Nebraskan* (US); 48 BU
Nemaha 46 *Orlando* (Hon)
Nevadan 43 *Jan Tomp* (Rus); 44 *Nevadan* (US); 49 BU
New Orleans 40 *Exton* (US); 41 *New Orleans* (US); 45–46 BU
New York 41 (Pan)
Nightingale 41 MoWT, *Empire Egret* (Br); 42 *Santa Isabel* (US); 1.44 WSA transport; 46 USMC, *Guiding Star* (US); 46 LU James R
Norfolk 46 *Hsin Hwa* (Chn)
Norman Bridge 40 *Esso Caracas* (Ven); 49 BU

Occidental 40 *Tennessee* (US)
Olean 14.3.42 Torpedoed by *U158*, damaged, salved; 13.6.42 WSA, *Sweep* (US); 44 USN, *Silver Cloud* (US)
Oradell 4.41 (Pan); 47 *Bharatbombay* (Ind)
Oriente 6.41–46 US Army transport *Thomas H Barry* (US); 46 LU James R
Orizaba 41 US Army transport; 6.41–45 USN, transport USS *Orizaba* (AP 24); 45 Brazilian navy, *Duque de Caxias* (Brz)
Oskawa 4.42 MoWT, *Empire Raven* (Br); 47 Sold (Br); 48 *Southern Raven* (Br)
Otsego 4.12.41 USMC transport; 45 *Ural* (Rus)

Pacific Oak 43 *Ingul* (Rus); 44 *Pacific Oak* (US); 45 *Taras Shevchenko* (Rus)
Pacific Redwood 40 MoWT, *Empire Chamois* (Br); 47 *Granview* (Br)
Pan America 2.39 US Army transport *Hunter Liggett*; 6.41–3.46 USN, USS *Hunter Liggett* (APA 14); 9.46 LU Olympia WA; 48 BU San Pedro CA
Pan Gulf 45 *Lermontov* (Rus)
Pan Pennsylvania 41 *Petrofuel* (US)
Panama 13.6.41–15.5.46 US Army transport *James Parker* (US); 46 *Panama* (US)
Panama City 45 *Novgorod* (Rus)
Panaman 47 *Marcella* (Ita)
Pastores 12.41 USN; 12.12.43–3.46 stores ship USS *Pastores* (AF 16); 3.46 USMC, LU Suisun Bay; 47 BU Oakland CA
Patrick Henry 40 MoWT, *Empire Steelhead* (Br); 42 *Crete* (Gre); 47 *Vernicos Nicolaos* (Gre)
Pennsylvania (6390gt) 44 WSA; 45 USN depot tanker *Sea Foam* (IX 210); 46 USMC, *Pennsylvania* (US); 47 BU Mobile
Phoenix 42 *Pacific* (Pan); 47 BU
Platte 40 Sold USN, USS *Platte* (AO 24)
Point Arena 40 *Arena* (Pan); 23.9.41 *Irish Plane* (Eir)
Point Bonita 40 *Bonita* (Pan)
Point Chico 40 *Alcoa Guard* (US); 45 *Saratov* (Rus)
Point Palmas 40 *Alcoa Pilot* (US)
Point Salinas 40 *Alcoa Scout* (US); 46 *Arctic* (Hon)
Ponce 41 (Pan); 46 *King Hsing* (Chn)
President Adams 6.41 USN, transport USS *President Adams* (AP 38); 2.43 APA 19; 6.50 LU
President Fillmore 2.40 *Panamanian* (Pan); 49 BU Hong Kong
President Garfield (10,501gt) 12.40 *President Madison* (US); 4.41 USN; 2.4.42 commd USS *President Madison* (AP 62); 42 *Kenmore* (AK 221); 2.44 hospital ship USS *Refuge* (AH 11); 29.6.46 *President Madison* (US); 46 LU; 48 BU Vancouver WA
President Garfield (9255gt) 5.42 USN, transport USS *Thomas Jefferson* (AP 60); 2.43 APA 30
President Grant 8.40 USN, transport USS *Harris* (APA 2); 48 BU Wilmington DE
President Hayes (10,533gt) 40 *President Tyler* (US); 1.42 WSA transport; 4.47 LU Hudson R
President Hayes (9255gt) 7.41–6.49 USN, USS *President Hayes* (AP 39); 2.43 APA 20; 6.49 USN Reserve
President Jackson 7.40 USN; 6.41 transport USS *Zeilin* (AP 37); 1.43 APA 3; 7.46 *President Jackson* (US); 48 BU Wilmington DE
President Jefferson 12.40 US Army transport *Henry T Allen*; 4.42 USN, transport USS *Henry T Allen* (APA 15); 2.45 amphibious training ship (AG 90); 2.47 *President Jefferson* (US); 47 LU Suisun Bay; 48 BU San Pedro
President Johnson 7.12.41 Req as USN transport; 14.1.46 decomm, LU; 47 *Santa Cruz* (Pan)
President Lincoln 40 *Maria del Carmen* (Spn); 40 *Cabo de la Esperanza* (Spn)
President McKinley (14,127gt) 10.40 US Army transport *J Franklin Bell*; 4.42 USN, transport USS *J Franklin Bell* (APA 16); 4.46 LU Suisun Bay; 48 BU San Pedro
President Monroe (10,533gt) 12.40 *President Buchanan* (US); 11.43 hospital ship *Emily H M Weder*; 11.45 transport *President Buchanan* (US); 6.46 LU Suisun Bay

President Monroe (9255gt) 1.42–1.46 USN, transport USS *President Monroe* (AP 104); 2.46 returned
President Polk 9.43–1.46 USN, transport USS *President Polk* (AP 103); 1.46 returned
President Roosevelt 10.40 US Army transport; 6.41 USN, transport USS *Joseph T Dickman* (APA 13); 3.46 LU Suisun Bay; 48 BU Oakland CA
President Taft 6.41 US Army transport *Willard A Holbrook*; 5.45 hospital ship *Armin W Leuschner*; 8.45 *Willard A Holbrook*; 11.49 LU James R
President Van Buren 2.41 *President Fillmore* (US); 2.42 WSA transport; 10.43 US Army, hospital ship *Marigold*; 46 *President Fillmore* (US), LU Suisun Bay; 48 BU Oakland CA
President Wilson 40 *Maria Pipa* (Spn); 40 *Cabo de Hornos* (Spn)

Quirigua 6.41–4.46 USN, stores ship USS *Mizar* (AF 12); 4.46 *Quirigua* (US)
Quistconck 40 MoWT, *Empire Falcon* (Br); 46 *Barnby* (Br)

Red Jacket 41 *Santa Monica* (US); 1.43 WSA transport; 5.46 *Bonita* (US); LU
Republic 7.41 USN, transport USS *Republic* (APA 33); 2.45 US Army hospital ship; 45 transport; 46 LU Olympia WA
Richmond 45 USMC (US); 47 BU Napa CA
Rio de la Plata 41 USN, escort carrier USS *Charger* (AVG 4); 24.1.42 AVG 30; 3.3.42 completed; 20.8.42 ACV 30; 15.7.43 CVE 30; 3.46 stricken; 3.46 USMC, LU
Rio Parana 41–42 Conv to escort carrier; 1.42 commd HMS *Biter* (D97); 4.45 *Dixmude* (Fra)
Robert Luckenbach 47 *Maria C* (Ita)
Robin Doncaster 41 MoWT, *Empire Curlew* (Br); 42 *Robin Doncaster* (US); 1.44 USN, transport; 4.46 USMC; 48 sold
Robin Kettering 5.41 USN, stores ship USS *Alhena* (AK 26); 43 AKA 9; 46 *Robin Kettering* (US)
Robin Sherwood 10.43 WSA transport; 46 returned
Robin Wentley 43 WSA transport; 46 returned
Royal Arrow 41 (Pan); 46 *Laura Corrado* (Ita)
Ruth Kellogg 41 MoWT, *Empire Dolphin* (Br); 47 BU Briton Ferry

S C T Dodd 43 *Mariupol* (Rus)
Saccarappa 41 *Alcoa Cutter* (US)
Sagua 40 (Hon)
San Benito 28.10.42 USN, stores ship USS *Taurus* (AF 25); 46 *San Benito* (Hon)
San Bernardino 40 *Atlantico* (Pan); 41 *Hokumei Maru* (Jpn); no further details
San Clemente 43 *Tobol* (Rus)
San Mateo 11.8.42 USN, stores ship USS *Delphinus* (AF 24); 46 *San Mateo* (Hon)
San Rafael 40 (Pan)
San Simeon (40) (Pan)
Santa Inez 3.40–1.47 USN, survey ship USS *Bowditch* (AGS 4); 6.48 LU James R
Santa Maria 8.40–46 USN, transport USS *Barnett* (APA 5)
Santa Rita 2.40–6.46 USN, transport USS *William Ward Burrows* (AP 6); LU Olympia WA
Santa Rosa 1.42 USMC, transport; 46 returned
Scanstates 40 *Cantuaria* (Brz)
Scanyork 40 *Maua* (Brz)
Sea Arrow 7.40 USN, seaplane tender USS *Tangier* (AV 8); 1.47 USN Reserve
Sea Fox 40 *Mormacport* (US); 43 WSA transport; 1.46 returned
Sea Hound 40 *Frederick Lykes* (US); 11.43 WSA transport; 2.46 returned
Sea Panther (I) 40 *Doctor Lykes* (US); 6.41 USN, stores ship USS *Hamul* (AK 30); 42 destroyer tender (AD 20)
Sea Panther (II) 41 *Mormacsea* (US); 2.42 WSA transport; 46 returned
Sea Star 1.41 Completed as *Mormacstar* (US); 9.42 transport *Elizabeth C Stanton* (AP 69); 3.46 USMC; 46 *Mormacstar* (US)
Sea Swallow 5.41 Completed as *Mormacpenn* (US); 5.41 USN, stores ship USS *Markab* (AK 31); 1.42 destroyer tender (AD 21); 1.47 USN Reserve
Sea Witch 12.42 WSA transport; 46 USMC; 47 *Axel Salén* (Swe)
Seakay .40 USN, *Santee* (AO 29); 24.8.42 completed conv to escort carrier USS *Santee* (CVE 29)
Seatrain Havana 41 USN, USS *Hammondsport* (APV); 43 AKV; 46 *Seatrain Havana* (US)
Seatrain New Jersey 10.42 USN, USS *Lakehurst* (APV 3); 12.42 APM; 8.43 US Army; 43 *Seatrain New Jersey* (US); 46 returned
Seatrain New York 42 USN, USS *Kitty Hawk* (APV); 43 AKV; 47 *Seatrain New York* (US)
Seminole (5896gt) 1.42 USMC, transport; 5.43 conv to US Army hospital ship; 2.46 LU James R
Shawnee 12.41–3.46 US Army transport; 3.46 returned; 10.46 *City of Lisbon* (Pan)
Shooting Star 11.40 USN, ammunition ship USS *Lassen* (AE 3); 1.47 USN Reserve
Siboney 6.41 US Army transport; 44 hospital ship *Charles A Stafford*; 46 LU James R
Siletz 43 *Vtoraya Pyatiletka* (Rus)
Southern Cross 11.39 USN, transport USS *Wharton* (AP 7); 47 LU Olympia WA
Southerner 40 *Imediato João Silva* (Brz)
Southfolk 40 *Rio Branco* (Brz)

Southland 40 *Comandante Lyra* (Brz)
Stag Hound 40 USN, stores ship *Aldebaran* (AF 10)
Standard 40 (Pan)
Standard Arrow 44 WSA; 44 USN, *Signal* (IX 142); 46 USMC, *Standard Arrow* (US)
Steel Exporter 43 *Fabritzius* (Rus); 44 *Steel Exporter* (US)
Steel Trader 45 *Kuzma Ninin* (Rus)
Surprise 4.41 Completed as USN ammunition ship USS *Kilauea* (AE 4); 43 *Mount Baker* (AE 4); 47 USN Reserve
Sweepstakes 8.41 Completed as USN stores ship USS *Procyon* (AK 19); 43 AKA 2; 7.46 USMC Reserve, Suisun Bay
Swiftarrow 45 Sold; 48 *Atlantic II* (Pan)
Swiftlight 46 *Yung Hung* (Chn)

Talamanca 41 USN; 1.42–11.45 stores ship USS *Talamanca* (AF 15); 46 *Talamanca* (US)
Tanamo 40 (Hon); 46 *Samaria* (Pan)
Tegucigalpa 41 (Pan); 17.7.41 *Chasseral* (Swi)
Tennesseean 40 MoWT, *Empire Penguin* (Br); 13.4.42 *Van de Velde* (Ne); 6.47 *Rijnland* (Ne)
Texas (6368gt) 43 *Apsheron* (Rus); 44 *Johren* (US); 12.44 USN, *Kenwood* (IX 179); 1.46 USMC, *Johren* (US)
Texas (5638gt) 45 *Kapitan Vislobokov* (Rus)
Texmar 45 *Irkutsk* (Rus)
Trento 4.41 Completed; 41 USMC, *Philae* (Pan); 48 *Thorscape* (Nor)
Tripp 40 *Île de Noirmoutier* (Fra); 40 taken over by VFr; 8.11.42 captured Casablanca by Allies; 45 returned (Fra), re-entered service

Ulua 5.43–4.46 USN, stores ship USS *Octans* (AF 26); 4.46 *Ulua* (US); 48 BU Baltimore
Unicoi 40 *Excelsior* (US); 42 *Unicoi* (US)
Vacuum 45 *Dawn* (US); 45 BU
Veragua 3.42 USN, stores ship USS *Merak* (AF 21); 6.46 *Veragua* (US)
Vermar 45 *Karaganda* (Rus)
Vermont 45 *Ismail* (Rus)
Virginia 45 WSA; 47 BU Mobile
Virginia (Hon) 41 Sold (Pan); 47 *Virginia May* (Br)

W C Fairbanks 43 *Emba* (Rus); 44 WSA, *W C Fairbanks* (US); 12.44–2.46 USN, depot tanker *Banshee* (US); 46 USMC, *W C Fairbanks* (US); 48 BU Shanghai
W H Libby 40 (Pan)
W M Irish 43 *Moskva* (Rus); 44 *W M Irish* (US)
W R Keever 45 *Cheliabinsk* (Rus)
Wallingford 40 *Limoges* (Fra)
Ward 40 *Exton* (US); 42 *Ward* (US)
Warwick 40 *Santa Maria* (Brz)
Washington 6.41 USN, transport USS *Mount Vernon* (AP 22); 1.46 *Washington* (US)
Waukau 40 *Alcoa Voyager* (US)
Waukegan 40 *John R R Hannay* (US)
West Camargo 43 *Desna* (Rus)
West Cape 40 MoWT, *Empire Woodcock* (Br); 42 *Epiros* (Gre)
West Celeron 44 *Vostok* (Rus); 44 *West Celeron* (US); 45 *Vostok* (Rus)
West Corum 40 *Will H Point* (US)
West Gotomska 43 *Andalien* (Chl)
West Modus 43 *Argun* (Rus)
West Raritans 10.3.41 MoWT; 22.3.41 *Empire Mavis* (Br); 24.7.42 *Jan van Goyen* (Ne); 46 *Stad Maastricht* (Ne)
West Saginaw 3.2.41 MoWT; 23.3.41 *Empire Cougar* (Br); 9.46 sold (Br); 49 *Cougar* (Pan)
West Wauna 24.12.40 MoWT; 22.3.41 *Empire Grebe* (Br); 22.8.46 sold; 47 *Inchmark* (Br)
Western Ocean 19.4.41 MoWT, *Empire Opossum* (Br); 2.11.44–31.3.47 ammunition store; 4.46 MoT (Br); 49 *Marianne Clunies* (Br)
Western World 2.39 US Army transport *Leonard Wood*; 6.41–3.46 USN, transport USS *Leonard Wood* (APA 12); 5.47 LU; 48 BU Vancouver WA
Westport 40 MoWT, *Empire Nightingale* (Br); 47 *Inchmull* (Br)
William C McTarnahan 16.5.42 Torpedoed by *U506*, damaged, salved; 43 *St James* (US)
Wm G Warden 43 (Pan); 44 WSA (US); 47 BU Newport News
William Luckenbach 47 *Maria C* (Ita)
William Penn 40 Sold, conv to tanker; 45 WSA (US); 25.7.45 LU James R
Wind Rush 45 *Kavkaz* (Rus)
Winona 45 *Akademik Pavlov* (Rus)

Yale 40 Accom ship, Sitka AK; 4.43 USN, USS *Greyhound* (IX 106); 48 LU; 49 BU Stockton CA
Yankee Arrow 7.43 War damaged, CTL; 25.9.43 WSA
Yapalaga 40 *Beauregard* (US); 45 *Mendelev* (Rus)

Yarmouth 6.42 US Army, transport; 2.46 returned, refit
Yucatan 40 Conv to general cargo; 41 *Agwileon* (US); 4.42 US Army transport; 8.43 hospital ship *Shamrock;* 2.46 LU Suisun Bay

Zoella Lykes 11.43 WSA transport; 3.46 returned

Yugoslavia

Most Yugoslavian vessels remained under that flag throughout the Second World War, but many were chartered to or transferred to the Ministry of War Transport and managed by British companies

Losses through marine hazard
Avala 3.2.39 Ashore 30m W of Cape Agulhas, South Africa; TL
Pavla 29.9.42 Stranded 1.5m ENE of Point Radix, E Trinidad; refloated, stranded L'Ebrauche Rocks, 9m away; TL
Petar 8.3.42 Collision with USN tanker, sank, 10 34N 59 10W (18†, 7 surv)
Sloga 16.10.43 Ashore off Long Point, Nfl; TL
Srebeno 17.12.40 Stranded in gale near Split, broke in two, sank
Talas 17.11.41 Stranded off Funk Is, Nfl; refloated, sank
Vidovdan 15.12.39 Wrecked Great Natuna, North Natuna Is, Malay archipelago
Zvir 15.11.42 Collision with *Skagerak* (4244gt, *qv*), sank, 37 27S 150 17E

Losses through war causes
Ante Matkovic 19.6.42 Shelled by *U159* 12 05N 72 30W (6†, 23 surv); sunk 11 35N 72 55W

Boka 40 (Pan); 20.9.40 torpedoed (in convoy OB216) by *U137*, sunk, 55 54N 07 24W (8†, 26 surv)
Bor 6.41 MoWT, *Radbury* (Br); 13.8.44 torpedoed by *U862*, sunk, 24 20S 41 45E (20†, 35 surv)
Bosiljka 19.6.42 Struck US mine, sunk, 25m NNW of Smith Shoal Lt, Florida, in 25N 81 55W (0†, 32 surv)

Carica Milica 18.11.39 Struck mine (laid 17.11.39 by *U19*), sunk, 52 05 05N 01 41 07E; wreck dispersed

Dinaric 40 MoWT (Br); 6.7.42 torpedoed (in convoy QS15) by *U132* 49 28N 65 38W; 9.7.42 sunk, 49 15N 66 43W (4†, 37 surv)

Ivo Racic 40 *Yewcrest* (Br); 25.8.40 shelled by *U37* 55 10N 25 02W (1†, 37 surv); 26.8.40 sunk
Ivo Matkovic 42 *Diocleziana* (Ita); 42 *Ivo Matkovic* (Yug); Italian control; 9.9.43 stranded Bisevo; bombed, on fire; 15.2.44 at Bari; CTL
Izgled 40 *Elmcrest* (Br); 4.7.40 torpedoed (in convoy OA178) by German E-boat *S19*, sunk, 50 11N 02 21W (16†, 22 surv)

Korana 40 *Oakcrest* (Br); 22.11.40 torpedoed (in convoy OB244) by *U123*, sunk, 53N 17W (35†, 6 surv)
Kralj Aleksandr I 43 *Re Alessandro* (Ita); end 9.43 stranded near Patras; 46 abandoned as TL (badly damaged by shelling from Patras)
Kraljica Marija 1.40 *Savoie* (Fra); 8.11.42 shelled by Allied warships and aircraft Casablanca during Opn 'Torch'; refloated, beached, BU
Kupa 15.5.42 Torpedoed by *U156*, sunk, 14 50N 52 20W (2†, 39 surv)

Labud 19.6.40 Torpedoed by *U32*, sunk, 51 06N 08 38W (0†, 34 surv)
Lina Matkovic 21.6.42 Struck US mine, sunk, entrance to Cristobal (5†, 23 surv)
Ljubica Matkovic 24.6.42 Torpedoed by *U404*, sunk, 34 30N 75 40W (0†, 30 surv)

Nemanja 8.4.42 Torpedoed by *U84*, sunk, 40 30N 64 50W (13†, 34 surv)
Niko Matkovic 41 *Pomo* (Ita); 23.6.43 torpedoed by subm HMS *Unshaken*, sunk, 37 10N 15 19E
Nikolina Matkovic 13.10.42 Torpedoed (in convoy SC104) by *U661*, sunk, 53 41N 41 23W (14†, 21 surv)

Orao 12.10.40 Torpedoed, shelled, by subm *Enrico Tazzoli* (Ita) 35 41N 10 53W (2†, 33 surv); sunk 35 34N 10 35W

Preradovic 40 *Fircrest* (Br); 25.8.40 torpedoed (in convoy HX65A) by *U124*, sunk, 58 52N 06 34W (40†, 0 surv)

Rad 3.8.40 Torpedoed, shelled, by *UA*, sunk, 11 20N 21W (0†, 29 surv)
Recina 11.4.43 Torpedoed (in convoy OC86) by subm *I-26* (Jpn), sunk, 37 24S 150 19E (31†, 10 surv)

Sava 41 MoWT, *Radhurst* (Br); 21.2.43 torpedoed (convoy ONS165 straggler) by *U525*, sunk, 48 50N 47W
Serafin Topic 41 Interned Oran by VFr; 11.42 *Cosala* (Ita); 10.2.43 torpedoed by subm HMS *Una* 38 52N 16 35E; beached 4200 metres from Marina di Badolato; TL
Slava 16.3.40 Struck mine, sunk, 51 19 53N 03 38 09W (1†, 33 surv)
Sud 14.8.41 Shelled (ind) by subm *Guglielmo Marconi* (Ita), damaged; torpedoed by *U126*, sunk, 41N 17 41W (0†, 33 surv)
Supetar 12.6.42 Torpedoed, shelled, by subm *I-16* (Jpn), sunk, 21 49S 35 50E (0†, 35 surv)
Susak 6.6.42 Torpedoed, shelled, by subm *I-16* (Jpn), sunk, 15 42S 40 58E (7†, 27 surv)

Tomislav 22.4.41 Boarded Shanghai by Italian marines, seized; 30.4.41 *Venezia Giulia* (Ita); 12.41 *Teian Maru* (Jpn); 9.1.42 torpedoed by subm USS *Pollack*, sunk, 35N 140 36E
Trepca 13.3.42 Torpedoed by *U332*, sunk, 37N 73 25W (4†, 33 surv)
Triglav 9.7.42 Torpedoed by *U66*, sunk, 26 47N 48 10W (24†, 19 surv)

Una 31.3.41 Seized Genoa by Italians; 11.10.42 torpedoed by subm HMS *Unruffled*, sunk, 5m S of Capri

Velebit 26.6.41 Shelled by aux cruiser *Kormoran*, Bay of Bengal (16†, 12 pow, 6 surv), on fire; 4.7.41 drifted ashore about 2m SW of North Reef Is, North Andaman Islands; back broken, CTL
Vid 41 MoWT, *Radchurch* (Br); 8.8.42 abandoned by crew (in convoy SC94) when in fact had not been torpedoed; torpedoed by *U176* 56 15N 32W; 9.8.42 torpedoed again by *U176*, sunk
Vido 6.10.40 Struck Russian mine, sunk, 18m N of Sulina Is, Black Sea (0†)
Vojvoda Putnik 8.3.43 Torpedoed (convoy SC121 straggler) by *U591*, sunk, 58 42N 31 25W (44†, 0 surv)

Zrinski 40 *Ashcrest* (Br); 7.12.40 reported in distress with broken rudder 54 35N 09 20W; 8.12.40 torpedoed by *U140*, sunk, 55 12N 10W (0 surv)

Sunk Mulberry Harbour, Normandy
Istok 40 *Maycrest* (Br); 30.6.44 Adm; 4.8.44 sunk as breakwater storm replacement
Njegos 5.44 MoWT (Br); 5.44 Adm; 9.6.44 sunk as breakwater Gooseberry 3, Gold Beach, Arromanches; raised, BU
Vicko Feric 42 USMC, *Flight Command* (Pan); 8.6.44 sunk as breakwater Gooseberry 2, Omaha Beach, St Laurent

Sunk postwar after striking mine
Vis 13.2.46 Struck mine, sunk, off Dalmatia

Changes of name, flag, role, disposals
Aleksandar I 46 *Biokovo* (Yug)
Balkan 41 *Armando* (Pan); 6.5.41 *St Gotthard* (Swi)
Bosanka 46 *Prenj* (Yug)
Dinara 46 *Split* (Yug)
Drava 46 *Podgora* (Yug)
Duba 41 *Leda* (Pan); 3.5.41 *Irish Elm* (Eir)
Dubac 29.3.41 Seized Genoa by Italians; 46 *Solta* (Yug)
Dubravka 46 *Plitvice* (Yug)
Dunav 46 *Ljubljana* (Yug)
Durmitor 21.10.40 Captured 08 30S 101 30E by aux cruiser *Atlantis*; sent Kismayu with pow; 2.41 retaken Mogadishu by HMS *Shropshire*; 41 MoWT; 43 *Radwinter* (Br); 46 *Durmitor* (Yug)
Federiko Glavic 41 MoWT, *Radport* (Br); 46 *Beograd* (Yug)
Ivan Topic 46 *Kragujevac* (Yug)
Jurko Topic 46 *Korenica* (Yug)
Karmen 46 *Tara* (Yug)
Kostrena 41 MoWT, *Radfield* (Br); 47 *Tuzla* (Yug)
Lucijana 46 *Livno* (Yug)
Marija Petrinovic 46 *Gorija* (Yug)
Milena 41 *Gloria* (Pan)
Nikola Pàsic 41 MoWT, *Radcombe* (Br); 46 *Kozara* (Yug)
Olga Topic 46 *Kosmaj* (Yug)
Perast 46 *Neretva* (Yug)
Plavnik 46 *Uzice* (Yug)
Princ Andrej 46 *Bihac* (Yug)
Princ Pavle 40 (Pan); 42 *Franka* (Yug); 46 *Kordun* (Yug)
Princesa Olga 40 *Serpa Pinto* (Por)

Rosina Topic 1.3.41 MoWT, *Picotee* (Br); 7.8.47 *Lika* (Yug)
Senga 46 *Korcula* (Yug)
Sréca 46 *Kornat* (Yug)
Sveti Vlaho 46 *Banija* (Yug)
Timok 46 *Sutjeska* (Yug)

Index